McGraw Hill Custom Publishing

ES175
Economics and Structure of Industry

University of Warwick

prepared by:

Ian Tuersley and Karen Bradbury

McGraw-Hill
A Division of The McGraw-Hill Companies

McGraw-Hill Custom Publishing

ISBN 13: 9780390169082

Texts:

Principles and Practice of Marketing, Fifth Edition
Jobber

Contemporary Management, European Edition
Meyer–Ashleigh–George–Jones

Operations and Supply Management, 12th Edition
Jacobs–Chase–Aquilano

Fundamentals of Management
Smith

and others . . .

McGraw-Hill Custom Publishing

http://www.primisonline.com

This McGraw-Hill Primis text may include materials submitted to McGraw-Hill for publication by the instructor of this course. The instructor is solely responsible for the editorial content of such materials.

Printed and bound in Great Britain by Bell & Bain Ltd., Glasgow

ISBN: 9780390169082

Economics and Structure of Industry

Contents

Chapter 1

What is the Business Environment?

CHAPTER OBJECTIVES

This chapter will explain:

- the elements that make up an organization's macro-, micro- and internal environments
- the complex interdependencies that exist in the business environment
- the concept of a value chain
- models for viewing the business environment as a system

1.1 Defining the business environment

What do we mean by the term business environment? In its most general sense, an environment can be defined as everything that surrounds a system. The environment of a central heating system, for example, comprises all those phenomena that impact on the system's ability to operate effectively. The environment would therefore include such factors as the external air temperature, the insulation properties of the rooms being heated, the quality and consistency of fuel supplied etc. A business organization can similarly be seen as a system, whose performance is influenced by a whole range of phenomena in its environment. However, while a central heating system may be said to be a *closed* system, the business organization and its environment is an *open* system. For the central heating system, all elements of the system can generally be identified, but for business organizations, it can be difficult to define what makes up the system, and even more difficult to define the elements of their environment. Some elements may seem quite inconsequential today, but may nevertheless have the potential to critically affect a business organization in future years. The test of a good business leader is to be able to read the environment and to understand not only how business systems and their environments work today, but also how they will evolve in the future. Society's rising expectations with regard to the ethical behaviour of business organizations is an example of an environmental factor that has emerged as an increasingly critical factor to the survival of business organizations. After studying this book, you should have a better idea of the complexity of the business environment.

Business organizations exist to turn inputs from their environment (e.g. materials, labour and capital) into goods and services that customers in the environment want to purchase. This **transformation process** adds value to the inputs, so that buyers are prepared to pay more to the business organization than the cost of resources that it has used up in the production process. This is the basis of a simple model of the organization in its environment, illustrated in Figure 1.1. This transformation process within the organization cannot be seen as a steady state, because external environmental influences have a tendency to be continually shifting, having the effect of undermining the current balance within the system. Just as the central heating thermostat has to constantly react to ensure a balance between its inputs (the energy source) and its outputs (the required amount of heat), so too organizations must constantly ensure that the system continues to transform inputs into higher-value outputs.

Of course, the organizations that form the centre of this transformation process take many shapes and forms, from a small sole trader through to a large multinational organization. The

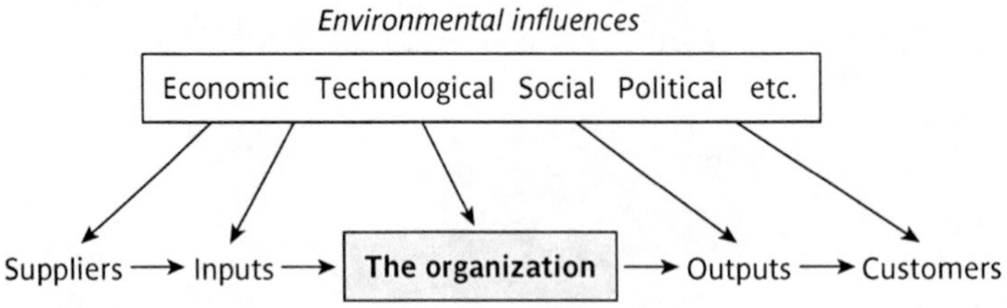

Figure 1.1 The organization in its environment

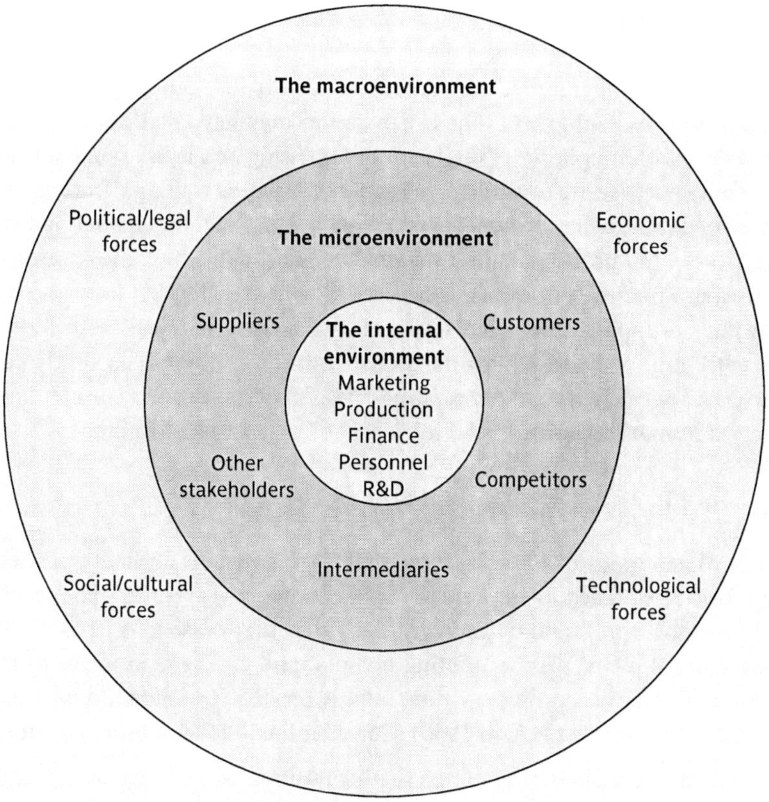

Figure 1.2 The principal elements of a business organization's environment

nature of the organization greatly affects the way in which it can adapt to its external environment. We will explore the great diversity of organizational types later, in the context of their ability to respond to environmental change.

Throughout this book, we are going to disaggregate a business organization's environment into a number of components. For now, we will introduce three important groups of components, which we will classify under the following headings:

- the macroenvironment
- the microenvironment
- the internal environment.

These are introduced schematically in Figure 1.2.

The external environment comprises all those forces and events outside the organization that impinge on its activities. Some of these events impinge directly on the firm's activities – these can be described as forming an organization's microenvironment. Other events that are beyond the immediate environment nevertheless affect the organization and can be described as the **macroenvironment**. As well as looking to the outside world, managers must also take account of factors within other functions of their own firm. This is referred to as the **internal environment**.

The macroenvironment comprises a whole set of factors that can indirectly affect an organization's relationship to its markets. The organization may have no direct relationships with legislators as it does with suppliers, yet their actions in passing new legislation may have profound effects on the markets that the organization is able to serve, as well as affecting its production costs. The macroenvironmental factors cover a wide range of nebulous phenomena. They represent general forces and pressures rather than institutions with which the organization relates.

The microenvironment, by contrast, is concerned with actual individuals and organizations (such as customers, suppliers and intermediaries) that a company deals with. It may currently deal directly with some of these, while others exist with whom there is currently no direct contact, but who could nevertheless influence its policies. An organization's competitors could have a direct effect on its market position, and form part of its microenvironment.

1.2 Why study the business environment?

History is full of examples of organizations that have failed to understand their operating environment, or simply failed to respond to change in the environment. The result has been a gradual decline in their profitability, and eventually they may cease to exist as a viable business unit. Theodore Levitt called this 'marketing myopia', and cited the example of railway companies that focused their vision on providing railway services, but failed to take account of the development of road transport (Levitt 1960). Consider the following more recent examples.

- The retailer Marks & Spencer assumed that its position was unassailable, but by the 1990s had failed to take account of the great improvements in value being offered by its competitors. The result was that many of Marks & Spencer's loyal customers deserted it, leading to a sharp fall in profitability, before a thwarted takeover bid led to new management bringing a new vision to the company.
- Healthy eating has become an important issue in the early twenty-first century. The profits of the fast-food company McDonald's fell and it was forced to close branches worldwide as consumers sought more healthy convenience food, before the company belatedly responded to change with healthier menu items.
- Music retailers such as HMV and EMI were accused of 'putting their head in the sand' and ignoring the threat to the sale of CDs posed by downloadable music sites. They adopted new distribution methods only after smaller, more aggressive companies had developed the online music market.

On the other hand, there have been many spectacular successes where organizations have spotted emerging trends in their business environment, and capitalized on these with new goods and services, or new ways of operating their business, in order to meet the new opportunities presented within the environment. Consider the following examples.

- In the airline market, companies such as Ryanair and easyJet spotted the opportunities represented by government deregulation and offered profitable low-cost 'no frills' air services, often aimed at people who would not previously have flown.

- Many supermarkets and farmers have noted consumers' concern for the purity of the food we eat, and this, combined with rising incomes, has led them to successfully develop ranges of organic foods.
- Many of the UK's pub operators have identified changing social behaviour, with fewer people using pubs as a regular venue primarily for beer drinking, but much greater levels of dining out for social purposes. This has led pub operators to increase their profits by reconfiguring their pubs as restaurants.

There is every indication that the pace of change in most organizations' business environment is speeding up and it is therefore increasingly important for organizations to have in place systems for monitoring their environment and, just as important, for responding appropriately to such change. There is evidence that successful organizations are not so much those that deliver value to customers today, but those that understand how definitions of value are likely to change in the future. A company may have been very good at creating value through the typewriters that it made, but it may nevertheless have failed to deliver value into the future had it not understood the impact of information technology. In the eyes of customers, the company's traditional products would no longer represent good value when compared with the possibilities presented by the new technologies.

Of course, it is much more difficult to predict the future than to describe the past. A stark indication of the rewards of looking forwards rather than backwards is provided by an analyst who studied stock market performance. If a cumulative investment of $1 had been invested from 1900 on 1 January each year in the stock that had performed best in the *previous* year, and then reinvested the following year, the accumulated value in 2000 would have been just $250. However, if it had been invested each year in the stock that performed best in the *year ahead*, the accumulated value would be over $1 billion. Successful companies have often been those that understand their business environment and have invested in growth areas, while cutting back in areas that are most likely to go into decline. Being first to market when trends are changing can be much more profitable than simply reacting to a market trend. However, predicting future trends can be very difficult and can involve a lot of risk. The aim of this book is to provide frameworks for making well-informed judgements about the likely future state of the business environment, based on a sound analysis of emerging trends.

1.3 The macroenvironment

While the microenvironment comprises the individuals and organizations with whom a company interacts, the macroenvironment is more nebulous. It comprises general trends and forces that may not immediately affect the relationships that a company has with its customers, suppliers and intermediaries but, sooner or later, macroenvironmental change will alter the nature of these relationships. As an example, change in the population structure of a country does not immediately affect the way in which a company does business with its customers but, over time, it may affect the numbers of young or elderly people with whom it is able to do business.

Most analyses of the macroenvironment divide the environment into a number of areas. The principle headings, which form the basis for chapters of this book, are described below. It must, however, be remembered that the division of the macroenvironment into subject areas does not

Thinking around the subject: 'Big Mac', big business, big problem?

Television images of young people joining protest marches against world capitalism have featured on our television screens. But just how hostile is the environment to business organizations? Large, successful companies, it seems, just have to accept that they will never please some people, who hold large corporate organizations responsible for all of the world's problems.

A report by the Future Foundation appeared to challenge the idea that young people are becoming more hostile towards big business. According to a 2001 study by the organization, 16- to 24-year-olds have more positive feelings towards multinationals than older groups, with the original protest generation, those who came of age in the 1960s, least likely of all to trust multinationals.

In the wake of violent protests surrounding World Trade Organization meetings, research revealed that younger generations are less inclined towards direct action than their parents and grandparents. Nearly half of all 16- to 34-year-olds claimed they would not demonstrate if a multinational company had done something wrong. Further confounding the myth of young people wanting to change the world was the statistic that fewer than one in twenty strongly agreed that they 'would not buy the products of a large multinational company that had done something wrong'. A third of teens and twentysomethings agreed to preserving the power of multinational companies and a further one in ten believed that multinationals are 'ultimately for the good of consumers' and should be encouraged to grow. By contrast, two-thirds of their grandparents – those aged 55 and above – claimed they would boycott goods to punish companies they considered guilty of corporate crimes. Even the issue of genetic engineering failed to provoke a strong response from young people, with only four in ten mistrusting the claims of the multinationals, compared to six in ten of their parents and grandparents.

Does this research indicate the ultimate supremacy for big business, where the golden arches of McDonald's and the Nike 'swoosh' are symbols of its global sovereignty? Should they feel safe in the knowledge of this study, or do they still need to be alert to possible trouble in the future? And even if a high proportion of young people support the idea of capitalism and big business, can such firms afford to ignore the vociferous and extreme minority whose direct action and boycotts can do costly and long-lasting harm to a firm's image?

result in watertight compartments. The macroenvironment is complex and interdependent, and these interdependencies will be brought out in later chapters. The subheadings of the sections that follow are also those that are commonly used in macroenvironmental analysis.

1.3.1 The political environment

Politicians are instrumental in shaping the general nature of the external environment, as well as being responsible for passing legislation that affects specific types of organization. The political environment can be one of the less predictable elements in an organization's marketing environment, and businesses need to monitor the changing political environment for a number of reasons.

- At the most general level, the stability of the political system affects the attractiveness of the business environment. Companies are likely to be reluctant to invest in a country with an unstable government, for fear that the law would not protect their investment.
- Governments pass legislation that, directly and indirectly, affects firms' business opportunities.
- There are many examples of the direct effects on business organizations – for example, laws giving consumers rights against the seller of faulty goods. At other times, the effects of legislative changes are less direct, as where legislation outlawing anti-competitive practices changes the nature of competition between firms within a market.
- In its broadest sense, the political environment includes pressure groups and trade associations, which can be influential in changing government policy.
- Government is responsible for formulating policies that can influence the rate of growth in the economy and hence the total amount of spending power. It is also a political decision as to how this spending power should be distributed between different groups of consumers and between the public and private sectors.
- Governments are responsible for protecting the public interest at large, imposing further constraints on the activities of firms (e.g. controls on pollution, which may make a manufacturing firm uncompetitive in international markets on account of its increased costs).
- Increasingly, the political environment affecting business organizations includes supranational organizations, which can directly or indirectly affect companies. These include trading blocs (e.g. the EU, ASEAN and NAFTA) and the influence of worldwide intergovernmental organizations (e.g. the World Trade Organization) and pressure groups (e.g. Greenpeace).

1.3.2 The social and cultural environment

Culture is concerned with a set of shared values that are passed down between generations. It is crucial for businesses to fully appreciate the cultural values of a society, especially where an organization is seeking to do business in a country that is quite different from its own. Attitudes to specific products change through time and at any one time can differ between groups in society.

Even in home markets, business organizations should understand the processes of gradual change in values and attitudes, and be prepared to satisfy the changing needs of consumers. Consider the following examples of contemporary social change in Western Europe and the possible responses of businesses.

- Leisure is becoming a bigger part of many people's lives, and businesses have responded with a wide range of leisure-related goods and services.
- Attitudes towards the work/life balance change. The nature of work relationships can affect company profits; for example, the formal clothing retailer Moss Bros claimed that the popularity of 'dress-down Friday' and more casual dressing in the workplace had badly affected its profits in 2002, as its customers switched to more casual clothes.
- The role of women in society is changing as men and women increasingly share expectations in terms of employment and household responsibilities. According to the Office for

National Statistics, women in 2006 represented 53 per cent of graduates in the UK and 45 per cent of the workforce (compared with 37 per cent in 1971) (Office for National Statistics 2008). Furthermore, a report by the Future Foundation predicted that women would be the major breadwinners in a quarter of families by 2030 (Doughty 2007). Examples of business responses include cars designed to meet the aspirational needs of career women, and ready prepared meals that relieve working women of their traditional role in preparing household meals.

- Many Western European countries are becoming ethnically and culturally much more diverse. In the UK, the large number of Polish people who entered the country from 2004 has led to the development of many retail and financial services aimed specifically at this group.
- Greater life expectancy is leading to an ageing of the population and a shift to an increasingly 'elderly' culture. This is reflected in product design that emphasizes durability rather than fashionability.
- The growing concern with the environment among many groups in society is reflected in a variety of 'green' consumer products.

In Chapter 3 we look in detail at consumers' values, attitudes and lifestyles, and the processes of gradual change in these. That chapter also explores the issue of 'cultural convergence', referring to an apparent decline in differences between cultures.

1.3.3 The demographic environment

Changes in the size and age structure of the population are critical to many organizations, for predicting both the demand for their products and the availability of personnel required for production. Analysis of the demographic environment raises a number of important issues. Although the total population of most Western countries is stable, their composition is changing. Most countries are experiencing an increase in the proportion of elderly people, especially the fit and active elderly. Organizations have monitored this growth and responded with the development of new goods and services to meet the aspirations of this growing group – for example, adventure holidays and 'gap years' for older people. At the other end of the age spectrum, the birth rate of most countries is cyclical. The decline in the birth rate in the United Kingdom in the late 1970s initially had a profound effect on those manufacturing and services organizations providing for the very young, such as maternity wards in hospitals, and kindergartens. Organizations that monitored the progress of this diminished cohort were prepared for the early 1990s when there were fewer teenagers requiring high schools or wanting to buy music from record shops. Companies that had previously relied on the supply of teenage labour to provide a cheap input to their production process would have been prepared for the downturn in numbers by substituting the quantity of staff with quality and by mechanizing many jobs previously performed by this group. The birth rate has since increased, continuing this cyclical trend.

Other aspects of the demographic environment that organizations need to monitor include the changing geographical distribution of the population (between different regions of the country and between urban and rural areas), changing ethnic composition and the changing composition of households (especially the growing number of single-person households).

Figure 1.3 Changing family structures and growing career orientation among women have led many people to seek outside childcare services, rather than caring for children entirely within the family unit. Some cultures may regard childcare as central to family life, and would therefore provide few opportunities for a commercial childcare service. Attitudes in Western countries have changed, and a growing proportion of people would regard it as quite normal to buy in professional help to look after their children. Many service providers, such as this one, have emerged to satisfy this growing market.

1.3.4 The technological environment

The pace of technological change is becoming increasingly rapid and marketers need to understand how technological developments might affect them in four related business areas.

1 New technologies can allow new goods and services to be offered to consumers – internet banking, mobile internet and new anti-cancer drugs, for example.

2 New technology can allow existing products to be made more cheaply, thereby widening their market through being able to charge lower prices. In this way, more efficient aircraft have allowed new markets for air travel to develop.

3 Technological developments have allowed new methods of distributing goods and services (for example, Amazon.com used the internet to offer book buyers a new way of browsing and buying books).

4 New opportunities for companies to communicate with their target customers have emerged, with many financial services companies using computer databases to target potential customers and to maintain a dialogue with established customers. The internet has opened up new distribution opportunities for many services-based companies. The development of mobile internet services offers new possibilities for targeting buyers at times and places of high readiness to buy.

1.3.5 The economic environment

Businesses need to keep an eye on indications of a nation's prosperity. There are many indicators of a nation's economic health, of which two of the most common are measures of gross domestic

Thinking around the subject: 'New man' for a 'new economy'?

In the late 1990s it became fashionable to talk about a 'new economy'. The environment of business organizations was to be changed for ever in a brave new world in which 'new' Britain was ruled by 'New' Labour, inhabited by 'new' man, who works in the 'new' economy and learns about the world through 'new' media. Electronic commerce would allow for almost infinite communication possibilities, breaking down international trade and cultural barriers in the process. Monopolies would be broken by the powerful forces of global competition facilitated by the internet, and our neighbours would become not the person who lives next door, but a person anywhere in cyberspace who shares our interests and lifestyle. As the world entered the new millennium, it seemed that the business environment would never be the same again, or at least that is what many people thought.

Of course, many 'big ideas' have a habit of imploding and we need to ask whether any of the promises of the 'new world' have been delivered, or were ever likely to be. The idea that the 'new economy' had banished the economic cycle of prosperity and recession appeared to be dubious as the United States economy slowed down in 2001 and recession finally set in during 2008 after a prolonged period of expansion. Many questioned the myth of 'new man' as something that was more talked about in glossy magazines than experienced in everyday life.

Many of the 'new' world phenomena that had helped to define the new economy soon began to lose their sparkle, leaving observers wondering whether there really was anything new. As an example, many commentators were excited by the prospects of new media advertising, and justified this by pointing to Procter & Gamble's decision to direct 80 per cent of its promotion budget to new media. But old media has a habit of fighting back hard, as witnessed by the huge amount of advertising by the new media owners themselves in traditional newspapers and on television channels.

It soon became recognized that the 'new' economy is very dependent upon the 'old' economy. Electronic communication may be fine in theory as a means of improving global competition, but somebody still has to manufacture goods and deliver them, invariably using 'old economy' methods.

Had the whole structure of the business environment changed, or was it simply transient details that had caused such excitement? Should we be wary of any proclamations of 'new' ways of doing business, or do we ignore changes in the business environment at our peril?

product (GDP) and household disposable income. Many of these indicators tend to follow cyclical patterns related to a general economic cycle of expansion followed by contraction.

Throughout the economic cycle, the consumption of most goods and services tends to increase during the boom period and to decline during recessionary periods. The difficulty in forecasting the level of demand for a firm's products is therefore often quite closely linked to the difficulty of forecasting future economic prosperity. This difficulty is compounded by the problem of understanding the relationship between economic factors and the state of demand – most goods and services are positively related to total available income, but some, such as bus services and insolvency practitioners, are negatively related. Furthermore, while aggregate changes in spending power may indicate a likely increase for goods and services in general, the actual distribution of spending power among the population will influence the pattern of demand for specific products. In addition to measurable economic prosperity, the level of perceived wealth and confidence in the future can be an important determinant of demand for some high-value goods and services.

An analysis of the economic environment will also indicate the level of competitor activity – an oversupply of products in a market sector normally results in a downward pressure on prices and profitability. Competition for resources could also affect the production costs of an organization, which in turn will affect its production possibilities and pricing decisions. Rising unemployment may put downward pressure on wage rates, favouring companies that offer a labour-intensive service.

1.4 The microenvironment

The microenvironment of an organization can best be understood as comprising all those other organizations and individuals who directly or indirectly affect the activities of the organization. The microenvironment comprises actual people and organizations. The company may be dealing with these organizations today, or may potentially deal with them in the future. It may have no intention of dealing with other companies in its microenvironment (such as competitors), but these can nevertheless have a major impact on the activities of an organization. Also, many of these other companies and individuals may feel that they have a such keen interest in the activities of the organization that they become **stakeholders** in it. We will return to the subject of stakeholders in organizations later. The following key groups can be identified in most companies' microenvironments.

1.4.1 Customers

Customers are a crucial part of an organization's microenvironment. Quite simply, in a competitive environment, no customers means no business. An organization should be concerned about the changing requirements of its customers and should keep in touch with these changing needs by using an appropriate information-gathering system. In an ideal world, an organization should know its customers so well that it is able to predict what they will require next, rather than wait until it is possibly too late and then follow.

But we need to think beyond this simplistic model of customers expressing their preferences and businesses then satisfying them. First, the people who buy a company's products are not necessarily the same as those who consume them. Any good book on consumer behaviour will describe a range of influencers, users, deciders and 'gatekeepers' who have a bearing on whether a company's product is bought.

Second, does the customer always know what is best for them, and should organizations think wider about their customers' long-term interests? There have been many examples of situations where customers' long-term interests have been neglected by companies, including the following.

- Fast-food companies, who have been accused of contributing to an 'epidemic' of obesity among young people by their promotion of high-fat food.
- Manufacturers of baby milk that failed to make mothers aware of the claimed long-term health benefits of using breast milk rather than manufactured milk products.
- Car manufacturers that add expensive music systems to cars as standard equipment but relegate vital safety equipment such as passenger airbags to the status of optional extras.

In each of these cases, most people might agree that, objectively, buyers are being persuaded to make a choice against their own long-term self-interest. Consumer groups have an increasing tendency to highlight mis-selling of products that are against the best long-term interests of customers, and the results of such actions range from bad publicity to expensive product recalls and litigation. We will return to the issue of ethical behaviour in Chapter 10.

1.4.2 Suppliers

Suppliers provide an organization with goods and services that are transformed by the organization into value-added products for customers. Very often, suppliers are crucial to an organization's marketing success. This is particularly true where factors of production are in short supply and the main constraint on an organization selling more of its product is the shortage of production resources. For example, in 2004, world steel prices rose following an increase in demand – especially from China – relative to the available capacity. Some businesses in the engineering sector were forced to reduce their production because of difficulties in obtaining supplies of steel. For companies operating in highly competitive markets where differentiation between products is minimal, obtaining supplies at the best possible price may be vital in order to be able to pass on cost savings in the form of lower prices charged to customers. Where reliability of delivery to customers is crucial, unreliable suppliers may thwart a manufacturer's marketing efforts.

There is an argument that companies should act in a socially responsible way to their suppliers. Does a company favour local companies rather than possibly lower-priced overseas producers? (For example, many UK supermarkets have gone out of their way to highlight locally grown farm produce, which supports local farmers and has not incurred a high level of 'food miles'.) Does it unfairly use its dominant market power over small suppliers (an accusation that has been made against UK supermarkets for their treatment of their small farm suppliers)? Does it divide its orders between a large number of small suppliers, or place the bulk of its custom with a small handful of preferred suppliers? Does it favour new businesses or businesses representing minority interests when it places its orders?

Taking into account the needs of suppliers is a combination of shrewd business sense and good ethical practice. In business-to-business marketing, one company's supplier is likely to be another company's customer, and it is important to understand how suppliers, manufacturers and intermediaries work together to create value. The idea of a value chain is introduced later in this chapter.

1.4.3 Intermediaries

These often provide a valuable link between an organization and its customers. Large-scale manufacturing firms usually find it difficult to deal with each one of their final customers individually, so they choose instead to sell their products through **intermediaries**. The advantages of using intermediaries are discussed below. In some business sectors, access to effective intermediaries can be crucial for marketing success. For example, food manufacturers who do not get shelf space in the major supermarkets may find it difficult to achieve large volume sales.

Channels of distribution comprise all those people and organizations involved in the process of transferring title to a product from the producer to the consumer. Sometimes, products will be transferred directly from producer to final consumer – a factory selling specialized kitchen units direct to the public would fit into this category. Alternatively, the producer could sell its output through retailers or, if these are considered too numerous for the manufacturer to handle, it could deal with a wholesaler that in turn would sell to the retailer. More than one wholesaler could be involved in the process.

Intermediaries may need reassurance about the company's capabilities as a supplier that is capable of working with intermediaries to supply goods and services in a reliable and ethical manner. Many companies have suffered because they failed to take adequate account of the needs of their intermediaries (for example, Body Shop and McDonald's have faced protests from their franchisees where they felt threatened by a marketing strategy that was perceived as being against their own interests).

1.4.4 Competitors

In highly competitive markets, keeping an eye on competitors and trying to understand their likely next moves can be crucial. Think of the manoeuvring and out-manoeuvring that appears to take place between competitors in such highly competitive sectors as soft drinks, budget airlines and mobile phones. But who are a company's competitors? *Direct* competitors are generally similar in form and satisfy customers' needs in a similar way. *Indirect* competitors may appear different in form, but satisfy a fundamentally similar need. It is the indirect competitors that are most difficult to identify and to understand. What is a competitor for a cinema? Is it another cinema? A home rental movie? Or some completely different form of leisure activity that satisfies similar underlying needs?

1.4.5 Government

The demands of government agencies often take precedence over the needs of a company's customers. Government has a number of roles to play as stakeholder in commercial organizations.

- Commercial organizations provide governments with taxation revenue, so a healthy business sector is in the interests of government.
- Government is increasingly expecting business organizations to take over many responsibilities from the public sector – for example, with regard to the payment of sickness and maternity benefits to employees.
- It is through business organizations that governments achieve many of their economic and social objectives – for example, with respect to regional economic development and skills training.

Given government's role as a regulator that impacts on many aspects of business activity, companies often go to great lengths in seeking favourable responses from such agencies. In the case of many UK private-sector utility providers, promotional effort is often aimed more at regulatory bodies than final consumers. In the case of the water industry, promoting greater use of water to final consumers is unlikely to have any significant impact on a water utility company, but influencing the disposition of the Office of Water Regulation, which sets price limits and service standards, can have a major impact.

1.4.6 Pressure groups

Pressure groups form part of the broadly defined political environment. Members of pressure groups may never have been customers of a company and are never likely to be. Yet a pressure group can detract seriously from the image that the company has worked hard to develop. Many businesses have learnt to their cost that they cannot ignore pressure groups. It seems that, in Britain, fewer people may be voting in elections but this is more than offset by a greater willingness of people to make their voices heard through pressure groups.

1.4.7 The financial community

This includes financial institutions that have supported, are currently supporting or may support the organization in the future. Shareholders – both private and institutional – form an important element of this community and must be reassured that the organization is going to achieve its stated objectives. Many market expansion plans have failed because the company did not adequately consider the needs and expectations of potential investors.

1.4.8 Local communities

Society at large has rising expectations of organizations, and market-led companies often try to be seen as a 'good neighbour' in their local communities. Such companies can enhance their image through the use of charitable contributions, sponsorship of local events and being seen to support the local environment. Again, this may be interpreted either as part of a firm's genuine concern for its local community, or as a more cynical and pragmatic attempt to buy favour where its own interests are at stake. If a fast-food restaurant installs improved filters on its extractor fans, is it doing so to genuinely improve the lives of local residents, or merely in an attempt to forestall prohibition action taken by the local authority?

1.5 The internal environment

We must remember that the structure and politics of an organization affect the manner in which it responds to environmental change. We are all familiar with lumbering giants of companies that, like a supertanker, have ploughed ahead on a seemingly predetermined course and had difficulty in changing direction. During the late 1990s such well-respected companies as Sainsbury's and Marks & Spencer were accused of having internal structures and processes that were too rigid to cope with a changing external environment. Simply having a strong marketing department is not necessarily the best way of ensuring adaptation to change. Such companies may in fact create internal tensions that make them less effective at responding to changing consumer needs than where marketing responsibilities in their widest sense are spread throughout the organization.

The internal culture of an organization can greatly affect the way it responds to organizational change. In the case of Sainsbury's, its culture was probably too much based on hierarchy and tradition, which can be a weakness in a rapidly changing external environment. **Organizational culture** concerns the social and behavioural manifestation of a whole set of values that are shared by members of the organization. Cultural values can be shared in a number of ways, including: the way work is organized and experienced; how authority is exercised and delegated; how people are rewarded, organized and controlled; and the roles and expectations of staff and managers.

For many organizations, employees are the biggest item of cost, and potentially the biggest cause of delay in responding to environmental change. Having the right staff in the right place at the right time can demand a lot of flexibility on the part of employees. Many organizations have sought to improve the effectiveness of their employees through programmes to increase their level of engagement with the organization. When the external environment calls for change, employees who share a sense of engagement with the organization are more likely to share in the threats and opportunities that environmental change presents, compared with employees who feel alienated from the organization. Change can be facilitated by a sense of teamwork, and effective communication between different groups of employees within an organization.

It is not uncommon to find organizations where communication between these different groups is characterized by distrust, and even hostility, making it difficult for the organization to respond to environmental change in a rapid and coordinated manner. In Chapter 9 we will look in more detail at the effects of internal management structure on an organization's ability to respond to external environmental change.

1.6 Contextual issues in a dynamic environment

So far in this introductory chapter, we have broken the business environment down into a number of component parts. These are the basic building blocks that we will come back to throughout the book. However, the key to analysing the business environment is to see the links between these component parts. A number of these linkages have already been mentioned – for example, how the political environment affects the nature of the economic environment that the business faces. Within the microenvironment, members of the local community may also be customers of an organization. Community groups may influence government agencies, which in turn affect the activities of business organizations.

As well as taking a snapshot of the interdependency between elements of the business environment, we also need to consider their dynamic interaction. Successful business organizations have spotted trends, especially the interaction between trends in the different environments. For example, one trend in the social environment has been an increasing fear of crime, especially against children. Another trend in the technological environment has been the falling cost and increasing sophistication of mobile phones. By putting these two trends together, businesses have developed novel products – for example, mobile phones that can track children and automatically send warning messages if the child strays beyond a predetermined zone.

We have introduced the main levels of the business environment in a manner that provides a foundation for the structure of this book. We will begin by looking at the macroenvironment before moving on to the micro- and internal environments. But the point cannot be stressed enough that the different elements of an organization's environment are very much interrelated and, in order to stress this interrelatedness, we will now briefly examine some common themes that run through all levels of the environment. We will focus on information and communication as two crucial elements that run through an organization's environment. We will then consider some simple frameworks that integrate the elements of the business environment, beginning with identification of the members of an organization's 'environmental set'. We will then integrate these within the concept of a 'value chain', and move on to take a dynamic look at these relationships and the emergence of power within them.

1.6.1 The interdependency of organizations in the business environment

No organization exists in a vacuum, and a crucial aspect of understanding the business environment lies in understanding the networks of formal and informal relationships that exist between a firm and its various stakeholders.

The people and organizations within a particular company's business environment that are of particular relevance to it are sometimes referred to as its **environmental set**. An example of an environmental set for a car manufacturer is shown in Figure 1.4.

Some of these relationships between members of an organization's environmental set will be latent rather than actual – for example, a company may currently have no dealings with a prospective customer, but knows that one day they could become an actual customer. Some actual relationships with set members may be casual, infrequent and relatively unimportant for the company, whereas others will be crucial and the company will seek to develop long-term relationships, rather than rely on casual transactions. It may have power over some set members, but other set members may have considerable power over it. Although the environmental set shown in Figure 1.4 depicts a network focused on one organization, in fact, networks can bring together these individual set members – for example, suppliers may have developed strategic alliances with the focal company's key competitors.

The relationship between set members is likely to be complex and constantly changing. Change can take a number of forms, including:

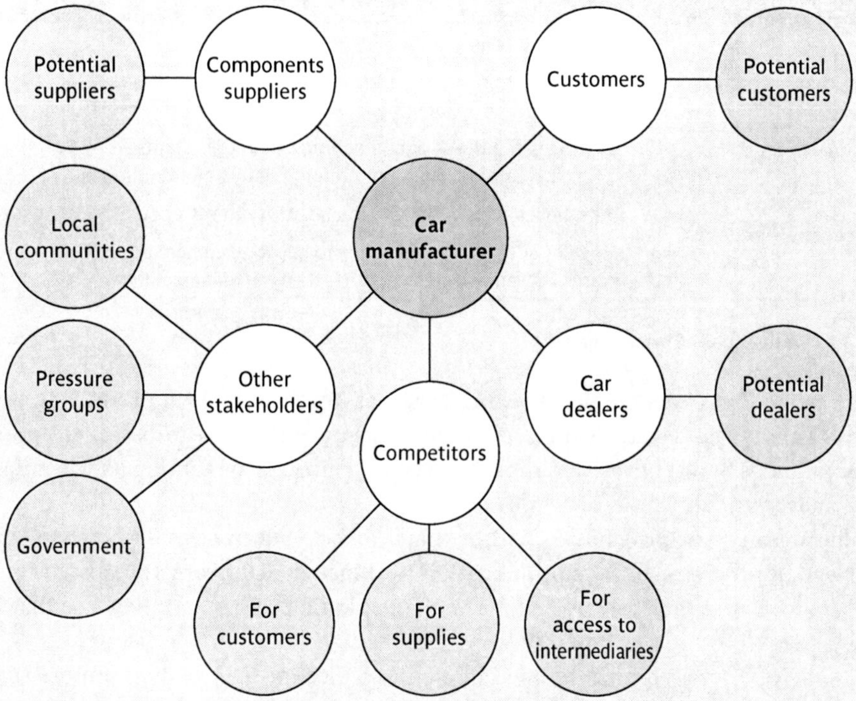

Figure 1.4 The 'environmental set' of a typical car manufacturer

- a tendency for firms to seek the stability of long-term relationships with key members of their environmental set, rather than treating them all on a fairly casual basis
- shifts in the balance of power between members of the environment (e.g. retailers becoming more dominant relative to manufacturers)
- the emergence of new groups of potential customers or suppliers
- fringe pressure groups may come to represent mainstream opinions, in response to changes in social attitudes.

Understanding the relationship between members of an organization's environmental set is a crucial part of environmental analysis, and in Chapter 7 we will return to look in more detail at the nature of relationships that bring companies together.

1.6.2 Value chains

It was noted at the beginning of this chapter that the purpose of organizations is to transform inputs bought from suppliers into outputs sold to customers. In carrying out such a transformation, organizations add value to resources. In fact, the buyer of one firm's output may

Value chain member	Functions performed
Farmer	Produces a basic commodity product - milk
Milk merchant	Adds value to the milk by arranging for it to be collected from the farm, checked for purity and made available to milk processors
Ice cream manufacturer	By processing the milk and adding other ingredients, turns raw milk into ice cream; through promotion, creates a brand image
Wholesaler	Buys bulk stocks of ice cream and stores in warehouses close to customers
Retailer	Provides a facility for customers to buy ice cream at a place and a time that is convenient to them rather than the manufacturer

Figure 1.5 A value chain for ice cream

be another firm that treats the products purchased as inputs to its own production process. It in turn will add value to the resources and sell on its outputs to customers. This process can continue as goods and services pass though several organizations, gaining added value as they change hands. This is the basis of a **value chain**.

An illustration of the principles of a value chain can be made by considering the value-added transformation processes that occur in the process of making ice cream available to consumers. Figure 1.5 shows who may be involved in the value-adding process and the value that is added at each stage.

The value of the raw milk contained in a block of ice cream may be no more than a few pennies, but the final product may be sold for over £1. Customers are happy to pay £1 for a few pennies' worth of milk because it is transformed into a product that they value and it is made available at a time and place where they want it. In fact, on a hot sunny day at the beach, many buyers would be prepared to pay even more to a vendor that brings ice cream to them. Value – as defined by customers – has been added at each stage of the transformation process.

Who should be in the value chain? The ice cream manufacturer might decide that it can add value at the preceding and subsequent stages better than other people are capable of doing. It may, for example, decide to operate its own farms and produce its own milk, or sell its ice cream direct to the public. The crucial question to be asked is whether the company can add value more cost-effectively than other suppliers and intermediaries. In a value chain, it is only value in the eyes of customers that matters. If high value is attached to having ice cream easily available, then distributing it through a limited number of company-owned shops will not add much value to the product.

The process of expanding a firm's activities through the value chain is often referred to as vertical integration where ownership is established. Backward vertical integration occurs where a manufacturer buys back into its suppliers. Forward vertical integration occurs where it buys into its outlets. Many firms expand in both directions.

With service being used as an increasingly important basis for differentiation between competing products, it is important that an organization looks not only outwards at the value chain, but also inwards at its own service–profit chain. The concept of the service–profit chain is based on the idea that employee satisfaction and productivity feeds into customer satisfaction and loyalty, thereby improving profitability. Profitability in turn can help create a more productive and satisfying work environment (see Figure 1.6).

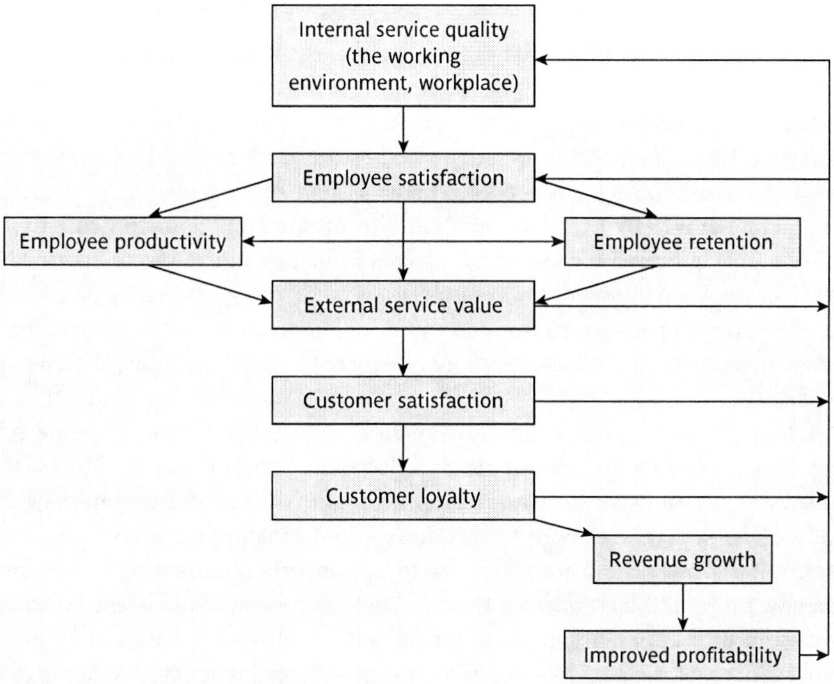

Figure 1.6 The service–profit chain
Source: adapted from Heskett *et al.* 2003

The growth of the internet has led to the development of a modified form of 'virtual value chain' to try to explain how information-based industries operate a value chain that is distinct from traditional models based on raw materials, production and distribution. While the traditional value chain may be applicable to industries involved in the movement of goods through a tangible, physical marketplace, other information-based industries (such as financial services) operate in a market 'space'. It has been argued that, for these companies, the value chain consists of content, infrastructure and context. The content is what is being offered, the infrastructure is what exists to enable transactions and the context is how the goods are offered.

1.6.3 The information environment

Information represents a bridge between the organization and its environment, and is the means by which a picture of the changing environment is built up within the organization. Knowledge is one of the greatest assets of most organizations and its contribution to sustainable competitive advantage has been noted by many. In 1991, Ikujiro Nonaka began an article in the *Harvard Business Review* with a simple statement: 'In an economy where the only certainty is uncertainty, the one sure source of lasting competitive advantage is knowledge' (Nonaka 1991). A firm's knowledge base is likely to include, among other things, an understanding of the precise needs of customers, how those needs are likely to change over time, how those needs are satisfied in terms of efficient and effective production systems, and an understanding of competitors' activities.

Information about the current state of the environment is used as a starting point for planning future strategy, based on assumptions about how the environment will change. It is also vital to monitor the implementation of an organization's corporate plans and to note the cause of any deviation from plan, and to identify whether these are caused by internal or external environmental factors. Information allows management to improve its strategic planning, tactical implementation of programmes, and its monitoring and control. In turbulent environments, having access to timely and relevant information can give a firm a competitive advantage. This can be manifested, for example, in the ability to spot turning points in the business cycle ahead of competitors; to respond more rapidly to customers' changing preferences; and to adapt manufacturing schedules more closely to demand patterns, thereby avoiding a build-up of stocks.

Information collection, processing, transmission and storage technologies are continually improving, as witnessed by the development of electronic point of sale (EPOS) systems. These have enabled organizations to greatly enhance the quality of the information they have about some aspects of their operating environment. However, information is becoming more accessible, not just to one particular organization, but also to its competitors. Attention is therefore moving away from how information is collected to who is best able to make use of the information.

Large organizations operating in complex and turbulent environments often use information to build models of their environment, or at least sub-components of it. Some of these can be quite general, as in the case of the models of the national economy that many large companies have developed. From a general model of the economy a firm can predict how a specific item of government policy (for example, increasing the rate of value added tax on luxury goods) will impact directly and indirectly on sales of its own products.

We look in more detail at the ways in which information technology influences firms' business environment in Chapter 4, and in Chapter 15 explore the implications of information for firms' responses to environmental change.

1.6.4 The communication environment

Communications bring together elements within a firm's environmental set. With no communication, there is no possibility for trading to take place. Although we talk today about a communications 'revolution', businesses in previous centuries have faced the challenge of rapid developments in communication. Consider the following historic developments in communications, and their impacts on businesses.

- The development of canals and railways during the industrialization of nineteenth-century England allowed manufacturers to communicate with customers who had previously been impossible or very expensive to reach. Manufacturers used improved communications to exploit emerging mass-production techniques that allowed them to compete in distant markets with relatively low-priced mass-produced goods.
- The development of steamships allowed companies to communicate with distant parts of the world, opening up new markets for their finished products and allowing new sources of

Thinking around the subject: The tiny spy that follows you home?

Big Brother may be following you home, reporting back where you go and how you use the product that you have just bought from a shop. RFId (Radio Frequency Identification) would seem like a blessing to companies keen to find out more about their products after they have left their shelves. But is their use ethical?

RFId involves placing a small radio transmitter on a product so that its movement can be tracked remotely. So far, RFId has mainly been applied to pallets and caseloads of goods, rather than individual consumer goods. The cost of tags, as well as the equipment needed to read them and process the data, means that item-level tagging may be still some way off. But the prospect of rapidly falling costs and greater miniaturization has alerted companies to the opportunities, and some consumer groups to the potential threats. In 2007, the EU's information society commissioner, Viviane Reding, called for a debate about the security and privacy issues surrounding RFId (*Financial Times* 2006).

Consumer groups and privacy campaigners have expressed concern that RFId tags could be used to build up massive databases of individuals' shopping, leisure and travel habits. These databases could be exploited by unscrupulous businesses and also become a target for cybercriminals. The fact that RFId tags track the actual items that people buy has led to fears that RFId data could be much more intrusive than the information retailers typically collect through bar code data and loyalty card programmes. As the cost of RFId tags falls and their versatility increases, they have the potential to be read at a distance without a consumer's knowledge. Would you want a bookshop 'spying' on how and where you read a book that you recently bought from the shop?

Not to be outdone, proponents of RFId have gone on the offensive to present the positive elements of the technology, such as its use in preventing counterfeit drugs reaching consumers, or in aviation, where tags have been fixed to aircraft spares and safety equipment. Retailers have attached RFId tags to goods to monitor thefts, and have argued that honest customers would have nothing to fear and would benefit from lower prices resulting from reduced shoplifting.

If you were a commercial organization contemplating the use of RFId, which way do you think the privacy debate will go? Are pressure groups being paranoid about the data that companies can keep on an individual, when in reality government agencies routinely collect much more information about us – for example, through vehicle number plate recognition? Will consumers be won over by the safety and security aspects of RFId, in much the same way as many people would readily accept the necessity for 'sinister' monitoring of their movements by CCTV? Would the most likely outcome of the EU review of RFId be a compromise, perhaps limiting how long RFId data could be kept and who would be allowed access to it?

supply of raw materials. British manufacturers of consumer goods exploited new markets in parts of the Empire served by the new shipping lines.

- The absence of a reliable postal and telephone system has often been cited as a reason for the failure of businesses to grow in less developed parts of the world.

Today, the internet has emerged as a versatile tool in an organization's relationship with its business environment, combining a communication function with a distribution function. The

Thinking around the subject: Firms face up to Facebook

In the old days, companies had research departments that listened to customers, and advertising departments that sent messages to them. Although customers may have learned about a company through word of mouth, this communication channel was essentially limited to small groups of friends. The communication environment has changed rapidly in recent years and the development of 'Web 2.0' has facilitated communication between customers themselves, as well as between companies and their customers. So-called 'social networking' sites, such as Facebook and YouTube, have led to many widely publicized problems for companies. For example, in 2005, the computer manufacturer Dell was hit by influential blogger Jeff Jarvis complaining about poor customer service provided by Dell. Fellow consumers, no longer passive in their dissatisfaction, joined in with comments of their own, and stories of 'Dell Hell' rapidly became mainstream news. Companies cannot afford simply to watch these sites – to do so could result in a minor irritation spiralling into a serious problem. Traditional media have sometimes picked up dissent, but social networking sites allow such dissent to gain momentum much more quickly (Bowen 2007).

Increasingly, companies have been mingling in social networking sites, and have sometimes created their own sites as community forums. Dell, for example, established the Dell2Dell blog, in an attempt to gain some control over communication about it. But on other occasions, companies have sponsored blogs without declaring their hand. The retailer Wal-Mart covertly sponsored a blog that was supposedly operated by a couple camping in the store's car parks. It had hoped to manipulate content to put the company in a good light, but eventually the exercise turned into a PR disaster when news broke that the company had in fact been controlling the blog.

A significant challenge for companies is the sometimes blurred distinction between communication that is internal and external to company. Social networking sites allow employees to spread stories of dissent about their company among their circle of friends. Using simpler communication technologies, a slanderous comment about a bad employer might have gone no further than a small circle of friends and family. But with large numbers of friends linked through Facebook, dissent can spread much more widely.

Do social networking sites change the rules of the communication environment? Or do they essentially require the same basic skills of listening and responding that have always been needed with more traditional communication media?

ability of companies to rapidly exchange information with their suppliers and intermediaries has allowed for the development of increasingly efficient supply chains, initially using EDI (electronic data interface) systems, but more recently using internet, intranet and extranet-based systems. Without efficient communication systems, attempts to introduce just-in-time production systems and rapid customer response are likely to be impeded.

The internet has an increasing role in allowing companies to communicate with their final consumers using email. Some companies have used the internet to cut out intermediaries altogether, through a process of 'disintermediation', although in reality the internet has allowed a new generation of 'information intermediary' (e.g. Expedia.com and esure.com) to appear in large numbers. As a promotional medium, a great strength of the internet is to target promotional messages that are directly relevant to the user, so, for example, the online retailer Amazon can present a selection of merchandise to a visitor to its site, based on what they had previously viewed or bought. Websites are increasingly being enabled to allow immediate fulfilment of a request, such as confirmation of a hotel booking or reservation of a plane ticket. Fixed-line and, increasingly, mobile internet services have narrowed the gap between a potential buyer receiving a message and being able to act upon it.

1.6.5 The ethical environment

All systems need rules if they are to operate efficiently and effectively. This can be observed in any marketplace, whether it is a fruit and vegetable market or a stock market. The market functions only because all participants conduct their actions according to a shared set of rules. These rules can be either informal or based on formal regulation. In many less developed economies, the dominant basis for rules is focused on embedded codes of trust. Increasingly in Western societies, commercial relationships are governed by formality and regulation. Of course, informal rules in a market may not always be in consumers' best interests, as sometimes happens when suppliers have formal or informal understandings about how they can restrict the level of competition between themselves.

In Western societies there is increasing concern that relationships between members of the environmental set should be conducted in an ethical manner. Ethics is essentially about the definition of what is right and wrong. However, it can be difficult to agree just what is right and wrong – no two people have precisely the same opinion. Culture has a great effect in defining ethics, and what is considered unethical in one society may be considered perfectly acceptable in another.

It can also be difficult to distinguish between ethics and legality – for example, it may not yet be strictly illegal to exploit the gullibility of children in advertisements, but it may nevertheless be unethical.

Today, ethical considerations are present in many business decisions. An example of a current issue is whether soft drinks and confectionery manufacturers should sponsor school activities. Is it ethical to expose children to subconscious positive messages about junk food at a time of increasing obesity?

With expanding media availability and an increasingly intelligent audience, it is becoming easier to expose examples of unethical business practice. Moreover, many television audiences appear to enjoy watching programmes that reveal the alleged unethical practices of household-name companies. To give one example, the media has on many occasions focused attention on the alleged exploitative employment practices of suppliers used by some of the biggest brand names in sportswear.

We return to the subject of ethics in Chapter 10.

1.6.6 The ecological environment

Issues affecting our natural ecology have captured the public imagination in recent years. The destruction of tropical rainforests and the depletion of the ozone layer, leading to global warming, have serious implications for our quality of life – not necessarily today, but for future

Figure 1.7 Like many bars, this one loudly promotes a 'happy hour' period during which alcohol is sold at a reduced price. For pub operators, such promotions may be vital to boost margins, especially if all bars in the area are offering equally low prices. Unfortunately, one consequence of cheap alcohol and 'buy one, get one free' offers is to increase 'binge drinking', with many town centres becoming noisy and violent areas at night time, fuelled by excessive drinking. For any individual pub, how does it balance the need for aggressive price promotion to customers with the need to appear socially responsible, for fear of further government regulation of the sector? Adverts for alcohol now routinely include warnings about the consequences for the customer of excessive drinking, but often in much smaller print than the main price information. Should a pub simply stop '2 for 1' offers and earn a higher margin on a smaller volume of sales? Although this may seem to be a responsible and profitable approach, it is unlikely to work if other pubs continue with their 2 for 1 offers – determined drinkers will simply make their way to the cheapest pub that has communicated the best offers. To illustrate the complexity of the task facing the sector, bar owners in some towns have voluntarily got together to try to agree collectively to stop price promotions that many believe lead to binge drinking. Agreement of all bar owners would be crucial, because otherwise drinkers would simply track down the cheapest outlet, and other bars would be forced to defensively cut their prices to retain business. But does government see this as a benign example of socially motivated cooperation? Not the Office of Fair Trading, which gave a veiled threat to a group of Essex bar owners that they could be prosecuted for operating a cartel and illegally fixing prices.

generations. Business organizations are often seen as being in conflict with the need to protect the natural ecology. It is very easy for critics of commercial organizations to point to cases where greed and mismanagement have created long-lasting or permanent ecological damage. Have rainforests been destroyed partly by our greed for more hardwood furniture? More locally, is our impatience for getting to our destination quickly the reason why many natural habitats have been lost to new road developments?

Only a few years ago, most business organizations in Western developed economies could have dismissed ecological concerns as something that only fanatical, minority groups in the population were concerned about. In the 1970s and 1980s, 'environmentalists' might have been ridiculed and associated with unrealistic dreams of the 'good life'. Today, the situation is very different, and just about all business organizations need to take the ecological environment seriously.

There are many good reasons why the ecological environment is rising up the agenda of business organizations.

- At its simplest, many organizations face segments of customers who prefer to make purchases that they believe to be ecologically responsible. For a variety of underlying psychological and sociological reasons, some consumers may feel better about their purchase if it is perceived to be 'good' for the planet. Of course, whether it is actually good or not may be another factor, and sometimes peer-group pressure may be at variance with the technical reality. As an example, the *Independent* newspaper reported in 2007 a case, probably not an isolated one, of a London house owner who had installed a solar panel on the north side of their house. Technically, the panel would be useless, because of the lack of direct sunlight, but for the house owner, the north side of the house could be seen by everybody. A panel on the south side of the house would not be visible, and would be less able therefore to make a statement about their 'green' credentials.
- Business organizations are dependent on the ecological environment for natural resources. If ecosystems are not managed carefully, resources that are affordable today and taken for granted may no longer be available in the future, and firms will have to pay higher prices for possibly inferior substitutes. As an example, the fishing industry in Britain has been greatly reduced in size through overfishing of the North Sea. Even companies further down the value chain of fish have been affected by this depletion of the ecological environment – for example, fish and chip shops have had to find alternative types of fish to replace the increasingly expensive cod.
- Firms can gain advantage in a market by leading in the use of alternative natural resources ahead of competitors, giving them a competitive advantage when the alternative becomes the only, or the most cost-effective, source available. However, it may be difficult for firms to evaluate not only what is going to be a better use of resources for the planet, but also one that is going to be better for their organization in particular. To illustrate this difficulty, many firms have been advocating a greater use of 'biofuels', which are derived from renewable crops, rather than fossil fuels. However, there is argument about the relative size of the ecological and social impacts of fossil fuels and renewable energy sources. The dilemma for business was illustrated in July 2007, when Virgin Group, never an organization to miss an opportunity for good publicity, announced that it would be greatly increasing the use of

biofuels for its fleet of trains. However, just a few weeks later, National Express Group, another UK operator of trains and buses, announced that it was abandoning its previous plan for increased use of biofuels. It had thought through the implications of farmers growing an increasing proportion of their crops for fuel rather than food, which could be expected to lead to progressively higher prices for biofuels, and sharply increasing food prices. The consumer appeal of biofuels was also wearing thin, with the scene set for the rich Western countries benefiting from a new source of fuel, while less developed countries could no longer afford basic food items because crops were being diverted to fuel the West's appetite for energy. In this scenario, biofuels became less cost-effective and socially acceptable.

- Markets are often incapable collectively of alleviating pending problems in ecosystems, and political intervention may be necessary to prevent a complete failure of the ecosystem. In the example above, individual fishermen may have had no incentive to limit their own fishing, until they reached the point where only government intervention could protect fish stocks from their own individual activities, and ultimately preserve long-term employment for companies and availability of supplies for consumers. Business organizations should be able to read the political environment and be prepared for politically imposed change in their business plans. See the case study at the end of this chapter – if you were running an airline, what level of future government taxation or restrictions on air travel would you factor into your future development plans, given current concerns about the effects of aircraft emissions?

We will return to the ecological environment in Chapter 10.

1.6.7 Systems theory, complexity and chaos

Systems theory was proposed in the 1940s by the biologist Ludwig von Bertalanffy. It is the interdisciplinary study of the abstract organization of phenomena, and investigates both the principles common to all complex entities and the models that can be used to describe them. More recently it has been applied to mathematics, computing and ecological systems. Some elements of systems theory have been applied to the modelling of relationships within the environmental sets of business organizations that we discussed earlier.

Although a number of attempts have been made to apply the principles of systems theory to the business environment, there are major differences between scientific models and the business environment. Very often, the natural sciences deal with **closed systems** in which all the parameters are known, and each can be monitored and controlled. Admittedly, this is not always true; for example, in some ecological studies it may not be possible to identify all life forms that might possibly migrate into a system. By contrast, the business environment is essentially an **open system** in which it is very difficult to place a boundary round the environment and to identify the complete set of components within the system. Elements may come or go from the system and a researcher generally has no control over these elements in the way that a laboratory-based scientist could carry out controlled experiments.

Two developments of systems theory are complexity theory and chaos theory. Complexity theory is concerned with the behaviour over time of certain kinds of complex system. The systems of interest to complexity theory, under certain conditions, perform in regular, predictable ways; under other conditions they exhibit behaviour in which regularity and predictability is lost. Almost undetectable differences in initial conditions lead to gradually diverging system reactions until eventually the evolution of behaviour is quite dissimilar.

Chaos theory describes the dynamics of sensitive systems that are mathematically deterministic but nearly impossible to predict, due to their sensitivity to initial conditions. The weather is an example of a chaotic system. In order to make long-term weather forecasts it would be necessary to take an infinite number of measurements, which would be impossible to do. Also, because the atmosphere is chaotic, tiny uncertainties would eventually overwhelm any calculations and defeat the accuracy of the forecast. One of the most widely quoted examples of chaos theory is the butterfly that flaps its wings and in so doing creates destabilizing forces that trigger subsequent events, resulting in a hurricane on the other side of the world.

Many business environments may be considered as chaotic in that it can be very difficult to predict the sequence of events following an initial disturbance to equilibrium. In Chapter 15 we return to the subject of risk and turbulence in the business environment.

1.6.8 Business cycles

The business environment is rarely in a stable state, and many phenomena follow a cyclical pattern. Companies are particularly interested in understanding business cycles and in predicting the cycle as it affects their sector. (We return to the subject of business cycles in Chapter 13.) Although the business cycle is widely talked about, there are other cyclical factors evident in the business environment. The interaction between supply and demand can result in a cycle of high prices, leading to new entrants coming into the market, which leads to lower prices, which makes the market less attractive, so companies leave the market, so prices begin to rise, which attracts new entrants to the market, and the cycle repeats itself.

As well as cycles affecting tangible resources, it is also possible to identify cycles in *ideas* about how the business environment operates. There have been many studies of how ideas grow to become mainstream, and the critical factors involved in this process. Chaos theory and the study of mimetics have offered an explanation of how, through random events, a small local idea can develop into a global paradigm. An analysis by Gladwell discusses how reaching a critical point is facilitated by the existence of 'connectors', 'mavens' and the 'stickiness' of an idea (Gladwell 2000). One such idea that took hold in the 1990s was 'relationship marketing' as a method of conducting exchanges between a company and its customers. It followed a long series of 'big new ideas' that have risen and fallen over time.

1.6.9 Risk and uncertainty

The business environment for most organizations is rarely in a stable state. There is no certainty that the future will follow the pattern of the recent past. For companies operating in a low-tech, low-scale environment, adaptation to change may be quite easy. But for a large organization, which has to invest heavily for the future, risks can be enormous. For very large projects, such as the construction of the European Airbus 'super jumbo' A380 aircraft, the risk and uncertainty was great not only for one company to take upon itself, but for the consortium of companies that makes up Airbus. Apart from uncertainty about the technology, and the risk of cost overruns, there is considerable risk concerning the business environment of airlines that would be customers for the Airbus. Will passengers want to fly between a small number of very large airports in very large aircraft? Or would they prefer the alternative model of the future, which sees larger numbers of smaller aircraft flying between a much bigger network of smaller airports? What will happen to fuel prices? Will long-term real increases in fuel prices put up air fares to the point where the long-term growth rate in passenger traffic is slowed down? Will governments introduce new taxation on aviation fuel, again possibly slowing down demand for air travel? And there is always the threat of terrorism, which caused such uncertainty following 11 September 2001 and could recur at any time.

All aspects of the business environment that have been introduced in this chapter carry an element of uncertainty. Within the microenvironment, what is the risk of a new, well-resourced competitor emerging? What if a strategic supplier goes out of business or is acquired by your competitor? What happens if government introduces new legislation or imposes new taxation? Within the macroenvironment, there is continual uncertainty for most companies about the future state of the economy and the impact of changes in disposable income on consumer expenditure. What would happen if a new government was elected with a radically different political agenda? And, in the internal environment, what is the risk of not being able to recruit the skilled employees the company needs? What would be the effect of new legislation on the recruitment and payment of employees?

There are many models for trying to comprehend the complexity of the business environment, and to attach risk levels to the different elements of it. In Chapter 15, we will look in more detail at some of these methods, including cross-impact analysis, and environmental threat and opportunity profiles. We will also discuss the development of scenarios, which is an attempt to paint a picture of the future. It may be possible to build a small number of alternative scenarios based on differing assumptions. This qualitative approach is a means of handling environmental issues that are hard to quantify because they are less structured, more uncertain and may involve very complex relationships. Scenarios may paint a picture of a major crisis or source of turbulence facing a company. For an airline, this could be a renewed terrorist threat elsewhere in the world, or the crash of one of its own aircraft. Although it may not be possible to predict the exact detail of the event, the company could establish a set of guidelines for what it should do in the event that a scenario comes true. For example, following 11 September 2001, the airline Virgin Atlantic rapidly downsized its fleet and laid off staff. It had seen the future, where a major incident caused a rapid fall in passenger traffic, before consumers regained confidence and returned in their previous numbers.

Case study: A war of words over green airline claims

Global warming has emerged as a major concern to consumers throughout the world. Initially, awareness of the causes and consequences of global warming was confined to a small part of the population, but linkages with the destructive tsunami of December 2004 and 2005's Hurricane Katrina brought home to many people the possible long-term harmful consequences of excessive emissions of CO_2 to the atmosphere. Global warming was no longer a humorous subject where people in the developed countries of northern Europe and the United States focused on the benign consequences of mild winters and the exotic new plants that they would be able to grow. Destructive winds, rising sea levels and devastation of low-lying areas were increasingly coming to be seen as a consequence of our prodigious use of fossil fuels.

The reduction of CO_2 emissions had already been taken on board by many manufacturing companies, the largest of which had seen reductions through a system of carbon trading initiated by the Kyoto treaty. But one business sector – civil aviation – had been quite notable for its failure to embrace the principles of reducing carbon emissions. Critics of the sector pointed out that as a result of worldwide agreements, aviation fuel was not taxed, in contrast to the steep taxation on most other forms of fuel. Although aircraft had become more efficient in their use of fuel during the 1990s, this was more than offset by booming demand for flights with no-frills airlines such as easyJet and Ryanair. It seemed that the budget airline companies were very effective in communicating their low price message to customers, who filled their planes, often with more thought about a cheap weekend break by the Mediterranean, rather than the unknown and remote possibilities of global warming. Indeed, the general public seemed to be somewhat hypocritical about the effects of global warming. Some still thought that the problem would go away, and may have recalled previous 'scares' such as the imminent depletion of fossil fuels and the effects of 'acid rain', neither of which had really affected most people's lives and had subsequently slipped down the news agenda. Even in respect of 'greenhouse gas' emissions, people may profess to being sympathetic to green causes, but then buy something that is anything but green. As an example, one survey of holidaymakers conducted in 2007 suggested that consideration of greenhouse gas emissions came way behind other evaluation criteria when choosing a holiday, including the ease of getting a sun lounger, proximity to the beach and the range of nightlife available.

How should airlines respond to the apparent threat to their business model that had been thrown up by the issue of global warming? Should they put their head in the sand and hope that the problem would go away? Should they concentrate on giving customers what they have repeatedly said they want – cheap flights – and hope that human hedonism will win out over feelings of social responsibility? Or should airlines be on their guard against possible government intervention that could undermine their business model? How could they prevent new legislation? And, if it was introduced, how could they respond to it?

Politicians were becoming increasingly frustrated by the airlines' seeming lack of willingness to address issues of climate change. Already, the Bishop of London had described air travel as 'immoral', for the way that wealthy Western travellers could inflict harm on people in the less developed world through climate change. Could a significant number of airline passengers really begin to feel guilty about flying away for a cheap weekend break, and cut back their purchases?

In January 2007, the communications battle was stepped up when a UK government minister described Ryanair as 'the irresponsible face of capitalism'. He had argued that while other industries and consumers were cutting down their emissions, Ryanair had expanded at a phenomenal rate, churning out more CO_2 into the atmosphere at a time when other industry sectors were reducing their emissions. Friends of the Earth, in a report entitled 'Aviation and global climate change', noted that commercial jets were adding 600 million tonnes of CO_2 a year to global warming, almost as much as for the whole of Africa. With such negative communication, would Ryanair suffer as people felt guilty about flying, and governments increasingly moved to regulate civil aviation and make it more expensive, especially for the price-sensitive segments that the no-frills airlines had been targeting?

Rarely known to be quiet, the chief executive of Ryanair, Michael O'Leary, went on a communications offensive. Dismissing the minister as 'knowing nothing', he presented Ryanair as a friend rather than an enemy of global warming. He argued that travellers should feel reassured that Ryanair used one of the world's most modern and fuel-efficient fleets of aircraft. Moreover, Ryanair's business model of filling seats at the lowest price really meant that carbon emissions per passenger were much lower than those of traditional full-service airlines, which often flew half-empty planes. And then there was the fact that budget airlines operated an extensive point-to-point network avoiding the costly and environmentally harmful effects of taking two indirect flights via a central hub airport.

The war of words that has ensued over airlines' contribution to global warming demonstrates the difficulty that many ordinary consumers have in evaluating rival claims. Many may have taken to heart governments' and church leaders' claims, which made them feel guilty about flying. But even if hypocritical consumers were happy to carry on flying and not backing their expressed concerns for climate change with changes in their behaviour, there was certainly a possibility that governments would intervene. Both the UK Government and EU Commission had floated the idea of taxing aviation fuel, and bringing aircraft emissions within the scope of the EU Emissions Trading Scheme. Some airlines, such as Ryanair, continued to sound off against the government, positioning them as the consumer's champion. But others, including easyJet, sensed the change in mood of the public and government bodies, and openly supported the idea of bringing aircraft emissions into the carbon trading regime. Was easyJet being philanthropic? Was it simply putting out a message that it thought its customers would want to hear, helping them salve their conscience and give easyJet a better image than arch-rival Ryanair? Or was there a shrewd underlying commercial advantage, in which the modern, efficient easyJet fleet may use less than its allotted share of carbon emissions, which it could then sell on to less efficient 'legacy' carriers? Should the company begin planning for higher taxes on flying, and be prepared for reducing its growth plans if some marginal customers decided that a weekend break by the Mediterranean was no longer a luxury that they could afford?

Source: based on Ben Hall and Kevin Done, Pearson brought to earth in airline row, *Financial Times*, 6 January 2007; Charles Starmer-Smith, Green travel: the winners and losers, *Daily Telegraph*, 12 January 2008; Jimmy Lee Shreeve, Green skies?, *Daily Telegraph*, 26 June 2007; Friends of the Earth, 'Aviation and global climate change', 2000

QUESTIONS

1 Discuss the possible policy options open to government to curb aircraft emissions, and assess their likely effects on 'budget' airlines.

2 The case study refers to the apparent hypocrisy of consumers, who may claim to be concerned about the environment, but nevertheless continue to fly. What might bring about a narrowing of this gap between what consumers think and what they actually do? How could a company such as easyJet measure and monitor consumers' attitudes?

3 What might be the consequences for a budget airline of government policy measures that have the effect of doubling air fares in real terms? Critically discuss how a budget airline might respond.

Summary

This chapter has reviewed the complex nature of an organization's business environment. The environment can be analysed at three levels: the microenvironment, comprising firms and individuals that an organization directly interacts with (or that directly affect its activities); the macroenvironment, comprising general forces that may eventually impact on the microenvironment; and the internal environment, comprising other functions within the organization.

This chapter has stressed the interrelatedness of all elements of the business environment. Although the social environment and technological environment are identified as separate elements, the two are closely linked (for example, technology has resulted in mass ownership of cars, which has in turn affected social behaviour).

Subsequent chapters pay attention to each of the elements of the business environment, but the complexity of linkages must never be forgotten. **Chapter 15** seeks to integrate these elements within dynamic analytical frameworks, which can be used to develop holistic forecasts of the future business environment.

Key terms

Channels of distribution (15)
Closed system (28)
Environmental set (18)
Intermediaries (15)
Internal environment (6)
Macroenvironment (6)
Microenvironment (5)
Open system (28)
Organizational culture (17)
Stakeholders (13)
Transformation process (4)
Value chain (20)

Chapter review questions

1 Discuss what you understand by the term 'business environment'.
2 Suppliers and intermediaries are important stakeholders in the microenvironment of business. Discuss the evolving role and functions of these stakeholders in business organizations.
3 Members of an environmental set are becoming increasingly interdependent. Identify examples of this interdependency, and discuss the reasons why it is happening.

Activities

1 Develop a checklist of points that you consider to be important indicators of whether an organization is responsive to changes in its business environment. Why did you choose these indicators? Now apply your checklist to three selected organizations: one a traditional manufacturing industry, the second a service-based commercial organization, and the third a government organization that serves the public. What, if anything, should your chosen organizations do to become more responsive to changes in their business environment?

2 Go back to Figure 1.4, which shows an environmental set for a car manufacturer. If you are studying at a college or university, repeat this diagram, but show the environmental set of your college/university.

3 Choose an industry sector with which you are familiar (e.g. mobile phones, grocery retail). Identify the elements in firms' macroenvironments that may affect their profitability during the next ten years.

Further Reading

A good starting point for understanding competitive advantage of firms and the role of value chains in achieving this is provided in Michael Porter's frequently cited book:

Porter, M.E. (1985) *Competitive Advantage: Creating and Sustaining Superior Performance*, Free Press.

There is now an extensive literature on the development of close buyer–seller relationships. A good summary of the principles can be found in the following texts.

Batonda, G. and Perry, C. (2003) 'Approaches to relationship development processes in inter-firm networks', *European Journal of Marketing*, Vol. 37, No. 10, pp. 1457–84.

Christopher, M., Payne, A. and Ballantyne, D. (2001) *Relationship Marketing: Creating Stakeholder Value*, London, Butterworth-Heinemann.

Donaldson, W.G. and O'Toole, T. (2007) *Strategic Market Relationships: From Strategy to Implementation* (2nd edn), Chichester, John Wiley.

Healy, M., Hastings, K., Brown, L. and Gardiner, M. (2001) 'The old, the new and the complicated: a trilogy of marketing relationships', *European Journal of Marketing*, Vol. 35, No. 1, pp. 182–93.

This chapter has provided a general overview of the components that make up the business environment. Suggestions for further reading on each of these components are given in later chapters.

References

Bowen, D. (2007) 'You can't stop them talking', *Financial Times*, 3 May, p. 13.

Doughty, S. (2007) 'Women to be the major breadwinners in a quarter of families by 2030', *Daily Mail*, 3 August, p. 17.

Financial Times (2006) 'Why the EU is worried about RFId', 30 May, p. 25.

Gladwell, M. (2000) *The Tipping Point: How Little Things Can Make a Big Difference*, New York, Little Brown & Co.

Heskett, J.L., Sasser, W.E. Jr, and Schlesinger, L.A. (2003) *The Value Profit Chain: Treat Employees Like Customers and Customers Like Employees*, New York, The Free Press.

Levitt, T. (1960) 'Marketing myopia', *Harvard Business Review*, July–August, pp. 45–56.

Nonaka, I. (1991) 'The knowledge-creating company', *Harvard Business Review*, Vol. 69, No. 6, pp. 96–104.

Office for National Statistics (2008) Social Trends No. 38, London, Office for National Statistics (available online at http://www.statistics.gov.uk/downloads/theme_social/Social_Trends38/Social_Trends_38.pdf).

CHAPTER 10
Strategic management

LEARNING OUTCOMES

By the end of this chapter, readers should be able to understand, explain and critically evaluate:

- the nature of strategic management
- characteristics of strategic decisions
- models of strategy – corporate planning and strategic management
- the elements of strategic management – analysis, choice and implementation
- vision, mission, values and objectives
- the nature and uses of mission statements
- the concept of core competence
- generic strategies and the strategy clock
- evaluation of strategic options – suitability, acceptability and feasibility.
- strategic implementation – transformational and incremental change
- models of change management
- the role of HR in change management
- change leadership.

INTRODUCTION

This chapter analyses the nature of strategic management, and identifies different models of strategy. It analyses the stages of strategic decision-making – analysis, choice and implementation. The last part of the chapter concentrates on the nature and practice of change management.

What is strategic management?

The origins of strategy are military, and concern the art of war. A *strategos* was a general in commend of a Greek army. Quinn (1980) identifies three elements of strategy:

- Goals or objectives. What is to be achieved, and when it is to be achieved? Major goals which affect an organisation's overall direction are strategic goals.
- Policies are guidelines which set out the limits within which action should occur. Major policies are strategic policies.
- Programmes lay down the sequence of actions necessary to achieve objectives. They set out how objectives will be achieved within the limits set by policies.

In other words:

- Where do we want to get?
- What actions should we take to get there?
- How can we carry out these actions?

The essence of a strategy is to build a position so strong that the organisation will achieve its objectives no matter what unforeseeable forces attack it (ie how can we win whatever the enemy does?). Effective strategies should:

- contain clear and decisive objectives – sub-goals may change in the heat of battle but the overriding objective provides continuity over time
- maintain the initiative
- concentrate power at the right time and place
- have built-in flexibility so that one can use minimum resources to keep opponents at a disadvantage
- have committed and co-ordinated leadership
- involve correct timing and surprise
- make resources secure and prevent surprises from opponents.

Strategic decisions have a number of characteristics:

- They are concerned with the scope of an organisation's activities – the boundaries which an organisation sets to its activities.
- They are concerned with matching the activities of an organisation to its environment.
- They are concerned with matching the activities of an organisation to its resource capability.
- They often have resource implications for an organisation – if current resources do not permit a particular strategy, can the necessary resources be acquired?
- They affect operational decisions – a whole series of implementing sub-decisions must flow from the making of a strategic decision.

- They are affected by the values and expectations of those who have power in an around the organisation – its stakeholders.
- They affect the long-term direction of an organisation (Johnson, Scholes and Whittington 2004).

Strategy can be seen at several levels:

- Corporate level, concerned with the overall scope of the operation, its financial performance, and the allocation of resources to different operations.
- Competitive or business unit level – how to compete within a particular market at the level of a strategic business unit (SBU).
- Operational level – how the different functions of the organisation contribute to the overall strategy. This level is often seen as tactical rather than in any real sense strategic, but it can equally be seen as the implementation stage of strategy.

Strategic management is about doing the right things. It is:

- ambiguous
- complex
- non-routine
- organisation-wide
- fundamental
- involving significant change
- environment or expectations driven.

Operational or tactical management is about doing things right. It is:

- routinised
- operationally specific
- involving small-scale change
- resource-driven.

MODELS OF STRATEGY

CORPORATE PLANNING

This was a product of the 1950s and 1960s, a period with a largely placid environment. Detailed corporate plans covering the whole organisation were drawn up by a central planning team and then agreed by top management. The details of the plan were extremely complex, as were the models used, but the planning process itself was relatively simple because the corporate future was seen as programmable since the future was expected to be a continuation of the past. The role of line management was to implement the plan. The main exponent of corporate planning was Igor Ansoff, although Ansoff has since modified his views on strategy. There are clear parallels with the system of central planning as used to run the Soviet Union.

The strength of the corporate planning approach is its rigour, and the vital information which is collected in the course of drawing up the plan. However, it has a number of weaknesses. It is inflexible – the plan is too vast and complex to cope with rapid change in the environment. However, some of the best corporate planners – such as those at Shell – coped with this by developing a range of scenarios about the future environment. One of these forecast exactly the huge rise in oil prices which happened in 1973, with the result that Shell could react very quickly to the new situation.

Centralised corporate planning is also demotivating. Nobody owns the plan except for the planners – the line managers who have to implement it have no commitment to it. At worst, corporate planning was an academic exercise, and the plan was put away in a drawer and quietly forgotten.

STRATEGIC MANAGEMENT

This model emphasises adaptability in the face of a turbulent environment. There is no rigid long-term plan, although there are long-term visions and values. Strategy becomes bottom-up, as line managers react to or anticipate changes in the environment. The organisation has to be very responsive to changes in the environment, which requires managers at all levels constantly to monitor the environment. The organisation becomes a learning organisation in the fullest sense of the term, as it is constantly scanning and learning from its environment.

Leading exponents of the strategic management concept are:

Tom Peters

In search of excellence in 1982 (Peters and Waterman 1982) stressed the importance of a number of attributes for excellence, which emphasised values, simplicity, quick reactions and understanding the customer:

- stick to the knitting
- close to the customer
- productivity through people
- autonomy and entrepreneurship
- hands on, value driven
- bias for action
- simple form, lean staff
- simultaneous loose-tight properties.

Peters followed this up with *Thriving on chaos* (1985), where he argued that the organisation should cope with chaos by becoming chaotic itself – being in a continual state of flux. He also stressed that chaos provides marvellous opportunities for the fleet of foot.

Michael Porter

Porter approached strategic management as an economist. He stressed the importance of the competitive position of an industry (the five forces) (1980), the nature of generic strategies, and the importance of the organisation's value chain in identifying its competitive advantage (1985).

Ralph Stacey

In *The chaos frontier* (1991) and *Strategic management and organisational dynamics* (1993), he developed the application of chaos theory to strategic management. The environment facing organisations is one of chaos. Multiple and ultimately unpredictable reactions follow from a single event – the classic example is the fluttering of a butterfly's wing ultimately leading to a hurricane. The environment facing an organisation is like that facing a weather forecaster – the patterns of weather are forecastable several days ahead, but the further the forecaster looks into the future, the more outcomes become possible. As a result the organisation must be highly responsive and reactive. The role of top management is to develop and support creativity and innovation.

Gary Hamel and C K Prahalad

In *Competing for the future* (1994), they stressed that the key role of management is to manage the organisation in such a way that it is flexible and able to respond to a changed environment. This means identifying and developing the core competencies of the organisation. We shall return to this later. Hamel later developed the 10 principles of revolutionary strategy (1996):

- Strategic planning isn't strategic – it assumed that the future will be more or less the same as the present.
- Strategy making must be subversive – strategy is about breaking rules and assumptions.
- The bottleneck is at the top of the bottle – top managers are most resistant to change.
- Revolutionaries exist in every company.
- Change is not the problem, engagement is – senior managers fail to give people responsibility for managing change.
- Strategy making must be democratic – senior managers must recognise that creativity is spread throughout an organisation.
- Anyone can be a strategy activist – senior managers must see activists as positive, not as anarchists.
- Perspective is worth 50 IQ points – organisations have to use all their knowledge to identify unconventional ideas.
- Top down and bottom up are not the alternatives – both are necessary.
- You can't see the end from the beginning – strategy can often throw up surprises.

James Quinn

In *Strategies for change: logical incrementalism* (1980), Quinn developed the concept of logical incrementalism, that strategy does not consist of a big bang, but rather of a series of small steps (incrementalism).

Say an organisation wants to get from A to E. It does not set out to go straight from A to E, but instead identifies intermediate steps on the road, B, C and D. It then concentrates first on getting from A to B, and experiments with ways of getting there. This may involve several false starts and blind allies, but eventually the firm gets to B. Then it follows the same process to get to C, and so on.

Henry Mintzberg and strategic management

One of the most trenchant critics of corporate planning has been the Canadian guru Henry Mintzberg. His writings include *The rise and fall of strategic planning* (1994). He argues that old-style corporate planning was all about left-brain activity – numbers, linearity, analysis. Strategic management is right-brain – ideas, patterns, relationships, intuition. He talks of crafting strategy, rather than planning strategy. Strategy emerges as a result of a whole series of decisions throughout an organisation.

Mintzberg is famous for his five Ps of strategy:

- Strategy as a plan for action. Here the strategy is made in advance of the actions to which they apply, and it is applied consciously and purposefully. However, as we shall see later, outcomes may not be as expected.
- Strategy as a ploy, a manoeuvre to outwit opponents.
- Strategy as a pattern. A pattern of behaviour becomes a strategy. If a particular course of action tends to lead to favourable results, a strategy emerges. The strategy is the result of events, rather than the cause of them. A variation on this he calls the umbrella strategy, where top management lays down broad principles, and line managers have autonomy to act within these principles. Here strategy is both planned and emergent.
- Strategy as position. Strategy here is about finding a niche in the market, a position which balances the pressures of the environment and the competition.
- Strategy as perspective. Here the strategy reflects how the organisation views the world and its place in it. A classic example is Hewlett-Packard's 'H-P way', where the whole approach of the organisation is based on engineering excellence and innovation. The important thing here is consistency in behaviour.

Planned strategies often require modification as they are implemented, as environmental or organisational factors change. It is very rare that a long-term strategic plan can be implemented over a period of years without modification. The intended strategy may not be realised in practice, and even if it is, it may not achieve the desired results.

There are six possible combinations of intended strategy, realised strategy and results:

CASE STUDY 10.1

THE EGG MCMUFFIN

One innovation introduced by McDonald's was the Egg McMuffin, basically an egg in a bun, the classic American breakfast. Mintzberg posed the question whether this was a strategic change for McDonald's. Some students argued that it was – McDonald's was moving into a new market, the breakfast market. Others argued that nothing had changed – all that had happened was that an egg had replaced a burger.

Mintzberg argued that both were right, and both wrong. McDonald's position had changed by moving into breakfasts, but the perspective was exactly the same – the product was classic McDonald's. The position could be changed easily because it was consistent with the perspective. Mintzberg suggested that a change in perspective would involve McDonald's entering the sophisticated evening dining market with a product like a 'McDuckling a l'Orange'.

Source: Mintzberg (1998).

- What is intended as a strategy is realised with desirable results.
- What is intended as a strategy is realised, but with less than desirable results.
- What is intended as a strategy is realised in some modified version because of an unanticipated environmental and/or internal requirement or change. The results are desirable.
- What is intended as a strategy is realised in some modified version because of an unanticipated environmental and/or internal requirement of change. The results are less than desirable.
- What is intended as a strategy is not realised. Instead, an unanticipated environmental and/or internal change requires an entirely different strategy. The different strategy is realised with desirable results.
- What is intended as a strategy is not realised. Instead, an unanticipated environmental and/or internal change requires an entirely different strategy. The different strategy is realised with less than desirable results.

THE ELEMENTS OF STRATEGIC MANAGEMENT

The analysis so far may seem extremely complex, but the important thing to remember is that the essence of strategic management is very simple. It consists of getting answers to four questions:

- Where are we?
- Where do we want to get?
- How can we get there?
- What do we have to do to get there?

From this we can derive the three elements of strategic management:

ACTIVITY

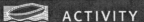

10.1 Honda and the US motorcycle market

When Honda established an American subsidiary in Los Angeles in 1959, its intended strategy was to push the sales of motorcycles with 250cc and 350cc engines, despite the fact that the much smaller 50cc model was a top seller in Japan. Honda's top managers believed that the American environment and the US consumer would prefer bigger models. However, Honda's 250cc and 350cc bikes did not sell well.

At this time, Honda's executives were using their own 50cc motorbikes to commute in traffic-congested Los Angeles. The convenience and appearance of the bikes began to be noticed. Orders for the 50cc model began to come in from motorbike retailers, but Honda was reluctant because it did not want its image in the United States to be associated with a small, no-frills motorbike. When the major US retailer Sears Roebuck expressed an interest, Honda management changed its mind. The move was overwhelmingly successful.

Honda's success in selling its 50cc bikes gradually convinced the firm to try again at developing a market for its bigger bikes. This was successful from the late 1960s to the mid-1980s. Honda's success was partially based on its reliable and sturdy products, but it was also successful because of weak competition. With the exception of a lethargic Harley-Davidson, Honda did not face any serious threat from American companies, and European and Japanese competitors had not matched Honda's investment in the US market.

This scenario began to change during the mid-1980s. Foreign competitors became more aggressive in the US market, particularly for small and medium-sized bikes, while following a management-led leveraged buyout in 1981, Harley-Davidson began to reassert its dominance in the large-bike market. Harley-Davidson increased its market share for the largest bikes from 23 per cent in 1983 to 60 per cent in 1990. Honda's overall share of the US market plunged from 58 to 28 per cent between 1985 and 1990. Hence, as the competitive situation changed rapidly, Honda's results deteriorated.

Identify episodes in the Honda experience which fit the intended and realised strategies outlined above.

- Strategic analysis – tackles the first two questions – what is our current position and where to do we want to go?
- Strategic choice – the third question – how can we get there, ie what strategy should we choose?
- Strategic implementation – what do we have to do to implement our chosen strategy?

STRATEGIC ANALYSIS

Strategic analysis is concerned with the strategic position of the organisation. What are the key characteristics of the organisation, what changes are going on in the environment, and how will these affect the organisation and its activities?

The aim is to form a view of the key influences on the present and future well-being of the organisation:

- Expectations of stakeholders, the culture of the organisation, and most important, the organisation's vision and values.
- The environment, as identified through a STEEPLE analysis and other techniques. Many of these variables will give rise to opportunities, and many will pose threats. The main problem is to distil out of the complexity the key environmental impacts for the purposes of strategic choice. I'm sure you will be delighted to hear that we have already covered the necessary techniques for this part of the analysis – the principles of STEEPLE and SWOT in Chapter 1, Porter's five forces and portfolio analysis in Chapter 2, and the detailed impact of the various elements of the environment throughout the book.
- Resources. Strategic capability is about identifying strengths and weaknesses by considering the key resource areas of the business such as physical plant, management, finance and products.

Classical corporate planning saw environmental analysis as the key element in strategic analysis, while strategic management sees culture and values as most crucial.

CASE STUDY 10.2

WHAT BUSINESS ARE WE IN?

In 2001, Hornby, the model railway company, was in trouble. Shareholders wanted to sell the company, but nobody wanted to buy it. The company was seen as staid and old-fashioned. Seventy per cent of its sales were to adult hobbyists, and 30 per cent to children, and marketing was heavily based on nostalgia for a vanished world of stream railways.

After the failure of the attempt to sell the company, new management was brought in, and Frank Martin became chief executive. He was horrified to find that the old management had just turned down the licence to make a Hogwarts Express set to tie in with *Harry Potter*, and he quickly reversed the decision.

What business is Hornby in? The old management felt that it was a hobby business, and should not be interested in products, like Hogwarts, aimed at children. Martin took the view that this was short-sighted. The hobbyist market was ageing, and unless a new segment of customers was attracted, the business would eventually die. Under his leadership, licensing of media tie-in properties has become an integral part of the business. This seems to have been the right strategic decision, as the share price is now eight times higher than when he first joined the business.

Source: Teather (2007).

GAP ANALYSIS

The extent to which there is a mismatch (a gap) between current strategy and the future environment is a measure of the strategic problem facing the organisation. As Figure 10.1 shows, over time the current strategy is likely to get more out of line with the environment, and a planning gap will grow.

Figure 10.1 Gap analysis

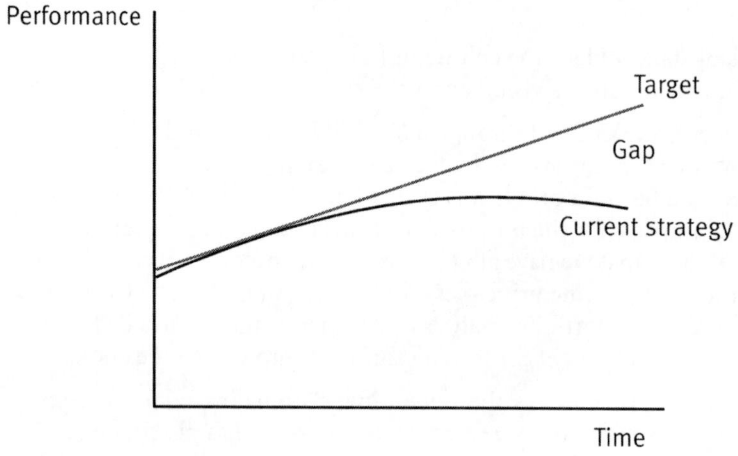

The organisation needs to choose a new strategy which will ensure that this gap is filled.

STRATEGIC CHOICE

Strategic choice involves three steps:

- Generation of strategic options. Three levels of analysis are involved here – what fundamental or generic strategy should be followed; within this generic strategy, what strategic directions are needed; and then what methods of strategic direction are most appropriate.
- Evaluation of strategic options. This involves testing options for suitability (do they fit the generic strategy, and will they provide the desired results?); feasibility (are resources available or obtainable?); and acceptability (do they fit the values of the stakeholders?).
- Selection of strategy – either logically, using some kind of weighting criteria, or politically.

STRATEGIC IMPLEMENTATION

Strategic implementation involves resource planning, organisational structure, systems, change management techniques, etc.

STRATEGIC ANALYSIS

VISION, MISSION, VALUES AND OBJECTIVES

Vision, mission, values and objectives are closely linked, and often confused. However, they are clearly distinguished by Peter Senge in *The fifth discipline* (1990).

- Vision is the what – the picture of the future we want to create, or the desired future state of the organisation (where do we want to get?).
- Mission is the why – the over-riding purpose of the organisation, its scope and boundaries (what business are we in, why do we exist?).
- Values are the how – the underlying beliefs and ethical stance which drives how the business behaves (how are we going to behave while we are getting there?).

Objectives operationalise all the other three – a precise statement of where we want to be and when, which turns the vision, mission and values into concrete quantifiable terms. It is frequently said that objectives should be SMART:

- Stretching
- Measurable
- Achievable
- Relevant
- Time limited.

CASE STUDY 10.3

CADBURY AND A FAILURE OF VALUES

The chocolate manufacturer Cadbury was founded in Birmingham in 1824 by John Cadbury, a local Quaker. Like other nineteenth-century Quakers, Cadbury was a committed social reformer. He campaigned against the use of climbing boys to clean chimneys, and he founded the Animals' Friend Society, which later became the RSPCA. The company remained true to its Quaker principles, and was a shining example of corporate social responsibility long before the term was invented. It took a leading role in promoting education in Birmingham, built the Bournville model village for its workers, was the first company in the country to introduce a half day on Saturday, and launched a pension fund as early as 1906 (Cadbury 2007).

The emphasis on Quaker values continued well into the twentieth century, as long as the company was directly controlled by the Cadbury family. It was a member of the family, Adrian Cadbury, who produced one of the first reports on corporate governance in the early 1990s.

It is clear from the Cadbury website that the company is still very proud of its Quaker heritage, and so it came as a great shock when the company was fined £1 million for a breach of safety regulations which led to a salmonella outbreak. What was worse was that the outbreak was a direct result of the company's own policy. In 2003, it had changed its policy on salmonella contamination from a 'zero tolerance' policy, where product was destroyed automatically if any trace of salmonella was detected on test, to a policy allowing a 'tolerable level' of salmonella. This was despite scientific opinion that no level of salmonella could be regarded as safe.

In January and February 2006 there were 36 positive tests for salmonella, but the company did nothing until it was linked to an outbreak of salmonella poisoning in June 2006, in which at least 42 people were infected (Williams 2007). It then recalled all the products concerned. It is estimated that the recall and the resultant bad publicity cost the company £40 million (Tait and Wiggins 2007).

In the company's trial under food hygiene regulations, it was claimed by the prosecution that the change in policy was a deliberate and cynical act of cost-cutting. The judge said the company had fallen 'seriously short' of its obligations, but accepted the company's defence that although it was negligent, it was not deliberately aiming to cut costs. Simon Baldry, the former managing director of Cadbury Trebor Bassett, was one of the casualties of a management shake-up which followed the product withdrawal (Elliott 2007).

What this case shows is that the higher an organisation's standards and values, the more serious are any shortcomings in failing to meet those standards.

The mission and objectives of the organisation are constrained by four main factors (Johnson, Scholes and Whittington 2004):

Corporate governance

External constraints on the organisation, set by company law; reports of investigations such as the Cadbury Report on non-executive directors or the Greenbury Report on directors' pay; regulatory bodies such as the Financial Services Authority, and targets and controls imposed by the government on public bodies (ie Best Value for local authorities).

Stakeholders

The rights and power of various stakeholder groups were discussed at length in Chapter 9, but basically stakeholders can influence the organisation's strategic direction through their power and/or their interest.

Business ethics

Again this was discussed at length in Chapter 9, but ethics can impact on an organisation at three levels: general ethical policy; how the organisation interprets its corporate social responsibility when it formulates its strategy; and the ethical behaviour of individuals within the organisation. Clearly ethics is all about values, particularly the values of top management.

Culture

Culture in organisations operates at three levels:

- Values, often written down as part of the mission statement, but often vague, like 'service to the community'.
- More specific beliefs, often expressed as policies.
- Taken for granted assumptions – the organisational paradigm – the 'way things are done here'. At grassroots level, these may often be in conflict with the values and beliefs officially expressed at a higher level. For example, the police force in the United Kingdom is totally committed to eradicating 'institutional racism', but at the level of 'canteen culture' there are still racist PCs.

ACTIVITY

10.2 London Zoo

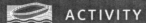

In 1993 *Management Today* published an article on the strategy of London Zoo (Sebag-Montefiore 1993). Although the case is an old one, it still deals with some fundamental issues in strategic management.

The zoo, owned by the learned society, the Zoological Society of London (ZSL), had been going through hard times. By 1992, it had lost money for a decade, and had only survived through drastic cost-cutting, including redundancies among keepers which many felt had reduced staffing to dangerous levels. The turnaround led to a small profit in the year ending March 1993.

However, the turnaround plan was only the start of a bitter battle for the soul of the zoo, between the zoo's commercial staff and their supporters – the 'suits', who wanted the zoo to become much more commercial, using high-tech computer displays and interactive technology, and a militant group on the Council of ZSL, the 'beards', who thought that the zoo should stick to its original aims of breeding and conserving endangered species. The suits were led by a property developer, David Laing, and the beards by a left-wing journalist, Colin Tudge. The centrepiece of the suits' plan was a giant interactive aquarium to be built at the zoo.

Each side was vitriolic about the other. The beards referred to the suits' plan as 'animal prostitution', and said that the animals would be reduced to 'bit part actors on a stage', while the suits described Tudge as 'that breeding fanatic' and his supporters as 'Leninists with their heads in the clouds'. However, both sides genuinely thought that their plan would make the zoo more attractive to visitors.

The job of resolving the quarrel fell to Jo Gipps, the director of the London Zoo. His business plan, revealed in 1993, was a compromise, but leaning more towards the beards.

Crucial to the argument was the mission statement of ZSL, which read:

> To achieve and promote the worldwide conservation of animals and their habitats.

Both sides could argue that this supported their argument. The beards pointed to the word 'conservation', while the suits pointed to the word 'worldwide' – in their view the zoo should be fully commercial, and raise money which could be used to support conservation elsewhere in the world, rather than specifically at London Zoo.

Question

What does this case tell you about the importance of vision, values and mission?

THE MISSION STATEMENT

This is the most generalised statement of organisational purpose. It sets the direction of the organisation, and provides a benchmark against which policies can be evaluated.

An effective mission statement should achieve the following:

- It should be visionary and long-term. It is meant to inspire and drive the organisation.
- It should clarify the main intentions and aspirations of the organisation and the reasons the organisation exists.

- It should describe the organisation's main activities and the position it wishes to attain in its industry.
- It should contain a statement of the key values of the organisation in relation to its stakeholders.
- It should be taken seriously within the organisation.
- It should be a focus for activity, which can serve as a continual guide, rather than a closed aim which can be fully achieved.

However, there are two great dangers with mission statements. The first is a risk that they can appear grandiose, or even ridiculous. Too many overblown mission statements have tended in the past to lead to the whole concept being treated with ridicule. Typical is the *Dilbert* website (www.dilbert.com), which contains a mission statement generator, which will produce randomly generated mission statements.

The other danger is that the mission statement may become set in concrete. The external environment may change in a way that renders the mission statement obsolete, and a hindrance rather than a help to strategy formulation (see the case study on Komatsu).

CASE STUDY 10.4

KOMATSU

Komatsu produces earth-moving equipment, an industry where the market leader is the American company Caterpillar. In the 1950s, it was a small company serving only its Japanese home market. In 1964, Yashinari Kawai became president of Komatsu, and announced the company's new mission statement – 'Maru C' or 'encircle Caterpillar'. This was to be the driving force of the company's strategy for the next 20 years.

The statement served Komatsu well – by the 1980s, it was the world's second largest producer of earth-moving equipment, although it had failed to overtake Caterpillar. Unfortunately, while Komatsu had been focusing all its attention and energy on Caterpillar, it had ignored changes in the environment. Demand for basic earth-moving equipment was falling, and new competitors in different but related industries were becoming an (unseen) threat.

Fortunately the new company president, Tetsuya Katada, spotted the danger in time. He decided that the company's new emphasis should be as a 'total technology enterprise', with the new mission statement 'Growth, Global, Groupwide'. Komatsu's sales decline was reversed, thanks entirely to an explosive growth in its non-construction equipment business.

RESOURCE ANALYSIS

Resource analysis is internal to the organisation. It is concerned with the strengths and weaknesses parts of SWOT analysis, and measures the efficiency and effectiveness of an organisation's resources, and their degree of fit with the external opportunities and threats also identified through SWOT. Ideally

ACTIVITY

10.3 THE WEA (NORTHERN IRELAND)

The Workers' Educational Association (WEA) in Northern Ireland publishes its mission statement and WEA values on its website (www.wea-ni.com), as follows:

The WEA Mission Statement

We will make learning accessible to all men and women, especially those removed from the educational experience. As well as offering opportunities to individuals we will assist those who wish to work collectively for the benefit of their communities and for the good of society as a whole.

The Value Base of the WEA

The WEA has been a catalyst for social change since it began in Belfast in 1910. The following values underpin our commitment to social change:

Social inclusion – we make special efforts to reach those most removed from the learning experience.

Voluntarism – we provide opportunities for people to volunteer to work both individually and collectively for the betterment of our society.

Active citizenship – we equip people to play a full role in the social, economic, cultural and political life of our society.

Building alliances – we work closely with others to improve opportunities for learning.

Sharing experience – we share good practice to promote mutual learning

Equality – we promote equality of opportunity through learning.

Evaluate the WEA mission statement against the six characteristics of an effective mission statement listed above.

strengths should support opportunities, and be able to counteract threats. Resources should be seen in the widest sense, to include the organisation's competitive position, as identified through techniques such as five forces and portfolio analysis. However, SWOT analysis has severe limitations. The most important of these is that it is subjective – different analysts will identify totally different strengths and weaknesses. Stevenson (1989) found no consensus among the managers in the companies he studied on the strengths and weaknesses of their companies. Higher-level managers tended to be more optimistic about the balance of strengths and weaknesses than lower-level managers.

Prahalad and Hamel in *The core competence of the corporation* (1990) identified the concept of the core competences of the organisation – those factors that give the organisation its key competitive advantages. Unlike resources, which are tangible, tradeable and easily replicable, competences are based on the accumulated knowledge and skills of the organisation, are unique to it, and difficult to copy. They are based on people rather than things. Examples are the way in which Dell Computer builds all computers individually to order, and the reputation of Body Shop as an ethical crusader. Other analysts have suggested that the crucial competence needed by all organisations is the ability to be nimble, flexible and responsive to rapid and unpredictable changes in the external environment.

Core competences can be based on:

- Cost efficiency. Many advantages based on cost efficiency are not really core competences, as they can relatively easily be copied by other organisations. One which may lead to a core competence is cost efficiency based on experience – the more experience an organisation has, the lower its costs tend to be.
- Value added. Is the organisation more effective than the competition? In the early stages of the quality movement in the 1970s and 1980s, quality could be a core competence. Now it is a given – it is expected of all organisations and does not in itself give a competitive advantage. Value added is more likely to be experienced by the customer through service than through the product itself – Dell does not necessarily sell a better computer, but it gives the customer a flexible computer configured to his or her requirements.
- Managing linkages, between different stages of production, or through alliances with other organisations. For example the low-cost airlines like easyJet and Ryanair pioneered the use of Internet-based ticket booking systems and paperless tickets, giving them both a cost and an effectiveness advantage, as well as allowing a very flexible pricing system. They also offer weblinks to suppliers of hotels and car hire.
- Robustness. How easy is it to ensure that the competences are difficult to copy?

If it can develop a number of core competences, an organisation can greatly strengthen its strategic position. However, there is the danger that over time the core competences may no longer match the external environment. If computing becomes based on mobile phones rather than PCs and laptops, Dell's core competence may prove to be a weakness rather than a strength.

ACTIVITY

10.4 Harry Potter and the Portents of Doom

Bloomsbury Publishing was founded in 1986 by Nigel Newton, still the company's chairman. His mission was to publish books of the highest quality, and to bring quality to the mass market (Bloomsbury 2007a). The company initially grew slowly, and by the early 1990s its turnover was barely £10 million. It then went public in 1994, raising £5.5 million, followed by a rights issue in 1998 which raised another £6.1 million.

By then Bloomsbury's fortunes had been transformed when it accepted a children's book from an unknown author, J K Rowling. This was published as *Harry Potter and the Philosopher's Stone* in 1997, and the rest is history. Bloomsbury owns the English-language rights to *Harry Potter* throughout the world except the United States (where the rights are owned by Scholastic). World-wide sales of the first six *Harry Potter* books totalled 325 million (Jordan 2007).

As the sales of *Harry Potter* soared, so did Bloomsbury's fortunes. Turnover rose from £20 million in 1999 to £109 million in 2005, while profit rose from £2.6 million in 1999 to £20.1 million in 2005 (Bloomsbury 2007b). However, events were then to show how dependent the company was on *Harry Potter*. The sixth book, *Harry Potter and the Half-Blood Prince*, was published in July 2005, and no *Potter* title appeared in 2006.

The result was that both sales and profits collapsed in 2006. 2006 turnover was £74 million, lower than 2003, while profits slumped to £5.2 million, the lowest figure since 2000. All the fall was due to a fall in turnover in the children's division (basically *Harry Potter*) (Shelley 2007).

Fortunately for Bloomsbury, the last book in the series was still in the pipeline, *Harry Potter and the Deathly Hallows*, published in July 2007. In the first 24 hours 2.6 million copies were sold in the United Kingdom, plus another 400,000 English language copies in Germany (Bloomsbury 2007c).

Clearly the success of the seventh and final title will generate healthy profits for Bloomsbury in 2007, but this boost is likely to be short-lived, because of the peculiar nature of the *Potter* market. The major supermarkets all see *Harry Potter* as an ideal vehicle for a short-term price war. The recommended retail price of *The Deathly Hallows* is £17.99, with a wholesale price of £9.89, but the supermarkets are selling the book for prices ranging from £5 to £8.99. It is cheaper for an independent bookseller to buy its stock from Tesco than from a wholesaler (Alberge 2007).

In a sense the fact that retailers make no money out of the book does not matter to Bloomsbury, because they get their £9.89 a copy anyway. But in another sense it does matter. The typical pattern with a best-selling book is that it is initially published in hardback at a high price, with only moderate but very profitable sales. Then a year later, a paperback edition appears, at a lower price, but with greater volume. The publisher has two bites at the apple.

This does not happen with *Harry Potter*. Because of the discounting and hype, people who might have waited for the paperback buy the hardback instead. As a result sales of *Harry Potter* are minimal after the year in which the title is published.

Bloomsbury is a classic example of an organisation whose success is resource-driven. Its key asset is the intellectual property embedded in the *Harry Potter* titles. Like a pharmaceutical company with a blockbuster drug, it must ensure that a stream of new products is developed to replace the blockbuster. If this is not done, as the blockbuster drug loses its patent protection, or the *Harry Potter* series comes to an end, profits collapse.

Question

How can Bloomsbury escape from *The Portents of Doom* and ensure its long-term future?

ACTIVITY

10.5 THE WATERSTONE'S TAKEOVER OF OTTAKAR'S

The bookselling industry comprises four broad types of outlet:

- **Specialist booksellers**, including retail chains such as Waterstone's, Ottakar's and Borders as well as independent booksellers.

  Waterstone's. Founded by Tim Waterstone in 1982, and owned by W H Smith until 1998, when it was acquired by HMV. On 31 December 2005 it had 190 bookshops in the UK, including 31 on university campuses. The range of book titles stocked varied between 30,000 and 40,000 per store. Its sales in the year ended 30 April 2005 were £446 million, but like-for-like sales fell in the year 2005–6 its market share in 2005 was 17 per cent.

  Ottakar's. Founded in 1987 by James Heneage and Philip Dunne. On 31 December 2005 it had 141 stores, with a typical store range of 20,000 to 30,000 titles. Its sales in the year ended 28 January 2006 were £176 million, a like-for-like fall of 3 per cent compared with the previous year. Ottakar's market share in 2005 was 7 per cent. The geographical overlap between Waterstone's and Ottakar's is fairly small, as Ottakar's has followed a deliberate strategy of entering small towns without significant competition.

  Borders. The US-based Borders is the second biggest book retailer in the world. It entered the United Kingdom in 1997 when it acquired Books Etc. It specialises in book superstores in out-of-town locations, carrying 50,000 to 80,000 titles. It thus does not directly compete with Waterstone's and Ottakar's, both of which are high-street based. Borders, Waterstone's and Ottakar's all generally provide a coffee shop in their stores.

  Blackwell's. A specialist university bookseller, with 56 stores in university towns, many on campus. Borders and Blackwell together have a 15 per cent market share.

- **Retail chains for which books are an important category.** The dominant company in this sector is WH Smith. WH Smith sells a wide range of newspapers, magazines, stationery and entertainment products as well as books. It has 545 high-street stores, of which 365 have a typical range of 5,000 to 10,000 book titles, and the remainder 10,000 to 20,000 titles. WH Smith is estimated to have around 10 per cent of the book market.

- **Retailers which sell books as part of a much wider range of goods** (the major supermarkets, plus Woolworths). Supermarkets specialise in best sellers and lifestyle books, particularly cookery and celebrity titles, and they discount heavily. Tesco increased its book sales by 52 per cent in the year to 25 February 2006. Supermarkets have a market share of 8 per cent, which is increasing rapidly, up from 4 per cent in 2001. Tesco alone has a target of 10 per cent of the market.

- **Distance sellers.** Amazon dominates the Internet market for books. It discounts, although not as extensively as the supermarkets (although unlike the supermarkets it offers discounts on non-best-selling books, making it more competitive against the high-street chains). It also has access to a much bigger backlist than any of the bricks and mortar retailers. The Internet had a 12 per cent of the market in 2005, up from 5 per cent in 2001. Other distance sellers are mainly book clubs, dominated by Book Club Associates, whose market share is 15 per cent, but falling rapidly, from 21 per cent in 2001 (Competition Commission 2006, Table 3, pC3).

Overall, market trends are that high-street retailers are slowly losing market share, book clubs are rapidly losing share, while Amazon and the supermarkets are rapidly increasing market share. Overall demand has risen over the past five years. Total sales in 2006 were £4.24 billion, an increase of 3.4 per cent (Keynote 2007), and are expected to grow by a total of 20 per cent over the period 2006–11.

The Waterstone's takeover

Ottakar's went public in 1998. In the spring of 2005, a management buy-out team headed by the founders of Ottakar's, James Heneage, then CEO, and Philip Dunne (then chairman), launched a bid to take the company private. They offered a price of £3.50 a share, increased to £4 on 6 September 2005. HMV then launched a rival bid at £4.50, and this was accepted by the Ottakar's directors on 13 September. The bid was notified to the Office of Fair Trading as, even though the combined market share was just below the referral threshold of 25 per cent, the size of the bid was sufficient to justify a referral.

On 6 December 2005, the OFT referred the bid to the Competition Commission. On 6 May 2006, the Competition Commission concluded that the merger should be allowed, as it would not be 'expected to result in a substantial lessening of competition ... at a local, regional or national level in the UK (Competition Commission 2006, p41).

The major source for this Activity is the Competition Commission report, *HMV Group plc and Ottakar's plc: proposed acquisition of Ottakar's plc by HMV Group plc through Waterstone's Booksellers Ltd* (12 May 2006), but also used was the Keynote report, *Book selling* (March 2007).

Question

1. Why do you think the Competition Commission allowed the merger?

As part of its research, the Competition Commission carried out a consumer survey to establish reasons why customers choose a bookshop. This came up with the following reasons (respondents could pick more than one answer):

Range of books	91%
Convenience	76%
Value for money	26%
Customer service	17%
Nice environment	12%

Converting these percentages to numbers, and scoring 'range of books' as 10, this gives the following reworked maximum scores

Range of books	10
Convenience	8
Value for money	3
Customer service	2
Nice environment	2
Total	25

The nearer a bookshop scored to 25, the more attractive it would be to customers.

We would give a (purely subjective) score to W H Smith as follows:

Range of books	4
Convenience	7
Value for money	1
Customer service	1
Nice environment	0
Total	13

Question

2. How would you (from your own experience) score Waterstone's/Ottakar's, Amazon and the supermarkets?

STRATEGIC CHOICE

GENERIC STRATEGIES

The concept of generic strategy was introduced by Michael Porter (1985). He identified possible strategies as being:

- Cost leadership. An organisation will succeed if it can achieve lower costs than its competitors, but sell its products at or near the industry average price.
- Differentiation. An organisation will succeed if it can produce a differentiated product which commands a premium price, but at the same time keep its costs to the industry average.
- Focus. An organisation will succeed if it concentrates on a niche market, in which it can achieve either cost focus or differentiation focus.

CASE STUDY 10.5

RYANAIR – A SUCCESSFUL FOCUSED COST LEADER

In 1991, Ryanair was a small, unsuccessful Irish airline, when its newly appointed CEO, Michael O'Leary, went to America to meet Herbert Kelleher, Southwest Airlines' founder. The low-cost carrier had transformed the economics of air travel in the United States. From Kelleher, O'Leary learned the importance of cost control, through the use of one type of plane, point-to-point flights only, and elimination of all frills (*Business Week* 2006).

Since then, Ryanair has pushed the Southwest business model even further, and has become the biggest and most profitable low-cost airline in Europe. Its success is based on three pillars – cut costs to the minimum ('nail down costs'), 'give nothing, sell everything', and efficiency.

Cost cutting

- Ryanair flies only one type of plane – the Boeing 737-800. This enables economies of scale in pilot training and maintenance.
- Ryanair's seat density on the 737 is 189, 15 per cent more than other airlines.
- Ryanair places its orders for aircraft in a counter-cyclical fashion, taking advantage of weak demand to wring better prices out of Boeing. For example, it placed a very big order in the immediate aftermath of 9/11. In 2007, it was rumoured by the *Financial Times* to be selling some of its planes secondhand for more than it had paid for them (Done 2007).
- The company's planes are stripped of all non-essentials – seats do not recline, there are no window blinds, and no seat-back pockets. This shaves several hundred thousand dollars off the cost of each plane.
- Like other low-cost airlines, Ryanair does not use travel agents, thus saving up to 15 per cent commission, but it has gone further than its rivals in promoting booking over the Internet, which minimises handling costs. By 2007, 98 per cent of bookings were made over the Internet.
- Ryanair does not use air bridges at airports – passengers must walk to the plane. This saves on airport charges.

- Ryanair is notorious for using secondary, but very cheap, airports. These are often some way from the city that they nominally serve. Brussels-Charleroi is 40 km from Brussels, Copenhagen-Malmo is actually in Sweden, not Denmark, and Frankfurt-Hahn is 140 km from Frankfurt. As easyJet repeatedly points out, this means that Ryanair's low fares are deceptive, as further transport costs are needed to reach the final destination. The secondary airports used are desperate for Ryanair's business, and are prepared to offer extremely good terms. In the case of Charleroi, allegedly illegal subsides were paid. In 2004, the European Commission ordered Ryanair to repay €4 million of subsidies.
- Advertising on planes is widespread (as well as liveries which attack other airlines).
- Extensive use is made of Eastern European (particularly Polish) cabin crew).

As a result of its rigorous cost-cutting programme, Ryanair's costs are two-thirds of those of easyJet, 60 per cent of UK holiday charter airlines, and half that of full-service carriers (Thompson 2005).

Charges

- Ryanair is notorious for charging its staff for perks normally seen as free: crew must pay for their own uniforms, they must pay for water drunk on flights, and they are banned from recharging their mobiles on company power sockets.
- Like other low-cost airlines, it charges passengers for refreshments on flights.
- Ryanair was the first airline to introduce a charge for baggage. This has the effect of raising revenue, and also of cutting the number of bags carried, so lowering baggage handling costs by an estimated £20 million a year (*Air Transport World* 2006a).
- In September 2007 it introduced a charge for checking in at the airport, which could only be avoided by checking in online (Milmo 2007b).
- In 2002 Ryanair was heavily criticised when it refused to provide wheelchairs for disabled passengers at Stansted. A court ruling in 2004 judged that the responsibility for disabled passengers was shared between the airport and the airline. Ryanair's response was to place a 33p surcharge on all its ticket prices (attacked by other airlines as a 'wheelchair levy'), which raised far more revenue for Ryanair than the costs it was claimed to cover (Starmer-Smith 2006).

Ryanair has made few friends. On the other hand, millions of travellers like its low fares. The airline is also unquestionably good at what it does.

Efficiency

As Ryanair gleefully points out on its website, the airline is extremely efficient. It claims:

- the best on-time record in Europe (91 per cent on time arrivals in 2003, compared with 83 per cent for British Airways and 82 per cent for easyJet)
- the lowest level of cancellations
- fewest lost bags – 0.6 bags per 1,000 passengers in 2003, compared with BA's 14.2) (Ryanair 2003).

Results

Ryanair's model seems to be successful. In 2005, it had the fourth-highest operating profit in Europe (behind BA, Air France-KLM and Lufthansa), and the 12th highest in the world, the 11th highest net profit in the world, and the 15th highest number of passengers carried (*Air Transport World* 2006b). In August 2005, for the first time it carried more passengers than the entire world-wide BA network (Ryanair 2007).

Conclusion

Ryanair seems to have the focused cost leadership business model cracked. However, there are three potential clouds on the horizon:

- In 2007, Ryanair operated 136 planes. However, it also had orders which would take its fleet size to 262 (Done 2007). Given Ryanair's flight pattern, it requires 250,000 passengers a year to operate a plane profitably. To fill all the planes on order, Ryanair would have to nearly double its present number of about 45 million passengers a year. Can the company's growth rate be maintained indefinitely?
- The full-service carriers are fighting back. They have cut their fares, increased their online bookings, and heavily marketed their own selling features – meals, free drinks, seat allocations, more convenient airports.
- There are ominous signs that O'Leary is being distracted from the business model. In 2006, he tried to take over the Irish state carrier Aer Lingus when it was privatised, with the intention of operating it as a going concern, including its long-haul flights, while in 2007, he announced plans to develop a new long-haul airline, to be called RyanAtlantic. Although this would be separate from Ryanair, it would sell tickets through the Ryanair website.

CASE STUDY 10.6

KwikSave: a failed cost leader

KwikSave was founded in Rhyl, North Wales in 1959, and floated on the stock exchange in 1970. At its peak in 1993 it had over 1,000 stores, made a profit of £135 million, was a member of the FTSE100, and in volume terms was the third-biggest food retailer in the United Kingdom, with a market share of over 10 per cent, more than Asda, and behind only Tesco and Sainsbury.

Its success was due to its aggressive pursuit of a strategy of cost leadership. It aimed directly at the bottom of the market. Its stores were in secondary high-street sites, which were cheap to acquire. It sold only branded tinned and packaged goods, which were sold direct from cardboard boxes, so cutting costs to the bone. It stocked only 1,000 lines, exploiting the 80:20 rule. As it pointed out in 1993, 80 per cent of typical supermarket sales came from only 20 per cent of its lines. KwikSave stocked only these fast-moving lines, ignoring the rest (Tempus 1993). As a result, its prices were more than 10 per cent lower than those of the major supermarkets (Gilchrist 1993a). In value added terms, KwikSave was the most successful retailer in the United Kingdom, with a value added return of 25 per cent, compared with Sainsbury's 10 per cent (Lord 1990).

However, even at the peak of KwikSave's success, small clouds were appearing on the horizon. Between 1990 and 1994 food sales in the United Kingdom grew much less quickly than floor space (Sivell and Dolan 1995). In the early 1990s the Danish discount retailer Netto entered the UK market, followed by the German companies Aldi and Lidl. All three had long experience in cut-throat European markets, and had deeper pockets than KwikSave. By 1993, Netto had a 2.5 per cent price advantage over KwikSave (Gilchrist 1993b), and KwikSave was warning that a price war would hit its profits (Gilchrist 1993b).

The response of KwikSave was twofold. It cut its prices further, and introduced a No Frills own brand, selling at or below cost. Simultaneously, it tried to move up-market by stocking fresh and chilled food, which had a higher profit margin. However, both proved to be mistakes. The low-price message was diluted, the price cuts provoked Tesco into retaliation, while KwikSave found that although fresh and chilled food could be more profitable, they also required specialised retailing skills which KwikSave did not possess (Sivell and Dolan 1995).

In 1994–5 profits were down from their peak, and like-for-like sales were down 2.5 per cent (Bagnall 1995). KwikSave shoppers were voting with their wallets, and deserting the high street for the out-of-town superstore.

KwikSave called in Andersen Consulting, whose solution was that KwikSave should become more like Tesco – widen its range, and widen its margins. The advice was disastrous – KwikSave shoppers had shopped at the chain because it was different from Tesco. If it became the same as Tesco, why not shop at Tesco? KwikSave also accelerated its store opening programme, spending money and lowering its return on capital. By 1996, KwikSave's profits were still falling, Tesco had matched its 3p price for a tin of baked beans, and the continental retailers were taking 1.5 per cent of the market, soon expected to rise to 5 per cent (Stevenson 1996, Cope 1996).

In February 1998 KwikSave merged with Somerfield in the hope that their greater combined size would enable them to overcome their trading problems. However, Somerfield was nearly as weak as KwikSave. The merger was described with ironic understatement as 'not quite the deal of the century', while an analyst said, 'Both of them would have hit a brick wall at some stage. Now they will just hit a bigger one' (Hollinger 1998).

Although it was nominally a merger, it soon became clear that Somerfield held the whip hand. The KwikSave head office in North Wales was scheduled for closure, and plans were announced to rebrand all the KwikSave stores as Somerfield. This proved a disaster, and within 18 months some ex-KwikSave stores were announcing falls in sales of up to 50 per cent (Cope 1999). At the end of 1999, 350 ex-KwikSave stores were put up for sale, only for the sale to be abandoned four months later when no realistic offers were received. The merger was described as 'one of the most disastrous in corporate history' (Finch 2000). Another U-turn saw the KwikSave brand resurrected. A further blow came late in 1999, when Asda was taken over by Wal-mart. Asda was even more aggressive on price than Tesco, and now had the bottomless pockets of Wal-mart behind it.

KwikSave-Somerfield sales continued to decline, and eventually in October 2005, the company was taken over by a private equity consortium headed by billionaire Robert Tchenguiz (Finch 2005). The new owners quickly off-loaded KwikSave to another company, Back to the Future, in February 2006 (Rigby 2006). By the end of 2006, KwikSave sales had collapsed to a market share of 0.2 per cent. By May 2007 the group was boycotted by its suppliers, by June it could not pay its staff, and in July it went into administration (Finch 2007).

What this case shows us is the very high risk associated with a cost leadership strategy. Caught in a vice between the continental discounters and Tesco and Asda, KwikSave was slowly squeezed to death.

CASE STUDY 10.7

Marks & Spencer Simply Food: a successful focused differentiator

In the late 1990s, Marks & Spencer's inexorable growth seemed to hit the buffers. Its clothes ranges were tired, and the company seemed to have run out of steam. However, this did not apply to its food ranges, which seemed to be exactly what the consumer wanted. Research showed that M&S was highly rated for the quality of its food, for offering more unusual items, for its high reputation, and its ready meals. It scored low on value for money and on convenience (Hamson 2004).

M&S decided to capitalise on its food reputation, and in July 2001 opened the first Simply Food outlet in Surbiton, Surrey. The store was aimed at commuters, with a high footfall but a low spend per customer, selling 4,000 food lines, plus newspapers and magazines. At 2,500 square feet, it qualified legally as a convenience store, and so is entitled to open extended hours on a Sunday (8 am to 6 pm). (Bruce 2001).

The format proved successful, and expansion was rapid. By the summer of 2003, 30 stores had opened, and there were plans to develop a further 40 stores on railway stations in partnership with Compass (Bruce 2003). The first Simply Food store on a motorway service station followed in August 2003. The stores were also made more flexible. Some went above the 3,000 square feet convenience store limit, while stores would now carry between 800 and 15,000 lines, depending on local demand, rather than the 4,000 lines per store originally planned (*Grocer* 2003).

The stores that proved most successful were those which generated annual turnover in excess of £3 million, and were situated well away from other M&S stores (Watson 2004).

It also became clear that the railway station and motorway service station stores served different types of customer. On the railway stations, customers were in a hurry, and their spend was lower. The priority here was to have an adequate number of tills to cope with the high footfall. Motorway service station customers were prepared to spend longer in store, and also almost by definition had cars, so their average shop was higher (Hamson 2005).

Expansion accelerated in 2006, when M&S acquired 28 ex-Iceland stores. The stores were cherry-picked with great care, using a number of key success criteria:

- strong footfall from high-street shoppers
- high penetration of affluent shoppers
- strong comparable premium retailer offering
- proximity to public transport
- large local resident population
- large work-based grocery expenditure.

Stores that scored highly on these criteria included Torquay and Hertford (*Grocer* 2006a). A trial with BP on BP petrol station forecourts in late 2005 also proved successful (*Grocer* 2006b).

Partly because of Simply Food, M&S has increased its share of UK food grocery sales to 4 per cent, with like for like sales in 2006 growing by up to 6 per cent (Durston 2006). By November 2006 M&S was operating more than 200 Simply Food stores, with a further 100 planned for 2007, of which 60 would be on BP forecourts (*Grocer* 2007).

Why has Simply Food been so successful? Because it:

- builds on the M&S high reputation for food quality
- successfully extends the M&S brand
- avoids cannibalisation by developing new types of site – railway stations, motorway service stations, smaller towns, petrol station forecourts

- had very careful site selection
- works with franchise partners (Compass and BP) which lowers risk and level of investment, and also brings in outside expertise
- has an offer that is carefully tailored to the type of outlet.

The result is that 50 per cent of Simply Food shoppers are in the 16–34 age band – a much younger demographic than for traditional M&S stores (Durston 2006).

CASE STUDY 10.8

NORTHERN ROCK: A FAILED FOCUSED DIFFERENTIATOR

Over a weekend in the middle of September 2007, the United Kingdom experienced the first serious run on a bank for a century. Hundreds of people queued for hours outside the branches of Northern Rock, desperate to withdraw their savings before the bank collapsed. How had a previously well-respected bank come to such a pass?

Northern Rock dates back to 1850, when the Northern Counties Permanent Building Society was formed, followed by Rock Building Society in 1865. The two merged to form the Northern Rock Building Society, based in Newcastle, in 1965. It was a typical building society – taking in deposits from its members, and lending them out as mortgages. It was safe, solid and respectable. Its share of the national mortgage market was 2 per cent. It was also very popular in the north-east because it had been very sympathetic to miners in mortgage arrears during the mining strike of the early 1980s.

In 1997 it demutualised, forming Northern Rock plc, and its status changed from a building society to a bank. As a public company its priorities changed. Rather than providing a service for its members, its priority was now to make profits for its shareholders. Within months, it showed a new face when it was criticised by the Office of Fair Trading of being 'cavalier' for unilaterally changing the terms offered to its depositors (Hughes and Tighe 2007).

Unlike some of the other demutualised ex-building societies, Northern Rock did not attempt to develop general banking services, but continued to specialise in mortgages. However, it was faced with problems in expanding in this area. First, it only had 79 branches, mainly concentrated in the relatively impoverished north-east. This limited its ability to raise funds from depositors (known as retail funds). By comparison, the leading building society, Nationwide, had over 700 branches, and the big high-street banks had thousands.

Northern Rock tacked this problem by raising funds through the interbank market, from other financial institutions (known as wholesale funds). As a building society, it would have been limited by law from raising more than 50 per cent of its funds from the wholesale market, but no such restrictions applied to banks (BBC2 2007). At its peak in the early autumn of 2007, Northern Rock raised more than three-quarters of its funds from the wholesale market, on terms ranging from overnight to three months.

Wholesale borrowing is generally regarded as more risky and volatile than retail borrowing. Although retail depositors can in theory withdraw many of their funds on demand, in practice they are highly unlikely to do so. On the other hand, other banks will move their money elsewhere if they think they can get a better return. Northern Rock's reliance on wholesale funds was described by one experienced banker as akin to overtaking a queue of traffic on the outside of a bend – 'everyone knows it works (for a time), but only fools or the inexperienced would attempt it' (Croggon 2007).

Even when Northern Rock obtained more funds, it still had to persuade people to take out more of its mortgages. It did this through aggressive lending policies. It became known as the bank which would lend even if you had a patchy credit record. It was also prepared to lend more than other banks or building societies. In 2002 it introduced its Together loan, which allowed a borrower to borrow up to 125 per cent of a property's valuation, or six times annual income. As other lenders were not prepared to lend more than four times income, borrowers flocked to Northern Rock. By the end of 2006, its share of the mortgage market was up to 7 per cent.

Massive expansion continued throughout the first half of 2007, at a time when increasing warnings were being issued of the frothy state of the UK housing market, and of a worrying level of consumer debt. In the first half of 2007 Northern Rock took a 25 per cent share of the new mortgage market, making it the biggest mortgage provider, shooting past traditional lenders such as the Halifax and the Nationwide (Collinson and Seager 2007).

With hindsight, it was clear that Northern Rock was over-trading, and taking unacceptable risks. In June 2007 it was forced to issue a profits warning, and its shares started to fall. Its strategy was described by Professor Willem Buiter, one of the founder members of the Bank of England's Monetary Policy Committee, as 'an extremely aggressive and high-risk strategy' (Duncan and Webster 2007).

Northern Rock might still have got away with it had it not been caught up in the backlash from a separate but related financial crisis, the sub-prime crisis in the United States. Here, US financial institutions had pursued a Northern Rock-style strategy of aggressive lending to poor credit risks (the sub-prime market), eventually leading to a collapse of the US housing market in the summer of 2007. One consequence of this was a freezing-up of the interbank lending market in the United Kingdom, as well as the United States. This meant that Northern Rock, which continually needed to roll over its wholesale borrowing, faced a liquidity crisis.

The crisis for Northern Rock came to a head on Thursday 13 September, when the bank applied to the Bank of England for emergency assistance (known as 'lender of last resort'). On Friday 14 September the Bank of England agreed to lend virtually unlimited funds to Northern Rock, but at a penal rate of interest, believed to be 7 per cent.

This should have been the end of the crisis, but Northern Rock retail depositors interpreted this as a sign that the bank was about to fail, and a run on the Bank's cash started and quickly accelerated. Bank deposits are guaranteed, but only up to a maximum of £35,000, and only up to 90 per cent. On Friday and Saturday, a sum estimated to be between £2 billion and £3 billion was withdrawn from Northern Rock branches. Eventually, to stop the run, the Chancellor, Alistair Darling, announced on Monday 16 September that the government would guarantee all deposits in Northern Rock, without limit. The immediate crisis was over.

This case illustrates several important points. One is that Northern Rock's strategy differentiated it from the rest of the mortgage industry, but only at the price of unacceptably high risk. Second, the case demonstrates the nature of moral hazard. The Bank of England was reluctant to intervene at an earlier stage in the crisis because of the risk of moral hazard – that in effect a rescue would reward Northern Rock for its reckless behaviour, and might encourage other institutions to be reckless in the future. Eventually, the Bank of England had no choice, and was forced to intervene to safeguard the stability of the whole banking system, as there was a risk that the panic might spread to other institutions. The bail-out safeguarded not only Northern Rock's depositors, who were innocent victims, but also the bank's management and shareholders, who should have known better (Davies 2007). Third, an ethical issue is involved. Northern Rock's depositors have a 100 per cent government guarantee for their funds, yet when the life assurance company Equitable Life failed in 2000, no such protection was extended to its policy-holders. Was this fair?

Porter's generic strategy concept has been further developed by Bowman (Bowman and Faulkner 1996), who proposes the strategy clock, based on a combination of price and perceived added value. He identified eight possible strategies:

- low price/low added value – not likely to be feasible in the long term unless the organisation operates in a protected niche
- low price/standard added value – equates to Porter's cost leadership
- low price/high added value (hybrid) – the strategy pursued by Japanese companies in the 1970s and 1980s, when they were gaining a foothold in European markets
- standard price/high added value (differentiation) – this would be a sensible strategy as a progression from the hybrid strategy
- high price/high added value (focused differentiation) – likely to be a niche strategy, similar to Porter's differentiation focus
- high price/standard added value – not a long-term viable strategy; why should customers pay more if they are not gaining added value?
- high price/low added value – only feasible for a monopoly in a market which is not contestable
- standard price/low added value – not viable in the long term; what is in it for the customer?

SELECTION OF STRATEGIES

This is concerned not with what strategies should be chosen, but how they should be chosen. Johnson and Scholes propose four models:

- Formal evaluation. Here the choice is based solely on analytical techniques. The decision process is impersonal and rational, and appears to be objective. This avoids the risk of taking decisions solely on gut feeling, but it should be remembered that a lot of the analytical techniques are themselves in practice subjective.
- Enforced choice. Here choice is imposed on the organisation from outside. This may be because of the dominant influence of an external stakeholder – for example, a supplier to Marks & Spencer has very little control over its own strategy. However, in the long term, even a firm in this situation does have some strategic choice – to widen its customer base, for example.
- Learning from experience. The emphasis here is on incremental change on a pilot basis with operating units, and then the application of the experience learned from this throughout the organisation. This method is increasingly used by government, which trials new policy initiatives through a pilot study before going for a national launch, and by many manufacturers, which test market new products before attempting a national launch. It is similar to Quinn's concept of logical incrementalism, which we discussed earlier. The advantage is that it pushes responsibility for strategic development down the organisation, but there is the possible disadvantage that there is never a

fundamental strategic rethink – the organisation can suffer from strategic drift.

- Command. Here the dominant stakeholder (who may be the CEO, the biggest shareholder or a government department) selects the strategic direction, and imposes it on the organisation. This has been the experience of the NHS, which has had fundamental strategic change imposed on it by successive governments at regular intervals.

EVALUATION OF STRATEGIES

Possible strategies should be evaluated on three levels, suitability, acceptability and feasibility.

SUITABILITY

Is this a strategy which will produce a sound fit between the organisation and its environment? Will it exploit opportunities in the environment and avoid or neutralise threats? Will it capitalise on the organisation's strengths and core competences and avoid or neutralise weaknesses? Various analytical techniques can be used to help answer these questions:

Life cycle analysis

The consultants Arthur D Little have identified the life cycle/portfolio matrix (see Johnson, Scholes and Whittington 2004). Here the strategies that should be adopted depend on the stage of the product/industry life cycle (embryonic, growing, mature or ageing), and the competitive position of the organisation (dominant, strong, favourable, tenable or weak). For example, the prescribed strategies for a strong firm in a growing industry are fast grow, catch-up, attain cost leadership or differentiation, while for a weak firm in an embryonic industry they are find niche, catch-up or grow with industry. The model is open to criticism, as the definition used are subjective (what is a favourable position in one environment may be a weak one in another), and because, like all models, it ignores all variables except those actually built into the model (stage of maturity and competitive position). For example, it ignores speed of technological development.

Portfolio analysis

We discussed the Boston matrix in Chapter 2. Briefly, this categorised product lines on a matrix of market share and market growth rate, as:

- cash cows: low market growth, high market share
- stars: high market growth, high market share
- question marks: high market growth, low market share
- dogs: low market growth, low market share.

Here the preferred strategic option is to attempt a balance to portfolio between stars and cash cows. Stars are profitable, but they do not generate much cash, while cash cows may be less profitable but are highly cash-generative. Hence use cash cows to finance stars. As with the life cycle model, this is superficially attractive, but again it ignores other variables.

Value chain analysis

Value chain analysis is yet another model developed by Michael Porter. He says that the activities of an organisation should be seen as a sequence of primary events:

- inbound logistics, deliveries, storage, etc
- operations
- outbound logistics (warehousing, wholesalers, deliveries, etc)
- marketing and sales
- service

while underpinning all of these are support activities:

- the firm's infrastructure
- human resource management
- technology
- procurement (purchasing, raising capital, recruitment).

All of these serve to add value for the organisation and form the value chain. The greater the synergies between the various elements, the greater the added value. Conversely, the whole value chain is only as strong as its weakest link. The aim of strategy should therefore be to strengthen the value chain as a whole, by building on existing strengths, or correcting weaknesses.

For example, the primary part of the chain might be strong, but the organisation might have problems caused by high turnover of staff. The strategic choice here would be to concentrate on improving staff turnover using HR techniques. Alternatively, the product might be strong, but its reputation is let down by poor after-sales service. After digging deeper, it might be discovered that the IT systems supporting service are inadequate.

The strength of the value chain technique is that it forces an analysis of how the organisation actually functions, and it avoids over-concentration on some of the more obvious strategic possibilities like merger or takeover. The weakness is that it is exclusively inward-looking. It should be combined with a rigorous analysis of fit with the environment.

ACCEPTABILITY

Strategies have to be acceptable to internal and external stakeholders. This can be assessed in three ways: return, risk and stakeholder reaction.

Return can be assessed using a range of standard accounting techniques, including profitability analysis (discounted cashflow etc), shareholder value analysis (looking at the overall increase in value for the shareholder), using techniques such as economic value added, or cost–benefit analysis (looking at non-financial as well as financial factors).

Risk can be assessed using techniques including:

- break-even analysis – if the break-even point for the new strategy is a very high percentage of capacity, the project is highly risky
- ratio analysis – if the new strategy will result in very low levels of liquidity, as measured by standard ratios, it is high risk
- sensitivity analysis – how sensitive is the profit of the project to a shortfall in any of the key financial variables?

Stakeholder reactions can be assessed using techniques such as stakeholder modelling (discussed in the Chapter 9). Stakeholders may well have strong views on risk, and these should be taken into account.

FEASIBILITY

Strategies have to be feasible in terms of resource availability. Techniques to measure this include:

- Funds flow analysis – what is the implication for future cashflows? If sufficient cash is not currently available, can it be acquired on reasonable terms?
- Break-even analysis – what is the break-even point given the present cost structure? If the break-even point is too high, can the cost structure be improved?
- Resource deployment analysis – what are the key resources and competences required for each strategy? Does the organisation already possess them? If not, can it reasonably acquire them?

STRATEGIC OPTION SCREENING

Several methods can be used to screen options to see whether they meet criteria on suitability, acceptability and feasibility. These include ranking, decision trees and scenario planning.

Ranking

Here options are assessed against key factors in the environment, resources and stakeholder expectations, and a score (or ranking) established for each option. To take a very simple example, assume that a company has two strategic options, A and B, and two success criteria, profitability and stakeholder acceptability. It has established that it regards profitability as more important, and has given this a weighting of 70. Stakeholder acceptability has a weighting of 30 (producing a total weighting of 100).

CASE STUDY 10.9

STAKEHOLDER ACCEPTABILITY

An acceptable strategy – Ben & Jerry's and Unilever

Ben & Jerry's ice cream was one of the leading lights of the ethical business movement. It was not only concerned to trade ethically, it also wanted to change the world. It donated heavily to radical causes, and was deeply involved in the anti-globalisation movement. These values were fully supported by its staff and customers, both key stakeholders.

In April 2000, Ben & Jerry's was taken over by the strait-laced Anglo-Dutch conglomerate Unilever, a classic representative of the globalisation that Ben & Jerry's had opposed. Although it had a good ethical reputation, Unilever was in no sense radical. Ben Cohen, the joint founder of Ben & Jerry's, forecast that the takeover would lead to the destruction of the company.

However, when Unilever appointed a 25-year Unilever man, Yves Couette, to run Ben & Jerry's, he was given the license to be a 'grain of sand in the eye' of Unilever. He abandoned his suit and tie, and followed a deliberate policy of empowerment and delegation. Tough profit targets were set, but Couette pointed out to staff that this would mean that more money would be donated to charity through the Ben & Jerry Foundation, which would continue to have a free hand to support any charity or movement which it chose (including the anti-globalisation movement).

An unacceptable strategy – Marconi

Throughout the 1980s and 1990s, GEC was seen as a safe, rather stolid company, dominated by the safety-first philosophy of its long-time chairman, Arnold (Lord) Weinstock. The company prospered in household electrical goods and defence electronics, and built up a bank balance of several billion pounds. It appealed to risk-averse shareholders.

In the late 1990s new management, headed by George Simpson, decided on a radical new strategy. The defence electronics business was sold to British Aerospace, most of the domestic electric businesses (Hotpoint etc) were sold, and the company, now renamed Marconi, began a dash for growth in the exciting new world of Internet electronics. The rationale was that Marconi would benefit from the dot.com boom which was raging at the time. The bank balances, plus several billions more, were used to buy up American Internet companies.

Unfortunately, the purchases were made right at the peak of the dot.com bubble, and when the bubble burst, many of the new acquisitions were effectively worthless. Marconi's share price plummeted, and when the company eventually went through a financial restructuring, shareholders effectively lost all their money.

Like all shareholders, the Marconi shareholders should have realised that any share investment is by its very nature risky, but they could legitimately argue that they had originally bought their shares in GEC precisely because it was seen as a low-risk company.

Strategy A scores 50 out of 70 for profitability, but only 10 out of 30 for stakeholder acceptability. Strategy B scores less well on profitability, 30 out of 70, but it scores 20 out of 30 for stakeholder acceptability.

This gives a total score for strategy A of 60/100 (50 + 10), and a total score for strategy B of 50/100 (30 + 20). Strategy A is thus the preferred option.

Decision trees

Here options are progressively eliminated by testing them against various criteria. For example, a company has two decision criteria, high growth (most important) and low cost (less important). It is considering four strategies:

Strategy W	high growth, high cost
Strategy X	high growth, low cost
Strategy Y	low growth, low cost
Strategy Z	low growth, high cost.

The first decision step would eliminate strategies Y and Z, because they are low growth, leaving W and X. The next decision step would eliminate W, leaving X as the preferred strategy.

Scenario planning

Here the options are evaluated against various scenarios for the future. For example, if the organisation thinks that the most likely future for the UK exchange rate is stability, this would favour a policy of manufacturing in the United Kingdom. If the most likely scenario is seen as a rising pound, this would favour manufacturing overseas.

ACTIVITY

10.6 STRATEGIC EVALUATION

A risk-averse firm with a strong current financial position, but little access to long-term capital, has decided that it must adopt a policy of unrelated diversification, in order to reduce its dependence on a declining industry. It has evaluated a number of areas for diversification, and decided on the appropriate industry to enter. It is now considering the best way to enter the new market.

Its options are:

A Develop and manufacture a new product.

B Manufacture an existing product under licence.

C Set up a joint venture with a firm that already has expertise in this field.

D Buy out a firm already in the industry.

E Market under its brand name an existing Taiwanese product not currently imported into the United Kingdom.

It has established the following criteria, and weighted them as follows:

		Weighting
a	Low risk	40
b	Speedy entry into the market	20
c	Low capital cost	20
d	Profitability	15
e	Short payback period	5

Activity

a. Discuss the advantages and disadvantages of each method of entry.

b. Using your own judgement, assign scores to each strategy and rank them.

STRATEGIC IMPLEMENTATION

The final stage in the strategy process is implementation – having decided on the chosen strategy, how is it put into practice? Frequently this will be the most difficult phase of the whole process. It involves a key competency of all managers – the ability to manage change.

INCREMENTAL AND TRANSFORMATIONAL CHANGE

Most of the writers on strategic implementation distinguish between incremental and transformational change, although their terminology varies. Johnson, Scholes and Whittington (2004) see strategic change on a two-by-two matrix, type of change and extent of change. A small change is incremental, a large change transformational. Each is of two types, dependent on whether the change is proactive or reactive. Proactive incremental change is tuning, reactive incremental change adaptation, while transformational change is divided into planned and forced change.

Walton (1999) defines transformational change as change which results in entirely new behaviour on the part of organisational members. He sees transformational change as in its very nature strategic. However, drawing on the work of Quinn on logical incrementalism, he sees incremental change as a possible route to strategic change. He also identifies transitional change, the process of carrying out change.

Porter (1999) concentrates on the outcome rather than the process. Changes such as the introduction of re-engineering or Total Quality Management are transformational, but they are not strategic. He sees them as improving operational effectiveness rather than changing the strategic position of the organisation. They are about doing better the same things as the competition are doing. Operational effectiveness is about running the same race faster, strategy is about running a different race.

MODELS OF CHANGE

The classic model of change was identified by Lewin in the 1950s and developed by Schein in the 1980s (Armstrong 1999; Walton 1999). They identified three stages in change management:

- Unfreezing – creating a readiness for change, through creation of a sense of anxiety about the present situation. The sequence here is to enable those involved to be convinced of the need for change.
- Movement – taking action that will encourage the desired new behaviour patterns. This involves doing things differently, based on access to new information, and identifying with new role models.
- Refreezing – embedding the new ways of working into the organisation.

Lewin also developed the concept of force field analysis – analysing the restraining and driving forces within the organisation which oppose or support the proposed change, and then taking steps to encourage the driving forces and decrease the restraining forces.

Beer took a different approach. He argued that the approach that tries to change attitudes in order to change behaviour is flawed. He argued that change should be approached in an opposite way – put people in new roles which require new behaviours, and this will change their attitudes. This is similar to the theory of cognitive dissonance. Beer proposed a six-stage model of change (CIPD 2004):

1. Mobilise commitment to change through joint analysis of problems.
2. Develop a shared vision.
3. Foster consensus and commitment to the shared vision.
4. Spread the word about the change.
5. Institutionalise the change through formal policies.
6. Monitor and adjust as needed.

The Lewin and Beer models both come out of relatively placid environments. They have been criticised for their assumption that it is possible to plan an orderly transition from one static state to another static state (Burnes 1996). In a more dynamic and chaotic environment like that experienced at present, a more continuous and open-ended change process is more appropriate. They also assume that a 'one size fits all' model of change is appropriate, whereas a more modern perspective would be to take a contingency approach and to argue that each organisation has a unique relationship with its environment. Its approach to change should reflect this.

The emergent approach to change as put forward by Burnes and Shaw (CIPD 2004) stresses that change is not linear. It is not a movement from state A to state B, it is continuous and messy. Just like its environment, an organisation is in a continuous state of flux, and the forces for change emerge as the organisation engages with its environment. Change in this model is bottom-up rather than top-down, and it emerges through experimentation. What is important is to ensure that the organisation is responsive to change, and the best way of doing this is to ensure that the organisation is a learning organisation.

MANAGING CHANGE

Kotter (1995) proposes an eight-step plan for transformation:

1. Establishing a sense of urgency – realising that change is needed.
2. Forming a powerful guiding coalition – a powerful and influential group of change leaders is needed.
3. Creating a vision – what will things be like after the change is achieved?
4. Communicating the vision.
5. Empowering others to act on the vision.
6. Planning for and creating short-term wins – a long change process that

appears to be getting nowhere can be demotivating. Building in some short-term wins can improve morale.

7. Consolidating improvements and producing still more change.
8. Institutionalising new approaches – similar to Lewin's refreezing process.

Bridges and Bridges (2000) identify three stages in a change programme:

1. Saying goodbye – letting go of the way that things used to be.
2. Shifting into neutral – the in-between stage when nothing seems to be happening, but everyone is in a stressful state of limbo. In the case of a major merger, this phase might take two years.
3. Moving forward – when people have to behave in a new way.

They describe seven steps in managing transition:

1. Describe the change and why it must happen – in one minute or less.
2. Make sure that the details of the change are planned carefully and that someone is responsible for each detail.
3. Understand who is going to have to let go of what.
4. Make sure that people are helped to let go of the past.
5. Help people through the neutral zone with communication, stressing the 'four Ps':

CASE STUDY 10.10

MOSES IN THE WILDERNESS

Bridges and Bridges discuss the change management techniques used by Moses on his way to the Promised Land:

- **Magnify the plagues.** Moses had to convince a key stakeholder (Pharaoh) that change was needed – that he had to let the Jews go. He did this through creating problems for Pharaoh – the seven plagues. The worse the current situation seems, the greater the impetus for change.
- **Mark the ending.** After the Jews crossed the Red Sea, there was (literally) no going back.
- **Deal with the 'murmuring'.** Don't be surprised when people lose confidence in the neutral zone. Moses faced lots of whingeing. He dealt with it by talking to people about their concerns.
- **Build up change champions.** Moses and his lieutenant Joshua appointed a new cadre of judges to champion the change.
- **Capitalise on creative opportunities.** It was in the Wilderness, not in the Promised Land, that the Ten Commandments were handed down.
- **Resist the urge to rush ahead.** Not much seems to be happening in the neutral zone, but it is where the true transformation takes place. Moses was in the Wilderness for 40 years!

Different stages need different leadership styles. Moses was an ideal leader for the neutral zone, but the Promised Land required a new type of leadership, provided by the conqueror of Jericho, Joshua.

the purpose – why we have to do this

the picture – what it will look and feel like when we get there

the plan – how we will get there

the part – what each person needs to do.

6. Create temporary solutions to the temporary problems found in the neutral zone.
7. Help people launch the new beginning.

RESISTANCE TO CHANGE

Resistance to change can be of two types: resistance to the content of change – ie opposition to the specific nature of the change – and resistance to the process of change – ie opposition to how to the change is introduced. Each might be a perfectly rational response to change, however inconvenient to management.

Armstrong (1999) identifies eight reasons that individuals might resist change:

- The shock of the new – people tend to be conservative, and they do not want to move too far from their comfort zones. To this we would add regret for the passing of the old.
- Economic fears – threats to wages or job security.
- Inconvenience.
- Uncertainty.
- Symbolic fears – the loss of a symbol, like a car parking space, may suggest that bigger and more threatening changes are on the way.
- Threats to interpersonal relationships.
- Threat to status or skill – a change may be seen as deskilling.
- Competence fears – concern about the ability to cope or acquire new skills.

THE ROLE OF HR IN CHANGE MANAGEMENT

The crucial role of HR in change management can be clearly identified using Beer's model of change. HR intervention is crucial at each stage of the model, as follows:

1. Mobilise commitment to change through joint analysis of problems. HR should play a leading role in benchmarking and other environment-scanning techniques, and so help to spot the need for change. HR staff are likely to be the organisers of the teams and workshops who are involved in problem identification and analysis. Underpinning this should be a learning organisation, in which HR should be a prime driver.
2. Develop a shared vision. This involves an understanding of the culture of the organisation, and the ability to support and direct the visions which underpin the culture.

3. Foster consensus and commitment to the shared vision. It is essential that those affected by the change should feel that they have ownership of it. Developing and supporting ownership is a key HR skill, as is the fostering and supporting of change champions.
4. Spread the word about the change. Here, as noted by McCarthy (2004), communication is key. McCarthy stresses that this should involve communication with, rather than communication at, those involved. He suggests the concept of 'conversation' as being appropriate here.
5. Institutionalise the change through formal policies. This may well include the development of new HR policies on recruitment, reward and development. It is crucial that the reward system supports the new ways of doing things, for example.
6. Monitor and adjust as needed. HR policy will need to be proactive after the change process is apparently completed. Development policies should be responsive to the need for any new competencies which become apparent.

Armstrong (1999) identifies a number of 'guidelines for change management', in most of which the role of HR is key. These include:

- commitment and visionary leadership from the top
- understanding the culture
- development of temperament and leadership skills at all levels which support change
- an environment conducive to change – a learning organisation
- full participation of those involved, so that they can own the change
- the reward system should recognise success in achieving change
- a willingness to learn from failure – a support culture rather than a blame culture
- support for change agents
- protection of those adversely affected by change.

Ridgeway and Wallace (1994) discuss the role of HR in managing a common strategic change – a takeover. Here matching the culture of the predator and the target are key. They quote from Furnham and Gunter (1993) on how such a match should be identified. It would involve:

- identifying the culture of the acquiring company
- deciding on any changes needed to ensure that culture supports the proposed strategy
- identifying potential acquisitions and their cultures
- isolating likely changes to those cultures
- designing a format for assessing other cultures
- establishing criteria by which to identify suitable acquisitions.

Crucial here is establishing how the senior management of the target company will fit with the acquirer's culture, and what senior staff gaps will be exposed.

The HR department of the acquiring company will also be responsible for ensuring that the procedures and systems of the two companies are compatible, or can be made compatible, including any industrial relations implications. During the takeover process, the HR department also needs to manage communication. This will involve close liaison with PR, as employees of the target company will get a lot of their information about the takeover via the media.

CASE STUDY 10.11

THE MORRISONS TAKEOVER OF SAFEWAY

The takeover of the supermarket chain Safeway by its rival Morrisons is an example of the most difficult type of takeover to manage – a takeover of a bigger company by its smaller rival. Safeway had three times as many stores as Morrisons, and a bigger turnover, when it was taken over in March 2004.

The cultures of the two companies were totally different. Morrisons was run as a family firm, dominated by the larger than life personality of Sir Ken Morrison, the son of the founder. It was aggressively northern, and prided itself on its 'call a spade a spade' philosophy – nothing subtle, pile it high and sell it cheap. Sir Ken even personally recorded all the store announcements used by the company. Safeway was very different. It had been formed from a number of mergers over the years, was impersonal and bureaucratic, and very southern. Although its stores were smaller than Morrisons it stocked a lot more lines. Its pricing policy was to draw customers in with a few drastic headline price reductions, but it had higher 'background' prices.

The merger also took a long time. Not only did Morrisons bid for Safeway, so did Tesco, Sainsbury and Asda. Because of a Competition Commission investigation, the whole process took 14 months, long enough for gloom and despondency to spread throughout Safeway. Perhaps reflecting this, or even a subconscious desire to sabotage Morrisons, Safeway introduced a totally new accounting system, incompatible with Morrisons, weeks before the takeover was completed.

Once the takeover was finalised, Morrisons did not handle things in the most tactful of ways. Except for one very small previous takeover, its managers had no experience of managing this kind of situation. The attitude was very much 'we know best', and surviving Safeway management was expected to adopt the Morrisons ways of doing things. The Safeway head office in Surrey was closed, and Morrisons was surprised when only 200 of its 1,600 staff wanted to transfer to Bradford. On the other hand, staffing in the old Safeway stores was increased, as although it stocked fewer lines, Morrisons did more activities in-store (bakeries etc). Although sales rose in the Safeway stores that were converted, they fell in those Safeway stores that were not yet converted, leading Morrisons to issue a profits warning in July 2004.

Morrisons also tended to alienate another important stakeholder, the City. The company was notoriously media-shy, and reluctant to talk to City analysts. This was tolerated before the takeover, as Morrisons was relatively small (a FTSE250 firm), and also very successful. As it was now in the FTSE100, it was much more in the media spotlight, and the City expected a much higher standard of communication.

The Morrisons share price has under-performed the market. From a peak of 256p in March, at the time of the takeover, it had fallen to a low of 171p in September, and had only recovered to 225p (on a rising market) by the end of November 2004. In 2007, however, it did achieve a high of 345p, although this was still a smaller rise than for the stock market as a whole.

The verdict: a takeover performance which illustrates Morrisons' lack of experience, failure to take the HR needs of ex-Safeway staff into consideration, and perhaps over-confidence.

ACTIVITY

10.7 Pearmount College

Pearmount College is a medium-sized further education (FE) college in the town of Hetherleigh (population 75,000). In many ways it is a typical FE college. In its Ofsted inspections, most aspects are rated as satisfactory (grade 3, the middle of the five grades available). A third of its courses are rated as above average, a third as below average. However, Pearmount is not typical in that it is a tertiary college. Unlike most FE colleges, it is responsible for all post-16 education in Hetherleigh. Except for a Catholic comprehensive, the secondary schools in Hetherleigh do not have sixth forms.

This gives the college a particular social responsibility. As the only post-16 provider, it cannot be selective in its recruitment policy. It is expected to provide educational opportunities for all of the post-16 population in the town.

There are four main types of post-16 providers, all of which compete to score highly in government league tables. These are school sixth forms, which are often selective, sixth form colleges, which are almost always selective, tertiary colleges, which are normally non-selective, and ordinary FE colleges, which tend to offer mainly vocational courses rather than A levels. The main league table competition is between sixth forms, sixth form colleges and tertiary colleges, and concentrates on A level results. Sixth form colleges tend to score more highly than school sixth forms and tertiary colleges. A recent Ofsted inspection of Pearmount noted that its A level results were at the FE college average, but below the average for sixth form colleges. It also criticised teaching as unimaginative, although it said that some vocational provision was excellent.

Post-16 education is funded by the Learning and Skills Council (LSC), under government guidance. Government funding policy is to concentrate on three main target areas – full time 16–19 education, adult basic literacy and numeracy skills, and adult level 2 qualifications (broadly GCSE grade A–C level). FE and tertiary colleges have responded to this by withdrawing from adult education, unless it fits into the funding priorities, or is fully funded by employers. Pearmount is typical in this. Over the last decade it has withdrawn from many advanced vocational and professional part-time programmes, and concentrated much more on full-time 16–19 programmes. The other continuing pressure from the LSC is to drive up the quality of further education provision, with the threat of withdrawing funding from courses within the priority areas that are deemed to be of low quality.

Jim Merryweather was appointed as the new

principal of Pearmount College in September 2006, following the retirement of his predecessor, who had taken an active role in the town. Within a month of taking up his post, he produced a new teaching and learning strategy for the college. This stressed individual daily targets for students, with daily assessment and measurement of achievement; all assignment work to be completed in college; and fortnightly reports to parents on progress and attendance. His aim was to make the college one of the best sixth forms in the country.

Although there was some concern that the new strategy seemed to focus solely on full-time 16–19 students, it was broadly welcomed by teaching staff, and rapid progress was made in its implementation.

However, Jim also faced the problem that many of his staff were ageing, while others, who mainly taught vocational programmes for adults, were seeing much of their workload disappear. Clearly the college staffing needed to be restructured. One way to do this could have been an early retirement programme, but what often happens in these programmes is that the people opting to take early retirement are the very people you do not want to lose. Another option could have been a programme of retraining and redeployment.

Jim's solution was to propose a radical restructuring, which was announced just before the Easter holidays in April 2007. A new staffing structure was proposed, with more higher-paid posts, but also some low-level posts with a salary ceiling well below that previously available to lecturers. All members of staff were expected to reapply for posts under the new structure, with the clear expectation that some would be unsuccessful.

In addition, holidays were reduced, and the normal working week was increased to 37 hours, all of which could in theory be spent teaching. The working week was also extended to five and a half days, and staff could be requested to work on Saturdays. Staff would no longer be entitled to overtime or time off in lieu.

The reaction of staff was one of horror, particularly as the new posts were immediately advertised internally, although the proposals came under the 90-day consultation period for major redundancies. Teaching staff held a number of one-day strikes, were fully supported by their union and the students union, and also attracted a lot of support within the town.

There was criticism that Jim had failed to consult adequately with stakeholders, and he seemed to have underestimated the affection the town held for the college. As Pearmount had been a tertiary college for over 20 years, virtually every family in Hetherleigh contained someone who had either attended the college themselves, or was the parent of someone who had been a college student.

By the end of the summer term in 2007, half the teaching staff had been made redundant, had found new posts or had taken early retirement. There was severe concern that college staffing would be inadequate to meet demand in 2007–8, and also that the adverse publicity would dissuade many potential students from attending the college.

Questions

1. Critically evaluate Jim's strategy for implementing change at Pearmount College.
2. What techniques do you think can be used to overcome resistance to change?

CHANGE LEADERSHIP

Ridgeway and Wallace (1994) identify a number of competencies required for effective change leadership. These are:

- intellectual skills: intellectually curious and able to handle ambiguity
- influencing skills: assertive, proactive and energetic
- counselling and people skills: sensitive, flexible and adaptable, with a high tolerance of pressure.

While this list is solid, we think that it misses the true essence of change leadership. A good change leader must above all be driven by a vision of the future, and be able to inspire others with that vision. This involves a high sense of values, exceptional communication abilities, a sense of inspiration, and the ability to empower others with the vision. All of these qualities are illustrated in our last case study.

CASE STUDY 10.12

NELSON MANDELA

Nelson Mandela is almost universally recognised as the last, and one of the greatest, inspirational leaders of the twentieth century. His career illustrates the characteristics of a brilliant change leader.

Mandela was born in 1918, a member of a chiefly clan in the Xhosa tribe. He trained as a lawyer, and was drawn at an early age into the struggle against white domination through his membership of the African National Congress (ANC). The political struggle intensified in the 1950s after the election of the white supremacist National Party government, and the establishment of the apartheid system of racial segregation.

In the early 1960s, Mandela was on trial for his life. His statement from the dock in his trial put forward his vision:

> I have fought against white domination. I have fought against black domination. I have cherished the ideal of a democratic and free society in which all persons live together in harmony and with equal opportunities. It is an ideal which I hope to live for and to achieve. But, if needs be, it is an ideal for which I am prepared to die.

Mandela was sentenced to life imprisonment on Robben Island, where he was to remain for 27 years. For much of this he was under a hard labour regime. A telling incident from his imprisonment throws more light on his vision. A particularly tough prison governor imposed a brutal regime on the prisoners, but when he was transferred, he wished Mandela and the other ANC leaders the best for the future. To Mandela, this illustrated the possibility of redemption. The man was brutal not because he had a brutal nature, but because he was conditioned by a brutal system. Like the Catholic Church, Mandela distinguished between the sin and the sinner. From this came his concept of redemption and reconciliation, which was to be a driving force of his presidency.

By the mid-1980s, another key player had entered the scene – F W de Klerk, the new National party leader. De Klerk recognised that the apartheid system must go, and that a settlement must be negotiated with the ANC. In Bridge's terms, this marked the end of the old system, and a move into the neutral transition zone. After lengthy negotiations, Mandela was released from prison in 1990. A new constitution was negotiated, leading to democratic elections in 1994, and the election of Mandela as the first democratic president of South Africa.

Mandela now faced his most severe test as a leader – how to hold the new South Africa together, and forge a new multiracial democratic state. He faced threats on all sides. A right-wing Afrikaner element was threatening civil war, and there was also an undeclared civil war between the ANC and the Zulu Inkatha Freedom Party. The Zulus were the largest tribe in South Africa, and resented the power held by the Xhosa Mandela.

Mandela's approach was to use symbolic acts of reconciliation. He visited the widow of the architect of apartheid, Hendrik Verwoerd. He also presented the rugby world cup to the victorious South African team wearing a South African rugby shirt. Rugby is an Afrikaner sport in South Africa, with almost totally white support. This action helped to reconcile the Afrikaner community to the new South Africa. He also pursued reconciliation with the Zulus. The Inkatha Freedom Party leader, Mangosuthu Buthelezi, was made minister for home affairs, and number three in the government, after Mandela and the vice-president Thabo Mbeki.

Mandela also used the idea of redemption through the Truth and Reconciliation Commission, which he launched with Archbishop Desmond Tutu. The idea here was that perpetrators of political crime could confess their involvement, and receive public absolution. Mandela insisted that this should apply as much to members of the ANC as to the agents of the apartheid regime.

Mandela's last great act of leadership was to recognise that by the end of his term as president in 1999, the transition phase had ended, and that South Africa was into the new beginning. Even his greatest admirers would not call Mandela a great administrator, and he recognised that a new type of more structured leadership was now needed. He therefore retired, leaving the way for Thabo Mbeki, a less charismatic but more structured politician, to succeed him.

When the sculptor Rodin was asked how he would sculpt an elephant, his reply was that he would start with a very large block of stone, and then remove everything which was not elephant. Mandela had a similar vision. Everything which was not part of his vision of a democratic, multicultural South Africa was irrelevant, including bitterness, revenge and recriminations.

CONCLUSIONS

This chapter has discussed the nature of strategy, and its transition from a corporate planning to a strategic management perspective, with a greater emphasis on contingency, experimentation and learning. We have identified the crucial role of change management and of the change leader in ensuring that strategy is implemented as planned.

KEY LEARNING POINTS

- Quinn identifies three elements of strategy – goals, policies and programmes.
- Strategy can be analysed at several levels – corporate, business unit and operational.
- Approaches to strategy are connected with the nature of the environment. In the 1950s and 1960s, a placid environment encouraged the rational, logical corporate planning approach, while a more turbulent environment since the 1970s encouraged the more contingent, experimental strategic management approach.
- The leading exponent of the corporate planning approach was Igor Ansoff, while the leading exponents of the strategic management approach are Tom Peters, Michael Porter, Ralph Stacey, Gary Hamel and C K Prahalad, James Quinn and Henry Mintzberg.
- It is important to distinguish between intended strategy and realised strategy.
- Strategic analysis is concerned with the strategic position of the organisation. What are the key characteristics of the organisation, what changes are going on in the environment, and how will these affect the organisation and its activities? This involves an analysis of the expectations of stakeholders, the culture of the organisation, the organisation's vision and values; the environment, as identified through a STEEPLE analysis; and the key resource areas of the business.
- The extent to which there is a mismatch (a gap) between current strategy and the future environment is a measure of the strategic problem facing the organisation.
- Vision, mission, values and objectives are closely linked, and often confused.
- The mission and objectives of the organisation are constrained by corporate governance, stakeholders, business ethics and culture.
- The mission statement provides a benchmark against which policies can be evaluated.
- Resource analysis is internal to the organisation. It is concerned with the strengths and weaknesses parts of SWOT analysis, and measures the efficiency and effectiveness of an organisation's resources.
- Prahalad and Hamel identify the concept of the core competences of the organisation – those factors that give the organisation its key competitive advantages.
- The concept of generic strategy was introduced by Michael Porter, and developed by Cliff Bowman.
- Possible strategies should be evaluated on three levels: suitability, acceptability and feasibility.
- Transformational change is change that results in entirely new behaviour on the part of organisational members, and is in its very nature strategic.
- Bridges and Mitchell identify three stages in a change programme: saying goodbye, shifting into neutral and moving forward.
- Resistance to change can be rational, and must be managed. This is one of the key functions of HR in change management.
- The critical role of a change leader is to be inspirational and visionary.

QUESTIONS

1. Explain what Quinn means by his three elements of strategy.
2. Why is the corporate planning approach inappropriate for a turbulent environment?
3. What is the role of gap analysis in strategic planning?
4. What are the differences between vision, mission, values and objectives?
5. What do you understand by the expression 'core competence'?
6. Explain the concept of generic strategy as developed by Michael Porter.
7. How can a proposed strategy be evaluated?
8. Why might individuals resist change?
9. What are the six stages in Beer's change model?
10. What are the key requirements for transformational leadership?

TRENDS TO WATCH

- The economic environment seems to be entering into an uneven more turbulent phase, with the surge in the oil price leading to a risk of stagflation – simultaneous rises in inflation and unemployment. Is this leading to a greater emphasis on flexibility and incrementalism in strategic decision making?
- In a more turbulent environment, leadership and change management skills are likely to become even more important. Watch out for examples of inspired leadership.

EXPLORE FURTHER

The leading UK text on strategic management is Gerry Johnson and Kevan Scholes, *Exploring corporate strategy*. A new edition (the seventh) was published in November 2004 (with Richard Whittington). Other valuable strategic management texts are John Thompson with Frank Martin, *Strategic management: awareness and change* (5th edn, 2005), Robert Clark, *Contemporary strategy analysis* (5th edn, 2005) and Bernard Burnes, *Managing change: a strategic approach to organisational dynamics* (4th edn, 2004). John Walton's *Strategic human resource development* (1999) is useful for the HR contribution to strategic management. Also useful is a CIPD factsheet on *Change management* (December 2004), available on the CIPD website.

SEMINAR ACTIVITY

THE SECOND WORLD WAR

Each major participant in the war had a different strategic approach to the war, which reflected their resource situation.

The United Kingdom

- Avoid war if possible.
- If war was inevitable, plan for a long war, and to involve the United States (UK resources were limited, but the United Kingdom could draw on the human and technological resources of the Empire, and hopefully the United States).
- Use the navy to keep supply routes open.
- Build up the defensive capacity of the RAF (fighter planes).

Germany

- Blitzkreig – go for quick, knock-out blows, exploiting the superior fighting ability of the German army.
- Avoid a long war, because of Germany's limited supply of raw materials, particularly oil.
- Avoid a war on two fronts – this made it essential that the USSR was knocked out of the war in 1941–2.

USSR

- Buy space and time (through the pact with Germany in 1939 which gained the USSR half of Poland and the Baltic States).
- Retreat into the interior of Russia to stretch the German lines of communication (just as in 1812).
- Exploit the USSR's vast reserves of manpower.
- Avoid war on two fronts – hence no declaration of war on Japan until August 1945.
- Press the western Allies to open a second front in Europe.

United States

- Avoid war.
- Exploit the mass production capacity of American industry to out-produce the Axis powers.

Japan

- Pre-emptive strike – to destroy the US navy at Pearl Harbour.
- Blitzkrieg.
- Seize oil supplies in Indonesia to make up for Japan's shortage of oil.
- Avoid war on two fronts – hence no declaration of war on the USSR.

France

- Avoid war if possible.
- Fight a defensive war, relying on the Maginot line to repel a German invasion.

Italy

- Initially avoid war, as Italy was militarily weak.
- Once the Germans appeared to have won in 1940, attack France and Britain to gain territory (Nice in France, which had been Italian until 1860, Egypt from Britain, to link up the Italian empire in North Africa).

Spain

- Avoid war with Britain and France, which could easily attack and/or blockade Spain.
- Resist German pressure to enter the war, but if this became impossible, only commit troops to the Eastern Front.

Once the United States had entered the war in 1941, the Anglo–American allies made the crucial corporate-level strategic decision that the war in Europe was to have first priority. In Asia, Japan was to be contained, particularly at sea.

Another corporate-level (but unsuccessful) strategic decision was to attempt to knock Germany out of the war through strategic bombing, exploiting the West's technological and material advantages, while leaving the USSR to defeat the German armies, using its manpower advantage.

Examples of business-unit-level decisions were the decisions to invade Sicily rather than the Balkans in 1943, and Normandy rather than Calais in 1944.

Operational tactical decisions were those to deploy particular national allied armies to particular beaches in the Normandy landings.

Questions

1. How far do the strategic decisions and approaches used in the war fit the characteristics of strategic decisions listed earlier?
2. How far do the strategic approaches taken by the war's participants reflect the core competencies of each country?

CHAPTER

The Marketing Function

❖ Learning Objectives

After reading this chapter you should understand some of the purpose and position of the marketing function within organisations. You should be familiar with ways of analysing markets and understand the ideas behind the marketing mix. You should also be familiar with some of the general criticisms of the marketing function. In particular you should be able to:

1. **define** both markets and marketing and be able to explain key terms within the definitions
2. **explain** concepts such as market size, niches, market segmentation and relationship marketing
3. **explain** at least two ways of categorising people into market segments
4. **explain** concepts such as competition, barriers to entry and exit and market dynamism
5. **discuss in detail** market strategy and market positioning
6. **draw** both a BCG matrix and a General Electric Matrix which might be useful for strategists in an organisation with which you are familiar
7. **draw** an imaginary product lifecycle for a consumer good that interests you
8. **contrast** briefly the difference between markets research and marketing research
9. **list** seven uses and four methods of market research
10. **discuss in detail** each of the five main components of the marketing mix
11. **explain** the concept of a "brand" in marketing
12. **differentiate** between marketing and public relations

13 **explain** the concepts of guerrilla marketing and cause-related marketing

14 **outline** some of the techniques and methods used in advertising

15 **evaluate** at least four criticisms that have been levelled against the marketing function

Definition and Introduction to Marketing

In theory at least, marketing has prime place in the sequence of management functions because it is concerned with identifying a need the organisation can exploit with a product or service. Once this need has been recognised, the other functions – operations, HRM, finance function – can work together to actually produce the product or service. In fact, the marketing function also plays an important part at the end of the process – selling the finished product. Some people find it difficult to distinguish between marketing and sales. As a simplification, marketing is "having something you can get rid of" while selling is "getting rid of what you have!" Many people have attempted to define marketing in more formal terms. Typical definitions assert that marketing is:

> "An organisational function and set of processes for creating, communicating and delivering value to customers and for managing customer relationships in ways that benefit the organisation and its stakeholders."
>
> *(American Marketing Association, 2004)*

> "Responsible for identifying, anticipating and satisfying customer requirements profitably."
>
> *(Hannagan, 2005)*

> "A management function which identifies, anticipates and supplies consumer requirements efficiently and effectively."
>
> *(Chartered Institute of Marketing [UK])*

Unfortunately each of the definitions has its disadvantages. The first is so megalomanic in its scope that it includes practically everything in an organisation. It does not differentiate between marketing and other essential functions such as production or finance. Two of the definitions imply, quite wrongly, that marketing only applies to commercial, profit-making, organisations. A definition which escapes these problems and which commands some consensus is:

> "A product or service's conception, pricing, promotion and distribution in order to create exchanges that satisfy consumers and organisational objectives and the interest of other stakeholders."
>
> *(see, for example, Pride and Farrell, 2000; Health Advantage, 2004; Quintessential Careers, 2004)*

This definition has a number of advantages.

- It is centred upon the exchange relationship between consumers (in the broadest sense) and organisations.
- It emphasises that these exchanges should be satisfactorily to all parties.
- It specifies the activities which constitute marketing.
- By implication it accepts that other functions in the organisation play an important part in a satisfactory exchange.

Many writers emphasise the importance of organisations adopting a marketing orientation. They contend that everyone in the organisation has a marketing role. For example, when a driver of a company van parks discourteously it tarnishes the company's image and affects its relationship with a customer. Similarly, an operative making a poor-quality product, an off-hand customer service assistant, a tardy accounts clerk and an arrogant chief executive all reflect badly on the organisation and affect its relationship with customers and clients. The management guru, Peter Drucker (1999) takes the view that:

> “The purpose of business is to create and keep customers ... it has only two functions – marketing and innovation. The basic function of marketing is to attract and retain customers at a profit.”

This view is probably overstated. It means that marketing and the organisation are almost synonymous and that one of the terms is therefore redundant. Furthermore, there are many non-profit organisations where the satisfaction of customers is not the only objective of the organisation. Nevertheless, most organisations need to have a *market orientation*. This is also called being *"consumer centred"* or being *"consumer driven"*. The marketing function can be discussed in five main sections:

Chapter contents

11.1 Markets

A *market* (in contrast to *marketing*) may be defined as:

> “The actual or potential buyers of a product.”

This means that a market is wider than individuals and it includes private and public sector organisations, supplier groups and purchasing groups. It is also wider than present or past buyers. It includes anyone or any organisation that is reasonably likely to buy a product in the future. Kotler (1986) defined a product broadly as:

> ". . . anything that can be offered to a market for attention, acquisition, use or consumption that might satisfy a want or need. It includes physical objects, services, persons, places, organisations and ideas."

An organisation that hopes to sell its product in a market needs to study the market very carefully and may commission extensive market research (see section 11.3). It will need to examine the characteristics of the market such as:

- the **people** and **organisations** that make up the market
- the **product** that it is bought
- the **purpose** for which it will be bought and the **needs** it will satisfy
- the **times** and **occasions** (e.g. birthdays, setting up a new home or everyday purchases) when the product is bought
- the **method** used to buy the product (e.g. visit to retail outlet, regular order, telephone order or Internet shopping)

It should be remembered that people and organisations do not buy products for their own sake. Products are bought because they *solve a problem* or confer *benefits* upon their owners. For example, organisations do not purchase a car for a sales representative because it is a good thing in itself. The car will be purchased because the organisation believes it will benefit from the sales representative's ability to visit more customers each day and because it can be sure that its image will not be damaged by the representative arriving at customers premises driving a clapped-out banger.

Markets can differ in many ways. The main differences are size, competition, barriers and dynamism.

Size, niches and market segmentation

Markets differ markedly in their size. Some markets, such as detergents and cleaning materials, are vast and international. Global companies such as Proctor and Gamble have developed to meet the needs of such markets. In principle, large markets are good and lead to very cost-effective products, because development costs are shared among millions of customers. However, these benefits accrue only if the large market is homogeneous and customers have similar needs. However, it is difficult to mount an effective marketing campaign for a large, heterogeneous market. It is usually better to target a smaller but more homogeneous group. A market can be made more homogeneous by focusing upon a restricted range of either products or consumers.

A market which focuses upon a restricted range of specialised products is generally called a "*niche market*". A niche market may be defined as "a portion of a market whose needs are met by a restricted range of specialised products". A classic example of an organisation that caters for a niche market is the Tie Rack chain. It operates within a wider market for clothing. However, it sells only ties, scarves, handkerchiefs and other accessories. Appropriately enough, many of Tie Rack's outlets are physical niches at airports or railway stations. WesternGeco, a subsidiary of the American company Schlumberger, also operates within a niche market. It provides seismic imaging services for oil companies. It operates on a worldwide basis from large, technically sophisticated premises. Catering for a niche market means that an organisation can develop highly specialised expertise and project a clear, distinctive image.

Another way to produce a homogeneous market is *market segmentation* where a wider market is divided into subgroups whose members have similar needs. Typical methods of market segmentation divide customers according to factors such as loyalty, age, gender, neighbourhood or social economic status.

Perhaps the most important way to segment a market is to divide it into *past customers* (i.e. loyal customers) and new customers. In the late 1990s there was a craze to focus upon past customers. The craze arose from the realisation that with the development of the Internet, customers had a much greater ability to "shop around" and become "promiscuous consumers". Many organisations therefore concentrated on establishing a dedicated base of existing customers and developing a long-term relationship that would prevent loyal customers switching to other suppliers. This is called *"relationship marketing"*. It was supported by claims such as:

- Costs of acquiring a new customer are ten times higher than keeping an existing customer.
- Loyal customers spend more than new customers.
- Past, satisfied customers tell others about their satisfaction.
- Past customers are more profitable because they are willing to pay a premium for a service they know.

Such principles were embraced by organisations that traded with other organisations. So, for example, a computer software company would develop a close marketing relationship with its customers. Specific programmers would be devoted to clients so that personalised help would be available if needed. It would hope that this would establish a deep, long-term and profitable relationship. Initially these concepts were applied to business organisations (*B2B transactions*). However, their relevance to retail transactions was quickly appreciated. Very successful examples of *customer management* and relationship marketing include the Tesco Clubcard scheme and Airmiles. A fundamental aspect of customer management is the concept of ***client life-cycle***. A new client needs to be welcomed, perhaps by email, and assured that they have made the correct choice of supplier. An established customer needs to be told that they are important and that the organisation wishes to attend to their needs. A long-established client needs to be made aware of new products. Unfortunately, some of these basic beliefs have not withstood scrutiny. For example, Werner and Kumar (2002) provided data that indicates loyalty is not as profitable as the gurus of the 1990s suggested. There are some advantages of encouraging customer loyalty but they are not as great as their advocates imply. Werner and Kumar note, for example, that long-term customers tend to demand more favourable contracts. Furthermore, many long-term customers make disproportionate demands in terms of customer support.

Market segmentation by *age* is also very common. Classic examples are the UK travel organisation Club 18–30 which markets lively Mediterranean holidays to youthful consumers, and the SAGA Group which markets holidays and financial products to people aged 50 years or more. Market segmentation by age is widespread in the fashion and entertainment industries.

Market segmentation by *gender* is widespread in the publishing industry. For example magazines such as *Woman's Weekly* and *Cosmopolitan* are marketed for women whilst *Playboy* and *What Car* are marketed for men. Similarly, the range of cars offered by major manufacturers will include at least one car designed to appeal to women and other cars that are designed to appeal to men.

Market segmentation by *neighbourhood* is very common. For example, billboards in prosperous areas will depict luxury goods purchased out of discretionary income whilst billboards in less affluent areas will advertise basic products. Probably the most extensive classification of residential areas is the ACORN system (CACI, 2005). Readers in the UK can obtain the ACORN classification of where they live by visiting the Internet site http://www.streetmap.co.uk . The ACORN classification starts with five major categories:

1 Wealthly Achievers
2 Urban prosperity
3 Comfortably off
4 Moderate means
5 Hard-pressed

These are then subdivided into 17 major groups. For example, the wealthy achievers are subdivided into groups such as wealthy executives, affluent greys and flourishing families. The hard-pressed are divided into four groups: struggling families, burdened singles, high-rise hardship and inner-city adversity. The groups are further divided into subgroups. For example, the affluent greys, who comprise 7.7 per cent of the British population, are subdivided into older affluent professionals (1.8 per cent), farming communities (2.0 per cent), old people in detached homes (1.9 per cent) and mature couples (2.0 per cent). The high-rise hardship group is subdivided into old people in high-rise flats (0.8 per cent) and singles in high-rise estates (0.9 per cent). A manager marketing sophisticated financial products such as shares or annuities would target neighbourhoods containing many affluent greys whilst a government department trying to ensure proper take-up of welfare benefits might target neighbourhoods containing many people experiencing high-rise hardship.

Markets are often segmented by *socio-economic status*. This system classifies markets according to the work performed by the head of the household. The categories are:

- A upper middle-class (e.g. directors, senior managers and senior civil servants)
- B middle-class (e.g. lawyers, doctors, middle managers and higher professional workers)
- C1 lower middle-class (e.g. teachers, nurses, junior managers and lower professional workers)
- C2 skilled workers including technologists and many engineering workers
- D working-class
- E subsistence workers and unemployed people

Market segmentation by socio-economic status is far from exact but it does help to group consumers who have similar spending power and preferences. This discussion covers only the most popular ways of dividing a large market into homogeneous groups. Many other methods exist. Markets are often segmented according to lifestyle using categories with cute acronyms such as "YUPPIES" (Young Upwardly Mobile Persons), "DINKIES" (Dual Income No Kids) or "GRUMPIES" (Grown Up Mature Persons)

Competition

In a totally captive market there is only one supplier and customers must purchase from this supplier or do without the product. From a supplier's viewpoint a captive market is ideal and very little effort is needed to sell products at a high price. Unfortunately, captive markets are very attractive to other organisations who then set up in competition. Captive markets are very rare. A market is generally regarded as being a captive when there are fewer than four suppliers. Sometimes captive markets are called *monopolies* or duopolies. A market which has, say, more than 12 suppliers is generally called a "*fluid market*".

Barriers to entry and exit

Captive markets tend to exist in situations when it is difficult for others to enter the market. For example, in the aerospace industry there are often only one or two suppliers. Few organisations can afford the immense costs of setting up huge and complicated factories or build up the technical knowledge and expertise needed. Barriers to entry also exist in the form of laws and regulations such as patent laws, copyright laws and planning permissions. Distribution channels can also constitute entry barriers. Commercial practices by competitors may present further entry barriers – especially the practice of *predatory pricing* (OECD, 1989). Predatory pricing occurs when a large, established business cuts its price below its costs so that new competitors must sell at a loss and are therefore eventually driven from a market. *Exit barriers* prevent organisations withdrawing from markets. Usually they wish to exit from a market because it is either unprofitable or it is no longer central to the organisation's strategy. Typical exit barriers include loss of capital already invested, the cost of making staff redundant, loss of prestige or government pressure.

CASE 11.1: ROCKEFELLER'S PREDATORY PRICING

A classic case of predatory pricing is given by John D. Rockefeller's oil interests (Tarbell, 1950). A new entrant, the Pure Oil Company, was driven out of business when Rockefeller's Standard Oil Company drastically lowered its price, knowing that its vast reserves could survive a short-term loss in order to reap a long-term benefit. Another example of predatory pricing is the way established airlines cut the price of their air fares in the 1970s to force a new entrant, Laker Airways, out of the transatlantic passenger market.

Dynamism

Markets differ in the rate at which they change. A growing market is called an *"expanding market"*. A market that is shrinking is called a *"declining market"* and one that stays the same is called a *"static"* or *"stagnant market"*. It is generally easiest to operate in an expanding market. Organisations operating in a declining market need to pay very close attention to costs in the hope that they will be able to drive less efficient competitors from the market.

These characteristics are not the only factors that differentiate markets. In order to predict and anticipate markets it is necessary to understand six further influences. They are the political, environmental, societal, technological, legal and economic (PESTLE) factors outlined in more detail when strategy was discussed in Chapter 3, p. 60. **Cultural factors** are also important characteristics of markets. For example, the French culture and traditions made it much more difficult for the McDonald's hamburger chain to penetrate the French market.

11.2 Market Strategy and Market Positioning

Once there is a clear understanding of market characteristics it is possible to choose the type of market an organisation would prefer to serve. This is called *"market strategy"*, *"market positioning"* or *"portfolio planning"*. Organisations and consultancies have devised schemes such as PESTLE analysis to aid market positioning. Additional schemes include the Boston matrix, the General Electric matrix and the Anscoff matrix.

The *Boston Matrix* (also known as the *BCG* matrix) focuses on two aspects of a market, its *dynamism* (growth rate) and a product's relative *share of a market*. This allows products, services or production units to be categorised into the four types shown in Figure 11.1.

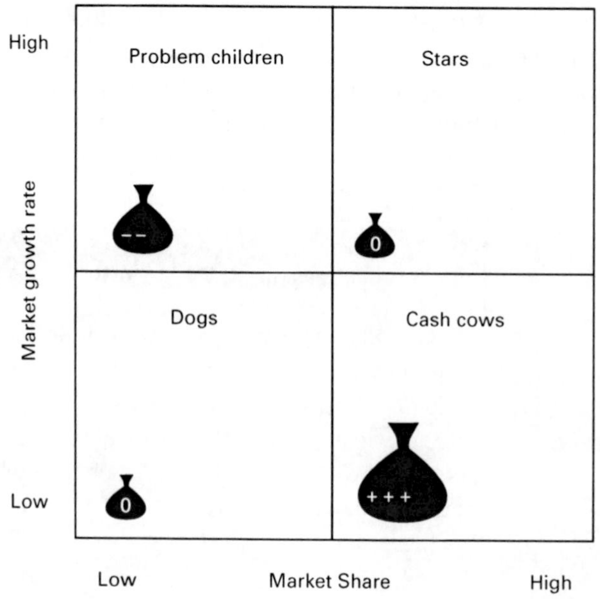

FIGURE 11.1 The BCG Matrix

If a product has a low market share in a slow-growing market, the product is classified as *"a dog"* since it is doing poorly in a weak market. The outlook for the product is poor and an organisation might be well advised to consider eliminating the product from its range – preferably by selling it to someone else, or in the worst case, shutting the product line down. If the product has a low market share but operates in an expanding market, the organisation has a problem because the outlook is mixed. The expanding market bodes well but the low market share implies a struggle to keep up with market leaders who will be able to obtain greater economies of scale. In these situations an organisation must decide whether to inject substantial resources to develop and promote the product. This may involve considerable risk. A product in this quadrant of the market is therefore categorised as *"a problem child"*. Sometimes, products categorised as "problem children" are called *"cash hogs"* because, while their profit potential is uncertain they often require large injections of cash to keep up. A product that commands a high share of a slowly growing market is categorised as a *"cash cow"*. Its high market share means that economies of scale are achieved and a lot of money is generated. This money can be used to promote other projects such as "a problem child" or a "star". Organisations may become complacent about their "cash cows" and pay more attention to new products (stars). Because of lack of investment the "cash cows" lose their competitiveness and turn into "dogs". A *"star"* is a product that has a high share of an expanding market. Generally, it will generate most of the funds needed for its own development and promotion but, from time to time, this may need supplementing by injections of resources from a "cash cow". The Boston Matrix provides a reasonable basis for the allocation of development funds. However, it has its disadvantages (Morrison and Wensley, 1991). It oversimplifies markets by focusing upon just two aspects: market growth and market share. This may lead an organisation to ignore other important aspects (Haspeslagh, 1982). Moreover, the Boston Matrix simplifies the two dimensions into just two crude categories; high and low.

The *General Electric Matrix* is also known as *"The Industry Attractiveness/Business Strength"* Matrix or the *"Directional Policy"* Matrix. It overcomes some of the disadvantages of the Boston Matrix by incorporating more factors and allowing three levels for each dimension. The General Electric Matrix has two composite dimensions: "industry attractiveness" and "business strength". *Industry attractiveness* is an amalgam of the following five characteristics of an industry:

- market forces – size, growth, price sensitivity and bargaining position
- competition – as types of competitors or substitution by new technology
- financial and economic factors – economies of scale, profits, entry and exit barriers
- technological factors – the maturity of the market, patents and copyrights together with the manufacturing technology needed
- socio-political factors – pressure groups, legal constraints and unionisation

A product is evaluated on a similar set of factors to arrive at a measure of *business strength*. Using these two measures the product is located on a matrix and an appropriate strategy is determined. In practice, this process is quite complicated because an intricate system of weights is applied to the characteristics of the industry and the strengths of the business or product. Figure 11.2 indicates the appropriate strategy for products or organisations positioned in each cell.

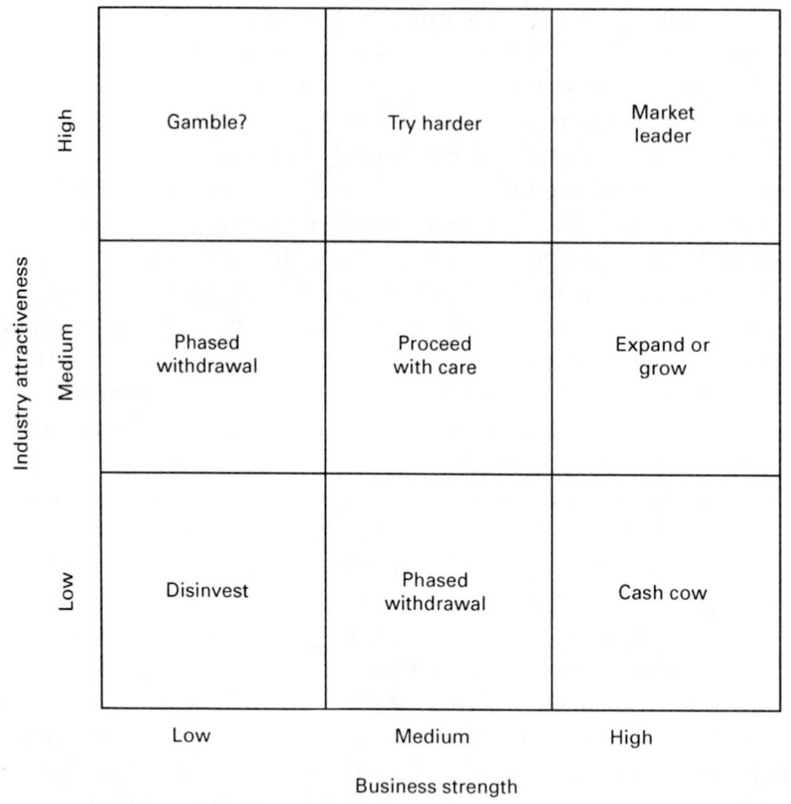

FIGURE 11.2 The General Electric Matrix

For example, a weak product in an unattractive market should be discontinued as quickly as possible, preferably by its sale to another organisation. A strong product in similarly unattractive market should be milked for all the cash it can generate. The case of a weak product in an attractive market is interesting. The organisation should either quit or take a gamble and invest many resources in the product's development in the hope that it can be made a market leader. It is similar to the "problem child" category of the BCG matrix.

Unfortunately, even a system as sophisticated as the General Electric Matrix does not capture the full complexity of positioning a product in a market. For example, a product which is an established market leader can be developed in a number of ways. Efforts could be made to obtain an even greater share of the market. Alternatively, the product can be adjusted so that it appeals to a new market. Ansoff (1989) developed a matrix to aid such decisions. This matrix focuses upon whether both the markets and the products are new or established and, as Figure 11.3 shows, it indicates an appropriate strategy for each combination.

Once a suitable market has been identified it is necessary to decide the organisation's role within that market. It is often assumed that organisations should aim to be market leaders or *pioneers*. In this role an organisation will devise new methods and campaigns

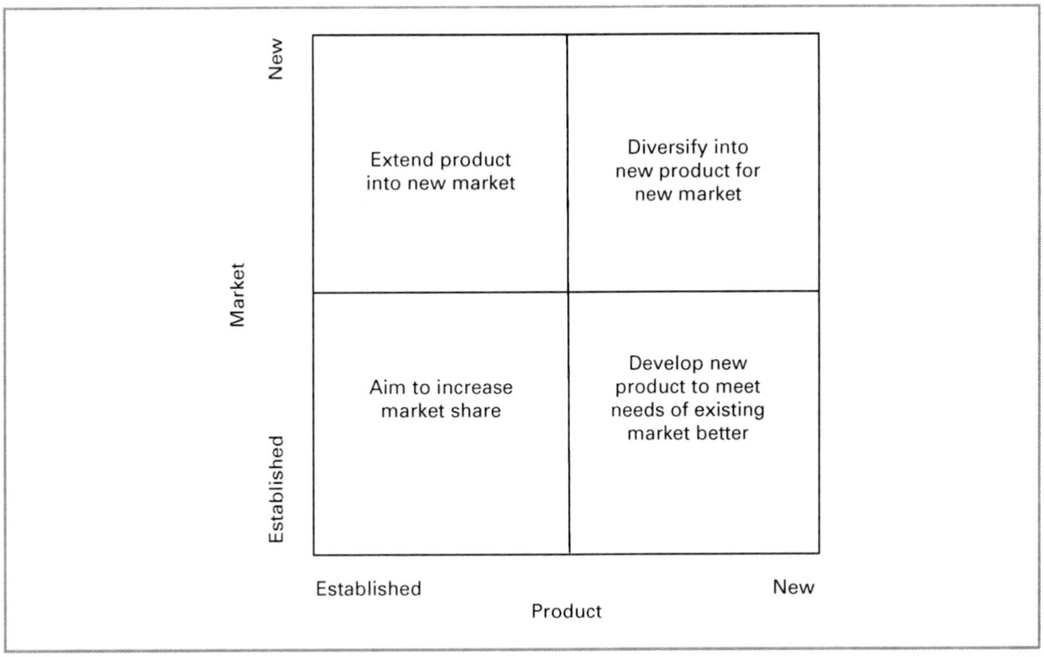

FIGURE 11.3 The Ansoff Matrix

(Pettinger, 1997). Pioneer organisations also open up new markets and devise new products. They frequently have a high esteem. However, being a pioneer can be risky because there may be unknown difficulties. Pioneers will need to carry substantial development costs. If the ideas are successful they can be copied more cheaply by other organisations. An alternative, and often more successful, marketing strategy is to adopt a *"follow the leader"* approach: keeping a keen eye on developments and maintaining a capability to quickly exploit the advances made by others. Other organisations adopt a strategy of building up *technical excellence*, or the *quality of their staff*, and they deploy these assets when and where an opportunity arises.

Organisations must also consider the maturity of their products or services and try to ensure their portfolios contain goods at different stages of the product life cycle. In general, product life cycles have five main phases as shown in Figure 11.4.

The continuous line shows the "natural" progression of sales. As a new product or service is being introduced, there is a period of slow growth. This is followed by rapid increase in sales as the product or service is adopted by opinion leaders and then a wider range of consumers. At maturity, growth is either slow or there is a small decline as the product loses some of its "novelty value". At this point the product has wide acceptance in the market. During the saturation phase, sales may decline somewhat because, although the market may be expanding, new competitors emerge. Finally, the product declines until sales are so low that they generate little cash. This pattern is an idealised generalisation. In practice, it varies greatly. In some cases, usually fashion items and children's toys, the whole life cycle is less than a year. In other cases such as "big ticket" items (e.g. televisions) the life cycle can be more than a decade. Organisations will try to predict the life cycle of their products or serv-

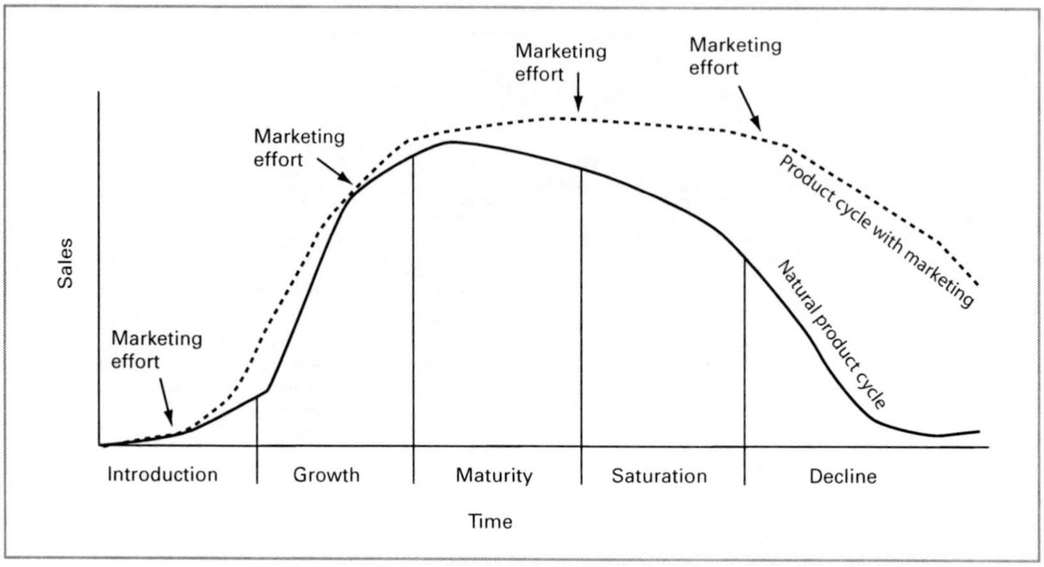

FIGURE 11.4 Product Life Cycle

ices to ensure that they have new products "in the pipeline" to replace the products that are in the saturation and decline phases. Predicting the life cycle of products is particularly important in industries such as pharmaceuticals where it can take years to develop new medicines. The marketing function will monitor the life cycles of products for a second reason. By mounting a marketing effort, such as advertising, new packaging or restyling at key times the marketing function can boost sales and extend the product life cycle. The effect of a marketing effort on a product life cycle is demonstrated by the dotted line in Figure 11.4.

11.3 Understanding Markets (Market Research)

Marketing decisions require a lot of information. The process of collecting and collating this information in a systematic and objective away is called **market research**. It is defined by the American Marketing Association as:

> ". . . the function that links the consumer, customer and public to the marketer through information – information used to identify and define marketing opportunities and problems; generate, refine and evaluate marketing actions; monitor marketing performance; and improve understanding of marketing as a process."

The terms "market research", "markets research" and "marketing research" sound very similar and are often used interchangeably. Technically, however, market research refers to *any* information about markets. *Markets research* is a part of market research and looks at the characteristics of markets. *Marketing research* deals with information relevant to marketing a specific product or service. To avoid confusion it is therefore helpful to divide market research into two main categories: *markets research* and *marketing research.*

Markets research

Research on markets is sometimes called "market intelligence". It obtains information, usually quantitative, on many of the market characteristics such as the size of a market, growth, use of technology, dynamism and level of competition (see Section 1 of this chapter). Often markets research is based on existing (secondary) data compiled by government and industry sources such as census figures, the retail price index and the value of certain imported goods. It may also use journal and newspaper articles to build up a picture of competitors.

Marketing research

Marketing research focuses upon the information that will be useful to organisations who wish to sell specific products. It is the research which, say, the brand manager for Coca-Cola would use to devise a campaign to increase Coca-Cola's market share. While marketing research has some overlap with research on markets, its focus is narrower and it is closer to the actual point of sale. Marketing research can, perhaps, the best considered under two headings: its uses and its methods.

Uses of marketing research

Marketing research can play a vital role in bringing to market a product that is valued by customers and which is presented to them in an enjoyable way. Marketing research's main uses include:

- **Product generation** – marketing research can be used to identify new products. These ideas can be obtained by listening to consumers or by holding brainstorming sessions with designers and marketing executives.
- **Product improvement and embellishment** – existing products can be improved or made more attractive. Again, the source of suggestions can be obtained from consumers or brainstorming sessions. Ideas may also be generated by examining competitors' products or even products and services in other markets.
- **Product testing and refinement** – prototypes of products and services can be tested on small groups of consumers. Their reactions and comments are usually incorporated in a modified product.
- **Consumer targeting** – marketing research can help pinpoint the people who are most likely to buy the product or use a service.
- **Sales forecasting.**
- **Packaging and advertising design** – various suggestions for packaging can be tested out on samples of consumers and the most effective packages or adverts chosen.
- **Point-of-sale displays and procedures** – marketing research can be used to develop and then refine point of sale displays, brochures and other factors that might influence the experience of a buyer.

Marketing research methods

Marketing research uses a wide range of techniques to collect data on customers and products. Some of the main methods are:

- **Existing internal data** – such as sales records, call reports from sales representatives and especially quotations for work that have been not been taking up by customers. Customer loyalty schemes such as Tesco's Clubcard routinely gather vast amounts of information on specific consumers. This information can give very detailed data on individuals and groups of customers.
- **Surveys** can take many forms. Perhaps the simplest is a questionnaire returned by a purchaser when she or he registers a guarantee. Many organisations also use questionnaire surveys. Archetypally, questionnaire surveys are administered by market researchers who approach customers, whose characteristics appear to meet their *quotas*, as they visit shopping malls or go about their daily life. Alternatively, questionnaire surveys may be administered in a slightly more rigorous way to a *random sample* of people in their own homes. Unfortunately, random samples are more expensive than quota samples. Questionnaires may also be distributed via the post but this method may result in a very poor response rate. The telephone and the Internet may also be used to administer questionnaires. However, the sample responding to this type of survey may not be representative of the whole market. Questionnaire surveys need to be constructed with care to ensure that the questions are "neutral". Sometimes a series of questionnaires are administered to the same group of people. Often these are called *consumer panels*. Consumer panels have the advantage that they can track changes in customer preferences over time. Unfortunately, the repeated questioning of the same people can sensitise them to issues so that they gradually become unrepresentative. Some unscrupulous organisations use questionnaires as a way of introducing themselves to people, getting them to divulge information and then attempting to sell them a product directly. This is called "SUGGING" (selling under the guise). Charities sometimes use surveys as a ruse to raise funds. This is called "FRUGGING" (fund raising under the guise). Both practices are unethical and should not be used.
- **Focus groups or group discussions** are frequently used in market research – especially when customers' underlying attitudes to new or changing situations are relevant. Focus groups consist of, say, eight people representing different types of consumers plus a leader who ensures they cover the required topics. Sometimes, focus groups attempt to assess "emotions" and "deep attitudes" towards a product or service. Some of the techniques are exotic and perhaps silly. Group members, for example, might be asked to nominate a type of tree that they associate with a certain public figure. In other situations, a focus group will be asked to taste a new drink and compare it to existing beverages. Focus groups can also be used to evaluate the clarity and impact of different ways of packaging a product.
- **Experiments** are used infrequently. Usually they are employed to study the impact of advertisements and packaging. For example, the technique of *pupilometry* may be used to monitor a consumer's eye movements and determine the parts of an advert that a consumer selects for attention. Sometimes experiments are used to observe buyer behaviour. For example, a supermarket may stock shelves in a different ways and videotape the behaviour of customers. The videotape will then be analysed to establish which shelf lay-out generates most purchases.

11.4 The Marketing Mix

Successful marketing of a product or service involves an appropriate combination of five main factors. This combination is called the marketing mix and is based on the *"5 Ps"* of: **p**roduct or service, **p**rice, **p**ackaging, **p**romotion and **p**lace of purchase.

Products

Section 2 of this chapter discussed the strategic marketing issues but many other factors must be taken into account. A product can be either a physical entity or a service. The main difference is that ownership of a physical entity changes hands when a *product* is purchased. When a *service* is purchased ownership is not transferred. From a marketing viewpoint, the most important feature of either is the *benefit* it bestows upon the customer. An engineer, a technologist, a production manager and a design specialist may eulogise about the product's features, its technical sophistication or its aesthetic appeal. However, these are only important if the consumer believes that they confer some benefit. The benefits may be a saving in time, the ability to perform a previously impossible task, a feeling of well-being and attractiveness or an increase in status. In other words a product or service must solve or ease a problem for the consumer. For example, consumers do not buy computers because they can add up numbers quickly or because they are an example of high technology. They buy computers because the machines solve problems such as communicating with others, keeping accounts or storing information. If a product or service confers benefits its competitors do not, the product has a *"unique selling-point"* that may increase sales.

Consumers frequently judge products on the basis of their *quality* – a freedom from imperfections and an implication of exclusivity or "class". Marketeers imply quality when they offer "fine wines", "prime beef", "select cheeses", "high-calibre education" and so on. Generally products must also offer *durability* – the ability to function satisfactorily for an acceptable time. However, there is a range of products (razors, pens, cameras, gloves, live entertainment, etc.) where durability is not expected.

A product's *brand* is an important feature. The marketing functions of organisations give their brand close attention. Brands started when farmers would burn distinctive marks into the flesh of their cattle so that they could be identified easily should they stray or be stolen. Farmers who produced good cattle were particularly keen on branding because their brand would be recognised at a market and their cattle would command a higher price. In early days of mass production good producers of products such as soap would mark their bars of soap with a distinctive mark so that consumers would know they were buying a better product. As the brands of soap became better known, manufacturers took steps to ensure other people could not use the same mark. They also began to promote brands via advertising that made them instantly recognisable and invoke positive associations in consumer's minds. Kellogg's, for example, developed a brand which is associated with freshness, sunshine and vitality. Today, most major products carry brands, some of which are so well-known that they are very valuable. Some of the most famous brands in the USA include Coca-Cola, Ford, McDonald's, Microsoft and GAP. Other world-famous brands include BP, Cadbury, IKEA, Mercedes, Myer, Nintendo, Qantas, Rip Curl and Toyota.

The major advantage of brands is that they add additional benefits to a product. A classic experiment by Penny, Hunt and Twyman as long ago as 1974 neatly demonstrates the point. They asked consumers who normally used brand B to try two products without knowing their brand. A majority (61 per cent) preferred brand A while 39 per cent preferred brand B. Another group also tried the same two products. For this group the brands were known. 35 per cent were found to prefer brand A while 65 per cent preferred brand B. A brand may be defined as:

> "A symbolic construct created by a marketeer to represent a collection of information about a product or group of products. This symbolic construct typically consist of a name, identifying mark, logo, visual images or symbols or mental concepts which distinguish the product or service."

A brand has connotations of a product's "promise" and differences from its competitors. A brand may attempt to give a product and a "personality" (Free-definition, 2005a). To be successful, a brand must have several characteristics (see iboost, 2005). These include:

- **Simple, clear messages**. A campaigning message or one which seems to go against the "Establishment" (e.g. the themes of the Bennetton and FCUK branding) are often a "cheap" way to success.
- **Projections of credibility** – so claims are believed.
- **Motivation of customers** which increases the enjoyment of purchasing products with the brand. This makes it more likely that purchases will actually take place.
- **Creation of strong user loyalty**. This is, perhaps, the most important aspect of branding.

Once a brand has been established, it can be extended to other products. This reduces the cost of a new project gaining a place in the market. However, the extension to weak or inappropriate new products can cause significant damage to the initial brand image.

Price

As a very broad generalisation, a marketing function will set the price of its goods at a low level but slightly above its costs so that it will sell many items, reap the economies of scale and deter competitors from entering the market.

Exceptions to this rule are almost as many as its adherents. The ability and willingness of consumers to pay for a product is important. It is pointless marketing a product or service at a price beyond the means of customers – unless the producer is willing to subsidise its manufacture for strategic reasons. The variation in supermarket and petrol prices from region to region or town to town is a clear example on how the ability of the consumer to pay influences prices: in affluent areas prices are usually higher than in poorer areas. Luxury goods are a classic example where people are willing to pay substantially more than the production costs. The price of diamonds, for example, has, for over a century, been maintained at an artificially high level. Superb branding (a diamond is forever) and a superb cartel (DeBeers) meant that the price of diamonds could be controlled so that the very affluent and starry-eyed people would pay very high prices (see *The Economist,* 2004).

The sales of some products respond very quickly to changes in price while the sales of other products change very little if the price increases or decreases (this is called *price sensitivity* or *elasticity of demand*). The price of vegetables such as broccoli is very price sensitive because people will switch to another vegetable such as cauliflower if there is even a small price increase. On the other hand, many medicines are price insensitive since people will cut back on other purchases in order to have money to buy medicines that save their lives. If a product or service has an inelastic demand, the marketing function of an organisation can engage in *price-skimming* – supplying only the upper fraction (those who can afford high prices) of the market. They can charge very high prices which quickly recover development and production costs. Price-skimming enables an organisation to build a considerable surplus so that, should a competitor enter the market they can afford to engage in predatory pricing (see p. 220).

Branding can also raise a product's price significantly. Classic examples are the pharmaceutical industry where branded, well-advertised products supported by an excellent sales force can cost several times more than an equally effective generic medication. For example, the branded drug Valium, which benefited from the usual periods of exclusivity provided by patents, is used to treat anxiety. It costs more than the equally effective generic drug Diazepam. However, the generic drug Diazepam does not have to bear the marketing, sales and advertising costs incurred by the branded version.

The price of products is heavily influenced by marketing strategy. For example, new products, such as plasma screen TVs, are introduced at a very high price to establish an aspirational position at the top of the market. This confers prestige that will help sustain a higher price among naive and impressionable consumers.

The price of a product or service may be concealed. For example, people can visit many tourist attractions such as museums, parks or educational "lectures" without any fee. However, someone – somewhere – will be paying higher taxes to sustain their enjoyment. In fact, a marketing function's dream is to separate the consumer from the person or organisation that pays for his or her consumption.

Packaging

Often packaging is not considered as a separate aspect of the marketing mix and it is usually subsumed under the heading of "promotion". It is described separately here because, in practice, the marketing function of most organisations will pay considerable attention to the way that their goods are packaged. Indeed, an item's packaging can make a very substantial difference to its sales. An item whose packaging is poor is less likely to be selected from among its competitors on a supermarket shelf. Packaging has the important functional value of ensuring that the product is delivered to the customer in prime condition. However, packaging can also be used to increase the perceived benefit to the consumer. For example, many items are packaged in an oversized box in an attempt to make the customer believe that the product is bigger than its actual size. Similarly, some products such as jewellery and watches, are packaged in grossly expensive cases made of embossed leather and silk in order to enhance the perceived value of their contents.

In general, an organisation's marketing function will try to ensure that the packaging of its products:

- Is distinctive from that used by its competitors.
- Uses colours appropriate to the product's benefits. For example, the packaging of a

valuable item is likely to be coloured in gold and silver while the packaging of a fun item is likely to be coloured in vivid reds, oranges and yellows.

- Displays the brand name in a prominent position.
- Contains a flattering picture of the product where happy people (or sometimes, animals) clearly enjoy the benefits of a purchase.

Promotion

Promotion is also called *"marketing communications"*. It may be defined as:

> "Any type of persuasive communication between the marketing function and one or more of its present customers, potential customers or stakeholder groups which aims, directly or indirectly, to increase the likelihood that time, product or service will be purchased."

This definition has four important components. First, it emphasises that the central concept of promotion as a persuasive communication. Second, the aim of communication is to increase purchases. Third, the communications are directed at a target that is wider than the organisation's present customers. Finally, some communications may be closely linked to the sales process in the short term whilst other communications may be designed to have an indirect, longer-term effect. This definition also covers a wide range of activities which include public relations, internal marketing, advertising and personal selling.

Public relations

Public relations is also known as "*Perception Management*" and its critics such as Chomsky (2002) have called it "*Manufacturing Consent*", "*Media Control*" and "*Spin*". It may be defined as:

> "A part of the promotional mix that communicates with stakeholders, the media and the public in general in order to achieve broadly, favourable and supportive attitudes towards a product, organisation or cause."

A shorter and less technical definition for public relations might be "the management of an organisation's image". Both definitions emphasise that public relations is a general activity and is only loosely tied to the sale of a specific product. It aims to obtain a generally favourable attitude so that subsequent, more specific communications are likely to succeed. Often, an organisation's marketing function will employ specialist public relations consultants to maintain its image. Public relations experts use six main methods (see Free-definition, 2005b):

- **Press conferences** are public or quasi-public events where speakers provide information on newsworthy items. Usually they are attended by selected journalists and TV reporters.
- **Press releases** are also called "news releases" and may consist of short fax statements that are sent to the media.
- **Publicity events** are contrived situations designed to attract media attention. Outrageous publicity events are sometimes called "**guerrilla marketing**".

- **The circuit** refers to the "talk-show circuit" where PR consultants attempt to get their clients or spokespersons to appear on these programmes.
- **Books, brochures** and other writings are sometimes commissioned and published on behalf of clients.
- **Press contacts** are developed assiduously so that they can be fed information about the organisation in the hope that the reporter will write a favourable story.

Public relations experts often identify opinion leaders and powerful people ("movers and shakers"). They then attempt to develop friendly relationships by offering corporate hospitality at events such as the Chelsea Flower Show, the Happy Valley racecourse in Hong Kong or Australia's prestigious Telstra motor rally.

The marketing function in some organisations also engages in "**cause-related marketing**". They undertake to give a certain proportion of their profits to a good cause in the hope that their generosity will reflect positively on their organisation.

Internal promotion

Internal promotion aims to alter the attitudes of the organisation's own workforce. It is particularly relevant when new products are being launched. Internal communications tend to foster the "team spirit" within an organisation. In addition, the staff of an organisation

CASE 11.2: GUERRILLA MARKETING

A good example of guerrilla publicity occurred in August 2002 when Vodafone arranged for two men to "streak" at an international rugby game with the Vodafone logo painted on their backs. The men's magazine *FHM* provides another good example of guerrilla marketing. The magazine cover featured a nude photograph of a former children's TV presenter. After doctoring the photograph to remove any suggestion of her nipples, FHM projected it onto one of the towers of the Houses of Parliament. Both stunts earned considerable free publicity (including in this book!).

CASE 11.3: CAUSE-RELATED MARKETING

A classic, and clever example of cause-related marketing is Tesco's "Computers for Schools" campaign in which shoppers are given vouchers to pass to their local school, which is then able to redeem them for computer equipment. This scheme is particularly ingenious because its customers are involved frequently and directly. Furthermore, the recipients are local and are clearly identified. However, such schemes can backfire. In 2003 Cadbury sold chocolate bars with tokens which a school could exchange for sports equipment. The scheme caused uproar and was criticised by the Food Commission since it was seen to encourage obesity rather than a healthy, sporty lifestyle.

become an unofficial sales force who talk about the new product with their relatives, friends and acquaintances.

Advertising

Advertising is a major method of *promoting specific goods and services.* It may be defined as:

> Attracting public attention to a product, service or issue using non-personal methods of communication with a view to persuading the targets to adopt certain behaviours or thought patterns. Usually the desired behaviour is to purchase a product and the advertising organisation usually pays for the advertisement to be put before the target audience.

It should be noted that advertising is impersonal. There is no one-to-one contact between buyer and seller. This distinguishes advertising from selling. Moreover, advertising concerns specific products or services. This distinguishes it from public relations.

An advertising campaign can have a number of objectives which will depend upon a product's position in the product life cycle. If the product is new, the campaign is likely to focus upon making target customers aware that the product exists. It may also try to establish the new product's position in the market and its brand. Advertising a new product is also likely to draw attention to its unique benefits and try to appeal to people's needs for novelty and the status of being an early adopter. During the growth stage, advertising may seek to reassure tentative purchasers and boost confidence in the product. In the maturity and saturation stages, advertising will seek to differentiate one brand from another. At this stage the main objective will be to increase, or at least preserve, market share at the expense of competitors. Organisations may engage in either defensive or offensive advertising. Offensive advertising (sometimes called "*knocking copy*") may point out disadvantages of competitors' products.

Advertisers use a very wide range of media which includes: billboards (also known as "poster hoardings"); posters on the sides of lorries, taxis and buses; leaflets (also known as "flyers") distributed in the street; direct mail leaflets; magazines and newspapers; skywriting; web-banners; radio, cinema and television. The exact choice will depend upon the product and the target audience. For example, luxury goods are unlikely to be advertised using leaflets distributed in the street. They are more likely to be advertised in posh magazines.

An advert's first job is to **a**ttract attention, then develop the **d**esire for the product and finally to encourage consumers to take **a**ction and purchase the product (ADA). Methods used to achieve these aims include:

- **Repetition** is very important with new products where the aim is to make people remember the name.
- **Bandwagon** campaigns imply that everyone is purchasing a product and to be without one would be odd. This tactic is frequently used during a product's growth stage.
- **Testimonials** appeal to people's propensity to obey authority. They may quote sources of authority such as "five out of six doctors eat product X".
- **Pressure** campaigns often take the form of "buy now, before stocks are gone" or "buy now, before a tax increase". This tactic is frequently used during a product's maturity stage.

- **Association** campaigns try to link products with desirable things and attractive or famous people. Association campaigns are often used in conjunction with testimonials.

Place

Place is the fifth and final component of the marketing mix. It is the location where the ownership of goods is transferred or where a service is performed. The place where a product is marketed depends on two main factors: distribution channels and customer expectations.

Distribution

Transporting goods to a market place, storing them until requested by a customer, employing sales staff and providing a setting which the customer finds conducive can cost almost as much as the production of an article or service. Few organisations can afford to provide these facilities on a national or regional basis; hence they need to rely upon other people, wholesalers and retailers, to provide them. Since wholesalers and retailers act on behalf of many producers the costs can be shared. Moreover, wholesalers and retailers develop specialist expertise which enables distribution costs to be minimised. Historically, the location of the transfer of goods and services happened in marketplaces at the centre of ancient towns and cities. Then it took place in shops in the centre of towns and cities. The rise of motor transport has meant that, nowadays, the location of the exchange of goods and services is often in purpose-built *shopping malls* and *retail parks* situated on the periphery of large towns – often at strategic points on a ring road.

However, a traditional *shop* or a *department store* is not the appropriate or most convenient place to sell all goods and services. *Catalogue sales*, for example, are more appropriate for people in isolated communities or those who are confined to their homes by disability. Some organisations have deliberately developed alternatives to the traditional chain of retail distribution. For example, Tupperware developed a new distribution structure by *selling its products in people's homes* at Tupperware parties. This gave a product a unique selling point, it reduced costs and it harnessed social pressures and friendships to increase sales. Catalogue showrooms, pioneered by Argos, reduce the need for space to display merchandise. Consequently *catalogue showrooms* can offer a wider range of products at a keen price. They do, however, require superb logistics to ensure that a replacement article is replaced from a central store on the same day that an item is sold. Since the development of the Internet a growing number of transactions take place in *cyberspace*. This is described in greater detail in Chapter 15.

The customer experience

Customers have clear images and expectations about where they will buy goods. If these expectations are not met they will make fewer purchases. They expect to buy cabbages at a greengrocer and not at a newsagent. They expect to buy expensive jewellery in a plush setting where they receive a great deal of personal attention. Such factors are carefully considered by retail stores who pay great attention to developing an appropriate image. A major factor determining a store's image is the range of goods it sells. This is known as the *"merchandise assortment"*. The merchandise assortment must be consistent with the ideas of the consumer otherwise they are unlikely to enter the store to find out whether a suitable article is in stock. Another important factor in determining a store's image is its *location*. People expect stores to be located among other stores selling similar or complementary products. For example, it is expected that a store selling chairs and tables will be near a store that sells carpets, which in turn will be near a store that sells curtains. Stores arranged in a line next to a large parking area are usually called a "*strip*". Stores that are arranged around a central area designed for sitting, strolling and perhaps taking light refreshments are called, especially in America, a "*mall*".

The interior of a store will be laid out with care so that it gives a customer a certain experience which is consistent with the image of the store and its products. The physical characteristics of a store's environment such as its decor, its displays and its layout are called "**atmospherics**" or "**ambiance**". Atmospherics indicate the merchandise assortment within the store. Most important, the exterior atmospherics exert a strong influence on a potential customer's willingness to enter. Interior atmospherics, which may include choice of music, influences a customer's movement and mood. A primary concern of a retail organisation's marketing function will be to draw potential consumers to the back of a store by using a particularly attractive display or moving image. Once drawn to the back of a store a customer will be encouraged, perhaps by appropriate music or exotic displays, to tarry. As they tarry, customers are more likely to make a purchase. A way for supermarkets to draw customers to the further reaches of their stores is to place essential items such as bread at the furthest distance from the entrance. Supermarkets have long appreciated the importance of layout. For example, sales are increased if items essential to customers are positioned either on high shelves or on low ones. Discretionary items are placed on shelves at eye level. As consumers reach for essential items they are likely to see, and purchase, discretionary products. Similarly, supermarkets have learned that the ends, between aisles, are positions where products are most likely to be selected.

11.5 Criticisms of Marketing

Marketing is more controversial than other management functions. Its intentions, interpreting and fulfilling customer demand, are impeccable. It also plays an undeniable role in creating mass markets which bring economies of scale that in turn drive prices down to the benefit of most people. However, its critics also have a strong case. The main charges include misleading advertisements, manipulation, encouragement of antisocial behaviour, creation of false markets and dumbing down.

Use of *misleading adverts* is a frequent criticism. The malpractice seems to be particularly prevalent in the pharmaceutical and food industry where adverts may claim that products provide spurious health benefits. In some countries the problem seems endemic. The marketing function is often accused of *underhand manipulation*. Adverts may not openly state a product's benefits. They may be implied by information of which the consumer is unaware. In other words, consumers are induced to buy products by messages outside their awareness or logical control. This reflects an imbalance in power and resources. A consumer buying an everyday product can only devote seconds to their choice. A multinational organisation marketing the same product can devote a team of a dozen or more experts for several months to devise ways to induce a consumer to make a purchase. One tactic is to target people with fewer evaluative powers. For example, makers of a breakfast cereal may *target adverts at children* knowing that, in turn, they will pressurise their parents.

Another tactic might be to use subliminal advertising. *Subliminal advertising* involves projecting a message at a very low level so that people are not conscious the message is there. For example, an advertiser might project a very faint advertisement during a soap opera programme. The advertisement is so faint that the viewer does not realise it is there but over the period of half an hour the message is subconsciously registered. Initial experiments showing subliminal advertising could be effective were seriously flawed. Modern research shows that subliminal advertising does not work. Furthermore, subliminal advertising is illegal in most countries. Underhand manipulation is not limited to the use of children or subliminal adverts. It can arise from non-verbal messages. An advertisement may not explicitly state that a product will bring wealth and power. However, it may imply these benefits by including images of wealthy and powerful people. For example, a business school might include photographs of successful business people boarding an aeroplane en route to a meeting to discuss international strategy. However, it may know, full well, that most of its MBAs work within the domestic economy. One of first people to note the manipulative aspect of the marketing function was Packard (1957).

Some people criticise marketing for *encouraging antisocial behaviour.* Attracting attention is a major problem for marketeers. There is so much advertising and so much media coverage that an organisation's message may get lost. One of the easiest solutions is shock tactics, but many shock tactics involve antisocial behaviour. For example, an organisation

CASE 11.4: MISLEADING ADVERTS

In 2002 the Chinese State Drug Administration estimated that 89 per cent of advertisements for drugs and medical services were illegal. Specific examples of misleading advert are found throughout the world. In 2003 the American Federal Drug Agency (FDA) ordered Purdue Pharma to withdraw its ads for a painkiller OxyCotin because they omitted to mention fatal side effects if the tablet was chewed rather than swallowed. A rather different criticism was levelled against the American milk industry's campaign "got milk" which featured celebrities with "milk moustaches". Physician groups complained that the advertisements ignored data linking high milk consumption with heart disease and prostate cancer. Their complaints were supported by the Department of Agriculture (USDA).

Criticisms of the marketing function for using misleading advertisements are by no means restricted to the pharmaceutical and food industry. In 2004 the British Advertising Standards Authority ordered the Internet service provider, Wanadoo, to withdraw its adverts for "full speed broadband", because the ads could mislead consumers into believing it was the fastest on the market. The travel industry, especially companies selling airfares, is frequently admonished for misleading, *bait and switch* tactics. Hectares of Sunday newspapers are covered with offers of cheap flights. Yet, when even the nimblest consumer telephones, there are no remaining seats at the cheapest rates. They are encouraged to switch to more expensive, and presumably more profitable, flights

producing crisps (chips) might draw attention to its product with an advert depicting a pupil successfully deceiving a teacher during a mathematics lesson to eat crisps. The advertisement would probably increase the sales of the crisp manufacturer. However, it would make classroom discipline more difficult. The impact on the skill base of a country might mean a significant reduction in its ability to provide social goods such as transport or healthcare.

The marketing function will usually seek to maximise the benefit for its own organisation rather than the community. It may benefit the organisation to develop and market a new product that is unnecessary and which will, in the long term, damage people and their society. In essence, this criticism accuses the marketing function of *developing and exploiting an unnecessary and dangerous* consumer need. For example, the market research of the company Masterfoods (MARS) revealed a marketing opportunity for a large wafer, chocolate caramel cream confectionary bar for women. It developed a product, Mars Delight, which was launched in Ireland. A marketing spend of £15 million was devoted to promoting this product. However, in the light of increasing obesity in the developed world, Mars was criticised for developing a needless and possibly dangerous product.

Perhaps the most important criticism against the marketing function is its impact on society. Because of its economic power and its expertise the influence of the marketing is very widespread and very pervasive. This leads to two further criticisms. First, it promulgates a capitalist, market ethos which ignores other social, cultural and aesthetic considerations. Probably more important is the impact on the intellectual standards – *dumbing down*. A manager in a marketing function of an individual organisation will wish to appeal to as many people as possible. This means that she or he will calculate the lowest common denominator of the market. Hence public standards will be diminished. This trend, combined with the tendency to encourage antisocial behaviour might lead to a society without standards.

Many of these criticisms may be unfair because they are directed at the image of the marketing function. The marketing function may be partly responsible as a victim of its own hype. Furthermore, many countries have enacted legislation that curb marketing's worst excesses.

Activities and Further Study

Essay Plans

Write essay plans for the following questions:

1 How might markets differ from each other?

2 What models might organisations use to locate a profitable market? To what extent are these models consistent with each other and how useful might they be in practice?

3 Why do organisations undertake market research? What methods could they use?

4 What is meant by "The Marketing Mix'?

5 What are the main criticisms against marketing? To what extent are these criticisms valid?

Web and Experiential Activities

Suggestions for Web exercises and experiential exercises for all functions are given at the end of Chapter 10 (p. 211).

Managing products: product life cycle, portfolio planning and product growth strategies

CHAPTER 10

Nothing can last for ever
Though the sun shines gold
It must plunge into the sea
The moon has also disappeared
Which but now so brightly gleamed.

Graffito from Pompeii

LEARNING OBJECTIVES

After reading this chapter, you should be able to:

1. describe the concept of the product life cycle
2. discuss the uses and limitations of the product life cycle
3. describe the concept of product portfolio planning
4. explain the Boston Consulting Group Growth-Share Matrix, its uses and the criticisms of it
5. explain the General Electric Market Attractiveness—Competitive Position Model, its uses and the criticisms of it
6. discuss the contribution of product portfolio management
7. discuss product strategies for growth

This chapter examines the application of a number of tools that can be used in the area of strategic product planning. Product lines and brands need to be managed over time. The product life cycle will be discussed as a tool for helping managers with this task. Its uses and limitations will be explored.

Marketing managers also need to manage brand and product line portfolios. Many companies are multi-product, serving multiple markets and segments. Managers need to address the question of where to place investment for product growth and where to withdraw resources. These and other questions will be dealt with in the second part of this chapter, which examines portfolio planning. The uses and criticisms of the Boston Consulting Group Growth-Share Matrix and the General Electric Market Attractiveness–Competitive Position Model will be explored.

Finally, this chapter discusses the Ansoff Matrix as a tool for analysing product strategies for growth. Whereas product portfolio planning focuses on existing sets of products, the Ansoff Matrix also considers new products and new markets as a means to achieve future growth.

MANAGING PRODUCT LINES AND BRANDS OVER TIME: THE PRODUCT LIFE CYCLE

No matter how wide the product mix, both product lines and individual brands need to be managed over time. A useful tool for conceptualizing the changes that may take place during the time that a product is on the market is called the **product life cycle.** It is quite flexible and can be applied to both brands and product lines.[1] For simplicity, in the rest of this chapter, brands and product lines will be referred to as products. We shall now look at the product life cycle, before discussing its uses and limitations.

The classic product life cycle has four stages (see Fig. 10.1): introduction, growth, maturity and decline.

Introduction

When first introduced on to the market a product's sales growth is typically low, and losses are incurred because of heavy development and promotional costs. Companies will be monitoring the speed of product adoption and, if this is disappointing, may terminate the

Figure 10.1 The product life cycle

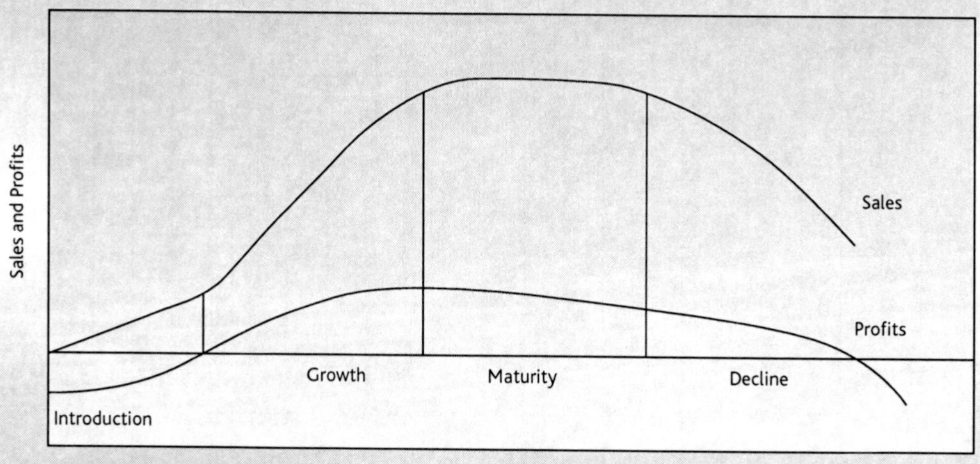

product at this stage. Samsung is one company that invests in new product development to create products that confer new features and benefits for consumers.

Growth

This stage is characterized by a period of faster sales and profit growth. Sales growth is fuelled by rapid market acceptance and, for many products, repeat purchasing. Profits may begin to decline towards the latter stages of growth as new rivals enter the market, attracted by the twin magnets of fast sales growth and high profit potential. The personal computer market was an example of this during the 1980s, when sales

10.1 Marketing in Action

Surviving a Shakeout

The change from booming growth to a static mature industry can prove traumatic for many companies. The growth phase may have been associated with entrepreneurial drive backed by a strong vision, such as that of Michael Dell who founded Dell Computers Corporation in 1984. With maturity comes the need to put a premium on operational efficiency, a greater sensitivity to customer needs and increased responsiveness to competitor threats For strong, well-positioned companies the looming shakeout provides an opportunity to stabilize the industry and gain market power. For such *adaptive survivors*, there is a need to face three key issues.

1 *Leadership and management style*: survival necessitates the recruitment of talented managers who have experience in large organizations and understand the systematic approach needed to manage a large company. Such a move by Dell Computers changed the orientation from 'growth, growth, growth' to 'liquidity, profitability and growth'.

2 *Resources*: much energy is required to critically evaluate options so that resources are allocated to the most attractive opportunities, and resources withdrawn from past mistakes. For example, Dell Computers invested to increase global sales while withdrawing from retail stores and dropping its failing line of note-book computers.

3 *Controls*: information systems need to be installed to identify such problems as excessive costs, bulging inventories and failure to meet promises to customers.

Smaller, also-ran companies are particularly vulnerable during a shake-out. They need to choose a buffer strategy to provide some protection during the crisis.

- *Market niching*: niches can serve as buffer zones when competitive pressures are not too strong and growth is possible. Managers need to accept a shrinking of aspirations and pruning of operations. Segments where the major companies are underperforming (perhaps because small segment size does not warrant heavy investment) are prime targets.

- *Strategic alliances*: small companies can buffer themselves by forming alliances to pool resources, access expensive assets and increase negotiating power.

If neither of these strategies is viable, then the also-ran company will need to face the decision to sell the company. An early sale may make sense if a buyer can be found who still has an optimistic view of the future. However, patience can be a virtue if the company can survive until prospective buyers have weathered the storm and have gained confidence in their new strategies.

Based on: Day (1997)[2]

growth was mirrored by a vast increase in competitors, and mobile phones experienced fast growth in the 1990s, with an accompanying increase in the number of competitors. The end of the growth period is often associated with *competitive shakeout*, whereby weaker suppliers cease production. How to survive a shakeout is discussed in Marketing in Action 10.1.

Maturity

Eventually sales peak and flatten as saturation occurs, hastening competitive shakeout. The survivors battle for market share by employing product improvements, advertising and sales promotional offers, dealer discount and price cutting; the result is strain on profit margins particularly for follower brands. The need for effective brand building is acutely recognized during maturity as brand leaders are in the strongest position to resist the pressure on profit margins.[3]

Decline

Sales and profits fall during the decline stages as new technology or changes in consumer tastes work to reduce demand for the product. Suppliers may decide to cease production completely or reduce product depth. Promotional and product development budgets may be slashed and marginal distributors dropped as suppliers seek to maintain (or increase) profit margins.

USES OF THE PRODUCT LIFE CYCLE

The product life cycle (PLC) concept is useful for product management in several ways, as described below.

Product termination

First, the PLC emphasizes the fact that nothing lasts forever. There is a danger that management may fall in love with certain products. Maybe a company was founded on the success of a particular product; perhaps the product champion of a past success is now the chief executive. Under such circumstances there can be emotional ties with the product that can transcend normal commercial considerations. The PLC underlines the fact that companies have to face the fact that products need to be terminated and new products developed to replace them. Without this sequence a company may find itself with a group of products all in the decline stage of their PLC.

Growth projections

The second use of the PLC concept is to warn against the dangers of assuming that growth will continue forever. Swept along by growing order books, management can fall into the trap of believing that the heady days of rising sales and profits will continue forever. The PLC reminds managers that growth will end, and suggests a need for caution when planning investment in new production facilities.

Marketing objectives and strategies over the PLC

The PLC emphasizes the need to review marketing objectives and strategies as products pass through the various stages. Changes in market and competitive conditions between the PLC stages suggests that marketing strategies should be adapted to meet them. Table

Table 10.1 Marketing objectives and strategies over the product life cycle

	Introduction	Growth	Maturity	Decline
Strategic marketing objective	Build	Build	Hold	Harvest/manage for cash/divest
Strategic focus	Expand market	Penetration	Protect share/ innovation	Productivity
Brand objective	Product awareness/ trial	Brand preference	Brand loyalty	Brand exploitation
Products	Basic	Differentiated	Differentiated	Rationalized
Promotion	Creating awareness/ trial	Creating awareness/ trial/repeat purchase	Maintaining awareness/repeat purchase	Cut/eliminated
Price	High	Lower	Lowest	Rising
Distribution	Patchy	Wider	Intensive	Selective

10.1 shows a set of stylized marketing responses to each stage. Note that these are broad generalizations rather than exact prescriptions but they do serve to emphasize the need to review marketing objectives and strategies in the light of environmental change.

Introduction

The strategic marketing objective is to build sales by expanding the market for the product. The brand objective will be to create product (as well as brand) awareness so that customers will become familiar with generic product benefits.

The marketing task facing pioneer video recorder producers was to gain awareness of the general benefits of the video recorder (e.g. convenient viewing through time-switching, viewing programmes that are broadcast when out of the house) so that the market for video recorders in general would expand. The product is likely to be fairly basic, with an emphasis on reliability and functionality rather than special features to appeal to different customer groups. Promotion will support the brand objectives by gaining awareness for the brand and product type, and stimulating trial. Advertising has been found to be more effective in the beginning of the life of a product than in later stages.[4] Typically price will be high because of the heavy development costs and the low level of competition. Distribution will be patchy as some dealers are wary of stocking the new product until it has proved to be successful in the marketplace.

Growth

The strategic marketing objective during the growth phase is to build sales and market share. The strategic focus will be to penetrate the market by building brand preference. To accomplish this task the product will be redesigned to create differentiation, and promotion will stress the functional and/or psychological benefits that accrue from the differentiation. Awareness and trial to acquire new customers are still important but promotion will begin to focus on repeat purchasers. As development costs are defrayed and competition increases, prices will fall. Rising consumer demand and increased salesforce effort will widen distribution.

Maturity

As sales peak and stabilize the strategic marketing objective will be to hold on to profits and sales by protecting market share rather than embark on costly competitive challenges. Since sales gains can only be at the expense of competition, strong challenges are likely to be resisted and lead to costly promotional or price wars. Brand objectives now focus on maintaining brand loyalty and customer retention, and promotion will defend the brand, stimulating repeat purchase by maintaining brand awareness and values. For all but the brand leader, competition may erode prices and profit margins, while distribution will peak in line with sales.

A key focus will be innovation to extend the maturity stage or, preferably, inject growth. This may take the form of innovative promotional campaigns, product improvements, and extensions and technological innovation. Ways of increasing usage and reducing repeat purchase periods of the product will also be sought. Digital Marketing 10.1 shows how mobile phone manufacturers and operators are seeking to revitalize sales in a mature market.

@ 10.1 Digital Marketing

Mobile Marketing in a Mature Market

The mobile phone market in western Europe has reached saturation. For example, ownership has reached 87 per cent in Germany, 83 per cent in the UK and 74 per cent in France. This means that mobile phone companies now operate in a mature market. No longer can profits be fuelled by explosive growth; instead attention has turned to competing for a relatively fixed market of consumers. In classic product life cycle style, this has meant a move from customer acquisition to retention, attempts to increase usage rates and lower repeat purchase periods, and heavy investment in innovation. It has also resulted in a period of falling prices and rationalization as all players—including Nokia, the market leader—have significantly reduced costs.

Increased usage of mobile phones has been stimulated by SMS (short message service). This allows users to send short text messages at relatively low cost. Usage has also been increased by adding on additional services such as cameras, video recording (see the ad for the Nokia N90), and the ability to download and play music.

Nokia was the leader in reducing repeat purchase periods: it made mobile phones a fashion item by introducing new, modified models with desirable design and colour features. Its crown was tarnished, however, by its slow adoption of the clamshell design, which allowed Motorola and Samsung to gain market share.

The aim of technological innovation has been to stimulate upgrading. Unfortunately, the first major innovation, Wireless Access Protocol (WAP), which was intended to allow Internet access from mobiles, proved irritatingly cumbersome and failed to attract customers. The pioneers of 3G technology failed to achieve mass-market access as the handset proved to be unreliable and bulky. However, heavy investment continues in the belief that consumers will upgrade to handsets capable of mobile TV, e-mail access, Internet search, video streaming and full multimedia messaging.

The name 'maturity' may conjure up images of tranquillity, but for incumbent companies, competitive and economic forces mean that they face a demanding and volatile marketplace.

Based on: Deere and Kilby (2005);[5] Lester (2005);[6] Odell (2006);[7] Wray (2006)[8]

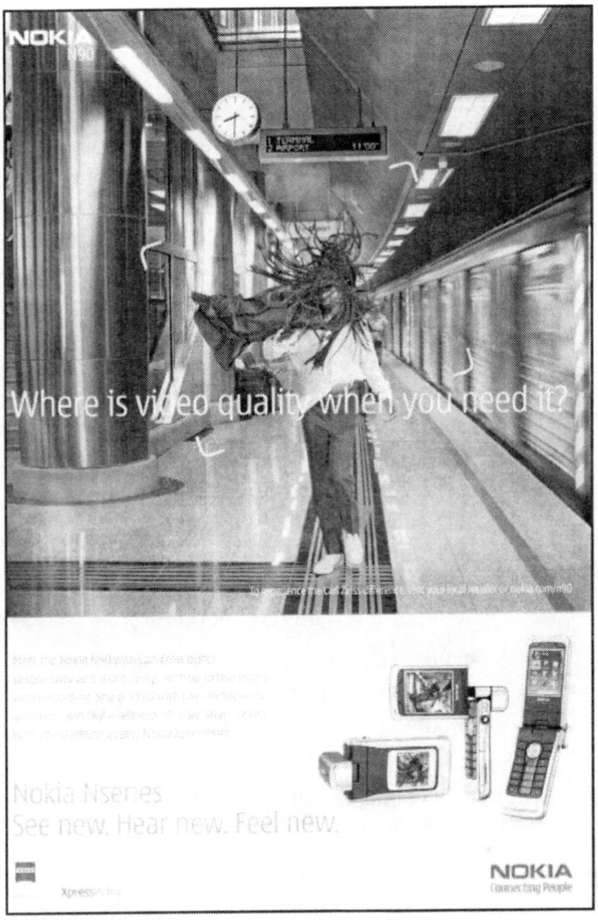

The versatile Nokia N90 is capable of video recording.

Decline

The conventional advice to companies managing products in the decline stage of the product life cycle is to harvest or divest. A harvest strategy would result in the raising of prices while slashing marketing expenditures in an effort to boost profit margins. The strategic focus, therefore, is to improve marketing productivity rather than holding or building sales. The brand loyalty that has been built up over the years is in effect being exploited to create profits that can be used elsewhere in the company (e.g. new products). Product development will cease, the product line cut to the bare minimum of brands and the promotional expenditure cut, possibly to zero. Distribution costs will be analysed with a view to selecting only the most profitable outlets. The Internet will be examined to explore its potential as a low-cost promotional and distribution vehicle.

Divestment may take the form of selling products to other companies, or, if there are no willing buyers, product elimination. The strategy is to extract any residual value in the products where possible, and to free up managerial time and resources to be redirected at more attractive products and opportunities. Occasionally, products are harvested and then divested. For example, Beecham harvested and then sold Brylcreem to the Health and Personal Care division of Sara Lee at a time when it was unfashionable for males to use hair cream. It proved a fortunate purchase as hair gel became fashionable and Sara Lee had the marketing expertise to reposition the brand in that market.

There are, however, two other strategies that can be applied at the decline stage: industry revitalization and the pursuit of a profitable survivor strategy.

Industry revitalization: some products go into decline not because they are inherently unpopular but because of lack of investment. In fact the application of conventional wisdom for strategy application in the decline stage could be the cause of accelerated sales and profit decline. Such was the case with the cinema market. Years of under-investment saw cinemas become drab affairs offering a very limited choice of films as cinema owners applied a classic harvest strategy. However, one company saw this scenario as a marketing opportunity. Showcase Cinemas was launched, offering a choice of around 12 films in modern purpose-built premises near large conurbations. This completely changed the experience of going to the cinema, resulting in revitalization of the industry and growth in cinema attendances and profits. Thus the classic PLC prescription of harvesting in the decline stage was rejected by a company that was willing to invest in order to reposition cinemas as an attractive means of offering evening entertainment.

Profitable survivor strategy: another alternative to harvesting or divestment is called the profitable survivor strategy.[9] This involves deciding to become the sole survivor in a declining market. This may involve being willing to incur losses while competitors drop out, or if it is thought that this process is likely to be lengthy and slow, to accelerate it by:

- further reducing the attractiveness of the market by such actions as price cuts or increases in promotional expenditures
- buying competitors (which may be offered at a low price due to the unattractive markets they operate in) or their product lines that compete in the same market
- agreeing to take over competitors' contracts (e.g. supplying spare parts or service contracts) in exchange for their agreement to drop out of the market.

Once in the position of sole supplier, the survivor can reap the rewards of a monopolist by raising prices and resuming profitable operations.

Product planning

The PLC emphasizes the need for *product planning*. We have already discussed the need to replace old products with new. The PLC also stresses the need to analyse the balance of products that a company markets from the point of view of the PLC stages. A company with all of its products in the mature stage may be generating profits today, but as it enters the decline stage, profits may fall and the company become unprofitable. A nicely balanced product array would see the company marketing some products in the mature stage of the PLC, a number in the growth stage, with the prospect of new product launches in the near future. The growth products would replace the mature products as the latter enter decline, and the new product successes would eventually become the growth products of the future. The PLC is, then, a stimulus to thinking about products as an interrelated set of profit-bearing assets that need to be managed as a group. We shall return to this theme when discussing product portfolio analysis later in this chapter.

The dangers of overpowering

The PLC concept highlights the dangers of overpowering. A company that introduces a new-to-the-world product may find itself in a very powerful position early in its PLC. Assuming that the new product confers unique benefits to customers there is an opportunity to charge a very high price during this period of monopoly supply. However, unless the product is patent-protected this strategy can turn sour when competition enters during the growth phase (as predicted by the PLC concept). This situation arose for the small components manufacturer that was the first to solve the technical problems associated with developing a seal in an exhaust recirculation valve used to reduce pollution in car emissions. The company took advantage of its monopoly supply position to charge very high prices to Ford. The strategy rebounded when competition entered and Ford discovered it had been overcharged.[10] Had the small manufacturer been aware of the predictions of the PLC concept it may have anticipated competitive entry during the growth phase, and charged a lower price during introduction and early growth. This would have enabled it to begin a relationship-building exercise with Ford, possibly leading to greater returns in the long run.

LIMITATIONS OF THE PRODUCT LIFE CYCLE

The product life cycle is an aid to thinking about marketing decisions, but it needs to be handled with care. Management needs to be aware of the limitations of the PLC so that it is not misled by its prescriptions.

Fads and classics

Not all products follow the classic S-shaped curve. The sales of some products 'rise like a rocket then fall like a stick'. This is normal for *fad* products such as skateboards, which saw phenomenal sales growth followed by a rapid sales collapse as the youth market moved on to another craze.

Other products (and brands) appear to defy entering the decline stage. For example, classic confectionery products and brands such as Mars bars, Cadbury's Milk Tray and Toblerone have survived for decades in the mature stage of the PLC. Nevertheless, research has shown that the classic S-shaped curve does apply to a wide range of products, including grocery food products, pharmaceuticals and cigarettes.[11]

Marketing effects

The PLC is the *result* of marketing activities not the cause. One school of thought argues that the PLC is not simply a fact of life—unlike living organisms—but is simply a pattern of sales that reflects marketing activity.[12] Clearly, sales of a product may flatten or fall simply because it has not received enough marketing attention, or has had insufficient product redesign or promotional support. Using the PLC, argue the critics, may lead to inappropriate action (e.g. harvesting or dropping the product) when the correct response should be increased marketing support (e.g. product replacement, positioning reinforcement or repositioning).

Unpredictability

The duration of the PLC stages is unpredictable. The PLC outlines the four stages that a product passes through without defining their duration. Clearly this limits its use as a forecasting tool since it is not possible to predict when maturity or decline will begin. The exception to this problem is when it is possible to identify a comparator product that serves as a template for predicting the length of each stage. Two sources of comparator products exist: first, countries where the same product has already been on the market for some time; second, where similar products are in the mature or decline stages of their life cycle but are thought to resemble the new product in terms of consumer acceptance. In practice, the use of comparator products is fraught with problems. For example, the economic and social conditions of countries may be so different that simplistic exploitation of the PLC from one country to another may be invalid; the use of similar products may offer inaccurate predictions in the face of ever-shortening product life cycles.

Misleading objective and strategy prescriptions

The stylized marketing objectives and strategy prescriptions may be misleading. Even if a product could accurately be classified as being in a PLC stage, and sales are not simply a result of marketing activities, the critics argue that the stylized marketing objectives and strategy prescriptions can be misleading. For example, there can be circumstances where the appropriate marketing objective in the growth stage is to harvest (e.g. in the face of intense competition), in the mature stage to build (e.g. when a distinct, defensive differential advantage can be developed), and in the decline stage to build (e.g. when there is an opportunity to dominate).

As was discussed earlier, the classic PLC advice concerning strategy in the decline stage is to harvest or divest, but other strategies—industry revitalization or the profitable survivor strategy—can be employed if the right conditions apply.

10.1 Pause for thought

On balance, how useful do you think the product life cycle is to strategic marketing thinking?

A summary of the usefulness of the product life cycle concept

Like many marketing tools, the product life cycle should not be viewed as a panacea to marketing thinking and decision-making but as an aid to managerial judgement. By emphasizing the changes that are likely to occur as a product is marketed over time, the concept is a valuable stimulus to strategic thinking. Yet as a prescriptive tool it is blunt. Marketing management must monitor the real-life changes that are happening in the marketplace before setting precise objectives and strategies.

MANAGING BRAND AND PRODUCT LINE PORTFOLIOS

So far in this chapter we have treated the management of products as separate, distinct and independent entities. However, many companies are multi-product, serving multiple markets and segments. Some of these products will be strong, others weak. Some will require investment to finance their growth, others will generate more cash than they need. Somehow companies must decide how to distribute their limited resources among the competing needs of products so as to achieve the best performance for the company as a whole. Specifically within a product line, management needs to decide which brands to invest in or hold, or from which to withdraw support. Similarly within the product mix, decisions regarding which product lines to build or hold, or from which to withdraw support need to be taken. Canon, for example, took the strategic decision to focus on its profitable products—mainly copiers, printers and cameras—while divesting personal computers, typewriters and liquid crystal displays.[13] Managers that focus on individual products often miss the bigger picture that helps ensure the company's entire portfolio of products fits together coherently rather than being a loose confederation of offerings that has emerged out of a series of uncoordinated historical decisions.[14] Philips finds itself in this position, marketing a sprawling

10.2 Marketing in Action

Portfolio Planning to the Core

The composition of a company's product portfolio is a vital strategic issue for marketers. Few companies have the luxury of starting with a clean sheet and creating a well-balanced set of products. An assessment of the strengths and weaknesses of the current portfolio is, therefore, necessary before taking the strategic decisions of which ones to build, hold, harvest or divest.

Major multinationals, like Nestlé, Cadbury Schweppes, Procter & Gamble, GE, IBM and Unilever, constantly review their product portfolios to achieve their strategic objectives. The trend has been to focus on core brands and product categories, and to divest minor, peripheral brands.

Nestlé, for example, has sold Crosse & Blackwell, whose portfolio of brands includes Branston Pickle, Gale's Honey and Sun-Pat Peanut Butter, to Premier International Foods as it focuses on key product categories where it can establish and maintain leadership. The focus is on the core categories of beverages, confectionery, chilled dairy, milks and nutrition. In line with this strategy Nestlé has acquired the Ski and Munch Bunch dairy brands from Northern Foods, propelling it into the number-two position behind Müller in the chilled dairy market.

Cadbury Schweppes is also concentrating on its core brands with the sale of its European soft drinks business, which includes brands such as Orangina, Oasis and Schweppes mixers, to an Anglo-American private equity consortium. The sale allows the company to concentrate on its higher growth and more profitable confectionery business and its regional drinks businesses in the USA and Australia. In line with this strategy, Cadbury Schweppes acquired Green & Black's, the organic chocolate maker, which operates under the fair trade banner.

This trend is not confined to the grocery business, however. For example, Adidas sold its ski and surf equipment firm Salomon to Amer Sports Corporation so that it could focus on its core strength in the athletic footwear and apparel market as well as the growing golf category. IBM sold its PC division to Lenovo to concentrate on software and services (see illustration overleaf).

One advantage of this strategy is to enable maximum firepower to be put behind core brands. This is the reason Carlsberg-Tetley has dropped minor brands to concentrate its marketing budget on Carlsberg, Carlsberg Export and Tetley Beer.

Based on: Mason (2002);[16] Tomlinson (2005);[17] Milner (2006)[18]

set of products, namely semiconductors, consumer electronics, medical equipment, lighting and small electrical appliances.[15]

Clearly, these are strategic decisions since they shape where and with what brands/product lines a company competes and how its resources should be deployed. Furthermore these decisions are complex because many factors (e.g. current and future sales and profit potential, cash flow) can affect the outcome. The process of managing groups of brands and product lines is called **portfolio planning**.

Key decisions regarding portfolio planning involve decisions regarding the choice of which brands/product lines to build, hold, harvest or divest. Marketing in Action 10.2 discusses several companies' approaches to portfolio planning.

In order to get to grips with the complexities of decision-making, two methods have received wide publicity. These are the Boston Consulting Group Growth-Share Matrix and the General Electric Market Attractiveness–Competitive Position portfolio evaluation models. Like the product life cycle these are very flexible tools and can be used at both the brand and product line levels. Indeed, corporate planners can also use them when making resource allocation decisions at the strategic business unit level.

IBM advertises its services capabilities.

Ad Insight

The Boston Consulting Group Growth-Share Matrix

A leading management consultancy, the Boston Consulting Group (BCG), developed the well-known BCG Growth-Share Matrix (see Fig. 10.2). The matrix allows portfolios of products to be depicted in a 2 × 2 box, the axes of which are based on market growth rate and relative market share. The analysis is based upon cash flow (rather than profits) and its key assumptions are:

- market growth has an adverse affect on cash flow because of the investment in such assets as manufacturing facilities, equipment and marketing needed to finance growth
- market share has a positive affect on cash flow as profits are related to market share.

The following discussion will be based on an analysis at the product line level.

Market growth rate forms the vertical axis and indicates the annual growth rate of the market in which each product line operates. In Figure 10.2 it is shown as 0–15 per cent although a different range could be used, depending on economic conditions, for example. In this example the dividing line between high and low growth rates is considered to be 7 per cent. Market growth rate is used as a proxy for market attractiveness.

Relative market share is shown on the horizontal axis and refers to the market share of each product relative to its largest competitor. It acts as a proxy for competitive strength. The division between high and low market share is 1. Above this figure a product line has a market share greater than its largest competitor. For example, if our product had a market share of 40 per cent and our largest competitor's share was 30 per cent this would

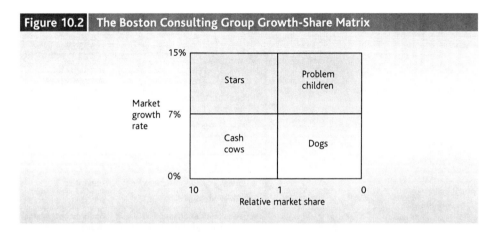

Figure 10.2 The Boston Consulting Group Growth-Share Matrix

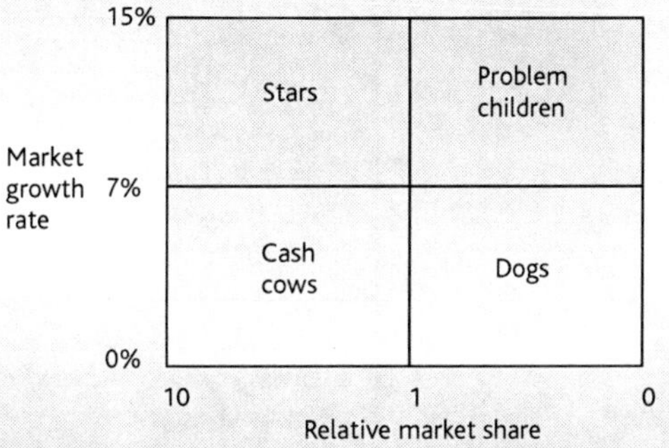

be indicated as 1.33 on the horizontal axis. Below 1 we have a share less than the largest competitor. For example, if our share was 20 per cent and the largest competitor had a share of 40 per cent our score would be 0.5.

The Boston Consulting Group argued that cash flow is dependent on the box in which a product falls. Note that cash flow is not the same as profitability. Profits add to cash flow but heavy investment in such assets as manufacturing facilities, equipment and marketing expenditure can mean that a company can make profits and yet have a negative cash flow.

Stars are likely to be profitable because they are market leaders but require substantial investment to finance growth (e.g. new production facilities) and to meet competitive challenges. Overall cash flow is therefore likely to be roughly in balance. *Problem children* are products in high-growth markets, which cause a drain on cash flow, but these are low-share products; consequently they are unlikely to be profitable. Overall, then, they are big cash users. *Cash cows* are market leaders in mature (low-growth) markets. High market share leads to high profitability and low market growth means that investment in new production facilities is minimal. This leads to a large positive cash flow. *Dogs* also operate in low-growth markets but have low market share. Except for some products near the dividing line between cash cows and dogs (sometimes called *cash dogs*) most dogs produce low or negative cash flows. Relating to their position in the product life cycle, they are the also-rans in mature or declining markets.

What are the strategic implications of the BCG analysis? It can be used for setting strategic objectives and for maintaining a balanced product portfolio.

Guidelines for setting strategic objectives

Having plotted the position of each product on the matrix, a company can begin to think about setting the appropriate strategic objective for each line. As you may recall from Chapter 2, there are four possible strategic objectives: build, hold, harvest and divest. Figure 10.3 shows how each relates to the star, problem children, cash cow and dog categories. However, it should be emphasized that the BCG matrix provides guidelines for strategic thinking and should not be seen as a replacement for managerial judgement.

- *Stars*: these are the market leaders in high-growth markets. They are already successful and the prospects for further growth are good. As we have seen when discussing brand building, market leaders tend to have the highest profitability so the appropriate strategic objective is to build sales and/or market share. Resources should be invested to maintain/increase the leadership position. Competitive challenges should be repelled. These are the cash cows of the future and need to be protected.

Figure 10.3 Strategic objectives and the 'Boston box'

Stars *Build* sales and/or market share Invest to maintain/increase leadership position Repel competitive challenges	**Problem children** *Build* selectively Focus on defendable *niche* where dominance can be achieved *Harvest* or *divest* the rest
Cash cows *Hold* sales and/or market share Defend position Use excess cash to support stars, selected problem children and new product development	**Dogs** *Harvest* or *Divest* or Focus on defendable niche

- *Problem children*: as we have seen these are cash drains because they have low profitability and need investment to keep up with market growth. They are called problem children because management has to consider whether it is sensible to continue the required investment. The company faces a fundamental choice: to increase investment (*build*) to attempt to turn the problem child into a star, or to withdraw support by either *harvesting* (raising price while lowering marketing expenditure) or *divesting* (dropping or selling it). In a few cases, a third option may be viable: to find a small market segment (*niche*) where dominance can be achieved. Unilever, for example, identified its speciality chemicals business as a problem child. It realized that it had to invest heavily or exit. Its decision was to sell and invest the billions raised in predicted future winners such as personal care, dental products and fragrances.[19]
- *Cash cows*: the high profitability and low investment associated with high market share in low-growth markets mean that cash cows should be defended. Consequently the appropriate strategic objective is to *hold* sales and market share. The excess cash that is generated should be used to fund stars, problem children that are being built, and research and development for new products.
- *Dogs*: dogs are weak products that compete in low-growth markets. They are the also-rans that have failed to achieve market dominance during the growth phase and are floundering in maturity. For those products that achieve second or third position in the marketplace (*cash dogs*) a small positive cash flow may result, and for a few others it may be possible to reposition the product into a defendable *niche*. (The problem with using the niche strategy is lack of economies of scale compared with bigger rivals, as MG Rover found.) But for the bulk of dogs the appropriate strategic objective is to *harvest* to generate a positive cash flow for a time, or to *divest*, which allows resources and managerial time to be focused elsewhere.

Maintaining a balanced product portfolio

Once all of the company's products have been plotted, it is easy to see how many stars, problem children, cash cows and dogs are in the portfolio. Figure 10.4 shows a product portfolio that is unbalanced. The company possesses only one star and the small circle indicates that sales revenue generated from the star is small. Similarly the two cash cows are also low revenue earners. In contrast the company owns four dogs and four problem

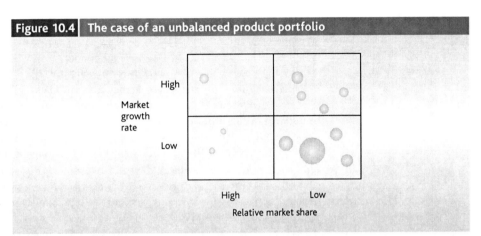

Figure 10.4 The case of an unbalanced product portfolio

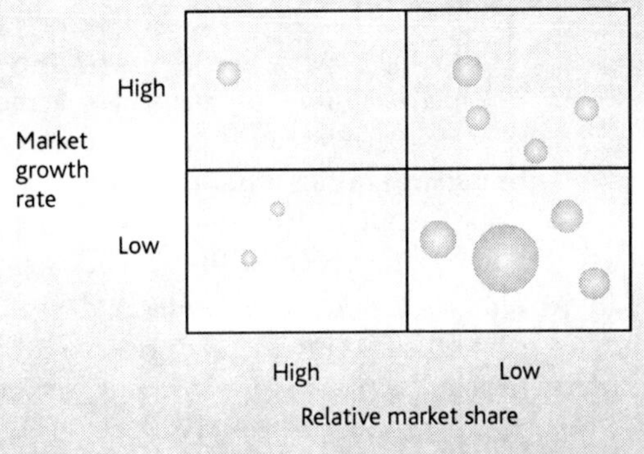

children. The portfolio is unbalanced because there are too many problem children and dogs, and not enough stars and cash cows. What many companies in this situation do is to spread what little surplus cash is available equally between the products in the growth markets.[20] To do so would leave each with barely enough money to maintain market share, leading to a vicious circle of decline.

The BCG remedy would be to conduct a detailed competitive assessment of the four problem children and select one or two for investment. The rest should be harvested (and the cash channelled to those that are being built) or divested. The aim is to build the existing star (which will be the cash cow of the future) and to build the market share of the chosen problem children so that they attain star status.

The dogs also need to be analysed. One of them (the large circle) is a large revenue earner, which despite low profits may be making a substantial contribution to overheads. Another product (on the left) appears to be in the cash dog situation. But for the other two, the most sensible strategic objective may be to harvest or divest.

Criticisms of the BCG Growth-Share Matrix

The simplicity, ease of use and importance of the issues tackled by the BCG Matrix saw its adoption by a host of North American and European companies that wanted to get a handle on the complexities of strategic resource allocation. But the tool has also attracted a litany of criticism.[21] The following list draws together many of the points raised by its critics.

1. The assumption that cash flow will be determined by a product's position in the matrix is weak. For example, some stars will show a healthy positive cash flow (e.g. IBM PCs during the growth phase of the PC market) as will some dogs in markets where competitive activity is low.
2. The preoccupation of focusing on market share and market growth rates distracts managerial attention from the fundamental principle in marketing: attaining a sustainable competitive advantage.
3. Treating the market growth rate as a proxy for market attractiveness, and market share as an indicator of competitive strength is oversimplistic. There are many other factors that have to be taken into account when measuring market attractiveness (e.g. market size, strengths and weaknesses of competitors) and competitive strengths (e.g. exploitable marketing assets, potential cost advantages), besides market growth rates and market share.

4 Since the position of a product in the matrix depends on market share, this can lead to an unhealthy preoccupation with market share gain. In some circumstances this objective makes sense (for example, brand building) but when competitive retaliation is likely, the costs of share building may outweigh the gains.

5 The matrix ignores interdependencies between products. For example, a dog may need to be marketed because it complements a star or a cash cow. For example, the dog may be a spare part for a star or a cash cow. Alternatively, customers and distributors may value dealing with a company that supplies a full product line. For these reasons, dropping products because they fall into a particular box may be naive.

6 The classic BCG Matrix prescription is to build stars because they will become the cash cows of the future. However, some products have a very short product life cycle, in which case the appropriate strategy should be to maximize profits and cash flow while in the star category (e.g. fashion goods).

7 Marketing objectives and strategy are heavily dependent on an assessment of what competitors are likely to do. How will they react if we lower or raise prices when implementing a build or harvest strategy, for example? This is not considered in the matrix.

8 The matrix assumes that products are self-funding. For example, selected problem children are built using cash generated by cash cows. But this ignores capital markets, which may mean that a wider range of projects can be undertaken so long as they have positive net present values of their future cash flows.

9 The matrix is vague regarding the definition of 'market'. Should we take the whole market (e.g. for confectionery) or just the market segment that we operate in (e.g. expensive boxed chocolates)? The matrix is also vague when defining the dividing line between high- and low-growth markets. A chemical company that tends to generate in lower-growth markets might use 3 per cent, whereas a leisure goods company whose markets on average experience much higher rates of growth might use 10 per cent. Also, over what period do we define market growth? These issues question the theoretical soundness of the underlying concepts, and allow managers to manipulate the figures so that their products fall in the right boxes.

10 The matrix was based on cash flow but perhaps profitability (e.g. return on investment) is a better criterion for allocating resources.

11 The matrix lacks precision in identifying which problem children to build, harvest or drop.

General Electric Market Attractiveness–Competitive Position model

As we have already noted, the BCG Matrix enjoyed tremendous success as management grappled with the complex issue of strategic resource allocation. Stimulated by this success and some of the weaknesses of the model (particularly the criticism of its oversimplicity) McKinsey & Co developed a more wide-ranging Market Attractiveness–Competitive Position (MA–CP) model in conjunction with General Electric (GE) in the USA.

Market attractiveness criteria

Instead of market growth alone, a range of market attractiveness criteria were used, such as:

- market size
- market growth rate
- beatable rivals

- market entry barriers
- social, political and legal factors.

Competitive strength criteria

Similarly, instead of using only market share as a measure of competitive strength, a number of factors were used, such as:

- market share
- reputation
- distribution capability
- market knowledge
- service quality
- innovation capability
- cost advantages.

Assessing market attractiveness and competitive strength

Management is allowed to decide which criteria are applicable for their products. This gives the MA-CP model flexibility. Having decided the criteria, management's next task is to agree upon a weighting system for each set of criteria, with those factors that are more important having a higher weighting. Table 10.2 shows a set of weights for market attractiveness. Management has decided that the key factors that should be used to assess market attractiveness are market size, market growth rate, beatable rivals and market entry barriers. Ten points are then shared between these four factors depending on their relative importance in assessing market attractiveness. Market size (weighting = 4.0) is considered the most important factor and market entry barriers (1.5) the least important of the four factors.

Next, management assesses the particular market for the product under examination on each of the four factors on a scale of 1 to 10. The market is rated very highly on size (rating = 9.0), it possesses beatable rivals (8.0), its growth rate is also rated highly (7.0) and there are some market barriers, although they are not particularly high (6.0). By multiplying each weighting by its corresponding rating, and then summing, a total score indicating the overall attractiveness of the particular market for the product under examination is obtained. In this case, the market attractiveness for the product achieves an overall score of 79 per cent.

Competitive strength assessment begins by selecting the strengths that are needed to compete in the market. Table 10.3 shows that market share, distribution capability, service quality, innovation capability, and cost advantages were the factors considered to be needed for success. Management then assigns a weight by sharing 10 points between each of these strengths according to their relative importance in achieving success. Innovation capability (weighting = 3.0) is regarded as the most important strength required to compete effectively. Distribution capability (1.0) is considered the least important of the five factors. The company's capabilities on each of the required strengths are rated on a scale of 1 to 10. Company capabilities are rated very highly on innovative capability (rating = 9.0), market share (8.0) and cost advantages (8.0), highly on distribution capability (7.0) but service quality (5.0) is mediocre. By multiplying each weighting by its corresponding rating, and then summing, a total score indicating the overall competitive strength of the company is obtained. In this example, the competitive strength of the company achieves an overall score of 76 per cent.

The market attractiveness and competitive strength scores for the product under appraisal can now be plotted on the MA-CP matrix (see Fig. 10.5). The process is repeated for each product under investigation so that their relative positions on the MA-CP matrix

Table 10.2 An example of market attractiveness assessment

Market factors	Relative importance weightings (10 points shared)	Factor ratings (scale 1–10)	Factor scores (weightings x ratings)
Market size	4.0	9.0	36
Market growth rate	2.0	7.0	14
Beatable rivals	2.5	8.0	20
Market entry barriers	1.5	6.0	9
			79%

Table 10.3 An example of competitive strength assessment

Strengths needed for success	Relative importance weightings (10 points shared)	Factor ratings (scale 1–10)	Factor scores (weightings x ratings)
Market share	2.5	8.0	20
Distribution capability	1.0	7.0	7
Service quality	2.0	5.0	10
Innovation capability	3.0	9.0	27
Cost advantages	1.5	8.0	12
			76%

can be established. Each product position is given by a circle, the size of which is in proportion to its sales.

Setting strategic objectives

The model is shown in Figure 10.5. Like the BCG Matrix the recommendations for setting strategic objectives are dependent on the product's position on the grid. Five zones are shown in Figure 10.5. The strategic objectives associated with each zone are as follows.[22]

- *Zone 1*: build—manage for sales and market share growth as the market is attractive and competitive strengths are high (equivalent to star products).
- *Zone 2*: hold—manage for profits consistent with maintaining market share as the market is not particularly attractive but competitive strengths are high (equivalent to cash cows).
- *Zone 3*: build/hold/harvest—this is the question-mark zone. Where competitors are weak or passive, a build strategy will be used. In the face of strong competitors a hold strategy may be appropriate, or harvesting where commitment to the product/market is lower. (Similar to problem children.)

Figure 10.5 The General Electric Market Attractiveness—Competitive Position model

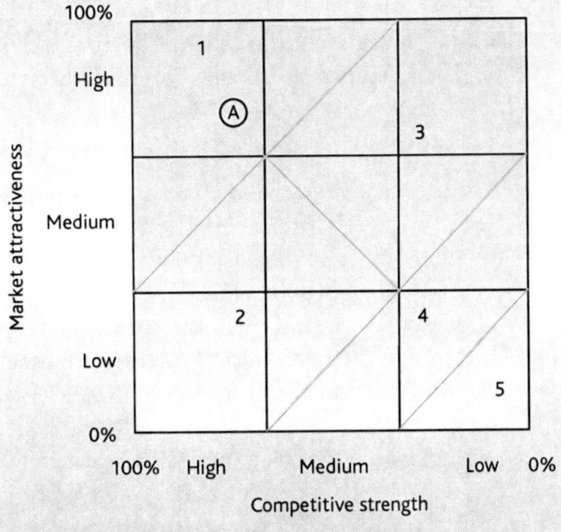

- *Zone 4*: harvest—manage for cash as both market attractiveness and competitive strengths are fairly low.
- *Zone 5*: divest—improve short-term cash yield by dropping or selling the product (equivalent to dog products).

In the example shown in Figure 10.5, the circle labelled A indicates the position of the product, which shows that it falls within zone 1 as it operates in an attractive market and its competitive strengths are high. This would suggest a build strategy that probably involves investing in raising service quality levels, which were found to be relatively weak.

Criticisms of the GE portfolio model

The proponents of the GE portfolio model argue that the analysis is much richer than BCG analysis—due to more factors being taken into account—and flexible. These are substantial advantages and the model is widely used, with companies such as BP, IBM, Honda, Nissan, Philips, Centrica, Mitsubishi and GE employing it to aid their strategic thinking. Critics argue, however, that it is harder to use than the BCG Matrix since it requires managerial agreement on which factors to use, their weightings and scoring. Furthermore, its flexibility provides a lot of opportunity for managerial bias to enter the analysis whereby product managers argue for factors and weightings that show their products in a good light (zone 1). This last point suggests that the analysis should be conducted at a managerial level higher than that being assessed. For example, decisions on which product lines to be built, held, and so on, should be taken at the strategic business unit level, and allocations of resources to brands should be decided at the group product manager level.

10.2 Pause for thought

On balance, how useful do you think the GE portfolio model is to strategic marketing thinking?

The contribution of product portfolio planning

Despite the limitations of the BCG and the GE portfolio evaluation models, both have made a contribution to the practice of portfolio planning. We shall now discuss this contribution and suggest how the models can usefully be incorporated into product strategy.

Different products and different roles

The models emphasize the important strategic point that *different products should have different roles* in the product portfolio. Hedley points out that some companies believe that all product lines and brands should be treated equally—that is, set the same profit requirements.[23] The portfolio planning models stress that this should not necessarily be the case, and may be harmful in many situations. For example, to ask for a 20 per cent return on investment (ROI) for a star may result in under-investment in an attempt to meet the profit requirement. On the other hand, 20 per cent ROI for a cash cow or a harvested product may be too low. The implication is that products should be set profitability objectives in line with the strategic objective decisions.

Different reward systems and types of manager

By stressing the need to set different strategic objectives for different products, the models, by implication, support the notion that *different reward systems and types of manager* should be linked to them. For example, managers of products being built should be marketing led, and rewarded for improving sales and market share. Conversely, managers of harvested (and to some extent cash cow) products should be more cost orientated, and rewarded by profit and cash flow achievement (see Fig. 10.6).

Aid to managerial judgement

Managers may find it useful to plot their products on both the BCG and GE portfolio grids as an initial step in pulling together the complex issues involved in product portfolio planning. This can help them get a handle on the situation and issues to be resolved. The models

Figure 10.6 Implications of portfolio planning

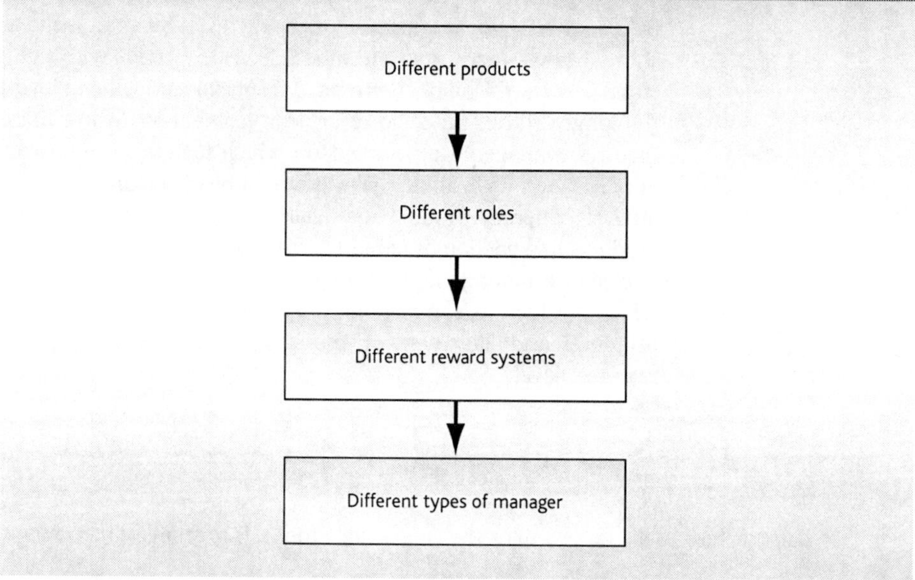

can then act as an *aid to managerial judgement* without in any way supplanting that judgement. Managers should feel free to bring into the discussion any other factors they feel are not adequately covered by the models. The models can therefore be seen as an aid to strategic thinking in multi-product, multi-market companies.

PRODUCT STRATEGIES FOR GROWTH

The emphasis in product portfolio analysis is on managing an *existing* set of products in such a way as to maximize their strengths, but companies also need to look to new products and markets for future growth. The Dyson DC08 vacuum cleaner is an example of a new product that is an addition to an existing line.

A useful way of looking at growth opportunities is the Ansoff Matrix, as shown in Figure 10.7.[24] By combining present and new products, and present and new markets into a 2×2 matrix, four product strategies for growth are revealed. Although the Ansoff Matrix does not prescribe when each strategy should be employed, it is a useful framework for thinking about the ways in which growth can be achieved through product strategy.

Figure 10.8 shows how the Ansoff Matrix can be used to implement a growth strategy.

The most basic method of gaining **market penetration** in existing markets with current products is by *winning competitors' customers*. This may be achieved by more effective use of promotion or distribution, or by cutting prices. Increasing promotional expenditure is another method of winning competitors' customers, as Cadbury Schweppes did by increasing expenditure by 87 per cent over a four-year period.[25] Another way of gaining market penetration is to *buy competitors*. An example is the Morrisons supermarket chain, which bought Safeway, a competitor, in order to gain market penetration. This achieves an immediate increase in market share and sales volume. To protect the penetration already gained in a market, a business may consider methods of *discouraging competitive entry*. *Barriers* can be created by cost advantages (lower labour costs, access to raw materials, economies of scale), highly differentiated products, high switching costs (the costs of changing from existing supplier to a new supplier, for example), high marketing expenditures and displaying aggressive tendencies to retaliate.

A company may attempt **market expansion** in a market that it already serves by converting *non-users to users* of its product. This can be an attractive option in new markets when non-users form a sizeable segment and may be willing to try the product given suitable inducements. Thus when Carnation entered the powdered coffee whitening market with Coffeemate, a key success factor was its ability to persuade hitherto non-users of powdered whiteners to switch from milk. Lapsed users can also be targeted. Kellogg's has

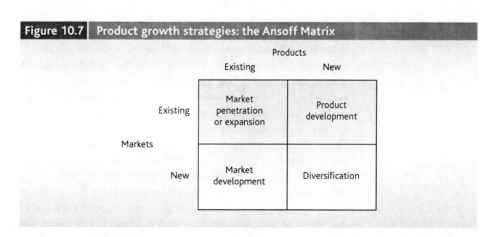

Figure 10.7 Product growth strategies: the Ansoff Matrix

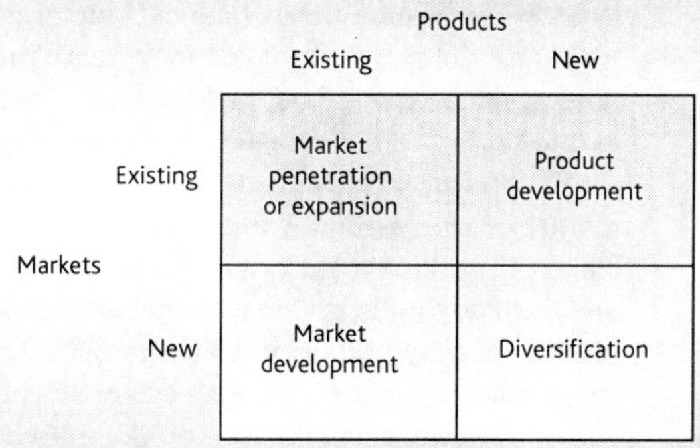

Products
Existing
New
Existing
Markets
New
Market penetration or expansion
Product development
Market development
Diversification

Figure 10.8 Strategic options for increasing sales volume

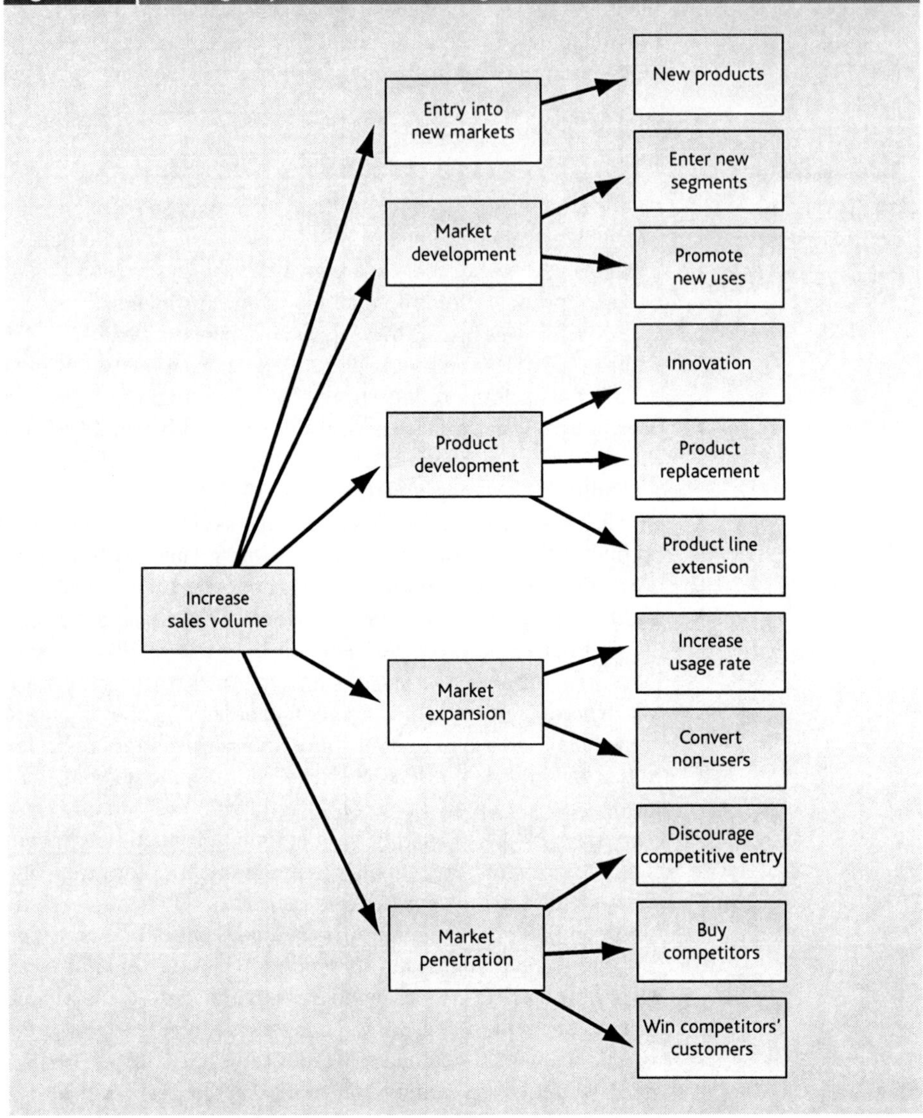

targeted lapsed breakfast cereal users (fathers) who rediscover the pleasure of eating cornflakes when feeding their children. Market expansion can also be achieved by *increasing usage rate*. Colman's attempted to increase the use of mustard by showing new combinations of mustard and food. Kellogg's has also tried to increase the usage (eating) rate of its cornflakes by promoting eating in the evening as well as at breakfast.

The **product development** option involves the development of new products for existing markets.[26] One variant is to *extend existing product lines* to give current customers greater choice. For example, the original iPod has been followed by the launches of the iPod nano and the iPod shuffle, giving its target market of young music lovers greater choice in terms of size, capacity and price. When new features are added (with an accompanying price rise) trading up may occur, with customers buying the enhanced-value product on repurchase. However, when the new products are cheaper than the original (as is the case with the iPod) the danger is cannibalization of sales of the core product. *Product replacement* activities involve the replacement of old brands/models with new ones. This is common in the car market and often involves an upgrading of the old model with a new (more expensive) replacement. A final option is the replacement of an old product with a fundamentally different one, often based on technology change. The business thus replaces an old product with an *innovation* (although both may be marketed side by side for a time). The development of the compact disc (CD) is an example.

Market development entails the promotion of new uses of existing products to new customers, or the marketing of existing products (and their current uses) to new market segments. The promotion of new uses accounted for the growth in sales of nylon, which was first marketed as a replacement for silk in parachutes but expanded into shirts, carpets, tyres, etc. Tesco, the UK supermarket chain, practised market development by marketing existing grocery products, which were sold in large out-of-town supermarkets and superstores, to a new market segment—convenience shoppers—by opening smaller grocery shops in town centres and next to petrol stations. Market development through entering new segments could involve the search for overseas opportunities. Andy Thornton Ltd, an interior design business, successfully increased sales by entering Scandinavia and Germany, two geographic segments that provided new expansion opportunities for its services. When Wagner, the German manufacturer of spray guns for painting, expanded to the USA in search of market development it found that it had to refocus on an entirely different market segment. In Europe it sells its products to professional painters but in the USA its products are bought by people who use spray guns in their own homes to paint interiors and outside surfaces such as fences.[27]

The **entry into new markets (diversification)** option concerns the development of *new products for new markets*. This is the most risky option, especially when the entry strategy is not based on the *core competences* of the business. However, it can also be the most rewarding, as exemplified by Honda's move from motorcycles to cars (based on its core competences in engines), Sony's move into 8 mm camcorders (based on its core competences in miniaturization and video technology)[28] and Apple Computer's launch of the iPod mobile music player, which can download music via a computer (based on its core competences in computer electronics). It is the lure of such rewards that has tempted the Internet networking equipment maker Cisco to venture into consumer electronics; and Intel, which manufactures microprocessors that power personal computers, to diversify into platforms combining silicon and software, which has led to new devices and technologies in consumer electronics, wireless communications and healthcare.[29]

REVIEW

1 The concept of the product life cycle

- A four-stage cycle in the life of a product illustrated as sales and profit curves; the four stages being introduction, growth, maturity and decline. It is quite flexible and can be applied to both brands and product lines.

2 The uses and limitations of the product life cycle

- Its uses are that it emphasizes the need to terminate old and develop new products, warns against the danger of assuming growth will last forever, stresses the need to review marketing objectives and strategies as products pass through the four stages, emphasizes the need to maintain a balanced set of products across the four stages, and warns against the damages of overpowering (setting too high prices early in the cycle when competition is low).
- The limitations are that it is wrong to assume that all products follow the classic S-shaped curve and it is misleading to believe that the product life cycle sales curve is a fact of life;

it depends on marketing activity. The duration of the stages are unpredictable, limiting its use as a forecasting tool, and the stylized marketing objectives and strategy prescriptions associated with each stage may be misleading in particular cases.

- Overall it is a valuable stimulus to strategic thinking but as a prescriptive tool it is blunt.

3 The concept of product portfolio planning

- This is the process of managing products as groups (portfolios) rather than separate, distinct and independent entities.
- The emphasis is on deciding which products to build, hold, harvest and divest (i.e. resource allocation).

4 The Boston Consulting Group Growth-Share Matrix, its uses and associated criticisms

- The matrix allows portfolios of products to be depicted in a 2 x 2 box, the axes of which are based on market growth rate (proxy for market attractiveness) and relative market share (proxy for competitive strength).
- Cash flow from a product is assumed to depend on the box in which a product falls.
- Stars are likely to have cash flow balance; problem children cause a drain on cash flow; cash cows generate large positive cash flow; and dogs usually produce low or negative cash flow.
- Its uses are that the matrix provides guidelines for setting strategic objectives (for example, stars should be built; problem children built selectively, harvested or divested; cash cows held; and dogs harvested or divested), and emphasizes the need to maintain a balanced portfolio with the cash generated by the cash cows being used to fund those being built.
- The criticisms are: the assumption that cash flow is determined by a product's position in the matrix is weak; it distracts management from focusing on sustainable competitive advantage; treating market growth rate and market share as proxies for market attractiveness and competitive strength is oversimplistic; it can lead to an unhealthy preoccupation with market share; it ignores interdependencies between products; building stars may be inappropriate; competitor reactions are ignored; the assumption that products are self-funding ignores capital markets; the theoretical soundness of some of the underlying concepts (e.g. market definition) is questionable; cash flow may not be the best criteria for allocating resources; and the matrix lacks precision in identifying which problem children to build, harvest or divest.

5 The General Electric Market Attractiveness–Competitive Position model, its uses and associated criticisms

- The model is based on market attractiveness (e.g. market size, market growth rate, strength of competition) and competitive strength (e.g. market share, potential to develop a differential advantage, cost advantages). By weighting the criteria and scoring products, these can be positioned on a matrix.
- Its advantages over the 'Boston Box' are that more criteria than just market growth rate and market share are used to determine the position of products in the matrix, and it is more flexible.
- Its uses are that the matrix provides guidelines for setting strategic objectives based upon a product's position in the matrix, and that the analysis is much richer than that of the Boston Box because more factors are being taken into account, leading to better resource allocation decisions.

- The criticisms are that it is harder to use than the Boston Box, and its flexibility can provide an opportunity for managerial bias.

6 The contribution of portfolio planning

- The models emphasize the important strategic point that different products should have different roles in a product portfolio, and different reward systems and managers should be linked to them.
- The models can be useful as an aid to managerial judgement and strategic thinking, but should not supplant that judgement and thinking.

7 Product strategies for growth

- A useful way of looking at growth opportunities is offered by the Ansoff Matrix as it is a practical framework for thinking about how growth can be achieved through product strategy.
- It comprises four general approaches to sales growth: market penetration/expansion, product development, market development and diversification.
- Market penetration and expansion are strategies relating to growing existing products in existing markets. Market penetration depends on winning competitors' customers or buying competitors (thereby increasing market share). Defence of increased penetration may be through discouraging competitive entry. Market expansion may be through converting non-users to users or increasing usage rate. Although market share may not increase, sales growth is achieved through increasing market size.
- Product development is a strategy for developing new products for existing markets. It has three variants: extending existing product lines (brand extensions) to give current customers greater choice; product replacement (updates of old products); and innovation (developing fundamentally different products).
- Market development is a strategy for taking existing products and marketing them in new markets. This may be through the promotion of new uses of existing products to new customers, or the marketing of existing products to new market segments (e.g. overseas markets).
- Diversification (entry into new markets) is a strategy for developing new products for new markets. It is the most risky of the four growth strategies but also potentially the most rewarding.

Key Terms

entry into new markets (diversification) the entry into new markets by new products

market development to take current products and market them in new markets

market expansion the attempt to increase the size of a market by converting non-users to users of the product and by increasing usage rates

market penetration to continue to grow sales by marketing an existing product in an existing market

portfolio planning managing groups of brands and product lines

product development increasing sales by improving present products or developing new products for current markets

product life cycle a four-stage cycle in the life of a product illustrated as sales and profits curves, the four stages being introduction, growth, maturity and decline

Study Questions

1. The product life cycle is more likely to mislead marketing management than provide useful insights. Discuss.

2. Evaluate the usefulness of the BCG Matrix. Do you believe that it has a role to play in portfolio planning?

3. What is the difference between product and market development in the Ansoff Matrix? Give examples of each form of product growth strategy.

4. How does the GE Matrix differ from the BCG Matrix? What are the strengths and weaknesses of the GE Matrix?

5. Evaluate the contribution of product portfolio planning models to product strategy.

Online LearningCentre

When you have read this chapter
log on to the Online Learning Centre at www.mcgraw-hill.co.uk/textbooks/jobber to explore chapter-by-chapter test questions, links and further online study tools for marketing.

REFERENCES

1. Polli, R. and V. Cook (1969) Validity of the Product Life Cycle, *Journal of Business*, October, 385–400.
2. Day, G. (1997) Strategies for Surviving a Shakeout, *Harvard Business Review*, March–April, 92–104.
3. Doyle, P. (1989) Building Successful Brands: The Strategic Options, *Journal of Marketing Management* 5(1), 77–95.
4. Vakratsas, D. and T. Ambler (1999) How Advertising Works: What Do We Really Know? *Journal of Marketing* 63, January, 26–43.
5. Deere, G. and N. Kilby (2005) White Heat or Lukewarm, *Marketing Week*, 18 August, 34–5.
6. Lester, R. (2005) 3 Sets Sights on Big Four, *Marketing Week*, 27 October, 26–7.
7. Odell, M. (2006) Mobile Television May Be the Answer, *FT Digital Business*, 13 February, 1.
8. Wray, R. (2006) Falling Prices Bring Nokia Handsets Below £70, *Guardian*, 27 January, 22.
9. Aaker, D. (2004) *Strategic Marketing Management*, New York: Wiley.
10. Cline, C. E. and B. P. Shapiro (1979) *Cumberland Metal Industries (A): Case Study*, Cambridge, Mass: Harvard Business School.
11. Polli and Cook (1969) op. cit.
12. Dhalia, N. K. and S. Yuspeh (1976) Forget the Product Life Cycle Concept, *Harvard Business Review*, Jan.–Feb., 102–12.
13. Rowley, I. and H. Tashiro (2005) Can Canon Keep Printing Money, *Business Week*, 5/12 September, 18–20.
14. Shah, R. (2002) Managing a Portfolio to Unlock Real Potential, *Financial Times*, 21 August, 13.
15. Marsh, P. and I. Bickerton (2005) Stewardship of a Sprawling Empire, *Financial Times*, 18 November, 13.

16. Mason, T. (2002) Nestlé Sells Big Brands in Core Strategy Focus, *Marketing*, 7 February, 5.
17. Tomlinson, H. (2005) Adidas Sells Ski and Surf Group for £329m, *Guardian*, 3 May, 5.
18. Milner, M. (2006) £1.2bn Sale of Schweppes' European Drinks Business Agreed, *Guardian*, 22 November, 26.
19. Brierley, D. (1997) Spring-Cleaning a Statistical Wonderland, *European*, 20–26 February, 28.
20. Hedley, B. (1977) Boston Consulting Group Approach to the Business Portfolio, *Long Range Planning*, February, 9–15.
21. See e.g. Day, G. S. and R. Wensley (1983) Marketing Theory with a Strategic Orientation, *Journal of Marketing*, Fall, 79–89; Haspslagh, P. (1982) Portfolio Planning: Uses and Limits, *Harvard Business Review*, Jan.–Feb., 58–73; Wensley, R. (1981) Strategic Marketing: Betas, Boxes and Basics, *Journal of Marketing*, Summer, 173–83.
22. Hofer, C. and D. Schendel (1978) *Strategy Formulation: Analytical Concepts*, St Paul, MN: West.
23. Hedley (1977) op. cit.
24. Ansoff, H. L. (1957) Strategies for Diversification, *Harvard Business Review*, Sept.–Oct., 114.
25. Mitchell, A. (2003) A Plea From the Top for a Marketing Revolution, *Marketing Week*, 20 March, 34–5.
26. Ansoff, I. (1957) Strategies for Diversification, *Harvard Business Review*, Sept.–Oct., 113–24.
27. Bolfo, B. (2005) The Art of Selling One Product to Two Markets, *Financial Times*, 10 August, 11.
28. Prahalad, C. K. and G. Hamel (1990) The Core Competence of the Corporation, *Harvard Business Review*, May–June, 79–91
29. See Palmer, M. (2006) Cisco Lays Plans to Expand into Home Electronics, *Financial Times*, 16 January, 21; and Edwards, C. (2006) Inside Intel, *Business Week*, 9 January, 43.

Case Nineteen

MIXING RED AND BLUE: LENOVO BUYS THE IBM PC DIVISION

Ad Insight

An unknown Chinese company buying the mighty IBM PC division would have been unheard of 10 years ago, but in December 2004 that is what happened when Lenovo paid $1.75 billion for the IBM personal computer business, which includes desktops, laptops and notebooks. Lenovo began life under the Legend company name, which was founded in 1984 by 11 scientists at a Chinese university. The business began as a distributor of foreign computer brands such as IBM and Hewlett-Packard in China: Legend first manufactured personal computers in 1990 and has grown into the leading PC maker in China with a 27 per cent market share. In 2003 the company changed its name to Lenovo to avoid confusion with other companies of the same name around the world. The new name is a mix of 'Le' from Legend and 'novo' which is Latin for 'new'.

IBM's resurgence

IBM became famous for being market leader in mainframe computers but saw mega-growth begin once it launched its first PC, priced at $1565 and backed by superior software, which gave it a major competitive advantage over rivals such as Apple. As competitors caught up in terms of software, PCs for the home became little more than commodities. IBM responded by focusing on large corporate clients where profit margins were more attractive. IBM reinvented itself again under the redoubtable Lou Gerstner in 1993 as IBM Global Services, which markets information technology outsourcing, consultancy and services (e.g. customer relationship management systems) and computer maintenance to companies.

Shortly before the change in direction IBM came close to collapse as its mainframe computer business, the star of the 1980s, faltered. Global Services has been the growth engine for IBM ever since, and now records annual sales revenues of over $46 billion, which account for over half the group total. It is also a high-margin business, which has enabled IBM to remain profitable in the face of stagnant demand for its computer hardware (PCs, mainframes and microprocessors), the sales of which were $30 billion in 1993 and $31 billion in 2004. In line with this move away from hardware, Gerstner also invested in the software side of the business; this has grown, albeit largely as a result of company acquisitions. It now accounts for about 40 per cent of group profits.

IBM has also built a fairly successful microprocessor business, although it has not met with the success accorded Intel. Its Power family of microprocessors has been successful within the corporate computing market and its collaboration with Sony and Toshiba has resulted in the development of the Cell processor. This has nine 'brains', seven more than Intel and AMD's dual-core processors, giving superior performance. It is used to power the PlayStation 3 games console, and IBM Power processors are also at the centre of Microsoft's Xbox and Nintendo's Revolution consoles. IBM's Powerchips are also at the heart of its successful Unix servers, the workhorses of most corporate data centres.

Current IBM chief executive Sam Palmiscano, who took over in 2002, further strengthened IBM's presence in consulting and services by buying PricewaterhouseCoopers Consulting for $3.5 billion. This made IBM the world's largest management consulting company. In PCs, however, the situation was different. At the time of the sale, IBM was a distant third in market share. It had around 6 per cent of the global PC market, behind Dell with 18 per cent and

Hewlett-Packard with 16 per cent. Internally, its share of group revenues had fallen to 12 per cent and was barely profitable. Growth in global sales of PCs was minimal.

Palmiscano's vision of the future is that in addition to selling hardware (mainframes and microprocessors), software and IT services, IBM would help its customers re-engineer their business processes and offer to run such activities as call centres, logistics and financial administration (e.g. invoicing). Big Blue would be a seller of 'business process transformation services' (BPTS) consisting of management consultancy, business process outsourcing and engineering services—a market estimated to be worth $500 billion worldwide. In so doing it is pitching itself against strong competitors such as Accenture, the management consulting group, Hewitt Associates, the human resources consultant, and Wipro, the India-based outsourcer.

Not all is well in Global Services, however. A trend towards shorter, lower-value service contracts is making it easier for smaller, low-cost rivals to challenge IBM. In doing so the market is more price sensitive, requiring IBM to cut costs to remain competitive. Consequently the company has announced a restructuring plan, eliminating 14,500 jobs (or 5 per cent of its workforce) mainly in services. This will cut $1 billion from costs per year.

Lenovo goes global

By buying the PC division of IBM, Lenovo hopes to create a third force to challenge the dominance of Dell and Hewlett-Packard. Fuelled by its success in China, where it is market leader with around 30 per cent market share, the purchase propels Lenovo from ninth position globally into the position of a global player with 7.7 per cent market share, and with 60 per cent of its sales overseas.

Much of Lenovo's success in China has been based on winning the loyalty of distributors. While overseas PC companies developed a reputation for squeezing distributors' margins when times were hard, Lenovo played fair by maintaining them. The result is a wide network of computer retailers, not only in large cities such as Beijing and Shanghai, but also in small provincial cities where China's growing middle class is beginning to buy PCs. This has meant that Lenovo's market reach far outstrips that of its competitors. Lenovo has also built a reputation for operational efficiency, allowing it to compete effectively on price, while designing machines specifically for the needs of the Chinese market.

Lenovo's Chinese headquarters are in Beijing but following the acquisition its headquarters for international operations are in New York. The company's chairman, Yang Yuanqing, has moved his base from Beijing to New York and an American from IBM is the chief executive officer. The deal allows Lenovo to use the IBM brand name on its machines for five years. In the USA, the IBM name will continue to be used, in the UK the company's Thinkpad notebooks are branded Lenovo, while in China IBM, Lenovo and Thinkpad will all be used.

Regarding after-sales support, IBM Global Services has been contracted to provide maintenance and support for PC products outside China. The idea is that IBM's current customers—mostly large corporations—would see no change. This is a major concern: when Hewlett Packard merged with Compaq it lost 20 per cent of its customers in the first year. For Lenovo, preserving business stability was a prime short-term goal.

The IBM salesforce is now incentivized to sell Lenovo machines in the same way as it has been with IBM-branded computers. The only overlap was in China, where the IBM salesforce has joined its former rival.

Lenovo's first objective is to duplicate its success in China in emerging markets such as India, Brazil and Mexico. Its second target is small and medium-sized businesses, where IBM did not have a strong presence.

References

Based on: Landon, S. (2005) Is Big Blue Fading Again?, *Financial Times*, 9 May, 19; Nuttall, C. (2005) IBM is the Only Certain Victor in New Console Wars, *Financial Times*, 16 May, 17; Landon, S. (2005) A Global Power Made in China, *Financial Times*, 9 November, 12; Landon, S. (2005) Your Rules and My Processes, *Financial Times*, 10 November, 13; Ritson, M. (2005) Lenovo is All Over the Place, *Marketing*, 8 June, 22; Anonymous (2005) A Tough Sell for Lenovo, *Business Week*, 12/19 December, 32.

Questions

1. Why did IBM sell its PC division? Relate your answer to the BCG and General Electric Market Attractiveness–Competitive Position models
2. Why was buying the IBM PC division an attractive proposition for Lenovo?
3. What are the challenges facing Lenovo in trying to make the acquisition work?
4. Do you think Lenovo will be successful?

This case was written by David Jobber, Professor of Marketing, University of Bradford.

Case Twenty

INTEL INSIDE OUT

Intel is one of the most famous business-to-business brand names in the world, with a value of over $35 billion. With sales of over $34 billion, profits of $7.5 billion and profit margins of 55 per cent, it is also one of the most successful. The foundation for its success was the development and marketing of microprocessors for PCs and servers. By investing billions in ever faster processors Intel has become the dominant force in this industry, with efficient plants that can produce more processors in a day than some rivals can in a year. The combination of low-cost production and ever faster chips was a powerful concoction that none of its rivals could match.

Much of the credit for Intel's success goes to Andy Grove, its former chief executive, who took the decision to leave the unprofitable memory chip business to focus on the fast-growing personal computer market, a move that enabled Intel to bury the competition. Intel's products were supported by powerful branding using the Pentium brand name and 'Intel inside' strap-line, bringing consumer awareness of a product hidden from sight in the heart of a computer. Intel's strategy was to work with Microsoft to appeal to PC industry giants such as Dell, HP, IBM and Compaq to be the first choice for microprocessors.

Under Grove, engineers dominated and the culture at Intel was summarized by his motto: 'Only the paranoid survive.' Managers often engaged in 'constructive confrontation', otherwise known as shouting at each other. Under Grove's successor, Craig R. Barrett, the company continued its successful path to ever greater sales and profits.

Things they are a' changin'

By 2005 the market for microprocessors was changing. Growth in PC demand was slowing as markets became saturated. No longer could Intel rely on double-digit market growth to fuel its sales and profit trajectory. Another change was occurring within Intel itself. A new chief executive, Paul Otellini, was at the helm. A non-engineer, Otellini joined Intel in 1974 straight out of business school at the University of California at Berkeley. A close working associate of Grove, who continued as chairman until 2005 after his departure as CEO in 1998, Otellini has a marketing background. Among his successes is the Centrino brand. When Otellini was head of product planning, he decided, against the wishes of Intel engineers, that rather than launch yet another fast processor, he would bundle it with a relatively new wireless Internet technology called WiFi. The combination enabled consumers to connect from their laptop to the Internet from such places as airport lounges and coffee shops. Supported by a $300 million marketing campaign, Centrino laptops caught on, revitalizing the PC market while encouraging consumers to purchase higher-margin products. Since launch, over $5 billion worth of Centrino chips have been sold.

Intel was also faced with an energetic competitor, Advanced Micro Devices, which had slowly been gaining ground in the battle of the microchip. A major competitive weapon of AMD was price, which prompted Intel to develop the low-priced Celeron microprocessor. AMD stole a march on Intel by being the first to launch a 64-bit chip, which held the competitive advantages of have greater power and lower power consumption. By 2005 AMD had increased its market share to 15 per cent of the PC microprocessor market and held 26 per cent of the market for the microprocessors that drive servers. Even more impressive was its 48 per cent share of the growing multi-core processor market, where two or more chips are put on to a single sliver of silicon. Such products consume less power, enabling laptops to run longer before recharge, and enhance performance without generating more heat, which was a problem with single chips. Using less power is especially important for business-to-business customers. For example, Google claimed that it cost more to run its computers than to buy them. A landmark came in 2005 when Dell, hitherto an Intel stronghold, moved to AMD chips for its servers. Its decision was influenced by the competitive advantage its rivals HP, Toshiba and Gateway were getting by using the more powerful AMD chips in their consumer and business systems, particularly servers.

A change of strategy

The promotion of Otellini to chief executive has heralded a change in strategic direction for Intel. The changing technological, competitive and market landscape is reflected in his desire to move the company away from its dependence on single microprocessor chips for the PC market. First, Intel has developed new dual-core chips for laptops (using the Core brand name), which place two microprocessors on one sliver of silicon. This allows laptops to run for five to ten hours rather than three to four, which was typical before. They also power the new Apple iMacs, allowing them to run at over twice the speed of the models (based on an IBM chip) they replaced without generating additional heat.

Second, Intel is focusing on 'complete technology platforms' rather than individual microprocessors. Platformization, as Intel calls it, means bundling a range of chips and the software needed to tie them all together, offering different features such as security, video, audio and wireless capabilities in a combination to suit a particular target market. This is recognition of the fact that computer manufacturers value the opportunity to buy a complete package of chips from one manufacturer rather than assemble components from several suppliers. It also means that Intel sells more components, and so takes a larger slice of the selling price of each PC. Whereas Intel can handle the process in-house, AMD requires partners to develop platforms.

Otellini has also announced plans to broaden Intel's target markets. Rather than focus only on PC manufacturers, Intel intends to be a major technological player in home entertainment, wireless communications and healthcare. In home entertainment, Otellini's vision is for the PC to be the central connection to individual entertainment devices. The company has developed the Viiv multicore chip, which allows PCs to connect to DVD players, TVs, stereo systems, and so on, so that consumers can move digital content around the home. This means that Viiv computers can act as an all-in-one DVD player, games console, CD player and television, and enable downloads of movies, music and games, which can then be moved around the home. Already Viiv has been chosen as the chip to power Windows Media Centre PCs.

In targeting wireless communications, Intel is hoping to make a breakthrough in an area where it has traditionally been weak. Hitherto, Intel's focus on PC microprocessors meant that investment in chips for mobile communications was considered secondary. Intel has yet to prove itself in the mobile handset market because of its poor record in producing radio chips. Intel is supporting WiMax, a new wireless broadband technology, and hopes to enter new markets such as smartphones and wireless broadband. Intel intends to manufacture chips to power mobile handsets and devices such as the BlackBerry and the Apple iPod.

Otellini is also hoping for breakthrough innovations in healthcare. His vision is for digital technology to help healthcare professionals. Ethnographers are employed to understand the problems of the elderly and people with specific diseases such as Alzheimer's. Currently, Intel is developing sensors that can communicate with computer networks, enabling care givers to monitor the health of the elderly remotely. One benefit of this would be to allow elderly people to remain in their own homes.

In line with his strategy, Otellini has reorganized Intel into platform-specific divisions: digital home (for consumer PCs and home entertainment), corporate (business PCs and servers), mobility (laptops and mobile devices) and healthcare, and scattered the processor engineers among them. New product development has also been reorganized. In the past engineers worked on ever faster chips and marketers were asked to sell them. Now new products are developed by teams of people: chip engineers, software developers and marketers all work together to design attractive new products. The type of person Intel hires has changed too. They include ethnographers, sociologists and software developers. Ethnographers, for example, are researching how people in emerging markets like China and India use technology.

Also—in a move that symbolizes Intel's break with the past—the Pentium brand name is being phased out and the 'Intel inside' strap-line dropped in favour of 'Intel leap ahead.' The change in branding strategy is being led by Eric Kim, chief marketing officer, recruited from Samsung and widely credited with raising its brand awareness and image as a leading consumer electronics company. Kim reports directly to Otellini. The company has spent $2 billion on a global marketing communications campaign to promote the new strap-line and logo. Intel has also become corporate technological partner with BMW, which sees its chips powering operations across BMW dealerships, the company and its cars. The partnership also makes Intel a major sponsor of BMW's Sauber Formula One motor racing team. The male-dominated F1 audience, with its keen interest in technology, is a core target market for Intel.

Not everyone at Intel is happy about the reorganization and the increased emphasis on marketing, however. Before Otellini's elevation to CEO anyone not working for the core PC business was considered a second-class citizen, and many high-level engineers working on PC products feel they have lost their star status. Some regard marketing as little more than gloss and glitz, and others have left to join rivals such as AMD. The competition is also critical of Intel's practice of offering volume-based rebates to computer manufacturers, which they claim acts as a barrier to entry. This view was supported by Japan's Fair Trade Commission, which found Intel guilty of using rebates to shut out its competitors.

References

Based on: Edwards, C. (2006) Inside Intel, *Business Week*, 9 January; Anonymous (2005) Intel's Right-hand Turn, *Economist*, 14 May, 67–9; Nuttall, C. (2005) Intel Ventures Beyond PCs, *Financial Times*, 12 November, 3; Kilby, N. (2006) Intel's Power Drive, *Marketing Week*, 5 January, 21; Durman, P. (2005) Intel Attacked for Stifling Competition, *Sunday Times*, 20 March, 10; Edwards, C. (2006) AMD: Chipping Away at Intel's Lead, *Business Week*, 12 June, 72–3.

Questions

1. Interpret Intel's move from its reliance on microprocessors for PCs into home entertainment, healthcare and mobile communications using (i) the product life cycle, (ii) the BCG, and (iii) the General Electric Market Attractiveness–Competitive Position models.

2. Locate each of Intel's moves (products and markets) since Otellini became CEO in the Ansoff product growth matrix. Justify your answer.

3. How has the corporate culture changed since Otellini became CEO? Support your answer with examples.

4. What challenges does Intel face as it moves into home entertainment, healthcare and mobile communications?

This case was prepared by David Jobber, Professor of Marketing, University of Bradford.

Developing new products

CHAPTER 11

I met R&D people who never left the lab ... and who were so snobbish about the salesforce that they wouldn't know a customer if they tripped over one. I saw financial controllers whose projections sounded exciting but who didn't have a clue about how to make a company grow with new products.

DON FREY, *Learning the Ropes: My Life as a Product Champion*

Learning Objectives

After reading this chapter, you should be able to:

1. define the different types of new products that can be launched
2. describe how to create and nurture an innovative culture
3. discuss the organizational options that apply to new product development
4. identify the methods of reducing time to market
5. explain how marketing and R&D staff can work together effectively
6. describe the stages in the new product development process
7. explain how to stimulate the corporate imagination
8. discuss the six key principles of managing product teams
9. describe the innovation categories and their marketing implications
10. discuss the key ingredients in commercializing technology quickly and effectively

The life-blood of corporate success is bringing new products to the marketplace. Changing customer tastes, technological advances and competitive pressures mean that companies cannot afford to rely on past product success. Instead they have to work on new product development programmes and nurture an innovation climate to lay the foundations for new product success. The 3M company, for example, places a heavy reliance on new product introduction. Each of its divisions is expected to achieve a quarter of its revenue from products that have been on the market for under six years.

The reality of new product development is that it is a risky activity: most new products fail. But, as we shall see, new product development should not be judged in terms of the percentage of failures. To do so could stifle the spirit of innovation. The acid test is the number of successes. Failure has to be tolerated; it is endemic in the whole process of developing new products.

To fully understand new product development, we need to distinguish between invention and innovation. **Invention** is the discovery of new ideas and methods. **Innovation** occurs when an invention is commercialized by bringing it to market. Not all countries that are good at invention have the capability to innovate successfully. For example, the UK has an excellent record of invention; among major UK inventions and discoveries are the steam engine, the steamboat, the locomotive, the steam turbine, the electric heater, the hydraulic press, cement, the telegraph, the stethoscope, rubber tyres, the bicycle, television, the

Table 11.1 The world's most innovative companies

Company	Reason
Apple	Outstanding design and innovative software platforms create an unrivalled user experience. iPod a major success
Google	Allows one of the world's brightest crops of engineers time to experiment Focuses on simplicity and the customer
3M	Revamped its vaunted R&D labs in 2003 to centralize basic research
Toyota	A master of manufacturing innovation and, now, hybrid technology New cost-cutting strategy calls for reducing vehicle system costs as a whole
Microsoft	Primes Windows and Office sales with innovations A new combo of Web and PC services, called Live, is off to a solid start
General Electric	Transforming from an efficiency powerhouse to one that values bold ideas Now rates managers on traits such as 'imagination and courage'
Procter & Gamble	Its 'connect and develop' model calls for 50 per cent of new products to come from outside Design and innovation executives are now part of the organizational chart
Nokia	Global handset leader. Diverse teams create future-orientated 'world maps' to track macro trends Designed low-cost phones for emerging markets
Starbucks	Would you like a movie with your latté? The creator of the $3 coffee has started marketing films Taps an army of baristas for customer insight
IBM	Donated 500 of its more than 40,000 patents to help build new technology ecosystems Co-invests in projects with clients and partners

Source: A 2006 survey of 1070 senior executives in 63 countries by the Boston Consulting Group, reported by McGregor (2006)[4]

computer, the radio valve, radar, celluloid, the hovercraft and the jet engine. In terms of innovation, however, the British fall far short of the Japanese, who have the ability to successfully market products by constantly seeking to improve and develop—a process called Kaizen (sometimes Kaisan).[1] The classic example is the Sony Walkman, which was not an invention in the sense that it was fundamentally new: rather its success (over 75 million have been sold worldwide) was based on the innovative marketing of existing technologies.

Scandinavian countries have many businesses built on a local invention. For example, Tetra Pak was founded by a person who conceived of 'pouring milk into a paper bag'. Lego bricks have revolutionized toys and Gambro invented a machine that can take the place of kidneys. In all these cases, the key was not just the invention but the capability to innovate by bringing the product successfully to market.[2]

The USA is a major source of innovation. The interest is dominated by US companies such as Amazon, Google, eBay and Yahoo! and, as Table 11.1 shows, US companies occupy eight out of the top 10 places in a survey of the world's most innovative companies.[3]

A key point to remember is that the focus of innovation should be on providing new solutions that better meet customer needs. Innovative solutions often do not require major breakthroughs in technology. For example, the growth of Starbucks was not fuelled by technological breakthroughs but by redefining what city-centre coffee drinking meant, and Ryanair has built its success by creating a different consumer appeal from traditional airlines based on low prices and strict cost control. The Body Shop's success was based on the modern woman's concern for the environment, and Dell became the most profitable computer company by becoming the first to market computers directly to its customers.[5]

Because many innovations fail, it is important to understand the key success factors. A study of 60 innovations launched by 34 companies and the PIMS database to determine the key success factors in innovation revealed the following major findings.[6]

Ad Insight

- *Innovation success is related to the creation and delivery of added consumer value.* Innovations that produce large improvements in consumer value perform much better than those that fail to show any change in consumer value. Unsurprisingly, radical innovation has greater potential for enhancing performance than small, incremental innovations. Incremental innovations, though, can be very successful provided they meet the first test: the creation and delivery of added consumer value (see the Whirlpool illustration).
- *Speed to market counts.* The most successful new products tend to be those that are launched within one year of the conception of the new idea. There are two reasons for this. First, delay increases the risk of others getting to market first; second, consumer priorities may change.
- *A product's inferior perceived value cannot be compensated for with high communications spending.* High expenditures on advertising and promotion only have a significant effect on performance where the product is already perceived to have high consumer value. High expenditures for inferior products actually worsen the performance: advertising makes bad products fail quicker.

In this chapter we shall ask the question 'What is a new product?' and examine three key issues in new product development, namely organization, developing an innovation culture and the new product development process. Then we shall examine the strategies involved in product replacement, the most common form of new product development. Finally, we shall look at the consumer adoption process, which is how people learn about new products, try them, and adopt or reject them. Throughout this chapter reference will be made to research that highlights the success factors in new product development.

Whirlpool's 'Sixth Sense' technology provides added consumer value by saving user time, energy and water.

WHAT IS A NEW PRODUCT?

Some new products are so fundamentally different from products that already exist that they reshape markets and competition. For example, the pocket calculator created a new market and made the slide rule obsolete. At the other extreme, a shampoo that is different from existing products only by means of its brand name, fragrance, packaging and colour is also a new product. In fact, four broad categories of new product exist.[7]

1. *Product replacements*: these account for about 45 per cent of all new product launches, and include revisions and improvements to existing products (e.g. the Ford Mondeo replacing the Sierra), repositioning (existing products such as Lucozade being targeted at new market segments) and cost reductions (existing products being reformulated or redesigned to cost less to produce).
2. *Additions to existing lines*: these account for about 25 per cent of new product launches and take the form of new products that add to a company's existing product lines. This produces greater product depth. An example is the launch by Weetabix of a brand extension, Fruitibix, to compete with the numerous nut/fruit/cereal product combinations that have been gaining market share. Another example is the addition to the Crest toothpaste brand of Crest Whitestripes, a tooth-whitening product, and the Crest Spinbrush line of inexpensive battery-powered toothbrushes.[8]

3 *New product lines*: these total around 20 per cent of new product launches, and represent a move into a new market. For example, in Europe, Mars has launched a number of ice cream brands, which is a new product line for this company. This strategy widens a company's product mix.
4 *New-to-the-world products*: these total around 10 per cent of new product launches, and create entirely new markets. For example, the video games console, the video recorder, camcorder and the Internet have created new markets because of the highly valued customer benefits they provide.

Clearly the degree of risk and reward varies according to the new product category. New-to-the-world products normally carry the highest risk since it is often very difficult to predict consumer reaction. Often, market research will be unreliable in predicting demand as people do not really understand the full benefits of the product until it is on the market and they get the chance to experience them. Furthermore, it may take time for the products to be accepted. For example, the Sony Walkman was initially rejected by marketing research since the concept of being seen in a public place wearing earphones was alien to most people. After launch, however, this behaviour was gradually accepted by younger age groups, who valued the benefit of listening to music when on a train or bus, walking down the street, and so on. At the other extreme, adding a brand variation to an existing product line lacks significant risk but is also unlikely to proffer significant returns.

Effective new product development is based on creating and nurturing an innovative culture, organizing effectively for new product development and managing the new product development process. We shall now examine these three issues.

CREATING AND NURTURING AN INNOVATIVE CULTURE

The foundation for successful new product development is the creation of a corporate culture that promotes and rewards innovation. Unfortunately many marketing managers regard their company's corporate culture as a key constraint to innovation.[9] Managers, therefore, need to pay more attention to creating a culture that encourages innovation. Figure 11.1 shows the kinds of attitudes and actions that can foster an innovation culture. People in organizations observe those actions that are likely to lead to success or punishment. The surest way to kill innovative spirit is to conspicuously punish those people who are prepared to create and champion new product ideas through to communication when things go wrong, and to reward those people who are content to manage the status quo. Such actions will breed the attitude 'Why should I take the risk of failing when by carrying on as before I will probably be rewarded?' Research has shown that those companies that have supportive attitudes to rewards and risk, and a tolerant attitude towards failure, are more likely to innovate successfully.[10] This was recognized as early as 1941 in 3M when the former president William McKnight said 'Management that is destructively critical when mistakes are made kills initiative, and it is essential that we have people with initiative if we continue to grow.'[11]

An innovation culture can also be nurtured by senior management visibly supporting new product development in general, and high-profile projects in particular.[12] British Rail's attempt to develop the ill-fated Advanced Passenger Train (APT), which involved new technology, was hampered by the lack of this kind of support. Consequently, individual managers took a subjective view on whether they were for or against the project. Beside sending clear messages about the role and importance of new product development, senior management should reinforce their words by allowing time off from their usual duties to people who wish to develop their own ideas, make available funds and resources for projects, and make themselves accessible when difficult decisions need to be taken.[13]

Figure 11.1 Creating and nuturing an innovative culture

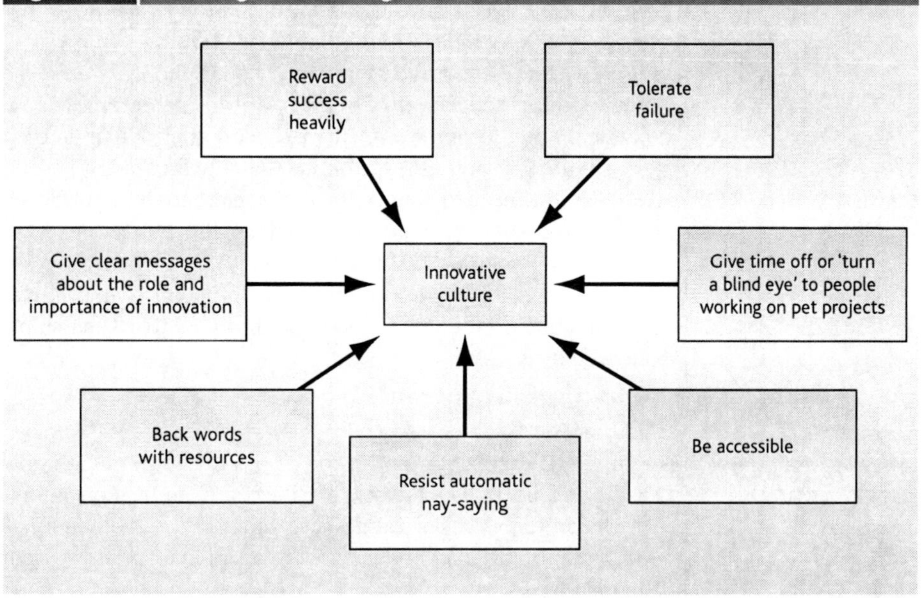

One company that displays its commitment to innovation is 3M. It invests around 7 per cent of its global sales of around £10 billion (€14.4 billion) in research and development and places a high value on staff input. This is formalized by allowing staff to spend 15 per cent of their work time on their own projects. By motivating staff to dedicate time to new product development, 3M generates 30 per cent of sales from products that are less than four years old.[14]

11.1 Marketing in Action

Creative Leadership and Innovation

The creation and nurturing of an innovative culture relies heavily on the kind of leadership than can release passions, imaginations and energy in a company. This type of creative leader has the following qualities.

- *They design cultures that support innovation*: people are encouraged to adapt continuously to constantly changing circumstances, reject the status quo and operate in a productive discomfort zone.
- *They inspire people*: they know how to electrify relationships between themselves and other people, and produce engagement that stimulates personal growth. They have a clear vision for the future and can motivate people to achieve the corporate mission.
- *They provide insights, not solutions*: they avoid simplistic answers to complex questions but provide support for exploration. In a complex environment, they recognize that there is a need to give form to what is unfolding by asking important questions.
- *They maintain focus, not control*: many organizations are tight on strategy but loose on vision. Creative leaders release the energy and potential of an organization by being tight on vision but looser on strategy. Rather than tight control, they encourage a healthy disequilibrium, and show in their actions how to tolerate uncertainty and live with paradox.

Based on: Francis (2000)[15]

Finally, management at all levels should resist the temptation of automatic 'nay-saying'. Whenever a new idea is suggested the tendency of the listener is to think of the negatives. For example, suppose you were listening to the first ever proposal that someone at Nokia made concerning a move into mobile phones. Your response might have been: 'We know nothing about that business', 'We are not strong enough to compete against the Americans and Japanese' and 'If we succeed they will undercut us on price.' All these perfectly natural responses serve only to demotivate the proposer. The correct response is to resist expressing such doubts. Instead, the proposer should be encouraged to take the idea further, to research and develop it. There will come a time to scrutinize the proposal but only after the proposer has received an initial encouraging response. Stifling new ideas at conception serves only to demotivate the proposer from trying again.

Marketing in Action 11.1 describes how creative leadership can help to foster an innovative culture.

ORGANIZING EFFECTIVELY FOR NEW PRODUCT DEVELOPMENT

The second building block of successful innovation is an appropriate organization structure. Most companies use one or a combination of the following methods: project teams, product and brand managers, new product departments and new product committees.

Project teams

Project teams involve the bringing together of staff from such areas as R&D, engineering, manufacturing, finance and marketing to work on a new product development project. Research has shown that assigning the responsibility of new product development to such cross-functional teams has a positive effect on new product performance.[16] Specialized skills

11.2 Marketing in Action

Razr-sharp Innovation Labs

The Razr, Motorola's sleek, ultra-light mobile phone was developed not in the company's sprawling research and development facility but in an innovation lab 50 miles away. There, engineers teamed up with designers and marketers in a building designed with open spaces and waist-high cubicles to foster teamwork and a breaking down of barriers. In an age where innovations grow stale fast, the aim was to speed the Razr to market quickly.

Innovation labs are a way of replacing the traditional system of new product development, which saw scientists or engineers work independently for years in pursuit of patents, then hand the work over to product developers who, in turn, passed it to designers and marketers for final commercialization work. By working as a team, these people can reduce time to market. Already Motorola has launched follow-on phones such as the Slvr and the Pebl to keep it ahead of the competition.

The need for cutting development time extends beyond high-tech companies with organizations as varied as Mattel, Boeing, Wrigley and Procter & Gamble using innovation labs to break down bureaucratic barriers. Teams of people from different backgrounds gather to focus on a problem. They bounce ideas around, brainstorm and generate possible solutions that can be tested on consumers and sped to market.

Based on: Weber et al. (2005)[17]

are combined to form an effective team to develop the new product concept. This organization form is in line with Kanter's belief that to compete in today's global marketplace, companies must move from rigid functional organizational structures to highly integrated ones.[18] People are assigned to the venture team as a major undertaking and the team is linked directly to top management to avoid having to communicate and get approval from several layers of management before progressing a course of action. This form of organization was used by IBM to successfully develop its first personal computer, and Unilever has also established a venture unit that focuses on developing new business targeted at areas not currently addressed by existing brands.[19] Its advantages include the fostering of a group identity and common purpose, fast decision-making, and the lowering of bureaucratic barriers.

Such teams meet in what are sometimes called 'innovation labs', located away from other employees, to work on a project free from bureaucratic intrusion. Marketing in Action 11.2 describes how these work in practice.

A similar organizational change that has reduced the product development cycle time is the bringing together of design and manufacturing engineers to work as a team. Traditionally, design engineers would work on product design and then the blueprint would be passed on to production engineers. By working together each group can understand the problems of the other and effectively reduce the time it takes to develop a new product. The process—**simultaneous engineering**—was pioneered in Japan but is being adopted by European companies. For example, Ford of Europe brings together design and production engineers, purchasing engineers, finance and quality control specialists, and support staff to work as teams to develop future Ford cars in long-term collaboration with component suppliers.[20] Being faster has been shown to result in better new product performance in terms of higher profits and market share.[21]

Product and brand managers

Product and brand management entails the assignment of product managers to product lines (or groups of brands within a product line) and/or brand managers to individual brands. These managers are then responsible for their success and have the task of coordinating functional areas (e.g. production, sales, advertising and marketing research). They are also often responsible for new product development, including the creation of new product ideas, improving existing products and brand extensions. They may be supported by a team of assistant brand managers and a dedicated marketing researcher. In some companies a new product development manager may help product and brand managers in the task of generating and testing new product concepts. This form of organization is common in the grocery, toiletries and drinks industries.

New product departments and committees

The review of new product projects is normally in the hands of high-ranking functional managers, who listen to progress reports and decide whether further funds should be assigned to a project. They may also be charged with deciding new product strategies and priorities. No matter whether the underlying structure is venture team, product and brand management or new product department, a new products committee often oversees the process and services to give projects a high corporate profile through the stature of its membership.

The importance of teamwork

Whichever method (or combination of methods) is used, effective cross-functional teamwork is crucial for success.[22] In particular, as the quotation by Frey at the beginning of this chapter implies, there has to be effective communication and teamwork between R&D and marketing.[23]

Although all functional relationships are important during new product development, the cultural differences between R&D and marketing are potentially the most harmful and difficult to resolve. The challenge is to prevent technical people developing only things that interest them professionally, and to get them to understand the realities of the marketplace.

The role of marketing directors

A study by Gupta and Wileman asked marketing directors of technology-based companies what they believed they could do to improve their relationship with R&D and achieve greater integration of effort.[24] Six major suggestions were made by the marketing directors.

1. *Encourage teamwork*: marketing should work with R&D to establish clear, mutually agreed project priorities to reduce the incidence of pet projects. Marketing, R&D and senior management should hold regular joint project review meetings.
2. *Improve the provision of marketing information to R&D*: one of the major causes of R&D rejecting input from marketing was the lack of quality and timely information. Many marketing directors admitted that they could do a better job of providing such information to R&D. They also believed that the use of information would be enhanced if R&D personnel were made part of the marketing research team so that the questions on their minds could be incorporated into studies. They also felt that such a move would improve the credibility and trust between marketing and R&D.
3. *Take R&D people out of the lab*: marketing should encourage R&D staff to be more customer aware by inviting them to attend trade shows, take part in customer visits and prepare customer materials.
4. *Develop informal relationships with R&D*: they noted that there were often important personality and value differences between the two groups, which could cause conflict as well as being a stimulus to creativity. More effort could be made to break down these barriers by greater socializing, going to lunch together, and sitting with each other at seminars and presentations.
5. *Learn about technology*: the marketing directors believed that improving their 'technological savvy' would help them communicate more effectively with R&D people, understand various product design trade-offs, and comprehend the capabilities and limits of technology to create competitive advantages and provide solutions to customer problems.
6. *Formalize the product development process*: they noted that marketing people were often preoccupied with present products to the neglect of new products, and that the new product development process was far too unstructured. They advocated a more formal process, including formal new project initiation, status reports and review procedures, and a formal requirement that involvement in the process was an important part of marketing personnel's jobs.

The role of senior management

The study also focused on marketing directors' opinions of what senior management could do to help improve the marketing–R&D relationship. We have already noted, when discussing how to create an innovative culture, the crucial role that senior management staff play in creating the conditions for a thriving new product programme. Marketing directors mentioned six major ways in which senior management could play a part in fostering better relations.

1. *Make organizational design changes*: senior management should locate marketing and R&D near to each other to encourage communication and the development of informal

relationships. They should clarify the roles of marketing and R&D in developing new products and reduce the number of approvals required for small changes in a project, which would give both R&D and marketing greater authority and responsibility.

2 *Show a personal interest in new product development*: organizational design changes should be backed up by more overt commitment and interest in innovation through early involvement in the product development process, attending product planning and review meetings, and helping to coordinate product development plans.
3 *Provide strategic direction*: many marketing directors felt that senior management could provide more strategic vision regarding new product/market priorities. They also needed to be more long term with their strategic thinking.
4 *Encourage teamwork*: senior management should encourage, or even demand, teamwork between marketing and R&D. Specifically, they should require joint R&D–marketing discussions, joint planning and budgeting, joint marketing research and joint reporting to them.
5 *Increase resources*: some marketing directors pointed to the need to increase resources to foster product development activities. The alternative was to reduce the number of projects. Resources should also be provided for seminars, workshops and training programmes for R&D and marketing people. The objective of these programmes would be to develop a better understanding of the roles, constraints and pressures of each group.
6 *Understand marketing's importance*: marketing directors complained of senior management's lack of understanding of marketing's role in new product development and the value of marketing in general. They felt that senior management should insist that marketing becomes involved with R&D in product development much earlier in the process so that the needs of customers are more prominent.

This research has provided valuable insights into how companies should manage the marketing–R&D relationship. It is important that companies organize themselves effectively since cross-functional teamwork and communication has proved to be a significant predictor of successful innovation in a number of studies.[25]

MANAGING THE NEW PRODUCT DEVELOPMENT PROCESS

There are three inescapable facts about new product development: it is expensive, risky, and time-consuming. For example, Gillette spent an excess of £100 million (€140 million) over more than 10 years developing its Sensor razor brand. The new product concept was to develop a non-disposable shaver that would use new technology to produce a shaver that would follow the contours of a man's face, giving an excellent shave (through two spring-mounted platinum-hardened chromium blades) with fewer cuts. This made commercial sense since shaving systems are more profitable than disposable razors and allow more opportunity for creating a differential advantage. Had the brand failed, Gillette's position in the shaving market could have been damaged irreparably. Nike is another company that invests heavily in new product development to maintain its lead in the specialist sports shoe market (see illustration overleaf).

Managing the process of new product development is an important factor in reducing cost, time and risk. Studies have shown that having a formal process with review points, clear new product goals and a strong marketing orientation underlying the process leads to greater success whether the product is a physical good or a service.[26]

An eight-step new product development process to provide these characteristics is shown in Figure 11.2 and consists of setting new product strategy, idea generation,

Nike continues to be at the forefront of the specialist sports shoe market.

screening, concept testing, business analysis, product development, market testing and commercialization. Although the reality of new product development may resemble organizational chaos, the discipline imposed by the activities carried out at each stage leads to a greater likelihood of developing a product that not only works, but also confers customer benefits. We should note, however, that new products pass through each stage at varying speeds: some may dwell at a stage for a long period while others may pass through very quickly.[27]

New product strategy

As we have already seen, marketing directors value strategic guidance from senior management about their vision and priorities for new product development. By providing clear guidelines about which products/markets the company is interested in serving, senior management staff can provide a focus for the areas in which idea generation should take place. Also by outlining their objectives (e.g. market share gain, profitability, technological leadership) for new products they can provide indicators for the screening criteria that should be used to evaluate those ideas. An example of a company with a clearly developed new product strategy is Mars, which developed ice-cream products that capitalized on the brand equity of its confectionery brand names, such as Twix, Mars and Milky Way.

Figure 11.2 The eight-stage new product development process

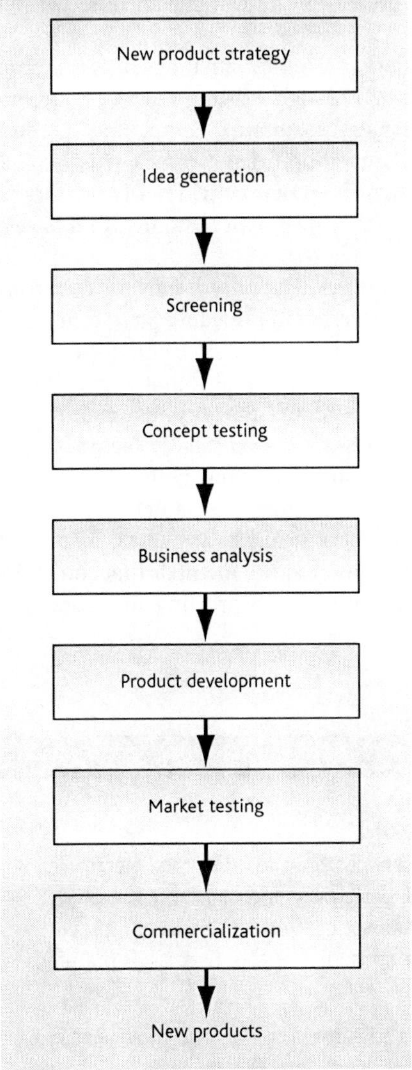

Idea generation

One of the benefits of developing an innovative corporate culture is that it sparks the imagination. The objective is to motivate the search for ideas so that salespeople, engineers, top management, marketers and other employees are all alert to new opportunities. Interestingly, questioning Nobel Prize winners about the time and circumstances when they had the important germ of an idea that led them to great scientific discovery revealed that it can occur at the most unexpected time: just before going to sleep, on waking up in the morning and at church were some of the occasions mentioned. The common factor seems to be a period of quite contemplation, uninterrupted by the bustle of everyday life and work.

Successful new product ideas are not necessarily based on technological innovation. Often, they are based on novel applications of existing technology (e.g. Velcro poppers on disposable nappies) or new visions of markets (e.g. Levi Strauss's vision of repositioning jeans, which were originally used as working clothes, as a fashion statement through its 501 brand).

The sources of new product ideas can be internal to the company: scientists, engineers, marketers, salespeople and designers, for example. Procter & Gamble is expert at this. It uses online networks to get in touch with thousands of experts to help it generate new product ideas. Nabil Sakkab, global leader of P&G's fabric and homecare research and development, commented, 'I pay 7000 scientists to work for me at P&G but there are 1.5 million scientists out there who do not work for P&G. I want to make my R&D department 1,507,000 strong.' This attempt to 'in-source' ideas and expertise is working: 45 per cent of the new ideas he is working on have come from outside the company.[28] Some companies use **brainstorming** as a technique to stimulate the creation of ideas, and use financial incentives to persuade people to put forward the ideas they have had. The 3M Post-it adhesive-backed notepaper was a successful product that was thought of by an employee who initially saw it as a means of preventing paper falling from his hymn book as he marked the hymns that were being sung. Because of the innovative culture within 3M, he bothered to think of commercial applications and acted as a product champion within the company to see the project through to become the commercial and global success it is today. In a survey of Dutch industrial goods, over 60 per cent of companies claimed to use brainstorming to generate new product ideas.[29]

11.1 Pause for thought

Try to think of a new product idea. The best time is during a period of quiet contemplation such as before going to sleep or after waking up. The idea does not have to be 'new to the world'. You could focus on a product that you use/consume regularly. What are its weaknesses? How could it be improved? Many new products are 'incremental' in the sense that they are small or medium-sized improvements on existing products.

Hamel and Prahalad argue that global competitive battles will be won by those companies that have the corporate imagination to build and dominate fundamentally new markets.[30] Introducing such products as speech-activated appliances, artificial bones and automatic language translators would effectively create new and largely uncontested competitive space.

Often, fundamentally new products/markets are created by small businesses that are willing to invent new business models or radically redesign existing models. Sources of new product ideas can also be external to the company. Examining competitors' products may provide clues to product improvements. Competitors' new product plans can be gleaned by training the sales-force to ask distributors about new activities. Distributors can also be a source of new product ideas directly since they deal with customers and have an interest in selling improved products.

A major source of good ideas is consumers themselves. Their needs may not be satisfied by existing products and they may be genuinely interested in providing ideas that lead to product improvement. Sometimes, traditional marketing research techniques such as focus groups can be useful. For example, marketing research revealed that young drinkers wanted great-tasting portable alcoholic drinks. A new product category – premium bottled spirits – was created as traditional spirits did not possess the portability factor. A prime example is Bacardi Breezer, which is a fruit-flavoured spirit in a small bottle.[31]

Other companies require a less traditional approach. Procter & Gamble, for example, has used ethnographic research to observe consumers using its products, in order to develop new and improved products. Others, like Philips, require methods that can foresee trends that can impact on their business in the future, as Marketing in Action 11.3 describes.

11.3 Marketing in Action

Philips Looks into the Future

Philips Design is a stand-alone unit of Philips that provides design services for the consumer electronics, lighting, medical equipment and semiconductor group. In the old days, design was focused more on internal production issues than on consumers: on standardization, manufacturability, cost-effectiveness and process. Although these issues still matter, the emphasis has moved towards the consumer as the market has matured and competition intensified.

Philips Design now employs anthropologists and cognitive psychologists to gather insights into the needs and expectations of consumers around the world. It conducts 'culture scan' research into shorter-term social, cultural and aesthetic trends, and 'strategic futures' research into trends over a five- to seven-year period. The findings play a major role in the parent company's decisions about which products should be developed and brought to market, and the design features that should be built into them.

One strong trend to emerge is consumers' desire for simplicity. Once consumer products like washing machines were packed with programmes in an effort to impress consumers with their technological complexity, even though very few of these were actually used, and audio systems were aglow with coloured lights. This has now changed, with consumers rejecting over-complex products. The focus is on simplicity of form and function, and is exemplified by the Philips Senseo Excel automatic coffee machine and the Philips Heart-Start home defibrillator, which is so compact and simple to use even a young child could save a parent from the effects of a sudden heart attack.

Based on: Tomkins (2005)[32]

In organizational markets, keeping in close contact with customers who are innovators and market leaders in their own marketplaces is likely to be a fruitful source of new product ideas.[33] These *lead customers* are likely to recognize required improvements ahead of other customers as they have advanced needs and are likely to face problems before other product users. For example, GE's healthcare division researches 'luminaries', who tend to be well-published doctors and research scientists from leading medical institutions. Up to 25 luminaries are brought together at regular medical advisory board sessions to discuss developments in GE's technology. GE then shares some of its advanced technology with a subset of these people. The result is a stream of new products that emerge from collaboration with these groups.

Marketing research can play a role in providing feedback when the product line is familiar to customers. For example, the original idea for Hewlett-Packard's successful launch of its Desk-Jet printer came from marketing research, which revealed that personal computer users would value a relatively slow-speed printer that approached the quality of a laser printer but sold at less than half the price.[34] However, for radically new products customers may be unable to articulate their requirements and so conventional marketing research may be ineffective as a source of ideas. In this situation, as can be seen in Marketing in Action 11.4, companies need to be proactive in their search for new markets rather than rely on customer suggestions.[35]

Screening

Having developed new product ideas, they need to be screened to evaluate their commercial worth. Some companies use formal checklists to help them judge whether the product idea should be rejected or accepted for further evaluation. This ensures that no important criterion is overlooked. Criteria may be used that measure the attractiveness of the market for the proposed product, the fit between the product and company objectives, and the capability of the company to produce and market the product. Texas Instruments focused on financial and market-based criteria when screening new semiconductor products. To pass its screen, a new product idea had to have the potential to sustain a 15 per cent compound sales growth rate, give 25 per cent return on assets, and be of a unique design that lowered costs or gave a performance advantage. Other companies may use a less systematic approach, preferring more flexible open discussion among members of the new product development committee to gauge likely success.

Concept testing

Once the product idea has been accepted as worthy of further investigation, it can be framed into a specific concept for testing with potential customers. In many instances the basic product idea will be expanded into several product concepts, each of which can be compared by testing with target customers. For example, a study into the acceptability of a new service—a proposed audit of software development procedures that would lead to the award of a quality assurance certificate—was expressed in eight service concepts depending on which parts of the development procedure would be audited (e.g. understanding customer needs, documentation, benchmarking, and so on). Each concept was evaluated by potential buyers of the software to gauge which were the most important aspects of software development that should be audited.[36] **Concept testing** thus allows the views of customers to enter the new product development process at an early stage.

Group discussion can also be used to develop and test product concepts. For example, a major financial services company decided it should launch an interest-bearing transaction account (product idea) because its major competition had done so.[37] Group discussions

11.4 Marketing in Action

Creating Radical Innovation

Many new products are incremental, such as Diet Coke from Coca-Cola or Persil detergent tables from Unilever; others fundamentally change the nature of a market and may be based on technological breakthroughs such as the development of mobile phones or the invention of new business models such as Dell selling customized computers direct to consumers or Starbucks' reinvention of city-centre coffee drinking. Radical innovation is risky but can bring huge rewards. The focus is on making the competition irrelevant by creating a leap in value for customers, and entry into new and uncontested market space.

Avoiding an incremental approach to new product development involves a sharpening of the corporate imagination to become more alive to new market opportunities. Five factors can aid this development.

1. *Escaping the tyranny of served markets*: looking outside markets that are currently served can be assisted by defining core competences and looking at products/markets that lie between existing business units. For example, Motorola's core competences in wireless technology led it to look beyond current products/markets (e.g. mobile phones) and towards global positioning satellite receivers. Looking for white space between business units led Kodak to envisage a market for storing and viewing photographs.
2. *Searching for innovative product concepts*: this can be aided by viewing markets as a set of customer needs and product functionalities. This has led to adding an important function to an existing product (e.g. Yamaha's electronic piano), creating a new way to deliver an existing function (e.g. electronic notepads), or creating a new functionality (e.g. the Internet).
3. *Weakening traditional price–performance assumptions*: traditional price–performance assumptions should be questioned. For example, it was Sony and JVC that questioned the price tag of £25,000 (€35,000) on early video recorders. They gave their engineers the freedom and the technology to design a video recorder that cost less than £500 (€720).
4. *Leading customers*: a problem with developing truly innovative products is that customers rarely ask for them. Successful innovating companies lead customers by imagining unarticulated needs rather than simply following them. They gain insights into incipient needs by talking in-depth to and observing closely a market's most sophisticated and demanding customers. For example, Yamaha set up a facility in London where Europe's most talented musicians could experiment with state-of-the-art musical hardware. The objective was not only to understand the customer but also to convey to the customer what might be possible technologically.
5. *Building a radical innovation hub*: a hub is a group of people who encourage and oversee innovation. It includes idea hunters, idea gatherers, internal venture capitalists, members of project evaluation committees, members of overseeing boards and experienced entrepreneurs. The hub's prime function is to nurture hunters and gatherers from all over the company to foster a stream of innovative ideas. At the centre of each project is a product champion who takes risks, breaks the rules, energizes and rescues, and re-energizes the project.

Based on: Hamel and Prahalad (1991);[38] Hamel (1999);[39] Leifer et al. (2001);[40] Hunt (2002);[41] Bartram (2004)[42]

were carried out to develop the product idea into a specific product concept (a chequebook feature was rejected in favour of a cash card) with a defined target market (the under-25s). This concept was then developed further using group discussions to refine the product features (a telephone banking service was added) and to select the lifestyle image that should be used to position the new product.

The concept may be described verbally or pictorially so that the major features are understood. Potential customers can then state whether they perceive any benefits accruing from the features. A questionnaire is used to ascertain the extent of liking/disliking what is liked/disliked, the kind of person/organization that might buy the product, how/where/when/how often the product would be used, its price acceptability, and how likely they would be to buy the product.

Considerable ingenuity is needed to research new concepts. For example, research into a new tea shop/tea bar concept avoided the mistake of asking people about it 'cold' (unprepared). This would have resulted in consumers saying negative things like 'only grannies like tea shops' or 'tea isn't fashionable like coffee is'. Instead, in order to establish the tea bar concept as contemporary in feel, a cuttings file of 'articles' about it in fashionable areas such as Soho and Brighton was produced and shown to participants before the market research session took place. Because they felt that the tea bar chain was already up and running and that it was contemporary, the participants became very enthusiastic about it. The research had successfully conveyed the correct concept to the participants and, therefore, their responses were more valid than if they had been asked about their reaction to the concept without the associated image.[43]

This example illustrates the use of a scenario to help the participant in the research visualise the new product concept. The scenario method is of particular use when researching radical innovation concepts which, if launched, produce new-to-the-world products. Traditional marketing research methods rely on asking target consumers what they want or asking them to rate the attractiveness of new product concepts. This can lead to less radical innovations being favoured because of the concept of *functional fixedness*, which is the tendency for people to evaluate new products in terms of what they already know. New products are evaluated by consumers in terms of already existing products and technologies rather than considering their needs in future situations. This can lead consumers to favour conventional new product concepts that are most likely the ones they already know.

The scenario method overcomes this problem by describing the new product in the the context of a future technological and market setting. Usually a short story is told in which a potential consumer uses the new product in a future setting. The scenario can also be accompanied by visual material that shows various design features of the product and its future environment. By portraying the new product concept in a new environment, scenarios help consumers to evaluate new products outside the usuage situations that are familiar to them, and encourages them to imagine what it would be like to use the portrayed product. The result is that judgements of radical innovations are less likely to suffer from the consumer's normal frame of reference, on the basis of which more conservative options are usually favoured.[44]

Often the last question (buying intentions) is a key factor in judging whether any of the concepts are worth pursuing further. In the grocery and toiletries industries, for example, companies (and their marketing research agencies) often use *action standards* (e.g. more than 70 per cent of respondents must say they intend to buy) based on past experience to judge new product concepts. Concept testing allows a relatively inexpensive judgement to be made by customers before embarking on a costly product development programme. Although not foolproof, obvious non-starters can be eliminated early on in the process.

Business analysis

Based on the results of the concept test and considerable managerial judgement, estimates of sales, costs and profits will be made. This is the **business analysis** stage. In order to produce sensible figures a marketing analysis will need to be undertaken. This will identify the target market, its size and projected product acceptance over a number of years. Consideration will be given to various prices and the implications for sales revenue (and profits) discussed. By setting a tentative price this analysis will provide sales revenue estimates.

Costs will also need to be estimated. If the new product is similar to existing products (e.g. a brand extension) it should be fairly easy to produce accurate cost estimates. For radical product concepts, costings may be nothing more than informal 'guesstimates'.

Break-even analysis, where the quantity needed to be sold to cover costs is calculated, may be used to establish whether the project is financially feasible. *Sensitivity analysis*, in which variations from given assumptions about price, cost and customer acceptance, for example, are checked to see how they impact on sales revenue and profits, can also prove useful at this stage. Optimistic, most likely and pessimistic scenarios can be drawn up to estimate the degree of risk attached to the project.

If the product concept appears commercially feasible, this process will result in marketing and product development budgets being established based on what appears to be necessary to gain customer awareness and trial, and the work required to turn the concept into a marketable product.

Product development

At this stage the new product concept is developed into a physical product. As we have seen, the trend is to move from a situation where this is the sole responsibility of the R&D and/or engineering department. Multi-disciplinary project teams are established with the task of bringing the product to the marketplace. A study by Wheelwright and Clark lays out six key principles for the effective management of such teams.[45]

1. *Mission*: senior management must agree to a clear mission through a project charter that lays out broad objectives.
2. *Organization*: the appointment of a heavyweight project leader and a core team consisting of one member from each primary function in the company. Core members should not occupy a similar position on another team.
3. *Project plan*: creation by the project leader and core team of a contract book, which includes a work plan, resource requirements and objectives against which it is willing to be evaluated.
4. *Project leadership*: heavyweight leaders not only lead, manage and evaluate other members of the core team, they also act as product champions. They spend time talking to project contributors inside and outside the company, as well as customers and distributors, so that the team keeps in touch with the market.
5. *Responsibilities*: all core members share responsibility for the overall success of the project as well as their own functional responsibilities.
6. *Executive sponsorship*: an executive sponsor in senior management is required to act as a channel for communication with top management and to act as coach and mentor for the project and its leader.

The aim is to integrate the skills of designers, engineers, production, finance and marketing specialists so that product development is quicker, less costly and results in a high-quality product that delights customers. For example, the practice of simultaneous engineering means that designers and production engineers work together rather than passing the project from one stage of development to another once the first department's work is finished. Costs are controlled by a method called *target costing*. Target costs are worked out on the basis of target prices in the marketplace, and given as engineering/design and production targets.

Cutting time to market by reducing the length of the product development stage is a key marketing factor in many industries. Allied to simultaneous engineering, companies are using computer-aided design and manufacturing equipment and software (CAD-CAM) to cut time and improve quality. In particular, the use of 3D solid modelling, which completely defines an object in three dimensions on a computer screen and has the ability to compute masses, is very effective in shortening the product development stage.[46] In addition, three-dimensional CAD system designs can be shared with suppliers and customers. For example, Boeing engages customers such as British Airways and United Airlines in an online design process that allows them to engage in debates over alternative cabin layouts.

There are two reasons why product development is being accelerated. First, markets such as personal computers, video cameras and cars change so fast that to be slow means running the risk of being out of date before the product is launched. Second, cutting time to market can lead to competitive advantage. This may be short-lived but is still valuable while it lasts. For example, Rolls-Royce gained an 18-month window of opportunity by cutting lead times on its successful Trent 800 aero-engine.[47]

Marketing has an important role to play in the product development stage. R&D and engineering may focus on the functional aspects of the product, whereas seemingly trivial factors may have an important bearing on customer choice. For example, the foam that appears when washing up liquid is added to water has no functional value: a washing-up liquid could be produced that cleans just as effectively but does not produce bubbles. However, the customer sees the foam as a visual cue that indicates the power of the washing-up liquid. Therefore, to market a brand that did not produce bubbles would be suicidal. Marketing needs to keep the project team aware of such psychological factors when developing the new product. Marketing staff need to make sure that the project team members understand and communicate the important attributes that customers are looking for in the product.

In the grocery market, marketing will usually brief R&D staff on the product concept, and the latter will be charged with the job of turning the concept into reality. For example, Yoplait, the French market leader in fruit yoghurts, found through marketing research that a yoghurt concept based on the following attributes could be a winner:

- top-of-the-range dessert
- position on a health–leisure scale at the far end of the pleasure range—the ultimate taste sensation
- a fruit yoghurt that is extremely thick and creamy.

This was the brief given to the Yoplait research and development team that had the task of coming up with recipes for the new yoghurt and the best way of manufacturing it. Its job was to experiment with different cream–fruit combinations to produce the right product—one that matched the product concept—and to do it quickly. Time to market was crucial in this fast-moving industry. To help them, Yoplait employed a panel of expert tasters to try out the new recipes and evaluate them in terms of texture, sweetness, acidity, colour, smell, consistency and size of the fruit.

Product testing focuses on the functional aspects of the product and on consumer acceptance. Functional tests are carried out in the laboratory and out in the field to check such aspects as safety, performance and shelf life. For example, a car's braking system must be efficient, a jet engine must be capable of generating a certain level of thrust and a food package must be capable of keeping its contents fresh. Product testing of software products by users is crucially important in removing any 'bugs' that have not been picked up by internal testers.

Besides conforming to these basic functional standards, products need to be tested with consumers to check acceptability in use. For consumer goods this often takes the form of in-house product placement. *Paired companion tests* are used when a new product is used alongside a rival, so that respondents have a benchmark against which to judge the new offering. Alternatively two (or more) new product variants may be tested alongside one another. A questionnaire is administered at the end of the test, which gathers overall preference information as well as comparisons on specific attributes. For example, two soups might be compared on taste, colour, smell and richness. In *monadic placement tests* only the new product is given to users for trial. Although no specific rival is used in the test, in practice users may make comparisons with previously bought products, market leaders or competitive products that are quickly making an impact on the market.

Another way of providing customer input into development is through *product clinics*. For example, prototype cars and trucks are regularly researched by inviting prospective drivers to such clinics where they can sit in the vehicle, and comment on its design, comfort and proposed features. For example, an idea to provide a hook for a woman's handbag in the Ford Mondeo was firmly rejected when researched in this way, and the feature discarded.

Experts can also be used when product testing. For example, the former world champion racing driver Jackie Stewart was used in the development work that led to the launch of the Ford Mondeo. Although there is a danger that expert views may be unrepresentative of the target market, it was found with the Mondeo that Stewart's opinion carried the necessary political clout to force changes in the design of the car that may not have been made without his input.

Information technology is assisting the product development process by allowing various combinations of product features to be displayed on a laptop so that customer preferences can be identified. For example, for a new mobile phone, various combinations of size, colour, screen display, keyboard layout and special facilities can be shown to consumers via a laptop, which enables them to construct their ideal product.

In organizational markets, products may be placed with customers free of charge or at below cost to check out the performance characteristics. Parkinson contrasted the attitudes of West German machine tool manufacturers with their less successful British competitors towards product development.[48] The West German companies sought partnerships with customers, and developed and tested prototypes jointly with them. British attitudes were vastly different: marketing research was seen as a way of delaying product development, and customers were rarely involved for fear that they would stop buying existing products.

Market testing

So far in the development process, potential customers have been asked if they intend to buy the product but have never been placed in the position of having to pay for it. **Market testing** takes measurement of customer acceptance one crucial step further than product testing by forcing consumers to 'put their money where their mouth is'. The basic idea is to launch the new product in a limited way so that consumer response in the marketplace can be assessed. Two major methods are used: the simulated market test and test marketing.

The *simulated market test* can take a number of forms, but the principle is to set up a realistic market situation in which a sample of consumers chooses to buy goods from a range provided by the organizing company, usually a marketing research company. For example, a sample of consumers may be recruited to buy their groceries from a mobile supermarket that visits them once a week. They are provided with a magazine in which advertisements and sales promotions for the new product can appear. This method allows measurement of key success indicators such as *penetration* (the proportion of consumers that buy the new product at least once) and *repeat purchase* (the rate at which purchasers buy again) to be made. If penetration is high but repeat purchase low, buyers can be asked why they rejected the product after trial. Simulated market tests are therefore useful as a preliminary to test marketing by spotting problems, such as in packaging and product formulation, that can be rectified before test market launch. They can also be useful in eliminating new products that perform so badly compared to competition in the marketplace that test marketing is not justified. Indeed, as techniques associated with simulated market tests become more sophisticated and distributors increasingly refuse to cooperate in test marketing, they have become an attractive alternative to a full test market.[49]

Test marketing involves the launch of the new product in one or a few geographical areas chosen to be representative of its intended market. Towns or television areas are chosen in which the new product is sold into distribution outlets so that performance can be gauged face to face with rival products. Test marketing is the acid test of new product development since the product is being promoted as it would during a national launch, and consumers are being asked to choose it against competitor products as they would if the new product went national. It is a more realistic test than the simulated market test and therefore gives more accurate sales penetration and repeat purchasing estimates. By projecting test marketing results to the full market, an assessment of the new product's likely success can be made.

Test marketing does have a number of potential problems. Test towns and areas may not be representative of the national market, and thus sales projections may be inaccurate. Competitors may invalidate the test market by giving distributors incentives to stock their product, thereby denying the new product shelf space. Also, test marketing needs to run over a long enough period to measure the repeat purchase rate for the product, since this is a crucial indicator of success for many products (e.g. groceries and toiletries). This can mean a delay in national launch stretching to many months or even years. In the meantime, more aggressive competitors can launch a rival product nationally and therefore gain market pioneer advantages. A final practical problem is gaining the cooperation of distributors. In some instances, supermarket chains refuse to take part in test marketing activities or charge a hefty fee for the service.

The advantages of test marketing are that the information it provides facilitates the 'go/no go' national launch decision, and the effectiveness of the marketing mix elements—price, product formulation/packaging, promotion and distribution—can be checked for effectiveness. Sometimes a number of test areas are used with different marketing mix combinations to predict the most successful launch strategy. Its purpose therefore is to reduce the risk of a costly and embarrassing national launch mistake.

Although commonly associated with fast-moving consumer goods, service companies use test marketing to check new service offerings. Indeed, when they control the supply chain, as is the case with banks and restaurants, they are in an ideal situation to do so. Companies selling to organizations can also benefit from test marketing when their products have short repeat purchase periods (e.g. adhesives and abrasives). For very expensive equipment, however, test marketing is usually impractical, although as we have seen product development with lead users is to be recommended.

On a global scale, many international companies roll out products (e.g. cars and consumer electronics) from one country to another. In so doing they are gaining some of the benefits of test marketing in that lessons learned early on can be applied to later launches.

11.2 Pause for thought

Why is market testing important in the new product development process? Is it practicable for all new products?

Commercialization

In this section we shall examine four issues: a general approach to developing a commercialization strategy for a new product, specific options for product replacement strategies, success factors when commercializing technology, and reacting to competitors' new product introductions.

Developing a commercialization strategy for a new product

An effective commercialization strategy relies upon marketing management making clear choices regarding the target market (where it wishes to compete), and the development of

Figure 11.3 The diffusion of innovation process

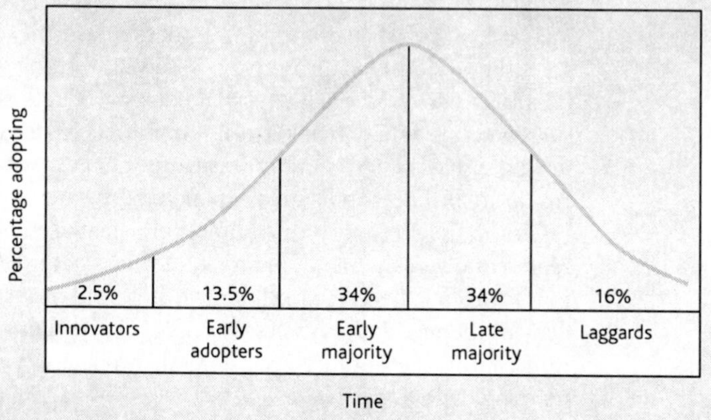

a marketing strategy that provides a differential advantage (how it wishes to compete). These two factors define the new product positioning strategy, as discussed in Chapter 8.

A useful starting point for choosing a target market is an understanding of the **diffusion of innovation process**.[50] This explains how a new product spreads throughout a market over time. Particularly important is the notion that not all people or organizations who make up the market will be in the same state of readiness to buy the new product when it is launched. In other words, different actors in the market will have varying degrees of innovativeness—that is, their willingness to try something new. Figure 11.3 shows the *diffusion of innovation* curve which categorizes people or organizations according to how soon they are willing to adopt the innovation.

The curve shows that those actors (*innovators* and *early adopters*) who were willing to buy the new product soon after launch are likely to form a minor part of the total number of actors who will eventually be willing to buy it. As the new product is accepted and approved by these customers, and the decision to buy the new product therefore becomes less risky, so the people that make up the bulk of the market, comprising the *early and late majority*, begin to try the product themselves. Finally, after the product has gained full market acceptance, a group suitably described as the *laggards* adopt the product. By the time the laggards have begun buying the product, the innovators and early adopters have probably moved on to something new.

These diffusion of innovation categories have a crucial role to play in the choice of target market. The key is to understand the characteristics of the innovator and early adopter categories and target them at launch. Simply thinking about the kinds of people or organizations that are more likely to buy a new product early after launch may suffice. If not, marketing research can help. To stimulate the thinking process, Rogers suggests the following broad characteristics for each category.[51]

- *Innovators*: these are often venturesome and like to be different; they are willing to take a chance with an untried product. In consumer markets they tend to be younger, better educated, more confident and more financially affluent, and consequently can afford to take a chance on buying something new. In organizational markets, they tend to be larger and more profitable companies if the innovation is costly, and have more progressive, better-educated management. They may themselves have a good track record in bringing out new products and may have been the first to adopt innovations in the past. As such they may be easy to identify.

- *Early adopters*: these are not quite so venturesome; they need the comfort of knowing someone else has taken the early risk. But they soon follow their lead. They still tend to have similar characteristics to the innovator group, since they need affluence and self-confidence to buy a product that has not yet gained market acceptance. They, together with the innovators, can be seen as opinion leaders who strongly influence other people's views on the product. As such, they have a major bearing on the success of the product. One way of looking at the early adopters is that they filter the products accepted by the innovator group and popularize them, leading to acceptance by the majority of buyers in the market.[52] The Internet can provide valuable information on this group, as Digital Marketing 11.1 explains.
- *Early and late majorities*: these form the bulk of the customers in the market. The early majority are usually deliberate and cautious in their approach to buying products. They like to see products prove themselves on the market before they are willing to part with cash for them. The late majority are even more cautious, and possibly sceptical of new products. They are willing to adopt only after the majority of people or organizations have tried the products. Social pressure may be the driving force moving them to purchase.
- *Laggards*: these are tradition-bound people. The innovation needs to be perceived almost as a traditional product before they will consider buying it. In consumer markets they are often the older and less well-educated members of the population.

These categories, then, can provide a basis for segmenting the market for an innovative product (see Chapter 8) and for target market selection.[53] For example, Samsung Electronics directs much of its marketing effort towards the innovator/early adopter segments by targeting what it calls 'high-life seekers'—consumers who adopt technology

11.1 Digital Marketing

Understanding Early Adopters Via the Internet

The link between the Internet, personal computers and home entertainment systems has been given significant attention over recent years, with many more technically minded consumers (early adopters) trying to access a multitude of multimedia content stored on their PCs from other areas of the home. This has led to a rise in the availability of equipment that can cater for such interests, ranging from Media PCs promoted by Microsoft and the Intel 'Viiv' brand, Xbox 360 games consoles and dedicated 'media servers' established by both traditional equipment providers such as Dlink and Pinnacle, to the more mainstream domestic electronics brands such as Sony and Philips.

As one such provider, Philips has produced and marketed a range of different products under the brand name Streamium. The Streamium product is designed to be placed with other consumer electronics next to the TV. Customers are able not only to 'stream' content from their own personal computers but also to access additional multimedia content from the Internet. In order to do this, customers must register the Streamium device with Philips via an Internet connection, which gives the added benefit of keeping the machine up to date with any new software enhancements.

The success of such technology relies on its ability to 'cross the chasm' from early adopters to the more mainstream 'early majority' and beyond. As part of this development it is not unusual to seek feedback from the user community, as in the case of www.streamiumcafe.com, a community forum dedicated to Philips Streamium users, initially instigated by Philips to gain feedback from early adopters. This technique should, however, be approached with some caution as the feedback at such an early stage of product development may not always prove positive if the community feels that its feedback is being ignored, as is the case with many postings on this particular website.

early and are prepared to pay a premium price for it.[54] Note that the diffusion curve can be linked to the product life cycle, which was discussed in Chapter 10. At introduction, innovators buy the product, followed by early adopters as the product enters the growth phase. Growth is fuelled by the early and late majority, and stable sales during the maturity phase may be due to repurchasing by these groups. Laggards may enter the market during late maturity or even decline. Thus promotion designed to stimulate trial may need to be modified as the nature of new buyers changes over time.

The second key decision for commercialization is the choice of marketing strategy to establish a differential advantage. Understanding the requirements of customers (in particular, the innovator and early adopter groups) is crucial to this process and should have taken place earlier in the new product development process. The design of the marketing mix will depend on this understanding and the rate of adoption will be affected by such decisions. For example, advertising, promotion and sales efforts can generate awareness and reduce the customer's search costs, sales promotional incentives can encourage trial, and educating users in product benefits and applications has been found to speed the adoption process.[55]

As we have seen, the characteristics of customers affect the rate of adoption of an innovation, and marketing's job is to identify and target those with a high willingness to adopt upon launch. The characteristics of the product being launched also affect the diffusion rate and have marketing strategy implications (see Fig. 11.4).

First, its differential advantage compared to existing products affects the speed of adoption. The more added customer benefits a product gives to a customer the more customers will be willing to buy. The high differential advantage of a fax machine over sending telegrams (e.g. convenience) or letters (e.g. speed) meant fast adoption. In turn, the convenience of e-mail over fax has meant rapid adoption. The differential advantage can be psychological, as when the handheld electronic personal organizer ousted the leather Filofax as a status symbol for the business elite.[56] More recently, the adoption of the BlackBerry can be explained by high functional (mobile e-mail access) and psychological (status symbol among businesspeople) benefits.

Figure 11.4 How the characteristics of a product affect its rate of diffusion

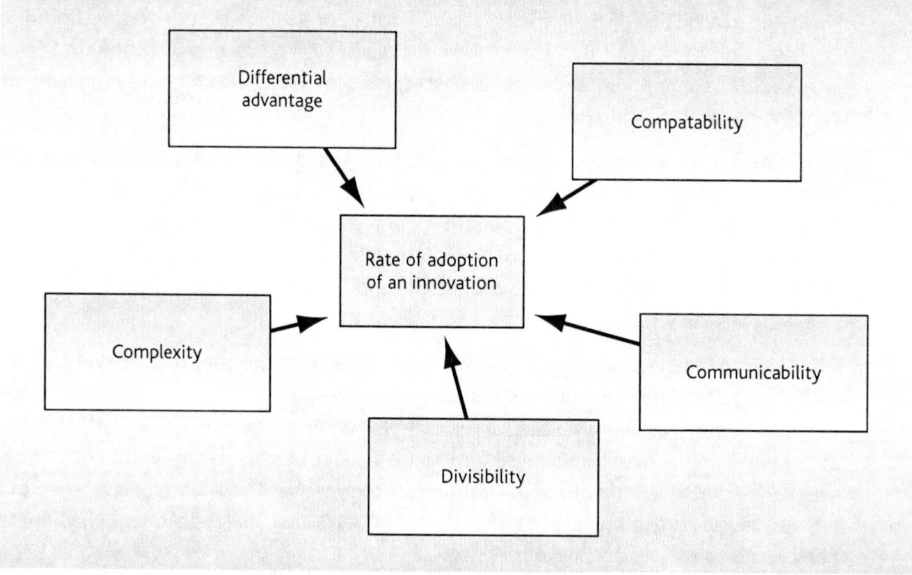

Second, there is the innovation's *compatibility* with consumers' values, experiences, lifestyles and behaviours. The congruence between mobile phones and the lifestyles of many young people helped their diffusion. The iPod's rapid diffusion was also aided by such compatibility. The new product also needs to be compatible with consumers' behaviour. If its adoption depends on significant behaviour change, failure or prolonged diffusion may result. For example, the unsuccessful Dvorak typing keyboard was supposed to modestly increase typing speed, but at the behavioural cost of having to 'unlearn' the QWERTY keyboard. Although the telephone is now part of our everyday lives, diffusion was slow because its adoption required significant behaviour change.[57]

A third factor affecting diffusion rate is the innovation's *complexity*. Products that are difficult to understand or use may take longer to be adopted. For example, Apple launched its Macintosh computer backed by the proposition that existing computers were too complex to gain widespread adoption. By making its model more user friendly, it hoped to gain fast adoption among the large segment of the population that was repelled by the complexity of using computers.

Fourth, an innovation's *divisibility* also affects its speed of diffusion. Divisibility refers to the degree to which the product can be tried on a limited basis. Inexpensive products can be tried without risk of heavy financial loss. The rapid diffusion of Google was aided by the fact that its functionality could be accessed free of charge.

The final product characteristic that affects the rate of diffusion of an innovation is its *communicability*. Adoption is likely to be faster if the benefits and applications of the innovation can be readily observed or described to target customers. If product benefits are long term or difficult to quantify, then diffusion may take longer. For example, Skoda's attempt to produce more reliable cars took time to communicate, as buyers' acceptance of this claim depended on their long-term experience of driving the cars. In service industries, marketing innovations like providing more staff to improve the quality of service are hard to quantify in financial terms (i.e. extra revenue generated) and therefore have a low adoption rate by the management of some companies. The marketing implications are that marketing management must not assume that what is obvious to them will be clear to customers. They need to devise a communications strategy that allows potential customers to become aware of the innovation, and understand and be convinced of its benefits.

11.3 Pause for thought

Explain the rapid diffusion of the iPod in terms of the characteristics of the product.

Product replacement strategies

As we found at the start of this chapter, product replacement is the most common form of new product introduction. A study of the marketing strategies used to position *product replacements* in the marketplace found eight approaches based on a combination of product change and other marketing modifications (i.e. marketing mix and target market changes).[58] Figure 11.5 shows the eight replacement strategies used by companies.

1 *Facelift*: minor product change with little or no change to the rest of the marketing mix or target market. Cars are often given facelifts midway through their life cycle by undergoing minor styling alterations, for example. Japanese companies constantly facelift current electronic products such as video recorders and camcorders by changing product features, a process known as **product churning**.

Figure 11.5 Product replacement strategies

Marketing \ Product	No change	Product modified	Technology change
No change	No change	Facelift	Inconspicuous technological substitution
Remix	Remerchandising	Relaunch	Conspicuous technological substitution
New market/ segment	Intangible repositioning	Tangible repositioning	Neo-innovation

Source: Saunders, J. and D. Jobber (1994) Strategies for Product Launch and Deletion, in Saunders, J. (ed.) The Marketing Initiative, *Hemel Hempstead: Prentice-Hall, 227.*

2 *Inconspicuous technological substitution*: a major technological change with little or no alteration of the other elements of the marketing mix. The technological change is not brought to the consumer's attention. For example, brand loyalty to instant mashed potatoes was retained through major technological process and product changes (powder to granules to flakes) with little attempt to highlight these changes through advertising.

3 *Remerchandising*: a modification of name, promotion, price, packaging and/or distribution, while maintaining the basic product. For example, an unsuccessful deodorant for men was successfully remerchandised with repackaging, heavier advertising, a higher price and new brand name: Brut.

4 *Relaunch*: both the product and other marketing mix elements are changed. Relaunches are common in the car industry where, every four to five years, a model is replaced with an upgraded version. The replacement of the Ford Sierra with the Mondeo is one example.

5 *Conspicuous technological substitution*: a major technological change is accompanied by heavy promotional (and other mix changes) to stimulate awareness and trial. An example is the replacement of the Rover Mini with the BMW Mini, which, despite remaining faithful to the character of the original, is technologically a fundamentally different car.

6 *Intangible repositioning*: the basic product is retained but other mix elements and target customers change. Lucozade is an example of a product that kept its original formulation but was targeted at different customer segments over time.

7 *Tangible repositioning*: both the product and target market change. Skoda is an example of the product being significantly improved to appeal to a more upmarket, wealthier target market.

8 *Neo-innovation*: a fundamental technology change accompanied by target market and mix changes. For example, Nokia practised neo-innovation when it moved from a conglomerate operating in such industries as paper, chemicals and rubber to being a marketer of mobile phones.

Companies, therefore, face an array of replacement options with varying degrees of risk. Figure 11.5 categorizes these options and provides an aid to strategic thinking when considering how to replace products in the marketplace.

Commercializing technology

Superior commercialization of technology has been, and will continue to be, a key success factor in many industries. Some companies, such as Canon, Sony, and Philips, already have the capability to bring sophisticated high-tech products to market faster than other companies that treat the commercialization process in a less disciplined manner. For example, Canon spends heavily on R&D (8 per cent of sales revenues) to maintain its leadership in the laser printer market by fast introduction of innovations such as colour improvements. Consistently beating the competition has been found to rest on four capabilities: being faster to market, supplying a wider range of markets, executing a larger number of product launches, and using a wider breadth of technologies.[59]

Many major market innovations appear in practice to be technologically driven: a technology seeking a market application rather than a market opportunity seeking a technology.[60] Marketing's input in such situations is to provide the insight as to how the technology may provide customer benefits within a prescribed target market. For example, an X-ray brain scanner was developed from a system used to X-ray metal. It was marketing insight that led to its application in medical diagnosis. As we have already discussed, traditional marketing research techniques have only a limited role to play when using technology to create new markets: people find it difficult to articulate their views on subjects that are unfamiliar, and acceptance may come only over time (the diffusion of innovation). Indeed, the price the customer will be asked to pay is usually unclear during the early stage of technological development. A combination of these factors may have been responsible for the first-ever forecast for computers, which predicted worldwide sales of 10 units.

The marketing of technological innovations, therefore, calls for a blend of technology and marketing. The basic marketing question, 'What potential benefits over existing products is this product likely to provide?', needs to be asked constantly during product development.

Furthermore the following lessons from the diffusion of innovation curve need to be remembered.

- The innovator/early adopter segments need to be identified and targeted initially.
- Initial sales are likely to be low: these groups are relatively small.
- Patience is required as the diffusion of an innovation takes time as people/organizations originally resistant to it learn of its benefits and begin to adopt it.
- The target group and message will need to be modified over time as new categories of customer enter the market.

COMPETITIVE REACTION TO NEW PRODUCT INTRODUCTIONS

New product launches may be in response to new product entries by competitors. Research suggests that when confronted with a new product entry by a competitor, incumbent firms should respond quickly with a limited set of marketing mix elements. Managers should rapidly decide which ones (product, promotion, price and place) are likely to have the most impact, and concentrate their efforts on them.[61]

Competitors' reaction times to the introduction of a new product have been found to depend on four factors.[62] First, response is faster in high-growth markets. Given the importance of such markets, competitors will feel the need to take action speedily in response to a new entrant. Second, response is dependent on the market shares held by the introducing firm and its competitors. Response time is slower when the introducing firm has higher market share and faster for those competitors who have higher market share. Third, response time is faster in markets characterized by frequent product changes. Finally, it is not surprising to find that response time is related to the time needed to develop the new product.

REVIEW

1 The different types of new product that can be launched

- There are four types of new product that can be launched: product replacements, additions to existing lines, new product lines and new-to-the-world products.

2 How to create and nurture an innovative culture

- Creating and nurturing an innovative culture can be achieved by rewarding success heavily, tolerating a certain degree of failure, senior management sending clear messages about the role and importance of innovation, their words being supported by allowing staff time off to develop their own ideas, making available resources and being accessible when difficult decisions need to be taken, and resisting automatic nay-saying.

3 The organizational options applying to new product development

- The options are project teams, product and brand managers, and new product departments and committees. Whichever method is used, effective cross-functional teamwork is essential for success.

4 Methods of reducing time to market

- A key method of reducing time to market is the process of simultaneous engineering. Design and production engineers, together with other staff, work together as a team rather than sequentially.
- Consumer goods companies are bringing together teams of brand and marketing managers, external design, advertising and research agency staff to develop simultaneously the brand and launch strategies.

5 How marketing and R&D staff can work together effectively

- A study by Gupta and Wileman suggests that marketing and R&D can better work together when teamwork is encouraged, there is an improvement in the provision of marketing information to R&D, R&D people are encouraged to be more customer aware, informal relationships between marketing and R&D are developed, marketing is encouraged to learn about technology, and a formal process of product development is implemented. Senior management staff have an important role to play by locating marketing and R&D close to each other, showing a personal interest in new product development, providing strategic direction, encouraging teamwork, increasing the resources devoted to new product development and enhancing their understanding of the importance of marketing in new product development.

6 The stages in the new product development process

- A formal process with review points, clear new product goals and a strong marketing orientation underlying the process leads to greater success.
- The stages are new product strategy (senior management should set objectives and priorities), idea generation (sources include customers, competitors, distributors, salespeople, engineers and marketers), screening (to evaluate their commercial worth), concept testing (to allow the views of target customers to enter the process early), product development (where the concept is developed into a physical product for testing), market testing (where the new product is tested in the marketplace) and commercialization (where the new product is launched).

7 How to stimulate the corporate imagination

- Four ways of stimulating the corporate imagination are: to encourage management to escape the tyranny of served markets by exploring how core competences can be exploited in new markets; to search for innovative product concepts—for example, by creating a new way to deliver an existing function (e.g. the electronic notepad); questioning traditional price–performance assumptions and giving engineers the resources to develop cheaper new products; and gaining insights by observing closely the market's most sophisticated and demanding customers.

8 The six key principles of managing product teams

- These are the agreement of the mission, effective organization, development of a project plan, strong leadership, shared responsibilities, and the establishment of an executive sponsor in senior management.

9 The diffusion of innovation categories and their marketing implications

- The categories are innovators, early adopters, early and late majorities, and laggards.
- The marketing implications are that the categories can be used as a basis for segmentation and targeting (initially the innovator/early adopters should be targeted). As the product is bought by different categories, so the marketing mix may need to change.
- The speed of adoption can be affected by marketing activities—for example, advertising to create awareness, sales promotion to stimulate trial, and educating users in product benefits and applications.
- The nature of the innovation itself can also affect adoption—that is, the strength of its differential advantage, its compatibility with people's values, experiences, lifestyles and behaviours, its complexity, its divisibility and its communicability.

10 The key ingredients in commercializing technology quickly and effectively

- The key ingredients are the ability of technologists and marketing people to work together effectively, simultaneous engineering, constantly asking the question 'What benefits over existing products is this new product likely to provide?', and remembering lessons from the diffusion of innovation curve (i.e. target the innovator/early adopter segments first).

Key Terms

brainstorming the technique where a group of people generate ideas without initial evaluation; only when the list of ideas is complete is each idea then evaluated

business analysis a review of the projected sales, costs and profits for a new product to establish whether these factors satisfy company objectives

concept testing testing new product ideas with potential customers

diffusion of innovation process the process by which a new product spreads throughout a market over time

innovation the commercialization of an invention by bringing it to market

invention the discovery of new methods and ideas

market testing the limited launch of a new product to test sales potential

Key Terms

product churning a continuous and rapid spiral of new product introductions

project teams the bringing together of staff from such areas as R&D, engineering, manufacturing, finance, and marketing to work on a project such as new product development

simultaneous engineering the involvement of manufacturing and product development engineers in the same development team in an effort to reduce development time

test marketing the launch of a new product in one or a few geographic areas chosen to be representative of the intended market

Study Questions

1. Try to think of an unsatisfied need that you feel could be solved by the introduction of a new product. How would you set about testing your idea to examine its commercial potential?

2. The Sinclair C5 was soon withdrawn from market in the UK. The three-wheeled vehicle was designed to provide electric-powered transport over short distances. If you can remember the vehicle, try to think of reasons why the product was a failure. On the other hand, video recorders and fax machines have been huge successes. Why?

3. Why is it difficult for a service company such as a bank to develop new products that have lasting success?

4. You are the marketing manager for a fast-food restaurant chain. A colleague returns from France with an idea for a new dish that she thinks will be a winner.

   How would you go about evaluating the idea?

5. What are the advantages and disadvantages of test marketing? In what circumstances should you be reluctant to use test marketing?

6. Your company has developed a new range of spicy-flavoured soups. They are intended to compete against the market leader in curry-flavoured soups. How would you conduct product tests for your new line?

7. What are the particular problems associated with commercializing technology? What are the key factors for success?

8. Discuss how marketing and R&D can form effective teams to develop new products.

Online LearningCentre

When you have read this chapter
log on to the Online Learning Centre at www.mcgraw-hill.co.uk/textbooks/jobber to explore chapter-by-chapter test questions, links and further online study tools for marketing.

REFERENCES

1. Pearson, D. (1993) Invent, Innovate and Improve, *Marketing*, 8 April, 15.
2. Richard, H. (1996) Why Competitiveness is a Dirty Word in Scandinavia, *European*, 6–12 June, 24.
3. McGregor, J. (2006) The World's Most Innovative Companies, *Business Week*, 24 April, 63–76.
4. McGregor (2006) op. cit.
5. Doyle, P. (1997) From the Top, *Guardian*, 2 August, 17.
6. A study conducted by Kashami, K. and T. Clayton, reported in Murphy, D. (2000) Innovate or Die, *Marketing Business*, May, 16–18.
7. Booz, Allen and Hamilton (1982) *New Product Management for the 1980s*, New York: Booz, Allen and Hamilton, Inc.
8. London, S. (2005) Floodgates Open Up to a Sea of Ideas, *Financial Times*, Special Report on Innovation, 8 June, 2.
9. Matthews, V. (2002) Caution Versus Creativity, *Financial Times*, 17 June, 12.
10. See Gupta, A. K. and D. Wileman (1990) Improving R&D/Marketing Relations: R&D Perspective, *R&D Management* 20(4), 277–90; Koshler, R. (1991) Produkt—Innovationasmanagement als Erfolgsfaktor, in Mueller-Boehling, D. *et al.* (eds) *Innovations—und Technologiemanagement*, Stuttgart: C. E. Poeschel Verlagi; Shrivastava, P. and W. E. Souder (1987) The Strategic Management of Technological Innovation: A Review and a Model, *Journal of Management Studies* 24(1), 24–41.
11. Aceland, H. (1999) Harnessing Internal Innovation, *Marketing*, 22 July, 27–8.
12. See Booz, Allen and Hamilton (1982) op. cit.; Maidique, M. A. and B. J. Zirger (1984) A Study of Success and Failure in Product Innovation: The Case of the US Electronics Industry, *IEEE Transactions in Engineering Management*, EM-31 (November), 192–203.
13. See Bergen, S. A., R. Miyajima and C. P. McLaughlin (1988) The R&D/Production Interface in Four Developed Countries, *R&D Management* 18(3), 201–16; Hegarty, W. H. and R. C. Hoffman (1990) Product/Market Innovations: A Study of Top Management Involvement among Four Cultures, *Journal of Product Innovation Management* 7, 186–99; Cooper, R. G. (1979) The Dimensions of Industrial New Product Success and Failure, *Journal of Marketing* 43 (Summer), 93–103; Johne, A. and P. Snelson (1988) Auditing Product Innovation Activities in Manufacturing Firms, *R&D Management* 18(3), 227–33.
14. Aceland, H. (1999) op. cit.
15. Francis, T. (2000) Divine Intervention, *Marketing Business*, May, 20–2.
16. Joshi, A. W. and S. Sharma (2004) Customer Knowledge Development: Antecedents and Impact on New Product Performance, *Journal of Marketing*, 68 (October), 47–9.
17. Weber, J., S. Holmes and C. Palmeri (2005) Mosh Pits of Creativity, *Business Week*, 7 November, 74–6.
18. Kanter, R. M. (1983) *The Change Masters*, New York: Simon & Schuster.
19. Mitchell, A. (2003) The Tyranny of the Brand, *Marketing Business*, January, 17.
20. Done, K. (1992) From Design Studio to New Car Showroom, *Financial Times*, 11 May, 10.
21. Carbonell, P. and A. I. Rodriguez (2006) The Impact of Market Characteristics and Innovation Speed on Perceptions of Positional Advantage and New Product Performance, *International Journal of Research in Marketing*, 23, 1–12.
22. See Hise, R. T., L. O'Neal, A. Parasuraman and J. U. NcNeal (1990) Marketing/R&D Interaction in New Product Development: Implications for New Product Success Rates, *Journal of Product Innovation Management* 7, 142–55; Johne and Snelson (1988) op. cit.; Walsh, W. J. (1990) Get the Whole Organisation Behind New Product Development, *Research in Technological Management*, Nov.–Dec., 32–6.
23. Frey, D. (1991) Learning the Ropes: My Life as a Product Champion, *Harvard Business Review*, Sept.–Oct., 46–56.
24. Gupta, A. K. and D. Wileman (1991) Improving R&D/Marketing Relations in Technology-based Companies: Marketing's Perspective, *Journal of Marketing Management* 7(1), 25–46.
25. See Dwyer, L. M. (1990) Factors Affecting the Proficient Management of Product Innovation, *International Journal of Technological Management* 5(6), 721–30; Gupta and

Wileman (1990) op. cit.; Adler, P. S., H. E. Riggs and S. C. Wheelwright (1989) Product Development Know-How, *Sloan Management Review* 4, 7–17.

26. Brentani, U. de (1991) Success Factors in Developing New Business Services, *European Journal of Marketing* 15(2), 33–59; Johne, A. and C. Storey (1998) New Source Development: A Review of the Literature and Annotated Bibliography, *European Journal of Marketing* 32(3/4), 184–251.

27. Cooper, R. G. and E. J. Kleinschmidt (1986) An Investigation into the New Product Process: Steps, Deficiencies and Impact, *Journal of Product Innovation Management*, June, 71–85.

28. Mitchell, A. (2005) After Some Innovation? Perhaps You Just Need to Ask Around, *Marketing Week*, 16 June, 28–9.

29. Nijssen, E. J. and K. F. M. Lieshout (1995) Awareness, Use and Effectiveness of Models and Methods for New Product Development, *European Journal of Marketing* 29(10), 27–44.

30. Hamel, G. and C. K. Prahalad (1991) Corporate Imagination and Expeditionary Marketing, *Harvard Business Review*, July–August, 81–92.

31. Bower, F. (2000) Latin Spirit, *Marketing Business*, October, 24–5.

32. Tomkins, R. (2005) Products that Aim Straight for Your Heart, *Financial Times*, 29 April, 13.

33. Parkinson, S. T. (1982) The Role of the User in Successful New Product Development, *R&D Management* 12, 123–31.

34. Nevens, T. M., G. L. Summe, and B. Uttal (1990) Commercializing Technology: What the Best Companies Do, *Harvard Business Review*, May–June, 154–63.

35. Johne, A. (1992) Don't Let your Customers Lead You Astray in Developing New Products, *European Management Journal* 10(1), 80–4.

36. Jobber, D., J. Saunders, G. Hooley, B. Gilding and J. Hatton-Smooker (1989) Assessing the Value of a Quality Assurance Certificate for Software: An Exploratory Investigation, *MIS Quarterly*, March, 19–31.

37. Edgett, S. and S. Jones (1991) New Product Development in the Financial Services Industry: A Case Study, *Journal of Marketing Management* 7(3), 271–84.

38. Hamel, G. and C. K. Prahalad (1991) Corporate Imagination and Expeditionary Marketing, *Harvard Business Review*, July–August, 81–92.

39. Hamel, G. (1999) Bringing Silicon Valley Inside, *Harvard Business Review*, Sept.–Oct., 71–84.

40. Leifer, R. G., C. O'Connor and M. Rice (2001) Implementing Radical Innovation in Mature Firms: The Role of Hubs, *Academy of Management Executives* 15(3) 61–70.

41. Hunt, J. W. (2002) Crucibles of Innovation, *Financial Times*, 18 January, 18.

42. Bartram, P. (2004) Why the Competition Doesn't Matter, *The Marketer*, April, 18–21.

43. Matthews, V. (2002) Caution Versus Creativity, *Financial Times*, 17 June, 12.

44. The author is indebted to Dr Dirk Snelders of Delft University, Netherlands, for supplying material on the scenario method. For further reading see Burt, G. and K. van der Heijden (2003) First Steps: Towards Purposeful Activities in Scenario Thinking and Future Studies, *Futures*, 35, 1011–26; Carroll, J. M. (2000) Scenario-based Design: A Brief History and Rationale in Eastman C., M. McCracken and W. Newsletter (eds), *Knowing and Learning to Design: Cognitive Perspectives in Design Education*. Amsterdam: Elsevier; Tauber, E. M. (1974) How Marketing Research Discourages Major Innovation, *Business Horizons*, 17 (June), 22–6; and Ulwick, A. W. (2002) Turn Customer Input Into Innovation, *Harvard Business Review*, (January), 91–7.

45. Wheelwright, S. and K. Clark (1992) *Revolutionizing Product Development*, New York: Free Press.

46. Baxter, A. (1992) Shifting to High Gear, *Financial Times*, 14 May, 15.

47. Pullin, J. (1997) Time is Money on the Way to Market, *Guardian*, 5 April, 99.

48. Parkinson (1982) op. cit.

49. Chisnall, P. (2005) *Marketing Research*, Maidenhead: McGraw-Hill.

50. Rogers, E. M. (1995) *Diffusion of Innovations*, New York: Free Press.

51. Rogers (1995) op. cit.

52. Zinkmund, W. G. and M. D'Amico (1999) *Marketing*, St Paul, MN: West.

53. Easingwood, C. and C. Beard (1989) High Technology Launch Strategies in the UK, Industrial *Marketing Management* 18, 125–38.

54. Pesola, M. (2005) Samsung Plays to the Young Generation, *Financial Times*, 29 March, 11.

55. See Mahajan, V., E. Muller and R. Kerin (1987) Introduction Strategy for New Product with Positive and Negative Word-of-Mouth, *Management Science* 30, 1389–404; Robertson, T. S. and H. Gatignon (1986) Competitive Effects on Technology Diffusion, *Journal of Marketing* 50 (July), 1–12; Tzokas, N. and M. Saren (1992) Innovation Diffusion: The Emerging Role of Suppliers Versus the Traditional Dominance of Buyers, *Journal of Marketing Management* 8(1), 69–80.

56. Daniel, C. (2001) Psion Quits Handheld Organiser Market, *Financial Times*, 12 July, 1.

57. Gourville, J. (2006) The Curse of Innovation: Why Innovative Products Fail, MSI Report No. 05-117.

58. Saunders, J. and D. Jobber (1994) Product Replacement Strategies: Occurrence and Concurrence, *Journal of Product Innovation Management* (November).

59. Nevens, Summe and Uttal (1990) op. cit.

60. Brown, R. (1991) Managing the 'S' Curves of Innovation, *Journal of Marketing Management* 7(2), 189–202.

61. Gatignon, H., T. S. Robertson and A. J. Fein (1997) Incumbent Defence Strategies Against New Product Entry, *International Journal of Research in Marketing* 14, 163–76.

62. Bowman, D. and H. Gatignon (1995) Determinants of Competitor Response Time to a New Product Introduction, *Journal of Marketing Research* 33, February, 42–53.

Case Twenty-one

THE DEVELOPMENT OF A NEW MOTORING ICON: THE LAUNCH OF THE MINI

Launched in 1959, the original Mini proved to be one of the most enduring fashion and motoring icons of the twentieth century, with production of the car finally coming to a halt in 1998. The announcement in 2000 by BMW, owner of the Mini brand, that it was to invest £200 million (€280 million) in the development and launch of the new Mini was therefore received both by the press and the public with enormous enthusiasm.

The small car market

The European car market is intensively competitive, with one of the most crowded parts of this being the so-called 'supermini' segment. With the sector being dominated by some of the mass-market players, such as Renault, Volkswagen, Nissan, Peugeot, Citroën, Ford and Toyota, but also featuring some of the luxury brands such as the Mercedes A-Class and the Audi A2, competition for the Mini was expected from the outset to be particularly tough. However, the attraction of the sector stems from the way in which demand for small city cars is forecast to grow faster than the overall market and far faster than any other sector of the car market. The target set for the Mini was to capture 4.6 per cent of this sector. In order to do this, a brand strategy was devised that set out 'to distance the Mini from what was viewed as comparatively bland competition and capture the car's unique personality in a modern context. References to the past were deliberately avoided.'[1]

The target market

Although a company spokesman said initially that they did not know exactly what kind of customer would be attracted to the new car, the expectation was that customers would probably fall within two main groups. A younger group, aged about 25–35, was expected to buy the Mini as their primary car and was expected to choose the car in preference to a similarly priced Toyota, Volkswagen, Renault or Smart Car. Older buyers, in their forties with grown-up children and with an urge for some youthful motoring fun, were expected to buy it as their second or third car.

The marketing strategy

BMW has described the Mini as central to its strategy of developing premium cars for every size segment of the car market. From the outset, therefore, the marketing team realized that the key to the Mini's success would be how the car was positioned in the market and how it could be differentiated from the competition. They therefore set out to develop an innovative and high-profile strategy. A key element of this in the UK was a £14.4 million (€20.16 million) television and cinema advertising campaign[2] designed to reflect the product's quirky looks and image, showing 'Mini adventures'. These adventures, which included finding lost cities and helping to save the world from a Martian invasion, led to the Mini achieving the highest awareness per £million spent and, in the case of the cinema, the highest levels of awareness ever recorded by Carlton Cinema. The ad campaign was supported, in turn, by an innovative Internet campaign that made use of Eyeblaster technology, which made it appear as if the site's home pages were being attacked by Martians and disgruntled zombies. The Mini, of course, then appeared and saved the day.

In the USA, the company ignored television and cinema advertising and opted instead for a guerrilla marketing campaign that included mounting Minis on top of a fleet of Ford Excursions, one of the world's largest sports utility vehicles (SUVs). The company also played to the growing backlash against the fuel-hungry SUV sector. With these vehicles accounting for a quarter of total US vehicle sales, the Mini ads featured the line 'Let's not use the size of our vehicle to compensate for other shortcomings.'

Distribution for the car was based initially on the parent company's BMW dealer network, with all 148 main BMW dealers in the UK (70 Mini-exclusive showrooms in the USA) selling the car either from a separate area in the showroom or from a separate building. Although the same mechanics service both BMW and Mini cars, sales of the Mini are made by dedicated sales teams, each of which were given an initial sales target of 149 cars.

Although the marketing team believed in the product's distinctiveness, they also recognized that one of the most important keys to success within their sector was price. The decisions about the pricing strategy would therefore be a pivotal part of the car's success. Although the original plan was to sell the Mini for about £14,000 (€19,600), the company made a point of learning from the mistakes that Volkswagen had made in adopting a premium pricing strategy for its new Beetle in 1998, but it was then forced to cut prices. BMW opted for a far more aggressive strategy, with the basic car—the Mini One—costing just over £10,000 (€14,000), rising to £11,600 (€16,240) for the Mini Cooper. However, profit margins for the car were then increased substantially through the series of options that included the roof of the car being painted as a flag, and leather-bound steering wheels, which have added 20 per cent on average to the car's price.

Sales targets and performance

The sales target for the first year was set at around 100,000 units. In the event, global sales proved to be far higher with 144,000 of the cars reaching the roads in 2002. In the United States, the Mini's largest market outside Britain, the response to the car was so strong that 25,000 Minis were sold in the first 12 months (the target was 18,000 cars) and waiting lists reached six months or more. The picture in the UK was broadly similar, with dealers not being able to meet demand.

The critics

Although the car has undoubtedly captured the hearts and minds of the motoring public, much of the pre-launch press coverage gave emphasis to the negative aspects of the German acquisition of a British icon. Subsequently, car industry analysts have expressed a number of reservations. Prominent among these have been that, where most companies update their models every two or three years, BMW has said that it does not intend to freshen the Mini for at least seven. Other critics have said that, as it is in effect a fashion item, customers will quickly get bored. Others have pointed to the relatively low levels of productivity (25 cars per employee, compared with Nissan's 94 cars per employee), the low selling price of the car and the UK currency base, all of which, it is suggested, will leave BMW struggling to make money from the car.[3]

Post-launch activities and performance

The launch of the Mini has proved to be one of the most successful launches ever of a car and has captured the hearts, minds and, most importantly, the wallets of an increasingly cynical and demanding car-buying public. The initial launch featured the basic car—the Mini One—and the Mini Cooper, and this was quickly followed by the high-performance Mini Cooper S and the Mini Convertible, which featured a soft top that could be folded back to allow open-air driving. Priced at £13,595 (€19,033) for the Mini One Convertible and £14,925 (€20,895) for the Mini Cooper Convertible, the range was positioned at a considerable price premium to the standard models.

The company's plans for the future cover both product and market development, with talk of the possibilities of a diesel-engined version and possibly a 4×4 version. At the same time, the company is moving into a variety of other geographic markets, including China, all of which look as if they too will fall in love with the Mini.

At the beginning of 2005, the company announced that sales of the car had exceeded all expectations and that by mid-2004 the 500,000th car had rolled off the production lines—two years ahead of schedule. When launched in 2001, the sales target had been 100,000 cars per year, but by 2004 this had risen to 180,000. However, the sheer scale of the success of the Mini—on sale in 73 countries around the world and voted 'car of the year' in the USA—had brought with it a number of problems, since the Oxford plant could not exceed its capacity of about 200,000 cars without substantial new investment. The company's management team was, therefore, faced with the decision of whether to invest in additional capacity that would allow for a further 100,000 cars a year: to be competitive in terms of economies of scale, the plant needs to be producing at least 250,000–300,000 cars a year. In the event, the decision was taken to invest £100 million (€140 million), not just to boost capacity and flexibility, which would allow the company to enter new markets such as India, Brazil and Indonesia, but also to make the plant ready for the launch of a revised model in 2007. In developing the new model, the design team applied the lessons developed by Porsche with its 911-like evolution: let successful design evolve in a subtle way. The next generation of Minis has therefore been designed to stay true to the Mini's strengths—driveability and design—by using the same proportions and details as the predecessor. The company also took to another level one of the real marketing coups of the earlier model: the telephone directory-sized options list that allowed for showroom personalization and helped to fuel the cult of the Mini and, in the process, made a major contribution to the company's profits.

Notes

[1] *marketingbusiness*, January 2003, 11.
[2] The advertising spend of £14.4 million (€20.16 million) compares with £19.5 million (€27.3 million) for Ford's Fiesta, £18.6 million (€26.04 million) for the Renault Clio and £11 million (€15.4 million) for the Volkswagen Polo.
[3] BMW Struggling to Get Max out of Mini, *Financial Times*, 26 August 2004, 4.

Questions

1. Assume that you are part of the marketing team for Mini. Using the concept of the diffusion of innovation developed by Rogers, show how your marketing strategy might need to change as you move from the innovators and early adopters that currently make up the market, to other buyer categories.

2. Several commentators have suggested that the Mini is essentially a fashion statement. What are the short- and long-term marketing implications of this?

3. Referring back to the chapters on branding and product life cycle management (Chapters 9 and 10), what lessons emerge from the Mini experience?

This case was written by Colin Gilligan, Professor of Marketing, Sheffield Hallam University.

Case Twenty-two

MICROSOFT'S XBOX 360 VERSUS SONY'S PLAYSTATION 3: THE BATTLE OF THE GAMES CONSOLES

The latest salvo in the video games console war has been launched with two giants of the industry, Microsoft (www.xbox.com) and Sony (www.playstation.com), releasing their latest devices: the Xbox 360 and PlayStation 3. Both have placed billion-dollar gambles on their machines becoming the dominant platform in the industry. The video games industry will be worth an estimated $46.5 billion by 2010. Video games are big business, with blockbuster games like *Tomb Raider* bringing in sales of between $200 million and $300 million, showing the industry's lucrativeness. Another example is Microsoft's hit game, *Halo*, which has sold in excess of 2,000,000 units.

Every five years or so, games console makers release their latest consoles, luring gamers with the latest technology improvements on previous iterations. Now Sony, Microsoft and Nintendo are contending the next generation games consoles battle, vying for the high-definition gaming market. These latest consoles utilize technological advancements promising pin-sharp photo-realistic environments and improved game play. In the previous battle for dominance, Microsoft was last to arrive in the market with its Xbox device, and it was a first timer in this hyper-competitive industry, with no video-gaming or hardware-manufacturing experience. This time it hopes to have the edge on its rivals by launching its latest platform a full year ahead of its nearest rivals. Will it succeed?

Games have been transformed over the last two decades; visuals have come a long way from Atari's *Pong* and *Pac-Man*. Now games possess photo-realism, astonishing 3D graphics, accompanied by Dolby Digital bombastic surround sound. The gaming industry is characterized by five-year cycles, where a games console has roughly a five-year life before being replaced with a new and improved device, making the old hardware obsolete. Many industry giants have come and gone in this very competitive arena. The pioneering firm Atari had enormous financial difficulties in the mid-1980s and went out of business. Sega, with its all-conquering *Sonic the Hedgehog* and Sega Megadrive, has retrenched from the games console market, and is now concentrating solely on becoming a games developer. Its last foray, the Sega Dreamcast machine, was an unmitigated failure despite being the most powerful console of its time and the company spending a huge marketing budget. Having the most advanced technology does not always guarantee industry success.

After this five-year cycle ends, the next generation of consoles is launched, with advanced technological features, usually faster processing speeds or larger memories. In 2006, this five-year cycle began once again with the launch of the Microsoft Xbox 360, Sony's PlayStation 3 and

Table C22.1 A brief history of games consoles

Launched	Game console
1977	Atari Video Computer System (VCS)
1982	Sinclair Spectrum
1984	Commodore 64
1985	Nintendo Entertainment System (NES)
1986	Commodore Amiga
1989	Nintendo Gameboy
1989	Sega Megadrive
1995	Sony PlayStation
1995	Sega Saturn
1996	Nintendo 64
1999	Sega Dreamcast
2000	Sony PlayStation 2 (PS2)
2002	Nintendo Gamecube
2002	Microsoft Xbox
2005	PlayStation Portable (PSP)
2005	Microsoft Xbox 360
2006	Nintendo Wii
2007	Sony PlayStation 3

Nintendo's Wii. Table C22.1 illustrates past video games consoles and their product life cycles. In the last round of games console wars, Microsoft Xbox captured the number two position with 18 per cent of the market, but it was way behind leader Sony PlayStation 2, which held 67 per cent; and Nintendo held just 15 per cent of the market. Sony's dominance is attributed to it superior games portfolio and its strong brand image. To counter this Microsoft engaged in a price war with Sony. It slashed the price of its console on several occasions, in a bid to boost market share.

Microsoft entered the games console market in 2002 with the Xbox. This was Microsoft's first time involved in hardware manufacturing. With the Xbox it received many industry plaudits, creating a very powerful games console, developing a strong online gaming experience with its 'Xbox Live' service, and had a strong portfolio of games. Microsoft invested a colossal \$3.8 billion into its Xbox project, and has yet to make a profit from the business. It is hoping to yield its first profit by 2008. The rationale to enter such a highly competitive industry, fraught with risks and huge costs, is puzzling for many. To any other company, this investment would seem sheer lunacy, but Microsoft has deep pockets, with an estimated \$42 billion in cash reserves, and makes \$10 billion in profit annually. Microsoft is estimated to be currently losing at least \$150 on every Xbox, which is probably more when shipping, advertising and development costs are factored in. The industry sells its consoles at below cost, hoping to get its money back on the sale of games for the consoles, which typically sell in the UK for £40 (€56). For every game sold, the console makers make roughly £8 (€11) in the form of licensing fees. So why gaming for Microsoft?

Microsoft dominates its core markets of operating systems and desktop application software, with monopoly status. Its revenues and profits are steady. However PC software revenues are not going to grow continually like they have over the past decade. Microsoft had to look for new avenues of future growth. It decided that the video-gaming industry was this avenue. The company wants to be in the centre of people's living rooms, and use this position as the platform for future home entertainment where consumers can play games, watch DVDs, listen to music, display photos, record TV programmes and browse the Internet. Sony has the exact same ambition. Microsoft poured millions into the development of its first Xbox. This games console was the most sophisticated ever released, allowing DVDs to be played and possessing broadband gaming capability. (Broadband is a high-speed network connection that allows for real-time Internet gaming and the ultra-quick downloading of software, games and films through an Internet broadband connection.) This is the real reason why Microsoft entered the games console industry: as a distribution platform. However, this has proved problematic. By launching titles online through its 'Xbox Live' service, its online gaming portal, it risks alienating retailers, which are crucial to the Xbox 360's ability to build market share. The traditional retail channels cannot be compromised just yet. Instead, Microsoft is using 'Xbox Live' to distribute content unlikely to upset retailers, such as interactive demos, games footage, very minor arcade titles, and digital videos. It hopes to use the Xbox 360 as a platform through which to distribute other Microsoft products and gain subscription fees from subscribers. The company sells its game console at a loss, hoping to build a large customer base of future potential subscribers and make money from licensing arrangements with games developers. The manufacturers really make their money through the amount of games sold, not the hardware. For every Xbox game developed, Microsoft receives a licensing fee from the games developer.

Microsoft launched the Xbox 360 simultaneously in the three core markets of the USA, Europe and Japan, with 20 titles initially available. Microsoft has learnt a lot since its initial foray into the gaming market. Its first console was large and chunky; its latest iteration has a more aesthetically pleasing sleek design, and comes with interchangeable covers. Gamers can now play games while listening to their favourite music. Microsoft's wireless controllers were an industry first, and a key selling feature. The company pinned much of its hopes on releasing the Xbox earlier than the much anticipated Sony PlayStation 3. It had hoped to get an initial six-month head start, but it gained a year's head start when Sony announced delays with its PlayStation 3 release. When the Xbox 360 was launched in the pre-Christmas market, it sold out. Many were sceptical, suggesting that Microsoft limited supply to hype up its launch and give the brand extra publicity. It launched the box on MTV. The head start has led the firm to develop a strong roster of exclusive games, which has added to its appeal. Over 160 high-definition games were launched in this intervening period. It hopes to sell an ambitious 12 million units by the middle of 2007. Sony now has to contend with a very serious rival, with strong financial clout.

Sony never envisaged how successful or important to the firm its PlayStation brand would become. The PlayStation brand is now over 10 years old, and over 100 million PlayStation 2 consoles were sold. Nearly 60 per cent of Sony's profits have been attributed to the success of the PlayStation brand. The development of the PlayStation games console series showed that adults were a very lucrative segment in the gaming market, and that video games were not just toys for kids. Sony desperately needs a hit product, as its electronics division has been in the doldrums, losing revenue. It has spent four years and close to £1 billion (€1.4 billion) in developing the PlayStation 3. Sony's revenues and profits from PlayStation 2 have fallen, as the technology has reached the end of its cycle, and as consumers wait until the next generation of consoles are released. Sony is banking on its brand appeal and technological features to entice the latest generation of gamers. The company is hoping that its much lauded and very powerful 'cell' processor technology, and its new high-definition Blu-Ray disc drives will push sales. PlayStation 2 incorporated DVD playback into its game console, which helped boost sales. Sony hopes that this will boost sales for its proprietary Blu-Ray disc technology, which it hopes will become an industry standard.

With PlayStation 3 incorporating the latest technology, this has led to long production delays and concerns over pricing. Component prices for the PlayStation are very high, since it is the latest in terms of technology. This has pushed up the price to very high levels. At launch it is priced at £425 (€595) in the UK, putting it out of reach for a large portion of the market and making it £150 (€210) more expensive than the Xbox 360 (see Table C22.2). Even at this high price, Sony is subsidizing the price, as the cost of the individual components is much higher. During a machine's five-year production life cycle, component prices fall rapidly, due to manufacturing improvements; more profit is earned in the later stages of its product life cycle. Subsidizing launch prices is nothing new in this market. All the games consoles are sold at a loss. Manufacturers hope to make profits from licensing and royalties from game software titles in the future, online subscriptions, and even online advertising with real-time online gaming. Sony hopes that its loyal fan base of PlayStation enthusiasts will invest in its latest machine. At stake is the battle to become the future hub for digital entertainment in the home. Both machines have strong online capabilities, and both Sony and Microsoft see this as the future platform for the distribution of digital content.

Japanese firm Nintendo is also in the fray. Its last console, the Gamecube, failed. It is launching the unusually titled Nintendo Wii, priced at £150 (€210) in the UK, hoping it will win the hearts and minds of gamers. Nintendo, along with the quirky name, has developed a truly unique product. The Wii is not aiming to be the most powerful games console, but hopes to develop a unique product offering that will entice both young and old with a unique gaming experience. Nintendo has developed groundbreaking motion-sensor technology, so that by physically moving the controller it interacts with the game play. For example, a gamer could play virtual tennis or have a swordfight by swinging the controller. This unique feature has wooed audiences and is deemed to be a killer feature. In the wake of this launch, Sony

Table C22.2 Comparison of the key players

	Microsoft Xbox 360	Sony PlayStation 3	Nintendo Wii
Specification	3 Power PC processors on one chip Two versions: the Core or Premium with 20 GB hard drive version	'Cell' processor, 35 times faster than PlayStation 2 Two versions: 20 GB or 60 GB	IBM Power PC 512 MB of internal Flash memory
DVD playback	Yes	Yes	Yes (optional)
Key features	Optional DVD-HD external drive Wireless joystick Online 'Xbox Live'	New Blu-Ray disc Entertainment Centre (Web, Video, Photos & Music) Motion sensing joystick Backward compatible	Innovative Wii Motion sensing controller Backward compatible, can play Nintendo classics Web browser
Key games titles	*Call of Duty 2* *Dead or Alive 4* *Halo 3*	*Grand Theft Auto 4* *Metal Gear Solid 4* *Gran Turismo HD*	*Super Mario* *Legend of Zelda* *Wii Sports*
Available since	December 2005	November 2006	Late 2006
Price	£275 (€385)	£425 (€595)	£150 (€210)

responded by copying the idea and placing a similar feature in its latest PlayStation 3 (PS3) console. Nintendo is aiming for a slightly different market, however. Many of its games are targeted towards children, utilizing kid-friendly games franchises such as Pokémon and SpongeBob. The Nintendo brand and its game catalogue are extremely popular with both males and females ranging from 7 to 18 years of age, whereas both Microsoft and Sony target the exact same 15–35-year-old male audience, promising sophisticated game play and high graphics performance.

Many view PS3 as having the edge in terms of technology, however the quality and number of games developed will ultimately decide who wins in this latest console war. Luring games developers to develop games for a particular platform is vital for any platform to succeed. Finding the right formula of great technology, with great features, a collection of great games, at a price that attracts gamers can prove an elusive mix. Others have failed, but those who succeed are rewarded with huge dividends.

Questions

1. Discuss what you believe to be the key success factors of launching a games console, using the marketing mix 4-Ps framework.
2. Debate the merits of Microsoft launching the Microsoft Xbox 360 several months before competing consoles, discussing first mover advantages in new product development.
3. Discuss what marketing strategies could be deployed as products enter their decline stage, using PlayStation 2 and the original Xbox as examples.

This case was written by Conor Carroll, Lecturer in Marketing, University of Limerick. Copyright © Conor Carroll (2006). The material in the case has been drawn from a variety of published sources.

Analysing competitors and creating a competitive advantage

CHAPTER 19

The race is not always to the swift, nor the battle to the strong, but that is the way to bet.

DAMON RUNYON

If you don't have a competitive advantage, don't compete.

JACK WELCH, FORMER CHIEF EXECUTIVE OF GENERAL ELECTRIC

LEARNING OBJECTIVES

After reading this chapter, you should be able to:

1. describe the determinants of industry attractiveness
2. explain how to analyse competitors
3. distinguish between differentiation and cost leader strategies
4. discuss the sources of competitive advantage
5. discuss the value chain
6. explain how to create and maintain a differential advantage
7. explain how to create and maintain a cost leadership position

Satisfying customers is a central tenet of the marketing concept, but it is not enough to guarantee success. The real question is whether a firm can satisfy customers better than the competition. For example, many car manufacturers market cars that give customer satisfaction in terms of appearance, reliability and performance. They meet the basic requirements necessary to compete. Customer choice, however, will depend on creating a little more value than the competition. This extra value is brought about by establishing a competitive advantage—a topic that will be examined later in this chapter.

Since corporate performance depends on both customer satisfaction and being able to create greater value than the competition, firms need to understand their competitors as well as their customers. By understanding its competitors, a firm can better predict their reaction to any marketing initiative that the firm might make, and exploit any weaknesses they might possess. Competitor analysis is thus crucial to the successful implementation of marketing strategy. The discussion will begin by examining competitive industry structure: rivalry between firms does not take place within a vacuum. For example, the threat of new competitors and the bargaining power of buyers can greatly influence the attractiveness of an industry and the profitability of each competitor.

ANALYSING COMPETITIVE INDUSTRY STRUCTURE

An **industry** is a group of firms that market products that are close substitutes for each other. In common parlance we refer to the car, oil or computer industry, indicating that the definition of an industry is normally product-based. It is a fact of life that some industries are more profitable than others. For example, the car, steel, coal and textile industries have had poor profitability records for many years, whereas the book publishing, television broadcasting, pharmaceuticals and soft drinks industries have enjoyed high long-run profits. Not all of this difference can be explained by the fact that one industry provides better customer satisfaction than another. There are other determinants of industry attractiveness and long-run profitability that shape the rules of competition. These are the threat of entry of new competitors, the threat of substitutes, the bargaining power of buyers and of suppliers, and the rivalry between the existing competitors.[1] Where these forces are intense, below-average industry performance can be expected; where these forces are mild, superior performance is common. Their influence is shown diagrammatically in Figure 19.1, which is known as the Porter model of competitive industry structure. Each of the 'five forces' in turn comprises a number of elements that, together, combine to determine the strength of each force and its effect on the degree of competition. Each force is discussed below.

The threat of new entrants

New entrants can raise the level of competition in an industry, thereby reducing its attractiveness. For example, in Denmark, foreign entrants such as Sweden's SE-Banken posed a threat to the largest banks, Den Danske Bank and Unibank, and Norway's Finax.[2] The threat of new entrants depends on the barriers to entry. High entry barriers exist in some industries (e.g. pharmaceuticals), whereas other industries are much easier to enter (e.g. restaurants). Key **entry barriers** include:

- economies of scale
- capital requirements
- switching costs
- access to distribution
- expected retaliation.

Figure 19.1 The Porter model of competitive industry structure

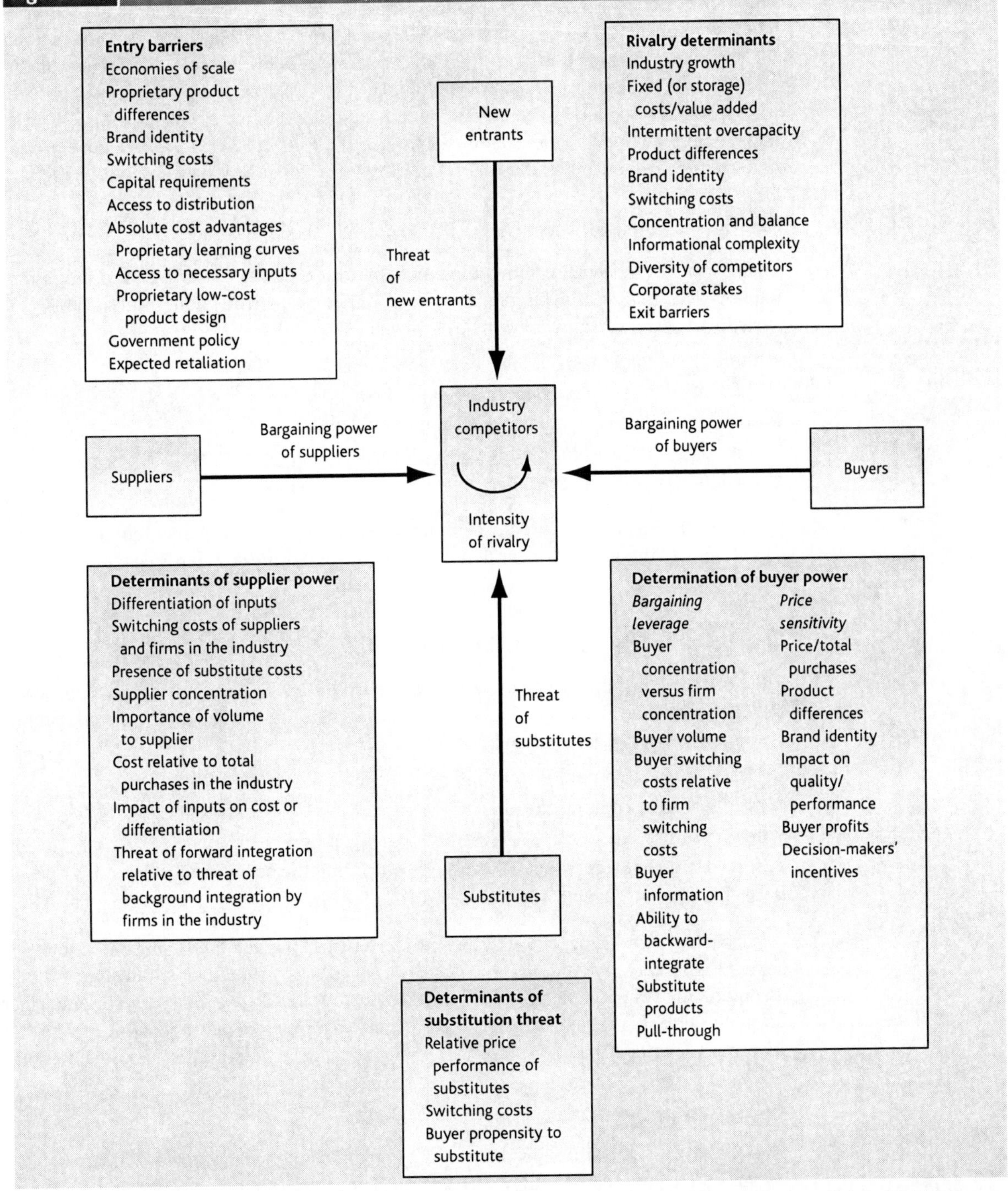

Source: adapted from Porter, M. E. (1998) Competitive Strategy, *New York: Free Press, 4. Reprinted with permission of the Free Press, an imprint of Simon and Schuster. Copyright © 1980 by Free Press.*

For present competitors, industry attractiveness can be increased by raising entry barriers. High promotional and R&D expenditures, and clearly communicated retaliatory actions to entry are some methods of raising barriers. One example of a company taking clear retaliatory action is that of Rotaprint, a US manufacturer of printing machines and accessories. The company made it common knowledge that it would retaliate if attacked. Despite this it was attacked by Toshiba in the USA. Rotaprint retaliated by launching an offensive against Toshiba in Japan where it cut its prices by 50 per cent. Toshiba matched the price cuts, only for Rotaprint to further reduce them by another 25 per cent. Shortly afterwards Toshiba left the USA, to be followed by Rotaprint's withdrawal from Japan. Other ways of raising barriers are by taking out patents and tying up suppliers and/or distributors. Some managerial actions can unwittingly lower barriers. For example, new product designs that dramatically lower manufacturing costs can ease entry for newcomers.

The bargaining power of suppliers

The cost of raw materials and components can have a major bearing on a firm's profitability. The higher the bargaining power of suppliers, the higher these costs. The bargaining power of suppliers will be high when:

- there are many buyers and few dominant suppliers
- there are differentiated highly valued products
- suppliers threaten to integrate forward into the industry
- buyers do not threaten to integrate backward into supply
- the industry is not a key customer group to the suppliers.

A firm can reduce the bargaining power of suppliers by seeking new sources of supply, threatening to integrate backward into supply, and designing standardized components so that many suppliers are capable of producing them.

The bargaining power of buyers

The concentration of European retailing has raised manufacturers' bargaining power. Benetton's use of many suppliers has increased its bargaining power. The bargaining power of buyers is greater when:

- there are few dominant buyers and many sellers
- products are standardized
- buyers threaten to integrate backwards into the industry
- suppliers do not threaten to integrate forwards into the buyer's industry.
- the industry is not a key supplying group for buyers.

Firms in the industry can attempt to lower buyer power by increasing the number of buyers they sell to, threatening to integrate forwards into the buyer's industry and producing highly valued, differentiated products. In supermarket retailing, the brand leader normally achieves the highest profitability partially because being number one means that supermarkets need to stock the brand, thereby reducing buyer power in price negotiations.

Threat of substitutes

The presence of substitute products can lower industry attractiveness and profitability because these put a constraint on price levels. For example, tea and coffee are fairly close substitutes in most European countries. Raising the price of coffee, therefore, would make tea more attractive. The threat of substitute products depends on:

- buyers' willingness to substitute
- the relative price and performance of substitutes
- the costs of switching to substitutes.

The threat of substitute products can be lowered by building up switching costs, which may be psychological—for example, by creating strong distinctive brand personalities—and maintaining a price differential commensurate with perceived customer values. If these tactics fail to deter a rival from launching a substitute product, the incumbent is faced with the following options: copy the substitute; copy but build in a differential advantage; form a strategic alliance with the rival; buy the rival; or move to a new market. An example of the last option is the case of Rockware Glass, which was threatened by the desire of supermarkets to move from glass beer containers to cans. Its response was to move to the production of wine bottles for the French market, where there was no threat of the substitute container.

Industry competitors

The intensity of rivalry between competitors in an industry will depend on the following factors.

- *Structure of the competition*: there is more intense rivalry when there are a large number of small competitors or a few equally balanced competitors, and less rivalry when a clear leader (at least 50 per cent larger than the second) exists with a large cost advantage.
- *Structure of costs*: high fixed costs encourage price-cutting to fill capacity.
- *Degree of differentiation*: commodity products encourage rivalry, while highly differentiated products that are hard to copy are associated with less intense rivalry.
- *Switching costs*: rivalry is reduced when switching costs are high because the product is specialized, the customer has invested a lot of resources in learning how to use the product or has made tailor-made investments that are worthless with other products and suppliers.
- *Strategic objectives*: when competitors are pursuing build strategies, competition is likely to be more intense than when playing hold or harvesting strategies.
- *Exit barriers*: when barriers to leaving an industry are high due to such factors as lack of opportunities elsewhere, high vertical integration, emotional barriers or the high cost of closing down plant, rivalry will be more intense than when exit barriers are low.

Firms need to be careful not to spoil a situation of competitive stability. They need to balance their own position against the well-being of the industry as a whole. For example, an intense price or promotional war may gain a few percentage points in market share but lead to an overall fall in long-run industry profitability as competitors respond to these moves. It is sometimes better to protect industry structure than follow short-term self-interest.

A major threat to favourable industry structure is the use of a no-frills, low-price strategy by a minor player seeking positional advantage. For example, the launch of generic products in the pharmaceutical and cigarette industries has lowered overall profitability.

Despite meeting customers' needs with high-quality, good-value products, firms can 'compete away' the rewards. An intensive competitive environment means that the value created by firms in satisfying customer needs is given away to buyers through lower prices, dissipated through costly marketing battles (e.g. advertising wars) or passed on to powerful suppliers through higher prices for raw materials and components.

In Europe the competitive structure of industries was fundamentally changed with the advent of the single European market. The lifting of barriers to trade between countries has radically altered industry structure by affecting its underlying determinants. For example, the threat of new entrants and the growth in buyer/supplier power through acquisition or merger are fundamentally changing the competitive climate of many industries.

COMPETITOR ANALYSIS

The analysis of how industry structure affects long-run profitability has shown the need to understand and monitor competitors. Their actions can spoil an otherwise attractive industry, their weaknesses can be a target for exploitation, and their response to a firm's marketing initiatives can have a major impact on their success. Indeed, firms that focus on competitors' actions have been found to achieve better business performance than those who pay less attention to their competitors.[3] Competitive information can be obtained from marketing research surveys, recruiting competitors' employees (sometimes interviewing them is sufficient), secondary sources (e.g. trade magazines, newspaper articles), distributors, stripping down competitors' products and gathering competitors' sales literature.

Competitor analysis seeks to answer five key questions.

1 Who are our competitors?
2 What are their strengths and weaknesses?
3 What are their strategic objectives and thrust?
4 What are their strategies?
5 What are their response patterns?

Figure 19.2 Competitor analysis

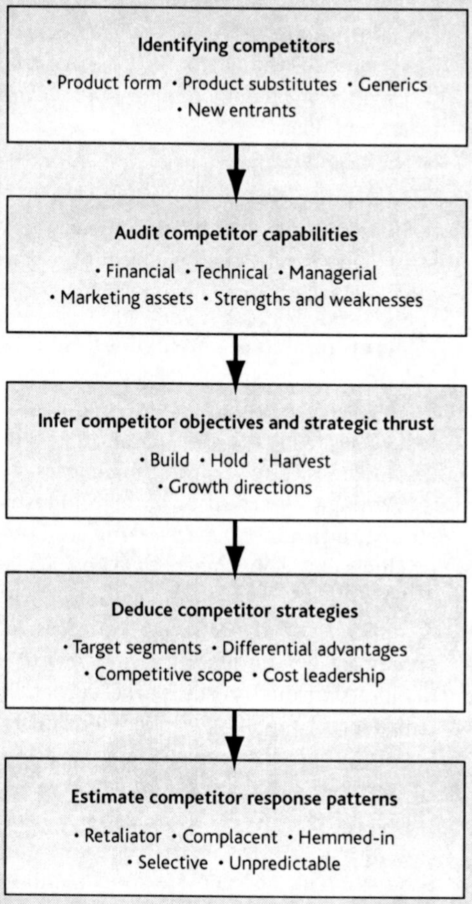

These issues are summarized in Figure 19.2. Each question will now be examined.

Who are our competitors?

The danger when identifying competitors is that competitive myopia prevails. This malady is reflected in a narrow definition of competition resulting in too restricted a view of which companies are in competition. Only those companies that are producing technically similar products are considered to be the competition (e.g. paint companies). This ignores companies purchasing substitute products that perform a similar function (e.g. polyurethane varnish firms) and those that solve a problem or eliminate it in a dissimilar way (e.g. PVC double-glazing companies). The actions of all of these types of competitors can affect the performance of our firm and therefore need to be monitored. Their responses also need to be assessed as they will determine the outcome of any competitive move that our firm may wish to make. For example, we need to ask how likely it would be that polyurethane varnish companies would follow any price move we might wish to make.

Beyond these current competitors the environment needs to be scanned for potential entrants into the industry. These can take two forms: entrants with technically similar products and those invading the market with substitute products. Companies with

Figure 19.3 Competitor identificaton

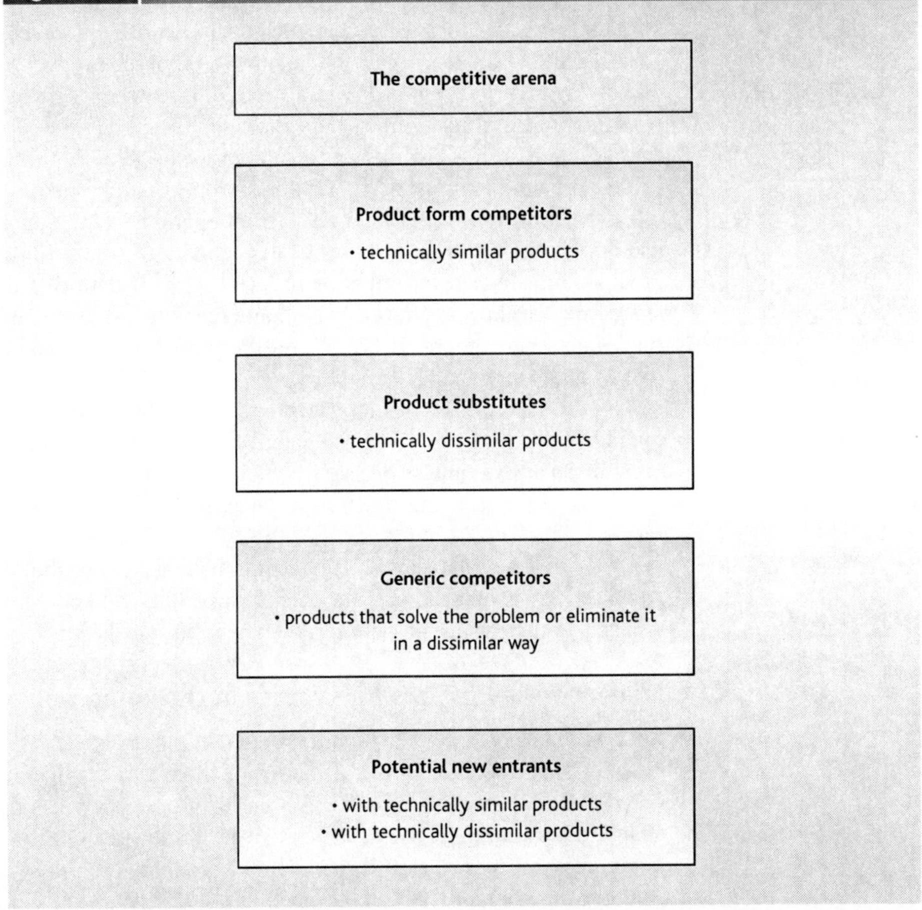

similar core competences to the present incumbents may pose the threat of entering with technically similar products. For example, Apple's skills in computer electronics provided the springboard for it to become market leader in the portable music player market with its iPod brand. The source of companies entering with substitute products may be more difficult to locate, however. A technological breakthrough may transform an industry by rendering the old product obsolete as when the calculator replaced the slide rule, or when the car replaced the horse-drawn buggy. In such instances it is difficult to locate the source of the substitute product well in advance. Figure 19.3 illustrates this competitive arena.

19.1 Pause for thought

Think of an airline with which you are familiar. Who/what are its product form competitors? Can you think of as many product substitute competitors as possible? What are the marketing implications of recognizing that competitors should be identified beyond just those that supply technically similar products.

What are their strengths and weaknesses?

Having identified our competitors the next stage is to complete a **competitor audit** in order to assess their relative strengths and weaknesses. A precise understanding of competitor strengths and weaknesses is an important prerequisite of developing competitor strategy. In particular, it locates areas of competitive vulnerability. Military strategy suggests that success is most often achieved when strength is concentrated against the enemy's greatest weakness.[4] This analogy holds true for business, as the success of Japanese companies in the car and motorcycle industries demonstrates.

The process of assessing competitors' strengths and weaknesses may take place as part of a marketing audit (see Chapter 2). As much internal, market and customer information should be gathered as is practicable. For example, financial data concerning profitability, profit margins, sales and investment levels, market data relating to price levels, market share and distribution channels used, and customer data concerning awareness of brand names, and perceptions of brand and company image, product and service quality, and selling ability may be relevant.

Not all of this information will be accessible, and some may not be relevant. Management needs to decide the extent to which each element of information is worth pursuing. For example, a decision is required regarding how much expenditure is to be allocated to measuring customer awareness and perceptions through marketing research.

This process of data gathering needs to be managed so that information is available to compare our company with its chief competitors on the *key factors for success* in the industry. A three-stage process can then be used, as follows.

1 Identify key factors for success in the industry

These should be restricted to about six to eight factors otherwise the analysis becomes too diffuse.[5] Their identification is a matter of managerial judgement. Their source may be functional (such as financial strength or flexible production) or generic (for example, the ability to respond quickly to customer needs, innovativeness, or the capability to provide other sales services). Since these factors are critical for success they should be used to compare our company with its competitors.

Figure 19.4 Company capability profiles

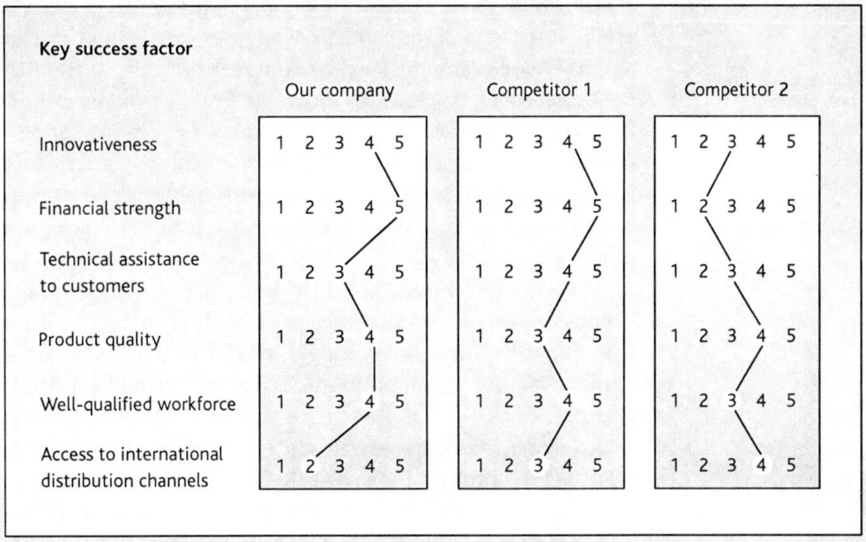

2 Rate our company and competitors on each key success factor using a rating scale

Each company is given a score on each success factor using a rating device. This may be a scale ranging from 1 (very poor) to 5 (very good); this results in a set of company capability profiles (an example is given in Fig. 19.4). Our company is rated alongside two competitors on six key success factors. Compared with our company, competitor 1 is relatively strong regarding technical assistance to customers and access to international distribution channels, but relatively weak on product quality. Competitor 2 is relatively strong on international distribution channels but relatively weak on innovativeness, financial strength and having a well-qualified workforce.

3 Consider the implications for competitive strategy

The competitive profile analysis is then used to identify possible competitive strategies. This analysis would suggest that our company should consider taking steps to improve technical assistance to customers to match or exceed competitor 1's capability on this factor. At the moment, our company enjoys a differential advantage over competitor 1 on product quality. Our strength in innovativeness should be used to maintain this differential advantage and competitor 1's moves to improve product quality should be monitored carefully.

Competitor 2 is weaker overall than competitor 1 and our company. However, it has considerable strengths in having access to international distribution channels. Given our company's weakness in this area, a strategic alliance with or take-over of competitor 2 might be sensible if our company's objective is to expand internationally. Our company's financial strength and competitor 2's financial weakness suggests that a take-over might be feasible.

What are their strategic objectives and thrust?

The third part of competitor analysis is to infer their *strategic objectives*. Companies may decide to build, hold or harvest products and strategic business units (SBUs). To briefly recap, a build objective is concerned with increasing sales and/or market share, a hold objective suggests maintaining sales and/or market share, and a harvest objective is followed when the emphasis is on maximizing short-term cash flow through slashing expenditure and raising prices whenever possible. It is useful to know what strategic objectives are being pursued by competitors because their response pattern may depend upon objectives. Looking at this topic from a product perspective, if we are considering building market share of our product by cutting price, a competitor who is also building is almost certain to follow; one who is content to hold sales and market share is also likely to respond, but a company following a harvest objective for its product is much less likely to reduce price because it is more concerned with profit margin than unit sales.

Conversely, if we are considering a price rise, a competitor pursuing a build strategy is not likely to follow; the price of a product subject to a hold objective is now likely to rise in line with our increase; and a company using a harvest objective will almost certainly take the opportunity to raise its product's price, maybe by more than our increase.

Knowing competitors' strategic objectives is also useful in predicting their likely strategies. For example, a build objective is likely to be accompanied by aggressive price and promotional moves, a hold objective with competitive stability, and a harvest objective with cost- rather than marketing-orientated strategies.

Strategic thrust refers to the future areas of expansion a company might contemplate. Broadly, a company can expand by penetrating existing markets more effectively with current products, launching new products in existing markets or by growing in new markets with existing or new products. Knowing the strategic thrust of competitors can help our strategic decision-making. For example, knowing that our competitors are considering expansion in North America but not Europe will make expansion into Europe a more attractive strategic option for our company.

What are their strategies?

At the product level, competitor analysis will attempt to deduce positioning strategy. This involves assessing a competitor product's target market and differential advantage. The marketing mix strategies (e.g. price levels, media used for promotion, and distribution channels) may indicate target market, and marketing research into customer perceptions can be used to assess relative differential advantages.

Companies and products need to be monitored continuously for changes in positioning strategy. For example, Volvo's traditional positioning strategy, based on safety, has been modified to give more emphasis to performance and style.

Strategies can also be defined in terms of competitive scope. For example, are competitors attempting to service the whole market or a few segments of a particular niche? If a niche player, is it likely that they will be content to stay in that segment or will they use it as a beachhead to move into other segments in the future? Japanese companies are renowned for their use of small niche markets as springboards for market segment expansion (e.g. the small car segments in the USA and Europe).

Competitors may be playing the cost-leadership game, focusing on cost-reducing measures rather than expensive product development and promotional strategies. (Cost leadership will be discussed in more detail later in this chapter.) If competitors are following this strategy it is more likely that they will be focusing research and development expenditure on process rather than product development in a bid to reduce manufacturing costs.

What are their response patterns?

A key consideration in making a strategic or tactical move is the likely response of competitors. As we have discussed, understanding competitor objectives and strategies is helpful in predicting competitor reactions. Indeed, a major objective of competitor analysis is to be able to predict competitor response to market and competitive changes. Competitors' past behaviour is also a guide to what they might do. Market leaders often try to control competitor response by retaliatory action. These are called *retaliatory* competitors because they can be relied on to respond aggressively to competitive challenges. Len Hardy, ex-chairman of Lever Brothers, explained the role of a retaliation as follows:

> A leader must enforce market discipline, must be ruthless in dealing with any competitive challenge. If you make a price move and a competitor undercuts it, then he should be shown that this action has been noticed and will be punished. If he is not punished he will repeat the move—and soon your leadership will be eroded.[6]

Thus by punishing competitor moves, market leaders can condition competitors to behave in predicted ways—for example, by not taking advantage of a price rise by the leader.

It is not only market leaders that retaliate aggressively. Where management is known to be assertive, and our move is likely to have a major impact on their performance, a strong response is usual.

The history, traditions and managerial personalities of competitors also have an influence on competitive response. Some markets are characterized by years of competitive stability with little serious strategic challenge to any of the incumbents. This can breed complacency, with predictably slow reaction times to new challenges. For example, innovation that offers superior customer value may be dismissed as a fad and unworthy of serious attention.

Another situation where competitors are unlikely to respond is where their previous strategies have restricted their scope for retaliation. An example of such a *hemmed-in competitor* was a major manufacturer of car number plates that were sold to car dealerships. A new company was started by an ex-employee who focused on one geographical area, supplying the same quality product but with extra discount. The national supplier could not respond since to give discount in that particular region would have meant granting the discount nationwide.

A fourth type of competitor may respond selectively. Because of tradition or beliefs about the relative effectiveness of marketing instruments a competitor may respond to some competitive moves but not others. For example, extra sales promotion expenditures may be matched but advertising increases (within certain boundaries) may be ignored. Another reason for selective response is the varying degree of visibility of marketing actions. For example, giving extra price discounts may be highly visible, but providing distributors with extra support (e.g. training, sales literature, loans) may be less discernible.

A final type of competitor is totally *unpredictable* in its response pattern. Sometimes there is a response and, at other times, there is no response. Some moves are countered aggressively; with others reaction is weak. No factors explain these differences adequately; they appear to be at the whim of management.

Some companies use role-play to assess competitor reactions: their most knowledgeable managers act out the roles of key competitors to aid prediction of their response to a proposed marketing initiative.[7] Interestingly, research has shown that managers tend to over-react more frequently than they under-react to competitors' marketing activities.[8]

COMPETITIVE ADVANTAGE

The key to superior performance is to gain and hold a *competitive advantage*. Firms can gain a competitive advantage through *differentiation* of their product offering, which provides superior customer value, or by managing for *lowest delivered cost*. Evidence for this proposition was provided by Hall, who examined the competitive strategies pursued by the two leading firms (in terms of return on investment) in eight mature industries characterized by slow growth and intense competition.[9] In each industry the two leading firms offered either high product differentiation or the lowest delivered cost. In most cases, an industry's return on investment leader opted for one of the strategies, while the second-placed firm pursued the other.

Competitive strategies

These two means of competitive advantage, when combined with the **competitive scope** of activities (broad vs narrow), result in four generic strategies: differentiation, cost leadership, differentiation focus, and cost focus. The differentiation and cost leadership strategies seek competitive advantage in a broad range of market or industry segments, whereas differentiation focus and cost focus strategies are confined to a narrow segment[10] (see Fig. 19.5).

Differentiation

Differentiation strategy involves the selection of one or more choice criteria that are used by many buyers in an industry. The firm then uniquely positions itself to meet these criteria. Differentiation strategies are usually associated with a premium price, and higher than average costs for the industry as the extra value to customers (e.g. higher performance) often raises costs. The aim is to differentiate in a way that leads to a price premium in excess of the cost of differentiating. Differentiation gives customers a reason to prefer one product over another and thus is central to strategic marketing thinking. Here are some examples of brands that have achieved success using a differentiation strategy.

- Nokia became market leader in mobile phones by being the first to realize that they were fashion items and to design stylish phones to differentiate the brand from its rivals.
- Toyota has built its success and reputation by targeting a broad market with highly reliable, high build quality, low running cost and stylish cars, which differentiate the brand from its competitors, such as GM, Ford and Fiat.

Figure 19.5 Competitive Strategy Options

		Competitive base: Differentiation	Competitive base: Cost
Scope	Broad	Differentiation leader	Cost leader
	Narrow	Differentiation focuser	Cost focuser

Source: Porter, M. E. (1985) Competitive Advantage, *New York: Free Press, 37. Reprinted with the permission of the Free Press, an imprint of Simon and Schuster: Copyright © 1985 by Michael E. Porter.*

- Dyson differentiated its vacuum cleaners by inventing a bagless version, which outperformed its rivals by providing greater suction and convenience, and by eliminating the need to buy and install dust bags. Its vacuum cleaners are also differentiated from other brands by their distinctive colours.
- Google created a differential advantage over its search engine rivals by enabling the most relevant websites to be ranked at the top of listings.

Cost leadership

This strategy involves the achievement of the lowest cost position in an industry. Many segments in the industry are served and great importance is attached to minimizing costs on all fronts. So long as the price achievable for its products is around the industry average, cost leadership should result in superior performance. Thus cost leaders often market standard products that are believed to be acceptable to customers. Heinz and United Biscuits are believed to be cost leaders in their industries. They market acceptable products at reasonable prices, which means that their low costs result in above-average profits. Wal-Mart is also a cost leader, which allows the company the option of charging lower prices than its rivals to achieve higher sales and yet achieve comparable profit margins, or to match competitors' prices and attain higher profit margins. Dell has also achieved success using a cost leadership strategy. It outsources manufacturing, sells direct to customers, does little R&D and keeps overheads to less than 10 per cent of sales. This has meant that it has been able to undercut Hewlett-Packard on price while achieving higher profit margins and forcing IBM out of the PC business.

Differentiation focus

With this strategy, a firm aims to differentiate within one or a small number of target market segments. The special needs of the segment mean that there is an opportunity to differentiate the product offering from the competition's, which may be targeting a broader group of customers. For example, some small speciality chemical companies thrive on taking orders that are too small or specialized to be of interest to their larger competitors. Differentiation focusers must be clear that the needs of their target group differ from those of the broader market (otherwise there will be no basis for differentiation) and that existing competitors are underperforming. Examples of differentiation focusers are Burberry, Bang & Olufsen, Mercedes and Ferrari; each of these markets differentiated products to one or a small number of target market segments.

Cost focus

With this strategy a firm seeks a cost advantage with one or a small number of target market segments. By dedicating itself to the segment, the cost focuser can seek economies that may be ignored or missed by broadly targeted competitors. In some instances, the competition, by trying to achieve wide market acceptance, may be overperforming (for example, by providing unwanted services) to one segment of customers. By providing a basic product offering, a cost advantage will be gained that may exceed the price discount necessary to sell it. Examples of cost focusers are easyJet and Ryanair, who focus on short-haul flights with a basic product trimmed to reduce costs. Lidl is also a cost focuser, targeting price-sensitive consumers with a narrow product line (around 300 items in stock) but with large buying power. Travelodge, the no-frills hotel chain, is another example with its focus on one market segment: price-conscious consumers.

Choosing a competitive strategy

The essence of corporate success, then, is to choose a generic strategy and pursue it with gusto. Below-average performance is associated with the failure to achieve any of these generic strategies. The result is no competitive advantage: a *stuck-in-the-middle position* that results in lower performance than that of the cost leaders, differentiators or focusers in any market segment. An example of a company that made the mistake of moving to a stuck-in-the-middle position was General Motors with its Oldsmobile car. The original car (the Oldsmobile Rocket V8) was highly differentiated, with a 6-litre V8 engine, which was virtually indestructible, very fast and highly reliable. In order to cut costs, this engine was replaced by the same engine that went into the 5-litre Chevrolet V8. This had less power and was less reliable. The result was catastrophic: sales plummeted.

Firms need to understand the generic basis for their success and resist the temptation to blur strategy by making inconsistent moves. For example, a no-frills cost leader or focuser should beware the pitfalls of moving to a higher cost base (perhaps by adding expensive services). A focus strategy involves limiting sales volume. Once domination of the target segment has been achieved there may be a temptation to move into other segments in order to achieve growth with the same competitive advantage. This can be a mistake if the new segments do not value the firm's competitive advantage in the same way.

In most situations differentiation and cost leadership strategies are incompatible: differentiation is achieved through higher costs. However, there are circumstances when both can be achieved simultaneously. For example, a differentiation strategy may lead to market share domination, which lowers costs through economies of scale and learning effects; or a highly differentiated firm may pioneer a major process innovation that significantly reduces manufacturing costs leading to a cost-leadership position. When differentiation and cost leadership coincide, performance is exceptional since a premium price can be charged for a low-cost product.

Grolsch's competitive advantage lies in its long history and core competence in the brewing process.

Sources of competitive advantage

In order to create a differentiated or lowest cost position, a firm needs to understand the nature and location of the potential *sources of competitive advantage*. The nature of these sources are the superior skills and resources of a firm. One key source of competitive advantage for Grolsch is its long-established skills in brewing (see illustration). Management benefits by analysing the superior skills and resources that are contributing, or could contribute, to competitive advantage (i.e. differentiation or lowest cost position). Their location can be aided by value chain analysis. A **value chain** is the discrete activities a firm carries out in order to perform its business.

Superior skills

Superior skills are the distinctive capabilities of key personnel that set them apart from the personnel of competing firms.[11] The benefit of superior skills is the resulting ability to perform functions more effectively than other firms. For example, superior selling skills may result in closer relationships with customers than competing firms achieve. Compaq Computers built strong relationships with corporate retailers by offering attractive margins and exclusive franchises.[12] Superior quality assurance skills can result in higher and more consistent product quality.

Superior resources

Superior resources are the tangible requirements for advantage that enable a firm to exercise its skills. Superior resources include:

- the number of sales people in a market
- expenditure on advertising and sales promotion
- distribution coverage (the number of retailers who stock the product)
- expenditure on R&D
- scale of and type of production facilities
- financial resources
- brand equity
- knowledge.

Core competencies

The distinctive nature of these skills and resources makes up a company's **core competencies**. For example, Canon's core competences lie in printer, copier and camera technologies. Canon invests 8 per cent of its sales revenues in these technologies to maintain and extend its competitive advantages in these fields.[13]

Value chain

A useful method for locating superior skills and resources is the value chain.[14] All firms consist of a set of activities that are conducted to design, manufacture, market, distribute and service its products. The value chain categorizes these into primary and support activities (see Fig. 19.6). This enables the sources of costs and differentiation to be understood and located.

Primary activities include in-bound physical distribution (e.g. materials handling, warehousing, inventory control), operations (e.g. manufacturing, packaging), out-bound physical distribution (e.g. delivery, order processing), marketing (e.g. advertising, selling, channel management) and service (e.g. installation, repair, customer training).

Figure 19.6 The value chain

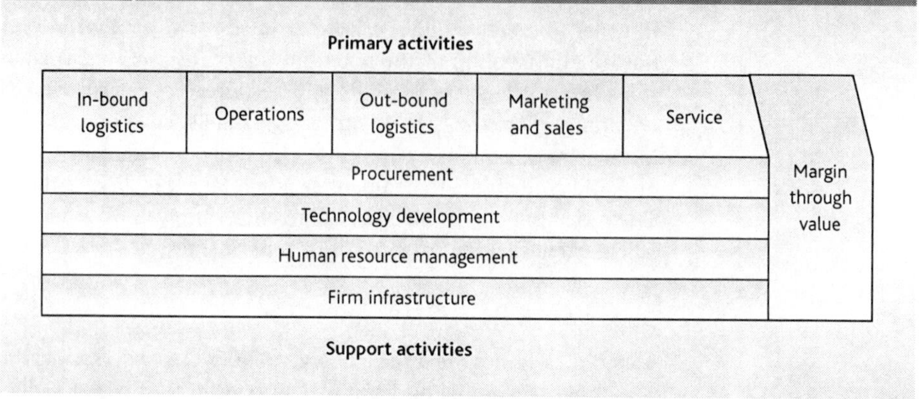

Source: Porter, M. E. (1985) Competitive Advantage, *New York: Free Press, 37. Reprinted with the permission of the Free Press, an imprint of Simon & Schuster: Copyright © 1985 by Michael E. Porter.*

Support activities are found within all of these primary activities, and consist of purchased inputs, technology, human resource management and the firm's infrastructure. These are not defined within a given primary activity because they can be found in all of them. Purchasing can take place within each primary activity, not just in the purchasing department; technology is relevant to all primary activities, as is human resource management; and the firm's infrastructure, which consists of general management, planning, finance, accounting and quality management, supports the entire value chain.

By examining each value-creating activity, management can look for the skills and resources that may form the basis for low-cost or differentiated positions.

To the extent that skills and resources exceed (or could be developed to exceed) those of the competition, they form the key sources of competitive advantage. Not only should the skills and resources within value-creating activities be examined, the *linkages* between them should be examined too. For example, greater coordination between operations and in-bound physical distribution may give rise to reduced costs through lower inventory levels.

Value chain analysis can extend to the value chains of suppliers and customers. For example, just-in-time supply could lower inventory costs; providing salesforce support to distributors could foster closer relations. Thus, by looking at the linkages between a firm's value chain and those of suppliers and customers, improvements in performance can result that can lower costs or contribute to the creation of a differentiated position.

Overall, the contribution of the value chain is in providing a framework for understanding the nature and location of the skills and resources that provide the basis for competitive advantage. Furthermore, the value chain provides the framework for cost analysis. Assigning operating costs and assets to value activities is the starting point of cost analysis so that improvement can be made, and cost advantages defended. For example, if a firm discovers that its cost advantage is based on superior production facilities, it should be vigilant in upgrading those facilities to maintain its position against competitors. Similarly, by understanding the sources of differentiation, a company can build on these sources and defend against competitive attack. For example, if differentiation is based on skills in product design, then management knows that sufficient investment in maintaining design superiority is required to maintain the firm's differentiated position. Also, the identification of specific sources of advantage can lead to their exploitation in new markets where customers place a similar high value on the resultant outcome. For example, Marks & Spencer's skills in clothing retailing were successfully extended to

Figure 19.7 Value Chain Reconfiguration

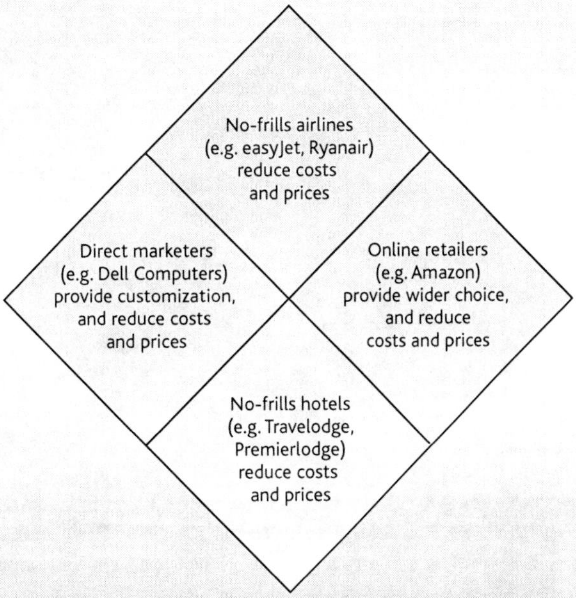

provide differentiation in food retailing. Finally, analysis of the value chain can lead to its reconfiguration to fundamentally change the way a market is served. Figure 19.7 provides some examples.

CREATING A DIFFERENTIAL ADVANTAGE

Although skills and resources are the sources of competitive advantage, they are translated into a **differential advantage** only when the customer perceives that the firm is providing value above that of the competition.[15] The creation of a differential advantage, then, comes with the marrying of skills and resources with the key attributes (choice criteria) that customers are looking for in a product offering. However, it should be recognized that the distinguishing competing attributes in a market are not always the most important ones. For example, if customers were asked to rank safety, punctuality and onboard service in order of importance when flying, safety would undoubtedly be ranked at the top. Nevertheless, when choosing an airline, safety would rank low because most airlines are assumed to be safe. This is why airlines look to less important ways of differentiating their offerings (e.g. by giving superior onboard service).

A differential advantage can be created with any aspect of the marketing mix. Product, distribution, promotion and price are all capable of creating added customer value (see Fig. 19.8). The key to whether improving an aspect of marketing is worthwhile is to know whether the potential benefit provides value to the customer. Table 19.1 lists ways of creating differential advantages and their potential impact on customer value.

Product

Product performance can be enhanced by such devices as raising speed, comfort and safety levels, capacity and ease of use, or improving taste or smell. For example, raising

Figure 19.8 Creating a differential advantage

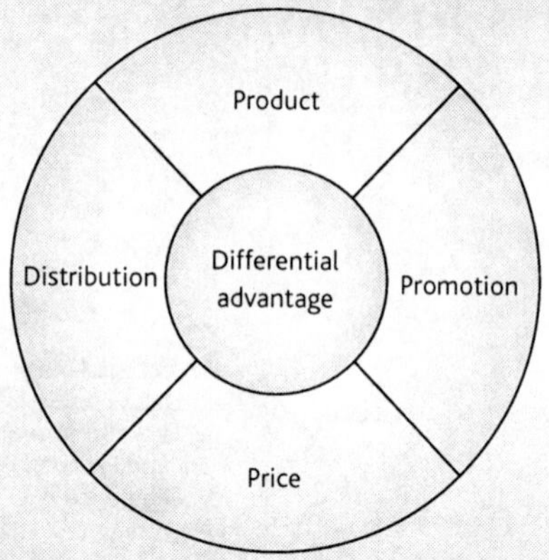

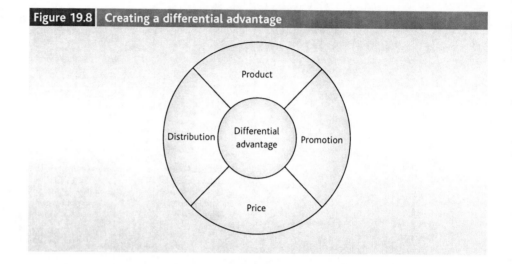

Table 19.1 Creating a differential advantage using the marketing mix

Marketing mix	Differential advantage	Value to the customer
Product	Performance	Lower costs; higher revenue; safety; pleasure; status
	Durability	Longer life; lower costs
	Reliability	Lower maintenance and production costs; higher revenue; fewer problems
	Style	Good looks; status
	Upgradability	Lower costs; prestige
	Technical assistance	Better-quality products; closer supplier–buyer relationships
	Installation	Fewer problems
Distribution	Location	Convenience; lower costs
	Quick/reliable delivery	Lower costs; fewer problems
	Distributor support	More effective selling/marketing; close buyer–seller relationships
	Delivery guarantees	Peace of mind
	Computerized reordering	Less work; lower costs
Promotion	Creative/more advertising	Superior brand personality
	Creative/more sales promotion	Direct added value
	Cooperative promotions	Lower costs
	Well-trained salesforce	Superior problem-solving and building close relationships
	Dual selling	Sales assistance; higher sales
	Fast, accurate quotes	Lower costs; fewer problems
	Free demonstrations	Lower risk of purchase
	Free or low-cost trial	Lower risk of purchase
	Fast complaint handling	Fewer problems; lower costs
Price	Lower price	Lower cost of purchase
	Credit facilities	Lower costs; better cash flow
	Low-interest loans	Lower costs; better cash flow
	Higher price	Price–quality match

Singapore Airlines differentiates by offering exceptional service.

the speed of operation of a scanner can lower the cost of treating hospital patients. Improving comfort levels (e.g. of a car), taste (e.g. of food), or smell (e.g. of cosmetics) can give added pleasure to consumption. Raising productivity levels of earth-moving equipment can bring higher revenue if more jobs can be done in a given period of time. The advertisement for Singapore Airlines (see illustration) highlights how it offers better performance through superior service.

The *durability* of a product has a bearing on costs since greater durability means a longer operating life. Improving product *reliability* (i.e. lowering malfunctions or defects) can lower maintenance and production costs, raise revenues through lower downtime and reduce the hassle of using the product. Product *styling* can also give customer value through the improved looks that good style brings. This can confer status to the buyer and allow the supplier to charge premium prices, as with Bang & Olufsen hi-fi equipment. Marketing in Action 19.1 discusses how style can be used as a differentiator.

19.1 Marketing in Action

Using Style to Differentiate Products

Two companies that have successfully used style to differentiate their products from those of the competition are Bang & Olufsen and Apple Computer. Bang & Olufsen has long been regarded as the style leader in audio and television equipment, and Apple created a stir in the computer world with the launch of its iMac.

Bang & Olufsen has built a worldwide reputation for quality and a fanatically loyal customer base. Its sleek, tastefully discrete designs and high standards of production have earned it elite status in the market. For decades, these factors have formed the basis of its advertising and marketing strategy. The company recognizes that style needs to be displayed distinctively in retail outlets. This has led to the creation of 'concept shops' where subtle images are projected on to walls and products displayed in free-standing areas constructed from translucent walls. The company's view is that you cannot sell Bang & Olufsen equipment when it is sandwiched between a washing machine and a shelf of videos. The concept shop gives the right look to make the most of the products. The company exemplifies the importance of style and aesthetics rather than technology or low prices in buying decisions. It trades on ambience as much as sound.

Although not the market leader overall, Apple's iMac leads the competition in the design, publishing and education segments. It also sells well in the consumer market: over 30 per cent of iMac buyers are first-time home computer owners. A key point of differentiation is its looks. As Steve Jobs, chief executive at Apple, explains, 'If you look at it, our industry has done a pretty poor job of listening to its customers in the consumer market. The industry sold big, ugly beige ... boxes that took up desks and everything else. The customers were saying "My God, I don't know how to connect all these cables", "My God, this thing is too noisy", "My God, this doesn't fit on my desk", and "My God, I have to hide it when visitors come over".' The result was the colourful, curvaceous all-in-one iMac. No consumer could mistake the distinctive design of the new model. The result was that over 2 million units have been sold and Apple's market share in the USA has risen to a respectable 11 per cent. So successful has Apple been in creating a strong brand identity with its iMac that the company has withstood the challenge of a flood of iMac lookalikes.

Based on: Pickford (1999);[16] Whiteling (2002);[17] Gapper (2005)[18]

The capacity to *upgrade* a product (to take advantage of technological advances) or to meet changing needs (e.g. extra storage space in a computer) can lower costs, and confer prestige by maintaining state-of-the-art features. The illustration featuring the Apple iMac computer shows how style can be used to create a differential advantage.

Products can be augmented by the provision of *guarantees* that give customers peace of mind and lower costs should the product need repair, as well as giving *technical assistance* to customers, so that they are provided with better-quality products. Both parties benefit from closer relationships and from the provision of product *installation*, which means that customers do not incur problems in properly installing a complex piece of equipment.

Distribution

Wide distribution coverage and/or careful selection of distributor *locations* can provide convenient purchasing for customers. *Quick and/or reliable delivery* can lower buyer costs by reducing production downtime and lowering inventory levels. Reliable delivery, in particular, reduces the frustration of waiting for late delivery. Providing distributors with *support* in the form of training and financial help can bring about more effective selling and marketing, and offers both parties the advantage of closer relationships. FedEx has

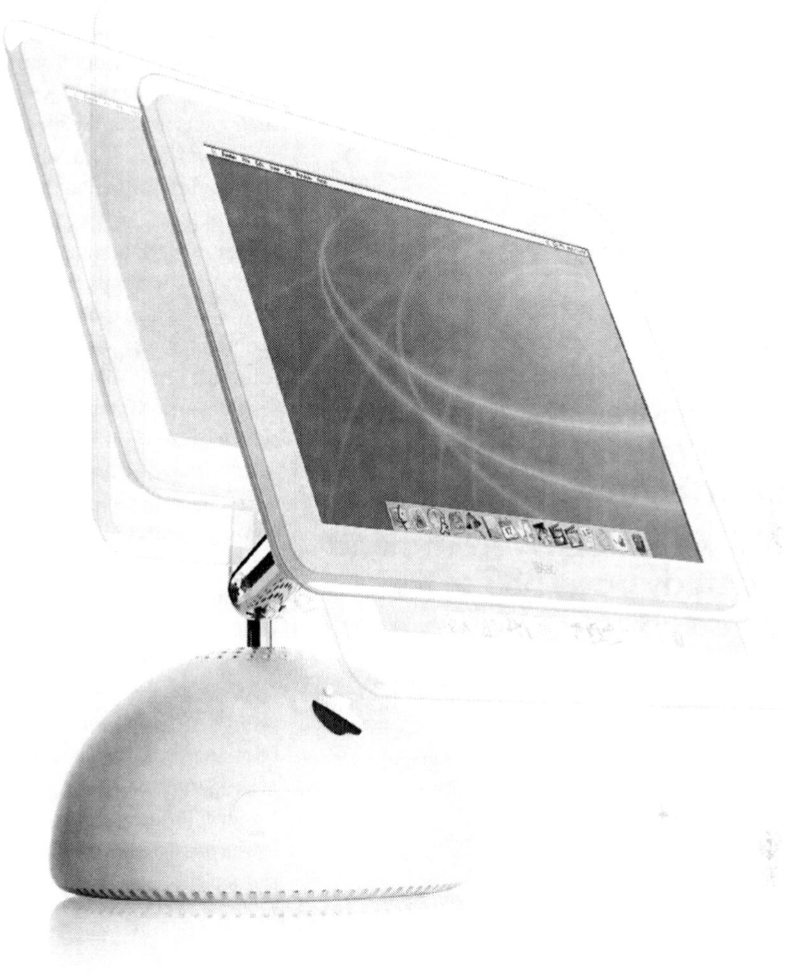

Apple uses style to create a differential advantage for its iMac computer.

continued to prosper by giving *delivery guarantees* of critical documents 'down to the hour'.[19] Working with organizational customers to introduce *computerized reordering* systems can lower their costs, reduce their workload and increase the cost for them of switching to other suppliers.

Promotion

A differential advantage can be created by the *creative use of advertising*. For example, Heineken was differentiated by the use of humour and the tag-line 'Heineken refreshes the parts other beers cannot reach' at a time when many other lagers were promoted by showing groups of men in public houses enjoying a drink together. The VW Polo advertisement creatively uses a *Which?* magazine product test endorsement to promote the superiority of the car over its competitors (see illustration overleaf). *Spending more on advertising* can also aid

We're not allowed to quote from 'Which?' magazine in an advertisement.
All we can do is recommend you study page 583 of the October issue.
Polo.

Indirect endorsement of VW Polo by Which? *magazine in this advert provides some credibility.*

differentiation by creating a stronger brand personality than competitive brands. Similarly, using *more creative sales promotional methods* or simply *spending more on sales incentives* can give direct added value to customers. By engaging in *cooperative promotions* with distributors, producers can lower their costs and build goodwill.

The salesforce can also offer a means of creating a differential advantage. Particularly when products are similar, a *well-trained salesforce* can provide superior problem-solving skills for their customers. Part of the success of IBM in penetrating the mainframe computer market in the early 1980s was due to its well-trained salesforce, which acted as problem solver and information consultant for its customers. As IBM has been transformed into a services-orientated company, its salesforce has been retrained to deliver consultancy services and, in so doing, *build close relationships* with its customers. *Dual selling*, whereby a producer provides salesforce assistance to distributors, can lower the latter's costs and increase sales. For example, a chemical company might supply product specialists who support a distributor's salesforce by providing technical expertise when required. Sales responsiveness in the form of *fast, accurate quotes* can lower customer costs by making transactions more efficient, and reduce the hassle associated with ordering supplies. Furthermore, *free demonstrations* and *free (or low cost) trial* arrangements can reduce the risk of purchase for customers. Finally, *superior complaint handling* procedures can lower customer costs by speeding up the process, and reduce the inconvenience that can accompany it.

Price

Using low price as a means of gaining differential advantage can fail unless the firm enjoys a cost advantage and has the resources to fight a price war. For example, Laker Airways challenged British Airways in transatlantic flights on the basis of lower price, but lost the battle when British Airways cut its prices to compete. Without a cost advantage and with fewer resources, Laker Airways could not survive BA's retaliation. Budget airlines such as Ryanair and easyJet have challenged more traditional airlines by charging low prices based on low costs, as Digital Marketing 19.1 discusses.

A less obvious means of lowering the effective price to the customer is to offer *credit facilities* or *low-interest loans*. Both serve to lower the cost of purchase and improve cash flow for customers. Finally, a *high price* can be used as part of a premium positioning strategy to support brand image. Where a brand has distinct product, promotional or distributional advantages, a premium price provides consistency within the marketing mix.

This analysis of how the marketing mix can be used to develop a differential advantage has focused on how each action can be translated into value to the customer. It must be remembered, however, that for a differential advantage to be realized, a firm needs to provide not only customer value but also value that is superior to that offered by the competition. If all firms provide distributor support in equal measure, for example, distributors may gain value, but no differential advantage will have been achieved. Finally, innovative

19.1 Digital Marketing

Low-cost Airlines: Using the Internet to Build Competitive Advantage

The model for budget, or 'no-frills', airlines was first developed in the USA by Southwest Airlines in the 1970s. The premise of this budget airline was to get passengers to their destination for less, with an 'adequate' level of service. This model, highly successful for Southwest, has since been copied by Ryanair, easyJet, and others.

The competitive advantage of budget airlines is in maintaining low operating costs while increasing revenue, and the Internet has helped them do both.

The majority of budget carriers use the Internet as the main distribution channel, while traditional airlines still rely on intermediaries. In fact, the sole order method of Ryanair (www.ryanair.co.uk) is online, where it takes over 600,000 bookings per week. In addition, the Internet enables e-ticketing and reduces other material costs as customers receive all information online.

The largest area of competitive advantage is in maximizing seat revenue, and all carriers have sophisticated yield management systems. Maximizing seat revenue involves charging just enough to fill the flight but not so little that margins are cut. It is impossible to optimize revenues when sales are achieved through the airline and a network of travel agencies—the flow of information is too slow. However, through sole use of the Internet, budget carriers can update prices instantaneously, maximizing flight profitability.

Technology provides huge advantages for these companies but (as Ryanair and others have proved) it is also easy to copy their advances. Competitors such as BA, bmibaby and Flybe are increasingly using technology to cut costs. These companies need to be aware of new ways of retaining their competitive advantage

Based on: Key Note (2002);[20] Choueke (2006)[21]

ways of creating a differential advantage have been developed by ethically minded companies in the tourism industry, as Marketing Ethics and Corporate Social Responsibility 19.1 describes.

Fast reaction times

In addition to using the marketing mix to create a differential advantage, many companies are recognizing the need to create *fast reaction times* to changes in marketing trends. For example, H&M and Zara have developed fast-reaction systems so that new designs can be delivered to stores within three weeks, and top-selling items are requested and poor sellers withdrawn from shops within a week. This is made possible by sophisticated marketing information systems that feed data from stores to headquarters every day.

19.2 Pause for thought

Consider a market-leading brand that you have bought in the last 12 months. Why did you buy it and why do you think it is so successful? Your answers will identify its differential advantage(s).

Sustaining a differential advantage

When searching for ways to achieve a differential advantage, management should pay close attention to factors that cannot easily be copied by the competition. The aim is to achieve a *sustainable differential advantage*. Competing on low price can often be copied by

19.1 Marketing Ethics and Corporate Social Responsibility in Action

Can Eco-tourism Save the Planet?

The tourism industry is booming: cheap flights and the 'democratization' of travel have put the jet-set lifestyle within reach of a far greater number of consumers. The World Tourism Organization estimates there were 760 million outbound trips of one night or more worldwide in 2004, a total spend of almost £350 billion (€490 billion). Over the next 10 years travel and tourism are expected to grow by an average of 4.5 per cent annually, particularly in the Asian market. While this is good news for the travel industry, environmentalists and climate change experts are less optimistic. Given the enthusiasm for ethical consumption, the alternative travel industry is setting out a new model of competitive tourism. The emphasis is now on eco-tourism, encouraging tourists to minimize the ecological footprint of their holiday. The International Ecotourism Society (www.ecotourism.org) defines ecotourism as 'responsible travel to natural areas that conserves the environment and improves the well being of local people'.

Responsible Travel (www.responsibletravel.com), an online travel agent, sells holidays that 'give the world a break', and is proving popular with the ethical holiday consumer. The market for 'responsible travel' is growing at an estimated three times the industry rate, and is predicted to account for 5 per cent of the market in the next 10 years. *Worlds Apart*, a recent ethical travel report, suggested that 52 per cent of people would be more likely to book a holiday with a tour company that has a responsible tourism policy; 65 per cent of people surveyed by Christian Relief and Tearfund said they wanted to be better informed about local customs, preserving the environment, supporting the local economy and how to behave more responsibly when on holiday.

In response to consumer demand, new environmentally and ethically aware hotels, travel agents, tour operators, campsites and websites have opened up. Travellers are interested in 'offsetting' their carbon dioxide emissions when they fly (e.g. by making a donation to plant a tree, a strategy supported by the Association of British Travel Agents), or by taking trains (Eurostar won the Responsible Travel Award for best mode of transport, providing a low-emissions alternative to flying) or a car instead of jetting off on cheap flights. An example of an eco-holiday destination is Whitepod, a 'zero impact' camp for 10 guests situated over 1700m in the Swiss Alps. It consists of five geodesic pods on platforms, which are removed in the spring, leaving no trace on the mountainside; it is comfortable, close to nature and has negative environmental impact. Eventually the owners plan to completely eliminate all the camp's carbon dioxide emissions, but they have already won the Responsible Tourism Award for Innovation. The Black Sheep Inn, high in the Andes, offers an eco-friendly sauna, and aims to be entirely self-sufficient in its use of water, energy and food.

Justin Francis, co-founder of Responsible Travel, recognizes that the 'dark green' traveller accounts for only 1 per cent of the overall market. What is now emerging is something he calls the 'light green' traveller, the type of person who maybe goes to farmers' markets, but also shops at the local supermarket. He believes the reason that eco-tourism is growing so quickly is not just because people want to 'do the right thing', it is also about finding a different kind of experience, a deeper connection to nature and the community. A further attraction is that today's eco-savvy operators are no longer polarized by either 'rough and ready, dirt-cheap campsites or ultra high-end luxury wilderness experiences'. Francis considers responsible tourism to be 'a sleeping giant', stating 'just as the organic food movement took off, responsible tourism will become a recognized consumer brand'. As a result, Responsible Travel offers a range of options including eco-hideaways in Sri Lanka, cycling in Sardinia and diving in the Red Sea.

Another related development is the backlash against budget air travel by a growing band of conscientious objectors who recognize that any effort to be green through recycling, saving energy, and so on, is totally wiped out by taking holidays by air. Many eco-tourist resorts are in South America, Asia and Africa, requiring travellers to expend vast amounts of fuel and carbon dioxide in order to reach their destinations. In response, Mark Ellingham, founder of the *Rough Guide* series of travel books, has stated that he will be limiting his trips by plane, and taking his summer holidays in the UK. Ellingham has just commissioned the *Rough Guide to Climate Change*, and from 2006 all *Rough Guides* will have a section warning readers about the negative environmental effects of flying.

Based on: BBC News (2002);[22] Baker (2005);[23] Hammond (2005);[24] Siegle (2005);[25] McKie et al. (2006);[26] Mills (2006);[27] Robbins

the competition, meaning that any advantage is short-lived. Means of achieving a longer-term advantage include:

- patent-protected products
- strong brand personality
- close relationships with customers
- high service levels achieved by well-trained personnel
- innovative product upgrading
- creating high entry barriers (e.g. R&D or promotional expenditures)
- strong and distinctive internal processes that deliver the above and are difficult to copy.[29]

Eroding a differential advantage

However, many advantages are contestable. For example, IBM's stronghold on personal computers was undermined by cheaper clones. Three mechanisms are at work that can erode a differential advantage:[30]

1 technological and environment changes that create opportunities for competitors by eroding the protective barriers (e.g. long-standing television companies are being challenged by satellite television)
2 competitors learn how to imitate the sources of the differential advantage (e.g. competitors engage in a training programme to improve service capabilities)
3 complacency leads to lack of protection of the differential advantage.

CREATING COST LEADERSHIP

Creating a cost-leadership position requires an understanding of the factors that affect costs. Porter has identified 10 major *cost drivers* that determine the behaviour of costs in the value chain (see Fig. 19.9).[31]

Figure 19.9 Cost drivers

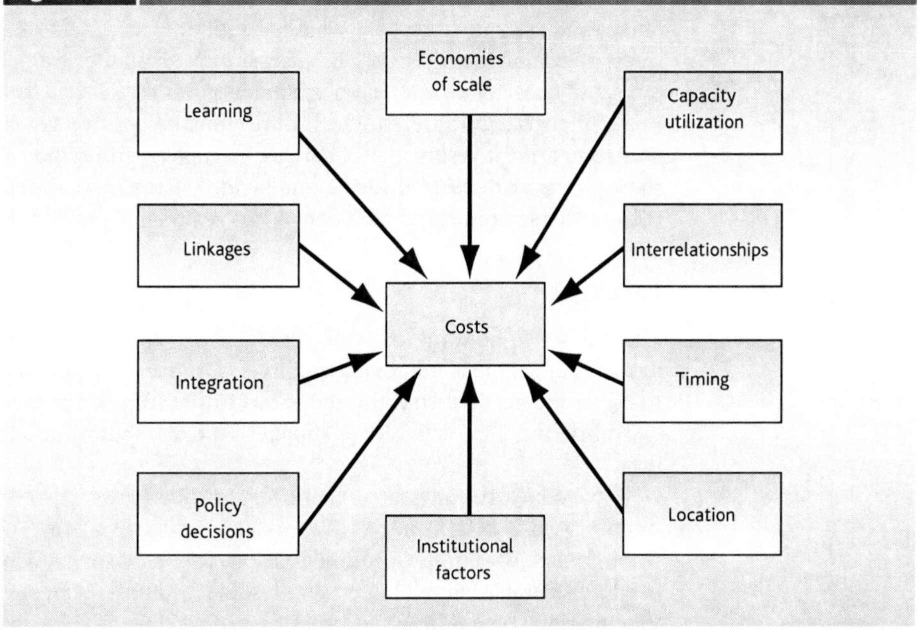

Economies of scale

Scale economies can arise from the use of more efficient methods of production at higher volumes. For example, United Biscuits benefits from more efficient machinery that can produce biscuits more cheaply than that used by Fox's Biscuits, which operates at much lower volume. Scale economies also arise from the less-than-proportional increase in overheads as production volume increases. For example, a factory with twice the floor area of another factory is less than twice the price to build. A third scale economy results from the capacity to spread the cost of R&D and promotion over a greater sales volume. Such scale economies mean that companies such as Coca-Cola, General Electric, Intel, Microsoft and Wal-Mart have a huge advantage over their competitors. However, economies of scale do not proceed indefinitely. At some point, diseconomies of scale are likely to arise as size gives rise to overcomplexity and, possibly, personnel difficulties.

Learning

Costs can also fall as a result of the effects of learning. For example, people learn how to assemble more quickly, pack more efficiently, design products that are easier to manufacture, lay out warehouses more effectively, cut driving time and reduce inventories. The effect of learning on costs was seen in the manufacture of fighter planes for the Second World War. The time to produce each plane fell over time as learning took place. The combined effect of economies of scale and learning as cumulative output increases has been termed the **experience curve**. The Boston Consulting Group has estimated that costs are reduced by approximately 15–20 per cent on average each time cumulative output doubles. This suggests that firms with greater market share will have a cost advantage through the experience curve effect, assuming all companies are operating on the same curve. However, a move towards a new manufacturing technology can lower the experience curve for adopting companies, allowing them to leap-frog more traditional firms and thereby gain a cost advantage even though cumulative output may be lower.

Capacity utilization

Since fixed costs must be paid whether a plant is manufacturing at full or zero capacity, underutilization incurs costs. The effect is to push up the cost per unit for production. The impact of capacity utilization on profitability was established by the PIMS (profit impact of marketing strategy) studies, which have shown a positive association between utilization and return on investment.[32] Changes in capacity utilization can also raise costs (e.g. through the extra costs of hiring and laying off workers). Careful production planning is required for seasonal products such as ice cream and fireworks, in order to smooth output.

Linkages

These describe how the costs of activities are affected by how other activities are performed. For example, improving quality-assurance activities can reduce after-sales service costs. In the car industry, the reduction in the number of faults on a new car reduces warranty costs. The activities of suppliers and distributors also link to affect the costs of a firm.

For example, the introduction of a just-in-time delivery system by a supplier reduces the inventory costs of a firm. Distributors can influence a firm's physical distribution costs through their warehouse location decision. To exploit such linkages, though, the firm may need considerable bargaining power. In some instances it can pay a firm to increase distributor margins or pay a fee in order to exploit linkages. For example, Seiko paid its US jewellers a fee for accepting its watches for repair and sending them to Seiko; this meant that Seiko did not need local services facilities and its overall costs fell.[33]

Interrelationships

Sharing costs with other business units is another potential cost driver. Sharing the costs of R&D, transportation, marketing and purchasing lower costs. Know-how can also be shared to reduce costs by improving the efficiency of an activity. Car manufacturers share engineering platforms and components to reduce costs. For example, Volkswagen does this across its VW, Skoda, Seat and Audi cars. Care has to be taken that the cars appearing under different brand names do not appear too similar, however, or this may detract from the appeal of the more expensive marques.[34]

Integration

Both integration and de-integration can affect costs. For example, owning the means of physical distribution rather than using outside contractors could lower costs. Ownership may allow a producer to avoid suppliers or customers with sizeable bargaining power. De-integration can lower costs and raise flexibility. For example, by using many small clothing suppliers, Benetton is in a powerful position to keep costs low while maintaining a high degree of production flexibility.

Timing

Both first movers and late entrants have potential opportunities for lowering costs. First movers in a market can gain cost advantages: it is usually cheaper to establish a brand name in the minds of customers if there is no competition. Also, they have prime access to cheap or high-quality raw materials and locations. However, late entrants to a market have the opportunity to buy the latest technology and avoid high market development costs.

Policy decisions

Firms have a wide range of discretionary policy decisions that affect costs. Product width, level of service, channel decisions (e.g. small number of large dealers vs large number of small dealers), salesforce decisions (e.g. in-company salesforce vs sales agents) and wage levels are some of the decision areas that have a direct impact on costs. Southwest Airlines, for example, cuts costs by refusing to waste time assigning seats and does not wait for late arrivals. The overriding concern is to get the aeroplane in and out of the gate quickly so that it is in the air earning money. Southwest flies only one kind of aircraft, which also keeps costs down.[35]

As we saw in Digital Marketing 19.1, no-frills airline operators are using the Internet to further reduce costs. Indeed, Ryanair accepts bookings only over the Internet, thus eliminating the need for an inbound telemarketing team and allowing e-ticketing, which cuts postage and paper costs. Other sectors, such as insurance, rail, banking, package holidays and hotels, encourage transactions over the Internet in order to reduce costs. Care must be taken, however, not to reduce costs with regard to activities that have a major bearing on customer value. For example, moving from a company-employed salesforce to sales agents may not only cut costs but also destroy supplier–customer relationships. Even high-technology companies such as Nokia and Ericsson have had to make policy decisions designed to cut costs in the face of intense competition and, for some undifferentiated car companies, cost cutting has been essential for survival, as Marketing in Action 19.2 describes.

19.2 Marketing in Action

US Car Companies Trim Their Wheels

For US car giants GM and Ford, taking tough policy decisions to cut costs is not an option: it has become essential to survive. Crippled by huge healthcare and pension costs, these two long-established car manufacturers are losing out to arch-rival Toyota. GM, for example, has more than 400,000 North American retirees and $1500 of the price of each of its cars goes towards meeting that financial burden. In response GM has struck a deal with the unions that will reduce its healthcare costs by $1 billion a year. It has also embarked on a massive plant closure programme, designed to reduce overcapacity. GM is also looking to low-cost economies such as China, South Korea and eastern Europe to build cars rather than high-wage US and western European countries.

Ford is following in GM's footsteps by engaging in negotiations with the unions to reduce its healthcare liabilities, and has announced 14 US plant closures by 2012. However, as we saw in Chapter 1, becoming more efficient without an accompanying improvement in effectiveness will only delay the inevitable, a point not missed by chief executive Bill Ford, who recently remarked that restructuring the business alone will not bring success because it is not something that customers care about: 'The customer wants the latest and greatest technology. The customer wants leadership in technologies that are going to make their lives better.'

Based on: Helmore (2005);[36] Simon and MacKintosh (2005);[37] Teather (2006)[38]

Location

The location of plant and warehouses affects costs through different wage, physical distribution and energy costs. Dyson, for example, manufactures its vacuum cleaners in Malaysia to take advantage of low wage costs.[39] Car manufacturers such as VW, Peugeot, Citroën and Fiat have moved production to eastern Europe to take advantage of low costs.[40] Locating near customers can lower out-bound distributional costs, while locating near suppliers reduces in-bound distributional costs.

Institutional factors

These include government regulations, tariffs and local content rules. For example, regulations regarding the maximum size of lorries affect distribution costs.

Firms employing a cost leadership strategy will be vigilant in pruning costs. This analysis of cost drivers provides a framework for searching out new avenues for cost reduction.

REVIEW

1 The determinants of industry attractiveness

- Industry attractiveness is determined by the degree of rivalry between competitors, the threat of new entrants, the bargaining power of suppliers and buyers, and the threat of substitute products.

2 How to analyse competitors

- Competitor analysis should identify competitors (product from competitors, product substitutes, generic competitors and potential new entrants); audit their capabilities; analyse their objectives, strategic thrust and strategies; and estimate competitor response patterns.

3 The difference between differentiation and cost leadership strategies

- Differentiation strategy involves the selection of one or more choice criteria used by buyers to select suppliers/brands and uniquely positioning the supplier/brand to meet those criteria better than the competition.
- Cost leadership involves the achievement of the lowest cost position in an industry.

4 The sources of competitive advantage

- Competitive advantage can be achieved by creating a differential advantage or achieving the lowest cost position.
- Its sources are superior skills, superior resources, and core competences. A useful method of locating superior skills and resources is value chain analysis.

5 The value chain

- The value chain categorizes the value-creating activities of a firm. The value chain divides these into primary and support activities. Primary activities are in-bound physical distribution, operations, out-bound physical distribution, marketing and service. Support activities are found within all of these primary activities, and consist of purchased inputs, technology, human resource management and the firm's infrastructure.
- By examining each value-creating activity, management can search for the skills and resources (and linkages) that may form the basis for low cost or differentiated positions.

6 How to create and maintain a differential advantage

- A differential advantage is created when the customer perceives that the firm is providing value above that of the competition.
- A differential advantage can be created using any element in the marketing mix: superior product, more effective distribution, better promotion and better value for money by lower prices. A differential advantage can also be created by developing fast reaction times to changes in marketing trends.
- A differential advantage can be maintained (sustained) through the use of patent protection, strong brand personality, close relationships with customers, high service levels based on well-trained staff, innovative product upgrading, the creation of high entry barriers (e.g. R&D or promotional expenditures), and strong and distinctive internal processes that deliver the earlier points and are difficult to copy.

7 How to create and maintain a cost leadership position

- Cost leadership can be created and maintained by managing cost drivers, which are economies of scale, learning effects, capacity utilization, linkages (e.g. improvements in quality assurance can reduce after-sales service costs), interrelationships (e.g. sharing costs), integration (e.g. owning the means of distribution), timing (both first movers and late entrants can have low costs), policy decisions (e.g. controlling labour costs), location, and institutional factors (e.g. government regulations).

Key Terms

competitive scope the breadth of a company's competitive challenge, e.g. broad or narrow

competitor audit a precise analysis of competitor strengths and weaknesses, objectives and strategies

core competencies the principal distinctive capabilities possessed by a company—what it is really good at

differential advantage a clear performance differential over the competition on factors that are important to target customers

differentiation strategy the selection of one or more customer choice criteria and positioning the offering accordingly to achieve superior customer value

entry barriers barriers that act to prevent new firms from entering a market, e.g. the high level of investment required

experience curve the combined effect of economies of scale and learning as cumulative output increases

industry a group of companies that market products that are close substitutes for each other

value chain the set of a firm's activities that are conducted to design, manufacture, market, distribute, and service its products

Study Questions

1. Using Porter's 'five forces' framework, discuss why profitability in the European textile industry is lower than in book publishing.
2. For any product of your choice identify the competition using the four-layer approach discussed in this chapter.
3. Why is competitor analysis essential in today's turbulent environment? How far is it possible to predict competitor response to marketing actions?
4. Distinguish between differentiation and cost-leadership strategies. Is it possible to achieve both positions simultaneously?
5. Discuss, with examples, ways of achieving a differential advantage.
6. How can value chain analysis lead to superior corporate performance?
7. Using examples, discuss the impact of the advent of the single European market on competitive structure.
8. What are cost drivers? Should marketing management be concerned with them, or is their significance solely the prerogative of the accountant?

Online LearningCentre

When you have read this chapter
log on to the Online Learning Centre at www.mcgraw-hill.co.uk/textbooks/jobber to explore chapter-by-chapter test questions, links and further online study tools for marketing.

REFERENCES

1. Porter, M. E. (1998) *Competitive Strategy: Techniques for Analysing Industries and Competitors*, New York: Free Press.
2. Graham, G. (1997) Competition is Getting Tougher, *Financial Times*, Special Report on Danish Banking, 9 April, 2.
3. Noble, C. H., R. K. Sinha and A. Kumar (2002) Market Orientation and Alternative Strategic Orientations: A Longitudinal Assessment of Performance Implications, *Journal of Marketing* 66, October, 25–39.
4. Von Clausewitz, C. (1908) *On War*, London: Routledge & Kegan Paul.
5. Macdonald, M. (2002) *Marketing Plans*, Oxford: Butterworth Heinemann.
6. Dudley, J. W. (1990) 1992: *Strategies for the Single Market*, London: Kogan Page.
7. Ross, E. B. (1984) Making Money with Proactive Pricing, *Harvard Business Review* 62, Nov.–Dec., 145–55.
8. Leeflang, P. H. S. and D. R. Wittink (1996) Competitive Reaction versus Consumer Response: Do Managers Over-react? *International Journal of Research in Marketing* 13, 103–19.
9. Hall, W. K. (1980) Survival Strategies in a Hostile Environment, *Harvard Business Review* 58, Sept.–Oct., 75–85.
10. Porter (1998) op. cit.
11. Day, G. S. and R. Wensley (1988) Assessing Advantage: A Framework for Diagnosing Competitive Superiority, *Journal of Marketing* 52, April, 1–20.
12. Day, G. S. (1999) *Market Driven Strategy: Processes for Creating Value*, New York: Free Press.
13. Anonymous (2002) Hard to Copy, *Economist*, 2 November, 79.
14. Porter, M. E. (1998) *Competitive Advantage*, New York: Free Press.
15. For methods of calculating value in organizational markets, see Anderson, J. C. and J. A. Narus (1998) Business Marketing: Understand What Customers Value, *Harvard Business Review*, Nov.–Dec., 53–65.
16. Pickford, J. (1999) Sounds Like a Better Vision, *Financial Times*, 1 December, 15.
17. Whiteling, I. (2002) Innovate Don't Imitate, *Marketing Week*, 2 May, 41–2.
18. Gapper (2005) When High Fidelity Becomes High Fashion, *Financial Times*, 20 December, 11.
19. Anonymous (2006) Business Week Top 50 US Companies, *Business Week*, 3 April, 82–100.
20. Key Note Report (2002) *The Airline Industry*.
21. Choueke, M. (2006) Taking Change on Board, *Marketing Week*, 4 May, 28–9.
22. *BBC News* (2002) Demand growing for ethical tourism, retrieved 25 January 2002, from http://news.bbc.co.uk/hi/english/uk/newsid_1769000/1769262.stm.
23. Baker, N. (2005) Know Your Greens, *Guardian*, 10 December, 23.
24. Hammond, R. (2005) Nurturing the Eco, *Guardian*, 10 December, 24.
25. Siegle, L. (2005) Tourists Keep Heads in the Sand, *Guardian*, 25 June, 26.
26. McKie, R., A. Hill, J. Jowit and N. Mathiason (2006) Can Our Way of Living Really Save the Planet?, *Observer*, 5 March, 24–5.
27. Mills, S. (2006) Gently Does It, *Guardian*, 25 February, 21.
28. Robbins, T. (2006) What is the Real Price of Cheap Air Travel?, *Guardian*, 29 January, 26.
29. De Chernatony, L., F. Harris and F. Dall'Olmo Riley (2000) Added Value: Its Nature, Roles and Sustainability, *European Journal of Marketing* 34(1/2), 39–56.
30. Day (1999) op. cit.
31. Porter (1998) op. cit.
32. Buzzell, R. D. and B. T. Gale (1987) *The PIMS Principles*, New York: Free Press.
33. Porter (1998) op. cit.
34. MacKintosh, J. (2005) Car Design in a Generalist Market, *Financial Times*, 6 December, 20.
35. McNulty, S. (2001) Short on Frills Big on Morale, *Financial Times*, 31 October, 14.
36. Helmore, E. (2005) Can US Carmakers Get Back on the Road, *Observer*, 27 November, 3.
37. Simon, B. and J. MacKintosh (2005) Ford Warns of Plant Closures After $284m Loss, *Financial Times*, 21 October, 21.

38. Teather, D. (2006) Ford to Cut 30,000 Jobs as Losses in North America Reach $1.6 bn, *Guardian*, 26 January, 22.
39. Marsh, P. (2002) Dismay at Job Losses as Dyson Shifts Production to Malaysia, *Financial Times*, 6 February, 3.
40. Milne, R. and H. Williamson (2005) BMW Ignores Signals and Puts its Faith in Germany, *Financial Times*, 13 May, 20.

Case Thirty-seven

GENERAL MOTORS: THE DECLINE OF AN AUTOMOTIVE GIANT

General Motors (www.gm.com) is the world's largest automobile maker, and has been leading the automotive business for over 75 years. The company owns several different automobile brands, which it markets around the world. It employs over 327,000 staff and builds nearly 9 million vehicles a year, making it an industry colossus. It is seen as the heartbeat of the American manufacturing industry. For decades it was viewed as an exemplar in the effective management, strategy and organization of a modern corporation. Yet trouble is brewing for this pillar of American industry, and more problems are looming on the horizon. Low-cost competition is eroding its market share. Toyota, Nissan and Hyundai have all reported record sales in the US market. Toyota is threatening its status as the world's largest car manufacturer. Most alarmingly, the company is over $300 billion in debt, and lost a staggering $10.5 billion (£5.7 billion/€7.98 billion) in 2005. Sales within its North American division have fallen by 25.9 per cent, with the pick-up truck market plummeting. The company has some fundamental problems that it needs to address in order to redesign its strategy.

General Motors has a huge product portfolio, and sells cars in nearly every single market. Under its 10 different car brands it manufactures 89 different car models. The company has a truly international manufacturing presence, with 11 assembly plants in Europe, 3 in Asia, 8 in South America, and 29 in North America. The company has set up a number of manufacturing centres in low-cost countries such as Mexico, India, South Africa and China. In addition, it has grown through a series of acquisitions and alliances, which it is hoped will strengthen its brand portfolio even further. In 2000, GM gained 100 per cent control over Swedish luxury car maker Saab. It has several joint ventures, such as that with Chinese car maker Shanghai Automotive Industry Corporation to build a family car for the Chinese market. In 2002, it took over troubled South Korean car maker Daewoo. This has proved to be one of GM's remarkable success stories. Now the firm produces low-cost cars under the Chevrolet brand in 140 different international markets, using low-cost manufacturing bases. The company dropped the Daewoo brand in 2004, in favour of the Chevrolet name, with the aim of turning it into a global brand.

It is attempting to strengthen its international presence by focusing on growth areas such as China, moving it away from its over-reliance on the North American market. A synopsis of GM's 10 main automotive brands is given in Table C37.1. The company uses these different brands to target different segments of the market in different countries. In America, its uses eight different car brands (Chevrolet, GMC, Pontiac, Buick, Cadillac, Saturn, Saab and Hummer), while in Europe it sells Opel/Vauxhall, Saab and Chevrolet.

One of the biggest difficulties for the GM stable of car brands is the lack of distinction between the various car marques. Car buyers view many of the models launched by GM as very similar to other cars in its range. Several industry analysts have suggested that GM adopt a 'euthanasia' policy on several of its underperforming brands, in an effort to quell costs and create a stronger brand proposition. They argue that the cars sold under the various brands confuse customers, and that better returns could be yielded by a coordinated branding strategy that communicates the true brand essence of each of the brands. For example, you can buy a similar saloon car under the Pontiac, Buick, Saturn and Chevrolet brand names with little or no discernible differences. GM suffers from the curse of sameness. Other companies have developed stronger reputations on a smaller repertoire of vehicles. Originally each of the GM brands had a strong distinctive image, with various brands focusing on different tiers of the market. For instance, Chevrolet focused on the value end,

Table C37.1 General Motors' main automotive brands

Chevrolet	Pontiac	Saab	Opel/ Vauxhall	GMC
The Chevrolet brand is the third biggest car brand in the world and GM's most important brand. It has offerings in nearly every sector of market. Focuses strongly in the SUV sector of the market.	Pontiac is a mid-level brand, aimed typically at a young market. Focuses on projecting an image of performance, sportiness and youthfulness. Available only in North America. Sells roadsters, saloons and SUVs.	Bought Swedish luxury car maker to boost its presence in that sector. Focuses on premium market, with sporty designs. Small niche brand.	Uses the Vauxhall brand for UK. Wide range of cars and vans in product range. Sells approx. 1.6 million vehicles a year. Its market share has declined to 7.6 per cent.	It focuses on producing SUVs, pick-up trucks and a range of commercial vehicles. Formerly known as GMC Truck. Sales are falling sharply, due to high oil prices.
Buick	**Cadillac**	**GM Daewoo**	**Hummer**	**Saturn**
A mid-tier brand, with several luxury saloon cars and SUV offerings. Criticized for lacking distinction and rationalizing its current car model portfolio. Focuses on safety, quality and premium interiors at attainable prices. Brand is huge success in China.	The luxury car brand in the GM stable. Sales rose 23 per cent for the revitalized car brand. The quintessential luxury American car brand, with an emphasis on luxury, comfort, performance, and technology.	Formerly South Korean Daewoo brand. GM now sells this brand in Asian and European markets under the Chevrolet brand. Focused on small and medium-sized cars that represent value for money. Changed to Chevrolet brand in January 2005.	The former military vehicle jeep has been transformed into a highly popular and ridiculously expensive 4 × 4 vehicle. Launched in 1999, it has earned a cool cachet. Sold only 630 in Europe.	Created Saturn brand in 1990 in response to low-cost Japanese imports in the subcompact sector, using plastic body styling. Saturn is now repositioning in several different sectors such as saloons, SUVs, roadsters and minivans.

while Cadillac focused on the premium end of the market. Now those clear distinctions are blurred. It has culled its product line in the past in an effort to rationalize its product portfolio: it scrapped the Oldsmobile brand in 2000. This famous US car brand suffered a perennial decline in its revenue, due to a poor product offering and the brand's lack of differentiation. GM has continually stated that it is determined to keep all its brands intact, however. Table C37.2 shows GM's global vehicle sales in 2005.

Mounting troubles

The company has been prone to difficulties throughout its history. It managed to stave off bankruptcy by just 40 minutes in 1992 during a credit crunch. During that turbulent period it bounced back by slashing 21 plants and cutting 70,000 jobs, eliminating corporate bureaucracy and improving productivity and quality. GM is heavily reliant on the North American market, where most of it problems reside. Excess capacity, diminishing margins, a rigid sales channel structure, confusing brand propositions, falling market share, labour problems and exorbitant legacy costs, all have made a serious impact. Over 57 per cent of its sales come from North America, making it very susceptible to market shocks within the US market (see Figure C37.1).

During recent years the firm has focused on churning out gas-guzzling SUVs (large sports utility vehicles) and pick-up trucks, diverting its attention from normal saloon cars. These vehicles were much sought after at the time by the market and yielded higher margins. The company lost sight of developing a solid saloon car range, whereas foreign competitors developed strong reputations in this sector. In the wake of rising oil prices, demand for these expensive-to-run SUVs has slumped, and consumers have turned to more fuel-efficient cars. With so much of GM's portfolio focused on large cars, it has been particularly

Table C37.2 GM Global vehicle sales, 2005

	Total market sales*	Total GM sales*	GM market share*
North America	20,542	5,246	25.5
Europe	21,050	1,983	9.4
Asia-Pacific	18,240	1,064	5.8
South America	2,790	632	22.6
Mid-East/Africa	2,189	249	11.4
Total Global	64,811	9,174	14.3

* Sales in thousand units, shares in %, rounded and preliminary figures.
Source: GM Europe, Facts & Figures (2006).

Figure C37.1 Market sales

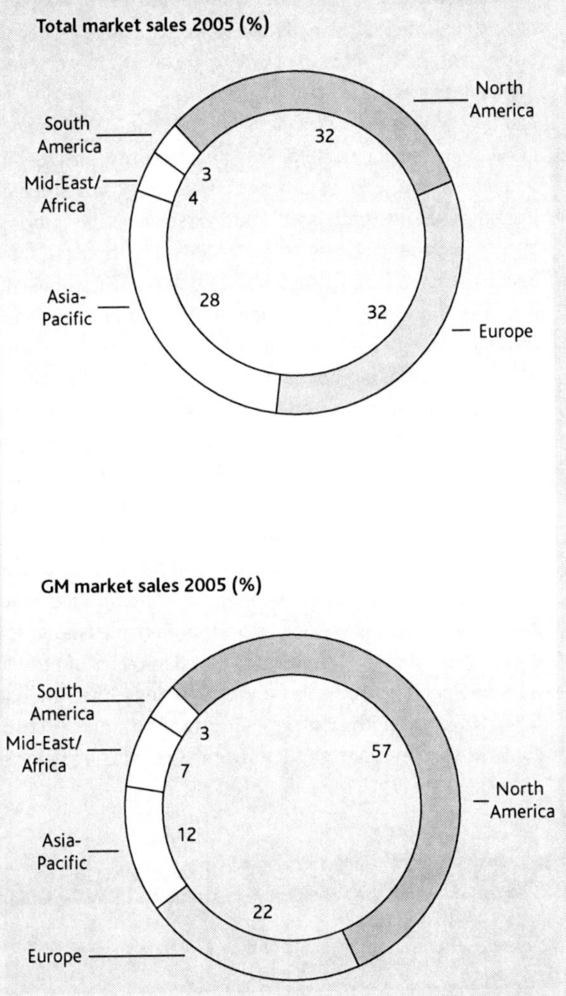

Source: GM Europe—Facts & Figures 2006

susceptible to rising petrol prices. While companies like Toyota and Honda developed environmentally friendly petrol/electric hybrid cars such as the Toyota Prius, GM focused on hydrogen-powered technology as the future for the car industry. However, this technology is years from providing a viable alternative, leaving GM without any foothold in this sector.

Its US market share is continuing to slide too. Where it once garnered 41 per cent of the market in 1985, it now accounts for only 23 per cent. In an effort to stave off the decline, the company has deployed an aggressive price-discounting strategy, which has devalued many of its venerable brands. The company on average offers cash rebates of nearly $1500 per vehicle off the ticket price. Some Buick models sell with 20 per cent discounts off the ticket price. It recently offered its cars at 'employee discount for everyone'. Sales drop when a promotion ends as consumers wait for the next rebate or promotional offer. The average price of a GM car is $18,900, which has remained static for several years. The company hopes to shift away from price promotions, and focus on building brands, through lower advertised prices, more advertising expenditure and extra equipment as standard.

General Motors is much derided in the business press as the 'world's biggest healthcare provider', rather than the 'world's biggest car manufacturer'. To put it into perspective, the firm's healthcare costs add nearly $1500 to the cost of each new GM vehicle produced. This is seen as totally untenable for the company. GM is severely curtailed by the legacy costs of former employees. Each GM worker must now produce enough profit to provide for the future healthcare of 2.5 former GM workers. The company has to spend a massive $61.5 billion on healthcare for its past and current employees. This commitment could rise even further, with the spiralling costs associated with the American healthcare system. This legacy of fixed costs contributes nothing to the future well-being of the company.

Key to GM's future survival is the efficiency and effectiveness of its manufacturing capabilities. GM factories have won several awards for quality processes. However, this is not reflected in the market, where consumers have poor quality perceptions toward GM brands. Continued improvement in its manufacturing capabilities is vital, focusing on quality, efficiency and costs. For instance, it takes 34 hours to build a typical GM car, while at Toyota it takes 28. The company has only recently focused on harmonizing production, and sharing parts and car platforms. With falling sales, GM has closed several plants, which is incurring the wrath of its unions. Trades unions are worried about the increasing concessions workers have had to make to stem the company's losses, including redundancies, reduced compensation and amendments to their own healthcare provisions. Strikes potentially loom. Also its main supplier of automotive parts, Delphi (spun off from GM in 1999), is in severe financial difficulty as well, which could have dangerous repercussions for GM's supply chain.

GM has been criticized for launching numerous new models under different brands, then subsequently ditching them if they are not proven to be a stellar success, creating huge levels of product churn. This has required substantial investment in terms of marketing expenditure, because of the need to constantly boost brand recognition for these new brands. Other car makers have several cornerstone car marques, which they frequently update with the latest technology and revamp with subtle stylistic changes. GM has increased the level of new product launches to unprecedented levels, placing an emphasis on getting newer models out on to the market very quickly. In addition, GM is seen as having too many dealers: it has five times more than Toyota and dealer margins have slipped to 1.6 per cent.

The turnaround strategy

The group has launched several initiatives in order to reverse its declining fortunes, namely reducing exorbitant fixed costs, maximizing manufacturing capacity and revitalizing a weak product offering through improved R&D. The company is aiming to reduce capacity by 1 million units to 4.2 million cars. Manufacturing plants that are not operating at full capacity really hurt the business, especially in high-cost manufacturing countries. At present GM factories are operating at about 85 per cent of their manufacturing capacity. Previously the company had allowed autonomous R&D within divisions, but now the firm is seeking to leverage engineering expertise across its global operations. This, it is hoped, will improve design, reduce costs and avoid the fruitless duplication of activities. It is spending nearly $8 billion on R&D every year, which equates to approximately 5 per cent of its revenue. It also hopes to eliminate lookalike products from its portfolio.

It is considering selling off its highly profitable financing division, GMAC. This financing arm provides commercial, residential and automotive finance packages in over 40 countries. The firm has sold equity stakes in several businesses. GM is now attempting to amalgamate several brands into one sales channel. For instance, in the USA, it is creating dealerships where Pontiac, Buick and GMC are sold under the same dealership. Similarly, in Europe, it is selling Vauxhall and Chevrolet (formerly Daewoo) car marques in the same dealer premises, creating strong sales propositions. Continued efforts to alter GM sales channels have been restricted due to franchised dealers' rights under US law. The only way to change a dealership contract is through paying expensive compensation to the franchisee. Also the company hopes to offer lower ticket prices, moving away from the endless stream of price promotions.

GM now has mounting debts and is rapidly losing its cash stockpile. The company has recently announced that it plans to eliminate over 30,000 jobs in the USA, with more to come. In addition, the firm is closing 12 of its North American plants. Alliances, mergers and bankruptcy remain distinct possibilities for General Motors. The firm has made indications that it is seeking to partner Renault-Nissan. It is hoped that synergies could be achieved in terms of production, engineering, and sales and marketing—the rationale being 'the bigger the better'—and that the newer entity could squeeze out better prices from suppliers due to larger orders.

Questions

1. Using Porter's 'five forces' framework, discuss the competitiveness of the global automobile market.
2. Identify and discuss the weaknesses associated with General Motors' marketing strategy.
3. What are GM's sources of competitive advantage? Discuss how it could achieve a differential advantage over competitors.

This case was written by Conor Carroll, Lecturer in Marketing, University of Limerick. Copyright © Conor Carroll (2006). The material in the case has been drawn from a variety of published sources and research reports.

Case Thirty-eight

THE GOING GETS TOUGH FOR WAL-MART AND ASDA

Ad Insight

In the spring of 1999, the shareholders of Kingfisher, the UK retail group, were smiling. They had just seen their share price rocket from around £5 (€7.2) to over £9 (€13) in less than a year with the news that Kingfisher was to take over Asda, the UK supermarket chain. Geoffrey Mulcahy, who headed Kingfisher, saw the move as another step towards his ambition of being a 'world-class retailer', where the efficiencies of buying merchandise in massive quantities, managing large stores, and achieving lower prices and higher sales turnover would reap further benefits for shareholders, employees and customers alike.

Mulcahy, the normally taciturn former Harvard MBA (he even calls his 40-foot boat *No Comment*), had turned around the ailing Woolworth's chain by selling off its city sites to release cash that could be used for investment. He discovered that Woolworth's owned a small do-it-yourself chain called B&Q. By building large retail 'sheds' backed up by service provided by ex-plumbers, electricians and the like, an advertising campaign based on the tag-line 'You can do it when you B&Q it!', and low prices, the chain became a success story of the 1990s, beating off me-too rivals such as Do It All, Sainsbury's Homebase and US invaders such as Texas. By adding the electrical goods retailer Comet and the health and beauty products chain Superdrug, Kingfisher was on the road to fulfilling Mulcahy's dream—taking over Asda was the next step. Sadly, his vision was to be shattered by Wal-Mart, the US predator that wanted to expand its European presence, which had already begun by the acquisition of the German warehouse chain Wertkauf.

Mulcahy was well aware that Wal-Mart was lurking in the wings, but all the talk was that the US retailer was cool about entering the UK market where retail competition was intense and planning restrictions made the likelihood of opening the kind of vast Supercentres it operates in the USA unlikely. All that changed one June Monday morning when he received a 7 am telephone call from Archie Norman, Asda's chief executive, to say that he had 'a bit of a problem'. The 'problem' was that Asda had agreed a deal with Wal-Mart.

Wal-Mart USA

Enter any Wal-Mart store in the USA and consumers are struck by the sheer scale of the operation. These are stores of over 200,000 square feet in which seven UK superstores could be accommodated. Next come the 'greeters', who welcome customers into the stores, give them their card in case they need help and put a smiley sticker on them. Then come the prices where, for example, a cotton T-shirt that would sell for the equivalent of around $15 (£9.40/€13.5) in a UK department store sells for $1 (£0.60/€0.90) in Wal-Mart. The choice of products is wide ranging, from clothes via groceries and pharmaceuticals to electrical goods. Stores are well organized with the right goods always available, kept neat and clean in appearance and with goods helpfully displayed.

At the heart of the Wal-Mart operation are its systems and information technology: 1000 information technologists run a 24-terabyte database; its information collection, which comprises up to 65 million transactions (by item, time, price and store), drives most aspects of its business. Within 90 minutes of an item being sold,

Wal-Mart's distribution centres are organizing its replacement. Distribution is facilitated by state-of-the-art delivery tracking systems. So effective is the system that when a flu epidemic hit the USA, Wal-Mart followed its spread by monitoring flu remedy sales in its stores. It then predicted its movement from east to west so that Wal-Mart stores were adequately stocked in time for the rise in demand.

Wal-Mart also uses real-time information systems to let consumers decide what appears in its stores. The Internet is used to inform suppliers what was sold the day before. In this way, it only buys what sells.

Its relationship with its suppliers is unusual in that they are only paid when an item is sold in its stores. Not only does this help cash flow, it also ensures that the interests of manufacturer and Wal-Mart coincide. Instead of the traditional system where once the retailer had purchased stock it was essentially the retailer's problem to sell it, if the product does not sell it hurts the manufacturer's cash flow more than Wal-Mart's. Consequently, at a stroke, the supplier's and retailer's interests are focused on the same measures and rewards. There is no incentive for the supplier to try to sell Wal-Mart under-performing brands since they will suffer in the same way as the retailer if they fail to sell in the store.

Wal-Mart staff are called 'associates' and are encouraged to tell top management what they believe is wrong with their stores. They are offered share options and encouraged to put the customer first.

Wal-Mart has enjoyed phenomenal success in the USA, but the sparkle has been taken out of its recent performance by its rival Target, which has built its business by selling similar basic consumable goods like soap at low prices, but also higher-margin, design-based items such as clothing and furnishings. The problem Wal-Mart faced was that consumers were buying groceries and toiletries at its stores but not its clothing, furnishing or electronics ranges. Target was stealing customers by positioning itself as an upmarket discounter using designers such as Isaac Mizraki and stylish lifestyle advertising to attract consumers to its clothing and furnishings. Wal-Mart, by contrast, was using mundane in-store advertising focusing on low prices.

Wal-Mart's response was to commission, for the first time, a marketing research survey. Hitherto it had believed marketing research was the province of its suppliers. The survey of its customers revealed that Wal-Mart's clothing was considered dull. This led to the launch in 2005 of a more upmarket fashion brand, Metro 7, targeted at the group Wal-Mart calls 'selective shoppers'—those who buy groceries and toiletries but who previously would not have bought clothing. The new clothing range was backed by a change in advertising, including a spread in *Vogue* magazine and a move to lifestyle advertising, designed to appeal to what the retailer terms 'fashion-savvy' female customers with an urban lifestyle.

Wal-Mart has also redesigned its electronics and furnishings departments and improved the product ranges to appeal to wealthier customers. In consumer electrics, for example, it has added high-end products from Sony LCD televisions and Toshiba laptops to Apple iPods, and is backing the new ranges with aggressive advertising campaigns. Departments have been redesigned with wider aisles and lower shelves.

Wal-Mart is not without its critics, though, who claim that its success has driven stores out of business, leaving derelict, boarded-up downtown streets. Christened 'Sprawl-Mart' by its critics, it has been accused of being anti-union and causing the demise of small shopkeepers.

Wal-Mart's overseas operations

Since 1992 Wal-Mart has moved into eight countries and trounced the competition. In Canada and Mexico it is already market leader in discount retailing. In Canada it bought Woolco in 1994, quickly added outlets, and by 1997 became market leader with 45 per cent of the discount store market—a remarkable achievement. In countries such as China and Argentina it has been surprisingly successful and, in 2005, achieved international sales of over £32 billion (€45 billion).

In 1998 it entered Europe with the buying of Germany's Wertkauf warehouse chain, quickly followed by the acquisition of 74 Interspar hypermarkets. It immediately closed stores, then reopened them with price cuts on 1100 items, making them 10 per cent below competitors' prices. Wal-Mart's German operation was not a success, however, because of the presence of more aggressive discounters such as Aldi. In 2006 it admitted failure by selling its 85 stores to a local rival, Metro, at a loss of £530 million (€740 million).

Wal-Mart's entry into the UK was the next step in its move into the European market. Asda was a natural target since it shared Wal-Mart's 'everyday low prices' culture. It was mainly a grocery supermarket but also sold clothing. Its information technology systems lagged badly behind those of its UK supermarket competitors, but it has acted as 'consumer champion' by selling cosmetics and over-the-counter pharmaceuticals for cheaper prices than those charged by traditional outlets. It has also bought branded products such as jeans from abroad to sell at low prices in its stores. Wal-Mart decided to keep the Asda store name rather than rebranding it as Wal-Mart. However, in 2002 the Wal-Mart name was incorporated on carrier bags, till receipts and lorries for the first time. The phrase 'part of the Wal-Mart Family' appeared under the Asda name, with 'Wal-Mart' in the strong blue colour associated with the supermarket's US owner. Asda also changed its tag-line, 'Permanently low prices', to Wal-Mart's 'Always low prices'. Although supermarket fascias continue to carry the Asda logo only, the largest store format was renamed Asda Wal-Mart Supercentre. (Most of Asda's stores are located in the north of the UK.)

The early signs were that the acquisition was a success with sales and profits rising. A major move was to create a speciality division that operates pharmacy, optical, jewellery, photography and shoe departments. The aim was to make store space work harder (i.e. improve sales revenue and profits per square metre). Asda has also benefited from the introduction of thousands of new non-food items across a wide range of home and leisure categories. Space has been made for these extra products in existing food-dominated supermarkets by decreasing the amount of shelf space devoted to food and reducing pack sizes.

The George line of clothing has been a huge success and was expanded to include a lower-priced version of the brand called Essentially George. In 2003, two stand-alone 10,000-square-foot clothing stores were opened, branded George, in Leeds and Croydon city centres. The stores carry the complete line of George-brand men's, women's and children's clothing at prices the same as those offered in the George departments in Asda supermarkets. By 2005, the total number had risen to 10. So impressed were Wal-Mart management at the success of George clothing that they introduced the range in their US stores.

Besides expanding its product lines, Asda has also focused on cutting prices, aided by its inclusion in the Wal-Mart stable, which brings it enormous buying power. For example, since the take-over, it has made 60 per cent savings on fabrics and 15 per cent on buttons. This has meant price reductions on such clothing items as jeans, ladies' tailored trousers, skirts, silk ties and baby pyjamas. In four years, the price of George jeans has fallen from £15 (€21.6) to £6 (€8.6).

Change of fortunes

Asda's initial success was reflected in its overtaking of Sainsbury's to become the UK's number two supermarket chain behind Tesco in 2004. Since then, however, Asda's fortunes have changed. Faced with a rampant Tesco and a resurgent Sainsbury's, the company lost market share. When Wal-Mart bought Asda the intention was to build huge US-style hypermarkets. Unfortunately, shortly after the acquisition, UK planning rules tightened to prevent out-of-town shopping developments. Tesco, and to a lesser extent Sainsbury's, entered the smaller store market, opening outlets in town and city centres and petrol stations where planning restrictions were much less severe. Asda kept its focus on large supermarkets.

In 2005, Andy Bond was promoted internally to replace Tony de Nunzio, who left to join Dutch non-food retailer Vendex. Faced with a dominant Tesco with over 30 per cent market share, and a more aggressive Sainsbury's under the leadership of Justin King, Bond faced an enormous challenge. His actions have been as follows.

- Remove 1400 managers: 200 jobs at Asda's head office and 1200 junior managerial positions in stores were cut. Part of the savings were invested in front-line customer service staff in stores.
- Open 10 more Asda Living stores to bring the total to 15 and to develop the Living range online: there are non-food stores offering such products as furnishings, electrical goods, DVDs and beauty items.
- Open two more George fashion stores, taking the total to 12.
- Open over 100 Asda Essentials stores: these are a small store format to challenge Tesco Express and Sainsbury's Local convenience stores. They stock a limited range of products, including fresh food, and are based on the French Leader Price chain, which sells fresh fruit, vegetables, meat, grocery products and cosmetics. The stores sell almost entirely Asda own-label products. At the same time, Tesco was planning to double the number of its 600 convenience stores by 2010.
- Improve the product line: healthier food sourced from local producers, and selling new products online such as contact lenses and airline tickets.
- Urge the Office of Fair Trading to open an inquiry into Tesco's landbank of 185 development sites with a view to preventing it buying land and opening stores close to existing outlets without reference to the OFT. But if an existing store was sold by one supermarket chain to another, the deal had to be scrutinized by the competition authority.

References

Based on: Merrilees, B. and D. Miller (1999) Defensive Segmentation Against a Market Spoiler Rival, *Proceedings of the Academy of Marketing Conference*, Stirling, July, 1–10; Mitchell, A. (1999) Wal-Mart Arrival Heralds Change for UK Marketers, *Marketing Week*, 24 June, 42–3; Voyle, S. (2000) Wal-Mart Expands Asda in Drive for Market Share, *Financial Times*, 10 January, 21; Anonymous (2002) Asda Reaps

Reward for International Division, *DSN Retailing Today*, 25 February, 1; Bowers, S. (2003) Hunter to Raise the Stakes, *Guardian*, 6 January, 17; Teather, D. (2003) Asda's £360m Plan Will Create 3,900 Jobs, *Guardian*, 19 February, 23; Troy, M. (2003) 'Buy' George! Wal-Mart's Asda Takes Fashion to UK's High Street, *DSN Retailing Today*, 23 June, 1; Finch, J. (2005) Asda to Open Hundreds of Discount Shops, *Guardian*, 10 December, 22; Finch, J. (2005) Asda Cuts 1400 Managers in Fight to Stay No 2 Grocer, *Guardian*, 6 July, 16; Birchall, J. (2005) What Wal-Mart Women Really Want, *Financial Times*, 10 October, 11; Birchall, J. (2005) Supermarket Sweep, *Financial Times*, 10 November, 17; Anonymous (2006) Wal-Mart Admits Defeat in Germany and Sells Stores, *Guardian*, 24 July, 32.

Questions

1. What are Wal-Mart's sources of competitive advantage? How do these sources manifest themselves in creating competitive advantage for Wal-Mart customers?
2. Does Wal-Mart's acquisition of Asda make competitive sense?
3. Why have Asda's fortunes worsened since 2004?
4. Assess the actions taken by Andy Bond to revive Asda.

This case was prepared by David Jobber, Professor of Marketing, University of Bradford.

Chapter 11

The Principles of Market Forces

CHAPTER OBJECTIVES

This chapter will explain:

- the concept of market structure and the range of structures from atomistic competition to pure monopoly
- the principles of atomistic competition as basic building blocks for understanding a firm's pricing and output decisions
- the interaction of demand and supply leading to price determination
- elasticity of demand and supply

11.1 Introduction

'Market forces' is a widely used term that implies some kind of external pressure on an organization, acting as a constraint (and an opportunity) for the goods and services that it buys and sells. A company may have to accept a lower price for the goods it sells because 'market forces' don't allow it to sell its goods at the higher price that it seeks. Similarly, a company may have to pay higher wages to its employees because market forces in the labour market have put upward pressure on wage rates, and if the company is going to be able to employ the staff that it seeks, it will have to pay market rates of pay.

Market forces are a crucial fact of life to most organizations operating in a commercial environment. They occur where companies seek to attract customers from rival companies by offering better products and/or lower prices. Market forces also have an effect in the acquisition of resources, and where these are scarce relative to the demand for them, rival buyers will bid up their price. However, competition in customer and resource markets can be complex and a full understanding of each market is needed if the effects of market forces on an organization are to be fully appreciated. This chapter begins by reviewing the fundamental building blocks on which markets are based. However, all **markets** are not equally aggressive in the way in which 'market forces' operate, and in many cases, an observer would be forgiven for doubting the existence of a market. So before we begin our microeconomic investigation of how markets operate in practice, we will review different types of market structure, to illustrate the very limited circumstances in which market forces are fully effective. In Chapter 12, we will explore the nature of imperfections to markets, which limit the effects of market forces that are described in this chapter.

11.1.1 Market structure

The market conditions facing suppliers of goods and services vary considerably. Customers of water supply companies may feel they are being exploited with high prices and poor service levels by companies that know that their customers have little choice of supplier. On the other hand, customers are constantly wooed by numerous insurance companies that are all trying to sell basically similar products in a market that provides consumers with a lot of choice. Differences in the characteristics and composition of buyers and sellers define the structure of a market.

The term **market structure** is used to describe:

- the number of buyers and sellers operating in a market
- the extent to which the market is concentrated in the hands of a small number of buyers and/or sellers
- the degree of collusion or competition between buyers and/or sellers.

An understanding of market structure is important to businesses, not only to understand the consequences of their own actions but also the behaviour of other firms operating in a market.

Market structures range from the theoretical extremes of perfect competition to pure monopoly. In practice, examples of the extremes are rare and most analysis therefore focuses on levels of market imperfection between the two extremes (Figure 11.1).

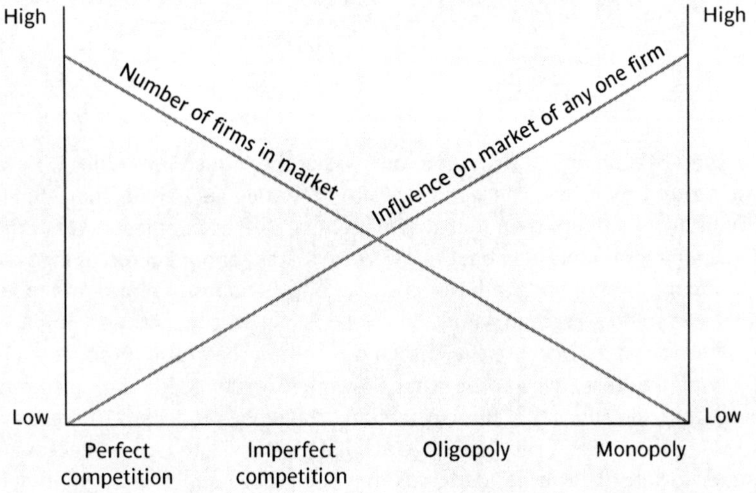

Figure 11.1 A continuum of market structures

It is easy to take a static view of market structure but, in reality, markets are often in transition. This has been most apparent in the economies of the former Soviet bloc countries, which until the late 1980s allocated resources according to their governments' central planning processes. Officially, market forces had little role to play, although they often existed informally, especially in the more liberal Soviet bloc countries such as Hungary. The collapse of communism brought about a major change in the way that resources were allocated in the national economy, with the interaction of supply and demand leading to the price mechanism being used as a means of allocating scarce resources, rather than government bureaucrats. In many countries that have emerged from communism, the transition to market forces has not been an easy one (see 'Thinking around the subject' on p. 372).

11.2 The characteristics of very competitive markets

Highly competitive market structures are often referred to as atomistic (or 'perfect') competition. This is the simplest type of market structure to understand and corresponds very much with most people's idea of what a very competitive market should be like. Government policy makers often pursue a vision of this as the ideal market structure. Although perfectly competitive markets in their theoretical extreme are rarely found in practice, a sound understanding of the way they work is essential for understanding competitive market pressures in general.

Perfectly competitive markets are attributed with the following key characteristics.

- There are a large number of small producers supplying to the market, each with similar cost structures and each producing an identical product.
- There are also a large number of buyers in the market, each responsible for purchasing only a small percentage of total output.

Thinking around the subject: From the queues of Communism to the high prices of market forces?

By most measures of economic activity, the countries of the former Soviet bloc were lagging well behind most Western countries. The level of wealth generated per person, indicated by GDP per head, was typically much less than half that of comparable economies in Western Europe. It seemed that central government bureaucrats were no match for market forces in stimulating the economy to produce more goods at lower cost. So long as factories and farms produced their quota of output, everybody seemed happy. The workers had little incentive to produce more output, and at a better quality, because they would not be rewarded for it. Producers simply didn't undertake any market research in order that they might make goods that customers actually wanted, rather than the goods that bureaucrats said should be produced. The result of this centralized planning process was a shortage of goods that people wanted, with 'black markets' often arising in order to satisfy customer demands that could not be met through an open market. Stories abounded of raw materials and agricultural produce left to rot on farms, either because there was little incentive to get them to consumers, or because the farms had simply grown too much of the produce that customers didn't want to buy.

The dismantling of Communist government planning processes and the introduction of market forces came as a shock to most people of Eastern Europe – both as producers and consumers. Producers were at first slow to learn the principles of marketing and the importance of understanding customers' needs. But, slowly, producers began to pick up signals from the market and started developing new and improved goods and services. In came modern bars and cafes to replace the previous dull outlets. Slowly, goods manufactured by Western companies began to appear in East European markets and were highly prized by those consumers who could afford them. The presence of Western competitors now gave manufacturers new standards they had to compete against if they were to stay in business.

For consumers, centralized planning had previously meant allocation of resources by queuing. It was not uncommon, for example, to have to wait 20 years from ordering for a new Lada car to be delivered to the buyer. A ten-year wait for a new washing machine was typical for many consumer durables. With the introduction of market forces, prices rather than queuing became the method for allocating scarce resources. So the prices of most goods and services shot up to a level way beyond that most consumers could afford. In any free-market economy, limited supply and strong demand for goods and services can only lead to higher prices. The paradox was that consumers now had much more freedom and choice in the marketplace but, at market-determined prices, the typical consumer did not have anywhere near enough money to pay for the goods and services that were now available. During the transition period, incomes struggled to keep up as factory closures led to rising unemployment. Meanwhile, inflation rates soared, and in many countries prices more than doubled each year.

A market-based economy was further frustrated by the presence in many countries of mafia-style groups that sought to control some aspect of the newly liberated markets. There were stories of gangsters and former Communist Party members using coercion to control the supply of many essential goods and services through the distribution chain. As an example, tomatoes grown in Bulgaria were being sold in shops in the country's capital, Sofia, for a higher price than those same tomatoes sold in export markets such as Britain and France. Retailing and distribution should have become a competitive business, helping to force down prices, but it seemed that the simple transition to a market-based economy was impeded by the presence of mafia-type groups. In the turmoil that accompanied the transition from centralized planning to market-based mechanisms, these groups saw a window of opportunity to re-establish a form of central power that had been lost with the demise of Communism.

Competitive market forces may be a fine ideal, but this chapter and the next demonstrate how economies have a tendency to develop anti-competitive practices that undermine the power of markets to produce more output at low price.

- Both buyers and sellers are free to enter or leave the market – that is, there are no barriers to entry or exit.
- In a perfectly competitive market, there is a ready supply of information for buyers and sellers about market conditions.

Some markets come close to having these characteristics – for example:

- wholesale fruit and vegetable markets
- the 'spot' market for oil products
- stock markets, where shares are bought and sold (see Figure 11.2).

In reality, very few markets fully meet economists' criteria for perfect competition and even those markets described above have imperfections (e.g. wholesale fruit and vegetable markets are increasingly influenced by the practice of large retailers contracting directly with growers or growers' intermediaries).

Perfect competition implies that firms are price *takers* in that competitive market forces alone determine the price at which they can sell their products. If a firm cannot produce its goods or services as efficiently as its competitors, it will lose profits and eventually go out of business. Customers are protected from exploitative high prices, because as long as selling a product remains profitable, companies will be tempted into the market to satisfy customers' requirements, thereby putting downward pressure on prices. Eventually, competition between firms will result in excessive profits being eliminated so that an equilibrium is achieved where loss-making firms have left the market and the market is not sufficiently attractive to bring new firms into it.

Probably the most important reason for studying perfect competition is that it focuses attention on the basic building blocks of competition: demand, supply and price determination.

11.2.1 Demand

Demand refers to the quantity of a product that consumers are willing and able to buy at a specific price over a given period of time. In economic analysis, demand is measured not simply in terms of what people would like to buy – after all, most people would probably want to buy

BANKS				↓ 5.17%		
1153½	222	Allied Irish	222	−27	27.7	1.5
821½	93¾	Anglo Irish	93¾	−8⅞	17.1	0.9
129½	97	BGI Endow Fd II ..	101½	...	–	–
790½	73¾	Bank of Ireland .	73¾	−21½	34.9	0.9
569	154	**Barclays**	154	−5	21.4	3.0
303	20	Bradford & Bing #♦ .	20	...	71.5	0.7
833	60	**HBOS**	74½	−12	36.4	0.9
927¾	663	**HSBC**	708¾	−10¼	6.5	10.6
504½	149	**Lloyds TSB**	149	−17	21.8	3.7
490	44¾	**Ryl Bk Scot** ...	44¾	−6¼	44.2	1.2
1134	507	Santander	507	−45½	10.4	5.0
1960	680	**Standard Chart**	722	−54½	5.3	6.8
BEVERAGES				↓ 0.68%		
354	165½	Britvic♦	221½	−½	5.2	10.3
1116	794	**Diageo**	910½	−7½	3.7	15.5
1448	799½	**SABMiller**	953½	−4½	4.1	10.4
CHEMICALS				↓ 1.77%		
715	451¾	Croda♦	484	−3¾	3.5	11.3
135	75	Delta Gp	78	−2	6.6	5.3
223½	18¾	Dyson	18¾	−¾	22.1	1.5
2093	763	**Johnson Mat**	763	−9½	4.7	8.6
297	191½	Treatt	191½	−2	5.6	9.9
829	508	Victrex♦	529	−27	3.2	12.2
205	80½	Yule Catto	82¼	−1¼	11.6	4.7
220	12	Uniq	12	−1¼	–	21.9
1927	1274	**Unilever**	1424	−60	3.7	11.8
1873	1311¼	Unilever N.V. ..	1507¾	−68⅞	–	–
GAS & WATER				↓ 1.63%		
371½	265	**Centrica**	301	−6¾	4.4	15.1
370	246½	Northumbrian♦	299¼	−5¾	4.0	11.4
694½	479¾	Pennon Gp♦ .	515	−11½	3.8	14.3
1582	1056	**Severn Trent** .	1276	+17	5.2	14.1
777½	547½	**Utd Utilities**	682	−12	6.6	14.9
GENERAL FINANCIAL				↓ 2.22%		
180	83¼	Aberdeen Asset♦	92½	+1½	6.3	7.2
126	14	Accident Exch ..	14	−6¾	12.1	1.3
316¼	125	Ashmore♦	125	−¾	9.5	6.0
175¾	95	Brewin Dolphin .	99¼	+¼	7.1	6.7
310½	23½	Cattles♦	46½	−1	41.3	1.7
316½	168	Charles Stanley	177½	−1½	4.8	8.6
995	460	Close Bros♦ .	578	−5	6.7	8.7
184¼	40½	Collins Stewart .	40½	−5	16.5	1.9
276½	162½	Equity Spec Sits ..	237½	...	–	5.2
212	31	F & C Asset Man♦ ..	54	−3	10.5	5.5
68½	32½	Guinness Peat .	36½	+1	2.6	8.4
220	132	Hargreaves Lans♦ ..	154¾	−2¾	3.5	17.3
401¼	82¼	Helphire	90	−2¾	13.3	3.8
155¼	50	Henderson Gp♦ .	52½	−1	11.8	4.3
728	238	**ICAP**	251½	+13½	6.6	7.6
1821	805½	ICG Group♦ .	805½	−79½	7.3	4.1
415	222¼	IG Group♦	256¼	−7¼	4.5	12.8

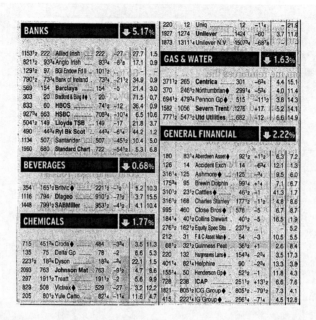

Figure 11.2 Stock markets come close to satisfying the requirements of perfect competition, with large numbers of people buying and selling shares, resulting in daily movement in share prices. Regulators of stock markets go to great lengths to preserve the competitiveness of their markets – for example, by requiring full disclosure by firms of information that might affect their share price, and punishing the misuse of 'insider' information, which can give some people an unfair advantage. Where a buyer builds up a significant holding of a company's shares, stock market rules may require this fact to be disclosed.

expensive holidays and cars. Instead, demand refers to how many people are actually *able and willing* to buy a product at a given price, and given a set of assumptions about the product and the environment in which it is being offered. Demand is also expressed in terms of a specified time period – for example, so many units per day.

In general, as the price of a product falls, so the demand (as defined above) can be expected to rise. Likewise, as the price rises, demand could be expected to fall. This relationship can be plotted on a simple graph. In Figure 11.3, a demand curve for medium-fat Cheddar cheese is shown by the line D1. This relates any given price, shown on the vertical axis, to the volume of demand, which is shown on the horizontal axis. Therefore, at a price of £8.00 per kg, demand is 10,000 units per period within a given area, while, at a price of £4.00, the demand rises to 12,000 units.

It is important to note that the demand curve drawn here refers to total market demand from all consumers and is not simply measuring demand for one producer's output. The importance of this distinction will become clear later, as the implication of this is that firms have to make their price decisions based on overall market conditions.

The demand curve D1 is based on a number of assumptions. These include, for example, assumptions that the price of substitutes for cheese will not change or that consumers will not

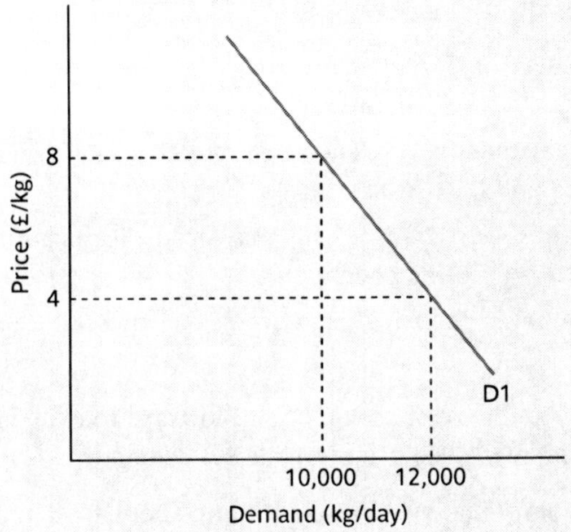

Figure 11.3 A demand curve for medium-fat Cheddar cheese

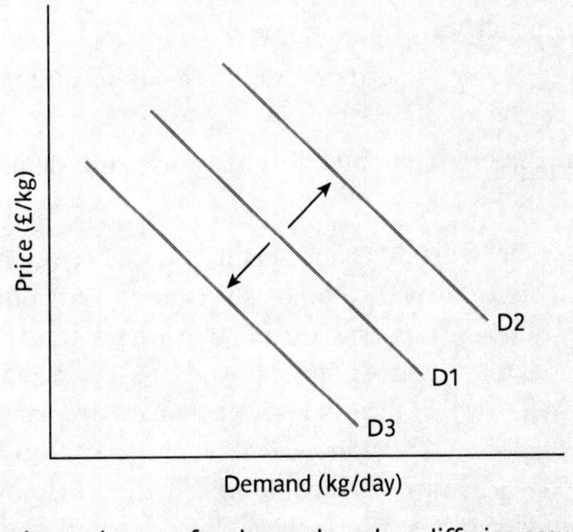

Figure 11.4 Alternative demand curves for cheese, based on differing assumptions

suddenly take a dislike to Cheddar cheese. Demand curve D1 measures the relationship between price and market demand for one given set of assumptions. When these assumptions change, a new demand curve is needed to explain a new relationship between price and quantity demanded.

In Figure 11.4, two sets of fresh assumptions have been made and new demand curves, D2 and D3, drawn based on these new sets of assumptions. For new demand curve D2, more cheese is demanded for any given price level (or, alternatively, this can be restated in terms of any given number of consumers demanding cheese being prepared to pay a higher price). There are a number of possible causes of the shift of the demand curve from D1 to D2.

- Consumers could have become wealthier, leading them to demand more of all goods, including cheese.
- The price of substitutes for Cheddar cheese (e.g. meat or other types of cheese) could have increased, thereby increasing demand for cheese.
- Demand for complementary goods (such as savoury biscuits) may increase, thereby leading to an increase in demand for Cheddar cheese.
- Consumer preferences may change. This may occur, for example, if Cheddar cheese is found to have health-promoting benefits.
- An advertising campaign for Cheddar cheese may increase demand for cheese at any given price.

Similarly, a number of possible reasons can be put forward to explain the shift from demand curve D1 to D3, where, for any given price level, less is demanded.

- Consumers could have become poorer, leading them to demand fewer of all goods, including cheese.
- The price of substitutes for Cheddar cheese (e.g. meat or other types of cheese) could have decreased, thereby making the substitutes appear more attractive and reducing demand for Cheddar cheese.
- Demand for complementary products may fall.
- Cheddar cheese may become associated with health hazards, leading to less demand at any given price.
- An advertising campaign for substitute products may shift demand away from Cheddar cheese.

The demand curves shown in Figures 11.3 and 11.4 have both been straight, but this is a simplification of reality. In fact, demand curves would usually be curved, indicating that the relationship between price and volume is not constant for all price points. There may additionally be significant discontinuities at certain price points, as where buyers in a market have psychological price barriers, above or below which their behaviour changes. In many markets, the difference between £10.00 and £9.99 may be crucial in overcoming buyers' attitudes that predispose them to regard anything over £10 as being unaffordable and anything below it as a bargain.

Actually collecting information with which to plot a demand curve poses theoretical and practical problems. The main problem relates to the cross-sectional nature of a demand curve – that is, it purports to measure the volume of demand across the ranges of price possibilities. However, this kind of information can often only be built up by a longitudinal study of the relationship between prices and volume over time. There is always the possibility that, over time, the assumptions on which demand is based have changed, in which case it is difficult to distinguish between a movement along a demand curve and a shift to a new demand curve. It is, however, sometimes possible for firms to conduct controlled cross-sectional experiments where a different price is charged in different regions and the effects on volume recorded. To be sure that this is accurately measuring the demand curve, there must be no extraneous factors in regions (such as differences in household incomes) that could partly explain differences in price/volume relationships.

The demand curves shown in Figures 11.3 and 11.4 slope downwards, indicating the intuitive fact that, as price rises, demand falls, and vice versa. While this is intuitively plausible, it is not always the case. Sometimes, the demand curve slopes upwards, indicating that, as the price of a product goes up, buyers are able and willing to buy more of the product. Classic examples of this phenomenon occur where a product becomes increasingly desirable as more people consume it. A telephone network that has only one subscriber will be of little use to the first customer, who will be unable to use a telephone to call anyone else. However, as more customers are connected, the value of the telephone network becomes greater to each individual, who is correspondingly willing to pay a higher price. This phenomenon helps to explain why large international airports can charge more than smaller regional airports for aircraft to land. As the number of possible aircraft connections increases, airlines' willingness to pay high prices for landing slots increases.

Upward-sloping demand curves can also be observed for some products sold for their 'snob' value. Examples include some designer-label clothes where high price alone can add to a product's social status. Upward-sloping demand curves can be observed over short time periods where a 'bandwagon' effect can be created by rapidly rising or falling prices. For example, in stock markets, the very fact that share prices are rising may lead many people to invest in shares.

11.2.2 Supply

Supply is defined as the amount of a product that producers are willing and able to make available to the market at a given price over a particular period of time. Like demand, it is important to note that at different prices there will be different levels of supply, reflecting the willingness and/or ability of producers to supply a product as prices change.

A simple supply curve for medium-fat Cheddar cheese is shown in Figure 11.5. The supply curve slopes upwards from left to right, indicating the intuitively plausible fact that, as market

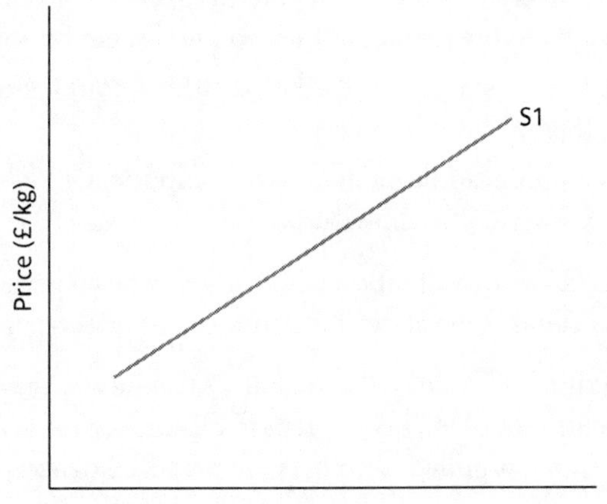

Figure 11.5 A supply curve for cheese

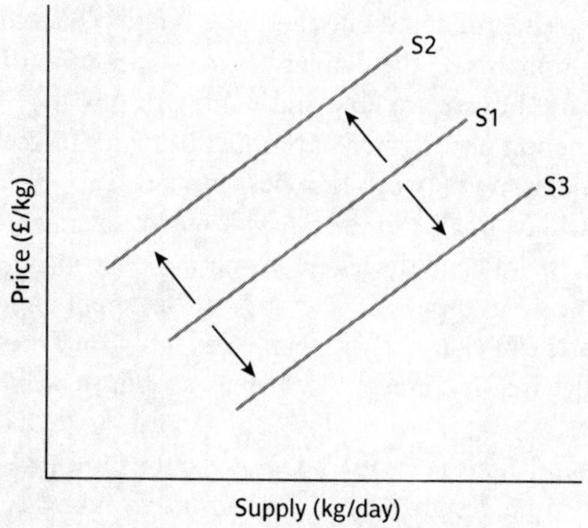

Figure 11.6 Alternative supply curves for cheese, based on differing assumptions

prices rise, more suppliers will be attracted to supply to the market. Conversely, as prices fall, marginal producers (such as those who operate relatively inefficiently) will drop out of the market, reducing the daily supply available.

It is again important to distinguish movements along a supply curve from shifts to a new supply curve. The supply curve S1 is based on a number of assumptions about the relationship between price and volume supplied. If these assumptions are broken, a new supply curve based on the new set of assumptions needs to be drawn. In Figure 11.6, two new supply curves, S2 and S3, are shown. S2 indicates a situation where, for any given price level, total supply to the market is reduced. This could come about for a number of reasons, including the following.

- Production methods could become more expensive – for example, because of more stringent health and safety regulations. Therefore, for any given price level, fewer firms will be willing to supply to the market as they will no longer be able to cover their costs.
- Extraneous factors (such as abnormally bad weather) could result in producers having difficulty in getting their produce to market.
- Governments may impose additional taxes on suppliers (e.g. extending the scope of property taxes to cover agricultural property).

The new supply curve S3 indicates a situation where, for any given price level, total supply to the market is increased. This could come about for a number of reasons, including the following.

- Changes in production technology that result in Cheddar cheese being produced more efficiently and therefore suppliers being prepared to supply more cheese at any given price (or, for any given volume supplied, suppliers are prepared to accept a lower price).
- Extraneous factors (such as favourable weather conditions) could result in a glut of produce that must be sold, and the market is therefore flooded with additional supply.
- Governments may give a subsidy for each kilogram of cheese produced by suppliers, thereby increasing their willingness to supply to the market.

11.2.3 Price determination

An examination of the demand and supply graphs indicates that they share common axes. In both cases the vertical axis refers to the price at which the product might change hands, while the horizontal axis refers to the quantity changing hands.

It is possible to redraw the original demand and supply lines (D1 and S1) on a single graph (Figure 11.7). The supply curve indicates that, the lower the price, the less cheese will be supplied to the market. Yet at these lower prices, customers are willing and able to buy a lot of cheese – more than the suppliers collectively are willing or able to supply. By following the supply curve upwards, it can be observed that suppliers are happy to supply more cheese, but at these high prices, there are few willing buyers. Therefore, at these high prices supply and demand are again out of balance.

Between the two extremes there will be a price where the interest of the two groups will coincide. This balancing of supply and demand is the foundation of the theory of market price, which holds that in any free market there is an 'equilibrium price' that matches the quantity that consumers are willing and able to buy (i.e. demand) with the quantity that producers are willing and able to produce (i.e. supply). Working out what this equilibrium price is, is called price determination.

In perfectly competitive markets, the process of achieving equilibrium happens automatically without any external regulatory intervention. Perfectly competitive markets do not need any complicated and centralized system for bringing demand and supply into balance, something that is difficult to achieve in a centrally planned economy, such as those that used to predominate in Eastern Europe.

In Figure 11.7, supply and demand are brought precisely into balance at a price of £6.00. This is the equilibrium price and, at this price, 11,000 kg of cheese per day will be bought and sold in the market. If a company wants to sell its cheese in the market, it can only do so at this price. In theory, if it charged a penny more, it would get no business because everybody else in

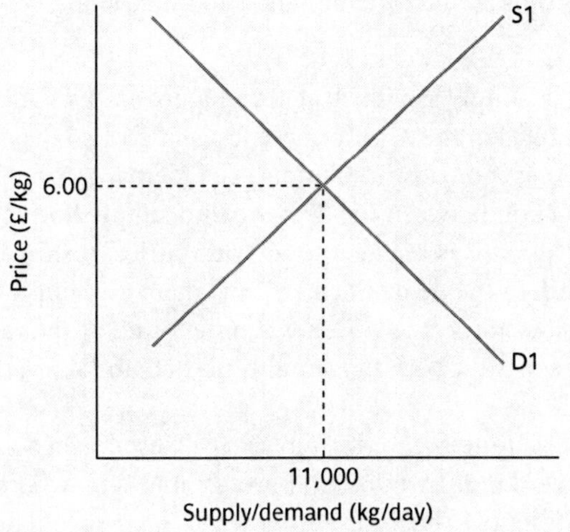

Figure 11.7 Supply and demand for cheese, showing the equilibrium market price

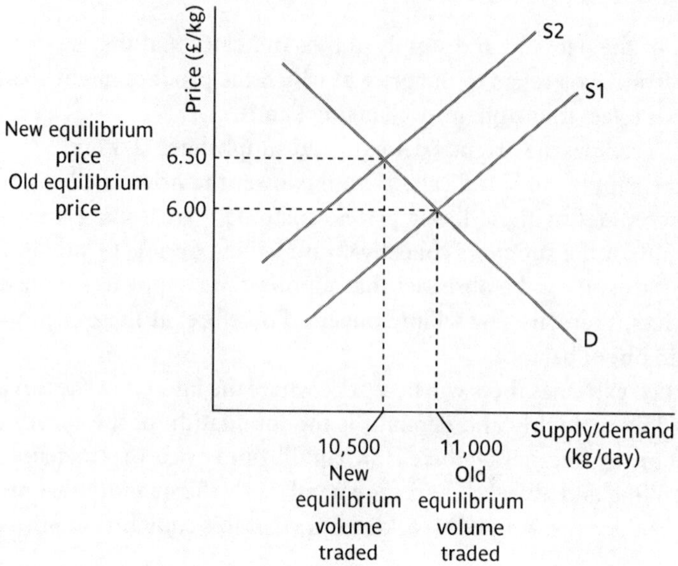

Figure 11.8 A shift in the supply curve for cheese, showing the new equilibrium market price

the market is cheaper. If it sells at a penny less, it will be swamped with demand, probably selling at a price that is below its production costs.

It is important to remember that in a perfectly competitive market, individual firms are price takers. The market alone determines the 'going rate' for their product. Changes in the equilibrium market price come about for two principal reasons:

1 assumptions about suppliers' ability or willingness to supply change, resulting in a shift to a new supply curve
2 assumptions about buyers' ability or willingness to buy change, resulting in a shift to a new demand curve.

The effects of shifts in supply are illustrated in Figure 11.8. From an equilibrium price of £6.00 and volume of 11,000 kg, the supply curve has shifted to S2 (perhaps in response to the imposition of a new tax on production). Assuming that demand conditions remain unchanged, the new point of intersection between the demand and supply lines occurs at a price of £6.50 and a volume of 10,500 kg. This is the new equilibrium price. A similar analysis can be carried out on the effects of a shift in the demand curve, but where the supply curve remains constant.

New equilibrium prices and trade volumes can be found at the intersection of the supply and demand curves. In practice, both the supply and demand curves may be changing at the same time.

The speed with which a new equilibrium price is established is dependent upon how efficiently a market is working. In pure commodity markets, where products are instantly perishable, rapid adjustments in price are possible. Where speculators are allowed to store goods, or large buyers and sellers are able to unduly influence a market, adjustment may be

Thinking around the subject: Effects of increased government regulation

Many industry sectors have complained of the burden of increased government regulation. But how are the effects reflected in demand/supply analysis? Consider the following recent examples.

- *EU Directive on Traditional Herbal Medicinal Products*: the directive requires traditional, over-the-counter herbal remedies to be made to assured standards of safety and quality. Some small-scale producers have not been able to justify the elaborate testing that the directive would require, and have therefore withdrawn from the market – their cost curve had effectively shifted upwards.
- *Financial Services and Markets Act 2000*: required all businesses selling insurance to be registered with the Financial Services Authority and to meet its criteria from January 2005. Some small travel agents, who previously sold travel insurance as an ancillary part of a holiday, decided that the cost of compliance was too great and withdrew from selling insurance.
- *Housing Act 1996*: introduced a discretionary local authority licensing scheme for houses in multiple occupation. To obtain a licence, landlords would need to satisfy a number of standards – for example, in relation to fire exits. Some landlords decided that the cost of improvements to their property could not be justified by the likely returns on their investment.
- *Disability Discrimination Act Part III – Access to Goods and Services*: from 2004, companies were required to take 'reasonable measures' to ensure equality of access to a company's goods and services for disabled people. Some organizations are reported to have closed facilities to the public rather than spend money in upgrading them.

The effects of these regulations can be assessed using supply–demand analysis. Each of these regulations may have the effect of increasing producers' costs – some producers more than others. This can be shown as an upward shift in the supply curve. How much of the increase in cost will be passed on to customers? This will depend on the elasticity of demand for the product in question. A highly elastic demand curve may result in customers buying substitute products instead – for example, buying mainstream medicines rather than herbal medicines. If the regulation applies to the whole sector, firms are likely to differ in their ability to absorb additional costs, and the least efficient producers may be forced out of the market because the market price for their product is now below their cost of production.

Try showing the effects of each of the regulations described above on a supply–demand graph, and observe what is likely to happen to the equilibrium price.

slower. The extent of changes in price and volume traded is also dependent on the elasticities of demand and supply, which are considered in the following sections.

11.3 Bartering and auctions

Bartering and auctions are traditional methods of determining prices based on interaction between buyer and seller. The practice of bartering is familiar to buyers in Eastern bazaars in which the seller opens with a high offer price and, through a process of negotiation, eventually finds out the maximum price that a buyer is prepared to pay.

Many companies have developed auction sites to sell off spare goods or surplus capacity to the highest bidder. If a company is short of cash and desperate to sell its surplus, it might be more willing to accept a low price for it, compared to a company that has a stronger bank balance and greater confidence that it will be able to sell its stock in the future. Similarly, some buyers may want to pay a relatively high price for the certainty of being able to obtain the product to their exact specification, at the right time and in the right place, whereas others would be happy to compromise on these conditions in return for a lower price. Popular auction sites such as eBay show many of the characteristics of competitive markets; eBay typically has many small-scale sellers and buyers, with no domination of the market by any individual. There is a good level of information about the organizations in the market, including ratings for sellers' previous performance. Goods and services offered for sale are classified so that a prospective buyer can immediately see what is available for any particular product category and assess whether it meets their requirements. Like any market, eBay requires rules to govern the conduct of buyers

Figure 11.9 In many town centres, clusters of restaurants offer a 'dish of the day' at roughly the same price. The meal is likely to be quite generic (such as fish and chips or chicken tikka masala) and prices for one restaurant will be established by reference to what other restaurants are charging. Restaurants may take a 'going price' from the market and design their meal offering around this price. Just what can they offer for the going rate of £6.00? Although the price of standard set menus may be very strongly determined by competitors' prices, each restaurant may nevertheless offer more specialized meals for which it faces less direct competition and therefore has greater discretion in setting its prices. Differentiation as a means of avoiding direct price competition is discussed later in this chapter.

and sellers, and the company has taken measures to ensure that the market works efficiently – for example, by reducing the possibilities for fraudulent trading.

As well as consumer sales, internet auctions have found a valuable role for business-to-business procurement (Timmins 2003). A company can put out a tender and invite suppliers to bid, following which it would choose the lowest-price bidder.

11.4 Going rate pricing

The principles of market forces are often seen in markets where competing businesses set their prices according to the 'going rate'. Here, demand may be so sensitive to price that a firm would risk losing most of its business if it charged just a small amount more than its competitors. On the other hand, charging any lower would result in immediate retaliation from competitors. Where cost levels are difficult to establish, charging a going rate can avoid the problems of trying to calculate costs. As an example, it may be difficult to calculate the cost of renting out a video film, as the figure will be very dependent upon assumptions made about the number of uses over which the initial purchase cost can be spread. It is much easier to take price decisions on the basis of the going rate among nearby competitors.

Thinking around the subject: Penny wise or pound foolish?

One of the assumptions of a competitive market is that buyers have a good awareness of prices within the market. But survey after survey has shown consumers in fact typically have a very distorted knowledge of prices, reflecting individuals' own experiences and background. For example, a survey carried out in 2005 by ICM Research asked young people to estimate the price of a range of goods and services. Two-thirds knew how much a 6GB Apple iPod Mini should cost, within just a few pounds of the actual price charged by most retailers. However, three-quarters of the people interviewed had no idea about the price of a pint of milk. An earlier survey by the telephone company BT had found knowledge of telephone prices to be particularly bad, probably reflecting the plethora of price plans that have emerged in recent years. Respondents gave the average price of a five-minute peak national call as £2.15, whereas in fact it was only 44p. Another sector with confusing price structures is railway travel. Here, respondents estimated the price of a second-class 'saver' ticket from London to Edinburgh at £54, compared to the actual price of £64.

Supermarkets have long known that consumers are typically only able to compare prices on a range of regularly purchased staple items, such as baked beans, potatoes and bread, so price cutting has often been focused on these items. Meanwhile, consumers are likely to be less knowledgeable about infrequently purchased items, and supermarkets may be tempted to let prices of these rise, in the knowledge that consumers would have little idea about whether the price was a good one or not. Of course, there are lots of other ways in which businesses may deliberately or inadvertently make prices difficult for consumers to understand, as witnessed by the complexity of pricing for gas and electricity supply. This reminds us again that it may be fine in theory to talk about competitive markets, but in practice, without consumers' knowledge of the prices available in a market, a market cannot work efficiently.

Many goods and service providers face 'price points' around which customers expect to pay for a service. The UK market for internet service providers (ISPs), for example, has developed a number of price points, and customer evaluation processes may begin with the question 'How much do I want to spend?'; comparison is then based on what level of service (e.g. connection speed, download limits, free telephone calls, helpline availability) they can obtain within this price. The service provider's task then becomes one of designing a profitable service around the price point, rather than designing the service and then fixing a price.

11.5 Elasticity of demand

Elasticity of demand refers to the extent to which demand changes in relation to a change in price or some other variable, such as income. What is important here is to compare the proportionate (or percentage) change in demand with the proportionate (or percentage) change in the other variable, over any given period of time.

The most commonly used measure of elasticity of demand is price elasticity of demand. Information on this is useful to business organizations to allow them to predict what will happen to the volume of sales in response to a change in price. This section is concerned with the responsiveness of a whole market to changes in price. It will be recalled that, in a perfectly competitive market, firms must take their selling price from the market, so the only elasticity that is of interest to them is the elasticity of the market as a whole.

Price elasticity of demand refers to the ratio of the percentage change in demand to the percentage change in price. In other words, it seeks to measure how the sales of a product respond to a change in its price. This can be expressed as a simple formula:

$$\text{Price elasticity of demand} = \frac{\text{change in demand (\%)}}{\text{change in price (\%)}}$$

Where demand is relatively unresponsive to price changes, it is said to be inelastic with respect to price. Where demand is highly responsive to even a small price charge, demand is described as being elastic with respect to price.

Two demand curves are shown in Figure 11.10. D1 is more elastic than D2, as indicated by the greater effect on volume of a change in price, compared with the effects of a similar price change with D2.

A number of factors influence the price elasticity of demand for a particular product. The most important is the availability of substitutes. Where these are readily available, buyers are likely to switch between alternative products in response to price changes. The absolute value of a product and its importance to a buyer can also influence its elasticity. For example, if infrequently purchased boxes of matches fell in price by 10 per cent from 11p to 10p, buyers would probably not increase their purchases. However, if the price of television sets came down by the same percentage, from £330 to £300, many buyers may enter the market.

For any measure of elasticity, it is important to consider the time period over which it is being measured. In general, products are much more inelastic to changes in price over the short term, when possibilities for substitution may be few. However, over the longer term, new possibilities for substitution may appear. This explains why petrol is very inelastic over the short term but much more so over the long term. Faced with a sudden increase in petrol prices (as

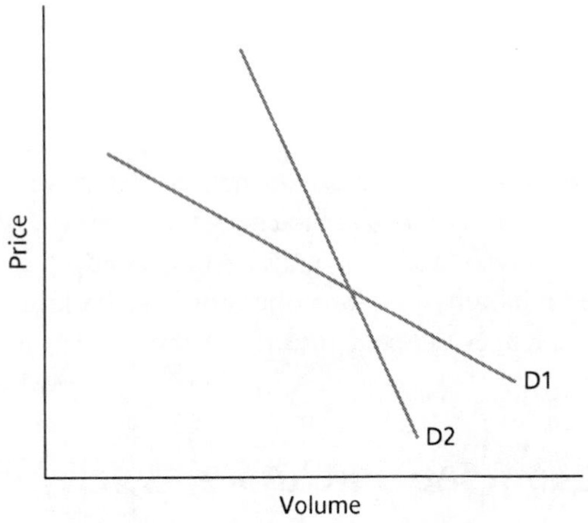

Figure 11.10 A comparison of a relatively elastic demand function (D1) with a relatively inelastic one (D2)

happened following the first Gulf War), motorists have little choice other than to pay the increased price. However, over the longer term, they can reduce their purchases of petrol by buying more fuel-efficient cars, rearranging their pattern of life so that they do not need to travel as much, or by sharing cars.

Further measures of elasticity of demand can be made by considering the responsiveness of demand to changes in the assumptions on which the demand curve is based. The most important of these is income elasticity of demand, which measures the responsiveness of demand to changes in buyers' combined incomes, and can be expressed in the following way:

$$\text{Income elasticity of demand} = \frac{\text{change in demand (\%)}}{\text{change in income (\%)}}$$

In general, as a population's income rises, the demand for most products rises, giving rise to a positive income elasticity of demand. Where there is a particularly strong increase in demand in response to an increase in incomes (or vice versa), a product can be said to have a high income elasticity of demand. This is true of luxuries such as long-haul air holidays and fitted kitchens, whose sales have increased during times of general economic prosperity, but declined during recessionary periods. On the other hand, there are some goods and services whose demand goes down as incomes increase. These are referred to as inferior goods; examples in most Western countries include local bus services and household coal.

It is useful for business organizations to understand income elasticity of demand in order to plan a response to anticipated changes in aggregate income. If, for example, a general rise in consumer income looks likely to reduce the sales of a product that has a negative income elasticity, a business may seek to shift its resources to making products with a positive income elasticity. In trying to plan for the future, businesses rely on their own historical information about sales/income relationships, and also government and private forecasts about current and future levels and distribution of income.

A third measure of demand elasticity to note is a product's cross-price elasticity of demand. This refers to the percentage change in demand for product A when the price of product B changes. Where products are very close substitutes, this may be a very important measure to understand consumer demand. For example, the price of butter can have a significant effect on demand for margarine.

It is possible to identify numerous other ad hoc measures of elasticity of demand. Firms may be interested in the responsiveness of demand to changes in some measure of the quality of their product. For example, a railway operator may be interested in the effects on demand of improvements in service reliability or a bus operator may be interested in establishing the percentage increase in passenger demand resulting from a given percentage increase in the frequency of a bus route.

11.6 Imperfect competition and elasticity of demand

The analysis of price decisions for firms in a competitive market indicates that, for any one firm, price is given by the market. An individual firm cannot increase profits by stimulating demand through lower prices, nor would it gain any benefit by seeking to raise its prices. This changes in an imperfectly competitive market where a firm acquires a degree of monopoly power over its customers. Each firm now has a demand curve for its own unique product.

Firms face a downward-sloping demand curve for each of their products, indicating that, as prices fall, demand increases, and vice versa. In fact, a number of demand curves describing a firm's market can be described, ranging from the general to the specific brand. For example, in the market for breakfast cereals, the demand curve for cereals in general may be fairly inelastic, on the basis that people will always want to buy breakfast cereals of some description (Figure 11.11). Demand for one particular type of cereal, such as corn flakes, will be slightly more elastic as people may be attracted to corn flakes from other cereals such as porridge oats on the basis

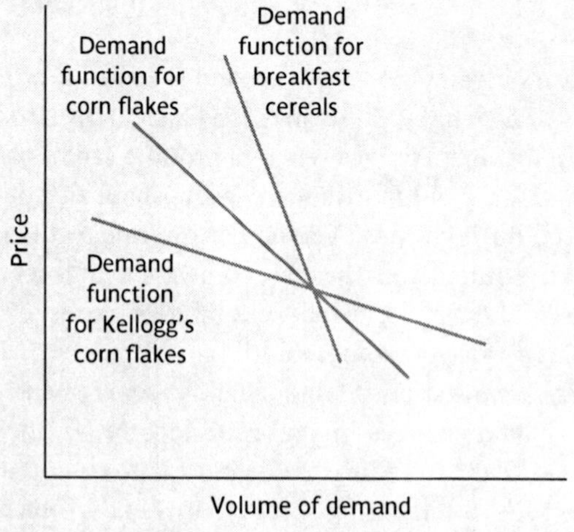

Figure 11.11 A comparison of elasticities of demand for breakfast cereals at different levels of product specificity

Price elasticity of demand	Price change	Revenue effect
High	–	–
(elastic demand)	–	+
Low	+	+
(inelastic demand)	–	–

Figure 11.12 Effects of elasticity of demand and price changes on total revenue

of their relative price. Price becomes more elastic still when a particular brand of cereals is considered. To some people, Kellogg's corn flakes can easily be substituted with other brands of corn flakes, so if a price differential between brands developed, switching may occur. By lowering its price, a firm may be able to increase its sales, but what is important to firms is that they increase their total revenue (and, thereby, profits). Whether this happens depends upon the elasticity of demand for the product in question.

Total revenue is a function of total sales multiplied by the selling price per unit. Figure 11.12 summarizes the effects on total revenue of changes in price, given alternative assumptions about elasticity.

11.7 Elasticity of supply

The concept of elasticity can also be applied to supply, so as to measure the responsiveness of supply to changes in price. Elasticity of supply is measured by the formula:

Thinking around the subject: Where's the veg?

In theory, high market prices act as a signal for companies to enter that market, or to increase the volume they supply to it. But in practice, there can be lengthy delays before firms are able to respond to these market signals, and the market for organic vegetables during the late 1990s illustrates this point. A combination of rising incomes, greater awareness of health issues and a string of food safety scares had led to rapid growth in demand for organic produce throughout Europe. But how can farmers grow organically on land that has been saturated by decades of artificial fertilizer use? The Soil Association, which operates a widely recognized accreditation scheme for organic produce, required that farmland should be free of artificial fertilizer for at least five years before any crops grown on it could be described as organic. So, despite the rapid growth in demand and the price premiums that customers were prepared to pay, retailers found it difficult to satisfy demand. Furthermore, with a difficult and intermittent supply, could retailers risk their brand name by being seen as an unreliable supplier of second-rate produce? Marks & Spencer launched a range of organic vegetables in 1997, only to withdraw them soon afterwards, blaming the difficulty in obtaining regular and reliable supplies. However, by 2004, producers that had earlier taken their signals from the market and prepared themselves for organic production were finally able to increase the volume supplied to the market. But with a sharp increase in supply relative to demand, the price premiums available for organic produce fell.

$$\text{Elasticity of supply} = \frac{\text{change in supply (\%)}}{\text{change in price (\%)}}$$

If suppliers are relatively unresponsive to an increase in the price of a product, the product is described as being inelastic with respect to price. If producers increase production substantially as prices rise, the product is said to be elastic.

As with price elasticity of demand, time is crucial in determining the elasticity of supply. Over the short term, it may be very difficult for firms to increase supply, making it very inelastic with respect to price. In the case of markets for agricultural products, elasticity is determined by the growing cycle, and new supply may be forthcoming only in time for the next season. For many manufacturing processes, supplies can eventually be increased by investing in new productive capacity and taking on additional workers. Over the longer term, supply is more elastic.

11.8 Limitations of the theory of perfect competition

Although government policy makers often view perfectly competitive markets as an ideal to aim towards, the automatic balancing of supply and demand at an equilibrium price, as described above, is seldom achieved in practice. The following are some of the more important reasons why perfect competition is rarely achieved in practice.

- Where economies of scale are achievable in an industry sector, it is always possible for firms to grow larger and become more efficient, and thereby able to exercise undue influence in a market. In general, perfect competition applies only where production techniques are simple and opportunities for economies of scale few.
- Markets are often dominated by large buyers that are able to exercise influence over the market. The domestic market for many specialized defence products may be competitive in terms of a large number of suppliers, but demand for their products is dominated by one government buying agency.
- It can be naive to assume that high prices and profits in a sector will attract new entrants, while losses will cause the least efficient to leave. In practice, there may be a whole range of barriers to entry that could cover the need to obtain licences for production, the availability of trained staff and access to distribution outlets. Also, there are sometimes barriers to exit where firms are locked into long-term supply contracts or where it would be very expensive to lay off resources such as labour.
- A presumption of perfectly competitive markets is that buyers and sellers have complete information about market conditions. In fact, this is often far from the truth. On the simple point of making price comparisons, much research has been undertaken to show that buyers often have little knowledge of the going rate for a particular category of product. For example, the use of bar code scanning equipment by retailers has resulted in many products no longer carrying a price label, weakening customers' retained knowledge of prices. Sometimes, as in the case of telephone call tariffs or credit card interest charges, prices are very difficult to comprehend.

In the following chapter, we will explore market situations that are in some sense 'imperfect', perhaps because a small number of companies dominate the market, or because products are so diverse that each product becomes unique in its own right, and therefore by implication doesn't face any direct competition.

It should be stressed again that, so far in this chapter, we have merely looked at the basic building blocks by which we begin to understand competition within markets. Although perfect competition may be an exception rather than the norm for markets, an understanding of basic market forces should allow us to assess the characteristics of less competitive market structures.

Thinking around the subject: **Marketing or markets?**

Is marketing a natural ally of free markets, or is it really an enemy? To many people, marketing is all about bringing together customers who want to buy with sellers who want to sell. By carefully studying what buyers want to buy, marketers contribute towards the efficient operation of a market. Advocates of marketing would contrast the benefits of having marketers controlled by market disciplines with the inefficiency of having a central bureaucracy making resource allocation decisions.

However, marketers are not always so benign in their thoughts about markets. While most marketers would publicly endorse the power of free markets, many of their activities, consciously or unconsciously, undermine the spirit of free markets. Consider three of the defining characteristics of competitive markets that were discussed above: a homogeneous product; freely available information; and freedom of entry to and exit from the market. Now consider some common marketing strategies.

The idea of all companies selling a homogeneous product is anathema to one of the basic philosophies of marketing, which is to add value to products through differentiation. The following chapter will discuss ways in which companies use branding to try to differentiate their products from those of the competitors. Faced with shelves of slightly differentiated bottled water carrying different brand names, can this be said to be a market in a homogeneous product? Is there any meaningful difference between many of the brands? How can buyers tell?

Information available in a market is often difficult to assimilate, and some people have accused marketers of making their information even more difficult to understand. Try comparing mobile phone calling plans, or the different tariffs offered by gas and electricity companies, and you could come to the conclusion that the companies' information may be freely available to all, but actually understood by very few. Some would accuse marketers of engaging in 'confusion marketing' to try to make informed comparisons more difficult.

Marketers often do their best to reduce the ease of entry to or exit from a market. One consequence of the recent trend towards 'relationship marketing' has been to try to tie customers to the company through a long-term contract. Customers of mobile phone companies cannot easily leave their existing supplier if they are committed to a 12-month contract. Many manufacturers have sought exclusivity contracts with retailers, which makes it difficult for new competitors to enter the market.

Karl Marx once observed that capitalism was essentially all about *reducing* risk rather than *taking* risk. Could marketing be more about trying to undermine the value of markets rather than trying to make them work more efficiently?

Case study: Can market mechanisms reduce global climate change?

To anti-capitalism protestors, the cause of global climate change can be attributed to market forces. A focus by individuals on buying goods and services for the lowest price, and a focus by producers producing those goods and services for the lowest cost has made full use of market forces. For many shoppers, the price of a pair of shoes is a very important basis for choosing between competing shoes, and market forces have helped to drive down the price of shoes, so that we can now regard shoes almost as a disposable fashion item, regardless of the impact of short-life shoes filling up landfill sites and using scarce natural resources. Similarly, shoe manufacturers have used market forces to ruthlessly cut their production costs, even if this means moving shoes and their component materials long distances round the world, adding to greenhouse gas emissions in the process. So, market forces may indirectly have contributed to current problems of global warming, but can those same market forces also be used to try to redress the problem? Backers of carbon trading hope so.

Greenhouse gases are blamed for causing climate change because they absorb infrared radiation and prevent it from being dispersed into space, thereby having the effect of warming the Earth. This not only increases global average temperatures, but is also claimed to lead to increasingly unpredictable weather. Probable results of climate change include more frequent and fiercer storms, droughts and floods. If warming causes enough of the world's ice to melt, rises in sea levels could occur, leading to flooding in coastal areas. It is also claimed that melting ice from the Arctic could disrupt the flow and direction of the Gulfstream, having the effect of cooling parts of Europe.

Very few businesses can claim not to be affected by climate change. Bad weather (such as hurricanes, floods and gale-force winds, which have been attributed to climate change) affects companies when they come to renew their insurance policies. The storms that hit the UK in autumn 2000 are estimated to have cost UK insurers more than £1 billion, and these costs will ultimately be passed on to businesses and consumers in the form of higher premiums. Damage caused to property by storms can close down a company's factories and disrupt the supply of its raw materials. If the weather becomes more unpredictable, risk will increasingly have to be factored into business planning.

As well as being affected by climate change, companies are increasingly being called upon to take some of the responsibility for slowing the rate of greenhouse gas emissions. An important focus for these efforts was the Kyoto Treaty, drawn up in 1997. This requires developed countries to reduce their dependence on fossil fuels, which produce the greenhouse gases blamed for causing climate change. Kyoto binds developed nations to cut emission levels by 2012, compared with those of 1990.

One outcome of the Kyoto Treaty was the introduction in 2005 of the European Union's Emissions Trading Scheme (ETS), which essentially sought to reduce carbon emissions through a system of quotas traded through market mechanisms. The scheme capped the amount of carbon dioxide that could be emitted from large installations, such as power generation and carbon-intensive factories, and covers almost half the EU's total CO_2 emissions. All businesses in the UK covered by the scheme were allocated a share of the 756 million tonnes of carbon dioxide that the UK was allowed to produce. Companies covered by the trading scheme were allocated a share of permitted total emissions, which represented their 'cap'. If they emitted above their cap, they would have to buy carbon permits in the specialist carbon trading market that emerged. On the other hand, if they did not need all their quota, they could sell surplus through these same markets. In principle, companies had a strong incentive to reduce their carbon emissions, as market forces would reward them with income from the sale of unused carbon permits.

However, market forces were not as straightforward as first appeared. The ETS commenced with excessive permits for emissions being issued, many would argue in response to political pressure to reduce the immediate effect on high-emissions sectors. There had been many loopholes and incentives for industries to exaggerate their emissions in order to increase the number of permits they were allocated. One consequence of the over-issue of quotas was that most firms had little difficulty in achieving emission levels below their cap, and were therefore able to sell their surplus quota on the open carbon market. Of course, with a generous allocation of quota, there were more sellers of carbon permits than buyers, with the result that the price of carbon permits fell by 60 per cent within the first year of operation of the scheme. The incentive for companies to reduce their emissions was, accordingly, much less than it could have been. Perversely, one estimate claimed that the UK's biggest polluters had earned a 'windfall' profit of nearly £1 billion as a result of over-generous allocation of carbon quotas, which they were able to sell.

The use of market mechanisms to solve the problem of global warming is an innovative way of trying to internalize companies' external costs. Rather than imposing a bureaucratic solution, a market-based system was seen by many as an attractive means by which businesses could overcome an ecological problem by doing what they are good at – trading. However, some argued that markets were inherently incapable of solving the pressing problems of climate change and more drastic action based on strict limits on emissions would bring about more rapid change. There was also the issue that without world agreement on permitted carbon emissions, manufacturers would simply shift production to countries with fewer restrictions on emissions. A perverse consequence of the ETS could be to shift production from relatively clean and modern European factories to relatively heavy-polluting factories in developing countries. Moreover, additional emissions may have been generated in the process of transporting raw materials and finished goods to take advantage of the favourable emissions regime. It follows therefore that the market-based ETS could actually have led to an increase in total carbon emissions.

In 2007, the United States, which is the world's largest producer of emissions (an estimated 20.6 per cent of the world total in 2000), appeared to become more amenable to the idea of globally agreed emissions limits imposed on its domestic manufacturers, linked to a trading scheme. It seemed that the US electorate had become concerned and impatient with its government's lack of action on what was perceived by Americans as an increasingly pressing problem. Or was the US Government's change of heart more to do with the opportunities that its business organizations saw in the market for reduced carbon emissions? With companies such as Boeing leading the world in wind energy generation, was it just cynicism that they supported the idea of markets only when they could see a clear benefit for themselves?

Meanwhile, concern remained about how to introduce developing economies into markets for emissions. The US-based Pew Center on Global Climate Change estimated that, in 2004, China was responsible for 17 per cent of the world's greenhouse gas emissions, and this figure was expected to climb rapidly. Persuading developing countries to sign up to emissions reduction has been difficult. Many resent the idea that the developed world grew rich, fuelled by coal and oil, while the developing world might now be denied the chance to catch up. How could they be persuaded that they could benefit from market forces? Or do market forces invariably help those who already have a strong position, at the expense of the relatively disadvantaged?

QUESTIONS

1. Critically assess the opportunities and challenges for energy-intensive businesses, such as a metal manufacturer, resulting from the introduction of carbon trading.
2. Show, using supply/demand analysis, the effects of the over-issuing of carbon quotas described in the case study.
3. Discuss the extent to which the carbon market represents a perfectly competitive market. What would be the most likely causes of market distortion?

Summary

This chapter has reviewed the variety of market structures that exist, and the effect market structure has on a firm's pricing and product decisions. Perfectly competitive markets are presumed to favour consumers, but can limit the revenues of profit-seeking firms. In its purest extreme, this market structure is unusual; however, the basic building blocks of demand, supply and price determination provide a foundation for understanding more complex market structures. We will return to these market structures in **Chapter 12**. The trend towards globalization of business (**Chapter 14**) is having the effect of making markets more competitive. This chapter has taken a microeconomic perspective on pricing and competition. Pricing is also affected by macroeconomic factors, and these are discussed in **Chapter 13**.

Key terms

Demand (373)
Elasticity of demand (384)
Elasticity of supply (387)
Market structure (370)
Markets (370)
Perfect competition (373)
Price determination (379)
Supply (377)

Chapter review questions

1 In the context of market structure analysis, what are the options available to firms in a highly competitive market to improve profitability? Select one of the options and discuss it, making clear how lasting the profit improvement is likely to be in the long run. (*Based on a CIM Marketing Environment Examination question*)

2 'Elasticity of demand is a fine theoretical concept of economists, but difficult for marketers to use in practice.' Critically assess this statement.

3 Show, using diagrams, what would happen to the price of whisky if a new technological development suddenly allowed whisky to be produced at a much lower cost than previously.

Activities

1 Collect information on prices charged for the following products: a top ten DVD film to buy; car insurance quotes; mobile phone charges. What do the prices tell you about the competitiveness of these markets? Identify strategies that companies in these markets have pursued in order to reduce the effects of direct competition.

2 Try to construct a demand curve for an item of consumer technology whose price is falling – for example, a mobile phone with a GPS system. Try to construct a demand curve on the basis of your friends' statements about their likelihood of buying the product at specified price levels. What limitations are there in this approach to determining the demand curve for the product?

3 Identify the impact and discuss the likely marketing response to the following environmental changes affecting a major oil refining and distributing company:

- the introduction of a carbon tax
- a breakthrough in cost-effective solar power stations
- a well-financed new entrant entering its main market
- teleconferencing and telecommunications growing rapidly.

(Based on a CIM Marketing Environment Examination question)

Further Reading

This chapter has provided only a very brief overview of the principles of economics as they affect pricing. For a fuller discussion, one of the following texts would be useful.

Begg, D. and Ward, D. (2006) *Economics for Business*, Maidenhead, McGraw-Hill.

Lipsey, R.G. and Chrystal, K.A. (2007) *Economics*, 11th edn, Oxford, Oxford University Press.

Sloman, J. and Hinde, K. (2007) *Economics for Business*, London, FT Prentice Hall.

Reference

Timmins, N. (2003) 'A bid to save money for the government: online auctions', *Financial Times*, 29 January, p. 12.

Chapter 5 Costs, supply and perfect competition

Learning outcomes

By the end of this chapter, you should understand:

- Total, average and marginal cost
- The law of diminishing returns
- Costs in the short run
- Technology and production techniques
- Returns to scale and average cost curves
- Long-run and short-run costs
- A firm's supply decision, in the short run and long run
- Temporary shutdown and permanent exit
- The concept of perfect competition
- Why a perfectly competitive firm's output equates price and marginal cost
- Incentives for entry and exit
- The supply curve of a perfectly competitive industry
- The effect of shifts in demand or costs

5-1 How costs affect supply in the short run

Chapter 3 introduced the bare bones of a theory of supply, which depended on both costs and revenue. Now we need to put more flesh on this theory. Chapters 5–6 deal with two ideas. First, adjusting production methods takes time. Given time, firms may be able to reduce costs by choosing more appropriate methods of production. This leads to a distinction between optimal behaviour in the short run, when some things cannot be changed, and in the long run when everything can be changed.

Second, the revenue obtained from selling any particular output depends on the extent of competition in that market. This means that the general theory of supply is affected by the context of the degree of competition in which firms find themselves. To begin the analysis of the general theory of supply, this chapter deals with the special case of perfect competition. Chapter 6 then examines the theory of supply in other market environments in which competition is more restricted.

New companies, such as Orange and Amazon, lost a lot of money before eventually starting to make profits. Existing companies, such as British Airways and British Telecom, made big losses in the cyclical downturn of 2001–02, despite previous periods of healthy profits; and banks made huge losses in 2007 as a result of overoptimistic lending decisions. But they kept going nevertheless. Firms don't always close down when they are losing money. They may keep going because they expect demand to rise, or costs to fall. We need to distinguish between the *short-run* and the *long-run* supply decisions of firms. In the short run, a firm can't fully adjust to new information. In the long run, full adjustment is possible. In this section, we focus on how costs affect the supply decision. We then turn to the influence of demand and revenue on supply decisions.

An **input** (sometimes called a *factor of production*) is any good or service used to make output. A **production technique** is a particular way of using inputs to make output. **Technology** is the list of production techniques known today.

Inputs are labour, machinery, buildings, raw materials and energy.

Land is the input supplied by nature; **capital** is the input that exists because of a previous production process, and still exists at the end of the production process. **Raw materials** are the physical inputs used up during the production process.

Thus, machinery and buildings are capital, because they were made previously, but now supply input services to the production processes in which they are now used; and they will still be there again next year. Power stations supply capital input services to making electricity and trains supply capital input services to the production of train journeys. For simplicity, economists often treat land as fixed in supply (even though meticulous application of fertilizer may increase its effective input a little). Capital services are usually fixed in the short run, but variable in the long run. Eventually we can produce more buildings and machinery (thereby increasing their input to future production), or allow them to depreciate (thereby reducing their input to future production).

Raw materials are things such as fertilizer in agriculture, or hops in the beer industry, inputs that are entirely used up during the production process. We get some raw materials largely from nature (fresh water, plants, easily collected minerals) but devote considerable amounts of production to making some raw materials for subsequent production processes (high-octane fuel for aircraft, specialist steel for buildings, silicon for computer chips).

Labour is the production input supplied by workers.

With slavery now abolished, firms don't own workers any more, but they do rent or hire the labour services of workers. We usually assume that labour is the most easily variable input in the short run. How productive these workers are depends on the quantities of other inputs with which they can work. In some countries, wheat is produced with few people using lots of machinery: these workers will produce a lot of output per worker. In other countries, the same crop is produced with lots of workers using little machinery: now output per worker will be lower because they have a lower quantity of non-labour inputs with which to co-operate.

Both are possible techniques with which to produce wheat. Which one is adopted will depend on the prices of the different inputs and the chosen scale of production.

Short-run costs and diminishing returns

In the short run, the firm has some fixed inputs.

A **fixed input** can't be varied in the short run. A **variable input** can be adjusted, even in the short run.

The short run varies from industry to industry. It may take ten years to build a new power station, but only days to create a new market stall. Having built a power station, the electricity supplier must treat this input as fixed in the short run – the input of power station services cannot quickly be augmented nor quickly reduced. The existence of fixed inputs in the short run has two implications.

First, in the short run the firm has some fixed costs, which must be paid even if output is zero. It has to pay rent on its premises even if it decides not to produce anything this month. Second, because the firm cannot make all the adjustments it would like, its short-run costs must exceed its long-run costs. If it behaves differently in the long run, this can only be because it prefers to switch to a cheaper production method once this opportunity arises.

Variable costs are the costs of hiring variable factors, typically labour, raw materials and energy. Although firms may have long-term contracts with workers, and with material or energy suppliers, in practice most firms retain some flexibility through overtime and short time, hiring or non-hiring of casual and part-time workers, and purchases of raw material and energy in the open market to supplement contracted supplies.

Fixed costs don't vary with output levels. **Variable costs** change with output.

Chapter 3 introduced the theory of supply. Marginal revenue is the extra revenue obtained from selling another unit of output. Marginal cost is the extra cost of producing another unit of output. A firm will increase its profit if it expands output further whenever marginal revenue exceeds marginal cost, and will also increase its profit if it contracts its output whenever marginal revenue is less than marginal cost. Hence, profits are maximized at the output at which marginal revenue is equal to marginal cost. This was summarized in Figure 3-3, which we show again below as Figure 5-1.

We now wish to understand in more detail what determines the costs of a firm in the short run. For simplicity, we will think about a firm whose only variable input in the short run is labour. To show we are explicitly focusing on the short run, we now draw the short-run marginal cost curve *SMC* available

Box 5-1 Sunk costs

If certain costs have *already* been incurred and can't be affected by your decision, ignore them. They shouldn't influence your future decisions. In deciding how much to produce in the short run, the firm ignores its fixed costs which must be incurred anyway.

It may seem a pity to abandon a project in which a lot of money has already been invested. Poker players call this throwing good money after bad. If you don't think it will be worth reading the rest of this book, you should not do it merely because you put a lot of effort into the first four chapters. Your optimal decision of how to spend your time, from now on, is to decide whether the benefits of reading the rest of the book outweigh the costs of reading the rest of the book.

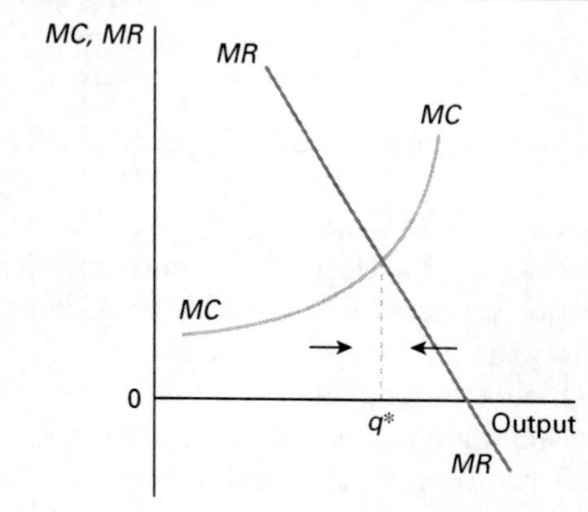

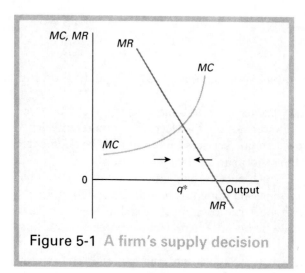

Figure 5-1 A firm's supply decision

to the firm while it has to treat its other inputs as fixed. It can increase output only by using more and more labour to work with fixed amounts of capital and other inputs.

The **marginal product** of a variable input (labour) is the *extra* output from *adding* 1 unit of the variable input, holding constant the quantity of all other inputs in the short run.

The first worker has a whole factory to work with and has too many jobs to do to produce much. A second worker helps, a lot, and so does a third. Suppose the factory has three machines and the three workers are now specializing in each running one of the factory's machines. The marginal product of a fourth worker is lower. With only three machines, the fourth worker gets a machine only when another worker is resting. A fifth worker only makes tea for the other four. By now there are diminishing returns to labour.

Holding all inputs constant except one, the **law of diminishing returns** says that, beyond some level of the variable input, further rises in the variable input steadily reduce the marginal product of that input.

Output is varied by using more labour input. Changes in the marginal product of labour affect the marginal cost of making output. The more productive a worker, the lower is the cost of making output. Figure 5-2 shows that, as output rises, short-run marginal costs initially fall as we move to the right along *SMC*; however, beyond some output, diminishing returns set in, additional workers add less and less to extra output, and hence marginal cost becomes higher and higher as the firm raises output further by adding to its variable labour input. While the marginal product of labour is rising, each worker adds more to output than the previous workers, and marginal cost is falling.

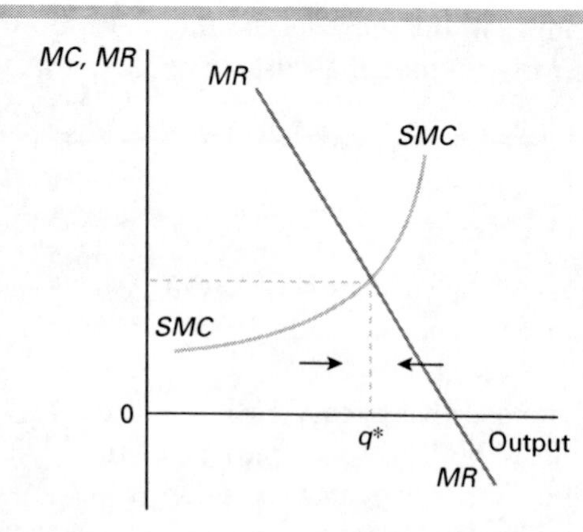

Figure 5-2 Short-run marginal cost and the optimal output level

Short-run marginal cost ***SMC*** is the extra cost of making one more unit of output in the short run while some inputs are fixed.

Once diminishing returns to labour set in, the marginal product of labour falls steadily as output is expanded, and marginal costs therefore rise with the level of output. This is the basic insight behind the shape of the marginal cost curve in Figure 5-2. Because other inputs are limited, it takes more and more extra workers to make each extra unit of output.

In Figure 5-2, the output q^* is the most profitable output to produce because it is the point at which $SMC = MR$. If SMC exceeded MR at that output, the firm could make even more profit by contracting output a little (the last unit of production cost more to produce than it added to revenue); if MR exceeded SMC, the firm could make even more profit by expanding output a little further (thereby making more in revenue than it costs to produce for that extra unit of production).

A firm's supply decision in the short run

The firm only has one thing left to check. Should it be producing at all? To answer this question, the firm calculates its total revenue from production and compares this with its total costs in the short run.

Total costs are total fixed costs plus total variable costs.

In the short run, the firm has to pay the costs of its fixed inputs whether or not its produces any output and earns any revenue. The only decisions it can make are whether to incur variable costs and, if so, how much to produce. (Total revenue *minus* variable costs) is therefore the financial benefit to the firm from deciding to produce, and producing at q^* at which $SMC = MR$ is guaranteed to maximize this financial benefit.

The firm's short-run supply decision is therefore simple to describe:

(a) If at output q^*, total revenue *exceeds* total variable costs, then produce output q^*.

(b) If, even at output q^*, total revenue is less than total variable costs, then produce zero output: shut down in the short run and hope for better times later.

Two final remarks. First, in the short run, even if the firm decides to produce, it may not be making profits. It is stuck with its fixed costs whatever it does. Ignoring these, it produces if it at least makes a profit on the variable part that it can affect. Either the profit from production is large enough to cover the fixed costs too, in which case the firm is in overall profit, or the profit from production is positive but less than the fixed costs, in which case the decision to produce is partially reducing the losses from the fixed (overhead) costs, even though in total the firm is still losing money.

Second, instead of comparing total revenues and total costs, we can divide both by output to get average revenues and average costs.

Average revenue is total revenue divided by output. But revenue is just output multiplied by price. So average revenue *is* the price the firm receives for its output. Average cost is total cost divided by output.

Since total cost = total fixed cost + total variable cost, dividing everything by the same output level we get

Average cost = average fixed cost + average variable cost

We can therefore restate the firm's supply decision as follows:

(a) If at the best production level q^*, price (hence average revenue) > average variable cost, then choose to produce q^*.

(b) If at output q^*, price < average variable cost, then shut down temporarily and produce 0.

Of course, private firms cannot be compelled to lose money indefinitely – they would rather quit the industry entirely. To examine when temporary shutdown makes sense and when permanent exit makes sense, we need to think about the long run as well as the short run.

5-2 Costs and supply in the long run

A technique is said to be **technically efficient** if no other technique could make the same output with fewer inputs. **Technology** is all the techniques known today. **Technical progress** is the discovery of a new technique that is more efficient than existing ones, making a given output with fewer inputs than before.

Technology relates volumes of inputs to volume of output. But costs are values. To deduce the cheapest way to make a particular output, the firm needs to know input prices as well as what technology is available. At each output level, the firm finds the lowest-cost technique. When labour is cheap, firms choose labour-intensive techniques. If labour is expensive, the firm will switch to more capital-intensive techniques that use less labour.

Faced with higher demand, the firm will want to expand output, but adjustment takes time. In the long run, the firm can adjust all input quantities and the choice of technique. In the short run, the firm can't change all inputs, and may also be unable to change technique. It may be years before a new factory is designed, built, and operational.

Long-run total cost *LTC* is the total cost of making each output level when a firm has plenty of time to adjust fully and produce this output level by the cheapest possible means. **Long-run marginal cost** *LMC* is the rise in total cost if output permanently rises by one unit. **Long-run average cost** *LAC* is *LTC* divided by the level of output *Q*.

In the long run, most firms face the U-shaped average cost curve shown in Figure 5-3. At higher output levels, the firm achieves efficiency gains and lower average costs. However, beyond some output level *Q**, life gets more difficult for the firm, and its average costs increase if output is higher.

There are **economies of scale** (or increasing returns to scale) if long-run average cost *LAC* falls as output rises, **constant returns to scale** if *LAC* is constant as output rises, and **diseconomies of scale** (or decreasing returns to scale) if *LAC* rises as output rises.

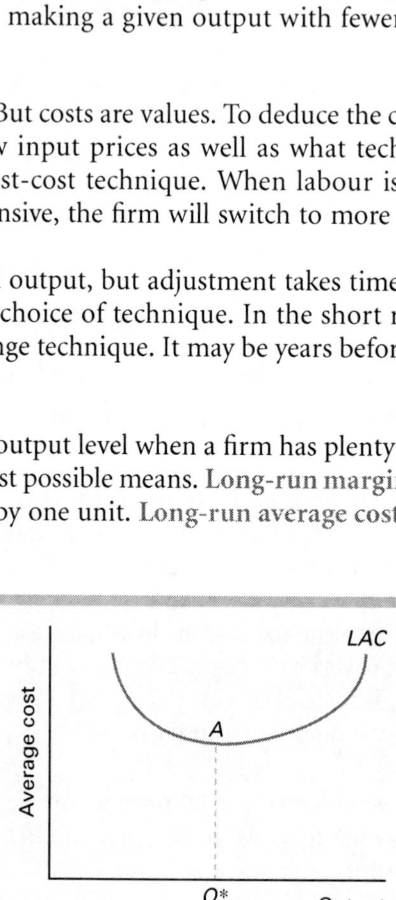

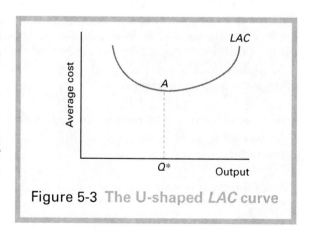

Figure 5-3 The U-shaped *LAC* curve

The U-shaped average cost curve in Figure 5-3 has scale economies up to point *A*, where average cost is lowest. At output levels above *Q**, there are decreasing returns to scale. Since *LAC* is horizontal at point *A*, there are constant returns to scale when output is close to *Q**.

Other shapes of cost curve are possible. Later, we shall see that in some industries with large-scale economies, *LAC* may fall over the entire output range. Conversely, the output *Q** may be so tiny that the *LAC* curve slopes up over most normal output ranges.

Scale economies

There are three reasons for economies of scale. Production may entail some *overhead costs* that do not vary with the output level.[1] A firm requires a manager, a telephone, an accountant and a market research survey. It can't have half a manager and half a telephone if output is low. From low initial output, rises in output allow overheads to be spread over more units of output, reducing average cost. Beyond some output level, the firm needs more managers and telephones. Scale economies end. The average cost curve stops falling.

A second reason for economies of scale is *specialization*. At low output levels, each of the few workers has to do many jobs and never becomes very good at any of them. At higher output and a larger workforce, each worker can focus on a single task and handle it more efficiently. The third reason for economies of scale is that large scale is often needed to take advantage of better machinery. Sophisticated but expensive machinery also has an element of indivisibility. A farmer with a small field may as well dig the field by hand. With a larger field, it becomes worth buying a tractor.

Diseconomies of scale

The main reason for diseconomies of scale is that management is hard once the firm is large: there are *managerial diseconomies of scale*. Large firms need many layers of management, which themselves have to be managed. Co-ordination problems arise, and average costs begin to rise. Geography may also explain diseconomies of scale. If the first factory is sited in the best place, a second factory has to be built in a less advantageous location, and the third in a less advantageous location still.

The shape of the average cost curve thus depends on two things: how long the economies of scale persist, and how quickly the diseconomies of scale occur as output rises.

The lowest output at which all scale economies are achieved is called **minimum efficient scale**.

In heavy manufacturing industries economies of scale are substantial. At low outputs, average costs are much higher than at minimum efficient scale. High fixed costs of research and development need to be spread over large output to reduce average costs. Hence, large markets are needed to allow low costs to be attained.

High transport costs used to mean that markets were small. For industries with large fixed costs, this meant that average costs were high. Globalization is partly a response to a dramatic fall in transport costs. By selling in bigger markets, some firms can enjoy large-scale economies and lower average costs.

In other industries, minimum efficient scale occurs at a low output. Any higher output raises average cost again. There is a limit to a hairdresser's daily output. A larger market makes little difference. Globalization has not had a big impact on hairdressing; but the Internet has always been global – admitting another user to Google hardly costs anything at all. Almost all the costs are fixed costs, the costs of setting up the website in the first place. Marginal cost is very low. And average cost falls as more users are admitted and the fixed costs are spread across more and more users.

We begin by discussing the output decision of a firm with a U-shaped average cost curve. Then we show how to amend this analysis when firms face significant economies of scale.

---

1 Some textbooks refer to these as fixed costs, because they must be paid anyway. We prefer to call them overhead costs, reserving the term 'fixed costs' for those which cannot be varied in the short run but could be altered if there is sufficient time to adjust production methods. In contrast, overhead costs have to be paid by any firm that remains in business, no matter how long it has to adjust.

Box 5-2 Scale economies and co-opetition

Competitors are often forced to co-operate in order to share in scale economies that each firm alone cannot enjoy. Arch rivals in the New York newspaper business, the *New York Post* and the *Daily News* compete over circulation, but, behind the scenes, are talking about working together in some areas, such as distribution, in an effort to slash costs. Nor are they the only rivals thinking the previously unthinkable.

Arrangements in which firms compete vigorously with one another, while also co-operating in specific areas – what Yale professor Barry Nalebuff calls 'co-opetition' – are not new. Car-makers have long collaborated on vehicle platforms, engines and so on to achieve economies of scale. And airlines have shared check-in, gate management and other facilities.

As firms get squeezed by recession and competition from lower-cost producers elsewhere in the global economy, such co-opetition is on the increase. In July 2008, BMW (which makes the Mini) and Fiat (which produces the rival MiTo under its Alfa Romeo brand) said they were considering joint production of components and systems for their vehicles.

Similarly, parcel-delivery companies watched their market shrinking and took action to cut costs. DHL and UPS are planning to collaborate in the express-delivery market in the US: UPS, which has some excess capacity in its American air-freight network, will carry DHL's packages on its planes inside America – and between the United States, Canada and Mexico – for a fee of up to $1 billion a year.

The impetus for the deal came from DHL, whose US express-delivery business was losing money. By working with UPS and restructuring its own ground-delivery network, the German-owned firm planned to cut its US losses from $1.3 billion in 2008 to $300 million by 2011. UPS could do with the cash from DHL: its second-quarter 2008 operating profit shrank by 18 per cent, owing to rising fuel costs and the stagnant American economy.

Co-opetition deals are tricky because firms need to be very clear about what will and will not be covered by them. Newspapers differentiate themselves by their editorial content and the quality of their advertising-sales operations. Editorial and advertising departments of rival papers must be kept separate if they are to retain their distinctive identities. But distribution, printing and back-office operations are easier to consolidate without blurring brands – which is why the *Post* and the *Daily News* explored such possibilities.

UPS and DHL stressed that their proposed deal just covered air freight – they would still compete in all the other parts of the express-parcel business, including ground collection and delivery. Frank Appel, the boss of Deutsche Post World Net, DHL's parent, was confident that a deal with UPS could be reached before 2009.

Source: Adapted from *The Economist*, 7 April 2008

Average cost and marginal cost

As output rises, average cost falls whenever marginal cost is below average cost; average cost rises whenever marginal cost is above average cost. Hence average cost is lowest at the output Q^* at which LAC and LMC cross. Figure 5-4 illustrates.

This relation between average and marginal is a matter of arithmetic, as relevant to football as to production. Suppose Wayne Rooney scores 3 goals in his first 3 games, thus averaging 1 goal per game. Two

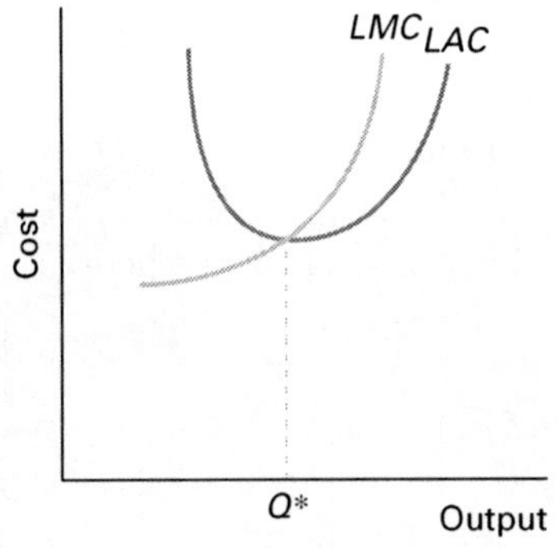

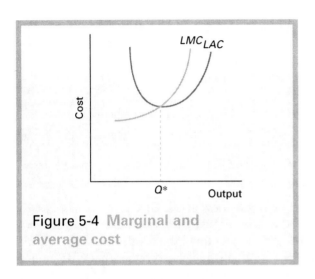

Figure 5-4 Marginal and average cost

goals in the next game, implying 5 goals from 4 games, raises the average to 1.25 goals per game. In the fourth game the marginal score of 2 goals exceeded the average score of 1 goal in previous games, thus raising the average. But if Wayne had not scored in the fourth game (a marginal score of 0), this would have dragged down his average per game from 1 (3 goals in 3 games) to 0.75 (3 goals in 4 games).

Similarly, when the marginal cost of making the next unit of output exceeds the average cost of making the existing units, making another unit *must* raise average cost. Conversely, if the marginal cost of the next unit is below the average cost of existing units, another unit *must* reduce average cost. When marginal and average cost are equal, making another unit leaves average cost unchanged.

Hence, in Figure 5-4, average and marginal cost curves cross at minimum average cost. At outputs below Q^*, *LMC* is below *LAC*, so average cost is falling. Above Q^*, *LMC* is above *LAC*, so average cost is rising. At output Q^*, average costs are at a minimum. As in Wayne's world, this relation rests purely on arithmetic.

Box 5-3 Scale economies and the Internet

Producing information products such as films, music and news programmes has a high fixed cost, but distributing these products digitally has almost a zero marginal cost and no capacity constraint. Scale economies are vast. Moreover, if marginal cost is close to zero, smart suppliers will price their products so that marginal revenue is also tiny.

EMI, a legend of the music industry, was formed in 1931. Its Abbey Road studios in London hosted giants such as the Beatles. Moving with the times, EMI has steadily withdrawn from the business of supplying records and CDs, and now operates largely online.

The firm's long-run output decision

We can now describe how a firm chooses its output level in the long run. This is a two-part decision. First, the firm evaluates its marginal cost and marginal revenue, thereby telling the firm the best output at which to produce in the long run. It should produce the output at which $LMC = MR$. If marginal revenue exceeds marginal cost at any particular output, the firm is still making a marginal profit by producing more, and should therefore raise production. If marginal cost exceeds marginal revenue, the firm has made a marginal loss on the last unit of production and should produce less. Only when marginal revenue equals marginal cost is there no scope to increase operating profits by changing the output level. The marginal condition tells us the best positive output level for maximizing profit, namely, where marginal revenue equals marginal cost.

Table 5-1 A firm's supply decisions

Output decision	Marginal condition: output at which	Produce this output unless
Short-run	*MR* = *SMC*	*P* < *Short-run average variable cost*; if it is, shut down temporarily
Long-run	*MR* = *LMC*	*P* < *LAC*; if it is, quit permanently

However, the firm also has to check that it should be in business at all. Given that it has chosen the most advantageous output level, is it making profits at this output? Or does it make losses at every output level, in which case the marginal condition has merely identified the least bad output to produce? It might be even better to give up completely and eventually make zero rather than lose money forever.

Suppose *Q*** is the output at which *LMC* = *MR*. If, at this output, the price for which this output can be sold (which we deduce from the demand curve) exceeds the average cost *LAC* of making this output, the firm is making permanent profits and should remain in the industry. However, if at the 'best' output *Q***, the firm is losing money because *LAC* exceeds the price for which *Q*** can be sold, the firm is better off by closing down completely.

Notice the two-stage argument. First we use the *marginal condition* (*LMC* = *MR*) to find the best output, *then* we use the *average condition* (comparing *LAC* at this output with the price or average revenue) to determine if the best output is good enough for the firm to stay in business in the long run. If the firm's best output yields losses, it should close down.

It is important to realize that the best output *Q*** is not, in general, the same as the output *Q** in Figure 5-4 at which long-run average costs are minimized. Figure 5-4 is purely an analysis of costs. What the firm wishes to do depends both on costs and revenues. If demand is strong enough, it is profitable to produce more than the minimum efficient scale *Q** because at this output level there are still further profits to be exploited by producing even more. Conversely, demand may be so weak that the firm chooses to produce less than minimum efficient scale. Any attempt to produce more would drive prices down too much. The firm would lose more from lower prices than it would gain from being able to reduce average costs. This completes our analysis of the supply decision, as demonstrated in Table 5-1.

Short-run and long-run costs

Even if losing money in the short run, a firm will stay in business if it at least covers its variable costs. In the long run it must cover all its costs to stay in business. A firm may reduce its costs in the long run, converting a short-run loss into a long-term profit. In the short run, its technique of production is fixed and it has some fixed inputs to production. In the long run, it can vary everything.

The firm will only wish to vary things where, by doing so, costs are reduced and hence profitability is increased.

Case study 5-1 Steel here?

Twenty-five years ago, British Steel was a state-owned monopoly, selling largely in the UK. Since then, four things have happened. First, the firm was privatized. Second, its market became global, in which British Steel was a relatively small player. Third, it decided to merge with a Dutch steel maker to form a new company, Corus. Even so, its UK plants continued to lose money. Partly, this reflected a continuing decline in the UK demand for steel, shrunk as UK manufacturing as a whole contracted. UK labour costs are now six times those in Brazil and ten times those in India, both countries now being capable of producing steel for the world market. If the UK wishes to be a high-wage producer within the global economy, it needs either to have massive investment to make UK factories ultra-modern and technically sophisticated or else to recognize that more basic production will be undertaken in lower-wage countries than the UK. Corus had to move upmarket into the niche of providing hi-tech steel that drew on the UK's science and technology base. But this entailed shutting down more basic capacity that was being outcompeted by cheaper producers abroad.

As competitive pressures mounted, loss-making Corus faced the classic choice: undertake expensive investment to restore competitiveness, shut down temporarily and hope for better demand conditions in the future, or exit the industry in order to avoid making permanent losses. If you had been a shareholder, would you have thought it worth contributing more money in the hope of saving the business, or concluded that it was more prudent to allow Corus to contract, saving your money for other, more profitable ventures with a greater prospect of international success?

In 2001, Corus announced plans for 6000 job losses and the closure of 3 million tons of steel capacity. It was beginning to exit the industry. The UK government offered to pay half the wage bill of these workers for a year if their jobs could be saved. Effectively, the government was betting either that costs could be reduced if the company had longer to adjust, or that demand would somehow improve within a year. In retrospect, this optimism was unjustified. Corus continued to lose money and further job losses ensued.

Sometimes, the firms that survive are not those with the lowest costs but those with the deepest financial pockets and the best relationships with the shareholders and bankers. As China has continued its rapid industrialization, it is now buying vast quantities of raw materials to fuel its continuing development. The result has been a dramatic upward shift in demand, and a corresponding rise in commodity prices, including the price of steel. Once Corus survived the tough years of 2000–03, its fortunes began to revive. Its uncompetitive capacity had been streamlined and reduced, it was focused increasingly on specialist steel, and it was able to raise prices by 10–20 per cent both because it was making higher-quality products and because the Chinese boost meant that world demand for steel rose by 8 per cent per annum during 2003–05. The table below shows the turnaround in output and profits.

Corus (£ billion)	2001	2002	2003	2004
Output and sales	7.7	7.2	8.0	9.3
Net profits	–0.4	–0.4	–0.2	0.4

While validating the Corus decision not to quit the industry earlier, the profits available by the middle of the decade brought their own dangers. In 2007, Corus became the target of a fierce takeover battle that was eventually won by the Indian conglomerate Tata.

Source: www.corus.group.com

5-3 Perfect competition

The previous two sections have explored how costs vary in the short run and in the long run, and how the firm therefore chooses whether to supply any output and, if so, what quantity of output is best. Throughout this analysis of costs and supply, we treated demand conditions as given.

We now switch our attention from costs to demand and revenue, for which we need to know about the structure of the industry in which the firm operates.

An **industry** is the set of all firms making the same product.

The output of an industry is the sum of the outputs of its firms. Yet different industries have very different numbers of firms. The UK has thousands of florists but only one producer of nuclear energy. We begin with perfect competition, a hypothetical benchmark against which to assess other market structures.

In **perfect competition**, actions of individual buyers and sellers have no effect on the market price.

This industry has many buyers and many sellers. Each firm in a perfectly competitive industry faces a horizontal demand curve, shown in Figure 5-5. Whatever output q the firm sells, it gets exactly the market price P_0, and the tiny firm can sell as much as it wants at this price. If it charges more than P_0, the firm loses all its customers. If it charges less than P_0, it attracts all the vast number of customers of other firms. This horizontal demand curve is *the* crucial feature of a perfectly competitive firm. We sometimes say such a firm is a *price-taker*. It has to treat the market price as given, independent of any decisions made by the individual firm. Next time you visit a fruit market, in which there are many stalls selling identical onions, you can think of each stall as a price-taker in the market for onions.

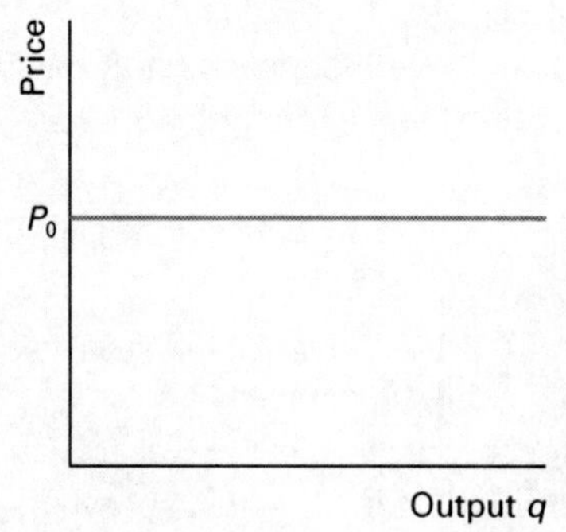

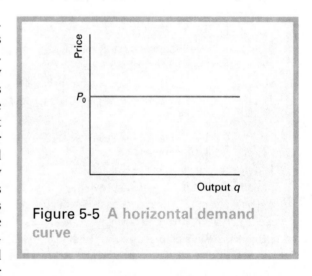

Figure 5-5 A horizontal demand curve

For each firm to face a horizontal demand curve, the industry must have four characteristics. First, there must be many firms, each trivial relative to the industry as a whole. Second, the firms must make a standardized product, so that buyers immediately switch from one firm to another if there is any difference in the prices of different firms. Thus, all firms make essentially the same product, *for which they all charge the same price.*

Why don't all the firms in the industry do what OPEC did, collectively restricting supply to raise the market price of their output? A crucial characteristic of a perfectly competitive industry is *free entry and exit.* Even if existing firms could organize themselves to restrict total supply and drive up the market price, the consequent rise in revenues and profits would attract new firms into the industry, raising total supply and driving the price back down. Conversely, when firms in a perfectly competitive industry are losing money, some firms close down. This reduces total supply and drives the price up, allowing the remaining firms to survive.

The firm's supply decision

We have already developed a general theory of the supply decision of a firm. First, the firm uses the marginal condition ($MC = MR$) to find the best positive level of output; then it uses the average condition to check whether the price for which this output is sold covers average cost. *The special feature of perfect competition is the relationship between marginal revenue and price.* Facing a horizontal demand curve, a competitive firm does *not* bid down the price as it sells more units of output. Since there is no effect on the revenue from existing output, the marginal revenue from an additional unit of output *is* its price: $MR = P$.

The firm's short-run supply curve

Firms in any industry choose the output at which short-run marginal cost SMC equals marginal revenue MR. In perfect competition, MR always equals the price P. Hence, a competitive firm produces the output at which price equals marginal cost, then checks whether zero output is better.

Figure 5-6 illustrates the firm's supply decision in the short run. P_1 is the shutdown price below which the firm fails to cover variable costs in the short run. At all prices above P_1, the firm chooses output to make $P = SMC$.

A competitive firm's **short-run supply curve** is that part of its short-run marginal cost curve above its shutdown price (the price that just covers its short-run average variable costs).

This shows how much the firm wants to make at each price it might be offered. For example, at a price P_4, the firm chooses to supply Q_4.

The firm's long-run supply curve

Similar reasoning applies in the long run. Figure 5-7 shows the firm's average and marginal costs in the long run. Facing a price P_4, equating price and long-run marginal cost, the firm chooses the long-run

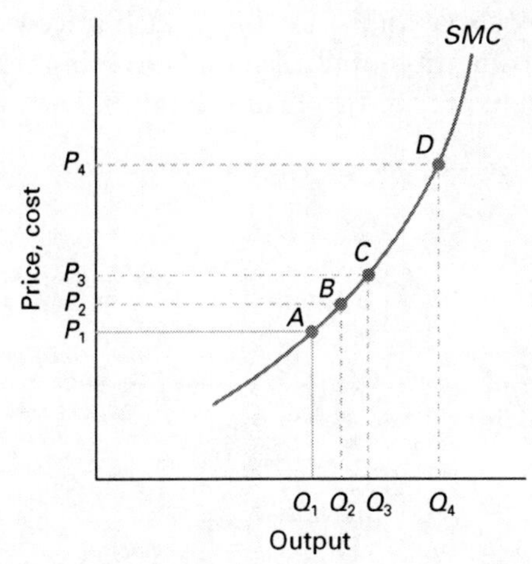

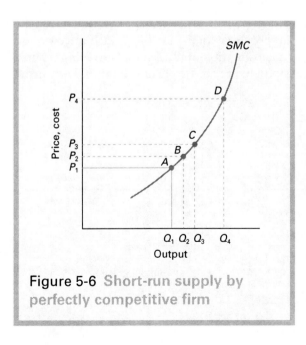

Figure 5-6 Short-run supply by perfectly competitive firm

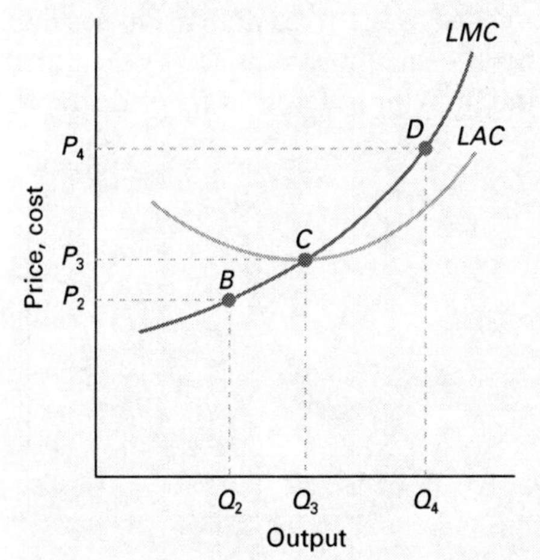

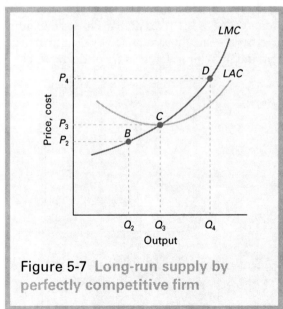

Figure 5-7 Long-run supply by perfectly competitive firm

output Q_4 at point *D*. Here it makes profits, since it is earning a price P_4 in excess of its average cost; equivalently, its total revenue exceeds its total cost.

In the long run, the firm exits from the industry only if, at its best positive output, price fails to cover long-run average cost *LAC*. At price P_2, the marginal condition leads to point *B* in Figure 5-7, but the firm is losing money and leaves the industry in the long run.

A competitive firm's **long-run supply curve** is that part of its long-run marginal cost *above* minimum average cost. At any price below P_3, the firm leaves the industry. At price P_3, the firm makes Q_3 and just breaks even after paying all its economic costs.

Entry and exit

The price P_3 corresponding to the minimum point on the *LAC* curve is called the *entry or exit price.* There is no incentive to enter or leave the industry. The resources tied up in the firm are earning just as much as their opportunity costs – what they could earn elsewhere. Any price less than P_3 will induce the firm to exit from the industry in the long run.

Entry is when new firms join an industry. **Exit** is when existing firms leave.

We can also interpret Figure 5-7 as the decision facing a potential entrant to the industry. At a price P_3, an entrant could just cover its average cost if it produced an output Q_3. Any price above P_3 yields economic profits and induces entry by other firms in the long run.

Industry supply curves

A competitive industry comprises many firms. In the short run, two things are fixed: the quantity of fixed factors used by each firm, and the number of firms in the industry. In the long run, each firm can vary all its factors of production, but the number of firms can also change through entry and exit.

The short-run industry supply curve

Just as we can add individual demand curves by buyers to get the market demand curve, we can add the individual supply curves of firms to get the industry supply curve. In Figure 5-8, at each price we add together the quantities supplied by each firm to get the total quantity supplied at that price. In the short run, the number of firms in the industry is given. Suppose there are two firms, A and B. Each firm's

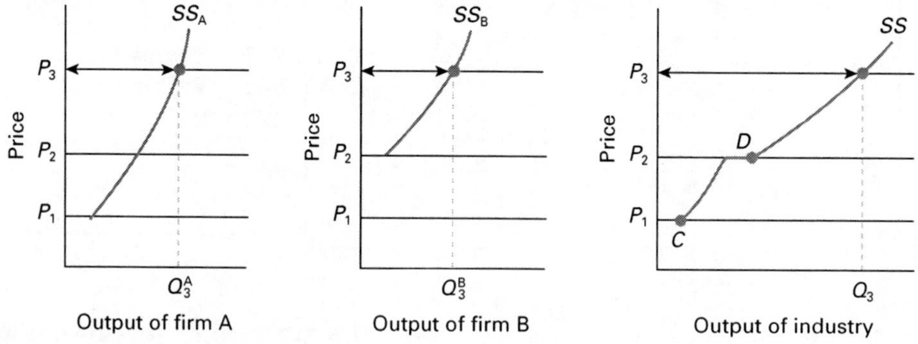

Figure 5-8 Deriving the industry supply curve

short-run supply curve is the part of its *SMC* curve above its shutdown price. Firm A has a lower shutdown price than firm B, perhaps because it has modern machinery. Each firm's supply curve is horizontal up to its shutdown price. At a lower price, no output is supplied.

The industry supply curve is the horizontal sum of the separate supply curves. Between P_1 and P_2 only the lower-cost firm, A, is producing. At P_2, firm B starts to produce too. When there are many firms, each with a different shutdown price, there are many small discontinuities as we move up the industry supply curve. Since each firm in a competitive industry is trivial relative to the total, the industry supply curve is in effect smooth.

The long-run industry supply curve

As the market price rises, the total industry supply rises in the long run for two distinct reasons: each existing firm moves up its long-run supply curve, and new firms find it profitable to enter the industry. Thus, total quantity rises both because each existing firm makes additional output and because new firms enter the industry and produce. Conversely, at lower prices, all firms move down their long-run supply curves, producing less output because prices are lower, and some firms may also leave the industry because they can no longer break even at the lower prices.

At any price, the industry supply is the horizontal sum of the outputs produced by the number of firms in the industry at that price. Hence, the long-run supply curve is flatter than the short-run supply curve for two reasons: each firm can vary its factors more appropriately in the long run; and higher prices attract *extra* firms into the industry. Both raise the output response to a price increase.

For each firm, the height of the minimum point on its *LAC* curve shows the critical price at which it can just survive in the industry. If different firms have *LAC* curves of different heights, they face different exit prices. At any price, there is a marginal firm only just able to survive in the industry, and a marginal potential entrant just waiting to enter if only the price rises a little.

The *long-run* industry supply curve normally slopes up, but in one special case it is horizontal. Suppose all existing firms and potential entrants have *identical cost curves*. In particular, they have the same long-run average cost curves *LAC* and thus the same price, shown as P_3 in Figure 5-7, at which they will enter or exit the industry in the long run. In this special case, if the market price ever exceeds P_3, new firms will enter the industry since they can make profits at any price above P_3. This flood of new entrants creates extra output, reduces scarcity, and bids down equilibrium prices until the price reverts to P_3, at which price there is no longer any incentive for firms to enter the industry. Conversely, if the price ever falls below this critical price, firms leave the industry, which makes output scarcer and raises the equilibrium price, until prices rise again to P_3, at which price there is no longer any pressure on firms to leave the industry.

Thus, in the long run, if all firms face identical cost curves, industry supply entails each individual firm producing at the output corresponding to the bottom of its average cost curve, and changes in industry output would be entirely accomplished by changes in the number of firms, via entry and exit. The industry supply curve in the long run is then *horizontal* at price P_3 corresponding to minimum average cost.

But this is a very special case. Normally, firms will have slightly different cost curves from one another for a whole host of reasons – differences in location, in expertise and knowledge, and in materials. Perfect competition does not require that firms are identical, merely that each firm is tiny relative to the market as a whole. Once firms are different, there is no possibility of expanding industry output indefinitely merely by attracting yet more of these identical firms.

On the plausible assumption that the lowest-cost producers are *already* in the market, inducing a rise in the quantity that an industry supplies generally requires higher prices, for two reasons: to induce existing firms to move along upward-sloping *LMC* curves and to attract new firms able at least to break even now that prices are higher than previously. Saying that higher prices are needed to induce the industry to supply more output is just to say that the industry supply curve slopes upwards.

Equilibrium in a competitive industry

Although each individual firm faces a horizontal demand curve for its output, the industry as a whole faces a downward-sloping demand curve for its total output. People will only buy a larger total quantity if the price is lower. To induce people as a whole to buy more flowers from flower stalls, the price of flowers needs to fall. Only then will romantic partners buy fewer boxes of chocolates and instead take home more roses for Valentine's Day.

Industry demand obeys the general laws of demand that we discussed in Chapter 2. Having now also discussed the industry supply curve, we can examine how supply and demand determine equilibrium price in the short run and the long run in a perfectly competitive industry.

In short-run equilibrium, the market price equates the quantity demanded to the total quantity supplied by the given number of firms in the industry when each firm produces on its short-run supply curve. In long-run equilibrium, the market price equates the quantity demanded to the total quantity supplied by the number of firms in the industry when each firm produces on its long-run supply curve. Since firms can freely enter or exit from the industry, the marginal firm must make only normal profits so that there is no further incentive for entry or exit.

Figure 5-9 shows long-run equilibrium for the industry. Demand is *DD* and supply is *SS*. At the equilibrium price *P**, the industry as a whole produces *Q**. This is the sum of the output of each tiny producer. At price *P**, the marginal firm is making *q** at minimum *LAC* and just breaks even. There is no incentive to enter or exit.

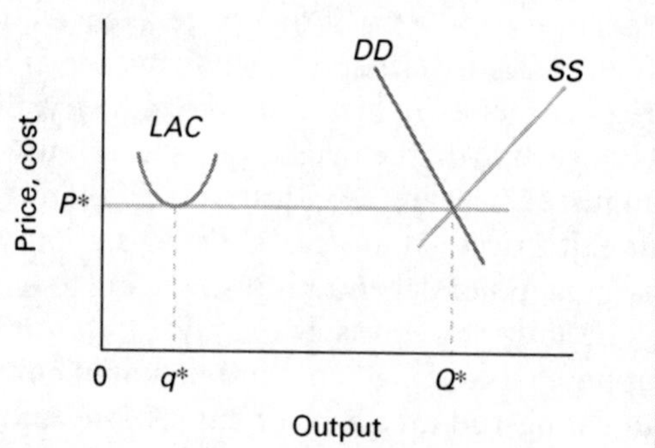

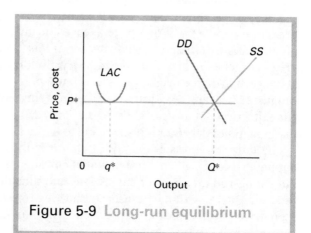

Figure 5-9 Long-run equilibrium

A rise in costs

Beginning from this equilibrium, suppose a rise in the price of raw materials raises costs for all firms in the industry. The average cost curve of every firm shifts up. The marginal firm is now losing money at the old price, *P**. Some firms eventually leave the industry. With fewer firms left, the industry supply curve *SS* shifts to the left. With less supply, the equilibrium price rises. When enough firms have left, and industry output falls enough, higher prices allow the new marginal firm to break even, despite an upward shift in *LAC*. Further incentives for entry or exit disappear.

Notice two points about the change in the long-run equilibrium that higher costs induce. First, the rise in average costs is eventually passed on to the consumer in higher prices. Second, since higher prices reduce the total quantity demanded, industry output must fall.

A rise in industry demand

The previous example discussed only long-term effects. We can of course discuss short-run effects as well. And we can examine changes in demand as well as changes in cost and supply. Figure 5-10 illustrates the effect of a shift up in the industry's demand curve from *DD* to *D′D′*.

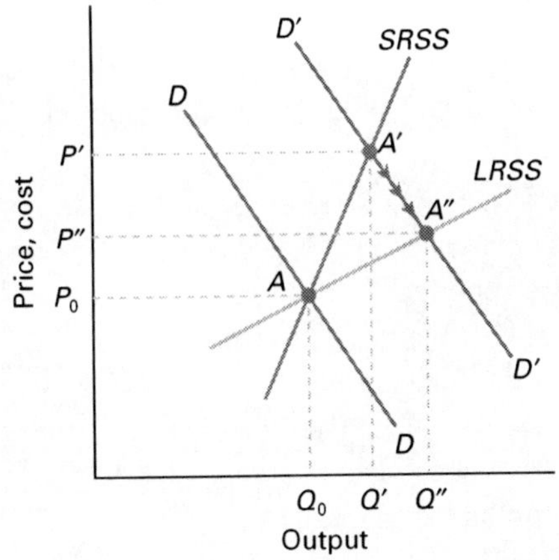

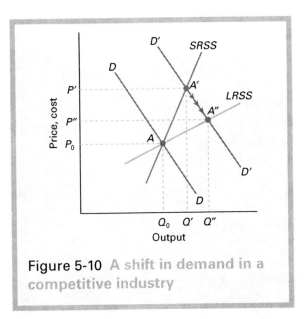

Figure 5-10 A shift in demand in a competitive industry

The industry begins in long-run equilibrium at *A*. Overnight, each firm has some fixed inputs, and the number of firms is fixed. Horizontally adding their short-run supply curves (the portion of their marginal cost curves above the shutdown price), we get the short-run industry supply curve *SRSS*. The new short-run equilibrium is at *A′*. When demand first rises, it needs a big price rise to induce individual firms to move up their steep short-run supply curves, along which some inputs are fixed.

In the long run, firms adjust all factors and move on to their flatter long-run supply curves. In addition, economic profits attract extra firms into the industry. The new long-run equilibrium is at *A″*. Relative to *A′* there is a further expansion of total output, but, with a more appropriate choice of inputs and the entry of new firms, extra supply reduces the market-clearing price.

Case study 5-2 Globalization, potential competition and price taking

The key feature of perfect competition is that each individual producer understands that it cannot affect the price by its production decisions. So what are these industries populated by trivially small firms? Some service industries provide good examples. There are no haircut hypermarkets. Most hairdressers are small because the technology does not yield large-scale producers any cost advantage. Because each operates on a small scale, but the market in the aggregate is large, each is therefore small relative to the market as a whole.

Perfect competitors can be producers of goods as well as services. There are also lots of small sheep farmers, each with a small patch of hillside, and lots of car washes, each having to charge similar prices.

Farms cultivating wheat usually operate on a much larger scale nowadays. If there were only 100 UK wheat farmers, would this mean that they would no longer be price-takers? Each is surely large enough to affect the price of UK wheat. Does this mean that wheat should not be viewed as a perfectly competitive industry? This argument would make sense if the UK did not trade with the rest of the world. But international trade is increasing all the time, as shown in the table below.

Imports as percentage of national output	1967	2007
Belgium	36	86
Netherlands	43	68
UK	18	29
France	14	29

UK firms have to compete not just with other UK firms but also with foreign firms who actually export to the UK or would like to do so. Potential entrants to the UK market are not merely UK firms but foreign firms that can sell to UK consumers not merely by building factories in the UK but simply by exporting goods from their factories abroad.

In theory, we could have a situation in which the entire UK market is supplied by a single UK firm but that firm is still a price-taker, and has no effect on UK prices at all. Suppose the whole of Norfolk became a giant wheat field supplying wheat to every UK bakery. If this superfarm thinks it faces no competition, it will be tempted to raise prices in order to make larger profits. It will try to do to wheat what OPEC did to oil: harvest a little less, make the good more scarce, force up the price (as with oil, the demand for wheat is inelastic – we all need our daily bread). So the superfarm has a small bonfire of its wheat crop to make the remaining wheat scarce. Imagine its disappointment when it subsequently discovers that high wheat prices then induce a flood of wheat imports as French and German farmers see profitable opportunities to sell their wheat in the UK!

Perhaps in the original situation, the UK superfarm faced only slightly cheaper costs of supplying the UK market than the costs faced by French and German farmers. For example, the only difference arose from the slightly higher transport costs of bringing wheat through the Channel Tunnel. Once UK wheat prices rise by more than the initial cost advantage of UK producers, suddenly there is a flood of new supply from abroad.

The more globalization takes place – national markets are increasingly integrated into a single world market – the more the relevant definition of the market is that global market itself and the prices that prevail in that market. We may therefore see situations in which even large UK firms have little ability to affect the price of their output because these firms are tiny *relative to the world market that sets the price.*

The fact that a UK firm looks large relative to the size of the UK market may not be an indication that the industry cannot be perfectly competitive. When products are standardized and can be shipped relatively easily (and therefore cheaply) from one country to another, national prices may in fact be set by international market forces.

In 2007, the high price of fuel led to protests by lorry drivers in the UK. But there were also protests in other European countries too. High prices were caused by the high world price for oil not by decisions taken by governments in the importing countries.

Recap

- The main production inputs are labour, capital, land, raw materials and energy. Land is supplied by nature and often treated as fixed in quantity. Capital is the input previously produced by people, and not used up during the current production process to which it is an input. Raw materials are used up during the production process to which they are an input. Labour is the service provided by use of workers.
- The short run is the period in which some inputs are fixed but some (especially labour, but perhaps also energy and raw materials) are variable. The production technique may also be fixed in the short run. In the long run, all input quantities and the choice of production technique can be varied if the firm wishes.

- The short-run marginal cost curve (*SMC*) rises because of diminishing returns to the variable input as output rises. Diminishing returns arise because more and more of the variable input(s) must be added to given quantities of the fixed input(s).
- Short-run total cost is short-run fixed cost + short-run variable cost. Hence, short-run average cost is short-run average fixed cost + short-run average variable cost, since in each case we simply divide the relevant total cost by the same output level.
- The firm sets output in the short run to equate *SMC* and *MR*, provided price covers short-run average variable cost. In the short run, the firm may produce at a loss if it recoups part of its fixed costs. Otherwise, it shuts down temporarily.
- In the long run, a firm can adjust all its inputs. In the short run, some inputs are fixed.
- The long-run total cost curve is the cheapest way to make each output level, when all inputs and the production technique are adjusted. It depends on technology and input prices. Technology is the set of all production techniques currently known.
- Average cost is total cost divided by output. The long-run average cost curve *LAC* is typically U-shaped. There are economies of scale on the falling bit of the U. The rising part reflects diseconomies of scale. Where the curve is horizontal, there are constant returns to scale and average cost is neither rising nor falling as output increases.
- When marginal cost is below average cost, average cost is falling. When marginal cost is above average cost, average cost is rising. Average and marginal cost are equal only at the lowest point on the average cost curve.
- In the long run, the firm supplies the output at which long-run marginal cost *LMC* equals *MR* provided price covers *LAC* at that output. If price is lower, the firm goes out of business.
- In a competitive industry, each buyer and seller is a price-taker, and cannot affect the market price.
- Perfect competition is most plausible when a large number of firms make a standard product, there is free entry and exit to the industry, and customers can easily verify that the products of different firms really are the same.
- For a competitive firm, marginal revenue and price coincide. Output is chosen to equate price to marginal cost. The firm's supply curve is its *SMC* curve above its short-run average variable cost. At any lower price, the firm temporarily shuts down. In the long run, the firm's supply curve is that part of its *LMC* curve above its *LAC* curve. At any lower price, the firm exits the industry.
- Adding, at each price, the quantities supplied by each firm, we get the industry supply curve. It is flatter in the long run both because each firm can fully adjust all factors and because the number of firms in the industry can vary.
- A rise in demand leads to a large price increase, but only a small rise in quantity. Existing firms move up their steep *SMC* curves. Price exceeds average costs. Profits attract new entrants. In the long run, output rises further but the price falls back a bit. In the long-run equilibrium, the marginal firm breaks even and there is no further change in the number of firms in the industry.
- A rise in costs for all firms reduces the industry's output and raises the price. In the long run, a higher price is needed to allow the firm that is now the marginal firm to break even. The price rise is achieved by exit from the industry, and a reduction in industry supply.

Review questions

To check your answers to these questions, go to page 335.

1 (a) Is it sufficient for a firm to know the set of available production techniques? (b) What other information is needed to run a firm?

2 (a) Why might scale economies exist? (b) The table below shows some production techniques. The cost of a worker is £5. A unit of capital costs £2. Complete the table and calculate the least-cost way to make 4, 8 and 12 units of output. (c) Are there increasing, constant or decreasing returns to scale in this output range? Which applies where?

Units of	Method 1	Method 2	Method 3	Method 4	Method 5	Method 6
Labour input	5	6	10	12	15	16
Capital input	4	2	7	4	11	8
Output	4	4	8	8	12	12
Total cost						
Average cost						

3 Suppose the cost of capital rises from 2 to 3 in the question above. (a) Would the firm change its method of production for any levels of output? Say which, if any. (b) How do the firm's total and average costs change when the cost of capital rises?

4 From the total cost curve shown below, calculate marginal and average cost at each output. Are these short-run or long-run cost curves? How can you tell?

Output	0	1	2	3	4	5	6	7	8
Total cost	12	25	40	51	60	70	84	105	128

5 Why does a marginal cost curve always pass through the minimum point on the average cost curve?

6 Why are these statements wrong? (a) Firms making losses should quit at once. (b) Big firms can always produce more cheaply than smaller firms. (c) Small is always beautiful.

7 The domestic economy has only one firm, but faces a flood of imports from abroad if it tries to charge more than the world price. Is this firm perfectly competitive?

8 Suppose an industry of identical competitive firms has a technical breakthrough that cuts costs for all firms. What happens in the short run and the long run? Explain for both the firm and the industry.

9 If every firm is a price-taker, who changes the price when a shift in demand causes initial disequilibrium?

10 Which industry has a more elastic long-run supply curve: coal mining or hairdressing? Why?

11 Harder question Since Ford and Vauxhall are very competitive with one another, should we view them as perfectly competitive firms?

12 Harder question Why are these statements wrong? (a) Since competitive firms break even in the long run, there is no incentive to be a competitive firm. (b) Competition prevents firms passing on cost increases.

13 Essay question 'Globalization means a larger market, less market power, and hence the increasing relevance of the economist's model of perfect competition.' Do you agree? What might prevent perfect competition being established in all industries?

Online LearningCentre

To help you grasp the key concepts of this chapter check out the extra resources posted on the Online Learning Centre at www.mcgraw-hill.co.uk/textbooks/begg

There are additional case studies, self-test questions, practice exam questions with answers and a graphing tool.

Chapter 6 Imperfect competition

Learning outcomes

By the end of this chapter, you should understand:

- Forms of imperfect competition
- How market structure affects the form of competition
- Pure monopoly
- How a monopolist chooses output
- How this output compares with that in a competitive industry
- How a monopolist's ability to price discriminate affects output and profits
- Monopolistic competition
- The tension between collusion and competition within a cartel
- Oligopoly and interdependence
- Games
- Commitment and credibility
- Why there is little market power in a contestable market
- Innocent entry barriers and strategic entry barriers

6-1 How market structure affects competition

Perfect competition is a useful benchmark, and represents one extreme in the spectrum of possible market structures. What determines the structure of a particular market? Why are there 10 000 florists but only a handful of chemical producers? How does the structure of an industry affect the behaviour of its constituent firms?

A perfectly competitive firm faces a horizontal demand curve at the going market price. It is a price-taker. Any other type of firm faces a downward-sloping demand curve for its product and is an *imperfectly competitive* firm.

An **imperfectly competitive** firm recognizes that its demand curve slopes down. To sell more of its own output, it needs to reduce its own price.

Within this general category are three particular examples.

For a **pure monopoly**, the demand curve for the firm is the industry demand curve itself. There is only one firm in the industry and it has no fear of entry by others.

Table 6-1 Market structure

Form of competition	Number of firms	Ability to affect price	Entry barrier	Example
Perfect competition	Many	Nil	None	Fruit stall
Imperfect competition				
Monopolistic competition	Many	Small	None	Corner shop
Oligopoly	Few	Medium	Some	Cars
Pure monopoly	One	Large	Huge	Post office

An industry with **monopolistic competition** has many sellers making products that are close but not perfect substitutes for one another. Each firm then has a limited ability to affect its output price.

Between these two lies **oligopoly**, an industry with only a few, interdependent producers.

Table 6-1 offers an overview of market structure. As with most definitions, the distinctions can get a little blurred. How do we define the relevant market? Was British Gas a monopoly in gas or an oligopolist in energy? Is Network Rail a monopoly in train lines or an oligopolist in transport infrastructure competing, for example, with the British Airports Authority.

We also have to be careful about the relevant definition of the market. When a small country trades in a competitive world market, even the sole domestic producer may have little influence on market price, which may be determined in the world market.

Why market structures differ

We now develop a general theory of how the economic factors of demand and cost interact to determine the likely structure of each industry. The car industry is not an oligopoly one day but perfectly competitive the next. It is long-run influences that induce different market structures. In the long run, one firm can hire another's workers and learn its technical secrets. In the long run, all firms or potential entrants to an industry essentially have similar cost curves.

Chapter 5 discussed minimum efficient scale, *MES*, the lowest output at which a firm's long-run average cost curve bottoms out. This is shown as the output Q^* in Figure 6-1.

When *MES* is tiny relative to the size of the market, the industry demand curve is drawn a long way to the right in Figure 6-1. There is room for

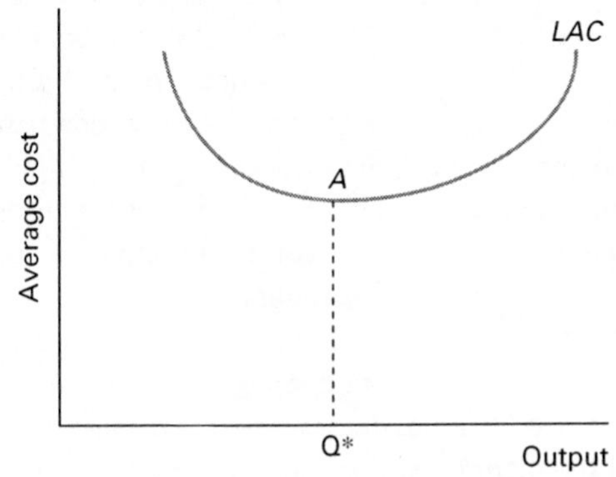

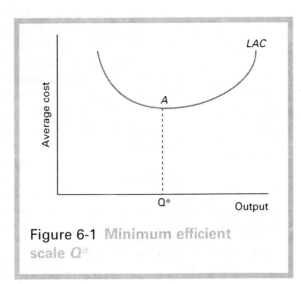

Figure 6-1 Minimum efficient scale Q^*

lots of little firms, each producing Q^* but trivial relative to the output of the whole industry, a good approximation to perfect competition. Conversely, when *MES* occurs at an output nearly as large as the entire market – imagine drawing a demand curve only just to the right of point *A* in Figure 6-1 – there is room for only one firm. A second firm trying to squeeze into the remaining space would have room only to produce a small output; but then its *LAC* curve would imply much higher average costs because it enjoys inadequate scale economies. So there is no room for a second firm to enter and make a profit. A natural monopoly enjoys sufficient scale economies to have no fear of entry by others.

When *MES* occurs at, say, a quarter of the market size as reflected by the position of the demand curve, the industry is an oligopoly, with each firm taking a keen interest in the behaviour of its small number of rivals.

Monopolistic competition lies midway between oligopoly and perfect competition. There is room for many small firms, but unlike perfect competition the firms are not identical to one another. Each corner shop is slightly closer to some customers than others. So each small firm has a little scope to affect the price it charges for its products.

Market structure thus reflects the interaction of two things: the shape and position of long-run average cost curves (and in particular the output corresponding to minimum efficient scale for a single firm) and the size of the market (as determined by the output levels consistent with the industry demand curve as a whole). Together, these determine how many firms are likely to survive in the industry and hence the type of competition that will then take place between them.

Perfect competition is one end of this spectrum, with *MES* so small relative to industry demand that each firm is insignificant. Next we look at the opposite case, in which only a single firm can survive.

Box 6-1 Facing the music

Recorded music, from albums to digital, is now a global business, owned by Sony–Bertelsmann 21.5 per cent, Universal Music 25.5 per cent, EMI 13.4 per cent, Warner Music 11.3 per cent, and independents taking the final 28.4 per cent. Why are there so few companies in the global music business? Because most of it is now digital and the marginal cost of connecting another user is tiny, whereas the fixed costs of developing playlists are large. These costs are independent of the subsequent number of users. This is a classic case in which economies of scale are huge. There is no point being a small producer. Actually, life is not that easy for the giants either: the value of the global recorded music market is falling every year because of price competition and endemic Internet piracy.

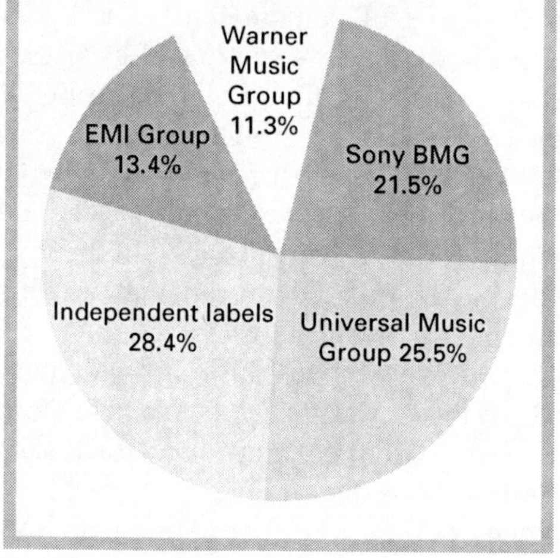

Source: http://en.wikipedia.org/wiki/Global_music_market

6-2 Pure monopoly

The perfectly competitive firm is too small to worry about the effect of its own decisions on industry output. In contrast, a pure monopoly *is* the entire industry.

A **monopolist** is the sole supplier or potential supplier of the industry's output.

A sole national supplier need not be a monopoly. If it raises prices, it may face competition from imports or from domestic entrants to the industry. In contrast, a pure monopoly does *not* need to worry about competition from either existing firms or from firms that could enter.

Profit-maximizing output

To maximize profits, a monopolist chooses the output at which marginal revenue *MR* equals marginal cost *MC*, then checks that it is covering average costs. Figure 6-2 shows the average cost curve *AC* with its usual U-shape.

Marginal revenue *MR* lies below the downward-sloping demand curve *DD*. The monopolist recognizes that, to sell extra units, it has to lower the price, even for existing customers. The more units the firm is already making and selling, the more any price reduction to sell a new unit has the effect of depressing revenue earned on existing units produced. Hence, as we move to the right and output increases, the marginal revenue schedule lies increasingly below the demand curve. Indeed, marginal revenue can become negative. In cutting the price to sell an additional output unit, the firm can lose more revenue on existing units than it gains in revenue by being able to sell an extra unit.

It is implicit in this argument that the firm has to charge a single price to all purchasers, and therefore has to reduce the price for which existing units are sold in order to sell an extra unit by inducing buyers to move downwards along their demand curve. Later, we analyse what happens when the monopolist can charge different prices to different customers. Initially, however, we assume that this is impossible.

Any firm maximizes profits choosing the output at which marginal revenue *MR* equals marginal cost *MC*. In Figure 6-2, the monopolist thus chooses the output Q_1. The demand curve *DD* implies that the monopolist sells Q_1 at a price P_1 per unit. Profit per unit is thus $[P_1 - AC_1]$, price minus average cost at the output Q_1. Total profit is the area $(P_1 - AC_1) \times Q_1$.

Even in the long run, the monopolist *continues* to make these monopoly profits. By ruling out the possibility of entry, we remove the mechanism by which profits are competed away in the long run by additional supply.

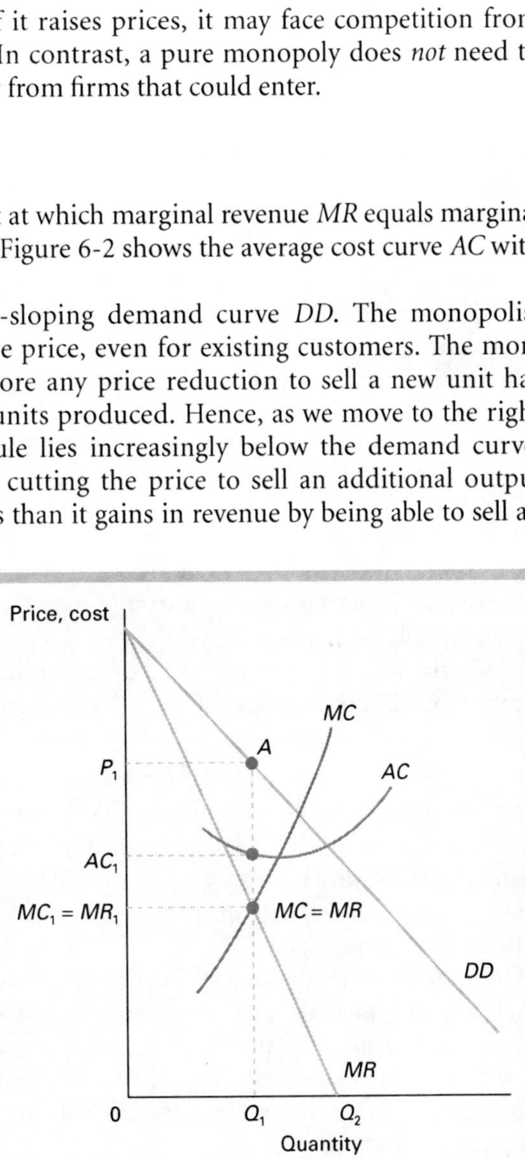

Figure 6-2 The monopolist's output decision

Price-setting

A competitive firm is a *price-taker*, taking as given the price determined by supply and demand at the industry level. In contrast, the monopolist is a *price-setter*. Having decided to make Q_1, the monopolist quotes a price P_1 knowing (from the demand curve) that the output Q_1 will be bought at this price.

When demand is elastic, lower prices increase revenue by raising quantity demanded a lot. When revenue rises, the marginal revenue from the extra output is positive. Conversely, when demand is inelastic, marginal revenue is negative. To raise output demanded, prices must be cut so much that total revenue falls.

To maximize profits, a monopolist sets $MC = MR$. Since MC is always positive, MR must also be positive at the profit-maximizing output. But this means that demand is elastic at this output. Hence, in Figure 6-1, the chosen output must lie to the left of Q_2. *A monopolist will never produce on the inelastic part of the demand curve where* MR *is negative, for then* MR *could not equal* MC, *which can never be negative.*

Monopoly power

At any output, price exceeds a monopolist's marginal revenue since the demand curve slopes down. In setting $MR = MC$, the monopolist sets a price above marginal cost. In contrast, a competitive firm equates price and marginal cost, since its price is also its marginal revenue. A competitive firm cannot raise price above marginal cost. It has no monopoly power.

Monopoly power is measured by price *minus* marginal cost at any output level.

Changes in profit-maximizing output

Figure 6-2 may also be used to analyse the effect of changes in costs or demand. Suppose higher input prices shift the MC and AC curves up. The higher MC curve must cross the MR curve at a lower output. The cost increase must reduce output. Since the demand curve slopes down, lower output induces a higher equilibrium price.

Similarly, with the original cost curves, an upward shift in demand and marginal revenue curves means that MR now crosses MC at a higher output. The monopolist raises output.

Monopoly versus competition

We now compare a perfectly competitive industry with a monopoly. Facing the same demand and cost conditions, how would the *same* industry behave if it organized as a competitive industry or as a monopoly? Cost differences are often the reason why some industries become competitive while others become monopolies. Only in special circumstances could the same industry be either perfectly competitive or a monopolist.

One case in which the comparison makes sense is when an industry has lots of *identical* firms. From Chapter 5 we know that, as a competitive industry, its long-run supply curve $LRSS$ is then horizontal. It can always expand or contract output by changing the number of firms, each producing at the bottom of its long-run average cost curve. If run as a competitive industry, long-run equilibrium occurs where this horizontal supply curve crosses the industry demand curve. In Figure 6-3 this occurs at A, where output is Q_C and the price P_C.

Now suppose two things happen. The different firms come under a single co-ordinated decision-maker, and all future entry is prohibited. Perhaps the industry is nationalized (but told to keep maximizing profits). Long-run costs, both marginal and average, are unaffected, but now the industry supremo recognizes that higher output bids down prices for everyone.

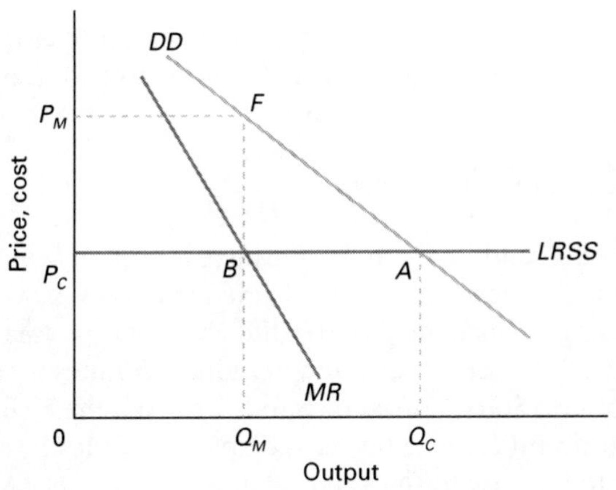

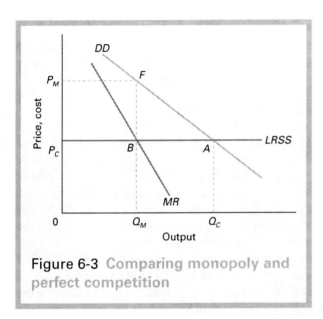

Figure 6-3 Comparing monopoly and perfect competition

In the special example, *LRSS* is also the marginal cost of output expansion by the multi-plant monopolist. In the long run the cheapest way to raise output is to build more of the identical plants, each operated at minimum average cost. Hence, equating marginal cost and marginal revenue, the multi-plant monopoly produces at *B*. Output Q_M is lower under monopoly than competition, and the price P_M is higher than the competitive price P_C.

The monopolist cuts output in order to create scarcity and raise the equilibrium price. In Figure 6-3 average cost and marginal cost are equal, since each plant is at the bottom of its *LAC* curve, where it crosses *LMC*. Hence, the monopolist's profits are the rectangle $P_M P_C BF$.

Without fear of entry, the consequent profits last forever. Notice the crucial role of blocking competition from entrants. Without this, the attempt to restrict output to raise prices is thwarted by a flood of output from new entrants.

Box 6-2 Barriers at the checkout

When the Morrisons supermarket chain took over its rival Safeway, Morrisons was catapulted from the supermarket minnow, with a 6 per cent market share, to a big league player with 17 per cent of the UK market; only marginally less than Sainsbury's, one-time leader of the supermarket industry. With its market position enhanced, Morrisons also competes for some of the biggest stars to advertise its products, from Alan Hansen to Lulu.

The takeover of Safeway was contested, with Tesco, Asda and Sainsbury's all mounting rival bids to Morrisons. At one stage, Philip Green, the owner of high-street retailer British Home Stores, also registered an interest in Safeway. Safeway was such an attractive target because it provided the last chance to enter the supermarket industry. Without access to land, and facing difficulty getting planning permission for new supermarkets, the only way in which to become a successful supermarket chain was to enter the industry by taking over a chain that already had all the distribution outlets required. With Safeway in the hands of Morrisons, and the industry consolidated into large players, the next takeover will be that much more difficult. The entry barriers are steadily rising.

For that reason, Britain's Big Four supermarkets have been subject to continuing scrutiny of their controversial practice of hoarding land. In May 2006, the Competition Commission began an investigation into potential anti-competitive practices of these firms. Preliminary findings released in October 2007 criticized supermarkets for using their land holdings in key locations to deter competition by others. Leaving key sites vacant impedes the ability of entrants to compete.

Discriminating monopoly

Thus far, all consumers were charged the same price. Unlike a competitive industry, where competition prevents any individual firm charging more than its competitors, a monopolist may be able to charge different prices to different customers.

A **discriminating monopoly** charges different prices to different buyers.

Consider an airline monopolizing flights between London and Rome. It has business customers whose demand curve is very inelastic. They have to fly. Their demand and marginal revenue curves are very steep. The airline also carries tourists whose demand curve is much more elastic. If flights to Rome are too dear, tourists can visit Athens instead. Tourists have much flatter demand and marginal revenue curves.

The airline will charge the two groups *different* prices. Since tourist demand is elastic, the airline wants to charge tourists a low fare to increase tourist revenue. Since business demand is inelastic, the airline wants to charge business travellers a high fare to increase business revenue.

Profit-maximizing output will satisfy two separate conditions. First, business travellers with inelastic demand will pay a fare sufficiently higher than tourists with elastic demand that the marginal revenue from the two separate groups is equated. Then there is no incentive to rearrange the mix by altering the price differential between the two groups. Second, the general level of prices and the total number of passengers are chosen to equate marginal cost to both these marginal revenues. This ensures that the airline operates on the most profitable scale, as well as with the most profitable mix.

When a producer charges different customers different prices, we say it *price discriminates*. There are many examples in the real world. Rail operators charge rush-hour commuters a higher fare than mid-day shoppers whose demand for trips to the city is much more elastic.

Price discrimination often applies to services, which must be consumed on the spot, rather than to goods, which can be resold. Price discrimination in standardized goods won't work. The group buying at the lower price resells to the group paying the higher price, undercutting the price differences. Effective price discrimination requires that the submarkets can be isolated from one another to prevent resale.

Figure 6-4 illustrates *perfect price discrimination*, where it is possible to charge every customer a different price for the same good. If the monopolist charges every customer the same price, the profit-maximizing output is Q_1, where *MR* equals *MC* and the corresponding price is P_1.

If the monopolist can perfectly price discriminate, the very first unit can be sold for a price *E*. Having sold this unit to the highest bidder, the customer most desperate for the good, the next unit is sold to the next highest

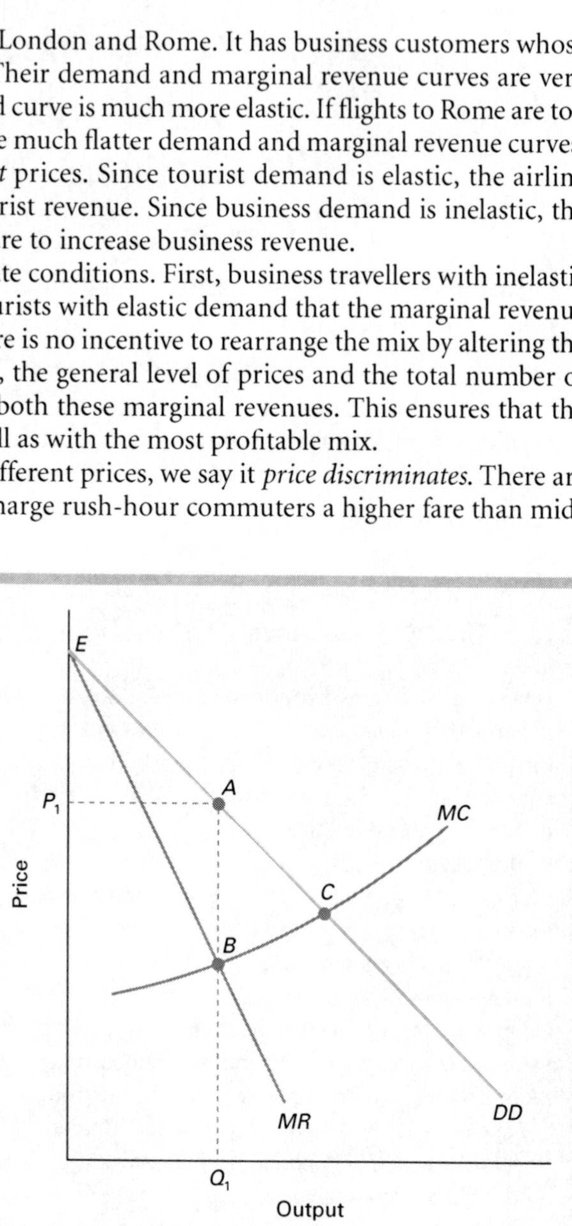

Figure 6-4 Perfect price discrimination

bidder, and so on. In reducing the price to sell that extra unit, the monopolist no longer reduces revenue from previously sold units. The demand curve *is* the marginal revenue curve under perfect price discrimination. The marginal revenue of the last unit is simply the price for which it is sold.

A perfectly price discriminating monopolist produces at *C*, where $MC = DD$, which is now marginal revenue. Price discrimination, if possible, is always profitable. In moving from the uniform pricing point *A* to the price discriminating point *C*, the monopolist adds the area *ABC* to profits. This is the excess of additional revenue over additional cost when output is higher.

The monopolist makes a second gain from price discrimination. Even the output Q_1 now brings in more revenue than under uniform pricing. The monopolist also gains the area EP_1A by charging different prices, rather than the single price P_1, on the first Q_1 units. Economic consultants often earn their fees by teaching firms new ways in which to price discriminate.

Notice, too, that whether or not the firm can price discriminate affects its chosen output by affecting its marginal revenue. In the extreme case, perfect price discrimination leads to the same price and output as under perfect competition, since in both cases the firm then sets $MC = MR = P$.

Monopoly and technical change

Joseph Schumpeter (1883–1950) argued that, even with uniform pricing, a monopoly may not produce a lower output and at a higher price than a competitive industry because the monopolist has more incentive than a competitive firm to shift its cost curves down. Technical advances reduce costs, and allow lower prices and higher output. A monopoly has more incentive to undertake research and development (R&D), necessary for cost-saving breakthroughs.

In a competitive industry a firm with a technical advantage has only a temporary opportunity to earn high profits to recoup its research expenses. Imitation by existing firms and new entrants soon compete away its profits. In contrast, by shifting down all its cost curves, a monopoly can enjoy higher profits forever. Schumpeter argued that monopolies are more innovative than competitive industries. Taking a dynamic long-run view, rather than a snapshot static picture, monopolists may enjoy lower cost curves that lead them to charge lower prices, thereby raising the quantity demanded.

This argument has some substance, but may overstate the case. Most Western economies operate a *patent* system. Inventors of new processes acquire a *temporary* legal monopoly for a fixed period. By temporarily excluding entry and imitation, the patent laws increase the incentive to conduct R&D without establishing a monopoly in the long run. Over the patent life the inventor gets a higher price and makes handsome profits. Eventually the patent expires and competition from other firms leads to higher output and lower prices. The real price of copiers and microcomputers fell significantly when the original patents of Xerox and IBM expired.

Case study 6-1 The value of a good patent

Why have food giants Unilever and Procter & Gamble withdrawn from the espresso coffee business? Not because they don't know where to find good coffee or how to manufacture home espresso machines. Rather, they have been defeated by the series of patents taken out by Nestlé.

The best cup of coffee requires that all coffee grounds are the same size, are stored in containers that do not allow the coffee to oxidize before it is used, and that it is brewed in hot water of exactly the optimal temperature and pressure. Nestlé's patents for grinding, packaging and delivering coffee through their famous Nespresso system (now licensed and retailed by other brand names) have effectively wiped out the competition. Nestlé's patent lawyers managed to preempt the key processes so accurately that Nestlé's competitors gave up trying to challenge the Nestlé monopoly. Now they are simply waiting for the patents to expire. Patents have become a key part of competitive strategy in the knowledge economy. You are probably aware of two other hotly contested patent issues in today's global economy.

The first is the patents of music companies such as EMI, who argued, successfully eventually, that Napster and other free Internet download music services were infringing the patent (usually called a copyright when it applies to music, writing and the arts) that EMI held over the artistes that it had produced. Without such protection, there is no incentive to remain in the industry: expensive investment never has any payback since Internet companies subsequently compete away all the profits. Foreseeing this, recording studios would go bankrupt and there would be no music for the Internet to download. This issue has now been resolved, and the music industry has received sufficient protection that it can now coexist with Napster and iPods, which have to pay a fee for the music to which they have access.

Another contentious issue is the price of drugs that combat HIV/Aids. Global pharmaceutical companies, such as GSK, Pfizer, and Merck, always argue that drug development is hugely costly, and that many drugs fail to succeed in the testing phase, so that the occasional winner has to earn lots of money to cover the cost of all the ones that fail, just as successful gamblers recognize that their winnings on the occasional horse that they pick has to cover all the losses on the plausible horses that nevertheless failed to win as expected. Yet poor countries, such as those in sub-Saharan Africa where HIV/Aids is a major social and economic problem, argue that they should not be forced to pay drug prices considerably in excess of current production costs merely so that pharmaceutical companies can repay their failed investment in other drugs that did not work out as planned.

Both sides of course are simultaneously correct. If pharmaceutical companies are deprived of profits on their winners, they will have to exit the industry since they will no longer be able to pay for their inevitable losers. Since the latter lose big, it also takes big winnings just to keep pharmaceutical companies in the industry. However, if they charge prices that poor Africans cannot afford, not only do many people find this ethically unattractive, it may even diminish the profits of drug companies themselves. You already know enough economics to appreciate that if the world price of drugs is substantially above the current production cost then even a lower price would yield a profit. If Africans could then afford to buy at this lower price, total drug company profits would rise *provided they did not have to reduce the price for which the drugs were sold in rich countries.* Hence, if all countries support this form of price discrimination – and if those allowed to import at lower prices undertake not to attempt to resell to richer countries at higher prices – poor countries will get the cheaper drugs that they need, and drug producers will find that they get the same revenue as before from the rich countries (where prices have not changed), plus some new sales to poor countries that were not taking place before because poor countries could not afford the high prices previously charged to them.

6-3 Monopolistic competition

The theory of monopolistic competition envisages a large number of quite small firms, each ignoring any impact its own decisions might have on the behaviour of other firms. There is free entry and exit from the industry in the long run. In these respects, the industry resembles *perfect* competition. What distinguishes monopolistic competition is that each firm faces a *downward*-sloping demand curve in its own little niche of the industry.

Different firms' products are only limited substitutes. An example is the location of corner grocers. A lower price attracts some customers from other shops, but each shop has some local customers for whom local convenience matters more than a few pence on the price of a jar of coffee. Monopolistically competitive industries exhibit *product differentiation.* For corner grocers, differentiation is based on location. In other cases, it reflects brand loyalty or personal relationships. A particular restaurant or hairdresser can charge a slightly different price from other producers in the industry without losing all its customers.

Monopolistic competition requires not merely product differentiation, but also few economies of scale. Hence there are many small producers, ignoring their interdependence with their rivals. Many examples of monopolistic competition are service industries.

Each firm produces where its marginal cost equals marginal revenue. If firms make profits, new firms enter the industry. That is the competitive part of monopolistic competition. As a result of entry, the downward-sloping demand curve of each individual firm shifts to the left. For a given market demand curve, the market share of each firm falls. With lower demand but unchanged cost curves, each firm makes lower profits. Entry stops when enough firms have entered to bid profits down to zero for the marginal firm.

Figure 6-5 shows long-run equilibrium once there is no further incentive for entry or exit. Each individual firm's demand curve *DD* has shifted enough to the left to just be tangent to its *LAC* curve at the output q^* the firm is producing. Hence, it makes zero economic profits. Price P^* equals average cost. For a perfectly competitive firm, its horizontal demand curve would be tangent to *LAC* at the minimum point on the average cost curve. In contrast, the tangency for a monopolistic competitor lies to the left of this, with both demand and *LAC* sloping down. The firm chooses output such that marginal revenue equals long-run marginal cost. That is the monopolistic part of monopolistic competition.

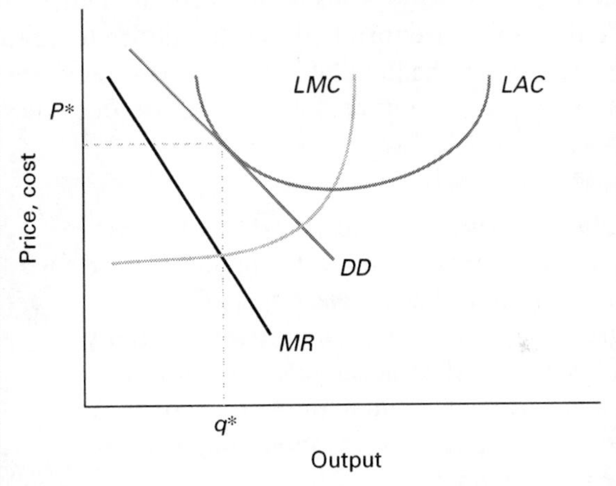

Figure 6-5 Tangency equilibrium in monopolistic competition

Notice two things about the firm's long-run equilibrium. First, the firm is *not* producing at the lowest point on its average cost curve. It could reduce average costs by further expansion. However, its marginal revenue would be so low as to make this unprofitable.

Second, the firm has some monopoly power because of the special feature of its particular brand or location. Price exceeds marginal cost. Hence, firms are usually eager for new customers prepared to buy more output at the *existing* price. It explains why we are a race of eager sellers and coy buyers. It is purchasing agents who get Christmas presents from sales reps, not the other way round.

6-4 Oligopoly and interdependence

Under perfect competition or monopolistic competition, there are so many firms in the industry that no single firm need worry about the effect of its own actions on rival firms. In pure monopoly the firm has no rivals. In contrast, the essence of an oligopoly is the need for each firm to consider how its actions affect the decisions of its relatively few rivals. The output decision of each firm depends on its guess about how its rivals will react. We begin with the basic tension between competition and collusion in such situations.

Collusion is an explicit or implicit agreement between existing firms to avoid competition.

Initially, for simplicity, we ignore entry and exit, studying only the behaviour of existing firms.

The profits from collusion

The existing firms maximize their *joint* profits if they behave like a multi-plant monopolist. A sole decision-maker would organize industry output to maximize total profits. By colluding to behave like a monopolist, oligopolists maximize their *total* profit. There is then a backstage deal to divide up these profits between individual firms.

Having cut back industry output to the point at which $MC = MR < P$, each firm then faces a marginal profit $(P - MC)$ if it can expand a little more. Provided its partners continue to restrict output, each individual firm now wants to break the agreement and expand!

Oligopolists are torn between the desire to collude, thus maximizing joint profits, and the desire to compete, in the hope of increasing market share and profits at the expense of rivals. Yet if all firms compete, joint profits are low and no firm does very well.

Cartels

Collusion between firms is easiest when formal agreements are legal. Such *cartels* were common in the late nineteenth century. They agreed market shares and prices in many industries. Such practices are now outlawed in Europe, the US and many other countries. However, secret deals in smoke-filled rooms are not unknown even today.

The kinked demand curve

In the absence of collusion, each firm's demand curve depends on how competitors react. Firms must guess these reactions. Suppose that each firm believes that its own price cut will be matched by all other firms in the industry but that an increase in its own price will induce no price response from competitors.

Figure 6-6 shows the demand curve DD each firm then faces. At price P_0, the firm makes Q_0. Since competitors do not follow suit, a price rise leads to a big loss of market share to other firms. The firm's demand curve

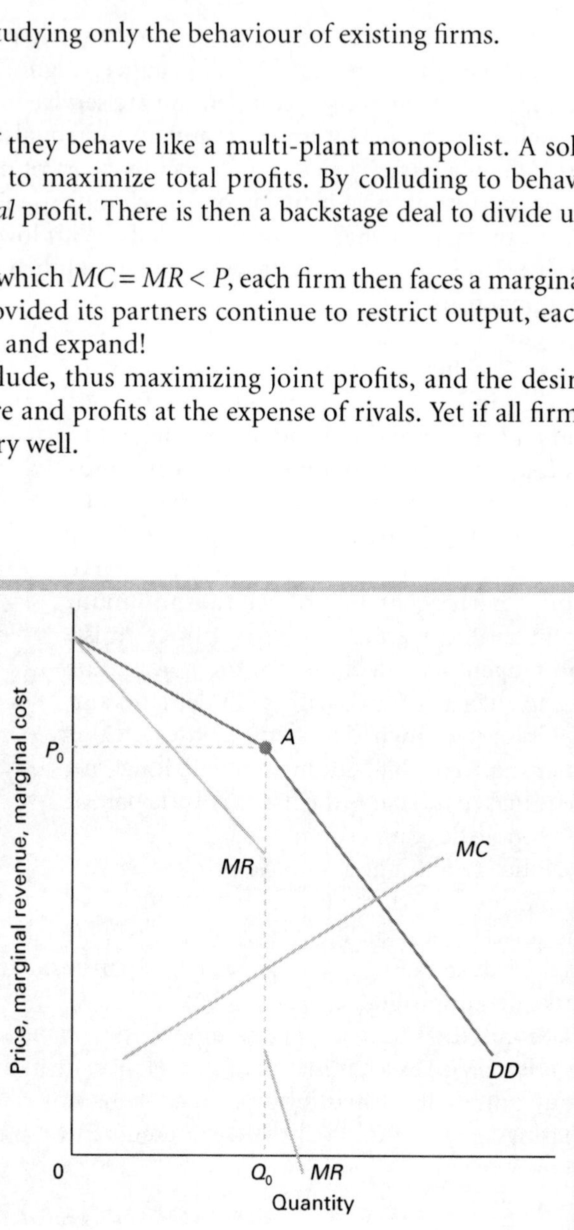

Figure 6-6 The kinked demand curve

is elastic above A at prices above P_0. However, a price cut is matched by its rivals, and market shares are unchanged. Sales rise only because the industry as a whole moves down the market demand curve as prices fall. The demand curve DD is much less elastic for price reductions from the initial price P_0.

Thus, marginal revenue MR is discontinuous at Q_0. Below Q_0 the elastic part of the demand curve applies, but at Q_0 the firm hits the inelastic portion of its kinked demand curve and marginal revenue suddenly falls. Q_0 is the profit-maximizing output for the firm, given its belief about how competitors will respond.

The model has an important implication. Suppose the MC curve of a single firm shifts up or down by a small amount. Since the MR curve has a discontinuous vertical segment at the output Q_0, it remains optimal to make Q_0 and charge a price P_0. The kinked demand curve model may explain the empirical finding that firms do not always adjust prices when costs change.

It does not explain what determines the initial price P_0. It may be the collusive monopoly price. Each firm believes that an attempt to undercut its rivals induces them to cut prices to defend market share. However, its rivals are happy for it to charge a higher price and lose market share.

There is a difference between the effect of a cost change for a single firm and a cost change for all firms together. The latter shifts the marginal cost curve up for the industry as a whole, raising the collusive monopoly price. Each firm's kinked demand curve shifts up since the monopoly price P_0 rises. Thus, we can reconcile the stickiness of a single firm's prices with respect to changes in its own costs alone, and the speed with which the entire industry marks up prices when all firms' costs are increased by higher taxes or wage rises in the whole industry.

Game theory and interdependent decisions

A good poker player sometimes bluffs. Sometimes you make money with a bad hand that your opponents misread as a good hand. Like poker players, oligopolists have to try to second-guess their rivals' moves to determine their own best action. To study how interdependent decisions are made, we use *game theory*.

A **game** is a situation in which intelligent decisions are necessarily interdependent.

The *players* in the game try to maximize their own *pay-offs*. In an oligopoly, the firms are the players and their pay-offs are their profits in the long run. Each player must choose a strategy.

A **strategy** is a game plan describing how the player will act or move in each situation.

Being a pickpocket is a strategy. Lifting a particular wallet is a move. As usual, we are interested in equilibrium. In most games, each player's best strategy depends on the strategies chosen by other players. It is silly to be a pickpocket in a police station.

In **Nash equilibrium**, each player chooses his best strategy, *given* the strategies chosen by other players.

This description of equilibrium was invented by John Nash, who won the Nobel Prize for Economic Science for his work on game theory, and was the subject of the film *A Beautiful Mind*, starring Russell Crowe. Sometimes, but not usually, a player's best strategy is independent of those chosen by others. If so, it is a *dominant strategy*. We begin with an example in which each player has a dominant strategy.

Box 6-3 War games

For years, Nintendo, Sony and Microsoft have pitted their video game consoles against each other, fighting for a global industry. The seventh-generation consoles began in 2005 with the launch of Microsoft's Xbox 360, followed by Sony's PlayStation 3 and Nintendo's Wii in 2006. Xbox 360 and PlayStation 3 emphasized high-definition graphics, whereas Wii focused on movement sensors and joysticks.

Microsoft's earlier launch won it initial market share, though it also experienced some technical problems. However, the Nintendo Wii subsequently proved popular, forcing Sony to drop the price of their relatively expensive PlayStation 3. The Xbox 360's advantage over its competitors has been its quantity and quality of games, winning more awards than its rivals. Although the last to launch, Nintendo has benefited from the distinctive joystick technology, clawing back the early lead of Xbox 360 and outselling PlayStation 3. Competition between the three rivals is fierce – in technology, in pricing strategy and in ancilliary support.

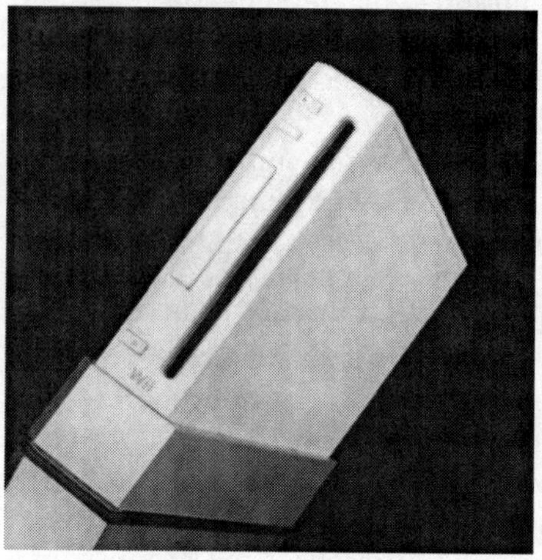

Nintendo Wii console
© Optikat/Alamy

Console	Million units shipped to retailers (worldwide) as at 30 June 2008
Wii	30
Xbox 360	20
PlayStation 3	14

Source: Adapted from http://en.wikipedia.org/wiki/History

Collude or cheat?

Figure 6-7 shows a game that we can imagine is between the only two members of a cartel like OPEC. Each firm can select a high-output or low-output strategy. In each box, the first number shows firm A's profits and the second number, firm B's profits for that output combination.

When both have high output, industry output is high, the price is low, and each firm makes a small profit of 1. When each has low output, the outcome is more like collusive monopoly. Prices are high and each firm does better, making a profit of 2. Each firm does best (a profit of 3) when it alone has high output; for, then, the other firm's low output helps hold down industry output and keep up the price. In this situation we assume the low-output firm makes a profit of 0.

Now we can see how the game will unfold. Consider firm A's decision. If firm B has a high-output strategy, firm A does better also to have high output. In the two left-hand boxes, firm A gets a profit of 1 by choosing high but a profit of 0 by choosing low. Now suppose firm B chooses a low-output strategy. From the two right-hand boxes, firm A still does better by choosing high, since this yields it a

		Firm B output	
		High	Low
Firm A output	High	1 1	3 0
	Low	0 3	2 2

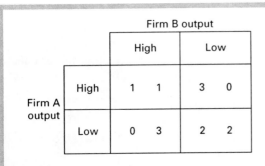

Figure 6-7 The Prisoners' Dilemma game

profit of 3, whereas low yields it a profit of only 2. Hence firm A has a dominant strategy. Whichever strategy B adopts, A does better to choose a high-output strategy. Firm B also has a dominant strategy to choose high output. Check for yourself that B does better to go high whichever strategy A selects. Since both firms choose high, the equilibrium is the top left-hand box. Each firm gets a profit of 1.

Yet both firms would do better, getting a profit of 2, if they colluded to form a cartel and both produced low – the bottom right-hand box. But neither can afford to take the risk of going low. Suppose firm A goes low. Firm B, comparing the two boxes in the bottom row, will then go high, preferring a profit of 3 to a profit of 2. And firm A will get screwed, earning a profit of 0 in that event. Firm A can figure all this out in advance, which is why its dominant strategy is to go high.

This is a clear illustration of the tension between collusion and competition. In this example, it appears that the output-restricting cartel will never get formed, since each player can already foresee the overwhelming incentive for the other to cheat on such an arrangement. How, then, can cartels ever be sustained? One possibility is that there exist binding commitments.

A **commitment** is an arrangement, entered into voluntarily, that restricts one's future actions.

If both players could simultaneously sign an enforceable contract to produce low output they could achieve the co-operative outcome in the bottom right-hand box, each earning profits of 2. Clearly, they then do better than in the top left-hand box, which describes the non-cooperative equilibrium of the game. Without any commitment, neither player can go low because then the other player will go high. Binding commitments, by removing this temptation, enable both players to go low, and both players gain. This idea of commitment is important, and we shall meet it many times. Just think of all the human activities that are the subject of legal contracts, a simple kind of commitment simultaneously undertaken by two parties or players.

This insight is powerful, but its application to oligopoly requires some care. Cartels within a country are illegal, and OPEC is not held together by a signed agreement that can be upheld in international law! Is there a less formal way in which oligopolists can commit themselves not to cheat on the collusive low-output solution to the game? If the game is played only once, this is hard. However, in the real world, the game is repeated many times: firms choose output levels day after day. Suppose two players try to collude on low output. Furthermore, each announces a *punishment strategy*. Should firm A ever cheat on the low-output agreement, firm B promises that it will subsequently react by raising its output. Firm A makes a similar promise.

Suppose the agreement has been in force for some time, and both firms have stuck to their low-output deal. Firm A assumes that firm B will go low as usual. Figure 6-7 shows that firm A will make a *temporary* gain today if it cheats and goes high. Instead of staying in the bottom right-hand box with a profit of 2, it can move to the top right-hand box and make 3. However, from tomorrow onwards, firm B will also go high, and firm A can then do no better than continue to go high too, making a profit of 1 for evermore.

However, if A refuses to cheat today it can continue to stay in the bottom right-hand box and make 2 forever. In cheating, A swaps a temporary gain for permanently lower profits. Thus, punishment strategies can sustain an explicit cartel or implicit collusion even if no formal commitment exists.

It is easy to say that you will adopt a punishment strategy in the event that the other player cheats; but this will affect the other player's behaviour only if your threat is credible.

A **credible threat** is one that, after the fact, it is still optimal to carry out.

In the preceding example, once firm A cheats and goes high, it is then in firm B's interest to go high anyway. Hence B's threat to go high if A ever cheats is a credible threat.

Entry and potential competition

So far we have discussed imperfect competition between existing firms. What about potential competition from new entrants? Three cases must be distinguished: where entry is trivially easy, where it is difficult by accident, and where it is difficult by design.

Contestable markets

Suppose we see an industry with few incumbent firms. Before assuming it is an oligopoly, we must think about entry and exit.

A **contestable market** has free entry and free exit.

Free exit means that there are no *sunk* or irrecoverable costs. On exit, a firm can fully recoup its previous investment expenditure, including money spent on building up knowledge and goodwill. A contestable market allows *hit-and-run* entry. If the incumbent firms, however few, are pricing above minimum average cost, an entrant can step in, undercut them, make a temporary profit, and exit. If so, even when incumbent firms are few in number, they have to behave as if they were perfectly competitive, setting $P = MC = AC$.

The theory of contestable markets is controversial. There are many industries in which sunk costs are hard to recover, or where expertise takes an entrant time to acquire. Nor is it safe to assume that incumbents will not change their behaviour when threatened by entry. But the theory does vividly illustrate that market structure and incumbent behaviour cannot be deduced by counting the number of firms in the industry. We were careful to stress that a monopolist is a sole producer *who can completely discount fear of entry.*

Innocent entry barriers

Entry barriers may be created by nature or by other rivals.

An **innocent entry barrier** is one made by nature.

Absolute cost advantages, where incumbent firms have lower cost curves than entrants, may be innocent. If it takes time to learn the business, incumbents have lower costs in the short run.

Scale economies are another innocent entry barrier. If minimum efficient scale is large relative to market size, an entrant cannot get into the industry without considerably depressing the price. It may be impossible to break in at a profit. The greater the innocent entry barriers, the more we can neglect potential competition from entrants. The oligopoly game then reduces to competition between incumbent firms, as we discussed in the previous section.

Where innocent entry barriers are low, incumbent firms may accept this situation, in which case competition from potential entrants prevents incumbent firms from exercising much market power, or else incumbent firms will try to design some entry barrier of their own.

Strategic entry deterrence

The word 'strategic' has a precise meaning in economics.

> Your **strategic move** influences the other player's decision, in a manner helpful to you, by affecting the other person's expectations of how you will behave.

Suppose you are the only incumbent firm. Even if limited scale economies make it feasible for entrants to produce on a small scale, you threaten to flood the market if they come in, causing a price fall and big losses for everyone. Since you have a fat bank balance and they are just getting started, they will go bankrupt. Entry is pointless. You get the monopoly profits. But is your threat credible? Without spare capacity, how can you make extra output to bid down the price a lot.

Seeing this, the potential entrant may call your bluff. Suppose, instead, you build a costly new factory which is unused unless there is no entry. If, at some future date, an entrant appears, the cost of the new factory has largely been paid, and its marginal cost of production is low. The entrant succumbs to your credible threat to flood the market and decides to stay out. Provided the initial cost of the factory (spread suitably over a number of years) is less than the extra profits the incumbent keeps making *as a result of having deterred entry*, this entry deterrence is profitable. It is strategic because it works by influencing the decision of *another* player.

> **Strategic entry deterrence** is behaviour by incumbent firms to make entry less likely.

Is spare capacity the only commitment available to incumbents? Commitments must be irreversible, otherwise they are an empty threat; and they must increase the chances that the incumbent will fight. Anything with the character of fixed and sunk costs may work. Fixed costs artificially increase scale economies, and sunk costs have already been incurred.

Box 6-4 Freezing out new entrants?

Unilever is a major player in many consumer products, from toothpaste to soap powder. One of its big winners is Wall's ice cream, which has two-thirds of the UK market and generates profits of £100 million a year; retailers' mark-ups can also be as high as 55 per cent. In addition to established rivals such as Nestlé (www.nestle.com) and Haagen Dazs, Unilever has faced new challenges from frozen chocolate bars such as Mars.

A critical aspect of these 'bar wars' is the freezer cabinets in which small shops store ice cream. As the leading incumbent, Unilever 'loaned' cabinets free of charge to small retailers. Unilever contended that its high market share reflected its marketing expertise ('just one Cornetto'); Mars argued that Unilever erected strategic barriers to entry, particularly effective in small shops with space for only one freezer cabinet, by requiring that only Unilever products were stocked in the cabinet they loaned to retailers. In January 2000, the UK government ordered Unilever to stop freezing out competitors.

Advertising to invest in goodwill and brand loyalty is a good example. So is product proliferation. If the incumbent has only one brand, an entrant may hope to break in with a different brand. If the incumbent has a complete range of brands or models, however, an incumbent will have to compete across the whole product range. Sometimes deterring entry costs incumbents too much money. Entry will then take place, as in the example of monopolistic competition.

Summing up

Few industries in the real world closely resemble the textbook extremes of perfect competition or pure monopoly. Most are imperfectly competitive. Game theory in general, and notions such as commitment, credibility and deterrence, let economists analyse many of the practical concerns of big business.

What have we learned? First, market structure and the behaviour of incumbent firms are determined *simultaneously*. At the beginning of the section, we argued that the relation between minimum efficient scale and market size would determine market structure, whether the industry was a monopoly, oligopoly or displayed monopolistic or perfect competition. However, these are not merely questions of the extent of innocent entry barriers. Strategic behaviour can also affect the shape of cost curves and the market structure that emerges.

Second, and related, we have learned the importance of *potential* competition, which may come from domestic firms considering entry, or from imports from abroad. The number of firms observed in the industry today conveys little information about the extent of the market power they truly exercise. The more globalization takes place, the more relevant this argument becomes.

Finally, we have seen how many business practices of the real world – price wars, advertising, brand proliferation, excess capacity, or excessive research and development – can be understood as strategic competition in which, to be effective, threats must be made credible by commitments.

Case study 6-2 Why advertise so much?

Evan Davis is host of the *Dragons' Den*. John Kay writes a fortnightly column on corporate strategy for the *Financial Times*. This case study is based on work they did together at the London Business School over 15 years ago, but which is still just as relevant today.

Advertising is not always meant to erect entry barriers to potential entrants. Sometimes, it really does aim to inform consumers by revealing inside information that firms have about the quality of their own goods.

When consumers can tell at a glance the quality of a product, even before buying it, there is little gain from advertising. Black rotten bananas cannot convincingly be portrayed as fresh and delicious. Information is freely available and attempts to deceive consumers are detected rapidly. However, for most goods, consumers cannot detect quality before purchase, and gradually discover quality only after using the good for a while.

The producer then has inside information over first-time buyers. A conspicuous (expensive) advertising campaign *signals* to potential buyers that the firm believes in its product and expects to make enough repeat sales to recoup the cost of the initial investment in advertising. Firms whose lies are quickly discovered by consumers do not invest much in advertising because they never sell enough to recoup their outlay on adverts. Consumers discover the poor quality and refrain from repeat purchasing. Foreseeing this, the firm that knows it will be quickly discovered never wastes money on expensive advertising in the first place. ▶

What about one-off purchases, such as refrigerators, that usually last a decade or more? Consumers would really benefit from truthful advertising but producers of high-quality goods have no incentive to advertise. It would pay producers of low-quality refrigerators to advertise too since it would be ages before gullible consumers needed to return for a repeat purchase. A willingness to advertise no longer signals how much the firm believes in its own product. Since high-quality firms do not bother advertising, and since low-quality firms mimic the behaviour of high-quality firms, low-quality firms do not advertise either.

The table below shows advertising spending as a fraction of sales revenue for the three types of good identified above. The theory fits the facts well.

Quality detected	Time till buy again	Example	Advertising as percentage of sales revenue
Before buy	Irrelevant	Bananas	0.4
Soon after buy	Soon	Biscuits	3.6
Long after buy	Much later	Refrigerator	1.8

Source: E. Davis, J. Kay and J. Star, 'Is advertising rational?', *Business Strategy Review*, 1991

Recap

- Market structure refers to the relative size of minimum efficient scale and the total size of the market as reflected by the position of the industry demand curve.
- Market structure is also affected by the shapes of these curves. The steeper the industry demand curve, the more an entrant's extra output will bid down the price, making it harder to enter; and the steeper the *LAC* curve at outputs below minimum efficient scale, the harder it is for an entrant to enter and produce a small output.
- A pure monopoly is the only seller or potential seller in an industry. The monopolist has a large minimum efficient scale relative to the size of the industry. Economies of scale are important.
- To maximize profits, a monopolist chooses the output at which $MC = MR$. The relation of price to MR depends on the elasticity of the demand curve.
- A monopolist cuts back output to force up the price. The gap between price and marginal cost is a measure of monopoly power.
- A discriminating monopoly charges higher prices to customers whose demand is more inelastic.
- Monopolies have more ability and incentive to innovate. In the long run, this is a force for cost reduction. Temporary patents achieve some of the same effect even in competitive industries.
- Imperfect competition exists when individual firms face downward-sloping demand curves.
- When minimum efficient scale is very large relative to the industry demand curve, this innocent entry barrier may produce a natural monopoly in which entry can be ignored.

- At the opposite extreme, entry and exit may be costless. The market is contestable, and incumbent firms must mimic perfectly competitive behaviour, or be undercut by a flood of entrants.
- Monopolistic competitors face free entry and exit, but are individually small and make similar though not identical products. Each has limited monopoly power in its special brand. In long-run equilibrium, price equals average cost. Each firm's downward-sloping demand curve is tangent to the downward-sloping part of its *LAC* curve.
- Oligopolists face a tension between collusion to maximize joint profits and competition for a larger share of smaller joint profits. Without credible threats of punishment by other collusive partners, each firm is tempted to cheat.
- Game theory describes interdependent decision making. In the Prisoners' Dilemma game, each firm has a dominant strategy but the outcome is disadvantageous to both players. With binding commitments, both are better off by guaranteeing not to cheat on the collusive solution.
- In Nash equilibrium, each player selects her best strategy, given the strategies selected by rivals.
- Innocent entry barriers are made by nature, and arise from scale economies or absolute cost advantages of incumbent firms. Strategic entry barriers are made in boardrooms and arise from credible commitments to resist entry if challenged.

Review questions

To check your answers to these questions, go to page 336.

1 A monopolist produces at constant marginal cost of £5 and faces the following demand curve:

Price (£)	8	7	6	5	4	3
Quantity	1	2	3	4	5	6

Calculate the *MR* curve. What is the equilibrium output? Equilibrium price? What would be the equilibrium price and output for a competitive industry? Why does the monopolist make less output and charge a higher price.

2 In addition to the data above, the monopolist also has a fixed cost of £2. What difference does this make to the monopolist's output, price and profits? Why?

3 Now suppose the government levies a monopoly tax, taking half the monopolist's profit. (a) What effect does this have on the monopolist's output? (b) What was the marginal profit on the last unit of output before the tax was levied? (c) Does this help you answer (a)?

4 Why do golf clubs have off-peak membership at reduced fees?

5 Why might a monopoly have more incentive to innovate than a competitive firm? Could a monopoly have less incentive to innovate?

6 Why are these statements wrong? (a) By breaking up monopolies we always get more output at a lower price. (b) A single producer in the industry is a sure sign of monopoly.

7 Vehicle repairers sometimes suggest that mechanics should be licensed so that repairs are done only by qualified people. (a) Evaluate the arguments for and against licensing car mechanics. (b) Are the arguments the same for licensing doctors?

8 An industry faces the demand curve:

Q	1	2	3	4	5	6	7	8	9	10
P	10	9	8	7	6	5	4	3	2	1

(a) As a monopoly, with $MC = 3$, what price and output are chosen? (b) Now suppose there are two firms, each with $MC = AC = 3$. What price and output maximize joint profits if they collude? (c) Why do the two firms have to agree on the output each produces? Why might each firm be tempted to cheat?

9 **Harder question** With the above industry demand curve, two firms, A and Z, begin with half the market each when charging the monopoly price. Z decides to cheat and believes A will stick to its old output level. (a) Show the demand curve Z believes it faces. (b) What price and output would Z then choose?

10 **Harder question** Why are these statements wrong? (a) Competitive firms should collude to restrict output and drive up the price. (b) Firms would not advertise unless it increased their sales.

11 **Essay question** A good-natured parent knows that children sometimes need to be punished, but also knows that, when it comes to the crunch, the child will be let off with a warning. Can the parent undertake any pre-commitment to make the threat of punishment credible?

Online LearningCentre

To help you grasp the key concepts of this chapter check out the extra resources posted on the Online Learning Centre at www.mcgraw-hill.co.uk/textbooks/begg

There are additional case studies, self-test questions, practice exam questions with answers and a graphing tool.

Chapter 6

Types of Business Organization

CHAPTER OBJECTIVES

This chapter will explain:

- the diversity of organizational types
- the advantages and disadvantages of sole traders, partnerships and limited companies
- the role of public-sector organizations and Non-Departmental Public Bodies
- the effects of organizational form and size on responsiveness to environmental change

6.1 Introduction: organizations and their environment

Previous chapters have focused on the external environment that affects business organizations. In this chapter we begin to turn our focus inward, to look at the nature of business organizations. We need to understand the factors that facilitate or inhibit an internal response to external environmental change.

But first, we need to ask a basic question: 'Why do organizations exist?' The main reason is that some forms of value creation can be carried out much more efficiently within organizations than by individuals acting alone. Imagine individuals trying to build an aircraft and you can appreciate that they will achieve their objective much more effectively if they come together in some form of organization. However, if a group of individuals want to go into business as household decorators, they might find that the costs of managing the organization put them at a competitive disadvantage compared to individuals acting on their own. Business organizations are extremely diverse in their forms and functions, even within a single business sector. It is therefore difficult to define an 'ideal' organization. Instead, all organizational forms have advantages and disadvantages relative to the environment in which they operate, and successful organizations capitalize on their advantages while recognizing their disadvantages. In a single business sector, there can be a role for both the one-person owner-managed business and the multinational organization. Both can adapt and find a role.

Analogies can be drawn between business organizations and their environment and the animal kingdom. In a natural habitat, the largest and most powerful animals can co-exist with much smaller species. The smaller species can avoid becoming prey for the larger ones by being more agile, or developing defences such as safe habitats that are inaccessible to their larger predators. Sometimes, a symbiotic relationship can develop between the two. In a bid to survive, animals soon learn which sources of food are easily obtainable and abandon those that are either inedible or cause them to face competition from more powerful animals. In Darwinian terms, the 'fittest' survive, and an ecosystem allows for co-existence of living organisms that have adapted in their own way to the challenges of their environment. As in the business environment, macro environmental change can affect the relationships between species – as, for example, has occurred with deforestation and the use of intensive farming methods.

Just as any study of the animal world may begin by examining the characteristics of the participants, so an analysis of the business environment could begin by looking at the characteristics of the organizations that make it up. Businesses need to understand the diversity of organizational types for a number of reasons.

- Different types of organization will be able to address their customers, suppliers and employees in different ways. Lack of resources could, for example, inhibit the development of expensive new products by a small business. Sometimes, the objectives of an organization – either formal or informal – will influence what it is able to offer the public.
- As a seller of materials to companies involved in further manufacture, a company should understand how the buying behaviour of different kinds of organization varies. A small business is likely to buy equipment in a different way to a large public-sector organization.
- We should be interested in the structure of business units at the macroeconomic level. Many economists have argued that a thriving small business sector is essential for an expanding economy, and that the effect of domination by large organizations may be to

reduce competition and innovation. We should therefore be interested in the rate of new business creation and trends in the composition of business units.

6.1.1 Classification of business organizations

There are many approaches to classifying organizations that would satisfy the interests identified above. Organizations are commonly classified according to their:

- size (e.g. turnover, assets, employees, geographical coverage)
- ownership (e.g. public, private, cooperative)
- legal form (e.g. sole trader, limited company)
- industry sector.

A good starting point for classifying business organizations is to look at their legal form. A business's legal form is often closely related to its size, objectives, and the level of resources it has available for marketing and for new product development (the issues of organizational size and objectives are considered in more detail in the next chapter).

This chapter will first consider private-sector organizations, which range from the small owner-managed sole trader to the very large public limited company. It will then review the diverse range of publicly owned organizations that operate as businesses. A third, and growing, group of organizations cannot be neatly categorized into private or public sector and includes Non-Departmental Public Bodies (NDPBs) (often referred to as quangos) and charities. To put the diversity of organizations into context, Figure 6.1 illustrates the types of organization that will be described in this chapter.

6.2 The sole trader

The most basic level of business organization is provided by the sole trader. In fact, the concept of a separate legal form does not apply to this type of organization, for the business and the individual are considered to be legally indistinguishable. The individual carries on business in his or her own name, with the result that the individual assumes all the rights and duties of the business. It follows that if the business is sued for breach of contract, this amounts to suing the individual. If the business does not have the resources to meet any claim, the claim must be met out of the private resources of the individual.

Becoming a sole trader requires the minimum of formality and for this reason it can be difficult to tell how many are being created or are in existence at any one time. The most commonly used indication is provided by VAT registrations, although this does not give a complete picture as businesses with a turnover of less than £64,000 (2007/08) do not need to register. Maintaining a business as a sole trader also requires a minimum of formality – for example, there is no obligation to file annual accounts, other than for the assessment of the individual's personal tax liability.

It has been estimated that about 80 per cent of all businesses in the United Kingdom are sole traders, although they account for only a small proportion of gross domestic product (GDP). In some sectors of the economy they are a very popular business form, and dominate sectors such as newsagents, window cleaners and hairdressers. Sole traders can grow by taking on additional

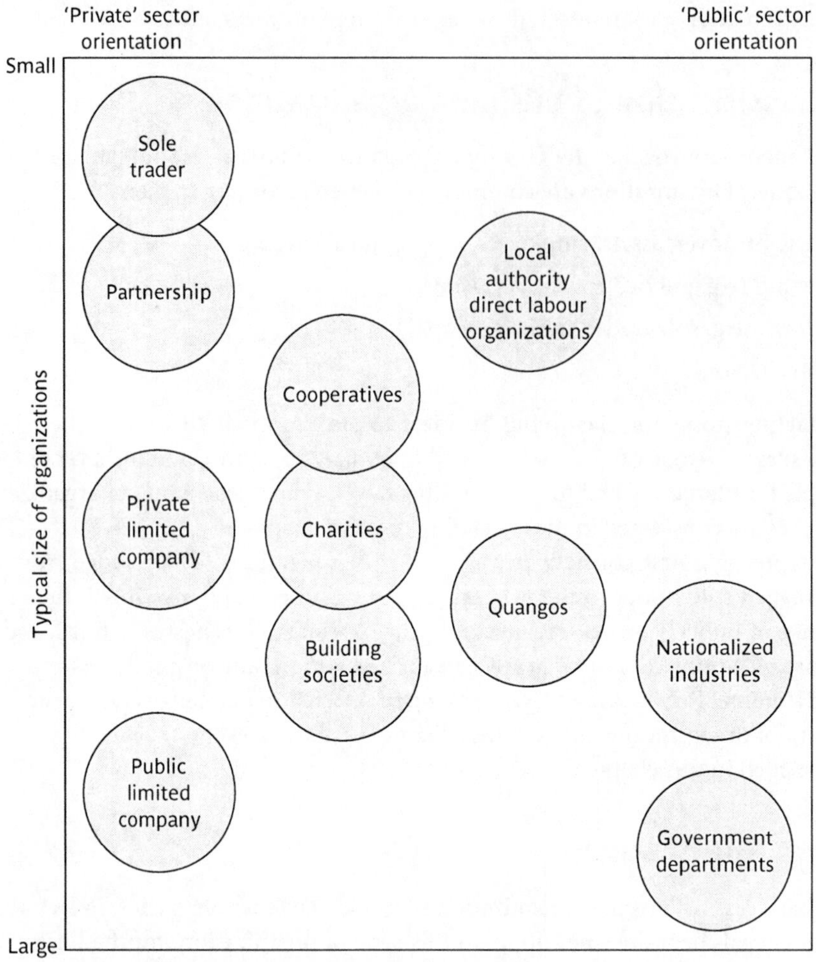

Figure 6.1 A schematic classification of organizational types

employees. There is no legal limit on the number of employees that a sole trader may have and there are many examples of sole traders employing over 100 people. At the other extreme, it is sometimes difficult to describe just when a sole trader business unit comes into existence, with many sole traders operating on a part-time basis – some 'moonlighting' without the knowledge of the tax authorities. Estimates of the annual value of this so-called 'black economy' are as high as £200 million per annum.

We should recognize a number of important characteristics of sole traders. First, they tend to have limited capital resources. Risk capital is generally provided only by the sole proprietor or close personal backers, and additional loan capital is often made available only against security of the individual's assets. In the field of new product development, this type of business has very often made discoveries, but has been unable to see new products through to production and launch on account of a lack of funds. If a new product does make it into a competitive market, this type of business may face competition in price, promotional effort or product offering from larger and better-resourced firms. The larger firm is likely to have greater resources to mount a campaign to see off a newer competitor.

Being relatively small, the sole trader may suffer by not being able to exploit the economies of scale available to larger firms. On the other hand, many sole traders aim for those sectors where economies of scale are either unimportant or non-existent – for example, painting and decorating, hairdressing and outside catering. In many personal services, smallness and the personal touch, plus the fact that many small businesses do not need to charge their customers VAT, can be a strong selling point.

The small sole trader could find that it is too small to justify having its own expertise in many areas. Many do not have specialists to look after the accounting or advertising functions, for example. Furthermore, the goals and policies of the business can become totally dominated by the owner of the business. Although goals can be pursued determinedly and single-mindedly, the sole trader presents a narrower view than may be offered by a larger board of directors. The goals of a sole trader may appear very irrational to an outsider; for instance, many individuals may be happy to continue uneconomic ventures on emotional grounds alone. Many very small caterers, for example, may be financially better off drawing unemployment benefit, but being a sole trader may satisfy wider goals of status or the pursuit of a leisure interest.

Many sole traders fail after only a short time, often because of the lack of management skills of an individual who may well be an expert in his or her own field of specialization. Others continue until they reach a point where lack of expertise and financial resources impose a constraint on growth. At this point, many sole traders consider going into partnership with another individual, or setting up a company with limited liability.

6.2.1 Sole trader or employee?

It can sometimes be difficult to decide whether a person is a self-employed sole trader or an employee of another organization. The distinction is an important one, because a trend in recent years has been for large organizations to outsource many of their operations, often buying in services from apparently self-employed individuals. There can be many advantages in classifying an individual as self-employed rather than an employee. For the self-employed person, tax advantages could result from being able to claim as legitimate some business expense items that are denied to the employee. The method of assessing income tax liability in arrears can favour an expanding small business. For the employer, designation as self-employed could save on National Insurance payments. It also relieves the employer of many duties that are imposed in respect of employees but not subcontractors, such as entitlement to sick pay, notice periods and maternity leave.

The problem of distinction is particularly great in the construction sector and for service sectors (such as market research), which employ large numbers of part-time workers. The courts would decide the matter, among other things, on the basis of the degree of control that the employer has over the employee and their level of integration within the organization. If the employer is able to specify the manner in which a task is to be carried out, and assumes most of the risk in a transaction, then an employment relationship generally exists. If, however, the required end result is specified but the manner in which it is achieved is left up to the individual, who also bears the cost of any budget overrun, then it is most likely that a contract for services will exist – in other words, self-employment.

Thinking around the subject: A mountain of paperwork

One of the biggest complaints from sole traders is the amount of paperwork that they are required by government to complete. Most small business owners have a vision of what they want to do: open a hairdressing salon, install kitchens, run a convenience store or exploit a new invention. But the reality is that they are likely to become bogged down in completing paperwork, some of which they may never have envisaged. According to a NatWest survey, conducted on a quarterly basis by the Open University Business School, the average small firm spent 23.3 hours a month in 2005 completing government paperwork. The burden of red tape fell hardest on small sole traders. Businesses with more than 25 staff spend 1.5 hours per employee on forms, whereas those with more than 50 staff spent 0.6 hours per employee. More than half the firms surveyed said the cost of employee regulation and paperwork had meant they employed fewer staff than they would like. More than a third said they would avoid employing more people, while 18 per cent said that growing levels of regulation had led them to reduce their workforce. After employment paperwork, main gripes concerned the paperwork associated with VAT, and the form-filling associated with health and safety assessments. The Small Business Council has been campaigning to keep paperwork simple and to reduce the time it takes to fill out forms. It has pointed out that, for every hour a sole trader spends filling out forms, they are not able to use the time to sell more products or develop new ones. While large companies may be able to employ specialists to cope with paperwork, for the small business, productivity suffers.

Governments continually say that they wish to reduce the paperwork burden on small businesses, but how can this be achieved in practice?

6.3 Partnerships

Two or more persons in partnership can combine their resources and expertise to form what could be a more efficient business unit. The Partnership Act 1890 defines a **partnership** as 'the relation which subsists between persons carrying on a business with a view to profit'. Partnerships can range from two builders joining together to a very large accountancy or solicitors' practice with hundreds of partners.

Partnerships are generally formed by contract between the parties, although, where this is not done, the Partnership Act 1890 governs relationships between the partners. Among the main items in a Partnership Agreement will be terms specifying:

- the amount of capital subscribed by each partner
- the basis on which profits will be determined and allocated between partners and the management responsibilities of each partner – some partners may join as 'sleeping partners' and take no active part in the management of the business
- the basis for allocating salaries to each partner and for drawing personal advances against entitlement to profits
- procedures for dissolving the partnership and distributing the assets of the business between members.

Despite this internal agreement between partners, partnerships in England and Wales have not had their own legal personality. As a consequence, the partners incur unlimited personal liability for the debts of the business. Furthermore, each partner is jointly liable for the debts incurred by all partners in the course of business. An added complication of a partnership is that the withdrawal of any one partner, either voluntarily or upon death or bankruptcy, causes the automatic termination of the partnership. A new partnership will come into being, as it would if an additional partner were admitted to the partnership.

Because of the lack of protection afforded to partners, this form of organization tends to be relatively uncommon, except for some groups of professional people, where business risks are low and for whom professional codes of practice may prevent the formation of limited companies. To overcome the problem of limited liability, the Limited Liability Partnerships Act 2000 created a new form of partnership with limited liability. The Act extends limited liability to partnerships in specified circumstances, and is most popular with professional partnerships of accountants, solicitors, dentists and opticians.

6.4 Limited companies

It was recognized in the nineteenth century that industrial development would be impeded if investors in business always ran the risk of losing their personal assets to cover the debts of a business over which very often they had no day-to-day control. At the same time, the size of business units had become larger, causing the idea of a partnership to become strained. The need for a trading company to have a separate legal personality from that of its owners was recognized from the Middle Ages, when companies were incorporated by Royal Charter. From the seventeenth century, organizations could additionally be incorporated by Act of Parliament. Both methods of incorporating a company were expensive and cumbersome, and a simpler method was required to cope with the rapid expansion of business enterprises that were fuelling the Industrial Revolution. The response to this need was the Joint Stock Companies Act 1844, which enabled a company to be incorporated as a separate legal identity by the registration of a Memorandum of Association and payment of certain fees. The present law governing the registration of companies is contained in the Companies Act 1985. Today, the vast majority of trading within the United Kingdom is undertaken by **limited companies**. The legislation of most countries allows for organizations to be created that have a separate legal personality from their owners. In this way, separate legal identity is signified in the United States by the title 'Incorporated' after a company's name, by 'Société Anonyme' (SA) in France, 'Gmbh' in Germany and 'Sdn. Bhd.' in Malaysia.

When a limited company is created under UK legislation, it is required to produce a Memorandum and Articles of Association. The Memorandum includes a statement as to whether the liability of its members is limited, and if so what the limit of liability will be in the event of the company being wound up with unpaid debts. The majority of companies are limited by shares – members' liability to contribute to the assets of the company is limited to the amount (if any) that is unpaid on their shares. Another important element of the Memorandum is the objects clause, which specifies the scope within which the company can exercise its separate legal personality. Any act that the company performs beyond its powers is deemed to be *ultra vires* and therefore void.

While the Memorandum regulates the relationships of the company with the outside world, the Articles of Association regulate the internal administration of the company, the relations between the company and its members, and between the members themselves. The Articles cover such matters as the issue and transfer of shares, the rights of shareholders, meetings of members, the appointment of directors, and procedures for producing and auditing accounts.

Most limited companies are registered as private limited companies, indicated in company names by the designation 'Limited'. However, a larger company may choose to register as a public limited company (plc) and will thus face tougher regulatory requirements. These are described later in this chapter.

6.4.1 Company administration

A company acts through its directors, who are persons chosen by shareholders to conduct and manage the company's affairs. The number of directors and their powers are detailed in the Articles of Association and, so long as they do not exceed these powers, shareholders cannot normally interfere in their conduct of the company's business. The Articles will normally give one director additional powers to act as managing director, enabling him or her to make decisions without reference to the full board of directors.

Every company must have a secretary on whom Companies Acts have placed a number of duties and responsibilities, such as filing reports and accounts with the Registrar of Companies. The secretary is the chief administrative officer of the company, usually chosen by the directors.

6.4.2 Shareholders

The shareholders own the company, and in theory exercise control over it. A number of factors limit the actual control that shareholders exercise over their companies. The Articles of a company might discriminate between groups of shareholders by giving differential voting rights. Even where shareholders have full voting rights, the vast majority of shareholders typically are either unable or insufficiently interested to attend company meetings, and are happy to leave company management to the directors, so long as the dividend paid to them is satisfactory. In the case of pension funds and other institutional holders of shares in a company, their concern may be mainly with the stability of the financial returns from the business. In most large organizations, private investors are in a distinct minority in terms of the value of shares owned. There has been a tendency in recent years for individual shareholders to use their privileged position to raise issues of social concern at companies' annual shareholders' meetings. For example, in 2007, Ben Birnberg, a retired solicitor and small shareholder in Tesco, amassed enough support to force the issue of ethical trading onto the agenda at Tesco's annual shareholders' meeting. Mr Birnberg, who was also the company secretary of the charity War on Want, won the support of more than 100 shareholders – enough to force Tesco to include a resolution to be put to shareholders requiring the supermarket to adopt higher standards in its dealings with suppliers and farmers in low-wage countries.

6.4.3 Company reports and accounts

A company provides information about itself when it is set up, through its Memorandum and Articles of Association. To provide further protection for investors and people with whom the company may deal, companies are required to provide subsequent information.

An important document that must be produced annually is the annual report. Every company having a share capital must make a return in the prescribed form to the Registrar of Companies, stating what has happened to its capital during the previous year – for example, by describing the number of shares allotted and the cash received for them. The return must be accompanied by a copy of the audited balance sheet in the prescribed form, supported by a profit and loss account that gives a true and fair representation of the year's transactions. Like the Memorandum and Articles of Association, these documents are available for public inspection, with the exception of unlimited companies, which do not have to file annual accounts. Also, most small companies need only file an abridged balance sheet and do not need to submit a profit and loss account.

As well as providing the annual report and accounts, the directors of a company are under a duty to keep proper books of account and details of assets and liabilities.

6.4.4 Liquidation and receivership

Most limited companies are created with a view to continuous operation into the foreseeable future (although, sometimes, companies are set up with an expectation that they should cease to exist once their principal objective has been achieved). The process of breaking up a business is referred to as liquidation. Voluntary liquidation may be initiated by members (for example, where the main shareholder wishes to retire and liquidation is financially more attractive than selling the business as a going concern). Alternatively, a limited company may be liquidated (or wound up) by a court under section 122 of the Insolvency Act 1986. Involuntary liquidation involves the appointment of a receiver, who has authority that overrides the directors of the company. An individual or company that has an unmet claim against a company can apply to a court for it to be placed in receivership. Most receivers initially seek to turn round a failing business by consolidating its strengths and cutting out activities that brought about failure in the first place, allowing the company to be sold as a going concern. The proceeds of such a sale are used towards repaying the company's creditors and, if there is a sufficient surplus, the shareholders of the company. However, many directors who have lost their businesses claim that receivers are too eager to liquidate assets, and unwilling to take any risks that may eventually allow both creditors and shareholders to be paid off. The Insolvency Act 1986 allows a period of 'administration' during which a company can seek to put its finances into order with its creditors, without immediate resort to receivership. Section 5.8 of the Act defines the circumstances in which an administration order may be made by a court.

In January 2005, the department store Allders was placed into administration. Like many administrative orders, this one followed poor trading (in this case, lower-than-expected levels of Christmas sales), which left the company short of cash. Krupp was appointed by Allders' bank as administrator, and its first task was to control unnecessary expenditure, resulting in redundancies of staff who were not essential to the continued operation of the chain. The administrator then set about selling the chain as a going concern. Despite expressions of interest from several companies, both trade buyers and venture capital firms, no offers for the whole chain were forthcoming. One complicating factor was the requirement for anybody taking over the whole company as a going concern to assume responsibility for Allders' pension fund deficit, and for making redundancy payments to any staff whom they no longer needed after taking over the business. Krupp was mindful that a prolonged search for a buyer would diminish the value of the company, as customers became disillusioned and staff morale sank. It therefore sold bundles of stores to British Home Stores, Debenhams and Primark. Some smaller stores attracted no bids, and the administrator proceeded to close these and to dispose of the assets for the best price possible.

6.4.5 Public limited companies

The Companies Act 1985 recognized that existing company legislation did not sufficiently distinguish between the small owner-managed limited company and the large multinational firm. Thus the concept of the public limited company – abbreviated to plc – came about. The basic principles of separate legal personality are similar for both private and public limited companies, but the Companies Act 1985 confers a number of additional duties and benefits on public limited companies.

The difference is partly one of scale – a plc must have a minimum share capital of £50,000 compared to the £100 of the private limited company. It must have at least two directors instead of the minimum of one for the private company. Before a public limited company can start trading, or borrow money, it must obtain a 'business certificate' from the Registrar of Companies, confirming that it has met all legal requirements in relation to its share capital.

Against these additional obstacles of the public limited company is the major advantage that it can offer its shares and debentures to the public, something that is illegal for a private company, where shares are more commonly taken up by friends, business associates and family. As a private limited company grows, it may have exhausted all existing sources of equity capital, and 'going public' is one way of attracting capital from a wider audience. During periods of economic prosperity, there has been a trend for many groups of managers to buy out their businesses, initially setting up a private limited company with a private placement of shares. In order to attract new capital, and often to allow existing shareholders to sell their holding more easily, these businesses have often been re-registered as public companies.

There are a number of additional strengths and weaknesses to plc status that can be noted. Many companies highlight plc status in promotional material in order to give potential customers a greater degree of confidence in the company. Another major strength is the greater potential ability to fund major new product developments. Against this, the plc is much more open to public examination, especially from the financial community. Management may develop business plans that will achieve long-term payback, bringing it into conflict with the (possibly short-term) objectives of City financial institutions. Indeed, a number of companies have recognized this problem of plc status and reverted to private status by buying back shares from the public – the Virgin airline business, for example, converted back to a private limited company after a few years as a plc (although the Virgin Mobile business was subsequently floated as a plc in 2004).

Larger limited companies can sometimes be described as multinational companies. They have operations in many countries, although subsidiaries would usually be registered locally in each country of operation. A multinational company based overseas may register a subsidiary in the UK as a private limited company in which it holds 100 per cent of the shares. UK-based companies which are holding companies for overseas subsidiaries are most likely to be registered as public limited companies.

Today, although public limited companies are in a numerical minority, they account for a substantial proportion of the equity of the limited company sector and cover a wide range of industries that typically operate on a large scale – for example, banking, car manufacture and property development.

6.4.6 Advantages and disadvantages of limited companies

To summarize, comparisons between sole traders and partnerships, on the one hand, and limited companies, on the other, can be made at a number of levels. First, formation of a limited company is relatively formal and time-consuming – for a sole trader there is the minimum of formality in establishing a business. The added formality continues with the requirement to produce an annual return and set of accounts. On the other hand, limited company status affords much greater protection to the entrepreneur in the event of the business getting into financial difficulty. Raising additional funds would usually be easier for a limited company, although personal guarantees may still be required to cover loans to the company. Additional funding, which limited company status makes possible, especially public limited company status, allows organizations to embark on more ambitious expansion plans. While a sole trader may concentrate on small, niche markets, a limited company may be in a better position to tackle mainstream mass markets.

6.5 Commercial and quasi-commercial organizations operating in the public sector

Government has traditionally been involved in providing goods and services that cannot realistically be provided by market forces – for example, defence, policing and basic health services. Government involvement has, however, developed beyond providing these basic public services to providing goods and services that could also be provided by private-sector organizations.

Public-sector organizations take a number of forms, embracing government departments and agencies, local government, nationalized industries and all other undertakings in which central or local government has a controlling interest. This chapter will focus on those public-sector organizations that supply goods and services to consumers. Those government organizations that are primarily policy making in nature were considered in more detail in Chapter 2, dealing with the political environment. In between those branches of government responsible for providing goods and services and those responsible for policy are an increasing number that are involved in both. For example, in the UK, many public services, such as National Health Service Trusts, are increasingly being required to compete for contracts to provide services, using the price mechanism to allocate resources, rather than centralized planning.

6.5.1 State-owned enterprises

Goods and services provided on a commercial basis have often been provided through state-owned enterprises, often referred to as **nationalized industries**. Most countries have a state-owned industry sector and the size of the sector generally reflects the political ideology of a nation. The United States has traditionally had very few government-owned business organizations, while in China, state ownership dominates many sectors, such as banking and manufacturing, which others would consider a prerogative of the private sector. In the UK, a once large state-owned industry sector has shrunk with changes in political ideology (UK state-owned industries accounted for less than 1 per cent of GDP in 2006, having fallen from 9 per cent in 1979). Throughout the EU, privatization of state-owned enterprises has been occurring, or at least these enterprises are being reorganized to behave more like private-sector organizations. An important item on the agenda of the World Trade Organization (WTO) is to reduce the power of state-owned industries, which can act as a barrier to global competition. This is increasingly the case for the services sector, where many 'utilities', such as gas, water and electricity supply, have traditionally been state controlled, preventing global competition in these services. Sceptics have been quick to point out the dangers of the WTO's agenda for developing countries – for example, privatization of the Indian Post Office might give new opportunities for Federal Express, but could the Indian Post Office realistically be expected to compete for mail business in the USA?

Governments first became involved in industry for largely pragmatic reasons. In 1913, a key shareholding in the Anglo-Iranian Oil Company – the precursor of British Petroleum – was acquired by the British Government to ensure oil supplies to the Royal Navy. During the inter-war years, the Central Electricity Generating Board, the British Broadcasting Corporation and the London Passenger Transport Board were created to fill gaps that the private sector had not been capable of filling. Whereas the reasons for the creation of these early nationalized industries were largely pragmatic, the early post-Second World War period saw a large number of nationalized industries created for increasingly ideological reasons. During the Labour government of the late 1940s, the state acquired control of the coal, electricity, gas, and iron and steel industries, and most inland transport. Some industries returned to the private sector during the Conservative government of the 1950s, while subsequent Labour governments added others.

The 1980s and 1990s saw a great decline in the role of nationalized industry, not just in the United Kingdom but also throughout the world. Post-war Europe may have needed centralized planning and allocation of resources to facilitate the reconstruction effort, but the mood had changed by the relatively affluent, consumer-orientated years of the 1980s. The view went around that governments were bad managers of commercial businesses and that private-sector organizations were much more capable of giving good value to consumers. In the rush to sell off state-owned industries, privatization was often confused with deregulation. Simply transferring a nationalized industry to the private sector could easily create a private monopoly that was unresponsive to consumers' needs. Consequently, most privatization has been accompanied by measures to deregulate sectors of the economy. Where this has been impractical, government intervention has been retained in the form of regulation of prices and service standards. Not all privatizations have been successful and, occasionally, private-sector organizations have been taken back into state control. This happened in the UK in 2001 when the privatized provider of railway infrastructure (Railtrack plc) was seen as failing and its duties subsequently given to the state-owned organization Network Rail. On occasions, governments have taken into state control private-sector organizations that have never been state owned, but are considered important to the national interest. In 1971 the Conservative government nationalized the Rolls-Royce aircraft engine company – which had got into financial difficulties – on the grounds that many high-technology jobs in the UK depended on the continued existence of the company, which no private-sector company had been prepared to rescue. In 2008, a Labour government took a number of banks into state control, including Northern Rock, Bradford & Bingley and Royal Bank of Scotland, arguing that a failure of a UK bank would harm the country's international reputation in financial services, and a public-sector solution offered better value to taxpayers than the private takeover bids put forward.

Governments have chosen a number of methods to transfer state-owned industries to the private sector (see Figure 6.2). The most common are described below.

- *Sale of shares to the public*: before shares in a state-owned organization can be sold to the public, a limited company with a shareholding must be formed. Initially, all of the new company's shares are owned by the government, and privatization subsequently involves

Organization	Date of privatization	Method of privatization
British Aerospace	1981	Public sale of shares
National Freight Corporation	1982	Employee/management buy-out
British Telecom	1984	Public sale of shares
Jaguar	1984	Public sale of shares
Sealink	1984	Trade sale
British Gas	1986	Public sale of shares
British Petroleum	1986	Public sale of shares
BA Helicopters	1986	Trade sale
National Bus Company	1986–91	Trade sales/management buy-outs
British Airports Authority	1987	Public sale of shares
British Airways	1987	Public sale of shares
Rolls-Royce	1987	Public sale of shares
Leyland Bus Company	1987	Trade sale
British Steel	1988	Public sale of shares
Rover Group	1988	Trade sale
Regional Water Companies	1989	Public sale of shares
Regional Electricity Companies	1990	Public sale of shares
Powergen/National Power	1991	Public sale of shares
Scottish Electricity Companies	1991	Public sale of shares
British Coal	1994	Trade sale
British Rail	1994–97	Public sale of shares/trade sales
National Air Traffic Services	2001	Sale of 51% of shares to airline consortium in public–private partnership
London Underground	2001	Franchise-type agreement with private-sector Metronet and Tube lines to operate and develop infrastructure
Qinetiq	2003	Sale to private equity company

Figure 6.2 Methods used in UK privatizations

Note: This is not a complete list. In some cases, the sale of shares was phased over a number of periods.

selling these shares to the public. For large privatizations, shares may be targeted at international investors in order to secure the substantial amounts of share capital sought. Sale to the general public has been undertaken where it would be considered politically unacceptable to exclude small investors from the benefits of privatization.

- *Trade sale*: smaller state-owned industries have often been easily sold to other private-sector companies as a complete entity. This happened, for example, in the sale of the then state-owned Rover car company to British Aerospace. Sometimes, parts of nationalized industries have been broken away for sale to private buyers (e.g. the shipping and hotel operations of British Railways were separated from the parent organization for sale to private-sector organizations long before the rail privatization of the 1990s). The administrative costs of this method of disposal are relatively low, but governments are open to allegations that they sold off a private-sector asset too cheaply to favoured buyers (an allegation that was made when British Aerospace subsequently sold Rover to BMW for a much higher price than it had paid for the company).
- *Management/employee buy-out*: this is often a popular option for people-intensive businesses for which financial institutions may have difficulty in deciding on a value, especially in industries with a history of poor industrial relations. It was used as a method of disposing of the National Freight Corporation and parts of the National Bus Company.
- *Public–private partnerships*: sometimes, it may be politically unacceptable, or just impractical, to dispose of government assets into the private sector. Instead, the government may retain ownership of the assets, but pay a contractor to provide services using those assets. Contracts would usually include an incentive for the contractor, so that as their performance improves, the payment that they receive increases. In the UK, much of the management of the motorway network and Royal Navy dockyards is now in the hands of private-sector consortia, which receive bonus-related payments in return for work undertaken.

Prior to their privatization, many state-owned organizations have been restructured to make them more attractive to potential buyers. This has typically involved writing off large amounts of debt and offering generous redundancy payments to workers who would not therefore become a liability to a new owner. In doing this, Conservative governments have been accused of providing subsidies for private buyers, although, very often, such action has been essential to provide a buyer with a competitive business proposition.

While governments may be ideologically committed to reducing the role of state-owned industries, it has proved difficult to sell many of them, for a variety of practical and ideological reasons. In the case of the Post Office, ideological objections have been raised at the prospect of the Royal Mail letter delivery monopoly being owned by a private-sector company. This has not, however, prevented the Post Office from being reorganized along business lines, with private limited companies being formed for the main business units, one of which – Girobank – was sold off to the Alliance & Leicester Building Society, while another – the parcel delivery service – was restructured to act more like one of the private parcel companies with which it is having to compete in an increasingly competitive market. The letter business was opened to competition in 2005, following EU measures to deregulate postal services.

It is also possible that attitudes towards privatization may be turning, and it is now possible to see the problems as well as the benefits. Very few people would advocate turning back the clock in sectors such as telecommunications, where privatization and deregulation have been associated with rapidly falling prices and improving service standards. However, it is more doubtful whether privatization of the bus or water supply industries has been entirely beneficial. Customers of newly privatized train companies have pointed out that punctuality fell sharply in the years immediately after privatization, while public subsidies more than doubled. The complex relationships between companies in the rail industry have led many people to suggest that gaps in safety coverage exist, and that the centralized 'command and control' approach of the former state-owned British Rail offered a safer railway at a lower cost.

The importance of a customer orientation within public corporations has been influenced by the nature of the market in which they operate. Following the nationalizations of the late 1940s, marketing was seen in many of the nationalized industries as being very secondary to production. The relative unimportance of marketing was often associated with some degree of monopoly power granted to the industry. In these circumstances, public corporations could afford to ignore marketing. However, as production of the basic industries caught up with demand and the economy became more deregulated during the 1980s, consumers increasingly had a choice between the suppliers offered to them. For example, the deregulation of the coach industry in 1981 and the growth in private car ownership placed increasing competitive pressure on British Rail, and hence an increasing importance for the organization to become customer-orientated. British Rail was increasingly set profit objectives rather than poorly specified social objectives.

What could be seen as either a strength or a weakness for the state-owned industries has been finance for investment and new product development. Investment comes from government – either directly or through guarantees on loans from the private sector. Profits earned have not necessarily been ploughed back into the business. The public sector has, since the 1930s, been seen as one instrument for regulating the economy, cutting back or increasing investment to suit the needs of the national economy rather than the needs of the particular market that the corporation is addressing. As well as limiting the amount of investment funds available, government involvement has also been accused of delay caused by the time it has taken to scrutinize and approve a proposal. By the time approval had been granted, the investment could be too late to meet changed market conditions.

State-owned industries are perceived as an instrument of government and although, theoretically, they may have an independent constitution, government is frequently accused of exercising covert pressure in order to achieve political favour. Electricity prices, rail fares and telephone charges have all at some time been subject to these allegations, which makes life more difficult for managers in nationalized industries because of confused objectives.

Britain is widely credited with having taken the lead in privatizing state-owned industries, and many countries have followed. The EU has taken action to reduce the anti-competitive consequences of having large subsidized public-sector organizations distorting markets. This has been particularly true in the case of airlines, where some European countries have continued to support loss-making state-owned carriers. In 2005, the EU Transport Commissioner investigated a proposal by the Italian Government to rescue the near-bankrupt state-owned airline Alitalia with public money. By EU rules, such funding had to be justified as part of a restructuring process with the objective of returning the airline to profitable private-sector ownership, and could not be allowed as a straightforward operating subsidy.

6.5.2 Local authority enterprise

In addition to providing basic services such as roads, education, housing and social services, local authorities have a number of roles in providing marketable goods and services in competitive markets. For a long time, local authorities have operated bus services and leisure facilities, among others. Initially they were set up for a variety of reasons – sometimes to provide a valuable public service, at other times to help stimulate economic development or to earn a profit to supplement the local authority's income. Sometimes, where a project was too large for one authority and benefited many neighbouring authorities, a joint board would be formed between the authorities. This sometimes happened with local authority-controlled airports – for example, East Midlands Airport was formed by a joint board comprising Leicester, Derby, Nottingham, Derbyshire and Nottinghamshire authorities.

UK local authorities have been required to turn their trading activities into business-like units, separately accountable from the rest of the local authority's activities. In the case of local authority bus and airport operations, the Local Government Act 1988 required local authorities to create limited companies into which their assets are placed. Like any limited company, local authority-owned companies are required to appoint a board of directors and to produce an annual profit and loss statement. By creating a company structure, it becomes easier to introduce private capital, or indeed to sell off the business in its entirety to the private sector. This has occurred in the case of a large number of local authority bus companies and airports (Nottingham East Midlands Airport was initially sold to the National Express group and is now owned by Manchester Airport Group).

Even where separate business units have not been created, local authority services are being exposed to increasing levels of competition. Operations in such areas as highway maintenance, refuse collection and street cleaning must now be assessed to ensure that they offer the 'best value' to the local authority. Local authorities have appointed best value units to monitor their activities against competitive benchmarks and, where necessary, have put the provision of services out to competitive tender. Where a private-sector company takes over the provision of services for a local authority and takes on its employees, the new employer will generally take on responsibilities for accrued rights to redundancy payments, among other things. Best value requirements were discussed in Chapter 2.

In other non-commercial local authority services, clients are being offered greater choice. With the development of locally managed foundation schools, the governing bodies of schools are adopting – if somewhat grudgingly – a marketing orientation to ensure that the service they are offering is considered better than neighbouring schools that pupils would have the choice of attending. Only by attracting clients can they ensure funding for their school.

6.5.3 Private-sector and public-sector organizations compared

Although public-sector organizations cover a wide range of services operating in diverse environments, a few generalizations can be made about the ways in which their business activities differ from those practised by the private sector.

- The aim of most private-sector organizations is to earn profits for the owners of the organization. By contrast to these quantifiable objectives, public-sector organizations operate with relatively diverse and unquantified objectives. For example, a museum may have qualitative scholarly objectives in addition to relatively quantifiable objectives, such as maximizing revenue or the number of visitors.

- The private sector is usually able to monitor the results of its marketing activity, as the benefits are usually internal to the organization. By contrast, many of the aims that public-sector organizations seek to achieve are external, and a profit and loss statement sometimes cannot be produced in the way that is possible with a private-sector organization operating to narrow internal financial goals.
- The degree of discretion given to a private-sector manager is usually greater than that given to a counterpart in the public sector. The checks and balances imposed on many of the latter reflect the fact that their organizations are accountable to a wider constituency of interests than the typical private-sector organization.
- Many of the marketing mix elements that private-sector organizations can tailor to meet the needs of specific groups of users are often not open to public-sector organizations. For non-traded public services, price – if it is used at all – is a reflection of centrally determined social values rather than the value placed on a service by consumers.
- Public-sector organizations are frequently involved in supplying publicly beneficial services where it can be difficult to identify just who the customer is. Should the customer of a school be regarded as the student, their parents or society as a whole, which is investing in the trained workforce of tomorrow?
- Just as the users of some public services may have no choice in who supplies their service, so too the suppliers may have no choice in who they can provide services to. Within the public sector, organizations may be constrained by statute from providing services beyond specified groups of users. On the other hand, some public-sector organizations may be required by law to supply services to specific groups, even though a market-led decision may lead them not to supply.

6.6 Non-departmental public bodies

There are many types of organization that do not fit neatly into the private or public sectors. Non-Departmental Public Bodies (NDPBs) is a title given to a type of organization that has traditionally been referred to as a quango ('quasi-autonomous non-governmental organization').

NDPBs have been around in their modern form since before the Second World War, and semi-independent public bodies of one sort or another have been part of British governance for 200 years. NDPBs are used to carry out a variety of trading and policy formulation roles. Their policy-formulation roles were discussed in Chapter 2 and so we briefly note here the reasons why they have become an important type of business-orientated organization.

The following are the most important characteristics of NDPBs.

- They provide services that are considered politically inappropriate for private companies to dominate.
- The assets of the organization are vested in a body whose constitution is determined by government, and cannot be changed without its approval.

- Management of an NDPB is generally by political appointees rather than directly elected representatives.
- In theory, NDPBs operate at 'arm's length' from government and are free from day-to-day political interference.
- NDPBs have structures and processes that resemble those of private-sector organizations in terms of their speed and flexibility.
- NDPBs are generally relatively small organizations compared to the larger bureaucracies from which they were separated. Because of their autonomous nature, NDPBs may be financially more accountable than a department within a large government departmental structure. However, many would argue that they are generally much less politically accountable where vital public services are concerned.
- Decisions can generally be made much more speedily by a self-governing organization compared to a unit of a large government department where approval must first be obtained from several layers of a hierarchy.

The following are examples of NDPBs that have recently been created in Britain.

- Housing Associations, which now own and maintain much of the housing stock previously owned by local authorities.
- Regional Development Agencies, which have been given, among other things, a remit to encourage inward investment to their areas.
- In many areas, organizations with the characteristics of NDPBs have been created to market the areas as tourism destinations.

In all the above examples, bodies are motivated to satisfy the needs of their users or stakeholders more effectively, as they usually have some element of choice. If a local housing association does not score highly on its performance indicators (such as speed of repairing faults or length of time that houses are unoccupied), it may lose funding for future house investment or maintenance.

In practice, the business activities of NDPBs are often highly constrained. Many continue to depend on central or local government for a large part of their income, with no realistic short-term threat of competition for resources. Managers cannot act with as much freedom as their equivalents in the private sector, because the public and local media often take a keen interest in vital public services and are ready to voice their opposition to the activities of a non-elected body responsible for essential services. Another issue that has not been significantly put to the test is what happens to an NDPB if it fails to attract clients and therefore funding. Government would generally not allow such bodies to 'go out of business' in a way that a private-sector organization can go into receivership. Instead, the tendency has been for the assets of a failing NDPB to be handed over to another NDPB whose management has proved itself to be more capable of meeting clients' needs efficiently and effectively.

6.7 Public–private partnerships

The concept of a public–private partnership (PPP) – already introduced in Chapter 2 – further blurs the distinction between private and public sector. Public–private partnerships take a number of forms, from a small-scale local tourism marketing initiative, through to major infrastructure projects, such as the construction and maintenance of roads and railway facilities. PPPs are based on the belief that government organizations can get better value for money by bringing in expertise from the private sector to vital public projects. It is also often believed that the private sector is better able to manage the risks associated with major infrastructure projects and, in support of this argument, it has been pointed out that many projects managed by the public sector alone have run massively over budget and been delivered late. The whole subject of public–private partnerships is controversial, and many critics have challenged their claimed benefits. It has been pointed out that, over the longer term, financial savings to government may not exist – the government may end up paying more by way of rental and service charges to the private-sector collaborators compared to the amount it would have paid had it managed the project entirely by itself. The idea of private-sector partners sharing risk has also been challenged. Some critics have claimed that partnership agreements still place the burden of unexpected risk on the public-sector partner, and the private-sector partners may put the collaborative venture into receivership, leaving the risk with the public sector. (This happened in 2007 when the Metronet public–private-sector partnership managing London's deep-level underground railway lines went into receivership.)

6.8 Other types of organization

6.8.1 Cooperative societies

Cooperatives can be divided into two basic types according to who owns them: consumer cooperatives and producer cooperatives.

Consumer cooperative societies date back to the mid-nineteenth century, when their aims were to provide cheap, unadulterated food for their members and to share profits among members rather than hand them over to outside shareholders. The number of retail cooperative societies in the UK grew during the latter half of the nineteenth century but has declined during recent years as a result of mergers, so that there were fewer than 50 in 2005. Nevertheless, cooperative societies collectively remain the fifth largest retailer in the United Kingdom. Food retail is by far the largest sector of the Co-op in the UK, accounting for almost half of all turnover, and the Co-operative Group accounts for more than 50 per cent of total cooperative trade. But although food stores are perhaps the most recognizable face of the Co-op, the cooperative societies also comprise travel agencies, funeral homes, the Co-operative Bank, Co-operative Insurance Service and car dealerships.

Each cooperative society is registered under the Industrial and Provident Societies Acts, and not the Companies Acts, and has its own legal personality, very much as a private limited company. The main contrast between the two comes in the form of control of the society – an individual can become a member of a cooperative by buying one share and is entitled to one vote. Further shares can be purchased, but the member still has only one vote, unlike the private limited company, where voting power is generally based on the number of shares held. The appeal of a shop owned by customers has declined of late, as customers have been attracted by competing companies offering lower prices and/or better service. So the cooperative movement has responded by taking on many of the values of the private sector – for example, through the abolition of 'dividend' payments and advertising low prices for all. However, the movement has tried to capitalize on its customer ownership by appealing to customers on the basis of its social responsibility. Promotion of cooperative retail stores has often sought to stress their 'green' credentials, while the Co-operative Bank has stressed that it does not lend for unethical purposes.

Producer cooperatives are formed where suppliers feel they can produce and sell their output more effectively by pooling their resources – for example, by sharing manufacturing equipment and jointly selling output. Producer cooperatives are popular among groups of farmers, allowing individual farmers to market their produce more effectively than they could achieve individually. An example is OMSCo (Organic Milk Supply Company), formed in 1994 when five like-minded organic dairy farmers joined forces to sell their organic milk. Now with around 300 members, OMSCo is the largest and longest-established UK organic milk supplier. For the marketing of a producer cooperative to be successful, members need to share a sense of vision and have clear leadership. Where this is lacking, many producer cooperatives may be successful in buying products for their members at a discount, but less successful at marketing their output. There are currently about 1000 producer cooperative societies within the UK, mainly in the farming and fishing sectors. Farmers' cooperatives are much more important in other EU countries, such as France, where there are many more local, regional and national farmers' cooperatives, the larger of which have diversified into non-farming activities such as banking and transport.

Producer cooperatives may fall foul of legislation to protect the competitiveness of markets where collectively the producers account for a high proportion of sales in the market. However, as most producer cooperatives tend to be quite local in their membership, there is usually the possibility of competition from producers located in other areas.

6.8.2 Charities and voluntary organizations

The aims of this group of organizations can be quite complex. Serving a good cause, such as famine relief or cancer research, is clearly very important. However, these organizations often also set trading objectives, as where charities run shops to raise funds. Often, the way in which such businesses are run is just as important as the funds generated. For example, Barnardo's runs coffee shops where providing training for disadvantaged staff is seen to be as important as providing a fast service for customers or maximizing the profits of the outlet.

In the UK, charities that are registered with the Registrar of Charities are given numerous benefits by the government, such as tax concessions (although recent changes in legislation have introduced stricter controls over their activities in order to reduce abuses of their status – for example, private schools have previously qualified as 'charities', benefiting parents who are arguably among the better-off members of society). Where a charity has substantial trading activities, it is usual for these to be undertaken by a separately registered limited company, which then hands over its profits to the charity.

In some respects, charities have become more like conventional trading organizations – for example, in their increasingly sophisticated use of direct marketing techniques. However, in other respects they can act very differently from private- and public-sector organizations. Customers may show a loyalty to the charity's cause, which goes beyond any rational economic explanation. Employees often work for no monetary reward, providing a dedicated and low-cost workforce, which can help the organization achieve its objectives.

Thinking around the subject: The National Health Service goes to market

The National Health Service (NHS) is Britain's largest employer and has traditionally operated with a command and control structure. Money was allocated by government and distributed between regions, then between hospitals, and then allocated between wards. There was a sense of security in this centralized planning, and hospitals – even wards – could reasonably expect that their budget in the following year would not be drastically different to that in the current year. Hospitals developed specialisms and tended to take on a steady workload of patients referred through an established network of consultants and primary care trusts. The development of 'Foundation'-status hospital trusts from 2003, and the introduction of a market for hospital services, were intended to improve the effectiveness and efficiency with which trusts operated. From 2004, the government introduced privately operated 'treatment centres' to provide a wide range of elective treatment, such as eye cataract operations and MRI scans. These effectively took 'business' away from NHS hospitals, which would in future have to compete for these patients. In the new NHS market, money followed the patients, and patients were given more choice, while family doctors were increasingly being encouraged to take control of their budgets.

But were managers of the traditionally bureaucratic command and control NHS ready for the uncertainty of a market economy? More worryingly, what would happen if a hospital with Foundation Trust status ran out of money? Could it 'go bust'? Foundation Trust hospitals are free-standing businesses that depend on government for their cash flow. Doubts were raised when Bradford Teaching Hospital, one of the first Foundation Trusts, went from a projected surplus of £1 million in 2005 to a potential deficit of £11 million in a matter of months of it coming into existence. At the same time, a number of other Foundation Trusts faced lesser financial difficulties.

The government claimed to have in place procedures for dealing with a failing Foundation Trust hospital. The first resort would be to put in new management. If the failing was more serious, it could be taken over by another Foundation Trust. Ultimately, the Trust could be returned to the Secretary of State's ownership. The government would doubtless be mindful of the political consequences of allowing a hospital trust to close down, or concentrating services in one centralized facility.

In many parts of the country, hospitals provide overlapping services, with very complex sets of relationships with Primary Care Trusts, which do the purchasing of hospital services. In the new NHS market, the financial skills of boards were called for if a chaotic and unstable environment was to be avoided. It was almost unheard of for a British hospital to go out of business but, as the government pursues a market discipline for the NHS, is going out of business a logical consequence that should be shared with the private sector?

6.8.3 Building societies

Building societies are governed by the Building Societies Acts, which have evolved over time to reflect their changing role. They were for some time seen as almost monopoly providers of money for house purchases, with strict regulations on the powers of societies in terms of their sources of funds and the uses for which loans could be advanced. With the liberalization of the home mortgage market, building societies now have wider powers of lending and borrowing, and face much greater competition. As a result of this, societies have had to embrace marketing activities more fully. The Building Societies Act 1986 further allowed building societies the possibility of converting to public limited company status, eliminating the remaining controls imposed by the Building Society Acts (Figure 6.3).

Figure 6.3 Public limited companies have grown in number in recent years and added a number of former building societies whose members voted for conversion. Although plc status does give numerous benefits over mutual status, there are also many benefits of remaining mutual. The Coventry Building Society has stressed the benefits of remaining mutual, arguing that it is achieving high levels of customer satisfaction and a financial performance that matches that of plcs and returns the benefits to members. Plc status gave newly converted building societies a lot more freedom, but it also exposed them to greater risk. Among the newly converted societies, Northern Rock and Bradford & Bingley failed and were subsequently taken into state control, while others, including Alliance & Leicester, saw their share prices fall sharply and were taken over by larger rivals. (Picture reproduced with permission of Coventry Building Society)

Case study: **Cooking by yourself or with company?**

The restaurant sector in Britain is dominated by thousands of small owner-managed businesses, which compete and co-exist with much larger managed enterprises. Many people dream about setting up their own restaurant, and a BBC television show in 2007 even saw the celebrity chef Raymond Blanc 'rewarding' the winner of a competition with their own restaurant. For somebody who loves food, the prospect of giving up a 9–5 office job and spending all their working life developing new menus may seem irresistible. Sadly, although thousands of people have ventured down the route to becoming a restaurateur, their success rate is low. Estimates vary, but it is generally reckoned that about three-quarters of all new restaurants are not a success and close within three years of opening (see Parsa *et al.* 2005). Large corporate restaurant chains generally do better, but it is the sole trader that is particularly likely to face problems. Instead of experimenting with new recipes for beef bourguignon or duck à l'orange, the small restaurant owner is likely to spend much of their time on more mundane matters: filling out the VAT return, recruiting staff, calculating their income tax and paying their National Insurance contributions, keeping abreast of new legislation concerning minimum wage levels, maternity leave and disability discrimination are all distractions from the kitchen. Then there is the never-ending task of promoting the restaurant. Many restaurateurs think that customers will beat a path to their door, but diners can be fickle and as soon as a new restaurant opens in town, they may be off to try it out. With so much to do in simply running the business, it is not surprising that many small restaurateurs become disillusioned and move on. Some fail simply because they hadn't developed a realistic business plan.

There are clearly many advantages to a restaurant that can operate on a larger scale and spread many of these burdensome administrative tasks over a larger volume of business. However, it can be very difficult for a small restaurant owner to establish a chain of outlets. With so much attention to detail needed, a potential chain could be harmed if the standard of service at one restaurant is not the same as the standards elsewhere. For example, a customer eating at a branch of Gordon Ramsay's restaurant may expect the celebrity chef's attention to detail to be present in all places at all times, but ensuring this actually happens demands a high level of management effort and a willingness to delegate.

Nevertheless, large chains of restaurants have prospered, and many have achieved international success. But how can this be done? One approach is a 'command and control' type of management, in which each restaurant is run by a manager who is paid a salary by the company. The successful manager will have earned a bonus and probably promotion within the organization. However, this type of approach can become very bureaucratic and may fail to inspire individuals in an industry where attention to detail can be vital.

One approach adopted by many restaurant chains is to incorporate small businesses within the umbrella of a large franchise organization. We will look in more detail at franchising in the next chapter, but essentially this allows the small entrepreneur to run their own business, while at the same time relying on the franchisor for promotional and administrative support, for which they pay a proportion of their turnover. Within the restaurant sector, franchising has been relatively slow to take hold at the gourmet end of the market, where the owner's individuality and style can add to the appeal of a restaurant. But in the convenience food sector, franchising has really taken hold and allows dedicated individuals to build a secure and profitable business.

The pizza chain Domino's has grown rapidly throughout the world by franchising out its operations to smaller businesses. In some cases, franchisees are sole traders, but can also take the form of large limited companies that operate many outlets. The company has used the energy of talented and hard-working individuals to deliver good financial rewards to its franchisees and quality pizzas to its customers.

In 2004, Domino's reported that ten of its 100-plus UK and Ireland franchisees owned businesses that were worth more than £1,000,000 each. These figures are based on a standard calculation of twice annual turnover. With a typical start-up cost of £250,000 per store this is a significant return on franchisees' initial investment. Only two years previously, one in ten of Domino's stores had a turnover of £10,000 a week; by 2004 this figure was one in three. In 2002, Domino's franchisees earned around £120,000 a year on average (although some considerably more), which was more than three times the average income of a typical business manager (£38,107). Furthermore, no Domino's franchise failed during the year, compared with over 22,000 business failures elsewhere in the UK economy.

Founded in 1960, Domino's makes and delivers nearly 6 million pizzas a week in more than 60 countries around the world. By 2006, it had 8190 stores serving a total of over 1 million pizzas a week. From humble beginnings in 1960, franchising has been a key element of the company's mission to bring pizza to the world. By 2006, 85 per cent of its outlets were owned by franchisees. The UK was an early target for Domino's expansion, and it established a subsidiary company, Domino's Pizza Group Limited, which holds the exclusive master franchise to own, operate and franchise Domino's Pizza stores in the UK and Ireland. In 2007, it operated 501 stores with a total sales turnover of £296.3 million and a profit before tax of £18.7 million.

Domino's research into the skills set and characteristics of the most successful franchisees, both in the UK and internationally, has uncovered the fact that the majority of franchisees believe the traditional corporate management career path failed to offer either the scope to succeed or the financial rewards within the timescale they want. Typical of the hard-working individuals attracted to a Domino's franchise was James Swift. As a 16-year-old delivery driver for Domino's Pizza, Swift spotted the potential to run his own business at an early age. He soon secured a position as the manager of Domino's branch in Swindon and learned everything there was to know about running a store. This operational experience was critical for learning everything from how to make a pizza to how to manage a team. It was about three years later that he got the chance to buy a share in the franchise. By the age of 24, he had become co-franchisee of three Domino's outlets in Swindon, Newbury and Bath. He put his success down to sheer hard work and determination, with the backing of a renowned brand and the commitment that only the owner of a business can give.

Maybe one day, James Swift would match the success of Richard P. Mueller Jr, Domino's Pizza's most successful global franchisee. Mueller joined Domino's in 1967 as a delivery driver and became a franchisee in 1970. By 2003 he owned 158 stores in the USA and employed over 3000 team members. His company sold over 10 million pizzas a year, as many as the entire UK Domino's business. That equated to 5 million pounds of dough, 5 million pounds of cheese and enough pizza sauce to fill a large swimming pool. In the process of growing his business, Mueller had become a millionaire.

Given the stressful, tedious conditions of most fast-food operations, it is vital that staff are motivated to succeed. While many part-time staff, such as students and parents of young school children, are happy to just do a few hours of work in return for a bit of extra cash, the business needs to be able to accommodate the ambitions of people who could make good leaders of people. A bureaucratic 'jobsworth' culture will not allow a pizza company to compete effectively with more agile and committed competitors.

Although franchising has figured prominently in Domino's growth, the company retains a proportion of directly managed outlets. As well as providing an internal benchmark against which franchisees can be judged, these outlets are useful for developing new product ideas that may be too risky for individual franchisees to undertake on their own. One outcome of this process has been the development of a bluetooth- and GPS-enabled system that can pinpoint a pizza delivery person's exact location via satellite. Information can then be transmitted to the delivery person's bluetooth headset, providing advice on the best route to take to their next customer via the GPS system based at the store. Would such developments be possible without the support of a strong centrally managed franchise?

Source: based on material provided on the Domino's (www.dominos.com) and British Franchise Association's (www.british-franchise.org) websites.

QUESTIONS

1 Summarize the relative advantages and disadvantages of the small sole trader, and the large limited company chain within the restaurant sector.

2 What problems does a franchisee such as Domino's face in trying to reconcile the individualism of entrepreneurial franchisees with the need for brand consistency?

3 Why do you think that 15 per cent of Domino's outlets are managed directly by the company, rather than by franchisees?

Summary

There are numerous ways of classifying business organizations. Classification based on legal status is useful because this is often related to other factors such as size, the ability to raise fresh capital and the level of constraints imposed on managers. Private-sector organizations range from the informality of the sole trader to the formality of the public limited company. In between is a diverse range of organizations, each of which has its role in the business environment. Some of these differences will become apparent in **Chapter 11**, which reviews competition within markets. While small sole traders may be associated with perfectly competitive markets, the reality of most markets is domination by a small number of public limited companies. This chapter explored the reasons behind the recent resurgence in small business units. The ability to keep in touch with customers and to react to changes in the marketing environment were noted as important advantages. There is also diversity within public-sector organizations, although this group as a whole has tended to diminish in relative importance in most Western countries. **Chapter 2** discussed organizational structures within the public sector by focusing on government bodies that are policy making rather than operational. **Chapter 8** will discuss how organizations grow. This chapter has laid the ground for **Chapter 8** by suggesting that there are differences in organizations' inherent ability to grow.

Key terms

Building societies (234)
Charities (232)
Cooperative societies (231)
Franchising (235)
Limited company 219)
Liquidation (221)
Multinational company (222)
Nationalized industry (223)
Non-Departmental Public Bodies (NDPBs) (229)
Partnership (218)
Privatization (224)
Public limited company (222)
Receivership (221)
Share capital (221)
Shareholders (220)
Sole trader (215)

Chapter review questions

1 For what reasons might a manufacturer of fitted kitchens seek plc status? What are the advantages and disadvantages of this course of action?

2 Why have governments found it difficult to privatize state-owned postal services? Suggest methods by which private-sector marketing principles can be applied to state-owned postal services.

3 Critically assess the benefits to the public of turning branches of the National Health Service into self-governing trusts.

Activities

1 Identify three Non-Departmental Public Bodies (NDPBs) operating in the following areas: education, housing and transport. Critically evaluate the suitability of NDPB status. Do you think these organizations' service to the public would be improved if they were either purely private-sector or purely public-sector organizations?

2 Choose one of the following business sectors: hotels; fashion retailers; restaurants. Identify a sample of small sole traders and larger limited companies within each sector, and critically examine the ways that their marketing efforts differ.

3 Examine the charges made by a public-sector hospital. These may typically include charges for car parking, telephones and catering. To what extent do you think the organization is business orientated in relation to these? How successfully has it managed to combine its social objectives with its business objectives?

Further Reading

A useful starting point for further reading is one of a number of books discussing the nature of different types of organizations.

Burns, P. (2006) *Entrepreneurship and Small Business*, 2nd edn, Basingstoke, Palgrave Macmillan.

Carnall, C. (2007) *Managing Change in Organizations*, 5th edn, London, FT Prentice Hall.

Clegg, S., Pitsis, T. and Kornverger, M. (2008) *Managing Organizations: An Introduction to Theory and Practice*, 2nd edn, London, Sage.

For a review of current statistics on the composition of business units, the following sources are useful.

Department of Trade and Industry, *SME Statistics*, London, The Stationery Office.

Office for National Statistics, *Annual Abstract of Statistics*, London, The Stationery Office.

The nature of public-sector organizations has changed considerably in recent years and the following provides an overview of this change.

Flynn, N. (2007) *Public Sector Management*, 5th edn, London, Sage.

Charities are becoming increasingly involved in business activities and their distinctive characteristics are discussed in the following text.

Sargeant, A. (1999) *Marketing Management for Non-Profit Organizations*, Oxford, Oxford University Press.

References

Parsa, H.G., Self, J.T., Njite, D. and King, T. (2005) 'Why restaurants fail', *Cornell Hotel and Restaurant Administration Quarterly*, Vol. 46, No. 3, pp. 304–322.

Chapter 2

The Political Environment

CHAPTER OBJECTIVES

This chapter will explain:

- the nature of the political environment
- the structure and processes of local, regional, national and supranational government
- political ideologies, and their effects on government policy and implications for business organizations
- the two-way influence between business organizations and government
- the role of pressure groups in the political process

2.1 Defining the political environment

All aspects of an organization's business environment are interrelated to some extent, and this is especially true of the political environment. Interlinkages occur in many ways. Here are some examples.

- Political decisions inevitably affect the economic environment – for example, in the proportion of gross domestic product (GDP) accounted for by the state and the distribution of income between different groups in society (Chapter 13).
- Political decisions also influence the social and cultural environment of a country (Chapter 3). For example, governments create legislation, which can have the effect of encouraging families to care for their elderly relatives or allowing shops to open on Sundays. In short, the actions of politicians are both a reflection of the social and cultural environment of a country and also help to shape it.
- Politicians can influence the pace at which new technologies appear and are adopted – for example, through tax concessions on research and development activity or through direct intervention such as the UK Government's decision to replace the analogue TV broadcast signal with digital only (Chapter 4).

The political environment is one of the less predictable elements in an organization's business environment. Although politicians issue manifestos and other policy statements, these have to be seen against the pragmatic need of governments to modify their policies during their period in office. Change in the political environment can result from a variety of internal and external pressures. The fact that democratic governments have to seek re-election every few years has contributed towards a cyclical political environment. Turbulence in the political environment can be seen by considering some of the major swings that have occurred in the political environment in the United Kingdom since the Second World War.

- During the late 1940s, the political environment stressed heavy government intervention in all aspects of the economy, including ownership of a substantial share of productive capacity.
- During the 1950s, there was a much more restrained hands-off approach in which many of the previously nationalized industries were deregulated and sold off.
- During the 1960s and 1970s the political environment oscillated in moderation between more and less government involvement in the ways businesses are run.
- The 1980s saw a significant change in the political environment, with the wholesale withdrawal of government from ownership and regulation of large areas of business activity.
- During the 1990s political commentators detected a shift away from the radicalism of the 1980s to more middle-of-the-road policies based on a social market economy.
- Since the election of a Labour government in 1997, there has been a gradual retreat from the free market idealism of previous Conservative governments.

In its widest sense, the political environment refers not just to those institutions, such as local and national government, that are responsible for developing and implementing policy. It also refers to forces in the environment comprising vested interests that, ultimately, politicians seek to serve. In this chapter we will begin by looking at how political systems work, and introduce lobbyists and pressure groups as part of the political environment.

2.2 Political systems

Throughout most of this chapter, we will be describing political systems based on the type of democracy that is prevalent in Western countries. However, there is great diversity in political systems. At one extreme is a political system based on an open system of government that is democratically elected by the population of a country. The other extreme may be represented by totalitarian systems of government in which power derives not from popular representation, but is acquired by a select group. This may be in the form of communism, or may be based on the interests of sectional groups, often militarily based, that acquire power through force or tradition.

The link between the dominant political system, economic growth and the nature of the business environment is an interesting and often complex one. There has been a lot of research into the relationship between democracy and economic prosperity. The idea that autocratic regimes have an advantage in economic development was once quite fashionable. The plausibility of such a notion lies in the advantages such regimes were said to have in forcing through development in the long term. There is some evidence for this in the way that countries go about the construction of major transport infrastructure projects. In Western countries with open democratic governance, a lengthy process of consultation is likely to take place before a new road is built, and there are likely to be extensive checks and balances to prevent the interests of individuals or groups being threatened or unduly favoured. In countries with less democratic traditions, government is more likely to go ahead regardless of objections. Some commentators have attributed part of the rapid economic development of South-east Asia during the 1980s and 1990s to the absence of democratic government in the Western tradition.

An alternative view is that democracy is likely to foster economic development. The political institutions critical to economic development are more likely to exist and function effectively in democratic systems. These institutions include a legal system that protects property rights, individual liberties that encourage creativity and entrepreneurship, the freedom of expression that facilitates the flow of information in an economy, and institutional checks and balances that prevent the theft of public wealth often observed in totalitarian systems. There is a suggestion of a non-linear relationship in which greater democracy enhances growth at low levels of political freedom but depresses growth when a moderate level of freedom has already been attained. Improvements in the standard of living, health services and education may subsequently raise the probability that political freedom will grow.

There are many variations in political systems and their links to economic development. The Chinese system, for example, is one of district, city, regional and state government, which is similar to an electoral college. There are elections at all levels but the system is not democratic on the Western model. Also it is interesting to note that there is now a split between political and economic systems. Previously communism was both a political and an economic system, but the modern Chinese system is much more subtle than this. Within a centralized state system are powerful regional governments, and individual free market systems in many sectors.

Corruption remains a barrier to economic development in many countries. Some companies may survive and prosper by bribing government officials, but the success and growth of such companies is not necessarily based on the value they create for consumers. In many cases, they have simply bought themselves a dominant position in a market that the government is happy to allow them to exploit, in return for a payment that is made. In government systems with poor accountability, such payments may not be made for the public good, but instead just add to the private wealth of government officials.

The statistical evidence of a link between democracy and economic growth is mixed. One study of economic growth data for 115 countries from 1960 to 1980 found that countries with high degrees of political openness achieved an average annual real per capita growth rate of 2.53 per cent, compared with 1.41 per cent in more closed political systems. This implies that more democratic countries may grow 80 per cent faster than less democratic countries. However, other studies have given more ambiguous results, including some that reported a weak negative overall effect of democracy on economic growth (Barro 1996).

Figure 2.1 reports data for a selection of countries, linking annual GDP per capita with an index of political freedom within the country (for example, the extent of universal voting rights), a ranking of economic freedom (for example, the ease with which new entrants can enter a market), and ranking of corruption. A casual glance at this table will reveal that many of the poorest countries of the world are associated with lower levels of political freedom and a high level of corruption.

A further intriguing issue concerns the role of political systems relative to transnational organizations. It has been suggested that the increasing volume of business transactions that take place across the borders of nation-states is eroding the efficiency of national governing structures, especially democratic ones. Many multinational corporations have a turnover that is much larger than that of small less-developed countries. When one of these countries relies on the multinational company for a lot of its income (a situation common in many economies dependent on natural resources), some would argue that the power of the people to control their government is less than the power of the multinational company (Rodrik 2002).

2.3 The importance of monitoring the political environment

We now move on to explore the reasons why business organizations should constantly monitor their political environment, whether this be a totalitarian or democratic system, or a system that is in the process of changing from one type of system to another. It must not be forgotten that within the past couple of decades businesses have observed and reacted to some dramatic changes in political systems – for example, the transformation of former communist Eastern European countries into fledgling democracies. Even here, the ending of communism was only the beginning of a process of political change. In many Eastern European countries, the early days of *laissez-faire* capitalism (described by Joseph Stiglitz as 'market bolshevism', in which unregulated free markets were forced on these countries) was replaced over time with calls for more rather than less state involvement. Governments gradually recognized the need to intervene to counteract market failures by creating enforceable laws and collectable taxes, among other things (Stiglitz 2000).

Countries	Per capita GDP $ (2006 estimate)	Index of freedom (2007)	Ranking of economic freedom (1999)	Ranking of corruption (1998)
Tanzania	800	3.5	103	94
Zambia	1,000	4	92	123
Nigeria	1,500	4	131	147
Zimbabwe	2,100	6.5	154	150
Pakistan	2,600	6.5	89	138
India	3,800	2.5	104	72
Philippines	5,000	3	97	131
China	7,800	6.5	119	72
Colombia	8,600	3	73	68
United Kingdom	31,800	1	6	12
Switzerland	34,000	1	9	7
Canada	35,700	1	10	9
Hong Kong	37,300	3.5	1	14
Ireland	44,500	1	7	17
Norway	46,300	1	30	9

Figure 2.1 National indices for selected countries linking GDP per capita, political freedom, economic freedom and corruption

Source: based on United Nations, *Human Development Report 1998*; World Bank, *World Development Report 1996*; Freedom House, *Freedom in the World 2007*; The Heritage Foundation, Index of Economic Freedom 2007 (http://www.heritage.org); Transparency International, Corruption Perceptions Index 2007; World Factbook 2007 (http://www.cia.gov)

Note: The measure of political freedom comprises a composite of two separate indicators: political rights and civil liberties. The combined score is between 1.0 and 7.0, 1.0 being the freest and 7.0 being the most unfree. The organization Freedom House considers countries with scores of between 1.0 and 2.5 'free'; those scoring between 3.0 and 5.0 as 'partly free'; those scoring between 5.5 and 7.0 as 'unfree'.

The ranking of economic freedom consists of one index in which the freest economy (Hong Kong) is ranked 1 and the least free economy (North Korea) ranks 157.

Ranking of corruption is based on data provided by Transparency International (2007), with the least corrupt country being ranked 1.

Change in the political environment can impact on business strategy and operations in a number of ways.

- At the most general level, the stability of the political system affects the attractiveness of a particular national market. While radical change rarely results from political upheaval in most Western countries, the instability of governments in many less developed countries leads to uncertainty about the economic and legislative framework in which goods and services will be provided.
- At a national level, governments pass legislation that directly affects the relationship between the firm and its customers, and relationships between itself and its suppliers, and between itself and other firms and individuals. Sometimes legislation has a direct effect on

the organization – for example, a law giving consumers rights against the seller of faulty goods. At other times, the effect is less direct, as where changes in legislation concerning anti-competitive practices alter an organization's relative competitive advantage in a market.

- As employers, governments see business organizations as an important vehicle for social reform through legislation that affects employment relationships. During the previous 30 years, organizations have been affected by a wide range of employment legislation, affecting, among other things, discrimination against disadvantaged groups, minimum wages, and more stringent health and safety requirements.
- The government is additionally responsible for protecting the public interest at large, imposing further constraints on the activities of firms – for example, where the government lays down design standards for cars to protect the public against pollution or road safety risks.
- The economic environment is influenced by the actions of government. It is responsible for formulating policies that can influence the rate of growth in the economy and hence the total amount of spending power. It is also a political decision as to how this spending power should be distributed between different groups of consumers and between the public and private sectors.
- Government at both a central and local level is itself a major consumer of goods and services, and accounts for about 40 per cent of the UK's gross domestic product.
- Government policies can influence the dominant social and cultural values of a country, although there can be argument about which is the cause and which the effect. For example, UK government policies of the 1980s emphasized wealth creation as an end in itself; these policies also had the effect of generating a feeling of confidence among consumers. This can be directly linked to an increase in consumer spending at a higher rate than earnings growth, and a renewed enthusiasm for purchasing items of ostentatious consumption.

It should be remembered that organizations not only monitor the political environment – they also contribute to it. This can happen where organizations feel threatened by change and lobby government to intervene to pass legislation that will protect their interests. The role of lobbying and pressure groups will be discussed later in this chapter.

2.4 Political ideologies

It was noted earlier that political ideologies in the UK have changed through a series of cycles during the post-Second World War period. It is important to consider the issue of dominant political ideologies, as they can have such a major impact on the business environment. At one extreme, the ideology of the immediate post-war Labour government placed great importance on the role of the state, and this resulted in many private-sector organizations being taken into state ownership. The political ideology of the incoming Conservative government in 1979 was very different on this and many other issues. As a consequence of this shift in ideology, large parts of state control of business were dismantled and nationalized industries sold off, a process commonly referred to as privatization. This process gave many ordinary people the opportunity to buy shares for the first time. For business organizations, understanding shifts in dominant ideologies can be crucial to understanding the future nature of their business environment. Two important and recurring ideological issues that affect business organizations are the distribution of wealth between different groups in society and the role of the state versus the private sector in delivering goods and services. Political parties represent the gathering of individuals who share a political ideology.

2.4.1 Political parties

Most Members of Parliament belong to a political party. In general, the views of members of political parties cross a range of policy issues, so political parties can be distinguished from single-interest groups such as the League Against Cruel Sports. The existence of political parties makes the management of parliamentary business more efficient, because party leaders can generally be assured of the support of their members when passing new legislation. Parties also provide a hierarchical organization through which MPs can become junior ministers and eventually take a place in the executive.

From the perspective of the electorate, belonging to a political party identifies an individual candidate with a known set of values. There is a lot of evidence that when voting for a Member of Parliament, a substantial proportion of voters are guided primarily by the party affiliation of a candidate, rather than the personal views and characteristics of the candidate.

Political parties represent an ideological point of view, although it has been noted that in recent years the ideological gap between the main UK parties has been reducing. Some cynics suggested that the incoming New Labour government in 1997 shared many ideological values of the previous Conservative government and was far removed from the ideological zeal with which the post-Second World War Labour government took office. The main parties have tended to converge on a relatively moderate ideology, leaving extreme parties such as the British National Party and Socialist Workers Party to pursue more radical ideologies. Of course, the prevalence of an ideology represents shifts in the value of society as a whole. The radical free market ideology of the incoming Conservative government of 1979 found a ready reception by an electorate that had come to see the shortcomings of the previous Labour government. This was seen by many as being too restrictive and closely aligned with the inflexible attitudes of trades unions. The fact that extreme ideologies have not found great recent support in the UK, and the fact that the difference between the two main parties has been narrowed, is a reflection of relatively moderate political values held by the population as a whole, and possibly contentment with increasing personal wealth and living standards.

Because political parties represent a diverse range of ideological issues, it is not surprising that party leaders often find it difficult to gain the unanimous support of all members on all issues. In the United Kingdom, members of the main political parties are divided on issues such as the level of involvement with the European Union, defence expenditure and educational policy. Nevertheless, a political party stands for a broad statement of ideological values with which its members can identify. In the United Kingdom, the Conservative Party has traditionally been identified with such core values as the self-reliance of individuals, less rather than more government, and the role of law and order. The Labour Party, by contrast, has traditionally stood for state intervention where market failure has occurred, protection of the weak in society from the strong, and efforts to reduce inequalities in wealth. The Liberal Democrat Party has traditionally appealed to people who believe in open democratic government in a market economy, with government intervention where market mechanisms have produced inequalities or inefficiencies.

The Conservative Party has traditionally been seen as the party of business and the Labour Party as the party of organized labour. This is largely true as far as the funding of the parties goes, with the Conservative Party receiving sizeable donations from business organizations while many Labour MPs are sponsored by trades unions (although the number of donations by business to Labour has increased in recent years). In general, the free market enterprise values of the Conservative Party would appear to favour the interests of businesses, while the socialist values of the Labour Party would appear to be against business interests. Historically, business has been worried at the prospect of a Labour government, as witnessed by the fall in stock market prices that has often followed a Labour Party election victory. However, the United Kingdom, like many Western countries, has seen increasing levels of convergence between parties, which makes business leaders very uncertain about just what makes a party's policies distinctive. For example, the UK Labour Party has traditionally been opposed to privatization of public utilities, but the Labour government elected in 1997 had no immediate plans to renationalize previously privatized companies, and indeed has subsequently privatized London Underground and the air navigation services. As political parties have targeted the crucial middle-ground 'floating voter', their underlying ideologies have become increasingly indistinguishable.

The UK political environment has traditionally been dominated at a national level by two major parties. By contrast, most other European countries have a long tradition of multiple parties that represent different shades of opinion, and each sends small numbers of members to its legislative body. The result is often that no one party is able to form an executive with an outright majority of members, so executives based on a coalition of parties must be formed. The difference in electoral outcomes between the two systems reflects the method by which the election is conducted. In the UK, the party with the most MPs elected within individual constituencies takes power. In most European countries it is the percentage of total votes that determines the number of representatives of each party. Within the Scottish Parliament (see below) proportional representation has resulted in a coalition of Green MSPs (Members of the Scottish Parliament) together with an ideological Scottish Socialist Party.

There is an argument that diversity of parties in the legislature (something that is generally favoured by 'proportional representation' electoral systems) allows for a wide range of political views to be represented in the government, in contrast to two-party systems where minority opinions can easily be lost. Against this, the reality is often that a minority party is able to hold power that is disproportionate to its size, by threatening to withhold its membership of a coalition. Coalition governments (which are common in some European countries such as Italy and Germany) also have a tendency to be unstable, and withdrawal of one party may bring down an executive. The radical change that occurred with the strong single-party governments of the Conservative Party in the 1980s may be much more difficult where a coalition government has to broker a compromise between all parties.

2.4.2 Social exclusion

Political parties have often based their principal ideology on a desire to see a more equitable distribution of wealth and life chances within society. Some great revolutions in history have been brought about by the socially excluded using force to overturn the power of an elite. The incoming Labour government of 1997 set about reducing social exclusion in a more low-key manner, but nevertheless as an important part of its election promise.

Social exclusion is a shorthand term for what can happen when people or areas suffer from a combination of linked problems such as unemployment, poor skills, low incomes, poor housing, high-crime environments, bad health and family breakdown. In the past, governments have had policies that tried to deal with each of these problems individually, but there has been little success at tackling the complicated links between them or preventing them from arising in the first place.

In response to these problems, the UK Government created the Social Exclusion Unit in 1997. Its remit has been to help improve government action to reduce social exclusion by producing 'joined-up solutions to joined-up problems'. Most of its work is based on specific projects, which the prime minister chooses following consultation with other ministers and suggestions from interested groups. The unit is staffed by a combination of civil servants and external secondees. They come from a number of government departments and from organizations with experience of tackling social exclusion – the probation service, housing, police, local authorities, the voluntary sector and business.

One of the unit's early reports focused on problems caused by housing estates that had become 'sink areas'. Numerous government agencies had tackled the problems but more concerted collective action was needed if significant results were to be achieved. The Social Exclusion Unit set up 18 Policy Action Teams (PATs) to work on solutions, bringing together civil servants and outside experts to develop a National Strategy for Neighbourhood Renewal.

2.4.3 Redistribution of wealth

Left to market forces, numerous studies have suggested that the wealthier members of a society would continue to get richer, while the poor would find it difficult to escape from their relative poverty. Karl Marx's analysis predicted the end of capitalism on the basis that, without the spending power of the poor, the wealthy owners of resources would have no markets for the products from which they made their profits. In reality, Marx's thesis was weakened by new overseas opportunities to recirculate capital owners' wealth. During the twentieth century, progress towards a more egalitarian distribution of wealth was slow and required intervention by governments.

Governments with socialist leanings have recognized that there is nothing inherently just in the pattern of market rewards that reflects the accidents of heredity and the labour skills that happen to be in demand at the time. A distinguishing feature of the Left in politics is often its belief in a positive role for government. However, redistribution has acquired a bad name because it has been associated with the politics of envy. It has also sometimes been carried out in such a way as to interfere unnecessarily with incentives. Adverse publicity can also easily be generated by the media, particularly at election time, with headline figures of high taxation rates.

Under previous Labour governments, taxation on marginal income has exceeded 90 per cent. This has invariably entrenched the position of those who already own wealth or who can take their rewards in the form of professional perks, while discouraging those who want to better themselves without the aid of tax advisers.

Actually getting benefits to lower-income groups can pose a challenge for policy makers. Minimum wage legislation, introduced in the UK in 1999, may provide guaranteed levels of income for the poorest members of society, but higher-earning individuals invariably seek to maintain differentials, leaving minimum-wage employees in a position of relative poverty, and possibly putting an employer at a competitive disadvantage compared to companies located in low-wage economies. An alternative approach to redistribution has been to increase the benefits paid to individuals who are not in work. But this has often led to a 'poverty trap' whereby it is not financially advantageous for an individual to enter employment, because the benefits that they are giving up are greater than the wages that they will earn. There are a number of structural issues that governments have sought to tackle in order to improve the relative economic

Thinking around the subject: **Will the poor always be with us?**

It seems that even a socialist government dedicated to reducing social inequality cannot easily eliminate inequality. According to a report by the Office for National Statistics, the income of the richest and poorest 10 per cent of the population had each grown by around 5 per cent between 1997 (the date when a Labour government was elected) and 2003. But, in absolute terms, the gap between rich and poor had widened. The poorest 10 per cent had seen a £28 a week rise, compared to the richest 10 per cent, which had seen a rise of £119. Furthermore, the wealthiest 1 per cent of the population had prospered. In 1991, they owned 17 per cent of the nation's wealth, but by 2003 the figure had grown to 21 per cent. A large part of this growth was attributed to a rise in house prices (Office for National Statistics 2008).

It has often been argued that the surest way out of inequality is through education, but the report found that children's chances of doing well in exams depended enormously on their parents' qualifications and jobs. In 2002, more than three-quarters of children with parents in higher professional occupations achieved five or more GCSEs at grades A to C. Less than a third of children with parents in manual or clerical jobs achieved this (Office for National Statistics 2004).

Even when the government takes proactive measures to help disadvantaged groups, these may backfire. In 2001, the government abolished entrance fees to national museums, arguing that high charges were deterring poor people from sharing the nation's heritage and learning from it. After the abolition of charges, museum attendance figures rose. However, a subsequent report by the National Audit Office indicated that it was relatively wealthy middle-class parents who were now making more visits to museums, and disadvantaged groups were still underrepresented in the admission figures. Worse still, many of the middle-class parents who were now making more visits to state-subsidized museums now made fewer visits to privately owned museums, many of which were forced to cut back their expenditure and reduce the number of staff they employed.

What policies can in practice be used to overcome social inequality? Given the importance of education as a means of reducing inequality, what can governments do to encourage people from disadvantaged backgrounds to take part in higher education? Even in higher education, is government policy sometimes contradictory, as evidenced by the introduction of tuition fees, which may deter groups in society that have traditionally been afraid of getting into debt?

standing of disadvantaged groups. As an example, many single parents have found it uneconomic to enter the labour market because the loss of benefits and costs of childcare are greater than their earnings.

Pursuing full employment may be an admirable goal as a means of reducing poverty. But public perceptions of government programmes to get people off benefits and into employment can very easily change from enlightenment to harassment once pressure is put on people, whether they be the well-meaning unmarried mother or the workshy who would rather claim benefits than work.

2.5 The structure of government

To understand the nature of the political environment more fully, and its impact on business organizations, it is necessary to examine the different aspects of government. Government influence on businesses in the United Kingdom can be divided into the following categories:

- central government
- regional government
- local government
- European Union (EU) government
- supranational government.

Most countries have hierarchical levels of government that follow a roughly similar pattern. The UK will be used to illustrate the principles of multi-level government influences on businesses, with reference to comparable institutions in other countries.

2.6 Central government

The central government system of most countries can be divided into four separate functions. The United Kingdom is quite typical in dividing functions of government between the legislature, the executive, the civil service and the judiciary. These, collectively, provide sovereign government within the United Kingdom although, as will be seen later, this sovereignty is increasingly being subjected to the authority of the European Union.

2.6.1 Parliament

Parliament provides the supreme legislative authority in the United Kingdom and comprises the monarch (the present Queen), the House of Commons and the House of Lords. The House of Commons is the most important part of the legislature as previous legislation has curtailed the authority in Parliament of the monarch and the House of Lords. It is useful to be aware of the procedures for enacting new legislation so that the influences on the legislative process can be fully understood (see Figure 2.2).

New legislation starts life as a Bill and passes through parliamentary processes to the point where it becomes an Act of Parliament. Most Bills that subsequently become law are government sponsored and often start life following discussion between government departments and

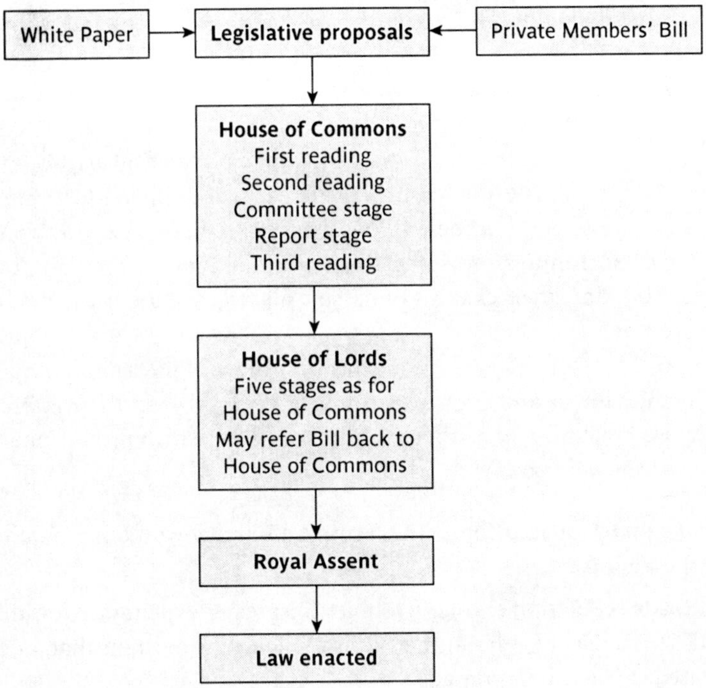

Figure 2.2 The progress of legislation through Parliament

interested parties. On some occasions these discussions may lead to the setting up of a Committee of Enquiry or (less frequently) a Royal Commission, which reports to the government. The findings of such a committee can be accepted, rejected or amended by the government, which puts forward ideas for discussion in a Green Paper. Following initial discussion, the government would submit definite proposals for legislation in the form of a White Paper. A Parliamentary Bill would then be drafted, incorporating some of the comments that the government has received in response to the publication of the White Paper. The Bill is then formally introduced to Parliament by a first reading in the House of Commons, at which a date is set for the main debate at a second reading. A vote is taken at each reading and, if it is a government Bill, it will invariably pass at each stage due to the government majority in the House of Commons. If it passes the second reading, the Bill will be sent to a Standing Committee for a discussion of the details. The Committee will in due course report back to the full House of Commons and there will be a final debate where amendments are considered, some of which originate from the Committee and some from members of the House of Commons in general. The Bill then passes to the House of Lords and goes through a similar five stages. The Lords may delay or amend a Bill, although the Commons may subsequently use the Parliament Act to force the Bill through. Finally, the Bill goes to the monarch to receive the Royal Assent, upon which it becomes an Act of Parliament.

This basic model can be changed in a number of ways. First, in response to a newly perceived problem, the government could introduce a Bill with very few clauses and, with the agreement of party managers, could cut short the consultation stages, speed up the passage of the Bill through its various stages and provide Royal Assent within a matter of days, instead of the months that it could typically take. This has occurred, for example, in the case of a one-clause Bill to prohibit trade in human organs, a measure that had received all-party support. A second variation on the basic model is provided by Private Members' Bills. Most Bills start life with government backing. However, backbench Members of Parliament can introduce their own Bills, although the opportunities for doing this are limited and if they do not subsequently receive government backing, their chances of passing all stages of the Parliamentary process are significantly reduced.

The **lobbying** of Members of Parliament has become an increasingly important activity, brought about by individuals and pressure groups to try to protect their interests where new legislation is proposed that may affect them. Typical tasks for which professional lobbyists have been employed in recent years are:

- a major campaign by tobacco companies against a Bill that would have limited their ability to sponsor sporting events
- the British Roads Federation regularly lobbies for greater expenditure on roads, and seizes opportunities presented by relevant new Bills to include provisions that are more supportive of increased expenditure on roads
- each year, prior to the Chancellor of the Exchequer's annual Budget speech (which forms the basis of a Finance Act), considerable lobbying is undertaken by vested interests that appeal for more public spending to be directed to their cause and/or less taxation to be imposed on it.

If organizations are to succeed in influencing their political environment, they need to identify the critical points in the passage of a Bill at which pressure can be applied and the critical members who should form the focus of lobbying (for example, the members of the Committee to which the Bill is sent for detailed examination). As we will see later, much legislation that passes through the UK Parliament is enacting EU legislation. At this stage it may be too late for lobbyists to achieve significant change in the overall policy underlying the Bill, although it may still be possible to amend details of its implementation.

Political parties typically make bold promises in their election manifestos. If elected, they may promptly enact legislation that formed the flagship of their campaign. However, after a honeymoon period, governments must set to work addressing structural issues in the economy, which will take some time to make good. This may involve painful economic measures in the short term, but the payoff is improved economic performance in a few years' time. With a five-year election cycle for Parliament in the United Kingdom, it is often claimed that voters have short memories and will forget the austere economic conditions of two or three years previously. What matters at election time is the *appearance* that economic conditions are getting better. Therefore, government economic planning may try to achieve falling unemployment, stable prices and a consumer boom just ahead of a general election. This may itself lead to structural problems that must be sorted out after the election, leading to a repeat of this cyclical

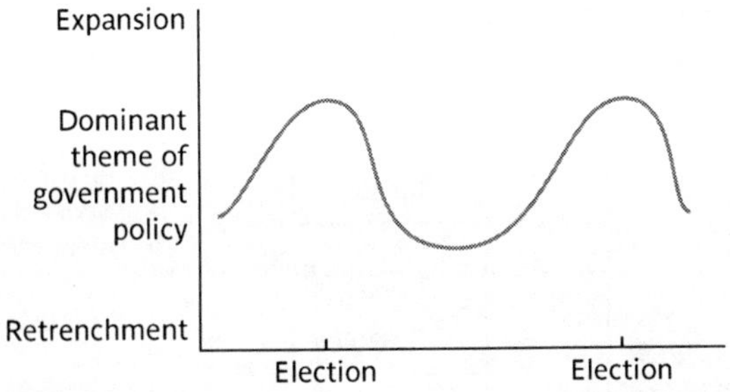

Figure 2.3 The political life cycle

process (see Figure 2.3). The existence of the political cycle frequently impacts on the economic environment, with periods of increased expenditure just before an election and reduced expenditure shortly after. Organizations may acknowledge this cycle by gearing up for a boom in sales just ahead of a general election.

2.6.2 The executive

Parliament comprises elected representatives whose decisions, in theory, are carried out by the executive arm of government. In practice, the executive plays a very important role in formulating policies, which Parliament then debates and invariably accepts. In the United Kingdom, the principal elements of the executive comprise the Cabinet and Ministers of State.

The Cabinet

The main executive element of central government is made up of the Prime Minister and Cabinet (comprising approximately 26 members), who determine policy and are responsible for the consequences of their policies. The Cabinet is headed by the Prime Minister, who has many powers, including the appointment and dismissal of ministers and determining the membership of Cabinet committees, chairing the Cabinet and setting its agenda, summarizing the discussions of the Cabinet and sending directives to ministers. The Prime Minister is also responsible for a variety of government and non-government appointments, and can determine the timing of a general election. Many have argued that Britain is moving towards a system of presidential government by the Prime Minister, given the considerable powers at his or her disposal. There are, however, a number of constraints on the power of the Prime Minister, such as the need to keep the loyalty of the Cabinet and the agreement of Parliament, which may be difficult when the governing party has only a small majority in the House of Commons.

In practice, the Prime Minister is particularly dependent upon the support of a small 'inner cabinet' of senior colleagues for advice and assistance in carrying policy through the party. In addition to this small inner cabinet surrounding the Prime Minister, recent years have seen the development of a small group of outside advisers on whose loyalty the Prime Minister can

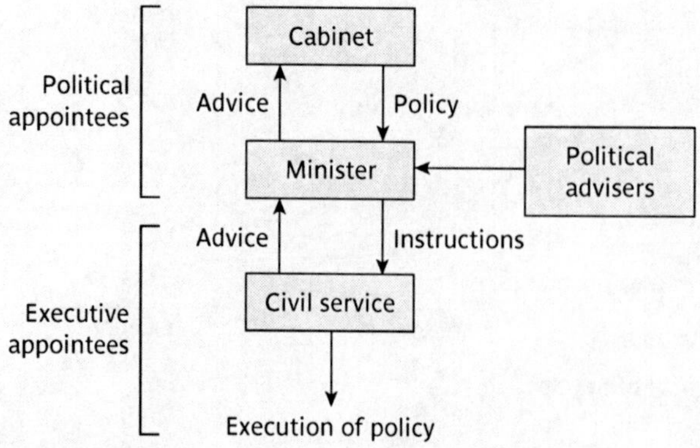

Figure 2.4 The UK Government system of departmental administration: a simplified diagram

totally rely. Some are likely to be party members sitting in Parliament, while others may be party loyalists who belong to the business or academic community. There have been occasions when it has appeared that the Prime Minister's advisers were having a greater influence on policy than their Cabinet colleagues.

The ideological background of the Prime Minister and the composition of the government may give some indication of the direction of government policy. On government attitudes towards issues such as competition policy and personal taxation, organizations should study the composition of the government to try to predict future policy.

Ministers of State

The government of the country is divided between a number of different departments of state (see Figure 2.4). Each department is headed by a Minister or Secretary of State who is a political appointee, usually a member of the House of Commons. They are assisted in their tasks by junior ministers. The portfolio of responsibilities of a department frequently changes when a new government comes into being. Ministers are often given delegated authority by Parliament, as where an Act may allow charges to be made for certain health services, but the minister has the delegated power to decide the actual level of the charges.

2.6.3 The civil service

The civil service is the secretariat responsible for implementing government policy. In the United Kingdom, civil servants are paid officials who do not change when the government changes, adding a degree of continuity to government (although in some countries, such as the United States, it is customary for senior officials to be political appointees and therefore replaced following a change of government). Although, legally, civil servants are servants of the Crown, they are technically employed by a separate government department and are responsible to a minister. Each department is generally headed by a Permanent Secretary, responsible to the Public Accounts Committee of Parliament. The Permanent Secretary is a professional administrator who gives advice to his or her minister, a political appointee who generally lacks expertise in the work of the department.

The fact that civil servants are relatively expert in their areas and generally remain in their posts for much longer than their minister gives them great power. A delicate relationship develops between the Permanent Secretary and the minister, based on sometimes conflicting goals. The minister may view an issue in terms of broader political opportunities while the civil servant may be more concerned about his or her status and career prospects resulting from a change affecting his or her department.

The nature of the career civil servant is changing with the emergence of Non-Departmental Public Bodies (NDPBs) to take over many of the activities of civil service departments (see below). In theory, these new executive agencies should be much freer of ministerial control, meeting longer-term performance standards with less day-to-day ministerial intervention as to how this should be achieved.

Organizations seeking to influence government policy must recognize the power that civil servants have in advising their minister, especially on the details of proposed legislation. Civil servants are usually involved in consultation exercises – for example, on the details of proposed food regulations. In some countries, business may seek to influence the policy-making process at this stage through overt or covert bribery. This is not a feature of most mature democracies such as Britain, and business seeks to exert influence in a more mutually cooperative manner. Civil servants require information on the background to policy and need to understand its possible implications. A close dialogue between the business community and civil servants can increase the chances of civil servants' policy recommendations being based on a sound understanding of business needs, rather than ignorance.

2.6.4 The judiciary

Most democratic systems of government provide a number of checks and balances against the abuse of executive power. The **judiciary** is independent of government, and judges in the United Kingdom are answerable to the Crown and not to politicians. Through the court system, citizens can have some redress against a legislature, executive or civil service that acts beyond its authority. If complainants believe that they have suffered because a government minister did not follow statutory consultation procedures, they may apply to the courts for a **judicial review** of the case. A court may order that ministers reconsider the matter by following statutory procedures.

Business organizations have become increasingly willing to use the courts to challenge allegedly incorrect government procedures that have put them at a disadvantage. The proliferation of industry-sector regulators in the UK has created many opportunities for aggrieved business organizations to challenge the processes of the regulator. As an example, the UK National Lottery regulator Oflot was challenged in the High Court during 2000 by Camelot – the existing Lottery franchise holder – when it alleged that it had been procedurally incorrect in the way that it granted a new franchise to the rival People's Lottery. The Court instructed the regulator to reconsider its decision.

Thinking around the subject: **Minister for Spin?**

Britain's system of government has often been held out as an example of good governance. Politicians decided policy and if the electorate didn't like their policies, they could be thrown out of office at the next election. Civil servants were the loyal servants of politicians who got on and implemented their masters' policies. Because the electorate could not throw out a civil servant directly, ministers took responsibility for the actions of their civil servants. Carefully honed sets of procedures and codes of conduct were developed, which made the UK civil service an example to the world of professionalism.

What, then, are we to make of recent developments that would appear to blur the distinction between elected politicians and an appointed civil service? The 1990s saw a big growth in policy advisers who report to the Prime Minister or other senior ministers, but who are still technically civil servants. These special advisers are overtly chosen by ministers on the basis of their political views, breaking the tradition of neutrality within the civil service. They have often been given the label of 'spin doctor' for the way in which they represent the views of their minister. Do these advisers debase the whole principle of a politically neutral civil service? Are they one step towards the development of a presidential style of government on the American model? Are 'spin doctors' merely providing a substitute for substantive actions by the politicians? Against this, isn't good government all about strong leadership? Could these special advisers be beneficial in the way that they cut through the delaying tactics of the civil service machinery in their efforts to see the politically accountable executive's wishes implemented?

The blurred distinction between functions doesn't end with special policy advisers. Governments have been increasingly enthusiastic about the use of 'task forces' and so-called policy 'czars' to implement policy in such areas as crime, education, housing and environmental protection. These may draw on individuals' special skills, or draw membership from a wide range of interests, but they are invariably political appointments and not democratically accountable in the way that a civil servant is accountable to their minister. Are the possible benefits for good government worth the possible price of less accountability to the electorate?

2.7 Regional and national government

Although many European countries, such as Germany and France, have historically had some degree of regional government, this has been largely absent in the UK. The end of the 1990s saw a potentially fundamental change in the structure of government in the UK with the emergence of regional elected government. However, this is only a partial system of regional government covering some parts of the United Kingdom, and the constitution and powers of each are very different.

2.7.1 Scotland

Scotland was granted devolution by the passing of the Scotland Act in 1998, which means that Scotland has a parliament with 'devolved' powers within the United Kingdom. Any powers that remain with the UK Parliament at Westminster are 'reserved', and set out in Schedule 5 of the Scotland Act. Essentially the powers of the Scottish Parliament are defined by what it does not have legislative competence in, rather than by what it can do. Devolved powers include matters such as education, health and prisons. Reserved powers comprise all other areas of decision making. Those decisions that have a UK-wide or an international impact are reserved and dealt with at Westminster.

The Scottish Parliament is made up of 129 members (MSPs), one of whom is elected by the Parliament to serve as the Presiding Officer. Like the UK Parliament, the Scottish Parliament passes laws. It also scrutinizes the work and policies of the Scottish Executive. The Scottish Parliament is staffed by civil servants who serve the Parliament and, like the Presiding Officer, they must remain neutral.

The Scottish Executive is the government in Scotland for all devolved matters. It is formed from the party or parties holding a majority of seats in the Parliament. The Executive is led by the First Minister, who appoints other ministers and is supported by six administrative departments staffed by civil servants.

The Scottish Assembly has powers to vary income tax by plus or minus up to 3p in the pound to spend as it wishes. This, combined with the Scottish Parliament's ability to alter Scots law, increasingly leads to disparities, such as on anti-smoking legislation, care of the elderly and higher education policy, particularly on student fees.

The UK Government continues to appoint a Secretary of State for Scotland, who remains a member of the UK Cabinet and is responsible for reserved items of government within Scotland.

2.7.2 Wales

In Wales, the National Assembly for Wales consists of 60 members elected throughout Wales. The Welsh Assembly is responsible for developing and implementing policies and programmes for all issues that have been devolved to Wales, which include agriculture, ancient monuments and historic buildings, culture, economic development, education and training, the environment, health services, highways, housing, industry, local government, social services, sport and leisure, tourism, town and country planning, transport and roads, and the Welsh language. The First Minister leads the Assembly and chairs a Cabinet of eight other ministers. All ministers are accountable to the Assembly and its committees for their actions. Unlike the Scottish Parliament, the Welsh Assembly has no tax-raising powers.

2.7.3 Northern Ireland

In Northern Ireland, an Assembly was established as part of the Belfast (or 'Good Friday') Agreement. Northern Ireland had previously had a high level of devolved administration through the UK Government's Northern Ireland Office, and the Good Friday Agreement sought to re-establish a form of Parliament that had previously been suspended during two decades of the 'Troubles'. The newly established Northern Ireland Assembly consists of 108 elected members – six from each of the 18 Westminster constituencies. Its role is primarily to scrutinize and make decisions on the issues dealt with by government departments, and to consider and make legislation. A First Minister and a Deputy First Minister are elected to lead the

Executive Committee of Ministers. Due to the history of divisions within Northern Ireland society, a complicated system was set up whereby the First Minister and Deputy First Minister must stand for election jointly and, to be elected, they must have cross-community support. Decisions in the Assembly are taken by a 'parallel consent formula', which means that a majority of both the members who have designated themselves Nationalists and those who have designated themselves Unionists, and a majority of the whole Assembly, must vote in favour. After a troubled start, the restored Northern Ireland Assembly has assumed responsibility for government functions previously handled by the UK Government's Northern Ireland Office, and is allocated its block allocation of government expenditure.

2.7.4 London

In London, a referendum established the Greater London Authority. This provides for a directly elected Mayor (Ken Livingstone was the first Mayor elected in 2000, and re-elected until 2008, when he was succeeded by Boris Johnson), who has the role of a policy leader and 'Champion for London'. The Mayor's office is the executive of London's government – managing a budget of over £8 billion and having revenue-raising powers (e.g. the London Congestion Charge is determined by the Mayor). The London Assembly – an elected body – scrutinizes the Mayor's policies, decisions and budget.

The Greater London Authority is made up of the Mayor, the London Assembly and a team of over 600 staff supporting their work to develop and implement London-wide policies in respect of transport, policing, fire and emergency services, economic development, planning, culture and the environment. The Mayor works closely with, and sets budgets for, Transport for London (TfL), the London Development Agency (LDA), the Metropolitan Police Authority (MPA), and the London Fire and Emergency Planning Authority (LFEPA). The Mayor also works closely with London's borough councils, which are responsible for providing many local services. The Mayor works with the boroughs to ensure that local and London-wide policies work together for maximum effect.

2.7.5 Other regional assemblies

The UK Government published a White Paper on regional governance in 2002. It proposed to strengthen the existing regional institutions in England and take forward the government's manifesto commitment on elected regional government in England. However, a number of anomalies have arisen with the piecemeal development of regional government in the UK. The parliamentary arrangements for Scotland, Wales, Northern Ireland and London are all different. While all the regions have power to make local legislation, they all still elect MPs to the UK national Parliament, which can vote on legislation affecting England. England remains the only region without its own parliament and legislator.

Advocates of regional government argue that it will allow legislation and economic policy to be developed that is better suited to the needs of their area. Critics would argue that regional government creates more bureaucracy, which will cost businesses time and money. Instead of devolving powers down from central government, a Local Government Association study in 2004 suggested regional assemblies would actually lead to the transfer of authority upwards

Thinking around the subject: Political vision helps win Olympic Games for London

It has been claimed that having an elected mayor and assembly greatly assisted London in its successful bid to host the 2012 Olympic Games. At a time when much of the country was ambivalent about bidding for the Games, the Mayor provided a focal point for championing the interests of London. The Games would bring more than 28 days of sporting activities, and provide a lasting legacy in terms of economic growth and social regeneration. The Games would also create opportunities for businesses, large and small, bringing thousands of new jobs in sectors ranging from construction, hospitality and media to environmental services. As well as stimulating the development of world-class sporting facilities, including swimming pools, a velodrome and hockey facilities, it was hoped that the Games would inspire a new generation to greater sporting activity and achievement.

The Mayor agreed with the government a funding package of up to £2.375 billion to help meet the costs of staging the Olympics. The first £2.050 billion would be met, with up to £1.5 billion from the Lottery and up to £550 million from London council tax, which would cost the average London household £20 a year, or 38p a week. Could the 2012 Olympic Games be won for London without the focal point provided by the Mayor of London and the Greater London Authority? Or had the two between them landed Londoners with an ever increasing bill for the Games, which they would be burdened with for many years to come?

from local authorities to the new regional government bodies. Some saw evidence of the effect of this in the Welsh Assembly Government budget for 2008, which critics claimed increased spending by the Assembly, but cut the funding allocated to local councils. There has been a muted response to proposals for further regional assemblies. In 2005, a referendum on a proposal to establish a regional assembly in north-east England was overwhelmingly rejected.

Delays in implementing policies may occur where the aims of national and regional governments differ, but cooperation between the two is essential if a regional policy is to be implemented successfully. Legal challenges by the London Assembly against the Department of Transport, Environment and Regions over privatization of the London Underground demonstrated that interdependencies between regional and national governments are likely to remain strong.

The likely effects of regional governments on business organizations are ambiguous. On the one hand, it can be argued that increasing amounts of UK legislation are merely enactments of

EU directives, which would need to be enacted regardless of whether it is the UK Parliament or a regional assembly that assumes the responsibility. On the other hand, there are many areas of discretion, which can lead to differences between regions. Where it has tax-raising powers, regional assembly funds can be directed towards what are considered to be regionally important social goals. As an example of the differences that can emerge, the Scottish Parliament voted in 2001 to fund long-term care for elderly people, something that was not available in England, and thereby opening up business opportunities in Scotland that were not available in England.

2.8 Local government

Local authorities in the United Kingdom are responsible for a wide range of services, from social services and education to refuse collection and street cleaning. The structure of local government that was implemented in 1974 divided the largely rural areas of England into counties ('shire counties'), each with a County Council. The chief responsibilities of these County Councils included education, social services, emergency services, highways and refuse disposal. Shire counties were further subdivided into District Councils (sometimes designated as Borough or City Councils), which had responsibilities for housing, leisure services and refuse collection. Districts in rural areas were usually further divided into parishes with a Parish Council (sometimes designated as a Town Council) responsible for local matters such as the maintenance of playing fields.

In the larger conurbations, Metropolitan District Councils had greater functions than their shire county counterparts – for example, they were additionally responsible for education and social services. Following the abolition of Metropolitan County Councils in 1986, responsibility for conurbation-wide services (such as public transport and emergency services) passed to a series of joint boards governed by the District Councils. In London, the pattern of government has been broadly similar to that of metropolitan areas, although there is now an assembly for the capital (see above). In Scotland, the structure of local government has been based on a two-tier system of Regional and District Councils.

From the mid-1990s, the basic structure of local government set up by the 1974 Act has been changed further by the appointment of commissions to study the needs of local government in individual areas. This has led to the emergence of 'unitary' authorities that combine the functions of District and County Councils. Many large urban areas, such as Leicester, Nottingham and Bristol, have gained their own unitary authorities, in the hope that previous duplication of facilities provided by District and Council Councils can be avoided. As an example, the new 'unitary' authority for Leicester combines previous City Council functions of housing, refuse collection and car parking (among others) with responsibilities transferred from Leicestershire County Council for education, social services and highways.

Arguments for large County Councils based on economies of scale and centralized provision have given way to a philosophy based on small, locally responsive units acting as enablers for services provided by subcontracted suppliers. Even a small, re-created county such as Rutland, it is argued, can provide many services previously considered too complex for such a small unit, by buying them in from outside suppliers, or by acting in partnership with other local authorities.

2.8.1 The relationship between central and local government

It has been argued that local government in Britain is losing its independence from central government, despite claims by successive governments that they support a philosophy of less government and a decentralization of powers. There is a great deal of evidence of this erosion of local autonomy.

- Over half of local government income now comes in the form of grants from central government.
- Local authorities have had the ability to set rates on business premises taken away from them altogether and these are now determined by central government.
- Furthermore, central government has the power to set a maximum permitted total expenditure for a local authority and to set a maximum amount for its council tax due from householders.

In addition, legislation setting performance standards in education and social services (among others) has limited the independence of local government to set locally determined standards. Local authorities now have less local discretion in determining what is an acceptable standard for services in its area and in deciding between competing priorities.

Local authorities have had increasing numbers of functions removed from their responsibility and placed with Non-Departmental Public Bodies (NDPBs) which are no longer answerable to the local authority (for example, colleges of further education now have their own governing bodies).

2.9 The European Union

The European Union (EU), formerly known as the European Community, was founded by the Treaty of Rome, signed in 1957 by France, West Germany, Italy, Belgium, the Netherlands and Luxembourg. Britain joined the EC in 1972, together with Ireland and Denmark, to be joined by Greece in 1981, Spain and Portugal in 1986, and Austria, Finland and Sweden in 1995. A more significant expansion to the EU occurred in May 2004 when ten countries of Central and Eastern Europe joined – Cyprus, the Czech Republic, Estonia, Hungary, Latvia, Lithuania, Malta, Poland, Slovakia and Slovenia. Romania and Bulgaria joined the EU in 2007 and these additions brought the EU's population to over 450 million people in 27 countries. Turkey has begun accession talks but membership still seems far from certain. Norway and Switzerland have always declined to join the EU but enjoy a similar freedom of movement of capital, goods, people and services, as part of the wider European Economic Area (EEA).

2.9.1 Aims of the EU

An important aim of the Treaty of Rome was the creation of a common market in which trade could take place between member states as if they were one country. The implication of a common market is the free movement of trade, labour and capital between member states. Agriculture was the first sector in which a genuinely common market was created, with a system of common pricing and support payments between all countries and free movement of produce between member states. Further development of a common market has been impeded by a range of non-tariff trade barriers, such as national legislation specifying design standards, the cost and risk of currency exchange and the underlying desire of public authorities to back their own national industries. The creation of the single European market in January 1993 removed many of these barriers, but many practical barriers to trade remain, of which differences in language and cultural traditions are probably the most intractable.

There is considerable debate about the form that future development of the EU should take and, in particular, the extent to which there should be political as well as economic union. Recent debate has focused on the following issues.

- The creation of a common unit of currency has been seen by many as crucial to the development of a single European market, avoiding the cost and uncertainty for business and travellers of having to change currencies for cross-border transactions. A strong single currency would also be able to act as a true international currency comparable to the US dollar, in a way that few individual national currencies could hope to achieve on their own. The launch of the euro (now adopted by all of the 15 pre-2004 EU countries except the UK and Denmark) in 1999 has reduced transaction costs for trade between member states and has allowed member states' central banks to reduce their holdings of foreign currency. Within the UK, opposition to monetary union has been based on economic and political arguments. Economically, a common currency would deny to countries the opportunity to revalue or devalue their currency to suit the needs of their domestic economy. This lack of flexibility implies a political sacrifice, as control of currency is central to government management of the economy (although it should be noted that the UK Government has handed over control of monetary policy to the Bank of England in an attempt to de-politicize financial policy). During 2001, so-called Eurosceptics seized on guidance given by the European Central Bank (ECB) to the Irish Government. Irish inflation was approaching the upper limits set by the ECB, and in asking the Irish government to take fiscal measures to reduce inflation, the ECB was seen as interfering in a very successful national economy.

  Regardless of whether the UK Government formally adopts the euro, businesses may start using the currency, in much the same way as non-US companies often trade in US dollars. The euro will gain acceptability if businesses perceive the currency as being stable and widely accepted.

- Argument continues about the amount of influence the EU should have in nation-states' social and economic policy. For example, previous UK governments have shown reluctance to agree to EU proposals that would harmonize personal taxation and social welfare benefits. The UK Government has supported the idea of 'subsidiarity', whereby decisions are taken at the most localized level of government that is compatible with achieving EU objectives. Cynics have, however, pointed out that the UK Government has not always been willing to practise this principle at home, as witnessed by the gradual erosion of the powers of local authorities in favour of central government.

- There is concern that enlargement of the EU to include the less developed economies of Central and Eastern Europe, and possibly Turkey, could put strains on EU budgets. Many have argued that enlargement should allow the EU to become a loose federation of states, rather than a centralizing bureaucracy, which many critics claim it has become.

- The principle of free movement of people across borders remains controversial in view of the possibility of large numbers of refugees or economic migrants being admitted by one state and then being automatically allowed to migrate to other member states. Following the entry of a number of former communist countries to the EU in 2004, an estimated 600,000+ people made their way from these relatively poor countries to find work in the UK during the first year of accession. This sudden influx made planning for public services such as schools and hospitals very difficult.
- Member states still have difficulty in formulating a coherent foreign policy for the EU as a whole, as has been seen in the fragmented approach taken towards the 2004 invasion of Iraq.
- There remains widespread concern about the lack of democratic accountability of EU institutions, not helped by allegations of excessive bureaucracy and corruption.
- In order to meet the challenges posed by growth in the EU, attempts have been made to formalize the rights and responsibilities of member states through some form of constitution. Inevitably, member states have widely differing experiences of written constitutions, and there has, not surprisingly, been a lot of debate about what such a constitution should cover (see below).

2.9.2 The structure of the EU

The Treaty of Rome (as modified by the Treaty of Maastricht) developed a structure of government whose elements reflect, in part, the structure of the UK government. The executive (or Cabinet) is provided by the European Council of Ministers; the secretariat (or civil service) is provided by the European Commission; while the legislature is provided by the European Parliament. The judiciary is represented by the European Court of Justice.

The Treaty of Rome places constraints upon the policies that the institutions of the EU can adopt. The European Court of Justice is able to rule that an action or decision is not in accordance with the Treaty. In some cases, such as competition policy, the Treaty is quite specific – for example, Articles 85 and 86, which define the basic approach to be adopted in dealing with cartels and monopoly power. On the other hand, the Treaty says little more on transport policy than that there should be a common policy, giving the community institutions considerable power to develop policies.

The activities of the EU are now directly funded from income received from customs duties and other levies on goods entering the EU from non-member countries. In addition, a value added tax collected by member states on purchases by consumers includes an element of up to 1.45 per cent that is automatically transferred to the EU budget. More recently, a new resource transfer payment between member states and the EU has been introduced, which is based on the gross domestic product of each member state. The United Kingdom remains a net contributor to the EU budget.

New legislation is increasingly the result of cooperation between the various institutions of the EU. The process of cooperation is illustrated in Figure 2.5 and the role of the principal institutions described below. There have been attempts to simplify this process following expansion of the EU from 15 to 27 members.

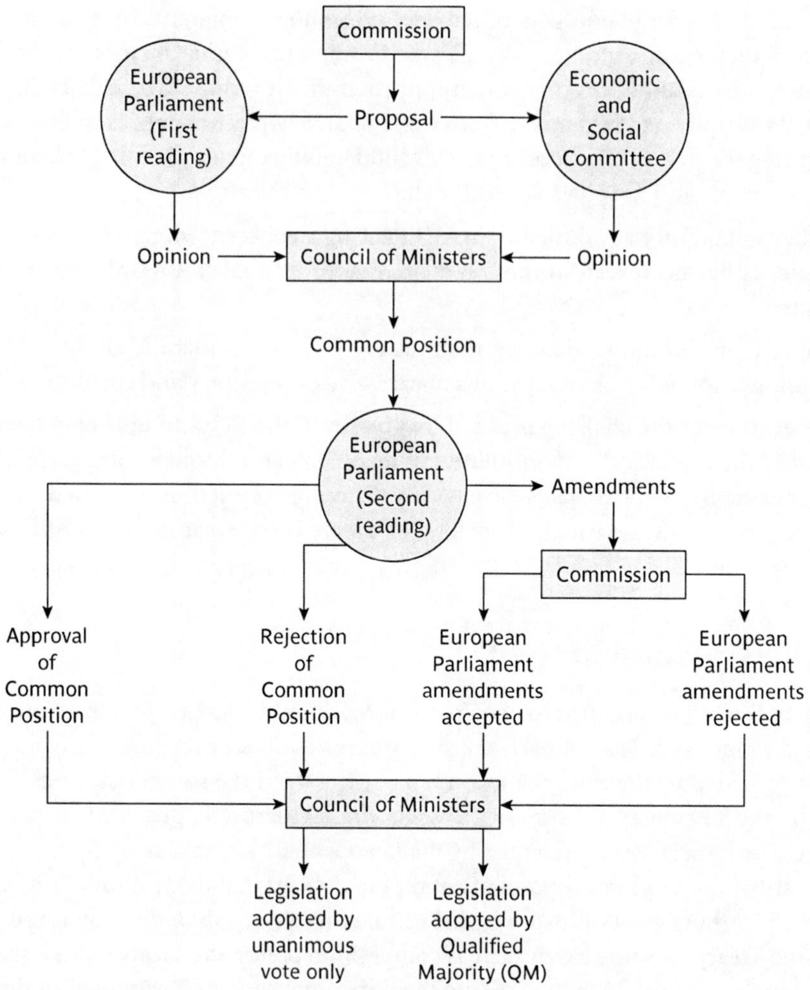

Figure 2.5 The process of cooperation in passing new European legislation

2.9.3 The Council of Ministers

The Council of Ministers represents the governments of member states and can be regarded as the principal lawmaker of the EU, although it can act only on proposals submitted by the Commission. It has powers to:

- adopt legislation
- ratify treaties after consultation with the European Parliament
- ask the Commission to undertake studies and to submit legislation
- delegate executive and legislative powers to the Commission.

Each member state sends one minister to the European Council of Ministers. Which minister attends will depend on the subject being discussed – for example, agriculture ministers would be sent if the Common Agricultural Policy were being discussed. The ministers of foreign affairs, of agriculture, and those with budgetary responsibilities meet more frequently, making a senior body within the Council, sometimes called the General Council. The chairmanship or presidency of the Council of Ministers rotates between countries in alphabetical order, with each period of presidency lasting for six months (see below for proposed constitutional changes in the method of selecting the President).

The Council of Ministers adopts new legislation either by simple majority, qualified majority or unanimity.

- Simple majority gives each minister one vote and is used for proposals such as procedural rules for the convening of intergovernmental conferences.
- Qualified majority voting is based on a weighted voting system where member states' votes are roughly proportional to their size and economic strength. Qualified majority voting prevents smaller states being consistently outvoted and eliminates the risk of two of the larger member states constituting a blocking majority. Examples of applications of this method of voting include legislation on completion of the internal market; the freedom to provide professional services across national borders; and measures to free up the movement of capital within the EU.
- Unanimity is required on issues that are fundamental to individual member states' interests, such as enlargement of the EU, harmonization of taxation and extension of EU powers.

In 2000 an intergovernmental conference of ministers agreed to reduce the number of areas in which unanimity was required, to be further codified by a proposed EU constitution (see below). With enlargement, achieving unanimity between all member states has become increasingly difficult.

The Council of Ministers can generally pass laws even if the European Parliament disagrees with them, unlike the practice within the UK and other national parliamentary systems where ministers must obtain the approval of a majority of Members of Parliament. There are two main exceptions to this authority of the Council. First, the European Parliament has power to approve or reject the EU budget (see below). Second, the Single European Act introduced a system of legislative cooperation between the Council and Parliament, obliging the Council and the Commission to take Parliament's amendments to proposals into consideration, although a unanimous vote by the Council of Ministers retains ultimate authority.

The Committee of Permanent Representatives (Coreper) complements the work of the Council of Ministers. Because ministers have responsibilities to their own national governments as well as to the European Union, they cannot give a continuing presence. To make up for this, each member state sends one ambassador to the Committee, which is based in Brussels. Proposals are discussed in Coreper and its subcommittees before they reach ministers. If Coreper reaches full agreement on the matter, it is empowered to pass it through the Council without further debate, but where disagreement occurs it is left for ministers to discuss.

2.9.4 The European Commission

Each member state sends one commissioner to the Commission (the larger members send two), each appointed by the member government for a renewable term of four years. They are supported in their work by a staff of civil servants, divided between 23 directorates-general and mainly based at the Commission's headquarters in Brussels. Each commissioner is given responsibility for a portfolio, which could be for a policy area, such as transport, or for administrative matters such as the Commission's relations with the Parliament, while others are given a combination of responsibilities in their portfolio. Unlike the Council of Ministers, all members of the Commission are supposed to act primarily for the benefit of the Union as a whole, rather than the country that they represent. This is spelt out in Article 157 of the Treaty of Rome, which states that commissioners 'shall neither seek nor take instruction from any other body'.

The Commission has an initiation, mediation and implementation role. As an initiator, it is the task of the Commission to draft proposals for legislation, which the Council of Ministers has to consider. If the Council does not accept a proposal, it can alter the draft only by a unanimous vote. If unanimity cannot be achieved, the proposal has to go back to the Commission for it to draft a revised proposal that will be acceptable to the Council of Ministers.

As a mediator, the Commission can intervene in disputes between member states to try to find a solution through negotiation. The Commission has frequently acted as mediator in trade disputes between members, avoiding recourse to the European Court of Justice. As an implementer, the Commission undertakes the day-to-day administration of the EU. This involves monitoring the activities of member states to ensure that they do not conflict with community policy. In addition, the Commission implements community policies such as the Regional Development Fund and Common Agricultural Policy.

2.9.5 The European Parliament

Unlike the UK Parliament, the European Parliament is primarily consultative and has relatively little power. Its main function is to monitor the activities of other EU institutions. It can give an opinion on Commission proposals but has powers only to amend, adopt or reject legislation, especially the EU budget. It also has the theoretical power to dismiss the entire Commission, for which a censure motion must be passed by a two-thirds majority of members. Although it can dismiss the entire Commission, the Parliament has no control over the selection of new commissioners to replace those who have been dismissed. It does not yet have the power to initiate and enact legislation.

Members of the European Parliament are now directly elected by the constituents of each country, with countries returning members roughly in proportion to their populations. Members of the European Parliament increasingly belong to political rather than national groupings (e.g. the European People's Party represents 74 parties from European countries).

2.9.6 The European Court of Justice

The supreme legislative body of the EU is the Court of Justice. It is the final arbiter in all matters of interpreting community treaties and rules on disputes between member states, between member states and the Commission, and between the Commission and business organizations, individuals or EU officials. Although the Court can condemn violations of the Treaty by member governments, it has no sanctions against them except goodwill. The European Court of Justice can investigate complaints that the Commission has acted beyond its powers and, if upheld, can annul the decisions of the Commission.

The European Court of Justice is composed of 15 judges, assisted by nine advocates-general. Each is appointed by common agreement between the member states on the basis of their qualifications and impartiality, for a renewable six-year term of office. Members of the Court must put European interests before national interests. The Court can be called upon to settle disputes where the persuasion and negotiations of the Commission have failed to yield results. For example, in the area of competition policy, the Commission may by decision forbid an anti-competitive practice or impose a fine. The companies concerned can appeal to the European Court of Justice for the decision to be set aside. In one case, several dye producers appealed to the European Court of Justice against the fines imposed on them for an alleged price cartel.

2.9.7 Towards an EU constitution?

The European Union is in a state of flux. Its main institutions – the Commission, the Council of Ministers and the European Parliament – remain widely unloved and vulnerable to charges of inefficiency and lack of transparency. But, paradoxically, the EU is in many respects more active than ever before.

The administration of the EU has changed subtly as the EU has matured. The initiative for many new proposals has come from the European Council – summits of EU leaders held three or four times a year. By contrast, the European Commission has tended to become more of an administrator of programmes rather than the bold innovator that launched the single market in the 1980s. It was badly demoralized in March 1999 when the 20-strong commissioners, headed by Jacques Santer, resigned after a critical report alleging nepotism, fraud and mismanagement. At the Nice summit in 2000, the leaders of member states identified the urgent task of defining how powers would be divided between Brussels and national governments, and aimed to achieve this at an intergovernmental conference in 2004. The result was a proposed constitution for the EU. This has become urgently needed because the expansion of the EU to 27 member states in 2007 had threatened to slow down the process of decision making to the speed of the slowest country.

The treaty to establish a constitution for Europe was agreed by EU heads of government in June 2004, but rejected in May 2005 by referenda of voters in France and the Netherlands. A revised constitution was proposed following the Lisbon summit in 2007. This has sought to apply the principle of voting by qualified majority, as it was recognized that, otherwise, getting the agreement of all 27 members would stifle progress. However, member states remain keen to retain a veto, especially in areas of foreign policy, defence and taxation. There is pressure for the European Parliament to have an equal say on decisions requiring majority voting.

There has also been pressure for the appointment of a President of the EU for a term longer than the current rotating six-month presidency. A permanent president would potentially have much greater influence inside and outside the EU.

2.9.8 The relationship between the EU and the UK Government

A distinction needs to be drawn between the primary and secondary legislation of the EU. Primary legislation is contained in the Treaty of Rome (and subsequent treaties agreed by an intergovernmental conference) and takes precedence over national legislation, although national legislation may be required to implement it. Primary legislation can be altered only by an intergovernmental conference of all members. Secondary legislation is made by the Council of Ministers and the Commission under authority delegated to them by the treaties. Secondary legislation affects member states in several forms.

- Regulations automatically form part of the law of member states and apply directly to every individual in the EU. They give rights and duties to individuals that national courts must recognize.
- Directives are mandatory instructions to member states, which must take steps to implement them through national legislation. For example, national laws concerning vehicle safety have varied from state to state and, as a result, trade across frontiers may be impeded. One solution has been to harmonize standards between all member states by means of a directive. The directive will require member states to amend their national legislation governing the design of cars. Individuals will then have to obey the modified national law.
- Decisions of the EU are directly binding on the specific individuals or organizations to whom they are addressed, as where the Commission intervenes in a proposed merger between organizations.

2.9.9 Effects of EU membership on UK business organizations

The EU is having an increasingly important effect on business organizations in the United Kingdom. The relationship between a company and its customers is increasingly being influenced by EU regulations and directives – for example, in the provision of safety features in cars and the labelling of foods. The influence extends to the relationship between the firm and the public at large, as where the EU passes directives affecting advertising standards and pollution controls. Business organizations must monitor proposed EU legislation not only to spot possible changes in legislation that will eventually be implemented through national legislation, but also to lobby to bring about a desired change in EU law. To an increasing extent, lobbying of the UK parliamentary process is becoming less effective as the United Kingdom is bound to implement legislation emanating from the EU.

The extent to which the single European market legislation will further affect business organizations is open to debate. The EU has already had the effect of removing tariff barriers within the Community, and great progress has been made on EU legislation specifying common product design standards. Firms are increasingly seeing Europe as one market and designing standardized products that appeal to consumers in a number of EU states. Many would argue that overseas investors, especially American firms, have always regarded Europe as one market, and developed products as varied as soft drinks and cars to satisfy the whole European market. However, no amount of legislation is likely to overcome the hidden barriers to trade provided

Thinking around the subject: EU directives cause a headache for manufacturers of herbal remedies

The importance of understanding the complexities and different levels of political environments was illustrated by the case of a new EU directive affecting food supplements and herbal remedies, which came into force in 2005.

The EU had earlier passed two directives that would place all herbal medicines and vitamin and mineral supplements on the same regulatory basis as medicines. More than 300 widely used 'natural remedies' would be banned altogether and the cost of licensing each product – estimated at up to £2000 per product – would be beyond the means of many of the small producers that dominated the market for natural remedies. The big pharmaceutical companies had been lobbying the EU hard to get such a change, citing 'adverse reactions' from many herbal remedies and vitamin supplements, such as vitamin B6. Of course, they knew that driving thousands of small herbal producers out of business would draw customers to the pharmaceutical companies' mass-produced products. The natural remedy producers were much more fragmented than the large pharmaceutical companies and were slow to get their lobbying together. In November 2002, the sector presented to the UK Government a petition protesting about the proposed changes. It contained over 1 million signatures, including those of Sir Paul McCartney and Sir Elton John, but it was too late because the directives had already been passed by the EU and there was now little discretion left for the UK Government. The lobbyists of the pharmaceutical industry seemed to have outsmarted the lobbyists of the natural remedy firms, and understood where and when to apply pressure.

In this case, the herbal remedy industry portrayed the EU as a remote and bureaucratic institution that was harming the interests not only of producers, but also the customers who bought its products. However, at other times, businesses have been avid supporters of greater European integration, although sceptics have pointed out that a lot of this may be opportunistic. As an example, brewers have in the past condemned the European Commission's plans for tighter control over the labelling of beer, claiming their national beer is unique, but this has not prevented them also campaigning for a harmonization of taxes where the tax paid in their own country is higher than the EU average.

The EU is accounting for an increasing proportion of the legislation that affects UK businesses. Should the herbal remedy producers have recognized this, and applied their pressure to the EU at an early stage in the drafting of the directives, rather than wait to apply pressure to the UK Government?

by language and by ingrained market characteristics such as the UK practice of driving on the left and using electrical plugs that are not used elsewhere in continental Europe.

2.10 Supranational governmental organizations

National governments' freedom of action is further constrained by international agreements and membership of international organizations. In general, although the treaties of the

EU impose duties on the UK government that it is obliged to follow, membership of other supranational organizations is voluntary and does not have binding authority on the UK government.

Probably the most important organization that affects UK government policy is the United Nations (UN). Its General and Security Councils are designed as fora in which differences between countries can be resolved through negotiation rather than force. In the field of international trade, the UN has sought to encourage freedom of trade through the United Nations Conference on Trade and Development (UNCTAD). In matters of national security, the United Kingdom is a member of the North Atlantic Treaty Organization (NATO), whose role is changing following the end of the 'Cold War'.

Because the importance to the United Kingdom of international treaties and organizations lies to such a great extent in their benefits for international trade, they are considered in more detail in Chapter 14.

Thinking around the subject: **EU takes on Microsoft**

Big multinational companies have often been accused of bullying the governments of small countries. The turnover of a large mining company such as Rio Tinto Zinc may be much greater than the GDP of a small African country in which it operates. A big, well-resourced car manufacturer can negotiate hard deals with a small country to get tax concessions that would not be available to citizens of that country. Too often, the power and resources of small countries with weak governments are no match for the large, well-managed and well-resourced multinational organization.

It should therefore not be surprising that, as the EU has grown, it has been prepared to stand up and fight large organizations in a way that individual member states might not have been able to do on their own. One of the biggest showdowns in recent times has occurred between the EU and the mighty Microsoft Corporation. The European Commission had long felt that Microsoft had abused its dominant market position – for example, by bundling additional software with its operating systems, and restricting access to source code for software developers, thereby restricting interoperability. The Commission was particularly concerned that Microsoft had a 95 per cent market share in desktop publishing and more than 70 per cent of work group server operating systems. In what seemed to be a long war of attrition, the EU Commission first began investigating Microsoft in December 1998. In 2004, the company was fined €497 million by the European Court, for market abuse. It was fined a further €280 million in 2006 for failing to comply with the court's decision that it should make its operating systems more accessible to competitors. In 2007, Microsoft finally gave way and agreed to make it easier and cheaper for rivals to link their products to some classes of its software. In the course of its spat with the EU, it had set aside €1.6 billion to cover fines that had been imposed on it.

Had Microsoft misjudged the political power and determination of the EU? Had it expected to be able to walk over EU institutions in a way that it might have been able to do with smaller countries? Or was this a case of the EU flexing its muscles, in which the Commission was hoping that by bashing an American organization, it would appeal to a greater sense of European unity?

2.11 Improving the standards of government administration

There have been a number of government initiatives to improve the standards of public-sector services that are provided in an environment where there is no market discipline. These generally use a combination of carrot and stick approaches, offering rewards to those public bodies that are performing well, while taking funds away from those that are failing.

In this section, we will consider a number of recent UK government initiatives – performance measures, 'best value indicators' and the sometimes elusive aim of bringing about 'joined-up government'.

2.11.1 Government performance targets

Government organizations have been set increasingly detailed performance targets – for example, the average waiting time for a hospital appointment, the percentage of household waste that is recycled, and the time taken to process a passport application. Managers are often paid a bonus based on their achievement of targets. Of course, such micromanagement by government through targets can lead to dysfunctional outcomes. It was famously noted that when the centralized Russian Government set output targets for state-owned nail factories by weight, the factories simply produced very large nails, which few people wanted. To overcome this problem, targets need to be specified in more detail, resulting in a greater data collection burden for managers, and the possibility of further dysfunctional consequences occurring as individual managers seek to maximize their own performance targets, regardless of their effects on other people's targets.

An alternative approach is to encourage public-sector organizations to achieve more general status labels based on their performance. The Charter Mark is a UK government award scheme that aims to recognize and encourage excellence in public service. A wide range of government organizations have been successful in applying for a Charter Mark, including branches of the Benefits Agency, NHS Trusts, the Courts services, and local HGV testing stations. In local government, the Beacon Council scheme was set up to facilitate the sharing of excellent practice among local authorities by holding out such authorities as exemplars to be followed by others. As an example, Bexley Council was chosen in 2004 as a Beacon Council for its success in cutting anti-social behaviour and crime.

The Local Government Act 1999 introduced the concept of 'best value' in specified local authorities. The Act places on authorities a duty to seek continuous improvement in the way they exercise their functions. At the heart of best value is a statutory performance management framework, which provides for a set of national performance indicators and standards set by central government.

2.11.2 Joined-up government

Central, regional and local government can at times seem an amorphous mass of departments, each not appearing to know what the others are doing. There have been many documented cases where different government departments have taken completely opposing policy directions, thereby cancelling each other out (see 'Thinking around the subject' on p. 73).

Thinking around the subject: How good is the National Health Service?

One of the recurring problems of public-sector services is monitoring their performance, in an environment where market mechanisms alone will not reward the good performers and punish the bad. The UK has prided itself on a centralized National Health Service (NHS), which is free to consumers and paid for largely out of government taxation. But how do you measure the performance of doctors, either individually or in teams? The NHS has focused its efforts on quality-of-service issues. It routinely monitors, for example, the waiting time to see a consultant or to have elective surgery undertaken. But even such apparently simple indicators can mask a lot of problems. What does it mean when one consultant is shown to keep their patients waiting for longer than another consultant? To many people, a long waiting list may be a sign of a top-rated consultant who is very popular with patients, rather than a failing professional who cannot keep up with the demands put on them. And then, of course, figures for waiting times can often be manipulated, scrupulously or unscrupulously. For example, Accident & Emergency departments use triage nurses to assess new patients upon arrival, thereby keeping within their Patients' Charter target for the time taken to initially see a new patient; however, the hospital may be slower to provide actual treatment. In 2003, a number of ambulance services were reprimanded for trying to make their response times appear better than they actually were, by measuring the response time from when an ambulance set out, rather than when a call for help was received.

Attempts to measure doctors' medical performance are much less developed, with debate about the most appropriate methodologies for assessing the efficacy of an operation or clinical diagnosis. Many medical outcomes cannot be assessed simply on the basis of success/failure, but require more subjective quality-of-life assessments to be taken into account. However, even the routine monitoring of patients' recovery rates could have unexpected dysfunctional consequences for patients. Some critics have argued that in order to keep their performance indicators up, consultants may refuse to treat patients who have complications and a high risk of failure, and instead concentrate on easier cases with more predictable outcomes.

Some doctors have expressed a concern that merely publishing performance indicators pushes up users' expectations of service delivery, so that in the end they may become more dissatisfied even though actual performance has improved. Is there a case for treating doctors as professionals whose professional ethics leads them to do their very best for their patients? Or is this inward-looking approach to professional standards becoming increasingly untenable in an era of well-informed consumers who know their rights and have high expectations?

The UK government sought to alleviate such problems with the publication in 1999 of a White Paper on modernizing government. As a result of this, a government task force asked groups of public-sector volunteers, called integrated-service teams, to put themselves in the position of a member of the public experiencing one of a number of major life events, such as leaving school, becoming unemployed, changing address, having a baby or retiring. Team members contacted the relevant departments and agencies direct, and their research gave insights into the problems resulting from the way services are organized, and what might be done to improve things. The study found, for example, that people had to give the same information more than once to different – or even the same – organizations: for example, Housing Benefit and Income Support forms both ask for very similar information.

Having identified the problems, Service Action Teams (SATs) were created to look into particular life episodes that caused most problems in dealing with multiple departments and agencies. Early evidence of the move to joined-up government was seen in the trial integration of previously separate agencies dealing with finding employment and the payment of unemployment benefits.

Creating 'joined-up' thinking is never easy, even within profit-orientated private-sector organizations. In seeking to achieve integration within government, the administration must balance the need to share responsibilities with the need to hold manageable-sized units accountable for their actions.

2.12 Impacts of government on business operations

We will now return to impacts of the political environment on business organizations and discuss three levels of effect:

1 the transformation of many government departments into 'Non-Departmental Government Bodies', so that they act more like a business organization rather than a government department
2 the outsourcing of many government functions, and collaboration with the private sector through public–private partnerships (PPPs)
3 the effects of government legislation on business operations.

2.12.1 Non-Departmental Public Bodies (NDPBs)

The 1990s saw significant developments in the delegation of powers from government organizations to 'arm's length' executive agencies, often referred to collectively as quasi-autonomous non-governmental organizations (quangos) or, more correctly, Non-Departmental Public Bodies (NDPBs). In Britain, quasi-governmental bodies exist because direct involvement by a government department in an activity is considered to be inefficient or undesirable, while leaving the activity to the private sector may be inappropriate where issues of public policy are concerned. The quasi-government body therefore represents a compromise between the constitutional needs of government control and the organizational needs of independence and flexibility associated with private-sector organizations.

There is nothing new in arm's length organizations being created by governments – for example, the Arts Council has existed since before the Second World War. As the size of the state increased in the early post-Second World War period, there was concern that government departments were becoming overloaded. In 1968 the Fulton Committee came out in favour of 'hiving off' some government activities and NDPBs were one means of doing this.

Many aspects of government have been devolved to NDPBs. These are some examples:

- regulatory bodies (e.g. Ofcom for communications industries, Ofwat for water supply and Ofgem for energy supplies)

Thinking around the subject: Does the left hand know what the right hand is doing?

The government of a large modern economy necessarily involves dividing responsibilities between departments, each of which is given increasingly clear aims and objectives, as well as what are usually vague objectives 'to coordinate their activities with other departments'. But despite talk about 'joined-up government', evidence of disjointed government is often all too clear to see. Consider the following cases.

Farming in Britain and the EU has traditionally relied on high levels of government intervention and farmers have often spotted inconsistencies in government policy. For a period during the 1990s, the Department of Agriculture was paying farmers to drain wetlands to turn into farmland. At the same time, the Department of Environment was paying landowners to create ponds and marshland from farmland in order to foster wildlife.

The Department of Education has promoted the recruitment of students from overseas, which is good for the national economy and the longer-term cultural benefits of having students study in the UK. However, in 2004, the Home Office announced that it was doubling the fee for issuing visas to overseas students, and the number of overseas student applications subsequently fell. Were the government and the country any better off as a result of these apparently conflicting actions?

In 2004, the problem of 'binge drinking' late at night in town centres became a priority area for the Home Office. It was particularly concerned by pubs' practice of offering a 'happy hour' in which drinks were sold at a reduced price, leading to problems of drunkenness. The Home Office urged pubs to drop their happy hours. In one Essex town, pub landlords met under the auspices of their local Licensed Victuallers Association and agreed with the Home Office that the happy hour should be abolished. The pub landlords realized that it would be pointless for just one pub to abolish it, because customers would simply go to those pubs that retained cheap drinks. They therefore agreed collectively to abolish the happy hour for all pubs in the town. But this upset another government agency, the Office of Fair Trading, which claimed that the pub landlords were in danger of prosecution for breaching competition law, which made any agreement between suppliers to fix prices illegal.

Some businesses have exploited gaps in government thinking to their own advantage – for example, in the example above, unscrupulous farmers may have sought government grants for both draining their land and creating wetland out of other land. However, to many businesses, such as the well-meaning pub landlords, the appearance that the left hand of government doesn't know what the right hand is doing can be very frustrating. But how in practice can such a large institution as a national government be made to be entirely consistent in the diverse objectives its departments set?

- Regional Development Agencies, which are now very big and in many ways a substitute for regional government, and a key part of the European structure
- the Driver and Vehicle Licensing Agency.

NDPBs enjoy considerable autonomy from their parent department and the sponsoring minister has no direct control over the activities of the body, other than making the appointment of the chairman. The minister therefore ceases to be answerable to Parliament for the day-to-day activities of the body, unlike the responsibility that a minister has in respect of a government department. The responsibilities of NDPBs vary from being purely advisory to making important policy decisions and allocating large amounts of expenditure. Their income can come from a combination of government grant, precepts from local authorities and charges to users.

The main advantage of delegation to NDPBs is that action can generally be taken much more quickly than may have been the case with a government department, where it would probably have been necessary to receive ministerial approval before action was taken. Ministers may have less time to devote to the details of policy application with which many NDPBs are often involved, and may also be constrained to a much greater extent by broader considerations of political policy. Being relatively free of day-to-day political interference, NDPBs are in a better position to maintain a long-term plan free of short-term diversions, which may be the result of direct control by a minister who is subject to the need for short-term political popularity.

Against the advantages, NDPBs have a number of potential disadvantages. It is often argued that NDPBs are not sufficiently accountable to elected representatives for their actions. This can become an important issue where an NDPB is responsible for developing policy or is a monopoly provider of an essential service. The actual independence of NDPBs from government has also been questioned, as many are still dependent on government funding for block grants. NDPBs can easily become unpopular with the public, especially where senior managers are seen paying themselves high salaries as they take 'business-like' decisions to cut back on the services that they provide to the public.

A major objective of delegation to NDPBs has been to ensure that services are provided more in line with users' requirements rather than political or operational expediency. High-level appointments to NDPBs have been made from the private sector with a view to bringing about a cultural change that develops a customer-focused ethos. For the marketing services industry, the development of NDPBs has resulted in many opportunities as they increasingly use the services of market research firms, advertising agencies and public relations consultants.

2.12.2 Public–private partnerships (PPPs)

Throughout Europe, collaborative partnerships between the public and private sectors have become increasingly popular. In the UK, **public–private partnerships (PPPs)** is the umbrella name given to a range of initiatives that involve the private sector in the operation of public services. The **Private Finance Initiative (PFI)** is the most common initiative but PPPs could also extend to other forms of partnership – for example, joint ventures. The key difference between PFI and conventional ways of providing public services is that the public sector does not own the assets. The authority makes an annual payment to the private company, which provides the building and associated services.

Traditionally, government has procured facilities and services that the private sector has supplied under contract to the public sector. For example, under the traditional route, a private-sector contractor would build a new school to a Local Education Authority's (LEA) specification, with associated maintenance and services then being provided by a range of private companies and the LEA itself. With PPPs, one contractor provides the school and then operates a range of specific services such as maintenance, heating and school meals on behalf of the LEA through a long-term contract. This new way of working allows the private sector to contribute its expertise to the process, so as to find innovative solutions and secure better value for money. A typical PFI project will be owned by a company set up especially to run the scheme. These companies are usually consortia including a building firm, a bank and a facilities management company. While PFI projects can be structured in different ways, there are usually four key elements: design, finance, build and operations. In the case of new hospitals funded by PFI schemes, the clinical, medical and nursing services continue to be provided by the NHS, while the private sector finances the building of the new hospital and runs the non-clinical services in it such as maintenance, cleaning, portering and security.

The most significant benefits to government of PPP come through transferring risk to the private sector. This means that should a project under the PPP overrun its budget, the government and taxpayers should not be left to pick up the bill. Contrast this with a major project taken forward under direct contract to the public sector, such as London Transport's Jubilee Line Extension. This overran its planned budget by around £1.4 billion and opened nearly two years late, forcing the government to use taxpayers' money and grant additional funds to get the project completed.

In principle, a PPP should result in a lower level of government borrowing and should also achieve best value. A public-sector comparator is developed in order to establish whether the PPP represents better value than government providing the service by itself. It will show the overall cost of raising the finance and actually doing the work under a wholly public-sector arrangement.

Critics of PPPs argue that the price of involvement by the private sector inevitably includes a high premium to cover the risk of a budget overrun, which could come about for a variety of extraneous reasons. Although the government is saved the initial capital expenditure, over the longer term it has to pay rental charges for the use of facilities, which could work out more expensive than undertaking the whole task itself. The private sector borrows at higher rates of interest than the public sector, and this cost has to be passed on to the purchasing government department. Audit Scotland has calculated these costs as adding £0.2–£0.3 million each year for every £10 million invested. PFI projects can also have high set-up costs due to lengthy negotiations involving lawyers and consultants employed by both sides. It has been reported that the first 15 NHS trust hospital PFIs spent £45 million on advisers, an average of 4 per cent of the capital value (Clark and Simpkins 2006).

There is growing evidence that PFI projects escalate both in scale and cost, reflecting not just inflation but the very nature of PFI itself. In many cases, the PFI agreement places some responsibility for cost overruns with the government rather than the private sector, especially where specifications have changed during the duration of the contract. The higher costs can lead to an affordability gap for the procuring authority that is met by reductions in services and capacity.

There have been casualties among PFI providers. In 2007, Metronet – a company set up to operate some of London's underground railway lines in a PPP with the government body Transport for London – was placed into administration. The companies behind the Metronet consortium – Bombardier, Balfour-Beatty and WS Atkins – came to the conclusion that they could not bear any further cost overruns, which had been disputed with the public-sector partner. They therefore left Transport for London to pick up responsibility for maintaining and renewing the underground lines concerned.

2.12.3 Impacts of government legislation on business operations

Very few governments, whether free market or interventionist, would claim to have made life more difficult for businesses to operate. Yet a frequent complaint of many businesses, especially small business owners, is that government expects them to do too much administration on behalf of the government. Despite frequent high-profile government campaigns against 'red tape', the volume of regulation continues to have a major impact on the costs of business organizations. While large organizations may be able to afford specialists to handle administrative matters and can spread the cost over large volumes of output, government regulation can hit small businesses very hard. Consider some of the following examples of regulations that have added to the costs of business organizations in recent years.

- Value added tax (VAT) effectively makes most business organizations tax collectors on behalf of government, and small business owners must become familiar with complex sets of regulations.
- Legislation to give additional rights to employees bears down particularly heavily on small businesses. Granting maternity rights to new mothers may easily be absorbed by large organizations, but a small business may experience great difficulties when one person who represents a large and critical part of the workforce decides to exercise their rights.
- The mounting volume of consumer protection and health and safety legislation has a particularly big impact on small businesses, which do not generally have the expertise to readily assimilate the provisions of new regulations.

A number of attempts have been made to quantify the costs to business organizations of government regulation. The British Chamber of Commerce's 'Burdens Barometer' is independently compiled by the London and Manchester Business Schools. Its Barometer for 2006 estimated that the cost of 46 major regulations introduced by the UK government since 1998 resulted in annual costs to business of over £50 billion. Figure 2.6 shows a sample of these 46 regulations and the estimated resulting financial burden on business (BCC 2008).

Even the internet, which was supposed to simplify many administrative tasks, has led to new government-imposed burdens on businesses. Worried at the prospect of organized crime using the internet, the government passed the controversial Regulation of Investigatory Powers (RIP) Act 2000. This was bitterly contested by business for its provisions enabling the interception of emails and electronic correspondence.

The incoming Labour government of 1997 set out – as with many previous governments – on a mission to reduce unnecessary regulation, by creating the Better Regulation Task Force. The task force has produced a number of recommendations to government about ways in which the administrative burden could be reduced, but in reaching its recommendations it has to balance efficiency improvements against the often opposing need for greater protection of individuals that regulations provide.

2.13 Influences on government policy formation

Political parties were described earlier as organizations that people belong to in order to influence government policy, generally over a range of issues. Political parties aim to work

Regulation	Year of first implementation	Estimated annual recurring cost to UK business (£m)	Cumulative cost to UK businesses from date of introduction to July 2008 (£m)
The Working Time Regulations 1999	1999	1795	16,005
Employment Act 2002	2002	219	1,302
Flexible Working (Procedural Arrangements) 2002	2003	296	1,588
The Maternity and Parental Leave (Amendment) Regulations 2001	2001	5	95
The Money Laundering Regulations 2003	2004	106	472
The Consumer Credit Regulations 2004	2005	102	681
The Tax Credit Acts 1999 and accompanying regulations	2000	100	865
The Part-time Workers (Prevention of Less Favourable Treatment) Regulations 2000	2000	27	218
The Stakeholder Pensions Schemes Regulations 2000 and 2005	2001	78	660
The Disability Discrimination (Providers of Services) (Adjustments to Premises) Regulations 2001	2004	189	1,721
The Animal By-products Regulations 2003	2003	100	540
The Electricity and Gas (Energy Efficiency Obligations) Order 2004	2005	467	1,401
Total for all government regulations on business			**65,993**

Figure 2.6 Estimated costs to UK businesses of compliance with selected regulations
Source: adapted from the British Chambers of Commerce 'Burdens Barometer', 2008

within the political system – for example, by having members elected as MPs or local councillors. A distinction can be drawn between political parties and pressure groups or interest groups. These latter groups seek to change policy in accordance with members' interests, generally advancing a relatively narrow cause. Unlike members of political parties, members of pressure groups generally work from outside the political system and do not become part of the political establishment.

2.13.1 Pressure groups

Pressure groups can be divided into a number of categories. In the first place there is a division between those that are permanently fighting for a general cause, and those that are set up to achieve a specific objective and are dissolved when this objective is met – or there no longer seems any prospect of changing the situation. Pressure groups set up to fight specific new road building proposals fit into the latter category.

Pressure groups can also be classified according to their functions. Sectional groups exist to promote the common interests of their members over a wide range of issues. Trades unions and employers' associations fall into this category. They represent their members' views to government on diverse issues such as proposed employment legislation, import controls and vocational training. This type of pressure group frequently offers other benefits to members such as legal representation for individual members and the dissemination of information to members. Promotional groups, on the other hand, are established to fight for specific causes, such as animal welfare, which is represented by, say, the League Against Cruel Sports.

Businesses themselves also frequently join pressure groups as a means of influencing government legislative proposals that will affect their industry sector. An example of a powerful commercial pressure group is the British Road Federation, which represents companies with interests in road construction and lobbies government to increase expenditure on new road building.

Pressure groups can influence government policy using three main approaches.

1 The first, propaganda, can be used to create awareness of the group and its cause. This can be aimed directly at policy formers, or indirectly by appealing to the constituents of policy formers to apply direct pressure themselves. This is essentially an impersonal form of mass communication.
2 A second option is to try to represent the views of the group directly to policy formers on a one-to-one basis. Policy formers frequently welcome representations that they may see as preventing bigger problems or confrontations arising in the future. Links between pressure groups and government often become institutionalized, such as where the Department for Transport routinely seeks the views of the RAC Foundation on proposals to change road traffic legislation. Where no regular contacts exist, pressure groups can be represented by giving evidence before a government-appointed inquiry, by approaching sympathetic MPs or by hiring the services of a professional lobbyist.
3 A third approach used by pressure groups is to carry out research and to supply information. This has the effect of increasing public awareness of the organization and usually has a valuable propaganda function. The British Road Federation frequently supplies MPs with comparative road statistics purporting to show reasons why the government should be spending more money on road building.

Pressure groups are most effective where they apply pressure in a low-key manner – for example, where they are routinely consulted for their views. The lobbying of MPs – which combines elements of all three methods described above – has become increasingly important over recent years.

Sometimes pressure groups, or sectional interests within them, recognize that they are unlikely to achieve their aims by using the channels described above. Recent years have seen an increase in 'direct action' by pressure groups, or breakaway sections of mainstream groups, against their target. Campaigners for animal rights, or those opposed to the use of genetically modified (GM) crops, have on occasion given up on trying to change the law and have instead sought to disrupt the activities of those organizations giving rise to their concerns. Organizations targeted in this way may initially put a brave face on such activities by dismissing them as inconsequential, but often the result has been to change the organization's behaviour, especially where the prospect of large profits is uncertain. Action by animal rights protestors contributed to the near collapse of Huntingdon Life Sciences (an animal testing laboratory), and many farmers were discouraged from taking part in GM crop trials by the prospect of direct action against their farms.

It is not only national governments to which pressure groups apply their attention – local authorities are frequently the target of pressure groups over issues of planning policy or the provision of welfare services. Increasingly, pressure is also being applied at EU level. Again, the European Commission regularly consults some groups while other groups apply direct pressure to members of the Commission.

Business organizations have achieved numerous reported triumphs in attempting to influence the political environment in which they operate. The pressure group representing the tobacco industry – the Tobacco Advisory Council – had a significant effect in countering the pressure applied by the anti-tobacco lobby, represented by Action on Smoking Health. Legislation to ban cigarette advertising was delayed, and the pressure group has lobbied against a proposed ban on smoking in public places.

Pressure groups themselves are increasingly crossing national boundaries to reflect the influence of international governmental institutions such as the EU and the increasing influence of multinational business organizations. Both industrial and consumer pressure groups have been formed at a multinational level to counter these influences – a good example of the latter is Greenpeace.

Thinking around the subject: Political apathy becomes militant online

A casual glance at the politics pages in many newspapers in Western Europe may lead to the conclusion that most people don't really care about politics. Most countries have seen a succession of broadly moderate political parties, with very few parties proclaiming extreme views that capture the support of large numbers of people. This has been matched by growing levels of apathy about the political process, evidenced in many countries by a declining number of people voting in elections. In the elections for the EU held in the UK in 2004, it was noted that more people voted in television's *Big Brother* contest than voted for European MEPs. But are we right to dismiss such disengagement from politics as evidence of individuals' lack of concern for political issues? While voting in elections may be declining, there is no sign of people staying silent when their cherished views are challenged. Some countries, such as France, have a tradition of popular protest on the streets. In Britain, a more consensual approach has been more traditional. But, even here, there are signs that frustration with the political process can spill over into the streets, witnessed by the nearly half a million people who marched in London in 2002 under the guise of the Countryside Alliance, to protest about government policy on the countryside. New technology has opened up new opportunities for people to express their political views without going to the ballot box. One example is the facility for any individual to initiate an online petition to 10 Downing Street. In 2007, Peter Roberts and a small group who were opposed to the idea of charging for the use of roads launched a petition that attracted 1.3 million signatures. Is this the true democratization of politics? For businesses, rather than looking at politicians to try to judge future policy, would it be just as good an idea to look at what really brings people on to the streets, or to an online petition, in order to understand the pressures that politicians will probably eventually respond to?

2.13.2 Role of the media

The media – press, radio, television and increasingly the internet – not only spread awareness of political issues but also influence policy and decision making by setting the political agenda and influencing public opinion. The broadcast media in the United Kingdom must by law show balance in their coverage of political events, but the press is often more openly partisan. Campaigns undertaken by the press frequently reflect the background of their owners – the *Daily Telegraph* is more likely to support the causes of deregulation in an industry, while the *Guardian* will be more likely to put forward the case for government spending on essential public services. It is often said that *The Times* and the BBC Radio 4 *Today* programme set the political agenda for the day ahead.

Case study: **Should government be running the railways?**

Railways throughout the world have traditionally been owned and operated by governments. There have been good social arguments for state ownership, especially in communities where a railway represents a vital lifeline. The sheer costs and risks involved in building and operating a railway have deterred private investors, mindful of the many bankruptcies that have occurred during earlier 'railway booms'.

Britain led the way in privatizing its railways during the 1990s, and many other governments have followed by loosening their countries' railway links with government. But, ten years on, Britain's railways have been treated as a political football, and questions have been raised about the relative merits of state ownership and privatization. Along the way, there have been many opportunities, and headaches, for private-sector organizations that have been attracted to the sector.

Britain's railways came into public ownership because they had ceased to make profits for their private owners in the 1920s and 1930s. They became starved of new investment and this was seen as a major hindrance for the post-war Labour government's national reconstruction plans. It is true that the great modernization plan of the post-war period did see a lot of new investment in the railways – for example, new signalling and the replacement of steam trains with diesel and electric trains. Unfortunately, much of this investment was not customer-focused and customers increasingly voted with their wallets by going elsewhere. Passengers deserted in large numbers to the private car, to coach services and, to an increasing extent, to domestic air services. Freight customers found the cost, speed and reliability of road haulage gaining an edge over the railways.

To the Conservative government of the 1990s, British railways were suffering from a lack of entrepreneurship, which could be overcome by replacing public-sector employees and finance with new ideas and new capital brought in from the private sector. Ownership and maintenance of the track passed to Railtrack, whose shares were offered to the public. Railtrack in turn subcontracted much of its maintenance work to other private companies. The train operation was sold off to 26 franchised companies, which leased trains from three privatized rolling stock companies. All these were regulated by the Office of the Rail Regulator (Ofrail).

Privatization, and opposition to it, appeared to be driven as much by dogma as the operational realities of running a railway. The fragmentation of the industry track operator, rolling stock owners and franchise operators was driven by a desire for competition. Even the idea of having integrated regional organizations, which would be responsible for the track, the rolling stock and operations, was seen by the Conservative government as inherently anti-competitive and avoided almost as a dogmatic belief. During discussion of rail privatization, the opposition Labour Party appeared to be equally dogmatically opposed to it. Some of the party's more left-wing members were opposed to any diminution in the role of the state. The party's transport spokesperson vowed to renationalize railways if and when it came back into government but, paradoxically, this simply frightened off potential investors who could pick up shares in railway assets at knock-down bargain-basement prices.

It didn't take long for the critics of privatization to argue that the railways were now in worse shape than they ever were under state ownership. There was often a suspicion that when things went wrong, companies simply put the blame on one another. Train operators accused Railtrack if a train was late and Railtrack may have blamed a train operator for causing a blockage on its lines. This fragmentation was felt most seriously where accidents occurred and it was difficult to pin down responsibility. Worryingly, it seemed that the service quality improvements sought from privatization had actually gone into reverse. During the year ended September 2004, just 76.4 per cent of Virgin Cross-Country trains arrived on time or within 10 minutes of the scheduled time. The UK rail sector as a whole achieved only 81.2 per cent on-time arrivals in that period, lower than pre-privatization levels of reliability (90 per cent in 1992–93), despite longer scheduled journey times on many routes. Astonishingly, an international comparison found the Pakistan Railways route from Lahore to Karachi achieving 88 per cent reliability. Even the steam-hauled trains operating from Accra to Kumasi in Ghana beat Virgin's reliability, at 85 per cent. Critics of privatization argued that private companies were too concerned with cutting costs in order to meet their shareholders' expectations. Cost cutting and poor communications between companies were highlighted following a number of serious rail crashes. With most companies having franchises of only around seven years, cost reduction rather than investment was seen as the best way of improving profitability.

At the same time as service quality was evidently deteriorating, the cost to the government of subsidizing train services had increased sharply. Research carried out by rail journalist Roger Ford, and published in *The Rising Cost of Britain's Railways* by pressure group Transport 2000, showed that total government subsidy to Britain's railways in 2003/04 was £3.84 billion. By comparison, in British Rail's last year as operator of an integrated railway (1993–94) the total subsidy was £1.32 billion (at 2003–04 prices).

The Labour Party, when in opposition, had failed to stop rail privatization. However, the incoming Labour government of 1997 realized that undoing the process would be prohibitively costly and the government had much more pressing priority areas on which to spend the billions of pounds that rail nationalization would have cost. Nationalization would probably cause even more disruption to travellers in the process. The track operator, Railtrack, had become a popular scapegoat for the railway's problems, despite investing record amounts of private capital in the network. In 2002, the government used its powers to place Railtrack in administration, and gave responsibility for the track to a new not-for-profit organization, Network Rail. Two years later, it sacked the operator of the South Central franchise – Connex – and replaced it with a new company directly answerable to the government's previously created Strategic Rail Authority. The Strategic Rail Authority, originally set up as a quango at arm's length from the government, was itself wound up in 2006 following the Railways Act 2005, and its functions transferred to civil servants at the Department for Transport. Was this evidence of Labour Party dogma about state control reasserting itself, or was it a simple realization that the private sector is not capable of running a complex system such as the rail network? Meanwhile, political uncertainty had caused a lot of harm in the rail sector. Faced with short-term franchises, most train operators were initially reluctant to order new rolling stock, resulting in a drastic reduction in the UK's train-building capacity as manufacturers closed down or relocated their facilities overseas. Many suppliers to the industry could survive happily in either a state-owned or a privatized system of ownership, but the worst situation for them was political uncertainty.

The rest of Europe had made little progress towards deregulating and privatizing its railways, although the EU had been trying since 1998 to deregulate the sector. Full-scale liberalization of EU rail freight transport was implemented from 2007, allowing railway operators across the EU to provide their services in other member states. In the process of privatizing UK rail services, an anomaly occurred when a number of European state rail operators joined consortia to bid for UK franchises. In 2007, the German state operator, Deutsche Bahn, acquired the UK freight operator, EWS, and one year later took control of the company that operates Chiltern Trains services between London and Birmingham. A decade after privatization, government influence seemed to be creeping back into the UK rail sector.

QUESTIONS

1 Summarize the effects of political ideology on the management and ownership of railways in Britain.

2 What public interest is served by government involvement in the management and ownership of railways?

3 What are likely to be the key differences between the objectives of a railway in private ownership and a railway in state ownership?

Summary

The political environment impinges on many other aspects of an organization's environment; for example, change in the dominant political ideology can result in significant changes in the economic environment. Businesses dislike uncertainty in the political environment, and monitoring and understanding it is useful to pick up early signs of change. This chapter has explored the basis of government in the United Kingdom, and the respective roles of national, regional, local and European government. Although examples have been taken from the UK, the elements of the political environment described here are similar in most Western democratic countries. A two-way interaction occurs between government and business, in which business organizations monitor changes in the political environment, but also seek to influence the environment through lobbying. Pressure groups represent an increasingly important element of the political environment, working from outside the formal political system.

The overlaps between the political environment and other aspects of a firm's marketing environment are covered in following chapters. Politicians have a significant impact on the national economic environment (**Chapter 13**) and indeed respond to changes in it. The level of competition within any market can be influenced by government policies on anti-competitive practices (**Chapter 12**). Government policy is translated into legislation (**Chapter 5**) and influences the standards of behaviour expected from business (**Chapter 10**).

Key terms

Act of Parliament (49)
Beacon Council (70)
Best value (70)
Cabinet (52)
Charter Mark (70)
Civil service (53)
Directives (52)
European Commission (62)
European Council of Ministers (62)
European Court of Justice (62)
European Economic Area (EEA) (60)
European Union (EU) (60)
Executive (52)
Ideology (44)
Judicial review (54)
Judiciary (54)
Legislature (49)
Lobbying (51)
Local government (59)
Non-Departmental Public Bodies (NDPBs) (72)
Outsourcing (72)
Political parties (45)
Pressure groups (77)
Private Finance Initiative (PFI) (74)
Public–private partnership (PPP) (74)
Quango (72)
Regional government (55)
Regulation (76)
Social exclusion (47)
Task force (71)

Chapter review questions

1 For a newspaper lobbying against government proposals to impose value added tax on newspaper sales, identify the key points within the government system to which lobbying could be applied.

2 For a British manufacturing company, briefly summarize the principal problems and opportunities presented by the development of closer economic and political union within the EU.

3 What measures can a large multinational business take to monitor the political environment in its various operating areas?

Activities

1 Take three of the recent regulatory burdens on business that are listed in Figure 2.6. Discuss whether these are unfair burdens on business, or a real and worthwhile net benefit for customers, employees and society as a whole.

2 Go to the website of the main political parties in your country, and assess the extent to which you consider their policies to be beneficial for small or medium-sized businesses. Try to distinguish between specific policies that affect business, and more general policies that shape the nature of the country, and may indirectly have an effect on businesses.

3 Try to identify a list of non-departmental public bodies (or 'quangos') that you may have had dealings with (for example, health services, the driver licensing agency, educational establishment). Critically assess the nature of control of these organizations. Is bureaucratic control preferable to control by customers exercising their choice of service provider? Is such choice feasible for your selected quango?

Further Reading

For an overview of how government is managed in the UK, the following texts provide a useful insight.

Bogdanor, V. (2005) *Joined-up Government*, Oxford, Oxford University Press.

The following provide a more specific focus on local government.

Heywood, A. (2008) *The Essentials of UK Politics*, Basingstoke, Palgrave Macmillan.

Moran, M. (2005) *Politics and Governance in the UK*, Basingstoke, Palgrave Macmillan.

Van Der Waldt, G. (2004) *Managing Performance in the Public Sector: Concepts, Considerations and Challenges*, Juta & Company, Ltd.

Wilson, D. and Game, C. (2006) *Local Government in the UK*, Basingstoke, Palgrave Macmillan.

For a discussion of devolved government in the UK, consult the following.

Adams, J. and Schmuecker, K. (2006) *Devolution in Practice: Public Policy Differences within the UK*, London, IPPR.

O'Neill, M. (2004) *Devolution and British Politics*, London, Pearson.

To many, the workings of the European Union are extremely complex and the following texts provide a general overview.

Bomberg, E., Peterson, J. and Stubb, A. (2008) *The European Union: How Does it Work?*, Oxford, Oxford University Press.

El-Agraa, A. (2007) *The European Union: Economics and Policies*, Cambridge, Cambridge University Press.

The following official publications of the EU are also useful for monitoring current developments.

Basic Statistics of the Community

Bulletin of the European Commission of the European Communities

Finally, there is extensive coverage of the functions of pressure groups. The following texts are useful for highlighting their relationship to business organizations.

Coxall, B. (2001) *Pressure Groups in British Politics*, Longman.

Watts, D. (2007) *Pressure Groups*, Edinburgh, Edinburgh University Press.

References

Barro, R.J. (1996) 'Democracy and growth', *Journal of Economic Growth*, Kluwer Academic Publishers, Vol. 1, No. 1, pp. 1–27.

BCC (2008) 'Burdens Barometer', London, British Chamber of Commerce.

Clark, R. and Simpkins, E. (2006) 'Buy now pay later (a lot more, a lot later)', *Daily Telegraph*, 7 May.

Office for National Statistics (2004) *Focus on Social Inequalities*, London.

Office for National Statistics (2008) *Social Trends*, No. 38, London.

Rodrik, D. (2002) *Feasible Globalization*, Working Paper, Harvard University, May.

Stiglitz, J. (2000) 'Whither reform? Ten years of the transition', in B. Pleskovic and J. Stiglitz (eds) *Annual World Bank Conference on Development Economics 1999*, Washington, DC, World Bank, pp. 27–56.

Chapter 5

The Legal Environment

CHAPTER OBJECTIVES

This chapter will explain:

- the key legal challenges and opportunities facing business organizations, in respect of their relationships with customers, suppliers, employees and intermediaries
- sources of law – common law and statute law
- the basic principles of law – contract and tort
- legal processes
- quasi-law based on voluntary codes of conduct
- legal protection of intellectual property

5.1 Introduction

It was noted in the first chapter that all societies need some form of rules that govern the relationship between individuals, organizations and government bodies. In the absence of rules, chaos is likely to ensue, in which the strongest people will survive at the expense of the weakest. Businesses do not like to operate in environments in which there are no accepted rules of behaviour, because there is no guarantee that their investments will be protected from unauthorized seizure. This may partly explain why some countries of central Africa, which have been regarded as lawless areas without proper government, have failed to attract significant inward investment by businesses.

However, a system of rules does not necessarily imply a formal legal system. Many less developed economies manage with moral codes of governance that exert pressure on individuals and organizations to conform to an agreed code of conduct. In such countries, the shame inflicted on the family of a trader who defrauds a customer may be sufficient to ensure that traders abide by a moral code of governance.

In complex, pluralistic societies, moral governance alone may be insufficient to ensure compliance from business organizations. The tendency therefore has been for legal frameworks to expand as economies develop. One observer has pointed out that the Ten Commandments – a biblical code for governing society – ran to about 300 words. The American Bill of Rights of 1791 ran to about 700 words. Today, as an example of the detailed legislation that affects our conduct, the Eggs (Marketing Standards) Regulations 1995 run to several pages. The law essentially represents a codification of the rules and governance values of a society, expressed in a way that allows aggrieved parties to use an essentially bureaucratic system to gain what the society regards as justice. The legal environment of Western developed economies is very much influenced by the political environment, which in turn is influenced by the social environment. In this sense, the law does not exist in a vacuum. Developments in the business environment have led to changes in the law affecting businesses, and the law in turn has affected the activities of business organizations.

In previous chapters we have considered the relationship between elements of an organization's micro- and macroenvironments at a fairly abstract level. In reality, these relationships are governed by a legal framework that presents opportunities and constraints for the manner in which these relationships can be developed.

We can identify a number of important areas in which the legal environment impinges on the activities of business organizations.

- The nature of the relationship between the organization and its customers, suppliers and intermediaries is influenced by the prevailing law. Over time, there has been a tendency for the law to give additional rights to buyers of goods and additional duties to the seller, especially in the case of transactions between businesses and private individuals. Whereas the nineteenth-century entrepreneur in Britain would have had almost complete freedom to dictate the terms of the relationship with its customers, developments in statute law now require, for example, the supplier to ensure that the goods are of satisfactory quality and that no misleading description of them is made. Furthermore, the expectations of an organization's customers have changed over time. Whereas previous generations may have resigned themselves to suffering injustice in their dealings with a business, today the expectation is increasingly for perfection every time. Greater awareness of the law on the part of consumers has produced an increasingly litigious society.

- In addition to the direct relationship that a company has with its customers, the law also influences the relationship that it has with other members of the general public. The law may, for example, prevent a firm having business relationships with certain sectors of the market, as where children are prohibited by law from buying cigarettes or drinking in public houses. Also, the messages that a company sends out in its advertising are likely to be picked up by members of the general public, and the law has intervened to protect the public interest where these messages could cause offence (adverts that are racially prejudicial, for example).
- Employment relationships are covered by increasingly complex legislation, which recognizes that employees have a proprietary interest in their job. Legislation seeks to make up for inequalities in the power between employers and employee.
- The legal environment influences the relationship between business enterprises themselves, not only in terms of contracts for transactions between them, but also in the way they relate to each other in a competitive environment. The law has increasingly prevented companies from joining together in anti-competitive practices, whether covertly or overtly.
- Companies need to develop new products, yet the rewards of undertaking new product development are influenced by the law. The laws of copyright and patent protect a firm's investment in fruitful research.
- The legal environment influences the production possibilities of an enterprise and hence the products that can be offered to consumers. These can have a direct effect – as in the case of regulations stipulating car safety design requirements – or a more indirect effect – as where legislation to reduce pollution increases the manufacturing costs of a product, or prevents its manufacture completely.

The legal environment is very closely related to the political environment. In the UK, law derives from two sources: common law and statute law.

1. The **common law** develops on the basis of judgments in the courts – a case may set a precedent for all subsequent cases to follow. The judiciary is independent of government and the general direction of precedents tends gradually to reflect changing attitudes in society.
2. **Statute law**, on the other hand, is passed by Parliament and can reflect the prevailing political ideology of the government.

We can draw a distinction between *civil* law and *criminal* law. Civil law provides a means by which one party can bring an action for a loss it has suffered as the direct result of actions by another party. A party who is injured by a defective vehicle, or has suffered loss because a promised order for goods has not been delivered, can use the civil law to claim some kind of recompense against the other party. By contrast, criminal law is invoked when a party causes harm to society more generally. In this case, it is the government that brings a claim against a wrongdoer and punishment generally takes the form of a fine or a prison sentence. Most of the subjects covered in this chapter are concerned with the civil law – that is, relationships between an organization and other individuals and organizations in their business environment.

However, business organizations are increasingly being prosecuted for breaches of criminal law. Cases discussed in this chapter include breaches of food safety law, breaches of health and safety law, and providing misleading price information.

The law is a very complex area of the business environment. Most businesses would call upon expert members of the legal profession to interpret and act upon some of the more complex elements of the law. The purpose of this chapter is not to give definitive answers on aspects of the law as it affects business organizations – this would be impossible and dangerous in such a short space. Instead, the aim is to raise awareness of legal issues in order to recognize in general terms the opportunities and restrictions that the law poses, and the areas in which business organizations may need to seek the specialized advice of a legal professional.

This chapter will begin by looking at some general principles of law: the law of contract, the law relating to negligence and the processes of the legal system in England. Although the detail will describe the legal system of England, many of the principles apply in other judicial systems. The chapter will then consider the following specific areas of applications of the law, which are of particular relevance to businesses:

- dealings between organizations and their customers for the supply of goods and services
- contracts of employment
- protection of intellectual property rights
- legislation relating to production processes
- legislation to prevent anti-competitive practices.

5.2 The law of contract

A contract is an agreement between two parties where one party agrees to do something (e.g. supply goods, provide a service, offer employment) in return for which the other party provides some form of payment (in money or some other form of value). A typical organization would have contracts with a wide range of other parties, including customers, suppliers, employees and intermediaries.

There can be no direct legal relationship between a company and any of these groups unless it can be proved that a contract exists. An advertisement on its own only very rarely creates a legal relationship. The elements of a contract comprise: offer, acceptance, intention to create legal relations, consideration and capacity. We will consider these in turn.

5.2.1 Offer

This a declaration by which the offeror indicates that they intend to be legally bound on the terms stated in the offer if it is accepted by the offeree. An offer must be distinguished from an invitation to treat, which can be defined as an invitation to make offers. Normally, advertisements are regarded as invitations to treat, rather than an offer. Similarly, priced goods on display in shops are invitations to treat. Therefore, if a leather jacket is priced at £20 (through error) in the shop widow, it is not possible to demand the garment at that price. As the display is an invitation to treat, it is the consumer who is making the offer, which the shopkeeper may accept or reject as he wishes.

5.2.2 Acceptance

This may be made only by the person(s) to whom the offer was made, and it must be absolute and unqualified (i.e. it must not add any new terms or conditions, for to do so would have the effect of revoking the original offer). Acceptance must be communicated to the offeror unless it can be implied by conduct. An offer may be revoked at any time prior to acceptance. However, if postal acceptance is an acceptable means of communication between the parties, then acceptance is effective as soon as it is posted, provided it is correctly addressed and stamped.

5.2.3 Intention to create legal relations

Generally, in all commercial agreements it is accepted that both parties intend to make a legally binding contract and therefore it is unnecessary to include terms to this effect. In some circumstances, however, there may be no intention on the part of one or both parties to create legal relations, as occurs where a donor casually gives money to a charity organization. In the absence of such intention, a contract cannot exist.

5.2.4 Consideration

This is essential in all contracts unless they are made 'under seal'. Consideration has been defined as some right, interest, profit or benefit accruing to one party, or some forbearance, detriment, loss or responsibility given, suffered or undertaken by the other (i.e. some benefit accruing to one party or a detriment suffered by the other). In commercial contracts generally, the consideration takes the form of a cash payment. However, in contracts of barter, which are common in some countries, goods are often exchanged for goods.

5.2.5 Capacity

Generally, any person or organization may enter into an agreement, which may be enforced against them. They are deemed to have the 'capacity' to do so. Exceptions include minors, drunks and mental patients; for this reason, companies usually exclude people under 18 from offers of goods to be supplied on credit. Limited companies must have the capacity to make a contract identified in their Objects clause within their Articles and Memorandum of Association (see Chapter 6).

5.2.6 Terms and representations

Finally, a distinction can be made between the terms of a contract and representations, which were made prior to forming the contract. Generally, it is assumed that statements that are made at the formation of a contract are terms of that contract, but many statements made during the course of negotiations are mere representations. If the statement is a term, the injured party may sue for breach of contract and will normally obtain damages that are deemed to put him or her in the position they would have been in if the statement had been true. If the statement is a mere representation, it may be possible to avoid the contract by obtaining an order – known as

Thinking around the subject: Is a business relationship a contract?

One of the trends in the business environment that we discussed in Chapter 1 is towards closer relationships between companies in a supply chain. So, instead of buying 'job lots' of components and raw materials from the cheapest buyer whenever they are needed, a buyer and seller will come to an arrangement for their supply over the longer term. The parties may not be able to specify the precise products or volumes that they will need to buy, but just by understanding each other's processes and likely future requirements, the supply chain can be made more efficient and effective.

Many of these business relationships are based on 'gentlemen's agreements' with little formal specification in writing. So is this a contract? Can either party unilaterally end a gentleman's agreement?

The question was tested in 2002 in the case of Baird Textile Holdings Ltd vs. Marks & Spencer plc (M&S). Baird had been making lingerie, women's coats and men's clothes for M&S for over 30 years, and had largely built its business round the retail chain's requirements. However, the parties had resisted formalizing the arrangement in order to maintain maximum flexibility in their relationship. But increased competition in the high street led M&S to look for cheaper sources of manufacturing overseas, and Baird was told that with immediate effect its goods were no longer required by M&S.

Baird argued that although there was no written contract governing their relationship, there was an implied term that either party would give reasonable notice of any change to the relationship. The supplier claimed for damages of £53.6 million, which included a £33 million charge to cover redundancy payments, and further amounts in respect of asset write-downs, including IT equipment it used to help fulfil its M&S clothing orders. The claim was intended to put Baird back into the position it would have been in had M&S given it three years' notice, rather than suddenly terminating its agreement. But did the agreement between the two constitute a contract?

The Court of Appeal held that the long-term arrangements between Baird and M&S did not constitute a contract. It stated that there was a clear mutual intent not to enter into a legal agreement and this view was supported by the absence of any precise terms. Both parties clearly wished to preserve flexibility in their dealings with each other. A contract existed only in respect of individual orders when they were placed, but there was no contract governing the continuity of orders.

rescission – which puts the parties back in the position they were in prior to the formation of the contract. Even though the essential elements of a contract are present, the contract may still fail to be given full effect.

5.3 Non-contractual liability

Consider now the situation where a consumer discovers that goods are defective in some way but is unable to sue the retailer from which they were supplied because the consumer is not a party to the contract (which may occur where the goods were bought as a gift by a friend). The product may also injure a completely unconnected third party. The only possible course of action here has been to sue the manufacturer. This situation was illustrated in 1932 in the case of Donaghue vs. Stevenson, where a man bought a bottle of ginger beer manufactured by the defendant. The man gave the bottle to his female companion, who became ill from drinking the contents, as the bottle (which was opaque) contained the decomposing remains of a snail. The consumer sued the manufacturer and won. The House of Lords held that on the facts outlined there was remedy in the **tort** of negligence.

To prove **negligence**, there are three elements that must be shown:

1 that the defendant was under a duty of care to the plaintiff
2 that there had been a breach of that duty
3 that there is damage to the plaintiff as a result of the breach, which is not too remote a consequence.

In the case, Lord Atkin defined a **duty of care** by stating that:

> You must take reasonable care to avoid acts or omissions which you can reasonably foresee would be likely to injure your neighbour. Who then is my neighbour? The answer seems to be persons who are so closely and directly affected by my act that I ought reasonably to have them in contemplation as being so affected when I am directing my mind to the acts or omissions which are called in question.

The law of negligence is founded almost entirely on decided cases, and the approach adopted by the courts is one that affords flexibility in response to the changing patterns of practical problems. Unfortunately, it is unavoidable that with flexibility comes an element of uncertainty. Whether or not liability will arise in a particular set of circumstances appears to be heavily governed by public policy, and it is not clear exactly when a duty of care will arise. At present, the principles, or alternatively the questions to be asked in attempting to determine whether a duty exists, are:

- is there foreseeability of harm and, if so . . .
- is there proximity – a close and direct relationship – and, if so . . .
- is it fair and reasonable for there to be a duty in these circumstances?

Having established in certain circumstances that a duty of care exists, defendants will be in breach of that duty if they have not acted reasonably. The question is 'What standard of care does the law require?' The standard of care required is that of an ordinary prudent man in the circumstances pertaining to the case. For example, in one case it was held that an employee owed a higher standard of care to a one-eyed motor mechanic and was therefore obliged to provide protective goggles – not because the likelihood of damage was greater, but because the consequences of an eye injury were more serious (Paris vs. Stepney BC, 1951). Similarly, a higher standard of care would be expected from a drug manufacturer than from a greetings cards manufacturer because the consequences of defective products would be far more serious in the former case.

Where a person is regarded as a professional (i.e. where people set themselves up as possessing a particular skill, such as a plumber, solicitor, surgeon) then they must display the type of skill required in carrying out that particular profession or trade.

With a liability based on fault, the defendant can be liable only for damages caused by him or her. The test adopted is whether the damage is of a type or kind that ought reasonably to have been foreseen even though the extent need not have been envisaged. The main duty is that of the manufacturer, but cases have shown that almost any party that is responsible for the supply of goods may be held liable. The onus of proving negligence is on the plaintiff. Of importance in this area is s. 2(1) of the Unfair Contract Terms Act 1977, which states: 'a person cannot by reference to any contract term or notice exclude or restrict his liability for death or personal injury resulting from negligence'. Also s. 2(2): 'in the case of other loss or damage, a person cannot so exclude or restrict his liability for negligence except in so far as the contract term or notice satisfies the test of reasonableness'. Thus, all clauses that purport to exclude liability in respect of negligence resulting in death or personal injuries are void, and other clauses (e.g. 'goods accepted at owner's risk') must satisfy the test of reasonableness.

5.4 Legal processes

It is not only changes in the law itself that should be of concern to businesses but also the ease of access to legal processes. If legal processes are excessively expensive or time-consuming, the law may come to be seen as irrelevant if parties have no realistic means of enforcing the law. In general, developed economies have seen access to the law widened, so that it is not exclusively at the service of rich individuals or companies. As well as individuals and companies having the right to protect their own legal interests, a number of government agencies facilitate enforcement of the law.

In England, a number of courts of law operate with distinct functional and hierarchical roles.

- The Magistrates' Court deals primarily with criminal matters, where it handles approximately 97 per cent of the workload. It is responsible for handling prosecutions of companies for breaches of legislation under the Trade Descriptions and the Consumer Protection Acts. More serious criminal matters are 'committed' up to the Crown Court for trial.
- The Crown Court handles the more serious cases that have been committed to it for trial on 'indictment'. In addition, it also hears defendants' appeals as to sentence or conviction from the Magistrates' Court.
- The High Court is responsible for hearing appeals by way of 'case stated' from the Magistrates' Court or occasionally the Crown Court. The lower court, whose decision is being challenged, prepares papers (the case) and seeks the opinion of the High Court.
- The Court of Appeal deals primarily with appeals from trials on indictment in the Crown Court. It may review either sentence or conviction.
- County Courts are for almost all purposes the courts of first instance in civil matters (contract and tort). Generally, where the amount claimed is less than £25,000, this court will have jurisdiction in the first instance, but between £25,000 and £50,000, the case may be heard here, or be directed to the High Court, depending on its complexity.
- When larger amounts are being litigated, the High Court will have jurisdiction in the first instance. There is a commercial court within the structure that is designed to be a quicker

and generally more suitable court for commercial matters; bankruptcy appeals from the County Court are heard here.

- Cases worth less than £5000 are referred by the County Court to its 'Small Claims' division, where the case will be heard informally under arbitration, and costs normally limited to the value of the issue of the summons.
- The Court of Appeals' Civil Division hears civil appeals from the County Court and the High Court.
- The House of Lords is the ultimate appeal court for both criminal and domestic matters.
- However, where there is a European Issue, the European Court of Justice will give a ruling on the point at issue, after which the case is referred back to the UK court.

In addition to the court structure (see Figure 5.1), there are numerous quasi-judicial tribunals that exist to reconcile disagreeing parties. Examples include Rent Tribunals (for agreeing property rents), Valuation Tribunals (for agreeing property values) and Employment Tribunals (for bringing claims covered by employment legislation).

Despite the existence of legal rights, the cost to an individual or a firm of enforcing its rights can be prohibitive, especially where there is no certainty that a party taking action will be able to recover its legal costs. For a typical inter-company dispute over a debt of £50,000, the party suing the debtor can easily incur legal expenses of several thousand pounds, not counting the cost of its employees' time. Where a case goes to the Court of Appeal, a company could be involved in inestimable costs. The legal process can also be very slow. In the case of an inter-company debt claim, a case may take up to ten years between the first issue of a writ and compensation finally being received.

Numerous attempts have been made to make the legal system more widely accessible, such as the small claims section of the County Court, which handles claims of up to £5000 in a less formal and costly manner than a normal County Court claim. There have also been attempts to reduce the risks to individuals by allowing, in certain circumstances, solicitors to charge their

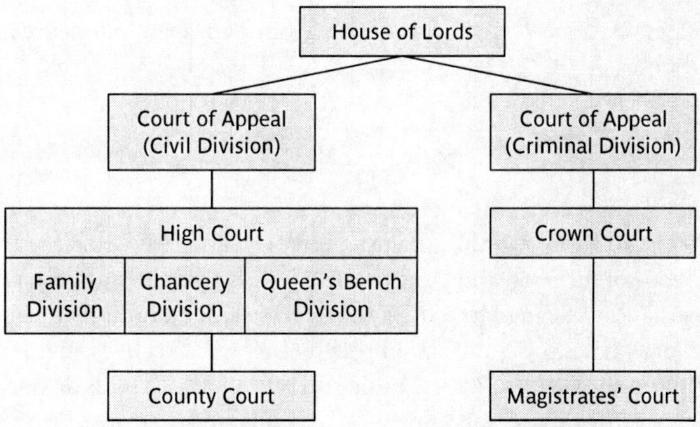

Figure 5.1 The structure of courts in England

clients depending upon results obtained in court (often referred to as a 'no win, no fee' system). There is a strong feeling that the costs of running the courts system could be cut by reducing many bureaucratic and restrictive practices within the legal profession.

Despite moves to make legal remedies more widely available, access to the law remains unequal. Among commercial organizations, a small under-resourced firm may be unable to put the money upfront to pursue a case against a larger company that could defend itself with an army of retained lawyers. Similarly, private consumers are unequal in their access to the law. It has often been suggested that easy access to the law is afforded to the very rich (who can afford it) and the very poor (who may be eligible to receive legal aid). An apparent paradox of attempts to make the law more accessible is that these attempts may themselves overwhelm courts with cases with which they are unable to cope. As an example, the Small Claims Court is reported to have been overwhelmed in 2007 by thousands of bank customers suing their banks for a refund of 'unreasonable' charges levied by the banks. The flood of litigants was assisted by the availability online of template letters promoted by consumer group sites and the ability of aggrieved customers to submit small claims online (www.moneyclaim.gov.uk).

Central and local government is increasingly being given power to act as a consumer champion and to bring cases before the courts which are in the interest of consumers in general. Bodies that pursue actions in this way include the following.

- Trading Standards Departments, which are operated by local authorities, have powers to investigate complaints about false or misleading descriptions of prices, inaccurate weights and measures, consumer credit and the safety of consumer legislation. Consumers' knowledge of their rights has often stretched the resources of Trading Standards Departments so that, at best, they can take action against bad practice only selectively.
- The Environmental Health Departments of local authorities deal with health matters such as unfit food and dirty shops and restaurants. A consumer who suspects that they have suffered food poisoning as a result of eating unfit food at a restaurant may lodge a complaint with the local Environmental Health Department, which may collate similar complaints and use this evidence to prosecute the offending restaurant or take steps to have it closed down.
- Utility regulators have powers to bring action against companies that are in breach of their licence conditions.

5.5 Legislation affecting the supply of goods and services

Prior to 1968, there was very little statutory intervention in the contractual relationship between business organizations and their customers, with a few exceptions such as those that came within the scope of the Food and Drugs Act 1955. Since the 1960s there has been an increasing amount of legislation designed to protect the interests of private consumers, who legislators have seen as unequal parties to a contract. In recent years EU directives have been incorporated into UK legislation to provide additional duties for suppliers of goods and services. It should be noted that much of the legislation applies only to business-to-consumer contracts and not business-to-business contracts. In the latter case, legislation has often presumed that parties have equal bargaining power and therefore do not need additional legislative protection.

Thinking around the subject: Who benefits from a 'compensation culture'?

Are we becoming a litigious society, dominated by a 'compensation culture'? Newspapers are continually reporting claims made by individuals that at first may seem quite trivial and not warranting legal intervention. Recent reported claims, which some would argue typify a compensation culture, include a teacher who won £55,000 after slipping on a chip, and the parents of a Girl Guide who sued after she was burnt by fat spitting from a sausage. Aggrieved parties may have been spurred on by the rise of 'personal injury advisers' who offer to take on a claim at no risk to the claimant. They have sometimes been referred to as 'ambulance chasers' for the way they pursue injured parties, making them aware of the possibility of claiming for a loss or injury, which they may otherwise have written off in their minds as just bad luck. If their claim is rejected by the court, the claimant will pay nothing. If it succeeds, they pay the company handling the claim a percentage of the damages awarded. Such companies have been accused of unrealistically raising clients' expectations of damages, and looking for confrontation where alternative methods of reconciliation may be more effective. The business practices of some companies have been criticized, and one company, the Accident Group, went out of business in 2004 after accumulating large debts and failing to deliver promised benefits to many of its customers.

Is the compensation culture necessarily a bad thing for society? Defending cases costs companies time and money, which will inevitably be passed on in the form of higher prices charged to consumers. Claims against companies sometimes even lead to goods or services no longer being made available to consumers because of an open-ended risk of being sued if there is a problem with the product.

But shouldn't consumers expect businesses to deliver their promises in a responsible manner? Is a compensation culture essentially about redressing the balance between relatively weak consumers and more powerful organizations? If those organizations did their job properly, would there be no case for even talking about a compensation culture? If the cost of obtaining justice made it difficult for aggrieved customers to bring a claim against a company, would the company simply carry on acting irresponsibly because it realized it was beyond reproach? In the case of very dubious claims, such as a customer who sued a restaurant because their cup of coffee was 'too hot', could the company attract sympathy from the majority of its customers, who might regard such a claim as frivolous?

In this section, we consider the following important pieces of statute law that have an impact on the relationship between an organization and its customers:

- the Trade Descriptions Act 1968
- the Sale of Goods Act 1979
- the Misrepresentation Act 1967
- the Consumer Protection Act 1987
- the Consumer Credit Act 1974.

In addition, this section reviews a number of quasi-legal codes of conduct operated by industry bodies.

5.5.1 Trade Descriptions Act 1968

The Trade Descriptions Act 1968 makes it an offence for a person to make a false or misleading trade description and creates three principal offences, as described below.

A false trade description to goods

Under s. 1, this states that 'a person who, in the course of business, applies false trade descriptions to goods or suppliers or offers to supply goods to which a false description has been applied is guilty of an offence'. Section 2 defines a false trade description as including 'any indication of any physical characteristics such as quantity, size, method of manufacture, composition and fitness for purpose'. A description is regarded as false when it is false or, by s. 3(2), misleading to a material degree. In some cases consumers are misled by advertisements that are economical with the truth. A car was advertised as having one previous 'owner'. Strictly this was true, but it had been owned by a leasing company, which had leased it to five different users. The divisional court held this was misleading and caught by s. 3(2) of the Trade Descriptions Act (R. vs. South Western Justices ex parte London Borough of Wandsworth, *The Times*, 20 January 1983).

A false statement of price

Section 11 makes a false statement as to the price an offence. If a trader claims that its prices are reduced, it is guilty of an offence unless it can show that the goods have been on sale at the higher price during the preceding six months for a consecutive period of 28 days (more specific requirements concerning pricing are contained in the Price Marking Order 2004).

A false trade description of services

Section 14 states that it is an offence to make false or misleading statements about services. An example of this is illustrated in the case of a store that advertised 'folding doors and folding door gear – carriage free'. This statement was intended to convey to the consumer that only the folding door gear would be sent carriage-free on purchase of the folding doors. It was held that the advert was misleading and that it was irrelevant that it was not intended to be misleading (MFI Warehouses Ltd vs. Nattrass, 1973, 1 All ER 762).

Traders can use a number of defences under the Act, set out in s. 24(i):

(a) that the commission of the offence was due to a mistake or to reliance on information supplied to the company or to the act or default of another person, an accident or some other cause beyond its control, and

(b) that the company took all reasonable precautions and exercised all due diligence to avoid the commission of such an offence by itself or any person under its control.

For the defence to succeed, it is necessary to show that both sub-sections apply. In a case concerning a leading supermarket, washing powder was advertised as being 5p less than the price marked in the store. The defendants said that it was the fault of the store manager who had failed to go through the system laid down for checking shelves. The court held that the defence applied; the store manager was 'another person' (s. 24(i)(a)) and the store had taken reasonable precautions to prevent commission of the offence (Tesco Supermarkets Ltd vs. Nattrass, 1971, 2 All ER 127).

5.5.2 Sale of Goods Act 1979

What rights has the consumer if he or she discovers that the goods purchased are faulty or different from those ordered? The Sale of Goods Act (SOGA) contains terms specifically to protect the consumer. The term 'consumer' is defined by s. 20(6) of the Consumer Protection Act 1987, and essentially covers situations where a purchase is made for private consumption, rather than for use in the course of a business.

Section 13 of the Sale of Goods Act 1979 states that, 'Where there is a contract for the sale of goods by description there is an implied condition that the goods will correspond with the description.' Goods must be as described on the package. If a customer purchases a blue long-sleeved shirt and on opening the box discovers that it is a red short-sleeved shirt, then he is entitled to a return of the price for breach of an implied condition of the contract.

Section 14(2), as amended by the Sale and Supply of Goods Act 1994, states that where a seller sells goods in the course of a business, there is an implied term that the goods supplied under the contract are of satisfactory quality. For the purposes of this Act goods are of satisfactory quality if they meet the standard that a reasonable person would regard as satisfactory, taking account of any description of the goods, fitness for all the purposes for which goods of the kind in question are commonly supplied, appearance and finish, safety, durability, freedom from minor defects, the price (if relevant) and all other relevant circumstances.

However, section 14(2C) states that the standard of satisfactory quality need not apply in respect of faults that are specifically drawn to the buyer's attention before the contract is made, which should be reasonably apparent to a buyer before purchase.

The implied term of unsatisfactory quality applies to sale goods and second-hand goods, but clearly the consumer would not have such high expectations of second-hand goods. For example, a clutch fault in a new car would make it unsatisfactory, but not so if the car were second-hand. In a second-hand car – again, depending on all the circumstances – a fault would have to be major to render the car unsatisfactory. Thus, the question to be asked is, 'Are the goods satisfactory in the light of the contract description and all the circumstances of the case?'

It is often asked for how long the goods should remain satisfactory. It is perhaps implicit that the goods remain satisfactory for a length of time reasonable in the circumstances of the case and the nature of the goods. If a good becomes defective within a very short time, this is evidence that there was possibly a latent defect at the time of the sale.

Under s. 14(3), there is an implied condition that goods are fit for a particular purpose where the seller sells goods in the course of a business and the buyer, expressly or by implication, makes known to the seller any particular purpose for which the goods are being bought. Thus, if a seller, on request, confirms suitability for a particular purpose and the product proves unsuitable, there would be a breach of s. 14(3); if the product is also unsuitable for its normal purposes, then s. 14(2) would be breached too. If the seller disclaims any knowledge of the product's suitability for the particular purpose and the consumer takes a chance and purchases it, then if it proves unsuitable for its particular purpose there is no breach of s. 14(3). The only circumstance in which a breach may occur is, again, if it were unsuitable for its normal purposes under s. 14(2).

In business contracts, implied terms in ss. 13–15 of the Sale of Goods Act 1979 can be excluded. Such exclusion clauses, purporting, for example, to exclude a term for reasonable fitness for goods (s. 14), are valid subject to the test of reasonableness provided that the term is incorporated into the contract. However, for consumer contracts, such clauses that purport to limit or exclude liability are void under s. 6(2) of the Unfair Contract Terms Act 1977.

The Supply of Goods and Services Act 1982 (SGSA) offers almost identical protection where goods and services are provided. Section 3 corresponds to s. 13 of SOGA and s. 4 corresponds to s. 14 of SOGA. Section 13 of SGSA provides that, where the supplier of a service under a contract is acting in the course of a business, there is an implied term that the supplier will carry out the service with reasonable care and skill. Reasonable care and skill may be defined as 'the ordinary skill of an ordinary competent man exercising that particular act'. Much will depend on the circumstances of the case and the nature of the trade or profession.

5.5.3 Misrepresentation Act 1967

The Misrepresentation Act 1967 provides remedies for victims of **misrepresentation**. For the purpose of the Act, an actionable misrepresentation may be defined as 'a false statement of existing or past fact made by one party to the other before or at the time of making the contract, which is intended to, and does, induce the other party to enter into the contract'.

Since the 1967 Act, it has been necessary to maintain a clear distinction between fraudulent misrepresentation, negligent misrepresentation and wholly innocent misrepresentation (Section 2(1)). Rescission of a contract is a remedy for all three types of misrepresentation. In addition to rescission for fraudulent misrepresentation, damages may be awarded under the tort of fraud, and in respect of negligent misrepresentation damages may be awarded under s. 2(1) of the 1967 Act. Under s. 2(2) damages may also be awarded at the discretion of the court, but, if so, these are in lieu of rescission.

The Property Misdescriptions Act 1991 built on the Misrepresentation Act and created a strict liability criminal offence of making, in the course of an estate agency or property development business, a false or misleading statement about a prescribed matter (s. 1(1)) to be specified in an order by the Secretary of State (s. 1(5)). The most common complaints from estate agents' (mis)descriptions include incorrect room sizes, misleading photographs and deceptive descriptions of local amenities. In one case, the agents blocked out in the photograph an ugly gasworks that overshadowed a house they were trying to sell.

5.5.4 The Consumer Protection Act 1987

The Consumer Protection Act 1987 came into force in March 1988 as a result of the government's obligation to implement an EU directive, and provides a remedy in damages for anyone who suffers personal injury or damage to property as a result of a defective product. The effect is to impose a strict (i.e. whereby it is unnecessary to prove negligence) tortious liability on producers of defective goods. The Act supplements the existing law; thus, a consumer may well have a remedy in contract, in the tort of negligence or under the Act if he or she has suffered loss caused by a defective product.

The producer will be liable if the consumer can establish that the product is defective and that it caused a loss. There is a defect if the safety of the goods does not conform to general expectations with reference to the risk of damage to property or risk of death or personal injury.

The general expectations will differ depending on the particular circumstances, but points to be taken into account include the product's instructions, warnings and the time elapsed since supply, the latter point to determine the possibility of the defect being due to wear and tear.

The onus is on the plaintiff to prove that loss was caused by the defect. A claim may be made by anyone, whether death, personal injury or damage to property has occurred. However, where damage to property is concerned, the damage is confined to property ordinarily intended for private use or consumption and acquired by the person mainly for his or her own use or consumption, thus excluding commercial goods and property. Damage caused to private property must exceed £275 for claims to be considered. It is not possible to exclude liability under the Consumer Protection Act.

The Act is intended to place liability on the producer of defective goods. In some cases the company may not manufacture the goods, but may still be liable, as outlined below.

- Anyone carrying out 'industrial or other process' to goods that have been manufactured by someone else will be treated as the producer where 'essential characteristics' are attributable to that process. Essential characteristics are nowhere defined in the Act, but processes that modify the goods may well be within its scope.
- If a company puts its own brand name on goods that have been manufactured on its behalf, thus holding itself out to be the producer, that company will be liable for any defects in the goods.
- Any importer who imports goods from outside EU countries will likewise be liable for defects in the imported goods. This is an extremely beneficial move for the consumer.

The Act is also instrumental in providing a remedy against suppliers who are unable to identify the importee or the previous supplier to them. If the supplier fails or cannot identify the manufacturer's importee or previous supplier, then the supplier is liable.

5.5.5 Consumer Credit Act 1974

This is a consumer protection measure to protect the public from, among other things, extortionate credit agreements and high-pressure selling off trade premises. The Act became fully operational in 1985, and much of the protection afforded to hire purchase transactions is extended to those obtaining goods and services through consumer credit transactions. It is important to note that contract law governs the formation of agreements coming within the scope of the Consumer Credit Act. Section 8(2) defines a consumer credit agreement as personal credit providing the debtor with credit not exceeding £25,000. Section 9 defines credit as a cash loan and any form of financial accommodation.

There are two types of credit. The first is a running account credit (s. 10(a)), whereby the debtor is enabled to receive from time to time, from the creditor or a third party, cash, goods and services to an amount or value such that, taking into account payments made by or to the credit of the debtor, the credit limit (if any) is not at any time exceeded. Thus, running account credit is revolving credit, where the debtor can keep taking credit when he or she wants it subject to a credit limit. An example of this is a credit card facility, e.g. Visa or MasterCard. The second type is fixed-sum credit, defined in s. 10(b) as any other facility under a personal credit agreement whereby the debtor is enabled to receive credit. An example here would be a bank loan.

The Act covers hire purchase agreements (s. 189), which are agreements under which goods are hired in return for periodical payments by the person to whom they are hired and where the property in the goods will pass to that person if the terms of the agreement are complied with – for example, the exercise of an option to purchase by that person. In addition to hire purchase agreements, also within the scope of the Act are conditional sale agreements for the sale of goods or land, in respect of which the price is payable by instalments and the property (i.e. ownership) remains with the seller until any conditions set out in the contract are fulfilled, and credit sale agreements, where the property (ownership) passes to the buyer when the sale is effected.

Debtor–creditor supplier agreements relate to the situation where there is a business connection between creditor and supplier (i.e. a pre-existing arrangement) or where the creditor and the supplier are the same person.

Section 55 and ss. 60–65 deal with formalities of the contract between debtor and creditor, their aim being that the debtor be made fully aware of the nature and the cost of the transaction and his or her rights and liabilities under it. The Act requires that certain information must be disclosed to the debtor before the contract is made. This includes total charge for credit, and the annual rate of the total charge for credit that the debtor will have to pay expressed in an approved format. All regulated agreements must comply with the formality procedures and must contain, among other things, the debtor's right to cancel and to pay off the debt early.

If a consumer credit agreement is drawn up off business premises, then it is a cancellable agreement designed to counteract high-pressure doorstep selling. If an agreement is cancellable, the debtor is entitled to a cooling-off period (i.e. to the close of the fifth day following the date the second copy of the agreement is received). If the debtor then cancels in writing, the agreement and any linked transaction is cancelled. Any sums paid are recoverable, and the debtor has a lien on any goods in his or her possession until repayment is made.

5.5.6 Codes of practice

Codes of practice do not in themselves have the force of law. They can, however, be of great importance to businesses. In the first place, they can help to raise the standards of an industry by imposing a discipline on signatories to a code not to indulge in dubious marketing practices, which – although legal – act against the long-term interests of the industry and its customers. Second, voluntary codes of practice can offer a cheaper and quicker means of resolving grievances between the two parties compared with more formal legal channels. For example, the holiday industry has its own arbitration facilities, which avoid the cost of taking many cases through to the courts. Third, business organizations are often happy to accept restrictions imposed by codes of practice as these are seen as preferable to restrictions being imposed by laws. The tobacco industry in the UK for a long time avoided statutory controls on cigarette advertising because of the existence of its voluntary code, which imposed restrictions on tobacco advertising.

The Director General of the Office of Fair Trading is instrumental in encouraging trade associations to adopt codes of practice. An example of a voluntary code is provided by the Vehicle Builders and Repair Association, which, among other items, requires members to: give clear estimates of prices; inform customers as soon as possible if additional costs are likely to be incurred; complete work in a timely manner. In the event of a dispute between a customer and a member of the Association, a conciliation service is available that reduces the need to resort to legal remedies. However, in April 2005, the National Consumer Council accused the motor industry of failing to adequately regulate itself, by providing 'shoddy services and rip-off charges'. The Council pledged to submit a 'super complaint' to the Office of Fair Trading (OFT), which would force the OFT to investigate its allegations, unless the industry took prompt remedial action. This raised the possibility of a licensing system for car repairers, something the industry had resisted so far and realized would be more onerous than a voluntary code of conduct.

Useful leaflets published by the OFT giving information regarding codes of practice can be obtained from local Consumer Advice Bureaux.

5.5.7 Controls on advertising

There are a number of laws that influence the content of advertisements in Britain. For example, the Trade Descriptions Act makes false statements in an advertisement an offence, while the Consumer Credit Act lays down quite precise rules about the way in which credit can be advertised. However, the content of advertisements is also influenced by voluntary codes. In the UK, the codes for advertising are the responsibility of the advertising industry through two Committees of Advertising Practice: CAP (Broadcast) and CAP (Non-broadcast). CAP (Broadcast) is responsible for the TV and radio advertising codes, and CAP (Non-broadcast) is responsible for non-broadcast advertisements, sales promotions and direct marketing. Both are administered by the Advertising Standards Authority (ASA). The Office of Communications (Ofcom) is the statutory regulator for broadcast advertising in the UK and has delegated its powers to the ASA, which deals with all complaints about such advertising.

The ASA codes are subscribed to by most organizations involved in advertising, including the Advertising Association, the Institute of Practitioners in Advertising, and the associations representing publishers of newspapers and magazines, the outdoor advertising industry and direct marketing.

The Code of Advertising Practice (Non-broadcast) requires that all advertisements appearing in members' publications should be legal, honest, decent and truthful. Two recent (2008) adjudications illustrate how the ASA interprets this. In one case, a national press advert for the retailer Lidl featured a Landmann Lava Rock Gas Barbecue and the message '£10 cheaper compared to B&Q'. It was held that the comparison was misleading, because the precise model sold by B&Q was not accurately specified, therefore the fact of '£10 cheaper' could not be established. In another case from 2008, an advert in the *Daily Mail* for Ryanair under the headline 'Hottest back to school fares . . . one way fares £10' featured a picture of a teenage girl or woman standing in a classroom and wearing a version of a school uniform consisting of a short tartan skirt, a cropped short sleeved shirt and tie, and long white socks. The ASA considered the model's clothing, together with the setting of the ad in a classroom strongly suggested she was a schoolgirl and considered that her appearance and pose, in conjunction with the heading 'Hottest', appeared to link teenage girls with sexually provocative behaviour. It considered the advert was likely to cause serious or widespread offence, and was in breach of the Code's sections governing social responsibility and decency.

Although the main role of the ASA is advisory, it does have a number of sanctions available against individual advertisers that break the code, ultimately leading to the ASA requesting its media members to refuse to publish the advertisements of an offending company. More often, the ASA relies on publicizing its rulings to shame advertisers into responding (although some critics would say that press coverage of companies breaching the code simply provides free awareness-grabbing publicity for the company).

The advertising codes are continually evolving to meet the changing attitudes and expectations of the public. Thus, restrictions on alcohol advertising have been tightened up – for example, by insisting that young actors are not portrayed in advertisements and by not showing them on television when children are likely to be watching. On the other hand, advertising restrictions for some products have been relaxed in response to changing public attitudes. Television adverts for condoms have moved from being completely banned to being allowed, but only in very abstract form, to the present situation where the product itself can be mentioned using actors in life-like situations.

Numerous other forms of voluntary control exist. As mentioned previously, many trade associations have codes that impose restrictions on how they can advertise. Solicitors, for example, were previously not allowed to advertise at all, but now can do so within limits defined by the Law Society.

The Control of Misleading Advertisements Regulations 1988 (as amended) provides the legislative back-up to the self-regulatory system in respect of advertisements that mislead. The Regulations require the Office of Fair Trading (OFT) to investigate complaints, and empower the OFT to seek, if necessary, an injunction from the courts against publication of an advertisement. More usually it would initially seek assurances from an advertiser to modify or not repeat an offending advertisement. Before investigating, the OFT can require that other means of dealing with a complaint, such as the ASA system mentioned above, have been fully explored. Action by the OFT therefore usually results only from a referral from the Advertising Standards Authority where the self-regulatory system has not had the required impact.

In general, the system of voluntary regulation of advertising has worked well in the UK. For advertisers, voluntary codes can allow more flexibility and opportunities to have an input to the code. For the public, a code can be updated in a less bureaucratic manner than may be necessary with new legislation or statutory regulations. However, the question remains as to how much responsibility for the social and cultural content of advertising should be given to industry-led voluntary bodies rather than being decided by government. Do voluntary codes unduly reflect the narrow financial interests of advertisers rather than the broader interests of the public at large? Doubtless, advertisers realize that if they do not develop a code that is socially acceptable, the task will be taken away from them and carried out by government in a process where they will have less influence.

5.6 Statutory legislation on employment

Employment law is essentially based on the principles of law previously discussed. The relationship between an employer and its employees is governed by the law of contract, while the employer owes a duty of care to its employees and can be sued for negligence where this duty of care is broken. Employers are vicariously liable for the actions of their employees, so if an employee is negligent and harms a member of the public during the course of their employment, the injured party has a claim against the employer as well as the employee who was the immediate cause of the injury.

The common law principles of contract and negligence have for a long time been supplemented with statutory intervention. Society has recognized that a contract of employment is quite different from a contract to buy consumer goods, because the personal investment of the employee in their job can be very considerable. Losing a job without good cause can have a much more profound effect than suffering loss as a result of losing money on the purchase of goods. Governments have recognized that individuals should have a proprietary interest in their jobs and have therefore passed legislation to protect employees against the actions of unscrupulous employers who abuse their dominant power over employees. Legislation has also recognized that employment practices can have a much wider effect on society through organizations' recruitment policies.

In this section we consider some of the areas in which statutory intervention has affected the environment in which organizations recruit, reward and dismiss employees. The information here cannot hope to go into any depth on particular legislative requirements, as legislation is complex, detailed and continually changing. There is also considerable difference between countries in terms of legislation that affects employment. The following brief summary can only aim to identify the main issues of concern covered by legislation, in England specifically. This chapter should also be read in conjunction with Chapter 9, on the internal environment. In that chapter we look in general terms at issues such as the need for flexibility in the workforce. This chapter identifies particular legal opportunities and constraints, which help to define an organization's internal environment.

5.6.1 When does an employment contract occur?

It is not always obvious whether a contract of employment exists between an organization and individuals providing services for it. Many individuals working for organizations in fact provide their services as self-employed subcontractors, rather than as employees. The distinction between the two is important, because a self-employed contractor does not benefit from the legislation, which only protects employees. There can be many advantages in classifying an individual as self-employed rather than as an employee. For the self-employed, tax advantages result from being able to claim as legitimate business expense items that in many circumstances are denied to the employee. The method of assessing National Insurance and income tax liability in arrears can favour a self-employed subcontractor. For the employer, designation as self-employed could relieve the employer of some duties that are imposed in respect of employees but not subcontractors, such as entitlement to sick pay, notice periods and maternity leave.

There was a great move towards self-employment during the 1990s, encouraged by the trend towards outsourcing of many non-core functions by businesses (see Chapter 7). Not surprisingly, the UK government has sought to recoup potentially lost tax revenue and to protect unwitting self-employed individuals, by examining closely the terms on which an individual is engaged. The courts have decided the matter on the basis of, among other things, the degree of control that the organization buying a person's services has over the person providing them, the level of integration between the individual and the organization, and who bears the business risk. If the organization is able to specify the manner in which a task is to be carried out, then an employment relationship generally exists. If, however, the required end result is specified but the manner in which it is achieved is left up to the individual, then a contract for services will exist – in other words, self-employment. There is still ambiguity in the distinction between employment and self-employment, which has, for example, resulted in numerous appeals by individuals against classification decisions made by the Inland Revenue.

5.6.2 Flexibility of contract

Organizations are increasingly seeking a more flexible workforce to help them respond more rapidly to changes in their external environment. In Chapter 9 we see some of the benefits to an organization of developing flexible employment practices.

Short-term employment contracts are becoming increasingly significant in a number of European countries, partly due to the existence of labour market regulations that make it difficult for employers to recruit and dismiss permanent staff. Within Europe, there has been a tendency for national legislation to reflect EU directives by imposing additional burdens on employers of full-time, permanent employees. This can affect the ease with which staff can be laid off or dismissed should demand fall – for example, in Germany, the Dismissals Protection Law (Kundigungsschutzgesetz) has given considerable protection to salaried staff who have been in their job for more than six months, allowing dismissal only for a 'socially justified' reason.

The move towards short-term contracts is a Europe-wide phenomenon. In 2005, about 34 per cent of the Spanish workforce was employed with contracts of limited duration compared to less than 16 per cent 20 years previously, while in France the proportion of employees with contracts of limited duration climbed from 6.7 per cent in 1985 to about 13 per cent by 2005 (Eurostat 2006–07). The spread of short-term contracts is most apparent among young workers employed in insecure and highly mobile areas of the labour market, such as the retail, distribution, communication and information technology sectors.

The percentage of persons working part-time increased persistently in the last decade. In the spring of 2005, 7 per cent of employed men in the EU-25 worked on a part-time basis, a share that rose considerably higher for women (33 per cent). Those countries with employment rates of 67 per cent or more also generally had higher proportions of part-time work, especially among women. In 2005, the Netherlands had the highest percentage of part-time employment, with 23 per cent of employed males and 75 per cent of females employed on a part-time basis (the latter figure rose from 71 per cent in 2001) (Eurostat 2006–07).

The European Union and most member state governments have been keen to ensure that workers on short-term contracts enjoy similar legal rights as those in full-time, permanent employment. In the UK, the Employment Relations Act 1999 requires appropriate secretary of state to make regulations to ensure that part-time workers are treated no less favourably than full-time workers. These regulations include provisions to implement the EU-level social partners' agreement and subsequent Council Directive on part-time work (97/81/EC).

Despite imposing additional burdens, many European governments have encouraged the greater use of short-term contracts as a way of improving the flexibility of their national economies – for example, through changes in welfare benefits that do not penalize short-term working.

5.6.3 Terms of the contract of employment

Under the Employment Rights Act 1996 it is required that an employer must issue its employees within 13 weeks of the date they start work the written terms and conditions of their employment in detail. The details can, however, be placed on a staff noticeboard at a point where every member of the workforce concerned can read them. In the statement there should be references to the following:

1. the job title
2. which individuals or groups the document is addressed to
3. the starting date of the employment
4. the scale of wages and the calculations used to work this out
5. the periods in which wages are paid
6. hours of work and the terms and conditions
7. holidays and holiday pay
8. sickness and sickness pay
9. pensions and pension schemes
10. how much notice the employee must give upon leaving and how much notice the company has to give the employee when terminating employment
11. rules for discipline procedures
12. to whom any grievances are to be made, and procedures.

The terms of contract cannot be altered until both parties have discussed and agreed the new conditions.

5.6.4 Minimum acceptable contract terms

Legislators have recognized that employee and employer often possess unequal bargaining power in the process of forming a contract of employment. Legislation therefore protects the interests of the weaker party – generally the employee – against the use of their power by unscrupulous employers. The following are examples of statutory intervention that protect employees' rights. Some would argue that intervention of this type has the effect of increasing the costs of businesses, thereby reducing their competitive advantage. However, as can be seen in Chapter 9, a lot of statutory intervention is merely spreading current best practice to all employees.

Health and safety legislation

There is a wide range of regulations governing employers' duty to provide a safe working environment. Most health and safety legislation is based on the Health and Safety at Work Act 1974, which provides a general duty to provide a safe working environment. The Act makes provision for specific regulations to be issued by government ministers and these detailed regulations can have significant impacts on businesses. The following are some recent examples of regulations:

Figure 5.2 Visitors to Bavaria's beer festivals come away with memories of the beer and barmaids. The event is made memorable by the distinctive dress worn by barmaids, which combines tradition with visual appeal (especially to men, who make up a large part of the festivals' market). The barmaids' dress, known as a 'dirndl', comprises a figure-hugging dress and apron with a tight, low-cut top. The sight of a barmaid dressed in a dirndl and carrying several glasses of beer helps to transform a drink into an experience. Customers love the dress, brewers love it, and apparently the barmaids do too. But this apparently happy service environment was threatened in 2006 by the EU's Optical Radiation Directive, by which employers of staff who work outdoors, such as those in Bavaria's beer gardens, must ensure that staff are protected against the risk of sunburn. The serious point underlying the EU legislation is that in the UK alone about 70,000 new cases of skin cancer are diagnosed each year. Faced with this directive, how should the provider of an outdoor service encounter react? If they leave scantily dressed employees exposed to the sun, they could face fines, and possible legal action by employees who subsequently develop skin cancer. But, contrary to many newspaper reports, the EU directive does not specifically require Bavarian barmaids (or outdoor workers elsewhere) to cover up their low-cut dresses. Management must undertake a risk assessment and consider what is appropriate to a specific service encounter. Perhaps the unique character of the Munich Oktoberfest could be preserved with the help of sun cream and by reducing each barmaid's hours of exposure to the sun.

- the Control of Major Accident Hazards Regulations 1999
- the Control of Substances Hazardous to Health Regulations 1999
- the Lifts Regulations 1997
- the Railway Safety (Miscellaneous Provisions) Regulations 1997.

The Health & Safety Executive oversees enforcement of these regulations.

Thinking around the subject: Take risks and go to jail?

One of the defining characteristics of a limited liability company (discussed in Chapter 6), is the separation of the company from its owners. So, in general, if the company breaks the law, whether civil law or criminal, the directors of the company can protect themselves behind a 'veil of incorporation'. Furthermore, many of the punishments available under the criminal law would at first sight seem to be inappropriate to business organizations. How, for example, can an organization be sent to prison for a serious breach of the criminal law? The question has arisen following a number of high-profile cases where a business has caused harm to the general public, but the directors of the company responsible for the wrongdoing have escaped relatively lightly. The *Herald of Free Enterprise* tragedy in 1987, and the Ladbroke Grove train accident of 1999, raised issues about senior management's culpability in these two serious transport accidents. In the first case, questions were raised about unreasonable pressures that management had put on staff loading vehicles on to ferries, one of which subsequently capsized. In the second case, questions were raised about the suitability of staff training programmes, which management, and ultimately the board of directors, was responsible for. Relatives of victims who died in both of these incidents claimed that they were not accidents at all, but the culmination of negligent actions by senior management. In both cases, initial blame was focused on relatively low-paid junior staff who made a mistake. But was senior management responsible for expecting too much of its junior staff? In both cases, attempts were made to bring charges of manslaughter against the directors of the companies involved, but due to the complexity of the cases, and the diffuse lines of responsibility within their organizations, there was insufficient evidence to successfully bring a case. According to the Centre for Corporate Accountability, only 11 directors were successfully prosecuted for manslaughter in the 30 years to 2005. Most of these have been small company directors; for example, in January 2005, the managing director of a building contractor was sentenced to 16 months in jail after a roofing worker died falling through a poorly protected roof light. Campaigners for a law on corporate manslaughter have argued that it is much more difficult to pin down responsibility in a large organization, but this is no reason for not trying to make senior staff personally accountable for their actions. Would directors of a company be so keen to pursue potentially dangerous efficiency-gaining strategies if they thought there was a risk that they might personally end up in prison? Or would a corporate manslaughter law stifle initiatives by directors, fearful that, if anything went wrong, there could be very serious consequences for them personally?

Minimum wage legislation

The national minimum wage came into force in the UK in 1999, implementing an earlier EU directive. In October 2007, this rate was set at £5.52 per hour for workers aged 22 and over, £4.60 for 18- to 21-year-olds, and £3.40 for 15- to 17-year-olds. There is provision for annual revision. Most adult workers in the UK must be paid at least the national minimum wage. This includes part-time workers, temporary or short-term workers, home workers, agency workers and casual labourers. An employee cannot be forced by an employer to accept a wage that is below the minimum wage, and can claim compensation if they are sacked or victimized because they sought to enforce their right to the national minimum wage.

Working hours

The EU's Working Time Directive of 1993 was implemented in the UK by the Working Time Regulations of 2000. According to these regulations, workers cannot be forced to work for more than 48 hours a week on average. However, there are various exclusions to this time and workers can cancel any opt-out agreement whenever they want, although they must give their employer at least seven days' notice, or longer (up to three months) if this has been agreed.

5.6.5 Discrimination at work

Companies sometimes find themselves being required to recruit their second choice of staff in order to comply with legislation against racial and sexual discrimination. For example, one UK airline found through its research that the majority of its customers preferred its cabin crew to be female and subsequently recruited predominantly female staff for this role. The airline was fined for unlawful discrimination against men, even though it had been innovative in appointing women to the traditionally male job of pilot. Legislation seeks to protect disadvantaged groups that may be discriminated against simply out of employers' ignorance.

The Sex Discrimination Act 1975 (SDA) prohibits discrimination against women, and men, on the grounds of sex or of being married. The SDA makes the distinction between the concepts of direct and indirect discrimination. Direct sex discrimination occurs when an employee is treated less favourably because of her, or his, sex. Indirect discrimination occurs when a requirement or condition – which may seem 'neutral' in terms of how it impacts upon men and women – in fact has an adverse effect on women, or men, in general (for example, specifying a dress code that is more onerous on women than men). The Equal Pay Act 1970 requires that a woman is entitled to the same pay (and other contractual conditions) as a man working for the same employer, provided they are doing similar work or work of equal value.

The legislation dealing with race discrimination derives from the Race Relations Act 1976 (RRA). By this Act, a person is guilty of race discrimination if 'on racial grounds he treats [a] person less favourably than he treats or would treat other persons'. Like the SDA, the RRA makes it illegal to discriminate directly or indirectly against a person on racial grounds. Research and official statistics demonstrate that people from ethnic minorities continue to experience severe discrimination in the field of employment. A report by the Joseph Rowntree Foundation found particularly high levels of unemployment among Africans, Pakistanis and Bangladeshis (Berthoud 2005).

5.6.6 Termination of contract

The proprietary interest of employees in their jobs is recognized by legislation that restricts the ability of an employer to terminate an employee's contract of employment.

Termination may come about because an individual's position is no longer required and the individual is declared redundant. The Employment Rights Act 1996 defines the circumstances in which redundancy takes effect and a sliding scale of payments which an employee is entitled to if they are made redundant by their employer.

In circumstances other than redundancy, employers may not terminate a contract in a way that constitutes unfair dismissal. Under the Employment Relations Act 1999, employees are not entitled to claim unfair dismissal until they have accumulated one year's service. Dismissal may be considered fair where an employee has not acted in good faith and/or has failed to observe previous warnings about poor conduct. Employment tribunals judge whether a dismissal is fair or not, and judgment frequently centres on procedural issues. A finding of unfair dismissal may lead to an order for compensation and a request for reinstatement.

5.6.7 Rights to workers' representation

The political environment and the dominant political ideology have had a very close bearing on legislation regulating the activities of trades unions. Traditionally, Labour governments have sought to advance the cause of organized labour, while Conservative governments have taken a more individualist approach to relationships between employers and employees. The incoming Conservative government of 1979 dismantled much of the legislation that had been passed by the previous Labour government to give greater rights for trades unions and greater duties for employers. The incoming Labour government of 1997 has gone some way to restoring trades union rights. This government inherited the Trade Union Reform and Employment Rights Act 1993 and the Trade Union and Labour Relations (Consolidation) Act 1992. The essence of this legislation was to make trades unions more accountable to their members and to reduce the risks to employers of loss resulting from politically inspired disputes. The following are key features that were covered by the legislation:

- individuals affected by industrial action are able to seek an injunction to prevent unlawful industrial action taking place
- seven days' notice must be given by trades unions of ballots and of industrial action
- individuals have a right to challenge collective agreements
- employers may refuse to recognize a trades union in specified circumstances
- all industrial action ballots must be postal and subject to independent scrutiny.

The Employment Relations Act 1999 amended a number of provisions of the previous legislation. For trades unions, the key element of the Act is a statutory procedure through which independent unions are able to seek recognition for collective bargaining from employers with more than 20 employees. The Act amended previous legislation to enable employees dismissed for taking part in lawfully organized official industrial action to take cases of unfair dismissal to an employment tribunal where the dismissal occurs within eight weeks of the start of the action.

The Transnational Information and Consultation of Employees Regulations 1999 came into force in the UK in 2000, implementing the EU Directive on European Works Councils. The Directive covers undertakings that have more than 1000 employees in member states and more than 150 employees in each of two member states, and sets out procedures for giving employees a statutory right to be consulted about a range of activities affecting the organization. From 2005, the legislation has given employees a legal right to know about, and be consulted on, an organization's plans that affect them. This can cover anything from the economic health of the business to decisions likely to cause redundancies or changes in how work is organized. This requirement applies initially only to larger organizations – those with 50 or more employees. However, from 2007, the threshold was lowered to 100 employees and, in 2008, lowered again to 50 or more employees.

5.7 The Human Rights Act

The Human Rights Act came into force in the UK in 2000 and has presented a number of new legal challenges for business organizations. The Act incorporates the European Convention on Human Rights into domestic law. The Convention is a 50-year-old code of basic rights drawn up in the aftermath of the Second World War, and covers such rights as that to a family life, to privacy and a fair trial. Prior to 2000, although UK courts could take note of the rights identified by the Convention, they could not be directly enforced, so aggrieved parties often had to take cases to the European Court of Human Rights for a remedy – a lengthy and costly process.

The Act incorporates only part of the European Convention and does not incorporate any of the procedural rights of the Convention. However, it does include all the following substantive rights:

- to life
- to freedom from torture or inhuman or degrading punishment
- to freedom from slavery, servitude, enforced or compulsory labour
- to liberty and security of the person
- to a fair trial
- to respect for private and family life
- to freedom of thought, conscience and religion
- to freedom of expression
- to freedom of assembly and association
- to marry and found a family
- to education in conformity with parents' religious and philosophical convictions
- to freedom from unfair discrimination in the enjoyment of these rights.

Many of the wider rights enshrined in the Human Rights Act are already protected by the UK's domestic legislation (e.g. the Sex Discrimination Act 1975). From 2000, courts in the UK have been able to issue injunctions to prevent violations of rights, award damages and quash unlawful decisions. Individuals are now able to use the Act to defend themselves in criminal proceedings.

The Act does not make Convention rights directly enforceable in proceedings against a private litigant, nor against a 'quasi-public' body, unless that body is acting in a public capacity. However, private individuals and companies have to take the Convention into account because the courts will be obliged to interpret the law so as to conform to it wherever possible.

In the early days of the Act a number of examples illustrated its possible impact on business organizations, including challenges about the legitimacy of local authority planning procedures and privacy of personal information. Despite early fears that the Human Rights Act would add significantly to business organizations' costs, it would appear that more recent cases have taken a balanced view on what is reasonable and in the public interest.

5.8 Protection of a company's intangible property rights

The value of a business enterprise can be measured not only by the value of its physical assets, such as land and buildings: increasingly, the value of a business reflects its investment in new product development and strong brand images. To protect a company from imitators benefiting from this investment, but bearing none of its cost, a number of legal protections are available. The most commonly used methods are patents and trademarks, which are described below. Intellectual property can also be protected through copyright (for example, the unauthorized copying and sale of DVD films is a breach of copyright).

5.8.1 Patents

We saw in Chapter 4 that a patent is a right given to an inventor that allows him or her exclusively to reap the benefits from the invention over a specified period. To obtain a patent, application must be made to the Patent Office in accordance with the procedure set out in the Patents Act 1977. To qualify for a patent, the invention must have certain characteristics laid down: it must be covered by the Act, it must be novel and it must include an inventive step. Some inventions would not qualify for a patent – for example, anything that has at any time before filing for the patent been made available to the public anywhere in the world by written or oral description, by use, or in any other way (s. 2(2)).

The effect of the Patents Act 1977 has been to bring UK patent law more into line with that of the EU in accordance with the provisions of the European Patent Convention. As a result of the implementation of the Convention, there are almost uniform criteria in the establishment of a patent in Austria, Belgium, Switzerland, Germany, France, the United Kingdom, Italy, Liechtenstein, Luxembourg, the Netherlands and Sweden. A European Patent Office has been set up in Munich, which provides a cheaper method to obtain a patent in three or more countries, but it should be noted that, if the patent fails as a result of an application to the European Patent Office, the rejection applies to all member states unless there is contrary domestic legislation that covers this part.

5.8.2 Trademarks

The Trade Marks Act 1994, which replaced the 1938 Act, implemented the Trade Marks Harmonization Directive No. 89/104/EEC, which provides protection for trademarks (they are also protected under the common law of passing off). A **trademark** is defined as any sign capable of being represented graphically that is capable of distinguishing goods or services of one undertaking from those of other undertakings (s. 1(1)).

Any trademark satisfying these criteria is registerable unless prohibited by s. 3; for example, an application may be refused if a trademark is devoid of any distinctive character, or is contrary to accepted principles of morality, or is of such a nature as to deceive the public.

If a trademark is infringed in any way, a successful plaintiff will be entitled to an injunction and to damages.

5.8.3 Law and the internet

The development of the internet does not change the basic principles of law, but the law has on occasions become ambiguous in the light of technological developments.

Unlawful copying of material downloaded from the internet (images, documents and particularly music) has focused attention on issues of ownership of intellectual property. Section 17 of the Copyright, Designs and Patents Act 1988 provides that: 'Copying in relation to a literary, dramatic, musical or artistic work means reproducing the work in any material form. This includes storing the work in any medium by electronic means.' Copying, therefore, includes downloading files from the internet or copying text into or attaching it to an email. Given the ability to copy material virtually instantaneously to potentially huge numbers, the internet presents a serious risk of copyright infringement liability. Just what constitutes 'public domain' information, and can therefore lawfully be copied, has been raised in a number of cases.

In addition to copyright issues, the international nature of communications on the internet makes it essential not to overlook questions such as where is the contract concluded, when is it concluded, what law governs it and where will any subsequent dispute be decided. Unexpected additional obligations may arise as a result of statements made during contract negotiations – for example, in an email from a salesperson to a customer. Even where the final written contract expressly excludes such representations, courts may be prepared to find that a collateral contract came into existence through the exchange of email messages.

EU countries have begun to introduce into national legislation a 1999 EU directive on electronic signatures. The directive comprises two major advances: the legal recognition of electronic signatures, which provide reliable identification of the parties engaged in an online transaction; and encryption, which enables companies to electronically protect documents liable to be intercepted during transmission, by wire or over the air. These measures will help companies doing business over the internet to verify with accuracy the identity of their contracting partners and to improve online security standards for international business.

The internet has also intensified concerns about data privacy. The misuse of personal data has always been an issue with traditional paper-based systems of recording information, but the internet increases the possibility for large amounts of data to be accidentally or deliberately misused. Chapter 4 reviewed some of the principal concerns, and you will recall that, in the UK, the Data Protection Commissioner is responsible for overseeing the provisions of the Data Protection Act 1988, which itself was based on an EU directive. The Act requires companies to keep accurate records that are not unnecessarily excessive in detail, and shall not be kept for longer than is necessary for the purpose of collecting them. Appropriate technical and organizational measures must be taken against unauthorized or unlawful processing of personal data, and against its accidental loss or destruction. Companies have been helped in their efforts to secure their data by the Computer Misuse Act 1990, which makes hacking and the introduction of viruses criminal offences.

Although the emphasis of the Data Protection Act has been on limiting the dissemination of data, the Act also provides individuals and companies with certain rights of access to data about them that are held by companies. There is also a more general provision under the Freedom of Information Act 2002, which allows individuals to request information.

Thinking around the subject: **Taking a punt online**

The internet has brought new challenges to the legal environment. Usually, it is quite easy to determine the jurisdiction of a transaction – for example, a British tourist eating in a Spanish restaurant would be covered by the laws of Spain. For exports, the parties can agree between themselves which legal jurisdiction should apply to their transaction – for example, a British exporter and a Spanish buyer may between them agree that British law will govern their contract. But many internet dealings may involve numerous nationalities – for example, a British buyer on holiday in France may use an American-based travel agent to buy tickets from an airline based in Hong Kong, using an internet service provider based in Belgium. Regulatory authorities have been keen to control some types of internet activity that are considered to be against the public interest, but have repeatedly come across the problem of defining legal jurisdiction. For service-based transactions, governments do not have the power or ability to stop such services coming into their country, as they could in the case of goods that need to pass through some kind of customs check. Service-based companies have sometimes moved their operations to jurisdictions that are friendly towards their activities, then 'export' their services to countries where they would otherwise be illegal.

One type of activity that has exercised the minds of lawyers is gambling. In many countries, gambling has been associated with a range of social problems, therefore countries have strict controls on individuals' access to gambling services. Betting shops have been strictly regulated in the UK and many other countries, and it has been made illegal for young people to enter them. But the internet can avoid many of these controls by slipping under regulators' radar and going direct from an offshore service provider to the punter's own home. This has annoyed regulators in the United States, where gambling laws tend to be quite strict. The United States by itself cannot legislate to stop online gambling companies selling their services from other countries in the world. In a free market economy where freedom of speech is valued, the US government is not predisposed to censoring the internet, in a way that the Chinese government has done in respect of political websites. So how can a government use the law to defend the interests of its citizens, when the borderless world of the internet allows many services to reach consumers unchallenged by national borders?

For online gambling companies, such as Partypoker.com and 888.com, the United States is a very attractive market, with a high disposable income and latent demand that has been suppressed by strict anti-gambling legislation. The online gambling companies could not operate legally if they were based in the United States, so most are based in countries with more lax regimes, including the Cayman Islands and the United Kingdom. Indeed, in 2007, the UK government expressed an aim to become the world's leading centre for the online gaming industry.

The US government, frustrated by the inability of its anti-gambling laws to control offshore internet operations, has resorted to a number of more indirect approaches to control these companies. Making it illegal for US-based companies to operate online gambling sites simply handed the business opportunity to overseas companies that had no such restriction. But, in 2007, the government sought to implement its laws through American-based banks, making it illegal for them to carry out transactions with online gambling companies. American customers of Partypoker.com suddenly found that their bank wouldn't allow them to pay for gambling using their credit card (although, not to be outdone, the gambling companies have attempted to facilitate payment through third-party mechanisms such as PayPal). The US government has also sought to extend its jurisdiction and prosecute the directors of offshore gambling companies. In 2006, the sector was shaken by the arrest of David Carruthers, a UK citizen and Chief Executive Officer of London Stock Exchange listed BetonSports, while in transit in Dallas from the UK to Costa Rica. He and ten other individuals and four corporations faced a 22-count indictment on various charges of racketeering, conspiracy and fraud.

Are the actions of the United States to control the internet intrusive, and beyond what should be its legal jurisdiction? Should there be a higher level of international law to govern an internet world that knows no political boundaries? Would it have any chance of succeeding? How would it reconcile the United States' aims for tighter legislation on gambling with the UK's aim of becoming the centre for the online gambling sector?

5.9 The law and production processes

As economies develop, there is a tendency for societies to raise their expectations about firms' behaviour, particularly where they are responsible for significant external costs (see Chapter 10). The result has been increasing levels of legislation that constrain the activities of firms in meeting buyers' needs. Some of the more important constraints that affect business decisions are described below.

- Pollution of the natural environment is an external cost that governments seek to limit through legislation such as the Environmental Protection Act 1995, the Environment Act 1990 and the Water Resources Act 1991. Examples of impacts on firms include requirements for additional noise insulation, and investment in equipment to purify discharges into watercourses and the atmosphere. These have often added to a firm's total production costs, thereby putting it at a competitive disadvantage, or made plans to increase production capacity uneconomic when faced with competition from companies in countries that have less demanding requirements for environmental protection.
- The rights of employees to enjoy safe working conditions have become increasingly enshrined in law as a country develops. In the United Kingdom, it was noted earlier in this

chapter that the Health & Safety at Work Act 1974 provides for large fines and, in extreme cases, imprisonment of company directors for failing to provide a safe working environment. Definitions of what constitutes an acceptable level of risk for employees to face change over time. As well as obvious serious physical injury, the courts in England now recognize the responsibility of firms to protect their employees against more subtle dangers such as repetitive strain injury. There has also been debate in cases brought before courts as to whether a firm should be responsible for mental illness caused by excessive stress in a job, and the courts have held that companies should be liable if the employee has suffered stress in the past of which the company was aware.

- In many cases it is not sufficient to rely on law to protect customers from the faulty outcomes of a firm's production. It is also necessary to legislate in respect of the quality of the *processes* of production. This is important where buyers are unable to fully evaluate a product without a guarantee that the method of producing it has been in accordance with acceptable criteria. An example of this is the Food Safety Act 1990, which imposes requirements on all firms that manufacture or handle food products to ensure that they cannot become contaminated (e.g. by being kept at too high a temperature during transport). Many small to medium-sized food manufacturers have closed down, claiming that they cannot justify the cost of upgrading premises. Laws governing production processes are also important in the case of intangible services, where customers may have little opportunity for evaluating the credentials of one service against another. For example, to protect the public against unethical behaviour by unscrupulous sales personnel, the Financial Services Act 1986 lays down procedures for regulating business practices within the sector.

The traditional view of legislation on production is that the mounting weight of legislation puts domestic firms at a cost disadvantage to those operating in relatively unregulated environments overseas. Critics of over-regulation point to Britain and the United States as two economies that have priced themselves out of many international markets.

Against this, it is argued that as the economy of a country develops, economic gains should be enjoyed by all stakeholders of business, including employees and the local communities in which a business operates. There are also many persuasive arguments why increasing regulation of production processes may not be incompatible with greater business prosperity.

- Attempts to deregulate conditions of employment may allow firms to be more flexible in their production methods and thereby reduce their costs. However, there is a suggestion that a casualized workforce becomes increasingly reluctant to make major purchases, thereby reducing the level of activity in the domestic economy. In the United Kingdom, moves during the 1990s to free employers of many of their responsibilities to employees resulted in a large number of casual workers who were reluctant or unable to buy houses, resulting in a knock-on effect on supplies of home-related goods and services.
- There is similarly much evidence that a healthy and safe working environment is likely to be associated with high levels of commitment by employees and a high standard of output quality. The law should represent no more than a codification of good practice by firms.
- Environmental protection and cost reduction may not be mutually incompatible, as Chapter 10 demonstrates.

5.10 Legislation to protect the competitiveness of markets

Finally, there are presumed benefits of having markets that are competitive and free of harmful monopolistic or collusive tendencies. Because of this, the law of most developed countries has been used to try to remove market imperfections where these are deemed to be against the public interest. We will discuss in Chapter 12 how the common law of England has developed the principle of restraint of trade, through which anti-competitive practices have been curbed.

As the economy has become more complex, common law has proved inadequate on its own to preserve the competitiveness of markets. Common law has therefore been supplemented by statutory legislation. One outcome of statutory intervention has been the creation of a regulatory infrastructure, which in the United Kingdom includes the Office of Fair Trading, the Competition Commission and regulatory bodies to control specific industries. However, much of the current regulatory framework in the UK is based on the requirements of Articles 85 and 86 of the Treaty of Rome.

In the UK, the Competition Act 1998 and the Enterprise Act 2002 reformed and strengthened competition law by prohibiting anti-competitive behaviour. The 1998 Act introduced two basic prohibitions: a prohibition of anti-competitive agreements, based closely on Article 85 of the EC Treaty; and a prohibition of abuse of a dominant position in a market, based closely on Article 86 of the EC Treaty. The Act prohibits agreements that have the aim or effect of preventing, restricting or distorting competition in the UK. Since anti-competitive behaviour between companies may occur without a clearly defined agreement, the prohibition covers not only agreements by associations of companies, but also covert practices.

Further discussion of the application of legislation concerning anti-competitive practices, and the task of defining the public interest, may be found in Chapter 12.

Case study: Legislation strengthened in a bid to end 'nightmare' holidays

Tour operators have probably felt more keenly than most businesses the effects of new legislation to protect consumers. Because holidays are essentially intangible, it is very difficult for a prospective customer to check out claims made by tour operators' advertising until their holiday is under way, when it may be too late to do anything to prevent a ruined holiday. Traditional attitudes of 'let the buyer beware' can be of little use to holidaymakers who have little tangible evidence on which to base their decision when they book a holiday.

Consumers have traditionally had very little comeback against tour operators that fail to provide a holiday that is in line with the expectations held out in their brochure. Their brochures have frequently been accused of misleading customers – for example, by showing pictures of hotels that conveniently omit the adjacent airport runway or sewerage works. The freedom of tour operators to produce fanciful brochures was limited by the Consumer Protection Act 1987. Part III of the Act holds that any person, who, in the course of a business of his, gives (by any means whatsoever) to any consumers an indication that is misleading as to the price at which any goods, services, accommodation or facilities are available shall be guilty of an offence. These provisions of the Act forced tour operators to end such practices as promoting very low-priced holidays, which in reality were never available when customers enquired about them – only higher-priced holidays were offered. Supplements for additional items such as regional airport departures could no longer be hidden away in the small print.

When a customer buys a package holiday through a travel agent, she or he is entering into a contract with the tour operator, and the travel agent is essentially a mediator that brings together the customer and tour operator. The tour operator itself enters into a series of contracts with service providers, including hotels, airlines and bus companies, among others. Although these suppliers are contracted to provide services, the tour operator in practice has no effective day-to-day control of its suppliers' operations. It has therefore been quite usual for tour operators to include in their booking conditions an exclusion clause absolving themselves of any liability arising from the faults of their subcontractors. If a customer was injured by a faulty lift in a Spanish hotel, a tour operator would deny any responsibility for the injury and could only advise the holidaymaker to sue the Spanish hotel themselves. For some time, the courts in England recognized that it would be unreasonable to expect UK tour operators to be liable for actions that were effectively beyond their management control. Anyone who had felt unfairly treated by a tour operator had to take the offending company to court personally, often at great expense and inconvenience to themselves.

EU legislation has strengthened the position of consumers. EU Directive 90/314/EEC is designed to protect consumers who contract package travel in the EU, and was implemented in the UK through the Package Travel Regulations 1992. It covers the sale of a pre-arranged combination of transport, accommodation and other tourist services ancillary to transport or accommodation and accounting for a significant proportion of the package. Consumers are covered only where at least two of these elements are sold or offered for sale at an inclusive price, and the service covers a period of more than 24 hours or includes overnight accommodation.

The Directive contains rules concerning the liability of package organizers and retailers, which must accept responsibility for the performance of the services offered. There are some exceptions – for example, cases of 'force majeure' or similar circumstances, which could be neither foreseen nor overcome. However, even in these cases the organizer must use its best endeavours to help consumers.

The Directive also prescribes rules on the information that must be given to consumers. It contains specific requirements with regard to the content of brochures, where these are issued. For example, any brochure made available to consumers must indicate clearly and accurately the price, destination, itinerary and the means of transport used, type of accommodation, meal plan, passport and visa requirements, health formalities, timetable for payment and the deadline for informing consumers in the event of cancellation.

The Regulations have sought to redress the balance by providing greater protection for customers of tour operators and making all tour operators liable for the actions of their subcontractors. In cases that have been brought before courts in England, tour operators have been held liable for illness caused by food poisoning at a hotel, injury caused by uneven tiles at a swimming pool, and loss of enjoyment caused by noisy building work. To emphasize the effects of the directive, one British tour operator was ordered to compensate a holidaymaker in respect of claims that she had been harassed by a waiter at a hotel that had been contracted by the tour operator.

In the space of less than a decade, the UK tour operating industry has been transformed from relying on exclusion clauses and seeking to govern its dealings with customers through voluntary codes of conduct (especially the code of the Association of British Travel Agents (ABTA)). Many would argue that voluntary regulation had failed to protect consumers in accordance with their rising expectations. Legislation, while it was initially resisted by tour operators, has undoubtedly increased consumers' confidence in buying package holidays, and lessened the chances of them buying a holiday from a rogue company, and thereby harming the reputation of the industry as a whole.

The effects of this and other legislation have borne down heavily on tour operators. Having grown rapidly during the 1970s and 1980s, their pace of growth has slowed considerably. This may be partly explained by consumers' greater confidence and willingness to make up their own packages independently, encouraged by cut-price hotel and flight deals offered by companies who are not bound by the packaged travel regulations. The internet has allowed consumers to easily 'pick and mix' the different parts of the package holiday, so that they can buy the cheapest airline ticket from one source, and the cheapest hotel room from another source, for example. However, if anything goes wrong with such a self-created package, the consumer has fewer statutory rights to rely on. So if a flight is delayed or rescheduled, causing a hotel booking to be wasted, or tickets to a sporting event to be rendered useless, the customer cannot rely on one single company to put things right. In fact, if the airline was at fault and caused them to waste a hotel booking and sports tickets, they may have only a limited claim for compensation against the airline, and almost certainly no claim for consequential loss of the hotel booking or sports tickets (although EU Regulation 261/2004 does require airline passengers to be compensated for delays and compensation in specified circumstances).

Increased legislation can undoubtedly be expensive for companies to comply with. But the legislation itself can add value to a product. In the case of package holidays, consumers could avoid the burden of costs imposed on tour operators by booking independently, but they would also lose many of the benefits provided by legislation.

QUESTIONS

1 What factors could explain the increasing amount of legislation that now faces tour operators?

2 Summarize the main consequences of the EU Directive referred to above on the marketing of package holidays in the UK.

3 Is there still a role for voluntary codes of conduct in preference to legislation as a means of regulating the relationship between a tour operator and its customers?

Summary

This chapter has noted the increasing effects that legislation is having on businesses. The principal sources of law have been identified. Statute law is becoming increasingly important, with more influence being felt from the EU. Legal processes and the remedies available to a firm's customers have been discussed.

Voluntary codes of conduct are often seen as an alternative to law, and offer firms lower cost and greater flexibility.

The discussion of business ethics in **Chapter 10** relates closely to the legal environment. To many people, law is essentially a formalization of ethics, with statute law enacted by government (**Chapter 2**). The competition environment (**Chapter 11**) is increasingly influenced by legislation governing anti-competitive practices. We saw in **Chapter 4** that legal protection for innovative new technologies is vital if expenditure on research and development is to be sustained. In addition to the aspects of law discussed in this chapter, legislation affects the status of organizations (**Chapter 6**) – for example, in the protection that is given to limited liability companies.

Key terms

Codes of practice (189)
Common law (176)
Contract (177)
Discrimination (197)
Dismissal (198)
Duty of care (180)
Intellectual property rights (177)
Misrepresentation (187)
Negligence (180)
Patents (200)
Statute law (176)
Tort (180)
Trademarks (201)

Chapter review questions

1 Discuss the main ways in which the legal environment impacts on the activities of the sales and marketing functions of business organizations.

2 Giving examples, evaluate the criticism that government legislation impacts primarily on those firms that can least afford to pay for it, mainly the small and the competitively vulnerable.

3 Using an appropriate example, evaluate the virtues and drawbacks of using voluntary codes of practice to regulate business activity.

Activities

1 Think back to a time when you had a problem with a good or service that didn't meet the agreed specification (e.g. a DVD you ordered didn't have as many tracks as advertised; the seats you ended up with at a rock concert were not as good as the ones you had ordered). Identify the methods of conflict resolution available to you, short of taking legal action. Did the supplier make it easy to resolve the problem? What more could it have done? Is there a voluntary code of conduct or arbitration service that you could have used? Is it easy to use? What factors would encourage or discourage you from taking legal action?

2 Philip, shopping at a large department store, sees a colourful spinning top, which he buys for his grandson Harry. While purchasing the toy, he sees a prominent notice in the store, which states: 'This store will not be held responsible for any defects in the toys sold.' The box containing the spinning top carries the description 'Ideal for children over 12 months, safe and non-toxic' (Harry is 15 months old). Within four weeks the spinning top has split into two parts, each with a jagged edge, and Harry has suffered an illness as a result of sucking the

paint. Philip has complained vociferously to the store, which merely pointed to the prominent notice disclaiming liability. Philip has now informed the store that he intends to take legal action against it.

Draft a report to the managing director setting out the legal liability of the store.

3 Zak runs his own painting and decorating business, and has been engaged to decorate Rebecca's lounge. While burning off layers of paint from the door with his blowtorch, Zak's attention is diverted by the barking of neighbour Camilla's Yorkshire terrier and, as he turns round, the flame catches a cushion on the sofa. Within seconds the room is filled with acrid smoke. Both the carpet and sofa are damaged beyond repair, and the dog, terrified, rushes into the road, where it is run over by a car. Consider Zak's legal liability.

Further Reading

The following texts provide a general overview of law as it affects commercial organizations.

Adams, A. (2006) *Law for Business Students*, 4th edn, London, Longman.

Keenan, D. and Riches, S. (2007) *Business Law*, 8th edn, London, Longman.

Woodroffe, G. and Lowe, R. (2007) *Consumer Law and Practice*, 7th edn, London, Sweet & Maxwell.

This chapter has discussed the basics of the law of contract and the following texts provide useful further reading.

Elliott, C. and Quinn, F. (2007) *Contract Law*, 6th edn, London, Longman.

Poole, J. (2006) *Textbook on Contract Law*, 8th edn, Oxford, Oxford University Press.

Trademarks and patent laws are discussed in the following text.

Hart, T., Fazzani, L. and Clark, S. (2006) *Intellectual Property Law*, 4th edn, Basingstoke, Palgrave Macmillan.

A valuable overview of employment law is provided in the following.

Lewis, D. and Sargeant, M. (2007) *Essentials of Employment Law*, 9th edn, London, Chartered Institute of Personnel and Development.

References

Berthoud, R. (2005) *Incomes of Ethnic Minorities*, Joseph Rowntree Foundation.

Eurostat (2006–07) *Eurostat Yearbook 2006–07*, Luxembourg, Statistical Office of the European Communities.

Chapter 13

The National Economic Environment

CHAPTER OBJECTIVES

This chapter will explain:

- the structure of national economies, distinguishing between consumer, producer and government sectors
- methods of measuring activity within the economy
- the business cycle – causes and consequences for business organizations
- government economic policy objectives
- methods used by governments to manage the national economy

13.1 Macroeconomic analysis

In the previous chapter, microeconomic analysis of a firm's competitive environment made a number of assumptions about the broader economic environment in which the firm operates. In the analysis of supply and demand in any given market, changes in household incomes or government taxation were treated as an uncontrollable external factor to which a market responded. For most businesses, a sound understanding of this broader economic environment is just as important as understanding short-term and narrow relationships between the price of a firm's products and demand for them.

An analysis of companies' financial results has often indicated that business people attribute their current success or failure to the state of the economy. For example, a retail store that has just reported record profit levels may put this down to a very high level of consumer confidence, while a factory that has just laid off workers may blame a continuing economic recession for its low level of activity. Few business people can afford to ignore the state of the economy because it affects the willingness and ability of customers to buy their products. It can also affect the price and availability of its inputs. The shop that reported record profits may have read economic indicators correctly and prepared for an upturn in consumer spending by buying in more stocks or taking on more sales assistants.

This chapter is concerned with what has often been described as macroeconomic analysis. Although the workings of the economy at a national level are the focus of this chapter, it must be remembered that even national economies form part of a larger international economic environment. Issues of international economic analysis are discussed in Chapter 14.

This chapter begins by analysing the structure of the national economy and the interdependence of the elements within this structure. The national economy is a complex system whose functioning is influenced by a range of planned and unplanned forces. While unplanned forces (such as turbulence in the world economic system) can have significant impacts on the national economic system, organizations are particularly keen to understand the planned interventions of governments that seek to influence the economy for a variety of social and political reasons.

13.2 The structure of the economy

Analyses of national economies have traditionally divided the productive sectors into three categories.

1. The *primary sector*, which is concerned with the extraction and production of basic raw materials from agriculture, mining, oil exploration, etc.
2. The *secondary sector*, which transforms the output of the primary sector into products that consumers can use (e.g. manufacturing, construction, raw material processing, etc.).
3. The *services sector*, which comprises intangible products such as hairdressing, and business services such as accounting.

Comparisons can be drawn between the three sectors described above and value chains (described in Chapter 1). In general, these three sectors add progressively higher levels of value to a product. In practice, most organizations are involved in two or more of these production categories; for example, the Ford car company manufactures cars, but it also produces a wide range of services, including financial services, extended warranties and insurance.

A further division in the economy occurs between the production sector and the consumption sector. The production sector creates wealth (e.g. making cars, providing meals in a restaurant), while the consumption sector essentially destroys wealth (using the car until it is worn out, eating the restaurant meal so that there is nothing left to show for it). Distinction is often made between government and private sectors of the economy. Government becomes involved in the economy as both a producer (e.g. educational services) and as a consumer on behalf of the public (e.g. through the purchase of equipment for schools)

The relationship between producers and consumers is the basis for models of the circular flow of income, discussed later in this chapter.

13.2.1 Measures of economic structure

The relative importance of the three productive sectors described above has been changing. Evidence of this change is usually recorded by reference to three key statistics:

1. the share of gross domestic product (GDP) that each sector accounts for
2. the proportion of the labour force employed in the sector
3. the contribution of the sector to a nation's balance of payments.

A key trend in Britain, as in most developed economies, has been the gradual decline in importance of the primary and manufacturing sectors and the growth in the services sector. The extent of the change in the UK economic structure, when measured by shifts in GDP and employment, is indicated in Figure 13.1.

While the statistics in Figure 13.1 appear to show a number of clear trends, the figures need to be treated with a little caution for a number of reasons.

	1969	1979	1989	1995	2000	2007
Primary						
GDP (%)	4.3	6.7	4.2	4.4	4.1	3.7
Workforce (%)	3.6	3.0	2.1	1.4	1.5	1.3
Secondary						
GDP (%)	42.0	36.7	34.5	29.4	25.5	24.5
Workforce (%)	46.8	38.5	28.9	18.3	20.8	19.2
Services						
GDP (%)	53.0	56.5	61.3	66.2	70.4	75.0
Workforce (%)	49.3	58.5	69.0	76.5	77.7	79.5

Figure 13.1 Composition of the UK productive sector
Source: compiled from 'Economic trends', *Employment Gazette*

- Fluctuations in the value of GDP for the primary sector often have little to do with changes in activity levels, but instead reflect changes in world commodity levels. Oil represents a major part of the UK's primary sector output, but the value of oil produced has fluctuated from the very high levels of the early 1980s to the very low levels of the 1990s, largely reflecting changes in oil prices.
- The level of accuracy with which statistics have been recorded has been questioned, especially for the services sector. The system of Standard Industrial Classifications (SICs) for a long while did not disaggregate the service sector in the same level of detail as the other two sectors.
- Part of the apparent growth in the services sector may reflect the method by which statistics are collected, rather than indicating an increase in overall service level activity. Output and employment is recorded according to the dominant business of an organization. Within many primary- and secondary-sector organizations, many people are employed in service-type activities, such as cleaning, catering, transport and distribution. Where a cook is employed by a manufacturing company, output and employment is attributed to the manufacturing sector. However, during recent years, many manufacturing firms have contracted out some of these service activities to external contractors. Where such contracts are performed by contract catering, office cleaning or transport companies, the output becomes attributable to the service sector, making the service sector look larger, even though no additional services have actually been produced – they have merely been switched from internally produced to externally produced.

Nevertheless, the figures clearly indicate a number of significant trends in the economy.

- The primary sector in the United Kingdom, as in most developed economies, has been contracting in relative importance. There are supply- and demand-side explanations for this trend. On the supply side, many basic agricultural and extractive processes have been mechanized, resulting in them using fewer employees and thereby consuming a lower proportion of GDP. Many primary industries have declined as suppliers have been unable to compete with low-cost producers in countries that are able to exploit poor working conditions. On the demand side, rising levels of affluence have led consumers to demand increasingly refined products. In this way, consumers have moved from buying raw potatoes (essentially a product of the primary sector) to buying processed potatoes (e.g. prepared ready meals), which involve greater inputs from the secondary sector. With further affluence, potatoes have been sold with the added involvement of the service sector (e.g. eating cooked potatoes in a restaurant).
- The output of the secondary sector in the United Kingdom fell from 42 per cent of GDP in 1969 to 26.7 per cent in 2006, reflecting the poor performance of the manufacturing industry (the comparable figure for the 25 EU countries was 25.8 per cent). This can again partly be explained by efficiency gains by the sector, requiring fewer resources to be used, but more worryingly by competition from overseas. The emergence of newly industrialized nations with a good manufacturing infrastructure and low employment costs, rigidities in the UK labour market, declining research and development budgets relative to overseas competitors, and the effects of exchange rate policy have all contributed to this decline.

- In respect of its share of GDP, the services sector saw almost continuous growth during the period 1969–99, with banking, finance, insurance, business services, leasing and communications being particularly prominent. In 2006, the services sector accounted for 75 per cent of UK GDP, up from 53 per cent in 1969.

13.2.2 Towards a service economy?

There is little doubt that the services sector has become a dominant force in many national economies. According to Eurostat, services accounted for 71.6 per cent of GDP in the 25 EU countries in 2005 (Eurostat 2006). Between 1970 and 1997, it is reported that about 1.5 million new jobs per year were created in the services sectors within the EU – twice the average for the rest of the economy (Eurostat 1998).

The United Kingdom, like many developed economies, has traditionally run a balance of trade deficit in manufactured goods (i.e. imports exceed exports), but has made up for this with a surplus in 'invisible' service 'exports'. In 2006, there was a trade surplus in services of £29,605 million, but this was more than offset by a deficit of £83,691 million in manufactured goods.

During periods of recession in the manufacturing sector, the service sector has been seen by many as the saviour of the economy. Many politicians have been keen to promote the service sector as a source of new employment to make up for the diminishing level of employment within the primary and secondary sectors. A common argument has been that the United Kingdom no longer has a competitive cost advantage in the production of many types of goods, and therefore these sectors of the economy should be allowed to decline and greater attention paid to those service sectors that showed greater competitive advantage. The logic of this argument can be pushed too far, as outlined below.

- A large part of the growth in the service sector during the 1980s and 1990s reflected the buoyancy of the primary and secondary sectors during that period. As manufacturing industry increases its level of activity, the demand for many business-to-business services, such as accountancy, legal services and business travel, increases. During periods of recession in the manufacturing sectors, the decline in manufacturing output has had an impact on the services sector, as evidenced, for example, through lower demand for business loans and export credits.
- The assumption that the United Kingdom has a competitive cost advantage in the production of services needs to be examined closely. In the same way that many sectors of UK manufacturing industry lost their competitive advantage to developing nations during the 1960s and 1970s, there is some evidence that the once unquestioned supremacy in certain service sectors is being challenged. High levels of training in some of Britain's competitor nations have allowed those countries to, first, develop their own indigenous services and then to develop them for export. Banking services that were once a net import of Japan are now exported throughout the world.
- Over-reliance on the service sector could pose strategic problems for the United Kingdom. A diverse economic base allows a national economy to be more resilient to changes in world trading conditions.

13.2.3 International comparisons

There appears to be a high level of correlation between the level of economic development in an economy (as expressed by its GDP per capita) and the strength of its services sector. Within the EU there is variation around the mean share of value added from services of 71.6 per cent, with more developed member-states being above this figure (e.g. UK 75 per cent, France 76 per cent), and less developed member-states below (e.g. Lithuania 55 per cent, Slovakia 63 per cent) (Eurostat 2006). According to the International Labour Organization, 71.5 per cent of the total workers from developed economies are employed in the services sector. Lower figures are found in many of the developing economies of Asia – for example, East Asia (34.7 per cent), South-east Asia and the Pacific (37 per cent), South Asia (30.3 per cent). The lowest level of services employment is found in the least developed countries for example, those in Sub-Saharan Africa (25.7 per cent) (ILO 2008).

It is debatable whether a strong services sector leads to economic growth or is a result of that economic growth. The debate can partly be resolved by dividing services into those 'consumer services' that are used up in final consumption and 'business to business' services that provide inputs to further business processes (see below).

13.2.4 Consumer, producer and government sectors

Consumer goods and services are provided for individuals who use up those goods and services for their own enjoyment or benefit. No further economic benefit results from the consumption of the product. In this way, the services of a hairdresser can be defined as consumer services. On the other hand, producer goods and services are those that are provided to other businesses in order that those businesses can produce something else of economic benefit. In this way, a road haulage company sells services to its industrial customers in order that they can add value to the goods that they produce, by allowing their goods to be made available at the point of demand.

The essential difference between production and final consumption sectors is that the former creates wealth while the latter consumes it. Traditionally, economic analysis has labelled these as 'firms' and 'households' respectively. The discussion later in this chapter will indicate the problems that may arise where an apparently prosperous household sector is not backed by an equally active production sector.

There has been continuing debate about the role of government in the national economy, which has led to shifts in the proportion of GDP accounted for by the public sector. During the 1980s, the UK government regarded the public sector as a burden on the country and set about dismantling much of the state's involvement in the economy. Privatization of public corporations and the encouragement of private pensions were just two manifestations of this. By the mid-1990s, the proportion of UK government expenditure as a proportion of total GDP appeared to have stabilized in the range 38–42 per cent, with increasing social security spending offsetting much of the reduction in expenditure accounted for by state-owned industries. Figure 13.2 illustrates the cyclical nature of public spending and taxation as a proportion of UK GDP.

Governments do not always take such a 'hands-off' approach. The economies of Eastern Europe have in the past been dominated by central planning in which the government determined the bulk of income and expenditure in the economy. Even in Britain shortly after the Second World War, the government assumed a very major role in the economy, with the

Thinking around the subject: **Services are not just about restaurants and hairdressers – they are vital to productivity in the whole economy**

The services sector includes businesses whose output is vital for improving the efficiency of other businesses within the national economy. Transport and communications are often cited as vital service activities, and the lack of transport infrastructure has held back many developing countries. The road haulage sector acts as part of many manufacturing firms' production process, moving raw materials and semi-manufactured components between factories. Road hauliers also add value for private households by making the goods of manufacturing companies available locally and, increasingly, delivering direct to their home. The road haulage sector does not exist in isolation from the government sector. Hauliers rely on government expenditure to provide adequate road capacity, and many would argue that cutbacks in government road expenditure have added to the operating costs of road hauliers, which are ultimately passed on to manufacturing companies and their customers. The government also collects taxation from the sector, only part of which is passed back to the sector, with the remainder being used to fund other government spending programmes.

nationalization of many essential industries. Even today, there are variations within Western Europe in the proportion of GDP accounted for by the government sector. Many Scandinavian countries, for example, have higher proportions than the UK, reflecting, among other things, a general acceptance by their populations that taxation revenues will be wisely spent on socially necessary expenditure.

Organizations need to keep their eyes on political developments that shift the balance of resources between public and private sectors. A company that is involved in the marketing of health service products, for example, will be very interested in the government's view about the respective roles to be played by the private sector and the National Health Service.

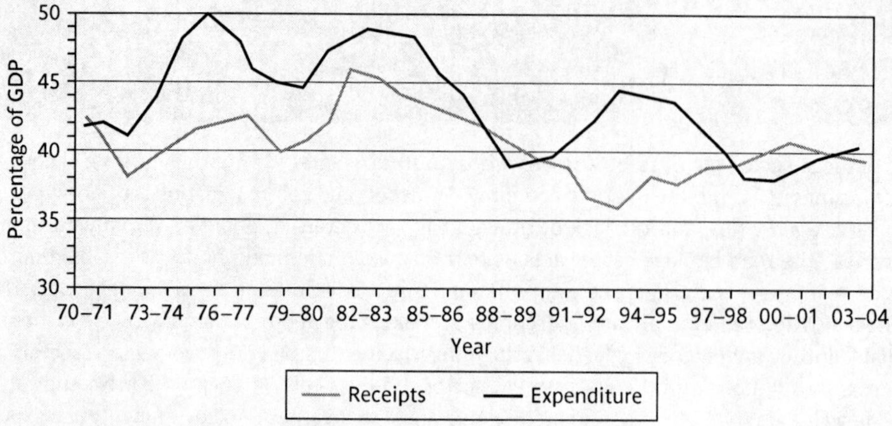

Figure 13.2 Trends in UK government taxation and spending as a proportion of GDP, 1970–2004
Source: based on HM Treasury Financial Statement and Budget Report, March 2001

13.3 The circular flow of income

Households, firms and government are highly interdependent and the level of wealth created in an economy is influenced by the interaction between these elements. To understand the workings of a national economy, it is useful to begin by developing a simple model of a closed economy comprising just two sectors – firms and households – which circulate money between each other.

The simplest model of a circular flow of income involves a number of assumptions.

- Households earn all their income from supplying their labour to firms.
- Firms earn all their income from supplying goods and services to households.
- There is no external trade.
- All income earned is spent (i.e. households and firms do not retain savings).

In this simple model, the income of households is exactly equal to the expenditure of firms, and vice versa. It follows that any change in income from employment is directly related to changes in expenditure by consumers. Similarly, any change in sales of goods and services by firms is dependent upon employment. In this simplified economy, income, output, spending and employment are all interrelated (Figure 13.3). Of course, this simplified model of the economy is almost impossible to achieve in practice, because most economies are affected by factors that upset this stable equilibrium pattern of income and expenditure.

Instability in this static model can come about for two principal reasons: additional money can be injected into the circular flow, while money currently circulating can be withdrawn. Injections have the effect of increasing the volume and speed of circulation of money within this flow, while withdrawals have the opposite effects.

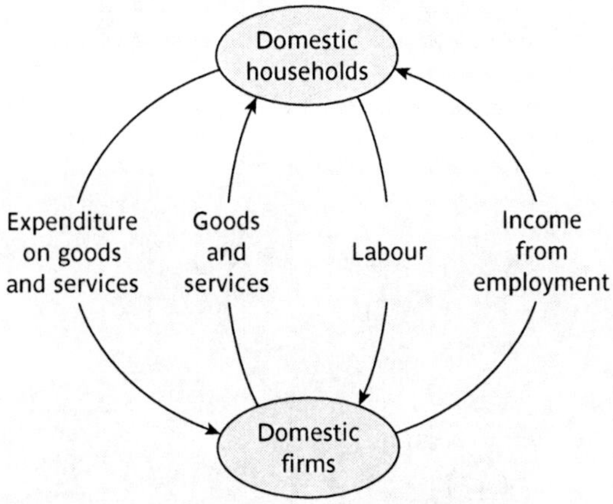

Figure 13.3 The circular flow of income, based on a simplified model of a national economy

Withdrawals can take a number of forms:

- savings by households that occur when income is received by them, but not returned to firms
- government taxation, which removes income received by households and prevents them from returning it to firms in the form of expenditure on goods and services; taxation of businesses diverts part of their expenditure from being returned to households
- spending on imported goods and services by households means that this money is not received by firms, which cannot subsequently return it to households in the form of wages.

The opposite of withdrawals are injections and these go some way to counterbalancing the effects described above, in the following ways.

- Firms may earn income by selling goods to overseas buyers. This represents an additional source of income that is passed on to households.
- Purchases by firms of capital equipment, which represents investment as opposed to current expenditure.
- Instead of reducing the flow of income in an economy through taxation, governments can add to it by spending on goods and services.

A revised model of the circular flow of income, incorporating these modifications, is shown in Figure 13.4.

This modified model of the economy still involves a number of fairly unrealistic assumptions (e.g. that consumers do not borrow money). In addition, it is unrealistic to assume that households earn income only from employment activity; they also receive it from returns on investments, property rentals and self-employment. However, it serves to stress the interdependence of the different sectors of the economy and the fact that, through this interdependence, changes in behaviour by one group can result in significant changes in economic performance

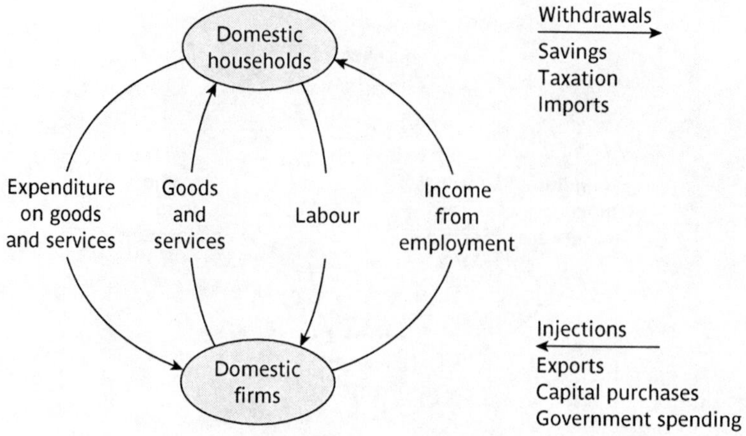

Figure 13.4 A modified circular flow of income, incorporating injections and withdrawals

as a whole. Of particular interest to government policy makers and businesses alike is the effect on total economic activity of changing just one element in the circular flow.

Another issue that is not fully reflected in this simple model is the role of the banking sector in circulating funds between and within the household and firm sectors. If firms rely on their own capital for growth, their growth would probably be very slow; therefore expanding economies have been associated with high levels of borrowing by firms. In the case of developing economies, this borrowing usually comes from overseas, representing a major injection to their national economies. If firms and banks do not feel confident about lending to each other (or do not feel confident about borrowing money), the circular flow of income will slow down. This was clearly seen in late 2007 when the so-called 'credit crunch' led to a liquidity crisis as banks became reluctant to lend money, both to firms and to private consumers. This led to a sharp downturn in consumer expenditure.

13.3.1 The multiplier effect

The multiplier effect can be compared to the effects of throwing a stone into a pool of water. The impact of the stone with the water will cause an initial wave to be formed, but beyond this will be waves of ever decreasing strength. The strength of these ripples will lessen with increasing distance from the site of original impact and with the passage of time. Similarly, injecting money into the circular flow of income will have an initial impact on households and businesses directly affected by the injection, but will also be indirectly felt by households and firms throughout the economy.

The multiplier effect can be illustrated by considering the effects of a major capital investment by private-sector firms or by government. The firm making the initial investment spends money buying in supplies from outside (including labour) and these outside suppliers in turn purchase more inputs. The multiplier effect of this initial expenditure can result in the total increase in household incomes being much greater than the original expenditure. A good example of the multiplier effect at work in the United Kingdom is provided by the Millennium Dome project at Greenwich, opened in 2000 (now known as the O_2). An important reason for the government supporting this project was the desire to regenerate an economically depressed part of London. Government expenditure initially created expenditure during the construction of the Dome and from employment within the Dome itself. This expenditure then rippled out to other business sectors, such as hotels and transport. The level of activity generated additional demand for local manufacturing industry – for example, visitors require food that may be produced locally, the producers of which may in turn require additional building materials and services to increase production facilities. On an even larger scale, the Mayor of London, supported by central government, successfully bid to host the 2012 Olympic Games, largely on the basis of the multiplier benefits that would result.

The extent of the multiplier effects of initial expenditure is influenced by a number of factors. Crucial is the extent to which recipients of this initial investment recirculate it back into the national economy. If large parts of it are saved by households or used to buy imported goods (whether by firms or by households), the multiplier effects to an economy will be reduced. In general, income that is received by individuals that have a high propensity to spend each additional pound on basic necessities is likely to generate greater multiplier benefits than the same money received by higher-income households that have a greater propensity to save it or to spend it on imported luxuries. The implications of this for government macroeconomic policy will be considered later.

The multiplier effect can be used to analyse the effects of withdrawals from the circular flow as well as injections. Therefore, if firms spend less on wages, household income will fall as a direct result, leading indirectly to lower spending by households with other domestic firms. These firms will in turn pay less to households in wages, leading to a further reduction in spending with firms, and so on.

Multiplier effects can be studied at a local as well as a national level. Government capital expenditure is often used with a view to stimulating areas of severe unemployment (as in the case of the Millennium Dome and grants given by Regional Development Agencies to support private-sector investment in Tyneside). The presence of a university in a town usually generates strong multiplier benefits – for example, one study in Wales estimated that the university in Newport, with a turnover of around £30 million per annum, and employing between 800 and 900 people, generated multiplier benefits to the local economy of around £80 million per annum in 2000. However, whether the local economy is helped will depend upon how much subsequent expenditure is retained within the area. In a study of the regional multiplier effects of siting a call centre for British Airways in a deprived part of Tyneside, it was found that a high proportion of the staff employed commuted in from other, more prosperous areas, thereby limiting the multiplier benefits to the deprived area.

As well as examining the general macroeconomic effects of spending by firms on household income, and vice versa, multiplier analysis can also be used to assess the impact of economic activity in one business sector upon other business sectors. Many economies suffer because vital economic infrastructure remains undeveloped, preventing productivity gains in other sectors. The availability of transport and distribution services has often had the effect of stimulating economic development at local and national levels – for example, following the improvement of rail or road services. The absence of these basic services can have a crippling effect on the development of the primary and manufacturing sectors – for instance, one reason for Russian agriculture not having been fully exploited has been the ineffective distribution system available to food producers.

One approach to understanding the contribution of one business sector to other sectors of the economy is to analyse input–output tables of production, and data on labour and capital inputs. In one study (Wood 1987), these were used to estimate the effects that productivity improvements in all the direct and indirect supply sectors had on the productivity levels of all other sectors. Thus, some apparently high-productivity sectors (such as chemicals) were shown to be held back by the low productivity of some of their inputs. On the other hand, efficiency improvements in some services, such as transport and distribution, were shown to have had widespread beneficial effects on the productivity contribution of other sectors. This is reflected in the common complaint among manufacturing businesses in the UK that their productivity is severely reduced by traffic congestion, which adds to their delivery costs and the costs of their supplies.

13.3.2 The accelerator effect

Changes in the demand for consumer goods can lead, through an accelerator effect, to a more pronounced change in the demand for capital goods. This accelerator effect occurs when, for instance, a small increase in consumer demand leads to a sudden large increase in demand for plant and machinery with which to satisfy that demand. When consumer demand falls by a small amount, demand for plant and machinery falls by a correspondingly larger amount.

The accelerator effect is best illustrated by reference to an example (Figure 13.5) based on consumers' demand for air travel and airlines' demands for new aircraft. In this simplified

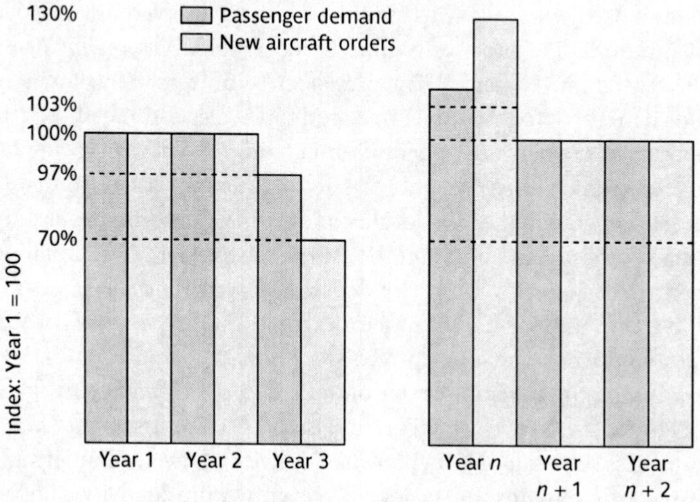

Figure 13.5 The accelerator effect on new aircraft orders of changes in passenger demand

example, an airline operates a fleet of 100 aircraft and, during periods of stable passenger demand, buys ten new aircraft each year and retires ten older aircraft, retaining a stable fleet size of 100 aircraft. Then, some extraneous factor (e.g. a decline in the world economy) may cause the airline's passenger demand to fall by 3 per cent per annum. The airline responds to this by reducing its capacity by 3 per cent to 97 aircraft (we will assume, perhaps unrealistically, that it can reschedule its aircraft so that it is able to accommodate all its remaining passengers). The easiest way to achieve this is by reducing its annual order for aircraft from ten to seven. If it continued to retire its ten oldest aircraft, this would have the effect of reducing its fleet size to 97, in line with the new level of customer demand. What is of importance here is that while consumer demand has gone down by just 3 per cent, the demand facing the aircraft manufacturer has gone down by 30 per cent (from ten aircraft a year to seven). If passenger demand settles down at its new level, the airline will have no need to cut its fleet any further, so will revert to buying ten new aircraft a year and selling ten old ones. If passenger demand picks up once more, the airline may seek to increase its capacity by ordering not ten aircraft but, say, 13.

13.3.3 Inflation

It should be apparent that multiplier effects are associated with injections to the circular flow of income, causing more money to chase a fixed volume of goods and services available for consumption. This leads to the classic case of demand-pull **inflation**, when excessive demand for goods and services relative to their supply results in an increase in their market price level. Demand-pull inflation can result from an increase in the availability of credit, excessive spending by government, and tax cuts that increase consumers' disposable incomes, so allowing them to buy more goods and services.

An alternative cause of inflation is referred to as cost-push inflation. On the supply side, increases in production costs (such as higher wage costs, rising raw material costs, higher overheads and additional costs of health and safety legislation) may push up the price at which companies are prepared to supply their goods to the market, unless they are offset by increases in productivity.

An inflationary spiral can be created where higher wages in an economy result in greater spending power, leading to demand-pull inflation. The resulting higher cost of consumer goods leads workers to seek wage increases to keep them ahead of inflation, but these increases in wage costs add a further twist to cost-push inflation, and so on. Because markets are seldom perfectly competitive and therefore unable to correct for inflation, governments are keen to intervene to prevent inflationary processes building up in an economy (see below).

13.3.4 Complex models of the economy

The simple **model** of the economy presented above is based on many assumptions, which need to be better understood if model making is to make a useful contribution to policy making. It is important for governments to have a reasonably accurate model of how the economy works so that predictions can be made about the effects of government policy. A model should be able to answer such questions as the following.

- What will happen to unemployment if government capital expenditure is increased by 10 per cent?
- What will happen to inflation if income tax is cut by 2p in the pound?
- What will be the net effect on government revenue if it grants tax concessions to firms investing in new capital equipment?

Companies supplying goods and services also take a keen interest in models of the economy, typically seeking to answer questions such as the following.

- What effect will a cut in income tax have on demand for new car purchases by private consumers?
- How will company buyers of office equipment respond to reductions in taxation on company profits?
- Will the annual budget create a feeling of confidence on the part of consumers, which is sufficiently strong for them to make major household purchases?

Developing a model of the economy is very different from developing a model in the natural sciences. In the latter case, it is often possible to develop closed models where all factors that can affect a system of interrelated elements are identifiable and can be measured. Predicting behaviour for any component of the model is therefore possible, based on knowledge about all other components. In the case of economic models, the system of interrelated components is open rather than closed. This means that not only is it difficult to measure components, but it can also be difficult to identify what elements to include as being of significance to a national economy. For example, few models accurately predicted that a sudden rise in oil prices by OPEC producers would have a major effect on national economies throughout the world. Furthermore, it is very difficult to develop relationships between variables that remain constant through time. Whereas the relationship between molecules in a chemistry model may be universally true, given a set of environmental conditions, such universal truths are seldom found in economic modelling. This has a lot to do with the importance of the attitudes of firms and consumers, which change through time for reasons that may not become clear until after the event. For example, a 2 per cent cut in income tax may have achieved significant increases in consumer expenditure on one occasion, but resulted in higher levels of savings or debt repayment on another. The first time round, factors as ephemeral as good weather and national success in an international football championship could have created a 'feel good' factor that was absent the next time round.

13.4 The business cycle

From the discussion in the previous sections, it should become quite apparent that national economies are seldom in a stable state. The situation where injections exactly equate with withdrawals can be described as a special case, with the normal state of affairs being for one of these to exceed the other. An excess of injections will result in economic activity increasing, while the opposite will happen if withdrawals exceed injections. This leads to the concept of the **business cycle**, which describes the fluctuating level of activity in an economy. Most developed economies go through cycles that have been described as:

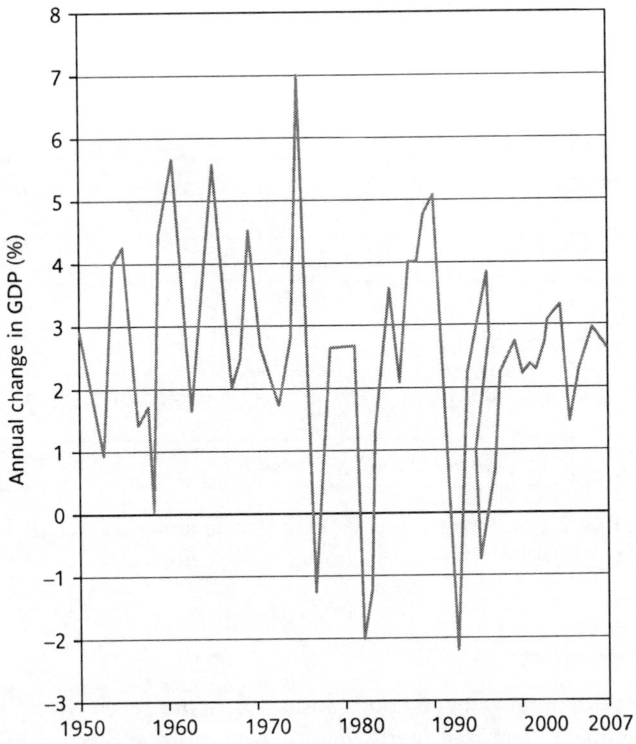

Figure 13.6 Annual rate of change of UK gross domestic product
Source: based on *Annual Abstract of Statistics*

- recession–prosperity
- expansion–contraction
- stop–go, and
- 'boom and bust'.

Figure 13.6 shows the pattern of the business cycle for the United Kingdom, as measured by fluctuations in the most commonly used indicator of economic activity – gross domestic product (described below).

13.4.1 Measuring economic activity

Gross domestic product (GDP) is just one indicator of the business cycle. In fact, there are many indicators of economic activity that may move at slightly different times to each other. Some 'leading' indicators may be used as early warning signs of an approaching economic recession, with other indicators – if not corrected by government intervention – following a similar trend in due course. Some of the more commonly used indicators of the business cycle are described below.

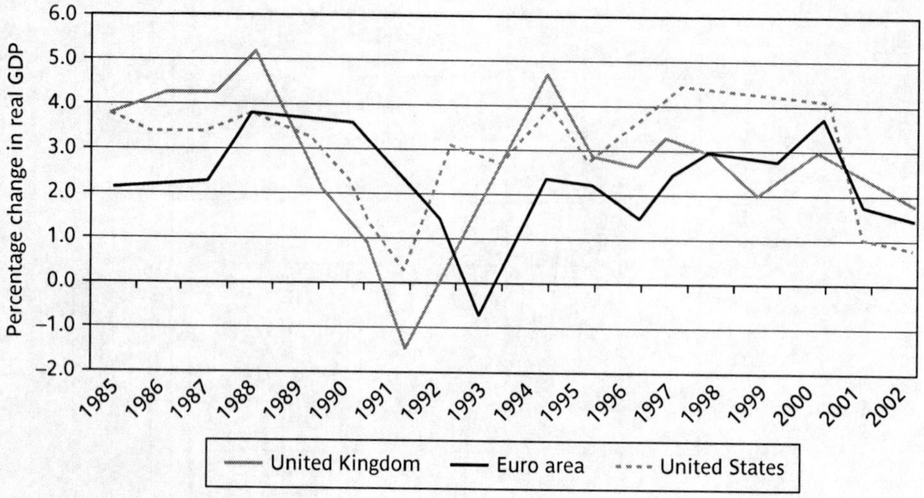

Figure 13.7 Annual GDP growth rate in the UK, Euro area countries and the USA
Source: based on European Commission data

Gross domestic product

This index measures the total value of goods and services produced within the economy, and can be used to compare economic performance over time and to compare performance between countries (see Figure 13.7). In a typical year, the economies of Western European countries may expand by 2–3 per cent per annum, although this has reached 4–5 per cent in boom years, while GDP has fallen during recessionary periods. Much more rapid growth in GDP has been seen in emerging economies, such as China, where annual growth in GDP in the early years of the twenty-first century was averaging about 9 per cent a year. One derivative of the crude GDP figure is a figure for GDP per capita. Therefore, if GDP is going up by 2 per cent a year and the population is constant, it means that, on average, everybody is 2 per cent better off. Whether this is true in reality, of course, depends not only on how the additional income is distributed but also on an individual's definition of being better off (GDP takes no account of 'quality of life'). Since GDP depends on both prices and quantities, an increase in prices will also increase GDP (this is also referred to as nominal GDP). This is not a particularly good measure of economic well-being, so a GDP deflator removes the effects of price changes by calculating real GDP, expressed using a constant set of prices.

Unemployment rates

Because of the profound social and economic implications of high levels of unemployment, governments normally monitor changes in unemployment levels closely. Unemployment tends to rise as the economy enters a general economic recession and falls as it enters a period of recovery. Unemployment occurs where firms are unable to sell their output and seek to scale back their workforce, either by laying off existing workers or not recruiting new ones. This results in less spending by the growing number of unemployed people, thereby exacerbating firms' sales difficulties. Actually measuring trends in unemployment over time can be difficult, as definitions used by governments frequently change. Cynics would say that this is done to hide the true level of unemployment – for example, by excluding people that are on job training schemes.

Output levels

The output of firms is an important indicator of the business cycle, and is closely watched because of its effects on employment, and the multiplier effects of firms producing less and therefore spending less with their suppliers. In the United Kingdom, the government's Business Monitor publishes regular indicators of outputs for different sectors. Another widely quoted source of data on output is the Confederation of British Industry (CBI), which publishes monthly and quarterly surveys on industry's output, investment and stock levels. This provides a good indication of changes in different sectors of the economy, and possible future business trends. In addition to these widely used and formalized methods of measuring output, a number of ad hoc approaches have been used, which it is claimed give early indicators of an economic recovery or downturn. Examples include the following.

- Sales of first-class tickets by train operating companies, where a fall in sales is often an early indication of firms cutting back expenditure ahead of major cuts in output.
- The number of commercial vehicles crossing the Severn Bridge between England and Wales has been correlated with the output of the manufacturing sector in general.
- Rising sales of Ford Transit vans have been associated with a revival in fortunes by the small business sector, and rising sales of heavy trucks with growing confidence by firms to invest in capital equipment.

Average earnings

Unemployment figures record the extreme case of workers that have no employment. However, underemployment can affect the national economy just as significantly as unemployment, as workers are put on short-time working or lose opportunities for overtime working. Conversely, average earnings may rise significantly during the early years of a boom as firms increase overtime working and bid up wage rates in an attempt to take on staff with key skills.

Disposable income

Average disposable income refers to the income that individuals have available to spend after taxation. It follows that, as taxes rise, disposable income falls. A further indicator of household wealth is discretionary income, which is a measure of disposable income less expenditure on the necessities of life, such as mortgage payments. Discretionary income can be significantly affected by sudden changes in the cost of mortgages and other items of expenditure, such as travel costs, which form a large component of household budgets.

Consumer spending

Trends in consumer spending may diverge from trends in discretionary income on account of changes in consumers' propensity to borrow or save. When consumer spending runs ahead of discretionary income, this can be explained by an increase in borrowing. Conversely, spending may fall faster than discretionary income, indicating that consumers are repaying debts and/or not borrowing additional money. There are numerous indicators of consumer spending, including the government's Family Expenditure Survey. More up-to-date information is supplied by the Credit Card Research Group (CCRG), an organization representing the main UK credit card issuers. After making a number of assumptions about changing card-using habits, CCRG is able to monitor changes in the volume of consumer spending using credit cards. It is also able to monitor consumer borrowing using credit cards and net repayments of credit card debts.

Savings ratio

The savings ratio refers to the proportion of individuals' income that is saved rather than spent. Saving/borrowing levels are influenced by a number of factors, including the distribution of income in society (poorer people tend to save less, therefore any redistribution of income to this group would have the effect of reducing net savings) and consumers' level of confidence about the future (see below). During periods of high consumer confidence, savings ratios tend to fall as consumer borrowing rises. This was true of the expansionary period of the late 1980s when the proportion of household income saved reached a low point of 2.8 per cent. During the recessionary years of the mid- to late 1990s, savings ratios increased sharply, reaching a high point of 12 per cent in 1996 before gradually falling again to 5.8 per cent in the more prosperous year of 2003. Businesses look to a fall in savings ratios as an early indicator of increasing consumer confidence.

Confidence levels

Private individuals and businesses may have a high level of income and savings, but there is no guarantee that they will spend that money or take on new debt in making purchases of expensive items. They may only be happy about making major spending decisions if they feel confident about the future. Higher confidence levels may result, for example, from consumers feeling that they are not likely to be made unemployed, that their pay is going to keep up with inflation and that the value of their assets is not going to fall. A number of confidence indices are now published – for example, by Chambers of Commerce and the CBI, covering both private consumers and businesses. The organization GfK publishes a monthly Consumer Confidence Barometer for the European Commission.

Inflation rate

Inflation refers to the rate at which prices of goods and services in an economy are rising. A commonly used general indicator of inflation in the United Kingdom is the Consumer Prices Index (CPI). In January 2004, the Bank of England's Monetary Policy Committee supplemented the Retail Prices Index (RPI) with this European-derived measure of inflation. Like the RPI, it is based on information collected about the prices of goods and services consumed by an average household. These are commonly used 'headline' rates of inflation, which are frequently used by employees as a basis for wage negotiations and by the UK government for adjusting the value of a number of social security benefits.

The problem with a general index such as the CPI is that it may be too general to be of relevance to the spending patterns of specific groups of individuals or organizations, so there are numerous alternative indices covering specific sectors. Many building societies, for example, produce indices of house price inflation, while specialized indices are available for new car purchases and construction costs, among others. The government publishes a monthly producer prices index, which measures changes in the prices of goods bought by manufacturing firms. A rise in this indicator can signal later increases in the CPI when the components are incorporated into finished goods bought by households. Inflation affects different groups of consumers in different ways. During a period of falling interest rates and fuel prices, a home-owning, car-using household may experience negative inflation, leaving it with greater discretionary income. At the same time, the cost of public transport and rented housing may be increasing, leaving groups dependent on public transport and paying rents to a Housing Association facing a high level of inflation, thereby leaving less discretionary income.

A 'normal' level of inflation is often considered to lie in the range of 1–3 per cent per annum. Where prices are falling, the opposite case of **deflation** occurs, which can have economic consequences just as serious as very high inflation. For several years from the mid-1990s, the Japanese economy experienced deflation, resulting in a reluctance of people to invest. Why invest today in an asset that will be cheaper in a year's time? Such attitudes can lead to a self-fulfilling prophecy.

Interest rates

Interest rates represent the price that borrowers have to pay to a lender for the privilege of using their money for a specified period of time. Interest rates tend to follow a cyclical pattern, which is partly a reflection of the level of activity in the economy. During periods of recession, the supply of funds typically exceeds demand for them (caused, for example, by consumers being reluctant to spend, thereby building up their savings, and by the unwillingness of consumers and firms to borrow to pay for major expenditure items). In these circumstances, interest rates have a tendency to fall. During a period of economic prosperity, the opposite holds true, and interest rates have a tendency to rise. Rates are also influenced by government intervention, as governments have frequently used them as a tool of economic management. In general, low interest rates are seen as desirable because they reduce the cost of firms' borrowings and increase consumers' level of discretionary income, especially through lower mortgage costs. However, during periods of unhealthily excessive demand in the economy, governments use high interest rates to try to dampen down demand from firms and consumers.

Overseas trade figures

The monthly overseas trade figures indicate the difference between a country's imports and exports. A lot of attention is given to the 'current account', which measures overseas transactions in goods and services but not capital (discussed further in Chapter 14). In general, a current account surplus is considered good for an economy, suggesting that an economy's production sector is internationally competitive. A detailed analysis of overseas trade figures indicates trends that can often be related to the business cycle and can be used to predict future levels of activity in the economy. At the height of a boom cycle, imports of manufactured goods may rise much faster than corresponding exports, possibly suggesting unsustainable levels of household consumption. Rising imports of capital equipment may give an indication that firms are ready to invest in additional domestic productive capacity following the end of a period of recession.

Exchange rates

The exchange rate is the price of one currency in terms of another (e.g. an exchange rate of £1 = $1.85 means that £1 costs $1.85). A number of factors influence the level of a country's exchange rate, but as an economic indicator the rate is often seen as an indication of the willingness of overseas traders and investors to hold that country's currency. Falling rates of exchange against other currencies may be interpreted as overseas investors losing their confidence in an economy or its government, leading them to sell their currency holdings and thereby depressing its price. The theory of exchange rate determination and the implications for business are discussed in more detail in Chapter 14.

Government borrowing

During periods of economic prosperity, government income streams from taxation tend to be buoyant, while many of its costs in respect of social welfare payment may be reduced, on account of lower levels of unemployment. The reverse tends to be true during periods of economic recession. In this sense, government borrowing is not so much an indicator of the business cycle, but rather a consequence of it. In recent years, UK governments have adopted a 'golden rule' on borrowing – to use borrowing only to finance investment and not to pay for day-to-day spending. Public-sector net debt, expressed as a percentage of gross domestic product (GDP), was 36.3 per cent at the end of October 2007. Debt peaked at 43.8 per cent of GDP in June 1997, its highest since the mid-1980s. The debt ratio then fell steadily as the economy and public-sector finances improved, reaching a low of 29.8 per cent in February 2002. It has since risen, coinciding with a downturn in the economy.

13.4.2 Tracking the business cycle

It is easy to plot business cycles with hindsight. However, businesses are much more interested in predicting the cyclical pattern in the immediate and medium-term future. If the economy is at the bottom of an economic recession, it is the ideal time for firms to begin investing in new productive capacity. In this case, accurate timing of new investment can have two important benefits.

1. Firms will be able to cope with demand as soon as the economy picks up. At the end of previous economic recessions, demand has often initially outstripped the restricted supply, leading many domestic firms and consumers to buy from overseas. Firms have often invested in new capacity only once overseas competitors have built up market share, and possibly created some long-term customer loyalty too.
2. At the bottom of the business cycle, resource inputs tend to be relatively cheap. This particularly affects wage costs and the price of basic raw materials such as building materials. Good timing can allow a firm to create new capacity at a much lower cost than it would incur if it waited until it was well into the upturn, when rising demand would push up resource costs.

Analysing turning points in the business cycle has therefore become crucial to marketers. To miss an upturn at the bottom of the recession can result in a firm missing out on opportunities when the recovery comes to fruition. On the other hand, reacting to a false signal can leave a

Thinking around the subject: **Boom and bust for ever?**

Throughout much of the later 1990s, growth of the US economy seemed almost unstoppable. In Britain it was described as the 'nice' decade (nice was an acronym for 'non inflationary continuous expansion'). Was this the dawn of the 'new economy' in which governments had managed to manipulate economies so effectively that the historical pattern of 'boom and bust' had become a thing of the past? Sadly, by 2007, the UK and US economies seemed to be coming back down to earth. By 2008, it seemed that the whole economy had gone into meltdown as share prices crashed, banks refused to lend to each other and GDP in most countries fell.

What causes such long and sustained booms, such as the UK and US economies had just enjoyed? Can we learn anything from previous booms that might help us to understand future business cycles?

The economic historian Angus Maddison undertook an analysis of the world economy over the past millennium and noted just three periods of rapid advance in incomes per head. The most rapid occurred from 1950 to 1973, when average global real incomes per head rose at a compound annual rate of 2.9 per cent. The other two periods were 1870–1913 and 1973 onwards. In the latter two periods, average real incomes per head rose at a compound average annual rate of 1.3 per cent.

Interestingly, these periods of prolonged economic boom appeared to have three things in common.

1 Each of these periods was associated with a process of rapid international economic integration, with trade and global capital flows growing faster than world output – for example, between 1973 and 1998, world exports rose from 10.5 per cent of world GDP to 17.2 per cent.
2 All three periods were associated with significant catching up by laggard economies with world-leading economies. Between 1870 and 1913, the catching up was by Western Europe, the USA and some former European colonies, on the UK; between 1950 and 1973, it was by Western Europe, Japan and a few small east Asian countries, on the USA; and from 1973, it was by much of the rest of Asia (including China), again on the USA. It was noted that the bigger the gap between the laggards and the leaders, the faster the rate of convergence has been.
3 The final feature of these periods has been a historically unprecedented rate of technological advance, generating rising real incomes per head in the world's most advanced economies.

The declining costs of transport and communications undoubtedly lie behind much of the development of the global economy over the last several centuries. The internet should be seen as just the latest innovation that continues a long historical sequence.

But what about the future? Over the past couple of decades, the world's two most populous countries, China and India, with 2.25 billion people between them (or just under 40 per cent of the total world population), have been growing faster than both the world as a whole and its economic leaders. Should this lead us to believe that economic growth will continue? Can the rate of technological advance be sustained? Between 1973 and 1995, the rate of US growth in labour productivity per hour fell to just under 1.5 per cent a year, from 3 per cent between 1950 and 1973. Even with the development of the internet, are rates of growth in productivity sustainable? Looking ahead, what new scientific and technological advances are likely to sustain a continued growth in productivity?

firm with expensive excess stocks and capacity on its hands. A similar problem of excess capacity can result when a firm fails to spot the downturn at the top of the business cycle.

It is extremely difficult to identify a turning point at the time when it is happening. Following the recession of the early 1990s, there were a number of false predictions of an upturn, some politically inspired by governments keen to encourage a 'feel good' factor ahead of an election. There was a widespread feeling in 1994 that the UK economy had reached a turning point, and many companies began investing in new stock and capacity in expectation of this upturn. When the predicted revival in domestic consumer expenditure failed to materialize, companies in product fields as diverse as cars, fashion clothing and electrical goods were forced to sell off surplus stocks at low prices.

Thinking around the subject: Spending cut as 'feel good' factor fades

What happens to consumers' spending patterns in the shops when recession sets in? After a number of years of sharp rises in house prices, the property market cooled towards the end of 2007, and Christmas 2007 saw many retailers reporting falling sales. It seemed that higher interest rates and a lessening of the 'feel good' factor had led shoppers to be more cautious in their spending. The more expensive retailers insisted that quality would always shine through, even in hard times, evidenced by strong sales figures from the upmarket department store and grocery group John Lewis. On the other hand, discount retailers argued that they would win business from more expensive competitors. The out-of-town shopping centres may claim that they are a natural destination for bargain hunters and will attract families that are watching their pennies. By contrast, their high-street rivals say that cash-strapped families will be spending in dribs and drabs and will make the occasional shopping trip to town but will not have enough discretionary income to justify a visit to an out-of-town centre.

Amid this hype and speculation, a survey by HSBC Bank had identified furniture, cars and DIY goods as the first casualties of a downturn. HSBC estimated that, for every 1 per cent drop in consumer spending, sales of vehicles would drop by 4.64 per cent, furniture and electrical goods by 1.87 per cent, and DIY sales by 1.61 per cent. The sectors most protected are utilities, which should suffer only a 0.32 per cent fall for every 1 per cent drop in spending, newspapers and books (0.32 per cent), and food (0.36 per cent). This is borne out in the financial performance of retailers during the recession of the early 1990s, when companies such as Harveys Furnishings, Dixons and Wickes DIY all suffered falls in profit, while Boots' and WHSmith's profits actually rose.

Despite the analysis of spending patterns during previous recessions, doubts often remain that things will be the same next time around. Could DIY stores actually benefit as people trade down from paying people to do their maintenance and building work for them? And what about food? Could people actually increase their spending as they substitute premium ready-prepared meals for more expensive eating out at restaurants?

Getting out of a trough in the business cycle is very dependent upon the confidence of firms and individuals about the future. Cynics may argue that governments are acting in a politically opportunistic way by talking about the onset of recovery. However, if the government cannot provide any confidence for the future, there is less likelihood of firms and individuals being prepared to invest their resources for the future.

Firms try to react to turning points as closely as possible in a number of ways.

- Companies that are highly dependent on the business cycle frequently subscribe to the services of firms that have developed complex models of the economy and are able to make predictions about future economic performance. Some of these models (such as those developed by major firms of stockbrokers) are general in their application and based on models of the economy used by government policy makers in the Treasury. Specialized models seek to predict demand for more narrowly defined sectors, such as construction.
- Companies can be guided by key lead indicators, which have historically been a precursor of a change in activity levels for the business sector. For a company manufacturing heavy trucks, the level of attendance at major truck trade exhibitions could indicate the number of buyers that are at the initial stages in the buying process for new trucks.
- Instead of placing all their hopes in accurate forecasts of the economy, companies can place greater emphasis on ensuring that they are able to respond to economic change very rapidly when it occurs. At the bottom of the cycle, this can be facilitated by developing flexible production methods – for example, by retaining a list of trained part-time staff that can be called on at short notice, or having facilities to acquire excess capacity from collaborating firms overseas at very short notice. At the top of the cycle, the use of short-term contracts of employment can help a company to downsize rapidly at minimum cost. The development of 'efficient customer response' systems seeks to simplify supply chains so that orders can be fulfilled rapidly without the need to carry large stockholdings.

13.5 Macroeconomic policy

The national economy has been presented as a complex system of interrelated component parts. To free-market purists, the system should be self-correcting and need no intervention from governments. In reality, national economies are not closed entities and equilibrium in the circular flow can be put out of balance for a number of reasons, such as:

- increasing levels of competition in the domestic market from overseas firms that have gained a cost advantage
- changes in a country's ratio of workers to non-workers (e.g. the young and elderly)
- investment in new technology, which may replace firms' expenditure on domestic wages with payments for capital and interest to overseas companies.

Most Western governments have accepted that the social consequences of free market solutions to economic management are unacceptable and they therefore intervene to manage the economy to a greater or lesser extent.

13.5.1 Policy objectives

This section begins by reviewing the objectives governments seek to achieve in their management of the national economy.

Maintaining employment

However unemployment is defined, its existence represents a waste of resources in an economy. Individuals who have the ability and willingness to work are unable to do so because there is no demand from employers for their skills. Workers' services are highly perishable in that, unlike stocks of goods, they cannot be accumulated for use when the economy picks up. Time spent by workers unemployed is an economic resource that is lost for ever. Most developed economies recognize that unemployed people must receive at least the basic means of sustenance, so governments provide unemployment benefit. Rising unemployment increases government expenditure. As well as representing a wasted economic resource, unemployment has been associated with widespread social problems, including crime, alcoholism and drug abuse. High levels of unemployment can create a divided society, with unemployed people feeling cut off from the values of society, while those in employment perceive many unemployed people as being lazy or unwilling to work.

In general, governments of all political persuasions seek to keep unemployment levels low in order to avoid the social and economic problems described above. However, many suspect that governments with right-wing sympathies are more likely to tolerate unemployment on the grounds that a certain amount of unemployment can bring discipline to a labour market that could otherwise give too much economic bargaining power to workers. An excess of labour supply over demand would result in wages paid to workers falling, at least in a free market. This may itself be seen as a desirable policy objective by lowering prices for consumers and increasing firms' competitiveness in international markets.

In their attempts to reduce unemployment, governments must recognize three different types of unemployment, each requiring a different solution.

1. Structural unemployment occurs where jobs are lost by firms whose goods or services are no longer in demand. This could come about through changing fashions and tastes (e.g. unemployment caused by the closure of many traditional UK seaside hotels); because of competition from overseas (for example, many jobs in the textile, shipbuilding and coal-mining industries have been lost to lower-cost overseas suppliers); or a combination of these factors. Where a local or national economy is very dependent upon one business sector and workers' skills are quite specific to that sector, the effects of structural employment can be quite severe, as can be seen in the former shipbuilding areas of Tyneside or coal-mining areas of South Wales. Governments have tackled structural employment with economic assistance to provide retraining for unemployed workers and Regional Assistance Grants to attract new employers to areas of high unemployment.

2. Cyclical unemployment is associated with the business cycle and is caused by a general fall in demand, which may itself be a consequence of lower spending levels by firms. Some business sectors, such as building and construction, are particularly prone to cyclical patterns of demand, and hence cyclical unemployment. The long-term cure for cyclical employment is a

pick-up in demand in the economy, which governments can influence through their macroeconomic policy.

3 Technological unemployment occurs where jobs are replaced by machines; it has had widespread implications in many industrial sectors, such as car manufacture, banking and agriculture. Governments have to accept this cause of unemployment, as failure to modernize will inevitably result in an industry losing out to more efficient competition. For this reason, attempts to subsidize jobs in declining low-technology industries are normally doomed as overseas competitors gain market share, and eventually lead to job losses that are greater than they would have been had technology issues been addressed earlier. Where a low-technology sector is supported by import controls, consumers will be forced to pay higher prices than would otherwise be necessary. Where the goods or services in question are necessities of life, consumers' discretionary income will effectively fall, leading to lower demand for goods and services elsewhere in the economy. Although technological unemployment may be very painful to the individuals directly involved, the increasing use of technology usually has the effect of making necessities cheaper, thereby allowing consumers to demand new goods and services. One manifestation of this has been the growth in services jobs, as consumers switch part of their expenditure away from food and clothing (which have fallen in price in real terms) towards eating out and other leisure pursuits.

Stable prices

Rapidly rising or falling prices can be economically, socially and politically damaging to governments.

Rapidly rising prices (inflation) can cause the following problems.

- For businesses, it becomes difficult to plan ahead when selling prices and the cost of inputs in the future are not known. In many businesses, companies are expected to provide fixed prices for goods and services, which will be made and delivered in the future at unknown cost levels.
- Governments find budgeting difficult during periods of high inflation. Although many government revenues rise with inflation (e.g. value added tax), this may still leave an overall shortfall caused by higher costs of employing government workers and higher contract costs for new capital projects.
- Inflation can be socially divisive as those on fixed incomes (e.g. state pensioners) fall behind those individuals who are able to negotiate wage increases to compensate for inflation. Inflation also discriminates between individuals that own different types of assets. While some physical assets, such as housing, may keep up with inflation, financial assets may be eroded by inflation rates that exceed the rate of interest paid. In effect, borrowers may be subsidized by lenders.
- High levels of inflation can put exporters at a competitive disadvantage. If the inflation level of the United Kingdom is higher than that of competing nations, UK firms' goods will become more expensive to export, while the goods from a low-inflation country will be much more attractive to buyers in the United Kingdom, all other things being equal. This will have an adverse effect on UK producers and on the country's overseas balance of trade (assuming that there is no compensating change in exchange rates).

High levels of inflation can create uncertainty in the business environment, making firms reluctant to enter into long-term commitments. Failure to invest or reinvest can ultimately be damaging for the individual firm as well as the economy as a whole.

This is not to say that completely stable prices (i.e. a zero rate of inflation) are necessarily good for a national economy. A moderate level of price inflation encourages individuals and firms to invest in stocks, knowing that their assets will increase in value. A moderate level of inflation also facilitates the task of realigning prices by firms. A price reduction can be achieved simply by holding prices constant during a period of price inflation. Where price inflation causes uncertainty for firms purchasing raw materials, this uncertainty can often be overcome by purchasing on the 'futures' market. Such markets exist for a diverse range of commodities, such as oil, grain and metals, and allow a company to pay a fixed price for goods delivered at a specified time in the future, irrespective of whether the market price for that commodity has risen or fallen in the meantime.

The opposite of inflation is deflation, and this too can result in social, economic and political problems.

- Individuals and firms that own assets whose value is depreciating perceive that they have become poorer and adjust their spending patterns accordingly. In Britain during the early 1990s, many individuals saw their most important asset – their house – falling in value as part of a general fall in property prices. In extreme cases, individuals felt 'locked' in to their house as they had borrowed more to buy it than the house was currently worth. They therefore had difficulty trading up to a larger house, thereby possibly also creating demand for home-related items such as fitted kitchens. More generally, falling property prices undermined consumer confidence, in sharp contrast to the 1980s when rising house prices created a 'feel good' factor, fuelling spending across a range of business sectors.
- Individuals and firms will be reluctant to invest in major items of capital expenditure if they feel that, by waiting a little longer, they could obtain those assets at a lower price.
- Deflation can become just as socially divisive as inflation. Falling house prices can lead many people who followed government and social pressures to buy their house rather than rent to feel that they have lost out for their efforts.

Economic growth

Growth is a goal shared by businesses and governments alike. It was suggested in Chapter 8 that businesses like to grow, for various reasons. Similarly, governments generally pursue growth in gross domestic product for many reasons.

- A growing economy allows for steadily rising standards of living, when measured by conventional economic indicators. In most Western economies, this is indicated by increased spending on goods and services that are considered luxuries. Without underlying growth in GDP, increases in consumer spending will be short-lived.
- For governments, growth results in higher levels of income through taxes on incomes, sales and profits. This income allows government to pursue socially and politically desirable infrastructure spending, such as the construction of new hospitals or road improvements.

Thinking around the subject: What value on quality of life?

One of the paradoxes of Western developed economies is that, despite increased prosperity, as measured by GDP, people appear to be more stressed and increasingly unhappy. Despite better healthcare, rising incomes and labour-saving devices, surveys repeatedly show people are no happier than they were in the 1950s. This seems far from the economist John Maynard Keynes' prediction in the 1930s that once the 'economic problem' of satisfying basic material needs was achieved, people would not have to work so hard and would devote their spare time to trying to live well.

People appear to be inconsistent in their statements about what would make them happy. They may say that a shorter travelling time to work would make them happy, yet more and more people travel longer distances to their place of employment in order to work harder to earn more money for more goods that, in the end, do not make them feel any better.

One explanation for this apparent paradox is that people compare themselves with others. If everyone is getting richer, people do not get happier – they do so only if they get richer relative to their peers. A BMW 3 series car can be a status symbol only if few people can afford it. When incomes rise and more people can afford the luxury brand, individuals become motivated to work harder to afford an even better model. This mechanism is a driving force behind economic growth, but it has the effect of constantly undermining the underlying benefit of economic progress.

Politicians tend to focus on economic growth figures, but should they instead be concentrating more on indices of happiness? Indices of depression and mental illness have been rising sharply in most Western countries in the past couple of decades, and seem to be closely correlated with economic growth. According to Lord Layard, author of a book on happiness, one in six people in the UK is thought to suffer from some form of mental illness. He has argued that a course of cognitive behavioural therapy can alleviate depression in 60 per cent of cases and typically costs about £1000. Is £1000 spent on relieving someone's depression, so they benefit in terms of happiness, a better investment by the government than £1000 spent increasing the competitiveness and efficiency of manufacturing industry?

- A growing economy creates a 'feel good' factor in which individuals feel confident about being able to obtain employment and subsequently feel confident about making major purchases.

Economic growth in itself may not necessarily leave a society feeling better off, as economic well-being does not necessarily correspond to quality of life. There is growing debate about whether some of the consequences of economic growth, such as increased levels of pollution and traffic congestion, really leave individuals feeling better off. There is also the issue of how the results of economic growth are shared out between members of a society.

Distribution of wealth

Governments, overtly and covertly, have objectives relating to the distribution of economic wealth between different groups in society. In the United Kingdom, the trend since the Second

World War has been for a gradual convergence in the prosperity of all groups, as the very rich have been hit by high levels of income, capital gains and inheritance tax, while the poorer groups in society have benefited from increasing levels of social security payments. During periods of Labour administrations, the tendency has been for taxes on the rich to increase, tilting the distribution of wealth in favour of poorer groups. However, the period of the Conservative governments in the 1980s saw this process put into reverse as high-income groups benefited from the abolition of higher rates of income tax and the liberalization of inheritance taxes. At the same time, many social security benefits were withdrawn or reduced in scope or amount, leaving many lower- or middle-income groups worse off. The post-1997 Labour government has tended to reverse this trend – for example, by introducing a statutory minimum wage and increasing a number of benefits paid to disadvantaged groups.

The effects of government policy objectives on the distribution of income can have profound implications for an organization's marketing activities. During most of the post-war years, the tendency was for mid-market segments to grow significantly. In the car sector, this was associated with the success of mid-range cars such as the Ford Focus and Mondeo. During periods of Labour administration, the sale of luxury cars had tended to suffer. The boom of the late 1980s and early 2000s saw the rapid rise in income of the top groups in society, resulting in a significant growth in luxury car sales. Manufacturers such as BMW, Mercedes-Benz and Jaguar benefited from this trend.

Improving productivity

Productivity growth, alongside high and stable levels of employment, is central to long-term economic performance and rising living standards. Increasing the productivity of the economy has become a key objective of successive UK governments. Government approaches to improving long-term productivity have followed two broad strands: maintaining macroeconomic stability to enable firms and individuals to plan for the future, and implementing microeconomic reforms to remove the barriers that prevent markets from functioning efficiently. These microeconomic reforms address historic weaknesses in competitiveness, investment, research and development, innovation and entrepreneurship.

Stable exchange rate

A stable value of sterling in terms of other major currencies is useful to businesses that are thereby able to accurately predict the future cost of raw materials bought overseas and the sterling value they will receive for goods and services sold overseas. Stable exchange rates can also help consumers – for example, in budgeting for overseas holidays. It is, however, debatable just what the 'right' exchange rate is that governments should seek to maintain (this is discussed further in Chapter 14).

An important contributor to maintaining a stable exchange rate is the maintenance of the balance of payments. Governments avoid large trade deficits, which can have the effect of lowering the exchange rate. From a business perspective, balance of trade surpluses tend to benefit the economy through the creation of jobs, additional economic growth and a general feeling of business confidence. Surpluses created from overseas trade can be used to finance overseas lending and investment, which in turn generate higher levels of earnings from overseas in future years.

Thinking around the subject: Pensions crisis – what pensions crisis?

To many commentators, a crisis is looming as retiring people find that their pensions are not sufficient to allow them to lead the lifestyle that they had expected. But research published by the Future Foundation in 2004 cast some doubt about the scale of any such 'crisis', and highlighted differences in wealth between different age groups. It found that the average amount of wealth for those aged 55 had reached a record £130,000. This was on top of the money they may have in their pension funds. The report challenged the traditional perception of all older people as needy, pointing out that a significant number of middle-aged people were 'over-saving' for their retirement. Increases in home ownership coupled with the house-price boom and greater participation in company and private pensions among those now in their forties and fifties were largely responsible for the emergence of the 'golden generation', with inequalities emerging between affluent, property-owning retirees and those who had low lifetime earnings and lived in rented accommodation.

The study also indicated that although levels of unsecured debt were high among younger people – peaking at £5000 to £6000 for those in their early twenties – by the age of 44 levels of consumer debt declined sharply as individuals prepared for retirement by paying off their loans, and building up their savings and investments. By retirement, very few individuals had any unsecured debt. The study also showed that the transition from being a mortgage-holder to an outright home owner occurs when people are aged between 55 and 59. People from 45 to 59 are the most likely to benefit from inherited wealth.

The Future Foundation had earlier reported that there is likely to be a significant growth in the wealth of the richest 20 per cent of the UK population, largely made up of '60s generation' people who are typically individualistic and liberal minded. Individuals with readily disposable assets (excluding houses and pension policies) of more than £50,000 have been dubbed the 'mass affluent', and their numbers have increased sharply. Typical members of this group are retired professionals, married but with no dependent children, who inherited property from parents, and received windfalls from privatized utilities and building society conversions. They are also likely to have a substantial occupational pension.

For businesses, the attractions of such a group are enormous and many financial services companies, for example, have targeted this group with products that meet their needs. For governments, the emergence of this mass affluent group raises a number of issues. Should policy seek to reduce the imbalances that are inherent in a society where some people have a good pension and others don't? Should this group be excluded from means-tested benefits, simply because they have saved for their retirement, whereas others have either chosen or not been able to save for theirs? Should this group be expected to provide its own healthcare, or should the state continue to provide a service for all, regardless of wealth?

Government borrowing

Government borrowing represents the difference between what it receives in any given year from taxation and trading sources and what it needs in order to finance its expenditure programmes. The difference is often referred to as public sector net borrowing (PSNB). The level of PSNB is partly influenced by political considerations, with right-wing free market advocates favouring a reduced role for the government, reflected in a low level of net borrowing. Advocates of intervention are happier to see the PSNB rise. Government borrowing tends to rise during periods of economic recession and fall during periods of boom. This can be explained by income (especially from income and profits taxes) rising relative to expenditure during a boom, and expenditure (especially on social security benefits) rising relative to income during a recession. Taxes and public spending tend to be quite cyclical, reflecting political ideology and the state of the national and international economy and trends, as discussed earlier (see Figure 13.7). Figure 13.8 shows a breakdown of total government budgeted income and expenditure by category for the year 2008–9.

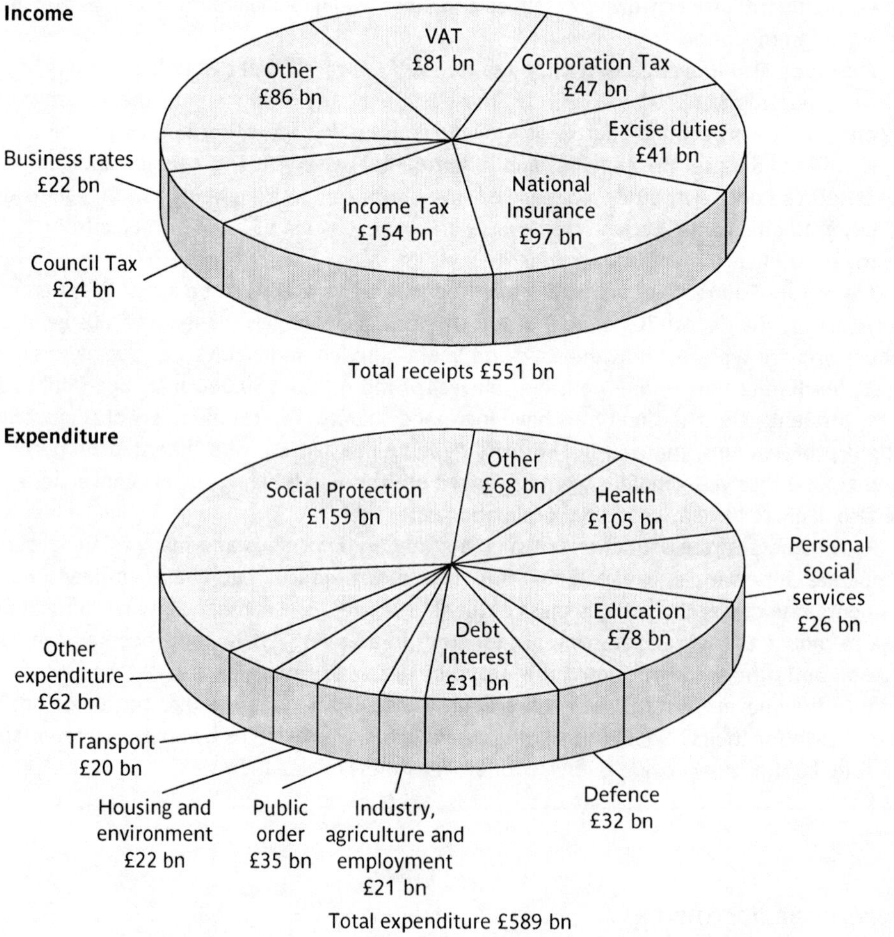

Figure 13.8 A comparison of UK government total revenues and expenditure for 2008–09
Source: based on Treasury Budget Statement, 2008

Policy goals

Possible effects of policy goals	Economy: steady increase in GDP	Employment: maintain full employment	Inflation: maintain stable currency
Economy	–	Full employment contributes to GDP growth	Desire to retain low level of inflation may curb economic growth
Employment	Rapid GDP growth can lead to 'over-full' employment and skill shortages	–	Desire to retain low level of inflation may limit employment opportunities
Inflation	Economic growth may lead to excessive demand relative to supply, resulting in inflation	Full employment can lead to an inflationary spiral of wage increases	–

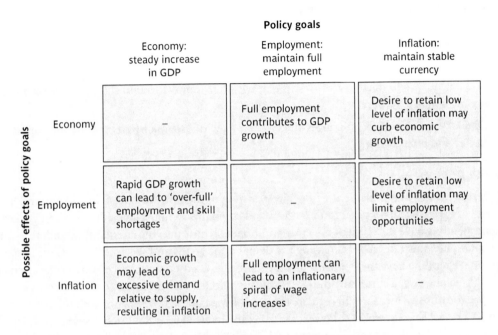

Figure 13.9 Problems in reconciling conflicting economic policy objectives

13.5.2 Government management of the economy

From government policy objectives come strategies by which these policy objectives can be achieved. This is an area where it can be possible to line up a dozen economists and get a dozen different answers to the same problem. Sometimes, political ideology can lead to the strategy being considered to be just as important as the policy objectives, with supporters of alternative strategies showing very strong allegiance to them.

In trying to reconcile multiple objectives, governments invariably face a dilemma in reconciling all of them simultaneously. Of the three principal economic objectives (maintaining employment, and controlling inflation and economic growth), satisfying objectives for any two invariably causes problems with the third (see Figure 13.9). It is therefore common for governments to shift their emphasis between policy objectives for political and pragmatic reasons. However, many surveys of business leaders have suggested that what they consider important above all else is stability in government policy. If the government continually changes the economic goalposts or its economic strategy, businesses' own planning processes can be thrown into confusion.

Sometimes, policy can be implemented in pursuit of one objective, only for adverse side effects to appear, leading to policy being directed to solving this second problem. During much of the 1990s, UK governments put the reduction in inflation as the top economic policy priority and achieved this through high interest rates and a strong value of sterling, among other things. However, high interest rates and a strong pound created recessionary conditions, signified by falling demand, rising unemployment and reduced levels of investment. Resolving these problems then became a priority for government policy.

Two commonly used approaches to economic management can be classified under the headings of:

1 *fiscal policy*, which concentrates on stimulating the economy through changes in government income and expenditure
2 *monetary policy*, which influences the circular flow of income by changes in the supply of money and interest rates.

Fiscal policy

Government is a major element of the circular flow of income, both as tax collector and as a source of expenditure for goods and services and payments to households. Increases in government spending have the effect of injecting additional income into the circular flow and, through the multiplier effect, thereby increasing the demand for goods and services. Reductions in government spending have the opposite effect. Changes in taxation can similarly affect the circular flow of income (e.g. a cut in income tax effectively injects more money into the economy).

The use of fiscal measures to regulate the economy achieved prominence with the economist John Maynard Keynes, whose followers are generally referred to as Keynsians. Keynes developed his ideas as a means of overcoming the high levels of unemployment and falling commodity prices that were associated with the Great Depression of the 1930s. Conventional economics had failed to return resource markets to equilibrium, largely because of rigidities that had built up in markets. Instead, Keynes advocated the use of fiscal policy to increase the level of aggregate demand within the economy. Through a multiplier effect, spending by workers employed on government 'pump-priming' projects would filter through to private-sector suppliers, who would in turn employ further workers, thereby eventually eradicating unemployment. If the economy showed signs of becoming too active, with scarcity in resource markets and rising price levels, suppression of demand through fiscal actions would have the effect of reducing inflationary pressures (Figure 13.10).

In the 1930s, fiscal measures were considered quite revolutionary and resulted in such projects as the electrification of railways and the construction of the National Grid being undertaken, not just for the end result but also for the multiplier benefits of carrying out the construction tasks. More recently, road-building and government-funded construction in general have been used as a regulator of the economy, on account of their high employment content and low levels of initial 'leakage' to imported supplies.

Critics of fiscal policy have argued that fiscal intervention is a very clumsy way of trying to return the economy to equilibrium and a method that achieves temporary rather than permanent solutions to underlying economic problems. Keynsian policies call for bureaucratic civil servants to make quasi-commercial decisions, which they are generally ill equipped to do. There is much evidence of failed fiscal policy at a local level where government grants and tax incentives have been given to attract industry to depressed areas, only for those industries to close down after a few years (e.g. car factories built in Northern Ireland, Merseyside and Glasgow with government grants and tax concessions have often proved to be commercial failures). The Keynesian notion that business cycles could be eliminated by fiscal policies of taxation and

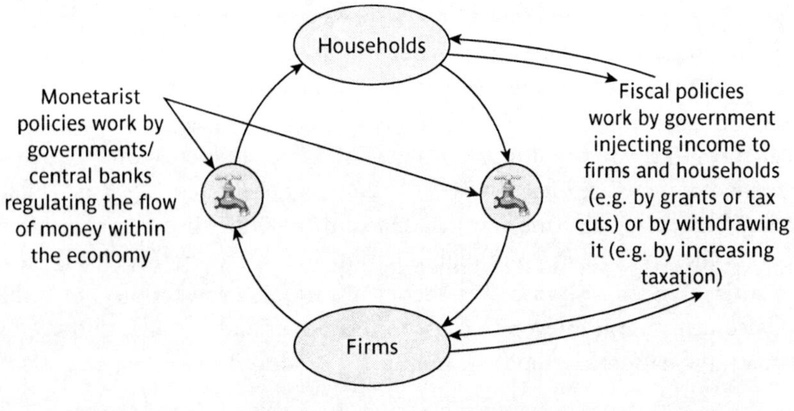

Figure 13.10 The monetarist and fiscal approaches to management of the economy

spending were severely challenged by the 'stagflation' of the late 1970s, when high inflation combined with rising levels of unemployment, despite policy makers seemingly doing all the right things according to Keynes.

Critics of fiscal policy look to monetarist policies as an alternative.

Monetary policy

Although Keynes' general theory influenced the world for decades, it has now largely been replaced by those of Adam Smith, Milton Friedman, Robert Lucas and Paul Samuelson, whose approach advocates change in the volume of money supply to influence aggregate demand in the economy. The basic proposition of monetarism is that government need only regulate the supply of money in order to influence the circular flow of income. From this, adjustments in the economy happen automatically by market forces without the need for intervention by government in the running of business organizations (Figure 13.10). If government wishes to suppress demand in the economy, it would do this by restricting the volume of money in circulation in the economy (e.g. by raising interest rates or restricting the availability of credit). It would do the opposite if it wished to stimulate the economy.

Monetarism appeals to free market purists because of the limited government hands-on intervention that is required. However, governments have found it politically unacceptable to pursue monetarist policies to their logical conclusion. Suppressing demand by controlling the availability of money alone could result in unacceptably high levels of interest rates.

13.5.3 Limitations of government intervention in the national economy

At a practical level, critics of both monetarist and fiscal approaches to economic management have pointed to their failure to significantly influence the long-term performance of an economy. More recently, the fundamental concept of government intervention has been challenged in an emerging body of theoretical and empirical research, which is commonly referred to as rational expectations theory. Proponents of the theory claim that it is too simplistic to regard government economic intervention in terms of simple stimulus–response models. It is naive, for example, to assume that private companies will take an increase in government capital spending as a cue to increase their own productive capacity. Instead, firms rationally assess the likely consequences of government intervention. Therefore, an increase in government capital expenditure may lead to an expectation of eventually higher interest rates and inflation. Faced with this rational expectation, firms may decide to cut back their own expenditure, fearing the consequences for their own business of high inflation and interest rates. This is the opposite of the government's intended response. The theory of rational expectations holds that business people have become astute at interpreting economic signals and, because of this, government's ability to manage the national economy is significantly reduced.

13.5.4 The central bank

A nation's central bank plays an important role in the management of the national economy. In the United Kingdom, the Bank of England has responsibility for regulating the volume of currency in circulation within the economy. Through its market operations, it intervenes to influence the exchange rate for sterling. It also has a supervisory role in respect of privately owned banks within the United Kingdom and acts as a lender of last resort to them. The role of the central bank was demonstrated in 2007 when a shortage of liquidity among commercial banks led to a reduction in banks' willingness and ability to give new loans to their customers. The resulting 'credit crunch' had serious implications for the business sector, which found expansion and the funding of working capital more difficult. This in turn had a generally deflationary effect on national economies, as employment was cut and consumers' spending fell. The US Federal Reserve Bank and the European Central Bank injected additional capital into the banking system in an attempt to lessen the effects of a credit shortage. In the UK, the Bank of England was faced with the prospect of a major bank – Northern Rock – having to close down because it could not obtain ongoing credit to fund mortgages that it had lent to its domestic customers. This would have seriously affected the stability of the banking sector, and the reputation of the City of London as a financial centre, so the Bank of England intervened with emergency loans to the UK banking sector, effectively taking many of the banks into state control.

Countries differ in the extent to which the powers of the central bank are separated from those of government. In the United States, for example, granting the central bank quasi-autonomous status and allowing it freedom to make decisions on monetary policy has for a long time been regarded as a means of guaranteeing prudent management of the money supply against political intervention for possibly short-term opportunistic objectives. Against this, the argument is put forward that central banks should be politically accountable, and should be influenced by the social and political implications of their actions and not just the more narrowly defined monetary ones. In the United Kingdom, the Bank of England has traditionally been influenced by the Treasury, and seen to be effectively a branch of government decision making. However, the incoming Labour government in 1997 decided to give autonomy to much of the Bank's activity through a newly formed Monetary Policy Committee (MPC), made up of a panel of eight economics experts plus the Governor of the Bank of England, who acts as Chair. The MPC is free to set interest rates at a level that it considers prudent and in the best interests of the country. Opinion remains divided on the relative merits of a politically influenced central bank and one that is above sectional political interests. While there is evidence that the MPC has acted with integrity, business leaders have sometimes accused it of being dominated by academics and financiers, who are unable to empathize with the problems faced by businesses. Employers' pressure groups, such as the CBI, feel less able to put pressure on the MPC than they previously could on Treasury ministers.

Throughout the EU, the development of a single currency has placed much greater control over monetary policy in the hands of the European Central Bank (ECB). The power of individual member states to determine their own interest rates and monetary policy is handed over to the ECB, which also handles member-states' currency reserves. The subject of the single European currency is discussed further in Chapter 14.

Case study: **Boom and bust in China?**

Ideas about the best way to manage national economies have changed over time. This chapter has discussed how Keynsian policies have tended to give way to monetarism as the favoured approach used by Western governments to manage their economies. Monetarist policies work best where markets are deregulated, and the effects of monetary change can rapidly be taken on board by firms and households through adjustments to their savings and expenditure. In reality, the economic framework of many emerging economies poses quite a different challenge for economic management, as a study of China demonstrates.

China is an emerging economy with a still relatively underdeveloped financial system. The period from the 1990s has been one of almost continuous boom, with the annual growth rate of GDP averaging about 9 per cent. The country has managed to combine very tight centralized political control by the Communist Party with thriving capitalism in its Special Economic Development Zones. But, by 2007, the strength of the Chinese economy was being questioned by some, and it seemed that the economy could already be overheating. Would this centralized control by the Communist Party be strong enough to prevent a Western-style boom and bust cycle? Or had the country gone down the route of economic liberalization, which laid it open to the type of economic cycle that the West had experienced repeatedly during the previous century?

China traditionally adopted the sort of approach to economic management favoured in the West in the 1950s and 1960s, when currencies were fixed to the dollar and credit controls were used to regulate unemployment and inflation. As a result, China has been less prone to economic or financial crises than those emerging countries where financial liberalization allowed hot money to flow in and out of the country quickly, precipitating a currency crisis that eventually impacts on the rest of the economy.

China has a very high level of savings by households, which are typically invested in government-owned banks. But these state-run banks lend mainly to state-run firms without being subject to market-based disciplines. As a result, there was an evident massive overinvestment in productive capacity, with little regard for return on capital. It seemed that the Chinese economy, where state planning co-exists with market forces, had difficulty in adjusting to change. In the case of privately owned companies, when demand begins to fall (for example, in response to a fall in demand from Western countries), the companies cut their investment. However, in the case of state-controlled companies, political factors can dominate and investment is not necessarily cut back when demand falls.

A feature of Chinese management of the economy has been a fixed exchange rate against major world currencies. Other countries, including the UK, have in the past tried to fix their exchange rates but eventually admitted defeat when market forces overcame their efforts. In the early post-war period, the UK maintained the value of sterling in terms of gold, but was eventually forced to come off the 'Gold standard' when the cost of supporting the currency became too great. A similar fate met the UK Government's attempt to peg the value of the pound to a basket of European currencies within the European Monetary System during the 1980s. The problem for China of seeking to maintain a fixed exchange rate for the renminbi was not downward pressure, but upward pressure. The renminbi had become increasingly strong as a result of China's huge trade surplus.

China's growing trade surplus – $262.2 billion in 2007 – has made its tightly managed currency the target of persistent complaints from the USA and Europe, where politicians claimed that the renminbi gives Chinese exporters an unfair advantage. China was angered by an International Monetary Fund decision in 2006 to establish a new currency surveillance mechanism by which the renminbi was categorized as 'fundamentally misaligned' in value. Although the renminbi was depegged from the US dollar in mid-2005, and rose in value against the dollar during the following two years by 13 per cent, many Western countries continued to complain that the renminbi was too strong.

Inflation in China began to creep up in the mid-2000s, at 4.1 per cent in 2007, up from 2.5 per cent in 2006. This reflected increased pressure on resources, as Chinese manufacturers' seemingly insatiable appetite for raw materials sent prices higher. Even wage costs – traditionally a source of China's competitive advantage – appeared to be edging up. In 2007, the *Financial Times* reported that growth in the financial services sector was being held back by a shortage of skilled staff. Gradual liberalization of the financial services sector, and the appearance of international banks in China, had squeezed the pool of available staff, forcing up wages and making it harder for companies to hire and retain qualified staff (*Financial Times* 2007).

Although the Chinese economic boom of the 1990s was based on export-led growth, by 2005 there were strong signs that the economy was becoming increasingly driven by domestic demand. A growing number of middle-class people were now earning a level of income that triggered a range of purchases that had previously been considered unaffordable luxuries. It seemed that the Chinese business cycle would increasingly be influenced by international and domestic market factors. The export-led nature of the economy had made the country quite dependent on the wealth of those countries that its manufacturers exported to. It was no coincidence that China's period of great economic growth also coincided with a period of great economic prosperity in the United States and Europe. But with the development of the domestic economy, an additional cyclical factor would set in. Faced with falling export orders, domestic employment would be likely to fall, and consequently the number of people earning a level of income that triggers 'luxury' purchases would fall. There would therefore be not only a primary effect of falling exports, but also a secondary effect from falling demand for domestic producers.

Should the outside world have been concerned about China's huge trade surplus and strong currency? Would these issues be corrected by market forces, regardless of the actions of the Chinese Government and international inter-governmental bodies? Over time, China's trade surplus will almost certainly go the same way as Britain's and the USA's once mighty surpluses, which were undermined by a combination of growing demand for imports and inflationary pressures that reduced the competitive edge of the countries' exporters. Some evidence of this beginning to happen was seen in China's overseas trade figures for the final quarter of 2007, when the pace of import growth outstripped that of exports for three consecutive months.

As for the high value of the renminbi, this may in due course fall as domestic inflation rises and the trade surplus is moderated. Experience elsewhere has suggested that, in an international economic environment, it can be very difficult for a country to manage the value of its currency.

QUESTIONS

1 To what extent is it possible, or desirable, for governments to manage a national economy through centralized planning systems of the type that have traditionally been practised in China?

2 Summarize the macroeconomic factors that will influence demand in China for consumer durables such as cars and televisions over the next decade.

3 What are the key consequences for the Chinese economy of the business cycle?

Summary

This chapter has reviewed the structure of national economies and the flow of income between different elements of the economy. Producers, consumers and government are interrelated in the circular flow of income. Business cycles occur because the speed of the circular flow of income temporarily increases or decreases. Although governments seek to limit the magnitude of the business cycle, the cycle can pose problems (and opportunities) for business organizations. The rate at which an organization can grow can be constrained by the rate at which the national economy is growing (**Chapter 8**). This chapter has reviewed economic indicators that companies can read in order to better understand and predict the environment in which they operate. A good information system (**Chapter 4**) should be able to analyse leading indicators of the economy rapidly and effectively.

The state of the economic environment is very much influenced by politicians, and the interaction between the economic and political environments is developed further in **Chapter 2**. This chapter has recognized that the national economic environment is part of the international economic environment and international economic issues are discussed in **Chapter 14.**

Key terms

Accelerator effect (430)
Borrowing (438)
Business cycle (432)
Central bank (452)
Circular flow of income (426)
Competitive cost advantage (423)
Confidence level (436)
Deflation (437)
Disposable income (435)
Economic structure (421)
Exchange rate (438)
Fiscal policy (450)
Gross domestic product (GDP) (433)
Inflation (431)
Injections (427)
Interest rates (437)
Invisibles (423)
Macroeconomic analysis (420)
Models (431)
Monetarism (451)
Monetary Policy Committee (MPC) (452)
Multiplier effect (428)
Public sector net borrowing (PSNB) (447)
Recession (423)
Retail Prices Index (RPI) (436)
Savings ratio (436)
Turning point (438)
Unemployment (434)
Withdrawals (427)

Chapter review questions

1 Identify some of the consequences for a UK vehicle manufacturer of a UK inflation rate of 5 per cent per annum, compared to an EU average of 2 per cent.
2 Contrast the effects of 'tight' fiscal and tight monetary policies on the construction sector.
3 In the context of 'rational expectations' theory, what evidence could you suggest to indicate that business people 'see through' the short-term implications of government economic policies?

Activities

1 You and your friends spend £200 on a night out at a nightclub, drinking beer, having a meal beforehand and taking a taxi home. Use a multiplier model to assess the effects on the local economy. What is the overall benefit locally? How much leaks out of the local economy?
2 Select a service sector from one of the following: restaurants; telecommunications; health services. Identify the effects of inflation on the sector. What steps could organizations take to try to overcome the effects of inflation?
3 Identify your government's current key economic policies. To what extent do you consider these policies to be good for business organizations?

Further Reading

Macroeconomics can be a complex subject and this chapter has reviewed only the key elements of the macroeconomic system. For a fuller discussion of the subject, the following texts are useful.

Blanchard, O. (2008) *Macroeconomics*, Pearson Education.

Burda, M. and Wyplosz, C. (2005) *Macroeconomics: A European Text*, 3rd edn, Oxford, Oxford University Press.

Griffiths, A. and Wall, S. (eds) (2007) *Applied Economics: An Introductory Course*, 11th edn, London, Prentice Hall.

Sawyer, M. (ed.) (2004) *The UK Economy: A Manual of Applied Economics*, Oxford, Oxford University Press.

For a review of the UK economy, the following statistical data are published regularly by the Office for National Statistics.

UK National Accounts (The Blue Book): the principal annual publication for national account statistics, covering value added by industry, the personal sector, companies, public corporations, central and local government.

Economic Trends: a monthly compendium of economic data, which gives convenient access from one source to a range of economic indicators.

References

Eurostat (1998) *Eurostat Yearbook 1998*, Luxembourg, Statistical Office of the European Communities.

Eurostat (2006) *Eurostat Yearbook 2006*, Luxembourg, Statistical Office of the European Communities.

Financial Times (2007) HSBC highlights China staffing woes, London, *Financial Times*, 3 April, p. 15.

Future Foundation (2004) *Asset Accumulation and Lifestage Report*, London, Future Foundation.

ILO (2008) *Global Employment Trends*, Geneva, International Labour Organization.

Wood, P.A. (1987) 'Producer services and economic change, some Canadian evidence', in *Technological Change and Economic Policy*, K. Chapman and G. Humphreys (eds), London, Blackwell.

Chapter 3

The Social and Demographic Environment

CHAPTER OBJECTIVES

This chapter will explain:

- how changing attitudes and lifestyles affect business organizations
- the changing demographic composition of society and its effects on business organizations
- change in family composition and household structure
- the effects on business of greater ethnic diversity
- the two-way relationship between society and business

3.1 Social change and its effects on business organizations

Consider the following recent social changes that have occurred in the UK and many other Western countries:

- an increasing ethnic diversity, which is manifested in Asian and Indian communities in many towns of the UK
- a rising divorce rate, which is manifested in a rising number of single-person households and single-parent families
- a desire for instant gratification, manifested in individuals' desire to obtain goods and services 24 hours a day
- a workforce whose cultural diversity brings new challenges and opportunities to the workplace.

These are typical of changes that have concentrated the minds of business organizations as they attempt to supply goods and services that are of continuing relevance to the population. Companies that continue to base their efforts on the assumption of a typical white family unit, which is prepared to wait for a long time before a product is delivered, may find themselves targeting an increasingly small market segment.

As a result of social change, we have seen many goods and services become redundant, as they no longer satisfy a population whose needs, attitudes, values and behaviour have changed. The following are typical of goods and services that have disappeared or been greatly reduced in sales as a result of social change.

- Traditional drinking pubs have reduced in number as patterns of social relationships change and individuals seek more family-friendly pubs, which serve food in a pleasant environment.
- The number of butchers' shops has been sharply reduced as consumers opt for a healthier lifestyle, based on foods that do not contain meat.
- Local and regional newspapers have seen declining sales as people increasingly turn to web-based news providers and social networking sites for their source of news and views.

On the other hand, social change has resulted in tremendous growth for some goods and services.

- Microwave cookers and portable televisions have benefited from a move towards 'cellular' households, in which each member of the family operates in a much more independent manner than has traditionally been the case.
- Gyms and leisure facilities have benefited from individuals' increasing concern for health and personal fitness.
- Sales of organically produced food have increased as more consumers become suspicious about the effects of intensive farming and additives in their food.

It is very easy for an individual to take for granted the way they live. Furthermore, young people may imagine that people have always lived their lives that way. From one year to the next, social change may seem quite imperceptible, but when life today is compared with what it was like ten

Thinking around the subject: Government's official shopping basket reflects social change

New evidence of changing lifestyles sometimes emerges from the most unlikely sources. One interesting insight comes from the regular updating of the UK's Retail Prices Index (RPI), which is used by many organizations as a benchmark for inflation in the national economy. In principle, it is quite easy to take a typical shopping basket of consumers' purchases and to monitor what happens to the price of this basket from one year to the next. A problem occurs, however, because the contents of the basket are constantly changing as consumers' preferences and spending patterns change. For example, the proportion of the average consumer's expenditure allocated to food has reduced over time, leading to the RPI weighting for food dropping from over a third in 1956 to 10.5 per cent in 2007.

In February 2007 the Office for National Statistics (ONS), which records the RPI (and also the related Consumer Prices Index (CPI)), carried out its annual updating of the average shopping basket, based on a survey of around 120,000 separate price quotations collected each month, covering some 650 representative consumer goods and services. The 2007 updating included a number of new items in the average shopping basket, partly reflecting the emergence of new products that did not exist in earlier baskets. New items included portable electric fans and mobile phone downloads. Three high-technology goods were introduced to the basket for the first time: DVD recorders, satellite navigation systems and DAB radios. In addition, credit card charges and mortgage arrangement fees were brought into the basket to increase the coverage of the heavily weighted financial services class. To make way for these new items, other items were removed from the basket, again reflecting changes in consumer spending patterns. For example, mail order developing and printing of photographic film was replaced with digital photographic processing. Car CD player/autochangers, children's wellington boots and decorative plant pots also left the basket, as it was judged that although these items continue to be sold, price changes for these goods remain adequately represented by those items that remain in the basket. Previously, the index had removed doorstep-delivered milk – a victim of the steady increase in supermarket sales of milk from the shelves – and the household bread bin. The disappearance of the bread bin may reflect a change in habits away from buying standard loaves of bread in favour of a desire to experiment with specialist bread such as baguettes.

It is not just changes in the actual products we buy that need to be reflected in the RPI index, but also how we buy them. The lowering of average grocery prices, which occurred as buyers moved from corner stores to supermarkets, and the lower prices available for many electrical goods bought online, are reflected in changes in the way the ONS samples points of purchase.

There still remains the problem that one person's shopping basket may be quite different to the next person's. Although the ONS weights its shopping basket according to the changing size of each population age group, an elderly person without a car and no satellite navigation system may think that the RPI – on which their annual pension increase is based – does not reflect their own spending habits.

years ago, noticeable changes begin to appear. If comparisons are made with 20 or 50 years ago, it may seem as if two entirely different societies are being compared. Simply by looking at an old movie, major differences become apparent, such as attitudes to the family, leisure activities and the items commonly purchased by consumers.

Change in society is also brought about by changes in its composition. Much recent attention has been given in many Western European countries to the effects of an ageing population on society. Some commentators have seen major problems ahead (or, for some, opportunities) as an increasingly large dependent population has to be kept by a proportionately smaller economically active group in society. Some see this as challenging basic attitudes that individuals have towards the community and the family. At the very least, business organizations should be concerned about the effects of demographic change on patterns of demand for goods and services, and the availability of a workforce to produce those goods and services.

It is bad enough not to recognize social change that has happened in the past. It is much worse to fail to read the signs of social change that is happening now and to understand the profound effect this could have on the goods and services that people will buy in the future.

This chapter begins by examining what can loosely be described as a society's social and cultural values. These are what make people in the United Kingdom different from how they were 20 years ago, or different from how people in Algeria or Indonesia are today. Social and cultural differences between countries focus on differences in attitudes, family structures and the pattern of interaction between individuals. Business organizations should understand the consequences of what may appear nebulous social changes for the types of things that consumers are likely to buy in the future.

3.1.1 Social influences on behaviour

The way an individual behaves as a consumer is a result of their unique physical and psychological make-up on the one hand, and a process of learning from experience on the other. The debate about the relative importance of nature and nurture is familiar to social psychologists. This chapter is concerned with the effects of learned behaviour on individuals' buying behaviour.

An individual learns norms of behaviour from a number of sources (see Figure 3.1):

- the dominant cultural values of the society in which they live
- the social class to which they belong
- important reference groups, in particular the family.

Culture can be seen as an umbrella within which social class systems exist and reference groups exert influence on individuals or groups of individuals. The following sections consider the effects of each of these influences.

3.2 The cultural environment

The *Oxford English Dictionary* defines culture as a 'trained and refined state of understanding, manners and tastes'. Central to culture is the concept of the learning and passing down of values

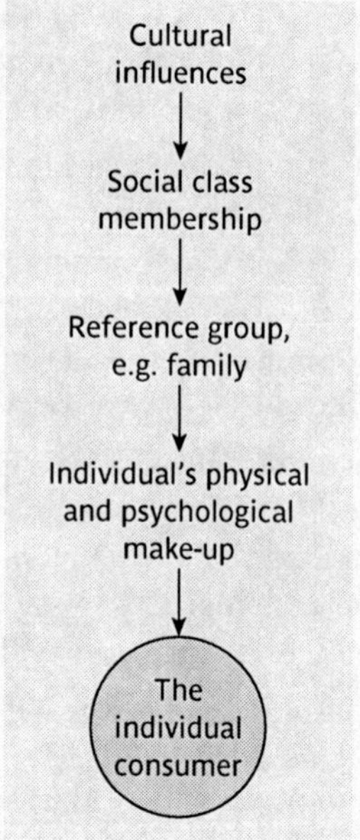

Figure 3.1 **Factors affecting the socialization process**

from one generation to the next. A culture's values are expressed in a complex set of beliefs, customs and symbols, which help to identify individuals as members of one particular culture rather than another. The following are typical manifestations of cultural identity.

- Shared attitudes – for example, towards the role of women or children in society.
- Abstract symbols and rituals, which can be seen in historic cultures by such events as religious practices, harvest festivals and maypole dancing, and in more modern times by support for local football teams.
- Material manifestations – for example, the literature and art of a culture, or the style of decoration used in private houses.

It is common to distinguish between 'core' and 'secondary' cultural values.

- Core cultural values tend to be very enduring over time. In Britain, for example, the acceptance of monogamy represents a core belief and one that very few people would disagree with.
- Secondary cultural values are more susceptible to change over time. While there may be a core belief in the family, this does not prevent changes in attitudes towards the form that families should take, as is evident from the growing incidence of divorce and the increasing number of single-parent families. It is shifts in these secondary cultural values that are particularly important for business organizations to monitor.

3.2.1 Effects of culture on business organizations

It is crucial for business organizations to fully appreciate the cultural values of a society, especially where an organization is seeking to do business in a country that is quite different from its own. The possible consequences of failing to do this can be illustrated by the following examples.

- When McDonald's entered the UK market, it initially found hostility from the British, who did not appreciate the brash, scripted, 'Have a nice day' mentality of its staff. The company subsequently adapted its style of business to cater for British preferences.
- The UK retailer Sainsbury's failed in its attempt to replicate supermarkets on the British model in Egypt, a country that had no tradition of supermarket shopping. Worse still, at the height of a Palestinian uprising, a story went round that Sainsbury's had Jewish connections, a rumour encouraged by local shopkeepers. After just two years, and losses of over £100 million, Sainsbury's pulled out of Egypt.
- Many UK businesses have set up operations overseas and gone about business in an open and above-board manner, only to find that corruption and the use of bribes is endemic in the local culture and essential for business success.

Cultural sensitivity affects many aspects of business planning and operations.

- Understanding processes of buyer behaviour (for example, the role of men in buying routine household goods varies between countries, leading sellers to adjust their product specification and promotional efforts to meet the needs of the most influential members of the buying unit).
- Some products may be unacceptable in a culture and must be adapted to be culturally acceptable (e.g. the original formulation for the McDonald's 'Big Mac' is unacceptable in Muslim cultures).
- Symbols associated with products, such as the design and colour of packaging, may be unacceptable in some cultures (e.g. the colour white is associated with pureness in most Western European cultures, but in other cultures it is associated with bereavement).
- Distribution channel decisions are partly a reflection of cultural attitudes and not just economics and land use. Retailers and wholesalers may be seen as a vital part of a culture's social infrastructure and individuals may feel a sense of loyalty to their suppliers. Although it may appear economically rational for shoppers to buy in bulk, small local shops opening for long hours may be seen by consumers as an extension of their pantry.
- Advertising messages do not always translate easily between different cultures, reflecting culturally influenced standards of what is considered decent and appropriate.
- Methods of procuring resources can vary between cultures. In some Far Eastern countries, it is essential to establish a trusting relationship with a buyer before the buyer will even consider placing an order. Sometimes, it is essential to personally know the key decision maker or to offer a bribe, which is considered routine business practice in some cultures.
- Obtaining good-quality staff can be influenced by cultural factors. The notion of punctual timekeeping and commitment to the employer is often an unfamiliar set of values in

cultures where commitment to the family comes very strongly first and timekeeping has little meaning.

Even in home markets, business organizations should understand the processes of gradual cultural change and be prepared to satisfy the changing needs of consumers. The following are examples of contemporary cultural change in Western Europe and the possible business responses.

- Women are increasingly being seen as equal to men in terms of employment expectations and household responsibilities. According to the Office for National Statistics, in 2006 women represented 53 per cent of graduates in the UK and 45 per cent of the workforce (compared with 37 per cent in 1971). Examples of business responses include variants of cars designed to appeal to career women, and ready prepared meals, which save time for busy working women who need to juggle work, family and social roles.
- Greater life expectancy is leading to an ageing of the population and a shift to an increasingly 'elderly' culture. This is reflected in product design, which reflects durability rather than fashionability.
- Leisure is becoming an increasingly important part of many people's lives, and businesses have responded with a wide range of leisure-related goods and services.
- Increasing concern for the environment is reflected in a variety of 'green' consumer products.

3.2.2 Cultural convergence

There has been much recent discussion about the concept of cultural convergence, referring to an apparent decline in differences between cultures. It has been argued that basic human needs are universal in nature and, in principle, capable of satisfaction with universally similar solutions. Companies have been keen to pursue this possibility in order to achieve economies of scale in producing homogeneous products for global markets. There is some evidence of firms achieving this – for example, the worldwide success of Coca-Cola and McDonald's. In the case of fast food, many Western chains have capitalized on the deep-seated habits in some Far Eastern countries of eating from small hawkers' facilities by offering the same basic facility in a clean and hygienic environment.

The desire of a subculture in one country to imitate the values of those in another culture has also contributed to cultural convergence. This is nothing new. During the Second World War, many individuals in Western Europe sought to follow the American lifestyle, and nylon stockings from the United States became highly sought-after cultural icons by some groups. The same process is at work today in many developing countries, where some groups seek to identify with Western cultural values through the purchases they make. Today, however, improved media communications allow messages about cultural values to be disseminated much more rapidly. The development of satellite television and the internet hastens the process of creating shared worldwide values.

It can be argued that business organizations are not only responding to cultural convergence, they are also significant contributors to that convergence. The development of global brands backed up by global advertising campaigns has contributed to an increasing uniformity in goods and services offered throughout the world. Many commentators have described an

Thinking around the subject: New magazines for new men?

Until a few years ago, the shelves of most newsagents would have been loaded with many general interest women's magazines (e.g. *Woman's Own*, *Woman's Weekly*, *Cosmopolitan*), but very few general interest magazines aimed at men. Why? Some cynics might have argued that women were more likely to have spare time at home and could sit around reading, while 'busy' men were out at work, in the pub or watching sport, and did not have time to read magazines. There may just have been a bit of truth in this, but the main reason has been that women's magazines have been popular with advertisers, who generally provide a high proportion of total income for a magazine publisher. In the traditional household, it has been women who have made decisions on a wide range of consumer goods purchases. Advertising the benefits of toothpaste, yoghurt or jam would have been lost on most men, who had little interest in which brand was put in front of them and may have played a very minor role in the buying process.

Take a look at the news-stand now and it will carry a wide range of men's general interest magazines, such as *FHM*, *Maxim*, *Nuts* and *Zoo*. Why have they suddenly mushroomed in number and in readership? Again, the answer lies in their attractiveness to advertisers. Talk of a male identity crisis may have spurred some sales. More importantly, it is evident that men are now involved in a much wider range of purchasing decisions than ever before, and therefore likely to be of much greater interest to advertisers. While some 'new men' may be taking a more active interest in the household shopping, many more are marrying later and indulging themselves in personal luxuries, an option that is less readily available to their married counterparts. With support from advertisers, the leading men's magazine in the UK, *FHM*, had a circulation of 371,263 copies per issue in 2006 (Audit Bureau of Circulation). In the late 1990s, it had even overtaken the leading women's monthly magazine, *Cosmopolitan*, although competition from the internet and a proliferation of men's titles, such as *Zoo* and *Nuts*, resulted in *Cosmopolitan* taking back the lead – in 2006, it had a circulation of 460,276. Advertising to men still looked very attractive.

'MTV' generation that views global satellite television channels, and who converge in their attitudes to consumption. The internet is contributing to this process of apparent global homogenization.

Critics of the trend towards cultural convergence have noted individuals' growing need for *identity* in a world that is becoming increasingly homogenized. Support for regional breakaway governments (e.g. by the Kurdish and Basque people) may provide some evidence of this. During the Iraq war in 2003, many consumers in Arab countries used purchases of Muslim products to identify themselves with an anti-American cause. Many Western service brands have become despised by some groups as symbols of an alien identity. Banks in many Muslim countries have reported increased interest in syariah-based banking services, and many UK banks have developed bank accounts specifically targeted at Muslims.

In some countries, cultural convergence has been seen as a threat to the sense of local identity that culture represents. Governments have therefore taken measures in an attempt to slow down this process of cultural homogenization. This has achieved significance in France

Figure 3.2 How can Coca-Cola be sure that its brand name and product offer will be the object of aspiration for the dominant groups in a country, rather than a hated symbol of an alien system of capitalism? Coca-Cola is often at the top of league tables of global brands, and most people in the world have access to the company's beverages. But Coca-Cola has been challenged by numerous functionally similar cola drinks, which seek to appeal to consumers' need for cultural identity. By rejecting Coca-Cola in favour of Mecca Cola (shown here), individuals have made a statement about their sense of cultural identity. Mecca Cola has donated 10 per cent of its profits to fund humanitarian projects in Palestine, and a further 10 per cent to charities in the countries in which the drink is sold – mainly Arab countries and European countries with significant Arab communities. An activist stance has been reflected in the company's slogan, which has appeared on all its products: 'Shake your Conscience', and in the company's pledge to support 'associations who work towards peace in the world and especially for peace in the conflict between Palestinians and fascist Zionist apartheid'.

where legislation requires the use of the French language – an important means of creating identity for any culture – in packaging and advertising for products.

3.2.3 Multicultural, multi-ethnic societies

The United Kingdom, like many Western countries, is increasingly becoming a culturally and ethnically diverse society (see Figure 3.3). By ethnicity, we are talking about groups based on their common racial, national, tribal, religious, linguistic or cultural origin. An important reason for increasing ethnic diversity in most Western countries is the growing numbers of immigrant people from overseas cultures, attracted by, among other things, economic prosperity in the host country, and motivated to leave their native country by the relative lack of available opportunities. Immigrants can bring with them a distinctive set of cultural and religious values, and adapting to the values of the host country can be a difficult task. In some countries, church and state may be closely linked, leading to an expectation that religious principles should be the basis for governance. For some religious groups, the power of a religious leader transcends any government institution. A lack of understanding from members of the host

Religion	Number (000)	% of total population	% of non-Christian religious population
Christian	37,046	71.8	
Muslim	1,547	2.8	51.9
Hindu	552	1.0	18.3
Sikh	329	0.6	11.0
Jewish	260	0.5	8.7
Buddhist	144	0.3	4.9
Others	89	0.3	5.2
All non-Christian religions			100.00
No religion	7,274	15.1	
Not stated	4,453	7.8	
Total	**57,100**	**100.00**	

Figure 3.3 Population of Great Britain by religion, 2001
Source: based on Census of Population, 2001

country may cause some immigrants to be seen as arrogant, lazy or lacking in humour by the standards of the host culture, but they may nevertheless be perfectly normal by the standards of their home culture. Where members of ethnic minorities are concentrated into distinct areas (within the UK this occurs in certain suburbs of London, Leicester and Bradford), their traditional cultural values may be strengthened and prolonged by mutual support and the presence of an infrastructure (such as places of worship and specialized shops) to support the values of the culture.

The presence of concentrations of ethnic subcultures in a town presents opportunities for businesses that cater for distinctive cultural preferences. In many towns catering for people of Asian origin, these include halal butchers, bureaux for arranged marriages and travel agents specializing in travel to India and Pakistan. In some cases, completely new markets have emerged specifically for minority ethnic groups, such as the market for black sticking plasters. It has sometimes proved difficult for established businesses to gain access to immigrant segments. Many established companies have not adequately researched the attitudes and buying processes of these groups, with the result that, in markets as diverse as vegetables, clothing and travel, ethnic minorities have supported businesses run by fellow members of their minority group.

A report entitled *Marketing to Ethnic Minorities*, published by Interfocus in 2001, identified a number of issues, such as differing household structures and value systems, that pose new challenges and opportunities for businesses arising from increasing cultural diversity. The report found that consumers from these groups are typically younger, more likely to own a business than others, tend to live in large urban centres – creating opportunities for cost-effective marketing – and are close-knit, making word-of-mouth recommendation a powerful force. However, they tend to be very fragmented, with intergenerational differences, requiring that businesses commission professional research to gain in-depth understanding of their target markets.

Members of ethnic minorities have contributed to the diversity of goods and services available to consumers in the host country. The large number of Indian restaurants in Britain, for example, can be attributed to the entrepreneurial skills of immigrants, while many food products (such as kebabs and Chinese food) have followed the example of immigrants.

Immigrants have tended to be of working age and have filled a vital role in providing labour for the economy. In 2004, the labour market in many parts of Britain was overheating, with labour shortages and a lack of people prepared to work in jobs involving unpleasant working conditions or anti-social hours. The opening of the UK labour market to migrants from the new EU member states of Eastern and Central Europe helped to alleviate these shortages with a supply of hard-working and flexible workers. Some ethnic groups have brought vital entrepreneurial skills to the economy, often at a high cost economically and socially to the less developed countries they have left.

It must be recognized that there are great differences between ethnic subgroups. Entrepreneurship is much greater among the Chinese group, where 21 per cent were classified as self-employed by the Office for National Statistics in the Annual Population Survey 2004, compared to 15 per cent for white Irish, 12 per cent for white British, but less than 10 per cent for mixed or black groups. The age structure of minority ethnic groups gives rise to differences in the proportion that are dependent. Within the Bangladeshi group, for example, 42 per cent are under 16 (compared to a figure of 20 per cent for whites), while only 20 per cent are in the economically most active group of 35–64 (compared with 37 per cent for whites). These figures are reversed for the Chinese community, where only 17 per cent are under 16 and 38 per cent are between 35 and 64.

3.2.4 Social class

In most societies, divisions exist between groups of people in terms of their access to privileges and status within that society. In some social systems, such as the Hindu caste system, the group that an individual belongs to exerts influence from birth and it is very difficult for the individual to change between groups. Western societies have class systems in which individuals are divided into one of a number of classes. Although the possibilities for individuals to move between social classes in Western countries are generally greater than the possibilities of movement open to a member of a caste system, class values tend to be passed down through families. The very fact that it is seen as possible to move classes may encourage people to see the world in a different way from that which has been induced in them during their years of socialization.

While some may have visions of a 'classless' society that is devoid of divisions in terms of status and privileges, the reality is that divisions exist in most societies, and are likely to persist in some form. It is common in Western societies to attribute individuals with belonging to groups that have been given labels such as 'working class' or 'middle class'. This emotional language of class is not particularly helpful to businesses that need a more measurable basis for describing differences within society, and later in this chapter we will look at some of the ways class is measured.

Why do business organizations need to know about the social grouping to which an individual belongs? The basic idea of a classification system is to identify groups that share common attitudes and behaviour patterns, and access to resources. This can translate into similar spending

Thinking around the subject: How far can halal food go?

One consequence of the increasing cultural diversity in the UK is the emergence of a market in halal fresh meat and processed foods, which Mintel estimated to be worth £460 million in 2001 (Mintel 2002). Halal means 'lawful and permitted', and, in food terms, products are not halal if they contain alcohol, any part of a pig, carnivorous animal meat or blood. Foods are also not halal if meat has not been slaughtered according to Islamic law.

The main market for halal food in the UK is the estimated 1.9 million Muslims who account for about 3.2 per cent of the population. However, Muslims have a varied ethnic background and in Britain are mainly drawn from Pakistan, Bangladesh, India and the Middle East, each with their own food preferences. Those from the Indian subcontinent are known to prefer hot, spicy food, while those from the Middle East have blander tastes, similar to those of native British people.

For butchers, who have had a hard time following a series of food scares and an increase in the number of vegetarian consumers, the emergence of the halal market is a welcome opportunity. Mintel estimated that halal fresh meat accounted for 11 per cent of the value of all meat sales in the UK, but it appeared that just 3.2 per cent of the population was accounting for a disproportionate volume of halal meat sales.

Small independent butchers' shops have dominated halal meat sales. There have been problems in verifying the authenticity of halal meat, so trust is an important element of fresh meat supply, and it is likely that independent butchers' shops are used regularly as consumers have learned to trust the meat that they buy there. This is particularly true of older and more traditional Asian shoppers, who are much less likely to use supermarkets. Mintel observed that a large proportion of Muslim women play the traditional role of home-maker, which means that they have more time available for shopping in independent outlets – particularly those where their native language is spoken – and for preparing meals from scratch. However, it is unlikely that third-generation Muslims onwards will be satisfied with such a lifestyle. Third-generation Muslim women are more likely to have careers, and their busy lifestyles are likely to lead them to seek the convenience of one-stop shopping at supermarkets and online rather than using specialist small suppliers. They are also more likely to seek the convenience of ready prepared meals, rather than cooking from raw ingredients as their parents did.

Already, halal brands have emerged, including Tahira (frozen, chilled, ambient foods) and Maggi (sauces and seasonings). Could other convenience food retailers further develop this market? Fast-food chains such as McDonald's are already experienced in catering for Muslim consumers in countries such as Malaysia – would there be a market for a halal burger in the UK?

Another intriguing question is whether the cultural traditions of Muslims may spread to the population generally. After all, Indian and Chinese restaurants now appeal to the UK population at large, rather than the narrow groups they initially served. Could halal food become mainstream rather than a niche market? One opportunity arises among the 3.4 million vegetarians in the UK, to whom meat-free halal foods are ideally placed to appeal.

patterns. There are, for example, many goods and services that are most heavily bought by people who can be described as 'working class', such as the *Daily Star* newspaper and betting services, while others are more often associated with 'upper-class' purchasers, such as Jaguar cars, the *Financial Times* and investment management services.

Businesses need to take note of the changing class structure of society. As the size of each class changes, so market segments, which are made up of people who are similar in some important respects, also change. In the United Kingdom during the 1960s and 1970s it has been observed that more people were moving into the 'middle classes'. The effects of taxation, the welfare state and access to education had flattened the class structure of society. For car manufacturers, this translated into a very large demand for mainstream middle-of-the-road cars. However, during the 1980s and 1990s, both the upper and lower classes tended to grow in what had become a more polarized society. In terms of car sales, there was a growing demand for luxury cars such as Jaguars and BMWs at one end of the market and cheaper cars such as Kias at the other.

3.3 The family

The family represents a further layer in the socialization process. It is important that business organizations understand changes in family structures and values because change in this area can impact on them in a number of ways. Consider the following impacts of families on business organizations.

- Many household goods and services are typically bought by family units – for example, food and package holidays. When family structures and values change, consumption patterns may change significantly.
- The family is crucial in giving individuals a distinctive personality. Many of the differences in attitude and behaviour between individuals can be attributed to the values that were instilled in them by their family during childhood. These differences may persist well into adult life.
- The family has a central role as a transmitter of cultural values and norms, and can exercise a strong influence on an individual's buying behaviour.

3.3.1 Family composition

Many people still live with the idea that the typical family comprises two parents and an average of 2.4 children. In many Western European countries this is increasingly becoming a myth, with single-person and single-parent households becoming increasingly common. The following factors have contributed to changes in family composition:

- an increasing divorce rate, with about one-third of all marriages in the United Kingdom now ending in divorce
- marriage and parenthood are being put off until later; the average age of first marriage has increased by around five years since 1961, to 30 for men and 28 for women (based on UK 2001 Census)

- the gap between people leaving school, settling down to get married and starting a family has grown steadily, and young people are now enjoying freedom from parental responsibility for longer than ever before
- more people are living on their own outside a family unit, either out of choice or through circumstances (e.g. divorce, widowhood)
- family role expectations have changed with an increasing number of career-orientated wives.

Changes in family composition have led firms to develop new goods and services that meet the changing needs of families, such as crèche facilities for working mothers and holidays for single parents. Advertising has increasingly moved away from portraying the traditional family group, which many individuals may have difficulty in identifying with. Recent examples that portray the new reality include an advertisement for McDonald's in which a boy takes his separated father to one of the company's restaurants, and one for Volkswagen in which a career-minded woman puts her car before her husband.

3.3.2 Family roles

As well as changing in composition, there is evidence of change in the way that families operate as a unit. Many household products have traditionally been dominated by either the male or female partner, but these distinctions are becoming increasingly blurred as family roles change.

A report by the Future Foundation showed that, in the UK, the proportion of couples in which the man has the final say in big financial decisions has fallen from 25 per cent in 1993 to 20 per cent in 2003 (Future Foundation 2004). This reflects an increase in the number of couples who claim that they have an equal say from 65 per cent to 69 per cent. The data also show that the number of couples where the female partner has the final say has risen from 10 per cent to 12 per cent. Men still make the major financial decisions in 40 per cent of couples aged over 65. Conversely, in couples under the age of 35, the woman is more likely to control major financial decisions. However, women still have the main responsibility for shopping in 47 per cent of couples, compared with 11 per cent of couples where men do it.

The scope for individual freedom of expenditure has increased significantly, and increasing affluence has widened the scope for discretionary spending in general. There are a number of markets, such as clothing, that benefit from this independent spending, although this finding is not consistent across the different age groups. Among couples aged over 65, a majority of men said their partner has at least an equal influence in the clothes they wear. This is lower in couples aged under 45, with only 19 per cent of men claiming that their partner mainly chooses their clothes for them. On the other hand, none of the women surveyed by Future Foundation said that their partner always chooses their clothes and a very small number indicated any significant influence.

The Future Foundation also highlighted a number of other changes in roles within family units.

- Cooking is still dominated by women, although men are increasingly sharing the task of preparing the main evening meal.

- Although men may say they believe household tasks should be shared, only 1 per cent say they always do the washing and ironing. Household cleaning is carried out mainly by women in nearly two-thirds of households, and this proportion has been falling gradually over the last two decades.
- The view that a man's task is to earn money, while a wife's job is to look after the family and home, has fallen consistently over the last decade.
- More women are stating that work and careers are more important than home and children.

There has been much debate about the fragmentation of families into **cellular households** in which family members essentially do their own activities independently of other members. This is reflected in individually consumed meals rather than family meals, and leisure interests that are increasingly with a family member's peer groups rather than other family members. Businesses have responded to the needs of the cellular household with products such as microwave cookers and portable televisions, which allow family units to function in this way. It can also be argued, however, that new product developments, combined with increasing wealth, are actually responsible for the fragmentation of family activities. The microwave cooker and portable television may have lessened the need for families to operate as a collective unit, although these possible consequences were not immediately obvious when they were launched. The family unit can expect to come under further pressures as new products, such as online entertainment and information services, allow individual members to consume in accordance with their own preferences rather than the collective preferences of the family.

Thinking around the subject: **Pocket-money pester power packs a punch**

What role do children play in the purchase of the goods and services that they ultimately consume? In the UK, children aged just 7 to 14 years old receive an estimated £1.5 billion in pocket money and financial handouts, according to a report by Mintel (Mintel 2004). There has been considerable debate about the extent of 'pester power', where parents give in to the demands of children. Increasingly, advertisers are aiming their promotional messages over the heads of adults and straight at children. The ethics of doing this have been questioned by many, and some countries have imposed restrictions on television advertising of children's products. However, even with advertising restrictions, companies have managed to get through to children in more subtle ways – for example, by sponsoring educational materials used in schools and paying celebrities to endorse their products. When it comes to items such as confectionery and toys, just what influence do children exert on the purchase decision? And when football clubs deliberately change their strip every season, is it unethical for the clubs to expect fanatical children to pester their parents to buy a new one so that they can keep up with their peer group? And does the role of children in influencing purchase decisions say a lot about the structure of a society? In some cultures, children should be 'seen but not heard', but in others children may be treated as responsible adults from a much earlier age.

3.4 Reference groups

The family is not the only influence on an individual as they develop a view of the world. Just as individuals learn from and mimic the values of parents and close relations, so too they also learn from and mimic other people outside their immediate family. Groups that influence individuals in this way are often referred to as **reference groups**. These can be one of two types.

1. Primary reference groups exist where an individual has direct face-to-face contact with members of the group.
2. Secondary reference groups describe the influence of groups where there is no direct relationship, but an individual is nevertheless influenced by the group's values.

3.4.1 Primary reference groups

These comprise people with whom an individual has direct two-way contact, including those with whom an individual works, plays football and goes to church. In effect, the group acts as a frame of reference for the individual. Small groups of trusted colleagues have great power in passing on recommendations about goods and services, especially those where a buyer has very little other evidence on which to base a decision. For many personal services, such as hairdressing, word-of-mouth recommendation from a member of a peer group may be a vital method by which a company gains new business. If an individual needs to hire a builder, the first thing they are likely to do is ask friends if they can recommend a good one on the basis of their previous experience. For many items of conspicuous consumption, individuals often select specific brands in accordance with which brand carries most prestige with its primary reference group.

3.4.2 Secondary reference groups

These are groups with whom an individual has no direct contact, but which can nevertheless influence a person's attitudes, values, opinions and behaviour. Sometimes, the individual may be a member of the group and this will have a direct influence on their behaviour patterns, with the group serving as a frame of reference for the individual member. Individuals typically belong to several groups that can influence attitudes and behaviour in this way – for example, university groups, trades unions and religious organizations. A member of a trades union may have little active involvement with the organization, but may nevertheless adopt the values of the union, such as solidarity.

At other times, an individual may not actually be a member of a group, but may aspire to be a member of it. Aspirational groups can be general descriptions of the characteristics of groups of people who share attitudes and behaviour. They range from teenage 'wannabes' who idolize pop stars through to businessmen who want to surround themselves with the trappings of their successful business heroes. It can be difficult to identify just which aspirational groups are highly sought after at any one time. Middle-aged marketers marketing youth products may find it difficult to keep up with which pop stars and fashion models are currently in favour with teenagers.

The influence of secondary groups on purchases tends to vary between products and brands. In the case of products that are consumed or used in public, group influence is likely to affect not only the choice of product but also the choice of brand. (For example, training shoes are often sold using a 'brand spokesperson' to create an image for the shoe. There are some people who are so influenced by the images developed by famous athletes wearing a particular brand that they would not want to be seen wearing anything else.) For mass-market goods that are consumed less publicly (e.g. many grocery items), the effects of reference groups are usually less.

3.5 Values, attitudes and lifestyles

Many organizations have recognized that traditional indicators of social class are poor predictors of buyer behaviour. An analysis of changing attitudes, values and lifestyles is considered to be more useful.

3.5.1 Values

Values represent an individual's core beliefs and tend to be deep-seated and relatively enduring. They tend to be learnt at an early age and passed on through generations. They form an underlying framework that guides an individual's construction of the world and their response to events in it. Typical underlying value systems may include the belief that it is wrong to get into debt; a belief that family is more important than work; and that it is important to be the winner in any competitive event.

The term values should be distinguished from value. Economists describe value as the ratio of the benefit arising from a product relative to its cost. The distinction between values and value is that an individual's value system influences the value they place on any particular object. A person with a value system that rates security and reliability highly may place a high value on a car that is solidly built but not particularly attractive. Another person whose value system ranks recognition by others as being more important may place a higher value on a car that is not necessarily reliable, but has 'street credibility'.

Although value systems tend to be deeply ingrained, they have a tendency to change through an individual's life cycle. So it follows that the value system of a teenager is likely to be different from that of a young adult parent, and different again from that of an elderly retired person.

3.5.2 Attitudes

Compared to values, **attitudes** are relatively transient sets of beliefs. Attitudes should be distinguished from the behaviour that may be manifested in a particular lifestyle. An individual may have an attitude about a subject, but keep their thoughts to themselves, possibly in fear of the consequences if these do not conform to generally accepted norms. A man may believe that it should be acceptable for men to use facial cosmetics, but be unwilling to be the first to actually change behaviour by using them.

It is important for businesses to study changes in social attitudes, because these will most likely eventually be translated into changes in buying behaviour. The change may begin with a small group of social pioneers, followed by more traditional groups who may be slow to change their attitudes and more reluctant to change their behaviour. They may be prepared to change only when something has become the norm in their society.

Businesses have monitored a number of significant changes in individuals' attitudes in Western Europe – for example:

- healthy living is considered to be increasingly important
- consumers have a tendency to want instant results, rather than having to wait for things
- attitudes are increasingly based on secular rather than religious values.

Business organizations have been able to respond to these attitude changes creatively – for example:

- demand for healthy foods and gymnasium services has increased significantly; at first, it was only a small group of people whose attitude towards health led them to buy specialist products – now it is a mainstream purchase
- the desire for instant gratification has been translated into strategies to make stock always available, next-day delivery for mail-order purchases, instant credit approval and instant lottery tickets
- supermarkets in England have capitalized on the secularization of Sunday by opening stores and doing increasing levels of business on Sundays.

3.5.3 Lifestyles

Lifestyles are the manifestation of underlying value systems and attitudes. Lifestyle analysis seeks to identify groups within the population based on distinctive patterns of behaviour. It is possible for two people from the same social class carrying out an identical occupation to have very different lifestyles, which would not be apparent if businesses segmented markets solely on the basis of easily identifiable criteria such as occupation. Consequently, product development and marketing communications have often been designed to appeal to specific lifestyle groups. This type of analysis can be very subjective and quantification of numbers in each category within a population at best can only be achieved through a small sample survey.

Studies have indicated a number of trends in lifestyles, which have impacts on business organizations.

- A growing number of individuals are becoming money rich, but time poor. Such individuals quite commonly seek additional convenience from their purchases, even if this means paying a premium price. Businesses have responded with products such as gourmet ready prepared meals.
- As individuals become financially more secure, their motivation to buy products typically changes from a need for necessities to a desire for the unusual and challenging. Businesses have responded with ranges of designer clothes, adventure holidays and personalized interior design services.

Figure 3.4 There can be a big difference between what people actually do; what they say they do; and what they would like to do. For businesses planning to offer new goods or services, it may be easy for a respondent to a survey to say that they would buy it, but when they have to get their money out, they may have other ideas. This gulf between attitudes and behaviour can be particularly great in the case of some health-related goods and services. Many people make 'New Year's resolutions' to change their lifestyle, often after a Christmas of overindulgence, but their best intentions are not always matched by their actions. Many people believe that they should be fitter, perhaps based on reports about the effects of overeating and sedentary lifestyles. Many of these will simply rationalize away reasons for doing nothing to make themselves fitter ('I don't have time'; 'I get enough exercise anyway'; 'I don't want to risk the possibility of an injury while exercising'). Some will take positive action – for example, by joining a local gym, and membership registrations rise sharply in January. However, industry research suggests that a high proportion of these people stop going to the gym after six months. Marketers face a dilemma, because what people actually do is the best guide to what they spend their money on, but businesses are also continually trying to understand latent needs that have not yet been expressed in the form of actual purchases. How can a researcher tell whether a consumer's wish will be transformed into an actual purchase? (Reproduced with permission of Fitness First)

- With the increase in numbers of single-person households, the symbolic meaning of the home has changed for many people. Businesses have responded with a range of home-related products such as widescreen home cinema systems and gas-fired barbecues.

Gaining knowledge of the current composition and geographical distribution of lifestyle segments is much more difficult than monitoring occupation-based segments, for which data are regularly collected by government and private-sector organizations. This is discussed again later in this chapter.

Thinking around the subject: A penny for your thoughts?

Businesses have become increasingly interested in individuals' deep-seated unconscious emotions, on the basis that these offer a much better guide to how they will actually behave than their considered responses to questions about their attitudes and beliefs. Enter the brave new world of 'neuro-marketing', which seeks to go straight to individuals' brains, rather than understanding them through what they say. One American organization, the Bright House Institute for Science, has used magnetic resonance imaging (MRI) to try to learn more about how marketing cues activate different parts of the brain.

The idea of trying to understand how people's brains function is not new, and has occupied scientists and criminologists, among others, for some time. The debate about the relative power of nature (a hard-wiring of the brain) versus nurture (the effects of socialization processes on our behaviour) is a long-running one. Marketers have already found some limited role for experimental methods of understanding deep-seated processing – for example, research into advertising effectiveness has used tachistoscopes to record individuals' conscious eye movements.

Should neuro-marketing be regarded as a great hope for the future? Or is it overhyped? Critics have been quick to argue that it is one thing being able to identify a pattern of brain activity but quite another to be able to infer causative links between brain patterns and buying behaviour. Some have dismissed neuro-marketing as a management fad, and a device used by research companies to get their foot in the door of the client, but then sell more conventional research.

Is neuro-marketing ethical? To many people, neuro-marketing sounds like an Orwellian nightmare, which could play straight into the hands of the 'thought police'. Could an understanding of people's deep-seated thought processes potentially allow companies to wrongly exploit emotions that are against a consumer's best interest? Could food companies exploit an emotional need for high-calorie 'comfort' food at the expense of a more considered need for healthy food? At a broader level, what are the implications for democracy if politicians can understand and manipulate individuals' deep-seated attitudes?

3.6 Identifying and measuring social groups

So far we have discussed the changing composition of society in general terms, but now we need to turn our attention to possible methods by which organizations can identify specific groups within society. This is important if business organizations are to be able to target differentiated goods and services at groups that have quite distinctive sets of attitudes and lifestyles.

The aim of any system of social classification is to provide a measure that encapsulates differences between individuals in terms of their type of occupation, income level, educational background and attitudes to life, among other factors. There are three theoretical approaches to measuring social groupings.

1 *By self-measurement:* researchers could ask an individual which of a number of possible groups they belong to. This approach has a number of theoretical advantages for organizations, because how an individual actually sees him or herself is often a more important

Thinking around the subject: Complicated lifestyles

Some indication of the minutiae of changing lifestyles, and their implications for marketing, was revealed in the report *Complicated Lives II – The Price of Complexity*, commissioned by Abbey National bank from the Future Foundation. The report brought together quantitative and qualitative research with extensive analysis of a range of trends affecting families and their finances. The findings show that, between 1961 and 2001:

- the average time women spent in a week doing cleaning and laundry fell from 12 hours and 40 minutes to 6 hours and 18 minutes
- the average time that parents spent helping their children with homework had increased from 1 minute a day to 15 minutes
- time spent caring for children increased from 30 minutes a day to 75 minutes
- the average amount of time spent entertaining went up from 25 minutes to 55 minutes per day
- time spent cooking has decreased for women, down from more than 1 hour and 40 minutes to just over an hour (73 minutes) per day; at the same time, men marginally increased their time in the kitchen from 26 to 27 minutes per day.

Figure 3.5 The growing number of money-rich, time-poor households presents new opportunities for businesses to provide convenient solutions to this group at a premium price. Sainsbury's was an early retailer to identify this opportunity and has developed a home delivery service that delivers customers' shopping to their home or place of work. The service has proved particularly popular with families who have difficulties in finding childminders, thereby avoiding the need to drag children round a supermarket. Nevertheless, such groups, for whom shopping has been transformed into a leisure experience, may enjoy shopping for non-household goods such as clothes.

determinant of behaviour than an objective measure. If people see themselves as working class, they are probably proud of the fact, and will choose products and brands that accord with their own self-image. The danger of this approach is that many people tend to self-select themselves for 'middle of the road' categories. In one self-assessment study, over two-thirds of the sample described themselves as 'middle class'.

2 *By objective approaches:* these involve the use of measurable indicators about a person, such as their occupation, education and spending habits, as a basis for class determination. A number of these are discussed below.
3 *By asking third parties:* this combines the objective approach of indicators described above with a subjective assessment of an individual's behaviour and attitudes.

Social scientists have traditionally used the second of these approaches as a basis for defining social groupings, largely on account of its objectivity and relative ease of measurement. However, organizations must also recognize that an individual's attitudes can be crucial in determining buying behaviour, and have therefore been keen to introduce more subjective and self-assessed bases for classification. In the following sections we will review some bases commonly used by businesses for identifying social groups.

3.6.1 IPA classification system

One of the most long-standing and still widely used bases for social classification is the system adopted by the Institute of Practitioners in Advertising (IPA). It uses an individual's occupation as a basis for classification, on the basis that occupation is closely associated with many aspects of a person's attitudes and behaviour. The classes defined range from A to E, and Figure 3.6 indicates the allocation of selected occupations to groups.

Such an attempt to reduce the multidimensional concept of social grouping to a single measure is bound to be an oversimplification, which limits its usefulness to business organizations. A person's occupation is not necessarily a good indicator of their buying behaviour – for example, an internet entrepreneur running a large business and a bishop would probably be put in the same occupational classification, but there are likely to be very significant differences in their spending patterns and the way they pass their leisure time. Nevertheless, the classification system described is widely used. Newspapers regularly analyse their readership in terms of

Class category	Occupation
A	Higher managerial, administrative or professional
B	Intermediate managerial, administrative or professional
C1	Supervisory or clerical, and junior managerial, administrative or professional
C2	Skilled manual workers
D	Semi- and unskilled manual workers
E	State pensioners or widows (no other earners), casual or lower-grade workers, or long-term unemployed

Figure 3.6 IPA basis for social classification

membership of these groups, and go out of their way to show how many of the highly prized A/B readers they have.

3.6.2 Classification used for the UK Census

The data sets used by many organizations import data collected by the UK's Census of population. Since 1921, government statisticians have divided the population into six classes, based simply on their occupation. But the expansion of the number of workers in traditionally middle-class jobs such as finance and management led the government to increase the number of classes and to look more critically at an occupational title in terms of the life opportunities that it offers.

The Standard Occupational Classification used for the Census was first published in 1990, and updated in 2000. It uses two main concepts for classifying individuals:

1 the kind of work performed (that, is the job description)
2 the competence level required for the tasks and duties (the skills required for the job).

Changes introduced in 2000 reflected the need to improve comparability with the International Standard Classification of Occupations and the changing needs of users of census data, who were becoming increasingly dubious about the existing bases of classification. Revisions were influenced by innovations associated with technological developments and the redefinition of work, reflecting the educational attainment of those entering the labour market.

The main features of the revision included:

- a tighter definition of managerial occupations
- a thorough overhaul of computing and related occupations
- the introduction of specific occupations associated with the environment and conservation
- changes linked to the de-skilling of many manufacturing processes
- the recognition of the development of customer service occupations, and the emergence of remote service provision through the operation of call centres.

The major occupational groups defined by the Census are shown in Figure 3.7.

1 Managers and senior officials
2 Professional occupations
3 Associate professional and technical occupations
4 Administrative and secretarial occupations
5 Skilled trades occupations
6 Personal service occupations
7 Sales and customer service occupations
8 Process, plant and machine operatives
9 Elementary occupations

Figure 3.7 Major occupational groups used in UK Census data collection

Each of these nine groups is broken down into further sub-groups so, for example, major group 2 (professional occupations) has a sub-major group (21) of science and technology professionals, which is broken down into a minor group (211) of science professionals, from which a unit (2111) of scientists can be identified.

In this revised system of classification there were risers and fallers. Teachers, librarians, nurses and police officers were among the risers, based on the skills and security of their job. Workers in call centres fell according to this system of classification.

3.6.3 Geodemographic classification systems

A lot of research has shown a correlation between where a person lives and their buying behaviour. The type of house and its location says much more about an individual than occupation alone can. Income, the size of the family unit and attitudes towards city life/country living, as well as occupation, are closely related to residence. The classification of individuals in this way has come to be known as **geodemographic analysis**. A number of firms offer a geodemographic segmentation analysis, which allows a classification of small geographical pockets of households according to a combination of demographic characteristics and buying behaviour.

A widely used classification system is ACORN (ACORN is an acronym of A Classification Of Residential Neighbourhoods). ACORN is a geodemographic segmentation method, using census data to classify consumers according to the type of residential area in which they live. Each postcode in the country can, therefore, be allocated an ACORN category. This classification has been found to be a more powerful differentiator of consumer behaviour than traditional socioeconomic and demographic indicators. The ACORN categories, and their components, are described in Figure 3.8.

Group A - Thriving [Approx 20% of population]	Wealthy achievers, suburban areas Affluent greys, rural communities Prosperous pensioners, retirement areas
Group B - Expanding [Approx 11% of population]	Affluent executives, family areas Well-off workers, family areas
Group C - Rising [Approx 8% of population]	Affluent urbanites, town and city areas Prosperous professionals, metropolitan areas Better-off executives, inner-city areas
Group D - Settling [Approx 25% of population]	Comfortable middle-agers, mature home-owning areas Skilled workers, home-owning areas
Group E - Aspiring [Approx 13% of population]	New home-owners, mature communities White-collar workers, better-off multi-ethnic areas
Group F - Striving [Approx 21% of population]	Older people, less prosperous areas Council estate residents, better-off homes Council estate residents, high unemployment Council estate residents, greatest hardship People in multi-ethnic, low-income areas

Figure 3.8 ACORN classifications

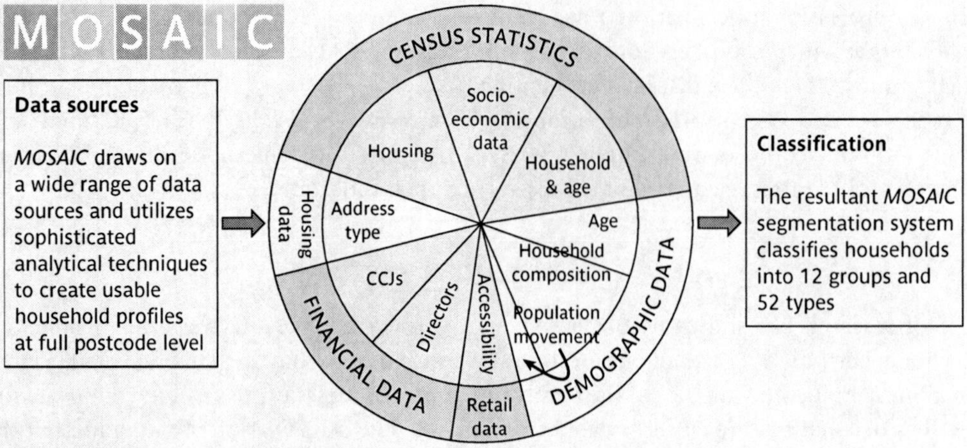

Figure 3.9 MOSAIC is a widely used geodemographic segmentation classification system (reproduced with permission of Experian Ltd)

Another widely used application of geodemographic analysis is MOSAIC, offered by Experian Ltd. By analysing a lot of sales data from people in each postcode area, it is possible to build up a good picture of the lifestyle and spending patterns associated with each classification. It is also possible to see how the distribution of the population between different classifications changes over time (see Figure 3.9).

3.6.4 Lifestyle bases of classification

Geodemographic classification systems tell business a lot more about individuals than their occupation alone can, but this still misses much detail about the lifestyle of particular individuals, or the size of groups that share a similar lifestyle. A starting point for lifestyle segmentation is to understand where an individual is located in the family life cycle. Traditional models of family life cycles have portrayed individuals as going through a number of distinct and sequential stages from dependent child, through young adults, adults with dependent children, then with no dependent children ('empty nesters'), to solitary survivors. However, such simple linear models are no longer considered relevant to an increasing number of individuals who break this pattern through divorce, single parenthood, remarriage etc. The research company Mintel, for example, has advanced from the traditional family life cycle model by identifying a number of special categories that typify consumer habits in the early 2000s (see Figure 3.10). Unlike the **life stage** groups, these groups represent only sections of the population and do not account for all adults.

Many research companies have developed much more subjective bases for defining lifestyle groups, which rely on a verbal description of the groups. Information to support the validity of these groups is hard to come by and generally relies on small sample surveys of the population. For this reason, such ideal-type classification systems are less well suited to monitoring social change than more objective systems based on quantifiable data.

Life stage groups	
Pre-family	those aged under 35 who are not parents
Family	those aged 15–54 with at least one child aged under 16 still at home
Empty nesters	no family/empty nesters aged 35–54 with no children [aged under 16]
Post-family	post-family/retired, those aged over 55/not working
Special category groups	
Benefit dependents	Es aged 35+ – those who are reliant solely on state benefits [around 10% of the adult population]
Families on a tight budget	working C2Ds with at least one child aged under 16 in the household – the majority have limited incomes that must be spent on a relatively large household [around 10% of the adult population]
Better-off families	working ABC1s with at least one child aged under 16 in the household [around 9% of the population]
Better-off empty nesters	ABC1s aged 35–64 who are working with no children [aged under 16] living at home. They are, therefore, the classic no family/empty nesters with probably a high income that can be spent on themselves rather than on family [around 8% of the adult population]
Working managers	working ABs [around 9% of the population]
Working women	women in part- or full-time employment [around 21% of the adult population]

Figure 3.10 Consumer life stage and special categories as identified by Mintel

Because of their subjectivity, there is a wide variety of lifestyle segmentation models, which tend to reflect the needs of the companies that created them. For example, one model developed by Young & Rubicam described four lifestyle groups to which members of a population could be allocated.

1 Conformers, comprising the bulk of the population, who typically may live in a suburban semi-detached house, drive a Ford Focus, shop at Sainsbury's and book a Thomsons package holiday.
2 Aspirers, a smaller group who are ambitious, innovative and keen to surround themselves with the trappings of success. This group may typically live in a trendy mews house, drive a sports utility vehicle, shop for brand-name clothes and take adventure holidays.
3 Controllers, by contrast, are comfortable in the knowledge that they have made it in life and do not feel the need to flaunt their success. They are more likely to live in a comfortable detached house, drive a Volvo, shop at Marks & Spencer and book their holiday through the local travel agent they trust.
4 Reformers have a vision of how life could be improved for everybody in society. At home they may be enthusiastic about DIY and energy conservation. They may see their car more as a means of transport than a status symbol, and buy own-label brands at the Co-op.

Of course, these are ideal types, and very few people will precisely meet these descriptions. However, they are a useful starting point for trying to understand who it is that a company is

Thinking around the subject: Sandwich statement

What does an individual's choice of sandwich say about them? The retailer Tesco undertook research that showed how complex the market for ready-made sandwiches had become, with clear segments emerging of people who sought quite different types of sandwich. In an attempt to define and target its lunch customers more precisely, the company found that well-paid executives invariably insisted on 'designer' sandwiches made from ciabatta and focaccia with sun-dried tomatoes and costing about £2.50. Salespeople and middle-ranking executives were more inclined to opt for meaty triple-deckers. Upwardly mobile women aged 25–40 chose low-calorie sandwiches costing around £1.49. Busy manual workers tended to grab a sandwich that looked affordable, simple and quick to eat, such as a ploughman's sandwich that Tesco sold for £1.15. Tesco's research claimed that sandwiches have become an important statement made by individuals and need to be targeted appropriately. What do your snack meals say about you?

targeting. The numbers in each category have undoubtedly risen and fallen in the recent past. Aspirers seem to appear in great numbers during periods of economic boom, but become less conspicuous at the onset of a recession.

Many more informal, almost tongue-in-cheek, bases for segmenting lifestyle groups are commonly used. It has in the past, for example, been common to talk about lifestyle groups that have been labelled yuppies (young, upwardly mobile professionals), dinkys (dual income, no kids yet) and bobos (burnt out, but opulent), to name but a few. New descriptions emerge to describe new lifestyles. Again, these classifications are not at all scientific, but they give marketers a chance to describe target markets.

3.7 Demography

Demography is the study of populations in terms of their size and characteristics. Among the topics of interest to demographers are the age structure of a country, the geographic distribution of its population, the balance between males and females, and the likely future size of the population and its characteristics.

3.7.1 The importance of demographic analysis to business organizations

A number of reasons can be identified why business organizations should study demographic trends.

- First, on the demand side, demography helps to predict the size of the market that a product is likely to face. For example, demographers can predict an increase in the number of elderly people living in the United Kingdom and the numbers living in the south-west region of the country. Businesses can use this information as a basis for predicting, for example, the size of the market for retirement homes in the south-west.

- Demographic trends have supply-side implications. An important aim of business organizations is to match the opportunities facing an organization with the resource strengths that it possesses. In many businesses, labour is a key resource and a study of demographics will indicate the human resources that an organization can expect to have available to it in future years. Thus a business that has relied on relatively low-wage, young labour, such as retailing, would need to have regard to the availability of this type of worker when developing its product strategy. A retailer might decide to invest in more automated methods of processing transactions and handling customer enquiries rather than relying on a traditional but diminishing source of relatively low-cost labour.
- The study of demographics also has implications for public-sector services, which are themselves becoming more marketing orientated. Changing population structures influence the community facilities that need to be provided by the government. For example, fluctuations in the number of children have affected the number of schools and teachers required, while the increasing number of elderly people will require the provision of more specialized housing and hospital facilities suitable for this group.
- In an even wider sense, demographic change can influence the nature of family life and communities, and ultimately affects the social and economic system in which organizations operate. The imbalance that is developing between a growing dependent elderly population and a diminishing population of working age is already beginning to affect government fiscal policy and the way in which we care for the elderly, with major implications for business organizations.

Although the study of demographics has assumed great importance in Western Europe in recent years, study of the consequences of population change dates back a considerable time. T.R. Malthus studied the effects of population changes in a paper published in 1798. He predicted that the population would continue to grow exponentially, while world food resources would grow at a slower linear rate. Population growth would be held back only by 'war, pestilence and famine' until an equilibrium point was again reached at which population was just equal to the food resources available.

Malthus's model of population growth failed to predict the future accurately and this only serves to highlight the difficulty of predicting population levels when the underlying assumptions on which predictions are based are themselves changing. Malthus failed to predict, on the one hand, the tremendous improvement in agricultural efficiency that would allow a larger population to be sustained and, on the other hand, changes in social and cultural attitudes that were to limit family size.

3.7.2 Global population changes

Globally, population has been expanding at an increasing rate. The world population level at AD 1000 has been estimated at about 300 million. Over the next 750 years, it rose at a steady rate to 728 million in 1750. Thereafter, the rate of increase became progressively more rapid, doubling

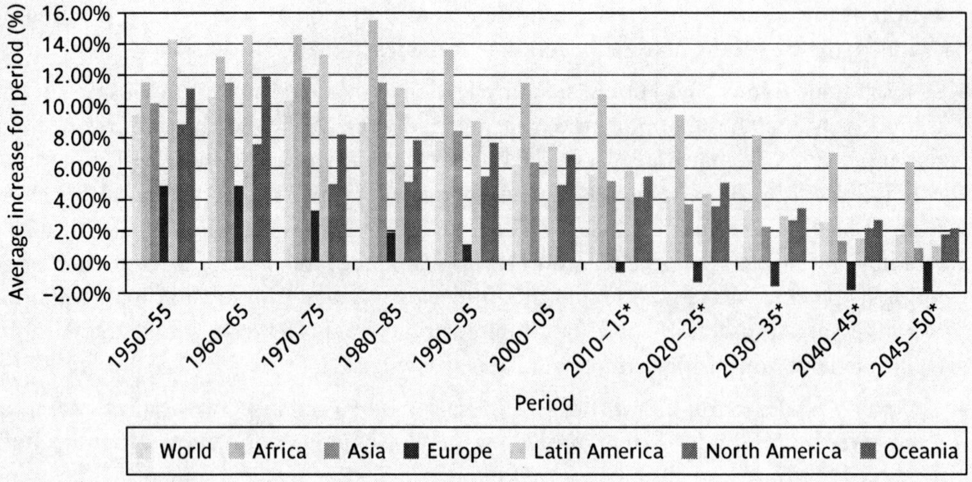

Figure 3.11 Growth in world population, by region
Source: based on UN estimates
Note: *denotes projections

in the following 150 years to 1550 million in 1900 and almost doubling again to 3000 million in the 62 years to 1962. The United Nations estimated total world population in 2007 to be 6.6 billion, and predicted that this would rise to 9.1 billion by 2050 (UNFPA 2007). The growth of world population has not been uniform, with recent growth being focused on the world's poorer countries, especially Korea and China, as well as South America. Within the EU countries, the total population in recent times has increased at a natural rate of about 1 per 1000 population (that is, for every 1000 deaths, there are 1001 births). However, this hides a range of rates of increase with, at each extreme, Ireland having a particularly high birth rate and Germany a particularly low one. This has major implications for future age structures and consumption patterns (see below). Much faster population growth is expected to occur in Africa and Latin America.

An indication of the variation in population growth rates is given in Figure 3.11. It should, however, be noted that there is still considerable debate about future world population levels, with many predictions being revised downwards.

A growth in the population of a country does not necessarily mean a growth in business opportunities, for the countries with the highest population growth rates also tend to be those with the lowest gross domestic product per head. Indeed, in many countries of Africa, total GDP is not keeping up with the growth in population levels, resulting in a lower GDP per head. On the other hand, the growth in population results in a large and low-cost labour force, which can help to explain the tendency for many European-based organizations to base their design capacity in Europe but relatively labour-intensive assembly operations in the Far East.

3.7.3 Changes in UK population level

The first British Census was carried out in 1801 and the subsequent ten-yearly census provides the basis for studying changes in the size of the British population. A summary of British population growth is shown in Figure 3.12.

The fluctuation in the rate of population growth can be attributed to three main factors: the birth rate, the death rate, and the difference between inward and outward migration. The fluctuation in these rates is illustrated in Figure 3.13. These three components of population change are described below.

Year	Population of England, Wales and Scotland (000)	Average increase per decade (%)
1801	10,501	13.9
1871	26,072	9.4
1911	40,891	4.5
1941	46,605	5.8
1971	54,369	0.8
1981	54,814	2.4
1991	55,831	2.8
2001	57,424	2.3
2011	58,794	1.7 (projected)
2031	58,970	0.5 (projected)

Figure 3.12 Population growth, England, Wales and Scotland, 1801–2031
Source: based on *Annual Abstract of Statistics*, Government Actuary's Department and population censuses

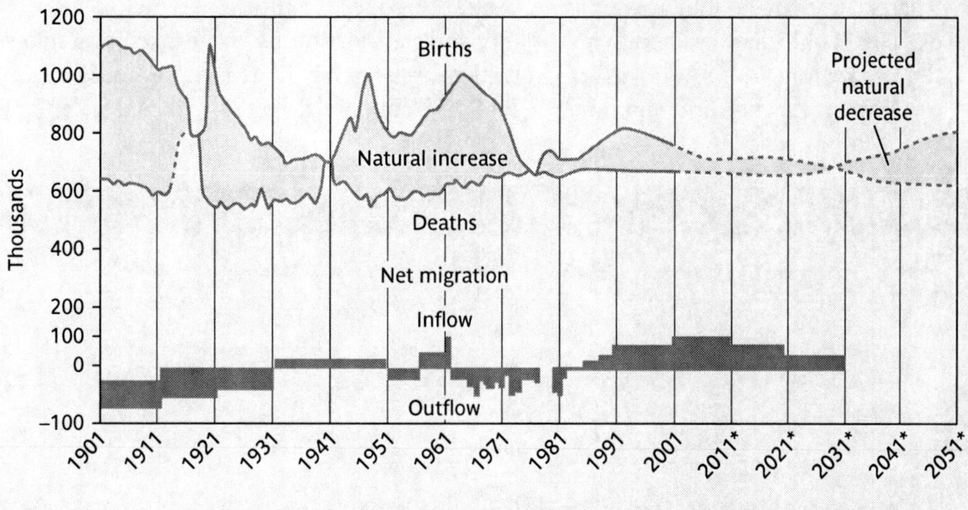

Figure 3.13 Changes in the UK birth rate, death rate and level of net migration, 1901–2051
Source: Office of Population Censuses and Surveys, Government Actuary's Department, © Crown copyright
Note: *denotes projections

3.7.4 The birth rate

The **birth rate** is usually expressed in terms of the number of live births per 1000 population. Since the Second World War, the birth rate of the UK has shown a number of distinct cyclical tendencies. The immediate post-war years are associated with a 'baby boom', followed by a steady decrease in the number of births until 1956. Following this, the rate rose again until the mid-1960s during a second, but lesser, baby boom. The birth rate then fell until the mid-1970s, rising again in recent years. Worldwide, the United Nations has estimated that the average birth rate per female has fallen from 5 in 1953 to 2.56 in 2007 (UNFPA 2007). Of the 44 countries in the developed world, all except Albania were reported to have birth rates below the natural replacement rate of 2.1 per female (the level needed to maintain a stable population level).

In order to explain these trends, it is necessary to examine two key factors:

1 the number of women in the population who are of childbearing age
2 the proportion of these women who actually give birth (this is referred to as the fertility rate).

The peak in the birth rate of the early 1960s could be partly explained by the 'baby boom' children of the immediate post-war period working through to childbearing age. Similarly, the children of this group have themselves reached childbearing age, accounting for some of the recent increase in the birth rate. Greater doubt lies over reasons for changes in the fertility rate, usually expressed in terms of the number of births per 1000 women aged between 16 and 44. This has varied from a peak of 115 at the beginning of the century to a low point of 56.8 in 1983 (see Figure 3.14).

There are many possible explanations for changes in fertility rates and it is our difficulty in understanding the precise nature of these changes that makes population forecasting a difficult task. Some of the more frequently suggested causes of the declining fertility rate are described below.

- A large family is no longer seen as an insurance policy for future parental security. The extended family has declined in importance and state institutions have taken over many of the welfare functions towards elderly members of the family that were previously expected of children. Furthermore, infant and child mortality has declined and consequently the

Year	Fertility rate
1900	115.0
1933	81.0
1951	73.0
1961	90.6
1971	84.3
1981	62.1
1991	64.0
2001	54.5

Figure 3.14 General fertility rate: total births per 1000 women aged 15–44, United Kingdom
Source: based on OPCS/Census of Population data

need for large numbers of births has declined. Alongside this falling need for large numbers of children has come a greater ability to control the number of births.

- Children use household resources that could otherwise be used for consumption. The cost of bringing up children has been increasing as a result of increased expectations of children and the raising of the school leaving age. Although in many Western countries this is partly offset by financial incentives for having children, the cost of child rearing has increased relative to consumer purchases in general. According to a study by the US Department of Agriculture, it costs a family earning \$54,100 (£28,000) a year \$178,000 (£93,000) at 2004 prices to raise a child from birth to 18 (US Department of Agriculture 2004).
- In addition to diverting household resources from the consumption of other goods and services, caring for children also has the effect of reducing the earning capacity of the household. Women may also seek additional status and career progression by having fewer children or spacing them over a shorter period of time.
- Birth rates tend to be related to current economic conditions, falling significantly in response to temporary economic recession and rising in response to a period of economic boom.

The effects of variation in birth rates can be felt for a long time after the variation itself. In the UK, a post-war peak in births resulted in a large 'baby boomer' generation having a high number of children in the 1960s, and their children in turn made up a large cohort of mothers who raised the birth rate again when they had children 20 to 30 years later. Although these cycles become progressively less pronounced over time, businesses should nevertheless be able to predict them and adjust their capacity accordingly.

3.7.5 The death rate

Death rates are normally expressed as the number of people in the country that die in a year per 1000 of the population. This is sometimes called the crude death rate; the age-specific death rate takes account of the age of death and is expressed as the number of people per 1000 of a particular age group that die in a year.

In contrast to the volatility of the birth rate during the post-war period, the death rate has been relatively stable and has played a relatively small part in changing the total population level. The main feature of mortality in the United Kingdom has been a small decline in age-specific death rates, having the effect of increasing the survival chances of relatively old people. The age-specific death rate of women has fallen more significantly than for men. The main reasons for the decline in age-specific death rates are improved standards of living, a better environment and better awareness of health issues, and an improvement in health services. While age-specific death rates have been falling in most advanced industrial countries, the United Kingdom has generally experienced a slower fall than most other EU member states.

3.7.6 Migration

If immigration is compared with emigration, a figure for net **migration** is obtained. In general, net immigration tends to be greatest during periods of economic prosperity, while net emigration tends to be greatest during periods of economic recession. During most periods of the twentieth century, the United Kingdom experienced a net outflow of population, the main exceptions being: the 1930s, caused by emigrants to the Commonwealth returning home during the depression; the 1940s when a large number of refugees entered the United Kingdom from Nazi Europe; and the late 1950s/early 1960s when the prosperity of the British economy attracted large numbers of immigrants from the new Commonwealth. Emigration has tended to peak at times of economic depression in the United Kingdom. The prosperity of the UK during the 1990s and 2000s increased the number of immigrants. The enlargement of the EU in 2004, to include former Eastern European countries, brought a large number of migrants to Britain from the new member states; some estimates put this as high as one million between 2004 and 2007. This has put pressure on public facilities in some areas, and provided

Country	Total population 1 Jan 2005 (000)	% aged 0–14	% aged 15–24	% aged 25–64	% aged 65+
Austria	8,206	16.1	12.3	55.6	16.0
Belgium	10,445	17.2	12.1	53.5	17.2
Bulgaria	7,761	13.8	13.7	55.3	17.1
Czech Republic	10,220	14.9	13.4	57.7	14.0
Cyprus	749	19.2	15.9	53.0	11.9
Denmark	5,411	18.8	11.0	55.1	15.0
Estonia	1,347	15.5	15.6	52.5	16.5
Finland	5,236	17.5	12.4	54.2	15.9
France	60,561	18.5	13.0	52.2	16.4
Germany	82,500	14.5	11.7	55.2	18.6
Greece	11,075	14.4	12.4	55.1	18.1
Hungary	10,097	15.6	13.1	55.6	15.6
Ireland	4,109	20.7	15.5	52.6	11.2
Italy	58,462	14.2	10.5	55.9	19.4
Latvia	2,306	14.8	15.6	53.1	16.5
Lithuania	3,425	17.1	15.4	52.5	15.1
Luxembourg	455	18.7	11.5	55.5	14.2
Malta	402	17.6	14.5	54.5	13.3
Netherlands	16,305	18.5	12.0	55.6	14.0
Poland	38,173	16.7	16.5	53.7	13.1
Portugal	10,529	15.6	12.6	54.7	17.0
Romania	21,658	15.9	15.5	53.9	14.7
Slovakia	5,384	17.1	16.1	55.2	11.6
Slovenia	1,997	14.4	13.4	56.9	15.3
Spain	43,038	14.5	12.3	56.4	16.8
Sweden	9,011	17.6	12.2	53.0	17.2
United Kingdom	60,034	18.1	13.1	52.9	16.0

Figure 3.15 A comparison of the population structure of EU member countries

Source: compiled from *Eurostat Yearbook 2006–07 (Population Statistics)*

opportunities for businesses targeting these new immigrants (for example, Lloyds TSB Bank announced in 2006 that it would open a business unit employing Polish-speaking staff, specifically to target Polish immigrants).

3.7.7 The age structure of the population

It was noted earlier that the total population of the United Kingdom – and indeed most countries of the EU – is fairly stable. However, within this stable total, there has been a more noted change in the composition of particular age groups, with Ireland having a particularly high birth rate and Germany a particularly low one (see Figure 3.15). This has major implications for future age structures and consumption patterns. By 2030, people over 65 in Germany will account for almost half the adult population, compared with one-fifth in 2000. And unless the country's birth rate recovers from its present low of 1.3 per woman, over the same period its population of under-35s will shrink about twice as fast as the older population will grow. The net result will be that the total population, now 82 million, will decline to 70–73 million, and the number of people of working age will fall by a quarter, from 40 million today to 30 million. In Japan, the population is expected to have peaked in 2005, at around 125 million and, by around 2030, the share of over-65s in the adult population will have grown to about half (*The Economist* 2001).

The changes that have affected the size of age-specific segments in the UK are illustrated in Figure 3.16.

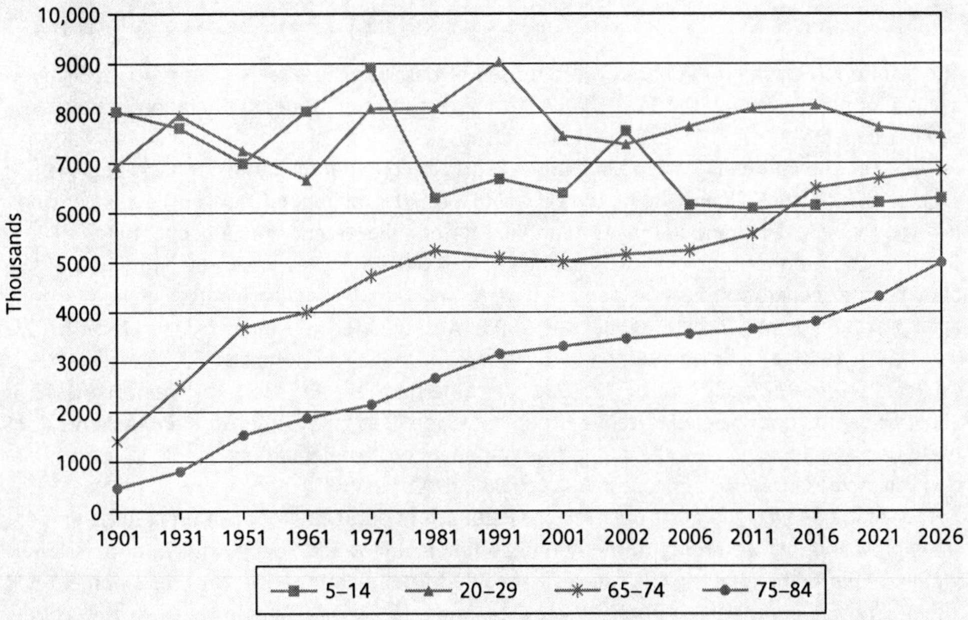

Figure 3.16 Size of selected age cohorts in United Kingdom, 1901–2026 (projected from 2006 onwards)
Source: based on Office of Population Censuses and Surveys estimates

What are the implications for business organizations of an ageing of the population structure?

- There is a growing imbalance between the shrinking size of the working population and an increasingly large dependent population. Government statistics show that, between 1961 and 2003, the number of people of working age in the UK available to support the retired population decreased from 4.1 per pensioner to 3.3. This figure is expected to fall again slightly to 2020 but then fall again sharply as those in the baby boom generation start to become eligible for their pensions. The ratio of those contributing to the pensions that sustain the retired population is smaller still, to take account of the fact that although many people of working age are available to work, many are either unemployed or pay no taxes. By 2020, each pensioner will be supported by the contributions of two tax-paying workers. This is expected to fall to 1.6 by 2040.
- For businesses that have offered their employees a 'final salary' pension scheme, the cost of paying pensions has increased markedly, as longevity has resulted in a lengthening stream of pension payments. The current profitability of many companies has been reduced as they divert profits to fill this pension gap.

Thinking around the subject: How to defuse a demographic time bomb

The term demographic time bomb is often used to describe the effects of the increasing average age of populations in the EU. What will the effects of this 'time bomb' be on the business environment?

In 2005, the European Commission published a Green Paper on demographic change, which claimed that, from 2005 until 2030, the EU would lose 20.8 million (6.8 per cent) people of working age. By 2030, Europe would have 18 million fewer children and young people than in 2005. By 2030, the number of 'older workers' (aged 55 to 64) would have risen by 24 million as the baby boomer generation become senior citizens, and the EU would have 34.7 million citizens aged over 80 (compared to 18.8 million in 2005). Average life expectancy has also risen by five years since 1960 for women and nearly four years for men. The number of people aged 80+ is expected to grow 180 per cent by 2050. At the same time, the EU's fertility rate fell to 1.48 in 2003, below the level needed to replace the population (2.1 children per woman). As a result of these demographic changes, the proportion of dependent young and old people in the population will increase from 49 per cent in 2005 to 66 per cent in 2030.

For many people, the most pressing consequence of an ageing population focuses on pensions provision, but according to the European Employment and Social Affairs Commissioner, Vladimir Spidla, the looming crisis raises issues that are much broader. 'This development will affect almost every aspect of our lives – for example, the way businesses operate and work is organized, our urban planning, the design of houses, public transport, voting behaviour and the infrastructure of shopping possibilities in our cities,' he said.

The EU report noted that modern Europe has never experienced economic growth without rising birth rates, and suggested that 'ever larger migrant flows may be needed to meet the need for labour and to safeguard Europe's prosperity'.

How can Europe increase the size of its working population to serve the growing proportion of the population that is dependent? One strategy is to ensure that all people who are of working age and able to work actually do so. This would entail eliminating unemployment through retraining and changes to government social payments. Another strategy to increase long-term employment levels is to promote a higher birth rate. But there is an apparent contradiction here, because there is evidence that pressure on families to work harder has been having the effect of reducing the birth rate. The EU report found that Europe's low birth rate is largely the result of constraints on families' choices – late access to employment, job instability, expensive housing and lack of family-focused incentives (such as parental leave and childcare). Incentives of this kind can have a positive impact on the birth rate and increase employment, especially female employment.

A further way of expanding the workforce is to rely on immigration, but this raises a number of issues. First, there is the emotive issue to many people of diluting a national culture. More significantly, from a demographic perspective, what happens when these immigrant workers themselves get old and become dependent? They will need yet more immigrants to look after them. There is also a moral issue associated with immigration, because a common source of immigrants is the developing world. Given that many immigrants are the better-educated members of the society that they come from, is it morally right for the prosperous West to deprive developing countries of trained staff, such as doctors and nurses?

In presenting the EU report, Commissioner Spidla noted that 'Politics alone cannot solve the problem . . . they have to go hand in hand with a picture in society that does not stamp women who re-enter the labour market after maternity leave as "bad mothers" and men that take care of children as "softies".' Why do some cultures find this challenge insurmountable, whereas others readily accept working mothers as a valuable addition to the workforce? Is this the best way to defuse the 'demographic time bomb'?

- With the number of younger people declining as a proportion of the workforce, employers are increasingly looking to older people to fill their vacancies.
- The growing proportion of older people in the population may change the values of a youth-orientated culture. For example, the emphasis on fashion and short-life products may give way to an emphasis on quality and durability as the growing numbers in the older age groups increasingly dominate cultural values.

3.7.8 Household structure

Reference was made earlier in this chapter to the changing role and functions of family units, and this is reflected in an analysis of **household structure** statistics. A number of important trends can be noted.

Thinking around the subject:
More elderly people, so why are homes for the elderly closing?

Ageing of the population is a major opportunity for many organizations. However, the link between growth in size of the elderly population and demand for a company's products can be complex. Nursing homes may expect a boom in demand as the population ages. However, during the period 1995 – 2004, the number of elderly people in residential care in the UK fell, and many care homes and their operators went out of business, despite a growth in the number of elderly people during this period. Trying to forecast future demand for care homes is complicated by uncertainty over the future health needs of elderly people – will the elderly people of the future be healthier and able to look after themselves for longer? Will they make greater efforts to live in their own homes, rather than in a residential care home? Some care homes, such as this one, have spotted this trend and now offer an outreach service to care for people in their own homes. Costs of operating residential care homes are likely to increase, fuelled by increasing government regulations, and wages rising in real terms, reflecting a scarcity of people of working age relative to the number of elderly people. How much will elderly people and their relatives be able or willing to pay for residential care home accommodation? How much will the government be prepared to pay towards care? The Scottish Parliament announced in 2003 that it would provide financial support for elderly people in residential care homes, making the sector more attractive to operators in Scotland compared with the rest of the UK.

- First, it was noted above that there has been a trend for women to have fewer children. From a high point in the 1870s, the average number of children for each woman born in 1930 was 2.35, 2.2 for those born in 1945 and it is projected to be 1.97 for those born in 1965. There has also been a tendency for women to have children later in life. In the United Kingdom, the average age at which women have their first child has moved from 24 years in 1961 to 28 in 2001. There has also been an increase in the number of women having no children. According to the Office of Population Census and Surveys, more than one-fifth of women born in 1967 are expected to be childless when they reach the age of 40, compared with 13 per cent of those born in 1947.
- Alongside a declining number of children has been a decline in the average household size. The total number of dwellings in the UK is estimated to have risen by 9 per cent between 1992 and 2002, significantly outstripping population growth, which was 2.3 per cent for the same period. The result is a reduction in the number of people per household, falling continuously from an average of 3.1 people in 1961 to 2.4 in 2001 (Mintel 2003). There has been a particular fall in the number of very large households with six or more people (down from 7 per cent of all households in 1961 to under 2 per cent in 2001) and a significant increase in the number of one-person households (up from 14 per cent to 30 per cent over the same period). A number of factors have contributed to the increase in one-person households, including the increase in solitary survivors, later marriage and an increased divorce rate. The business implications of the growth of this group are numerous, ranging from an increased demand for smaller units of housing to the types and size of groceries purchased. A single-person household buying for him or herself is likely to use different types of retail outlet compared to the household buying as a unit – the single person may be more likely to use a niche retailer than the (typically) housewife buying for the whole family, whose needs may be better met by a department store. Mintel showed a number of ways in which the spending patterns of single-person households deviate from the average. For example, compared to the British average, a person living in a single-person household spends 49 per cent more on tobacco, 26 per cent more on household services and 23 per cent less on meat (Mintel 2003).
- There has been an increase in other non-traditional forms of household. Households comprising lone parents with children have increased, and in 2001, 20 per cent of all households in England and Wales with dependent children comprised only one adult. Further variation is provided by house sharers, who live independent lives within a household, pragmatically sharing the cost of many household items, while retaining the independence of mind more typical of a single-person household. The number of shared households has increased as young people find themselves priced out of the property market, and shared ownership (or shared rental) offers lifestyle opportunities that may otherwise be closed to a single person. In some cases, two families have shared the cost of a house, living as separate units within it.
- Very significant differences occur throughout the EU in home ownership patterns, with implications for demand for a wide range of home-related services. The proportion of households living in owned accommodation ranges from 57 per cent in Germany to 74 per cent in the United Kingdom and Belgium (Eurostat 2007).

3.7.9 Geographical distribution of population

The population density of the United Kingdom of 231 people per square kilometre is one of the highest in the world. However, this figure hides the fact that the population is dispersed very unevenly between regions and between urban and rural areas. The distribution of population is not static.

Regional distribution

The major feature of the regional distribution of the United Kingdom population is the dominance of the south-east of England with 30 per cent of the population. By contrast, the populations of Scotland, Wales and Northern Ireland account in total for only 17 per cent of the UK population.

Movement between the regions tends to be a very gradual process. In an average year, about 10 per cent of the population will change address, but only about one-eighth of these will move to another region. Nevertheless, there have been a number of noticeable trends. First, throughout the twentieth century there has been a general drift of population from the north to the Midlands and south. More recently, there has been a trend for population to move away from the relatively congested south-east to East Anglia, the south-west and the Home Counties. This can be partly explained by the increased cost of industrial and residential location in the south-east, the greater locational flexibility of modern industry and the desire of people for a pleasanter environment in which to live. The inter-regional movement of population is illustrated in Figure 3.17.

Urban concentration

Another trend has been a shift in the proportion of the population living in urban areas. Throughout most of Western Europe, the nineteenth and twentieth centuries have been associated with a drift from rural areas to towns. In the United Kingdom, this has resulted in the urban areas of Greater London, Greater Manchester, Merseyside, Greater Glasgow, the West Midlands, West Yorkshire and Tyneside having just one-thirtieth of the United Kingdom's surface area, but nearly one-third of the total population. From the 1960s, the trend towards urbanization was partly reversed, with many of the larger conurbations experiencing a decline in population, combined with a deterioration in many inner-city areas. Those moving out have tended to be the most economically active, leaving behind a relatively elderly and poor population. Much of the movement from the conurbations has been towards the rural areas just beyond the urban fringe. For example, London has lost population to the Home Counties of Berkshire, Buckinghamshire, Hertfordshire and Essex. The increasingly large dormitory population of these areas remains dependent on the neighbouring conurbation. Movement from urban to rural areas has brought about a change in lifestyle, which has implications for businesses. Higher car ownership in rural areas has led more households to make fewer shopping trips for household goods, to travel further to the shop that best suits their lifestyle and to spend more on each trip. In this changed shopping pattern, the decision-making unit may comprise more members of the household than in an urban area where the (typically) wife may have made more frequent trips to the local supermarket by herself.

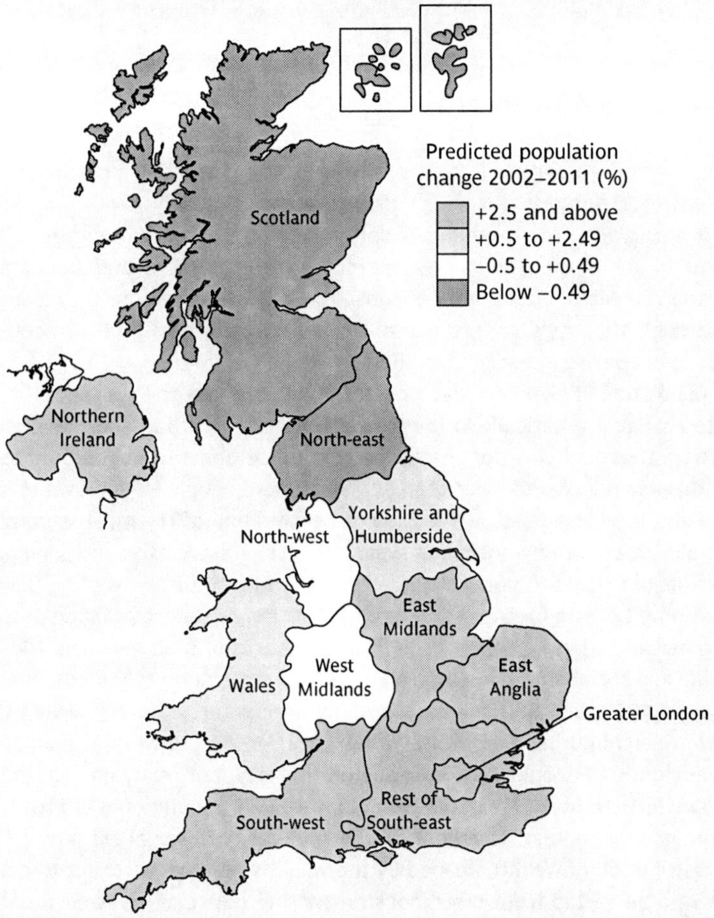

Figure 3.17 Percentage population change by region, 2002–2011 projections
Source: based on information published by the Office of Population Censuses and Surveys, General Register Office (Scotland) and General Register Office (Northern Ireland)

More recently, there has been a trend for young professional people to move back into town centres. For this group, having the facilities of a town centre close at hand without the need for increasingly expensive and time-consuming commuting has proved attractive. Town centres, which were once deserted in the evening, have often been brought back to life, helped by this group's patronage of wine bars, restaurants and all-night convenience stores.

The geographical distribution of the population differs between EU member states. For example, EU statistics show that the proportion of the population living within metropolitan areas varies from 13 per cent in Italy to 44 per cent in France. The resulting differences in lifestyles can have implications for goods and services as diverse as car repairs, entertainment and retailing.

Case study: A journey through Liverpool – European Capital of Culture 2008

By Damian Gallagher, Aberystwyth University

To many people, Liverpool's culture is characterized by the 'Scouser', an individual with a jovial, happy-go-lucky sense of humour, a strong, distinct accent and sense of community spirit. The Scouser's love of music and entertainment is epitomized by Liverpool being the birthplace of the Beatles, and home to one of the world's greatest football teams. But scratch beneath the surface of Scouser culture and you will find a number of subcultures. It has always been that way, and a historical excursion through the city's culture demonstrates how the evolution of Scouser culture has influenced the business environment of Liverpool.

In 1660, the population of Liverpool was a modest 1200, but over the course of the next three centuries this was to change dramatically in the face of unrelenting urban and commercial growth. By 1775 the culture of Liverpool was dominated by commerce and the population had increased to 35,000; by 1801 this had doubled to more than 82,295 as more people were drawn to its ever developing port facilities and transport links, and it grew to become one of the most important ports in the world, trading in almost everything, including sugar, tobacco, grain, cotton and even people.

As well as growing in size, the population had grown in its cultural diversity. Between 1830 and 1930 Liverpool became a centre for transcontinental migration as almost 9 million people used its port as a gateway to a new life. Many sought escape from the events of their own countries of origin, such as the Irish Famine and social unrest in Eastern Europe, via emigration to Canada, the USA, Australia, New Zealand, South Africa and South America. Many immigrant seafarers settled in the area and others moved from neighbouring agricultural areas attracted by the work available. Between 1845 and 1849, 1.25 million Irish people used Liverpool in this way, but many had to stay, as they could not afford to go any further. By 1851, 25 per cent of Liverpool's population was Irish.

By the mid-nineteenth century, Liverpool had become a city of social extremes. There was a distinctly unequal distribution of wealth, headed by the wealthy elite of merchant traders, bankers and shipping agents who benefited from Liverpool's prospering port and invested heavily in the city's architecture, but very little in the education, housing or healthcare of its workers. This allowed for ghetto-like segregation to develop in the city, with lots of poverty and deprivation. As the population increased, the city's boundaries expanded but its infrastructure struggled to cope with the sheer number of people, and many poor Irish, Caribbean, Chinese, Dutch, German, Jewish, Welsh, Filipino and African working-class slum areas developed around the Scotland Road and Sebastapol Dock areas. Houses built to accommodate 19 were often found to contain over 90 people, where typhus, dysentery, cholera and lack of adequate sanitation saw average life expectancy at only 38 for women and 37 for men compared to the national averages of 42 and 40 respectively.

In the years prior to the Second World War, Liverpool's population peaked at 867,000. However, the twentieth century saw massive changes in the world's economic order, with many political and commercial changes having a negative impact upon Liverpool. As the century drew to a close, the last of the working docks had closed and the once thriving port was a shadow of its former self. The population fell to 439,473, with many having chosen to leave the city in the face of rising unemployment.

High unemployment has often played a major role in the life of Liverpool. Manufacturing, which had boomed in the early post-war years, declined in the 1970s and 1980s. The docks were also shrinking rapidly and many of the inner-city docks closed, with the once strong workforce being replaced by machinery and new technologies. This led to much social and political unrest as answers and solutions were sought by the 22 per cent of the male population who were unemployed (compared to the national average of 10 per cent). In some areas of Liverpool, unemployment was as high as 90 per cent. In 1981, social unrest exploded into the notorious Toxteth riots. While racial tensions between the police and black youths provided the spark, it is now widely accepted that this was not a 'race riot'. Many underlying social issues lay at the heart of the problems in the form of chronic unemployment, bad housing and poor education. Many white youths from neighbouring areas saw the riots as an excuse to vent their frustrations and joined in the fierce battles that raged for most of that summer, causing millions of pounds' worth of damage and leading to over 500 arrests.

Many people in these areas also blamed the recently elected Thatcher government for making their problems worse, seeing no role for the working classes in its policies of free market enterprise and the reduced role of trades unions. This gave birth in the mid-1980s to a radical militant local government in the city. Based on the Far Left of the Labour Party, it was seen by many as a revolt against Thatcherism as it embarked upon largely confrontational policies that were detached from the central Conservative government. In challenging the Conservative government's house-building policies, among others, the socialist government of Liverpool appeared to be riding on a wave of popular support from the disadvantaged Scousers who had lost out in the economic and social reforms of the Thatcher government.

This militancy was seen by many as a hangover from the working-class labour organizations of the docks that were opposed to the aims of the Conservative government. Negative media images of a city with many social and economic problems did little to attract inward investment to the city or alleviate the sense of decline felt by its inhabitants.

By the 1990s, while the extremes of wealth and poverty still existed in Liverpool, though perhaps not as pronounced as in earlier years, a substantial middle-class population had also emerged. A new generation of young affluent and well-educated professionals with ambition and drive for success helped to fuel the social and economic regeneration of the city – some even point out with irony that these were the products of the Thatcherism that was once so reviled by the traditional Scouser. The smart coffee bars that this group gravitates to today are in another world compared with the rough pubs and ale houses of their predecessors.

An aerial view of Liverpool today reveals a city that is symbolized by its two cathedrals, one Catholic and one Anglican, standing at opposite ends of Hope Street. However, this hides the underlying multicultural make-up of the city, which remains from its days as a successful trading port. The Irish influence on the city remains strong, with many Scousers being fourth- and fifth-generation Irish, and the city often being referred to as the 'capital of Ireland'! Muslims, Jews, Hindus, Sikhs, Buddhists and Taoists of Europe's second-largest Chinese community still play a substantial role in the city. From 2004 onwards, many Poles headed for Liverpool, following the expansion of the EU to Eastern Europe. Many businesses specifically target these ethnic and cultural groups, whose cultures are celebrated in events such as the annual Chinese New Year celebrations, the Irish Festival, the Caribbean Carnival and the Liverpool Welsh Choral Union, as well as the recent Gay, Lesbian, Bisexual and Transsexual Homotopia festivals.

In 2008, the city of Liverpool was named European Capital of Culture. Liverpool was looking to its Capital of Culture celebrations as a key driver for economic and social regeneration in the same way as previous hosts had experienced (e.g. Glasgow in 1990). With unemployment at its lowest rate for 30 years as a good starting point, the city saw many benefits to be obtained before, during and after 2008; 11.1 million tourists were projected to visit and spend £547 million, leading to the creation of 14,000 new jobs. The docks area that temporarily lay derelict has been subject to regeneration and redevelopment, and is now home to many expensive luxury apartments and trendy bars, shops, restaurants and cafes, art galleries and museums. In 2004, Liverpool's Pier Head was even designated a UNESCO World Heritage site. Will such an influx bring about further change in the composition of Liverpool's cultural groups? And will the traditional working-class solidarity derived from the days of the docks survive in an era of consumerism and competitive service industry employment?

QUESTIONS

1 Summarize the changes in the cultural composition of Liverpool that have occurred during the last two centuries, and explain why business organizations should be interested in understanding these changes.

2 The case describes periods of social unrest in Liverpool that resulted from rising levels of unemployment following the decline of many traditional industries. Should business organizations seek to address issues of social exclusion such as that which occurred in Liverpool in the 1980s? If so, how could they help?

3 Identify the possible effects on businesses in Liverpool resulting from its nomination as European Capital of Culture 2008.

Summary

Societies are not homogeneous and this chapter has explored the processes by which individuals develop distinct social and cultural values. The concepts of social class, lifestyles, reference groups, family structure and culture are important reference points for businesses, and change in these must be monitored and addressed. Population totals and structures change and this chapter has reviewed the impact of demographic change on the marketing of goods and services. A changing population structure also has implications for the availability of employees.

There is a close link between this chapter and **Chapter 10**, where we look at the social responsibility of businesses. As attitudes change, there has been a trend for the public to expect business organizations to act in a socially more acceptable manner. There are close links between the social environment and the political environment (**Chapter 2**), with the latter reflecting changes in the former. It has also been noted that technology can have a two-way effect with the social environment, and understanding the complexity of society's changing needs calls for an information system that is comprehensive and speedy (**Chapter 4**). When a company enters an overseas market, it is likely to face a quite different set of cultural values (**Chapter 14**).

Key terms

Age structure (119)
Attitudes (102)
Birth rate (116)
Cellular household (100)
Census of population (108)
Cultural convergence (92)
Culture (89)
Demography (112)
Ethnic minorities (95)
Family roles (99)
Geodemographic analysis (109)
Household structure (121)
Life stages (110)
Lifestyle (103)
Migration (117)
Reference groups (101)
Role (99)
Social class (96)
Subculture (92)
Values (102)

Chapter review questions

1 Examine the ways in which the different culture of a less developed country may affect the marketing of confectionery that has previously been marketed successfully in the United Kingdom.

2 In what ways are the buying habits of a household with two adults and two children likely to change when the children leave home?

3 Critically assess some of the implications of an increasingly aged population on the demand for hotel accommodation in the United Kingdom.

Activities

1 Postcodes can reveal a lot about the social and economic composition of an area. If you live in the UK, go to the Up My Street website (www.upmystreet.com) and enter a selection of postcodes that you are familiar with. You will be given a range of information about each area – for example, house prices, nearby schools and crime levels. Click on the demographics button and you will be presented with a description of the area based on its ACORN code classification. How well do the ACORN classifications match the characteristics of inhabitants that you are familiar with?

2 If you live in a multi-ethnic area, examine advertising material for businesses catering for distinctive ethnic groups. What, if any, differences can you spot in how these businesses have differentiated their product, compared to similar goods and services offered by other companies to the indigenous population? To what extent do you see evidence of common underlying needs, but distinct cultural manifestations?

3 Consider a recent case when you went out with a group of friends to a restaurant, a bar or cinema. Critically examine the processes involved in deciding between the alternatives available. Explore the effects of the attitudes, values and lifestyles of the individuals concerned. What was the effect of social pressure on the final decision?

Further Reading

Social classification has been discussed widely and the following texts are useful in a marketing context.

Devine, F., Savage, M., Scott, J. and Crompton, R. (2004) *Rethinking Class: Cultures, Identities and Lifestyles*, Basingstoke, Palgrave Macmillan.

Mihić, C. and Čulina, G. (2006) 'Buying behavior consumption: social class versus income', *Management*, Vol. 11, No. 2, pp. 77–92.

For further discussion of market segmentation methods, the following texts show practical application of methods to identify groups within society which have similar consumption patterns.

Dibb, S. and Simkin, L. (2007) *Market Segmentation Success: Making it Happen!*, New York, Haworth Press.

Yankelovich, D. and Meer, D. (2006) 'Rediscovering market segmentation', *Harvard Business Review*, February, pp. 1–10.

For statistics on the changing structure of UK society and its habits, the following regularly updated publications of the Office for National Statistics provide good coverage.

Family Expenditure Survey: a sample survey of consumer spending habits, providing a snapshot of household spending, published annually.

Population Trends: statistics on population, including population change, births and deaths, life expectancy and migration.

Regional Trends: a comprehensive source of statistics about the regions of the UK, allowing regional comparisons.

Social Trends: statistics combined with text, tables and charts, which present a narrative of life and lifestyles in the UK, published annually.

References

Economist, The (2001) 'The new demographics', Vol. 361, No. 8246, 11 March, Special Section, pp. 5–8.

Eurostat (2007) *Eurostat Yearbook 2006–07*, Luxembourg, Statistical Office of the European Communities.

Future Foundation (2004) *Changing Lives*, London, Future Foundation.

Mintel (2002) *Halal Foods – UK*, London, Mintel.

Mintel (2003) *British Lifestyles*, London, Mintel.

Mintel (2004) *Pocket Money – Food and Drink in the UK 2004*, London, Mintel.

UNFPA (2007) *State of World Population Report 2007*, New York, United Nations Population Fund.

US Department of Agriculture (2004) *Annual Report*, 'The cost of raising a child', Washington, DC, US Department of Agriculture.

Chapter 4

The Technological and Information Environment

CHAPTER OBJECTIVES

This chapter will explain:

- the diversity of technological impacts on business
- the increasing speed of technological development
- innovation as a source of companies' and countries' competitive advantage
- the effects of the social environment on technology acceptance
- the impact of the internet on communication between organizations, and their environment

4.1 What is technology?

The word 'technology' can easily be misunderstood as simply being about computers and high-tech industries such as aerospace. In fact, technology has a much broader meaning and influences our everyday lives. It impacts on the frying pan (Teflon-coated for non-stick), the programmable central heating timer, cavity wall insulation, the television, DVD player, washing machine, car – in fact, just about everything in the home. The impact at work can be even greater, as technology changes the nature of people's jobs, creating new jobs and making others redundant. It influences the way we shop, our entertainment, leisure, the way we work, how we communicate and the treatment we receive in hospital. The aim of this chapter is to explore the many ways in which technology impacts on business, and will focus on:

- the development of new or better products
- reduction in the cost of making existing products
- improvements in the distribution of goods and services
- new methods of communicating with customers and suppliers.

Technology is defined in the *Longman Modern English Dictionary* as 'the science of technical processes in wide, though related, fields of knowledge'. Technology therefore embraces mechanics, electrics, electronics, physics, chemistry and biology, and all the derivatives and combinations of them. The **technological fusion** and interaction of these sciences is what drives the frontiers of achievement forward. It is the continuing development, combination and application of these disciplines that give rise to new processes, materials, manufacturing systems, products, and ways of storing, processing and communicating data. The fusion and interaction of knowledge and experience from different sciences is what sustains the 'technological revolution' (see Figure 4.1).

The term **demand-technology life cycle** is used to help explain the relevance to businesses of technological advances. Products are produced and marketed to meet some basic underlying need of individuals. An individual product or group of products may be only one way of meeting this need, however, and indeed is likely to be only a temporary means of meeting this need. The way in which the need is met in any period is dependent on the level of technology prevailing at that time. Kotler (1997) cited the need of the human race for calculating power. The need has grown over the centuries with the growth of trade and the increasing complexity of life. This is depicted by the 'demand life cycle' in Figure 4.2, which runs through the stages of emergence (E), accelerating growth (G_1), decelerating growth (G_2), maturity (M) and decline (D).

Over the centuries, the need for calculating power has been met by finger-counting, abacuses, ready-reckoners, slide rules, mechanical adding machines (as big as an office desk), electrical adding machines (half the size of an office desk), electric calculators (half the size of a typewriter), battery-powered hand calculators and now palm-sized computers. Kotler suggests that 'each new technology normally satisfies the need in a superior way'. Each technology has its own 'demand-technology life cycle', shown in Figure 4.2 as T_1 and T_2, which serves the demand cycle for a period of time. Each demand-technology life cycle will have a history of emergence, rapid growth, slower growth, maturity and decline, but over a shorter period than the more sustainable longer-term demand cycle.

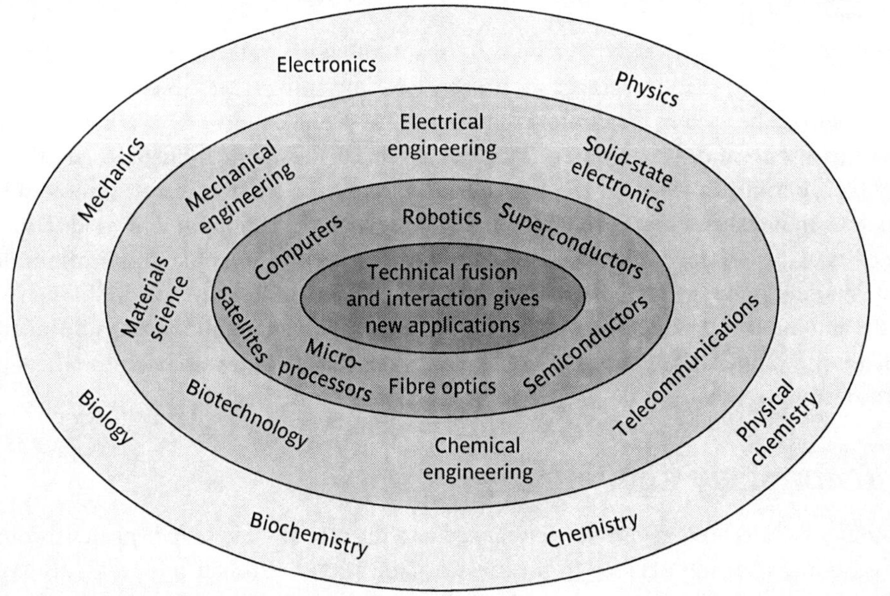

Figure 4.1 Technology fusion

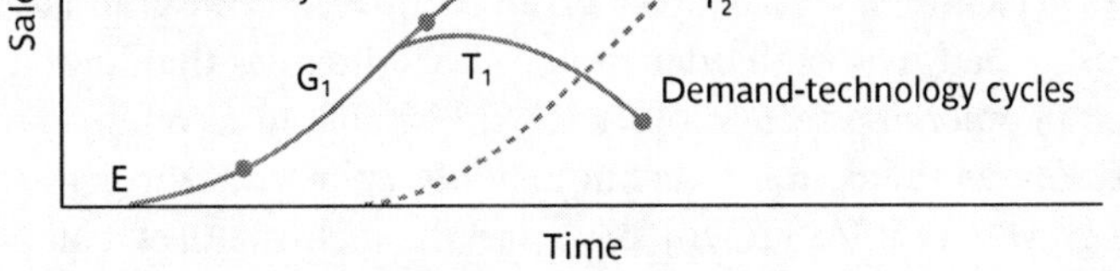

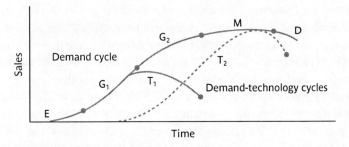

Figure 4.2 The demand-technology life cycle

Business organizations should watch closely not only their immediate competitors but also emerging technologies. Should the demand technology on which their product is based be undermined by a new demand technology, the consequences may be dire. If the emerging demand technology is not recognized until the new and superior products are on the market, there may be insufficient time and money available for the firm to develop its own products using the competing technology. Companies making mechanical typewriters, slide rules, gas lights and radio valves all had to adjust rapidly or go out of business. One way executives can scan the technological environment in order to spot changes and future trends is to study technology transfer.

The term technology transfer can be used in a number of contexts. It is used to refer to the transfer of technology from research establishments and universities to commercial applications. It may also be used in the context of transfers from one country to another, usually from advanced to less advanced economies. Transfers also occur from one industry to another; technology then permeates through the international economy from research into commercial applications in industries that can sustain the initially high development and production costs. As the costs of the new technology fall, new applications become possible. Applications of technology first developed for the US space programme, for example, may now be found in many domestic and industrial situations. NASA (the National Aeronautics and Space Administration) established nine application centres in the United States to help in transferring to other applications the technology that was developed for space exploration.

4.2 Technology and society

The rate at which technology is being enhanced and the rate at which it permeates through the world economy is of importance to business organizations. Product life cycles are typically becoming shorter. Expertise in a particular technology may no longer be a barrier preventing competitors from entering an industry. New entrants into an industry may benefit from the falling costs of technology or may be able to bypass the traditional technology by using some new and alternative technology.

Businesses managers should be interested in the degree to which technology influences their business. Consider some historical antecedents: Bic produces a disposable plastic razor to challenge Wilkinson and Gillette; the fountain pen is challenged by the ballpoint, and in turn the ballpoint is challenged by the fibre-tip. Failure to identify changes in technology soon enough may cause severe and sometimes terminal problems for companies. Although there can be sudden changes in technology that impact on an industry, it is the gradual changes that creep through the industry that may be harder to detect. Companies that anticipate, identify and successfully invest in emerging technologies should be able to develop a strategic advantage over the competition; as the demand-technology life cycle goes through the stage of rapid growth, they will grow with it. As growth slows and the cycle matures, competitors will find it increasingly hard to gain a foothold in the new and by now dominant technology.

Our lives are affected by the interaction between technological changes and the social, economic and political systems within which we live and work. Over the last half-century the life of a mother has changed dramatically. With washing machines, tumble dryers, dishwashers, fridge-freezers and microwave cookers, modern textiles that are easier to wash and iron, convenience foods and possibly the use of a car, the time devoted to household chores is much reduced. Partly as a result of these innovations, women are better educated and more likely to be in paid employment and thus contributing to an increased disposable income. Also flowing from these developments, shopping patterns change from daily shopping in small local shops, limited to what can be carried and with transport via the bus, to weekly shopping (perhaps even on a Sunday or in the middle of the night) using the car, or online grocery shopping with home delivery. The lives of schoolchildren also change, with even the youngest being introduced to the computer. Business people now have a truly mobile office with a laptop computer, PDA and mobile phone, which in turn are being integrated into a single unit. They may be working from the car, from home or even from a client's office. We are experiencing the casualization of communications, with people using personal phones, faxes, email and SMS text messages, and expecting immediate responses but of a less formal nature. Within the family, life can become more dysfunctional as individual members pursue their own lives and activities. With more TV channels and choice, there is a greater need for additional TVs, at least one of which is likely to be linked to a games console. Space will also need to be found for at least one computer.

4.2.1 Technology and consumer adoption

Many new technologies experience initial scepticism from consumers. At first, many thought that the technology of bank ATM machines would never become popular with bank customers, who would prefer to deal with bank staff face to face. Of course, ATMs have now become the routine method of withdrawing cash from a bank account. Similar voices of scepticism were raised with internet banking. So how does a company try to predict the take-up of new technologies by consumers?

Models of technology adoption have their origins in the disciplines of psychology, information systems and sociology. The Technology Acceptance Model (TAM) (Davis, Bagozzi and Warshaw 1989), based on the Theory of Reasoned Action (Ajzen and Fishbein 1980; Fishbein and Ajzen 1975), has become well established as a model for predicting acceptance of new IT-based services. The model (Figure 4.3) introduces two specific beliefs that are relevant for technology usage, namely perceived usefulness (U) and perceived ease of use (E). Actual behaviour is determined by behavioural intention (BI); however, behavioural intention is jointly determined by the individual's attitude towards a technology (A) and perceived usefulness (U). Finally, perceived ease of use (E) is a direct determinant of attitude (A) and perceived usefulness (U). In the case of older bank customers, where there is often nothing to be gained by switching to computer-mediated banking because other banking methods are available, it is likely that perceived ease of use would have a stronger influence on behavioural intentions than would perceived usefulness. However, in a business banking context, perceived usefulness is likely to be a stronger predictor of behavioural intention than attitude. There is considerable evidence that young people have been more ready than older people to adopt new technologies (O'Cass and Fenech 2003).

In some newly industrializing countries people would view the rush in Western economies to automated self-service as perplexing. In India and other Asian countries, where labour is relatively cheap, the rising incomes of the middle classes may be used to employ more domestic help rather than buying a washing machine or vacuum cleaner, for example. Consumers in different parts of the world will have different priorities according to wealth and circumstances. In China, where the opportunity to buy your own home or car is more limited than in the UK, consumers with rising incomes are more likely to spend on TVs and mobile phones.

Sometimes, consumers are faced with the simultaneous emergence of two new competing technologies, and it can be difficult at the outset to predict which new technology will win out. In the 1970s, video recording became a mass-market possibility, but although the Betamax

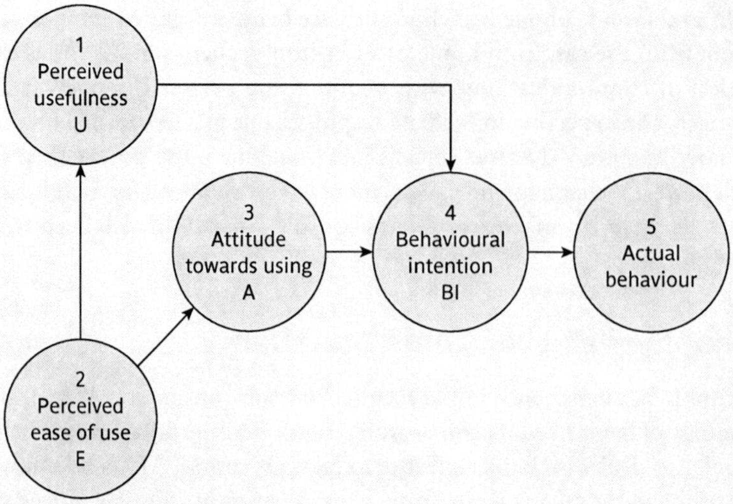

Figure 4.3 Services companies often encourage their customers to adopt new self-service technologies, thereby reducing their costs, especially staffing costs. They may also promote the fact that service users can obtain additional benefits by using an automated form of service delivery. However, many service users may remain deeply sceptical, failing to see the benefits to themselves, and influenced by horror stories in the media of how the new technology has previously let customers down (for example, many people remain cautious about giving their credit card details over the internet, although, rationally, this is safer than giving details over the telephone). When planning the expansion of self-service facilities, companies need to be able to estimate the take-up rate, so that queues do not form or capacity remain unused. This model has been developed to explain the influences of perceived usefulness and attitude on consumers' intention to use, and actual use of, new technology.
Source: based on Davis, Bagozzi and Warshaw 1989, p. 985

format was claimed to offer higher quality, it was the VHS format that eventually became dominant. Once a new technology passes a tipping point, with backing from key stakeholders, it can acquire an unstoppable momentum. The battle of technology formats came to a head again in 2008 in the struggle between two alternative versions of high-definition DVD recorders. Walt Disney, 20th Century Fox and Metro Goldwyn Mayer had lined up behind Blu-ray, while Universal supported the competing HD-DVD format. The costlier Blu-ray accounted for an estimated three-quarters of worldwide sales in 2007, but how long could this last? The film-makers were desperate for a new format to emerge in order to revive sales of DVDs, which had begun to slow down. However, they were concerned that consumers' confusion could lead to deferred purchases, and eventually high-definition DVD technology could lose out to digital downloads or video-on-demand. In this war of the formats, the winner would be the format with support from the majority of film studios and equipment manufacturers. The losing format would probably become increasingly marginalized and eventually go the way of Betamax.

Thinking around the subject: Too many chips in the kitchen?

How does a company developing high-technology consumer products predict whether a new product is going to be a hit with consumers or a miserable failure? One very simple, but naive, solution would be to ask target consumers whether they would purchase the proposed new product. But, for radically new technologies, consumers may have very little idea of what the product involves and how it would fit into their lives. They would probably have difficulty articulating their thoughts about the product to a researcher. Is it any wonder then that an estimated 80 per cent of new products fail?

One method used by companies to try to better predict the likely take-up of new products is based on ethnographic research. This involves supplying participating households with prototype versions of the product and watching how they actually use and interact with it. In return for an incentive, a family may be filmed and a diary recorded of their activities, typically over a two- or three-week period.

Researchers have been curious to understand how automation, and the internet, can be brought into the domestic kitchen. The Korean firm LG developed an 'intelligent fridge' that used bar code readers to record items put into the fridge, and then taken from it and used up. This was linked to a simple stock control programme, which drew up a shopping list for the household, which in turn could be sent through the internet to the household's preferred online grocer. In principle, the household need not worry about shopping or running out of any of its favourite grocery items. But the developers of the intelligent fridge didn't take account of the loss of a sense of control felt by the household. Ethnographic researchers pointed out that what appeared to be a technologically neat solution did not meet the lifestyle requirements of households.

The electronics companies Electrolux and Ericsson joined forces for another study involving human guinea pigs and their use of domestic refrigerators. They wanted to test the concept of a 'screen fridge', which allowed the user to download recipe ideas from the internet, store shopping lists and had a built-in video camera to record messages. Among the questions to which they sought answers were: To what extent are households adventurous in their use of recipes? What is the typical number of recipes that a household relies on when cooking family meals? Who would show most interest in the technology – male members of the household who like gizmos, or the women who do most of the cooking?

The idea of being watched by television cameras throughout the house might seem very Orwellian. However, a rash of reality television shows such as *Big Brother* has made many people more open to the idea of being watched. But the question is often asked – as it has been for the *Big Brother* series – whether what is being seen is reality or the actions of a self-selecting idiosyncratic group who like to be watched. There is apparently no shortage of individuals and households who are willing to be filmed, and stories abound of semi-professional people who make a decent part-time living through such research. But is this really research that represents the population as a whole?

Source: based on Jones 2004

4.3 Expenditure on research and development

Research and development (R&D) expenditure is often classified into three major types: basic, applied and experimental.

1 Basic or fundamental research is work undertaken primarily for the advancement of scientific knowledge, without a specific application in view.
2 Applied research is work undertaken with either a general or specific application in mind.
3 Experimental development is the development of fundamental or applied research with a view to the introduction of new, or the improvement of existing, materials, processes, products, devices and systems.

Classification is also often carried out on a sectoral basis, e.g. public or private, and by type of industry. The International Standard Industrial Classification Code (ISIC) is often used.

International comparisons of R&D expenditure should be used with caution. Difficulties in comparing statistics stem from:

- differences in the basic definitions of R&D and the boundaries between R&D and education, training, related scientific expenditure and administration costs
- differences in counting numbers employed in R&D; e.g. definitions of full-time/part-time, directly or indirectly employed, qualifications and occupation
- discrepancies in the sources and destination of funds; e.g. private and commercial organizations receive some public funds, but public bodies also receive some funding from private sources; this makes it difficult to calculate the proportion of R&D expenditure financed by governments as compared to that financed by the private sector; university expenditure is typically a mix of the two, for instance
- difficulties in distinguishing the R&D element of large-scale defence programmes
- difficulties in assessing R&D funds flowing between countries, particularly between the components of multinational firms (Young 1993); the consolidated accounts of a multinational may show R&D expenditure, but in which country was it spent?
- R&D expenditure undertaken by small firms is not usually recorded by government agencies (Lopez-Bassols 1998).

In order to overcome these difficulties, economists at the Organization for Economic Co-operation and Development (OECD) issue guidelines in the form of the *Frascati Manual* for use by government statisticians. This helps to ensure that statistics are collected by each country on a similar basis, thereby aiding international comparison. The manual is also updated regularly to take account of new issues, such as software R&D expenditure, for example. However, caution still needs to be exercised when using international comparative statistics. Variations in exchange rates, the purchasing power of the currency in the domestic market, and the reliability and comparability of the statistics all give grounds for caution.

R&D expenditure across all OECD countries averaged 2.25 per cent of GDP in 2005, which is higher than the average for just the EU countries (1.57 per cent) (OECD 2007). Some emerging countries have robust and growing budgets for R&D; for example, according to the OECD, China increased its R&D spending from 0.5 per cent of GDP in 1995 to 1.34 per cent by 2005, a growth of 18 per cent per year in real terms.

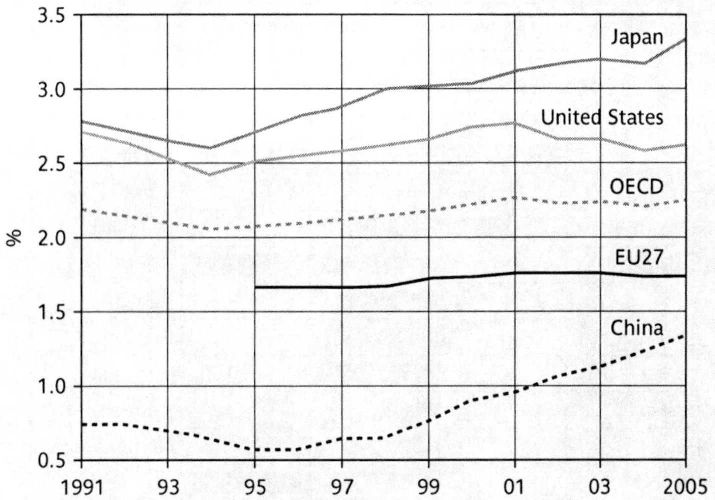

Figure 4.4 Gross domestic expenditure on research and development as a percentage of GDP for selected countries and regions
Source: based on *OECD in Figures*, 2007 edition (www.oecd.org/publications)

The UK's R&D figures do not make happy reading for the country's industrialists and politicians, with expenditure in manufacturing being particularly bad, and declining R&D expenditure in almost every sector. In real terms the UK's R&D expenditure has declined in recent years in mechanical engineering, electronics, electrical engineering, motor vehicles and aerospace. Increases in expenditure have occurred in chemicals, other manufactured products and non-manufactured products. The United Kingdom is well down the international league table on expenditure. Add to this the controversy surrounding cuts in science research budgets affecting UK universities and the picture looks even worse. Research and development is the seedcorn for the new technologies, processes, materials and products of the future. Failure in this area is likely to mean that UK companies are less competitive in the future.

According to the OECD the UK's expenditure on R&D between 1981 and 2005 declined from 2.4 per cent of gross domestic product (GDP) to 1.78 per cent (EU average 1.57 per cent) (OECD 2007). The United Kingdom's ranking against other major industrial nations (Group of Seven, or G7, nations) has slipped (see Figure 4.5).

Spending on research and development is not the only indicator of technological innovation. The number of patents registered in a country is also a reflection of a healthy R&D culture and advanced economy. As might be expected, the USA and Japan lead the way in patent registrations but Europe is also a significant contributor via the European Patent Office. However, with multinationals conducting research in many countries, and with multiple international registrations, it is becoming more difficult to track expenditure and patents by country. The OECD also collects data on the wider 'investment in knowledge', which includes public and private spending on higher education and software development, as well as expenditure on R&D (Figure 4.5).

Having taken the broad macro view of technology, the rest of this chapter looks more specifically at how technology impacts on a business and where it may be applied to improve

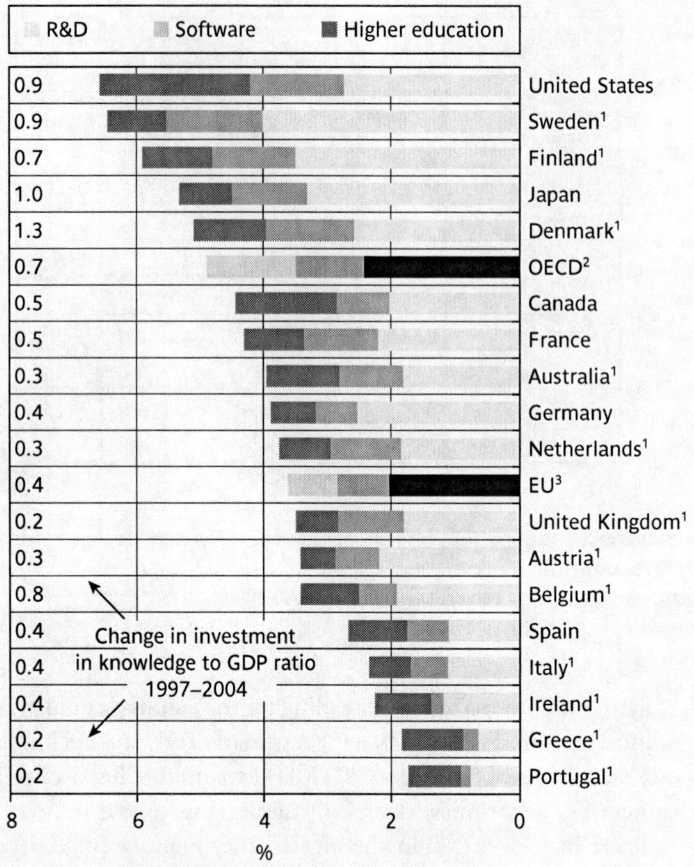

Figure 4.5 Investment in knowledge, as a percentage of GDP, 2004

Source: based on *OECD in Figures*, 2007 edition (www.oecd.org/publications)

Notes: 1. For all countries, investment in education refers to 2003. For Belgium, Australia and Austria the period of reference is 1998–2003. Data on machinery and equipment for Belgium concern total gross fixed capital investment.

2. OECD excludes Greece, Australia and Austria from the group of reporting countries.
3. EU excludes Greece from the group of reporting countries.

business operations. The following areas of technology application will be discussed: product design, manufacturing and processing systems, storage and distribution, order and payment processing, materials handling, document handling, computerized information and communications, and office automation (see Figure 4.6).

4.4 Forecasting new technologies

It can be very difficult to forecast the development and take-up of new technologies. Those nations and companies that are first to develop a technological lead will grow as the technology

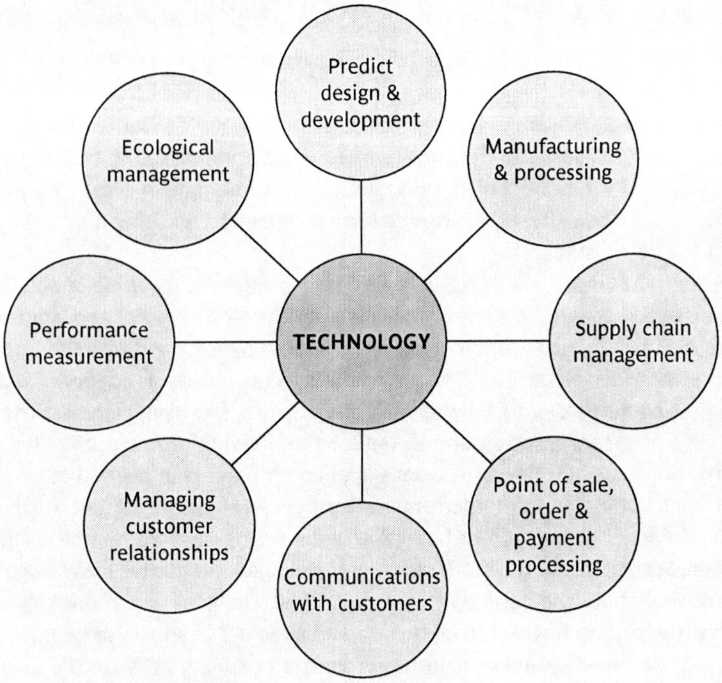

Figure 4.6 Impact of technological change on company operations

is embedded in new industries and products. Early developments in biotechnology in the USA and UK, for example, in the mid-1980s have developed into a billion-dollar global industry impacting on agriculture, pharmaceuticals, health and chemicals. Developments in the software industry transformed Silicon Valley, California, in the 1980s and 1990s, just as the car industry transformed Detroit, USA, in the 1950s. The interaction between a favourable political and social climate, higher education and research, and entrepreneurial individuals, may transform a whole economy and have a global impact.

One attempt at developing a multidisciplinary approach to forecasting the future is the UK government's 'Foresight Programme', which brings together industry, academia and government to consider how the UK can take advantage of opportunities to promote wealth creation through innovation. Foresight, and its associated 'horizon scanning centre', aims to provide challenging visions of the future, and to develop effective strategies for meeting them. It does this by providing a core of skills in science-based future projects, and access to leaders in government, business and science. Foresight operates through a rolling programme that looks at three or four areas at any one time. The starting point for a project area is either a key issue where science holds the promise of solutions, or an area of cutting-edge science where the potential applications and technologies have yet to be considered and articulated. In 2008, active projects included 'mental capital and well-being', sustainable energy management and the built environment, and tackling problems of obesity.

Thinking around the subject: Soap powder companies – all washed up?

The soap powder companies are popularly attributed with having invented modern marketing, and have continuously been at the forefront of new sales and marketing techniques. But could their progress be undone by recent developments in technology? A South Korean company, Kyungwon Enterprise Company, is reported to have developed a washing machine that does not use detergent to clean clothes.

According to the company, a device inserted into a washing machine is able to transform water into electrically charged liquid that cleans with the same results as a conventional synthetic detergent. Water is transformed inside the machine by forcing it through layers of special catalysts planted between electrodes. The system utilizes the natural tendency of water to return to a stable state, and harnesses it for laundering, deodorizing and killing viruses. The system also promises to cut water consumption and to reduce the growing problem of water pollution by detergents. The developers of the system have applied for patents in over 60 countries. How are existing washing machine and detergent manufacturers likely to react? The washing machine manufacturer Hotpoint is reported to have been monitoring developments closely and would doubtless seek a licence to use the technology, or develop an alternative technology not covered by patent. But what about the detergent manufacturers? Their market is unlikely to disappear overnight. The new system has still to be proven and even if it is shown to be effective, important segments for detergent could remain out of inertia or simply because the new technology does not cope with all tasks as well as traditional methods. The detergent companies may also embrace the new technology by developing ranges of complementary products, such as fragrant conditioners. Another possibility is that the detergent companies might seek to buy the patents to the new process and then not use them. The inventor of the technology would receive a payout and the detergent companies would continue to sell detergent, but what would be the effects on consumers?

4.5 Impacts of technology on business operations

From the previous discussion, it should be clear that technology has widespread impacts on business organizations. In extreme cases, technological development could be the reason for companies coming into existence in the first place (think of start-up companies created in the field of biotechnology), or the reason for a company's death (e.g. UK-based car manufacturers which, among other things, were slower than their Japanese competitors in adopting low-cost, high-quality manufacturing systems). In the following sections, we are going to look at a number of themes for analysing the impacts of technology on business operations:

- product design and development
- manufacturing and processing
- supply chain management
- point of sale, order and payment processing
- communicating with customers

- managing customer relationships
- performance measurement
- the ecological environment.

Of course, many of these themes overlap – for example, performance measurement is an important aspect of most companies' efforts at managing relationships with customers (databases allow the company to identify who are its most profitable customers). In the following sections we will introduce general principles for assessing technology. In a later section, we will specifically look at the impact of the internet.

4.6 Product design and development

It is often argued that the life expectancy of products has tended to shorten as technology has advanced. It took radio 30 years, from 1922 to 1952, to reach 50 million users. Television required 13 years to do the same thing. Cable television became available in 1974 and achieved this level of worldwide take-up in ten years. It took the internet approximately five years to reach an estimated 100 million users (Harris Interactive: www.harrisinteractive.com). The increasingly rapid pace of technological change means that nearly all companies must have a strategy for developing new products, to replace those that become redundant. Typewriter manufacturers who did not embrace the move towards electronic word processing eventually saw their sales decline sharply. Central to companies' understanding of change in their technological environment is the concept of the product life cycle (PLC). This is a means of plotting the sales and profits of a product over time (see Figure 4.7) in such a way that different stages in the life cycle can be identified and appropriate marketing strategies applied.

Five stages in the product life cycle can be identified.

1. *Product development prior to launch*: at this point, sales are zero and development and investment costs are rising. The new technology may as yet be unproven, so this can be a very risky stage.
2. *Introduction of the product into the market*: this means expensive launch costs and promotion. Profitable sales may take some time to develop.

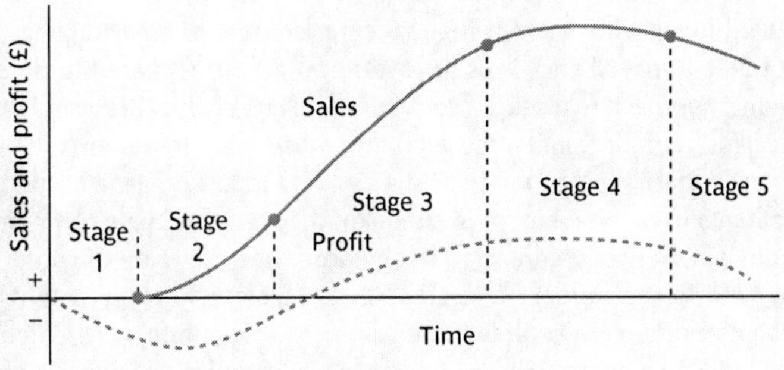

Figure 4.7 The product life cycle

3 *Growth stage*: this is when the product is fully accepted into the market and healthy profits begin to materialize on the strength of increasing sales.

4 *Maturity*: this refers to the period over which sales growth begins to slow and eventually stop. Profits may begin to decline as increasing competition puts pressure on prices and forces up promotional expenses to defend market share. New technologies are now mature and easy for competitors to copy. Patents may have expired.

Thinking around the subject: **Do patents encourage or stifle innovation in business?**

Patents grant their owner a limited monopoly on the 'idea' defined by the patent. Such monopoly rights restrict competition for the length of the patent, which some may argue is socially harmful (the example of drugs companies pricing AIDS-related drugs out of the reach of most people in developing countries is often mentioned). On the other hand, a patent helps the owner to achieve a return on the research expenditures that went into the discovery of the patented idea. This makes large expenditures for easily copied products, such as pharmaceuticals, easier to justify, arguably increasing research and development activity throughout an industry.

But could the granting of patents slow down, rather than encourage, technological development? And are there cases where it may be considered immoral to grant patents for knowledge that should be freely available to all?

One of the biggest public concerns voiced in recent times against the patent system is in relation to the granting of patents by the United States Patent Office (USPTO) for inventions in biotechnology, especially those based on genetic information. The Human Genome Project has sought to identify the structure of DNA, sometimes referred to as the building blocks of life. An understanding of human genes offers the prospect of new medical treatments. But can and should gene sequences be patented? It is reported that, by 2005, four leading private companies had already patented about 750 human genes between them and had applications for a further 20,000 pending. If all these pending patents were awarded (which is unlikely), those four private companies could own half the human genome.

There have been conflicting results in studies of the impact on research of gene patents. Is there a risk that a lack of reasonable access to the genetic codes will stifle further basic research? Will it slow down the development of commercial products? In one study, it is reported that 25 per cent of United States university and commercial laboratories were refraining from providing genetic tests or continuing with some of their research for fear of breaching patents or because they lacked the funds to pay licence fees or royalties. Patents appeared to be challenging the traditional academic approach to a shared community of knowledge (Press and Washburn 2000).

On the other hand, turning genetic research into marketable treatments implies a long-term investment, for which there is no certainty of success. In a report on genetics patents, the OECD suggested that patents have the effect of making 'knowledge a tradeable commodity which both encourages the circulation of new information and promotes a division of labour'. It found little evidence that growth in the number and complexity of biotechnology patents had caused a breakdown in the patent system or prevented access to inventions by researchers and health service providers. In fact, patents and licences for genetic inventions appeared to have stimulated research, knowledge flows and the entry of new technology into markets (OECD 2002).

5 *Decline*: at this point, sales begin to fall off and profits decline due to a lower volume of production. New technologies are likely to have appeared that take sales away from the product.

A distinction can be made between product category (say computers), product forms (e.g. networked, desktop PC, laptop, notebook and PDA) and brands (individual product brands offered by particular manufacturers such as Dell, Toshiba and Apple). Product categories tend to have the longest life cycles and stay in the mature stage for very long periods. They may begin to decline only with significant and fundamental changes in technology (as when typewriters came to be replaced by personal computers) or major shifts in consumer preferences. Product forms tend to show a more classical PLC, with each subsequent form showing a similar history to the previous one. For example, manual typewriters moved through the stages of introduction, growth and maturity, and entered decline as electronic typewriters were introduced. These then followed a similar history until they began to decline as personal computers were introduced. The old product category entered a decline stage as the new product category of personal computers went through a growth stage, and indeed has since gone into maturity. Individual brands follow the shortest life cycle, as companies are constantly attempting to update their products to keep abreast of changes in technology, fashion, customer preferences and competitors' offerings. Rapid advances in technology may mean shortening product life cycles in some industries. In consumer electronics, for example, advances in technology have allowed manufacturers to add more and more product features and to reduce prices as costs have fallen. Consumer electronic products may have a life expectancy of only 18 months before they are withdrawn and replaced.

Managing the development of new products is a complex and risky business. While many textbooks will identify a linear process, usually comprising about five stages, the reality involves a complex interaction between a number of forces. These external forces comprise technological developments, market demand, competitor activity, and possibly government influence. The internal organizational factors include management culture, research and development capabilities, engineering skills, production experience, management competence, access to finance, and marketing ability.

The linear model of the **new product development (NPD) process** can be seen in Figure 4.8.

The process starts with idea generation, which involves the search for new ideas. The next step is evaluation and screening, during which the ideas are assessed for potential. If the company has a short-term planning horizon and a conservative culture then revolutionary and innovative ideas may be dropped at this stage. As the company focuses on the short term and operates in its comfort zone it may reduce risks but it may also be producing 'me too' products. In doing so it may also miss innovative developments and technological shifts and, as a result, jeopardize its long-term competitive position or even its survival. The purpose of this stage is to

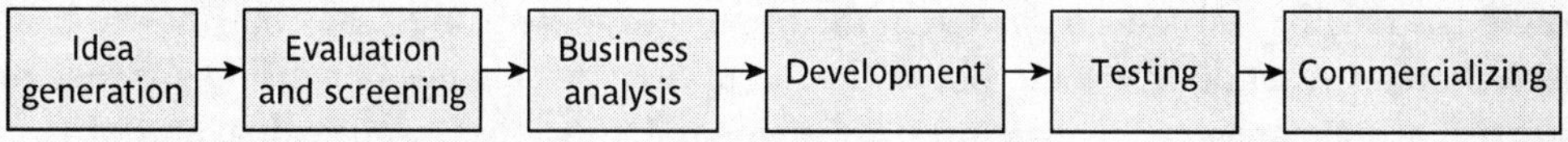

Figure 4.8 The new product development process

reduce the number of ideas and to focus on further development of those with potential. Before engaging in expensive research and development an initial business analysis should be undertaken to assess the market potential of new ideas. For products involving minor innovation, and aimed at an existing well-defined market, estimating total market potential should be relatively straightforward. But what will be the share taken by a completely new product, especially if it is aimed at a new group of buyers? How will consumers take to the new product? Will distributors like the product? How will competitors react? Will competitors launch a similar product? What price should be charged and how will this affect demand? Is the new product likely to cost more, the same or less to make than the existing product? These are all questions that need to be considered when calculating the potential sales and profit.

For those products remaining, the next stage is development. This is where the expenses, mainly associated with research and development and/or engineering, are heaviest. Can the idea and new technology be developed into a workable product that can be produced in volume, at a reasonable cost, and that is practicable for the consumer? The testing stage may involve a number of activities. Testing the functional capabilities of the product may include technical tests, reliability tests and performance tests. Market testing involves testing consumers' and dealers' attitudes to the product. The final decision as to whether to launch the product is made at this stage.

Commercializing is the last stage, and can involve the highest expenditure as the product is prepared for manufacture and launch into the market. Decisions on expected sales, what volume to manufacture, what to contract out and what to manufacture in-house can all be critical. Product decisions such as the final form of the product, the number of variants to offer, features, size, colours, branding and packaging all have to be made, as have decisions on pricing and dealer margins. Promotional strategies have to be finalized, and the timing and logistics of the launch planned.

These stages are often presented as sequential linear activities with one stage being completed before the next commences. In reality not all of the new product ideas come together and start the process at the same time. Ideas are generated at odd times and come from a wide variety of sources. The company needs to capture and evaluate these as and when they arise. From here on the company will have a number of products at different stages in the process at any one time. The development of some may be speeded up or slowed down as priorities are reassessed. Neither is the process completed in separate and distinct stages as described above. Some new ideas may come from the company's blue-sky (speculative) research, so a certain amount of 'development' will have been done before the 'evaluation and screening' stage. 'Testing' is likely to begin before the 'development' stage is finished, and planning for 'commercialization' will commence before 'testing' is finished. The important point to note is that there should be formal reviews and reappraisal at regular intervals. Transition periods between the stages identified in the NPD process are appropriate times for such reviews.

There are of course internal barriers to the adoption of new technology-based products. Individuals may be resistant to change in the organizational setting. They may have a fear of new technology itself, or for their job, or the disruption that change may bring. Change may disturb existing management structures, departmental power bases, individual authority and working relationships.

Products should be designed with a view to keeping material, manufacturing, handling and storage costs to a minimum. These issues should be considered at the outset of the design brief and not as an afterthought. Reducing product costs by 5 or 10 per cent can mean huge savings over the life of a product. In many industries computer-aided design (CAD) gives more flexibility and a speedier response to customer needs. As production methods may now give greater flexibility, it is possible to produce a wider variety of styles, colours and features based on a basic product. These planned variations should be designed in at the initial design stages, even though they may not be offered for sale until much later.

The new product development process can be extremely complex, with many examples of cost overruns and delayed results (Kim and Wilemon 2003). A key to more effective new product development activity is close working relationships between marketing and operational functions. Even simple administrative matters such as rapid communication following the results of one stage can help to speed up the process. The complexity of the new product development process has often led to companies outsourcing the whole process to specialist companies that have developed an expertise in product development and market testing (Howley 2002). Bringing in an outside consultancy can also be useful where a company's ethos is production orientated and it seeks to bring on board broader marketing skills. It has been noted that brilliant inventors do not necessarily make good marketers of a new product (Little 2002).

4.7 Manufacturing and processing

Technology impacts on manufacturing and processing systems, particularly in computerized numerical control (CNC) machine tools, computer-aided manufacturing (CAM), integrated manufacturing systems (IMS) and just-in-time (JIT) systems. With CNC, a machine tool is directly linked to a computer so that the instructions can be stored and repeated. This gives greater reliability and quicker changeover times. CAM involves linking computers to a number of machine tools and assembly robots that are interfaced with computer-controlled material handling systems. Sections of the manufacturing process are thus integrated into the same production control system. CAD/CAM (computer-aided design/computer-aided manufacturing) is where parts designed on the computer can be programmed directly into the machine tool via the same computer system. These systems can save many hours over previous methods involving the separate activities of design, building models and prototypes and then programming separate machines for production.

Integrated manufacturing systems (IMS) enable a number of CAM sub-systems to be integrated together within a larger computer-controlled system. A number of manufacturers are attempting to integrate the total manufacturing process. This, however, is very difficult to do in practice, as plant and equipment are often of different ages, were designed by different companies and use different control systems. While it is possible to design a total IMS from scratch, the investment costs are likely to be prohibitive for most companies.

JIT systems are designed to limit stockholding and handling costs. A supplier is often expected to deliver components to the right delivery bay, at a specific day and time. There may be heavy penalties for failing to deliver on time. Components can then be moved directly on to the production floor ready for use on the line. This requires close cooperation between the manufacturer and supplier, and usually is made possible only by the use of computerized information systems and data links.

These developments in technology impact on small companies and large, and on traditional industries such as textiles and shoes, as well as on new ones. Generally speaking, modern manufacturing systems allow production lines to be run with greater flexibility and higher quality, making it easier to produce product variations and allowing a speedier changeover between products, thus minimizing downtime.

Developments in production technology present companies with a number of opportunities for gaining a competitive advantage. First, developments in these areas are likely to contribute to a reduction in costs. Aiming to be a low-cost manufacturer should help in achieving a higher return on investment by allowing a higher margin and/or a higher volume of sales at lower prices. Second, modern manufacturing techniques allow for greater flexibility in production; thus, a wider variety of product variations may be produced without incurring onerous cost penalties. Recent advances in integrated manufacturing systems using computer-controlled industrial robots have meant that car markers, for example, can produce totally different models on the same production line. Third, lead times between orders and delivery can be improved. Finally, it is possible to ensure that the quality of the products is more consistent and of a higher standard.

4.8 Supply chain management

The storage and distribution of goods has also benefited from advances in technology. In particular, the increased capacity and reliability of computerized data processing and storage, combined with improved data transmission and computer-controlled physical handling systems, have led to reductions in costs and improvements in service. It is now possible to hold less stock at all stages in the distribution chain for a given product variety. From a retailer's perspective the amount of stock kept on the sales floor and in the back room can be greatly reduced.

As companies come to rely very heavily on IT systems, any problems in the system can have an adverse effect on logistical and financial operations. During 2001, the children's goods retailer Mothercare opened a new UK distribution centre at Daventry. The aim was to increase the efficiency and effectiveness of deliveries to the company's nationwide store network. In reality, poor implementation of IT systems caused stock to be lost within its system. Instead of getting 'hot' products quickly to the shelves where customers were eager to buy them, they arrived at the shop only after market preferences had changed and the goods had to be sold at discounted 'clearance' prices. As a direct result of its distribution problems, the company was forced to issue a series of profit warnings and its share price slumped, threatening the continued independent existence of the company (Keers 2002).

Retail groups acquiring competitor companies now face a much more difficult task in integrating the newly acquired stores. Previously the takeover focused on re-branding with the new company's logo and house style, selling off old stock and replacement with new, and refurbishment of some stores. Now all tills and local computer systems are likely to need replacing, the newly acquired stores must be networked into the group computer, information and communication systems, and staff need to be trained in the new systems (see Figure 4.9).

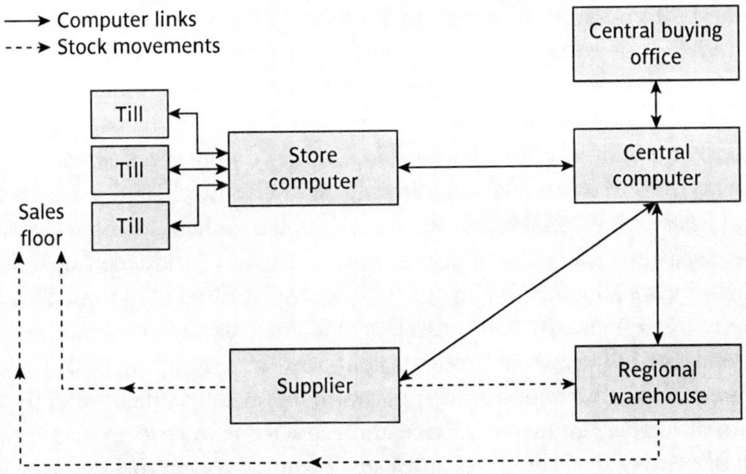

Figure 4.9 Systems linking retail stores, warehouse and head office

4.8.1 Efficient consumer response

Partnerships between producers and intermediaries are evident in the Efficient Consumer Response (ECR) initiative. This involves members of the total supply chain working together to respond to customers' purchasing patterns, thereby ensuring the right products are delivered to store shelves at the right time. Rather than seeing one retailer competing against another, it may be more realistic to see one supply chain competing against another supply chain. The implications of ECR for IT in enhancing the flow of information between participants are discussed later in this chapter. However, it should be noted that the implementation of ECR could require considerable investment from manufacturers to change corporate structures and culture, and to improve IT links between participants. Efficient consumer response can be further facilitated by just-in-time (JIT) methods of production, which require close cooperation between firms and rapid sharing of data. We will return to JIT relationships in Chapter 7.

4.8.2 Article numbering/bar codes

Efficient response to consumer demands depends on each individual product having a unique code number and the equipment at the point of sale being able to read that number. Manufacturers, retailers and other interested parties cooperated under the auspices of the global umbrella of GS1 (formed from an alliance of the Article Number Association, Electronic Commerce Association and e-Centre UK) to devise an **article numbering** system, to allocate numbers and set standards for the use of what have become known as 'bar codes'. GS1 is a non-profit-making member organization with representation globally. According to GS1, over 1 million organizations in 133 countries adhere to its standards. Recently the organization has also extended its work to radio frequency identification (RFId) for use in tracking goods in transit.

GS1 issues its members with sets of globally unique numbers, which form the basis of this identification and communication system. Each product item is allocated a unique global traded item number (referred to as the GTIN), so that each product variation by size and colour can be identified by the manufacturer. For example, a 430g can of peas has a different number from a 300g can. Nearly all grocery products now carry a bar code on the packaging. A product is simply passed over the scanner at the checkout so that the computerized till can read its bar code.

Developments in RFId technology are allowing tags to be attached to products, transmitting information to nearby receivers without the need for a bar code to be manually scanned. RFId tags were first used to track bulk containers and cartons of products, but falling costs and improved reliability are allowing individual products to be fitted with tags. This has potential to remove the need to manually scan groceries at a supermarket checkout, as the tag would immediately transmit full details of products contained in a shopping basket. However, RFId tags are still too expensive for widespread application to low-value, high-volume products.

For a national retailer, improved service and reductions in costs are achieved by linking computerized tills to a central computer and a stock control system that connects all stores and warehouses (Figure 4.10). In many cases large suppliers are also linked directly into the system. At the end of the day's trading, or periodically during the day, the central computer checks on the sales through each till. Replacement orders can then be placed with the nearest warehouse and, if necessary, the warehouse stock will be replenished by calling off further orders from the supplier. In the warehouse, orders can be processed overnight or the next day and delivered the following evening or early the next morning. Fast-selling lines can be identified using sales data

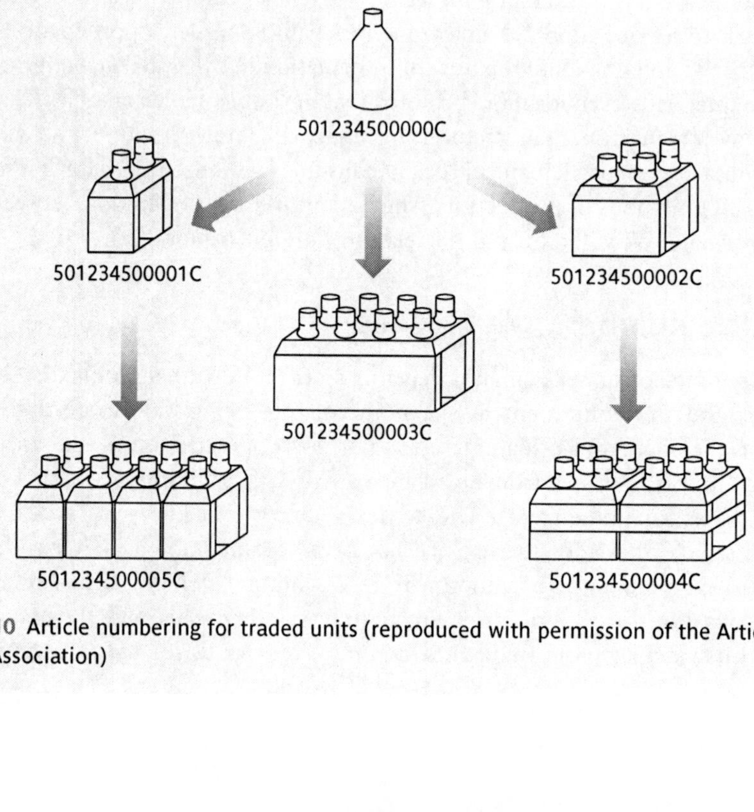

Figure 4.10 Article numbering for traded units (reproduced with permission of the Article Number Association)

and projections of sales made; further orders can then be placed with the supplier. This may be based on the first few days of a line being placed on sale. On delivery to the store, most of the items will be placed directly on to the sales floor, thus considerably reducing the need for back-room storage. This allows for a greater range of items to be stocked in a given floor space, as the stock held for each item is reduced. Stockholding by the individual store may be as low as two days' sales, compared with a week in the late 1970s. The space previously given over to back-room storage can now be opened up as part of the sales floor. Thus, the total selling space is increased, sales turnover per square metre is increased and the range of items carried is increased. There is less overstocking, fewer out-of-stock situations and less shrinkage. The tighter financial control, higher sales turnover and increased profits help pay for the investment in computers, new out-of-town warehousing, transport and physical handling systems. Electronic point of sale (EPOS) systems, which are an important source of information for the supply chain, are discussed later in this chapter.

Bar code scanning systems are used throughout the distribution chain. Outer cases are referred to as 'traded units' and can include pallets. GS1 coordinates the allocation of numbers that are used for traded units as well as consumer units. These bar codes for the 'traded units' are also machine readable, so the outer case can be monitored more at every stage in the distribution channel, from the manufacturer to the retailer or customer; every traded unit that differs by the nature or quantity of its contents must have a different number (see Figure 4.10).

At each stage of the distribution process, electronic communications between seller, distributor and buyer keep all the individual organizations' systems up to date. Electronic despatch documents, shipping documents and goods received documents form the basis of electronic invoicing and payment systems (see below). These systems are not only invaluable in tracking items through the supply chain but can be used to trace products in the event of a product recall. This is known as 'traceability' and is an essential requirement in a world of global trade. With products and processed food manufactured from components and ingredients sourced throughout the world, traceability back through the supply chain is necessary to isolate the cause of any problems.

4.9 Point of sale, order and payment processing

This chapter continues to explore specific methods by which technology has been used to improve the efficiency and effectiveness of transactions within a supply chain. In particular, organizations must aim to cut the cost of stockholding, yet still be able to respond efficiently and effectively to customers' requests.

In the previous section we considered the impact of computer systems and data links on storage and distribution. The combination of bar codes, laser scanners, computerized tills, data links and powerful computers with remote terminals has much improved control of stock. Systems are constantly being improved, as is the reliability and speed with which the systems operate. These systems are also expensive to install and run. However, as the technology improves and competition increases between suppliers of systems, we can expect the costs to come down.

EPOS (electronic point of sale) systems allow each till to total the goods purchased by individual customers and record the transaction in the normal way. In addition to the daily cash

Figure 4.11 It is not just the supply chains of manufacturing companies that have been radically improved by improved technology. Services companies do not generally need to move large volumes of physical stock, but they nevertheless often deal with their final consumers through intermediaries. For a typical insurance broker or travel agent, this may have meant handling and storing large volumes of documents as policies and tickets passed from the service principal, to the agent and on to the customer. Electronic forms of communication have greatly speeded up this process, and reduced the amount of paper needing to be moved. More significantly, for some highly intangible services, the internet has allowed a company to deal directly with its customers, rather than having to deal with them through intermediaries. An airline such as easyJet now has the technology to deal directly with millions of individual customers quickly and cheaply, something that might have been unthinkable in earlier paper-based systems of distribution. Credit cards and electronic ticketing have allowed easyJet to simplify its distribution channel, so that now over 90 per cent of its tickets are sold directly, rather than through an agent. However, such 'disintermediation' is not universal, because technology has also allowed internet-based intermediaries to flourish. Instead of booking directly with airlines such as easyJet, some travellers may prefer to use an intermediary such as Expedia or Opodo, which offers a choice of airlines. By linking airlines' and agents' databases, a customer can rapidly compare prices and availability for a selection of airlines. (Reproduced with permission of easyJet Airline Company Ltd)

Improved management information
Store-by-store comparison of states
Direct product profitability analysis
Sales-promotion effectiveness
Operational efficiency
Better stock control
Quicker stocktaking
Reduced shrinkage
No item pricing
Faster price changes
Improved customer service
Faster checkout service
Fewer queues
Itemized sales receipts
Reduced operator error

Figure 4.12 Benefits of EPOS
Source: adapted from Fletcher 1995, p. 367

analysis, however, EPOS systems may provide stock reports and an analysis of sales figures, and improve control over each till and the staff using it. The retailer no longer has to price each individual item, as the price needs to be displayed only on the shelf or the rack. This saves labour and allows for easier price changes. The customer benefits from itemized till receipts, a faster checkout, greater choice and fewer items out of stock (Figure 4.12).

EFTPOS (electronic funds transfer at point of sale) extends the benefits of EPOS to include electronic funds transfer. This means that the computerized till is now fitted with a card reader, and data links into the banking system can transfer funds electronically. The convenience for customers and retailers is enhanced, the accuracy of transactions is increased, cash handling is reduced and the costs of processing the sale are also significantly reduced (Figure 4.13).

Benefits to retailers
Reduced paperwork
Single system for all cards
Reduction in volume and cost of cash handling
Reduced security risk
Reduction in fraud
Faster checkout time
Faster payment into retailer's account
Benefits to customers
Less need to carry large amounts of cash
More choice in methods of payment
No £50 limit as with cheques
Itemized receipts and statements easy to check
Faster checkout time

Figure 4.13 Benefits of EFTPOS
Source: adapted from Fletcher 1995, p. 367

In business-to-business transactions the speed at which orders can be captured and processed by a company's systems is related to the speed at which orders and invoices can be despatched and payment collected. Closely associated with and inseparable from the ordering system is a document handling system, which includes orders, manufacturing dockets, picking notes, despatch/delivery notes, invoices and statements.

4.10 Communicating with customers

In a simple, pre-industrialized economy, companies tended to communicate with their customers personally, face to face. With the Industrial Revolution, economies of scale led to centralized manufacturing, while improved transport allowed a company to sell its goods to a much more geographically dispersed market than was previously possible. Customers who could not have direct contact with the manufacturer now had to rely on impersonal forms of communication through which they could learn about the product. It was following this process of industrialization that many of the great brands that we still know today were developed. If the local brewer was to take its beer beyond its local market, it had to communicate the brand values of its beer in markets that were distant from its brewery, and increasingly in competition with other brewers who were targeting a regional or national market, rather than a purely local one. Fortunately, just as the Industrial Revolution was associated with improvements in manufacturing and distribution, it also brought about improvements in communication. Mass-market newspapers, and later radio and television, allowed companies to spread their messages to increasingly large and dispersed audiences, at a falling cost per message received.

A number of long-term trends in the technological impacts on communication can be noted.

- There has been a gradual proliferation of communication media available for companies to send messages to customers. In the early twentieth century, advertisers' choices were largely limited to printed media, but since then, a variety of alternative media have become available, including radio, television and the internet.
- There has been a long-term reduction in the cost of communicating with customers – for example, internet communication reduces the need for costly printing and physical distribution of messages.
- The time taken to get a message to its audience has been reduced. Instead of waiting for the next daily, weekly or monthly edition of a newspaper or magazine, electronic media allow almost instantaneous generation and distribution of messages. This can be particularly important in dynamic environments – for example, airlines routinely update the price message they send to individual enquirers at their websites, depending upon the current level of availability of seats.
- Communication has become increasingly two-way rather than one-way. Printed and broadcast media, which essentially send a message from a company to its customers, with no opportunity for direct feedback, are being supplemented with interactive media, such as the telephone and internet, by which a company can engage in a dialogue with customers.

- Technology has allowed much more precise targeting of messages. In the early days of printed media, targeting was essentially limited to the regional geographical coverage of local newspapers, or the readership profile of national dailies. Modern database marketing allows companies to send quite different messages to individuals, depending upon their interests. A company such as Amazon makes very little use of impersonal broadcast media, but instead builds up a picture of its customers and uses this to send quite specific messages. For example, a customer who has a long record of buying Harry Potter books is likely to be particularly receptive to a message about a new book by the author J.K. Rowling.

Thinking around the subject: Telecoms companies are particularly bad at communicating, says report

The phenomenal development of telecommunications over the past couple of decades should have opened up tremendous new opportunities for two-way communication between a company and its customers – actual and potential. But there is still evidence that companies can be slow to embrace the interactive communication abilities of the telephone and internet. Research undertaken in 2006 by the e-services provider Transversal showed that the UK telecoms sector, which should have been at the forefront of the telecommunications revolution, was actually performing badly at communication. The report found phone companies to be among the slowest at answering their phones, with some, such as Carphone Warehouse, apparently being overwhelmed at their call centres. Answering a phone is generally more expensive than having customers communicating through a website, entering all data themselves and using their time rather than a call centre operator's time to search for results. But the phone companies didn't seem to do well here either. The report found that only a third provided an online customer search function, down from 70 per cent in 2005. Furthermore, the telephone companies' websites could answer an average of just two out of ten most basic customer questions, such as 'How do I upgrade my phone?' Online users who sent an email to the company to resolve a problem would typically wait 48 hours for a reply, and many email requests for information simply did not get answered.

It is easy to say that telecommunications improve the ability of companies to communicate with their customers, but technology alone will not improve communication. Telecommunications companies should be at the leading edge when it comes to the enabling technology, but did they have the management abilities to put the technology to good use? Or were they simply victims of their own success and, as they grew, their capacity to handle calls continually lagged behind customer demand? Had the communications revolution led to higher expectations by customers, who may have been happy to wait several days for an answer, but now want an instant response, 24/7? And, with communication costing money, could facilitating easier communication simply result in more calls from customers, adding to a company's costs and putting it at a disadvantage in a price-sensitive market?

4.11 Managing customer relationships

The information-gathering and analysis power of the internet has allowed companies to build a much clearer picture of their markets in general, and individual customers in particular. This has resulted in improvements in efficiency (for example, fewer wasted mailshots sent to uninterested target buyers), as well as improvements in effectiveness (improving the content of the mailshot so that it addresses specific target buyers' principal concerns).

Whatever the reason for a customer first making a purchase from a company, an important role in sustaining an ongoing business relationship is likely to be played by the information held about customers. A small business owner, such as a small shopkeeper or guest house owner, may have the ability to keep in their head all the information that they need in order to deliver a high quality of relationship. But in a large organization, information about individual customers must be shared, so that, for example, a customer of a hotel chain will find their personal details readily available every time they deal with one of the chain's hotels or reservations office. We are probably all familiar with companies where customer information seems to be very poor – the hotel reservation that is mixed up, the delivery that does not happen as specified, or junk mail that is of no interest at all. On the other hand, customers may revel in a company that delivers the right service at the right time and clearly demonstrates that it is knowledgeable about all aspects of the transaction.

Customer relationship management (CRM) has become a generic term to describe processes that essentially seek to join up a company's customer-focused information systems and to track dealings with individual customers throughout the relationship life cycle. Many companies offer technological solutions that promise integrated information management. However, technology is of little value if management does not give the leadership and create a culture that is conducive to integrated systems. Indeed, it is not uncommon to find firms that have invested heavily in IT systems to handle customer information, only to find that the information may actually hinder, rather than help, the task of creating more effective customer relationships.

There are many definitions of customer relationship management, which reflect the varying scope of CRM within different companies. It is defined here as:

> The systems and processes used by an organization to integrate all sources of information about a customer so that the organization can meet individual customers' needs more effectively and efficiently.

One reason for the variation in definitions is that organizations may pay differing levels of attention to the different components of CRM. The basic, but interrelated, components can be described as follows.

- Data collection and management – ensuring that data are captured accurately and speedily during all points of contact with a customer. Data collection can also include buying in records from third-party sources.
- Customer analysis and profiling – developing algorithms to analyse a customer database and identify customer/product profitability, and to identify opportunities for new product development (see the 'Thinking around the subject' box on p. 157).

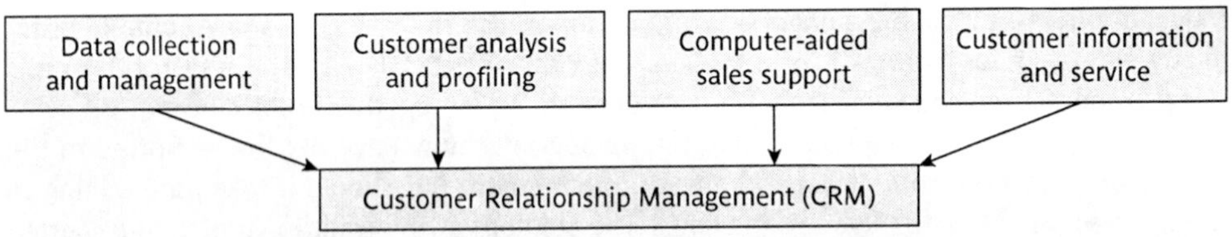

Figure 4.14 The components of customer relationship management (CRM)

- Computer-aided sales support – providing members of the salesforce with information about an actual or prospective customer so that they can conduct sales negotiations from a position of knowledge about the customer's history and preferences.
- Customer information and service – providing information to customers about a product that they have bought, or may be considering buying – for example, a warranty claim or a product recall.

How much data should a company collect about its customers? A trade-off has to be made between the cost and inconvenience of collecting information and the associated benefits to the company. Is it really worthwhile for a company to ask questions of prospective customers the first time they call? Will this be regarded as too intrusive? Will it add to costs by slowing up the process of taking customers' orders? Will the information actually be used to profitably improve sales and service delivery? Or is the information crucial to ensure that the prospective customers' needs – crucial for the long-term development of a relationship – are correctly diagnosed?

Thinking around the subject: Any excuse for a pint?

Companies are able to capture ever increasing amounts of information in order to build up a better picture of their customers' buying behaviour. The retailer Tesco is one of many companies that gather large volumes of data from till receipts, loyalty card data and other bought-in data, to give previously unimaginable insights into consumer behaviour. The story has frequently been told of an exercise undertaken by the company using data-mining techniques, which apparently discovered a correlation between sales of beer and sales of nappies. The two products were not in any way complementary to each other, so why should their sales appear to be associated? Was this just another spurious correlation, to be binned along with other gems of information such as a previously reported correlation between an individual's shoe size and their propensity to use a gym? The company didn't give up, and refined its analysis to study the correlation for different categories of store and by different times of day. Where it also had details of customers' demographic characteristics (gathered through its Clubcard loyalty programme) it was able to probe for further insights. The company was edging towards a better understanding of why the sales of these two products should be closely correlated, but it took further qualitative analysis techniques to provide a fuller explanation. It appeared that men were offering to run a household errand to the shops in order to buy babies' nappies. This was an excuse to leave the family home in order to buy more beer for their own consumption. The company is claimed to have learnt from this exercise and subsequently positioned the two products closer together in selected stores.

The story of Tesco's analysis of beer and nappy sales may have become distorted in the telling, and may even come close to being an urban myth. But should it take data mining to reveal these insights into buyers' behaviour? The landlord of the traditional Irish pub spotted this type of behaviour long ago, with pubs doubling up as the local post office, bookseller or grocer, giving the Irish drinker plenty of good excuses to visit the pub. He would have had none of the technology available to today's businesses, just a good set of ears and eyes. Do we sometimes look for complex technological solutions to understand buyer behaviour when the answer might be much easier to find using more traditional judgements?

Merging and updating databases can be a very complex task, especially where a company has multiple points of access by customers. It is quite common to find telephone sales and internet sales databases, for example, not linked to each other. The problem of linkages is particularly great where companies have merged or been acquired, and the resulting 'legacy' systems do not interface easily with each other. It is reported that when Lloyds Bank merged with Trustee Savings Bank (TSB), it took over two years for both banks' customer databases to be effectively integrated.

4.12 Performance measurement

It has been suggested that measurability – an inherent aspect of IT applications in business – has led to a change in organizational culture, from one based on a great deal of intuition and judgement, to one where measurement of targets, processes and outcomes is key. IT makes it increasingly easy for companies to measure their:

- efficiency – that is, the extent to which they are performing their activities using the minimum amount of inputs relative to outputs (e.g. what proportion of banner ads results in a click-through or a sale?)
- effectiveness – that is, the extent to which the company is doing the right things in the first place (e.g. how satisfied are its customers with the products they buy?).

Shared information through a distribution channel can also help to improve each member's measurement of business performance. Intermediaries can conduct direct product profitability (DPP) analysis of individual items, through the use of EPOS data. DPP attempts to identify all the costs that are attached to a product or an order as it moves through the distribution channel. Thus, after the gross margin has been calculated, costs such as warehousing, transportation, retail space allocation and stocking labour are subtracted to give the product's net profit contribution to a business. It is in a manufacturer's interest to determine how it might lower the cost element to the retailer by, say, redesigning a product's packaging, and thus influencing the retailer's purchase decision more favourably. Because shelf space is often a limiting factor, the key performance measure becomes DPP per square metre. A typical store may find that the figure for ready prepared meals is over twice that of basic items such as rice.

4.13 Technology and the ecological environment

Increasingly, there is concern about the ecological environment, but is technology a friend or enemy of the environment? In many people's minds, technology may be associated with ecological problems. The Industrial Revolution that took place in England in the nineteenth century is associated with harmful ecological effects, including pollution of water courses and the emission of noxious substances into the atmosphere. Industrialization has been associated with many techniques that have depleted natural resources in an unsustainable manner. Instead of small-scale fishing, trawlers with large nets and detecting equipment are able to locate and quickly catch large volumes of fish, contributing to a decline in fish stocks available in the North Sea.

The harmful ecological consequences of industrialization are not confined to Western countries during their periods of rapid industrial development; similar effects can be seen today in rapidly developing economies such as India and China. In these countries, standards of ecological protection tend to be lower than in the developed West, with manufacturers able to undertake production processes that would no longer be allowed in the developed West. Some in the West have sought measures to restrict emerging countries from polluting the ecological environment, although others have argued that it is morally wrong for the West, which has already made its wealth, to seek to restrict the activities of emerging economies that have yet to fully develop their wealth. Furthermore, it has been argued that much of the damage in emerging economies is indirectly caused by Western consumers demanding cheap manufactured goods from their polluting industries.

It is not just in the traditional manufacturing industries where harmful ecological effects have been observed. Critics of many modern technologies have argued that they are likely to have harmful effects on the ecological environment – for example, genetically modified (GM) crops may harm natural ecosystems.

Technology can help solve ecological problems, as well as add to them. Of the examples given above, it could be argued that some of the problems could in fact be solutions. In the case of GM crops, the ability to improve yields could be seen as a solution to the problem of finite farming resources, against a background of rising population. There are many examples of technology leading to the development of substitute products that have reduced demand for finite supplies of natural resources – for example, composite materials have provided an alternative to scarce ivory.

Whether a technological development is good or bad for the environment can be the subject of endless debate, with uncertain facts often being mixed with personal and political prejudice. Debate over nuclear power typifies this dilemma. In Britain, early development of nuclear power was generally seen as harmful to the environment, and emphasis was placed on the risk of emissions into the atmosphere and watercourses. Incidents involving nuclear power plants, such as that at Chernobyl in 1986, heightened concerns about the harmful effects of nuclear power generation. However, in recent years, nuclear power plants have been seen as a solution to problems of global warming. With fewer CO_2 emissions than electricity generated from gas or coal, nuclear energy has been rehabilitated in many people's minds, including some elements of the 'green' movement that have traditionally been vehemently opposed to nuclear power. Recall also the case study in Chapter 1 about the ecological impacts of civil aviation. While many would see cheap 'no-frills' airlines as an enemy of the ecological environment, the chief executive of Ryanair nevertheless claimed that his airline was a friend of the environment, by using the latest technology in its engines and control systems in order to cut down emissions.

4.14 The internet and electronic business

We may be tempted to think that the use of information technology to communicate between organizations began with the development of the internet. In fact, organizations had already developed proprietary systems through which orders and payments could be processed. In this section, we will explore the diversity of forms of electronic business. One underlying theme of the development of electronic business has been the reduced cost of handling transactions electronically, rather than through paper-based systems. Alongside this, the speed of communication has allowed business to be transacted at a faster speed, and the data generated through electronic business systems have given managers a much better understanding of the marketing and operational aspects of their organization.

4.14.1 The internet

The internet, or World Wide Web (www), is an open system that anyone can access via a computer and a modem. No one person, organization or government controls or owns the internet. It developed as a means of transferring large volumes of information between academic and government research centres in the USA. Soon people were sending messages via electronic mail (email). More universities hooked up and commercial companies became involved. As the personal computer developed so did the software, netware, browsers, search engines etc., to interface between the user and the internet. Messages and information are relayed quickly via servers and hubs to their final destination.

Initially the system was used by technical experts to send data, and text messages followed subsequently. Commercial companies began to post web pages on the internet so that those interested could browse through the information. Soon websites were developed that provided more information and this eventually led to the development of interactive sites. With the development of protocols for encoding financial and other sensitive information, the internet can now be used to purchase services and products using a credit card. The latest developments mean that the screen can be integrated with a telephone call so that the web page can be viewed at the same time as using the phone to talk to the telesales operator.

Of course, it is not just in business-to-consumer markets that the internet is reshaping distribution channels. In business-to-business channels, the internet (and intranets and extranets) has replaced previous **electronic data interchange (EDI)** systems for handling transactions between businesses. Government and not-for-profit organizations have also incorporated the internet into their distribution channels, both for procuring purchases (Timmins 2003) and for making services available to users (e.g. NHS Direct makes medical advice available to the public through call centres and the internet).

Intranet systems are private internal systems (as opposed to open and public systems) constructed using internet technology. They are internal to an organization and can be accessed and used only with permission and passwords. These systems provide a similar function to the older EDI systems, but are more flexible and user-friendly. A company's intranet system can link together an organization that is geographically dispersed, and facilitate links between an organization and its business partners, such as suppliers and distributors. Such a system is often described as an 'extranet'.

The deregulated nature of the internet, operating across international boundaries, has posed new challenges as it developed from an information service, to a promotional tool, and finally a sales and distribution channel. Concerns have been expressed in four areas: confidentiality of individual information; consumer protection for those purchasing goods and services; under which legal system a transaction takes place; and the difficulty of governments collecting sales taxes.

Some people have argued that the internet has represented a step-change in methods of conducting business, whereas others would place the internet that we know today in a more gradual process of evolution. The processes of industrialization using electronic methods, including some of those described earlier in this chapter, provided an evolutionary basis for modern internet service delivery. So, in the case of banking, ATM machines provided some of the benefits to customers (e.g. 24/7 access to account information and availability in a wide range of locations) and to banks (reduced cost of face-to-face contacts), which have evolved into online banking. Insurance companies that had moved from distribution through branches to distribution through call centres saw the development of online sales as a natural evolution. Even the whole concept of the internet has evolved during its so far still brief history. Early internet applications using the internet were relatively static, and largely sought to replicate the telephone and printed media they replaced. As the internet has developed into what has become known as 'Web 2.0', there has been much greater interactivity between service providers and consumers, and between fellow consumers. There has been a lot of discussion about whether further developments in the interactive consumer-to-consumer abilities of the internet will lead to consumers setting the agenda for the internet environment, rather than commercial organizations. The development of peer-to-peer sites such as YouTube and Facebook has challenged many assumptions about the role of traditional advertising, for example. Customer review sites are increasingly becoming an important source of evaluation in the buying decision process, yet such sites are much more difficult to control than conventional paid-for advertising. There is also some evidence of websites being used to 'educate' a customer prior to a face-to-face encounter with an organization. For example, one study of medical practitioners showed how patients engaged in virtual, parallel service encounters through the internet, changing the nature of their appointment with the doctor and presenting challenges to medical professionals both in terms of doctor–patient relationships and their professional judgement (Hogg, Laing and Winkelman 2003).

In this evolving role for the internet, some see a greater need for government control, or at least influence in the development of the internet. The OECD's Sacher Report identified three priority areas for governments. The first is for governments to actively support the development of electronic commerce by encouraging the development of the infrastructure. Governments have traditionally controlled telecommunications and television industries by either direct ownership or licensing. Technologies in computing, telecommunications, data networks and television are now converging rapidly. The report recommends that governments should encourage this by modifying regulatory regimes where necessary and by working to commonly agreed international protocols.

The second recommendation was that all governments should 'raise the visibility of electronic commerce and promote new partnerships with the private sector in order to coordinate technical, economic and political choices'. It is suggested that governments may seek to appoint a Chief Information Officer to coordinate these activities.

The third recommendation was that governments themselves should acquire the skills to participate in the electronic information age. Regulatory issues need to be dealt with urgently and as they arise. Legal issues surrounding the 'definitions, practices and structures' of electronic commerce are now being addressed. International protocols need to be further developed for dealing with consumer protection, fraud, crime prevention, the protection of intellectual property, electronic identity, definitions of residence, liability, auditing, and the control, unauthorized use and protection of databases. The issue of taxation is also of concern, particularly for taxes based on sales. Sales taxes are often refunded to exporters at despatch but re-applied on receipt in the country of importation. These issues have not been fully resolved for internet transactions.

The Economist Intelligence Unit (EIU), working in collaboration with IBM, publishes annual 'E-Readiness' ratings for countries. It defines E-readiness as the extent to which a country is conducive to internet-based opportunities, and takes into account a wide range of factors, including the quality of its information technology infrastructure, the ambition of government initiatives and the degree to which the internet is helping businesses to become commercially efficient. Its 2007 ranking showed Sweden in first place, and a generally strong performance by Scandinavian countries, which occupied first, second (joint) and tenth places (Figure 4.15). It seemed that what set Scandinavia apart was a wholehearted embrace of the information society. Sweden also had among the lowest broadband prices in Europe and the highest levels of broadband internet access.

Country	Rank
Sweden	1
Denmark	2=
USA	2=
Hong Kong	4
Switzerland	5
Singapore	6
UK	7
Netherlands	8
Australia	9
Finland	10

Figure 4.15 E-readiness of top ten ranked countries, 2007
Source: based on Economist Intelligence Unit E-readiness rankings, 2007

4.14.2 The EU and the development of a knowledge-based economy

At the 2000 summit of EU leaders held in Nice, they stated their intention for Europe 'to become the most competitive and dynamic knowledge-based economy in the world'. A programme of action included the creation of a fully integrated and liberalized telecoms market by the end of 2001; a single market for financial services by 2005; making all EU public services, including tenders, available on the internet; an EU regulatory framework and common security standards for e-commerce; connecting all schools and training centres to the internet; and creating an IT 'passport' of specific skills.

Since the summit, there has been a flurry of activity: an accelerated effort to boost national programmes for promoting e-business and getting schools online; and new laws and directives governing e-business. However, although the pace of change may be more brisk than before, those used to the rapid speed of developments in the internet world still find EU processes very slow. Business is particularly frustrated by EU-wide government inaction in terms of creating a better environment for e-commerce to flourish in.

Can the EU rhetoric be matched by reality? A report by the UK research and consultancy group Gartner identified a number of pressing challenges for the EU in its attempts to create an e-commerce-friendly environment.

- Anti-trust authorities will have to resolve, more rapidly than at present, complex competition issues raised by mergers in the media and telecoms sectors, electronic marketplaces, wireless portals and public service providers.
- Enterprises will need more flexible employment schemes and laws to cope with skills shortages in the information technology sector. Employers need the ability to import and outsource skills as required and a clearer legislative framework for teleworking.
- Tax regulations need to be brought up to date to recognize the presence of internet transactions. The Gartner study predicted that the difference between European and US internet tax schemes would become a major source of friction in international trade.
- In order to boost consumers' trust in e-commerce and reduce legal uncertainty for enterprises, governments need to develop privacy laws that are relevant to the internet.

The report painted a picture of national governments throwing money at the microenvironment of electronic commerce (e-commerce), such as grants for computer training, often displacing money that could readily be provided by the private sector. Developing the macroenvironment for e-commerce throughout the EU is a much bigger challenge. The question remains as to just what it is possible for governments to do to create an e-commerce-friendly environment. Is responsibility for achieving it best left to the EU rather than national governments? Or is even the EU too small a unit for making decisions, when the internet is progressively breaking down national boundaries?

4.14.3 E-retailing

The trend towards direct delivery from producer to consumer has been speeded up by the growth of internet access. As a communication medium with customers, email (and SMS text messaging) extends the profiling and interactivity features of direct mail. An accurate database of customers' preferences is essential if email messages are not to be discarded as junk. The capacity to send email to individuals' mobile phones raises the prospect of a huge amount of low-cost messages being targeted at individuals, and senders of messages must ensure that their messages stand out from those of competitors and have immediate relevance to the recipient.

Although 'bricks and mortar' companies may have been a little late into the fray, they are now doing well compared to some dotcom start-ups. According to websites that list the top UK retail sites, traditional bricks and mortar retailers are still very well represented. Many high-street names have transformed themselves into 'clicks and mortar' companies, including Argos

Thinking around the subject: The internet and the law of unintended consequences

'The world will never be the same again.' This was the bold message being proclaimed by many pundits at the dawn of the internet age. In one sense, these pundits were quite right, because the internet has had a significant effect on how individuals have gone about their lives. Business processes have been transformed, often resulting in great cost savings and improvements in service to customers. But, in many respects, the nature of the change that has resulted from the development of the internet has not quite been what was expected. The complex interaction between the technological, social and economic environments has produced some unexpected consequences of technological development.

Consider the following predictions, which were made in 2000 when 'dotcom' mania was at its height.

- Predictions were made that there would be less commuting as people work from home using the internet to communicate with their work colleagues. Traffic congestion would disappear and commuter rail services would lose customers. In fact, technology has allowed many people to choose a pleasant residential environment and to live much further away from their work, because they now have to travel to the office on only a couple of days each week rather than every day. Overall, the travelling distances of many people in this situation have actually increased, resulting in more rather than less total commuting.
- Conferences were predicted to disappear in favour of videoconferencing. Why bother travelling to a meeting or conference when you can meet 'virtually' from the comfort of your own desk or armchair, and at lower cost? However, face-to-face conferences have continued to prosper. The technology that causes many people to work in isolation may have indirectly contributed to a desire to counter this with more face-to-face meetings with a greater social content.
- High-street shops were being written off in 2000 when, quite extraordinarily, the pure internet company lastminute.com had a market capitalization value far in excess of the 110-outlet Debenhams store. The convenience of shopping in the high street or at out-of-town shopping centres and the problems of arranging the home deliveries of internet suppliers were underestimated by advocates of internet-based shopping.

- Pre-dating all these predictions has been the expectation that we will need to work fewer hours, as we live in a world of leisure where machines do the work, leaving consumers with more leisure time. In reality, average working hours have tended to increase in recent years, not fall.

We seem to have an inherent tendency to overstate the short-term effects of technological change, but to understate the long-term effects on our behaviour. With the development of new technologies enabling high-speed mobile internet services, further predictions were being made in 2008. Would we really want to download full-length feature films to watch on our mobile phones? Would we really want to surf the net while travelling on a train? Would there be unforeseen 'killer applications' such as SMS text messaging, which was almost left out of the specification of first-generation mobile phones because no useful role for it was foreseen? Perhaps the long-term effects of the internet may be more subtle by contributing to individuals' sense of connectedness with narrowly selected commercial and social groups, no matter where they may be located, while the sense of community with diverse groups of people forced to live together in close proximity may be reduced.

The unforeseen consequences of the internet emphasize how difficult it can be for organizations to understand the consequences of new technologies. These examples demonstrate the importance of understanding the linkages between different elements of the business environment, so developments in the technological environment can be sensibly understood only in conjunction with changes in the social environment.

(general household goods), Tesco (groceries), Comet (electrical appliances), PC World (computers), WHSmith (books and stationery). Many offer a variety of options, including 'buy online and pick up from store', which gives them an advantage. Although research estimates and sales forecasts vary widely, most agree that travel is the largest e-retailing sector by far.

The traditional problems of home shopping and delivery remain:

- small orders
- high transport costs
- goods not compatible with the letter/mail box
- difficulty in offering a timed delivery window
- the most economical delivery times for companies are 9 am to 5 pm, Monday to Friday, when the customer is most likely to be out
- difficulty of returning goods.

The delivery of goods to the final consumer has not shown the productivity gains that internet-based ordering has achieved (see Yrjölä 2001). This is probably not surprising when it is remembered that home delivery remains a labour-intensive activity in which two of the main costs – labour and transport – are likely to continue to increase in real terms. We should not forget that, in the UK, the milkman has almost disappeared because efficiency of delivery could not be improved relative to the cost of consumers collecting milk from large, efficient supermarkets.

There are also many high-involvement goods where buyers feel more comfortable being able to see and feel the goods before they commit to a purchase. The failed internet clothes retailer boo.com encountered the reality that many people would probably find it much easier and reassuring to try on clothes in a shop rather than rely on a computer image, thereby ensuring a continuing role for traditional high-street retailers (although 'bricks and clicks' retailers such as Next have quietly developed a substantial level of clothes sales via their websites).

In addition, customer expectations of 'e-tailers' have risen. When ordering online, customers expect to have prices and stock confirmed as well as a delivery date and preferably the time. Customers are also expecting to be told of any delays, particularly when they are waiting in for the delivery.

Some retailers have closed a number of branches or reduced their salesforce and instead offer customers access to their product range via a website. Several UK suppliers of books, music, computer games and flowers have the logistical support to develop their business on the internet. In the longer term, it is possible that fmcg suppliers may use the internet to regain some of their lost power in channel relationships. Car manufacturers are recognizing the impact of the internet on their traditional dealership-based channels of distribution, with evidence that the internet is increasingly being used for selecting new cars (Morton 2003).

However, while the internet may facilitate direct communication between producers and end consumers, the chances of dialogue actually taking place are lessened by the proliferation of content on the internet, which presents a bewildering array of choice to consumers. The response has been the development of a new breed of information intermediary, or 'infomediary'. This type of channel intermediary gathers information about customers and sells access to them to companies seeking to promote their products. The new generation of infomediaries has effectively become a new form of value-adding member in a virtual value chain. Within the travel and financial services sectors, airlines' and insurance companies' attempts to create direct dialogue with customers have often been overshadowed by the development of powerful infomediaries such as lastminute.com, expedia.com and e-sure.com

4.15 Data security and privacy

Technology has undoubtedly allowed businesses to do things that, previously, were unimaginable – for example, in the way that data are handled and analysed. While much of this development has been beneficial to companies and their customers, some commentators have pointed to more harmful consequences for personal privacy and security.

Data protection has become a very big issue, as it is not just companies that can easily collect and manipulate information, so too can criminals. There is also concern on the part of some consumers that their personal data may be misused, if not in a criminal way, certainly in a way that they would consider unethical. These concerns have grown with developments in technology. When personal records were entirely paper based, it was difficult to appropriate data for improper uses. If paper records were lost, they were probably only likely to turn up in a rubbish skip or a place to which only a small number of people have access. The bank customer could be reasonably confident that their personal information would not get out of their local branch, and it would be difficult for anybody else to get hold of their records. Today, their personal information is likely to be held on servers that are accessible remotely by a range of authorized employees.

Unfortunately, unauthorized people may be able to access personal information held on databases. Instead of having to laboriously break into several bank branches to obtain large volumes of customer data, there have been many reported cases (and probably many more unreported cases) of skilled hackers being able to get into a bank's database and view the records of thousands or even millions of customers. Where customer information is held on transportable discs, huge amounts of data can accidentally or deliberately end up in the wrong hands. In November 2007, many people in the UK were concerned to hear that the government had 'lost' two CDs containing the personal information of 25 million recipients of government benefits. There was concern that this information could be used by criminals to wrongly impersonate another person and obtain credit or benefits to which they were not entitled.

Within the EU, the 1981 European Convention for Individuals with Regard to Automatic Processing of Personal Data, implemented through Directive 95/46/EC, provides a framework for data privacy and security. This has been implemented in the UK in the 1988 Data Protection Act, and policed by the Data Protection Commissioner. The Act covers electronically stored data, which can be used to identify a living person, including names, birthday and anniversary dates, addresses, telephone numbers, fax numbers, email addresses etc. A number of principles guide companies' use of data, and require, among other things, that personal data shall be processed fairly and lawfully, and shall not be used for any purpose that is not compatible with the original purpose. There is a requirement for companies to keep accurate records, which are not unnecessarily excessive in detail and shall not be kept for longer than is necessary for the purpose of collecting it. Appropriate technical and organizational measures must be taken against unauthorized or unlawful processing of personal data, and against its accidental loss or destruction. The Data Protection Act 1988 and the Freedom of Information Act 2000 give some rights of access to data.

The internet has created problems for consumers in verifying who they are actually dealing with. There have been many cases of sham online companies that have set up in business with enticing offers, but have rapidly disappeared without trace. Some have been set up to obtain customers' personal information, which has then been used fraudulently after the company had disappeared. But it is not just customers who need be wary of rogue companies; companies also need to be wary of rogue customers. In a real-life environment, a company can see who is coming into its site and remove visibly disruptive elements, such as drunks disturbing the atmosphere of a restaurant. In the case of online service processes, it can be much more difficult to judge whether visitors to a company's website are benign or malicious. Malicious visitors may disrupt a company's service processes by planting viruses, bombing it with mass emails or disrupting the codes of its operating system. The reasons for this action may be a grudge against the company, or simply the challenge for a computer hacker of beating a system. Where a company is dependent on online transactions for the bulk of its revenue, the effects of such malicious intrusions can be devastating, resulting not only in a short-term loss of revenue, but long-term harm to its brand reputation where customers' details are obtained or used in an unauthorized way. In designing the online environment, companies must strike a balance between making a site easily accessible to all, and difficult for those with malicious intentions.

Case study: Will 3G phone company learn from a Rabbit?

The mobile telephone sector hardly existed just 20 years ago, but during its short history it has grown phenomenally to the point where in 2006 over two-thirds of the UK population owned a mobile phone. The pace of growth posed enormous risks for the companies involved, especially where new technologies displaced the technologies that went before them, calling for ever increasing capital investment and no chance of a return from consumers until long after the initial investment had been made in new capacity.

Many commentators saw third-generation (or '3G') technology as the key to a whole new world of mobile telephony in which the mobile phone would be positioned not just as a device for voice communication, but a vital business, leisure and information tool. In 2000 the UK government held an auction for five new 3G mobile phone licences, and the mobile phone companies paid a total of £22 billion for licences. Would they get back their huge investment, not only in licence fees paid, but also the infrastructure that was needed to support the new 3G networks?

During 2003, the Hong Kong-based Hutchison Whampoa became the first company to launch a 3G service in the UK, with its '3' network. The launch was accompanied by endless hype about how the world was going to be transformed by the streaming of video and football clips live to customers' mobile phones, and a whole new world of mobile advertising media would open up. Location-based services (LBS) had been a small but growing sector of the mobile phone industry. A report by Concise Insight (2004) noted that Vodafone UK's mobile content reached 1.9 per cent of total service revenue for March 2004, almost double the 1.0 per cent a year before. It seemed that location technology was underpinning value-added data services. Even the emergency services stood to benefit from 3G's ability to precisely pinpoint a caller's location. By 2004, 60 per cent of calls to the UK emergency services were made from mobiles, but in many instances callers didn't know exactly where they were, and ambulances and fire brigades had only very approximate locations.

But after long delays in rolling out the new phones and networks, followed by sluggish uptake of the early services, 3 found itself in 2004 focusing on more mundane marketing issues, such as the cost of old-fashioned voice calls. The costs of recruiting new customers were high, with Mark James, telecoms analyst at Japanese investment bank Nomura, estimating that 3's customer acquisition costs in its first year were £600 per customer – around four times the European average.

Initially, technical glitches, the high price of handsets and poor customer service were compounded by a shortage of handsets. But 3 was on a mission to grab market share ahead of the launch of its rivals' 3G services, seemingly almost regardless of the cost. During 2003 its 'land grab' programme received a boost with the launch of a highly desirable lightweight silver clamshell-style phone manufactured by LG. Just a year previously, one of these cost more than £400, but now 3 was giving them away for free on the back of generous tariffs that offered consumers 500 or 750 voice minutes to any network for £25 or £35 a month respectively.

Analysts estimated that Hutchison, which had placed a US$22 billion bet on the fledgling technology, was seeing a worldwide 3G cash-burn of about HK$100 million (US$12.8 million) per day during 2003/4, and market concern about its 3G exposure was beginning to depress the group's share price. By June 2004, the company had already lost one of its key shareholders – Japanese heavyweight NTT DoCoMo, which sold its 20 per cent stake in 3 UK back to Hutchison at a 90 per cent loss on its initial investment. However, Hutchison Whampoa had deep pockets to fund an expensive launch – although it had net borrowings, most of those were long-term debts, and disposals during 2003/4 meant it had HK$111 billion (£8 billion) of cash on its balance sheet.

More worrying to many commentators was the effect of Hutchison's tactics on the fledgling 3G industry. At the time of launch, 3 emphasized its 'gee-whiz' features. But, after only a year, it was increasingly emphasizing the more mundane affordability of its calling plans. Rival operators that were preparing their own 3G launches would aim to start by pricing the technology at a premium. But their problem was that 3 was already pricing its phones and services – which offered ITN news and premiership football clips, among other features – at cut-throat prices. Their best hope was that 3's model would prove unsustainable. After all, anyone can get customers if they effectively give their product away.

Hutchison is not new to taking big risks in the mobile phone market. It was behind the 'Rabbit' network of semi-mobile Telepoint phones launched in the UK in the 1980s. These allowed callers to use a compact handset to make outgoing calls only, when they were within 150 metres of a base station, these being located in public places such as railway stations, shops, petrol stations etc. As in the case of many new markets that suddenly emerge, operators saw the advantages of having an early market share lead. Customers who perceived that one network was more readily available than any other would – all other things being equal – be more likely to subscribe to that network. Operators saw that a bandwagon effect could be set up – to gain entry to the market at a later stage could become a much more expensive market challenger exercise.

Such was the speed of development that the Telepoint concept was not rigorously test-marketed. To many, the development was much too product led, with insufficient understanding of buyer behaviour and competitive pressures. Each of the four companies forced through their own technologies, with little inclination or time available to discuss industry-standard handsets, which could eventually have caused the market to grow at a faster rate and allowed the operators to cut their costs.

The final straw for the Rabbit network came with the announcement by the UK government of its proposal to issue licences for a new generation of Personal Communications Networks – these would have the additional benefit of allowing both incoming and outgoing calls, and would not be tied to a limited base station range. While this in itself might not have put people off buying new Rabbit handsets, it did have the effect of bringing new investment in the network to a halt, leaving the existing networks in a state of limbo.

Could the point about leapfrogging technology – which had wiped out Hutchison's Rabbit network – happen again with 3G technology? By 2006 the next generation of mobile phone services was under development, with Japanese trials of 4G well under way and already promising even greater functionality and transfer rates. The International Telecommunication Union (ITU) defined 4G as providing a minimum stationary data rate of 1 Gbps and a moving (say in a car or a train) data rate of around 100 Mbps. In field tests held in Kanagawa, the Japanese telephone company NTT achieved up to 300 Mbps at 30 kmh and an average moving transfer rate of 135 Mbps up to 1 kilometre from the base station.

More pragmatically, 3G phone technology was challenged by the development of alternative wireless access services, notably WiFi. Many companies, such as T-Mobile, had begun offering mobile WiFi services, which allow users to log on to local access points, and gain access to their email and browse the internet. Subscribers to 'VOIP' telephony services could also effectively make free phone calls from a WiFi access point. For many business travellers, using their laptop, WiFi access seemed a more attractive and less expensive option than using a 3G phone connection to check for email. It was likely to become even more attractive, with development of longer-range WiMax services that extended beyond the very limited 50-metre or so range of WiFi. The pressure on 3G services was intensified when the UK government announced in 2006 that it would license the development of a national WiFi network.

Could 3G become old hat before it had even had a successful and profitable launch? Would the history of the short-lived Rabbit network be repeated? Had the owners of the '3' network, Hutchison, failed to learn from the Rabbit failure? Or should Hutchison point to its record with another of its previous ventures – the launch of the UK Orange network in the early 1990s, which critics initially dismissed as a costly failure, but went on to become one of the UK's strongest mobile phone brands? ▶

QUESTIONS

1 Review the launch of Telepoint in the context of the 'demand-technology life cycle'. Where would 3G mobile phones fit in this life cycle?

2 Summarize the environmental factors that contributed to the demise of Telepoint services. What are the main environmental challenges facing 3G phones?

3 How might the launch of 3G services differ in a less developed country with a less sophisticated telecommunications infrastructure?

Summary

This chapter has considered technological change from the macro perspective, and examined the impact of technology on different aspects of business at the micro level. In both instances the relevance of technological change to business success has been stressed. At the macro level of technological change, the key points to remember concern the demand-technology life cycle. This will be influenced by the level of research and development expenditure, not only in a particular industry but also in related and sometimes unrelated industries. The fusion and interaction of different technologies results in new applications and processes, which may eventually give rise to whole new industries. Technology permeates through from academic and research institutions into industry, from one industry to another, and from one economy to another.

At the micro level, this chapter has considered the impact of technology on a company's products and operations: product design and development, manufacturing and processing; storage and distribution; order and payment processing; and information and communication systems via electronic business. Managers should seek to improve the efficiency of business operations and also to ensure that the benefits are passed on to the customer. These customer benefits may include better pre-order services, such as product availability and specification, information, faster quotations, quicker design customization and shorter delivery times.

The technological environment is a constantly changing one. In many industries during the 2000s and beyond, change will be the norm rather than the exception. Companies that focus on customer needs, competitor activity and technological developments, rather than simply aim to sell what the factory makes, are more likely to succeed.

There is a close link between this chapter and **Chapter 7**, which looks at networks and relationships between companies. The use of technology to improve supply chain efficiency is often a key element of business-to-business relationships. The interrelationship between technology and society is emphasized in **Chapter 3**, and this chapter explores not only technology's response to changes in society, but also the effects of changing technology on social values.

Technology has opened up many opportunities for businesses to enter global markets, and these are discussed in more detail in **Chapter 14**.

Finally, issues of privacy and security surrounding new technologies have attracted the attention of the law (**Chapter 5**) and raised ethical concerns (**Chapter 10**).

Key terms

Article numbering (149)
Computer-aided design (CAD) (147)
Computer-aided manufacturing (CAM) (147)
Demand-technology life cycle (132)
Electronic commerce (e-commerce) (163)
Electronic data interchange (EDI) (160)
Electronic point of sale (EPOS) (151)
Internet (135)
Just-in-time (JIT) systems (147)
New product development (NPD) process (145)
Product life cycle (143)
Research and development (R&D) (138)
Technological fusion (132)
Technology transfer (134)

Chapter review questions

1 Discuss the extent to which marketing managers should be involved in the R&D process. What should their role be?

2 Critically discuss the role of governments in fostering an R&D culture and in encouraging technological development.

3 Using examples, discuss ways in which new technologies have altered social relationships.

Activities

1 Assume you are working for a multinational manufacturer of electrical goods. Your main retailer in the UK has had a number of your vacuum cleaners returned recently with a serious malfunction. It appears to be a problem with the on/off switch. The product is assembled at the company's plant in Spain, but the on/off switch is manufactured in China. However, the miniature circuit board in the vacuum could have been made in Japan or Korea (two suppliers). It may be just one batch of switches or circuit boards that was faulty. To recall all the products sold in the UK in recent months would be extremely expensive. Also it is not known as yet if the vacuum cleaners sold in other countries are affected, or if other products (such as hair dryers) use the same switch or other switch designs with the same circuit board.

How would you trace the identity of the batch of vacuum cleaners and other products affected before enacting a product recall?

2 In the pub one Friday evening two men were overheard discussing electronic shopping. Both men worked in the computer industry, had lots of 'kit' at home, and had been connected to the World Wide Web for some time. They were exchanging views about the latest developments on the internet, and getting quite excited about the possibilities of buying their weekly groceries over the net and having them delivered. This would take the drudgery out of supermarket shopping, they agreed. Both men worked long hours and when asked the last time ▶

they had seen the inside of a supermarket, neither could remember. Both were married. One wife, although quite capable of holding a good job, did not work at all, had no need to work, and was quite happy to look after the family (two children) and do the supermarket shopping. The other was in a very similar position, although she had taken up part-time work, as the children were a little older. Neither woman was much taken with computers and thought that being tied to a computer all day and half the evening would be a life of drudgery.

Discuss the advantages and limitations of online grocery shopping in the social context described above.

3 Now revisit the case of online shopping and identify the technological innovations that have made this method of shopping a sustainable business model. Think carefully about technology innovation at all points in the supply chain.

Further Reading

The following texts provide contemporary insights into the role of innovation in organizations and the relationship between business and R&D.

Christensen, C.M., Anthony, S.D. and Roth, E.A. (2004) *Seeing What's Next: Using the Theories of Innovation to Predict Industry Change*, Harvard Business School Press.

Dodgson, M., Gann, D. and Salter, A. (2008) *Management of Technological Innovation: Strategy and Practice*, Oxford, Oxford University Press.

Trott, P. (2008) *Innovation Management and New Product Development*, 4th edn, London, FT Prentice Hall.

There are now lots of books about e-business, ranging from textbooks to quick 'how to' books, including the following.

Chaffey, D. (2006) *E-business and E-commerce Management*, 3rd edn, London, FT Prentice Hall.

Damani, C. and Damani, R. (2007) *Ecommerce 2.0: The Evolution of Ecommerce*, London, Imano.

Laudon, K. and Traver, C. (2006) *E-Commerce: Business, Technology, Society*, Englewood Cliffs, NJ, Prentice Hall.

References

Ajzen, I. and Fishbein, M. (1980) *Understanding Attitudes and Predicting Social Behaviour*, Englewood Cliffs, NJ, Prentice Hall.

Concise Insight (2004) *European Location-Based Services 2004 Report*, http://www.itelogy.com/downloads/European%20Location%20%20Based%20Services%202003%20%20Operator%20Status%20and%20Market%20Drivers.pdf

Davis, F.D., Bagozzi, R.P. and Warshaw, P.R. (1989) 'User acceptance of computer technology: a comparison of two theoretical models', *Management Science*, Vol. 35, No. 8, pp. 982–1003.

Economist Intelligence Unit (2007) E-readiness rankings, London, EIU.

Fishbein, M. and Ajzen, I. (1975) *Belief, Attitude, Intention and Behaviour: An Introduction to Theory and Research*, Reading, Massachusetts, Addison-Wesley.

Fletcher, K. (1995) *Marketing Management and Information Technology*, 2nd edn, Prentice-Hall International, London.

Hogg, G., Laing, A. and Winkelman, D. (2003) 'The professional service encounter in the age of the internet: an exploratory study', *Journal of Services Marketing*, Vol. 17, No. 5, pp. 476–94.

Howley, M. (2002) 'The role of consultancies in new product development', *Journal of Product and Brand Management*, Vol. 11, No. 6/7, pp. 447–58.

Jones, H. (2004) 'Up close and personal', *The Marketer*, No. 7, November.

Keers, H. (2002) 'Mothercare slips into red as warehouse woes grow', *Daily Telegraph*, 22 November.

Kim, J. and Wilemon, D. (2003) 'Sources and assessment of complexity in NPD projects', *R&D Management*, Vol. 33, No. 1, pp. 16–30.

Kotler, P. (1997) *Marketing Management: Analysis, Planning, Implementation and Control*, 9th edn, Englewood Cliffs, NJ, Prentice-Hall.

Little, G. (2002) 'Inventors don't always make great marketers', *Design Week*, Vol. 17, No. 27, p. 15.

Lopez-Bassols, V. (1998) *The OECD Observer*, No. 213, August–September, pp. 16–19.

Morton, R. (2003) 'Some pick-up in online sales . . . however, most customers still prefer to buy from showrooms', *Financial Times*, 4 March, p. 5.

O'Cass, A. and Fenech, T. (2003) 'Web retailing adoption: exploring the nature of Internet users' web retailing behaviour', *Journal of Retailing and Consumer Services*, Vol. 10, No. 2, pp. 81–94.

OECD (2002) *Short Summary of the Workshop on Genetic Inventions, Intellectual Property Rights and Licensing Practices*, Paris, OECD.

OECD (2007) *OECD in Figures 2007*, Paris, OECD.

Press, E. and Washburn, J. (2000) 'Secrecy and Science', *The Atlantic Online*, www.theatlantic.com/issues/2000/03/press2.htm, accessed April 2005.

Timmins, N. (2003) 'A bid to save money for the government: online auctions', *Financial Times*, 29 January, p. 12.

Young, A. (1993) 'What goes into R&D?', *OECD Observer*, No. 183, August–September.

Yrjölä, H. (2001) 'Physical distribution considerations for electronic grocery shopping', *International Journal of Physical Distribution and Logistics Management*, Vol. 31, No. 10, pp. 25–38.

chapter

PROJECT MANAGEMENT

3

APPLE'S IPOD HAS ITS OWN PRODUCT DEVELOPMENT TEAM

How does Apple develop the innovative products it sells? Apple has separate product development teams for each major product. By organizing this way, Apple can precisely focus resources on its amazingly successful products. The iPod and the iPhone have reinvigorated Apple and its bottom line over the past few years.

Much of the underlying iPod design was performed by outside companies. Consumer electronics is a fast-moving area, and using established experts linked together in what could be called a design chain, Apple was able to quickly bring the iPod to market. Apple developed a layered project that relied on a platform created by a third party, PortalPlayer, of Santa Clara, California. PortalPlayer had developed a base platform for a variety of audio systems, including portable digital music devices, general audio systems, and streaming audio receivers.

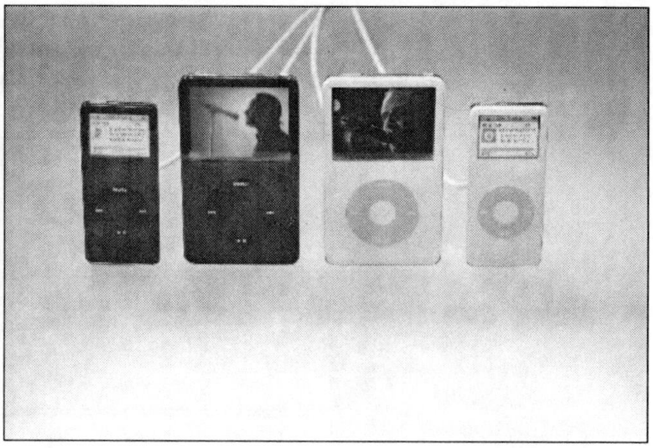

Apple started with a vision of what the player should be and what it should look like. The subsequent design parameters were dictated by its appearance and form factor. That outside-in perspective helped determine a number of the components, including the planar lithium battery from Sony and the 1.8-inch Toshiba hard drive. The essential units—battery, hard drive, and circuit board—are layered, one on top of the next. The rest of the device uses a dedicated MP3 decoder and controller chip from PortalPlayer, a Wolfson Microelectronics Ltd. stereo digital-to-analog converter, a flash memory chip from Sharp Electronics Corp., a Texas Instruments 1394 firewire interface controller, and a power management and battery charging integrated circuit from Linear Technologies, Inc.

Working with these partners, the iPod design project was completed in a few months of iterative loops. Managing activities among the multiple partners was extremely difficult since Apple needed to make sure that its suppliers' development schedules matched the product introduction schedule. No doubt subsequent versions of the iPod will depend on this dynamic design chain as different components and optimizations are discovered. Apple's iPod product has been wildly successful due in large part to successful project management efforts, the topic of this chapter.

> *"The high-impact project is the gem . . . the fundamental nugget . . . the fundamental atomic particle from which the new white collar world will be constructed and/or reconstructed. Projects should be, well WOW!"*
>
> —Tom Peters

Although most of the material in this chapter focuses on the technical aspects of project management (structuring project networks and calculating the critical path), as we see in the opening vignette, the management aspects are certainly equally important. Success in project management is very much an activity that requires careful control of critical resources. We spend much of the time in this book focused on the management of nonhuman resources such as machines and material; for projects, however, the key resource is often our employees' time. Human resources are often the most expensive, and those people involved in the projects critical to the success of the firm are often the most valuable managers, consultants, and engineers.

At the highest levels in an organization, management often involves juggling a portfolio of projects. There are many different types of projects ranging from the development of totally new products, revisions to old products, new marketing plans, and a vast array of projects for better serving customers and reducing costs.

Most companies deal with projects individually—pushing each through the pipeline as quickly and cost-effectively as possible. Many of these same companies are very good at applying the techniques described in this chapter in a manner where the myriad of tasks are executed flawlessly, but the projects just do not deliver the expected results. Worse, what often happens is the projects consuming the most resources have the least connection to the firm's strategy.

The vital big-picture decision is what mix of projects is best for the organization. A firm should have the right mix of projects that best support a company's strategy. Projects should be selected from the following types: derivative (incremental changes such as new product packaging or no-frills versions), breakthrough (major changes that create entirely new markets), and platform (fundamental improvements to existing products). Projects can be categorized in four major areas: product change, process change, research and development, and alliance and partnership (see Exhibit 3.1).

exhibit 3.1 Types of Development Projects

More ← Change → Less

	Breakthrough Projects	Platform Projects	Derivative Projects
Product Change	New core product	Addition to product family	Product enhancement
Process Change	New core process	Process upgrade	Incremental change
Research & Development	New core technology	Technology upgrade	Incremental change
Alliance & Partnership	Outsource major activity	Select new partner	Incremental change

In this chapter, we only scratch the surface in our introduction to the topic of project management. Professional project managers are individuals skilled at not only the technical aspects of calculating such things as early start and early finish time but, just as important, the people skills related to motivation. In addition, the ability to resolve conflicts as key decision points occur in the project is a critical skill. Without a doubt, leading successful projects is the best way to prove your promotability to the people who make promotion decisions. Virtually all project work is team work, and leading a project involves leading a team. Your success at leading a project will spread quickly through the individuals in the team. As organizations flatten (through reengineering, downsizing, outsourcing), more will depend on projects and project leaders to get work done, work that previously was handled within departments.

WHAT IS PROJECT MANAGEMENT?

Project
Project management

A **project** may be defined as a series of related jobs usually directed toward some major output and requiring a significant period of time to perform. **Project management** can be defined as planning, directing, and controlling resources (people, equipment, material) to meet the technical, cost, and time constraints of the project.

Although projects are often thought to be one-time occurrences, the fact is that many projects can be repeated or transferred to other settings or products. The result will be another project output. A contractor building houses or a firm producing low-volume products such as supercomputers, locomotives, or linear accelerators can effectively consider these as projects.

STRUCTURING PROJECTS

Before the project starts, senior management must decide which of three organizational structures will be used to tie the project to the parent firm: pure project, functional project, or matrix project. We next discuss the strengths and weaknesses of the three main forms.

Cross Functional

PURE PROJECT

Pure project

Tom Peters predicts that most of the world's work will be "brainwork," done in semipermanent networks of small project-oriented teams, each one an autonomous, entrepreneurial center of opportunity, where the necessity for speed and flexibility dooms the hierarchical management structures we and our ancestors grew up with. Thus, out of the three basic project organizational structures, Peters favors the **pure project** (nicknamed *skunkworks*), where a self-contained team works full time on the project.

ADVANTAGES

- The project manager has full authority over the project.
- Team members report to one boss. They do not have to worry about dividing loyalty with a functional-area manager.
- Lines of communication are shortened. Decisions are made quickly.
- Team pride, motivation, and commitment are high.

DISADVANTAGES

- Duplication of resources. Equipment and people are not shared across projects.
- Organizational goals and policies are ignored, as team members are often both physically and psychologically removed from headquarters.
- The organization falls behind in its knowledge of new technology due to weakened functional divisions.

BREAKTHROUGH

THE MOTOROLA RAZR CELL PHONE

The new Motorola RAZR was incubated and "hatched" in colorless cubicles in Libertyville, a northern Chicago suburb. It was a skunkworks project whose tight-knit team repeatedly flouted Motorola's own company rules for developing new products. They kept the project top-secret, even from their colleagues. They used materials and techniques Motorola had never tried before. After contentious internal battles, they threw out accepted models of what a mobile telephone should look and feel like. In short, the team that created the RAZR broke the mold, and in the process rejuvenated the company.

To design the look and feel as well as the internal configuration of a telephone takes a team of specialists, in the case of the RAZR about 20 people. The full team met daily at 4 P.M. in a conference room in Libertyville to hash over the previous day's progress as they worked down a checklist of components: antenna, speaker, keypad, camera, display, light source, battery, charger port, and so on. Scheduled for an hour, the meetings frequently ran past 7 P.M. The "thin clam" project became a rebel outpost. Money wasn't an object or a constraint, but secrecy and speed were. The team prohibited digital pictures of the project so that nothing could be inadvertently disseminated by e-mail. Models of the phone could leave the premises only when physically carried or accompanied by a team member.

There were two key innovations that allowed the team to make quantum leaps in thinness, one of the key design features they aimed at. The first was placing the antenna in the mouthpiece of the phone instead of at the top. While this had not been done in cell phones before, it was also a technical challenge. The second brainstorm was rearranging the phone's innards, primarily by placing the battery next to the circuit board, or internal computer, rather than beneath it. That solution, however, created a new problem: width. Motorola's "human factors" experts had concluded that a phone wider than 49 millimeters wouldn't fit well in a person's hand. The side-by-side design yielded a phone 53 millimeters wide. But the RAZR team didn't accept the company's research as gospel. The team made its own model to see how a 53-millimeter phone felt, and in the end, the team members decided on their own that the company was wrong and that four extra millimeters were acceptable.

The company sold its 50-millionth RAZR in June 2006! Motorola will sell more RAZRs this year than Apple will iPods. Several key players from the RAZR development team were asked to appear at a meeting of top executives at company headquarters. They weren't told why. Then, as the team members filed in, the Motorola brass awaiting them rose in applause, delivering a standing ovation. Team members were also told they would be rewarded with a significant bonus of stock options.

SOURCE: ADAPTED FROM "RAZR'S EDGE," *FORTUNE MAGAZINE*, JUNE 1, 2006.

- Because team members have no functional area home, they worry about life-after-project, and project termination is delayed.

The Motorola RAZR cell phone was developed using a pure project team (see Breakthrough box).

FUNCTIONAL PROJECT

Functional project

At the other end of the project organization spectrum is the **functional project**, housing the project within a functional division.

ADVANTAGES
- A team member can work on several projects.
- Technical expertise is maintained within the functional area even if individuals leave the project or organization.

- The functional area is a home after the project is completed. Functional specialists can advance vertically.
- A critical mass of specialized functional-area experts creates synergystic solutions to a project's technical problems.

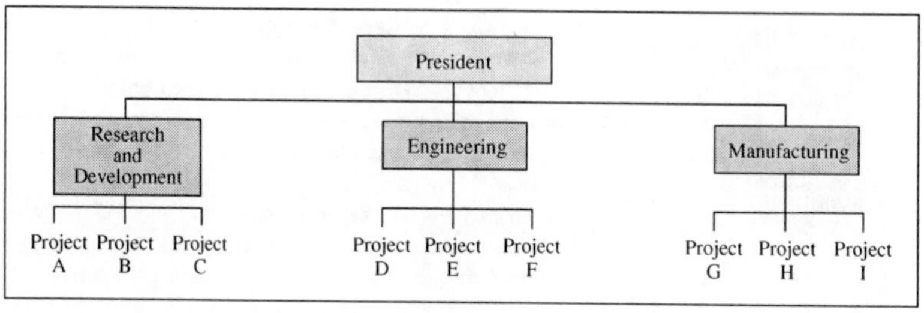

DISADVANTAGES

- Aspects of the project that are not directly related to the functional area get short-changed.
- Motivation of team members is often weak.
- Needs of the client are secondary and are responded to slowly.

MATRIX PROJECT

The classic specialized organizational form, "the **matrix project**," attempts to blend properties of functional and pure project structures. Each project utilizes people from different functional areas. The project manager (PM) decides what tasks and when they will be performed, but the functional managers control which people and technologies are used. If the matrix form is chosen, different projects (rows of the matrix) borrow resources from functional areas (columns). Senior management must then decide whether a weak, balanced, or strong form of a matrix is to be used. This establishes whether project managers have little, equal, or more authority than the functional managers with whom they negotiate for resources.

Matrix project

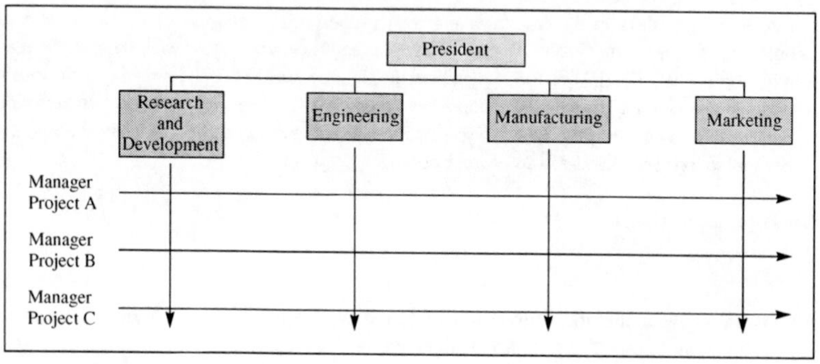

ADVANTAGES

- Communication between functional divisions is enhanced.
- A project manager is held responsible for successful completion of the project.
- Duplication of resources is minimized.
- Team members have a functional "home" after project completion, so they are less worried about life-after-project than if they were a pure project organization.
- Policies of the parent organization are followed. This increases support for the project.

DISADVANTAGES

- There are two bosses. Often the functional manager will be listened to before the project manager. After all, who can promote you or give you a raise?
- It is doomed to failure unless the PM has strong negotiating skills.

- Suboptimization is a danger, as PMs hoard resources for their own project, thus harming other projects.

Note that regardless of which of the three major organizational forms is used, the project manager is the primary contact point with the customer. Communication and flexibility are greatly enhanced because one person is responsible for successful completion of the project.

WORK BREAKDOWN STRUCTURE

A project starts out as a *statement of work* (SOW). The SOW may be a written description of the objectives to be achieved, with a brief statement of the work to be done and a proposed schedule specifying the start and completion dates. It also could contain performance measures in terms of budget and completion steps (milestones) and the written reports to be supplied.

A *task* is a further subdivision of a project. It is usually not longer than several months in duration and is performed by one group or organization. A *subtask* may be used if needed to further subdivide the project into more meaningful pieces.

A *work package* is a group of activities combined to be assignable to a single organizational unit. It still falls into the format of all project management; the package provides a description of what is to be done, when it is to be started and completed, the budget, measures of performance, and specific events to be reached at points in time. These specific events are called **project milestones**. Typical milestones might be the completion of the design, the production of a prototype, the completed testing of the prototype, and the approval of a pilot run.

Project milestone

Work breakdown structure

The **work breakdown structure** (WBS) defines the hierarchy of project tasks, subtasks, and work packages. Completion of one or more work packages results in the completion of a subtask; completion of one or more subtasks results in the completion of a task; and, finally, the completion of all tasks is required to complete the project. A representation of this structure is shown in Exhibit 3.2.

Exhibit 3.3 shows the WBS for an optical scanner project. The WBS is important in organizing a project because it breaks the project down into manageable pieces. The number of levels will vary depending on the project. How much detail or how many levels to use depends on the following:

- The level at which a single individual or organization can be assigned responsibility and accountability for accomplishing the work package.
- The level at which budget and cost data will be collected during the project.

exhibit 3.2 An Example of a Work Breakdown Structure

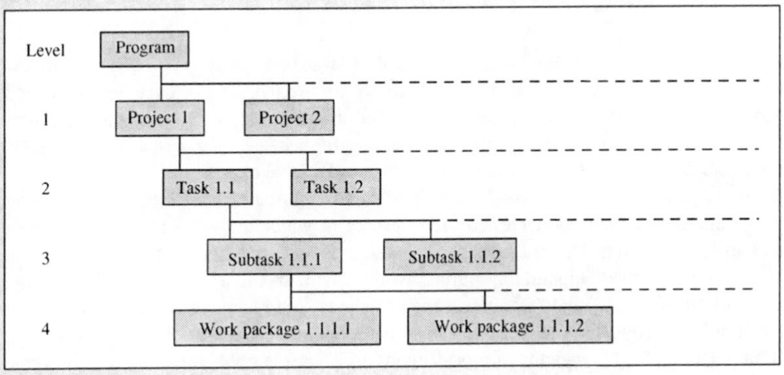

Work Breakdown Structure, Large Optical Scanner Design

exhibit 3.3

Level 1	Level 2	Level 3	Level 4		
x				1	Optical simulator design
	x			1.1	Optical design
		x		1.1.1	Telescope design/fab
		x		1.1.2	Telescope/simulator optical interface
		x		1.1.3	Simulator zoom system design
		x		1.1.4	Ancillary simulator optical component specification
	x			1.2	System performance analysis
		x		1.2.1	Overall system firmware and software control
			x	1.2.1.1	Logic flow diagram generation and analysis
			x	1.2.1.2	Basic control algorithm design
		x		1.2.2	Far beam analyzer
		x		1.2.3	System inter- and intra-alignment method design
		x		1.2.4	Data recording and reduction requirements
	x			1.3	System integration
	x			1.4	Cost analysis
		x		1.4.1	Cost/system schedule analysis
		x		1.4.2	Cost/system performance analysis
	x			1.5	Management
		x		1.5.1	System design/engineering management
		x		1.5.2	Program management
	x			1.6	Long lead item procurement
		x		1.6.1	Large optics
		x		1.6.2	Target components
		x		1.6.3	Detectors

There is not a single correct WBS for any project, and two different project teams might develop different WBSs for the same project. Some experts have referred to project management as an art rather than a science, because there are so many different ways that a project can be approached. Finding the correct way to organize a project depends on experience with the particular task.

Activities are defined within the context of the work breakdown structure and are pieces of work that consume time. Activities do not necessarily require the expenditure of effort by people, although they often do. For example, waiting for paint to dry may be an activity in a project. Activities are identified as part of the WBS. From our sample project in Exhibit 3.3, activities would include telescope design and fabrication (1.1.1), telescope/simulator optical interface (1.1.2), and data recording (1.2.4). Activities need to be defined in such a way that when they are all completed, the project is done.

Activities

PROJECT CONTROL CHARTS

The U.S. Department of Defense (one of the earliest large users of project management) has published a variety of helpful standard forms. Many are used directly or have been modified by firms engaged in project management. Computer programs are available to quickly generate the charts described in this section. Charts are useful because their visual presentation is easily understood. Exhibit 3.4 shows a sample of the available charts.

Exhibit 3.4A is a sample **Gantt chart**, sometimes referred to as a *bar chart,* showing both the amount of time involved and the sequence in which activities can be performed. The chart is named after Henry L. Gantt, who won a presidential citation for his application of this type of chart to shipbuilding during World War I. In the example in Exhibit 3.4A, "long lead procurement" and "manufacturing schedules" are independent activities and can occur simultaneously. All other activities must be done in the sequence from top to bottom. Exhibit 3.4B graphs the amounts of money spent on labor, material, and overhead. Its value is its clarity in identifying sources and amounts of cost.

Gantt chart

exhibit 3.4 A Sample of Graphic Project Reports

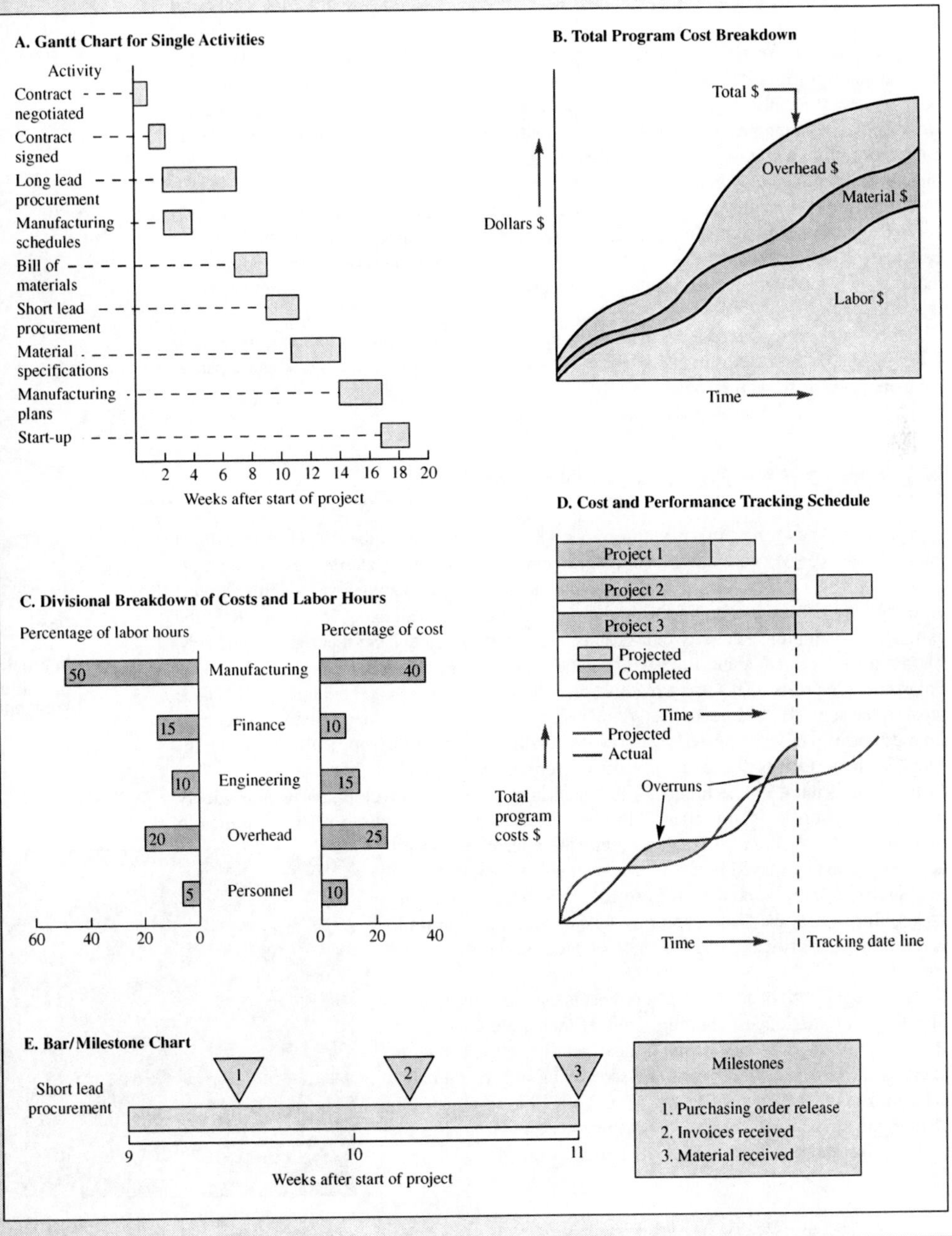

Exhibit 3.4C shows the percentage of the project's labor hours that comes from the various areas of manufacturing, finance, and so on. These labor hours are related to the proportion of the project's total labor cost. For example, manufacturing is responsible for 50 percent of the project's labor hours, but this 50 percent has been allocated just 40 percent of the total labor dollars charged.

The top half of Exhibit 3.4D shows the degree of completion of these projects. The dotted vertical line signifies today. Project 1, therefore, is already late because it still has work to be done. Project 2 is not being worked on temporarily, so there is a space before the projected work. Project 3 continues to be worked on without interruption. The bottom of Exhibit 3.4D compares actual total costs and projected costs. As we see, two cost overruns occurred, and the current cumulative costs are over projected cumulative costs.

Exhibit 3.4E is a milestone chart. The three milestones mark specific points in the project where checks can be made to see if the project is on time and where it should be. The best place to locate milestones is at the completion of a major activity. In this exhibit, the major activities completed were "purchase order release," "invoices received," and "material received."

Other standard reports can be used for a more detailed presentation comparing cost to progress (such as cost schedule status report—CSSR) or reports providing the basis for partial payment (such as the earned value report).

NETWORK-PLANNING MODELS

The two best-known network-planning models were developed in the 1950s. The Critical Path Method (CPM) was developed for scheduling maintenance shutdowns at chemical processing plants owned by Du Pont. Since maintenance projects are performed often in this industry, reasonably accurate time estimates for activities are available. CPM is based on the assumptions that project activity times can be estimated accurately and that they do not vary. The Program Evaluation and Review Technique (PERT) was developed for the U.S. Navy's Polaris missile project. This was a massive project involving over 3,000 contractors. Because most of the activities had never been done before, PERT was developed to handle uncertain time estimates. As years passed, features that distinguished CPM from PERT have diminished, so in our treatment here we just use the term CPM.

Interactive Operations Management

In a sense, the CPM techniques illustrated here owe their development to the widely used predecessor, the Gantt chart. Although the Gantt chart is able to relate activities to time in a usable fashion for small projects, the interrelationship of activities, when displayed in this form, becomes extremely difficult to visualize and to work with for projects that include more than 25 activities. Also, the Gantt chart provides no direct procedure for determining the critical path, which is of great practical value to identify.

Critical path

The **critical path** of activities in a project is the sequence of activities that form the longest chain in terms of their time to complete. If any one of the activities in the critical path is delayed, then the entire project is delayed. Determining scheduling information about each activity in the project is the major goal of CPM techniques. The techniques calculate when an activity must start and end, together with whether the activity is part of the critical path.

NEW ZEALAND'S TE APITI WIND FARM PROJECT CONSTRUCTED THE LARGEST WIND FARM IN THE SOUTHERN HEMISPHERE, WITHIN ONE YEAR FROM COMMISSION TO COMPLETION, ON TIME AND WITHIN BUDGET. EMPLOYING EFFECTIVE PROJECT MANAGEMENT AND USING THE CORRECT TOOLS AND TECHNIQUES, THE MERIDIAN ENERGY COMPANY PROVIDED A VIABLE OPTION FOR RENEWABLE ENERGY IN NEW ZEALAND, AND ACTS AS A BENCHMARK FOR LATER WIND FARM PROJECTS.

CRITICAL PATH METHOD (CPM)

Here is a procedure for scheduling a project. In this case, a single time estimate is used because we are assuming that the activity times are known. A very simple project will be scheduled to demonstrate the basic approach.

Consider that you have a group assignment that requires a decision on whether you should invest in a company. Your instructor has suggested that you perform the analysis in the following four steps:

A Select a company.
B Obtain the company's annual report and perform a ratio analysis.
C Collect technical stock price data and construct charts.
D Individually review the data and make a team decision on whether to buy the stock.

Your group of four people decides that the project can be divided into four activities as suggested by the instructor. You decide that all the team members should be involved in selecting the company and that it should take one week to complete this activity. You will meet at the end of the week to decide what company the group will consider. During this meeting, you will divide your group: two people will be responsible for the annual report and ratio analysis, and the other two will collect the technical data and construct the charts. Your group expects it to take two weeks to get the annual report and perform the ratio analysis, and a week to collect the stock price data and generate the charts. You agree that the two groups can work independently. Finally, you agree to meet as a team to make the purchase decision. Before you meet, you want to allow one week for each team member to review all the data.

This is a simple project, but it will serve to demonstrate the approach. The following are the appropriate steps.

1. **Identify each activity to be done in the project and estimate how long it will take to complete each activity.** This is simple, given the information from your instructor. We identify the activities as follows: A(1), B(2), C(1), D(1). The number is the expected duration of the activity.
2. **Determine the required sequence of activities and construct a network reflecting the precedence relationships.** An easy way to do this is to first identify the **immediate predecessors** associated with an activity. The immediate predecessors are the activities that need to be completed immediately before an activity. Activity A needs to be completed before activities B and C can start. B and C need to be completed before D can start. The following table reflects what we know so far:

Immediate predecessors

Activity	Designation	Immediate Predecessors	Time (Weeks)
Select company	A	None	1
Obtain annual report and perform ratio analysis	B	A	2
Collect stock price data and perform technical analysis	C	A	1
Review data and make a decision	D	B and C	1

Here is a diagram that depicts these precedence relationships:

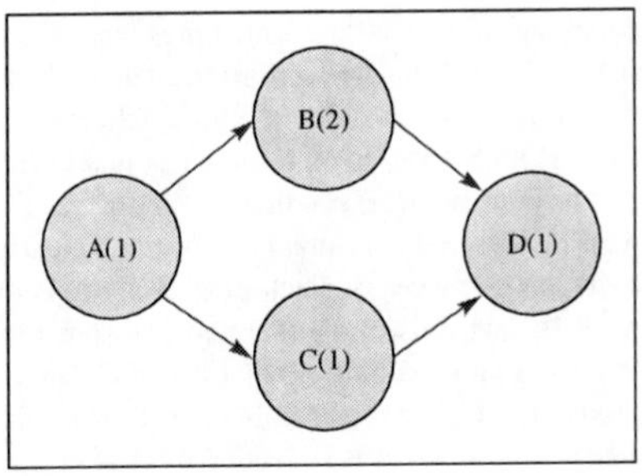

3. **Determine the critical path.** Consider each sequence of activities that runs from the beginning to the end of the project. For our simple project, there are two paths: A–B–D and A–C–D. The critical path is the path where the sum of the activity times is the longest. A–B–D has a duration of four weeks and A–C–D a duration of three weeks. The critical path, therefore, is A–B–D. If any activity along the critical path is delayed, then the entire project will be delayed.
4. **Determine the early start/finish and late start/finish schedule.** To schedule the project, find when each activity needs to start and when it needs to finish. For some activities in a project, there may be some leeway in when an activity can start and finish. This is called the **slack time** in an activity. For each activity in the project, we calculate four points in time: the early start, early finish, late start, and late finish times. The early start and early finish are the earliest times that the activity can start and be finished. Similarly, the late start and late finish are the latest times the activities can start and finish. The difference between the late start time and early start time is the slack time. To help keep all of this straight, we place these numbers in special places around the nodes that represent each activity in our network diagram, as shown here.

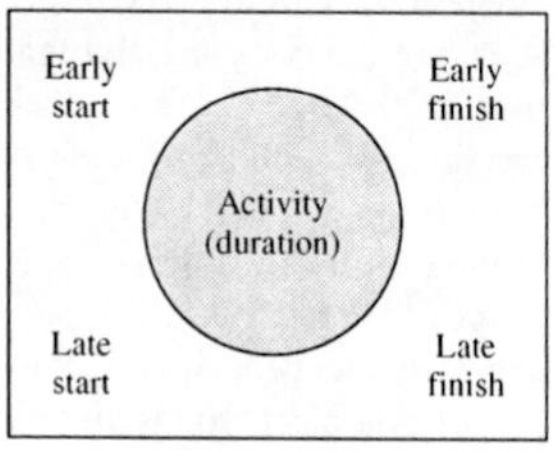

Slack time

To calculate numbers, start from the beginning of the network and work to the end, calculating the early start and early finish numbers. Start counting with the current period, designated as period 0. Activity A has an early start of 0 and an early finish of 1. Activity B's early start is A's early finish or 1. Similarly, C's early start is 1. The early finish for B is 3, and the early finish for C is 2. Now consider activity D. D cannot start until both B and C are done. Because B cannot be done until 3, D cannot start until that time. The early start for D, therefore, is 3, and the early finish is 4. Our diagram now looks like this.

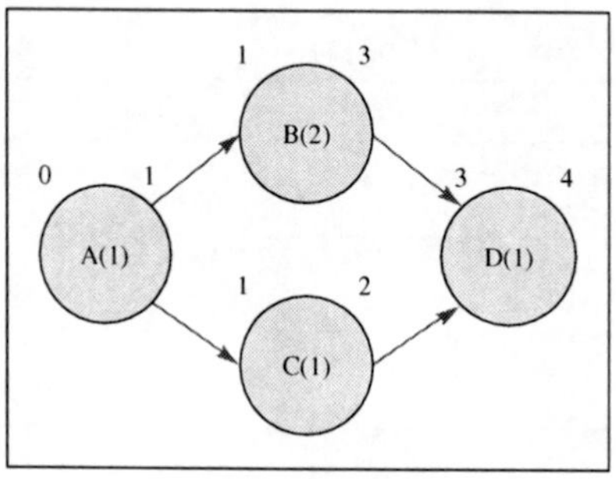

To calculate the late finish and late start times, start from the end of the network and work toward the front. Consider activity D. The earliest that it can be done is at time 4; and if we do not want to delay the completion of the project, the late finish needs to be set to 4. With a duration of 1, the latest that D can start is 3. Now consider activity C. C must be done by time 3 so that D can start, so C's late finish time is 3 and its late start time is 2. Notice the difference between the early and late start and finish times: This activity has one week of slack time. Activity B must be done by time 3 so that D can start, so its late finish time is 3 and late start time is 1. There is no slack in B. Finally, activity A must be done so that B and C can start. Because B must start earlier than C, and A must get done in time for B to start, the late finish time for A is 1. Finally, the late start time for A is 0. Notice there is no slack in activities A, B, and

D. The final network looks like this. (Hopefully the stock your investment team has chosen is a winner!)

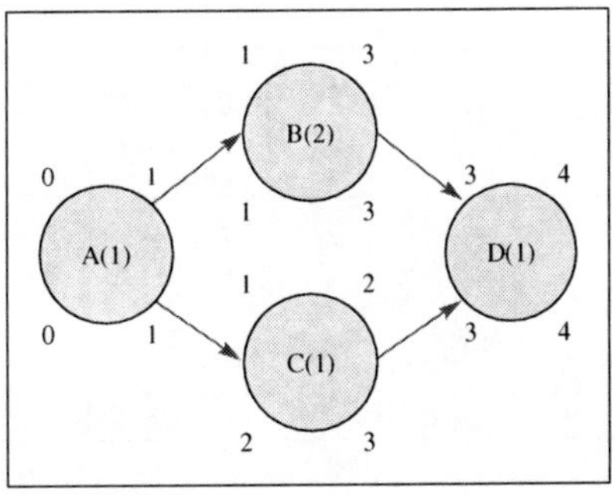

EXAMPLE 3.1: Critical Path Method

Excel: Project Management

Many firms that have tried to enter the notebook computer market have failed. Suppose your firm believes that there is a big demand in this market because existing products have not been designed correctly. They are too heavy, too large, or too small to have standard-size keyboards. Your intended computer will be small enough to carry inside a jacket pocket if need be. The ideal size will be no larger than 5 inches × 9½ inches × 1 inch with a folding keyboard. It should weigh no more than 15 ounces and have an LCD display, a micro disk drive, and a wireless connection. This should appeal to traveling businesspeople, but it could have a much wider market, including students. It should be priced in the $175–$200 range.

The project, then, is to design, develop, and produce a prototype of this small computer. In the rapidly changing computer industry, it is crucial to hit the market with a product of this sort in less than a year. Therefore, the project team has been allowed approximately eight months (35 weeks) to produce the prototype.

SOLUTION

The first charge of the project team is to develop a project network chart and estimate the likelihood of completing the prototype computer within the 35 weeks. Let's follow the steps in the development of the network.

1. **Activity identification.** The project team decides that the following activities are the major components of the project: design of the computer, prototype construction, prototype testing, methods specification (summarized in a report), evaluation studies of automatic assembly equipment, an assembly equipment study report, and a final report summarizing all aspects of the design, equipment, and methods.

2. **Activity sequencing and network construction.** On the basis of discussion with staff, the project manager develops the precedence table and sequence network shown in Exhibit 3.5. When constructing a network, take care to ensure that the activities are in the proper order and that the logic of their relationships is maintained. For example, it would be illogical to have a situation where Event A precedes Event B, B precedes C, and C precedes A.

3. **Determine the critical path.** The critical path is the longest sequence of connected activities through the network and is defined as the path with zero slack time. This network has four different paths: A–C–F–G, A–C–E–G, A–B–D–F–G, and A–B–D–E–G. The lengths of these paths are 38, 35, 38, and 35 weeks. Note that this project has two different critical paths; this might indicate that this would be a fairly difficult project to manage. Calculating the early start and late start schedules gives additional insight into how difficult this project might be to complete on time. ●

Early start schedule

Early Start and Late Start Schedules An **early start schedule** is one that lists all of the activities by their early start times. For activities not on the critical path, there is slack time between the completion of each activity and the start of the next activity. The early start schedule completes the project and all its activities as soon as possible.

CPM Network for Computer Design Project

exhibit 3.5

CPM ACTIVITY DESIGNATIONS AND TIME ESTIMATES

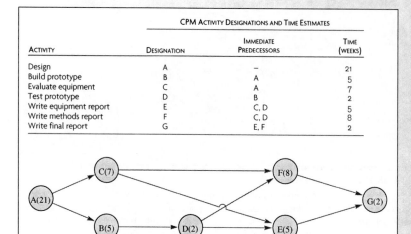

ACTIVITY	DESIGNATION	IMMEDIATE PREDECESSORS	TIME (WEEKS)
Design	A	–	21
Build prototype	B	A	5
Evaluate equipment	C	A	7
Test prototype	D	B	2
Write equipment report	E	C, D	5
Write methods report	F	C, D	8
Write final report	G	E, F	2

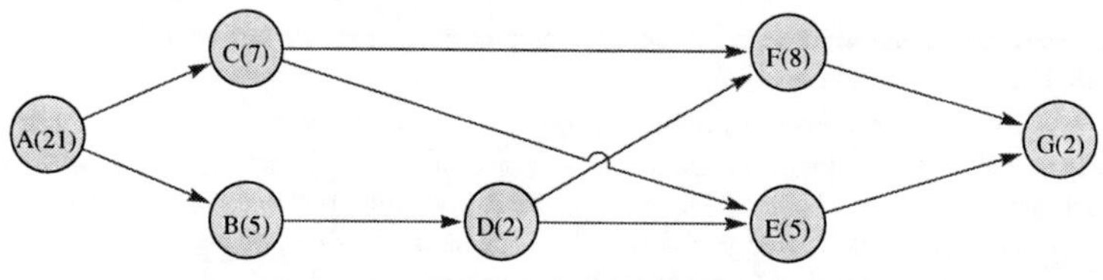

CPM Network for Computer Design Project

exhibit 3.6

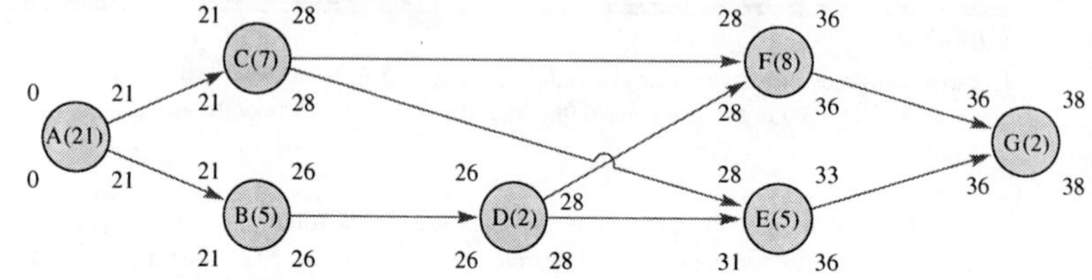

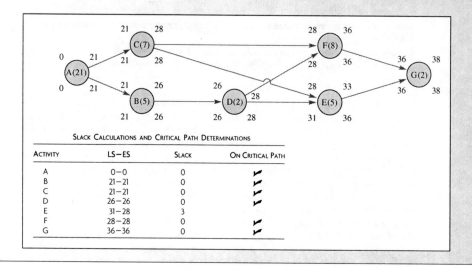

SLACK CALCULATIONS AND CRITICAL PATH DETERMINATIONS

ACTIVITY	LS–ES	SLACK	ON CRITICAL PATH
A	0–0	0	✓
B	21–21	0	✓
C	21–21	0	✓
D	26–26	0	✓
E	31–28	3	
F	28–28	0	✓
G	36–36	0	✓

A **late start schedule** lists the activities to start as late as possible without delaying the completion date of the project. One motivation for using a late start schedule is that savings are realized by postponing purchases of materials, the use of labor, and other costs until necessary. These calculations are shown in Exhibit 3.6. From this we see that the only activity that has slack is activity E. This certainly would be a fairly difficult project to complete on time.

Late start schedule

CPM WITH THREE ACTIVITY TIME ESTIMATES

If a single estimate of the time required to complete an activity is not reliable, the best procedure is to use three time estimates. These three times not only allow us to estimate the activity time but also let us obtain a probability estimate for completion time for the entire network. Briefly, the procedure is as follows: The estimated activity time is calculated using a weighted average of a minimum, maximum, and most likely time estimate. The expected completion time of the network is computed using the procedure described above. Using estimates of variability for the activities on the critical path, the probability of completing the project by particular times can be estimated. (Note that the probability calculations are a distinguishing feature of the classic PERT approach.)

EXAMPLE 3.2: Three Time Estimates

We use the same information as in Example 3.1 with the exception that activities have three time estimates.

SOLUTION

1. Identify each activity to be done in the project.
2. Determine the sequence of activities and construct a network reflecting the precedence relationships.
3. The three estimates for an activity time are

   a = Optimistic time: the minimum reasonable period of time in which the activity can be completed. (There is only a small probability, typically assumed to be 1 percent, that the activity can be completed in less time.)

   m = Most likely time: the best guess of the time required. Since m would be the time thought most likely to appear, it is also the mode of the beta distribution discussed in step 4.

   b = Pessimistic time: the maximum reasonable period of time the activity would take to be completed. (There is only a small probability, typically assumed to be 1 percent, that it would take longer.)

   Typically, this information is gathered from those people who are to perform the activity.
4. Calculate the expected time (ET) for each activity. The formula for this calculation is

   [3.1] $$\text{ET} = \frac{a + 4m + b}{6}$$

   This is based on the beta statistical distribution and weights the most likely time (m) four times more than either the optimistic time (a) or the pessimistic time (b). The beta distribution is extremely flexible. It can take on the variety of forms that typically arise; it has finite end points (which limit the possible activity times to the area between a and b); and, in the simplified version, it permits straightforward computation of the activity mean and standard deviation.
5. Determine the critical path. Using the expected times, a critical path is calculated in the same way as the single time case.
6. Calculate the variances (σ^2) of the activity times. Specifically, this is the variance, σ^2, associated with each ET and is computed as follows:

   [3.2] $$\sigma^2 = \left(\frac{b - a}{6}\right)^2$$

   As you can see, the variance is the square of one-sixth the difference between the two extreme time estimates. Of course, the greater this difference, the larger the variance.
7. Determine the probability of completing the project on a given date, based on the application of the standard normal distribution. A valuable feature of using three time estimates is that it enables the analyst to assess the effect of uncertainty on project completion time. (If you are not familiar with this type of analysis, see the box titled "Probability Analysis.") The mechanics of deriving this probability are as follows:

   a. Sum the variance values associated with each activity on the critical path.

b. Substitute this figure, along with the project due date and the project expected completion time, into the Z transformation formula. This formula is

[3.3]
$$Z = \frac{D - T_E}{\sqrt{\sum \sigma_{cp}^2}}$$

where

D = Desired completion date for the project
T_E = Expected completion time for the project
$\sum \sigma_{cp}^2$ = Sum of the variances along the critical path

c. Calculate the value of Z, which is the number of standard deviations (of a standard normal distribution) that the project due date is from the expected completion time.

d. Using the value of Z, find the probability of meeting the project due date (using a table of normal probabilities such as Appendix E). The *expected completion time* is the starting time plus the sum of the activity times on the critical path.

Following the steps just outlined, we developed Exhibit 3.7 showing expected times and variances. The project network was created the same as we did previously. The only difference is that the activity times are weighted averages. We determine the critical path as before, using these values as if they were single numbers. The difference between the single time estimate and the three times (optimistic, most likely, and pessimistic) is in computing probabilities of completion. Exhibit 3.8 shows the network and critical path.

Activity Expected Times and Variances

exhibit 3.7

Activity	Activity Designation	Time Estimates a	m	b	Expected Times (ET) $\frac{a+4m+b}{6}$	Activity Variances (σ^2) $\left(\frac{b-a}{6}\right)^2$
Design	A	10	22	28	21	9
Build prototype	B	4	4	10	5	1
Evaluate equipment	C	4	6	14	7	$2\frac{7}{9}$
Test prototype	D	1	2	3	2	$\frac{1}{9}$
Write report	E	1	5	9	5	$1\frac{7}{9}$
Write methods report	F	7	8	9	8	$\frac{1}{9}$
Write final report	G	2	2	2	2	0

Excel: Project Management

Computer Design Project with Three Time Estimates

exhibit 3.8

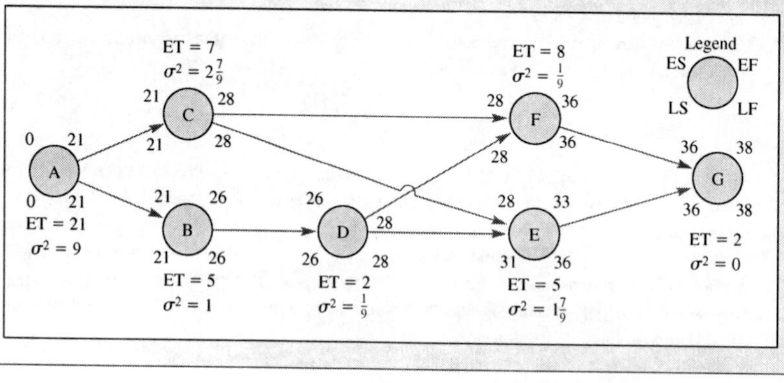

PROBABILITY ANALYSIS

The three-time-estimate approach introduces the ability to consider the probability that a project will be completed within a particular amount of time. The assumption needed to make this probability estimate is that the activity duration times are independent random variables. If this is true, the central limit theorem can be used to find the mean and the variance of the sequence of activities that form the critical path. The central limit theorem says that the sum of a group of independent, identically distributed random variables approaches a normal distribution as the number of random variables increases. In the case of project management problems, the random variables are the actual times for the activities in the project. (Recall that the time for each activity is assumed to be independent of other activities, and to follow a beta statistical distribution.) For this the expected time to complete the critical path activities is the sum of the activity times.

Likewise, because of the assumption of activity time independence, the sum of the variances of the activities along the critical path is the variance of the expected time to complete the path. Recall that the standard deviation is equal to the square root of the variance.

To determine the actual probability of completing the critical path activities within a certain amount of time, we need to find where on our probability distribution the time falls. Appendix E shows the areas of the cumulative standard normal distribution for different values of Z. Z measures the number of standard deviations either to the right or to the left of zero in the distribution. Referring to Appendix E, the $G(z)$ values are the area under the curve representing the distribution. The values correspond to the cumulative probability associated with each value of Z. For example, the first value in the table, −4.00, has a $G(z)$ equal to .00003. This means that the probability associated with a Z value of −4.0 is only .003 percent. Similarly, a Z value of 1.50 has a $G(z)$ equal to .93319 or 93.319 percent. The Z values are calculated using Equation (3.3) given in Step 7b of the "Three Time Estimates" example solution. These cumulative probabilities also can be obtained by using the NORMSDIST (Z) function built into Microsoft Excel.

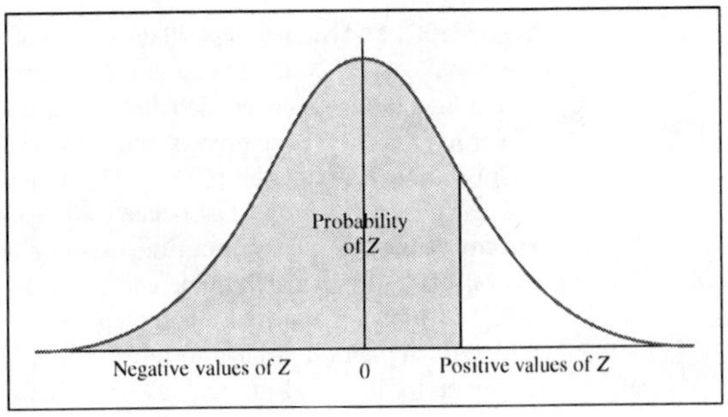

Because there are two critical paths in the network, we must decide which variances to use in arriving at the probability of meeting the project due date. A conservative approach dictates using the path with the largest total variance to focus management's attention on the activities most likely to exhibit broad variations. On this basis, the variances associated with activities A, C, F, and G would be used to find the probability of completion. Thus $\Sigma\,\sigma_{cp}^2 = 9 + 2\frac{7}{9} + \frac{1}{9} + 0 = 11.89$. Suppose management asks for the probability of completing the project in 35 weeks. D, then, is 35. The expected completion time was found to be 38. Substituting into the Z equation and solving, we obtain

$$Z = \frac{D - T_E}{\sqrt{\Sigma\,\sigma_{cp}^2}} = \frac{35 - 38}{\sqrt{11.89}} = -0.87$$

Looking at Appendix E, we see that a Z value of −0.87 yields a probability of 0.1922, which means that the project manager has only about a 19 percent chance of completing the project in 35 weeks. Note that this probability is really the probability of completing the critical path A–C–F–G. Because there is another critical path and other paths that might become critical, the probability of completing the project in 35 weeks is actually less than 0.19. ●

TIME–COST MODELS

Time–cost models

In practice, project managers are as much concerned with the cost to complete a project as with the time to complete the project. For this reason, **time–cost models** have been devised. These models—extensions of the basic Critical Path Method—attempt to develop a minimum-cost schedule for an entire project and to control expenditures during the project.

Minimum-Cost Scheduling (Time–Cost Trade-Off) The basic assumption in minimum-cost scheduling is that there is a relationship between activity completion time and the cost of a project. On one hand, it costs money to expedite an activity; on the other, it costs money to sustain (or lengthen) the project. The costs associated with expediting activities are termed *activity direct costs* and add to the project direct cost. Some may be worker-related, such as overtime work, hiring more workers, and transferring workers from other jobs; others are resource-related, such as buying or leasing additional or more efficient equipment and drawing on additional support facilities.

The costs associated with sustaining the project are termed *project indirect costs:* overhead, facilities, and resource opportunity costs, and, under certain contractual situations, penalty costs or lost incentive payments. Because *activity direct costs* and *project indirect costs* are opposing costs dependent on time, the scheduling problem is essentially one of finding the project duration that minimizes their sum, or, in other words, finding the optimum point in a time–cost trade-off.

The procedure for finding this point consists of the following five steps. It is explained by using the simple four-activity network shown in Exhibit 3.9. Assume that the indirect costs remain constant for eight days and then increase at the rate of $5 per day.

1. **Prepare a CPM-type network diagram.** For each activity, this diagram should list
   a. Normal cost (NC): the lowest expected activity costs. (These are the lesser of the cost figures shown under each node in Exhibit 3.9.)
   b. Normal time (NT): the time associated with each normal cost.
   c. Crash time (CT): the shortest possible activity time.
   d. Crash cost (CC): the cost associated with each crash time.
2. **Determine the cost per unit of time (assume days) to expedite each activity.** The relationship between activity time and cost may be shown graphically by plotting CC and CT coordinates and connecting them to the NC and NT coordinates by a concave, convex, or straight line—or some other form, depending on the actual cost structure of activity performance, as in Exhibit 3.9. For activity A, we assume a linear relationship

Example of Time–Cost Trade-Off Procedure

exhibit 3.9

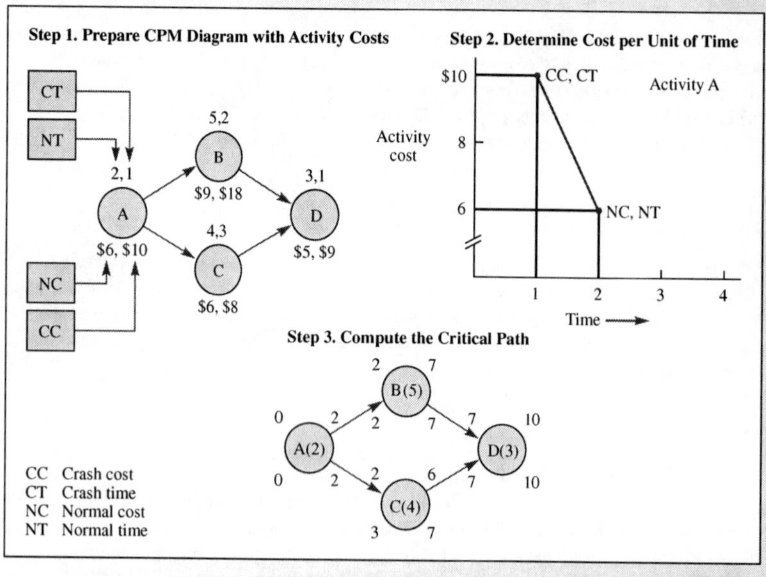

Excel: Project Management

exhibit 3.10 Calculation of Cost per Day to Expedite Each Activity

ACTIVITY	CC − NC	NT − CT	$\frac{CC - NC}{NT - CT}$	COST PER DAY TO EXPEDITE	NUMBER OF DAYS ACTIVITY MAY BE SHORTENED
A	\$10 − \$6	2 − 1	$\frac{\$10 - \$6}{2 - 1}$	\$4	1
B	\$18 − \$9	5 − 2	$\frac{\$18 - \$9}{5 - 2}$	\$3	3
C	\$8 − \$6	4 − 3	$\frac{\$8 - \$6}{4 - 3}$	\$2	1
D	\$9 − \$5	3 − 1	$\frac{\$9 - \$5}{3 - 1}$	\$2	2

exhibit 3.11 Reducing the Project Completion Time One Day at a Time

CURRENT CRITICAL PATH	REMAINING NUMBER OF DAYS ACTIVITY MAY BE SHORTENED	COST PER DAY TO EXPEDITE EACH ACTIVITY	LEAST-COST ACTIVITY TO EXPEDITE	TOTAL COST OF ALL ACTIVITIES IN NETWORK	PROJECT COMPLETION TIME
ABD	All activity times and costs are normal.			\$26	10
ABD	A–1, B–3, D–2	A–4, B–3, D–2	D	28	9
ABD	A–1, B–3, D–1	A–4, B–3, D–2	D	30	8
ABD	A–1, B–3	A–4, B–3	B	33	7
ABCD	A–1, B–2, C–1	A–4, B–3, C–2	A*	37	6
ABCD	B–2, C–1	B–3, C–2	B&C†	42	5
ABCD	B–1	B–3	B‡	45	5

*To reduce the critical path by one day, reduce either A alone or B and C together at the same time (either B or C by itself just modifies the critical path without shortening it).

†B&C must be crashed together to reduce the path by one day.

‡Crashing activity B does not reduce the length of the project, so this additional cost would not be incurred.

between time and cost. This assumption is common in practice and helps us derive the cost per day to expedite because this value may be found directly by taking the slope of the line using the formula Slope = (CC − NC) ÷ (NT − CT). (When the assumption of linearity cannot be made, the cost of expediting must be determined graphically for each day the activity may be shortened.)

The calculations needed to obtain the cost of expediting the remaining activities are shown in Exhibit 3.10.

3. **Compute the critical path.** For the simple network we have been using, this schedule would take 10 days. The critical path is A–B–D.
4. **Shorten the critical path at the least cost.** The easiest way to proceed is to start with the normal schedule, find the critical path, and reduce the path time by one day using the lowest-cost activity. Then recompute and find the new critical path and reduce it by one day also. Repeat this procedure until the time of completion is satisfactory, or until there can be no further reduction in the project completion time. Exhibit 3.11 shows the reduction of the network one day at a time.

   Working though Exhibit 3.11 might initially seem difficult. In the first line, all activities are at their normal time and costs are at their lowest value. The critical path is A–B–D, cost for completing the project is \$26, and the project completion time is 10 days.

The goal in line two is to reduce the project completion time by one day. We know it is necessary to reduce the time for one or more of the activities on the critical path. In the second column, we note that activity A can be reduced one day (from two days to one day), activity B can be reduced three days (from five to two days), and activity D can be reduced two days (from three days to one day). The next column tracks the cost to reduce each of the activities by a single day. For example, for activity A, it normally costs \$6 to complete in two days. It could be completed in one day at a cost of \$10, a \$4 increase. So we indicate the cost to expedite activity A by one day is \$4. For activity B, it normally costs \$9 to complete in five days. It could be completed in two days at a cost of \$18. Our cost to reduce B by three days is \$9, or \$3 per day. For C, it normally costs \$5 to complete in three days. It could be completed in one day at a cost of \$9; a two-day reduction would cost \$4 (\$2 per day). The least expensive alternative for a one-day reduction in time is to expedite activity D at a cost of \$2. Total cost for the network goes up to \$28 and the project completion time is reduced to nine days.

Our next iteration starts in line three, where the goal is to reduce the project completion time to eight days. The nine-day critical path is A–B–D. We could shorten activity A by one day, B by three days, and D by one day (note D has already been reduced from three to two days). Cost to reduce each activity by one day is the same as in line two. Again, the least expensive activity to reduce is D. Reducing activity D from two days to one day results in the total cost for all activities in the network going up to \$30 and the project completion time coming down to eight days.

Line four is similar to line three, but now only A and B are on the critical path and can be reduced. B is reduced, which takes our cost up \$3 to \$33 and reduces the project completion time to seven days.

In line five (actually our fifth iteration in solving the problem), activities A, B, C, and D are all critical. D cannot be reduced, so our only options are activities A, B, and C. Note that B and C are in parallel, so it does not help to reduce B without reducing C. Our options are to reduce A alone at a cost of \$4 or B and C together at a cost of \$5 (\$3 for B and \$2 for C), so we reduce A in this iteration.

In line six, we take the B and C option that was considered in line five. Finally, in line seven, our only option is to reduce activity B. Since B and C are in parallel and we cannot reduce C, there is no value in reducing B alone. We can reduce the project completion time no further.

5. **Plot project direct, indirect, and total-cost curves and find the minimum-cost schedule.** Exhibit 3.12 shows the indirect cost plotted as a constant \$10 per day for eight days and increasing \$5 per day thereafter. The direct costs are plotted from Exhibit 3.11, and the total project cost is shown as the total of the two costs.

Plot of Costs and Minimum-Cost Schedule

exhibit 3.12

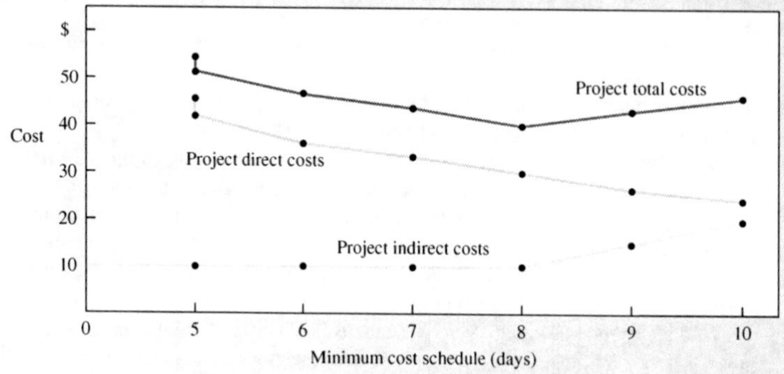

Summing the values for direct and indirect costs for each day yields the project total cost curve. As you can see, this curve is at its minimum with an eight-day schedule, which costs \$40 (\$30 direct + \$10 indirect).

MANAGING RESOURCES

In addition to scheduling each task, we must assign resources. Modern software quickly highlights overallocations—situations in which allocations exceed resources.

BREAKTHROUGH

PROJECT MANAGEMENT INFORMATION SYSTEMS

Interest in the techniques and concepts of project management has exploded in the past 10 years. This has resulted in a parallel increase in project management software offerings. Now there are over 100 companies offering project management software. For the most up-to-date information about software available, check out the Web site of the Project Management Institute (**www.pmi.org**). Two of the leading companies are Microsoft, with Microsoft Project, and Primavera, with Primavera Project Planner. The following is a brief review of these two programs:

The Microsoft Project program comes with an excellent online tutorial, which is one reason for its overwhelming popularity with project managers tracking midsized projects. This package is compatible with the Microsoft Office Suite, which opens all the communications and Internet integration capability that Microsoft offers. The program includes features for scheduling, allocating, and leveling resources, as well as controlling costs and producing presentation-quality graphics and reports.

Finally, for managing very large projects or programs having several projects, Primavera Project Planner is often the choice. Primavera was the first major vendor of this type of software and has possibly the most sophisticated capability.

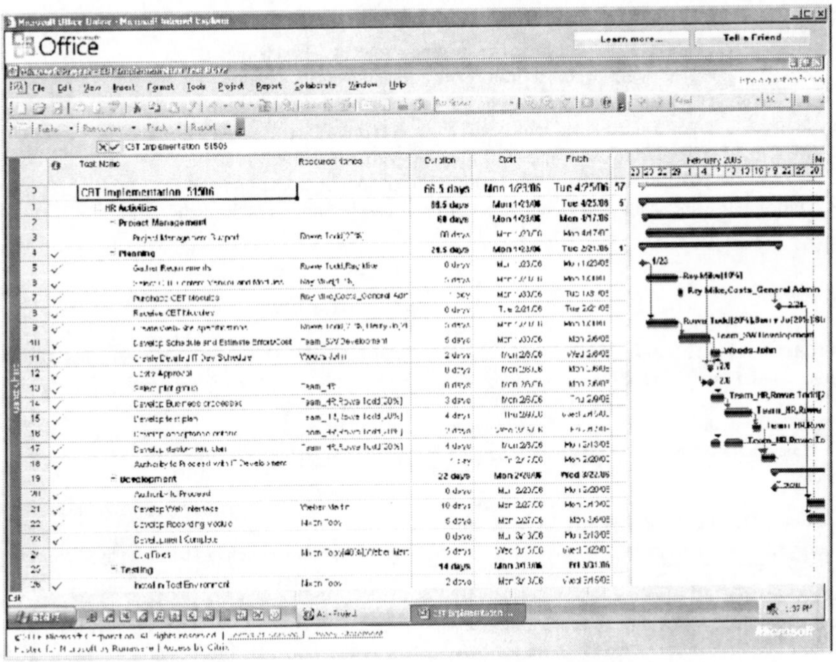

Internet

To resolve overallocations manually, you can either add resources or reschedule. Moving a task within its slack can free up resources.

Mid- to high-level project management information systems (PMIS) software can resolve overallocations through a "leveling" feature. Several rules of thumb can be used. You can specify that low-priority tasks should be delayed until higher-priority ones are complete, or that the project should end before or after the original deadline.

PARAMOUNT INVESTED OVER $17 MILLION IN THIS PROJECT AT GREAT AMERICA IN SANTA CLARA. THE PROJECT INCLUDED A UNIQUE USE OF COMPUTERS FOR LAYOUT, DESIGN, AND SIMULATION IN ORDER TO COMPLY WITH RIGID SAFETY STANDARDS FOR THE WORLD'S FIRST "FLYING COASTER."

TRACKING PROGRESS

The real action starts after the project gets under way. Actual progress will differ from your original, or baseline, planned progress. Software can hold several different baseline plans, so you can compare monthly snapshots.

A *tracking Gantt chart* superimposes the current schedule onto a baseline plan so deviations are easily noticed. If you prefer, a spreadsheet view of the same information could be output. Deviations between planned start/finish and newly scheduled start/finish also appear, and a "slipping filter" can be applied to highlight or output only those tasks that are scheduled to finish at a later date than the planned baseline.

Management by exception also can be applied to find deviations between budgeted costs and actual costs. (See the Breakthrough box titled "Project Management Information Systems.")

CONCLUSION

This chapter provides a description of the basics of managing projects. The chapter first describes how the people involved with a project are organized from a management viewpoint. The scope of the project will help define the organization. This organization spans the use of a dedicated team to a largely undedicated matrix structure. Next, the chapter considers how project activities are organized into subprojects by using the work breakdown structure. Following this, the technical details of calculating the shortest time it should take to complete a project are covered. Finally, the chapter considers how projects can be shortened through the use of "crashing" concepts.

KEY TERMS

Project A series of related jobs usually directed toward some major output and requiring a significant period of time to perform.

Project management Planning, directing, and controlling resources (people, equipment, material) to meet the technical, cost, and time constraints of a project.

Pure project A structure for organizing a project where a self-contained team works full time on the project.

Functional project A structure where team members are assigned from the functional units of the organization. The team members remain a part of their functional units and typically are not dedicated to the project.

Matrix project A structure that blends the functional and pure project structures. Each project uses people from different functional areas. A dedicated project manager decides what tasks need to be performed and when, but the functional managers control which people to use.

Project milestone A specific event in a project.

Work breakdown structure The hierarchy of project tasks, subtasks, and work packages.

Activities Pieces of work within a project that consume time. The completion of all the activities of a project marks the end of the project.

Gantt chart Shows in a graphic manner the amount of time involved and the sequence in which activities can be performed. Often referred to as a *bar chart.*

Critical path The sequence of activities in a project that forms the longest chain in terms of their time to complete. This path contains zero slack time. Techniques used to find the critical path are called CPM or Critical Path Method techniques.

Immediate predecessor Activity that needs to be completed immediately before another activity.

Slack time The time that an activity can be delayed; the difference between the late and early start times of an activity.

Early start schedule A project schedule that lists all activities by their early start times.

Late start schedule A project schedule that lists all activities by their late start times. This schedule may create savings by postponing purchases of material and other costs associated with the project.

Time–cost models Extension of the critical path models that considers the trade-off between the time required to complete an activity and cost. This is often referred to as "crashing" the project.

FORMULA REVIEW

Expected Time

$$ET = \frac{a + 4m + b}{6}$$

Variance (σ^2) of the activity times

$$\sigma^2 = \left(\frac{b - a}{6}\right)^2$$

Z transformation formula

$$Z = \frac{D - T_E}{\sqrt{\sum \sigma_{cp}^2}}$$

SOLVED PROBLEMS

SOLVED PROBLEM 1

A project has been defined to contain the following list of activities, along with their required times for completion:

Excel: PM_solved problem.xls

ACTIVITY	TIME (DAYS)	IMMEDIATE PREDECESSORS
A	1	—
B	4	A
C	3	A
D	7	A
E	6	B
F	2	C, D
G	7	E, F
H	9	D
I	4	G, H

a. Draw the critical path diagram.
b. Show the early start and early finish times.
c. Show the critical path.
d. What would happen if activity F was revised to take four days instead of two?

Solution

The answers to *a*, *b*, and *c* are shown in the following diagram.

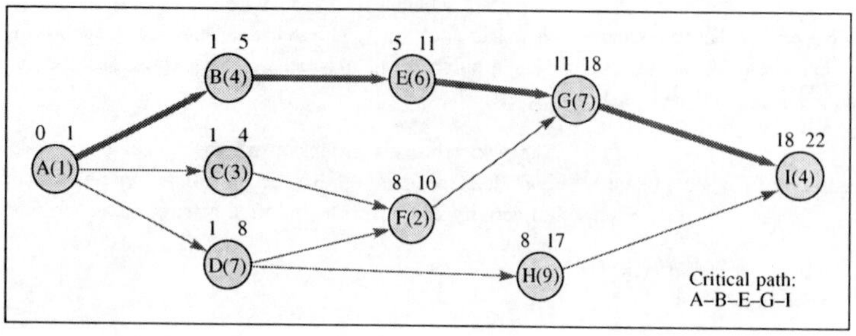

d. New critical path: A–D–F–G–I. Time of completion is 23 days.

SOLVED PROBLEM 2

A project has been defined to contain the following activities, along with their time estimates for completion,

ACTIVITY	TIME ESTIMATES (WK) *a*	*m*	*b*	IMMEDIATE PREDECESSOR
A	1	4	7	—
B	2	6	7	A
C	3	4	6	A, D
D	6	12	14	A
E	3	6	12	D
F	6	8	16	B, C
G	1	5	6	E, F

Excel: PM_solved problem.xls

a. Calculate the expected time and the variance for each activity.
b. Draw the critical path diagram.
c. Show the early start, early finish times and late start, late finish times.
d. Show the critical path.
e. What is the probability that the project can be completed in 34 weeks?

Solution

a.

ACTIVITY	EXPECTED TIME $\frac{a+4m+b}{6}$	ACTIVITY VARIANCE $\left(\frac{b-a}{6}\right)^2$
A	4.00	1
B	5.50	$\frac{25}{36}$
C	4.17	$\frac{1}{4}$
D	11.33	$1\frac{7}{9}$
E	6.50	$2\frac{1}{4}$
F	9.00	$2\frac{7}{9}$
G	4.50	$\frac{25}{36}$

b.

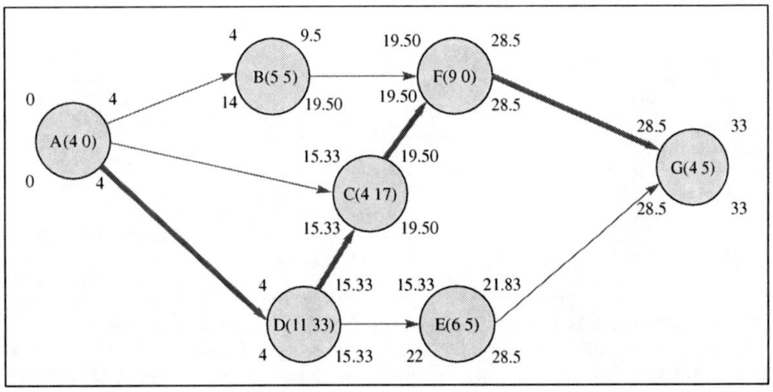

c. Shown on diagram.
d. Shown on diagram.

e. $Z = \frac{D - T_E}{\sqrt{\sum \sigma_{cp}^2}} = \frac{34 - 33}{\sqrt{1 + 1\frac{7}{9} + \frac{1}{4} + 2\frac{7}{9} + \frac{25}{36}}} = \frac{1}{2.5495} = .3922$

Look up that value in Appendix E and we see that there is about a 65 percent chance of completing the project by that date.

SOLVED PROBLEM 3

Here are the precedence requirements, normal and crash activity times, and normal and crash costs for a construction project:

		Required Time (weeks)		Cost	
Activity	Preceding Activities	Normal	Crash	Normal	Crash
A	—	4	2	$10,000	$11,000
B	A	3	2	6,000	9,000
C	A	2	1	4,000	6,000
D	B	5	3	14,000	18,000
E	B, C	1	1	9,000	9,000
F	C	3	2	7,000	8,000
G	E, F	4	2	13,000	25,000
H	D, E	4	1	11,000	18,000
I	H, G	6	5	20,000	29,000

a. What are the critical path and the estimated completion time?
b. To shorten the project by three weeks, which tasks would be shortened and what would the final total project cost be?

Solution

The construction project network is shown below:

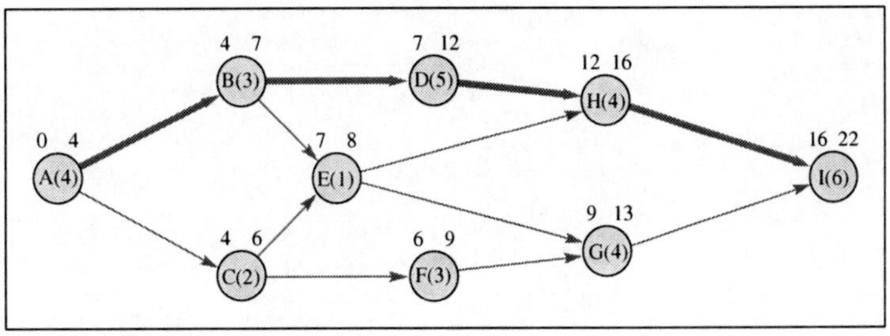

a. Critical path A–B–D–H–I.
Normal completion time is 22 weeks.

b.

ACTIVITY	CRASH COST	NORMAL COST	NORMAL TIME	CRASH TIME	COST PER WEEK	WEEKS
A	$11,000	$10,000	4	2	$ 500	2
B	9,000	6,000	3	2	3,000	1
C	6,000	4,000	2	1	2,000	1
D	18,000	14,000	5	3	2,000	2
E	9,000	9,000	1	1		0
F	8,000	7,000	3	2	1,000	1
G	25,000	13,000	4	2	6,000	2
H	18,000	11,000	4	1	2,333	3
I	29,000	20,000	6	5	9,000	1

(1) 1st week: CP = A–B–D–H–I. Cheapest is A at $500. Critical path stays the same.
(2) 2nd week: A is still the cheapest at $500. Critical path stays the same.
(3) 3rd week: Because A is no longer available, the choices are B (at $3,000), D (at $2,000), H (at $2,333), and I (at $9,000). Therefore, choose D at $2,000.

Total project cost shortened three weeks is

A	$ 11,000
B	6,000
C	4,000
D	16,000
E	9,000
F	7,000
G	13,000
H	11,000
I	20,000
	$97,000

REVIEW AND DISCUSSION QUESTIONS

1 What was the most complex project that you have been involved in? Give examples of the following as they pertain to the project: the work breakdown structure, tasks, subtasks, and work package. Were you on the critical path? Did it have a good project manager?
2 What are some reasons project scheduling is not done well?
3 Discuss the graphic presentations in Exhibit 3.4. Are there any other graphic outputs you would like to see if you were project manager?
4 Which characteristics must a project have for critical path scheduling to be applicable? What types of projects have been subjected to critical path analysis?
5 What are the underlying assumptions of minimum-cost scheduling? Are they equally realistic?
6 "Project control should always focus on the critical path." Comment.
7 Why would subcontractors for a government project want their activities on the critical path? Under what conditions would they try to avoid being on the critical path?

PROBLEMS

1 For the project given in the table below, what is the duration of the project?

ACTIVITY	PREDECESSORS	DURATION (DAYS)
A	none	7
B	none	23
C	A	10
D	A	9
E	C	11
F	C, D	12
G	B, F	6
H	E, F	4
I	G, H	5

2 The following activities are part of a project to be scheduled using CPM:

ACTIVITY	IMMEDIATE PREDECESSOR	TIME (WEEKS)
A	—	6
B	A	3
C	A	7
D	C	2
E	B, D	4
F	D	3
G	E, F	7

a. Draw the network.
b. What is the critical path?
c. How many weeks will it take to complete the project?
d. How much slack does activity B have?

3 Schedule the following activities using CPM:

ACTIVITY	IMMEDIATE PREDECESSOR	TIME (WEEKS)
A	—	1
B	A	4
C	A	3
D	B	2
E	C, D	5
F	D	2
G	F	2
H	E, G	3

a. Draw the network.
b. What is the critical path?
c. How many weeks will it take to complete the project?
d. Which activities have slack, and how much?

4 The R&D department is planning to bid on a large project for the development of a new communication system for commercial planes. The accompanying table shows the activities, times, and sequences required:

ACTIVITY	IMMEDIATE PREDECESSOR	TIME (WEEKS)
A	—	3
B	A	2
C	A	4
D	A	4
E	B	6
F	C, D	6
G	D, F	2
H	D	3
I	E, G, H	3

a. Draw the network diagram.
b. What is the critical path?
c. Suppose you want to shorten the completion time as much as possible, and you have the option of shortening any or all of B, C, D, and G each one week. Which would you shorten?
d. What is the new critical path and earliest completion time?

5 A construction project is broken down into the following 10 activities:

ACTIVITY	IMMEDIATE PREDECESSOR	TIME (WEEKS)
1	—	4
2	1	2
3	1	4
4	1	3
5	2, 3	5
6	3	6
7	4	2
8	5	3
9	6, 7	5
10	8, 9	7

a. Draw the network diagram.
b. Find the critical path.
c. If activities 1 and 10 cannot be shortened, but activities 2 through 9 can be shortened to a minimum of one week each at a cost of $10,000 per week, which activities would you shorten to cut the project by four weeks?

6 The following represents a project that should be scheduled using CPM:

ACTIVITY	IMMEDIATE PREDECESSORS	TIMES (DAYS)		
		a	*m*	*b*
A	—	1	3	5
B	—	1	2	3
C	A	1	2	3
D	A	2	3	4
E	B	3	4	11
F	C, D	3	4	5
G	D, E	1	4	6
H	F, G	2	4	5

a. Draw the network.
b. What is the critical path?
c. What is the expected project completion time?
d. What is the probability of completing this project within 16 days?

7 There is an 82% chance the project below can be completed in X weeks or less. What is X?

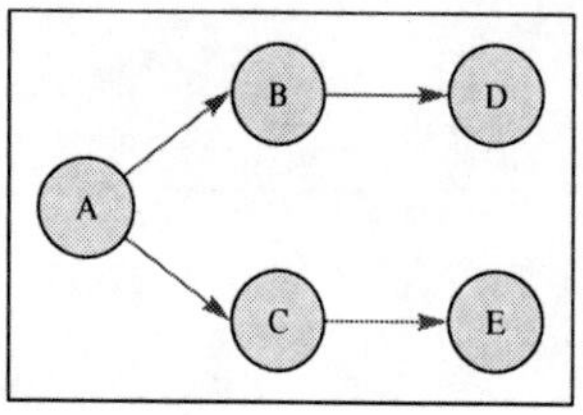

ACTIVITY	MOST OPTIMISTIC	MOST LIKELY	MOST PESSIMISTIC
A	2	5	11
B	3	3	3
C	1	3	5
D	6	8	10
E	4	7	10

8 Here is a CPM network with activity times in weeks:

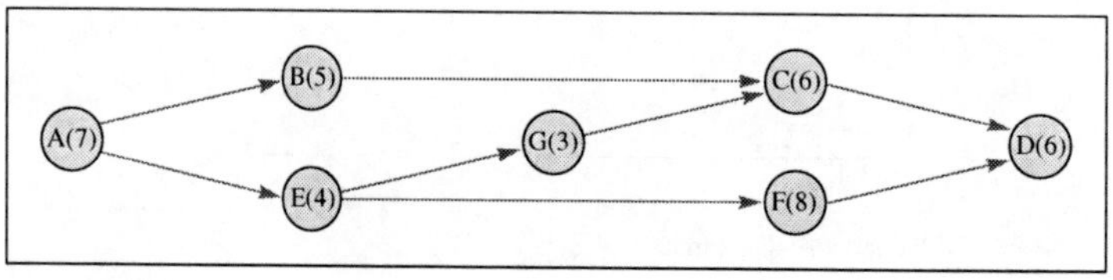

a. Determine the critical path.
b. How many weeks will the project take to complete?
c. Suppose F could be shortened by two weeks and B by one week. How would this affect the completion date?

9 The following table represents a plan for a project:

		Times (Days)		
Job No.	Predecessor Job(s)	*a*	*m*	*b*
1	—	2	3	4
2	1	1	2	3
3	1	4	5	12
4	1	3	4	11
5	2	1	3	5
6	3	1	2	3
7	4	1	8	9
8	5, 6	2	4	6
9	8	2	4	12
10	7	3	4	5
11	9, 10	5	7	8

a. Construct the appropriate network diagram.
b. Indicate the critical path.
c. What is the expected completion time for the project?
d. You can accomplish any one of the following at an additional cost of $1,500:
(1) Reduce job 5 by two days.
(2) Reduce job 3 by two days.
(3) Reduce job 7 by two days.
If you will save $1,000 for each day that the earliest completion time is reduced, which action, if any, would you choose?
e. What is the probability that the project will take more than 30 days to complete?

10 A project has an expected duration of 34 weeks with a critical path variance of 6. What is the probability the project can be completed in 32 weeks or less?

11 Here is a network with the activity times shown in days:

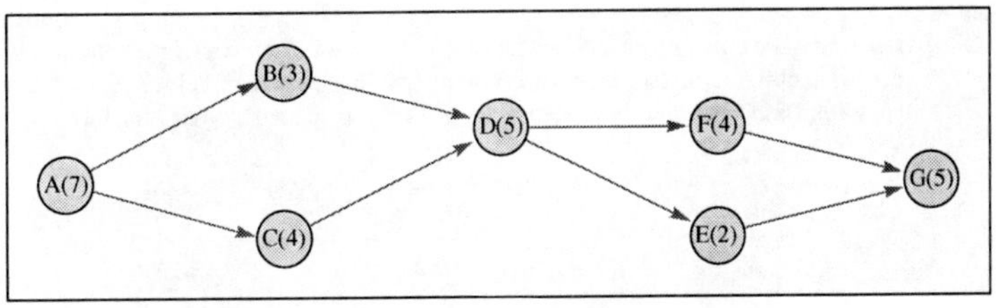

a. Find the critical path.
b. The following table shows the normal times and the crash times, along with the associated costs for each activity.

Activity	Normal Time	Crash Time	Normal Cost	Crash Cost
A	7	6	$7,000	$ 8,000
B	3	2	5,000	7,000
C	4	3	9,000	10,200
D	5	4	3,000	4,500
E	2	1	2,000	3,000
F	4	2	4,000	7,000
G	5	4	5,000	8,000

If the project is to be shortened by four days, show which activities, in order of reduction, would be shortened and the resulting cost.

12 The home office billing department of a chain of department stores prepares monthly inventory reports for use by the stores' purchasing agents. Given the following information, use the critical path method to determine

a. How long the total process will take.

b. Which jobs can be delayed without delaying the early start of any subsequent activity.

	Job and Description	Immediate Predecessors	Time (hours)
a	Start	—	0
b	Get computer printouts of customer purchases	a	10
c	Get stock records for the month	a	20
d	Reconcile purchase printouts and stock records	b, c	30
e	Total stock records by department	b, c	20
f	Determine reorder quantities for coming period	e	40
g	Prepare stock reports for purchasing agents	d, f	20
h	Finish	g	0

13 For the network shown:

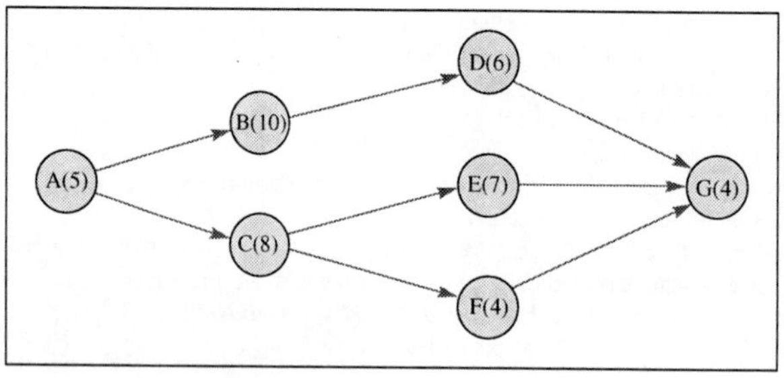

a. Determine the critical path and the early completion time in weeks for the project.

b. For the data shown, reduce the project completion time by three weeks. Assume a linear cost per week shortened, and show, step by step, how you arrived at your schedule.

Activity	Normal Time	Normal Cost	Crash Time	Crash Cost
A	5	$ 7,000	3	$13,000
B	10	12,000	7	18,000
C	8	5,000	7	7,000
D	6	4,000	5	5,000
E	7	3,000	6	6,000
F	4	6,000	3	7,000
G	4	7,000	3	9,000

14 The following CPM network has estimates of the normal time in weeks listed for the activities:

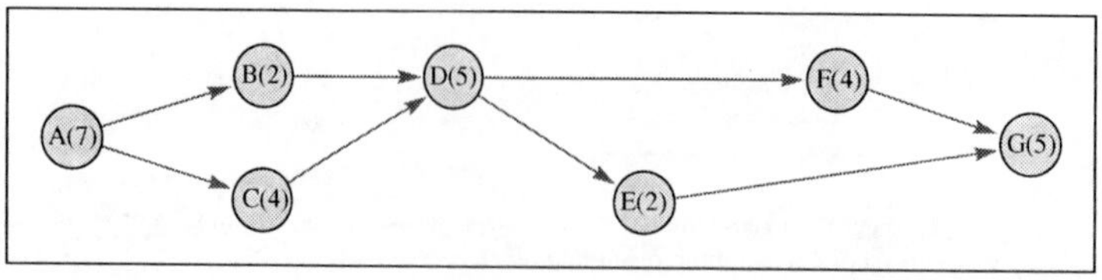

a. Identify the critical path.
b. What is the length of time to complete the project?
c. Which activities have slack, and how much?
d. Here is a table of normal and crash times and costs. Which activities would you shorten to cut two weeks from the schedule in a rational fashion? What would be the incremental cost? Is the critical path changed?

Activity	Normal Time	Crash Time	Normal Cost	Crash Cost	Possible Number of Weeks Decrease	Cost/Week to Expedite
A	7	6	$7,000	$ 8,000		
B	2	1	5,000	7,000		
C	4	3	9,000	10,200		
D	5	4	3,000	4,500		
E	2	1	2,000	3,000		
F	4	2	4,000	7,000		
G	5	4	5,000	8,000		

15 A project has been defined to contain the following activities, along with their time estimates for completion.

Activity	Time Estimates (wk) *a*	*m*	*b*	Immediate Predecessor
A	2	5	8	—
B	1	5	9	—
C	4	6	9	A
D	2	2	2	B
E	1	2	9	A
F	2	4	5	C, D
G	3	8	10	C, E
H	1	2	3	F, G

a. Calculate the expected time and the variance for each activity.
b. Draw the critical path diagram. Show the early start, early finish times and late start, late finish times.
c. Show the critical path.
d. What is the probability that the project can be completed in 19 weeks?

16 Hungry Henry's is building a new restaurant. In order to complete the project, the following activities, along with their time estimates, are given below.

Activity	Time Estimates (wk) *a*	*m*	*b*	Immediate Predecessor
A	2	4	7	—
B	1	4	9	A
C	3	6	9	A
D	2	3	5	B, C
E	1	3	9	B
F	2	4	5	C, D
G	3	8	10	E
H	1	2	3	F, E
I	3	5	7	G, H

a. Calculate the expected time and the variance for each activity.
b. Draw the critical path diagram. Show the early start, early finish times and late start, late finish times.
c. Show the critical path.
d. What is the probability that the project can be completed in 26 weeks? What is the probability it will take longer than 26 weeks?
e. Are there any other paths that can interfere with completing this project on time?

17 Bragg's Bakery is building a new automated bakery in downtown Sandusky. Here are the activities that need to be completed to get the new bakery built and the equipment installed.

ACTIVITY	PREDECESSOR	NORMAL TIME (WEEKS)	CRASH TIME (WEEKS)	EXPEDITING COST/WEEK
A	—	9	6	$3,000
B	A	8	5	$3,500
C	A	15	10	$4,000
D	B, C	5	3	$2,000
E	C	10	6	$2,500
F	D, E	2	1	$5,000

a. Draw the project diagram.
b. What is the normal project length?
c. What is the project length if all activities are crashed to their minimum?
d. Bragg's loses $3,500 in profit per week for every week the bakery is not completed. How many weeks will the project take if we are willing to pay crashing cost as long as it is less than $3,500?

ADVANCED PROBLEM

18 Assume the network and data that follow:

ACTIVITY	NORMAL TIME (WEEKS)	NORMAL COST	CRASH TIME (WEEKS)	CRASH COST	IMMEDIATE PREDECESSORS
A	2	$50	1	$70	—
B	4	80	2	160	A
C	8	70	4	110	A
D	6	60	5	80	A
E	7	100	6	130	B
F	4	40	3	100	D
G	5	100	4	150	C, E, F

a. Construct the network diagram.
b. Indicate the critical path when normal activity times are used.
c. Compute the minimum total direct cost for each project duration based on the cost associated with each activity. Consider durations of 13, 14, 15, 16, 17, and 18 weeks.
d. If the indirect costs for each project duration are $400 (18 weeks), $350 (17 weeks), $300 (16 weeks), $250 (15 weeks), $200 (14 weeks), and $150 (13 weeks), what is the total project cost for each duration? Indicate the minimum total project cost duration.

CASE: THE CAMPUS WEDDING (A)

On March 31 of last year, Mary Jackson burst into the family living room and announced that she and Larry Adams (her college boyfriend) were going to be married. After recovering from the shock, her mother hugged her and asked, "When?" The following conversation resulted:

Mary: April 22.

Mother: What!

Father: The Adams–Jackson wedding will be the social hit of the year. Why so soon?

Mary: Because on April 22 the cherry blossoms on campus are always in full bloom! The wedding pictures will be beautiful.

Mother: But honey, we can't possibly finish all the things that need to be done by then. Remember all the details that were involved in your sister's wedding? Even if we start tomorrow, it takes a day to reserve the church and reception hall, and they need at least 17 days' notice. That has to be done before we can start decorating the church, which takes three days. An extra $100 contribution on Sunday would probably cut that 17-day notice to 10 days, though.

Father: Ugh!

Mary: I want Jane Summers to be my maid of honor.

Father: But she's in the Peace Corps, in Guatemala, isn't she? It would take her 10 days to get ready and drive up here.

Mary: But we could fly her up in two days, and it would cost only $500. She would have to be here in time to have her dress fitted.

Father: Ugh!

Mother: And catering! It takes two days to choose the cake and table decorations, and Jack's Catering wants at least 10 days' notice prior to the rehearsal dinner (the night before the wedding).

Mary: Can I wear your wedding dress, Mom?

Mother: Well, we'd have to replace some lace, but you could wear it, yes. We could order the lace from New York when we order the material for the bridesmaids' dresses. It takes eight days to order and receive the material. The pattern needs to be chosen first, and that would take three days.

Father: We could get the material here in five days if we paid an extra $25 to airfreight it.

Mary: I want Mrs. Watson to work on the dresses.

Father: But she charges $120 a day!

Mother: If we did all the sewing, we could finish the dresses in 11 days. If Mrs. Watson helped, we could cut that down to six days, at a cost of $120 for each day less than 11 days.

Mary: I don't want anyone but her.

Mother: It would take another two days to do the final fitting. It normally takes two days to clean and press the dresses, but that new cleaner downtown could do them in one day if we pay the $30 charge for express service.

Father: Everything should be completed by rehearsal night, and that's only 21 days from now. I bet that will be a busy day.

Mother: We've forgotten something. The invitations.

Father: We should order the invitations from Bob's Printing Shop, and that usually takes 12 days. I'll bet he would do it in five days if we slipped him an extra $35.

Mother: It would take us three days to choose the invitation style before we could order them, and we want the envelopes printed with our return address.

Mary: Oh! That will be elegant.

Mother: The invitations should go out at least 10 days before the wedding. If we let them go any later, some of the relatives would get theirs too late to come, and that would make them mad. I'll bet that if we didn't get them out until eight days before the wedding, Aunt Ethel couldn't make it, and she would reduce her wedding gift by $200.

Father: Ugh!

Mother: We'll have to take them to the post office to mail them, and that takes a day. Addressing would take four days unless we hired some part-time help, and we can't start until the printer is finished. If we hired someone, we could probably save two days by spending $25 for each day saved.

Mary: We need to get gifts to give to the bridesmaids at the rehearsal dinner. I can spend a day and do that.

Mother: Before we can even start to write out those invitations, we need a guest list. Heavens, that will take four days to get in order, and only I can understand our address file.

Mary: Oh, Mother, I'm so excited. We can start each of the relatives on a different job.

Mother: Honey, I don't see how we can do it. Why, we've got to choose the invitations and patterns and reserve the church and . . .

Father: Why don't you just take $1,500 and elope. Your sister's wedding cost me $1,200, and she didn't have to fly people up from Guatemala, hire extra people, use airfreight, or anything like that.

QUESTIONS

1 Given the activities and precedence relationships described in the (A) case, develop a network diagram for the wedding plans.
2 Identify the paths. Which are critical?
3 What is the minimum-cost plan that meets the April 22 date?

CASE: THE CAMPUS WEDDING (B)

Several complications arose during the course of trying to meet the deadline of April 21 for the Adams–Jackson wedding rehearsal. Because Mary Jackson was adamant about having the wedding on April 22 (as was Larry Adams, because he wanted her to be happy), the implications of each of these complications had to be assessed.

1 On April 1 the chairman of the Vestry Committee at the church was left unimpressed by the added donation and said he wouldn't reduce the notice period from 17 to 10 days.
2 A call to Guatemala revealed that the potential bridesmaid had several commitments and could not possibly leave the country until April 10.
3 Mother came down with the four-day flu just as she started on the guest list.
4 The lace and dress materials were lost in transit. Notice of the loss was delivered to the Jackson home early on April 10.
5 There was a small fire at the caterer's shop on April 8. It was estimated that the shop would be closed two or three days for repairs.

Mary Jackson's father, in particular, was concerned about expenses and kept offering $1,500 to Mary and Larry for them to elope.

QUESTION

1 Given your answers to the (A) case, describe the effects on the wedding plans of each incident noted in the (B) case.

SOURCE: ADAPTED FROM A CASE ORIGINALLY WRITTEN BY PROFESSOR D. C. WHYBANK, UNIVERSITY OF NORTH CAROLINA, CHAPEL HILL, NORTH CAROLINA.

Work Breakdown Structure and Activities for the Cell Phone Design Project

exhibit 3.13

MAJOR PROJECT TASKS/ACTIVITIES	ACTIVITY IDENTIFICATION	DEPENDENCY	DURATION (WEEKS)
Product specifications (P)			
Overall product specifications	P1	—	4
Hardware specifications	P2	P1	5
Software specifications	P3	P1	5
Market research	P4	P2, P3	2
Supplier specifications (S)			
Hardware	S1	P2	5
Software	S2	P3	6
Market research	S3	P4	1
Product design (D)			
Circuits	D1	S1, D7	3
Battery	D2	S1	1
Display	D3	S1	2
Outer cover	D4	S3	4
User interface	D5	S2	4
Camera	D6	S1, S2, S3	1
Functionality	D7	D5, D6	4
Product integration (I)			
Hardware	I1	D1, D2, D3, D4, D6	3
Software	I2	D7	5
Prototype Testing	I3	I1,I2	5
Subcontracting (V)			
Vendor selection	V1	D7	10
Contract negotiation	V2	I3, V1	2

Excel: Cell_Phone Design.xls

CASE: CELL PHONE DESIGN PROJECT

You work for Motorola in their global cell phone group. You have been made project manager for the design of a new cell phone model. Your supervisors have already scoped the project, so you have a list showing the work breakdown structure and this includes major project activities. You must plan the project schedule and calculate project duration and project costs. Your boss wants the schedule and costs on his desk tomorrow morning!

You have been given the information in Exhibit 3.13. It includes all the activities required in the project and the duration of each activity. Also, dependencies between the activities have been identified. Remember that the preceding activity must be fully completed before work on the following activity can be started.

Your project is divided into five major tasks. Task "P" involves developing specifications for the new cell phone. Here decisions related to such things as battery life, size of the phone, and features need to be determined. These details are based on how a customer uses the cell phone. These user specifications are redefined in terms that have meaning to the subcontractors that will actually make the new cell phone in Task "S" supplier specifications. These involve engineering details for how the product will perform. The individual components that make up the product are the focus of Task "D." Task "I" brings all the components together, and a working prototype is built and tested. Finally in Task "V," vendors are selected and contracts are negotiated.

QUESTIONS

1. Draw a project network that includes all the activities.
2. Calculate the start and finish times for each activity and determine how many weeks is the minimum for completing the project. Find the critical set of activities for the project.
3. Identify slack in the activities not on the project critical path.
4. Your boss would like you to suggest changes that could be made to the project that would significantly shorten it. What would you suggest?

SELECTED BIBLIOGRAPHY

Gray, C. F., and E. W. Larson. *Project Management: The Managerial Process*. 3rd ed. New York: Irwin/McGraw-Hill, 2005.

Project Management Institute (PMI). www.pmi.org.

Wysocki, Robert K. *Effective Project Management: Traditional, Adaptive, Extreme*. 4th ed. New York: Wiley, 2007.

Chapter 13

Motivation and Performance

LEARNING OBJECTIVES

After studying this chapter, you should be able to:

- ☑ Explain what motivation is, and why managers need to be concerned about it.
- ☑ Describe from the perspectives of expectancy theory and equity theory what managers should do to have a highly motivated workforce.
- ☑ Explain how goals and needs motivate people, and what kinds of goals are especially likely to result in high performance.
- ☑ Identify the motivation lessons that managers can learn from operant conditioning theory and social learning theory.
- ☑ Explain why and how managers can use pay as a major motivation tool.

A Manager's Challenge

Consistently Ranking as a Best Company to Work For: Sandwell Community Caring Trust

How can managers motivate employees in an industry known for high levels of turnover and low levels of motivation?

Sandwell Community Caring Trust was founded in 1996. The trust, which is a registered charity, looks after people in three of the most deprived areas of the Midlands. The charity serves more than 350 severely disabled adults and children, and also runs a residential home for the elderly. The services offered include residential care, day care and support for people in their own home, and the trust actively helps in building specialist properties for disabled people.

Geoff Walker, CEO of the Trust, believes that it is important to treat its most important resource, the trust's staff, well for the charity to deliver the best service. His opinion is that 'they [staff] are mirror images. How you treat your workforce is the experience the service users get.' This motto includes an appreciation that in order to empower service users, treat them with dignity and make them feel good about themselves requires that the staff experiences a similar treatment.

This attitude has been rewarded by a continuous ranking as one of the best organisations to work for within the UK. So how does Geoff Walker manage to retain staff in an industry that is usually plagued by high staff turnover and low morale?

Sandwell Community Caring Trust ranks highest in a *Times* survey for delivering the best work–life balance. The charity offers a generous holiday allowance of up to 39 days and staff are extremely satisfied with the pay that they receive. Salaries for staff within the Trust are higher than the industry average, a deliberate choice to attract only the best people. The excellent pay packages offered by the charity are further enhanced by bonus schemes which, in effect, increase the salary by 6 per cent for an average member of staff. Staff turnover within the Trust is less than half of the industry's average.

But these rewards are just part of the Trust's success. The survey showed that most of the staff felt that the management of the charity was excellent and that senior managers were good role models. The staff also trusted the leadership that was given by the charity's senior managers. All this is underlined by the attitude of Geoff Walker and his team, who have reduced administration and thus kept a large proportion of their diaries free to work 'out there' where leadership is needed. Geoff Walker, for example, remains very hands-on. He performs care duties or drives the minibus, just like any other employee.[1]

Overview

Even with the best strategy in place and an appropriate organisational architecture, an organisation will be effective only if its members are motivated to perform at a high level. Walker clearly realises this. One reason why leading is such an important managerial activity is that it entails ensuring that each member of an organisation is motivated to perform highly and help the organisation achieve its goals. When managers are effective, the outcome of the leading process is a highly motivated workforce. A key challenge for managers of organisations both large and small is to encourage employees to perform at a high level.

This chapter describes what motivation is, where it comes from and why managers need to promote high levels of it for an organisation to be effective and achieve its goals. It examines important theories of motivation – expectancy theory, need theories, equity theory, goal-setting theory and learning theories. Each provides managers with important insights about how to motivate organisational members and the theories are complementary in that each focuses on a somewhat different aspect of motivation. Considering all of the theories together helps managers gain a rich understanding of the many issues and problems involved in encouraging high levels of motivation throughout an organisation. The chapter finally considers the use of pay as a motivation tool. By the end of this chapter, you will understand what it takes to have a highly motivated workforce.

The Nature of Motivation

Motivation may be defined as the psychological forces that determine the direction of a person's behaviour in an organisation, a person's level of effort and a person's level of persistence in the face of obstacles.[2] The *direction of a person's behaviour* refers to the many possible behaviours that a person could engage in. Employees at Sandwell Community Caring Trust know that they should do whatever is required to meet a customer's needs and don't have to ask permission to do something out of the ordinary.[3] *Effort* refers to how hard people work. Employees at the Trust exert high levels of effort to provide superior customer service. *Persistence* refers to whether, when faced with roadblocks and obstacles, people keep trying or give up.

Motivation is central to management because it explains *why* people behave the way they do in organisations[4] – why employees at the Trust provide such excellent customer service, and enjoy doing so. Motivation also explains why a waiter is polite or rude and why a kindergarten teacher really tries to get children to enjoy learning or just goes through the motions. It explains why some managers truly put their organisation's best interests first whereas others are more concerned with maximising their salaries and why – more generally – some workers put forth twice as much effort as others.

Motivation can come from *intrinsic* or *extrinsic* sources. **Intrinsically motivated behaviour** is behaviour that is performed for its own sake. The source of motivation is actually performing the behaviour, and motivation comes from doing the work itself. Many managers are intrinsically motivated; they derive a sense of accomplishment and achievement from helping the organisation to achieve its goals and gain competitive advantage. Jobs that are interesting and challenging or high on the five characteristics described by the job characteristics model in Chapter 9 are more likely to lead to intrinsic motivation than are jobs that are boring or do not make use of a person's skills and abilities. An elementary school teacher who really enjoys teaching children, a computer programmer who loves solving programming problems and a commercial photographer who relishes taking creative photographs are all intrinsically motivated. For these individuals, motivation comes from performing their jobs whether it be teaching children, finding bugs in computer programmes or taking pictures.

Extrinsically motivated behaviour is behaviour that is performed to acquire material or social rewards or to avoid punishment. The source of motivation is the consequences of the behaviour, not the behaviour itself. A salesperson who is motivated by receiving a commission on units sold, a lawyer who is motivated by the high salary and status that go along with the job and a factory worker who is motivated by the opportunity to earn a secure income are all extrinsically motivated. Their motivation comes from the consequences they receive as a result of their work behaviours.

People can be intrinsically motivated, extrinsically motivated, or both intrinsically and extrinsically motivated.[5] A senior manager who derives a sense of accomplishment and achievement from managing a large corporation and strives to reach year-end targets to obtain a hefty bonus is both intrinsically and extrinsically motivated. Similarly, a nurse who enjoys helping and taking care of patients and is motivated by having a secure job with good benefits is both intrinsically and extrinsically motivated. At the Trust, employees are both extrinsically motivated because they receive relatively high salaries and generous benefits and intrinsically motivated because they genuinely enjoy and get a sense of satisfaction out of doing their work and serving customers and look forward to coming to work each day: a senior care assistant, for example is excited about the change that he can observe in the people he works with, their growing confidence and happiness. Whether workers are intrinsically motivated, extrinsically motivated or both depends on a wide variety of factors. First of all, a worker's *own personal characteristics* (such as their personalities, abilities, values, attitudes and needs) are factors to be considered. Secondly, the *nature of the jobs* that are performed need to be taken into consideration – such as whether they have been enriched or where they are on the five core characteristics of the job characteristics model. Lastly, the *nature of the organisation* (such as its structure, its culture, its control systems, its HRM system and the ways in which rewards such as pay are distributed to employees) are likely to play a role in the way individuals are motivated.

Regardless of whether people are intrinsically or extrinsically motivated, they join and are motivated to work in organisations to obtain certain **outcomes**. An outcome is anything a person gets from a job or organisation. Some outcomes, such as autonomy, responsibility, a feeling of accomplishment and the pleasure of doing interesting or enjoyable work, result in intrinsically motivated behaviour. Other outcomes, such as pay, job security, benefits and annual leave allowances, result in extrinsically motivated behaviour.

Organisations hire people to obtain important **inputs**. An input is anything a person contributes to the job or organisation – such as time, effort, education, experience, skills, knowledge and actual work behaviours. Inputs such as these are necessary for an organisation to achieve its goals. Managers strive to motivate members of an organisation to contribute inputs – through their behaviour, effort and persistence – that help the organisation achieve its goals. How do managers do this? They ensure that members of an organisation obtain the outcomes they desire when they make valuable contributions to the organisation. Managers use outcomes to motivate people to contribute their inputs to the organisation: giving people outcomes when they contribute inputs and perform well aligns the interests of employees with the goals of the organisation as a whole because when employees do what is good for the organisation, they personally benefit.

This alignment between employees and organisational goals as a whole can be described by the *motivation equation* depicted in Fig. 13.1. Managers seek to ensure that people are motivated to contribute important inputs to the organisation, that these inputs are put to good use or focused in the direction of high performance and that high performance results in workers obtaining the outcomes they desire.

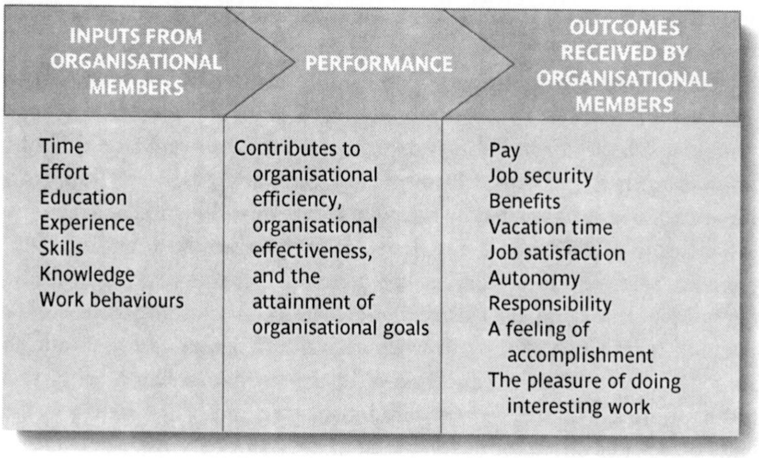

INPUTS FROM ORGANISATIONAL MEMBERS
PERFORMANCE
OUTCOMES RECEIVED BY ORGANISATIONAL MEMBERS
Time
Effort
Education
Experience
Skills
Knowledge
Work behaviours
Contributes to organisational efficiency, organisational effectiveness, and the attainment of organisational goals
Pay
Job security
Benefits
Vacation time
Job satisfaction
Autonomy
Responsibility
A feeling of accomplishment
The pleasure of doing interesting work

Figure 13.1 The Motivation Equation

Each of the theories of motivation discussed in this chapter focuses on one or more aspects of this equation. Each theory concentrates on a different set of issues that managers need to address to have a highly motivated workforce. Together, the theories provide a comprehensive set of guidelines for managers to follow in promoting high levels of employee motivation. Effective managers, such as Geoff Walker, tend to follow many of these guidelines, whereas ineffective managers often fail to follow them and seem to have trouble motivating organisational members.

Expectancy Theory

Expectancy theory, formulated by Victor H. Vroom in the 1960s, posits that motivation is high when workers believe that high levels of effort lead to high performance and high performance leads to the attainment of desired outcomes. Expectancy theory is one of the most popular theories of work motivation because it focuses on all three parts of the motivation equation: *inputs*, *performance* and *outcomes*. Expectancy theory identifies three major factors that determine a person's motivation: expectancy, instrumentality and valence (Fig. 13.2).[6]

Expectancy

Expectancy is a person's perception about the extent to which effort (an *input*) results in a certain level of performance. A person's level of expectancy determines whether he or she believes that a high level of effort results in a high level of performance. People are motivated to exert a

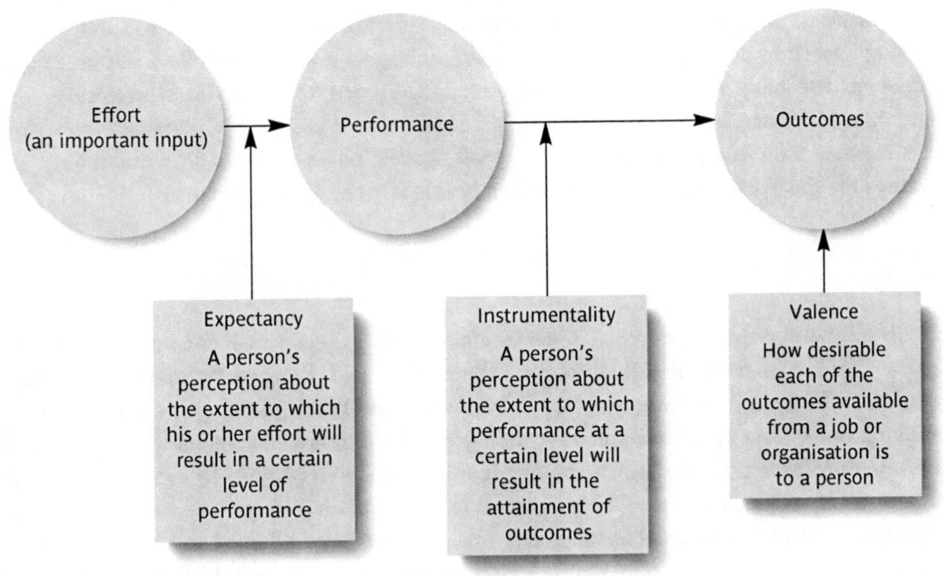

Figure 13.2 Expectancy, Instrumentality and Valence

lot of effort on their jobs only if they think that their effort will pay off in high performance – that is, if they have high expectancy. Think about how motivated you would be to study for a test if you thought that no matter how hard you tried, you would get a low mark. Think about how motivated a marketing manager would be who thought that no matter how hard he or she worked, there was no way to increase sales of an unpopular product. In these cases, expectancy is low, so overall motivation is also low.

Members of an organisation are motivated to put forth a high level of effort only if they think that doing so leads to high performance.[7] In other words, in order for people's motivation to be high, expectancy must be high. Thus, in attempting to influence motivation, managers need to make sure that their subordinates believe that if they try hard, they can actually succeed. One way managers can boost expectancies is through expressing confidence in their subordinates' capabilities.

One way for managers to boost subordinates' expectancy levels and motivation is by providing training so that people have all the expertise needed for high performance.

Instrumentality

Expectancy captures a person's perceptions about the relationship between effort and performance. *Instrumentality*, the second major concept in expectancy theory, is a person's perception about the extent to which performance at a certain level results in the attainment of outcomes (Fig. 13.2). According to expectancy theory, employees are motivated to perform at a high level only if they think that high performance will lead to (or is *instrumental* for attaining) outcomes such as pay, job security, interesting job assignments, bonuses or a feeling of accomplishment. In other words, instrumentalities must be high for motivation to be high – people must perceive that because of their high performance they will receive outcomes.[8]

Managers promote high levels of instrumentality when they clearly link performance to desired outcomes. In addition, managers must clearly communicate this linkage to subordinates. By making sure that outcomes available in an organisation are distributed to organisational members on the basis of their performance, managers promote high instrumentality and motivation. When outcomes are linked to performance in this way, high performers receive more outcomes than low performers. CEO Geoff Walker raises levels of instrumentality and motivation for the Trust employees by linking a bonus scheme to performance.

Valence

Although all members of an organisation must have high expectancies and instrumentalities, expectancy theory acknowledges that people differ in their preferences for outcomes. For many people, pay is the most important outcome of working. For others, a feeling of accomplishment or enjoying one's work is more important than pay. The term *valence* refers to how desirable each of the outcomes available from a job or organisation is to a person. To motivate organisational members, managers need to determine which outcomes have high valence for them – are highly desired – and make sure that those outcomes are provided when members perform at a high level. It appears that not only pay but also intrinsic rewards such as a stimulating work environment, observable change in patients and generous benefits are highly important outcomes for many employees at the Trust.

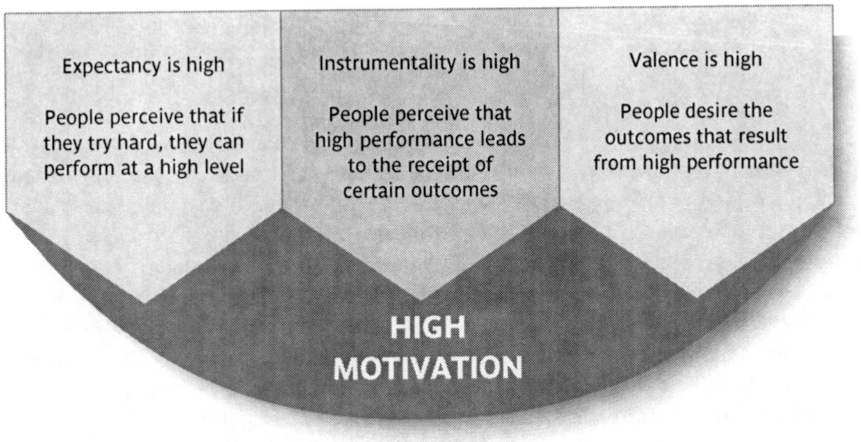

Figure 13.3 Expectancy Theory

Bringing it All Together

According to expectancy theory, high motivation results from high levels of expectancy, instrumentality and valence (Fig. 13.3). If any one of these factors is low, motivation is likely to be low. No matter how tightly desired outcomes are linked to performance, if a person thinks that it is practically impossible to perform at a high level, then motivation to perform at a high level is exceedingly low. Similarly, if a person does not think that outcomes are linked to high performance, or if a person does not desire the outcomes that are linked to high performance, then motivation to perform at a high level is low.

A key challenge for managers is encouraging high levels of motivation when trying to expand into new markets or trying out new products. Change needs enthusiastic people who drive the change and make it happen – even if similar attempts have been unsuccessful. As indicated in Case 13.1, maintaining high levels of expectancy, instrumentality and valence and learning from past failures are essential.

Case 13.1: Nike's efforts to appeal to diverse customers

Nike had some failures in the 1980s and 1990s trying to make inroads into new markets. Bowling shoes that left bowlers sliding down bowling alleys, a commercial for women's clothing that turned women off rather than on to Nike, and a golf shoe that was so uncomfortable employees nicknamed it 'air-blister' were among Nike's missteps in trying to appeal to diverse customers in new markets.[9] Fast-forward to 2004, and Nike was once again trying to win over diverse customers in new markets. But this time around, managers had learned from their mistakes and were taking a new approach.[10]

A key element of Nike's new approach was motivating employees to develop products in non-traditional markets (for Nike) in ways that would lead to high expectancy and instrumentality as well as to products that diverse customers would want to buy. Nike is a huge brand, embraced both by athletes playing team sports and consumers young and old looking for athletic clothing ▶

and gear.[11] However, skateboarder or other extreme and alternative sporting groups would loathe having the Nike *swoosh* adorning their shoes or clothes. Skateboarders, for example, have their own subculture and brands.[12]

How could employees be motivated to enter this challenging market and woo diverse customers who prided themselves on having their individual style and were unconventional? Nike tried the approach of working in a small 'company' that knew the skateboarding subculture. This group's task was to take time to develop products that they were confident would appeal to skateboarders. Nike Skate, headed by a Vice President, a ski-racing coach, was an autonomous unit that began with 11 skateboarding employees. They took their time to develop products that would appeal to skateboarders, such as URL, E-Cue, Dunk SB and Air Angus shoes.[13] They also took pains to win over owners of skate shops who were initially reluctant to carry Nike merchandise out of fear that they would ultimately lose some of their customers when discount stores started selling the same Nike merchandise at lower prices. Offering skate shops exclusive rights to stock Nike's skate products helped to disperse such fears.[14]

Nike Skate employees were immersed in the skateboarding culture, listening to music and paging through skateboarding magazines on the job. Managing the new product development process in this manner helped managers and employees alike have high expectancy that they would be able to develop products that appealed to skateboarders, products instrumental for the growth and revenues of the unit.

Need Theories

A need is a requirement or necessity for survival and well-being. The basic premise of *need theories* is that people are motivated to obtain outcomes at work that will satisfy their needs. Need theory complements expectancy theory by exploring in depth which outcomes motivate people to perform at a high level. Need theories suggest that to motivate a person to contribute valuable inputs to a job and perform at a high level, a manager must determine what needs the person is trying to satisfy at work and ensure that the person receives outcomes that help to satisfy those needs when the person performs at a high level and helps the organisation achieve its goals.

There are several need theories. The chapter discusses Maslow's hierarchy of needs, Alderfer's ERG theory, Herzberg's motivator-hygiene theory and McClelland's needs for achievement, affiliation and power. These theories describe needs that people try to satisfy at work; in doing so, they provide managers with insights about what outcomes motivate members of an organisation to perform at a high level and contribute inputs to help the organisation achieve its goals.

Maslow's Hierarchy of Needs

One of the most widely used theories about needs is by psychologist *Abraham Maslow*, who proposed that all people seek to satisfy five basic kinds of needs: *physiological needs*, *safety needs*, *belongingness needs*, *esteem needs* and *self-actualisation needs* (Table 13.1).[15] He suggested that these needs constitute a *hierarchy of needs* (Fig. 13.4), with the most basic or compelling needs – physiological and safety needs – at the bottom. Maslow argued that these lowest-level needs must be met before a person strives to satisfy needs higher up in the hierarchy, such as self-esteem needs. Once a need is satisfied, Maslow proposed, it ceases to operate as a source of motivation. The lowest level of unmet needs in the hierarchy is the prime motivator of behaviour; if and when this level is satisfied, needs at the next-highest level in the hierarchy motivate behaviour.

Table 13.1 Maslow's hierarchy of needs

	Needs	Description	Examples of how managers can help people satisfy these needs at work
Highest-level needs ↑	**Self-actualisation needs**	The needs to realise one's full potential as a human being	By giving people the opportunity to use their skills and abilities to the fullest extent possible
	Esteem needs	The needs to feel good about oneself and one's capabilities, to be respected by others, and to receive recognition and appreciation	By granting promotions and recognising accomplishments
	Belongingness needs	Needs for social interaction, friendship, affection and love	By promoting good interpersonal relations and organising social functions such as company picnics and holiday parties
↓	**Safety needs**	Needs for security, stability and a safe environment	By providing job security, adequate medical benefits and safe working conditions
Lowest-level needs (most basic or compelling)	**Physiological needs**	Basic needs for things such as food, water and shelter that must be met in order for a person to survive	By providing a level of pay that enables a person to buy food and clothing and have adequate housing

The lowest level of unsatisfied needs motivates behaviour; once this level of needs is satisfied, a person tries to satisfy the needs at the next level

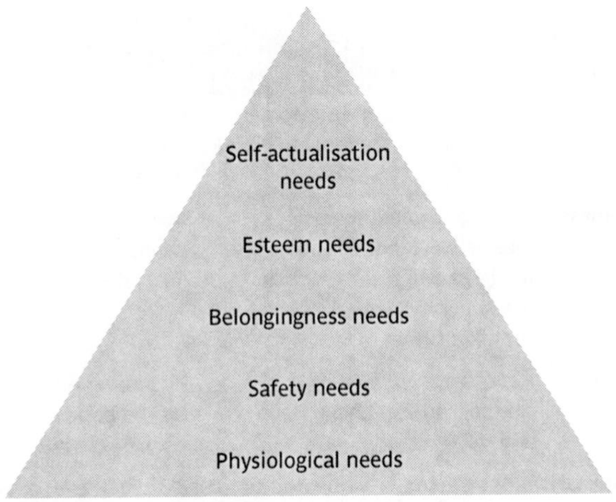

Figure 13.4 Maslow's Hierarchy of Needs

Although Maslow's theory identifies needs that are likely to be important sources of motivation for many people, research does not support his contention that there is a *need hierarchy* or his notion that only one level of needs is motivational at a time.[16] Nevertheless, a key conclusion can be drawn from Maslow's theory: individuals try to satisfy different needs at any one time – at work or in their private life. In the workplace, managers must determine which needs employees are trying to satisfy and then make sure that individuals receive outcomes that satisfy their needs when they perform at a high level and contribute to organisational effectiveness. By doing this, managers align the interests of individual members with the interests of the organisation as a whole. By doing what is good for the organisation (that is, performing at a high level), employees receive outcomes that satisfy their needs.

In our increasingly global economy, managers must realise that citizens of different countries may differ in the needs they seek to satisfy through work. Some research suggests, for example, that people in Greece and Japan are especially motivated by safety needs and that people in Sweden, Norway and Denmark are motivated by belongingness needs.[17] In less developed countries with low standards of living, physiological and safety needs are likely to be the prime motivators of behaviour. As countries become wealthier and have higher standards of living, needs related to personal growth and accomplishment (such as esteem and self-actualisation) become important as motivators of behaviour.

Alderfer's ERG Theory

Clayton Alderfer's ERG theory collapses the five categories of needs in Maslow's hierarchy into three universal categories – *existence*, *relatedness* and *growth* – also arranged in a hierarchy (Table 13.2). Alderfer agrees with Maslow that as lower-level needs become satisfied, a person seeks to satisfy higher-level needs. Unlike Maslow, however, Alderfer believes that a person can be motivated by needs at more than one level at the same time. A cashier in a supermarket, for

Table 13.2 Alderfer's ERG theory

	Needs	Description	Examples of how managers can help people satisfy these needs at work
Highest-level needs ↑	**Growth needs**	The needs for self-development and creative and productive work	By allowing people to continually improve their skills and abilities and engage in meaningful work
↓	**Relatedness needs**	The needs to have good interpersonal relations, to share thoughts and feelings and to have open two-way communication	By promoting good interpersonal relations and by providing accurate feedback
Lowest-level needs	**Existence needs**	Basic needs for food, water, clothing, shelter and a secure and safe environment	By promoting enough pay to provide for the basic necessities of life and safe working conditions

As lower-level needs are satisfied, a person is motivated to satisfy higher-level needs; when a person is unable to satisfy higher-level needs (or is frustrated), motivation to satisfy lower-level needs increases

example, may be motivated both by existence needs and by relatedness needs. The existence needs motivate the cashier to come to work regularly and not make mistakes so that his job will be secure and he will be able to pay his rent and buy food. The relatedness needs motivate the cashier to become friends with some of the other cashiers and have a good relationship with the store manager. Alderfer also suggests that when people experience *need frustration* or are unable to satisfy needs at a certain level, they will focus all the more on satisfying the needs at the next-lowest level in the hierarchy.[18]

As with Maslow's theory, research does not support some of the specific ideas outlined in ERG theory, such as the existence of the three-level need hierarchy that Alderfer proposed.[19] However, for managers, the important message from ERG theory is the same as that from Maslow's theory: determine what needs your subordinates are trying to satisfy at work, and make sure that they receive outcomes that satisfy these needs when they perform at a high level to help the organisation achieve its goals.

Herzberg's Motivator–Hygiene Theory

Adopting an approach different from Maslow's and Alderfer's, *Frederick Herzberg* focuses on two factors: (1) outcomes that can lead to high levels of motivation and job satisfaction and (2) outcomes that can prevent people from being dissatisfied. According to Herzberg's *motivator–hygiene theory*, people have two sets of needs or requirements: *motivator needs* and *hygiene needs*.[20]

Motivator needs are related to the *nature of the work itself* and how challenging it is. Outcomes, such as interesting work, autonomy, responsibility, being able to grow and develop on the job and a sense of accomplishment and achievement, help to satisfy motivator needs. To have a highly motivated and satisfied workforce, Herzberg suggests, managers should take steps to ensure that employees' motivator needs are being met.

Hygiene needs are related to the *physical* and *psychological context* in which the work is performed. Hygiene needs are satisfied by outcomes such as pleasant and comfortable working conditions, pay, job security, good relationships with co-workers and effective supervision. According to Herzberg, when hygiene needs are not met, workers are dissatisfied, and when hygiene needs are met, workers are not dissatisfied. Satisfying hygiene needs, however, does not result in high levels of motivation or even high levels of job satisfaction. For motivation and job satisfaction to be high, motivator needs must be met.

Many research studies have tested Herzberg's propositions and, by and large, the theory has failed to receive support.[21] Nevertheless, Herzberg's formulations have contributed to our understanding of motivation in at least two ways. First, Herzberg helped to focus researchers' and managers' attention on the important distinction between *intrinsic* motivation (related to *motivator needs*) and *extrinsic* motivation (related to *hygiene needs*), covered earlier in the chapter. Second, his theory prompted researchers and managers to study how jobs could be designed or redesigned so that they were *intrinsically motivating.*

McClelland's Needs for Achievement, Affiliation and Power

Psychologist *David McClelland* has extensively researched the needs for achievement, affiliation and power.[22] The *need for achievement* is the extent to which an individual has a strong desire to perform challenging tasks well and to meet personal standards for excellence. People with a high need for achievement often set clear goals for themselves and like to receive performance feedback. The *need for affiliation* is the extent to which an individual is concerned with establishing and maintaining good interpersonal relations, being liked and having the people around him or her get along with each other. The *need for power* is the extent to which an individual desires to control or influence others.[23]

While each of these needs is present in each of us to some degree, their importance in the workplace depends upon the position one occupies. Research suggests that high needs for achievement and for power are assets for first-line and middle managers and that a high need for power is especially important for upper-level managers.[24] One study found that US presidents with a relatively high need for power tended to be especially effective during their terms of office.[25] A high need for affiliation may not always be desirable in managers and other leaders, because it may lead them to try too hard to be liked by others (including subordinates), rather than doing all they can to ensure that performance is as high as it can and should be. Although most research on these needs has been done in the US, some studies suggest that the findings may be applicable to people in other countries as well, such as India and New Zealand.[26]

Other Needs

Clearly more needs motivate workers than the needs described by the above four theories. More and more workers, for example, are feeling the need for a work–life balance and time to take care of their loved ones while simultaneously being highly motivated at work. Interestingly enough, research suggests that being exposed to nature (even just being able to see some trees from your office window) has many salutary effects and a lack of such exposure can actually impair well-being and performance.[27] Having some time during the day when one can at least see nature may thus be another important need.

Managers of successful companies often strive to ensure that as many of their valued employees' needs as possible are satisfied in the workplace. This is illustrated by Case 13.2, concerning an Essex-based fresh produce supplier.

Case 13.2: High motivation rules at Hart Worldwide

Hart Worldwide is a small privately owned business that still has representatives of the founder among its senior management team. The company is based in Harlow, Essex, UK, and has some 50 staff. The current Managing Director uses a 'one-team' approach, which means that staff support each other not only in the workplace but also in their home lives.

Hart Worldwide addresses the various needs of its employees by using different approaches. Extrinsic award is offered with excellent pay packages and a profit-sharing scheme of 10 per cent of basic salary. Staff are also entitled to free private health care and gym membership. The latter two address some of the basic needs, which make staff feel safe and secure. This feeling is also apparent when looking at the staff turnover rate; Hart Worldwide has only 10 per cent staff turnover.

However, as outlined above, not all employees are purely motivated by external, financial rewards. Hart Worldwide also offers a wide range of other incentives to motivate their staff. One of the initiatives that encourage staff to aim for self-actualisation is the heavy investment of the company in off-the-job training. The Managing Director also runs a scheme that allows employees to take any course that they think might be relevant as part of their 'try new things' initiative. Hart Worldwide gives each employee £100 to spend on any type of training course the employee might be interested in. Such schemes allow employees to do things that they feel are important to themselves.

But Hart Worldwide goes even further. A *Times* survey on the best SME to work for shows that Hart Worldwide has managed to create an organisational culture that fosters needs for belonging. More than 90 per cent of the employees say they care for their team mates and enjoy working with them. The employees also spend time together at social gatherings that are as diverse as paintballing and opera.

It thus seems that Hart Worldwide has been able to balance the provision of incentives for staff that have diverse needs – catering for basic needs, extrinsically and intrinsically motivated staff.[28]

Equity Theory

Equity theory is a theory of motivation that concentrates on people's perceptions of the fairness of their work *outcomes* relative to, or in proportion to, their work *inputs*. Equity theory complements expectancy and need theories by focusing on how people perceive the relationship between the outcomes they receive from their jobs and organisations and the inputs they contribute. Equity theory was formulated in the 1960s by *J. Stacy Adams*, who stressed that what is important in determining motivation is the *relative* rather than the *absolute* levels of outcomes a person receives and inputs a person contributes. Specifically, motivation is influenced by the comparison of one's own outcome–input ratio with the outcome–input ratio of a referent.[29] The *referent* could be another person or a group of people who are perceived to be similar to oneself; the referent also could be oneself in a previous job or one's expectations about what outcome–input ratios should be. In a comparison of one's own outcome–input ratio to a referent's outcome–input ratio, one's *perceptions* of outcomes and inputs (not any objective indicator of them) are critical.

Equity

Equity exists when a person perceives his or her own outcome–input ratio to be equal to a referent's outcome–input ratio. Under conditions of equity (Table 13.3), if a referent receives more outcomes than you receive, the referent contributes proportionally more inputs to the organisation, so his or her outcome–input ratio still equals your outcome–input ratio. Surinda Partel and Claudia King, for example, both work in a shoe shop. Partel is paid more per hour than King but also contributes more inputs, including being responsible for some of the shop's bookkeeping, closing the shop and periodically depositing cash in the bank. When King compares her outcome–input ratio to Partel's (her referent's), she perceives the ratios to be equitable because Partel's higher level of pay (an outcome) is proportional to her higher level of inputs (bookkeeping, closing the shop and going to the bank).

Similarly, under conditions of equity, if you receive more outcomes than a referent, then your inputs are perceived to be proportionally higher. Continuing with our example, when Partel compares her outcome–input ratio to King's (her referent's) outcome–input ratio, she perceives them to be equitable because her higher level of pay is proportional to her higher level of inputs.

When equity exists, people are motivated to continue contributing their current levels of inputs to their organisations to receive their current levels of outcomes. If people wish to increase their outcomes under conditions of equity, they are motivated to increase their inputs.

Inequity

Inequity, lack of fairness, exists when a person's outcome–input ratio is not perceived to be equal to a referent's. Inequity creates pressure or tension in people and motivates them to restore equity by bringing the two ratios back into balance.

There are two types of inequity: underpayment inequity and overpayment inequity (Table 13.3). Under-payment inequity exists when a person's own outcome–input ratio is perceived to be *less* than that of a referent. In comparing yourself to a referent, you think that you are *not* receiving the outcomes you should be, given your inputs. Over-payment inequity exists when a person perceives that his or her own outcome–input ratio is *greater* than that of a referent. In comparing yourself to a referent, you think that you are receiving *more* outcomes than you should be, given your inputs.

Table 13.3 Equity theory

Condition	Person		Referent	Example
Equity	Outcomes / Inputs	=	Outcomes / Inputs	An engineer perceives that he contributes more inputs (time and effort) and receives proportionally more outcomes (a higher salary and choice job assignments) than his referent
Under-payment inequity	Outcomes / Inputs	< (less than)	Outcomes / Inputs	An engineer perceives that he contributes more inputs but receives the same outcomes as his referent
Over-payment inequity	Outcomes / Inputs	> (greater than)	Outcomes / Inputs	An engineer perceives that he contributes the same inputs but receives more outcomes than his referent

Ways to Restore Equity

According to equity theory, both under-payment inequity and over-payment inequity create a tension that motivates most people to restore equity by bringing the ratios back into balance.[30] When people experience *under-payment* inequity, they may be motivated to lower their inputs by reducing their working hours, putting forth less effort on the job, or being absent, or they may be motivated to increase their outcomes by asking for a rise or a promotion. Susan Richie, a financial analyst at a large corporation, noticed that she was working longer hours and getting more work accomplished than a co-worker who had the same position, yet they both received the exact same pay and other outcomes. To restore equity, Richie decided to stop coming in early and staying late. Alternatively, she could have tried to restore equity by trying to increase her outcomes – say, by asking her boss for a rise.

When people experience under-payment inequity and other means of equity restoration fail, they can change their perceptions of their own or the referent's inputs or outcomes. For example, they may realise that their referent is really working on more difficult projects than they are, or that they really take more time off from work than their referent does. Alternatively, if people who feel that they are underpaid have other employment options, they may leave the organisation. John Steinberg, a deputy head of a secondary school, experienced under-payment inequity when he realised that all of the other deputy head teachers of secondary schools in his local authority (LA) had received promotions to the position of head teacher, even though they had been in their jobs for a shorter time than he had been. Steinberg's performance had always been appraised as being high, so after his repeated requests for a promotion went unheeded, he found a job as a head teacher in a different LA.

When people experience *over-payment* inequity, they may try to restore equity by changing their perceptions of their own or their referent's inputs or outcomes. Equity can be restored when people realise that they are contributing more inputs than they originally thought. Equity also can be restored by perceiving the referent's inputs to be lower or the referent's outcomes to be higher than one originally thought. When equity is restored in this way, actual inputs and outcomes are unchanged and the person being over-paid takes no real action. What is changed is how people think about or view their or the referent's inputs and outcomes. Mary McMann experienced over-payment inequity when she realised that she was being paid £1.50 an hour more than a co-worker who had the same job as she did in a record store and who contributed the same amount of inputs. McMann restored equity by changing her perception of her inputs. She recognised that she worked harder than her co-worker and solved more problems that came up in the store.

Experiencing either over-payment or under-payment inequity, you may decide that your referent is not appropriate because, for example, it is too different from yourself. Choosing a more appropriate referent may bring the ratios back into balance. Angela Martinez, a middle manager in the engineering department of a chemical company, experienced over-payment inequity when she realised that she was being paid quite a bit more than her friend who was a middle manager in the marketing department of the same company. After thinking about the discrepancy for a while, Martinez decided that engineering and marketing were so different that she should not be comparing her job to her friend's job even though they were both middle managers. Martinez restored equity by changing her referent; she picked a fellow middle manager in the engineering department as a new one.

Motivation is highest when as many people as possible in an organisation perceive that they are being equitably treated – their outcomes and inputs are in balance. Top contributors and performers are motivated to continue contributing a high level of inputs because they are receiving the outcomes they deserve. Mediocre contributors and performers notice that if they want to increase their outcomes, they have to increase their inputs. Managers of effective organisations are aware of the importance of equity for motivation and performance and continually strive to ensure that employees believe that they are being equitably treated.

The dot-com boom, subsequent bust and a recession, along with increased global competition, have resulted in some workers putting in longer and longer working hours (i.e. increasing their inputs) without any kind of increase in their outcomes. For those whose referents are not experiencing a similar change, perceptions of inequity are likely. According to a 2001 study, people in the UK work the longest hours in Europe with an average of 44.7 hours per week, compared to 39.9 in Germany and 38.0 in Belgium.[31] Moreover, advances in IT, such as email and cell phones, have resulted in work intruding on home time, vacation time and even special occasions.[32]

Goal-setting Theory

Goal-setting theory focuses on motivating workers to contribute their inputs to their jobs and organisations; in this way, it is similar to expectancy theory and equity theory. But goal-setting theory takes this focus a step further by considering as well how managers can ensure that organisational members *focus their inputs* in the direction of high performance and the achievement of organisational goals.

Ed Locke and Gary Latham, the leading researchers on goal-setting theory, suggest that the goals that organisational members strive to attain are prime determinants of their motivation and subsequent performance. A *goal* is what a person is trying to accomplish through his or her efforts and behaviours.[33] Just as you may have a goal to get a good mark in your university courses, so do members of an organisation have goals that they strive to meet. Salespeople at Dyson strive to meet sales targets, while senior managers at HP pursue market share and profitability goals.

Goal-setting theory suggests that to stimulate high motivation and performance, goals must be *specific* and *difficult*.[34] Specific goals are often quantitative – a salesperson's goal to sell £500 worth of merchandise per day, a scientist's goal to finish a project in one year, a Managing Director's goal to reduce debt by 40 per cent and increase revenues by 20 per cent, a restaurant manager's goal to serve 150 customers per evening. In contrast to specific goals, vague goals such as 'doing your best' or 'selling as much as you can' do not have much motivational impact.

Difficult goals are hard but not impossible to attain. In contrast, easy goals are those that practically everyone can attain and moderate goals are goals that about half of the people can attain. Both easy and moderate goals have less motivational power than difficult goals.

Regardless of whether specific, difficult goals are set by managers, workers or teams of managers and workers, they lead to high levels of motivation and performance. When managers set goals for their subordinates, they must accept the goals or agree to work toward them; they should also be committed to them or really want to attain them. Some managers find having subordinates participate in the actual setting of goals boosts their acceptance of, and commitment to, them. A *participative approach* to goal-setting can be advocated as it is likely to result in higher levels of *ownership* from the subordinates. A study in the automotive industry found that participative goal-setting had a significant influence on performance.[35] Organisational members also need to receive *feedback* about how they are doing; this can often be provided by the performance appraisal and feedback component of an organisation's HR management system (Chapter 12). Goals and feedback are integral components of performance management systems in organisations, such as MBO (Chapter 11).

Specific, difficult goals affect motivation in two ways. First, they motivate people to contribute more inputs to their jobs. Specific, difficult goals cause people to put forth high levels of effort: just as you would study harder if you were trying to get 80 per cent or an A in a course instead of a getting below 40 per cent or a C, so will a salesperson work harder to reach a £500 sales goal instead of a £250 goal. Specific, difficult goals also cause people to be more persistent than easy, moderate or vague goals when they run into difficulties. Salespeople who are told to sell as much as possible might stop trying on a slow day, whereas having a specific, difficult goal to reach causes them to keep trying.

A second way in which specific, difficult goals affect motivation is by helping people focus their inputs in the right direction. These goals let people know what they should be focusing their attention on – be it increasing the quality of customer service or sales or lowering new product development times. The fact that the goals are specific and difficult also frequently causes people to develop *action plans* for reaching them.[36] Action plans can include the strategies to attain the goals and timetables or schedules for the completion of different activities crucial to goal attainment. Like the goals themselves, action plans also help ensure that efforts are focused in the right direction and that people do not get sidetracked along the way.

When senior managers take over troubled companies, it is often important for them to set specific, difficult goals for themselves and their employees in order to focus and direct their own efforts and the efforts of the company.

Although specific, difficult goals have been found to increase motivation and performance in a wide variety of jobs and organisations, research suggests that they may *detract from performance* under certain conditions. When people are performing complicated and very challenging tasks that require a considerable amount of learning, specific, difficult goals may actually impair performance.[37] All of a person's attention needs to be focused on learning complicated and difficult tasks. Striving to reach a specific, difficult goal may detract from performance because some of a person's attention is directed away from learning about the task and toward trying to figure out how to achieve the goal. Once a person has learned the task and it no longer seems complicated or difficult, then the assignment of specific, difficult goals is likely to have its usual effects. Specific, difficult goals may also be detrimental for work that is very creative and uncertain.

Learning Theories

The basic premise of *learning theories* as applied to organisations is that managers can increase employee motivation and performance by the ways they link the outcomes that employees receive to the performance of desired behaviours in an organisation and the attainment of goals. Learning theory focuses on the linkage between performance and outcomes in the motivation equation (Fig. 13.1).

Learning can be defined as a relatively permanent change in a person's knowledge or behaviour that results from practice or experience.[38] Learning takes place in organisations when people learn to perform certain behaviours to receive certain outcomes. A person learns to perform at a higher level than in the past or to come to work earlier because he or she is motivated to obtain the outcomes that result from these behaviours, such as a pay rise or praise from a supervisor. The emphasis on training by Hart Worldwide (Case 13.2) ensures that all employees continue their learning throughout their careers.

Of the different learning theories, operant conditioning theory and social learning theory provide the most guidance to managers in their efforts to have a highly motivated workforce.

Operant Conditioning Theory

According to *operant conditioning theory*, developed by psychologist B. F. Skinner, people learn to perform behaviours that lead to desired consequences and learn not to perform behaviours that lead to undesired consequences.[39] Skinner's theory means that people will be motivated to perform at a high level and attain their work goals to the extent that high performance and goal attainment allow them to obtain outcomes they desire. Similarly, people avoid performing behaviours that lead to outcomes they do not desire. By linking the performance of *specific behaviours* to the attainment of *specific outcomes*, managers can motivate organisational members to perform in ways that help an organisation achieve its goals.

Operant conditioning theory provides four tools that managers can use to motivate high performance and prevent workers from engaging in absenteeism and other behaviours that detract from organisational effectiveness. These tools are **positive reinforcement**, **negative reinforcement**, **extinction** and **punishment**.[40]

Positive reinforcement

Positive reinforcement gives people outcomes they desire when they perform organisationally functional behaviours. These desired outcomes, called *positive reinforcers*, include any outcomes that a person desires, such as pay, praise or a promotion. Organisationally functional behaviours are behaviours that contribute to organisational effectiveness; they can include producing high-quality goods and services, providing high-quality customer service and meeting deadlines. By linking positive reinforcers to the performance of functional behaviours, managers motivate people to perform the desired behaviours.

Negative reinforcement

Negative reinforcement also can encourage members of an organisation to perform desired or organisationally functional behaviours. Managers using negative reinforcement actually eliminate or remove undesired outcomes once the functional behaviour is performed. These undesired outcomes, called *negative reinforcers*, can range from a manager's constant nagging or criticism to unpleasant assignments to the ever-present threat of losing one's job. When negative reinforcement is used, people are motivated to perform behaviours because they want to stop receiving or avoid undesired outcomes. Managers who try to encourage salespeople to sell more by threatening them with being fired are using negative reinforcement. In this case, the negative reinforcer is the threat of job loss, which is removed once the functional behaviour is performed.

Whenever possible, managers should try to use positive reinforcement. Negative reinforcement can create a very unpleasant work environment and even a *negative culture* in an organisation. No one likes to be nagged, threatened or exposed to other kinds of negative outcomes. The use of negative reinforcement sometimes causes subordinates to resent managers and try to get back at them.

Identifying the right behaviours for reinforcement

Even managers who use positive reinforcement (and refrain from using negative reinforcement) can get into trouble if they are not careful to identify the *right behaviours to reinforce* – behaviours that are truly functional for the organisation. Doing this is not always as straightforward as it may seem. First, it is crucial for managers to choose behaviours over which subordinates have control; in other words, subordinates must have the freedom and opportunity to perform the behaviours that are being reinforced. Second, it is crucial that these behaviours contribute to organisational effectiveness.

Extinction

Sometimes members of an organisation are motivated to perform behaviours that actually detract from organisational effectiveness. According to operant conditioning theory, all behaviour is controlled or determined by its consequences; one way for managers to curtail the performance of dysfunctional behaviours is to eliminate whatever is reinforcing the behaviours. This process is called *extinction*.

Suppose a manager has a subordinate who frequently stops by his office to chat – sometimes about work-related matters but more often about various topics ranging from politics to last night's football game. The manager and the subordinate share certain interests and views, so these conversations can get quite involved, and both seem to enjoy them. The manager, however, realises that these frequent and sometimes lengthy conversations are actually causing him to stay at work later in the evenings to make up for the time lost during the day. The manager also recognises that he is actually reinforcing his subordinate's behaviour by showing interest in the topics the subordinate brings up and responding at length to them. To extinguish this behaviour, the manager stops acting interested in these non-work-related conversations and keeps his responses polite and friendly but brief. No longer being reinforced with a pleasurable conversation, the subordinate eventually ceases to be motivated to interrupt the manager during working hours to discuss non-work-related issues.

Punishment

Sometimes managers cannot rely on extinction to eliminate dysfunctional behaviours because they do not have control over whatever is reinforcing the behaviour or because they cannot afford the time needed for extinction to work. When employees are performing dangerous behaviours or behaviours that are illegal or unethical, the behaviour needs to be eliminated immediately. Sexual harassment, for example, is an organisationally dysfunctional behaviour that cannot be tolerated. In such cases managers often rely on *punishment*, administering an undesired or negative consequence to subordinates when they perform the dysfunctional behaviour. Punishments used by organisations range from verbal reprimands to pay cuts, temporary suspensions, demotions and firings. Punishment, however, can have some unintended side-effects – resentment, loss of self-respect, a desire for retaliation – and should be used only when absolutely necessary.

To avoid the unintended side-effects of punishment, managers should keep in mind three guidelines:

- Downplay the *emotional element* involved in punishment. Make it clear that you are punishing a person's performance of a dysfunctional behaviour, not the person himself or herself.
- Try to punish dysfunctional behaviours as soon after they occur as possible, and make sure the negative consequence is a source of punishment for the individuals involved. Be certain that organisational members know exactly *why* they are being punished.
- Try to avoid punishing someone in front of others, as this can hurt a person's self-respect and lower esteem in the eyes of co-workers as well as make co-workers feel uncomfortable.[41] Even so, making organisational members aware that an individual who has committed a serious infraction has been punished can sometimes be effective in preventing future infractions and teaching all members of the organisation that certain behaviours are *unacceptable*. For example, when organisational members are informed that a manager who has sexually harassed subordinates has been punished, they learn or are reminded of the fact that sexual harassment is not tolerated and illegal.

Both managers and students often confuse negative reinforcement and punishment. To avoid such confusion, keep in mind the two major differences between them. First, negative reinforcement is used to *promote* the performance of functional behaviours in organisations; punishment is used to *stop* the performance of dysfunctional behaviours. Second, negative reinforcement entails the *removal* of a negative consequence when functional behaviours are performed; punishment entails the *administration* of negative consequences when dysfunctional behaviours are performed.

Organisational behaviour modification

When managers systematically apply operant conditioning techniques to promote the performance of organisationally functional behaviours and discourage the performance of dysfunctional behaviours, they are engaging in organisational behaviour modification (OB MOD).[42] OB MOD has been successfully used to improve productivity, efficiency, attendance, punctuality, safe work practices, customer service and other important behaviours in a wide variety of organisations such as banks, department stores, factories, hospitals and construction sites.[43] The five basic steps in OB MOD are described in Fig. 13.5.

OB MOD works best for behaviours that are specific, objective and countable – such as attendance and punctuality, making sales or putting telephones together – all of which lend themselves to careful scrutiny and control. OB MOD may be questioned because of its lack of relevance to certain work behaviours (for example, the many work behaviours that are not specific, objective and countable). Some people also have questioned it on ethical grounds. Critics of OB MOD suggest that it is overly controlling and robs workers of their dignity, individuality, freedom of choice and even creativity. Supporters counter that OB MOD is a highly effective means of promoting organisational efficiency. There is some merit to both sides of this argument; what is clear, however, is that when used appropriately OB MOD provides managers with a technique to motivate the performance of at least some organisationally functional behaviours.[44]

Social Learning Theory

Social learning theory proposes that motivation results not only from the direct experience of rewards and punishments but also from a person's thoughts and beliefs. Social learning theory extends operant conditioning's contribution to managers' understanding of motivation by explaining (1) how people can be motivated by observing other people perform a behaviour and be reinforced for doing so (vicarious learning), (2) how people can be motivated to control their behaviour themselves (self-reinforcement) and (3) how people's beliefs about their ability to successfully perform a behaviour affect motivation (self-efficacy).[45] We now look briefly at each of these motivators.

Vicarious learning

Vicarious learning, often called *observational learning*, occurs when a person (the *learner*) becomes motivated to perform behaviour by watching another person (the *model*) perform the behaviour and be positively reinforced for doing so. Vicarious learning is a powerful source of motivation on many jobs in which people learn to perform functional behaviours by watching others. Salespeople learn how to be helpful to customers, medical school students learn how to treat patients, junior lawyers learn how to practise law and non-managers learn how to be managers, in part, by observing experienced members of an organisation perform these behaviours properly and be reinforced for them. In general, people are more likely to be motivated

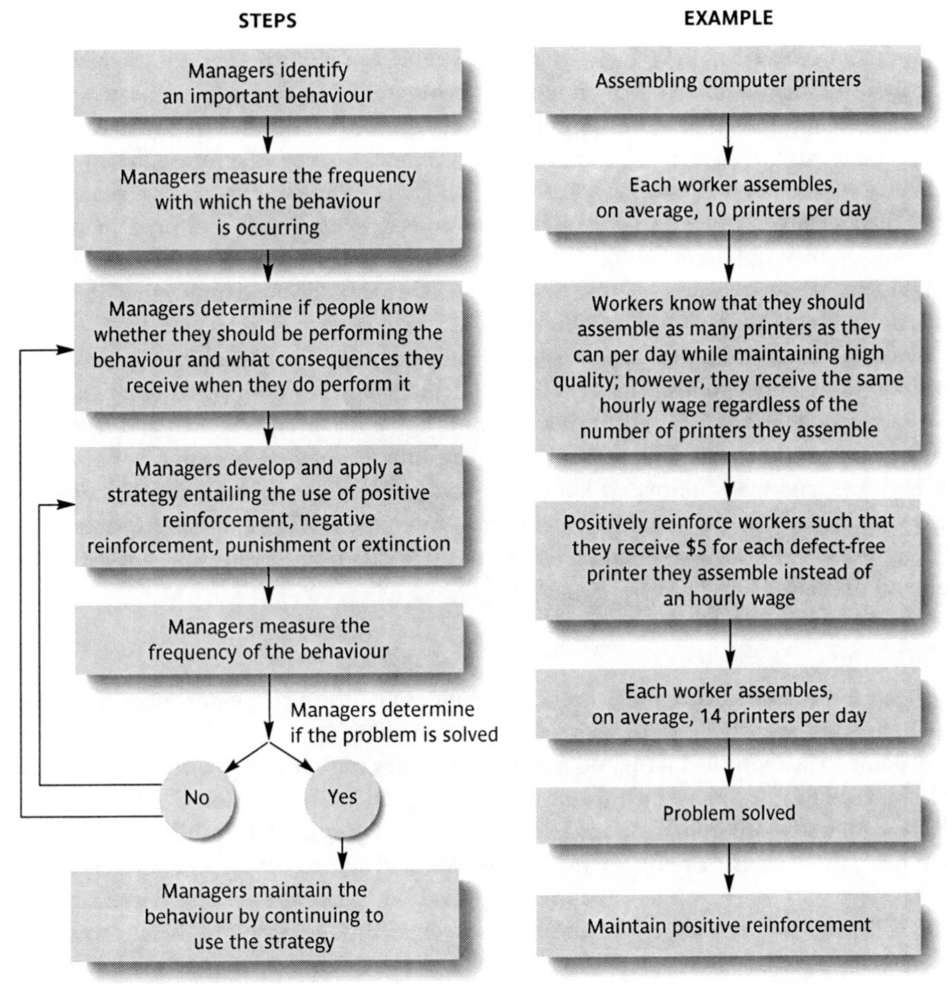
STEPS
EXAMPLE
Managers identify an important behaviour
Managers measure the frequency with which the behaviour is occurring
Managers determine if people know whether they should be performing the behaviour and what consequences they receive when they do perform it
Managers develop and apply a strategy entailing the use of positive reinforcement, negative reinforcement, punishment or extinction
Managers measure the frequency of the behaviour
Managers determine if the problem is solved
No
Yes
Managers maintain the behaviour by continuing to use the strategy
Assembling computer printers
Each worker assembles, on average, 10 printers per day
Workers know that they should assemble as many printers as they can per day while maintaining high quality; however, they receive the same hourly wage regardless of the number of printers they assemble
Positively reinforce workers such that they receive $5 for each defect-free printer they assemble instead of an hourly wage
Each worker assembles, on average, 14 printers per day
Problem solved
Maintain positive reinforcement

Figure 13.5 Five Steps in OB MOD

Source: Adapted from F. Luthans and R. Kreitner, *Organisational Behaviour Modification and Beyond* (Scott, Foresman, 1985). With permission of the authors.

to imitate the behaviour of models who are highly competent, are (to some extent) experts in the behaviour, have high status, receive attractive reinforcers and are friendly or approachable.[46]

To promote vicarious learning, managers should strive to have the learner meet five key conditions:

- The learner observes the model performing the behaviour.
- The learner accurately perceives the model's behaviour.
- The learner remembers the behaviour.
- The learner has the skills and abilities needed to perform the behaviour.
- The learner sees or knows that the model is positively reinforced for the behaviour.[47]

Self-reinforcement

Although managers are often the providers of reinforcement in organisations, people sometimes motivate themselves through self-reinforcement. People can control their own behaviour by setting goals for themselves and then reinforcing themselves when they achieve the goals.[48] Self-reinforcers are any desired or attractive outcomes or rewards that people can give to themselves for good performance, such as a feeling of accomplishment, going to a movie, having dinner out, buying a new CD, or taking time out for a golf game. When members of an organisation control their own behaviour through self-reinforcement, managers do not need to spend as much time as they ordinarily would trying to motivate and control behaviour through the administration of consequences because subordinates are controlling and motivating themselves. In fact, this self-control is often referred to as the *self-management of behaviour*.

Chinese students at the prestigious Jiaotong University in Shanghai exemplify how strong motivation through self-control can be. These students, many of whom are aspiring engineers, live in spartan conditions (a barely lit small room is home for seven students) and take exceptionally heavy course loads. They spend their spare time reading up on subjects not covered in their classes, and many ultimately hope to obtain engineering jobs overseas with high-tech companies. 22-year-old Yan Kangrong spends his spare time reading computer textbooks and designing software for local companies: 'We learn the basics from teachers . . . But we need to expand on this knowledge by ourselves.'[49]

Self-efficacy

Self-efficacy is a person's belief about his or her ability to perform behaviour successfully. Even with all the most attractive consequences or reinforcers hinging on high performance, people are not going to be motivated if they do not think that they can actually perform at a high level. Similarly, when people control their own behaviour, they are likely to set for themselves difficult goals that will lead to outstanding accomplishments only if they think that they have the capability to reach those goals. Self-efficacy thus influences motivation both when managers provide reinforcement and when workers themselves provide it.[50] The greater the self-efficacy, the greater is the motivation and performance. In companies such as Hart Worldwide (Case 13.2), where managers believe and openly declare that employees are responsible and trustworthy enough to handle their workload, self-efficacy is boosted. Such verbal persuasion, as well as a person's own past performance and accomplishments and the accomplishments of other people, plays a role in determining a person's self-efficacy.

Pay and Motivation

Chapter 12 discussed how managers establish a pay level and structure for an organisation as a whole. Here the focus is on how, once a pay level and structure are in place, managers can use pay to motivate employees to perform at a high level and attain their work goals. Pay is used to motivate at all levels of an organisation, from entry-level personnel to senior managers. Pay can be used to motivate people to perform behaviours that help an organisation achieve its goals, and it can be used to motivate people to join and remain with an organisation.

Each of the theories described in this chapter alludes to the importance of pay and suggests that pay should be based on performance:

- *Expectancy theory* Instrumentality, the association between performance and outcomes such as pay, must be high for motivation to be high. In addition, pay is an outcome that has high valence for many people
- *Need theories* People should be able to satisfy their needs by performing at a high level; pay can be used to satisfy several different kinds of needs
- *Equity theory* Outcomes such as pay should be distributed in proportion to inputs (including performance levels)
- *Goal-setting theory* Outcomes such as pay should be linked to the attainment of goals
- *Learning theories* The distribution of outcomes such as pay should be contingent on the performance of organisationally functional behaviours.

As these theories suggest, to promote high motivation managers should base the distribution of pay to organisational members on performance levels so that high performers receive more pay than low performers (other things being equal).[51] There are companies in which the pay of all employees, ranging from post room staff to senior managers, is based, at least in part, on performance.[52] A compensation plan basing pay on performance is often called a merit pay plan. Once managers have decided to use a merit pay plan, they face two important choices: whether to base pay on individual, group or organisational performance or to use salary increases or bonuses. Before commencing the discussion on pay as a motivator, caution is necessary: financial reward is an *extrinsic motivator* and thus not all people will be motivated this way. Financial rewards should be seen as a contributing factor to a motivated workforce, not the only way in which to motivate employees.

Basing Merit Pay on Individual, Group or Organisational Performance

Managers can base merit pay on individual, group or organisational performance. When individual performance (such as the value of merchandise a salesperson sells, the number of loudspeakers a factory worker assembles and a lawyer's billable hours) can be accurately determined, individual motivation is likely to be highest when pay is based on *individual performance*.[53] When members of an organisation work closely together and individual performance cannot be accurately determined (as in a team of computer programmers developing a single software package), pay cannot be based on individual performance, and a group- or organisation-based plan must be used. When the attainment of organisational goals hinges on members working closely together and co-operating with each other (as in a small construction company that builds custom homes), group- or organisation-based plans may be more appropriate than individual-based plans.[54]

It is possible to combine elements of an individual-based plan with a group- or organisation-based plan to motivate each individual to perform highly and, at the same time, motivate all individuals to work well together, co-operate with one another and help one another as needed. Lincoln Electric, a very successful company and a leading manufacturer of welding machines, uses a combination of individual- and organisation-based plans.[55] Pay is based on individual performance; in addition, each year the size of a bonus fund depends on organisational performance. Money from the bonus fund is distributed to people on the basis of their contributions to the organisation, attendance, levels of co-operation and other indications of performance. Lincoln Electric employees are motivated to co-operate and help one another because when the firm as a whole performs well, everybody benefits by having a larger bonus fund. Employees also are motivated to contribute their inputs to the organisation because their contributions determine their share of the bonus fund.

Salary Increase or Bonus?

Managers can distribute merit pay to people in the form of a salary increase or a bonus on top of regular salaries. Although the monetary amount of a salary increase or bonus may be identical, bonuses tend to have more motivational impact, for at least three reasons. First, salary levels are typically based on performance levels, cost-of-living increases and so forth, from the day people start working in an organisation, which means that the absolute level of the salary is based largely on factors unrelated to *current* performance: a 5 per cent merit increase in salary, for example, may seem relatively small in comparison to one's total salary. Second, a current salary increase may be affected by other factors in addition to performance, such as cost-of-living increases or across-the-board market adjustments. Third, because organisations rarely reduce salaries, salary levels tend to vary less than performance levels do. Bonuses also give managers more flexibility in distributing outcomes. If an organisation is doing well, bonuses can be relatively high to reward employees for their contributions. However, unlike salary increases, bonus levels can be reduced when an organisation's performance lags. Bonus plans have more motivational impact than salary increases because the amount of the bonus can be directly and exclusively based on performance.[56]

Consistent with the lessons from motivation theories, bonuses can be linked directly to performance and vary from year to year and employee to employee. Another organisation that successfully uses bonuses is Hart Worldwide (Case 13.2) and with low staff turnover and extremely satisfied employees, it is possible to argue that their success is based on receiving bonuses.

In addition to receiving pay rises and bonuses, high-level managers and executives are sometimes granted employee stock options. *Employee stock options* are financial instruments that entitle the bearer to buy shares of an organisation's stock at a certain price during a certain period of time or under certain conditions.[57] Stock options are sometimes used to attract high-level managers. The exercise price is the stock price at which the bearer can buy the stock, and the vesting conditions specify when the bearer can actually buy the stock at the exercise price. The option's exercise price is generally set equal to the market price of the stock on the date it is granted, and the vesting conditions may specify that the manager has to have worked at the organisation for 12 months or perhaps met some performance target (increase in profits) before being able to exercise the option. In high-technology firms and startups, options are sometimes used in a similar fashion for employees at various levels in the organisation.

From a motivation standpoint, stock options are used not so much to reward past individual performance but rather to motivate employees to work in the future for the good of the company as a whole. Stock options issued at current stock prices have value in the future only if an organisation does well and its stock price appreciates; giving employees stock options should thus encourage them to help the organisation improve its performance over time. At high-technology startups and dot-coms, stock options have often motivated potential employees to leave promising jobs in larger companies and work for the startups. In the late 1990s and early 2000s, many dot-commers were devastated to learn not only that their stock options were worthless, because their companies went out of business or were doing poorly, but also that they were unemployed.

Reaction Time

1. Discuss why two people with similar abilities may have very different expectancies for performing at a high level.
2. Describe why some people have low instrumentalities even when their managers distribute outcomes based on performance.
3. Analyse how professors can try to promote equity to motivate students.
4. Describe three techniques or procedures that managers can use to determine whether or not a goal is difficult.
5. Discuss why managers should always try to use positive reinforcement instead of negative reinforcement.

Summary and Review

The nature of motivation Motivation encompasses the psychological forces within a person that determine the direction of the person's behaviour in an organisation, the person's level of effort and the person's level of persistence in the face of obstacles. Managers strive to motivate people to contribute their inputs to an organisation, to focus these inputs in the direction of high performance and to ensure that people receive the outcomes they desire when they perform at a high level.

Expectancy theory According to expectancy theory, managers can promote high levels of motivation in their organisations by taking steps to ensure that expectancy is high (people think that if they try, they can perform at a high level), instrumentality is high (people think that if they perform at a high level, they will receive certain outcomes) and valence is high (people desire these outcomes).

Need theories Need theories suggest that to motivate their workforces, managers should determine what needs people are trying to satisfy in organisations and then ensure that people receive outcomes that satisfy these needs when they perform at a high level and contribute to organisational effectiveness.

Equity theory According to equity theory, managers can promote high levels of motivation by ensuring that people perceive that there is equity in the organisation, or that outcomes are distributed in proportion to inputs. Equity exists when a person perceives that his or her own outcome–input ratio equals the outcome–input ratio of a referent. Inequity motivates people to try to restore equity.

Goal-setting theory Goal-setting theory suggests that managers can promote high motivation and performance by ensuring that people strive to achieve specific, difficult goals. It is important for people to accept the goals, be committed to them and receive feedback about how they are doing.

Learning theories Operant conditioning theory suggests that managers can motivate people to perform highly by using positive reinforcement or negative reinforcement (positive reinforcement being the preferred strategy). Managers can motivate people to avoid performing dysfunctional behaviours by using extinction or punishment. Social learning theory suggests that people can also be motivated by observing how others perform behaviours and receive rewards, by engaging in self-reinforcement and by having high levels of self-efficacy.

Pay and motivation Each of the motivation theories discussed in this chapter alludes to the importance of pay and suggests that pay should be based on performance. Merit pay plans can be individual-, group- or organisation-based and can entail the use of salary increases or bonuses.

Topic for Action

- Interview three people who have the same kind of job (such as salesperson, waiter/waitress or teacher), and determine what kinds of needs they are trying to satisfy at work.
- Interview a manager in an organisation in your community to determine the extent to which he or she takes advantage of vicarious learning to promote high motivation among subordinates.

Applied Independent Learning

Building Management Skills

Diagnosing Motivation

Think about the ideal job that you would like to obtain upon graduation. Describe this job, the kind of manager you would like to report to, and the kind of organisation you would be working in. Then answer the following questions:

1. What would be your levels of expectancy and instrumentality on this job? Which outcomes would have high valence for you on this job? What steps would your manager take to influence your levels of expectancy, instrumentality and valence?
2. Whom would you choose as a referent on this job? What steps would your manager take to make you feel that you were being equitably treated? What would you do if, after a year on the job, you experienced under-payment inequity?
3. What goals would you strive to achieve on this job? Why? What role would your manager play in determining your goals?
4. What needs would you strive to satisfy on this job? Why? What role would your manager play in helping you satisfy these needs?
5. What behaviours would your manager positively reinforce on this job? Why? What positive reinforcers would your manager use?
6. Would there be any vicarious learning on this job? Why or why not?

7. To what extent would you be motivated by self-control on this job? Why?
8. What would be your level of self-efficacy on this job? Why would your self-efficacy be at this level? Should your manager take steps to boost your self-efficacy? If not, why not? If so, what would these steps be?

Managing Ethically

Sometimes pay is so contingent upon performance that it creates stress for employees. Imagine a salesperson who knows that if sales targets are not met, she or he will not be able to make a house mortgage payment or pay the rent.

Questions

1. Either individually or in a group, think about the ethical implications of closely linking pay to performance.
2. Under what conditions might contingent pay be most stressful, and what steps can managers take to try to help their subordinates perform effectively and not experience excessive amounts of stress?

Small Group Breakout Exercise

Increasing Motivation

Form groups of three or four people, and appoint one member as the spokesperson who will communicate your findings to the whole class when called on by the instructor. Then discuss the following scenario.

You and your partners own a chain of 15 dry-cleaning stores in a medium-size town. All of you are concerned about a problem in customer service that has surfaced recently. When any one of you spends the day, or even part of the day, in a particular store, clerks seem to provide excellent customer service, spotters are making sure all stains are removed from garments and pressers are doing a good job of pressing difficult items such as silk blouses. Yet during those same visits customers complain to you about such things as stains not being removed and items being poorly pressed in some of their previous orders; indeed, several customers have brought garments in to be redone. Customers also sometimes comment on having waited too long for service on previous visits. You and your partners are meeting today to address this problem.

1. Discuss the extent to which you believe that you have a motivation problem in your stores.
2. Given what you have learned in this chapter, design a plan to increase the motivation of clerks to provide prompt service to customers even when they are not being watched by a partner.
3. Design a plan to increase the motivation of spotters to remove as many stains as possible even when they are not being watched by a partner.
4. Design a plan to increase the motivation of pressers to do a top-notch job on all clothes they press, no matter how difficult.

Exploring the World Wide Web

If you had the chance to choose which well-known corporation you would like to work for, which would it be? Now go to the website of that company and find out as much as you can about how it motivates employees. Also, using Google and other search engines, try to find articles in the news about this company. Based upon what you have learned, would this company still be your top choice? Why or why not?

Application in Today's Business World

Coverup at Boeing?

More than a decade ago, Boeing Co. quietly began investigating a sensitive internal issue: whether female employees were paid less than men. Several sophisticated salary studies concluded that the answer was 'yes'. One 1998 report said: 'Men are more likely to be hired into the high paying positions.' A statistical analysis completed the same year noted that the pay gap for entry-level managers was $3,741.04.

Although she knew nothing of these sensitive analyses, Carol Jensen would not have found them surprising. The 64-year-old technical drafter had long complained that women were under-paid. 'We were treated with little respect,' recalls the mother of nine, who started working at Boeing in 1967 and was laid off in 2000. 'The men believed that the only work for women at Boeing was behind a desk as a secretary.'

In 2000, 38 women filed a class action in Seattle for pay discrimination against the company. The potential cost to Boeing exceeded $100 million. All of those salary studies Boeing had done through the years, of course, would have been dynamite evidence for the aggrieved women. But when their lawyers made routine pre-trial requests for any statistical data the company might have compiled on gender pay differentials, the aerospace giant said it had no obligation to turn the studies over. Why? Because they had allegedly been prepared at the direction of Boeing's lawyers and were therefore protected by attorney–client privilege, a legal doctrine that shields confidential communications between executives and their attorneys from public disclosure. It's intended to allow managers to be candid with their legal team.

Behind the scenes, meanwhile, Boeing employees removed payroll-planning documents about pay discrimination from the company's files. In an email dated 27 August 2001, compensation manager Paul A. Wells advised colleagues to get rid of drafts of these types of documents on the Salary Administration server because 'that which is retained can potentially be subpoenaed and . . . those with access [to] the files can be called on to testify about the content'. Wells declined to comment.

Systematic Campaign

It's a classic scenario – the type of confrontation that has served as dramatic fodder for countless movies: a big, powerful company bullies small, weak individuals. *Erin Brockovich, A Civil Action* and many other legal thrillers tell this tale from the point of view of the victims. But *BusinessWeek* obtained a rare view of the other side of the story: what takes place at the company. The federal judge overseeing the class action, Marsha J. Pechman, agreed to unseal more than 12,000 pages of internal Boeing documents on 11 February after *BusinessWeek* attorneys argued that they should be disclosed. This hidden corporate history raises questions as to whether the company and its lawyers had engaged in a systematic campaign to hide evidence and take advantage of attorney–client privilege.

Having witnessed Boeing's intransigence for more than four years, highlighted by a ferocious battle to avoid disclosure of its salary studies, Judge Pechman dropped an even bigger bombshell on the company on 11 May. Citing 'an evolving awareness, as more facts come to light, of how Boeing had inappropriately tried to shield [the documents] from discovery', she ordered Boeing to hand over the series of salary analyses it had fought hardest to withhold – those that left little room for doubting the company's knowledge of its pay disparities. That was only one of several rebukes Boeing received from the judge, as well as from a special master assigned to referee discovery disputes, during the course of the lawsuit. Though many questions remain about the company's conduct during the case, and a complete picture of the role played by Boeing's various managers and lawyers is still unavailable, Judge Pechman's rulings suggest that the company went beyond standard aggressive legal defence tactics.

Now that Boeing was faced with the prospect of telling jurors why its own internal documents seemingly contradicted its legal theory, the company suddenly became accommodating. Two days before the case was scheduled to go to trial, on 17 May, Boeing made a settlement offer. While the two teams hammer out the details of the deal, which neither side will discuss, the case has been postponed. . . .

Spokesman Kenneth B. Mercer says Boeing is committed to honest business practices and equal opportunity. Because settlement talks in the Beck lawsuit aren't complete, he refuses to discuss the underlying facts of the case, the conduct of the company's attorneys, or any of the individual documents obtained by *BusinessWeek* – beyond saying that Boeing thinks that its hiring and promotion practices are fair. Mercer adds that the statistical studies Judge Pechman forced the company to turn over were intended to help eliminate pay disparities and that they 'can't capture all of the critical factors that go into pay or promotion decisions'.

Boeing's Mercer also noted that federal judges tossed out three similar gender-discrimination class actions filed against Boeing in Southern California, Kansas and Missouri. A fourth suit, in Oklahoma, has been granted class-action status. The company says its high batting average against female pay-discrimination suits is proof that its compensation practices were legal. But the plaintiffs' attorneys claim Boeing won mainly because it successfully suppressed the evidence that ultimately entered the Beck case.

Record Output of Jets

Troubling headlines are a comparatively new problem for Boeing. A company dominated by engineers, it traditionally focused on innovation and design. Executives believed that profits would naturally follow. During the Pentagon over-billing scandals of the late 1980s, Boeing was the least tarnished of the major contractors. But the culture started to change after its merger with the more aggressive McDonnell Douglas in 1997. That deal, along with tougher competition for government dollars in the Clinton years, shifted Boeing's emphasis to the bottom line.

Women first entered Boeing's workforce in large numbers during the Second World War – and they enabled the company to roll out record fleets of B-17 bombers. But when the war ended, Boeing's male-dominated culture returned in full force. When Carol Jensen joined in 1967, she was one of the first females to draw technical blueprints. 'Men were getting the plum designing assignments,' recalls Jensen. 'It was out-and-out discrimination, and a woman couldn't do anything about it.'

Despite the anger of Jensen and others, female pay did not become a serious concern at Boeing until 1996, when the US Labor Department's Office of Federal Contract Compliance Programme (OFCCP) ran a routine investigation of Boeing's mammoth Philadelphia plant. Under government contracting rules, the OFCCP has the right to audit whether federal contractors are complying with anti-discrimination laws. The agency does this by using a statistical method known as 'median analysis'. In broad terms, it compares the relationship between the median pay of male and female employees and their median job experience.

After informing Boeing that the OFCCP had discovered 'a prima facie case of systemic discrimination concerning compensation of females and minorities' in Philadelphia, the agency audited nine other plants nationwide. The stakes for Boeing, the country's Number Two federal contractor, were huge. With defence and space representing nearly half of its revenues and growing, the loss of federal contracts would be devastating.

Recognizing the seriousness of the inquiry, Boeing wasted no time launching a counter-attack. It hired Jon A. Geier, a partner in the Washington (DC) office of Paul, Hastings, Janofsky & Walker LLP. One of his top priorities, he said in a declaration submitted in the Beck case, was developing a 'legally defensible' statistical analysis of Boeing's pay practices to counter the one OFCCP used to evaluate pay discrimination. But there was one big problem: the findings of Geier's own Diversity Salary Analysis project, or DSA, also found pay disparities. Its 1997 report determined that females 'are paid less'. The 1998 report noted that 'gender differences in starting salaries generally continue and often increase as a result of salary planning decisions'. Geier did not respond to requests for comment. . . .

'There Was a Lot More'

Despite Boeing's 'extensive efforts', in the words of one in-house lawyer, not to forfeit the attorney–client privilege, the company did do a few things to jeopardise its eligibility for that legal protection. Its attorneys, for instance, gave DSA documents to managers outside their tightly guarded legal team. These executives used the information not just to fight the OFCCP inquiry but also to make broader salary decisions.

The OFCCP settled with Boeing for $4.5 million in November 1999. Boeing did not admit liability. On 1 December, relieved HR executives and attorneys gathered to discuss their victory over the federal government, according to a meeting transcription obtained by *BusinessWeek*. Boeing's former director for employee relations, Marcella Fleming, declared that the company got off easy. 'We thought that there was a lot more potential financial liability out there,' Fleming told her colleagues. 'And so, what we're paying for this deal in the long run is a lot less than we think we could have potentially paid.' Fleming declined to comment for this story.

Boeing officials had little time to dwell on their triumph. On 25 February 2000, Seattle attorney Michael D. Helgren filed the *Beck* v. *Boeing* class action after some female employees told him their stories. The company enlisted the help of its chief outside law firm, Seattle-based Perkins Cole LLP. . . .

Almost immediately, the company resumed the aggressive strategies that had worked so well in the OFCCP investigation. After being deposed by attorney Helgren in September 2000, Boeing compensation manager Jeffrey K. Janders told colleagues in a memo that he wanted the Salary Planning Team to 'delete the concept of target salaries' – the hypothetical pay increases Boeing executives believed would be necessary to create salary parity – 'to prevent an audit trail where a substantial difference exists between target and planned salaries'. Because Janders could not be reached for comment, *BusinessWeek* does not know the full context of the email.

Helgren did not find out about these manoeuvres until years later, but from the start he suspected that the company was not turning over all of the salary infromation it had. After Boeing's Hannah claimed that many of the pay-related documents his rival wanted were covered by attorney–client privilege, Helgren requested a so-called privilege log – a list containing a brief description of every document the company was withholding. A common tool in US courts, these logs are intended to give plaintiffs' attorneys an idea of what material the defendant is holding back and why it is privileged without revealing any sensitive secrets. . . .

Suspecting that many of these documents did not deserve attorney–client privilege, Helgren asked for a judicial review of those covered by the privilege log. Judge Pechman assigned retired state court judge George Finkle the job of managing the pre-trial discovery disputes. After studying a 1,400-page sample of Boeing's DSA documents, Finkle rejected the claim that the studies were protected simply because attorneys were involved in producing them. The documents 'served business purposes extending well beyond providing assistance in . . . anticipation of litigation', Finkle ruled on 25 October 2000. 'Legal departments are not citadels in which public business or technical information may be placed to defeat discovery and thereby ensure confidentiality.'

That should have been the end of Helgren's quest. Still, Boeing dragged its feet. The documents Judge Finkle ordered Boeing to give to plaintiffs' attorneys came slowly and in small batches. It wasn't until early 2004 that Boeing attorneys handed over some damning internal statistical salary studies that executives had not even previously acknowledged. For Helgren, these late-released documents proved that Boeing not only knew about the pay discrimination but refused to take serious steps to eliminate it. 'These pay disparities were caused by their own practices,' Helgren says. 'None of this was by chance. And they continued for years and years to avoid the problem.'

Suddenly Amenable

In a last-ditch effort to prevent a jury from seeing these potential smoking guns, Boeing attorneys appealed Finkle's discovery order. They claimed that disclosing these documents would 'materially and unfairly' bias the case. On 11 March, Pechman denied Boeing's appeal. It was a huge boost for Helgren, who started gearing up for the trial, scheduled to begin on 17 May. But on 13 May, he got an unexpected call. A third party representing Boeing phoned to say the company was willing to talk settlement. Negotiations proceeded almost continuously until the next day at noon, when the two sides reached a tentative settlement.

While she is happy about the potential deal, plaintiff Jensen is reserving judgement about the company. Among her nine children are six adult daughters, and she currently 'wouldn't let any of them work at Boeing'. The pay gap there may disappear one day. But one thing Boeing will never be able to erase is its long history of under-paying women.

Questions

1. What inequities did women and minorities at Boeing experience?
2. What were the consequences of these inequities?
3. When managers became aware of the inequities, what did they do? Why didn't they do more?
4. What are the broader implications of the discrimination suits for Boeing and its future?

Source: S. Holmes and M. France, 'Coverup at Boeing?', adapted and reprinted from *BusinessWeek*, June 28, 2004 by special permission. Copyright © 2004 by the McGraw-Hill Companies, Inc.

Notes and References

1 *The Times*, 100 Best Companies, 5 March 2006, TimesOnline; www.tridos.co.uk.

2 R. Kanfer, 'Motivation Theory and Industrial and Organizational Psychology', in M. D. Dunnette and L. M. Hough, eds., *Handbook of Industrial and Organizational Psychology*, 1, 2nd ed. (Palo Alto, CA: Consulting Psychologists Press, 1990), 75–170.

3 T. A. Stewart, 'Just Think: No Permission Needed', *Fortune*, January 8, 2001.

4 G. Latham, 'The Study of Work Motivation in the 20th Century', in L. Koppes, ed., *The History of Industrial and Organizational Psychology* (Hillsdale, NJ: Laurence Erlbaum, 2006).

5 N. Nicholson, 'How to Motivate Your Problem People', *Harvard Business Review*, January 2003, 57–65.

6 J. P. Campbell and R. D. Pritchard, 'Motivation Theory in Industrial and Organizational Psychology', in M. D. Dunnette, ed., *Handbook of Industrial and Organizational Psychology* (Chicago: Rand McNally, 1976), 63–130; T. R. Mitchell, 'Expectancy-Value Models in Organizational Psychology', in N. T. Feather, ed., *Expectations and Actions: Expectancy-Value Models in Psychology* (Hillsdale, NJ: Erlbaum, 1982), 293–312; V. H. Vroom, *Work and Motivation* (New York: Wiley, 1964).

7 N. Shope Griffin, 'Personalize Your Management Development', *Harvard Business Review* 8 (10) (2003), 113–19.

8 T. J. Maurer, E. M. Weiss and F. G. Barbeite, 'A Model of Involvement in Work-Related Learning and Development Activity: The Effects of Individual, Situational, Motivational, and Age Variables', *Journal of Applied Psychology* 88 (4) (2003), 707–24.

9 B. Stone, 'Nike's Short Game', *Newsweek*, January 26, 2004, 40–41.

10 Holloway, 'The Man Who Put the Boing in Nike', *CB Media Limited*, March 15, 2004.

11 D. Edwards, 'Adultescents: The Over-40s Trying to Be Teens', *The Mirror*, February 3, 2004.

12 R. A. Martin, 'The Rebirth of the New York Sneakerhead', *The New York Times*, July 11, 2004, www.nytimes.com; R. J. Moody, 'Nike Puts Faith in Savier', *American City Business Journal* 20 (52) (February 20, 2004), 1.

13 Stone, 'Nike's Short Game'.

14 *Ibid.*

15 A. H. Maslow, *Motivation and Personality* (New York: Harper & Row, 1954); Campbell and Pritchard, 'Motivation Theory in Industrial and Organizational Psychology'.

16 Kanfer, 'Motivation Theory and Industrial and Organizational Psychology'.

17 N. J. Adler, *International Dimensions of Organizational Behavior*, 2nd ed. (Boston: P.W.S.-Kent, 1991); G. Hofstede, 'Motivation, Leadership and Organization: Do American Theories Apply Abroad?', *Organizational Dynamics*, Summer 1980, 42–63.

18 C. P. Alderfer, 'An Empirical Test of a New Theory of Human Needs', *Organizational Behavior and Human Performance* 4 (1969), 142–75; C. P. Alderfer, *Existence, Relatedness, and Growth: Human Needs in Organizational Settings* (New York: Free Press, 1972); Campbell and Pritchard, 'Motivation Theory in Industrial and Organizational Psychology'.

19 Kanfer, 'Motivation Theory and Industrial and Organizational Psychology'.

20 F. Herzberg, *Work and the Nature of Man* (Cleveland: World, 1966).

21 N. King, 'Clarification and Evaluation of the Two-Factor Theory of Job Satisfaction', *Psychological Bulletin* 74 (1970), 18–31; E. A. Locke, 'The Nature and Causes of Job Satisfaction', in M. D. Dunnette, ed., *Handbook of Industrial and Organizational Psychology* (Chicago: Rand McNally, 1976), 1297–1349.

22 D. C. McClelland, *Human Motivation* (Glenview, IL: Scott, Foresman, 1985); D. C. McClelland, 'How Motives, Skills, and Values Determine What People Do', *American Psychologist* 40 (1985), 812–25; D. C. McClelland, 'Managing Motivation to Expand Human Freedom', *American Psychologist* 33 (1978), 201–10.

23 D. G. Winter, *The Power Motive* (New York: Free Press, 1973).

24 M. J. Stahl, 'Achievement, Power, and Managerial Motivation: Selecting Managerial Talent with the Job Choice Exercise', *Personnel Psychology* 36 (1983), 775–89; D. C. McClelland and D. H. Burnham, 'Power Is the Great Motivator', *Harvard Business Review* 54 (1976), 100–10.

25 R. J. House, W. D. Spangler and J. Woycke, 'Personality and Charisma in the US Presidency: A Psychological Theory of Leader Effectiveness', *Administrative Science Quarterly* 36 (1991), 364–96.

26 G. H. Hines, 'Achievement, Motivation, Occupations, and Labor Turnover in New Zealand', *Journal of Applied Psychology* 58 (1973), 313–17; P. S. Hundal, 'A Study of Entrepreneurial Motivation: Comparison of Fast- and Slow-Progressing Small Scale Industrial Entrepreneurs in Punjab, India', *Journal of Applied Psychology* 55 (1971), 317–23.

27 R. A. Clay, 'Green Is Good for You', *Monitor on Psychology*, April 2001, 40–42.

28 *The Times*, 'Hart Worldwide', 6 March 2005, TimesOnline.

29 J. S. Adams, 'Toward an Understanding of Inequity', *Journal of Abnormal and Social Psychology* 67 (1963), 422–36.

30 *Ibid.*; J. Greenberg, 'Approaching Equity and Avoiding Inequity in Groups and Organizations', in J. Greenberg and R. L. Cohen, eds., *Equity and Justice in Social Behavior* (New York: Academic Press, 1982), 389–435; J. Greenberg, 'Equity and Workplace Status: A Field Experiment', *Journal of Applied Psychology* 73 (1988), 606–13; R. T. Mowday, 'Equity Theory Predictions of Behavior in Organizations', in R. M. Steers and L. W. Porter, eds., *Motivation and Work Behavior* (New York: McGraw-Hill, 1987), 89–110.

31 Health & Safety Executive, 'Working Long Hours', 2003, HSL/2003/02.

32 A. Goldwasser, 'Inhuman Resources', ecompany.com, March 2001, 154–55.

33 E. A. Locke and G. P. Latham, *A Theory of Goal Setting and Task Performance* (Englewood Cliffs, NJ: Prentice Hall, 1990).

34 J. J. Donovan and D. J. Radosevich, 'The Moderating Role of Goal Commitment on the Goal Difficulty–Performance Relationship: A Meta-Analytic Review and Critical Analysis', *Journal of Applied Psychology* 83 (1998), 308–15; M. E. Tubbs, 'Goal Setting: A Meta-Analytic Examination of the Empirical Evidence', *Journal of Applied Psychology* 71 (1986), 474–83.

35 C. O. Longenecker, J. A. Scazzero and T. T. Stansfield, 'Quality Improvement through Team Goal Setting, Feedback, and Problem Solving: A Case Study', *International Journal of Quality & Reliability Management*, 11 (4) (1994), 45–52.

36 E. A. Locke, K. N. Shaw, L. M. Saari and G. P. Latham, 'Goal Setting and Task Performance: 1969–1980', *Psychological Bulletin* 90 (1981), 125–52.

37 P. C. Earley, T. Connolly and G. Ekegren, 'Goals, Strategy Development, and Task Performance: Some Limits on the Efficacy of Goal Setting', *Journal of Applied Psychology* 74 (1989), 24–33; R. Kanfer and P. L. Ackerman, 'Motivation and Cognitive Abilities: An Integrative/Aptitude–Treatment Interaction Approach to Skill Acquisition', *Journal of Applied Psychology* 74 (1989), 657–90.

38 W. C. Hamner, 'Reinforcement Theory and Contingency Management in Organizational Settings', in H. Tosi and W. C. Hamner, eds., *Organizational Behavior and Management: A Contingency Approach* (Chicago: St Clair Press, 1974).

39 B. F. Skinner, *Contingencies of Reinforcement* (New York: Appleton-Century-Crofts, 1969).

40 H. W. Weiss, 'Learning Theory and Industrial and Organizational Psychology', in M. D. Dunnette and L. M. Hough, *Handbook of Industrial and Organizational Psychology*, 1, 2nd ed. (Palo Alto, CA: Consulting Psychologists Press, 1990), 171–221.

41 Hamner, 'Reinforcement Theory and Contingency Management'.

42 F. Luthans and R. Kreitner, *Organizational Behavior Modification and Beyond* (Glenview, IL: Scott, Foresman, 1985); A. D. Stajkovic and F. Luthans, 'A Meta-Analysis of the Effects of Organizational Behavior Modification on Task Performance, 1975–95', *Academy of Management Journal* 40 (1997), 1122–49.

43 A. D. Stajkovic and F. Luthans, 'Behavioral Management and Task Performance in Organizations: Conceptual Background, Meta-Analysis, and Test of Alternative Models', *Personnel Psychology* 56 (2003), 155–94.

44 *Ibid.*; F. Luthans and A. D. Stajkovic, 'Reinforce for Performance: The Need to Go Beyond Pay and Even Rewards', *Academy of Management Executive* 13 (2) (1999), 49–56; G. Billikopf Enciina and M. V. Norton, 'Pay Method Affects Vineyard Pruner Performance', www.cnr.berkeley.edu/ucce50/ag-labor/7research/7calag05.htm.

45 A. Bandura, *Principles of Behavior Modification* (New York: Holt, Rinehart & Winston, 1969); A. Bandura, *Social Learning Theory* (Englewood Cliffs, NJ: Prentice Hall, 1977); T. R. V. Davis and F. Luthans, 'A Social Learning Approach to Organizational Behavior', *Academy of Management Review* 5 (1980), 281–90.

46 A. P. Goldstein and M. Sorcher, *Changing Supervisor Behaviors* (New York: Pergamon Press, 1974); Luthans and Kreitner, *Organizational Behavior Modification and Beyond.*

47 Bandura, *Social Learning Theory*; Davis and Luthans, 'A Social Learning Approach to Organizational Behavior'; Luthans and Kreitner, *Organizational Behavior Modification and Beyond.*

48 A. Bandura, 'Self-Reinforcement: Theoretical and Methodological Considerations', *Behaviorism* 4 (1976), 135–55.

49 P. Engardio, 'A Hothouse of High-Tech Talent', *BusinessWeek/21st Century Capitalism* (1994), 126.

50 A. Bandura, 'Self-Efficacy Mechanism in Human Agency', *American Psychologist* 37 (1982), 122–27; M. E. Gist and T. R. Mitchell, 'Self-Efficacy: A Theoretical Analysis of Its Determinants and Malleability', *Academy of Management Review* 17 (1992), 183–211.

51 E. E. Lawler, III, *Pay and Organization Development* (Reading, MA: Addison-Wesley, 1981).

52 'The Risky New Bonuses', *Newsweek*, January 16, 1995, 42.

53 Lawler, III, *Pay and Organization Development.*

54 *Ibid.*

55 J. F. Lincoln, *Incentive Management* (Cleveland: Lincoln Electric Company, 1951); R. Zager, 'Managing Guaranteed Employment', *Harvard Business Review* 56 (1978), 103–15.

56 Lawler, III, *Pay and Organization Development.*

57 'Stock Option', *Encarta World English Dictionary*, www.dictionary.msn.com.

Chapter 15

Effective Groups and Teams

LEARNING OBJECTIVES

After studying this chapter, you should be able to:

- Explain why groups and teams are key contributors to organisational effectiveness.
- Identify the different types of groups and teams that help managers and organisations achieve their goals.
- Explain how different elements of group dynamics influence the functioning and effectiveness of groups and teams.
- Explain why it is important for groups and teams to have a balance of conformity and deviance and a moderate level of cohesiveness.
- Describe how managers can motivate group members to achieve organisational goals and reduce social loafing in groups and teams.

A Manager's Challenge

Teams Excel at Louis Vuitton and Nucor Corporation

How can managers use teams in different kinds of organisations and work environments to gain a competitive advantage?

Groups and teams are relied on in all kinds of organisations, from those specialising in heavy industrial manufacturing to those in high-tech fields ranging from computer software development to biotechnology. Relying on groups and teams to accomplish work tasks is one thing; managing groups and teams in ways that enable them to truly excel and help an organisation gain and maintain a competitive advantage is another, much more challenging endeavour. Managers at Louis Vuitton, the most profitable luxury brand in the world, and managers at Nucor Corporation, the largest producer of steel and biggest recycler in the US, have succeeded in effectively using teams to produce their goods. Teams at both companies are truly effective and excel, having helped to make the companies leaders in their respective industries.[1]

The LVHM group, which includes Louis Vuitton, had £9.7 billion in revenues in 2005, which was 11 per cent more than in 2004.[2] Louis Vuitton has an operating margin of 45 per cent and is the largest and most profitable producer of high-end luxury accessories.[3] Impeccable quality and high standards are an imperative for Louis Vuitton; when customers purchase a handbag such as the Boulogne Multicolour, which appeared in stores for the first time in March 2004 with a £850 price tag, they expect only the best. Teams at Louis Vuitton are so effective at making handbags and other accessories that not only are customers never disappointed but Vuitton's profit margins are much higher than those of its competitors such as Prada and Gucci.[4]

Teams with between 20 and 30 members make Vuitton handbags and accessories. The teams work on only one particular product at a time. A team with 24 members might produce about 120 handbags per day. Team members are empowered to take ownership for the goods they produce, are encouraged to suggest improvements and are kept up to date on key facts such as products' selling prices and popularity. As Thierry Nogues, a team leader at a Vuitton factory in Ducey, France, puts it: 'Our goal is to make everyone as multi-skilled and autonomous as possible.'[5]

In the case of the Boulogne Multicolour, a team found out that some of the studs on the handbag were interfering with the smooth operation of the zipper. The team's discovery led to a small design change that completely eliminated the problem. By being involved in all aspects of the goods they produce, and having the skills and autonomy to ensure that all products live up to the Vuitton brand name, employees take pride in their work and are highly motivated.

Similar success can also be seen across the Atlantic. Headquartered in Charlotte, NC, Nucor has operations in 14 states manufacturing all kinds of steel products ranging from steel joists, bars and beams to steel decks and metal building systems.[6] Nucor has over 9,900 employees and over £3.6 billion in annual sales.[7]

Production workers at Nucor are organised into teams ranging in size from 8 to 40 members, depending on the kind of work the team is responsible for, such as rolling steel or operating a furnace. Team members have considerable autonomy to make decisions and creatively respond to problems and opportunities. The organisational structure has relatively few layers and supports the empowerment of teams.[8] Teams develop their own informal rules of behaviour and make their own decisions. As long as team members follow organisational rules and policies (e.g. for safety) and meet quality standards, they are free to govern themselves. Managers act as coaches or advisers rather than supervisors, helping teams when they need some additional outside assistance.[9]

To ensure that production teams are motivated to help Nucor achieve its goals, team members are eligible for weekly bonuses based on the team's performance. Essentially, these production workers receive a base pay that does not vary and are eligible to receive weekly bonus pay that can average from 80 to 150 per cent of their regular pay.[10] The bonus rate is predetermined by the work a team performs and the capabilities of the machinery they use. Given the immediacy of the bonus and its potential magnitude, team members are highly motivated to perform at a high level, develop informal rules that support high performance and strive to help Nucor reach its goals. Moreover, because all members of a team receive the same amount of weekly bonus money, they are motivated to do their best for the team, co-operate and help one another out.

Crafting a luxury handbag and making steel joists couldn't be more different from each other in certain ways and work ethics and national culture distinguish the two examples. Yet the highly effective teams at Louis Vuitton and Nucor share certain fundamental qualities.

These teams take ownership of their work and are highly motivated to perform effectively. Team members have the skills and knowledge they need to be effective, they are empowered to make decisions about their work and they know that their teams are making vital contributions to their organisations.[11]

Overview

Louis Vuitton and Nucor are not alone in using groups and teams to produce goods and services that best meet customers' needs. Not only do managers in large companies rely on teams, but the positive effects of successful team work can also be observed in small companies.[12] This chapter looks in detail at how groups and teams can contribute to organisational effectiveness and the types of groups and teams used in organisations. It will discuss how different elements of group dynamics can influence the functioning and effectiveness of groups, and describe how managers can motivate group members to achieve organisational goals and reduce slack performance in groups and teams. By the end of this chapter, you will appreciate why the effective management of groups and teams is a key ingredient for organisational performance and a source of competitive advantage.

Groups, Teams and Organisational Effectiveness

A **group** may be defined as two or more people who interact with each other to accomplish certain goals or meet certain needs.[13] A **team** is a group whose members work intensely with one another to achieve a specific common goal or objective. As these definitions imply, all teams are groups but not all groups are teams. The two characteristics that distinguish teams from groups are the *intensity* with which team members work together and the presence of a *specific, overriding team goal or objective*.

Members of production teams in Louis Vuitton work intensely together to achieve their goals – crafting high-quality handbags. In contrast, accountants who work in a small firm are a group: they may interact with one another to achieve goals such as keeping up to date on the latest changes in accounting rules and regulations, maintaining a smoothly functioning office, satisfying clients and attracting new clients. But they are not a team because they do not work intensely with one another. Each accountant concentrates on serving the needs of his or her own clients.

Because all teams are also groups, whenever we use the term *group* in this chapter, it refers to both groups *and* teams. Because members of teams work intensely together, teams can sometimes be difficult to form and it may take time for members to learn how to effectively work together. Groups and teams can help an organisation gain a competitive advantage because they can (1) enhance its performance, (2) increase its responsiveness to customers, (3) increase innovation and (4) increase employees' motivation and satisfaction (Fig. 15.1). In this section, we shall look at each of these contributions in turn.

Groups and Teams as Performance Enhancers

One of the main advantages of using groups is the opportunity to obtain a type of *synergy*: people working in a group are potentially able to produce more or higher-quality outputs compared to

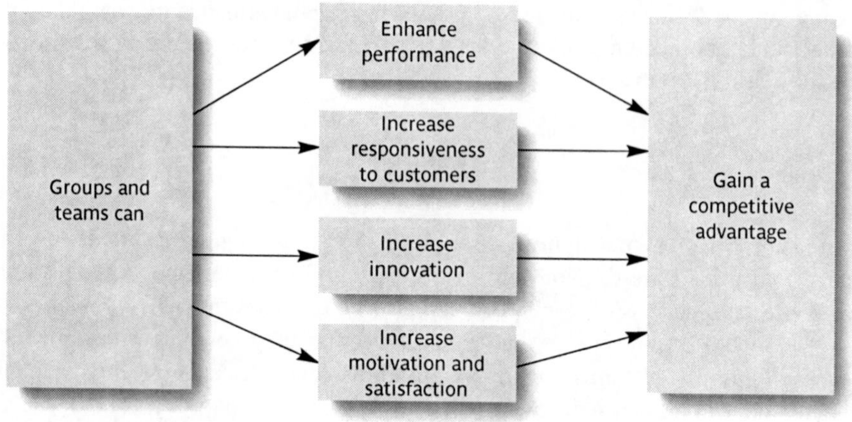

Figure 15.1 Groups' and Teams' Contributions to Organisational Effectiveness

individual outputs that are combined at a later stage. The essence of synergy is captured in the saying 'The whole is more than the sum of its parts', that has its origins in systems theory, discussed in Chapter 2. Factors that can contribute to synergy in groups include the ability of group members to bounce ideas off one another, to correct one another's mistakes, to solve problems immediately as they arise, to bring a diverse knowledge base to bear on a problem or goal and to accomplish work that is too big for any one individual to achieve on his or her own. At Louis Vuitton, the kinds of work the production teams are responsible for could not be performed by an individual acting alone; it is only through the *combined efforts* of team members that luxury accessories and products can be produced efficiently and effectively.

To take advantage of the potential for synergy in groups, managers need to make sure that groups are composed of members who have complementary skills and knowledge relevant to the group's work. At Hallmark Cards, synergies are created by bringing together all the different functions needed to create and produce a greeting card in a *cross-functional team* (a team composed of members from different departments or functions, see Chapter 10). Artists, writers, designers and marketing experts all work together as members of a team to develop new cards.[14]

At Hallmark, the skills and expertise of the artists complement the contributions of the writers and vice versa. Managers also need to give groups enough *autonomy* so that the groups, rather than the manager, are solving problems and determining how to achieve goals and objectives, as is true in the cross-functional teams at Hallmark and the production teams at Louis Vuitton. Every process needs to be owned by the team, not just individuals in the team. To promote synergy, managers need to empower their subordinates and be coaches, guides and resource providers for groups while refraining from playing a more directive or supervisory role, as is true at Louis Vuitton. The potential for synergy in groups may be the reason why more and more managers are incorporating empowerment into their personal leadership styles (see Chapter 14).

When tasks are complex and involve highly sophisticated and rapidly changing technologies, achieving synergies in teams often hinges on having the appropriate mix of backgrounds and areas of expertise represented on the team. In large organisations with operations in many countries it is often difficult for managers to determine which employees may have the expertise needed on a particular team or for a certain project, or create appropriate connections between dispersed team members. One way of creating those relationships among globally dispersed groups is to create *databases of expertise*. IBM has successfully implemented such a system in its consulting business: by entering employees onto the system, IBM was able to match consulting projects with the appropriate individuals and teams. As IBM says, it has already saved the company around £280 million.[15]

A different way to connect teams with appropriate expertise is to map the *interaction* of individuals and teams. MWH Global, an engineering and environmental consulting company operating in more than 36 countries,[16] has created such a map for its IT manager, who was relocated from Cheshire, UK, to New Zealand to manage the global network and systems of MWH Global. The map was created to understand who teams or individuals turn to for expertise. A computer program mapped the information and helped the IT manager to understand where expertise was located globally. This idea has also been adopted by the German pharmaceutical company Merck.[17]

Other practices to foster collaboration are the use of new and evolving IT. Some companies use wikis or blogs to form communities that are physically dispersed across the globe. The often very successful aim is to connect individuals and create 'virtual teams'.[18]

Groups, Teams and Responsiveness to Customers

Being responsive to customers is not always easy. In manufacturing organisations, for example, customers' needs and desires for new and improved products have to be balanced against engineering constraints, production costs and feasibilities, government safety regulations and marketing challenges. In service organisations such as health providers, being responsive to patients' needs and desires for prompt, high-quality medical care and treatment has to be balanced against meeting physicians' needs and desires and keeping health care costs under control – especially at a time when the NHS is in extreme financial difficulties. The same, however, applies to private health care providers, who have to see their business as a profit-making organisation. Being responsive to customers often requires the wide variety of skills and expertise found in different departments and at different levels in an organisation's hierarchy. Sometimes, for example, employees at lower levels in an organisation's hierarchy, such as sales representatives for a computer company, are closest to its customers and most attuned to their needs. However, salespeople often lack the technical expertise needed to come up with new product ideas; such expertise is found in the R&D department. Bringing salespeople, R&D experts and members of other departments together in a group or cross-functional team can enhance responsiveness to customers. When managers form a team, they need to make sure that the diversity of expertise and knowledge needed to be responsive to customers exists within the team; this is why cross-functional teams are so popular.

In a cross-functional team, the expertise and knowledge in different organisational departments is brought together in the skills and knowledge of the team members. Managers of high-performing organisations are careful to determine which types of expertise and knowledge are required for teams to be responsive to customers, and they use this information in forming teams.

Teams and Innovation

Innovation, the creative development of new products, new technologies, new services, or even new organisational structures, is a topic that is examined in more detail in Chapter 18. Often, an individual working alone does not possess the extensive and diverse set of skills, knowledge and expertise required for successful innovation. Managers can better encourage innovation by creating teams of diverse individuals who together have the knowledge relevant to a particular type of innovation rather than by relying on individuals working alone.

Using teams to innovate has other advantages. First, team members can often uncover one another's errors or false assumptions; an individual acting alone would not be able to do this. Second, team members can critique one another's approaches when needed. Using devil's advocacy and dialectical inquiry (discussed in Chapter 7) may help the team to use each other's strengths while compensating for any weaknesses.

Teams should also be empowered and feel fully responsible and accountable for the innovation process. The manager's role is to provide guidance, assistance, coaching and the resources for team members and not to closely direct or supervise their activities. Teams should be formed so that each member brings some unique resource to the team – such as engineering prowess, knowledge of production, marketing expertise or financial savvy. Successful innovation sometimes requires that teams comprise members from different countries and cultures.

Amazon uses teams to spur innovation, and many of the unique features on its website that enable it to be responsive to customers and meet their needs have been developed by teams, as indicated in Case 15.1.

Case 15.1: Pizza teams at Amazon

Jeff Bezos, founder and CEO of Amazon, is a firm believer in the power of teams to spur innovation. At Amazon, teams have considerable autonomy to develop their ideas and experiment without interference from managers or other groups. Teams are kept deliberately small: according to Bezos, no team should need more than two pizzas to feed its members. If more than two pizzas are needed to nourish a team, the team is too large. Teams at Amazon typically have no more than about five to seven members.[19]

'Pizza teams' have come up with unique and popular innovations that individuals working alone might never have thought of. A team developed the 'Bottom of the Page Deals' – low-priced offers ranging from electronics to CDs. The sign-up required 'Search Inside the Book', a massive undertaking that allows customers to search and read content from over 100,000 books, had its origins in a team.[20]

While Bezos gives teams autonomy to develop and run with their ideas, he also believes in the careful analysis and testing of ideas. A great advocate of the power of facts, data and analysis, Bezos feels that whenever an idea can be tested through analysis, analysis should rule. When an undertaking is just too large or too uncertain, or when data are lacking and hard to come by, Bezos and other experienced senior managers make the final call. But in order to make such judgment calls about implementing new ideas (either by data analysis or expert judgment), what really is needed are truly creative ideas. To date, teams have played a very important role in generating the ideas that have helped Amazon be responsive to its customers, have a widely known Internet brand name, survive through the dot-com bust and be the highly successful and innovative company it is today.[21]

Groups and Teams as Motivators

Managers often decide to form groups and teams to accomplish organisational goals and then find that using them brings additional benefits. Members of groups, and especially members of teams (because of the higher intensity of interaction), are likely to be more satisfied than they would have been if they had been working on their own. The experience of working alongside other highly charged and motivated people can be very stimulating. Working on a team can also be very motivating: team members more readily see how their efforts and expertise directly contribute to the achievement of team and organisational goals, and they feel personally responsible for the outcomes or results of their work. This has been the case at Louis Vuitton, Nucor and Hallmark Cards.

The increased motivation and satisfaction that can accompany the use of teams can also lead to other outcomes, such as lower turnover. This has been the experience of Pegasus Security Group, a privately owned guarding company located in London. To provide high-quality customer service, the core values of Pegasus Security Group include teamwork as a vital component, emphasising that mutual respect and understanding are vital to deliver excellence. Motivation and satisfaction levels seem to be higher than in other security firms, and turnover is believed to be the lowest in the contractual industry.[22]

Working in a group or team can also satisfy organisational members' needs for engaging in *social interaction*. For workers who perform highly stressful jobs, such as hospital emergency and operating room staff, group membership can be an important source of social support and motivation. Family members or friends may not be able to fully understand or appreciate the work stress that these group members experience first-hand. Group members may cope better with work stress when they are able to share it with other members of their group. Groups often devise techniques to relieve stress, such as the telling of jokes among hospital operating room staff.

Why do all kinds of organisations rely so heavily on groups and teams? Effectively managed groups and teams can help managers in their quest for high performance, responsiveness to customers and employee motivation. Before explaining how managers can effectively manage groups, however, we shall describe the types of groups that are formed in organisations.

Types of Groups and Teams

To achieve their goals of high performance, responsiveness to customers, innovation and employee motivation, organisations can use various types of groups and teams (Fig. 15.2). **Formal groups** are those that are established to achieve organisational goals. The formal work groups are *cross-functional* teams composed of members from different departments, such as those at Hallmark Cards, and *cross-cultural* teams composed of members from different cultures or countries, such as the teams at global car makers.

Organisational members, managers or non-managers, sometimes form groups because they feel that they will help them achieve their own goals or meet their own needs (for example, the need for social interaction). Groups formed in this way are **informal groups**. Four nurses who work in a hospital and have lunch together twice a week constitute an informal group.

The Senior Management Team

A central concern of the CEO or managing director of a company is to form a *senior management team* to help the organisation achieve its mission and goals. Such teams are responsible for

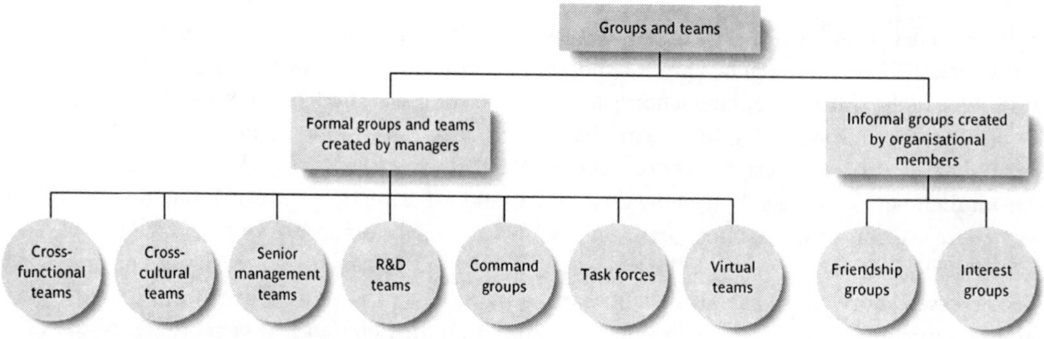

Figure 15.2 Types of Groups and Teams in Organisations

developing the strategies that result in an organisation's competitive advantage; most have between five and seven members. In forming their teams, CEOs are well advised to stress diversity – in expertise, skills, knowledge and experience. Many senior management teams are thus also cross-functional teams: they are composed of members from different departments, such as finance, marketing, production and engineering. Diversity helps ensure that the team will have all the background and resources it needs to make good decisions. Diversity also helps guard against *groupthink*, faulty group decision making that results when group members strive for agreement at the expense of an accurate assessment of the situation (see Chapter 7).

Research and Development Teams

Managers in pharmaceuticals, computers, electronics, electronic imaging and other high-tech industries often create **research and development (R&D) teams** to develop new products. The German pharmaceutical company Merck, the oldest pharmaceutical company in the world, assigns much of its success to its dynamic R&D agenda and to the way it has an employee-focused team structure.[23] Managers select R&D team members on the basis of their expertise and experience in a certain area. R&D teams are sometimes cross-functional teams with members from departments such as engineering, marketing and production in addition to members from the R&D department itself.

Command Groups

Subordinates who report to the same supervisor compose a **command group**. When senior managers design an organisation's structure and establish reporting relationships and a chain of command, they are essentially creating command groups. Such groups, often called *departments* or *units*, perform a significant amount of the work in many organisations. In order to have command groups that help an organisation gain a competitive advantage, managers not only need to motivate group members to perform at a high level but also need to be effective leaders. Examples of command groups include the sales assistants in a large John Lewis department store who report to the same department or floor supervisor, the employees of a small business who report to a general manager, or the workers on an automobile assembly line who report to the same first-line manager.

Task Forces

Task forces are formed to accomplish specific goals or solve problems in a certain time period; task forces are sometimes also called *ad hoc committees*. When an incident occurs in a company's or government's operations – such as the drug trial in 2006 in which six men ended up in hospital[24] – task forces may be formed to assess how it could have happened. Task forces may be given a set amount of time to achieve a specific goal; once the task force completes its report and reaches a conclusion, it is likely to be disbanded. Task forces can be a valuable tool for busy managers in the private or public sector who do not have the time to personally explore an important issue in depth.

Sometimes managers need to form task forces whose work is *never done*. The task force may be addressing a long-term or enduring problem or issue facing an organisation, such as how to most usefully contribute to the local community or how to make sure that the organisation provides opportunities for potential employees with disabilities. Task forces that are relatively permanent are often referred to as *standing committees*. Membership in standing committees changes over time – members may have a two- or three-year term, and memberships expire at varying times so that there are always some members with experience on the committee. Managers often form and maintain standing committees to make sure that important issues continue to be addressed.

Self-managed Work Teams

Self-managed work teams are teams in which team members are empowered and have the responsibility and autonomy to complete identifiable pieces of work. On a day-to-day basis, team members decide what the team will do, how it will do it and which team members will perform which specific tasks.[25] Managers provide self-managed work teams with their overall goals (such as assembling defect-free computer keyboards) but let team members decide how to meet them. Self-managed work teams are usually used to improve quality, increase motivation and satisfaction and lower costs. By creating self-managed work teams, tasks that individuals working separately used to perform are combined, so the team is responsible for a whole set of tasks that yields an identifiable output or end product.

In response to increasing competition, Johnson Wax (maker of well-known household products including Pledge furniture polish and Glade air freshener) formed self-managed work teams to find ways to cut costs. Traditionally, Johnson Wax used assembly-line production, in which workers were not encouraged or required to do much real thinking on the job, let alone determine how to cut costs. Things could not be more different at Johnson Wax now. A nine-member self-managed work team is responsible for moulding plastic containers. Team members choose their own leader, train new members, have their own budget to manage and are responsible for figuring out how to cut the costs of moulding plastic containers. Kim Litrenta, a 17-year veteran in one of the plants, sums up the effects of the change from assembly-line production to self-managed work teams this way: 'In the past you'd have no idea how much things cost because you weren't involved in decisions. Now it's amazing how many different ways people try to save money.'[26]

Managers can take a number of steps to ensure that self-managed work teams are effective and help an organisation gain a competitive advantage:[27]

- Give teams enough responsibility and autonomy to be truly *self-managing*. Refrain from telling team members what to do or solving problems for them even if you (as a manager) know what should be done.

- Make sure that a team's work is sufficiently complex so that it entails a number of different steps or procedures that must be performed and results in some kind of *finished end product*.
- Carefully *select* members of self-managed work teams. Team members should have the diversity of skills needed to complete the team's work, have the ability to work with others and want to be part of a team.
- As a manager, realise that your role *vis-à-vis* self-managed work teams calls for guidance, coaching and supporting, *not supervising*. You should be a resource for teams to turn to when needed.
- Analyse what type of training team members need and provide it. Working in a self-managed work team often requires employees to have extensive technical and interpersonal skills.

Managers in a wide variety of organisations have found that self-managed work teams help the organisation achieve its goals, as is certainly true at Louis Vuitton.[28] However, self-managed work teams can also run into trouble. Members are often reluctant to discipline one another by withholding bonuses from members who are not performing as well as others, or by firing members.[29]

An insurance company experimented with having members of self-managed teams evaluate one another's performance and determine pay levels. Team members did not feel comfortable assuming this role, however, and managers ended up evaluating performance and determining rewards.[30] One reason for team members' discomfort may be the close personal relationships they sometimes develop with one another. Members of self-managed work teams may also actually take longer to accomplish tasks, particularly when team members have difficulties co-ordinating their efforts.

Virtual Teams

Virtual teams are teams whose members rarely or never meet face-to-face but interact by using various forms of IT such as email, computer networks, telephone, fax and videoconferences; technology is constantly being developed, such as wikis and blogs, or podcasting, which are additional ways to communicate. As organisations become increasingly global, with operations in far-flung regions of the world, and as the need for specialised knowledge increases through advances in technology, managers can create virtual teams to solve problems or explore opportunities without being limited by the fact that team members need to be working in the same geographic location.[31]

Take the case of an organisation that has manufacturing facilities in Germany, the Czech Republic and Mexico and is encountering a quality problem in a complex manufacturing process. Each of its manufacturing facilities has a *quality control team* headed by a quality control manager. The Vice President for production does not try to solve the problem by forming and leading a team at one of the four manufacturing facilities; instead, a virtual team is formed, composed of the quality control managers of the four plants and the plants' general managers. When these team members communicate via email and videoconferencing, a wide array of knowledge and experience is brought to bear to solve the problem.

The principal advantage of virtual teams is that they enable managers to disregard geographic distance and form teams whose members have the knowledge, expertise and experience to tackle a particular problem or take advantage of a specific opportunity.[32] Virtual teams can also include members who are not actually employees of the organisation itself; a virtual team might include members of a company that is used for outsourcing. More and more companies, including Compaq-Hewlett-Packard, Motorola,[33] BP, Kodak, Whirlpool and VeriFone, are either using or exploring the use of virtual teams.[34]

Virtual teams rely on two forms of IT – *synchronous technologies* and *asynchronous technologies*.[35] Synchronous technologies enable virtual team members to communicate and interact with one another in real time simultaneously and include videoconferencing, teleconferencing and electronic meetings. Asynchronous technologies delay communication and include email, electronic bulletin boards and Internet websites. Many virtual teams use both kinds of technology, depending on the projects they are working on.

Increasing globalisation is likely to result in more organisations relying on virtual teams.[36] One of the major challenges members of virtual teams face is building a sense of camaraderie and trust among team members who rarely, if ever, meet face-to-face. To address this challenge, some organisations schedule recreational activities, such as ski trips, so that virtual team members can get together. Other organisations make sure that virtual team members have a chance to meet in person soon after the team is formed and then schedule periodic face-to-face meetings to promote trust, understanding and co-operation in the teams.[37] The need for such meetings is underscored by research that suggests that while some virtual teams can be as effective as teams that meet face to face, virtual team members may be less satisfied with teamwork efforts and have fewer feelings of camaraderie or cohesion. (Group cohesiveness is discussed in more detail later in the chapter.)[38]

Research also suggests that it is important for managers to keep track of virtual teams and intervene when necessary by, for example, encouraging members of teams who do not communicate often enough to monitor their team's progress and make sure that team members actually have the time, and are recognised for, their virtual teamwork.[39] When virtual teams are experiencing downtime or rough spots, managers may try to schedule face-to-face team time to bring team members together and help them focus on their goals.[40]

Friendship Groups

The groups described so far are *formal groups*, usually created by managers. **Friendship groups** are *informal groups* composed of employees who enjoy one another's company and socialise with one another. Members of friendship groups may have lunch together, take breaks together, or meet after work for meals, sports or other activities. Friendship groups help satisfy employees' needs for interpersonal interaction, can provide needed social support in times of stress and can contribute to people feeling good at work and being satisfied with their jobs. The informal relationships that are built in friendship groups can often help them solve work-related problems because members of these groups typically discuss work-related matters and offer advice.

Interest Groups

Employees form informal **interest groups** when they seek to achieve a common goal related to their membership in an organisation. Employees may form interest groups, for example, to encourage managers to consider instituting flexible working hours, providing on-site child care, improving working conditions, or more proactively supporting environmental protection. Interest groups can provide managers with valuable insights into the issues and concerns that are foremost in employees' minds. They also can signal the need for change. However, interest groups can also be external. An engineer in a small company, for example, may not have many colleagues whom he or she could approach to ask questions or exchange ideas with; so this engineer may join an interest group that specifically focuses on the type of area in which the engineer is interested. Virtual interest groups are now common and are likely to become an even more important source for expertise in the future.

Group Dynamics

The ways in which groups function – and, ultimately, their effectiveness – depend on group characteristics and processes known collectively as *group dynamics*. In this section, we discuss five key elements of group dynamics: group size, tasks and roles; group leadership; group development; group norms; and group cohesiveness.

Group Size, Tasks and Roles

Group size, group tasks and group roles all need to be taken into account if they are to create and maintain high-performing groups and teams.

Group size

The number of members in a group can be an important determinant of members' motivation, commitment and performance. There are several advantages to keeping a group relatively small – between two and nine members. Compared with members of large groups, members of small groups tend to (1) interact more with each other and find it easier to co-ordinate their efforts, (2) be more motivated, satisfied and committed, (3) find it easier to share information and (4) be better able to see the importance of their personal contributions for group success. A disadvantage of small rather than large groups, however, is that members of small groups have fewer resources available to accomplish their goals.

Large groups – with 10 or more members – also offer some advantages. They have more resources at their disposal to achieve group goals than small groups do – including the knowledge, experience, skills and abilities of group members as well as their actual time and effort. Large groups also enable managers to obtain the advantages stemming from the *division of labour* – splitting the work to be performed into particular tasks and assigning tasks to individual workers. Workers who specialise in particular tasks are likely to become skilled at performing them and contribute significantly to high group performance.

The disadvantages of large groups include the problems of communication and co-ordination and the lower levels of motivation, satisfaction and commitment that members sometimes experience. It is clearly more difficult to share information with, and co-ordinate the activities of, 16 people rather than 8 people. Members of large groups may also not think that their efforts are really needed, and sometimes may not even feel a part of the group.

In deciding on the appropriate size for any group, managers attempt to gain the advantages of small-group size and, at the same time, form groups with sufficient resources to accomplish their goals and have a well-developed division of labour, as is true at Louis Vuitton and Nucor. As a general rule of thumb, groups should have no more members than necessary to achieve a division of labour and provide the resources needed to achieve group goals. In R&D teams, for example, group size is too large when (1) members spend more time communicating what they know to others than applying what they know to solving problems and creating new products, (2) individual productivity decreases and (3) group performance suffers.[41]

Group tasks

The appropriate size of a high-performing group is affected by the kind of tasks the group is to perform. An important characteristic of group tasks that affects performance is task interdependence, the degree to which the work performed by one member of a group influences the work performed by others.[42] As task interdependence increases, group members need to interact more frequently and intensely with one another, and their efforts have to be more closely co-ordinated if they are to perform at a high level. Management expert James D. Thompson identified three types of task interdependence: pooled, sequential, and reciprocal (Fig. 15.3).[43]

Pooled task interdependence

Pooled task interdependence exists when group members make separate and independent contributions to group performance; overall group performance is the sum of the performance of

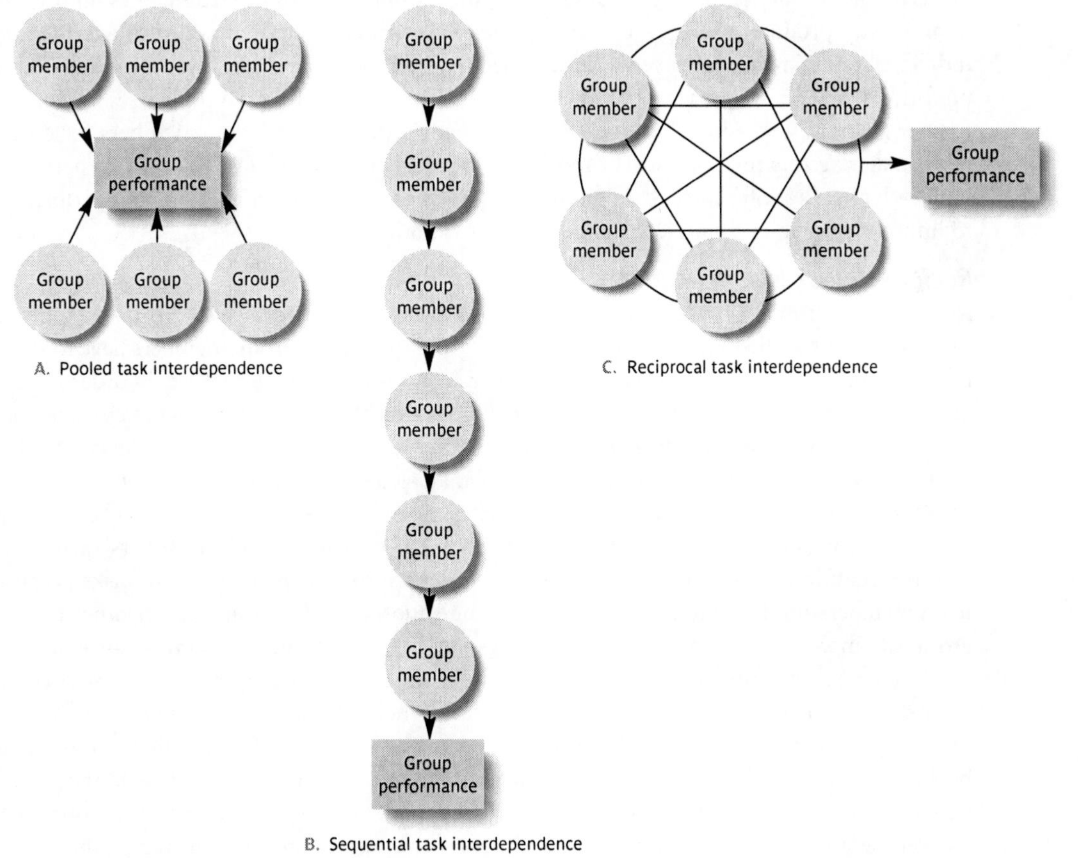

Figure 15.3 Types of Task Interdependence

the individual members (Fig. 15.3A). Examples of groups that have pooled task interdependence include a group of teachers in a primary school, a group of sales assistants in a department store, or a group of secretaries in an office. In these examples, group performance – whether it is the number of children who are taught and the quality of their education, the value of sales or the amount of secretarial work completed – is determined by *summing the individual contributions* of group members.

For groups with pooled interdependence, managers should determine the appropriate group size primarily from the amount of work to be accomplished. Large groups can be effective because group members work independently and do not have to interact frequently with one another. Motivation in groups with pooled interdependence will be highest when managers reward group members based on individual performance.

Sequential task interdependence

Sequential task interdependence exists when group members must perform specific tasks in a predetermined order: certain tasks have to be performed before others. The performance of one worker affects the work of others (Fig. 15.3B). Assembly lines and mass-production processes are characterised by sequential task interdependence.

When group members are sequentially interdependent, group size is usually dictated by the needs of the production process – for example, the number of steps needed in an assembly line to efficiently produce a CD player. With sequential interdependence, it is difficult to identify individual performance because one group member's performance depends on how well others perform their tasks. A slow worker at the start of an assembly line, for example, causes all workers further down to work slowly. Managers are often advised to reward group members for group performance: group members will be motivated to perform highly because if the group performs well, each member will benefit. In addition, group members may put pressure on poor performers to improve so that group performance and rewards do not suffer.

Reciprocal task interdependence

Reciprocal task interdependence exists when the work performed by each group member is fully dependent on the work performed by other group members: group members have to share information, intensely interact with one another, and co-ordinate their efforts in order for the group to achieve its goals (Fig. 15.3C). In general, reciprocal task interdependence characterises the operation of teams, rather than other kinds of groups. The task interdependence of R&D teams, senior management teams and many self-managed work teams is reciprocal.

When group members are reciprocally interdependent, managers are advised to keep group size relatively small because of the necessity of co-ordinating team members' activities. Communication difficulties can arise in teams with reciprocally interdependent tasks because team members need to interact frequently with one another and be available when needed. As group size increases, communication difficulties increase and can impair team performance.

When a group's members are reciprocally interdependent, managers also are advised to reward group members on the basis of group performance. Individual levels of performance are often difficult for managers to identify, and group-based rewards help ensure that group members will be motivated to perform at a high level and make valuable contributions to the group. Of course, if a manager can identify instances of individual performance in such groups, they too can be rewarded to maintain high levels of motivation. Microsoft and many other companies reward group members for their individual performance as well as for the performance of their group.

Group roles

A group role is a set of behaviours and tasks that a member of a group is expected to perform because of his or her position in the group. Members of cross-functional teams, for example, are expected to perform roles relevant to their special areas of expertise. At Hallmark Cards, it is the role of writers on the teams to create verses for new cards, the role of artists to draw illustrations and the role of designers to put verse and artwork together in an attractive and appealing card design. The roles of members of senior management teams are shaped primarily by their areas of expertise – production, marketing, finance, R&D – but members of such teams also typically draw on their broad-based expertise as planners and strategists.

In forming groups and teams, managers need to clearly communicate to group members the expectations for their roles in the group, what is required of them and how the different roles in the group fit together to accomplish group goals. Managers also need to realise that group roles often *change and evolve* as a group's tasks and goals change and as group members gain experience and knowledge. To get the performance gains that come from experience or 'learning by doing', managers should encourage group members to take the initiative to assume additional responsibilities as they see fit and modify their assigned roles. This process, called role making, can enhance individual and group performance.

In self-managed work teams and some other groups, group members themselves are responsible for creating and assigning roles. Many self-managed work teams also pick their own team leaders. When group members create their own roles, managers should be available to group members in an advisory capacity, helping them effectively settle conflicts and disagreements.

Team Roles

Various researchers (such as R. M. Belbin)[44] have tried to identify the *informal roles* people play in groups. These focus on the relationship of each member to other members and to the group task. Belbin's roles are categorised as Team leaders, Creative thinkers, Negotiators or Company workers:[45]

- *Team leaders*: Co-ordinators and shapers
- *Creative thinkers*: Monitor/evaluators, plant and specialists
- *Negotiators*: Implementers and completer/finishers
- *Company workers*: Resource/investigators and team workers.

Each role has both strengths and allowable weaknesses:

- *Co-ordinators* – usually respected leaders who help everyone focus on their task; at times can be seen as excessively controlling
- *Shapers* – tend to have lots of energy and action, challenge others to move forwards but can be insensitive
- *Monitor/evaluators* – see the big picture; think carefully and accurately about things, but may lack energy or ability to inspire others
- *Plants* – solve difficult problems with original and creative ideas; can be poor communicators and may ignore the details
- *Specialists* – have expert knowledge/skills in key areas and will solve many problems but can often be disinterested in all other areas

- *Implementers* – well-organised and predictable; take basic ideas and make them work in practice; can be slow and indecisive at times
- *Completer/finishers* – Reliably see things through to the end, ironing out the wrinkles and ensuring everything works well; can worry too much and not trust others
- *Resource investigators* – explore new ideas and possibilities with energy and with others; good networkers but can often be too optimistic and lose energy after the initial surge of motivation
- *Team workers* – care about people and how the team is getting on together, good listeners and work to resolve social problems; can have problems making difficult decisions.

Belbin's work is used extensively in organisations to identify team roles today, although there is still ambiguity among researchers as to whether these roles are valid. In trying to relate such roles to the division of labour within teams, Belbin does not maintain that these roles are 'types', as in personality traits, but that each role is related to identifiable *behaviours and competencies* that people can bring to the team, together with highlighting the allowable weaknesses of those roles. People can hold more than one role in a team but in degrees (one member may show 70 per cent Shaper (leader/coordination skills), 20 per cent Plant competencies and 10 per cent Completer/finisher skills, for example).

These roles should therefore be used as guidelines, not thought of as stable characteristics; team roles may differ according to the type of task that is performed and the team of which one is currently a part.

Group Leadership

All groups and teams need leadership. Indeed, as discussed in detail in Chapter 14, effective leadership is a key ingredient for high-performing groups, teams and organisations. Sometimes managers assume the leadership role in groups and teams, as is the case in many command groups and senior management teams. Or a manager may appoint a member of a group who is not a manager to be group leader or chairperson, as is the case in a task force or standing committee. In other cases, group or team members may choose their own leaders, or a leader may emerge naturally as members of a group work together to achieve shared goals. When managers empower members of self-managed work teams, they often let group members choose their own leaders. Some self-managed work teams find it effective to rotate the leadership role among their members. Whether leaders of groups and teams are managers or not, and whether they are appointed by managers or emerge naturally in a group, they play an important role in ensuring that groups and teams perform up to their potential. Leadership in R&D teams has been highlighted as a significant issue in driving forward effective and successful innovation.[46]

Group Development over Time

As many facilitators of self-managed teams have learned, it can take a self-managed work team two or three years to perform up to its true capabilities.[47] What a group is capable of achieving depends in part on its stage of development. Knowing that it takes considerable time for self-managed work teams to get up and running has helped managers have realistic expectations for new teams and know that they need to provide new team members with considerable training and guidance.

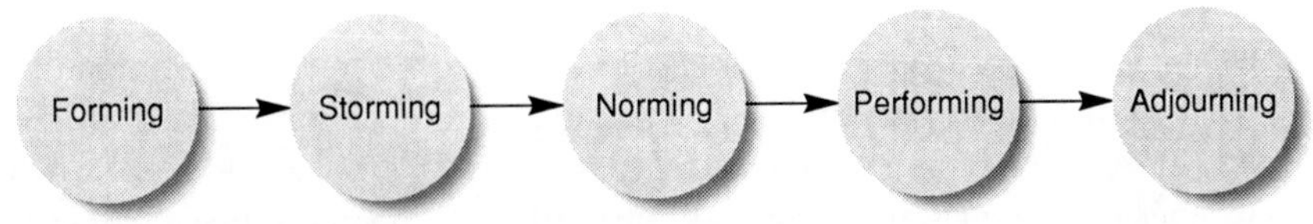

Figure 15.4 Five Stages of Group Development

Although every group's development over time is unique, researchers have identified five stages of group development that many groups seem to pass through (Fig. 15.4).[48]

Forming

In the first stage, *forming*, members try to get to know each other and reach a common understanding of what the group is trying to accomplish and how group members should behave. During this stage, managers should strive to make each member feel that he or she is a valued part of the group.

Storming

In the second stage, *storming*, group members experience conflict and disagreements because some members do not wish to submit to the demands of other group members. Disputes may arise over who should lead the group. Self-managed work teams can be particularly vulnerable during the storming stage. Managers need to keep an eye on groups at this stage to make sure that conflict does not get out of hand.

Norming

During the third stage, *norming*, close ties between group members develop, and feelings of friendship and camaraderie emerge. Group members arrive at a consensus about what goals they should be seeking to achieve, and how group members should behave toward one another.

Performing

In the fourth stage, *performing*, the real work of the group gets accomplished. Depending on the type of group in question, managers need to take different steps at this stage to help ensure that groups are effective. Managers of command groups need to make sure that group members are motivated and that they are effectively leading group members. Coaches overseeing self-managed work teams have to empower team members and make sure that teams are given enough responsibility and autonomy.

Adjourning

The last stage, *adjourning*, applies only to groups that are eventually broken up, such as task forces. During adjourning, a group is dispersed. Adjourning often takes place when a group completes a finished product, such as when a task force evaluating the pros and cons of providing on-site child care produces a report and recommendations.

Managers should have a flexible approach to group development and should keep attuned to the different needs and requirements of groups at various stages.[49] Above all else, and regardless of the stage of development, managers need to think of themselves as *resources* for groups. Managers always should be striving to find ways to help groups and teams function more effectively.

Group Norms

All groups, whether senior management teams, self-managed work teams or command groups, need to control their members' behaviours to ensure that the group performs effectively and efficiently and meets its goals. Assigning roles to each group member is one way to control behaviour in groups. Another important way in which groups influence members' behaviour is through the development and enforcement of group norms.[50] Group norms are shared guidelines or rules for behaviour that most group members follow. Groups develop norms concerning a wide variety of behaviours, including working hours, the sharing of information among group members, how certain group tasks should be performed and even how members of a group should dress. In the UK, such norms are often visible, as staff in banks or department stores wear uniforms.

Managers should encourage members of a group to develop norms that contribute to group performance and the attainment of group goals. Group norms that dictate that each member of a cross-functional team should always be available for the rest of the team when his or her input is needed, return phone calls as soon as possible, inform other team members of travel plans and give team members a phone number at which he or she can be reached when travelling on business help to ensure that the team is efficient, performs highly and achieves its goals. A norm in a command group of secretaries that secretaries who have a light workload in any given week should help out secretaries with heavier workloads helps to ensure that the group completes all assignments in a timely and efficient manner. A norm in a senior management team that dictates that team members should always consult with one another before making major decisions helps to ensure that good decisions are made with a minimum of errors and a maximum of consent.

Conformity and deviance

Group members conform to norms for three reasons: (1) they want to *obtain rewards* and *avoid punishments*, (2) they want to *imitate* group members whom they like and admire, (3) they have *internalised* the norm and believe it is the right and proper way to behave.[51] Consider the case of Robert King, who conformed to his department's norm of attending a charity event for raising money to provide food for homeless people. King's conformity could be due to (1) his desire to be a member of the group in good standing and to have friendly relationships with other group members (rewards), (2) his copying the behaviour of other members of the department whom he respects and who always attend the charity event (imitating other group members), or (3) his belief in the merits of supporting the activities of the charity (believing that is the right and proper way to behave).

Failure to conform, or *deviance*, occurs when a member of a group violates a group norm. Deviance signals that a group is not in control of one of its member's behaviours or that the deviant member is unsatisfied with one or more of the group's norms. Groups generally respond to members who behave defiantly in one of three ways:[52]

1. The group might try to get the member to change his or her deviant ways and conform to the norm. Group members might try to convince the member of the need to conform, or they might ignore or even punish the deviant. For example, in a food production plant Liz Senkbiel, a member of a self-managed work team responsible for weighing sausages, failed to conform to a group norm dictating that group members should periodically clean up an untidy room used to interview prospective employees. Because Senkbiel refused to take part in the team's cleanup efforts, team members reduced her monthly bonus for a two-month period.[53] Senkbiel clearly learned the costs of deviant behaviour in her team.

2. The group might expel the member.
3. The group might change the norm to be consistent with the member's behaviour.

That last alternative suggests that some deviant behaviour can be functional for groups. Deviance is functional for a group when it causes group members to evaluate norms that may be dysfunctional but are taken for granted by the group. Often, group members, like any individual, do not think about why they behave in a certain way or why they follow certain norms. Deviance can cause group members to reflect on their norms and change them when appropriate.

Take the case of a group of receptionists in a beauty salon who followed the norm that all appointments would be handwritten in an appointment book and at the end of each day the receptionist on duty would enter the appointments into the salon's computer system, which would print out the hairdressers' daily schedules. One day, a receptionist decided to enter appointments directly into the computer system at the time they were being made, bypassing the appointment book. This deviant behaviour caused the other receptionists to think about why they were using the appointment book in the first place, since all appointments could be entered into the computer directly. After consulting with the owner of the salon, the group changed its norm. Now appointments are entered directly into the computer, which saves time and cuts down on scheduling errors.

Encouraging a balance of conformity and deviance

To effectively help an organisation gain a competitive advantage, groups and teams need to have the right balance of conformity and deviance (Fig. 15.5). A group needs a certain level of conformity to ensure that it can control members' behaviour and channel it in the direction of high performance and group goal accomplishment. A group also needs a certain level of deviance to ensure that dysfunctional norms are discarded and replaced with functional ones. Balancing conformity and deviance is a pressing concern for all groups, whether they are senior management teams, R&D teams, command groups or self-managed work teams.

The extent of conformity and reactions to deviance within groups are determined by group members themselves. The three bases for conformity described above are powerful forces that more often than not result in group members conforming to norms. Sometimes these forces are so strong that deviance rarely occurs and, when it does, it is stamped out.

Managers can take several steps to ensure that there is enough tolerance of deviance in groups so that group members are willing to deviate from dysfunctional norms and, when deviance occurs in their group, reflect on the appropriateness of the violated norm and change it if necessary. First, managers or coaches can be *role models* for the groups and teams they oversee. When managers encourage and accept employees' suggestions for changes in procedures, do not rigidly insist that tasks be accomplished in a certain way and admit when a norm that they once supported is no longer functional, they signal to group members that conformity should not come at the expense of necessary changes and improvements. Second, managers should let employees know that there are always ways to improve group processes and performance levels and thus opportunities to *replace* existing norms with norms that will better enable a group to achieve its goals and perform at a high level. Third, managers should encourage members of groups and teams to periodically assess the *appropriateness* of their existing norms.

Managers in the innovative design firm Ideo, which has its UK office in London (Ideo's culture is described in Chapter 3) have excelled at ensuring that design teams have the right mix of conformity and deviance, resulting in Ideo's designing products in fields ranging from medicine to

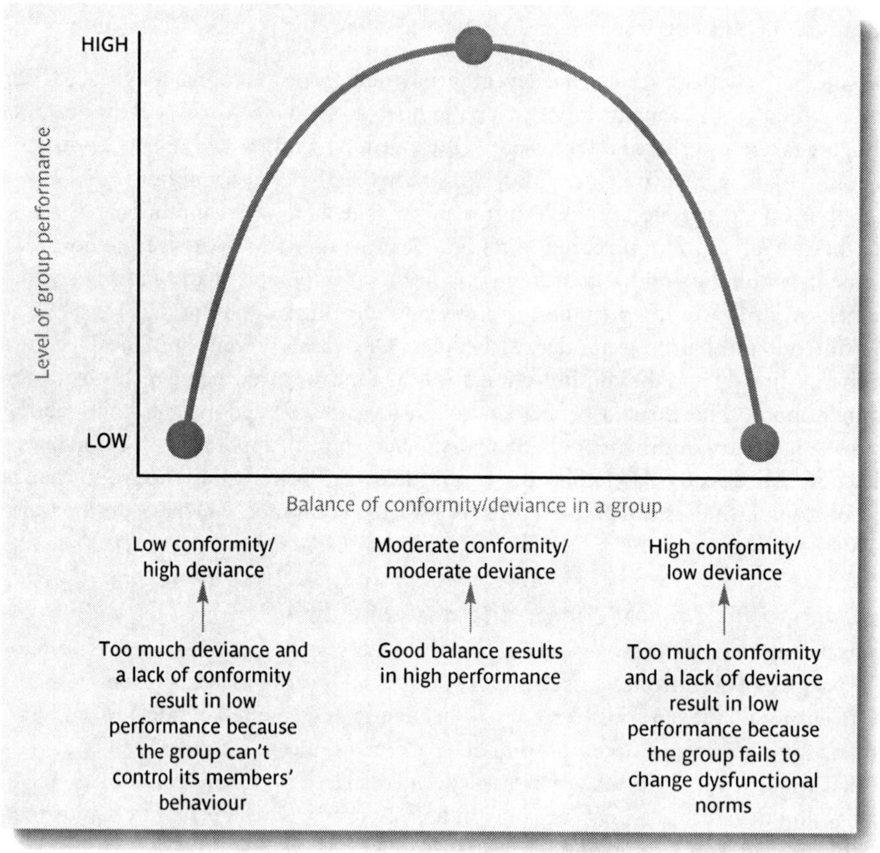

Figure 15.5 Balancing Conformity and Deviance in Groups

space travel to computing and personal hygiene, as indicated in Case 15.2. Its products are already labelled as antiques of the future; one of their design innovations that will be remembered is the BBC's interactive radio service.

Reaction Time

1. Why do all organisations need to rely on groups and teams to achieve their goals and gain a competitive advantage?
2. What kinds of employees would prefer to work in a virtual team? What kinds of employees would prefer to work in a team that meets face to face?
3. Think about a group that you are a member of, and describe that group's current stage of development. Does the development of this group seem to be following the forming, storming, norming, performing and adjourning stages?

Case 15.2: Diversity of thought and respect for ideas

Ideo designed many products we now take for granted – the first Apple mouse, the Palm handheld organiser, stand-up toothpaste containers, parts of the Oral-B toothbrush, flexible shelving for offices, self-sealing drink bottles for sports, blood analysers and even equipment used in space travel.[54] Managers and designers at Ideo pride themselves on being experts at the process of innovation in general, rather than in any particular domain. Of course, the company has technical design experts, such as mechanical and electrical engineers, who work on products requiring specialised knowledge, but on the same teams with the engineers might be an anthropologist, a biologist and a social scientist.[55]

Essentially, a guiding principle at Ideo is that innovation comes in many shapes and sizes and it is only through diversity in thought that people can recognise opportunities for innovation. To promote such diversity in thought, new product development at Ideo is a team effort.[56] Moreover, both conformity and deviance are encouraged in Ideo teams.

Deviance, thinking differently, and not conforming to expected ways of doing things and mind-sets are encouraged at Ideo. Innovative ideas often flow when designers try to see things as they really are and are not blinded by thoughts of what is appropriate, what is possible or how things should be. Often, constraints on new product design are created by designers themselves conforming to a certain mind-set about the nature of a product or what a product can or should do and look like. Ideo designers in their design teams are encouraged to actively break down these constraints.[57]

Managers at Ideo realise the need for a certain amount of conformity so that members of design teams can work effectively together and achieve their goals. Conformity to a few very central norms is emphasised in Ideo teams. These norms include understanding what the team is working on (e.g. the product, market or client need), observing real people in their natural environments, visualising how new products might work and be used, evaluating and refining product prototypes, encouraging wild ideas and never rejecting an idea simply because it sounds too crazy.[58] As long as these norms are followed, diversity of thought and even deviance serve to promote innovation. Another norm at Ideo is to study 'rule breakers' – people who don't follow instructions for products, for example, or who try to put products to different uses – as these individuals may help designers identify problems with existing products and consumer needs that are not satisfied.[59] Ideo's focus on encouraging both deviance and conformity in design teams has benefited all of us as we use Ideo-designed products that seem so familiar we take them for granted. We forget these products weren't in existence until a design team at Ideo was called on by a client to develop a new product or improve an existing one.[60]

Group Cohesiveness

Another important element of group dynamics that affects group performance and effectiveness is group cohesiveness – the degree to which members are attracted to or loyal to their group or team.[61] When group cohesiveness is high, individuals strongly value their group membership, find the group very appealing and have strong desires to remain a part of the group. When group cohesiveness is low, group members do not find their group particularly appealing and have little desire to retain their membership. Research suggests that managers should strive to have a moderate level of cohesiveness in the groups and teams they manage because that is most likely to contribute to an organisation's competitive advantage.

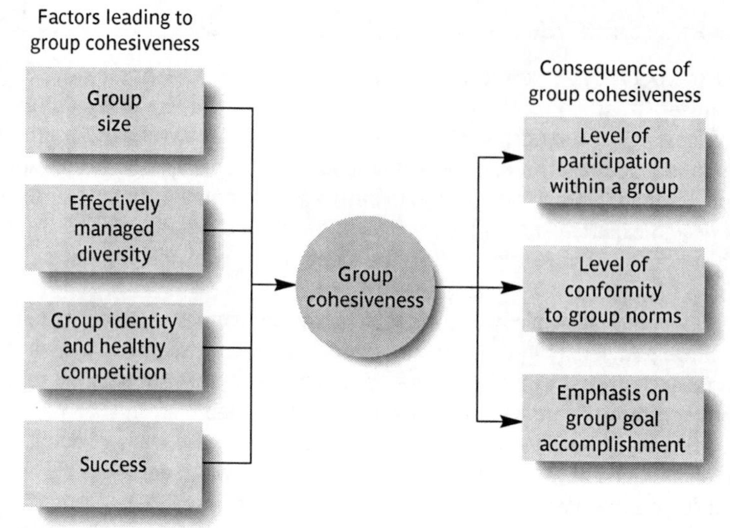

Figure 15.6 Sources and Consequences of Group Cohesiveness

Consequences of group cohesiveness

There are three major consequences of group cohesiveness: *level of participation* within a group, *level of conformity* to group norms and emphasis on group *goal accomplishment* (Fig. 15.6).[62]

Level of participation within a group

As group cohesiveness increases, the extent of group members' participation within the group increases. Participation contributes to group effectiveness because group members are actively involved in the group, ensure that group tasks get accomplished, readily share information with each other and have frequent and open communication (the important topic of communication is discussed in Chapter 16).

A moderate level of group cohesiveness helps to ensure that group members actively participate in the group and communicate effectively with one another. The reason why managers may not want to encourage high levels of cohesiveness is illustrated by the example of two cross-functional teams responsible for developing new toys. Members of the highly cohesive Team Alpha often have lengthy meetings that usually start with non-work-related conversations and jokes, meet more often than most of the other cross-functional teams in the company and spend a good portion of their time communicating the ins and outs of their department's contribution to toy development to other team members. Members of the moderately cohesive Team Beta generally have efficient meetings in which ideas are communicated and discussed as needed, do not meet more often than necessary and share the ins and outs of their expertise with one another only to the extent needed for the development process. Teams Alpha and Beta have both developed some top-selling toys. However, it generally takes Team Alpha 30 per cent longer to do so than Team Beta. This is why too much cohesiveness can be too much of a good thing.

Level of conformity to group norms

Increasing levels of group cohesiveness result in increasing levels of conformity to group norms, and when cohesiveness becomes high there may be so little deviance in groups that group members conform to norms even when they are dysfunctional. In contrast, low cohesiveness can result in too much deviance and undermine the ability of a group to influence its members' behaviours to get things done.

Teams Alpha and Beta both had the same norm for toy development. It directed that members of each team would discuss potential ideas for new toys, decide on a line of toys to pursue and then have the team member from R&D design a prototype. Recently, a new animated movie featuring a family of rabbits produced by a small film company was an unexpected hit, and major toy companies were scrambling to reach licensing agreements to produce toy lines featuring the rabbits. The senior management team in the toy company assigned Teams Alpha and Beta to develop the new toy lines and to do so quickly to beat the competition.

Members of Team Alpha followed their usual toy development norm even though the marketing expert on the team believed that the process could have been streamlined to save time. The marketing expert on Team Beta urged the team to deviate from its toy development norm. She suggested that the team not ask R&D to develop prototypes but, instead, modify top-selling toys the company already made to feature rabbits and then reach a licensing agreement with the film company based on the high sales potential (given the company's prior success). Once the licensing agreement was signed, the company could take the time needed to develop innovative and unique rabbit toys with more input from R&D.

As a result of the willingness of the marketing expert on Team Beta to deviate from the norm for toy development, the toy company obtained an exclusive licensing agreement with the film company and had its first rabbit toys on the shelves of stores in a record three months. Groups need a balance of conformity and deviance, so a moderate level of cohesiveness often yields the best outcome, as it did in the case of Team Beta.

Emphasis on group goal accomplishment

As group cohesiveness increases within a group, the emphasis placed on group goal accomplishment also increases. A very strong emphasis on group goal accomplishment, however, does not always lead to organisational effectiveness. For an organisation to be effective and gain a competitive advantage, the different groups and teams in the organisation must co-operate with one another and be motivated to achieve *organisational goals*, even if doing so sometimes comes at the expense of the achievement of group goals. A moderate level of cohesiveness motivates group members to accomplish both group and organisational goals. High levels of cohesiveness can cause group members to be so focused on group goal accomplishment that they may strive to achieve group goals no matter what – even when doing so is not in line with organisational performance.

At the toy company, the major goal of the cross-functional teams was to develop new toy lines that were truly innovative, utilised the latest in technology and were in some way fundamentally distinct from other toys on the market. When it came to the rabbit project, Team Alpha's high level of cohesiveness contributed to its continued emphasis of its group goal of developing an innovative line of toys; thus, the team stuck with its usual design process. Team Beta, in contrast, realised that developing the new line of toys quickly was an important organisational goal that should take precedence over the group's goal of developing groundbreaking new toys, at least in the short run. Team Beta's moderate level of cohesiveness contributed to team members doing what was best for the toy company in this case.

Factors leading to group cohesiveness

Four factors contribute to the level of group cohesiveness (Fig. 15.6).[63] By influencing these *determinants of group cohesiveness*, managers can raise or lower the level of cohesiveness to promote moderate levels in groups and teams.

Group size

As we mentioned earlier, members of small groups tend to be more motivated and committed than members of large groups. To promote cohesiveness in groups, when feasible, managers should form groups that are small-to-medium in size (about 2–15 members). If a group is low in cohesiveness and large in size, one way could be to divide the group in two and assign different tasks and goals to the two newly formed groups.

Effectively managed diversity

In general, people tend to like and get along with others who are similar to themselves. It is easier to communicate with someone, for example, who shares your values, has a similar background and has had similar experiences. However, as discussed in Chapter 5, diversity in groups, teams and organisations can help an organisation gain a competitive advantage. Diverse groups often come up with more innovative and creative ideas. One reason why cross-functional teams are so popular in organisations like Hallmark Cards is that the diversity in expertise represented in the teams results in higher levels of team performance.

In forming groups and teams, managers need to make sure that the diversity in knowledge, experience, expertise and other characteristics necessary for group goal accomplishment is represented in the new groups. Managers then have to make sure that this diversity in group membership is effectively managed so that groups will be cohesive.

Group identity and healthy competition

When group cohesiveness is low, managers can often increase it by encouraging groups to develop their own identities or personalities and to engage in healthy competition. Self-managed teams may be encouraged to perform better if they are publicly compared to one another – for example, by displaying their results in a common room.

If groups are too cohesive, managers can try to decrease cohesiveness by promoting organisational (rather than group) identity and making the organisation as a whole the focus of the group's efforts. Organisational identity can be promoted by making group members feel that they are valued members of the organisation as a whole and by stressing co-operation across groups to promote the achievement of organisational goals. Excessive levels of cohesiveness also can be reduced by limiting or eliminating competition among groups and rewarding co-operation.

Success

When it comes to promoting group cohesiveness, there is more than a grain of truth in the saying 'Nothing succeeds like success'. As groups become more successful, they become increasingly attractive to their members and their cohesiveness tends to increase (see Case 15.3). When cohesiveness is low, managers can increase it by making sure that a group can achieve some noticeable and visible successes.

Take the case of a group of sales assistants in the homeware department of a medium-sized department store. The homeware department was recently moved to a corner of the store's basement. Its remote location resulted in low sales because of infrequent customer traffic in that part of the store. The sales assistants, who were generally evaluated favourably by their supervisors and were valued members of the store, tried various initiatives to boost sales, but to no avail. As a result of this lack of success and the poor performance of their department, their cohesiveness started to plummet. To increase and preserve the cohesiveness of the group, the store manager implemented a group-based incentive across the store. In any month, members of the group with the best attendance and punctuality records would have their names and pictures posted on a bulletin board in the cafeteria and would each receive a gift certificate. The homeware group frequently had the best records, and their success on this dimension helped to build and maintain their cohesiveness. Moreover, this initiative boosted attendance and discouraged lateness throughout the store. The cohesiveness of teams at Louis Vuitton is enhanced by their success at producing high-quality accessories.

Case 15.3: Cohesiveness and success with Innocent and Virgin

Innocent Drinks have made a name for themselves by providing healthy and fun-looking fruit drinks. The company is also known for having one of the most innovative and successful business concepts. Part of the success is the way that the founders of Innocent treat their staff.

People and teams are greatly appreciated at Innocent, the company prides itself on providing an informal and enjoyable working environment. The founders aim to treat their staff well and believe that providing ample space for relaxation and doing things as a group make perfect business sense. Three-quarters of the offices of Innocent are *social spaces* – even table football is provided.

But it is not just social space during work time that encourages people to be together. Every year, all the staff are treated to a snowboarding holiday. Innocent also encourages the feeling of a family by providing ample support for a new parent, giving £2,000 for the birth of each child.

Cohesiveness and success is also formed by being content that what is given to the company is somehow returned. Innocent encourages staff to think outside the box, and be different. In order to keep staff motivated, Innocent offers scholarships of £1,000 to every staff member so people can do something different, something they have always wanted to do – such as recording a CD or taking flying lessons.

The continued success of Innocent speaks for itself. Innocent has taken its people and team issue seriously and has managed to encourage a family feel.[64]

Another company that has successfully been able to create cohesive teams that bring forward the business is Virgin Atlantic. The fun-loving, down-to-earth, friendly atmosphere associated with the brand has been adopted in its Cargo business. The business is divided into various parts, but all are organised around a team structure. Virgin's cargo service has won several awards that suggest that it got it right in encouraging teams.[65] Virgin Group's enthusiastic chairman, Richard Branson, summarises this by saying: 'The people who make up Virgin Atlantic make Virgin Atlantic.'

Managing Groups and Teams for High Performance

Now that you have a good understanding of why groups and teams are so important for organisations, the types of groups that managers create and group dynamics, we can consider some additional steps that managers can take to make sure that groups and teams perform highly and contribute to organisational effectiveness. Managers striving to have top-performing groups and teams need to (1) motivate group members to work toward the achievement of organisational goals, (2) reduce social loafing, and (3) help groups to manage conflict effectively.

Motivating Group Members to Achieve Organisational Goals

When work is difficult, tedious or requires a high level of commitment and energy, managers cannot assume that group members will always be motivated to work toward the achievement of organisational goals. Consider the case of a group of house painters who paint the interiors and exteriors of new homes for a construction company and are paid on an hourly basis. Why should they strive to complete painting jobs quickly and efficiently if doing so will just make them feel more tired at the end of the day and they will not receive any tangible benefits? It makes more sense for the painters to adopt a more relaxed approach, to take frequent breaks and to work at a leisurely pace. This relaxed approach, however, impairs the construction company's ability to gain a competitive advantage because it raises costs and increases the time needed to complete a new home.

Managers can motivate members of groups and teams to achieve organisational goals and create a competitive advantage by making sure that the members themselves benefit when the group or team performs highly, as is true at Luis Vuitton, Amazon or Innocent Drinks. If members of a self-managed work team know that they will receive a weekly bonus based on team performance, they will be highly motivated to perform at a high level. However, as described in earlier chapters, individuals are not motivated only by *extrinsic rewards* that promise financial bonuses in order to perform well within teams. Companies such as Innocent offer some financial rewards to achieve organisational goals, but also offer more *intrinsic rewards*.

Managers often rely on some combination of individual and group-based incentives to motivate members of groups and teams to work toward the achievement of organisational goals and a competitive advantage. When individual performance within a group can be assessed, pay is often determined by individual performance or by both individual and group performance. When individual performance within a group cannot be accurately assessed then group performance should be the key determinant of pay levels. Approximately 75 per cent of companies that use self-managed work teams base team members' pay in part on team performance.[66] A major challenge within self-managed teams is to develop a fair and equitable pay system that will lead to both high individual motivation and high group or team performance.

Other benefits that managers can make available to high-performance group members – in addition to monetary rewards – include extra resources such as equipment and computer software, awards and other forms of recognition and choice of future work assignments. Members of self-managed work teams that develop new software at companies like Microsoft often value working on interesting and important projects; members of teams that have performed highly are rewarded by being assigned to interesting and important new projects.

At Ideo, managers motivate team members by making them feel important: 'When people feel special, they'll perform beyond your wildest dreams.'[67] To make Ideo team members feel special, Ideo managers plan unique and fun year-end parties, give teams the opportunity to take time off if they feel they need or want to, encourage teams to take field trips and see pranks as a way to incorporate fun into the workplace.[68]

Reducing Social Loafing in Groups

We have focused on the steps that managers can take to encourage high levels of performance in groups. Managers, however, need to be aware of an important downside to group and team work: the potential for *social loafing*, which reduces group performance. Social loafing is the tendency of individuals to put forth less effort when they work in groups than when they work

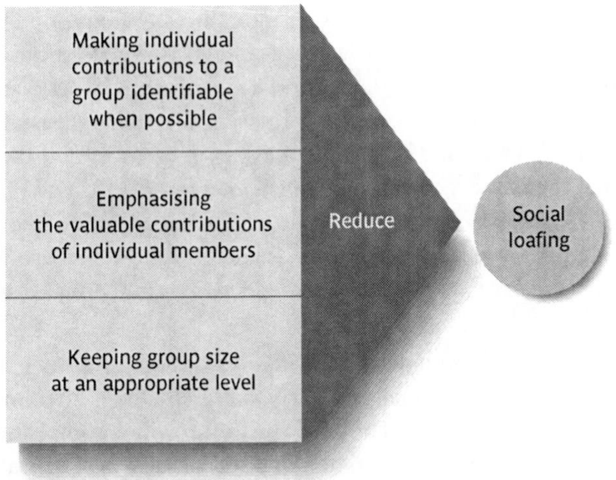

Figure 15.7 Three Ways to Reduce Social Loafing

alone.[69] Have you ever worked on a group project in which one or two group members never seemed to be pulling their weight? Have you ever worked in a student society or committee in which some members always seemed to be missing meetings and never volunteer for activities? Have you ever had a job in which one or two of your co-workers seemed to be doing less because they knew that you or other members of your work group would make up for their low levels of effort? If you have, you have witnessed social loafing in action.

Social loafing can occur in all kinds of groups and teams and in all kinds of organisations. It can result in lower group performance and may even prevent a group from attaining its goals. Fortunately, there are steps managers can take to reduce social loafing and sometimes completely eliminate it; we shall look at three (Fig. 15.7).

1. *Make individual contributions to a group identifiable* Some people may engage in social loafing when they work in groups because they think that they can hide in the crowd – that no one will notice if they put forth less effort than they should. Other people may think that if they put forth high levels of effort and make substantial contributions to the group, their contributions will not be noticed and they will receive no rewards for their work – so why bother?[70]

   One way in which managers can effectively eliminate social loafing is by making individual contributions to a group *identifiable* so that group members perceive that low and high levels of effort will be noticed and individual contributions evaluated.[71] Managers can accomplish this by assigning specific tasks to group members and holding them *accountable* for their completion. Take the case of a group of eight employees responsible for reshelving returned books in a large public library. The head librarian was concerned that there was always a backlog of seven or eight carts of books to be reshelved, even though the employees never seemed to be particularly busy and some even found time to sit down in the current-periodicals section to read newspapers and magazines. The librarian decided to try to eliminate the apparent social loafing by assigning each employee sole responsibility for reshelving a particular section of the library. Because the library's front-desk employees sorted the books by section on the carts as they were returned, holding the shelvers responsible for particular sections was easily accomplished. Once the shelvers knew that the librarian could identify their effort or lack of effort, there were rarely any backlogs of books.

Sometimes the members of a group can co-operate to eliminate social loafing by making individual contributions identifiable. Members of a self-managed work team in a small security company who assemble control boxes for home alarm systems start each day by deciding who will perform which tasks, and how much work each member and the group as a whole should strive to accomplish. Each team member knows that, at the end of the day, the other team members will know exactly how much he or she has accomplished. With this system in place, social loafing never occurs in the team. Remember, however, that in some teams – as in teams whose members are reciprocally interdependent – individual contributions cannot be made identifiable.

2. *Emphasise the valuable contributions of individual members* Another reason why social loafing may occur is that people sometimes think that their efforts are unnecessary or unimportant when they work in a group. They feel the group will accomplish its goals and perform at an acceptable level whether or not they personally perform at a high level. To counteract this belief, when managers form groups they should assign individuals to groups on the basis of the valuable contribution that *each* person can make to the group as a whole. Clearly communicating to group members why each person's contribution is valuable to the group is an effective means by which managers, and group members themselves, can reduce or eliminate social loafing.[72] This is most clearly illustrated in cross-functional teams where each member's valuable contribution to the team derives from a personal area of expertise. By emphasising why each member's skills are important, managers can reduce social loafing.
3. *Keep group size at an appropriate level* Group size is related to the causes of social loafing we have just described. As size increases, identifying individual contributions becomes increasingly difficult and members are more likely to think that their individual contributions are not very important. To overcome this, managers should form groups with no more members than are needed to accomplish group goals and perform highly.[73]

Helping Groups to Manage Conflict Effectively

At some point, practically all groups experience conflict either within the group (*intra-group* conflict) or with other groups (*inter-group* conflict). In Chapter 17 an in-depth discussion and exploration of conflict, and ways to manage it effectively, is presented. You will learn that managers can take several steps to help groups manage conflict and disagreements.

TIPS FOR PRACTICE

1. Try to ensure that the benefits of team work and group work benefit individuals' needs.
2. Think about being able to control the size of teams or groups – make the size relevant for the task at hand.
3. Try to understand your own role in a team and the roles of others. Help others to clarify each individual's role and how different roles can help in achieving a goal.
4. Challenge group norms if you feel that they are inappropriate. Assessing group and team norms frequently is vital for a healthy team or group.

Reaction Time

1. Think about a group of employees who works in a fast food restaurant. What type of task interdependence characterises this group? What potential problems in the group should the restaurant manager be aware of, and take steps to avoid?
2. Discuss the reasons why too much conformity can hurt groups and their organisations.
3. Why do some groups have very low levels of cohesiveness?

Summary and Review

Groups, teams and organisational effectiveness A group is two or more people who interact with each other to accomplish certain goals or meet certain needs. A team is a group whose members work intensely with one another to achieve a specific common goal or objective. Groups and teams can contribute to organisational effectiveness by enhancing performance, increasing responsiveness to customers, increasing innovation and being a source of motivation for their members.

Types of groups and teams Formal groups are groups that managers establish to achieve organisational goals; they include cross-functional teams, cross-cultural teams, senior management teams, R&D teams, command groups, task forces, self-managed work teams and virtual teams. Informal groups are groups that employees form because they believe that they will help them achieve their own goals or meet their needs; they include friendship groups and interest groups.

Group dynamics Key elements of group dynamics are group size, tasks and roles; group leadership; group development; group norms; and group cohesiveness. The advantages and disadvantages of large and small groups suggest that managers should form groups with no more members than are needed to provide the group with the HR it needs to achieve its goals and use a division of labour. The type of task interdependence that characterises a group's work gives managers a clue about the appropriate size of the group. A group role is a set of behaviours and tasks that a member of a group is expected to perform because of his or her position in the group. All groups and teams need leadership.

Five stages of development that many groups pass through are forming, storming, norming, performing and adjourning. Group norms are shared rules for behaviour that most group members follow. To be effective, groups need a balance of conformity and deviance. Conformity allows a group to control its members' behaviour to achieve group goals; deviance provides the impetus for needed change.

Group cohesiveness is the attractiveness of a group or team to its members. As group cohesiveness increases, so, too, does the level of participation and communication within a group, the level of conformity to group norms and the emphasis on group goal accomplishment. Managers should strive to achieve a moderate level of group cohesiveness in the groups and teams they manage.

Managing groups and teams for high performance To make sure that groups and teams perform highly, managers need to motivate group members to work toward the achievement of organisational goals, reduce social loafing and help groups to effectively manage conflict. Managers can motivate members of groups and teams to work toward the achievement of organisational goals by making sure that members personally benefit when the group or team performs highly.

Topic for Action

- Interview one or more managers in an organisation in your local community to identify the types of groups and teams that the organisation uses to achieve its goals. What challenges do these groups and teams face?

Applied Independent Learning

Building Management Skills

Diagnosing Group Failures

Think about the last dissatisfying or discouraging experience you had as a member of a group or team. Perhaps the group did not accomplish its goals, perhaps group members could agree about nothing, or perhaps there was too much social loafing. Now answer the following questions:

1. What type of group was this?
2. Were group members motivated to achieve group goals? Why or why not?
3. How large was the group, what type of task interdependence existed in the group and what group roles did members play?
4. What were the group's norms? How much conformity and deviance existed in the group?
5. How cohesive was the group? Why do you think the group's cohesiveness was at this level? What consequences did this level of group cohesiveness have for the group and its members?
6. Was social loafing a problem in this group? Why or why not?
7. What could the group's leader or manager have done differently to increase group effectiveness?
8. What could group members have done differently to increase group effectiveness?

Managing Ethically

Some self-managed teams encounter a vexing problem: One or more members engage in social loafing, and other members are reluctant to try to rectify the situation. Social loafing can be especially troubling if team members' pay is based on team performance and social loafing reduces the team's performance and thus the pay of all members (even the highest performers). Even if managers are aware of the problem, they may be reluctant to take action because the team is supposedly self-managing.

Questions

1. Either individually or in a group, think about the ethical implications of social loafing in a self-managed team.
2. Do managers have an ethical obligation to step in when they are aware of social loafing in a self-managed team? Why or why not? Do other team members have an obligation to try to curtail the social loafing? Why or why not?

Small Group Breakout Exercise

Creating a Cross-Functional Team

Form groups of three or four people, and appoint one member as the spokesperson who will communicate your findings to the whole class when called on by the instructor. Then discuss the following scenario.

You are a group of managers in charge of food services for a large state university in the Midwest. Recently a survey of students, faculty and staff was conducted to evaluate customer satisfaction with the food services provided by the university's eight cafeterias. The results were disappointing, to put it mildly. Complaints ranged from dissatisfaction with the type and range of meals and snacks provided, operating hours and food temperature to frustration about unresponsiveness to current concerns about low-carbohydrate diets and the needs of vegetarians. You have decided to form a cross-functional team that will further evaluate reactions to the food services and will develop a proposal for changes to be made to increase customer satisfaction.

1. Indicate who should be on this important cross-functional team, and explain why.
2. Describe the goals the team should be striving to achieve.
3. Describe the different roles that will need to be performed in this team.
4. Describe the steps you will take to help ensure that the team has a good balance between conformity and deviance, and has a moderate level of cohesiveness.

Exploring the World Wide Web

Many consultants and organisations provide team-building services to organisations. While some managers and teams have found these services to be helpful, others have found them to be a waste of time and money – another consulting fad that provides no real performance benefits. Search online for team-building services, and look at the websites of a few consultants/companies in depth. Based on what you have read, what might be some of the advantages and disadvantages of team-building services? For what kinds of problems/issues might these services be beneficial, and when might they have little benefit or perhaps even do more harm than good?

Application in Today's Business World

This Volvo Is Not a Guy Thing

Burning rubber, roaring engines. Grease and gas. Cars are a guy thing, right? The industry sure seems to think so. Auto ads tend to emphasise big, fast models, usually driven by a man – with a woman at his side, if at all – over user-friendly touches such as ergonomic seats. It's no surprise the crowd that designs, develops, builds and sells autos remains a boys' club.

Yet on the other side of the sales desk, women sway a disproportionate share of car sales. According to industry studies, women purchase about two-thirds of vehicles and influence 80 per cent of all sales. It's this gender gap that Volvo was trying to bridge with a concept car unveiled at the Geneva Auto Show on 2 March 2004. Shaped by all-female focus groups drawn from Volvo's workforce, the two-door hatchback was created by an all-woman management team. Dubbed Your Concept Car, or YCC, the resulting show car cost some $3 million to design and build and was packed with thoughtful design twists that attracted a big, spirited crowd in Geneva. 'We found that by meeting women's expectations, we exceeded those of most men,' said Hans-Olov Olsson, president and CEO of Volvo Cars, a unit of Ford Motor Co.

There's no guarantee the YCC will ever make it to a showroom. The auto industry uses concept cars as test beds for designs and technical innovations, and to gauge the public's reactions. Packed as it is with the latest gizmos, the YCC would be expensive: Volvo estimates a road version would cost about $65,000 and compete with luxury coupés built by the likes of Audi and Mercedes.

More James Bond than Soccer Mom, the YCC may just create enough buzz to hit the roads. Its gull-wing doors – which resemble the line of a bird's extended wings – are there as much for convenience and accessibility as for design chic. A button on the key fob stirs the YCC to life, raising the whole chassis a few inches to meet the driver, just as the upper door lifts hydraulically and the sill – the lower part of the door – slides under the car. The oversize opening makes stepping in and out a breeze, says Maria Widell Christiansen, the YCC's design manager. And because they're motor-driven, 'the driver doesn't even need to touch the car to get in', she adds.

This hands-off approach is deliberate and consistent. Rather than a dirty, tough-to-unscrew gas cap, the YCC borrows a technology from race cars: when the gas button is pressed in the cockpit, a ball valve on the outside of the car rotates, exposing an opening for the fuel pump. Ditto for windshield-wiper fluid. Body panels are low-maintenance, too. Clad in a non-stick paint, they repel dirt.

Smart Parking

Much of the advanced technology in the YCC is hidden from view. Women in Volvo's focus group weren't willing to give up power but wanted cleaner, more efficient performance. Hence the 215-horsepower, five-cylinder, near-zero emissions gas engine, which shuts off when not in motion and then fires up instantly with the help of an electric motor. This delivers a 10 per cent boost in mileage, says Olsson. There's also a nifty parallel parking aid. When the car is aligned in front of an empty spot, sensors can confirm that, yes, it's big enough. Then, while the driver controls the gas and brake, the system self-steers the car into the spot.

In the cockpit, the design team focused on ergonomics and styling. 'Access for women, in particular, can be difficult,' says Jennifer Stockburger, an automotive-test engineer at *Consumer Reports*, who has been testing vehicle ergonomics into her ninth month of pregnancy. For small women, especially, 'reaching out to shut a heavy door, or adjusting pedals, can be tough'.

To tailor the cockpit to drivers, the YCC team developed and applied for a patent on the Ergovision system. At a dealership, the driver's body is laser-scanned in a booth. Volvo then calculates optimal positions for the seat belt, pedals, headrest, steering wheel and seat, all of which is saved in the key fob. Each driver is 'automatically custom-fitted' when they get in the car, says Camilla Palmertz, YCC's project manager.

Whether or not the YCC is eventually built, some of its design innovations are likely to show up in future Volvo models, says Olsson. The concept car made its US debut on 7 April 2004 at the New York International Auto Show. And no doubt plenty of gearhead guys were there to admire its feminine wiles.

Questions

1. Why do men design most cars even though women are very influential in terms of actual car sales?
2. Why did Volvo rely on focus groups and a management team composed of women to design the Volvo YCC?
3. Designed by women, does the YCC appeal to men? Why or why not?
4. What lessons can other auto makers learn from Volvo's experience with the design of the YCC?

Source: A. Aston and G. Edmondson, 'This Volvo Is Not a Guy Thing', adapted and reprinted from *BusinessWeek*, March 15, 2004 by special permission. Copyright © 2004 by the McGraw-Hill Companies, Inc.

Notes and References

1 C. Matlack, R. Tiplady, D. Brady, R. Berner and H. Tashiro, 'The Vuitton Machine', *BusinessWeek*, March 22, 2004, 98–102; 'America's Most Admired Companies', *Fortune.com*, August 18, 2004, www.fortune.com/fortune/mostadmired/snapshot/0,15020,383,00.html; 'Art Samberg's Ode to Steel', *Big Money Weekly*, June 29, 2004, trading.sina/com/trading/rightside/bigmoney_weekly_040629.b5.shtml; 'Nucor Reports Record Results for First Quarter of 2004', www.nucor.com/financials.asp?finpage=newsreleases, August 18, 2004; 'Nucor Reports Results for First Half and Second Quarter of 2004', www.nucor.com/financials.asp?finpage=newsreleases; J. C. Cooper, 'The Price of Efficiency', *BusinessWeek Online*, March 22, 2004, www.businessweek.com/magazine/content/04_12/b3875603.htm.

2 http://webbolt.ecnext.com/coms2/news_58767_RET.

3 Matlack *et al.*, 'The Vuitton Machine'.

4 *Ibid.*

5 *Ibid.*

6 www.nucor.com.

7 'About Nucor', www.nucor.com/aboutus.htm, August 18, 2004.

8 M. Arndt, 'Out of the Forge and into the Fire', *BusinessWeek*, June 18, 2001.

9 S. Baker, 'The Minimill That Acts Like a Biggie', *BusinessWeek*, September 30, 1996, 101–04; S. Baker, 'Nucor', *BusinessWeek*, February 13, 1995, 70; S. Overman, 'No-Frills at Nucor', *HR Magazine*, July 1994, 56–60.

10 www.nucor.com.

11 Matlack *et al.*, 'The Vuitton Machine'; 'About Nucor'; 'America's Most Admired Companies'; 'Art Samberg's Ode to Steel'; 'Nucor Reports Record Results for First Quarter of 2004'; 'Nucor Reports Results for First Half and Second Quarter of 2004'.

12 W. R. Coradetti, 'Teamwork Takes Time and a Lot of Energy', *HR Magazine*, June 1994, 74–77; D. Fenn, 'Service Teams That Work', *Inc.*, August 1995, 99; 'Team Selling Catches On, but Is Sales Really a Team Sport?' *The Wall Street Journal*, March 29, 1994, A1.

13 T. M. Mills, *The Sociology of Small Groups* (Englewood Cliffs, NJ: Prentice Hall, 1967); M. E. Shaw, *Group Dynamics* (New York: McGraw-Hill, 1981).

14 R. S. Buday, 'Reengineering One Firm's Product Development and Another's Service Delivery', *Planning Review* (March–April 1993), 14–19; J. M. Burcke, 'Hallmark's Quest for Quality Is a Job Never Done', *Business Insurance*, April 26, 1993, 122; M. Hammer and J. Champy, *Reengineering the Corporation* (New York: HarperBusiness, 1993); T. A. Stewart, 'The Search for the Organization of Tomorrow', *Fortune*, May 18, 1992, 92–98.

15 *BusinessWeek Online Extra*, 'Six Best Web-Smart Practices', November 21 2005.

16 www.mwhglobal.com.

17 *BusinessWeek*, 'The Office Chart that Really Counts', January 26 2006.

18 *BusinessWeek Online Extra*, 'Six Best Web-Smart Practices'.

19 A. Deutschman, 'Inside the Mind of Jeff Bezos', *Fast Company*, August 2004, 50–58.

20 *Ibid.*

21 'Online Extra: Jeff Bezos on Word-of-Mouth Power', *BusinessWeek Online*, August 2, 2004, www.businessweek.com; R. D. Hof, 'Reprogramming Amazon', *BusinessWeek Online*, December 22, 2003, www.businessweek.com.

22 http://www.pegasus-security.co.uk/_pages/personnel.htm.

23 http://www.merck-pharmaceuticals.co.uk/files/Merck%20CIV(7.2).pdf.

24 www.bbc.co.uk/news March 15 2006.

25 J. A. Pearce II and E. C. Ravlin, 'The Design and Activation of Self-Regulating Work Groups', *Human Relations* 11 (1987), 751–82.

26 R. Henkoff, 'When to Take on the Giants', *Fortune*, May 30, 1994, 111, 114.

27 B. Dumaine, 'Who Needs a Boss?' *Fortune*, May 7, 1990, 52–60; Pearce and Ravlin, 'The Design and Activation of Self-Regulating Work Groups'.

28 Dumaine, 'Who Needs a Boss?'; A. R. Montebello and V. R. Buzzotta, 'Work Teams That Work', *Training and Development*, March 1993, 59–64.

29 T. D. Wall, N. J. Kemp, P. R. Jackson and C. W. Clegg, 'Outcomes of Autonomous Work Groups: A Long-Term Field Experiment', *Academy of Management Journal* 29 (1986): 280–304.

30 J. S. Lublin, 'My Colleague, My Boss', *The Wall Street Journal*, April 12, 1995, R4, R12.

31 W. R. Pape, 'Group Insurance', *Inc.* (Inc. Technology Supplement), June 17, 1997, 29–31; A. M. Townsend, S. M. DeMarie and A. R. Hendrickson, 'Are You Ready for Virtual Teams?' *HR Magazine*, September 1996, 122–26; A. M. Townsend, S. M. DeMarie and A. M. Hendrickson, 'Virtual Teams: Technology and the Workplace of the Future', *Academy of Management Executive* 12(3) (1998) 17–29.

32 Townsend *et al.*, 'Virtual Teams'.

33 J. Lipnack and J. Stamps, *Virtual Teams: People Working Across Boundaries with Technology* (Chichester: John Wiley, 2000).

34 Pape, 'Group Insurance'; Townsend *et al.*, 'Are You Ready for Virtual Teams?'.

35 D. L. Duarte and N. T. Snyder, *Mastering Virtual Teams* (San Francisco: Jossey-Bass, 1999); K. A. Karl, 'Book Reviews: *Mastering Virtual Teams*', *Academy of Management Executive*, August 1999, 118–19.

36 B. Geber, 'Virtual Teams', *Training* 32(4), 36–40; T. Finholt and L. S. Sproull, 'Electronic Groups at Work', *Organization Science* 1 (1990), 41–64.

37 Geber, 'Virtual Teams'.

38 E. J. Hill, B. C. Miller, S. P. Weiner and J. Colihan, 'Influences of the Virtual Office on Aspects of Work and Work/Life Balance', *Personnel Psychology* 31 (1998), 667–83; S. G. Strauss, 'Technology,

Group Process, and Group Outcomes: Testing the Connections in Computer-Mediated and Face-to-Face Groups', *Human–Computer Interaction* 12 (1997), 227–66; M. E. Warkentin, L. Sayeed and R. Hightower, 'Virtual Teams Versus Face-to-Face Teams: An Exploratory Study of a Web-Based Conference System', *Decision Sciences* 28(4), 975–96.
39 S. A. Furst, M. Reeves, B. Rosen and R. S. Blackburn, 'Managing the Life Cycle of Virtual Teams', *Academy of Management Executive* 18(2), 6–20.
40 *Ibid.*
41 A. Deutschman, 'The Managing Wisdom of High-Tech Superstars', *Fortune*, October 17, 1994, 197–206.
42 J. D. Thompson, *Organizations in Action* (New York: McGraw-Hill, 1967).
43 *Ibid.*
44 R. M. Belbin, *Management Teams: Why They Succeed or Fail* (Oxford: Butterworth-Heinemann, 1996).
45 R. M. Belbin, *Team Roles at Work* (London: Butterworth-Heinemann, 1993).
46 J. K. Wang, M. J. Ashleigh and E. Meyer, 'Knowledge Sharing and Team Trustworthiness: It's all about Social Ties', *Knowledge Management Research & Practice*, forthcoming.
47 R. G. LeFauve and A. C. Hax, 'Managerial and Technological Innovations at Saturn Corporation', *MIT Management*, Spring 1992, 8–19.
48 B. W. Tuckman, 'Developmental Sequences in Small Groups', *Psychological Bulletin* 63 (1965), 384–99; B. W. Tuckman and M. C. Jensen, 'Stages of Small Group Development', *Group and Organizational Studies* 2 (1977), 419–27.
49 C. J. G. Gersick, 'Time and Transition in Work Teams: Toward a New Model of Group Development', *Academy of Management Journal* 31 (1988), 9–41; C. J. G. Gersick, 'Marking Time: Predictable Transitions in Task Groups', *Academy of Management Journal* 32 (1989), 274–309.
50 J. R. Hackman, 'Group Influences on Individuals in Organizations', in M. D. Dunnette and L. M. Hough, eds., *Handbook of Industrial and Organizational Psychology* 3, 2nd ed., (Palo Alto, CA: Consulting Psychologists Press, 1992), 199–267.
51 *Ibid.*
52 *Ibid.*
53 Lublin, 'My Colleague, My Boss'.
54 T. Kelley and J. Littman, *The Art of Innovation* (New York: Doubleday, 2001).
55 B. Nussbaum, 'The Power of Design', *BusinessWeek*, May 17, 2004, 86–94.
56 *Ibid.*
57 *Ibid.*
58 Kelley and Littman, *The Art of Innovation.*
59 *Ibid.*; www.ideo.com; '1999 Idea Winners', *BusinessWeek*, June 7, 1999.
60 Nussbaum, 'The Power of Design'.
61 L. Festinger, 'Informal Social Communication', *Psychological Review* 57 (1950), 271–82; Shaw, *Group Dynamics.*
62 Hackman, 'Group Influences on Individuals in Organizations'; Shaw, *Group Dynamics.*
63 D. Cartwright, 'The Nature of Group Cohesiveness', in D. Cartwright and A. Zander, eds., *Group Dynamics*, 3rd ed. (New York: Harper & Row, 1968); L. Festinger, S. Schacter and K. Black, *Social Pressures in Informal Groups* (New York: Harper & Row, 1950); Shaw, *Group Dynamics.*
64 www.mybusiness.co.uk; www.innocentdrinks.co.uk.
65 www.virgin-atlantic.com.
66 Lublin, 'My Colleague, My Boss'.
67 Kelley and Littman, 'The Art of Innovation', p. 93
68 Kelley and Littman, 'The Art of Innovation'.
69 P. C. Earley, 'Social Loafing and Collectivism: A Comparison of the United States and the People's Republic of China', *Administrative Science Quarterly* 34 (1989), 565–81; J. M. George, 'Extrinsic and Intrinsic Origins of Perceived Social Loafing in Organizations', *Academy of Management Journal* 35

(1992), 191–202; S. G. Harkins, B. Latane and K. Williams, 'Social Loafing: Allocating Effort or Taking It Easy', *Journal of Experimental Social Psychology* 16 (1980), 457–65; B. Latane, K. D. Williams and S. Harkins, 'Many Hands Make Light the Work: The Causes and Consequences of Social Loafing', *Journal of Personality and Social Psychology* 37 (1979), 822–32; J. A. Shepperd, 'Productivity Loss in Performance Groups: A Motivation Analysis', *Psychological Bulletin* 113 (1993), 67–81.

70 George, 'Extrinsic and Intrinsic Origins'; G. R. Jones, 'Task Visibility, Free Riding, and Shirking: Explaining the Effect of Structure and Technology on Employee Behaviour', *Academy of Management Review* 9 (1984), 684–95; K. Williams, S. Harkins and B. Latane, 'Identifiability as a Deterrent to Social Loafing: Two Cheering Experiments', *Journal of Personality and Social Psychology* 40 (1981), 303–11.

71 S. Harkins and J. Jackson, 'The Role of Evaluation in Eliminating Social Loafing', *Personality and Social Psychology Bulletin* 11 (1985), 457–65; N. L. Kerr and S. E. Bruun, 'Ringelman Revisited: Alternative Explanations for the Social Loafing Effect', *Personality and Social Psychology Bulletin* 7 (1981), 224–31; Williams *et al.*, 'Identifiability as a Deterrent to Social Loafing'; Harkins and Jackson, 'The Role of Evaluation in Eliminating Social Loafing'; Kerr and Bruun, 'Ringelman Revisited'.

72 M. A. Brickner, S. G. Harkins and T. M. Ostrom, 'Effects of Personal Involvement: Thought-Provoking Implications for Social Loafing', *Journal of Personality and Social Psychology* 51 (1986), 763–69; S. G. Harkins and R. E. Petty, 'The Effects of Task Difficulty and Task Uniqueness on Social Loafing', *Journal of Personality and Social Psychology* 43 (1982), 1214–29.

73 B. Latane, 'Responsibility and Effort in Organizations', in P. S. Goodman, ed., *Designing Effective Work Groups* (San Franciso: Jossey-Bass, 1986); Latane *et al.*, 'Many Hands Make Light the Work'; I. D. Steiner, *Group Process and Productivity* (New York: Academic Press, 1972).

Chapter 1

Managers and Managing

LEARNING OBJECTIVES

After studying this chapter, you should be able to:

- ☑ Describe what management is, why management is important, what managers do, and how managers utilise organisational resources efficiently and effectively to achieve organisational goals.
- ☑ Distinguish among planning, organising, leading and controlling (the four principal managerial functions), and explain how managers' ability to handle each one can affect organisational performance.
- ☑ Differentiate among levels of management, and understand the responsibilities of managers at different levels in the organisational hierarchy.
- ☑ Identify the roles managers perform, the skills they need to execute those roles effectively, and the way new information technology is affecting these roles and skills.
- ☑ Discuss the principal challenges managers face in today's increasingly competitive global environment.

A Manager's Challenge

The Rise of Siemens

Werner von Siemens was born in Germany in a small town near Hannover in December 1816. No one could then know that the fourth child of a poor farmer's family would become the founder of one of the world's best-known companies.

While showing ample potential in science and engineering, Werner was denied a university education due to the financial constraints of his family. He thus chose the security of the Army as a profession. It was quickly noticed that he was inventive and apt at engineering problems and this aptitude also translated into business acumen. During his time in the army, Werner and his brother registered their first patent and sold the rights to it – leaving them financially comfortable and allowing Werner to research further into his main interest – telegraphy. This field was at the time relatively underdeveloped, but Werner showed truly managerial foresight in predicting it to be the 'technology of the future'. Through developing a superior product, Werner finally opened his first business with a skilled mechanical engineer, Johann Georg Halske, in Berlin in 1847.

The success of this company was rapid and Werner soon had to dedicate his entire time to the business. Werner realised that the technology that Telegraphen-Bau-Anstalt Siemens & Halske was providing would predominantly be bought by governments and large corporations. Thus, in order to advance the company, Werner internationalised and opened the first two offices outside Prussia (then a distinct part of the German empire), showing entrepreneurial spirit ahead of his time. The first international office opened was in London in 1850 with a second office in St Petersburg in 1855 and a third in Austria three years later. To maintain close control over the foreign subsidiaries, Werner's brothers managed the branches in London and St Petersburg. Within 10 years of operating, Siemens had already become a truly global company due to Werner's instinct and managerial abilities to spot developing and new markets.

Werner continued his innovation and astute management of the business. His biggest success was the invention of the dynamo-machine, with which he coined the term 'electrical engineering'.

However, it was not just Werner's innovations or his entrepreneurial spirit that made the company what it is today. Werner was a manager who cared for his employees, noticing that 'the firm could only be made to develop satisfactorily if one could further its interest by ensuring that all employees work together in a cheerful and efficient manner'. Werner negotiated social benefits that were ahead of their time. Siemens & Halske had a company pension scheme by 1872, a 9-hour working day (the norm was 10–12 for labour) and a profit-sharing scheme called 'stocktaking bonus' which was launched in 1866.

After Werner's retirement the company re-formed as a stock corporation in 1897 and developed to be one of the largest international companies by 1914, with 10 foreign subsidiaries and branch offices in another 49 countries.

The astute management of the company was taken forward by Werner's descendents, who managed the firm through rising competition and two world wars. It was Werner's third son, Carl Friedrich, who continued in his father's tradition of being ahead of his time in business. Carl started to rebuild the company after the First World War by concentrating and focusing the company direction based on its expertise and withdrawing from non-traditional areas of business. Carl was also responsible for various strategic alliances, mergers and acquisitions during his time at the helm. Siemens was the first company that ever posted sales figures in excess of 1 billion Marks. In the 1930s and 1940s Siemens was the largest electrical company in the world despite the Great Depression.

Due to its strong family values Siemens managed to survive the devastating Second World War in which nearly 80 per cent of its assets were lost and through some decisive management and its belief in people the company turned into the largest employer in Germany in the 1960s and 1970s.

Today Siemens operates in 190 countries, has nearly half a million employees and still believes that employees and innovation are its strongest assets. The success speaks for the effective management of the company, which had sales exceeding €75 billion and profits exceeding €2 billion in 2005.

Overview

The history of Siemens' ups and downs through competition, political instabilities and industrial volatilities illustrates many of the challenges facing people who become managers. Managing a large company is a complex activity, and effective managers must possess many skills, knowledge and abilities. Management is an unpredictable process. Making the right decision is difficult; even effective managers often make mistakes, but the most effective managers are the ones who learn from their mistakes and continually strive to find ways to help their companies increase their competitive advantage, improve performance and essentially survive in the volatile business environment.

This chapter looks at what managers do, and what skills and abilities they must develop if they are to manage their organisations successfully over time. It also identifies the different kinds of managers that organisations need, and the skills and abilities they must develop if they are to be successful. Finally, some of the challenges that managers must address if their organisations are to grow and prosper are addressed.

What Is Management?

When you think of a 'manager', what kind of person comes to mind? Do you see someone who, like Werner von Siemens, can determine the future prosperity of a large for-profit company? Or do you see the administrator of a not-for-profit organisation, such as a school, library or charity, or the person in charge of your local supermarket or McDonald's restaurant, or the person *you* answer to if you have a part-time job? What do all these managers have in common?

First, they all work in organisations. **Organisations** are collections of people who work together and co-ordinate their actions to achieve a wide variety of *goals*, or desired future outcomes.[1] Second, as managers, they are the people responsible for supervising the use of an organisation's social capital and other, more tangible, resources to achieve its goals. This use of resources needs to be co-ordinated over time. **Management**, then, is the planning, organising, leading and controlling of social capital and other resources to achieve organisational goals efficiently and effectively. An organisation's *resources* include assets such as people and their skills, know-how and knowledge; machinery; raw materials; computers and IT; and financial capital.

Achieving High Performance: A Manager's Goal

One of the most important goals that organisations and their members try to achieve is to provide some kind of product or service that *customers desire*. The principal goal of any **Chief Executive Officer (CEO)** is to manage an organisation so that a new stream of products and services are created that customers are willing to buy. For Werner von Siemens, these were generators, and for Siemens now it is medical devices, for example. The principal goal of doctors, nurses and hospital administrators is to increase their hospital's ability to make sick people well. Likewise, the principal goal of each McDonald's restaurant manager is to produce burgers, fries and shakes that people want to pay for and eat. All these activities have to be undertaken within set standards, rules, regulations and codes of practice. The achievements of such organisational goals and functions is called **organisational performance**.

EFFICIENCY

EFFECTIVENESS	LOW	HIGH
HIGH	Low efficiency/ High effectiveness Manager chooses the right goals to pursue, but does a poor job of using resources to achieve these goals Result: A product that customers want, but that is too expensive for them to buy	High efficiency/ High effectiveness Manager chooses the right goals to pursue and makes good use of resources to achieve these goals Result: A product that customers want at a quality and price that they can afford
LOW	Low efficiency/ Low effectiveness Manager chooses wrong goals to pursue and makes poor use of resources Result: A low-quality product that customers do not want	High efficiency/ Low effectiveness Manager chooses inappropriate goals, but makes good use of resources to pursue these goals Result: A high-quality product that customers do not want

High-performing organisations are efficient *and* effective.

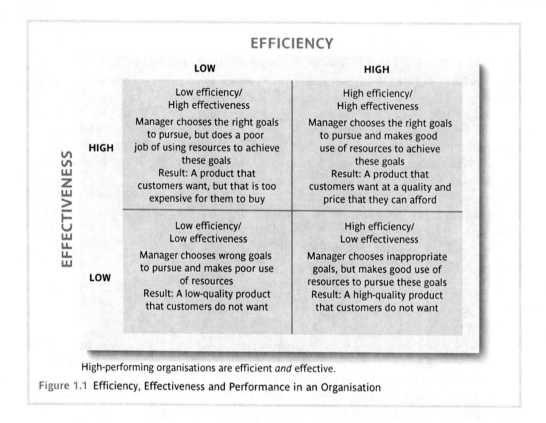

Figure 1.1 Efficiency, Effectiveness and Performance in an Organisation

Organisational performance is a measure of how efficiently and effectively managers use resources to *satisfy customers* and *achieve organisational goals.* Organisational performance increases in direct proportion to increases in efficiency and effectiveness (Fig. 1.1).

Efficiency is a measure of how well or how productively resources are used to *achieve a goal.*[2] Organisations are efficient when managers minimise the amount of input resources (such as labour, raw materials and component parts) or the amount of time needed to produce a given output of products or services. For example, McDonald's developed a more efficient deep fryer that not only reduced the amount of oil used in cooking by 30 per cent but also speeded up the cooking of French fries. Werner von Siemens invented the first dynamo that allowed the cheaper production of electricity. A manager's responsibility is to ensure that an organisation and its members perform as efficiently – i.e. with as few resources as possible – all the activities needed to provide goods and services to customers.

Effectiveness is a measure of the *appropriateness* of the goals that managers have selected for the organisation to pursue, and of the degree to which the organisation achieves those goals. Organisations are effective when managers choose appropriate goals and then achieve them. Some years ago, for example, managers at McDonald's decided on the goal of providing breakfast service to attract more customers. The choice of this goal has proved very smart, for sales of breakfast food now account for more than 30 per cent of McDonald's revenues. High-performing organisations, such as Siemens, McDonald's, ASDA, Intel, IKEA and Accenture, are simultaneously efficient and effective, as shown in Fig. 1.1. Effective managers are those who choose the right organisational goals to pursue, and have the skills to utilise resources efficiently.

Why Study Management?

Today, more and more students than ever before are enrolling for places in business courses. The number of people wishing to pursue Master of Business Administration (MBA) degrees – today's passport to an advanced management position – either on campus or from online universities, is at an all-time high. Student numbers are also increasing at an undergraduate level – including a growing demand for business courses. Why is the study of management currently so popular?[3]

First, *resources* in the twenty-first century are *valuable* and *scarce*, so the more efficient and effective use that organisations can make of them, the greater the benefit for all. In addition, the efficient and effective use of resources has a direct impact on the socio-economic situation and prosperity of people in society. Because managers are the people who decide how to use many of a society's resources – its skilled employees, raw materials like oil and land, computers and information systems and financial assets – their decisions directly impact the socio-economic situation of a society and the people in it. Understanding what managers do, and how they do it, is of central importance to understanding how a society works, and how it creates prosperity.

Second, although most people are not managers, and many may never intend to become managers, almost all of us encounter managers because most people have jobs and bosses. Moreover, many people today are working in groups and teams and have to deal with co-workers. Studying management helps people to understand how to deal with their bosses and their co-workers: it reveals how other people *behave* and *make decisions at work* that enable organisations to work in harmony and drive forward the achievement of organisational goals. Management also teaches people not yet in positions of authority how to lead co-workers, solve conflicts between them and increase team performance.

Third, in today's society people often feel that they are in competition for a well-paying job and an interesting and satisfying career in a volatile labour market. Understanding management is one important path towards obtaining such a position. Complexity and increasing responsibility often provide more stimulating and interesting jobs; any person who desires a motivating job that changes over time might therefore do well to develop management skills and become promotable. A person who has been working for several years and then returns to university for an MBA can usually, after earning the degree, significantly enhance their career prospects.

Indeed, once one reaches the top echelons within an organisation, rewards can be immense. The CEOs and other top executives or managers of companies, for example, receive millions in salary, bonuses and share options each year.[4] What is it that managers actually do to receive such rewards?[5]

Managerial Functions

The job of management is to help an organisation make the best use of its resources to achieve its goals. How do managers accomplish this objective? They do so by performing four essential managerial functions: **planning**, **organising**, **leading** and **controlling** (Fig. 1.2). The arrows linking these functions in Fig. 1.2 suggest the sequence in which managers typically perform these functions. The French manager Henri Fayol first outlined the nature of these managerial activities around the turn of the twentieth century in *General and Industrial Management*, a book that remains the classic statement of what managers must do to create a high-performing organisation.[6]

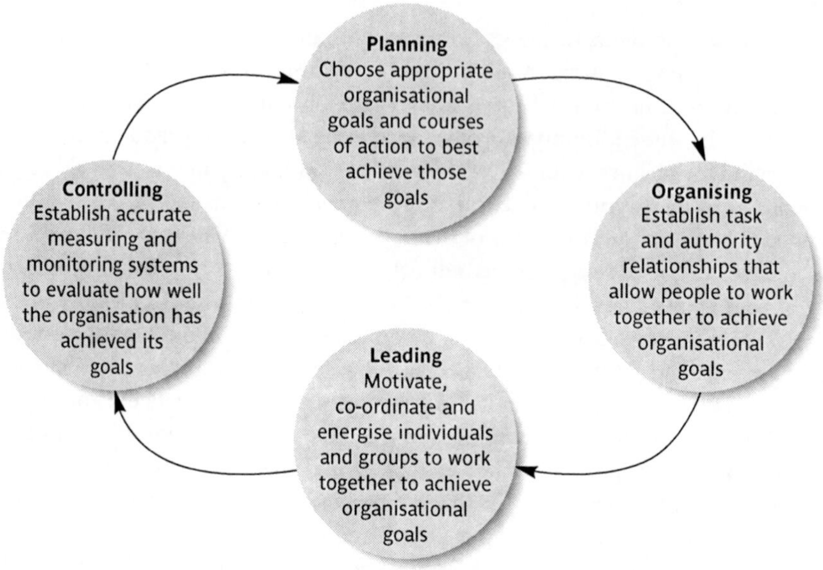

Figure 1.2 Four Functions of Management

Managers at all levels and in all departments – whether in small or large organisations, for-profit or not-for-profit organisations, or organisations that operate in one country or throughout the world – are responsible for performing these four functions, which we look at next. How well managers perform these functions determines how *efficient* and *effective* their organisations are.

Planning

Planning is a process that managers use to identify and select *appropriate goals and courses of action*. The three steps in the planning process are (1) deciding which goals the organisation will pursue, (2) deciding what actions to adopt to attain these goals and (3) deciding how to allocate organisational resources to accomplish them. The performance level is determined by how effective managers are at planning.[7]

As an example of planning in action, consider the situation confronting Michael Dell, CEO of Dell Computer, the very profitable PC maker.[8] In 1984, the 19-year-old Dell saw an opportunity to enter the PC market by assembling PCs and then selling them directly to customers. Dell began to plan how to put his idea into practice. First, he decided that his goal was to sell an inexpensive PC, to undercut the prices of companies such as Compaq. Second, he had to decide on a course of action to achieve this goal. He decided to sell directly to customers by telephone and to bypass expensive computer stores that sold Compaq or Apple PCs. He also had to decide how to obtain low-cost components and how to tell potential customers about his products. Third, he had to decide how to allocate his limited funds (he had only £2,750) to buy labour and other resources. He chose to hire three people and work with them around a table to assemble his PCs.

To put his vision of making and selling PCs into practice, Dell had to *plan*. Despite organisational growth or complexity (both of which Dell experienced), the process of planning remains a constant. This does not mean that plans themselves are not subject to change, as change is a part of any organisation. Dell and his managers continually plan how to maintain its position as the biggest and highest-performing PC maker that sells predominantly online and through the telephone. In 2003, Dell announced it would begin to sell printers and personal digital assistants (PDAs); this brought it into direct competition with Hewlett-Packard (HP), the leading printer maker, and Palm One, the maker of the Palm Pilot. In the same year, Dell also brought out its own Internet music player, the Digital Jukebox, to compete against Apple's iPod, and in 2004 it reduced the price of its player to compete more effectively against Apple. In April 2004, Dell's player was selling at a significantly lower price than Apple's, and analysts were wondering what effect this would have on iPod sales and Apple's future performance.

Such continuous and stringent planning results in a **strategy**: a cluster of decisions concerning what organisational goals to pursue, what actions to take and how to use resources to achieve goals. The decisions that were the outcome of Michael Dell's planning formed a *low-cost strategy*. A low-cost strategy is a way of obtaining customers' loyalty by making decisions that allow the organisation to make its products or services cheaper than its competitors so that prices can be kept low. Dell has constantly refined this strategy and explored new ways to reduce costs. Dell has become the most profitable PC maker as a result of its low-cost strategy, and it is hoping to repeat its success in the music player business. By contrast, Apple's strategy has been to deliver new, exciting and different computer and digital products, such as the iPod, to its customers – a strategy known as **differentiation**. The mini iPod was developed for people on the go, for example; it is as small as a (thick) credit card, has unique, easy-to-use controls and comes in a variety of bright contemporary colours.[9]

Planning is a difficult activity because normally the goals that an organisation should pursue and how best to pursue them – which strategies to adopt – are not immediately clear. Managers take risks when they commit organisational resources to pursue a particular strategy: both success or failure are possible outcomes of the planning process. Dell succeeded spectacularly, but many other PC makers either went out of business (such as Packard Bell and Digital) or lost huge sums of money (like IBM) trying to compete in this industry. In Chapter 8 we focus on the planning process and the strategies organisations can select, and also how these strategies can help organisations to respond to the opportunities or threats in an industry. The story of Rolf Eriksen (Case 1.1) highlights how planning and strategising can lead a company forward.

Case 1.1: New CEO brings change at H&M

One global company that required new and innovative thinking to take it forward was Swedish clothing retailer H&M. Hennes & Mauritz, as it was known when it was established in 1947 by Erling Persson, has moved from being a solely Nordic player to a global fashion retailer. This was achieved mainly through the appointment of the Dane Rolf Eriksen as CEO in 2000. Prior to this role, Eriksen had been responsible for the Danish and Swedish operation of H&M. Within his first year of being CEO he managed to increase net income by 49.5 per cent, to £211.3 million; sales rose by 29 per cent, to £2.61 billion. In the first quarter of 2002, earnings rose by 33 per cent. By 2005 it was argued that H&M had benefited from a constant growth of 21 per cent per ▶

year over the previous decade, and it was expected that sales figures would exceed £4.4 billion in 2006. H&M has now 1,200 stores in more than 20 countries, and by 2007 Eriksen expects to manage another 100 stores worldwide.

Achieving such a successful growth was a result of Eriksen's management of the company: he has shown that he can respond to opportunities. H&M was the pioneer of affordable, fashionable clothing. The company's strength under Eriksen is to quickly translate current trends into products for the masses, aided by the CEO's realisation that 'The world is becoming smaller and smaller, especially for the young customers'. Eriksen has been able to slash costs, streamline distribution and broaden H&M's lines by assuming a similar taste in fashion around the world, whether be it New York, Paris, Stockholm or Berlin. With his vision, he has been able to position H&M as a growing rival of well-established brands such as GAP or Benetton. Eriksen has been successful in realigning H&M's target group to middle-class customers, away from a 'cheap and cheerful' image towards affordable clothing that can be changed according to trends in fashion.

One of Eriksen's most successful ventures in driving forward H&M as a leading fashion retailer was the commissioning of one-off clothing lines with Chanel designer Karl Lagerfeld in 2004. The collection sold out within three days of the launch and stores reported a 12 per cent increase in sales in that month. Such a special edition was repeated, with a one-off 40-piece line from Stella McCartney, a member of the Gucci fashion group. H&M is hoping to appeal to fashion-conscious people who cannot afford the signature line: a stroke of genius in exploiting the current climate for branded fashion.

Eriksen has the ability to see potential growth, such as Eastern European and Asian markets, or collaborations with upmarket designers – a vision that has made H&M the global company it is today. For Eriksen as CEO, planning and organising are vital functions that must be continuously worked on by managers at all levels of the company.

Organising

Organising is a process that managers use to establish a *structure of working relationships* that allow organisational members to interact and co-operate to achieve organisational goals. Organising involves grouping people into departments according to the kinds of job-specific tasks they perform. In organising, managers also lay out the *lines of authority* and *responsibility* between different individuals and groups, and decide how best to co-ordinate organisational resources, particularly human resources.

The outcome of organising is the creation of an **organisational structure**, a formal system of task and reporting relationships that co-ordinates and motivates members so that they work together to achieve organisational goals. Organisational structure determines how an organisation's resources can be best used to create products and services. As Siemens grew, for example, Werner von Siemens faced the issue of how to structure the organisation. Early on, Siemens was hiring new employees at a staggering rate, and deciding how to design the **managerial hierarchy** (the structure of the reporting relationships) to best motivate and co-ordinate managers' activities was important. As Siemens grew and internationalised, more complex kinds of organisational structures needed to be created to achieve its goals. The aspects that influence organisational structure and the process of organising this structure will be examined in more detail in Chapters 9–11.

Leading

The concept of leadership is both a complex and interdependent process involving leaders and followers in a *reciprocal relationship*. The various theoretical frameworks and concepts available to explain this phenomenon are examined in more detail in Chapter 14. However as leadership is one of the four principal functions of management, it is briefly described here within the context of performing these functions. A key facet of leadership is to articulate a *clear vision* for organisational members to follow. This should enable organisational members to understand the role they play in achieving organisational goals. Leadership can depend on the use of power, influence, vision, persuasion and communication skills to co-ordinate the behaviours of individuals and groups so that their activities and efforts are in harmony. The ideal outcome of good leadership is a high level of motivation and commitment among organisational members. Employees at Dell Computer, for examples, responded well to Michael Dell's 'hands-on' leadership style, which resulted in a hardworking, committed workforce.

Controlling

In controlling, managers evaluate how well an organisation is *achieving* its goals, and take action to maintain or improve performance. Managers monitor the performance of individuals, departments and the organisation as a whole, for example, to see whether they are meeting desired performance standards. If standards are not being met, managers must take action to improve performance.

The outcome of the control process is the ability to measure performance accurately and regulate organisational efficiency and effectiveness. To exercise control, managers must decide *which goals to measure* – perhaps goals pertaining to productivity, quality, or responsiveness to customers – and then they must design *information and control systems* that will provide the data they need to assess performance. The controlling function also allows managers to evaluate how well they themselves are performing the other three functions of management – planning, organising and leading – and to take corrective action where necessary. This relies on organisational feedback mechanisms.

Michael Dell had difficulty establishing effective control systems because his company was growing so rapidly and he lacked experienced managers. In 1988 Dell's costs soared because no controls were in place to monitor inventory, which had built up rapidly. In 1993 financial problems arose because of ill-advised foreign currency transactions. In 1994 Dell's new line of laptop computers crashed because poor quality control resulted in defective products, some of which caught fire. To solve these and other control problems, Dell hired experienced managers to put the correct control systems in place. As a result, by 1998 Dell was able to make computers for about 10 per cent less than its competitors, creating a major source of competitive advantage. By 2001 Dell had become so efficient it was driving its competitors out of the market because it had realised a 15–20 per cent cost advantage over them.[10] By 2003 it was the biggest PC maker in the world. Controlling, like the other managerial functions, is an ongoing, dynamic, ever-changing process that demands constant attention and action. Because controlling is a function essential to organisational survival, the influence and impact of this function on all aspects of organisational behaviour will be revisited throughout the text.

The four managerial functions – planning, organising, leading and controlling – are all essential to a manager's job. At all levels in a managerial hierarchy, and across all departments in an organisation, effective management means making decisions and managing these four activities successfully.

Types of Managers

To perform efficiently and effectively, organisations employ different types of managers – for example, first-line managers, middle managers and senior managers, who are arranged in a hierarchy (Fig. 1.3). Typically, first-line managers report to middle managers and middle managers report to senior managers. Managers at each level have different but related responsibilities for utilising organisational resources to increase efficiency and effectiveness. Within each department, various levels of management may exist that reflect this particular categorisation and organisational hierarchy. A department, such as manufacturing, accounting or engineering, is a group of people who work together and may possess similar skills or use the same kind of knowledge, tools or techniques to perform one function that helps to achieve the overall organisational goal. The chapter next examines the reasons why organisations use a hierarchy of managers and group them into departments. We then examine some recent changes taking place in managerial hierarchies.

Levels of Management

As just discussed, organisations normally have various levels of management. Figure 1.3 is one possible example.

First-line managers

At the base of the managerial hierarchy are first-line managers, often called *supervisors*. They are responsible for the *daily supervision* of the non-managerial employees who perform many of the

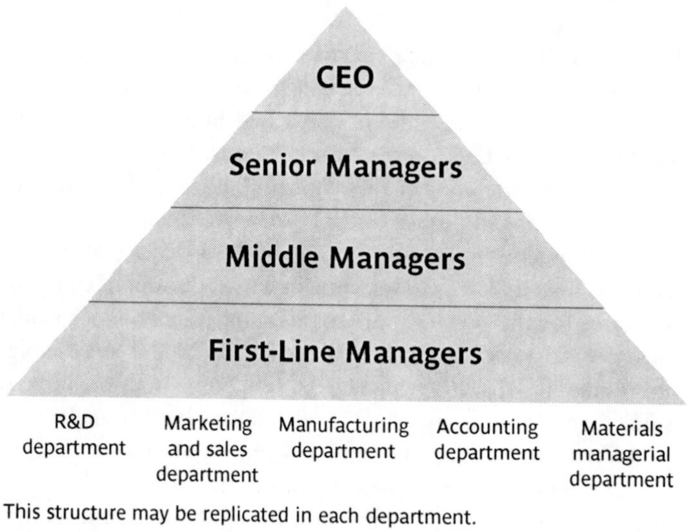

Figure 1.3 Types of Managers

specific (primary) activities necessary to produce goods and services. First-line managers work in all departments or functions of an organisation.

Examples of first-line managers include the supervisor of a work team in the manufacturing department of a car plant, the ward sister in an obstetrics ward of a hospital, or the foreman overseeing a crew of labourers on a construction site. At Dell Computer, first-line managers include the supervisors responsible for controlling the quality of Dell computers or the level of customer service provided by Dell's telephone salespeople. When Michael Dell started his company, he personally controlled the computer assembly process and thus performed as a first-line manager or supervisor.

Middle managers

Middle managers are responsible for finding the best way to *organise human and other resources* to achieve organisational goals. To increase efficiency, middle managers find ways to help subordinates better to utilise resources to reduce manufacturing costs or improve customer service. To increase effectiveness, middle managers evaluate whether the goals that the organisation is pursuing are appropriate and suggest to senior managers ways in which goals should be changed. Very often, the suggestions that middle managers make to senior managers can dramatically increase organisational performance. A major part of the middle manager's job is developing and fine-tuning *skills* and *know-how*, such as manufacturing or marketing expertise, that allow the organisation to be efficient and effective. Middle managers make thousands of specific decisions about the production of goods and services. Some of the decisions a middle-manager may face are:

- Which supervisor should be chosen for a particular project?
- Where can we find the highest-quality resources?
- How should employees be organised to allow them to make the best use of resources?

Behind any successful and committed team, department or individual employee, there will usually be a first-class middle manager, who is able to motivate, lead and reward staff to find ways to obtain the resources they need to do outstanding and innovative jobs in the workplace.

Senior managers

In contrast to middle managers, senior managers are responsible for the performance of *all* departments:[11] they have *cross-departmental responsibility*. Senior managers establish organisational goals, such as which products and services the company should produce; they decide how the different departments should interact; and they monitor how well middle managers in each department utilise resources to achieve goals.[12] Senior managers are ultimately responsible for the success or failure of an organisation, and their performance (like Werner von Siemens or Rolf Eriksen of H&M) is continually scrutinised by people inside and outside the organisation, such as other employees and investors.[13]

The *CEO* is a company's most senior manager, the one to whom all other senior managers report. Together, the CEO and the chief operating officer (COO) – also called Managing Director (MD) – are responsible for developing good working relationships among the senior managers of various departments (for example, manufacturing and marketing). A central concern of the CEO is the creation of a smoothly functioning senior-management team, a group composed of the CEO, the COO/MD and the department heads of an organisation to help to achieve organisational goals.[14]

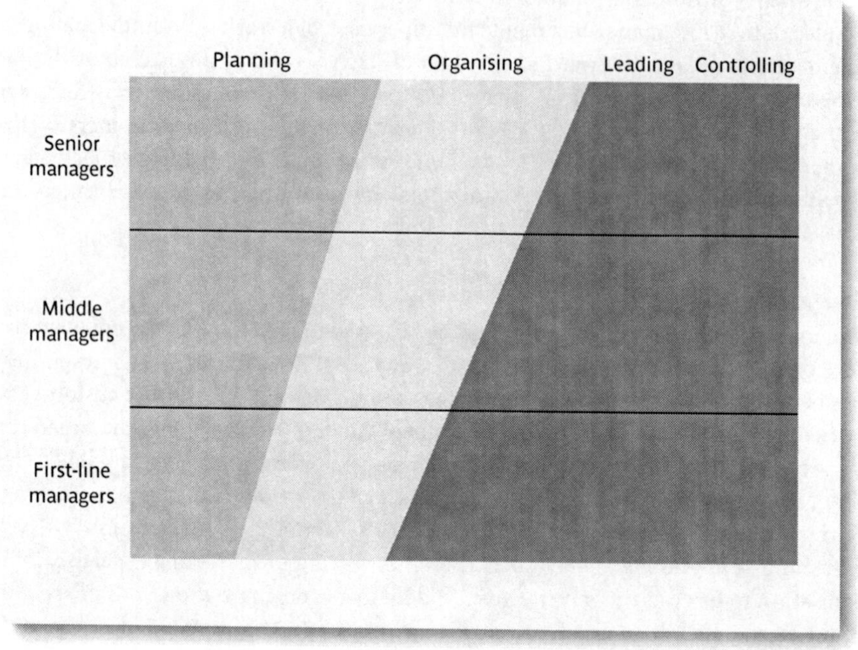

Figure 1.4 Relative Amount of Time That Managers Spend on the Four Managerial Functions

The relative importance of planning, organising, leading and controlling – the four managerial functions – to any particular manager depends on their position in the managerial hierarchy.[15] The amount of time that managers spend planning and organising the resources to maintain and improve organisational performance increases as they ascend the hierarchy (Fig. 1.4).[16] Senior managers usually devote most of their time to planning and organising, the functions so crucial to determining an organisation's long-term performance. The lower that managers' positions are in the hierarchy, the more time the managers tend to spend leading and controlling first-line managers or non-managerial employees.

The Managerial Hierarchy

Because so much of a manager's responsibility is to acquire and develop critical resources, managers are typically members of specific departments.[17] Managers inside a department possess job-specific skills and are known, for example, as marketing managers or manufacturing managers. As Fig. 1.3 indicates, first-line, middle and senior managers, who differ from one another by virtue of their job-specific responsibilities, are found in each of an organisation's major departments. Inside each department, a *managerial hierarchy* thus emerges.

At Dell Computer, for example, Michael Dell hired experts to take charge of the marketing, sales and manufacturing departments and to develop work procedures to help first-line managers control the company's explosive sales growth. The head of manufacturing quickly found that he had no time to supervise computer assembly, so he recruited manufacturing middle managers from other companies to assume this responsibility.

Reaction Time

1. Describe the difference between efficiency and effectiveness, and identify any real organisations that you think are, or are not, efficient and effective.
2. Identify an organisation that you believe is high-performing and one that you believe is low-performing. Give five reasons why you think the performance levels of the two organisations differ so much.
3. Try to identify the managerial hierarchy of your university department.

Recent Changes in Managerial Hierarchies

The tasks and responsibilities of managers at different levels have been changing dramatically in recent years. Three major factors that have led to these changes are global competition and advances in new IT and in e-commerce. Intense competition for resources from organisations, both nationally and internationally, has put increased pressure on all managers to improve efficiency, effectiveness and organisational performance. Increasingly, senior managers are encouraging lower-level managers to look beyond the goals of their own departments and take a *cross-departmental view* to find new opportunities to improve organisational performance. New ITs give managers at all levels access to more and better information and improve their ability to plan, organise, lead and control; this has also revolutionised the way the managerial hierarchy works.[18]

Restructuring and Outsourcing

To take advantage of IT and e-commerce and their ability to reduce operating costs, CEOs and senior management teams have been restructuring organisations and outsourcing specific organisational activities to reduce the number of employees on the payroll.

Restructuring

Restructuring involves the use of IT to *downsize* an organisation or *shrink its operations* by eliminating the jobs of large numbers of top, middle or first-line managers and non-managerial employees. In some industries, for example car manufacturing, IT allows fewer employees to perform a given task because it increases each person's ability to process information and make decisions more quickly and accurately. UK overall investment into information and communication technology (ICT) has increased by 133 per cent since 1992, to £25.7 billion in 2001.[19] In the US, companies are spending over £27.3 billion a year on advanced IT, and it is likely that a large part of this investment has been made to improve efficiency and effectiveness. Some of the effects of IT on management are discussed in Chapter 18.

Restructuring, however, can produce some powerful *negative outcomes*. IT can reduce the morale of the remaining employees, who are worried about their own job security, and senior managers of many downsized organisations can come to realise that they have downsized too far, because employees complain they are overworked and because more customers complain about poor-quality service.[20] Some more recent restructuring initiatives – for example in the National Health Service (NHS) in the UK – are about creating more effective and efficient job descriptions to streamline the delivery of a service. The Department of Health (DoH) in England has created new levels of qualifications, such as associate practitioner roles, to restructure its service delivery.[21]

Outsourcing

Outsourcing involves contracting with another company, usually in a low-cost country abroad, so that it can perform an activity – such as manufacturing or marketing – the organisation previously performed itself. Outsourcing promotes efficiency by reducing costs and by allowing an organisation to make better use of its remaining resources. The need to respond to low-cost global competition has speeded up outsourcing dramatically since 2000: 3 million US jobs in the manufacturing sector have been lost as companies moved their operations to countries such as China, Taiwan and Malaysia. Tens of thousands of high-paying jobs in IT have moved to countries such as India and Russia, where programmers work for one-third the salary of those in the US. In the UK, an ongoing decline in manufacturing industry has seen a decrease in manufacturing jobs of nearly 4 per cent per annum since 2000, which is more than double the EU–25 average. This means that manufacturing jobs now account for approximately 14.9 per cent of employment in the UK:[22] in 2004 approximately 3.5 million people were employed in manufacturing compared to over 7 million in the late 1970s.[23] While some of this decline may be due to natural wastage, the majority can be assigned to the move away from expensive western European labour to workers in cheaper countries.

Large for-profit organisations today typically employ 10–20 per cent fewer employees than they did 10 years ago because of restructuring and outsourcing. Siemens, IBM, HP, Dell and Du Pont are among the thousands of organisations that have streamlined their operations to increase efficiency and effectiveness. The argument is that the managers and employees who have lost their jobs will find employment in new and growing organisations where their skills and experience will be better utilised. The millions of manufacturing jobs that have been lost overseas are expected to be replaced by higher-paying jobs in the service sector that are made possible because of the growth in global trade. However, the downside of outsourcing and reengineering is an *overreliance on technology*. This can prove to be detrimental to organisational performance, especially in light of the emerging discipline of knowledge management (KM) where loss of staff may also mean *loss of expertise* and *performance-enhancing knowledge*. The issues surrounding the retaining of knowledge and information will be further examined in Chapter 18.

Empowerment and Self-managed Teams

Another major change in management has taken place at the level of first-line managers, who typically supervise the employees engaged in producing goods and services. Many companies have taken two key steps to reduce costs and improve quality. One is the empowerment of their workforces to expand employees' knowledge, tasks and responsibilities. The other is the creation of self-managed teams – groups of employees given responsibility for supervising their own activities and for monitoring the quality of the goods and services they provide.[24] Members of self-managed teams assume many of the responsibilities and duties previously performed by first-line managers.[25]

What is the role of the first-line manager in this new work context? First-line managers act as *coaches* or *mentors* whose job is not to tell employees what to do but to provide advice and guidance and help teams find new ways to perform their tasks more efficiently.[26] Both self-managed teams and empowerment are concepts that will be discussed as part of the leadership debate and effective team working in Chapters 14 and 15.

TIPS FOR PRACTICE

1. Think about how customers perceive the products and services that your organisation offers, if these adequately meet their needs and how they might be improved.
2. Explore whether your organisation can be better at obtaining or using resources to increase efficiency and effectiveness.
3. Think about how the skills and know-how of departments is helping your organisation to achieve its competitive advantage. Take steps to improve these skills whenever possible.

IT and Managerial Roles and Skills

A **managerial role** is a set of specific tasks that a manager is expected to perform because of the position he or she holds in an organisation. One well-known model of managerial roles was developed by Henry Mintzberg, who detailed 10 specific roles that effective managers undertake. Although Mintzberg's roles overlap with Fayol's model (p. 41) they are useful because they focus on what managers do in a typical hour, day or week in an organisation as they go about the job of managing.[27] We now discuss these roles and the skills managers need to develop to perform effectively.

Managerial Roles Identified by Mintzberg

Henry Mintzberg developed a model of managerial behaviours that reduces the thousands of specific tasks that managers need to perform as they plan, organise, lead and control organisational resources to 10 roles.[28] Managers assume each of these roles to influence the behaviour of individuals and groups inside and outside the organisation. The people who are directly or indirectly affected by what the organisation does are called *organisational stakeholders*, and they can be identified as internal or external. People inside the organisation (internal stakeholders) include other managers and employees. People outside the organisation (external stakeholders) can include shareholders, customers, suppliers, the local community in which an organisation is located and any local or government agency that has an interest in the organisation and what it does.[29] Mintzberg grouped the 10 roles into three broad categories: *decisional*, *informational* and *interpersonal*, as described in Table 1.1. Managers often perform many of these roles from minute to minute while engaged in the more general functions of planning, organising, leading and controlling.

Decisional roles

Decisional roles are closely associated with the methods managers use to *plan strategy and utilise resources*. The role of the **entrepreneur** is to provide more and better information to use in deciding which projects or programmes to initiate and resources to invest to increase organisational performance. As a *disturbance handler*, a manager has to move quickly to manage the unexpected event or crisis that may threaten the organisation and to implement solutions quickly. As a *resource allocator*, a manager has to decide how best to use people and other resources to increase organisational performance. While engaged in that role, the manager must also be a *negotiator*, reaching agreements with other managers or groups or with the organisation and

Table 1.1 Managerial roles identified by Mintzberg

Type of role	Specific role	Examples of role activities
Decisional	**Entrepreneur**	Commit organisational resources to develop innovative goods and services; decide to expand internationally to obtain new customers for the organisation's products
	Disturbance handler	Move quickly to take corrective action to deal with unexpected problems facing the organisation from the external environment (such as a crisis like an oil spill), or from the internal environment (such as producing faulty goods or services)
	Resource allocator	Allocate organisational resources among different functions and departments of the organisation; set budgets and salaries of middle and first-level managers
	Negotiator	Work with suppliers, distributors and labour unions to reach agreements about the quality and price of input, technical and human resources; work with other organisations to establish agreements to pool resources to work on joint projects
Informational	**Monitor**	Evaluate the performance of managers in different functions and take corrective action to improve their performance; watch for changes occurring in the external and internal environments that may affect the organisation in the future
	Disseminator	Inform employees about changes taking place in the external and internal environments that will affect them and the organisation; communicate the organisation's vision and purpose to employees
	Spokesperson	Launch a national advertising campaign to promote new goods and services; give a speech to inform the local community about the organisation's future intentions
Interpersonal	**Figurehead**	Outline future organisational goals to employees at company meetings; open a new corporate headquarters; state the organisational ethical guidelines and the principles of behaviour that employees should follow in their dealings with customers and suppliers
	Leader	Provide an example for employees to follow; give direct commands and orders to subordinates; make decisions concerning the use of human resource and technical resources; mobilise employee support for specific organisational goals
	Liaison	Co-ordinate the work of managers in different departments; establish alliances between different organisations to share resources to produce new goods and services

outside groups such as suppliers or customers. The advancement of IT may enable managers to perform these roles more efficiently and effectively.

Informational roles

Informational roles are closely associated with the tasks necessary to *obtain and seek information*, which is the monitor role. Acting as a *disseminator*, a manager should be able to transmit information to employees to influence their work attitudes and behaviour. As a *spokesperson* a manager should be able to promote the organisation so that people inside and outside it respond positively. While these roles may be influenced by IT, the function of those roles more specifically relates to the brokering of internal and external knowledge sources, and developments in IT may facilitate this process.

Interpersonal roles

Managers assume interpersonal roles to provide *direction and supervision* for both employees and the organisation as a whole. The role of a figurehead is to inform employees and other interested parties, such as shareholders, about what the organisation's mission is, and what it is seeking to achieve. At all levels managers can act as figureheads and role models who establish appropriate ways to behave in the organisation. In order to perform better as leaders, managers should focus on training, counselling and mentoring subordinates to help them reach their full potential. Finally, as a *liaison*, a manager should be able to show his or her ability to link and co-ordinate the activities of people and groups both inside and outside the organisation. As with the other roles, IT may prove to be a useful tool in facilitating these functions.

Being a Manager

Our discussion of managerial roles may seem to suggest that a manager's job is highly orchestrated and that management is a logical, orderly process in which managers rationally calculate the best way to use resources to achieve organisational goals. In reality, being a manager often involves acting emotionally and relying on intuition and instinct. Quick, immediate reactions to situations, rather than deliberate thought and reflection, are an important aspect of managerial action.[30] Managers are often overloaded with responsibilities and do not have time to spend on analysing every nuance of a situation. Managers therefore make decisions in uncertain conditions and often without all the necessary and appropriate information, leaving the outcome ambiguous.[31] For senior managers, in particular, the situation is constantly changing, and a decision that seems right today may prove to be wrong tomorrow. In addition, the job of a manager involves constant interaction with other individuals; Chapter 5 will discuss the diversity of human beings and will show that people are not predictable and thus may cause managers at times to act in a non-rational and subjective manner.

Managers have to face a range of problems (*high variety*). Managers frequently must deal with many problems simultaneously (*fragmentation*), often must make snap decisions (*brevity*) and must frequently rely on experience gained throughout their careers to do their jobs to the best of their abilities.[32] It is no small wonder that many managers claim that they are performing their jobs well if they are right just half of the time, and it is understandable why experienced managers should accept failure by their subordinates as a normal part of the learning experience. Managers and their subordinates learn from both their successes and their failures.

Managerial Skills

Both education and experience enable managers to recognise and develop the personal skills they need to put organisational resources to their best use. Michael Dell realised from the start that he lacked sufficient experience and technical expertise in marketing, finance and planning to guide his company alone. He recruited experienced managers from other IT companies, such as IBM and HP, to help him build his company. Research has shown that education and experience help managers acquire three principal types of skills: conceptual, human, and

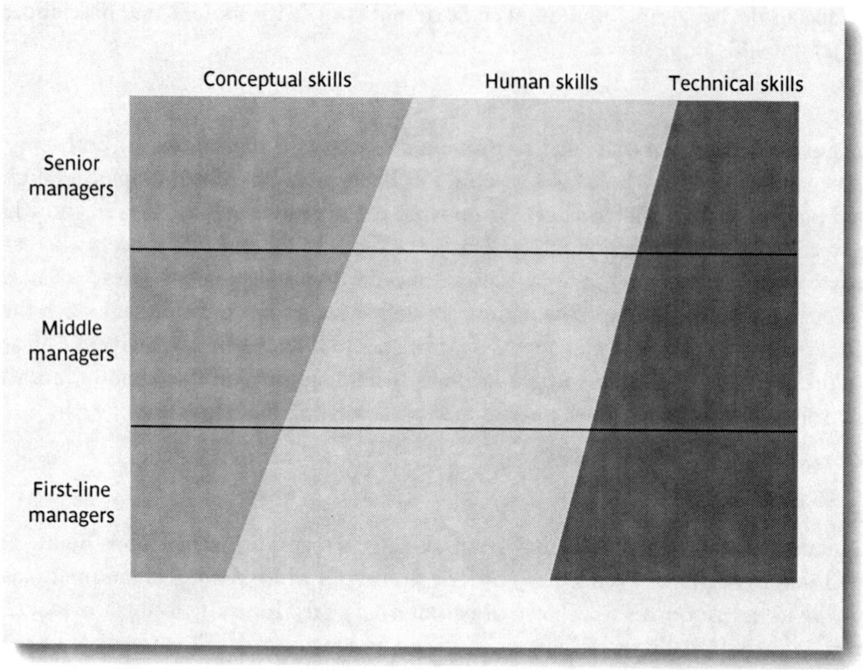

Figure 1.5 Conceptual, Human and Technical Skills Needed by the Three Levels of Management

technical.[33] As you might expect, the level of these skills that managers need depends on their level in the managerial hierarchy. Typically planning and organising require higher levels of conceptual skills, while leading and controlling require more human and technical skills (Fig. 1.5).

Conceptual skills

Conceptual skills are demonstrated in the ability to *analyse* and *diagnose* a situation and to distinguish between cause and effect. Senior managers require the best conceptual skills because their primary responsibilities are planning and organising.[34] By all accounts, Werner von Siemens' success came from his ability to identify new opportunities and mobilise resources to take advantage of them.

Formal education and training can be very important in helping managers develop conceptual skills, by introducing the variety of conceptual tools (theories and techniques in marketing, finance and other areas) that managers need to perform their roles effectively. The study of management helps to develop the skills that allow managers to understand the bigger picture confronting an organisation. The ability to focus *holistically* on the organisational context enables managers to see beyond the situation immediately at hand and consider choices, while keeping in mind the organisation's long-term goals.

Continuing management education and training, including training in advanced IT, is now an integral step in building managerial skills, because new theories and techniques, such as business-to-business (B2B) networks, are constantly being developed to improve organisational effectiveness. A quick scan through a magazine such as *The Economist* or *Management Today* reveals a host of seminars on topics such as advanced marketing, finance, leadership and human resources management (HRM) that are offered to managers at many levels in the organisation, from the most senior corporate executives to middle managers. Within the private sector many companies – Shell, British Airways or Motorola, and many other organisations, for example – designate a budget for attending management development programmes. The public sector also invests large amounts of money in developing the managerial capabilities of their staff.

In addition, many non-managerial employees who are performing at a high level (because they have studied management) are often sent to intensive management training programmes to develop their management skills and to prepare them for promotion to higher management positions.

Human skills

Human skills include the ability to understand, alter, lead and control the behaviour of other individuals and groups. The ability to communicate, to co-ordinate, to motivate people and to mould individuals into cohesive teams, distinguishes effective from ineffective managers.

Like conceptual skills, human skills can be learned through education and training, as well as be developed through experience.[35] Organisations increasingly utilise advanced programmes in leadership skills and team training as they seek to capitalise on the advantages of *self-managed teams*.[36] To manage personal interactions effectively, each person in an organisation needs to learn how to empathise with other people – to understand their viewpoints and the problems they face. One way to help managers understand their personal strengths and weaknesses is to have their superiors, peers and subordinates provide feedback about their performance. Thorough and direct feedback allows managers to develop their human skills: in some contexts, such feedback is known as a '360 degree approach', in which superiors, subordinates and peers comment on an individual's behaviour. There are a variety of tools available to assess an individual's skill set, but providing the feedback generated by such tools needs to be carefully managed for it to be constructive.

Technical skills

Technical skills are the *job-specific knowledge and techniques* required to perform an organisational role. Examples include a manager's specific manufacturing, accounting, marketing – and, increasingly, IT – skills. Managers need a range of technical skills to be effective. The array of technical skills managers need depends on their position in their organisation. The manager of a restaurant, for example, may need accounting and bookkeeping skills to keep track of receipts and costs and to administer the payroll, and aesthetic skills to keep the restaurant looking attractive for customers.

Effective managers need all three kinds of skills – conceptual, human and technical. The absence of even one of these can lead to failure. One of the biggest problems that people who start small businesses confront is their lack of appropriate conceptual and human skills. Someone who has the technical skills to start a new business does not necessarily know how to manage the venture successfully. Similarly, one of the biggest problems that scientists or engineers who switch careers from research to management confront is their lack of effective human skills. Management skills, roles and functions are closely related, and wise managers or prospective managers are constantly in search of the latest educational contributions to help them develop the conceptual, human and technical skills they need to function in today's changing and increasingly competitive global environment.

Today, the term competencies is often used to refer to a specific set of skills, abilities and experiences that gives one manager the ability to perform at a higher level than in a particular organisational setting. Developing such competencies through education and training has become a major priority for both aspiring managers and the organisations they work for. As we discussed earlier, many people are enrolling in advanced management courses, but companies such as IBM have established their own colleges to train and develop their employees and managers at all levels. Every year, for example, General Electric (GE) puts thousands of its employees through management programmes designed to identify the employees whom the company believes have superior competencies and whom it can develop to become its future senior managers. In many organisations promotion is closely tied to a manager's ability to acquire the competencies that a particular company believes are important.[37] At 3M, the company that developed the Post-it note, for example, the ability to successfully lead a new product development team is viewed as a vital requirement for promotion; at IBM, the ability to attract and retain clients is viewed as a vital competency its consultants must possess. We discuss specific kinds of managerial competencies throughout this book.

TIPS FOR PRACTICE

1. Think about how much time managers spend performing each of the four tasks of planning, organising, leading and controlling. Decide if managers are spending the appropriate amount of time on each.
2. To compare how well managers perform their different roles, you may want to use Mintzberg's model and compare a manager against it to assess his or her behaviour.
3. Find out whether managers possess the right levels of conceptual, technical and human skills to perform their jobs effectively.

Challenges for Management in a Global Environment

Because the world has been changing more rapidly than ever before, managers and other employees throughout an organisation need to perform at higher and higher levels.[38] In the last 20 years, competition between organisations nationally and internationally has increased dramatically. The rise of global organisations – organisations that operate and compete in more than one country – has put severe pressure on many organisations to improve their performance and to identify better ways to use their resources. The successes of the German chemical companies Schering and Hoechst, Italian furniture manufacturer Natuzzi, Korean electronics companies Samsung and LG, Brazilian plane maker Embraer and Europe's Airbus Industries are putting pressure on organisations in other countries to raise their level of performance to compete successfully.

Even in the not-for-profit sector, global competition is driving change. Schools, universities, police forces and government agencies are re-examining their operations. Some English universities now have a campus in other countries, for example. European and Asian hospital systems have learned much from the very effective US model.

Managers who make no attempt to learn and adapt to changes in the global environment will find themselves *reacting* rather than innovating, and their organisations often become uncompetitive and fail.[39] Four major challenges stand out for managers in today's world:

- Building a competitive advantage
- Maintaining ethical standards
- Managing a diverse workforce
- Utilising new information systems and technologies.

All of these topics will be discussed in more detail in later chapters and all these factors play an important role in understanding both modern management and its practices.

Building Competitive Advantage

What are the most important lessons for managers and organisations to learn if they are to reach, and remain at, the top of the competitive business environment? The answer relates to the use of organisational resources to build a competitive advantage. Competitive advantage is the ability of one organisation to outperform others because it produces desired products or services more efficiently and effectively than its competitors. One model of competitive advantage is the 'four building blocks' that advocates superior *efficiency*; *quality*; *speed*, *flexibility* and *innovation*; and *responsiveness to customers* (Fig. 1.6).

Increasing efficiency

Organisations increase their efficiency when they reduce the quantity of resources (such as people and raw materials) they use to produce goods or services. In today's competitive environment, organisations constantly are seeking new ways of using their resources to improve efficiency.

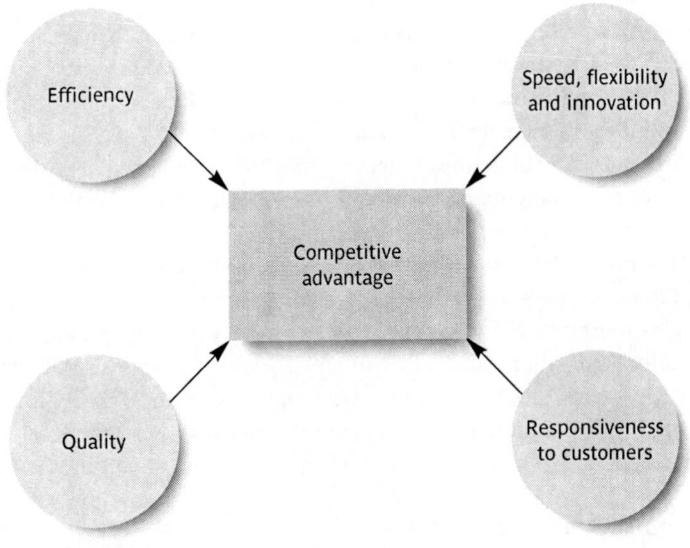

Figure 1.6 Building Blocks of Competitive Advantage

Many organisations are training their workforces in the new skills and techniques that are needed to operate within today's sophisticated technologically advanced working environment. Similarly, *cross-training* gives employees the range of multi-tasking skills and organising employees in new ways (such as in self-managed teams, see p. 14) allows them to make good use of their skills. These are all key steps in the effort to improve productivity. Japanese and German companies invest far more in training employees than do American or Italian companies. In the UK in 2002, 90 per cent of employers provided some form of training to their staff, with 62 per cent providing off-the-job training.[40]

Managers must improve efficiency if their organisations are to compete successfully with companies operating in India, Malaysia, China and other countries where employees are paid comparatively low wages. New methods must be devised either to increase efficiency or to gain some other competitive advantage – higher-quality products, for example – if outsourcing and the loss of jobs to low-cost countries are to be prevented.

Increasing quality

The challenge from global organisations such as Korean electronics manufacturers, Mexican agricultural producers and European marketing and financial firms has also increased pressure on companies to improve the skills and abilities of their workforce in order to improve the quality of their products and services. One major way to improve quality has been to introduce different techniques to ensure tighter quality controls. One of these quality-enhancing techniques is known as total quality management (TQM). Employees involved in TQM are often organised into *quality control teams* responsible for continually finding new and better ways to perform their jobs; they also must monitor and evaluate the quality of the products they produce at all stages of the development and production cycle. TQM is based on a significant new philosophy of managing behaviour in organisations; a detailed discussion of this approach, and ways of managing TQM successfully, can be found in Chapter 9.

Increasing speed, flexibility and innovation

Today, companies can win or lose the competitive race depending on their *speed* – how fast they can bring new products to market – or their *flexibility* – how easily they can change or alter the way they perform their activities to respond to the actions of their competitors. Companies that have speed and flexibility are *agile competitors*: their managers have superior planning and organising abilities; they can think ahead, decide what to do and then speedily mobilise their resources to respond to a changing environment. We examine how managers can build speed and flexibility in their organisations in Chapters 7 and 8.

Innovation – the process of creating new or improved products and services that customers want or developing better ways to produce or provide goods and services – poses a particular challenge. Managers must create an organisational setting in which people are encouraged to be innovative. Typically, innovation takes place in small groups or teams. Management decentralises control of work activities to team members and creates an organisational culture that rewards risk taking. Understanding and managing innovation and creating such a work setting are among the most difficult of managerial tasks. Chapter 18 discusses innovation in more detail.

Increasing responsiveness to customers

Organisations compete for customers with their products and services, so training employees to be responsive to customers' needs is vital for all organisations, and particularly for service organisations. Retail stores, banks and hospitals, for example, depend entirely on their employees to provide high-quality service at a reasonable cost.[41] As many countries (like the UK) move toward a more service-based economy (in part because of the loss of manufacturing jobs to China, Malaysia and other countries with low labour costs), managing behaviour in service organisations is becoming increasingly important. Many organisations are empowering their customer service employees and giving them the authority to take the lead in providing high-quality customer service. As noted previously, the empowering of non-managerial employees changes the role of first-line managers, and often leads to the more efficient use of organisational resources.

Maintaining Ethical and Socially Responsible Standards

Managers at all levels are under considerable pressure to increase the level at which their organisations perform.[42] For example, senior managers receive pressure from shareholders to increase the performance of the entire organisation to boost the stock price, improve profits, or raise dividends. In turn, senior managers may then pressure middle managers to find new ways to use organisational resources to increase efficiency or quality, and thus attract new customers and earn more revenues.

Pressure to increase performance can be healthy for an organisation because it causes managers to question the way the organisation is working and it encourages them to find new and better ways to plan, organise, lead and control. However, too much pressure to perform can be harmful.[43] It may induce managers to behave unethically in dealings with stakeholders both inside and outside the organisation.[44] For example, a purchasing manager for a large retail chain might buy inferior clothing as a cost-cutting measure; or to secure a large foreign contract, a sales manager in a large defence company might offer bribes to foreign officials. The issue of **corporate social responsibility** concerns the obligations that a company should have toward all stakeholders within the communities in which they operate. An example of companies that act in a socially irresponsible and unethical way is now described (Case 1.2).

Case 1.2: Death through painkillers

On 30 September 2004 the painkiller Vioxx, manufactured by Merck, one of the largest German pharmaceutical companies, was banned after it had been claimed that more than 60,000 people had died from the drug worldwide. This case caused a series of investigations in Britain, where 103 deaths had been officially linked to the use of Vioxx, although it was believed that the actual figure of Vioxx-related deaths is close to 2,000.

The drug had been sold since 1999 and it was believed that worldwide it had been prescribed to nearly 20 million patients. In the UK the drug had been prescribed to 400,000 patients as it was believed to be a 'miracle drug' treating everything from severe arthritis pain to minor injuries – but without the nasty side-effects of stomach ulcers commonly associated with other painkillers. However, as it turned out, this was not the case: many people died of heart attacks, strokes, or related illnesses.

In their attempts to obtain and maintain market share in an increasingly competitive industry, Merck behaved in an unethical and socially irresponsible way. Investigations uncovered evidence that the cardiovascular problems associated with the drug had been identified by the ▶

head of research, Edward Scolnick, in 2000. Merck was accused of deliberately withholding information about fatal side-effects in both the US and the UK. A review of confidential material and consent forms for a trial of the drug in the UK showed that many patients had not been told about the risks and concerns related to the use of the drug.

While the UK Legal Service Commission has decided not to fund law suits against Merck, many British relatives of people who died from Vioxx-related side-effects are now considering joining US proceedings against the company, supported by a landmark ruling in Texas where Merck was found negligent and the widow of a Vioxx patient was awarded £141 million.

Unethical behaviour of pharmaceutical companies has already been costly to the industry; Eli Lilly – a research-based pharmaceutical company also operating in the UK – had to pay settlements of more than £380 million when one of its drugs was found to increase the risk of diabetes. However, the company earned more than £2.4 billion from the drug in 2004. Do companies – for profit reasons – take such dangers to patients to be a calculated risk worth taking?!

Managing a Diverse Workforce

Another challenge for managers is to recognise the need to treat human resources in a fair and equitable manner. Today, the age, gender, race, ethnicity, religion, sexual preference and socio-economic makeup of the workforce present new challenges. Managers must establish employment procedures and practices that are legal and fair and do not discriminate against any organisational members.[45]

In the past, white male employees dominated the ranks of management. Today increasing numbers of organisations are realising that to motivate effectively and take advantage of the talents of a diverse workforce, they must make promotion opportunities available to all employees, including women and minorities.[46] Managers must also recognise the performance-enhancing possibilities in the ability to take advantage of the skills and experiences of different kinds of people.[47]

Managers who value their diverse employees not only invest in developing these employees' skills and capabilities but also link rewards to their performance. They are the managers who succeed in promoting performance in the long term.[48] Today, more and more organisations are realising that people are their most important resource and that developing and protecting human resources is an important challenge for management in a competitive global environment. We discuss the complex issues surrounding the management of a diverse workforce in Chapter 5.

Utilising IT and E-Commerce

As has already been discussed, another important challenge for managers is the efficiency of new IT and e-commerce.[49] New technologies such as computer-controlled manufacturing and information systems that link and enable employees in new ways are continually being developed. In a setting that uses self-managed teams, for example, sophisticated computer information systems link the activities of team members so that each member knows what the others are doing. This co-ordination helps to improve quality and increase the pace of innovation. Microsoft, Hitachi, IBM and other companies make extensive use of information systems such as email, the Internet and videoconferencing, accessible by means of PCs, to build a competitive advantage. The importance of IT is discussed in detail in Chapters 16 and 18.

Reaction Time

1. What are the building blocks of competitive advantage? Why is obtaining a competitive advantage important to managers?
2. In what ways do you think managers' jobs have changed the most over the last 10 years? Why have these changes occurred?

Summary and Review

What is management? A manager is a person responsible for supervising the use of an organisation's resources to meet its goals. An organisation is a collection of people who work together and co-ordinate their actions to achieve a wide variety of goals. Management is the process of using organisational resources to achieve organisational goals effectively and efficiently through planning, organising, leading and controlling. An efficient organisation makes the most productive use of its resources. An effective organisation pursues appropriate goals and achieves them by using its resources to create the goods or services that customers want.

Managerial functions The four principal managerial functions are planning, organising, leading and controlling. Managers at all levels of the organisation and in all departments perform these functions. Effective management means managing these activities successfully.

Types of managers Organisations typically have three levels of management. First-line managers are responsible for the day-to-day supervision of non-managerial employees. Middle managers are responsible for developing and utilising organisational resources efficiently and effectively. Senior managers have cross-departmental responsibility. The senior manager's job is to establish appropriate goals for the entire organisation and to verify that department managers are utilising resources to achieve those goals. To increase efficiency and effectiveness, some organisations have altered their managerial hierarchies by restructuring, empowering their workforces, utilising self-managed teams and utilising new IT.

IT and managerial roles and skills According to Mintzberg, managers play 10 different roles: figurehead, leader, liaison, monitor, disseminator, spokesperson, entrepreneur, disturbance handler, resource allocator and negotiator. Three types of skills help managers perform these roles effectively: conceptual, human and technical skills. IT is changing both the way managers perform their roles and the skills they need to perform these roles because it provides richer and more meaningful information.

Challenges for management in a global environment Today's competitive global environment presents many interesting challenges to managers. One of the main challenges is building a competitive advantage by increasing efficiency; quality; speed, flexibility and innovation; and customer responsiveness. Others are behaving ethically toward people inside and outside the organisation; managing a diverse workforce; and utilising new information systems and technologies.

Topic for Action

- Choose an organisation such as a school or a bank; visit it; then list the different organisational resources it uses.
- Visit an organisation, and talk to first-line, middle and senior managers about their respective management roles in the organisation and what they do to help the organisation be efficient and effective.
- Ask a middle or senior manager, perhaps someone you already know, to give examples of how he or she performs the managerial functions of planning, organising, leading and controlling. How much time does he or she spend in performing each function?
- Like Mintzberg, try to find a co-operative manager who will allow you to follow him or her around for a day. List the roles the manager plays, and indicate how much time he or she spends performing them.

Applied Independent Learning

Building Management Skills

Thinking About Managers and Management

Think of an organisation that has provided you with work experience and of the manager to whom you reported (or talk to someone who has had extensive work experience); then answer these questions.

1. Think of your direct supervisor. Of what department is he or she a member, and at what level of management is this person?
2. How do you characterise your supervisor's approach to management? For example, which particular management functions and roles does this person perform most often? What kinds of management skills does this manager have?
3. Do you think the functions, roles and skills of your supervisor are appropriate for the particular job he or she performs? How could this manager improve his or her task performance? How can IT affect this?
4. How did your supervisor's approach to management affect your attitudes and behaviour? For example, how well did you perform as a subordinate, and how motivated were you?
5. Think of the organisation and its resources. Do its managers utilise organisational resources effectively? Which resources contribute most to the organisation's performance?
6. Describe the way the organisation treats its human resources. How does this treatment affect the attitudes and behaviours of the workforce?
7. If you could give your manager one piece of advice or change one management practice in the organisation, what would it be?
8. How attuned are the managers in the organisation to the need to increase efficiency, quality, innovation or responsiveness to customers? How well do you think the organisation performs its prime goals of providing the goods or services that customers want or need the most?

Managing Ethically

Think about an example of unethical behaviour that you observed in the past. The incident could be something you experienced as an employee or a customer or something you observed informally.

1. Either by yourself or in a group, give three reasons why you think the behaviour was unethical. For example, what rules or norms were broken? Who benefited or was harmed by what took place? What was the outcome for the people involved?
2. What steps might you take to prevent such unethical behaviour in the future and encourage people to behave in an ethical way?

Small Group Breakout Exercise

Opening a New Restaurant

Form groups of three or four people, and appoint one group member as the spokesperson who will communicate your findings to the entire class when called on by the instructor. Then discuss the following scenario.

You and your partners have decided to open a large, full service restaurant in your local community; it will be open from 7 a.m. to 10 p.m. to serve breakfast, lunch and dinner. Each of you is investing £50,000 in the venture, and together you have secured a bank loan for an additional £300,000 to begin operations. You and your partners have little experience in managing a restaurant beyond serving meals or eating in restaurants, and you now face the task of deciding how you will manage the restaurant and what your respective roles will be.

1. Decide what each partner's managerial role in the restaurant will be. For example, who will be responsible for the necessary departments and specific activities? Describe your managerial hierarchy.
2. Which building blocks of competitive advantage do you need to establish to help your restaurant succeed? What criteria will you use to evaluate how successfully you are managing the restaurant?
3. Discuss the most important decisions that must be made about (a) planning, (b) organising, (c) leading and (d) controlling, to allow you and your partners to utilise organisational resources effectively and build a competitive advantage.
4. For each managerial function, list the issue that will contribute the most to your restaurant's success.

Exploring the World Wide Web

Use the Internet to find a company or a manager and discover how he or she deals with the four principles of management. Online resources you may want to consider are *The Economist*, *BusinessWeek*, the *Financial Times*, *Management Today* or other current periodicals, newspaper business sections, or professional magazines.

Application in Today's Business World

Can A US-Style Boss Rev Up Siemens?

CEO-designate Kleinfeld cut his teeth in America, but he may meet resistance from labour and polls at home

It's safe to say Klaus Kleinfeld didn't have much trouble adjusting to life in America after Siemens (**SI**) made him chief operating officer of its US units in 2001. Kleinfeld soon won invitations to join the boards of a dozen prestigious organisations including the Metropolitan Opera and Alcoa, Inc. (**AA**) He ran two New York marathons and frequented the city's jazz clubs. Under Kleinfeld, who was promoted to CEO of Siemens' US unit in 2002, the company played a big role in building Houston's Reliant Stadium, scene in February of that most American of events, the Super Bowl.

Now, Kleinfeld, 46, is set to become the latest German manager to parlay US experience and attitude into a top job at a German corporate icon. On 7 July, Siemens announced that, effective in January, Kleinfeld would succeed Heinrich von Pierer as CEO of the $89 billion Munich conglomerate, which makes everything from light bulbs and power plants to trains and mobile phones. The question is whether the energetic Kleinfeld will fare better than some other German bosses who tried to import US-style management techniques, with their emphasis on speed and profit. 'Kleinfeld stands for the modern approach in German industry, of trying to cope with globalisation and move out of the old, well-trodden path,' says Jens van Scherpenberg, head of the Americas Research Unit at the German Institute for International & Security Affairs, a Berlin think tank.

The Right Stuff?

Trouble is, others who fit that description haven't always fared so well. Remember Thomas Middelhoff, the self-styled 'American with a German passport'? He was ousted as CEO of media giant Bertelsmann in 2002 after disagreeing with the controlling family over plans to go public. Then there was Ulrich Schumacher, CEO of chipmaker Infineon Technologies (**IFX**), who led a successful initial public offering on Wall Street but lost his job in March. Schumacher alienated board members and labour representatives with his inclination to act without consulting others – a no-no in consensus-driven Germany.

Kleinfeld, a member of Siemens' corporate executive committee, seems to be a different breed. By choosing Kleinfeld as his successor, von Pierer clearly hopes his young protégé will be more in the mould of Deutsche Telekom (**DT**): CEO Kai-Uwe Ricke, 42, has led a turnaround at the telecom giant. Kleinfeld isn't talking to the press, waiting at least until 28 July, when the Siemens supervisory board is expected to ratify his appointment. But those who know Kleinfeld, who joined Siemens in 1987, say he combines an ability to push change with an antenna for human nature. 'He's young, and he belongs to another generation, but he's also a Siemens guy who knows Siemens culture,' says Roland Berger, chairman of Munich-based Roland Berger Strategy Consultants.

The CEO-designate has already begun to make changes. His fingerprints were on Siemens' decision, also announced on 7 July, to merge the mobile phone division with the land-line telecom unit. In the US, Kleinfeld managed to get Siemens' disparate fiefdoms to co-operate more on marketing. One result was the contract to provide everything from telecom equipment to computer networks for Houston's $750 million Reliant Park convention and sporting complex.

In fact, Kleinfeld probably won the top job because he showed he could get Siemens divisions to work together to win big orders. The company has struggled for years to prove that synergies among branches justify the inherent unwieldiness of a far-flung conglomerate. He also got Siemens' legions of proud engineers to see things more from their customers' point of view. After a $553 million loss in 2001, Siemens reported an $810 million profit for its US units in 2002 and a $561 million profit in 2003, after which he returned to Germany. 'He was instrumental in getting it working,' says Gerhard Schulmeyer, Kleinfeld's predecessor as CEO of Siemens in the US.

Back home, Kleinfeld will have to spend a lot of time smoothing out relations with politicians and unions. In the US, where Siemens had sales of $16.6 billion in 2003, the company cut staff by 15,000 to 65,000, by selling or closing unprofitable units but also by shifting work to lower-wage countries such as India. Von Pierer has reduced the German workforce by more than 50,000 (to 167,000) since becoming CEO in 1992.

Investor Pressure

But by imposing cuts gradually, the diplomatic von Pierer managed to avoid serious confrontation with Germany's powerful labour unions and their allies in Parliament. That is becoming more difficult. Labour leaders are sore that they were forced recently to give in to demands that workers at a mobile phone factory put in extra hours without extra pay: Siemens threatened to shift the work to Hungary. 'Siemens has damaged its image with that kind of action,' says Wolfgang Müller, a worker on the supervisory board.

Siemens' shareholders are another restive constituency. The company's shares have fallen 8.9 per cent this year, vs. a 6.9 per cent gain for their rival the General Electric Co. (**GE**). While Siemens is profitable, earning $1.45 billion on sales of $21 billion in the last quarter, there are problem areas. The telecommunications equipment businesses have wobbly margins, and the transportation unit is in the midst of a costly recall of defective streetcars. Kleinfeld will face pressure from investors to slim down the company. Some analysts also say it would make sense for Siemens to put its mobile-handset business into a **joint venture (JV)** with another manufacturer such as Samsung Electronics Co.

Kleinfeld will have to do a lot of creative thinking. But people who have worked with him say he's good at that. 'He was exceptionally exact but not narrow-minded; on the contrary, very independent and creative,' says Peter Fassheber, a retired professor at Georg-August University in Göttingen who supervised Kleinfeld's research in the early 1980s. Kleinfeld focused on the intersection of psychology and economics. If Kleinfeld can reconcile human nature with economic reality at Siemens, he might just succeed.

Questions

1. How would you describe Klaus Kleinfeld's approach to managing?
2. What skills and abilities helped him rise to become Siemen's CEO?

Source: Jack Ewing, 'Can a US-Style Boss Rev Up Siemens?', adapted and reprinted from *BusinessWeek*, July 26, 2004 by special permission. Copyright © 2004 by the McGraw-Hill Companies, Inc.

Notes and References

1 G. R. Jones, *Organizational Theory, Design, and Change* (Upper Saddle River, NJ: Pearson, 2003).
2 J. P. Campbell, 'On the Nature of Organizational Effectiveness', in P. S. Goodman, J. M. Pennings *et al.*, *New Perspectives on Organizational Effectiveness* (San Francisco: Jossey-Bass, 1977).

3 M. J. Provitera, 'What Management Is: How It Works and Why It's Everyone's Business', *Academy of Management Executive* 17 (August 2003), 152–54.

4 J. McGuire and E. Matta, 'CEO Stock Options: The Silent Dimension of Ownership', *Academy of Management Journal* 46 (April 2003), 255–66.

5 J. G. Combs and M. S. Skill, 'Managerialist and Human Capital Explanations for Key Executive Pay Premium: A Contingency Perspective', *Academy of Management Journal* 46 (February 2003), 63–74.

6 H. Fayol, *General and Industrial Management* (New York: IEEE Press, 1984). Fayol actually identified five different managerial functions, but most scholars today believe that these four capture the essence of his ideas.

7 P. F. Drucker, *Management Tasks, Responsibilities, and Practices* (New York: Harper & Row, 1974).

8 D. McGraw, 'The Kid Bytes Back', *U.S. News & World Report*, December 12, 1994, 70–71.

9 www.apple.com, press release, 2003.

10 G. McWilliams, 'Lean Machine – How Dell Fine-Tunes Its PC Pricing to Gain Edge in a Slow Market', *The Wall Street Journal*, June 8, 2001, A1.

11 J. Kotter, *The General Managers* (New York: Free Press, 1992).

12 C. P. Hales, 'What Do Managers Do? A Critical Review of the Evidence', *Journal of Management Studies*, January 1986, 88–115; A. I. Kraul, P. R. Pedigo, D. D. McKenna and M. D. Dunnette, 'The Role of the Manager: What's Really Important in Different Management Jobs', *Academy of Management Executive*, November 1989, 286–93.

13 A. K. Gupta, 'Contingency Perspectives on Strategic Leadership', in D. C. Hambrick, ed., *The Executive Effect: Concepts and Methods for Studying Top Managers* (Greenwich, CT: JAI Press, 1988), 147–78.

14 D. G. Ancona, 'Top Management Teams: Preparing for the Revolution', in J. S. Carroll, ed., *Applied Social Psychology and Organizational Settings* (Hillsdale, NJ: Erlbaum, 1990); D. C. Hambrick and P. A. Mason, 'Upper Echelons: The Organization as a Reflection of Its Top Managers', *Academy of Management Journal* 9 (1984), 193–206.

15 T. A. Mahony, T. H. Jerdee and S. J. Carroll, 'The Jobs of Management', *Industrial Relations* 4 (1965), 97–110; L. Gomez-Mejia, J. McCann and R. C. Page, 'The Structure of Managerial Behaviors and Rewards', *Industrial Relations* 24 (1985), 147–54.

16 W. R. Nord and M. J. Waller, 'The Human Organization of Time: Temporal Realities and Experiences', *Academy of Management Review* 29 (January 2004), 137–40.

17 R. Stewart, 'Middle Managers: Their Jobs and Behaviors', in J. W. Lorsch, ed., *Handbook of Organizational Behavior* (Englewood Cliffs, NJ: Prentice Hall, 1987), 385–91.

18 K. Labich, 'Making over Middle Managers', *Fortune*, May 8, 1989, 58–64.

19 Office for National Statistics, Information, Communications, and Technology, Economic Trends 603, February 2004.

20 B. Wysocki, 'Some Companies Cut Costs Too Far, Suffer from Corporate Anorexia', *The Wall Street Journal*, July 5, 1995, A1.

21 Department of Health, *Agenda for Change*, 2004.

22 Statistics in Focus, Science, and Technology, 'European Employment Increasing in Services and Especially in Knowledge-Intensive Services', EUROSTAT, 10/2004.

23 National Office for Statistics, Time Series Data.

24 V. U. Druskat and J. V. Wheeler, 'Managing from the Boundary: The Effective Leadership of Self-Managing Work Teams', *Academy of Management Journal* 46 (August 2003), 435–58.

25 S. R. Parker, T. D. Wall and P. R. Jackson, 'That's Not My Job: Developing Flexible Work Orientations', *Academy of Management Journal* 40 (1997), 899–929.

26 B. Dumaine, 'The New Non-Manager', *Fortune*, February 22, 1993, 80–84.

27 H. Mintzberg, 'The Manager's Job: Folklore and Fact', *Harvard Business Review*, July–August 1975, 56–62.

28 H. Mintzberg, *The Nature of Managerial Work* (New York: Harper & Row, 1973).
29 *Ibid.*
30 R. H. Guest, 'Of Time and the Foreman', *Personnel* 32 (1955), 478–86.
31 L. Hill, *Becoming a Manager: Mastery of a New Identity* (Boston: Harvard Business School Press, 1992).
32 *Ibid.*
33 R. L. Katz, 'Skills of an Effective Administrator', *Harvard Business Review*, September–October 1974, 90–102.
34 *Ibid.*
35 P. Tharenou, 'Going Up? Do Traits and Informal Social Processes Predict Advancing in Management?', *Academy of Management Journal* 44 (October 2001), 1005–18.
36 C. J. Collins and K. D. Clark, 'Strategic Human Resource Practices, Top Management Team Social Networks, and Firm Performance: The Role of Human Resource Practices in Creating Organizational Competitive Advantage', *Academy of Management Journal* 46 (December 2003), 740–52.
37 S. C. de Janasz, S. E. Sullivan and V. Whiting, 'Mentor Networks and Career Success: Lessons for Turbulent Times', *Academy of Management Executive*, 17 (November 2003), 78–92.
38 H. G. Baum, A. C. Joel and E. A. Mannix, 'Management Challenges in a New Time', *Academy of Management Journal* 45 (October 2002), 916–31.
39 A. Shama, 'Management Under Fire: The Transformation of Management in the Soviet Union and Eastern Europe', *Academy of Management Executive* 10 (1993), 22–35.
40 National Statistics First Release, SFR 02/2003.
41 K. Seiders and L. L. Berry, 'Service Fairness: What It Is and Why It Matters', *Academy of Management Executive* 12 (1998), 8–20.
42 T. Donaldson, 'Editor's Comments: Taking Ethics Seriously – A Mission Now More Possible', *Academy of Management Review* 28 (July 2003), 363–67.
43 C. Anderson, 'Values-Based Management', *Academy of Management Executive* 11 (1997), 25–46.
44 W. H. Shaw and V. Barry, *Moral Issues in Business*, 6th ed. (Belmont, CA: Wadsworth, 1995); T. Donaldson, *Corporations and Morality* (Englewood Cliffs, NJ: Prentice Hall, 1982).
45 S. Jackson *et al.*, *Diversity in the Workplace: Human Resource Initiatives* (New York: Guilford Press, 1992).
46 G. Robinson and C. S. Daus, 'Building a Case for Diversity', *Academy of Management Executive* 3 (1997), 21–31; S. J. Bunderson and K. M. Sutcliffe, 'Comparing Alternative Conceptualizations of Functional Diversity in Management Teams: Process and Performance Effects', *Academy of Management Journal* 45 (October 2002), 875–94.
47 D. Jamieson and J. O'Mara, *Managing Workforce 2000: Gaining a Diversity Advantage* (San Francisco: Jossey-Bass, 1991).
48 T. H. Cox and S. Blake, 'Managing Cultural Diversity: Implications for Organizational Competitiveness', *Academy of Management Executive*, August 1991, 49–52.
49 D. R. Tobin, *The Knowledge Enabled Organization* (New York: AMACOM, 1998).

Chapter 10

Managing Organisational Structure

LEARNING OBJECTIVES

After studying this chapter, you should be able to:

- ☑ Identify the factors that influence managers' choice of an organisational structure.
- ☑ Explain how managers group tasks into jobs that are motivating and satisfying for employees.
- ☑ Describe the types of organisational structures managers can design, and explain why they choose one structure over another.
- ☑ Explain why there is a need to both centralise and decentralise authority.
- ☑ Explain why managers must co-ordinate and integrate among jobs, functions and divisions as an organisation grows.
- ☑ Explain why managers who seek new ways to increase efficiency and effectiveness are using strategic alliances and network structures.

A Manager's Challenge

Nokia, Dow and the LEGO Company Revamp Their Global Structures to Raise Performance

How should managers organise to improve performance?

In 2004, suffering from its worst-ever annual losses, caused by a 25 per cent decline in global sales (see p. 248), the LEGO company decided that it needed to restructure its European operations.[1] Until 2004, the LEGO company had operated with three global subdivisions inside its European division – central, northern and southern. Many problems had arisen with this structure: first, each subdivision was performing many of the same activities, so the duplication was raising operating costs. Second, the subdivisions often did not co-operate and share information on new product developments or changes in customer needs. As a result, many opportunities were being lost, especially because this structure made it even more difficult to communicate with LEGO's US and Asian divisions.

The LEGO company's solution was to abolish these subdivisions and reunite them all into one European division under the control of its former top global marketer, Henrik Poulsen.[2] Poulsen reports to the LEGO company's CEO, just as do the heads of the LEGO company's other global divisions, and the company is hoping that this will lead to an increase in co-operation among its divisions around the world. The goal of the reorganisation is to help LEGO's global divisions to learn from one another and work together to develop toys that better suit the changing needs of customers throughout the world.

While the LEGO company is trying to solve its problem by combining its three European units into one, in 2004 US giant Dow Chemicals decided that the best way to leverage the skills and resources of its global chemicals division was to split it into three different global product groups – the plastics, chemicals and intermediates and performance chemicals groups.[3] Dow believes that when each group acts as a self-contained unit, this will make it easier for managers to focus on one range of chemical products that can then be delivered to customers around the world.[4] Note that in Dow's case the issue was to create more product divisions, while the issue facing the LEGO company was to reduce the number of its market divisions.

Finally, Nokia, the Finnish company that is the world's leader in cellular phones, also made a change to its global structure in 2004. Nokia recognised that it had an important weakness in its product line, wireless business communications, by means of which a company can communicate with its workforce through some form of wireless communication such as laptops, Palms and other PDAs, or wireless phones that allow employees to share information and communicate.

Since this part of the wireless market was rapidly growing, Nokia chairman Jornma Ollila decided to create a new global division to innovate wireless communication products and a new global product division, the Enterprise Solutions group. To give the new divisions the autonomy to innovate products quickly, he set them up in New York and appointed a former Hewlett-Packard (HP) manager, Mary McDowell, to develop an entry technology that would offer everything from server software to handsets and compete with giants like HP and IBM. Since the potential market in this area was expected to grow from £15.5 to £24 billion by 2007, Nokia hoped to obtain a significant share of this lucrative market to help boost its performance.[5]

Overview

The challenge facing managers in all three companies was to identify the best way to operate in a new, more competitive environment. Managers in all three companies were forced to radically change the way they organised their employees and other resources to meet that challenge.

Managers need to know how to organise and control human and other resources to create high-performing organisations. To organise and control (two of the four managerial functions), managers must design an **organisational architecture** that makes the best use of resources to produce the goods and services customers want. Organisational architecture is the combination of organisational structure, control systems, culture and human resource management

(HRM) systems that together determine how efficiently and effectively organisational resources are used.

By the end of this chapter, you will be familiar with various organisational structures and with a range of factors that determine the organisational design choices that managers make. In Chapters 11–12 the issues surrounding the design of an organisation's control systems, culture and HRM systems will be explored.

Designing Organisational Structure

Organising is the process by which managers establish the structure of *working relationships* among employees to allow them to achieve *organisational goals* efficiently and effectively. *Organisational structure* is the formal system of task and job reporting relationships that determines how employees use resources to achieve organisational goals.[6] **Organisational design** is the process by which managers make specific organising choices about tasks and job relationships that result in the construction of a particular organisational structure.[7]

As noted in Chapter 2, according to *contingency theory* managers design organisational structures to fit the factors or circumstances that are impacting the company the most and causing them the most uncertainty.[8] Thus, there is no one best way to design an organisation. Design reflects each organisation's specific situation, and researchers have argued that in some situations stable, mechanistic structures may be most appropriate while in a different industry or a different situation, flexible, organic structures may be the most effective. Four factors are important determinants of the type of organisational structure or organising method managers select: the nature of the organisational environment, the type of strategy the organisation pursues, the technology (this includes the IT) the organisation uses and the characteristics of the organisation's HR (Fig. 10.1).[9]

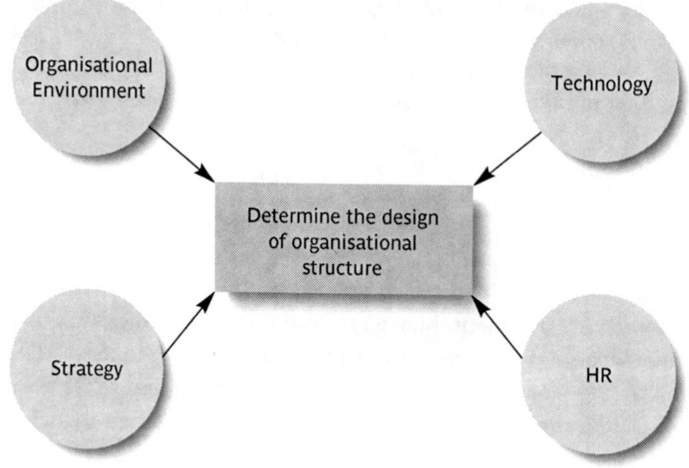

Figure 10.1 Factors Affecting Organisational Structure

The Organisational Environment

In general, a causal relationship can be found between the *speed of change* within an organisation's environment and the speed in which an organisation has to *adapt* to these changes. The quicker an external environment is changing, the greater the uncertainty. This results in greater problems for managers to gain access to scarce resources. To accelerate decision making and communication, and make it easier to obtain resources, managers typically make organising choices that bring *flexibility* to the organisational structure.[10] They are likely to decentralise authority and empower lower-level employees to make important operating decisions – a more *organic structure*. In contrast, if the external environment is stable, resources are readily available and uncertainty is low, then less co-ordination and communication among people and functions is needed to obtain resources. Managers can make organising choices that bring more *stability* or *formality* to the organisational structure. Managers in this situation prefer to make decisions within a clearly defined hierarchy of authority and use extensive rules and standard operating procedures to govern activities – a more *mechanistic structure*.

As we discussed in Chapter 6, change is rapid in today's marketplace, and increasing competition both at home and abroad is putting greater pressure on managers to attract customers and increase efficiency and effectiveness. Interest in finding ways to structure organisations – such as through empowerment and self-managed teams – to allow people and departments to behave flexibly has been rapidly increasing.

Strategy

As discussed in Chapter 8, once managers decide on a strategy, they must choose the right means of *implementing* it. Different strategies often call for the use of different organisational structures: a differentiation strategy, for example, aimed at increasing the value customers perceive in an organisation's products and services, usually succeeds best in a flexible structure. Flexibility facilitates a differentiation strategy because managers can develop new or innovative products quickly – an activity that requires extensive co-operation among functions or departments. In contrast, a low-cost strategy, aimed at driving down costs in all functions, usually sits best in a more formal structure, which gives managers greater control over the expenditures and actions of the organisation's various departments.[11]

In addition, at the corporate level, when managers decide to expand the scope of organisational activities by vertical integration or diversification, for example, they need to design a flexible structure to provide sufficient co-ordination among the different business divisions.[12] As discussed in Chapter 8, many companies have been *divesting* businesses because managers have been unable to create a competitive advantage to keep them up to speed in fast-changing industries. By moving to a more flexible structure, such as a product division structure, divisional managers gain more control over their different businesses. Expanding internationally and operating in many different countries challenges managers to create organisational structures that allow organisations to be flexible on a global level.[13] As will be discussed in this chapter, managers can group their departments or functions and divisions in several ways to allow them to effectively pursue an international strategy, or sell parts of their business to make them more successful ventures. The Motorola example in Case 10.1 shows that restructuring can sometimes mean selling off parts of an organisation for the business to retain its strength.

Case 10.1: Motorola succeeds in Freescale spin-off

In 2004, Motorola spun off one of its businesses in a move to make this 'redheaded stepchild'[14] a large, independent company even though it had been part of the Motorola family for 50 years. The move to restructuring was led by Freescale's (a £3.3 billion semiconductor business) poor performance as part of the Motorola Group. In the early 2000s Motorola downsized the business by closing nearly half of Freescale's plants and making 13,000 people redundant. After all this effort, Freescale still did not produce the desired results and was operating at a non-profitable margin of 29 per cent and making losses of up to £210 million. What could be done?

Motorola had to decide if spinning off Freescale was a viable option, considering that spin-offs are not always a successful way of restructuring an organisation. However, Motorola, which makes up 25 per cent of Freescale's revenue, needed the company to be a strong contender in the market in order to maintain a sustainable strategic partnership. Motorola's decision to distribute all shares and not retain any ownership was one important decision to Freescale's success. However, the most cunning decision was to hire the energetic Frenchman Michel Mayer who managed to turn around Freescale's performance within 15 months of his arrival. One of the major changes Mayer introduced was the refocusing of an engineering-led company to a customer focused and responsive one. Mayer also adapted the company's manufacturing to include technology and smarter operations. Mayer also retained the Motorola spirit by encouraging strong communication across its plants to ensure everyone was pulling in the same direction. For example, if production fell behind in order to respond to an emergency order in one plant, this was considered acceptable in order to be customer-focused. Mayer's arrival saw Freescale's performance soaring: its earnings jumped threefold and the share price rose by nearly 70 per cent.[15]

Technology

Technology is the combination of skills, knowledge, tools, machines, computers and equipment that is used in the design, production and distribution of goods and services. As a rule, the more complicated the technology that an organisation uses, the more difficult it is for managers and workers to impose strict control on it or to regulate it efficiently. The more complicated the technology, the greater is the need for a flexible structure to enhance managers' ability to respond to unexpected situations and give them the freedom to work out new solutions to the problems they encounter. In contrast, the more routine the technology, the more appropriate is a formal structure, because tasks are simple and the steps needed to produce goods and services have been worked out in advance.

What makes a technology routine or complicated? One researcher who investigated this issue, Charles Perrow, argued that two factors determine how complicated or non-routine technology is: *task variety* and *task analysability*.[16] Task variety is the number of new or unexpected problems or situations that a person or function will encounter in performing tasks or jobs. Task analysability is the degree to which programmed solutions are available to people or functions to solve the problems they encounter. Non-routine or complicated technologies are characterised by high task variety and low task analysability; this means that many varied problems occur and that solving them requires significant non-programmed decision making. In contrast, routine technologies are characterised by low task variety and high task analysability; the problems encountered do not vary much and are easily resolved through programmed decision making.

Examples of non-routine technology are found in the work of R&D units which develop new drugs or new compound materials, such as new forms of carbon fibre or plastic. Examples of routine technology include typical mass-production or assembly operations, where workers perform the same task repeatedly and where managers have already identified the programmed solutions necessary to perform a task efficiently. Similarly, in service organisations such as fast-food restaurants, the tasks that crew members perform in making and serving fast food are very routine.

The extent to which the process of actually producing or creating goods and services is dependent on people or machines, is another factor that determines how non-routine a technology is. The more the technology used to produce goods and services is based on individuals' skills, knowledge and abilities of working together on an ongoing basis and not on automated machines that can be programmed in advance, the more complex the technology is. Joan Woodward, a professor who investigated the relationship between technology and organisational structure, differentiated among three kinds of technology on the basis of the relative contribution made by people or machines.[17]

Small-batch technology is used to produce small quantities of customised, one-of-a-kind products and is based on the skills of people who work together in small groups. Examples of goods and services produced by small-batch technology include custom-built cars, such as Lamborghinis and Rolls Royces, highly specialised metals and chemicals that are produced by the pound rather than by the ton and the process of auditing in which a small team of auditors is sent to a company to evaluate and report on its accounts. Because small-batch goods or services are customised and unique, workers need to respond to each situation as required. A structure that decentralises authority to employees and allows them to respond flexibly is most appropriate with small-batch technology.

Woodward's second kind of technology, mass-production technology, is based primarily on the use of automated machines that are programmed to perform the same operations time and time again. Mass production works most efficiently when each person performs a repetitive task; there is less need for flexibility, and a formal organisational structure is the preferred choice because it gives managers the most control over the production process. Mass production results in an output of large quantities of standardised products such as tin cans, washing machines and light bulbs, or even services such as a car wash or dry cleaning.

The third kind of technology that Woodward identified, continuous-process technology, is almost totally mechanised. Goods are produced by automated machines working in sequence and controlled through computers from a central monitoring station. Examples of continuous-process technology include large steel mills, oil refineries, nuclear power stations and large-scale brewing operations. The role of workers in continuous-process technology is to watch for problems that may occur unexpectedly and cause dangerous or even deadly situations. The possibility of a machinery or computer breakdown, for example, is a major source of uncertainty associated with this technology. If an unexpected situation occurs, employees must be able to respond quickly and appropriately to prevent a disaster from resulting. An example could be a technological fault in a nuclear power station's cooling system, which could result in a potentially fatal accident. The need for a flexible response makes a flexible organisational structure the preferred choice for this kind of technology.

Information technology

As seen in previous chapters, new technologies have profound effects on the way an organisation operates. At the level of organisational structure, IT is changing methods of organising. An *IT-enabled organisational structure* allows for new kinds of tasks and job reporting relationships among electronically connected people that promotes superior communication and co-ordination. One type of IT-enabled organisational relationship is *knowledge management*, the sharing and integrating of expertise within and between functions and divisions through real-time, interconnected IT.[18] Some benefits from these arrangements include the development of synergies that may result in competitive advantage in the form of product or service differentiation – something LEGO, Dow and Nokia were seeking to achieve. Unlike the case with more rigid, bureaucratic organising methods, new IT-enabled organisations can respond more quickly to changing environmental conditions such as increased global competition.

Other examples include more flexible, interactive ways for teams to interact. For example, Dresdner Kleinwort Wasserstein, a financial services firm, has encouraged the use of interactive technologies, such as wikis and blogs (virtual spaces), after realising that email is not an effective tool for collaborative working. Since its introduction, this technology has been used by 1,500 employees. The email volume on projects is down by three-quarters, meeting times have halved and a general increase in productivity has been recorded.[19]

The nature of an organisation's technology is an important determinant of its structure. Today, many companies are trying to use IT in innovative ways to make their structures more flexible and to take advantage of its value-creating benefits. Many of the ways in which IT affects organising are discussed in this and later chapters.

Human Resources

A final important factor affecting an organisation's choice of structure are the characteristics of the *human resources* (HR) it employs. In general, the more highly skilled an organisation's workforce is, and the more people are required to work together in groups or teams to perform tasks, the more likely an organisation is to use a flexible, decentralised structure. Highly skilled employees or employees who have internalised strong professional values and norms of behaviour as part of their training usually desire freedom and autonomy and dislike close supervision. Accountants, for example, have learned the need to report company accounts honestly and impartially, and doctors and nurses have absorbed the obligation to give patients the best care possible.

Flexible structures, characterised by decentralised authority and empowered employees, are well suited to the needs of highly skilled people. Similarly, when people work in teams, they must be allowed to interact freely, which also is possible in a flexible organisational structure. When designing an organisational structure, managers must pay close attention to both the *workforce* and to the *work itself*.

An organisation's external environment, strategy, technology and HR are all factors to be considered by managers in seeking to design the best structure for an organisation. The greater the level of uncertainty in the organisation's environment, the more complex its strategy and technologies and the more highly qualified and skilled its workforce, the more likely managers are to design a structure that is flexible and that can change quickly. The more stable the organisation's environment, the less complex and more well understood its strategy or technology and the less skilled its workforce, the more likely managers are to design an organisational structure that is formal and controlling.

How do managers design a structure to be either flexible or formal? The way an organisation's structure works depends on the organising choices managers make about four issues:

- How to group tasks into *individual jobs*
- How to group jobs into *functions* and *divisions*

- How to *allocate authority* in the organisation among jobs, functions and divisions
- How to co-ordinate or integrate among jobs, functions and divisions.

Grouping Tasks into Jobs: Job Design

The first step in organisational design is job design, the process by which managers decide how to divide into specific jobs the tasks that have to be performed to provide customers with products and services. Managers at McDonald's, for example, have decided how best to divide the tasks required to provide customers with fast, cheap food in each McDonald's restaurant. After experimenting with different job arrangements, McDonald's managers decided on a basic division of labour among chefs and food servers. Managers allocated all the tasks involved in actually cooking the food (putting oil in the fat fryers, opening packages of frozen french fries, putting beef burgers on the grill, making salads and so on) to the job of chef. They allocated all the tasks involved in giving the food to customers (such as greeting customers, taking orders, putting fries and burgers into bags, adding salt, pepper and napkins and taking money) to food servers. In addition, they created other jobs – the job of dealing with drive-in customers, the job of keeping the restaurant clean and the job of overseeing employees and responding to unexpected events. The result of the job design process is a *division of labour* among employees, one that McDonald's managers have discovered through experience.

Establishing an appropriate division of labour among employees is a critical part of the organising process, vital to increasing efficiency and effectiveness. At McDonald's, the tasks associated with chef and food server were split into different jobs because managers found that, for the kind of food McDonald's serves, this approach was most efficient: when each employee is given fewer tasks to perform (so that each job becomes more *specialised*), employees become more productive at performing the tasks that constitute each job.

At the US Subway sandwich shops, however, managers chose a different kind of job design. At Subway, there is no division of labour among the people who make the sandwiches, wrap the sandwiches, give them to customers and take the money. The roles of chef and food server are combined into one. This different division of tasks and jobs is efficient for Subway and not for McDonald's because Subway serves a limited menu of mostly submarine-style sandwiches that are prepared to order. Subway's production system is far simpler than McDonald's, because McDonald's menu is much more varied and its chefs must cook many different kinds of foods.

Managers of every organisation need to analyse the range of tasks to be performed and then create the jobs that best allow the organisation to give customers the products and services they want. In deciding how to assign tasks to individual jobs, however, managers must be careful not to take job simplification – the process of reducing the number of tasks that each worker performs – too far.[20] Too much job simplification may reduce efficiency rather than increase it: if workers find their simplified jobs boring and monotonous, they become demotivated and unhappy, and as a result, perform at a low level.

Job Enlargement and Job Enrichment

In an attempt to create a division of labour and design individual jobs to encourage workers to perform at a higher level and be more satisfied with their work, several researchers have proposed two other ways to group tasks into jobs: job enlargement and job enrichment.

Job enlargement is increasing the number of different *tasks* in a given job by changing the division of labour.[21] For example, because Subway food servers make the food as well as serve it, their jobs are 'larger' than the jobs of McDonald's food servers. Increasing the range of tasks performed by a worker will reduce boredom and fatigue and may increase motivation to perform at a high level – increasing both the quantity and the quality of products and services provided.

Job enrichment is increasing the degree of *responsibility* a worker has over a job by, for example, (1) empowering workers to experiment to find new or better ways of doing the job, (2) encouraging workers to develop new skills, (3) allowing workers to decide how to do the work and giving them the responsibility for deciding how to respond to unexpected situations and (4) allowing workers to monitor and measure their own performance.[22] Increasing workers' responsibility increases their involvement in their jobs and thus increases their interest in the quality of the products they manufacture, or the services they provide.

In general, managers who make design choices that increase job enrichment and job enlargement are likely to increase the degree to which people behave flexibly rather than rigidly or mechanically. Narrow, specialised jobs are likely to lead people to behave in predictable ways; workers who perform a variety of tasks and who are allowed and encouraged to discover new and better ways to perform their jobs are likely to act flexibly and creatively. Managers who enlarge and enrich jobs create a flexible organisational structure, and those who simplify jobs create a more formal structure. If workers are grouped into self-managed work teams, the organisation is likely to be flexible because team members provide support for each other and can learn from one another.

The Job Characteristics Model

J. R. Hackman and G. R. Oldham's *job characteristics model* is an influential model of job design that explains in detail how managers can make jobs more interesting and motivating.[23] Hackman and Oldham's model (Fig. 10.2) also describes the likely *personal* and *organisational* outcomes that will result from enriched and enlarged jobs.

According to Hackman and Oldham, every job has five characteristics that determine how motivating the job is. These characteristics determine how employees *react to* their work and lead to outcomes such as high performance and satisfaction, low absenteeism and turnover:

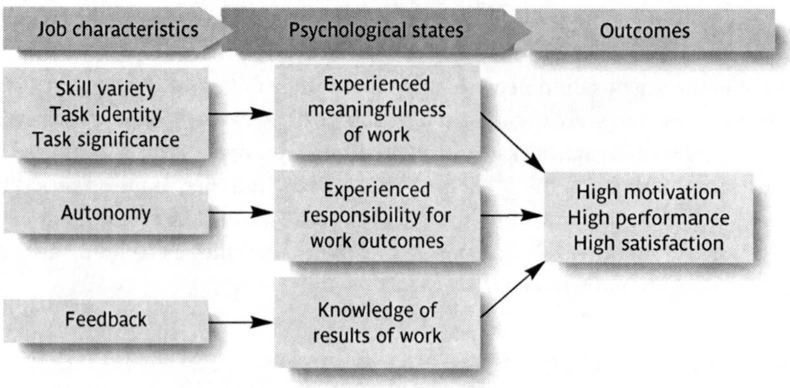

Figure 10.2 The Job Characteristics Model

Source: Adapted from J. R. Hackman and G. R. Oldham, *Work Redesign* (Reading, MA: Addison-Wesley, 1980).

- *Skill variety* The extent to which a job requires that an employee use a wide range of different skills abilities or knowledge. *Example*: the skill variety required by a family doctor is higher than that called for by the job of a McDonald's food server.
- *Task identity* The extent to which a job requires that a worker perform all the tasks necessary to complete the job from the beginning to the end of the production process. *Example*: a crafts worker who takes a piece of wood and transforms it into a custom-made piece of furniture such as a desk has higher task identity than does a worker who performs only one of the numerous operations required to assemble a television.
- *Task significance* The degree to which a worker feels that their job is meaningful because of its effect on people inside the organisation such as co-workers or on people outside the organisation such as customers. *Example*: a teacher who sees the effect of their efforts in a well-educated and well-adjusted student enjoys high task significance compared to a dishwasher who monotonously washes dishes as they come to the kitchen.
- *Autonomy* The degree to which a job gives an employee the freedom and discretion needed to schedule different tasks and decide how to carry them out. *Example*: salespeople who have to plan their schedules and decide how to allocate their time among different customers have relatively high autonomy compared to assembly-line workers whose actions are determined by the speed of the production line.
- *Feedback* The extent to which actually doing a job provides a worker with clear and direct information about how well they have performed the job. *Example*: an air traffic controller whose mistakes may result in a mid-air collision receives immediate feedback on job performance; a person who compiles statistics for a business magazine often has little idea of when he or she makes a mistake or does a particularly good job.

Hackman and Oldham argue that these five job characteristics affect an employee's motivation because they affect three critical psychological states (Fig. 10.2). The more employees feel that their work is *meaningful* and that they are *responsible for work outcomes* and *responsible for knowing how those outcomes affect others*, the more motivating work becomes, and the more likely employees are to be satisfied and to perform at a high level. Moreover, employees who have jobs that are highly motivating are called on to use their skills more and to perform more tasks. Usually, they are given more responsibility for doing their job. These are all characteristics of jobs and employees in flexible structures where authority is decentralised and where employees commonly work with others and must learn new skills to complete the range of tasks for which their group is responsible.

TIPS FOR PRACTICE

1. Be aware that the organisational structure should be appropriate for the organisational environment, strategy, technology and HR.
2. Formal structures require detail: if this is the preferred structure, remember to draw up specific job descriptions and evaluate performance.
3. If a flexible structure is more appropriate, then concepts such as job enrichment and enlargement, which encourage collaboration, should be employed.
4. Think about how you could make every job as motivating and satisfying as possible. Try to use the job characteristic model or other tools to think about this.

Grouping Jobs into Functions and Divisions

Once managers have decided which tasks to allocate to which jobs, they face the next organising decision: how to *group jobs together* to best match the needs of the organisation's environment, strategy, technology and HR. Most senior management teams decide to group jobs into *departments* and develop a *functional structure* to use organisational resources. As the organisation grows, managers design a *divisional structure* or a more complex *matrix or product team structure.*

Choosing a structure and then designing it so that it works as intended is a significant challenge. As noted earlier, managers reap the rewards of a well-thought-out strategy only if they choose the right type of structure to implement and execute the strategy. The ability to make the right kinds of organising choices is often what differentiates effective from ineffective managers.

Functional Structure

A *function* is a group of people, working together, who possess similar skills or use the same kind of knowledge, tools or techniques to perform their jobs. Manufacturing, sales and R&D are often organised into functional departments. A functional structure is an organisational structure composed of all the departments that an organisation requires to produce its goods or services. Figure 10.3 shows the functional structure of Telehouse Europe, a London-based IT housing and management service.[24]

Telehouse's main functions are finance, technical services and European sales and marketing. Each job inside a function exists because it helps the function perform the activities necessary for high organisational performance. Within the Sales and Marketing department, for example, are all the jobs necessary to efficiently distribute the service, to increase business awareness and to market the service appropriately.

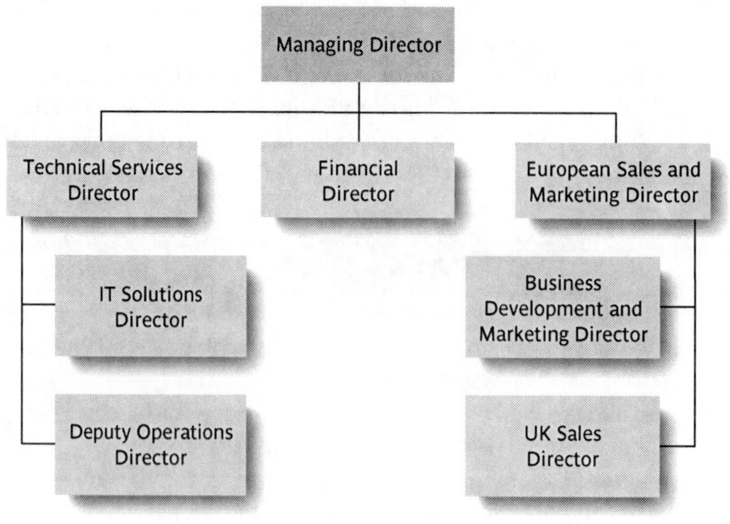

Figure 10.3 The Functional Structure of Telehouse Europe
Source: Taken from www.telehouse.net

There are several advantages to grouping jobs according to function. First, when people who perform similar jobs are grouped together, they can learn from observing one another and thus become more *specialised* and can perform at a higher level. The tasks associated with one job often are related to the tasks associated with another, which encourages *co-operation* within a function.

Second, when people who perform similar jobs are grouped together, it is easier for managers to *monitor* and *evaluate their performance.*[25] Imagine if marketing experts, purchasing experts and real-estate experts were grouped together in one function and supervised by a manager from merchandising. Obviously, the merchandising manager would not have the expertise to evaluate all these different people appropriately. However, a functional structure allows co-workers to evaluate how well their colleagues are performing their jobs, and if some are performing poorly, more experienced co-workers can help them develop new skills.

Finally, managers appreciate a functional structure because it allows them to create the set of functions they need in order to *scan and monitor the competitive environment* and obtain information about the way it is changing. With the right set of functions in place, managers are in a good position to develop a strategy that allows the organisation to respond to its changing situation. Employees in marketing, for example, can specialise in monitoring new marketing developments that will allow Telehouse Europe to better target its customers.

As an organisation grows, and particularly as its task environment and strategy change because it is beginning to produce a wider range of goods and services for different kinds of customers, several problems can make a functional structure less efficient and effective.[26] First, managers in different functions may find it more difficult to *communicate* and *co-ordinate* with one another when they are responsible for several different kinds of products, especially as the organisation grows both domestically and internationally. Second, functional managers may become so preoccupied with supervising their own specific departments and achieving their departmental goals that they lose sight of *organisational goals.* If that happens, organisational effectiveness will suffer because managers will be viewing issues and problems facing the organisation only from their own, relatively narrow, departmental perspectives.[27] Both of these problems can reduce efficiency and effectiveness.

Reaction Time

1. Would a flexible or a more formal structure be appropriate for these organisations: (a) a large department store, (b) a 'Big Five' accountancy firm, (c) a biotechnology company? Explain your reasoning.
2. Using the job characteristics model as a guide, discuss how a manager can enrich or enlarge subordinates' jobs.
3. How might a sales assistant's job or a secretary's job be enlarged or enriched to make it more motivating?

Divisional Structures: Product, Market and Geographic

As the problems associated with growth and diversification increase over time, managers must search for new ways to organise their activities to overcome the problems associated with a functional structure. Most managers of large organisations choose a divisional structure and create a series of business units to produce a specific kind of product for a specific kind of customer. Each division is a collection of functions or departments that work together to produce the product. The goal behind the change to a divisional structure is to create smaller, more manageable units within the organisation. There are three forms of divisional structure (Fig. 10.4).[28] When managers organise divisions according to the type of product or service they provide, they adopt a product structure. When managers organise divisions according to the area of the country or world they operate in, they adopt a geographic structure. When

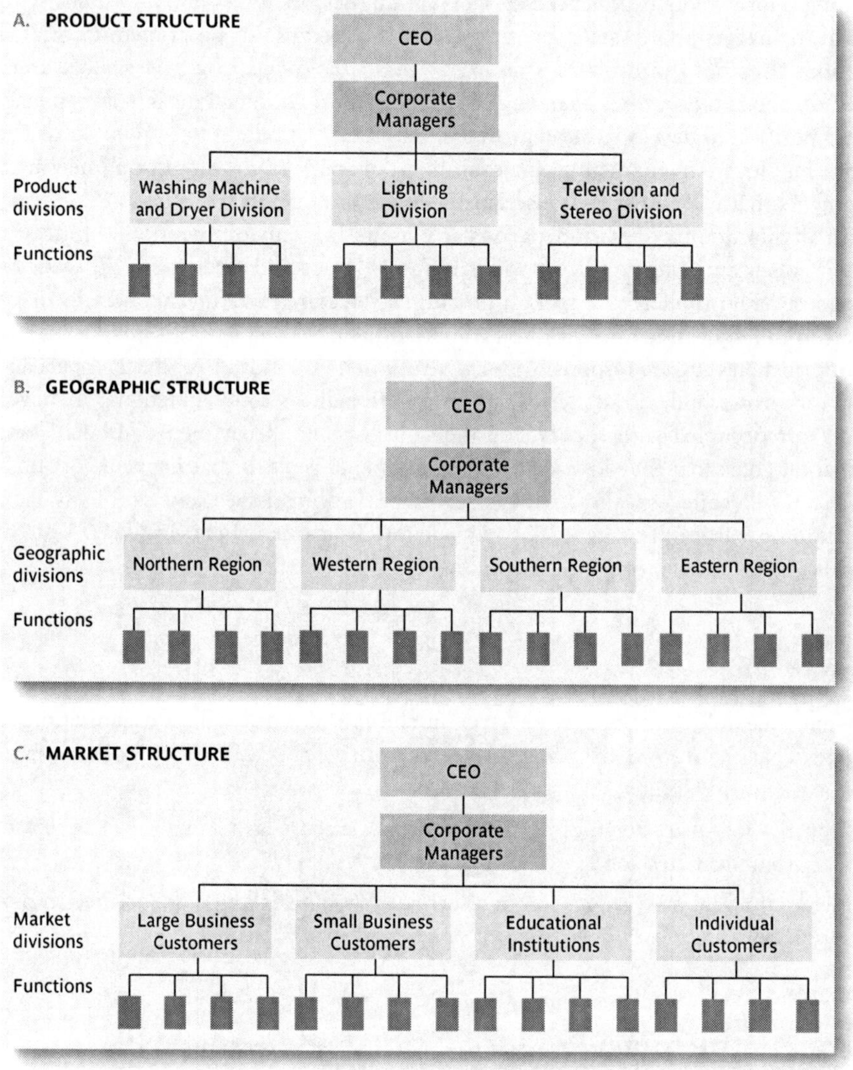

Figure 10.4 Product, Market and Geographic Structures

managers organise divisions according to the type of customer they focus on, they adopt a market structure.

Product structure

Imagine the problems that managers at IKEA would encounter if they decided to diversify into producing and selling cars, PCs and health insurance – in addition to home furnishings. They could try to use their existing set of functional managers to oversee the production of all four kinds of products. However, no manager would have the necessary skills or abilities to oversee them all. No individual marketing manager, for example, could effectively market cars, PCs, health insurance and home furnishings at the same time. To perform a functional activity successfully, managers must have experience in specific markets or industries. Consequently, if managers decide to diversify into new industries or to expand their range of products, they commonly design a *product structure* to organise their operations (Fig. 10.4A).

Using a *product structure*, managers place each distinct product line or business in its own self-contained division and give divisional managers the responsibility for devising an appropriate business-level strategy to allow the division to compete effectively in its industry or market.[29] Each division is self-contained because it has a complete set of all the functions – marketing, R&D, finance and so on – that it needs to produce or provide goods or services efficiently and effectively. Functional managers report to divisional managers, and divisional managers report to senior or corporate managers.

Grouping functions into divisions focused on particular products has several advantages for managers at all levels in the organisation. First, a product structure allows functional managers to specialise in only one product area, so they are able to build expertise and refine their skills in this particular area. Second, each division's managers can become experts in their industry; this expertise helps them choose and develop a business-level strategy to differentiate their products or lower their costs while meeting the customer needs. Third, a product structure frees corporate managers from the need to supervise each division's day-to-day operations directly. This latitude allows corporate managers to create the best corporate-level strategy to maximise the organisation's future growth and ability to create value. Corporate managers are likely to make fewer mistakes about which businesses to diversify into, or how best to expand internationally, for example, because they are able to take an organisationwide view.[30] Corporate managers also are likely to evaluate better how well divisional managers are doing, and they can intervene and take corrective action as needed.

The extra layer of management – the divisional management layer – can improve the use of organisational resources. A product structure also puts divisional managers close to their customers and lets them respond quickly and appropriately to the changing task environment. Consider how Viacom, the huge media entertainment company which owns Paramount Pictures and MTV, created a product structure.

Sumner Redstone, the billionaire chairman of Viacom, is continually making acquisitions that add to the range of entertainment products the company provides to its customers. Under Redstone, Viacom started in the cable and television business and expanded into several fields: entertainment, networks and broadcasting, video, music, theme parks, publishing and television. In 2000, for example, Viacom acquired CBS television and BET.[31]

To manage Viacom's many different businesses effectively, Redstone decided to design a product structure (Fig. 10.5). He put each business in a separate division and gave managers in each division responsibility for making their business the Number One performer in its

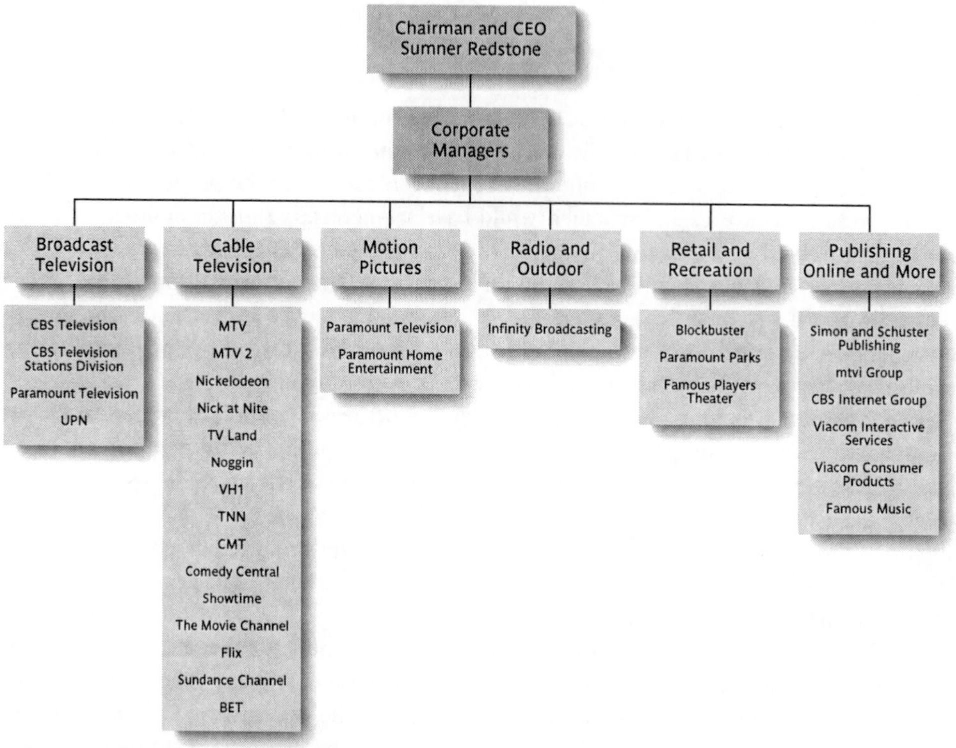

Figure 10.5 Viacom's 2001 Product Structure

industry. Redstone recognised, however, that the different divisions could help each other and create *synergies* for Viacom by sharing their skills and resources. Blockbuster, for example, could launch a major advertising campaign to publicise the movies that Paramount makes and thus boost the visibility of both divisions' products. Simon & Schuster, a publisher, could produce and publish specific books to tie in with the opening of a movie and thus boost ticket and book sales. To achieve these synergies, Redstone created a team of corporate managers who were responsible for working with the different divisional managers to identify new opportunities to create value. So far, this method of organising has served Viacom well, and it has become one of the 'Top Four' media and entertainment companies.[32]

A pharmaceutical company that has recently adopted a new product structure to better organise its activities is profiled in Case 10.2.

Geographic structure

When organisations expand rapidly both at home and abroad, functional structures can create special problems because managers in one central location may find it increasingly difficult to deal with the different problems and issues that may arise in each of the regions – whether these are countries or areas of the world. In these cases, a *geographic structure*, in which divisions are broken down by geographic location, is often chosen (Fig. 10.4B). To achieve the corporate mission of providing a next-day postage service, Fred Smith, CEO of Federal Express, chose a

Case 10.2: GlaxoSmithKline's new product structure

The need to innovate new kinds of prescription drugs in order to boost performance is a continual battle for pharmaceutical companies. In the 2000s, many of these companies have been merging to try to increase their research productivity, and one, GlaxoSmithKline, was created from the merger between Glaxo Wellcome and SmithKline Beechum.[33] Prior to the merger, both companies had experienced a steep decline in the number of new prescription drugs that their scientists were able to invent. The problem facing the new company's senior managers was how to best use and combine the talents of the scientists and researchers from both of the former companies to allow them to quickly innovate exciting new drugs.

Senior managers realised that after the merger there would be enormous problems associated with co-ordinating the activities of the thousands of research scientists who were working on hundreds of different kinds of drug research programmes. Understanding the problems associated with large size, the senior managers decided to group the researchers into eight smaller product divisions to allow them to focus on particular clusters of diseases, such as heart disease or viral infections. The members of each product division were told that they would be rewarded based on the number of new prescription drugs they were able to invent and the speed with which they could bring these new drugs to the market.

To date, GlaxoSmithKlein's new product structure has worked well. The company claimed that by 2004 research productivity had more than doubled since the reorganisation. The number of new drugs moving into clinical trials had doubled from 10 to 20, and the company had 148 new drugs that were being tested.[34] Moreover, the company claimed that the morale of its researchers had increased and turnover had fallen because the members of each division enjoyed working together and collaborating to innovate lifesaving new drugs. The company expected to have the best new drug pipeline in its industry in the next three to four years.

geographic structure and divided up operations by creating a division in each region. Since the needs of retail customers differ by region a geographic structure gives retail regional managers the flexibility they need to choose the range of products that best meets the needs of regional customers. Tesco has adopted such a structure to ensure that local customers are provided with the goods they need – for example, the product range in Malaysia differs from the product range in the UK.

In adopting a *global geographic structure*, such as shown in Fig. 10.6A, managers locate different divisions in each of the world regions where the organisation operates. Managers are most likely to do this when they pursue a *multi-domestic strategy*, because customer needs vary widely by country or world region. For example, if products that appeal to US customers do not sell in Europe, the Pacific Rim or South America, then managers must customise the products to meet the needs of customers in those different world regions; a global geographic structure with global divisions will allow them to do this.

In contrast, to the degree that customers abroad are willing to buy the same kind of product, or slight variations of it, managers are more likely to pursue a global strategy. In this case they are more likely to use a *global product structure*. In such a structure, each product division, not the country and regional managers, takes responsibility for deciding where to manufacture its products and how to market them in foreign countries worldwide (Fig. 10.6B). Product division managers manage their own global value chains and decide where to establish foreign

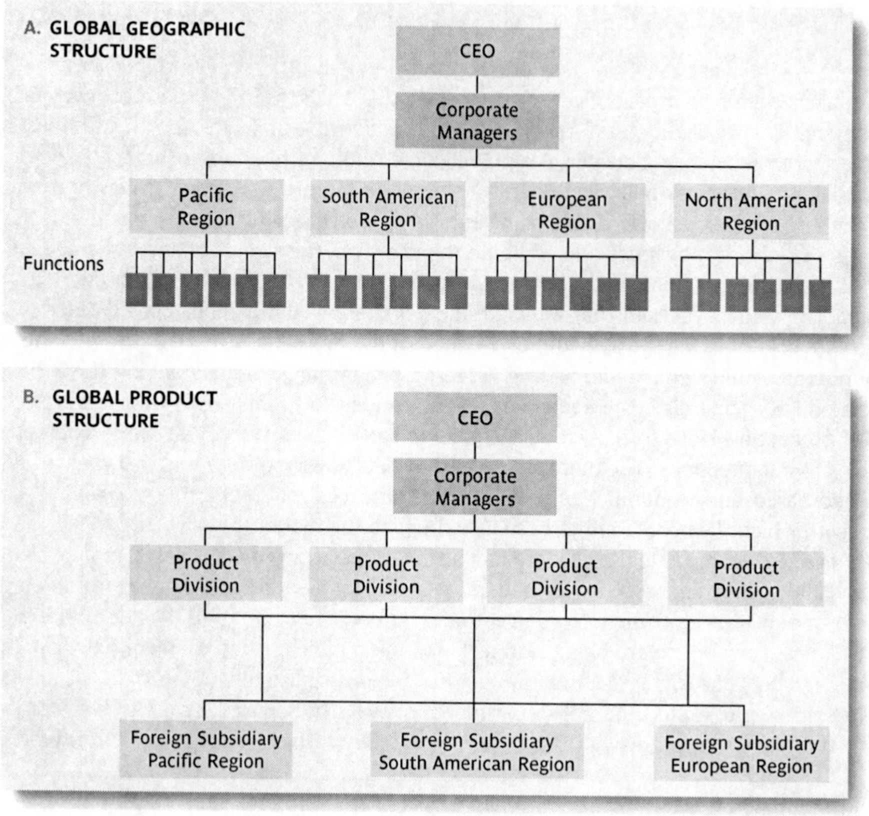

Figure 10.6 Global Geographic and Global Product Structures

subsidiaries to distribute and sell their products to customers in foreign countries. As we noted at the beginning of this chapter, an organisation's strategy is a major determinant of its structure both at home and abroad.

Market structure

Sometimes the pressing issue facing managers is to group functions according to the type of customer buying the product, in order to tailor the products the organisation offers to each customer's unique demands. A computer company like Dell, for example, has several kinds of customers, including large businesses (which might demand networks of computers linked to a mainframe computer), small companies (which may need just a few PCs linked together), educational users in schools and universities (which might want thousands of independent PCs for their students) and individual users (who may want a high-quality multimedia PC so that they can play the latest video games).

To satisfy the needs of diverse customers, a company might adopt a *market structure* (also called a *customer structure*), which groups divisions according to the particular kinds of customers they serve (Fig. 10.4C). A market structure allows managers to be responsive to the needs of their customers and allows them to act flexibly in making decisions in response to customers' changing needs.

Matrix and Product Team Designs

Moving to a product, market or geographic divisional structure allows managers to respond more quickly and flexibly to the particular set of circumstances they confront. However, when the environment is dynamic and changing rapidly and uncertainty is high, even a divisional structure may not provide managers with enough flexibility to respond to the environment quickly. When customer needs or IT is changing rapidly, and the environment is very uncertain, managers must design the most flexible kind of organisational structure available: a matrix structure or a product team structure (Fig. 10.7).

Matrix structure

In a *matrix structure*, managers group people and resources in two ways simultaneously: by function and by product.[35] Employees are grouped by *functions* to allow them to learn from one another and become more skilled and productive. In addition, employees are grouped into *product teams* in which members of different functions work together to develop a specific product. The result is a complex network of reporting relationships among product teams and functions that make the matrix structure very flexible (Fig. 10.7A). Each person in a product team reports to two bosses: (1) a functional boss, who assigns individuals to a team and evaluates their performance from a functional perspective, and (2) the boss of the product team, who evaluates their performance on the team. Thus, team members are known as *two-boss employees* because they report to two managers. The functional employees assigned to product teams change over time as the specific skills that the team needs change. At the beginning of the product development process, for example, engineers and R&D specialists are assigned to a product team because their skills are needed to develop new products. When a provisional design has been established, marketing experts are assigned to the team to assess how customers will respond to the new product. Manufacturing personnel join when it is time to find the most efficient way to produce the product. As their specific jobs are completed, team members leave and are reassigned to new teams. In this way the matrix structure makes the most use of HR.

To keep the matrix structure flexible, product teams are empowered and team members are responsible for making most of the important decisions involved in product development.[36] The product team manager acts as a *facilitator*, controlling the financial resources and trying to keep the project on time and within budget. The functional managers try to ensure that the product is the best that it can be in order to maximise its differentiated appeal.

High-tech companies that operate in environments where new product development takes place on a regular basis have used matrix structures successfully for many years, and the need to innovate quickly is vital to the organisation's survival. The flexibility afforded by a matrix structure allows managers to keep pace with a changing and increasingly complex environment.[37]

Product team structure

The dual reporting relationships that are at the heart of a matrix structure have always been difficult for managers and employees to deal with. The functional boss and the product boss often make conflicting demands on team members, who do not know which boss to satisfy first. Functional and product team bosses may also come into conflict over precisely who is in charge

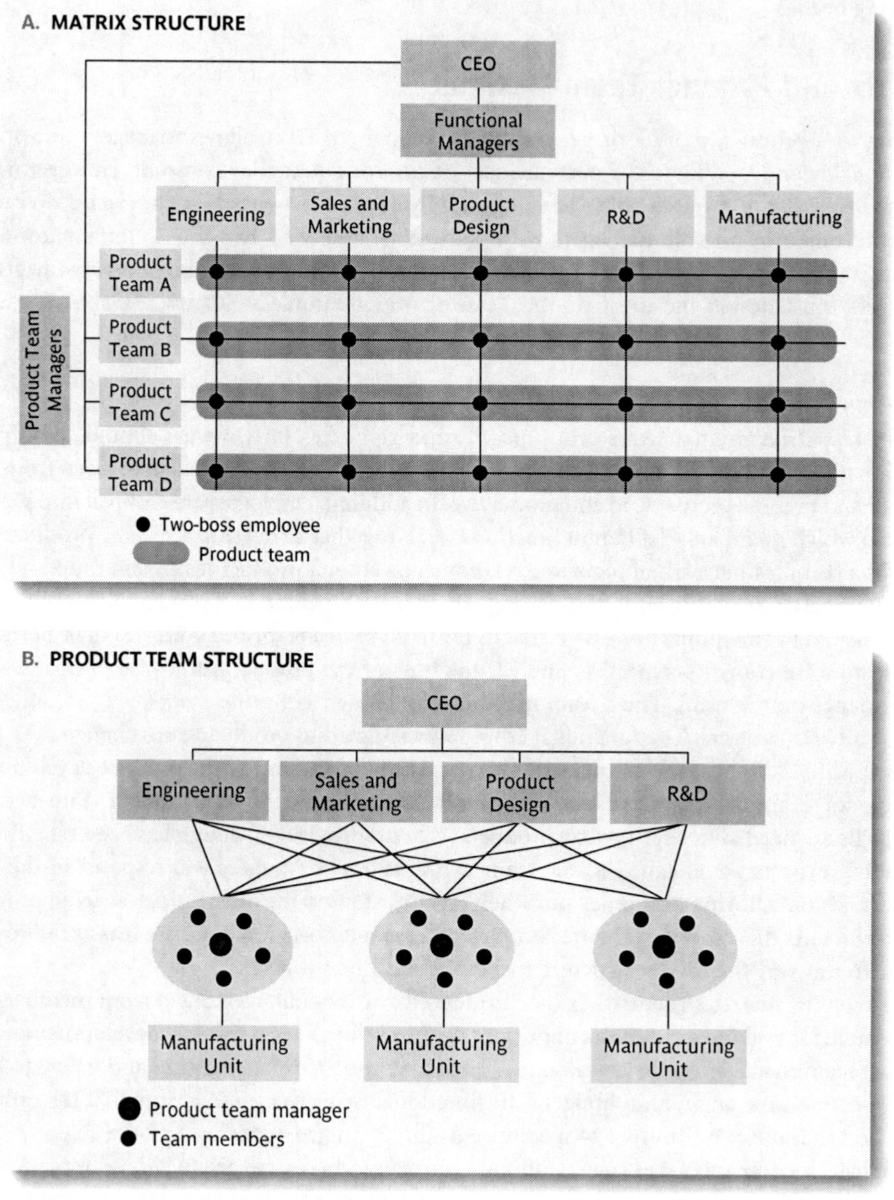

Figure 10.7 Matrix and Product Team Structures

of which team members, and for how long. To avoid these problems, managers have devised a way of organising people and resources that still allows an organisation to be flexible but make its structure easier to operate: a product team structure.

The *product team structure* differs from a matrix structure in two ways: (1) it eliminates dual reporting relationships and two-boss employees, and (2) functional employees are permanently assigned to a cross-functional team that is empowered to bring a new or redesigned product to market. A *cross-functional team* is a group of managers brought together from different departments to perform organisational tasks. When managers are grouped into cross-departmental teams, the artificial boundaries between departments disappear, and a narrow focus on departmental goals is replaced with a general interest in working together to achieve organisational goals. The results of such changes have been dramatic: DaimlerChrysler can now introduce a new model of car in two years, down from five; Black & Decker can innovate new products in months, not years; Hallmark Cards can respond to changing customer demand for types of cards in weeks, not months.

Members of a cross-functional team report only to the *product team manager* or to one of his or her direct subordinates. The heads of the functions have only an informal, advisory relationship with members of the product teams – the role of functional managers is only to counsel and help team members, share knowledge among teams and provide new technological developments that can help improve each team's performance (Fig. 10.7B).[38]

Organisations are increasingly making empowered cross-functional teams an essential part of their organisational architecture to help them gain a competitive advantage in fast-changing organisational environments. Newell Rubbermaid, for example, the maker of more than 5,000 household products such as Parker Pens or Rotring writing implements, moved to a product team structure because its managers wanted to speed up the rate of product innovation. Managers created 20 cross-functional teams composed of five–seven people from marketing, manufacturing, R&D, finance and other functions.[39] Each team focuses its energies on a particular product line, such as garden products, bathroom products or kitchen products. These teams develop more than 365 new products a year. Case 10.3 describes developments at Oxford University, which is facing a long-term commitment to change and restructure.

Case 10.3: Oxford faces its toughest challenge in its 900-year history

The university sector is changing. Global competition for academics, students and money has replaced the idealistic notion of an eternally curious and scholarly search for knowledge and scientific advancement. While these ideas are still alive, universities are now facing increasing pressure to maintain financial viability and expand. This development does not even stop at the gates of such prestigious institutions as Oxford. For the fourth year running, Oxford held the Number One spot in the UK's league tables for universities in 2005.[40] In a 2004 review of the top 200 universities in the world, Oxford was placed at Number 5.[41] However, its current Vice-Chancellor was employed in 2004 to overhaul and restructure the university.[42]

John Hood, who prior to his appointment was Vice-Chancellor at the University of Auckland, has a reputation for turning around conflict-ridden institutions and obtaining substantial investments; in the case of the University of Auckland he managed to lay the foundations for a £290 million investment. His aim of initiating and achieving change at Oxford is different from commercial companies. Hood argues he holds little power other than the 'power of persuasion'. His job is to move Oxford to an improved standing in the globalised academic market and achieve outstanding leadership in research by attracting international scientists. Oxford, like many other organisations, be they universities or private companies, is now competing against American counterparts: for Oxford, these are Yale, Harvard, or Stanford.

In order to achieve this, Hood plans, among other things, to restructure both finances and governance.

However, restructuring a 900-year-old institution is challenging. Oxford is extremely decentralised, with the Congregation, a 3,500-body strong institution of academics and administrators, at its centre. This Congregation can call votes on important decisions within the university. Alongside this structure are some 39 autonomous colleges that are trying to ensure their independence. These colleges at present control their finances, student admissions, etc.

Another area that Hood feels needs restructuring is Oxford's 28-member council, that includes only four external members, to provide a more objective viewpoint. Hood plans to restructure the council into two boards. One will be responsible for all academic and scholarly matters that arise at Oxford University. The second will resemble a more business-oriented board of directors. It is anticipated that this board will be 15 strong, comprising seven outside trustees, seven internal members and the University Chancellor as the Chair. These suggestions, nevertheless, did not receive positive feedback, as some people felt that it was undermining the democracy of Oxford University and that Hood was managing the institution like a large corporation.

Few, however, doubt that Hood will be able to restructure Oxford in time, as he has good intentions and knows where Oxford needs to be to compete successfully with its national and international rivals.[43]

Hybrid Structure

A large organisation that has many divisions and simultaneously uses many different structures has a **hybrid structure**. Most large organisations use product division structures and create self-contained divisions; each division's managers then select the structure that best meets the needs of the particular environment, strategy and so on. One product division may choose to operate with a functional structure, a second may choose a geographic structure and a third may choose a product team structure because of the nature of the division's products or the desire to be more responsive to customers' needs. Target, a US-based retailer which has very similar characteristics to the UK-based Argos, uses a hybrid structure based on grouping by customer and by geography.

As shown in Fig. 10.8, Target operates its different store chains as four independent divisions in a market division structure. Its four market divisions are Mervyn's and Marshall Field's, which cater to the needs of affluent customers; Target Stores, which competes in the low-price segment; and target direct, Target's Internet division, which manages online sales.

Beneath this organisational layer is another layer of structure because both Target Stores and Marshall Field's operate with a geographic structure that groups stores by region. This applies also to Argos, which is organised in a similar way. Individual stores are under the direction of a regional office, which is responsible for co-ordinating the market needs of the stores in its region and for responding to regional customer needs. The regional office feeds information back to divisional headquarters, where centralised merchandising functions make decisions for all Target or Marshall Field's stores.

Organisational structure may thus be likened to the layers of an onion. The outer layer provides the overarching organisational framework – most commonly a product or market division structure – and each inner layer is the structure that each division selects for itself in response to

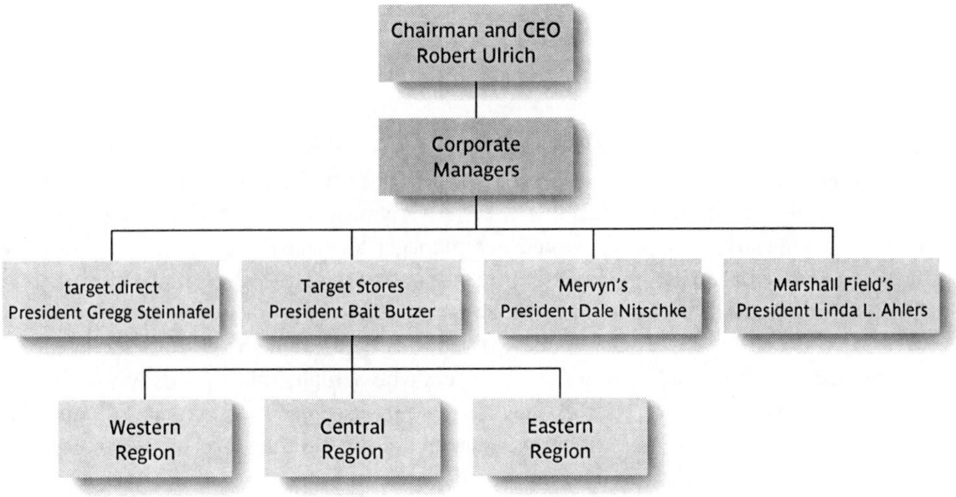

Figure 10.8 Target's Hybrid Structure

the contingencies it faces – such as a geographic or product team structure. The ability to break a large organisation into smaller units or divisions makes it much easier for managers to change structure when the need arises – for example, when a change in technology or an increase in competition in the environment necessitates a change from a functional to a product team structure.

Reaction Time

1. When and under what conditions might managers change from a functional to (a) a product, (b) a geographic, or (c) a market structure?
2. How do matrix structure and product team structure differ? Why is product team structure more widely used?

Co-ordinating Functions and Divisions

In organising, managers have several tasks. The first is to group functions and divisions and create the organisational structures best suited to the contingencies they face. The next task is to ensure that there is sufficient co-ordination or integration among functions and divisions so that organisational resources are used efficiently and effectively. Having discussed how managers divide organisational activities into jobs, functions and divisions to increase efficiency and effectiveness, we now need to look at how they put the parts back together.

We look first at the way in which managers design the hierarchy of authority to co-ordinate functions and divisions so that they work together effectively. Then we focus on *integration*, and examine the many different integrating mechanisms that managers can use to co-ordinate functions and divisions.

Allocating Authority

As organisations grow and produce a wider range of goods and services, the size and number of their functions and divisions increase. To co-ordinate the activities of people, functions and divisions and to allow them to work together effectively, managers must develop a clear hierarchy of authority.[44] Authority is the power vested in a manager to make decisions and use resources to achieve organisational goals by virtue of his or her position in an organisation. The *hierarchy of authority* is an organisation's chain of command – the relative authority that each manager or employee has – extending from the CEO at the top, down through the middle managers and first-line managers, to the non-managerial employees who actually make goods or provide services. Every manager, at every level of the hierarchy, supervises one or more subordinates. The term span of control refers to the number of subordinates who report directly to a manager.

Figure 10.9 shows a simplified picture of the hierarchy of authority and the span of control of managers in McDonald's in 2004. At the top of the hierarchy is Charlie Bell, CEO and chairman of McDonald's board of directors, who took control in 2004.[45] Bell is the manager who has ultimate responsibility for McDonald's performance, and he has the authority to decide how to use organisational resources to benefit McDonald's stakeholders.[46] Both Mike Roberts and Jim Skinner report directly to Bell. Roberts is the CEO of McDonald's domestic operations; Vice Chairman Skinner is the head of McDonald's overseas operations. They are next in the chain of command under Bell. Of special mention is Ralph Alvarez, who in July 2004 was appointed as president of domestic operations, reporting to Roberts. Also depicted is CFO Mathew Paull, who also reports directly to Bell; however, unlike the others, he is not a line manager, someone in the direct line or chain of command who has formal authority over people and resources. Rather, Paull is the staff manager, responsible for one of McDonald's specialist functions, finance.

Managers at each level of the hierarchy give managers at the next level down the authority to make decisions about how to use organisational resources. Accepting this authority, those lower-level managers then become responsible for their decisions and are accountable for how well they make them. Managers who make appropriate, sustainable and effective decisions are typically promoted. Organisations often motivate managers with the prospects of promotion and increased responsibility within the chain of command.

Below Roberts are the other main levels or layers in the McDonald's chain of command – executive vice presidents, zone managers, regional managers and supervisors. A hierarchy is also evident in each company-owned McDonald's restaurant. At the senior is the store manager; at lower levels are the first assistant, shift managers and crew personnel. McDonald's managers have decided that this hierarchy of authority best allows the company to pursue its business-level strategy of providing fast food at reasonable prices.

Tall and flat organisations

As an organisation grows in size (normally measured by the *number of employees*), its hierarchy of authority normally lengthens in order to decrease the span of control, making the organisational structure taller. A *tall* organisation has many levels of authority relative to company size; a *flat* organisation has fewer levels relative to company size (Fig. 10.10).[47] As a hierarchy becomes

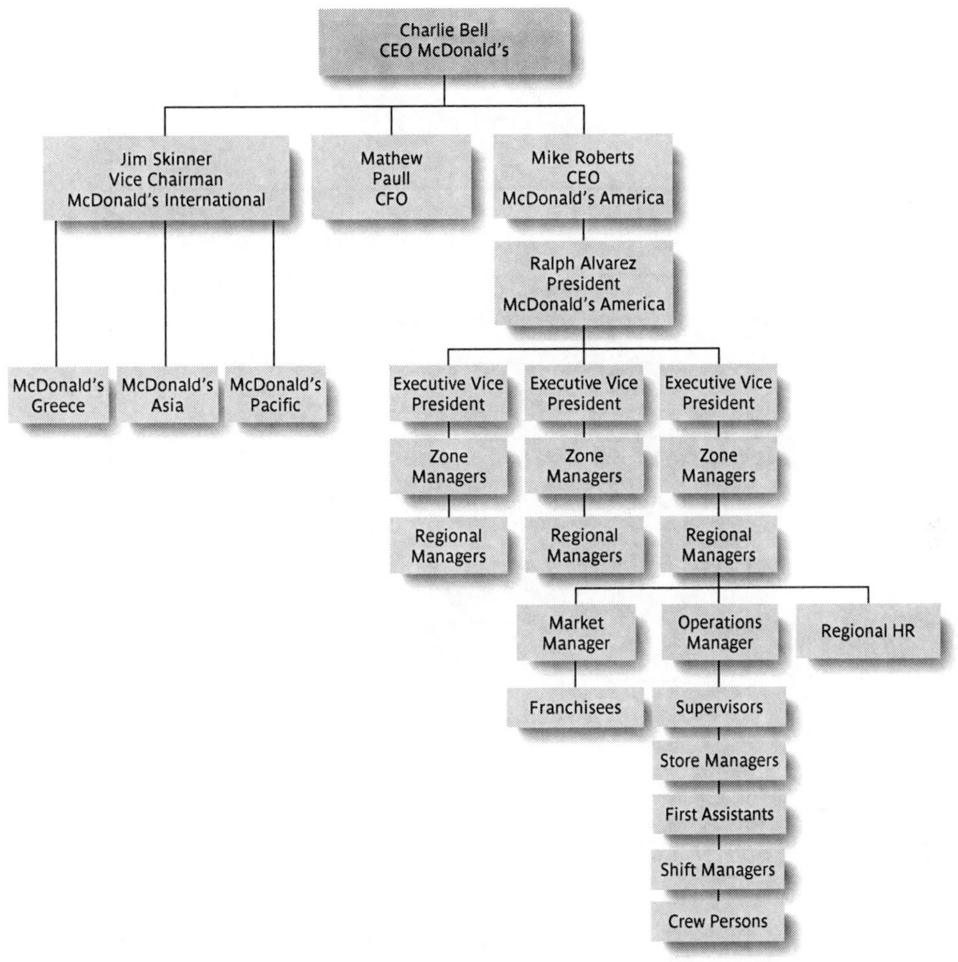

Figure 10.9 The Hierarchy of Authority and Span of Control at McDonald's Corporation

taller, an organisation's structure is likely to become less flexible and a slower response from managers to changes in the organisational environment may be the result.

Communication problems may arise when an organisation has many levels in the hierarchy: it can take a long time for the decisions and orders of upper-level managers to reach managers further down. It can also increase the time for senior managers to learn how well their decisions have worked. Feeling out of touch, senior managers may want to verify that lower-level managers are following orders and may require written confirmation from them. Middle managers, who know they will be held strictly accountable for their actions, start devoting more time to the process of decision making to improve their chances of making appropriate decisions; they may even try to avoid responsibility by making senior managers decide what actions to take.

Another communication problem that can result is the distortion of commands and orders being transmitted up and down the hierarchy, which may cause managers at different levels to

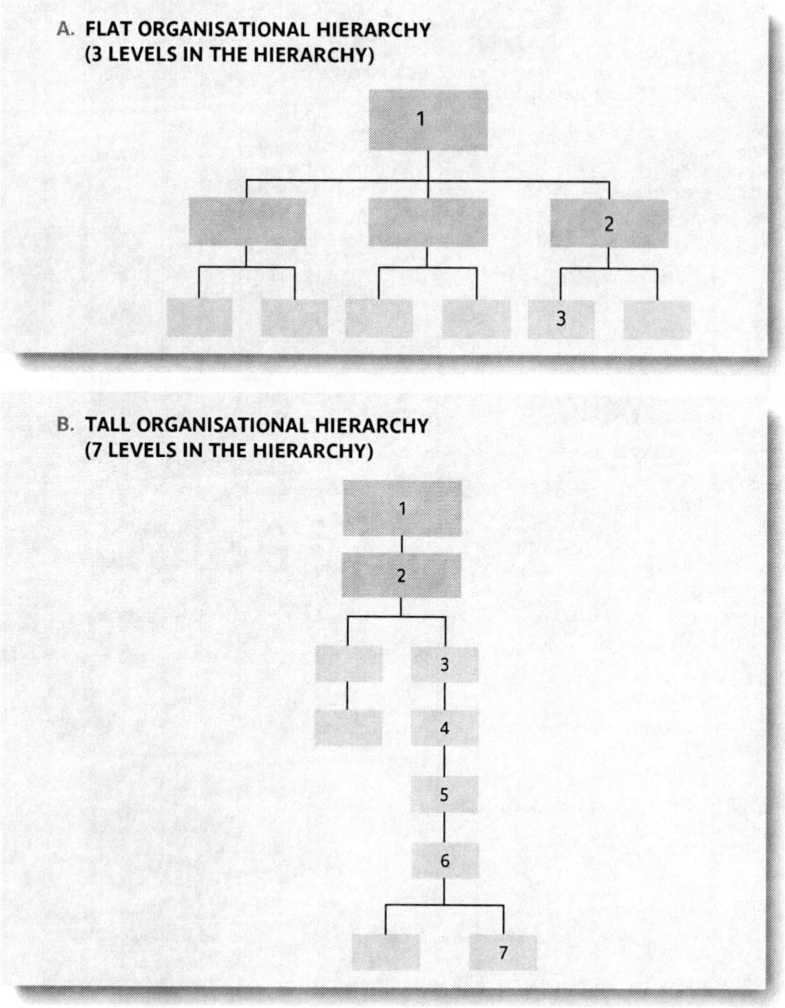

Figure 10.10 Tall and Flat Organisations

interpret the messages differently. Distortion of orders and messages can be accidental, occurring because different managers interpret messages from their own narrow, functional perspectives. Distortion may even be intentional, because managers lower in the hierarchy decide to interpret information in a way that increases their own personal advantage.

Another problem with tall hierarchies is that they usually indicate that an organisation is employing many managers, and managers are expensive. Managerial salaries, benefits, offices and secretaries are a huge expense. Large companies such as IBM and GM pay their managers billions of dollars a year. In the early 2000s, hundreds of thousands of middle managers were laid off as dot-coms collapsed and high-tech companies such as Hewlett-Packard, or manufacturers such as Volkswagen, attempted to reduce costs by restructuring and downsizing their workforces.

The minimum chain of command

To protect against the problems that result when an organisation becomes too tall and employs too many managers, senior managers need to ascertain whether they are employing the right number of middle and first-line managers, and whether they can redesign their organisational architecture. Senior managers may well follow a basic organising principle – the principle of the minimum chain of command – which states that senior managers should always construct a hierarchy with the *fewest levels of authority necessary* to efficiently and effectively use organisational resources.

Effective managers constantly scrutinise their hierarchies to see whether the number of levels can be reduced – for example, by eliminating one level and giving the responsibilities of managers at that level to the managers above and empowering the employees below. This practice has become increasingly common across the developed world as companies that are battling low-cost foreign competitors search for new ways to reduce costs. One manager who is constantly trying to empower employees and keep the hierarchy flat is Richard Branson of the Virgin Group. Branson is well known for continually reaffirming the message that employees should feel free to go above and beyond their prescribed roles to provide better customer service. His central message is that Virgin values and trusts its employees, who are empowered to take responsibility.

Centralisation and decentralisation of authority

Another way in which managers can keep the organisational hierarchy flat is by decentralising authority to lower-level managers and non-managerial employees.[48] If managers at higher levels give lower-level employees the responsibility of making important decisions and manage by exception, then the problems of slow and distorted communication we saw previously are kept to a minimum. Moreover, fewer managers are needed because their role is not to make decisions but to act as *coaches* and *facilitators* to help other employees make the best decisions. In addition, when decision making is low in the organisation and nearer the customer, employees are better able to recognise and respond to customer needs.

Decentralising authority allows an organisation and its employees to behave in a flexible way even as the organisation grows and becomes taller. This is why managers are so interested in empowering employees, creating self-managed work teams, establishing cross-functional teams and even moving to a product team structure. These design innovations help keep the organisational architecture flexible and responsive to complex task and general environments, complex technologies and complex strategies.

Although more and more organisations are taking steps to decentralise authority, *too much decentralisation* may also have negative impacts. If divisions, functions or teams are given too much decision-making authority, they may begin to pursue their own goals at the expense of organisational goals. Managers in engineering design or R&D, for example, may become so focused on making the best possible product that they fail to realise that the best product may be so expensive that few people will be willing or able to buy it. With too much decentralisation, lack of communication among functions or among divisions may also prevent possible synergies among them from ever materialising, and organisational performance suffers.

Senior managers must seek the balance between centralisation and decentralisation of authority that best meets the four major contingencies an organisation faces (Fig. 10.1). If managers are in a stable environment, are using well-understood technology and are producing staple kinds of products (such as cereal, canned soup, books or televisions), then there is no pressing need to decentralise authority, and managers at the top can maintain control of much of the organisational decision making.[49] However, in uncertain, changing environments where high-tech companies are producing state-of-the-art products, senior managers must empower employees and allow teams to make important strategic decisions so that the organisation can keep up with the changes taking place.

Case 10.4: Decentralisation to become one of the UK's best DIY stores

Homebase is the Number Two DIY retailer in the UK, serving more than 1.5 million customers weekly. Homebase has approximately 300 stores and a 12 per cent current market share.[50] In order to get to this position, Homebase had to adapt to new ways of organising its stores.

Homebase employees are organised into teams. Each team has a team leader who is responsible for holding regular team meetings, team building exercises and fun activities. These bonding activities are used to encourage employees to contribute to all kinds of decisions about the company and its processes, improvement of sales or improvements to customer service. Homebase emphasises the knowledge and expertise held by its shop floor workers, who are closest to customer needs. Empowerment in Homebase means that employees are not only encouraged to make their own decisions, but are expected to. The empowerment and team work is underpinned by a simple but effective philosophy. Employees go beyond simple decisions – they take full responsibility for their actions. They are expected to act confidently on problems they encounter and appreciate each other's contribution to the company's overall achievements.

But Homebase does not only place expectations on its employees. Part of the decentralisation is a Recognition Award that is given to employees who deliver outstanding customer service and go beyond their call of duty.[51]

Types of Integrating Mechanisms

Much co-ordination takes place through the hierarchy of authority. In addition, managers can use various *integrating mechanisms* to increase communication and co-ordination among functions and divisions. The greater the complexity of an organisation's structure, the greater is the need for co-ordination among people, functions and divisions to make the organisational structure work efficiently and effectively.[52] Thus, when managers choose to adopt a divisional, matrix or product team structure, they must use complex kinds of integrating mechanisms to achieve organisational goals. UPS and FedEx, for example, have complex geographic structures that need an enormous amount of co-ordination among regions to achieve the goal of next-day package delivery. They achieve this through the innovative use of integrating mechanisms such as computer-controlled tracking equipment and customer-liaison personnel to manage transactions quickly and efficiently.

Six integrating mechanisms are available to managers to increase communication and co-ordination.[53] These mechanisms – arranged on a continuum from simplest to most complex – are listed in Fig. 10.11, with examples of the individuals or groups that might use them. In the remainder of this section we examine each one.

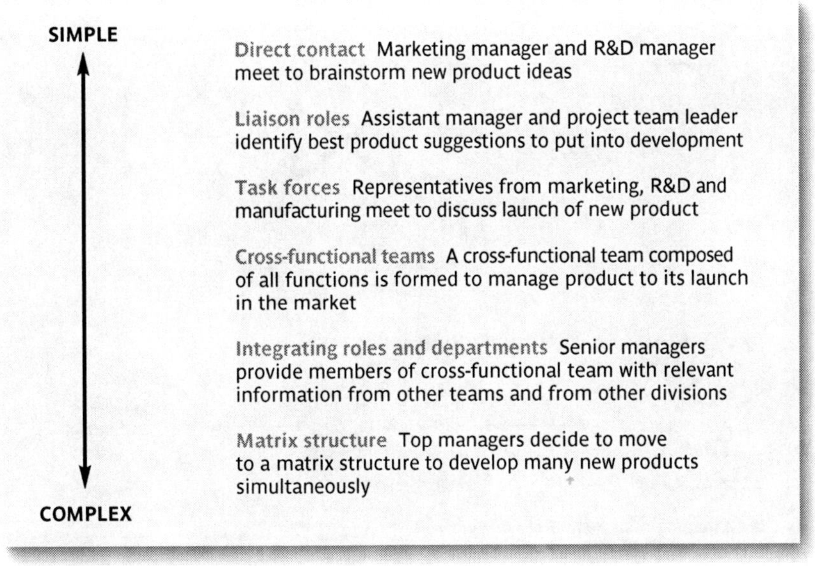
SIMPLE
Direct contact Marketing manager and R&D manager meet to brainstorm new product ideas
Liaison roles Assistant manager and project team leader identify best product suggestions to put into development
Task forces Representatives from marketing, R&D and manufacturing meet to discuss launch of new product
Cross-functional teams A cross-functional team composed of all functions is formed to manage product to its launch in the market
Integrating roles and departments Senior managers provide members of cross-functional team with relevant information from other teams and from other divisions
Matrix structure Top managers decide to move to a matrix structure to develop many new products simultaneously
COMPLEX

Figure 10.11 Types and Examples of Integrating Mechanisms

Direct contact

Direct contact among managers creates a context within which managers from different functions or divisions can work together to solve mutual problems. However, several problems are associated with establishing contact among managers in different functions or divisions. Managers from different functions may have different views about what must be done to achieve organisational goals. But if the managers have equal authority (as functional managers typically do), the only manager who can tell them what to do is the CEO: if functional and divisional managers cannot reach agreement, no mechanism exists to resolve the conflict apart from the authority of the boss. The need to solve everyday conflicts, however, wastes senior management time and effort and slows decision making. In fact, one sign of a poorly performing organisational structure is the number of problems sent up the hierarchy for senior managers to solve. To increase co-ordination among functions and divisions and to prevent these problems from emerging, senior managers can incorporate more complex integrating mechanisms into their organisational architecture.

Liaison roles

Managers can increase co-ordination among functions and divisions by establishing liaison roles. When the volume of contacts between two functions increases, one way to improve co-ordination is to give one manager in each function or division the responsibility for co-ordinating with the other. These managers may meet daily, weekly, monthly or as needed. Figure 10.12A depicts a liaison role; the small dot represents the person within a function who has responsibility for co-ordinating with the other function. The responsibility for co-ordination is part of the liaison

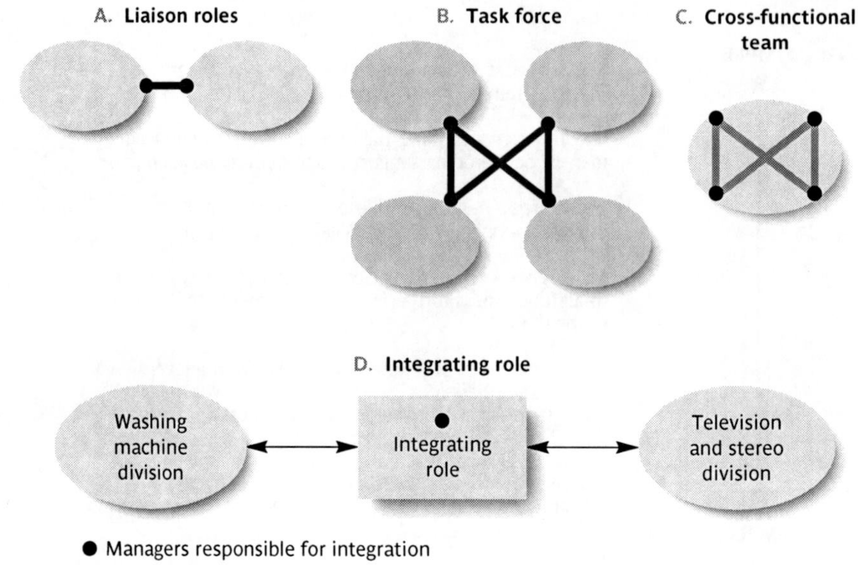

Figure 10.12 Forms of Integrating Mechanisms

person's full-time job, and usually an informal relationship forms between the people involved, greatly easing strains between functions. Furthermore, liaison roles provide a way of transmitting information across an organisation, which is important in large organisations whose employees may know no one outside their immediate function or division.

Task forces

When more than two functions or divisions share many common problems, direct contact and liaison roles may not provide sufficient co-ordination. In these cases, a more complex integrating mechanism, a task force, may be appropriate (Fig. 10.12B). One manager from each relevant function or division is assigned to a task force that meets to solve a specific, mutual problem; members are responsible for reporting back to their departments on the issues addressed and the solutions recommended. Task forces are often called ad hoc committees because they are temporary: they may meet on a regular basis or only a few times. When the problem or issue is solved, the task force is no longer needed; members return to their normal roles in their departments or are assigned to other task forces. Typically, task force members also perform many of their normal duties while serving on the task force.

Cross-functional teams

In many cases, the issues addressed by a task force are recurring problems, such as the need to develop new products or find new kinds of customers. To address recurring problems effectively, managers are increasingly using permanent integrating mechanisms such as cross-functional teams (Fig. 10.12C). An example of a cross-functional team is a new product development committee that is responsible for the choice, design, manufacturing and marketing of a new product. Such an activity obviously requires a great deal of integration among functions if new products are to be successfully introduced, and using a complex integrating mechanism such as a cross-functional team accomplishes this. Intel, for instance, emphasises cross-functional teamwork. Its structure consists of over 90 cross-functional groups that meet regularly to set functional strategy in areas such as engineering and marketing and to develop business-level strategy.

The more complex an organisation, the more important cross-functional teams become. As discussed previously, the product team structure is based on cross-functional teams to speed products to market. These teams assume responsibility for all aspects of product development.

Integrating roles and departments

An integrating role is a role whose only function is to increase co-ordination and integration among functions or divisions to achieve performance gains from *synergies* (Fig. 10.12D). Usually, managers who perform integrating roles are experienced senior managers who can envisage how to use the resources of the functions or divisions to obtain new synergies. One study found that Du Pont, the giant chemical company, had created 160 integrating roles to provide co-ordination among the different divisions of the company and improve corporate performance. Once again, the more complex an organisation and the greater the number of its divisions, the more important are integrating roles.

Matrix structure

When managers must be able to respond quickly to a task and general environment, they often use a matrix structure. The reason for choosing a matrix structure is clear. It contains many of the integrating mechanisms already discussed: the two-boss managers integrate between functions and product teams; the matrix is built on the basis of temporary teams or task forces; and each member of a team performs a liaison role. The matrix structure is flexible precisely because it is formed from *complex integrating mechanisms*.

To keep an organisation responsive to changes in its task and general environments as the organisation grows and becomes more complex, managers must increase co-ordination among functions and divisions by using complex integrating mechanisms. Managers must decide on the best way to organise their structures to create an organisational architecture that allows them to make the best use of organisational resources.

Strategic Alliances, B2B Network Structures and IT

Increasing globalisation and the use of new IT have brought about two innovations in organisational architecture that are sweeping through European companies: *strategic alliances* and business-to-business (B2B) network structures. A strategic alliance is a formal agreement that commits two or more companies to exchange or share their resources in order to produce and market a product.[54] Most commonly, strategic alliances are formed because the companies share similar interests and believe that they can benefit from co-operating. Japanese car companies such as Toyota and Honda for example, have formed many strategic alliances with particular suppliers of inputs such as car axles, gearboxes and air-conditioning systems. Over time, these car companies work closely with their suppliers to improve the efficiency and effectiveness of the inputs so that the final product – the car produced – is of higher quality and can very often be produced at lower cost. Toyota and Honda have also established alliances with suppliers throughout the world, because both companies now build several models of cars in other countries.

Throughout the 1990s, the growing sophistication of IT, with global intranets and teleconferencing, has made it much easier to manage strategic alliances and allow managers to share information and co-operate. One outcome of this has been the growth of strategic alliances into a **network structure**. A network structure is a series of global strategic alliances that one or several organisations create with suppliers, manufacturers and/or distributors to produce and market a product. Network structures allow an organisation to manage its global value chain in order to find new ways to reduce costs and increase the quality of products – without incurring the high costs of operating a complex organisational structure (such as the costs of employing many managers). More and more European companies are relying on *global network structures* to gain access to low-cost foreign sources of inputs, as discussed in Chapter 6. Shoe makers such as Nike and Adidas are two companies that have extensively used this approach.

Nike is the largest and most profitable sports shoe manufacturer in the world. The key to the company's success is the network structure that Nike founder and CEO Philip Knight created to allow his company to produce and market shoes. As noted in Chapter 8, the most successful companies today are trying to pursue simultaneously *low-cost* and a *differentiation* strategy. Knight decided early that to do this at Nike he needed an organisational architecture that would allow his company to focus on some functions (such as design) and leave others (such as manufacturing) to other organisations.

By far the largest function at Nike's headquarters is the design function, composed of talented designers who pioneered innovations in sports shoe design such as the air pump and Air Jordans that Nike introduced so successfully. Designers used computer-aided design (CAD) to design Nike shoes, and they electronically stored all new product information, including manufacturing instructions. When the designers finished their work, they electronically transmitted all the blueprints for the new products to a network of Southeast Asian suppliers and manufacturers with which Nike had formed strategic alliances.[55] Instructions for the design of a new sole may be sent to a supplier in Taiwan; instructions for the leather uppers to a supplier in Malaysia. The suppliers produce the shoe parts and send them for final assembly to a manufacturer in China with which Nike has established another strategic alliance. From China, the shoes are shipped to distributors throughout the world: 99 per cent of the 99 million pairs of shoes that Nike makes each year are made in Southeast Asia.

This network structure gives Nike two important advantages. First, Nike is able to respond to changes in sports shoe fashion very quickly. Using its global IT system, Nike can literally change the instructions it gives each of its suppliers overnight, so that within a few weeks its foreign manufacturers are producing new kinds of shoes.[56] Any alliance partners that fail to perform up to Nike's standards are replaced with new ones.

Second, Nike's costs are very low because wages in Southeast Asia are a fraction of what they are in developed countries, and this difference gives Nike a low-cost advantage. Also, Nike's ability to **outsource** and use foreign manufacturers to produce all its shoes abroad allows Knight to keep the organisation's structure flat and flexible. Nike is able to use a relatively inexpensive functional structure to organise its activities. However, sports shoe manufacturers' attempts to keep their costs low have led to many charges that Nike and others are supporting sweatshops that harm foreign workers, as Case 10.5 suggests.

Case 10.5: Of shoes and sweatshops

As the production of all kinds of goods and services is being increasingly outsourced to poor regions and countries of the world, the behaviour of companies that outsource production to subcontractors in these countries has come under increasing scrutiny. Nike, the giant sports shoe maker, with sales of more than £5.2 billion a year, was one of the first to experience a backlash when critics revealed how workers in these countries were being treated. Indonesian workers were stitching together shoes in hot, noisy factories for about 50 pence a day or about £10 a month.[57] Workers in Vietnam and China fared better; they could earn approximately £1 a day. In all cases, however, critics charged that at least £1.75 a day was needed to maintain an adequate living standard.

These facts generated an outcry, and Nike was attacked for its labour practices; a backlash against sales of Nike products forced Phil Knight, Nike's billionaire owner, to re-evaluate. Nike announced that henceforth all the factories producing its shoes and clothes would be independently monitored and inspected. After its competitor Reebok, which also had been criticised for similar labour practices, announced that it was raising wages in Indonesia by 20 per cent, Nike raised them by 25 per cent to over £13 a month.[58] Small though this may seem, it was a huge increase to workers in these countries.

In Europe, another sportswear company, Adidas, largely escaped such criticism, but in 1999 it was reported that in El Salvador a Taiwan-based Adidas subcontractor was employing girls as young as 14 in its factories and making them work for more than 70 hours a week. They were allowed to go to the restroom only twice a day, and if they stayed longer than three minutes, they lost a day's wages.[59] Adidas moved swiftly to avoid the public relations nightmare that Nike had experienced, by announcing that henceforth its subcontractors would be required to abide by more strict labour standards.

What happened in the sports shoe industry happened throughout the clothing industry as well as other industries like electronics and toys in the 2000s. Companies such as ASDA, Gap, Sony and Mattel were all forced to re-evaluate the ethics of their labour practices and to promise to keep a constant watch on subcontractors in the future. A statement to this effect can be found on many of these companies' Web pages – for example, Nike (www.nikebiz.com) and Unilever (www.unilever.co.uk/ourvalues), as mentioned in Chapter 4.

The ability of managers to develop a network structure to produce or provide the goods and services customers want, rather than create a complex organisational structure to do so, has led many researchers and consultants to popularise the idea of a **boundaryless organisation**. Such an organisation is composed of people linked by IT – computers, faxes, CAD systems and video teleconferencing – who may rarely, if ever, see one another face to face. People are utilised when their services are needed, much as in a matrix structure, but they are not formal members of an organisation; they are *functional experts* who form an alliance with an organisation, fulfil their contractual obligations and then move on to the next project.

Large consulting companies, such as PricewaterhouseCooper and McKinsey & Co., utilise their global consultants in this way. Consultants are connected by laptops to an organisation's **knowledge management system**, its company-specific information system that systematises the knowledge of its employees and provides them with access to other employees who have the expertise to solve the problems that they encounter as they perform their jobs.

The use of outsourcing and the development of network structures are increasing rapidly as organisations recognise the opportunities they offer to reduce costs and increase organisational flexibility. The current push to lower costs has led to the development of electronic *business-to-business (B2B) networks* in which most or all of the companies in an industry (for example, car makers) use the same software platform to link to each other and establish industry specifications and standards. These companies then jointly list the quantity and specifications of the inputs they require and invite bids from the thousands of potential suppliers around the world. Suppliers also use the same software platform, so that electronic bidding, auctions and transactions are possible between buyers and sellers around the world. The idea is that high-volume standardised transactions can help drive down costs at the industry level.

Today, with advances in IT, designing organisational architecture is becoming an increasingly complex management function. To maximise efficiency and effectiveness, managers must assess carefully the relative benefits of having their own organisation perform a functional activity versus forming an alliance with another organisation to perform the activity. It is still not clear how B2B networks and other forms of electronic alliances between companies will develop in the future.

TIPS FOR PRACTICE

1. Always ensure that the organisation you are working for adapts its structure to its business – i.e. if you diversify your product range, move to a product structure; if you diversify geographically, move to a geographic structure, etc.
2. Remember that there are a variety of structures available that have an impact on efficiency, quality, innovation and responsiveness, such as matrix or product teams, or a decentralised or centralised structure.
3. Do not allow organisations to become too tall. Assess the hierarchy frequently and check if alliances or networks can improve your structure.

Summary and Review

Designing organisational structure The four main determinants of organisational structure are the external environment, strategy, technology and HR. In general, the higher the level of uncertainty associated with these factors, the more appropriate is a flexible, adaptable structure as opposed to a formal, rigid one.

Grouping tasks into jobs: job design Job design is the process by which managers group tasks into jobs. To create more interesting jobs, and to get workers to act flexibly, managers can enlarge and enrich jobs. The job characteristics model provides a tool managers can use to measure how motivating or satisfying a particular job is.

Grouping jobs into functions and divisions Managers can choose from many kinds of organisational structures to make the best use of organisational resources. Depending on the specific organising problems they face, managers can choose from functional, product, geographic, market, matrix, product team and hybrid structures.

Co-ordinating functions and divisions No matter which structure managers choose, they must decide how to distribute authority in the organisation, how many levels to have in the hierarchy of authority and what balance to strike between centralisation and decentralisation to keep the number of levels in the hierarchy to a minimum. As organisations grow, managers must increase integration and co-ordination among functions and divisions. Six integrating mechanisms are available to facilitate this: direct contact, liaison roles, task forces, cross-functional teams, integrating roles and the matrix structure.

Strategic alliances, B2B network structures and IT To avoid many of the communication and co-ordination problems that emerge as organisations grow, managers are attempting to use IT to develop new ways of organising. In a strategic alliance, managers enter into an agreement with another organisation to provide inputs or to perform a functional activity. If managers enter into a series of these agreements, they create a network structure. A network structure, most commonly based on some shared form of IT, can be formed around one company, or a number of companies can join together to create an industry B2B network.

Topic for Action

- Compare the pros and cons of using a network structure to perform organisational activities and performing all activities in-house or within one organisational hierarchy.
- What are the advantages and disadvantages of B2B networks?
- Find a manager, and identify the kind of organisational structure that his or her organisation uses to co-ordinate its people and resources. Why is the organisation using that structure? Do you think a different structure would be more appropriate? Which one?
- With the same or another manager, discuss the distribution of authority in the organisation. Does the manager think that decentralising authority and empowering employees is appropriate?

Applied Independent Learning

Building Management Skills

Understanding Organising

Think of an organisation with which you are familiar, perhaps one you have worked in – such as a shop, restaurant, office, church or school. Then answer the following questions:

1. Which contingencies are most important in explaining how the organisation is organised? Do you think it is organised in the best way?

2. Using the job characteristics model, how motivating do you think the job of a typical employee in this organisation is?
3. Can you think of any ways in which a typical job could be enlarged or enriched?
4. What kind of organisational structure does the organisation use? If it is part of a chain, what kind of structure does the entire organisation use? What other structures discussed in the chapter might allow the organisation to operate more effectively? For example, would the move to a product team structure lead to greater efficiency or effectiveness? Why or why not?
5. How many levels are there in the organisation's hierarchy? Is authority centralised or decentralised? Describe the span of control of the senior manager and of middle or first-line managers.
6. Is the distribution of authority appropriate for the organisation and its activities? Would it be possible to flatten the hierarchy by decentralising authority and empowering employees?
7. What are the principal integrating mechanisms used in the organisation? Do they provide sufficient co-ordination among individuals and functions? How might they be improved?
8. Now that you have analysed the way this organisation is organised, what advice would you give its managers to help them improve the way it operates?

Managing Ethically

Suppose an organisation is downsizing and laying off many of its middle managers. Some senior managers charged with deciding who to terminate might decide to keep the subordinates they like, and who are obedient to them, rather than the ones who are difficult or the best performers. They might also decide to lay off the most highly paid subordinates even if they are high performers. Think of the ethical issues involved in designing a hierarchy, and discuss the following issues.

Questions

1. What ethical rules (see Chapter 4) should managers use to decide which employees to terminate when redesigning their hierarchy?
2. Some people argue that employees who have worked for an organisation for many years have a claim on the organisation at least as strong as that of its shareholders. What do you think of the ethics of this position – can employees claim to 'own' their jobs if they have contributed significantly to its past success? How does a socially responsible organisation behave in this situation?

Small Group Breakout Exercise

Bob's Appliances

Form groups of three or four people, and appoint one member as the spokesperson who will communicate your findings to the whole class when called on by the instructor. Then discuss the following scenario.

Bob's Appliances sells and services household appliances such as washing machines, dishwashers, ovens and refrigerators. Over the years, the company has developed a good reputation for the quality of its customer service, and many local builders patronise the store.

Recently, some new appliance retailers, including Comet and Dixons, have opened stores that also provide numerous appliances. In addition to appliances, however, to attract more customers these stores carry a complete range of consumer electronics products – televisions, stereos and computers. Bob Lange, the owner of Bob's Appliances, has decided that if he is to stay in business he must widen his product range and compete directly with the chains.

In 2002, he decided to build a 20,000 ft^2 store and service centre, and he is now hiring new employees to sell and service the new line of consumer electronics. Because of his company's increased size, Lange is not sure of the best way to organise the employees. Currently, he uses a functional structure; employees are divided into sales, purchasing and accounting and repair. Bob is wondering whether selling and servicing consumer electronics is so different from selling and servicing appliances that he should move to a product structure (see below) and create separate sets of functions for each of his two lines of business.

You are a team of local consultants whom Bob has called in to advise him as he makes this crucial choice. Which structure do you recommend? Why?

FUNCTIONAL STRUCTURE

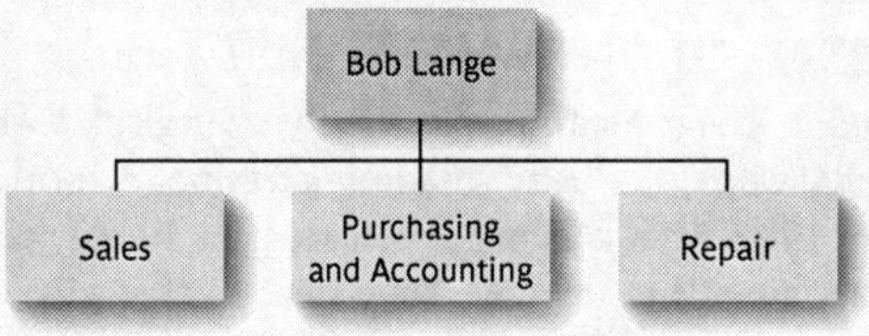

PRODUCT STRUCTURE

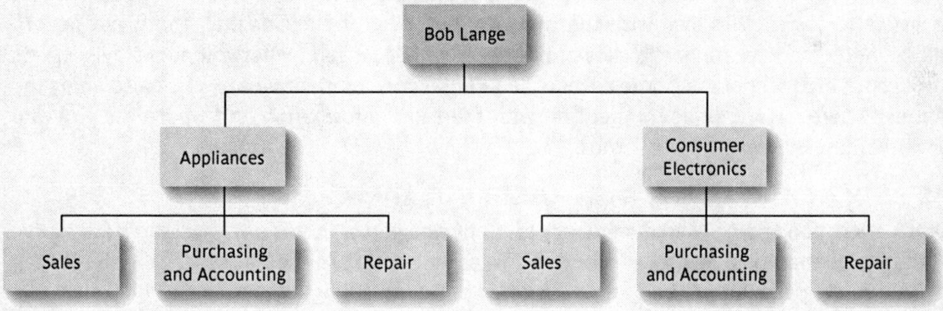

Exploring The World Wide Web

Go to the website of Kraft, the food services company (www.kraft.com). Click on 'brands', and then click on 'Europe' and answer the following questions:

1. What kind of international structure do you think Kraft uses to manage its food operations?
2. What kind of organisational structure do you think Kraft uses to manage its European operations? Why do you think it uses this structure?
3. What do you think are the main challenges Kraft faces in managing its food business to improve performance?

Application in Today's Business World

Making Barclays Sparkle

Bob Diamond discusses how he restructured the venerable institution's investment-banking unit, turning it into a leading fixed-income firm

One of the reasons London now rivals New York as a financial centre is the city's openness to a diverse, talented group of people. Bob Diamond, 54, is one of those Americans who has made a big impression in the UK. Diamond, a graduate of Colby College in Maine and the University of Connecticut School of Business, first came to London in early 1988 to run Morgan Stanley's Europe and Asia fixed-income trading business. But he found his calling in 1996 when he was recruited to reverse the fortunes of the floundering investment banking wing, then known as BZW, of Barclays PLC, one of Britain's largest banks.

Diamond survived the turmoil unleashed by the restructuring of the investment bank, and went on to forge its successor, Barclays Capital, into a world-class fixed-income player. Last year he also took on the additional title of president of the parent company. He talked in his Canary Wharf office to *BusinessWeek*'s London bureau chief, Stanley Reed. Edited excerpts from their conversation follow:

How did you get started on Wall Street?

After business school, I took a job at a company called US Surgical. I worked for a guy who is still a good friend, named Bill Cook, the head of administration. After two years, Bill Cook was hired by Morgan Stanley, in 1979. That was just when Morgan Stanley was moving from a pure advisory firm into secondary sales and trading. They needed someone to build all the IT and systems. Bill was hired for that, and he asked me to join him.

After a year as assistant to the CFO, I took a job on the fixed-income floor. It would be a bit excessive to say I fell in love with the markets. But given my personality, that's not far off. Although the markets are harsh, they are a very, very fair judge of what you do. I played sports throughout high school and some college, and I enjoy the competitive aspects. I also enjoy the fairness where we are all in competition with the same information and where the guy who works hardest or works smartest wins.

As long as the coach puts them out there . . .

That's a very good point. Markets are very fair, but who gets a shot is not necessarily fair. Some of the things that make me most proud of this organisation are the meritocracy – the feeling that we really put a lot of time and a lot of process into giving all people an equal shot and measuring them based on how they perform – not who they know or how long they have been here or what connections they have.

I made a decision in early 1996 to leave Credit Suisse First Boston. What was intriguing to me about the discussions I had with Martin Taylor (then-CEO of Barclays PLC) were that I believed very strongly in the single currency. It was going to be a reality – and change the balance of power between Europe and the US. The second thing was that [the] Glass–Steagall [the law separating commercial and investment banking] was eroding. Frankly, European and British banks were more comfortable with the universal banking, integrated model and would benefit big-time by that shift.

You found yourself in a pretty tough situation

It was clear pretty quickly that the all-singing, all-dancing, US bulge-bracket lookalike model was unsustainable. I knew it had to change, and Martin knew it had to change. But it was very important that we restructure quietly as opposed to announcing to the market that were going to sell M&A and equities. Frankly, that ended up hurting the organisation, because we didn't get the price we should have gotten for it, and it created a lot of internal drama. What was happening was that at the parts of the business that were for sale, everyone was out interviewing; no one was working.

How was the decision to sell made?

There were always four choices. One, ignore all these problems and just keep going. I wasn't going to be part of that, because it simply wasn't sustainable.

The second was to buy a US firm. My feeling was that Barclays couldn't manage that integration at that time, and, frankly, the success rates of deals in investment banking are very poor. The third option was to sell everything, but to sell the entire organisation would be ludicrous because we would be selling our access to clients and the capital markets. The fourth view, which I supported, was to dramatically restructure and take advantage of the fact that we are Barclays and that we are European. We have one of the world's best brands, AA+ credit rating, and a huge balance sheet. Take advantage of being in [Britain] and European time zones, and create a structure that we know will work.

That was the beginning of financing and risk management. We don't have to compete with the US firms in M&A. We don't have to have a large-scale cash equity business, where the model doesn't work and where one after another foreign firm and one after another US firm went through the same thing – trying and failing to mimic the US bulge-bracket firms. It was pouring good money after bad.

Why is the business working so well now?

The model of investment banking has changed radically to a more integrated model. It is the best of commercial banking and the best of investment banking. It is not just Barcap any more, but UBS, BNP Paribas, JP Morgan, Citigroup – most of the successful firms now have the integrated model. Goldman, too, has changed its model as a result of not doing a deal with a bank, which would have allowed it to adopt an integrated model.

The best example I can give you is virtually any league table of capital raising for corporates: ten years ago, Goldman, Merrill and Morgan Stanley would dominate. Now the top players are Deutsche Bank (DB), Barclays Capital, JP Morgan, Citigroup – all universal banks. Goldman is not even in the top 15. That doesn't mean it is not a great firm, but the model has changed.

So the direction of interest rates doesn't matter that much?

Our business is risk management. If you look at our results with value at risk down, corporate issuance down and the yield curve trade gone, you would say, 'How the hell did you drive up revenues?' The answer is what we have been preaching: relentless, rigorous focus on clients around risk management. If you are a German car manufacturer selling in the US, your exposure to the dollar is enormous. You may need to hedge your income. You may need to hedge the price of steel. If you are an airline you have a massive exposure to the price of fuel. All of the large corporates now manufacture in multiple locations. They have people in multiple locations. They sell in multiple locations. They have exposure to a multiplicity of risks, which they have to manage.

When you try to fix a business, what is your approach?

The thing that is most important of all is being very clear about the strategy and keeping it pretty simple. Once that is established, you need to make the tough decisions and implement them quickly. My style has been to spend an awful lot of time with the business until I have tremendous confidence that I have the right people, who understand the plan. At that point, it is equally important to step away and delegate.

Questions:

1. What were the main influences to change the structure of Barclay's investment bank?
2. What does Bob Diamond think are the most important aspects that make the structure effective?

Source: Online Extra, 'Making Barclay's Sparkle', adapted and reprinted from *Business Week*, April 10 2006.

Notes and References

1 www.lego.com.
2 B. Carter, 'Lego Centralizes European Activity to Combat Losses', *Marketing*, January 15, 2004, 1.
3 'Dow Revamps Its Corporate Structure', *Chemical Market Reporter*, December 15, 2003, 3.
4 www.dow.com.
5 A. Reinhardt, 'Can Nokia Capture Mobile Workers?', *BusinessWeek*, February 9, 2004, 80.
6 G. R. Jones, *Organizational Theory, Design and Change: Text and Cases* (Upper Saddle River: Prentice Hall, 2003).
7 J. Child, *Organization: A Guide for Managers and Administrators* (New York: Harper & Row, 1977).
8 P. R. Lawrence and J. W. Lorsch, *Organization and Environment* (Boston: Graduate School of Business Administration, Harvard University, 1967).
9 R. Duncan, 'What Is the Right Organizational Design?', *Organizational Dynamics*, Winter 1979, 59–80.
10 T. Burns and G. R. Stalker, *The Management of Innovation* (London: Tavistock, 1966).
11 D. Miller, 'Strategy Making and Structure: Analysis and Implications for Performance', *Academy of Management Journal* 30 (1987), 7–32.
12 A. D. Chandler, *Strategy and Structure* (Cambridge, MA: MIT Press, 1962).
13 J. Stopford and L. Wells, *Managing the Multinational Enterprise* (London: Longman, 1972).
14 *BusinessWeek* November 14, 2005.
15 *BusinessWeek* November 14, 2005.
16 C. Perrow, *Organizational Analysis: A Sociological View* (Belmont, CA: Wadsworth, 1970).
17 J. Woodward, *Management and Technology* (London: Her Majesty's Stationery Office, 1958).
18 *Ibid.*
19 *BusinessWeek* November 21, 2005.
20 F. W. Taylor, *The Principles of Scientific Management* (New York: Harper, 1911).
21 R. W. Griffin, *Task Design: An Integrative Approach* (Glenview, IL: Scott, Foresman, 1982).
22 *Ibid.*
23 J. R. Hackman and G. R. Oldham, *Work Redesign* (Reading, MA: Addison-Wesley, 1980).
24 http://www.telehouse.net/company_profile.asp.
25 J. R. Galbraith and R. K. Kazanjian, *Strategy Implementation: Structure, System, and Process*, 2nd ed. (St. Paul, MN: West, 1986).
26 Jones, *Organizational Theory, Design and Change.*
27 Lawrence and Lorsch, *Organization and Environment.*

28 R. H. Hall, *Organizations: Structure and Process* (Englewood Cliffs, NJ: Prentice Hall, 1972); R. Miles, *Macro Organizational Behavior* (Santa Monica, CA: Goodyear, 1980).
29 Chandler, *Strategy and Structure.*
30 G. R. Jones and C. W. L. Hill, 'Transaction Cost Analysis of Strategy-Structure Choice', *Strategic Management Journal* 9 (1988), 159–72.
31 www.viacom.com.
32 *Ibid.*
33 www.gsk.com.
34 *Ibid.*
35 S. M. Davis and P. R. Lawrence, *Matrix* (Reading, MA: Addison-Wesley, 1977); J. R. Galbraith, 'Matrix Organization Designs: How to Combine Functional and Project Forms', *Business Horizons* 14 (1971), 29–40.
36 L. R. Burns, 'Matrix Management in Hospitals: Testing Theories of Matrix Structure and Development', *Administrative Science Quarterly* 34 (1989), 349–68.
37 C. W. L. Hill, *International Business* (Homewood, IL: Irwin, 2003).
38 Jones, *Organizational Theory.*
39 A. Farnham, 'America's Most Admired Company', *Fortune*, February 7, 1994, 50–54.
40 www.timesonline.co.uk.
41 http://www.ccer.pku.edu.cn/ss/world-rankingsUnis.pdf.
42 *BusinessWeek*, December 5, 2005.
43 *Ibid.*
44 P. Blau, 'A Formal Theory of Differentiation in Organizations', *American Sociological Review* 35 (1970), 684–95.
45 S. Grey, 'McDonald's CEO Announces Shifts of Top Executives', *The Wall Street Journal*, July 16, 2004, A11.
46 www.mcdonalds.com.
47 Child, *Organization.*
48 P. M. Blau and R. A. Schoenherr, *The Structure of Organizations* (New York: Basic Books, 1971).
49 Jones, *Organizational Theory.*
50 www.homebase.co.uk.
51 http://www.thetimes100.co.uk/case_study.
52 Lawrence and Lorsch, *Organization and Environment*, 50–55.
53 J. R. Galbraith, *Designing Complex Organizations* (Reading, MA: Addison-Wesley, 1977), Chapter 1; Galbraith and Kazanjian, *Strategy Implementation*, Chapter 7.
54 B. Kogut, 'Joint Ventures: Theoretical and Empirical Perspectives', *Strategic Management Journal* 9 (1988), 319–32.
55 G. S. Capowski, 'Designing a Corporate Identity', *Management Review* (June 1993), 37–38.
56 J. Marcia, 'Just Doing It', *Distribution*, January 1995, 36–40.
57 'Nike Battles Backlash from Overseas Sweatshops', *Marketing News*, November 9, 1998, 14.
58 J. Laabs, 'Mike Gives Indonesian Workers a Raise', *Workforce*, December 1998, 15–16.
59 W. Echikson, 'It's Europe's Turn to Sweat About Sweatshops', *BusinessWeek*, July 19, 1999, 96.

7

Types of cost and their behaviour

Contents

Learning objectives

Completion of this chapter will enable you to:

- outline the additional accounting concepts that relate to management accounting
- explain what is meant by the term cost, its nature and limitations
- identify the bases for allocation and apportionment of costs
- determine the costs of products, services or activities using the techniques of absorption costing and marginal costing
- critically compare the techniques of absorption costing and marginal costing
- outline the more recently developed technique of activity based costing (ABC).

Introduction

The first six chapters of this book are primarily concerned with financial accounting, with particular emphasis on the three key financial statements: balance sheet; profit and loss account; cash flow statement. This has necessarily focused on the historical aspect of accounting. To use the car-driving analogy introduced earlier, we have made far more use of the rear view mirror than the view through the windscreen. We have concentrated on the accumulation of data and the reporting of past events, rather than the consideration of current and future activities.

We have previously identified accounting as having the three roles of maintaining the scorecard, problem solving, and attention directing. The scorecard role, although primarily a financial accounting role, remains part of the responsibility of management accounting. However, its more important roles are those of problem solving and attention directing. These roles focus on current and future activities, with regard to the techniques involved in decision-making, planning and control that will be covered in this and subsequent chapters.

This chapter introduces management accounting by looking at some further concepts to those that were introduced in Chapter 1. Management accounting is concerned with costs. We will look at what cost is, how costs behave and how costs are ascertained. This will include some of the approaches used to determine the costs of products and services. Management accountants may be involved in the preparation of financial information that frequently requires senior management attention, resulting in decisions that are not always popular, for example down-sizing of businesses. They may also be involved in many more positive ways in the development of businesses, as illustrated in the extract below from *Financial Management*, the journal of the Chartered Institute of Management Accountants.

We can see from the Figleaves example below that the management accounting function is extremely important in adding value to the business through its involvement in:

- investment decision-making
- scorecard design
- development of budgetary control systems
- capacity planning.

The importance of management accounting

Internet lingerie retailer Figleaves.com is expanding its management accounting function in recognition of the key contribution it made to the firm's first break-even result.

In December 2002 the company reported break-even at EBITDA on net sales of £1 million. This compares with Amazon.com's break-even on turnover of £550 million in September 2002.

'We are in rarefied territory for dotcoms,' said Figleaves.com's finance director, Howard Bryant ACMA. 'The management accounting team is crucial to that success, continually adding value to the business. The unique role of management accountants, experts in everything from investment to general management, makes them ideal for a smaller firm such as Figleaves.'

Over the past year the management accounting team has been involved in projects including the introduction of a scorecard design covering key metrics and interrelationships for discussion at company meetings; the development of budget and forecast control mechanisms; and the integration of rolling sales forecasts with inventory capacity planning.

Uplifting growth for on-line underwear company, by Cathy Hayward

© *Financial Management*, March 2003

The management accounting function may also be involved in many more important areas of business activity, for example:

- planning and preparation of business plans
- directing attention to specific areas and providing proposed solutions to actual and anticipated problems
- formulation of cost-cutting proposals and the evaluation of their impact on current and future operations
- preparation of forecasts
- negotiation with bankers for funding
- analysis and interpretation of internal and external factors in support of strategic decision-making.

Management accounting concepts

Management accounting is an integral part of management, requiring the identification, generation, presentation, interpretation and use of information relevant to the activities outlined in Fig. 7.1:

- formulating business strategy involves setting the long-term objectives of the business
- planning and controlling activities deal with short-term objectives and investigations into the differences that may arise from actual outcomes against the plan and the recommendation and implementation of remedial actions
- decision-making includes identification of those items of information relevant to a particular decision and those items that may be ignored
- efficient resource usage may be determined from the process of setting short-term budget plans and in their implementation
- performance improvement and value enhancement includes cost reduction and profit

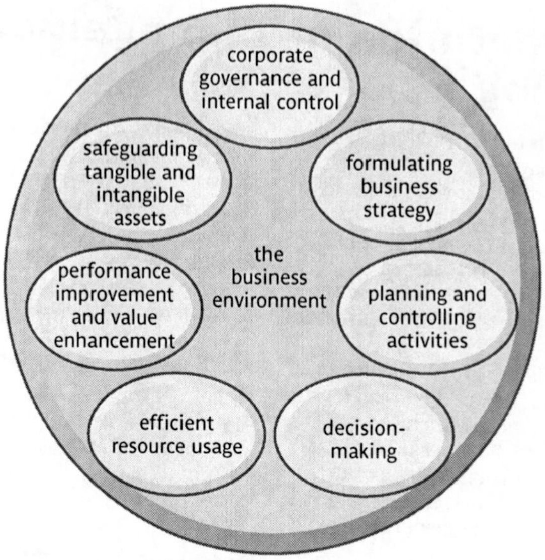

Figure 7.1 The areas of business activity supported by management accounting

improvement exercises and the implementation of improvement initiatives such as quality costing, continuous improvement, and benchmarking

- safeguarding tangible and intangible assets – the management of fixed assets, and working capital (which we shall look at in more detail in Chapter 12) are key accounting responsibilities in ensuring that there is no undue diminution in the value of assets such as buildings, machinery, stocks and debtors, as a result, for example, of poor management, and weak physical controls, and to ensure that every endeavour is made to maximise returns from the use of those assets
- corporate governance and internal control were considered in Chapter 6 and are concerned with the ways in which companies are controlled, the behaviour and accountability of directors and their levels of remuneration, and disclosure of information.

Therefore, it can be seen that management accounting, although providing information for external reporting, is primarily concerned with the provision of information to people within the organisation for:

- product costing
- forecasting, planning and control
- decision-making.

> Progress check 7.1 **Outline what is meant by management accounting and give examples of areas of business activity in which it may be involved.**

In addition to the fundamental accounting concepts that were introduced in Chapter 1, there are further fundamental management accounting concepts (see Fig. 7.2). These do not represent any form of external regulation but are fundamental principles for the preparation of internal management accounting information. A brief outline of these principles is as follows.

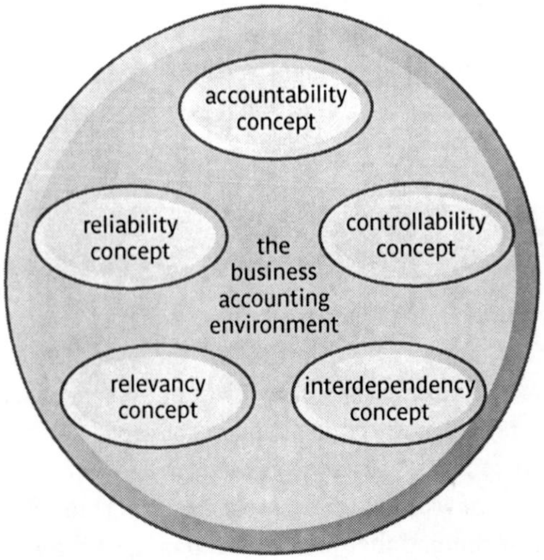

Figure 7.2 Management accounting concepts

The accountability concept

Management accounting presents information measuring the achievement of the objectives of an organisation and appraising the conduct of its internal affairs in that process. In order that further action can be taken, based on this information, the **accountability concept** makes it necessary at all times to identify the responsibilities and key results of individuals within the organisation.

The controllability concept

The **controllability concept** requires that management accounting identifies the elements or activities which management can or cannot influence, and seeks to assess risk and sensitivity factors. This facilitates the proper monitoring, analysis, comparison and interpretation of information which can be used constructively in the control, evaluation and corrective functions of management.

The interdependency concept

The **interdependency concept** requires that management accounting, in recognition of the increasing complexity of business, must access both internal and external information sources from interactive functions such as marketing, production, personnel, procurement and finance. This assists in ensuring that the information is adequately balanced.

The relevancy concept

The **relevancy concept** ensures that flexibility in management accounting is maintained in assembling and interpreting information. This facilitates the exploration and presentation, in a clear, understandable and timely manner, of as many alternatives as are necessary for impartial and confident decisions to be taken. This process is essentially forward-looking and dynamic. Therefore, the information must satisfy the criteria of being applicable and appropriate.

The reliability concept

The reliability concept requires that management accounting information must be of such quality that confidence can be placed on it. Its reliability to the user is dependent on its source, integrity and comprehensiveness.

Worked Example 7.1

During 1999 the UK Government promoted the building of the Dome in Greenwich, London, to celebrate the Millennium. It was opened on time for 31 December 1999. The projected number of visitors during the year was 12 million. That target was not reached. We can consider the Dome and its visitor targets with regard to the controllability concept.

The visitor numbers proved to be a major problem from the outset. Various attempts were made to increase the number of visitors, for example free tickets to schools. The visitor numbers were frequently reported in the national press. The management was changed to try and get somewhere near the targets. All measures taken and effort expended throughout the year unfortunately failed. The Internet is a rich source of information about the Dome, for example www.telegraph.co.uk, which you may use for further research.

Progress check 7.2 **Explain in what ways the additional concepts have been developed to support the profession of management accounting.**

The nature of costs

Costs and revenues are terms that are inextricably linked to accounting. Revenues relate to inflows of assets such as cash and accounts receivable from debtors, or reductions in liabilities, resulting from trading operations. Costs generally relate to what was paid for a product or a service. It may be a past cost:

- a particular use of resources forgone to achieve a specific objective
- a resource used to provide a product or a service
- a resource used to retain a product or a service.

A cost may be a future cost in which case the alternative uses of resources other than to meet a specific objective may be more important, or relevant, to the decision whether or not to pursue that objective.

Cost is not a word that is usually used without a qualification as to its nature and limitations. On the face of it cost may obviously be described as what was paid for something. Cost may, of course, be used as a noun or a verb. As a noun it is an amount of expenditure (actual or notional) incurred on, or attributable to, a specified thing or activity; it relates to a resource sacrificed or forgone, expressed in a monetary value. As a verb, we may say that to cost something is to ascertain the cost of a specified thing or activity.

A number of terms relating to cost are regularly used within management accounting. A comprehensive glossary of key terms appears at the end of the book. These terms will be explained as we go on to discuss each of the various topics and techniques.

Progress check 7.3 What does 'cost' mean?

Cost accumulation relates to the collection of cost data. Cost data may be concerned with past costs or future costs. Past costs, or historical costs, are the costs that we have dealt with in Chapters 2, 3 and 4, in the preparation of financial statements.

Costs are dependent on, and generally change with, the level of activity. The greater the volume or complexity of the activity, then normally the greater is the cost. We can see from Fig. 7.3 that there are three main elements of cost:

- fixed cost
- variable cost
- semi-variable cost.

Fixed cost is a cost which is incurred for an accounting period, and which, within certain manufacturing output or sales turnover limits, tends to be unaffected by fluctuations in the level of activity (output or turnover). An example of a fixed cost is rent of premises that will allow activities up to a particular volume, but which is fixed regardless of volume, for example a car production plant. In the

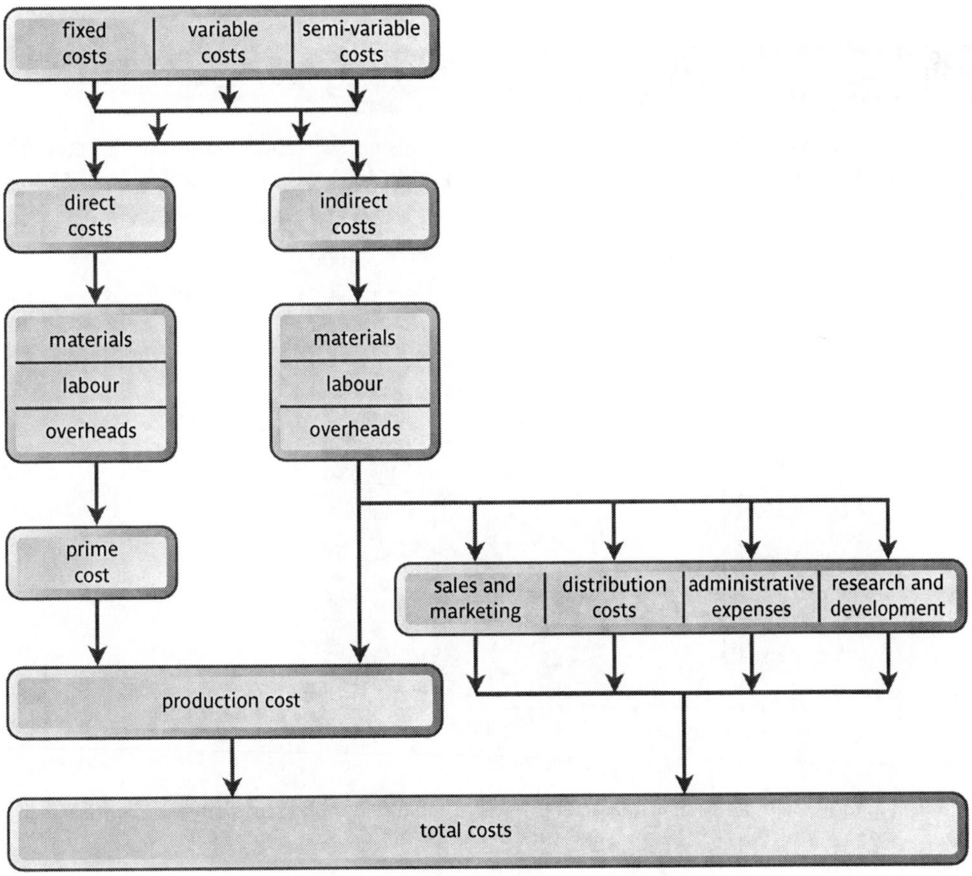

Figure 7.3 The elements of total costs

longer term, when volumes may have increased, the fixed cost of rent may also increase from the need to provide a larger factory. Discussion on fixed overheads invariably focuses on when the fixed costs should no longer be 'fixed'. Since most businesses these days need to be dynamic and constantly changing, changes to fixed costs inevitably follow changes in their levels of activity.

A variable cost varies in direct proportion to the level, or volume, of activity, and again strictly speaking, within certain output or turnover limits. The variable costs incurred in production of a car: materials; labour costs; electricity costs; and so on, are the same for each car produced and so the total of these costs varies as volume varies. The relationship holds until, for example, the cost prices of materials or labour change.

Progress check 7.4 **Discuss whether or not knowledge of labour costs can assist management in setting prices for products or services.**

A semi-variable cost is a cost containing both fixed and variable components and which is thus partly affected by a change in the level of activity, but not in direct proportion. Examples of semi-variable costs are maintenance costs comprising regular weekly maintenance and breakdown costs, and telephone expenses that include line and equipment rental in addition to call charges.

Worked Example 7.2

Quarterly telephone charges that may be incurred by a business at various levels of call usage are shown in the table below, and in the chart in Fig. 7.4. If the business makes no calls at all during the quarter it will incur costs of £200, which cover line rentals and rental of equipment.

Calls (units)	1,000	2,000	3,000
Call charges	£700	£1,400	£2,100

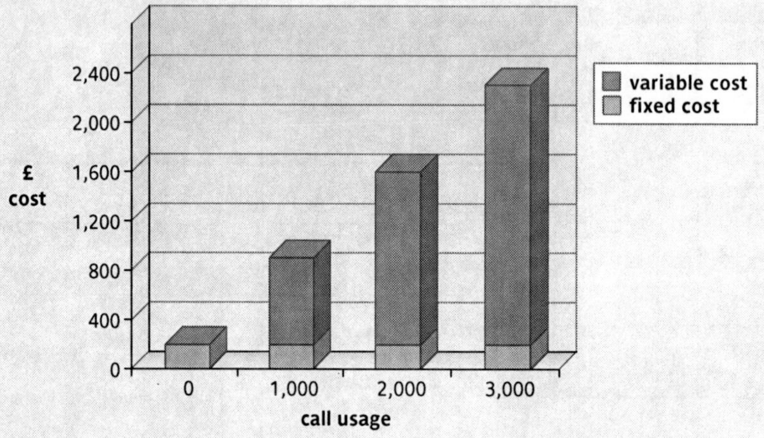

Figure 7.4 An example of how a quarterly semi-variable telephone cost comprises both fixed and variable elements

The total costs of an entity comprise three categories:

- staff costs, the costs of employment which include
  - gross pay
  - paid holidays
  - employer's contributions to National Insurance
  - pension schemes
  - sickness benefit schemes
  - other benefits, for example protective clothing and canteen subsidies
- materials, which include
  - raw materials purchased for incorporation into products for sale
  - consumable items
  - packaging
- expenses, relating to all costs other than materials and labour costs.

Each of the above three categories may be further analysed into:

- direct costs
- indirect costs.

Progress check 7.5 Are managers really interested in whether a cost is fixed or variable when assessing cost behaviour within an organisation?

Direct costs are those costs that can be traced and identified with, and specifically measured with respect to, a relevant cost object. A cost object is the thing we wish to determine the cost of. Direct costs include direct labour, direct materials, and direct overheads. The total cost of direct materials, direct labour and direct expenses, or overheads, is called prime cost.

Indirect costs, or overheads, are costs untraceable to particular units (compared with direct costs). Indirect costs include expenditure on labour, materials or services, which cannot be identified with a saleable cost unit. The term 'burden' used by American companies is synonymous with indirect costs or overheads.

Indirect costs may relate to:

- the provision of a product
- the provision of a service
- other 'sales and administrative' activities.

Total indirect costs may therefore be generally categorised as:

- production costs
- sales and marketing costs
- distribution costs
- administrative costs
- research and development costs.

Indirect costs relating to production activities have to be allocated, that is, assigned as allocated overheads to any of the following:

- a single cost unit
  a unit of product or service in relation to which costs are ascertained

- a cost centre
  a production or service location, function, activity or item of equipment for which costs are accumulated
- a cost account
  a record of the expenditure of a cost centre or cost unit
- a time period.

Worked Example 7.3

Are managers really interested in whether a cost is fixed or variable when assessing cost behaviour within their departments?

A manager should know how a cost will behave when setting a departmental budget. As time goes by and the manager routinely reports actual compared to budget, several differences will be caused by the behaviour of the cost. For example, certain wage costs may be greater per hour for hours worked after 6.00 pm each day.

Progress check 7.6 Explain costs in terms of the hierarchy of costs that comprise the total costs of a business.

Cost allocation and cost apportionment

The indirect costs of service departments may be allocated both to other service departments and to production departments. An idea of the range of departments existing in most large businesses can be gained by simply looking at the newspaper job advertisements of major companies, where each department may represent an 'allocation of costs' problem.

Allocation of overheads is the charging to a cost centre of those overheads that result solely from the existence of that cost centre. Cost assignment defines the process of tracing and allocating costs to the cost object. Overheads are allocated where possible, but allocation can only be done if the exact amount incurred is known without having to carry out any sort of sharing. For example, a department in a factory may have a specific machine or a type of skilled labour that is only used in that department. The depreciation cost of the specific machine and the cost of the skilled labour would be allocated to that department. If the amount is not known and it is not possible to allocate costs then the total amount must be apportioned.

Worked Example 7.4

A degree of subjectivity is involved in the allocation of expenses to a department, or cost centre, which can frequently cause problems. However, the allocation of wage costs to the Millennium Dome project should have been fairly straightforward.

The Dome was very unusual since it was a large capital project with a very short life, starting on 31 December 1999 and finishing 31 December 2000. The ticket office would also have a very short life – it would have had no tickets to sell after 31 December 2000! The costs of staff working in the ticket office would also be easy to identify.

Apportionment is the charging to a cost centre of a fair share of an overhead on the basis of the benefit received by the cost centre in respect of the facilities provided by the overhead. For example, a factory may consist of two or more departments that occupy different amounts of floor space. The total factory rent cost may then be apportioned between the departments on the basis of floor space occupied.

Therefore, if an overhead cannot be allocated then it must be apportioned, involving use of a basis of apportionment, a physical or financial unit, so that the overhead will be equitably shared between the cost centres. Bases of apportionment, for example, that may be used are:

- area – for rent, heating and lighting, building depreciation
- number of employees – for personnel and welfare costs, safety costs
- weights or sizes – for materials handling costs, warehousing costs.

The basis chosen will use the factor most closely related to the benefit received by the cost centres.

Worked Example 7.5

The Millennium Dome had many areas that were financed by outside companies, which had signed contracts for the year. The contracts would have included clauses regarding recovery of certain costs from them, by the Millennium Company. It is likely that different bases of apportionment would need to have been chosen for the costs of cleaning and security.

The cleaning costs would have been fairly straightforward to apportion, probably on a surface area basis (square metres).

The security costs may have been more problematical, for example using a basis of value of contents, area of concession and so on.

Once overheads have been allocated and apportioned, perhaps via some service cost centres, ultimately to production cost centres, they can be charged to cost units. For example, in a factory with three departments the total rent may have been apportioned to the manufacturing department, the assembly department, and the goods inwards department. The total overhead costs of the goods inwards department may then be apportioned between the manufacturing department and the assembly department. The total costs of the manufacturing department and the assembly department may then be charged to the units being produced in those departments, for example television sets, or cars. The same process may be used in the service sector, for example theatre seats, and hospital beds. A cost unit is a unit of product or service in relation to which costs are ascertained. A **unit cost** is the average cost of a product or service unit based on total costs and the number of units.

Worked Example 7.6

The unit cost ascertainment process illustrated in Fig. 7.5 involves taking each cost centre and sharing its overheads among all the cost units passing through that centre.

This example considers one cost centre, the manufacturing department, which is involved with the production of three different products, A, B, and C. The process is similar to apportionment but in this case cost units (which in this case are products) are charged instead of cost centres. This process of charging costs to cost units is absorption and is defined as the charging of overheads to cost units.

Manufacturing department

	Number of units	Production time	Rate per hour	Total charge on the basis of hours		Charge per unit
Overhead costs	3,000 product A	1,000 hours	£5	£5,000	[£5,000/3,000]	£1.67
for January	2,000 product B	4,000 hours	£5	£20,000	[£20,000/2,000]	£10.00
£50,000	5,000 product C	5,000 hours	£5	£25,000	[£25,000/5,000]	£5.00
	10,000 units	10,000 hours		£50,000		

Figure 7.5 An example of unit cost ascertainment

The cost of converting material into finished products, that is, direct labour, direct expense and production overhead, is called the conversion cost. An example of this may be seen in the manufacture of a car bumper, which may have started out as granules of plastic and 'cans of paint'. After the completion of carefully controlled processes that may use some labour and incur overhead costs, the granules and paint are converted into a highly useful product.

Progress check 7.7 What is cost allocation and cost apportionment? Give some examples of bases of cost apportionment.

Within the various areas of management accounting there is greater interest in future costs. The future costs that result from management decisions are concerned with relevant costs and opportunity costs, which are described briefly below but which will be illustrated in greater detail when we consider the techniques of decision-making in Chapter 8.

Relevant costs (and revenues) are the costs (and revenues) appropriate to a specific management decision. They are represented by future cash flows whose magnitude will vary depending upon the outcome of the management decision made. If stock is sold to a retailer, the relevant cost, used in the determination of the profitability of the transaction, would be the cost of replacing the stock, not its original purchase price, which is a sunk cost. Sunk costs, or irrecoverable costs, are costs that have been irreversibly incurred or committed prior to a decision point and which cannot therefore be considered relevant to subsequent decisions.

An opportunity cost is the value of the benefit sacrificed when one course of action is chosen in preference to an alternative. The opportunity cost is represented by the forgone potential benefit from the best of the alternative courses of action that have been rejected.

Worked Example 7.7

A student may have a Saturday job that pays £7 per hour. If the student gave up one hour on a Saturday to clean the car instead of paying someone £5 to clean it for them, the opportunity cost would be:

One hour of the student's lost wages	£7
less: **Cost of car cleaning**	£5
Opportunity cost	£2

Absorption costing

In this section we are looking at profit considered at the level of total revenue less total cost. If a CD retailer, for example, uses absorption costing it includes a proportion of the costs of its premises, such as rent and utilities costs, in the total unit cost of selling each CD. The allocation and apportionment process that has been outlined in the past few paragraphs is termed absorption costing, or full costing. This process looks at costing in terms of the total costs of running a facility like a hospital, restaurant, retail shop, or factory, being part of the output from that facility. This is one method of costing that, in addition to direct costs, assigns all, or a proportion of, production overhead costs to cost units by means of one or a number of overhead absorption rates. There are two steps involved in this process:

- computation of an overhead absorption rate
- application of the overhead absorption rate to cost units.

The basis of absorption is chosen in a similar way to choosing an apportionment base. The overhead rate is calculated using:

$$\textbf{overhead absorption rate} = \frac{\textbf{total cost centre overheads}}{\textbf{total units of base used}}$$

Worked Example 7.8

Albatross Ltd budgeted to produce 44,000 dining chairs in the month of January, but actually produced 48,800 dining chairs (units). Its sales were 40,800 units at a price of £100 per unit.

Budgeted costs for January:	
Direct material	£36 per unit
Direct labour	£8 per unit
Variable production costs	£6 per unit
Fixed costs	
Production costs	£792,000
Administrative expenses	£208,000
Selling costs	£112,000

Sales commission is paid at 10% of sales revenue. There was no opening stock and budgeted costs were the same as actual costs.

We can prepare the profit and loss account for January using absorption costing techniques, on the basis of the number of budgeted units of production.

$$\text{Overhead absorption rate} = \frac{\text{budgeted fixed production cost}}{\text{budgeted units of production}}$$

$$= \frac{£792{,}000}{44{,}000} = £18 \text{ per unit}$$

Over-absorption of fixed production overheads
= (actual production – budgeted production) × fixed production overhead rate per unit
= (48,800 – 44,000) × £18 per unit = £86,400

Production costs per unit

	£	
Direct material	36	
Direct labour	8	
Variable production overhead	6	
Variable production cost	50	
Fixed production overhead	18	see above
Full production cost per unit	68	

Profit and loss account

	£	£	
Sales (40,800 × £100)		4,080,000	
Full production costs (48,800 × £68)	3,318,400		
plus Opening stock	–		
less Closing stock (8,000 units × £68)	(544,000)		
Cost of sales		2,774,400	
Gross profit		1,305,600	
less Other expenses			
Sales commission (£4,080,000 × 10%)	408,000		
Administrative expenses	208,000		
Selling costs	112,000		
		728,000	
		577,600	
plus			
Over-absorbed fixed production overheads		86,400	see above
Net profit for January, before tax		664,000	

Under/over-absorbed overheads represent the difference between overheads incurred and overheads absorbed. Over-absorbed overheads are credited to the profit and loss account, increasing the profit, as in the above example. Under-absorbed overheads are debited to the profit and loss account, reducing the profit. In this example, the over-absorption of overheads was caused by the actual production level deviating from the budgeted level of production. Deviations, or variances, can occur due to differences between actual and budgeted volumes and/or differences between actual and budgeted expenditure.

There are many bases that may be used for calculation of the overhead absorption rate, for example:

- units of output
- direct labour hours
- machine hours.

Desktop IT systems can assist in these calculations and provide many solutions to the problem of the 'overhead absorption rate', allowing consideration of a number of 'what-if' scenarios before making a final decision.

It can be seen that absorption costing is a costing technique whereby each unit of output is charged with both fixed and variable production costs. The fixed production costs are treated as part of the actual production costs. Stocks, in accordance with SSAP 9, are therefore valued on a full production cost basis and 'held' within the balance sheet until the stocks have been sold, rather than charged to the profit and loss account in the period in which the costs of the stocks are incurred. When the stocks are sold in a subsequent accounting period these costs are matched with the sales revenue of that period and charged to the profit and loss account. The objective of absorption costing is to obtain an overall average economic cost of carrying out whatever activity is being costed.

In order for costings to be carried out from the first day of operations, overhead rates are invariably calculated on the basis of expected future or budgeted overheads and the number of units of manufacturing capacity. Actual overheads and levels of production are unlikely to exactly equal budgeted amounts and so the use of budgeted overhead absorption rates will inevitably lead to an overhead over- or under-absorption (as we have seen in Worked Example 7.8), which is transferred (usually) monthly to the profit and loss account, for internal management accounting reporting.

Progress check 7.8 What is absorption costing and how is it used? Give some examples of bases that may be used for the calculation of overhead absorption rates applied to cost units.

Worked Example 7.9

The total costs for one specific manufacturing process have been incurred at various levels of output as shown in the table below. We can assume that the fixed costs and the variable cost per unit remain constant over this range of output, that is to say there is a linear relationship between total costs and output.

Output units	Total cost £
28,750	256,190
30,000	261,815
31,250	267,440
32,500	273,065
33,750	278,690
35,000	284,315

From the table above we can use a high–low analysis to determine:

(i) the variable costs per unit for the process

(ii) the fixed cost of the process

(i)

	Total cost	Units output
	£	
High	35,000	284,315
Low	28,750	256,190
Difference	6,250	28,125

Variable cost per unit:

$$\frac{£28{,}125}{6{,}250} = £4.50$$

(ii) Using the answer from (i) we can calculate the total variable costs at any level of output, for example at 30,000 units we have:

Variable costs = 30,000 units × £4.50 = £135,000

We can now use this to determine fixed costs:

Total costs at an output level of 30,000 units	= £261,815
Less: variable cost element	= £135,000
Therefore fixed overhead	= £126,815

Alternatively, you may like to try and achieve the same result for Worked Example 7.9 using a graphical approach. If you plot the data in the table you should find that at the point where the graph crosses the y-axis (total costs) output is zero. At that point total costs are £126,815, which is the fixed cost – the cost incurred even when no output takes place. The slope of the graph represents the variable cost per unit, which may be calculated as £4.50 per unit.

We shall now consider another costing technique, **marginal costing**, which is also known as variable costing or **period costing**. We will return to Worked Example 7.8 later, using the marginal costing technique and contrast it with the absorption costing technique.

Marginal costing

We have considered above a costing method that looks at profit considered at the level of total revenue, or total sales, less total cost. We will now look at another way of considering profit, called **contribution**, and its corresponding costing system called marginal costing (see Fig. 7.6).

contribution = total revenue – variable costs

Marginal costing, variable costing, or period costing, is a costing technique whereby each unit of output is charged only with variable production costs. The costs which are generated solely by a given cost unit are the variable costs associated with that unit, including the variable cost elements of any associated semi-variable costs. Marginal cost ascertainment includes all unit direct costs plus the variable overhead cost per unit incurred by the cost unit. The marginal cost of a unit may be defined as the additional cost of producing one such unit. The marginal cost of a number of units is the sum

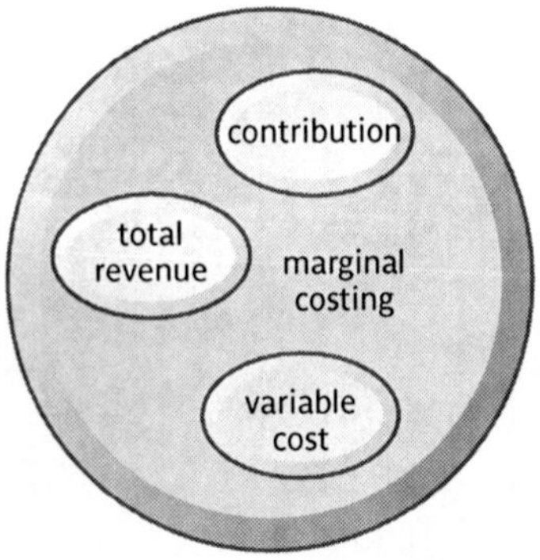

Figure 7.6 The elements of marginal costing

of all the unit marginal costs. Whereas absorption costing deals with total costs and profits, marginal costing deals with variable costs and contribution. Contribution is defined as the sales value less the variable cost of sales. Contribution may be expressed as:

- total contribution
- contribution per unit
- contribution as a percentage of sales.

If a business provides a series of products that all provide some contribution, the business may avoid being severely damaged by the downturn in demand of just one of the products. Fixed production costs are not considered to be the real costs of production, but costs which provide the facilities, for an accounting period, that enable production to take place. They are therefore treated as costs of the period and charged to the period in which they are incurred against the aggregate contribution. Stocks are valued on a variable production cost basis that excludes fixed production costs.

Marginal cost ascertainment assumes that the cost of any given activity is only the cost that that activity generates; it is the difference between carrying out and not carrying out that activity. Each cost unit and each cost centre is charged with only those costs that are generated as a consequence of that cost unit and that cost centre being a part of the company's activities.

We will now return to Worked Example 7.8 and consider the results using marginal costing techniques, and contrast them with those achieved using absorption costing in Worked Example 7.10.

Worked Example 7.10

Using the information for Albatross Ltd from Worked Example 7.8, we may prepare a profit and loss account for January using marginal costing.

The variable (marginal) production costs per unit from Worked Example 7.8 are:

	£
Direct material	36
Direct labour	8
Variable production overhead	6
Variable production cost	50

Profit and loss account

	£	£
Sales (40,800 × £100)		4,080,000
Variable production costs (48,800 × £50)	2,440,000	
plus Opening stock	–	
less Closing stock (8,000 units × £50)	(400,000)	
Cost of sales		2,040,000
Gross contribution		2,040,000
less Sales commission (£4,080,000 × 10%)		408,000
Net contribution		1,632,000
less Fixed costs		
Production costs	792,000	
Administrative expenses	208,000	
Selling costs	112,000	
		1,112,000
Net profit for January, before tax		520,000

It can be seen that profit calculated using the marginal costing technique is £144,000 less than that using the absorption costing technique, because under absorption costing stock is valued at full production costs, the fixed production costs being carried forward in the stock to the next period instead of being charged to the current period as under marginal costing.

Note: The activity is the same regardless of the costing technique that has been used. It is only the method of reporting that has caused a difference in the profit.

Stock valuation difference

Closing stock units × (absorption cost per unit – marginal cost per unit) = profit difference

8,000 units × (£68 – £50) = £144,000

Some specific features of the marginal costing technique are:

- its recognition of cost behaviour, providing better support for sales pricing and decision-making
- it allows better control reports to be prepared because contribution is based on, and varies with, the sales level
- fixed costs may be addressed within the period that gives rise to them.

However, marginal costing is not suitable for stock valuation in line with accounting standard SSAP 9, because there is no fixed cost element included. SSAP 9 requires closing stocks to consist of direct materials, direct labour and appropriate overheads. A great many companies, large and small, adopt marginal costing for monthly management reporting and stocks valuation for each of their accounting periods throughout their financial year. Such companies overcome the problems of non-compliance with SSAP 9 by making an adjustment to their stocks valuation and their profit and loss accounts to include an allowance for fixed overhead costs, in the final accounting period at their year end.

Absorption costing versus marginal costing

A more comprehensive list of the advantages and disadvantages of both techniques is summarised in Figs 7.7 and 7.8.

Progress check 7.9 Should managers participate in the accounting exercise of allocation of fixed costs?

(Hint: You may wish to consider the cyclical nature of the building industry as an example that illustrates the difficulty of allocating fixed costs.)

In the long run, over several accounting periods, the total recorded profit of an entity is the same regardless of whether absorption costing or marginal costing techniques are used. The difference is one of timing. The actual amounts of the costs do not differ, only the period in which they are charged against profits. Thus, differences in profit occur from one period to the next depending on which method is adopted.

Figure 7.9 illustrates and contrasts the formats of the trading and profit and loss account using absorption costing and marginal costing.

Marginal costing is a powerful technique since it focuses attention on those costs which are affected by, or associated with, an activity. It is also particularly useful in the areas of decision-making and relevant costs.

Management accounting continues to change and develop as it meets the needs presented by:

- changing economic climates
- globalisation
- information technology
- increasing competition.

Marginal costing developed from absorption costing in recognition of the differences in behaviour between fixed costs and variable costs. In most industries, as labour costs continue to become a smaller and smaller percentage of total costs, traditional costing methods, which usually absorb costs on the basis of direct labour hours, have been seen to be increasingly inappropriate.

The following are some management accounting techniques that have been developed more recently in response to some of the criticisms of traditional costing methods:

- ➡ activity based costing (ABC)
- ➡ throughput accounting (TA)
- ➡ life cycle costing
- ➡ target costing
- benchmarking
- ➡ *kaizen*.

Progress check 7.10 What is marginal costing and in what ways is it different from absorption costing?

advantages	disadvantages
it is simple to use, and based on a formula that uses an estimated or planned fixed overhead rate included in the calculation of unit costs of products and services	fixed costs are not necessarily avoidable and they have to be paid regardless of whether sales and production volumes are high, low or zero
it is easy to apply using cost or a percentage mark-up to achieve a reasonable profit	fixed costs are not variable in the short run
apportionment and allocation of fixed costs to cost centres makes managers aware of costs and services provided and ensures that they remember that all costs need to be covered for the company to be profitable	there are different alternative bases of overhead allocation which therefore result in different interpretations
cost price or full cost pricing ensures that all costs are covered	the capacity levels chosen for overhead absorption rates are based on historical information and are therefore open to debate
it conforms with the accrual concept by matching costs with revenue for a particular accounting period, as in the full costing of stocks	activity must be equal to or greater than the budgeted level of activity or else fixed costs will be under-absorbed
stock valuation complies with SSAP 9, as an element of fixed production costs is absorbed into stocks	if sales are depressed then profits can be artificially increased by increasing production thus increasing stocks
it avoids the separation of costs into fixed and variable elements, which are not easily and accurately identified	
analysis of over- and under-absorbed overheads highlights any inefficient utilisation of production resources	

Figure 7.7 Advantages and disadvantages of absorption costing

advantages	disadvantages
it is market based not cost based; exclusion of fixed production costs on a marginal basis enables the company to be more competitive	pricing at the margin may lead to underpricing with too little contribution and non-recovery of fixed costs, particularly in periods of economic downturn
it covers all incremental costs associated with the product, production and sales	stock valuation does not comply with SSAP 9, as no element of fixed production costs is absorbed into stocks
it enables the analysis of different market price/volume levels to allow selection of optimal contributions and it enables strategic analysis of competitors and customers	
it enables the company to determine break-even points and plan profit, and to use the opportunity cost approach	
it avoids the arbitrary apportionment of fixed costs and avoids the problem of determining a suitable basis for the overhead abortion rate, e.g. units, labour hours, machine hours etc.	
most fixed production overheads are periodic, or time-based, and incurred regardless of levels of production, and so should be charged to the period in which they are incurred, e.g. factory rent, salaries and depreciation	
fixed production costs may not be controllable at the departmental level and so should not be included in production costs at the cost centre level – control should be matched with responsibility	
profits cannot be manipulated by increasing stocks in times of low sales because stocks exclude fixed costs and profits therefore vary directly with sales	
it facilitates control through easier pooling of separate fixed costs and variable costs totals, and preparation of flexible budgets to provide comparisons for actual levels of activity	
stock valued on a variable cost basis supports the view that the additional cost of stock is limited to its variable costs	
marginal costing is prudent because fixed costs are charged to the period in which they are incurred, not carried forward in stock which may prove to be unsaleable and result in earlier profits having been overstated	

Figure 7.8 Advantages and disadvantages of marginal costing

Absorption costing		**Marginal costing**	
	Net turnover		**Net turnover**
less:		**less variable costs:**	
Direct materials		Direct materials	
Direct labour		Direct labour	
Production overhead		Variable production overhead	
		Variable selling and distribution overhead	
	Production cost of sales		Production cost of sales
	Gross profit		**Contribution**
less:		**less fixed costs:**	
		Production costs	
Selling costs		Selling costs	
Distribution costs		Distribution costs	
Administrative expenses		Administrative expenses	
Research and development costs		Research and development costs	
	Non-production costs		Total fixed costs
	Net profit before tax		**Net profit before tax**

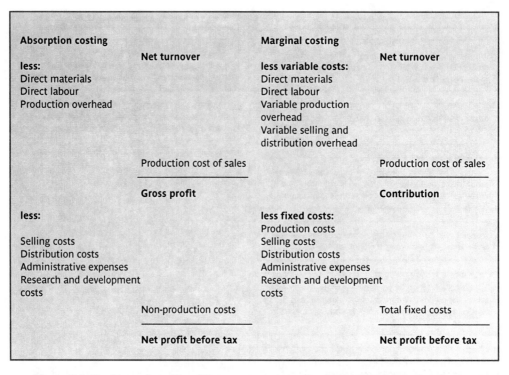

Figure 7.9 Trading and profit and loss account absorption and marginal costing formats

Worked Example 7.11

Management accounting provides information to various departments within a business. Fast-moving businesses need this information very quickly. Hotel groups have invested in central booking systems and these systems are used to reveal times of the year when reservations are down because of national and local trends. Let's consider how the marketing department and the management accounting function might work together to generate extra bookings.

The marketing department may assess the periods and times in which each hotel has gaps in its reservations. The management accountant may assess the direct costs associated with each reservation, for example the costs of cleaning and food. The two departments may then suggest a special offer for a fixed period of time (for example, Travelodge special offers in the press during January and February 2001). The special offer may allow for local conditions by varying the price within a range, for example £20 to £30 per night.

Activity based costing (ABC)

The activities of businesses across the entire chain of value-adding organisational processes have a considerable impact on costs and therefore profit. A recently developed management accounting approach to evaluating the extent of this impact and to dealing with the root causes of costs is activity based costing (ABC).

Activity based costing provides an alternative approach to the costing of products in response to some of the criticisms that have been aimed at the more traditional approaches. Before we examine the concept of ABC let us look at a simple example, which puts these criticisms in context.

Worked Example 7.12

Traditional Moulding Ltd manufactures two plastic fittings, the RX-L and the RX-R. Both products are produced in the Moulding2 department, which has total overheads of £5,000 for the month of March. Moulding2 uses 4,000 hours of direct labour to produce the RX-L (2,000) and RX-R (2,000). The other activities within the Moulding2 department are 10 machine set-ups (eight to produce the RX-L and two to produce the RX-R) which cost £3,200, and the processing of 90 sales orders (50 for the RX-L and 40 for the RX-R) costing £1,800.

The costs charged to each product may be determined using absorption costing on a direct labour hours basis, and alternatively they may be determined on the basis of the other activities within the department.

Absorption costing basis

Cost per labour hour = £5,000/4,000 hours = £1.25 per direct labour hour

	RX-L	RX-R	Total
	£	£	£
2,000 hours at £1.25	2,500		2,500
2,000 hours at £1.25		2,500	2,500
	2,500	2,500	5,000

Alternative activities basis

	RX-L	RX-R	Total	
Machine set-ups	8	2	10	(cost £3,200)
Sales orders	50	40	90	(cost £1,800)
				(total cost £5,000)

	RX-L	RX-R	Total
	£	£	£
Machine set-ups at £320 each	2,560	640	3,200
Sales orders at £20 each	1,000	800	1,800
	3,560	1,440	5,000

There is obviously a considerable difference between the overhead costs attributed to each of the products, depending on which basis we have used. We may question whether or not the absorption basis is fair and whether or not the activity basis provides a fairer method.

Increasing competition is a fact of life within any industry, public or private, and whatever product or service is being offered to customers in the marketplace. Globalisation has brought increased pressures of competition. Pressures on a company's profit margins inevitably follow from the increasing pace of technological change, which results in shortened life cycles of products that have been manufactured by the company as they are replaced by completely new models. Thus, the obsolescence of capital equipment is accelerated. This all means that the basis of competition has changed.

The effects on businesses are significant, and those that do not respond successfully may fail, or be acquired by other companies. Costs such as development costs and costs of capital equipment must be recovered over a shorter time period. The phases within the product life cycle must be managed more effectively and efficiently. The faster pace of business and the need for quick decisions and action mean that effective computerised information systems are required to provide relevant and timely information.

The above changes in the manufacturing business environment have led to changes in the patterns of cost behaviour. Technological and other changes have meant a lowering of the percentage of direct labour costs as a proportion of total manufacturing costs. An indication of the trend and the scale of this reduction in percentage of direct labour cost are shown in Fig. 7.10. In many industries materials and components costs have become an increasingly large proportion of total manufacturing costs. Automation and decreasing equipment life spans have led to capital equipment costs forming a higher percentage of total costs. The costs of information technology and other overhead and indirect costs have also increased as a percentage of total cost. There has therefore been increasing dissatisfaction with traditional costing and decision-making techniques and the search for other, perhaps more relevant and meaningful methods.

Traditional decision-making and control have looked at cost/volume relationships and the splitting of fixed and variable costs. The consideration of 'other characteristics' has not been emphasised. Activity based costing (ABC) was developed by Kaplan and Cooper in 1984 and was aimed to get accountants to consider 'other characteristics' in terms of the causes of cost, or what are defined as the cost drivers.

Kaplan and Cooper said that one cost system was not enough, and that three were needed:

- for stock valuation
- for operational control
- for product cost measurement.

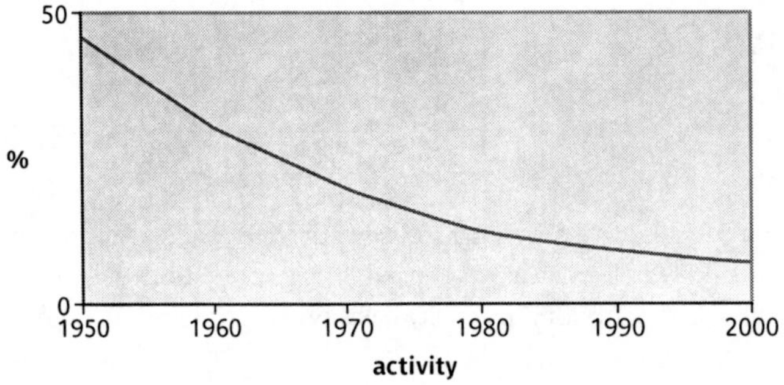

Figure 7.10 Estimated UK direct labour costs as % of manufacturing costs over the past 50 years

Together with Cooper, Kaplan proposed ABC as a method for dealing with the latter two requirements. ABC involves the examination of activities across the entire chain of value-adding organisational processes underlying the causes, or drivers, of cost and profit. Kaplan and Cooper have defined ABC as an approach to costing and monitoring of activities which involves tracing resource consumption and costing final outputs. Resources are assigned to activities and activities to cost objects based on consumption estimates. The latter utilise cost drivers to attach activity costs to outputs.

Progress check 7.11 **Why does traditional analysis of fixed and variable costs within a fast moving company (for example, a company that supplies computer hardware, software and helpline services) not appear to provide managers with enough information?**

An activity driver is defined as a measure of the frequency and intensity of the demands placed on activities by cost objects. An example is the number of customer orders which measures the consumption of order entries by each customer. A cost driver is defined as any factor which causes a change in the cost of an activity. For example, the quality of parts received by an activity is a determining factor in the work required by that activity and therefore affects the resources required. An activity may have multiple cost drivers associated with it.

If a company produces only one product then all overheads may be allocated to that product. The unit cost of the product is then the average cost. The difficulty of allocation of overheads arises when the company produces many products using many different resources consumed in different proportions by products. It is the sharing of overheads and the feasibility of monitoring the costs that causes the difficulty.

Traditional cost allocation approaches allocate overheads, for example, on the basis of direct labour hours, or units produced. They are therefore volume driven, based on a scientific management basis of mass production with standard design, a high labour content percentage of total costs, large volumes, low fixed costs, and with demand greater than supply. This incidentally resulted in competitive advantage gained from cost leadership.

ABC starts by considering four different groups of activities giving rise to overheads: movement, production demands, quality, and design, rather than the volume of production. ABC is based on the premise that activities consume resources, and products consume activities. There is a need to identify how labour and machinery is actually used through:

- interview
- questionnaire
- observation
- process activity mapping.

Activities are often cross-functional, for example a company buying function that involves purchasing, finance, administration, and personnel (human resources) departments in the whole procurement process. This speeds up and improves communication and may avoid a great deal of unnecessary and duplicate clerical and administrative tasks.

ABC requires the analysis of total overhead costs into variable costs and fixed costs, with variable costs split into short-term and long-term variable costs. Within an ABC system it is assumed that fixed costs do not vary with any measure of activity volume for a given time period. Short-term variable costs – volume-based costs – are defined in the same way as traditional volume-driven variable costs – materials and direct labour. Long-term variable costs – activity based costs – are defined as those costs which vary with the level of activity, which may be non-productive, and the variation may

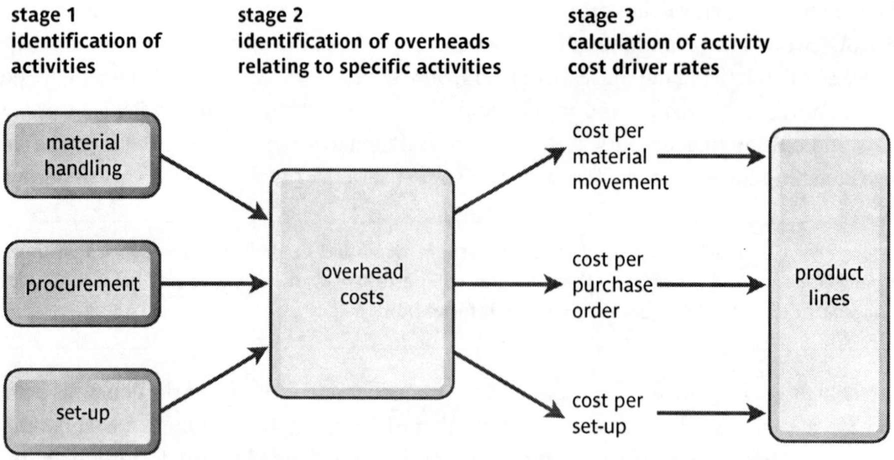

Figure 7.11 Framework of activity based costing (ABC)

not be instant. Examples of these are machine set-up costs, and goods receiving costs, which are driven by the activities of the number of production runs and number of customer orders, respectively.

The diagram in Fig. 7.11 represents an example of the framework of ABC. The bases of ABC are:

- it is activities that cause costs, not products
- it is activities and not costs that can be managed
- control of costs is best achieved through the management of activities
- each cost driver, or activity, is evaluated by setting up its own individual cost centre, to see if it is worth undertaking or buying in, and to see how it may be managed, reported on and evaluated.

The search for alternative methods such as ABC also highlights many weaknesses in traditional cost accounting methods. Indiscriminate use of a single performance measure can lead to misleading conclusions about profit and cost performance. Traditional cost accounting methods can lead to a failure to understand the activities that are causing costs, and a compartmentalised approach to costing which does not look at the processes and activities that cross departmental boundaries.

Progress check 7.12 **Use an example of a media group to provide the basis for a discussion on how ABC analysis considers departmental activities as the causes of costs rather than the products that are being produced.**

These weaknesses result in:

- pricing and profitability errors
- misidentified cause and effect relationships
- improper make or buy decisions
- improper design initiatives
- irrelevant and untimely variance analysis
- misallocations of capital and resources
- non-productive activities.

The ABC methodology requires all cost types to be identified and classified into those that are volume based, those that are activity based, and those that may have some other basis.

Worked Example 7.13

Let's consider how the costs of a wine-bottling process, for example, for supply to one large customer, may be classified into those that are volume based, activity based, or on some other basis.

The bottle-filling process costs may be totally volume related. The labelling and corking processes may be related to stocking and handling of materials and the set-up of the processes required to align labels and corks. Alternatively, costs may in some way be related to the different grades of product, perhaps the perceived quality of the wine as 'cheap plonk' or fine wine.

Volume-based costs are then computed on a product unit costs basis, for example, materials costs. Activity based costs are computed relative to each activity. For each product the cost of using each activity for the output level is calculated. The total costs for each product are then calculated and divided by the output volume in order to calculate the unit cost for each product.

The ABC accounting system may be used to develop an activity based management (ABM) system. This is a system of management, which uses activity based information for a variety of purposes including cost reduction, cost modelling and customer profitability analysis. The system involves four key operations: activity analysis; activity costings; activity costs per product; activity performance measurement and management. A good ABM system should promote more effective cross-function management.

Major companies involved with providing consumers with customer service and advice found the resources required on site were quite expensive, both in capital and management time. As a result of various experiments during the latter part of the 1990s, the UK has seen a major move towards the out-sourcing of these services to specialist call centres located in 'low cost' areas, away from 'high cost' city centres. This illustrates the ABM process applied to the customer service activity. Decisions are taken following analyses of activities and their costs, followed by the evaluation of various alternative options that might be available, their implementation and subsequent management. In a similar way, many companies have investigated the out-sourcing of a number of routine accounting functions to specialist contractors.

The activity analysis identifies all activities and analyses all inputs and outputs of each activity. Activity costings identify all relevant and important costs of all activities. The activity volume that is chosen is the one that most directly influences costs, and the total costs are expressed in terms of activity per unit of activity volume.

Next, the activity costs per product are calculated by identifying the activity, which each product consumes, and measuring the consumption rates of activities per product. Using the unit activity cost consumption rates, costs are then allocated to each product.

The final step is activity performance measurement and management. This involves evaluation of the major elements in the performance of an activity. Changes in activity levels are then evaluated and performance reviewed which may then result in re-engineering of the methods used in that activity. The results are evaluated by:

- measuring, and
- monitoring, and
- controlling the re-engineered activity.

Worked Example 7.14

Let's assume that Traditional Moulding Ltd (from Worked Example 7.12) had achieved improvements in the processes, which resulted in a reduction in the costs and number of machine set-ups required. We can calculate the revised costs that would result if the RX-L and the RX-R each required only one set-up and the total cost of set-ups was only £640.

	RX-L	RX-R	Total	
Machine set-ups	1	1	2	(cost £640)
Sales orders	50	40	90	(cost £1,800)

	RX-L	RX-R	Total
	£	£	£
Machine set-ups at £320 each	320	320	640
Sales orders at £20 each	1,000	800	1,800
	1,320	1,120	2,440

There is another considerable difference between the overhead costs attributed to each of the products. We have used the same basis as previously, but an improvement in one of the processes has brought the costs attributed to each product virtually in line with each other whereas previously one product bore almost three times the cost of the other product.

A full worked example will clarify the ABC accounting concepts we have discussed and show the results obtained using ABC compared with those using an alternative traditional absorption costing method.

Worked Example 7.15

A clothing manufacturer, Brief Encounter Ltd, manufactures two products, the Rose and the Rouge, using the same equipment and similar processes. Activities have been examined to identify the relevant cost drivers as machine hours, set-ups and customer orders. August budget data has been provided relating to the cost drivers, in addition to material, labour and overhead costs and quantities produced.

August budget ABC data	**Rose**	**Rouge**
Budgeted number of units manufactured	20,000	10,000
Direct material cost per unit	£5	£20
Direct labour hours per unit	0.5	0.5
Direct labour cost per hour	£8	£8
Machine hours per unit	2	4
Set-ups during the month	30	70
Customer orders handled in the month	40	160

Overhead costs for the month:	relating to machine activity	£300,000
	relating to set-ups of production runs	£50,000
	relating to order handling	£70,000

We can use the above data to illustrate ABC and to provide a comparison with traditional costing methods. The full production cost of each unit of the Rose and the Rouge using both a traditional absorption costing approach and an ABC costing approach may be compared and illustrated in both tabular and graphical form.

Absorption costing

Using a traditional absorption costing approach the full production cost of each unit of Rose and Rouge may be calculated:

Budget direct labour hours (20,000 units × 0.5 hours) + (10,000 units × 0.5 hours)
= 15,000 hours
Overhead absorption rate per direct labour hour

$$= \frac{\text{machine activity costs + set-up costs + order handling costs}}{\text{direct labour hours}}$$

$$= \frac{(£300{,}000 + £50{,}000 + £70{,}000)}{315{,}000 \text{ hours}} = £28 \text{ per direct labour hour}$$

Full unit production costs of the Rose and the Rouge:

		Rose		Rouge
		£		£
Direct materials		5.00		20.00
Direct labour	(0.5 hours × £8)	4.00	(0.5 hours × £8)	4.00
Factory overhead	(0.5 hours × £28)	14.00	(0.5 hours × £28)	14.00
Unit production costs		23.00		38.00

Total costs (20,000 × £23) + (10,000 × £38) = £840,000

ABC

Using an ABC costing approach the full production cost of each unit of the Rose and the Rouge may be calculated:

Planned for the month of August:

Machine hours (20,000 units × 2 hours) + (10,000 × 4 hours)		= 80,000 hours
Machine costs		= £300,000
Machine rate per hour		= £3.75
Number of set-ups	(30 + 70)	= 100 set-ups
Set-up costs		= £50,000
Cost per set-up		= £500
Number of orders handled	(40 + 160)	= 200 orders
Order handling costs		= £70,000
Cost per order handled		= £350

Overhead costs per unit of the Rose and the Rouge on an ABC basis:

		Rose £		Rouge £
Machine activity	(2 hours × £3.75)	7.50	(4 hours × £3.75)	15.00
Set-ups	(30 × £500)/20,000	0.75	(70 × £500)/10,000	3.50
Order handling	(40 × £350)/20,000	0.70	(160 × £350)/10,000	5.60
Unit overhead costs		8.95		24.10

ABC unit production costs of the Rose and the Rouge:

		Rose £		Rouge £
Direct materials		5.00		20.00
Direct labour	(0.5 hours × £8)	4.00	(0.5 hours × £8)	4.00
Factory overhead		8.95		24.10
Unit production costs		17.95		48.10

Total costs (20,000 × £17.95) + (10,000 × £48.10) = £840,000

Summary of unit product costs

	Rose £	Rouge £
Full absorption cost per unit	23.00	38.00
ABC cost per unit	17.95	48.10

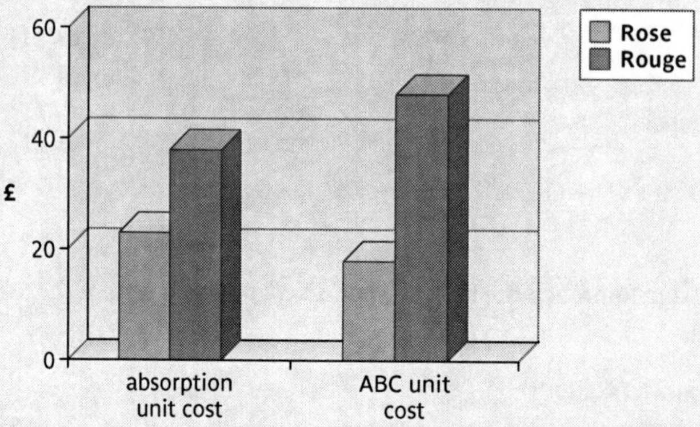

Figure 7.12 Unit costs for the Rose and Rouge using absorption costing and ABC

There are large differences between the two alternative calculations of unit costs. In practice, this can have a significant impact on pricing policies adopted by companies, and on other decision-making, for example with regard to discontinuation of apparently unprofitable products.

It can be seen from Worked Example 7.15 that all costs have been accounted for and included in the unit costs for the Rose and the Rouge using both the absorption costing and ABC methods. However, using absorption costing, the Rose has been shown to be far less profitable, and the Rouge shown to be far more profitable than by using the ABC approach. In this brief example, the ABC approach has probably shown the more correct and realistic unit costs applying to the Rose and the Rouge because it has identified the activities, the causes of costs, directly related to the manufacture of each product. The pooling of the costs associated with each activity has enabled costs to be attributed directly to each product, rather than using an estimate based on, say, direct labour costs. Therefore, a more informed approach may be taken to improving machine set-up, and order-handling performance, and their cost reduction and better pricing decisions may be made regarding both the Rose and the Rouge.

There are benefits to be gained from the use of ABC:

- it facilitates improved understanding of costs
- it enables improvements and overhead savings to be made
- it focuses on activities and not production volumes
- it examines the profitability of products
- it identifies loss-making products
- it leads to development of activity based management systems.

However, there are also many problems associated with the implementation and use of an ABC system:

- it does not comply with statutory stock valuation requirements
- it is as subjective as absorption costing
- it is historical
- it uses cost pooling (points of focus for the costs relating to particular activities), but also requires the use of apportionment, which involves the same problems of subjectivity identified in the use of absorption costing
- it requires identification of cost drivers, the right ones; it requires the measurement of cost drivers and activity costs
- it requires the relating of activities to products
- it requires the measurement of cross-product drivers, which are factors that cause changes in costs of a number of activities and products
- there are always other consequences that ABC does not address
- there is a novelty, or flavour of the month, factor associated with ABC which is questionable
- it is an expensive and time-consuming exercise.

Despite the problems associated with the implementation of ABC, its acceptance is becoming more widespread in the UK. Nevertheless, there is as yet little evidence as to improved profitability resulting from the implementation of ABC. Dr Stephen Lyne and Andy Friedman from Bristol University carried out research into 11 companies to study the impact of activity based techniques in real-life situations over a six-year period up to 1999 (*Success and Failure of Activity Based Techniques*).

The Lyne/Friedman research involved defining exactly what was meant by success and failure, and using the researchers' criteria five companies failed, and six were deemed a partial success. Interestingly, the research highlighted some key factors that influenced the success or otherwise of implementing ABC:

- the positive and negative roles of individuals
- the degree to which ABC was an embedded system
- the degree of integration with information technology systems
- the use of consultants
- relations between accountants and operational managers.

ABC should perhaps not be regarded totally as the panacea, the answer to all the problems associated with cost accounting. ABC, no doubt, represents an enlightened approach and adds something more meaningful than traditional costing methods. Its implementation requires very large and complex data-collection exercises in which involvement of all activities throughout the whole organisation is necessary. ABC is very time-consuming and costly. Care needs to be taken in evaluation of the results of ABC. It is very useful for identification and management of the activities that cause costs. It is a useful tool to assist in product pricing decisions. It is not yet a costing method which may replace absorption costing for use in financial reporting.

Progress check 7.13 **Describe the activity based costing (ABC) process and in what ways it may be most effectively used.**

Summary of key points

- There are a number of additional accounting concepts that relate to management accounting.
- Cost (as a noun) is an amount of expenditure attributable to a specified thing or activity, but also relates to a resource sacrificed or forgone, expressed in a monetary value.
- Cost (as a verb) may be used to say that to cost something is to ascertain the cost of a specified thing or activity, but cost is not a word that is usually used without a qualification as to its nature and limitations.
- Direct costs are directly identified with cost objects.
- Indirect costs have to be allocated or apportioned to cost units, cost centres, or cost accounts using appropriate bases for allocation and apportionment.
- Unit costs of products, services or activities may be determined using the traditional costing techniques of absorption costing and marginal costing.
- There are many arguments for and against the use of the techniques of both absorption costing and marginal costing, revolving mainly around the basis chosen for allocation and apportionment of overheads.
- The more recently developed technique of activity based costing (ABC) is an approach that attempts to overcome the problem of allocation and apportionment of overheads.

Questions

Q7.1 (i) What are the main roles of the management accountant?

(ii) How does management accounting support the effective management of a business?

Q7.2 (i) What are the differences between fixed costs, variable costs and semi-variable costs?

(ii) Give some examples of each.

Q7.3 (i) Why do production overheads need to be allocated and apportioned, and to what?

(ii) Describe the processes of allocation and apportionment.

Q7.4 (i) Which costing system complies with the provisions outlined in SSAP 9?
(ii) Describe the process used in this technique.

Q7.5 What is marginal costing and how does it differ from absorption costing?

Q7.6 What are the main benefits to be gained from using a system of marginal costing?

Q7.7 (i) What are the principles on which activity based costing (ABC) is based?
(ii) How does ABC differ from traditional costing methods?

Discussion points

D7.1 Surely an accountant is an accountant! Why does the function of management accounting need to be separated from financial accounting and why is it seen as such an integral part of the management of the business? Discuss.

D7.2 Do the benefits from using marginal costing outweigh the benefits from using absorption costing sufficiently to replace absorption costing in SSAP 9 as the basis for stock valuation and the preparation of financial statements? Discuss.

D7.3 Is activity based costing (ABC) a serious contender to replace the traditional costing methods? What are some of the drawbacks in implementing this?

Exercises

Solutions are provided in Appendix 3 to all exercise numbers highlighted in colour.

Level I

E7.1 *Time allowed – 45 minutes*

Bluebell Woods Ltd produces a product for which the following standard cost details have been provided based on production and sales of 4,300 units in a four-week period:

Direct material cost	£0.85 per kg
Direct material usage	2 kg per unit
Direct labour rate	£4.20 per hour
Direct labour time per unit	42 minutes
Selling price	£5.84 per unit
Variable production costs	£0.12 per unit
Fixed production costs	£3,526 per four-week period

Prepare a standard profit statement for a four-week period using:

(i) absorption costing

(ii) marginal costing.

E7.2 *Time allowed – 45 minutes*

A manufacturing company, Duane Pipes Ltd, uses predetermined rates for absorbing manufacturing overheads based on the budgeted level of activity. A total rate of £35 per direct labour hour has been calculated for the Assembly Department for March 2004, for which the following overhead expenditure at various activity levels has been estimated:

Total manufacturing overheads	Number of direct labour hours
£	
465,500	12,000
483,875	13,500
502,250	15,000

You are required to calculate the following:

(i) the variable overhead absorption rate per direct labour hour

(ii) the estimated total fixed overheads

(iii) the budgeted level of activity for March 2004 in direct labour hours

(iv) the amount of under/over-recovery of overheads, and state which, if the actual direct labour hours were 13,850 and actual overheads were £509,250

and

(v) outline the reasons for and against using departmental absorption rates as opposed to a single blanket factory-wide rate.

Level II

E7.3 *Time allowed – 75 minutes*

Square Gift Ltd is located in Wales, where the national sales manager is also based, and has a sales force of 15 salesmen covering the whole of the UK. The sales force, including the national sales manager, all have the same make and model of company car. A new car costs £16,000, and all cars are traded in for a guaranteed £6,000 when they are two years old.

The salesman with the lowest annual mileage, of 18,000 miles, operates in the South East of England.
The salesman with the highest annual mileage, of 40,000 miles, operates throughout Scotland.
The annual average mileage of the complete sales team works out at 30,000 miles per car.

The average salesman's annual vehicle running cost is:

	£
Petrol and oil	3,000
Road tax	155
Insurance	450
Repairs	700
Miscellaneous	300
Total	4,605

Annual vehicle repair costs include £250 for regular maintenance.
Tyre life is around 30,000 miles and replacement sets cost £350.
No additional repair costs are incurred during the first year of vehicle life because a special warranty agreement exists with the supplying garage to cover these, but on average £200 is paid for repairs in the second year – repair costs are averaged over the two years with regular maintenance and repairs being variable with mileage rather than time.
Miscellaneous vehicle costs include subscriptions to motoring organisations, vehicle cleaning costs, parking, and garaging allowances.

Analyse the total vehicle costs into fixed costs and variable costs separately to give total annual costs for:

(i) the lowest mileage per annum salesman

(ii) the highest mileage per annum salesman.

You may ignore cost of capital, and possible impacts of tax and inflation.
(Hints: Assume that insurance costs are the same for each area.
Assume that miscellaneous operating costs are fixed.
Repairs are based on amount of mileage.)

E7.4 *Time allowed – 75 minutes*

Rocky Ltd manufactures a single product, the budget for which was as follows for each of the months July and August 2005:

		Total		Per unit
		£		£
Sales (6,000 units)		60,000		10.00
Production cost of sales:				
Variable overhead	45,000		7.50	
Fixed overhead	3,000	48,000	0.50	8.00
		12,000		2.00
Selling and distribution costs (fixed)		4,200		0.70
Administrative expenses (fixed)		3,000		0.50
Profit		4,800		0.80

Actual units produced, sold and in stock in July and August were:

	July	August
Opening stock	–	900
Production	5,300	4,400
Sales	4,400	5,000
Closing stock	900	300

Prepare profit and loss accounts for each of the months July and August, assuming that fixed production overhead is absorbed into the cost of the product at the normal level shown in the monthly budget.

(Hint: This is the absorption costing approach.)

E7.5 *Time allowed – 75 minutes*

Using the data for Rocky Ltd from Exercise E7.4, prepare profit and loss accounts for each of the months July and August, assuming that fixed production overhead is not absorbed into the cost of the product, but is treated as a cost of the period and charged against sales.

(Hint: This is the marginal costing approach.)

E7.6 *Time allowed – 75 minutes*

Using your answers to Exercises E7.4 and E7.5, explain why the profits for July and August are different using the two costing methods, and support your explanation with an appropriate reconciliation of the results.

E7.7 *Time allowed – 75 minutes*

Abem Ltd produces three products, using the same production methods and equipment for each. The company currently uses a traditional product costing system. Direct labour costs £8 per hour. Production overheads are absorbed on a machine hour basis and the rate for the period is £25 per machine hour. Estimated cost details for the next month for the three products are:

	Hours per unit		Materials	Volumes
	Labour hours	Machine hours	per unit £	(units)
Product A	$\frac{1}{2}$	$1\frac{1}{2}$	20	750
Product B	$1\frac{1}{2}$	1	10	1,975
Product C	1	3	25	7,900

An ABC system is being considered by Abem Ltd, and it has been established that the total production overhead costs may be divided as follows:

	%
Costs relating to set-ups	35
Costs relating to machinery	20
Costs relating to materials handling	15
Costs relating to inspection	30
	100

The following activity volumes are associated with the production for the period:

	Number of set-ups	Number of movements of materials	Number of inspections
Product A	70	10	150
Product B	120	20	180
Product C	480	90	670
	670	120	1,000

Required:

(i) Calculate the cost per unit for each product using the traditional method of absorption costing.
(ii) Calculate the cost per unit for each product using ABC principles.
(iii) Comment on any differences in the costs in your answers to (i) and (ii).

8

Cost analysis and decision-making

Contents

Learning objectives

Completion of this chapter will enable you to:

- explain cost/volume/profit (CVP) relationships and break-even analysis
- identify the limitations of CVP analysis
- explain the scope and importance of decision-making to an organisation
- outline the decision-making process
- explain the significance of the concept of relevant costs
- apply marginal costing techniques to decision-making
- evaluate shut-down or continuation decisions
- critically compare make or buy alternatives
- consider the problem of product mix, scarce resources and limiting factors
- consider the wide range of sales pricing options
- use a decision tree to determine expected values of alternative outcomes.

Introduction

In Chapter 7 we introduced costs, contribution and profit. This chapter develops the importance of contribution as a measure of profitability and begins with an examination of the relationship between costs, volumes of activity, and profit, or CVP analysis. We will look at a particular application of CVP analysis in break-even analysis, and consider some of the advantages and limitations of its use.

This chapter will further develop the relationship between costs, activity levels, contribution and profit and introduce some additional ways of looking at costs. One of the most important uses of accounting and financial information is as an aid to decision-making. There are many categories of business decisions. The costs and benefits that result from each type of decision may be very different and so it is useful to identify the different categories of decisions. Broadly, decisions are to do with:

- problem solving
- planning
- control
- investment.

This chapter outlines what decision-making means and considers the different types of decision that may be assisted by various accounting techniques. A later chapter has been devoted to the whole area of capital investment decision-making.

We will outline the various types and levels of decision and the process of decision-making. The concept of relevant costs is explored in some detail and we will consider its significance in assessing the information that should be used in calculations to support decision-making.

This chapter will look at the following specific types of decision:

- whether or not to shut down a factory or a department, in a manufacturing or service environment
- whether to buy a component or part used in manufacturing from an outside supplier or to make it internally

- decisions on product or service mix and the constraints of limiting factors
- pricing policy and the alternative sales pricing options available to an entity
- decisions in which risk is a key factor, and the use of decision trees.

Cost/volume/profit (CVP) relationships and break-even analysis

It is sometimes said that accountants think in straight lines whereas economists think in curves. We can see this in the way that economists view costs and revenues. Generally, economists are looking at the longer term when they consider a company's total costs and total revenues.

We can see from Fig. 8.1 that the total revenue curve starts where the volume is zero and therefore the total revenue is zero (nothing is sold and so there is no sales value). The economist says that as the selling price (which the economist calls marginal revenue) is increased then total revenue will continue to increase, but by proportionately less and less. This continues up to a point where the decrease in selling price starts to have less and less impact on volume and so total revenue starts to decline. The result of this is a total revenue curve that increases but which becomes gradually less steep until it eventually flattens out and then falls away.

The total cost curve starts some way up the £ axis because fixed costs are incurred even when sales are zero. Total costs are comprised of fixed costs and variable costs (or marginal costs). As volumes increase then total costs increase. The economist assumes that fixed costs continue to be unchanged, and when volumes increase unit costs decrease because the fixed cost is spread amongst a greater number of products. Therefore, the total costs increase but proportionately less and less. In addition, the economist says that the total costs further benefit from decreases in variable costs as volume increases. This happens as a result of economies of scale:

- as labour becomes more experienced then less is required for a given level of output
- materials cost prices reduce as purchasing power increases from greater volumes.

Economies of scale continue until further economies are not possible, and we begin to see diminishing returns. This happens when variable costs start to increase, which may be due to the overloading of processes at high volumes, leading to possible malfunctions, breakdowns, and bottlenecks.

Initially the total cost curve does not rise steeply because of the fixed costs effect and the positive

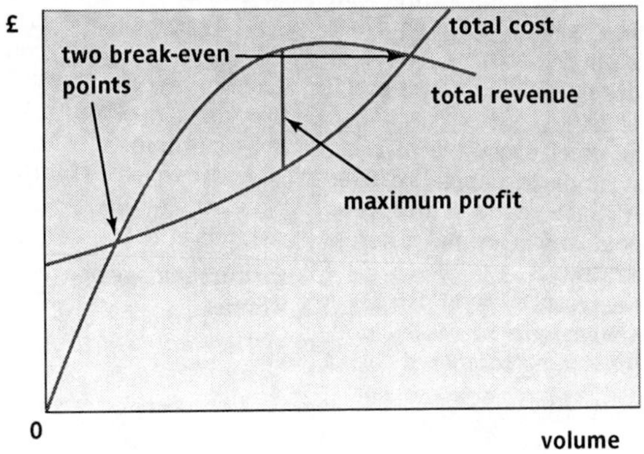

Figure 8.1 Economist's cost and revenue curves

impact of economies of scale on variable costs. As the business reaches its most efficient volume level further economies of scale are not possible and the total cost curve quickly becomes very steep as a result of the adverse impact of diminishing returns on variable costs.

It can be seen from Fig. 8.1 that profit is maximised at a specific point shown where the gap between the two curves is greatest. Also, because of the shapes of the economist's longer-term total cost and total revenue curves, it can be seen that they cross at two points. At these points total costs are equal to total revenues and so for the economist there are two break-even points. This contrasts with the accountant's view of costs, volumes, and break-even, which is explained below. This chapter will focus on the accountant's view of CVP analysis and break-even.

The break-even point is an important measure for NTL, the largest British cable company (see the press extract below):

- the company had needed to be able to determine the point at which it would break even
- one of the company's initial targets is likely to have been to be able to reach break-even within a given number of years from start-up.

NTL reported in May 2004 that it had reached a milestone in its development in breaking even at its operating income (profit) level for the first time in the company's history.

When does a company break even?

NTL, Britain's largest cable company, today said losses in the first three months of the year fell by 63% as over 61,000 new customers joined its NTL Home internet, phone and TV service.

The cable giant said the performance of NTL Home, combined with increased profitability in its other divisions, meant it had reached break-even in terms of operating income for the first time in its history.

Operating income in the first quarter rose to £2.2m compared with a £54.1m loss in the same period last year, as turnover rose 7% to £585m.

The cable group, which is expected to merge with Telewest once a lengthy financial restructuring process is completed, said net losses for the quarter fell by over 62% to £65.4m compared with the £174.7m it lost in the first three months of 2003.

Simon Duffy, the chief executive of NTL, said the company's complex financial restructuring, coupled with last year's share issue, had reduced the company's annual interest charges by 37% to £235m.

'The first quarter results demonstrate a strong start to the year with increased profitability across all divisions compared to the first quarter of 2003. The progress made in the first quarter positions NTL well for continued revenue growth and sustainable margin expansion over the balance of the year,' said Mr Duffy.

NTL added 61,500 subscribers to NTL Home, a quarterly record according to the company. It has 2.9 million subscribers who each spent just under £42 in the first three months of 2004 on either TV, telephone, internet or a mix of all three.

The cable company, which recently announced free speed upgrades for its broadband customers, said it had added 81,000 new high speed internet customers since December, taking the total to 1.03 million.

The number of people taking its TV services also rose, reversing consecutive quarters of decline. It added 16,600 TV subscribers in the first three months, boosting overall numbers to 2.05 million.

It also revealed for the first time that churn – the rate by which customers sign off services – stands at 13.2% annually, or 1.1% per month.

Customer drive boosts NTL hopes, by Dominic Timms

For the accountant the total cost and total revenue functions are not represented as curves, but as straight lines. There are a number of assumptions made by the accountant that support this, as follows:

- fixed costs may remain unchanged over a specific range of volumes but they increase in steps over higher ranges of volumes, because when volumes are significantly increased additional fixed costs are incurred on items like new plant and machinery, factories, etc. – the accountant considers a short-term relevant range of volumes over which fixed costs remain unchanged
- over the short term the selling price may be considered to be constant
- over the short term the unit variable cost may be considered to be constant.

The result of these assumptions is that, unlike the economist, the accountant views income from sales (total revenue) and total cost as straight lines over the relevant short-term period. This means that profit continues to increase as volume increases. Profit is maximised at the volume where maximum capacity is reached. Also, there is only one point where the total revenue and total cost lines cross and so for the accountant there is only one break-even point.

Cost/volume/profit (CVP) analysis studies the effects on future profit of changes in fixed costs, variable costs, volume, sales mix and selling price. The relationship between fixed costs and total costs is called operating gearing. Break-even (B/E) analysis is one application of CVP, which can be useful for profit planning, sales mix decisions, production capacity decisions and pricing decisions.

There are three fundamental cost/revenue relationships which form the basis of CVP analysis:

total costs = variable costs + fixed costs

contribution = total revenue – variable costs

profit (or operating income) = total revenue – total costs

The break-even point is the level of activity at which there is neither profit nor loss. It can be ascertained by using a break-even chart or by calculation. The break-even chart indicates approximate profit or loss at different levels of sales volume within a limited range. Break-even charts may be used to represent different cost structures and also to show contribution break-even positions and profit-volume relationships (see Figs. 8.2, 8.3, 8.4, and 8.5). Computerised spreadsheets can be used to convert profit/volume relationship 'what-ifs' into either charts or tables that may be used for presentation or decision-making purposes. They provide the means of exploring any area within fixed costs, variable costs, semi-variable costs, and sales, in terms of values and volumes.

The slopes of the total cost lines in Fig. 8.2 and Fig. 8.3 represent the unit variable costs. The break-even chart shown in Fig. 8.2 shows a relatively low level of fixed costs with variable costs rising quite steeply as the level of activity increases. Where the total sales (or income) line intersects the total cost line is the point at which total sales or total revenue equals total costs. This activity of 40 units is the break-even point.

The break-even chart shown in Fig. 8.3 shows the impact of a higher level of fixed costs with a higher break-even point at around 60 units, even though variable costs are lower than the cost structure shown in Fig. 8.2. If variable costs had stayed the same, the break-even point would be even higher at over 80 units of activity.

The margin of safety shown in each of these charts will be explained when we look a little further at some break-even relationships.

Figure 8.4 shows a contribution break-even chart, which is just a variation of the previous charts. In this chart, variable costs are shown starting from the zero x/y axes in the same way as sales. The effect of adding fixed costs to variable costs (or marginal costs) is shown in the total costs line. Where the sales line intersects the total costs line there is zero profit. This is the break-even point.

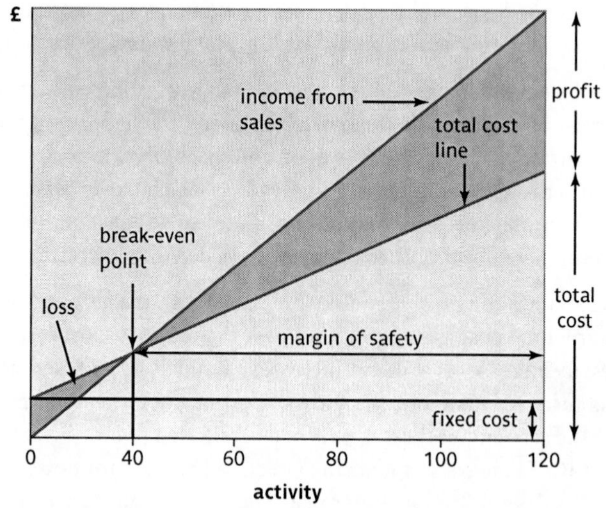

Figure 8.2 Break-even chart – low fixed costs, high variable costs

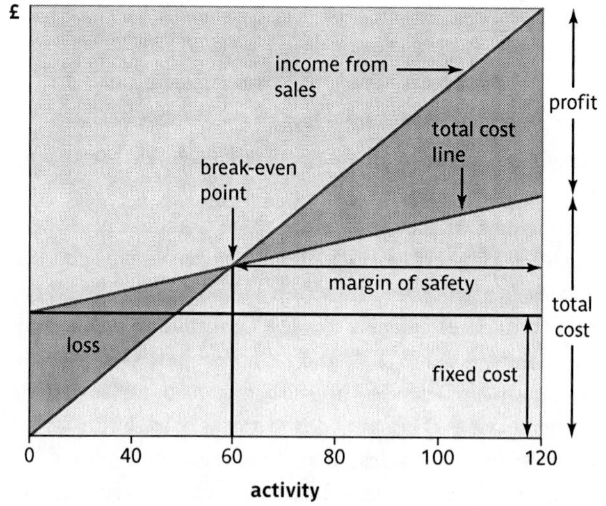

Figure 8.3 Break-even chart – high fixed costs, low variable costs

> **Progress check 8.1 Explain how a break-even analysis could be used within the planning of a 'one-off' event that involves:**
>
> - **the sales of tickets**
> - **provision of hotel accommodation**
> - **live music.**

Figure 8.5 shows a profit volume chart. The horizontal line represents fixed costs and the diagonal line represents the total contribution at each level of activity. The break-even point, where total sales equals total costs, is also where total contribution equals fixed costs.

We will look at why the break-even point is where total contribution equals fixed costs and also

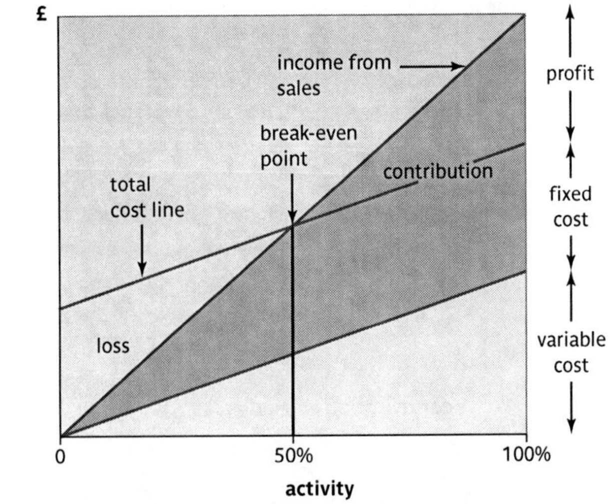

Figure 8.4 Contribution break-even chart

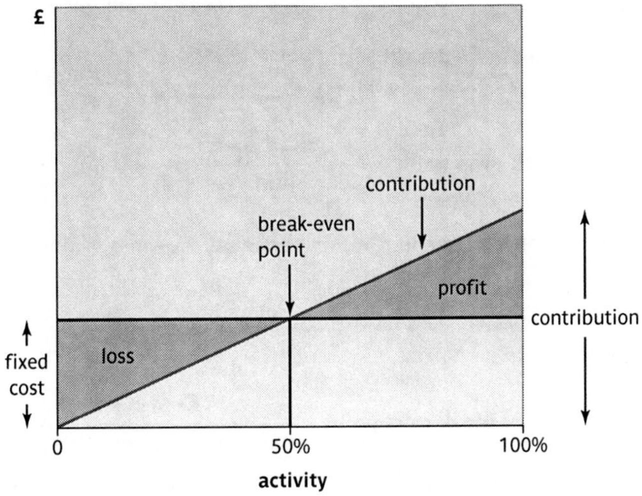

Figure 8.5 Profit volume (PV) chart

consider some further break-even relationships.

Consider:

Total revenue = R
Variable costs = V
Fixed costs = F
Profit = P
Contribution = C

Profit equals total revenue less total costs (variable costs and fixed costs)

$$P = R - V - F$$

Contribution equals total revenue less variable costs

$$C = R - V$$

Therefore, substituting C for R – V, profit equals contribution less fixed costs

$$P = C - F$$

At the break-even point total revenue equals totals costs, and profit is zero, therefore

$$0 = C - F$$

Or at the break-even point

$$C = F$$

$$\text{contribution} = \text{fixed costs} \qquad \textbf{(BE1)}$$

It follows that the:

Number of units at the break-even point × contribution per unit = fixed costs, or

$$\text{number of units at break-even point} = \frac{\text{fixed costs}}{\text{contribution per unit}} \qquad \textbf{(BE2)}$$

Therefore the break-even point in £ sales value is:
Number of units at the break-even point × selling price per unit, or

$$\text{£ sales value at break-even point} = \frac{\text{fixed costs}}{\text{contribution per unit}} \times \text{selling price per unit}$$

But the selling price per unit divided by contribution per unit is the same as total sales revenue divided by total contribution, which is:

The reciprocal of the contribution to sales ratio percentage
So, an alternative expression is:

$$\text{£ sales value at break-even point} = \frac{\text{fixed costs}}{\text{contribution to sales ratio \%}} \qquad \textbf{(BE3)}$$

The term 'margin of safety' is used to define the difference between the break-even point and an anticipated or existing level of activity above that point. (BE4)

In other words, the margin of safety measures the extent to which anticipated or existing activity can fall before a profitable operation turns into a loss-making one (see Figs. 8.2 and 8.3).

Progress check 8.2 **Discuss how departmental stores might use the concept of contribution and break-even analysis when analysing their financial performance.**

The following worked example uses the relationships we have discussed to illustrate the calculation of a break-even point.

Worked Example 8.1

	£
Sales (1,000 units)	10,000
Variable costs (direct materials and direct labour)	6,000
Contribution	4,000
Fixed costs	2,000
Profit	2,000

From the above table of sales and cost data we can find the break-even point in number of units and the sales value at that point.

Number of units sold 1,000

Therefore, contribution/unit $\frac{£4{,}000}{1{,}000} = £4$ per unit

And, contribution to sales ratio % $= \frac{£4{,}000}{£10{,}000} \times 100\% = 40\%$

Using BE2 number of units at break-even point $= \frac{\text{fixed costs}}{\text{contribution per unit}}$

$= £2{,}000/£4$

$= 500$ units

Using BE3 £ sales value at break-even point $= \frac{\text{fixed costs}}{\text{contribution to sales ratio \%}}$

$= £2{,}000/40\%$

$= £5{,}000$

The CVP technique may also be used to derive a target cost estimate, by subtracting a desired margin or target profit from a competitive market price. This cost may be less than the planned initial product cost, but will be a cost that is expected to be achieved by the time the product reaches the mature production stage. Sales volumes or sales values may be calculated that are required to achieve a range of profit targets.

Worked Example 8.2

Bill Jones, who had worked for many years as an engineer in the automotive industry, had recently been made redundant. Bill, together with a number of colleagues, now had the opportunity to set up a business to make and sell a specialised part for motor vehicle air-conditioning units. Bill had already decided on a name for the company. It would be called Wilcon Ltd. Bill had some good contacts in the industry and two automotive components manufacturers had promised him contracts that he estimated would provide sales of 15,000 units per month, for the foreseeable future.

The business plan was based on the following data:

Selling price per unit	£17.50
Variable costs per unit	£13.00

Fixed costs for month — £54,000 including salaries for 5 managers @ £1,500 each

Bill and his colleagues are very interested in determining the break-even volume and sales value for Wilcon Ltd.

Contribution/unit

	£
Selling price	17.50
Variable cost	13.00
Contribution/unit	4.50

Break-even volume

If the number of units sold is n — Total contribution = $n \times$ £4.50

At the break-even point fixed costs equal total contribution (see BE1)

£54,000 = £4.50 × n

Therefore, n = £54,000/£4.50 = 12,000 units

Sales value at break-even point = number of units at break-even point × selling price per unit

= 12,000 × £17.50 = £210,000

Bill and his colleagues are also interested in looking at the break-even points at different levels of sales, costs and profit expectation, which are considered in Worked Examples 8.3 to 8.7.

Worked Example 8.3

The data from Worked Example 8.2 can be used to find the margin of safety (volume and value) for Wilcon Ltd if the predicted sales volume is 12,500 units per month.

Margin of safety (volume and value) if the predicted sales volume is 12,500 units per month

The predicted or forecast volume is 12,500 units, with a sales value of 12,500 × £17.50

= £218,750

The margin of safety is predicted volume – break-even volume (see BE4)

= 12,500 – 12,000 = 500 units

Margin of safety sales value = £218,750 – £210,000

= £8,750

Worked Example 8.4

The data from Worked Example 8.2 can be used to find the reduction in break-even volume if one less manager were employed by Wilcon Ltd.

Reduction in break-even volume if one less manager were employed

Fixed costs become £54,000 – £1,500

= £52,500

If the number of units sold is n

$$£52{,}500 = £4.50 \times n$$

Therefore, $n = £52{,}500/£4.50 = 11{,}667$ units

Therefore reduction in volume from break-even is 12,000 – 11,667, or 333 units

Worked Example 8.5

The data from Worked Example 8.2 can be used to find the volume of units to be sold by Wilcon Ltd to make £9,000 profit per month.

Volume of units to be sold to make £9,000 profit

Profit = contribution – fixed costs

If n equals the number of units, for a profit of £9,000

$$£9{,}000 = (n \times £4.50) - £52{,}500\ [54{,}000 - 1{,}500]$$

Or, $n = £61{,}500/£4.50 = 13{,}667$ units

Worked Example 8.6

The data from Worked Example 8.2 can be used to find the revised break-even volume if fixed costs are reduced by 10% and variable costs are increased by 10% by Wilcon Ltd.

Revised break-even volume if fixed costs are reduced by 10% and variable costs are increased by 10%

If fixed costs are 90% × £54,000 = £48,600

And variable costs are 110% × £13 = £14.30

Then unit contribution becomes £17.50 – £14.30 = £3.20

$$£48{,}600 = £3.20 \times n$$

Therefore, $n = £48{,}600/£3.20 = 15{,}188$ units

Worked Example 8.7

The data from Worked Example 8.2 can be used to find the revised selling price that must be charged by Wilcon Ltd to show a profit of £6,000 on 10,000 sales units.

Revised selling price that must be charged to show a profit of £6,000 on 10,000 sales units

Profit = contribution – fixed costs
If total contribution is TC

$$£6{,}000 = TC - £54{,}000$$
$$TC = £60{,}000$$

Therefore
Contribution/unit = £60,000/10,000 = £6 per unit
Variable cost is £13 per unit
Therefore revised selling price is

$$£13 + £6 = £19 \text{ per unit}$$

Worked Examples 8.3 to 8.7 have used the technique of sensitivity analysis. We have considered the sensitivity of the break-even point against expected volumes of activity. We have also considered the impact on the break-even point of changes to fixed costs and variable costs, and how costs and price levels need to change to achieve a planned level of profit. Sales price sensitivity may be considered in terms of volume through analysis of fixed labour and overhead costs, and variable material, labour and overhead costs.

CVP analysis may therefore be used in:

- profit planning
- project planning
- establishing points of indifference between projects
- make or buy decision-making
- shut down or continuation decisions
- product mix decisions
- sales pricing.

We shall consider many of these applications of CVP analysis later in this chapter when we look at decision-making.

Progress check 8.3 **What is a break-even point? Why is it important for a business to know its break-even point, and what types of sensitivity can it be used to analyse?**

Limitations of CVP analysis

We have seen that break-even analysis is just one of the applications of CVP analysis that may be viewed differently by the economist and the accountant. The many assumptions made by the accountant, on which CVP analysis relies, include:

- that output is the only factor affecting costs – there may be others including inflation, efficiency, economic and political factors

- the simplistic approach to cost relationships: that total costs are divided into fixed and variable costs – in reality costs cannot be split easily, even into variable and fixed costs
- the likelihood that fixed costs do not remain constant beyond certain ranges
- the behaviour of both costs and revenue is linear – linearity is rare with regard to costs and revenue
- there is no uncertainty – there is much uncertainty involved in the prediction of costs and sales
- there is a single product – businesses usually provide more than one product and sales mix is not constant but continually changes due to changes in demand
- that stock levels do not change
- the time value of money is ignored (see Chapter 10)
- that these assumptions hold over the relevant range (the activity levels within which assumptions about cost behaviour in break-even analysis remain valid: it is used to mitigate the impact of some of the limitations of CVP analysis mentioned above).

In real-life situations the above assumptions clearly do not hold because, as has been noted previously, cost relationships are not simple and straightforward. Factors affecting the costs and volumes of products and services do change frequently. Such factors do not usually change only one at a time but more usually change all at once. The above limitations to CVP analysis are very real and should be borne in mind when using the technique, for example, to consider alternative pricing options that use both the marginal and full absorption costing approach. Nevertheless, the principles of CVP analysis continue to hold true, and some of the above limitations may be overcome.

Multiple product break-even analysis

The break-even analyses that we have considered thus far have assumed that only one product or service is being provided. In practice however this is rarely the case. Businesses usually offer a range of products or services.

In the same way as we have calculated for a single product, the weighted average contribution may be used for two or more products to calculate the selling prices required to achieve targeted profit levels, and revised break-even volumes and sales values resulting from changes to variable costs and fixed costs.

Worked Example 8.8

Curtis E. Carr & Co provides a range of three limousines for hire. The proprietor, Edna Cloud, has prepared the following details of estimated activity for 2005.

Limousine	**Elvis**	**JR Ewing**	**Madonna**
Estimated number of hours of hire	600	900	500
Hire price per hour	£25	£20	£24
Variable costs per hour of hire	£5	£3	£4

Fixed costs for the year £5,595

Edna would like to know what is the break-even position for the firm in total hours of hire and sales value.

We can summarise the estimated sales, contribution and profit from the information given by Edna, as follows:

Limousine	Elvis	JR Ewing	Madonna	Total
Contribution per hour of hire	£20 (£25 – £5)	£17 (£20 – £3)	£20 (£24 – £4)	
Estimated number of hours of hire	600	900	500	2,000
Total sales	£15,000	£18,000	£12,000	£45,000
Total contribution	£12,000	£15,300	£10,000	£37,300
Fixed costs for 2005				£5,595
Estimated profit for 2005				£31,705

To calculate the break-even position we need to weight the level of activity of each of the products, the hours of hire of each of the limousines:

	Hours	% of total hours
Elvis	600	30
JR Ewing	900	45
Madonna	500	25
	2,000	100

The weighting percentages of each product may then be used to calculate a weighted average contribution per hour:

	Contribution per hour	Weighting %	Weighted contribution
Elvis	£20	30	£6.00
JR Ewing	£17	45	£7.65
Madonna	£20	25	£5.00
Weighted average contribution per hour			£18.65

The multiple product break-even point is derived from:

$$\frac{\text{total fixed costs}}{\text{weighted average contribution}} = \frac{£5,595}{£18.65} = 300 \text{ hours}$$

The break-even level of activity (300 hours) may then be used to calculate the proportion of total hours for each product and the contribution for each product and the business.

		Break-even hours	Contribution per hour	Total contribution
Elvis	30% × 300 hours	90	£20	£1,800
JR Ewing	45% × 300 hours	135	£17	£2,295
Madonna	25% × 300 hours	75	£20	£1,500
		300		£5,595

The total contribution can be seen to equal total fixed costs at the break-even point.

Break-even sales may be calculated by first calculating the:

$$\text{weighted average contribution to sales ratio \%} = \frac{\text{total contribution}}{\text{total sales}} = \frac{£37,300}{£45,000}$$

$$= 0.8289$$

$$£\text{ sales value at the break-even point} = \frac{\text{total fixed costs}}{\text{contribution to sales ratio \%}}$$

$$= \frac{£5,595}{0.8289} = £6,750$$

for the total 300 hours of hire.

A greater degree of sophistication may be achieved from more dynamic and complex models, and using computerised simulation models. Uncertainty will always remain, but the impact of the results of the occurrence of uncertain events, within given constraints, may be evaluated using sensitivity analysis. Spreadsheets like Excel can provide very sensitive 'what-if' solutions, and the linking features in modelling systems can speedily provide a range of alternative values.

Progress check 8.4 Discuss the usefulness of a sensitivity analysis of the factors used in calculation of the break-even point of a national chain fast food outlet that uses television advertising campaigns.

In addition to break-even analysis, cost/volume/profit (CVP) analysis techniques may be used in a number of decision-making scenarios. Very often, for example, in a decision-making scenario there are two or more limiting factors, in which case a linear programming model would need to be used to determine optimum solutions. Linear programming is not covered in this book.

Progress check 8.5 What is CVP analysis and on what assumptions is it based?

The scope of decision-making

The management accountant is involved with providing financial and non-financial information and analysis to enable managers to evaluate alternative proposals and to determine which courses of action they should take. However, decisions are made by managers, not by the management accountant, and the levels of authority within the management hierarchy are determined by company policy. Companies normally establish limits at each management level for each type of decision, and the level of expenditure allowed. The approval of one or more directors is normally required for all capital expenditure. Strategic decision-making is carried out at board level. Operational decisions are normally made at the middle manager level, and tactical decisions made at the junior manager level.

There are obviously different levels of decision-making and different levels and types of decisions. The decision by the chairman of Corus (formerly British Steel) about whether he should wear a blue tie or a red tie is of less significance (although perhaps not to tie-makers) than his decision on whether or not to shut down a steel-producing plant. Indeed, decisions on factory closures by Corus and many other companies have unfortunately been all too common in the UK over the past 20 or 30

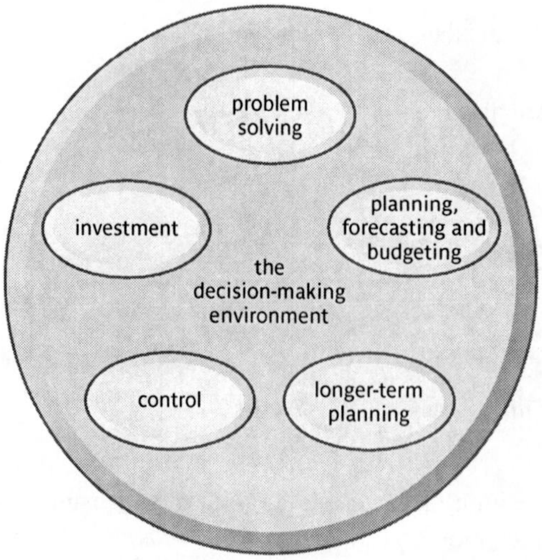

Figure 8.6 The scope of decision-making

years (see the Royal Doulton press extract below) as the manufacturing sector of the economy has shrunk to a fraction of its former size.

Royal Doulton has followed the closures of many other potteries in the areas around Stoke-on-Trent over the past few years. The impact of these factory closures is not just on the companies themselves, having much wider economic and social consequences for both the immediate areas in which the potteries are located and for UK manufacturing in general.

The scope of decision-making includes the areas of problem solving, planning, control, and investment (see Fig. 8.6).

Problem solving decisions

Decision-making relating to problem solving considers relevant costs (and revenues) which are the costs (and revenues) appropriate to a specific management decision. These include incremental or

Closing down a factory

Royal Doulton is to close its last remaining major UK factory with the loss of 525 jobs – 17pc of the group's workforce.

The loss-making fine china group will transfer work from its Nile Street factory in Stoke-on-Trent to a site in Indonesia as part of a restructuring programme.

However, production of Royal Doulton's high-value items, such as the collectable figurines, will continue at a new smaller factory and visitor centre in Festival Park, Stoke-on-Trent.

About 50 staff will transfer to the new facility, with the remaining 525 facing redundancy 'in stages' before June 2005.

The cost of the closure, redundancies and new site is expected to be reflected in an £8.5m exceptional charge in the group's 2004 accounts. Royal Doulton made a £5m pre-tax loss last year.

Geoff Bagnall, general secretary of The Ceramic and Allied Trades Union, claimed the management had broken every assurance made to the union and called for them to resign.

End of an era for Royal Doulton, by Tessa Thorniley

© *Daily Telegraph*, 27 March 2004

differential costs and benefits, and opportunity costs. They are represented by future cash flows whose magnitude will vary depending upon the outcome of the management decision made. If stock is sold to a retailer, the relevant costs used in the determination of the profitability of the transaction would be the cost of replacing the stock, not its original purchase price, which is a sunk cost. Sunk costs, or irrecoverable costs, are costs that have been irreversibly incurred or committed to prior to a decision point and which cannot therefore be considered relevant to subsequent decisions.

An opportunity cost is the value of the benefit sacrificed when one course of action is chosen in preference to an alternative. The opportunity cost is represented by the forgone potential benefit from the best of the alternative courses of action that have been rejected.

Planning, forecasting and budgeting decisions

Planning, forecasting and budgeting decisions require best estimates of costs and the use of cost/volume/profit (CVP) analysis.

Long-term planning decisions

Longer-term planning decisions assume that in the long run all costs are variable and that scarce resources, and over- or under-capacity, are problems that can be overcome.

Control decisions

Control decisions use historical information and comparisons such as variance analysis and actual/budget comparisons.

Investment decisions

Investment decisions tend to be longer term, and cash flow and the time value of money are important appraisal factors.

Decision-making is a crucially important process within any organisation. It is used to select, hopefully, the correct future course of action in, for example:

- whether to make or buy equipment
- levels of order quantities and stock holding
- whether or not to replace an asset
- determination of selling prices
- contract negotiation.

Decisions also have to be made as to whether or not to invest in capital projects and on choices between investments in alternative projects, which are competing for resources. Such decisions will be examined in Chapter 10 which deals with capital investment decisions.

Routine planning decisions, including budgeting, commonly analyse fixed and variable costs, together with revenues, over one year. These costs are often estimated and may support the use of cost/volume/profit (CVP) analysis. The usefulness of the analysis will almost certainly be enhanced by the speed and sophistication of IT spreadsheets. An example may be seen from special offers and weekend breaks seen within the UK hotel sector. Spreadsheet 'what-ifs' linked to current bookings suggest the capacity available to be offered at a special rate for specific periods (note the Travelodge 'book by 23 January 2001 – stay by 15 February 2001' offer).

Decisions on short-run problems are of a non-recurring nature, where costs are incurred and benefits are obtained all within a relatively short period. An example is whether or not a contract should be accepted or rejected. These types of decision need identification of incremental or differential costs and revenues and a distinction between sunk costs and opportunity costs.

Investment and disinvestment decisions, such as whether to buy a new machine, or shut down a department, often have long-term consequences, and so ideally the time value of money should be allowed for, using discounted cash flow (DCF) techniques. The long-term consequences may span several accounting periods and the economies of more than just one country may be involved, for example international motor manufacturers with plants established throughout the world.

Longer-range decisions are made once and reviewed infrequently. They are intended to provide a continuous solution to a continuing or recurring problem. They include decisions about selling and distribution policies, for example whether to sell direct to customers or through an agent. In the long run all costs are variable. In the short-term, fixed costs, or resource and capacity problems that may be encountered, can be changed or overcome over time.

Such changes may be determined by the board of directors at the strategic level, where the priorities of the business may be changed, or at the operational and tactical levels where change may be achieved through, for example, bottom-up continuous improvement initiatives. The process may therefore take several months or even years (especially, for example, when trying to sell a site or a building). The timespan may however be shorter; for example, UK retailers are able to announce the impact of their Christmas trading results very early in January, which suggests that analyses of variances are undertaken on a daily, or even perhaps an hourly, basis.

Control decisions involve deciding whether or not to investigate disappointing performance, and expected benefits should exceed the costs of investigation and control. Historical information such as comparison of costs, revenues or profits to budget, is used to carry out variance analysis to indicate what control decisions need to be taken. Variance analysis can be used to look at just one factory, or several factories. Manufacturers will often locate new plant and equipment in subsidiaries where there are few 'disappointing performances'.

Worked Example 8.9

The UK motor manufacturer Vauxhall began producing police cars and rally cars based on its 'family saloons'.

Let's consider the short-term problems that may have been encountered by Vauxhall during the decision-making process relating to these products.

The specification of the police car was customer driven and the changes to the standard saloons could be costed in order that a price could be proposed to the customer. The operatives on the production line could easily modify the existing model to the new specification.

The rally car was almost certainly going to create problems because the specification may need to change throughout the season. Production-line disruptions would inevitably ensue. The rally car would probably require specialists amongst the work force to design and produce it.

Progress check 8.6 Why is decision-making so important to any organisation and what types of decision do they face?

The decision-making process

We have seen that it is possible to analyse decisions into five main categories:

- short-term problem decisions
- routine planning decisions
- long-range decisions
- control decisions
- investment and disinvestment decisions.

This is useful because the relevant costs and benefits are likely to differ between each type of decision. The decision-making process comprises the seven steps outlined in Fig. 8.7.

First, the objectives, either long-term or short-term, need to be identified. Short-term objectives may be financial, such as:

- profit maximisation
- loss avoidance
- profit growth
- sales growth

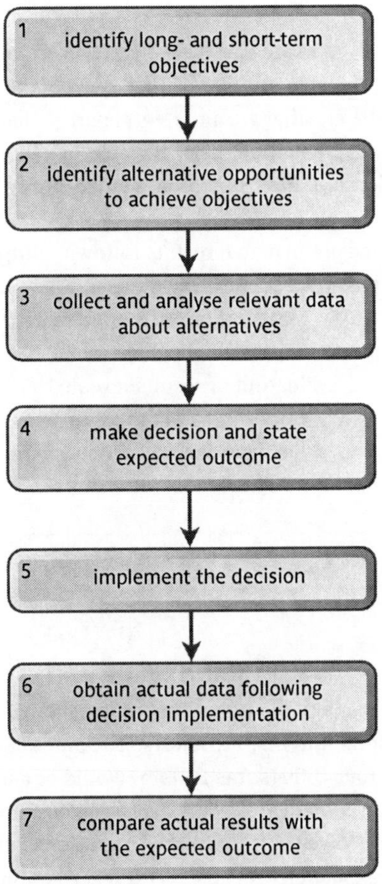

Figure 8.7 The seven steps of the decision-making process

or non-financial, such as:

- improved product quality
- customer service
- employee welfare
- environmental friendliness.

Long-term objectives may be more to do with:

- the financial risk of the company
- long-term growth
- debt/equity financing
- dividend growth
- the relationships between these factors.

Second, alternative opportunities must be identified which might contribute to achieving the company's objectives. The ability to identify opportunities, or things to do which might help the company reach its objectives, is a major test of how good management is. Failure to recognise opportunities that exist may result in decisions not taken and/or opportunities missed.

Third, the relevant data about each of the alternatives must be collected and analysed. For example, this may relate to decisions on whether to manufacture or buy from an external supplier, or to use an existing site or establish a new site.

Fourth, the decision must then be made and the expected outcome stated. If a board of directors, for example, makes a decision, then the minute of that decision should formally refer back to the various documentation, forecasts, etc. that are an integral part of that decision.

Fifth, the decision must be implemented. The minutes of meetings of the board of directors should confirm that a specific decision has been implemented, along with an overview of progress to date.

Sixth, data needs to be obtained about actual results following implementation of the decision.

Finally, the actual results are compared with the expected outcome, and the achievements that have resulted from the decision are evaluated. It must be appreciated that not every decision will generate achievements, as a UK major retailer found out when it launched a new range of clothes in 1999 and again in 2000. The subsequent evaluation of results revealed a series of disappointments.

Of course, in practice things rarely work out as planned, or in an orderly way. In reality the decision-making process often appears to be overtaken by events, requiring a very quick response and usually without the time for perhaps a more considered response.

Progress check 8.7 **Outline the decision-making process.**

Relevant costs

The Millennium Dome project in 2000 illustrated the importance of (the lack of) appropriate planning and control of cash to be sunk into major projects. The amount that was expected to have been spent on the attraction by December 2000 (some £800m) would be a past cost already committed and spent and would therefore not be considered in any decision about to whom the attraction may ultimately be sold or for how much. However, if future cash outlays were proposed, on which a sale was dependent, then these costs would be relevant costs with regard to the sale decision.

Worked Example 8.10

During the year 2000 a car manufacturer evaluated two proposals regarding the production of a new car. The car could be built in France or England. In 2001 the company chose England.

Both relevant costs and opportunity costs would have been considered by the company in making its decision.

The relevant costs were those of setting up the production line of the new car in England and these costs could be linked back to the decision made by the board of directors. The opportunity cost was the projected profit of the alternative French production facility.

Accounting information used in absorption costing, for example, may be different from relevant information used in decision-making. Relevant information may relate to costs or revenues; compared with accounting information, it may be qualitative as well as quantitative.

Relevant costs are costs that arise as a direct consequence of a decision. These may differ between the alternative options. They are sometimes referred to as incremental or differential costs.

Relevant costs are future costs, not past costs. A decision is about the future and it cannot alter what has been done already. A cost incurred, or committed to, in the past is irrelevant to any decision that is made now.

Relevant costs are cash flows, not accounting costs. All decisions are assumed to maximise the benefit to the shareholders. The time value of money impacts on longer-term decisions but all short-term decisions are assumed to improve shareholder wealth if they increase net cash flows.

Only cash flow information is required for a decision and so costs or charges that do not reflect additional cash spend are ignored for the purpose of decision-making. It should be appreciated that depreciation is not a cash-based expense, but an entry in the accounts of the business that reflects an estimate for 'wear and tear' of the particular item of capital expenditure.

Worked Example 8.11

If a hotel group with a central booking system is required to make a decision on whether to market empty rooms at a special offer through the press, or other media such as television or the Internet, cash outflow information might have an important influence on the final decision.

Almost certainly the major cash outflow will be the cost of the advertising itself. There is an element of a 'gamble' for the company, even if it has used this strategy in the past. However, if the company follows this strategy each year then it may gain experience and an understanding of the relationship between advertising and extra bookings. It will also be able to determine the relationship between the discounts and volume of bookings and type of advertising options.

Relevant costs may also be referred to as opportunity costs. An opportunity cost is the benefit forgone by choosing one option instead of the next best alternative. A car manufacturer is constrained to making a maximum number of cars in a particular period. Regardless of whether they are saloons or estates, there is always a maximum. A waiting list may have to be instituted, with the factory deciding which type of vehicle and which of the models to produce. The decision may result in lost sales and/or lost benefits in production.

Worked Example 8.12

An opportunity cost is the benefit forgone by choosing one option instead of the next best alternative.

Opportunity costs would have been considered by the managers of the Millennium Dome in their decision to embark on a policy of offering thousands of heavily discounted tickets to schools.

The managers knew how much cash they would lose on certain days if the tickets were sold at the discounted price. They knew how much they would lose if no discounted tickets were sold. On the basis of their current tickets sold they knew how many they would sell on a particular day in the future. It was obvious to them that the only way to build up ticket sale numbers was to discount tickets in a very formal way, generating cash, even at a lower rate per head.

Unless there is some evidence to the contrary, it is always assumed that variable costs are relevant costs and that fixed costs are not relevant to a decision. However, some variable costs may include some non-relevant costs. For example, direct labour costs are normally accounted for as variable costs, but if the workforce is paid a fixed rate per person per week, in some circumstances this may be a committed cost and therefore not relevant to decision-making.

Depreciation cost per hour may be accounted for as a variable cost. But depreciation is never a relevant cost because it is a past cost and does not represent cash flow that will be incurred in the future.

There are several costs: sunk costs; committed costs; notional costs, that are termed irrelevant to decision-making because they are either not future cash flows or they are costs which will be incurred anyway, regardless of the decision that is taken.

A sunk cost is a cost which has already been incurred and which cannot now be recovered. It is a past cost which is not relevant to decision-making. Such costs may be, for example, the costs of dedicated fixed assets and development costs already incurred. Most consumer goods currently being sold are the final version of earlier versions, which will have cost considerable sums of money to develop.

A committed cost is a future cash outflow that will be incurred, whatever decision is taken about alternative opportunities. Committed costs may exist because of contracts already entered into by the company. During the year 2000 Internet providers in the UK found themselves in loss-making contracts with their customers. Several providers closed their operations, incurring considerable bad publicity.

A **notional cost**, or imputed cost, is a hypothetical accounting cost to reflect the use of a benefit for which no actual cash expense is incurred. Examples are notional rents charged by a company to its subsidiary companies, or to cost centres, for the use of accommodation that the company owns, and notional interest charged on capital employed within a cost centre or profit centre of the company.

There are many examples of the use of relevant costs in decision-making: profit planning – for example, the contribution implications of pricing and advertising decisions, and the sales mix and contribution implications of constraints on resources; profit and product mix planning – for example with regard to the contribution per limiting factor.

The following sub-sections illustrate the general rules for identifying relevant costs.

Materials

The relevant cost of raw materials is generally their current replacement cost, unless the materials are already owned and would not be replaced if used. If the materials are already owned, the relevant cost is the higher of the current resale value and the value obtained if the materials were put to alternative use. The higher of these costs is the opportunity cost. If there is no resale value and there is no other use for the materials then the opportunity cost is zero.

Depreciation

Depreciation on equipment that has already been purchased is not a relevant cost for decision-making.

Capital expenditure

The historical cost of equipment that has already been purchased is not a relevant cost for decision-making. If the capital equipment has not already been purchased, and the decision would involve such a purchase, the situation is different. The relevant cost of equipment, of which the purchase would be a consequence of the decision, can be measured in two alternative ways, using the discounted cash flow (DCF) method:

- the cost of the equipment treated as an initial cash outlay in year zero, with the relevant costs and benefits of the decision assessed over the life of the project
- the cost of the equipment converted into an annual charge to include both the capital cost and a notional interest charge over the expected life of the equipment.

Future cash costs

Future cash costs are relevant if they have a direct consequence on the decision. These are costs not yet incurred or committed to. For example, you may have an old car which you would like to sell. The price you paid for it is irrelevant to your sale decision. However, if you needed to pay out large sums for a garage to work on the car to make it saleable, then those future cash costs would be very relevant to your decision to sell, or not, and at what price.

Differential costs

The relevant differential cash costs are the differences between two or more optional courses of action. If we return to the example of the sale of your old car, we may find that the cost of the work required to make it saleable is prohibitive and that you may be forced to keep the car rather than sell it. However, the difference between the price quoted by the garage may be undercut sufficiently by another garage to prompt you to reverse your decision.

Worked Example 8.13

A machine requires repair and the relevant costs of two different repair options are as follows:

	£
Repair machine on site	
Cost of spares	1,250
Labour cost	750
Reduction to contribution resulting from lost production	4,200

Take machine away to workshop for repair

Cost of spares	1,250
Labour cost	400
Reduction to contribution resulting from lost production	5,800

We can prepare a statement of differential costs:

		£
Statement of differential costs		
Additional labour cost of repair on site	[750 – 400]	(350)
Lower reduction to contribution from repair on site	[5,800 – 4,200]	1,600
Differential benefit of repair on site		1,250

Opportunity costs

The benefit forgone in choosing one option over the next best alternative is relevant. Many successful businesses find themselves in an expanding market, where most of their products are selling well, and each new product is becoming profitable. Inevitably, competing products from within the same company may have to be weeded out. Therefore, the company will have to forgo current benefits as a result of culling a profitable product.

The UK motor industry has several examples of product options that were dropped in favour of others. The German motor industry has seen two products dropped, only for them to reappear: the Beetle (VW) car and Boxer (BMW) motor cycle. In these cases, management decided to forgo the benefit of producing the products in favour of new models. Eventually they had to change their minds as the benefits forgone needed to be reassessed and updated versions were eventually brought back.

Sunk costs, committed costs and notional costs

None of these costs are relevant. They include, for example, costs of dedicated fixed assets and development costs already incurred.

Worked Example 8.14

A company bought a computer system two years ago for £57,000. After allowing for depreciation its book value is now £19,000. Because computer technology moves so quickly, resulting in obsolescence and price reductions, this equipment has no resale value. Although the company may continue to use the computer system for another year, with the limited facilities it provides, it would prefer to scrap it now and replace it with a much enhanced system providing many more functions.

Let's consider the implications of the company's decision to replace its computer system.

The original computer system initial cost of £57,000, which now has a net book value of £19,000, is a sunk cost, and therefore ignored in terms of decisions made to replace the computer system. The money has been spent and the asset has no alternative use.

Fixed costs

Fixed costs are not relevant costs, unless they are a direct consequence of the decision. For example, the cost of employing an extra salesman would normally be categorised as a fixed cost. Conceptually, fixed costs stay at the same level irrespective of the changes in level of activity. In practice, management needs to make decisions regarding future fixed costs. Longer-term forecasts and budgets may indicate that changes in activity levels require changes to levels of fixed costs. For example, if higher education in the UK saw the falling-off of student numbers in certain courses then that might result in the universities cutting back on their fixed overheads, such as premises and staff numbers.

Worked Example 8.15

The UK saw two attractions open in London in 2000: the Millennium Dome and the London Eye.

What should we consider to be the fixed costs of the two attractions?

One basic difference between the two attractions is that the Dome was to remain open for one year and the London Eye would remain open for a number of years. Obviously the majority of the Dome's fixed costs would cease with its closure, but charges like insurance would need to continue to be paid. The London Eye became popular and fully booked very quickly. Unlike the Dome, its capacity is limited to the number of passengers each gondola can hold. In the Eye's case an analysis of the fixed costs should reveal that the costs are indeed genuinely fixed and there will be little 'movement' from year to year, whereas the headlines during 2000 would suggest that most of the Dome's expenses were varying throughout the year!

Variable costs

Variable costs are generally relevant costs but care must be taken with regard to the provisos outlined above. Variable costs may be non-relevant costs in some circumstances, for example where a variable cost is also a committed cost.

Worked Example 8.16

A company is planning a small new project that requires 1,000 hours of direct labour, costing £9 per hour. However, the company pays its direct labour workforce a fixed wage of £342 per person for a 38-hour week.

The company has a 'no redundancy' agreement, and has enough spare capacity to meet the additional hours required for the project.

What should we consider are the relevant costs relating to the new project?

The direct labour cost for accounting purposes is regarded as a variable cost of £9 per hour. But it is really a committed cost, and therefore a fixed cost of £342 per week. The relevant cost of the new project for direct labour is therefore zero.

It should be noted that the company may similarly treat depreciation of say £2.40 per hour as an accounting variable cost. However, for decision-making, depreciation is never considered as a relevant cost. It is a past cost, and therefore not a cash flow to be incurred in the future.

Attributable costs

We may consider fixed costs as comprising divisible fixed costs, and indivisible fixed costs. A fixed cost is divisible if significant changes in activity volumes require increases or decreases in that cost.

An **attributable cost** is the cost per unit that could be avoided, on average, if a product or function were discontinued entirely without changing the supporting organisational structure. An attributable cost consists of:

- short-run variable costs
- divisible fixed costs
- only those indivisible fixed costs that are traceable.

Worked Example 8.17

A company employs 55 people, who are paid fixed monthly wages, within four departments in its factory. Each department is headed by a departmental manager who is paid a salary.

How should each of the staff costs be regarded in a decision relating to the possible shutdown of one of the departments?

The direct labour costs of the 55 operators are divisible fixed costs (if there were only one operator, then the direct labour cost would be an indivisible fixed cost).

Each departmental manager's salary is an indivisible fixed cost that is traceable to their department. This is because if a department were to be shut down, the manager would no longer be required and therefore no cost would be incurred.

Scarce resources

The relevant cost of a scarce resource to be included in a decision-making calculation is the benefit forgone (the opportunity cost) in using the resource in another way, in addition to the direct cost of purchasing the resource. Let's look at an example.

Worked Example 8.18

Mr and Mrs Green are willing to pay £22,000 to Steamy Windows Ltd to build a conservatory. The general manager of Steamy Windows estimates that the job requires the following materials:

Material	Total units required	Units in stock	Book value of units in stock £/unit	Realisable value £/unit	Replacement cost £/unit
A	1,000	0	0.0	0.0	6.0
B	1,000	600	2.0	2.5	5.0
C	1,000	700	3.0	2.5	4.0
D	200	200	4.0	6.0	9.0

B is regularly used by Steamy Windows Ltd and if it is required for this job it needs to be replaced to meet other production demands.

C and D are in stock because of previous overbuying, and have restricted use. No other use can be found for C, but D could be used as a substitute for 300 units of E, which currently costs £5/unit and Steamy Windows Ltd currently has none in stock.

Steamy Windows Ltd needs to determine the relevant costs of the project to assist the company in its decision on whether or not it should take the job.

Relevant costs:

		£	
A	1,000 × £6/unit	6,000	replacement cost because these materials have not yet been purchased
B	1,000 × £5/unit	5,000	replacement cost because these materials are used regularly and so the stock items would have to be replaced
C	(300 × £4/unit) + (700 × £2.50/unit)	2,950	300 must be bought at the replacement cost of £4/unit – 700 will not be replaced but could have been sold for £2.50 per unit
D	(300 E × £5/unit)	1,500	200 could be sold for £6/unit, but this is less than the opportunity cost of substitution of E
		15,450	

The relevant costs of the job are £15,450. If the difference of £6,550 is an acceptable level of profit to Steamy Windows Ltd, before allowing for labour and overhead costs, then the job should be accepted.

Progress check 8.8 Outline three examples of costs that are usually relevant, and three costs that are not usually relevant in decision-making.

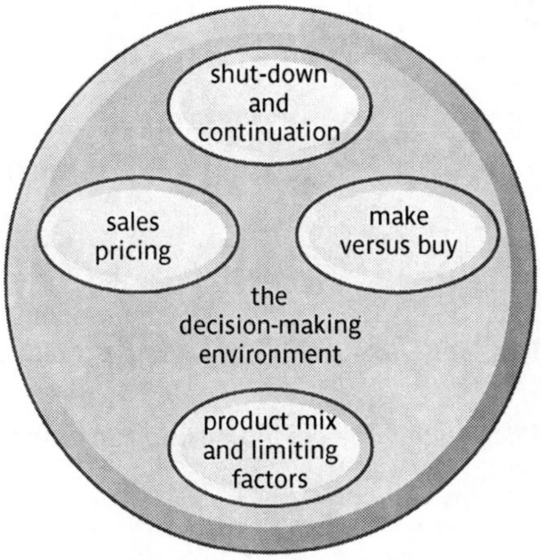

Figure 8.8 Practical areas of decision-making

We will now look at examples of four specific areas of decision-making, outlined in Fig. 8.8.

Shut-down or continuation decisions

We have already discussed the importance of the marginal costing technique as an aid to costing and break-even decision-making. In the UK, during December 2000 a major car manufacturer decided that production of cars would cease at its Luton (Bedfordshire) plant. The company explained that over-capacity forced it to cut back on production. The employees on the second shift were sent home on full pay in February 2001 since there was no point in producing cars that would not sell. It was quite obvious from the public announcements that the company had carried out many 'what-ifs' on the corporate spreadsheets. However, it was apparently unable to justify continuation of production at the Luton site, despite its presence in the town for the past 90 years or so. The following example looks at the use of marginal costing in a decision regarding the possible closure of an apparent loss-making activity.

Worked Example 8.19

Ron G Choice Ltd has three departments: C chairs; D desks; T tables, manufacturing three separate ranges of office furniture. Choice Ltd's sales manager, Jim Brown, has just started a course on cost accounting and has reviewed the company's accounts for last year with renewed interest.

	C	D	T
	£	£	£
Sales	60,000	80,000	40,000
Variable costs	40,000	60,000	34,000
Fixed costs allocated	6,000	10,000	8,000

It appeared to Jim that all was not well with the table department T. He was about to recommend to the managing director that department T should be closed down because it appeared to be making a loss. However, Jim felt he should first run his ideas past the company's accountant, Tony White, to check his figures and gain some support.

Jim provided the following analysis, using an absorption costing basis:

	C	D	T	**Total**
	£	£	£	**£**
Sales	60,000	80,000	40,000	180,000
Total costs	46,000	70,000	42,000	158,000
Profit/(loss)	14,000	10,000	(2,000)	22,000

On this basis, Jim said, department T was making a loss and should be closed.

Tony asked Jim if he had considered the position using a marginal costing basis. Jim said he had not and so Tony provided the following analysis:

	C	D	T	Total
	£	£	£	£
Sales	60,000	80,000	40,000	180,000
Variable costs	40,000	60,000	34,000	134,000
Contribution	20,000	20,000	6,000	46,000
less: Fixed costs				24,000
Profit				22,000

Tony explained to Jim that the profit for the company was the same using both techniques because there is no closing-stock adjustment involved.

However, Tony said that the way in which the fixed costs had been allocated to each department was fairly arbitrary and so perhaps they could consider the position of Choice Ltd following the closure of department T on a marginal costing basis.

The result was as follows:

	C	D	T	Total
	£	£	£	£
Sales	60,000	80,000	–	140,000
Variable costs	40,000	60,000	–	100,000
Contribution	20,000	20,000	–	40,000
less: Fixed costs				24,000
Profit				16,000

Jim could see that closure of the tables department T would result in a reduction in total company profit by £6,000 to £16,000, compared with the original £22,000. Tony explained that this was caused by the loss of contribution of department T.

Jim thanked Tony for helping him avoid an embarrassing visit to the managing director's office. He would now also be better prepared for the next part of his costing course – on marginal costing!

This simple example shows that despite what the absorption costing approach indicated, department T should be kept open because it yields a contribution towards covering the fixed costs.

The marginal costing approach, as we have seen previously, focuses on the variable costs which are affected by the decision and separates them from the fixed costs which are unaffected by the decision and are therefore irrelevant to it. In Worked Example 8.19, the closure of department T would not save any of the allocated fixed costs – they would then have to be shared amongst departments C and D. If the fixed costs had been directly attributable to each department rather than allocated then there would have been an £8,000 saving by closing department T. Since that is higher than the department's contribution of £6,000, then Jim's advice would have been correct to close department T.

Progress check 8.9 In what way is marginal costing useful in shut-down decisions?

Make versus buy

Make versus buy decisions are made when a component used in one of the manufacturing processes to produce a product may either be bought in from outside suppliers or manufactured within the factory. It would seem that the choice is simply a straightforward comparison between the extra cost to make the component, the marginal cost, and the price charged by suppliers. In fact, the decision involves consideration of a number of other factors, for example:

- cost price sensitivity to changes in volumes
- accuracy of data
- reliability of bought-in and/or self-manufactured components
- supplier switching costs
- reliability of suppliers in terms of delivery and financial stability
- length of time the cost price will be held
- opportunity cost.

If the component were not made in-house what activities would be carried out using the relevant facilities? If other manufacturing activities have to be forgone so as to make the component in-house then there is a loss of the contribution that this work would otherwise have earned. The contribution sacrificed is the opportunity cost of not carrying out the alternative activities. The opportunity cost must be added to the marginal cost of making the component to compare with suppliers' prices in making a make versus buy decision. The technique usually used to determine loss of contribution is contribution per unit of a key factor (limiting factor) of production.

Worked Example 8.20

Procrastinate Ltd makes a product A, which takes 30 hours using the Dragon machine. Its marginal cost and selling price are £1,400 and £2,000 respectively. Component X, which is used in the manufacture of product A, could be made on the Dragon machine in five hours with a marginal cost of £400. The best outside supplier price for one component X is £450.

Procrastinate have to decide whether to make or buy component X.

Contribution of product A	= £2,000 – £1,400	= £600
Contribution per hour of use of the Dragon machine	= £600/30	= £20

If component X is made in five hours then 5 × £20, or £100 contribution would be lost. Opportunity cost plus marginal cost = £100 + £400 = £500, which is greater than the best outside supplier price of £450 so component X should be bought rather than made in-house.

In this example, we have assumed that the Dragon machine is working at full capacity in order to calculate the opportunity cost of lost production. If this were not so and the Dragon machine were idle for a significant amount of time then there would be no loss of contribution. The only cost of making component X would then be its marginal cost of £400 which, being less than the best supplier price of £450, would indicate a decision to make in-house rather than buy.

Progress check 8.10 Illustrate the process used to make a make/buy decision.

Product mix decisions and limiting factors

An organisation may not have access to an unlimited supply of resources to allow it to exploit every opportunity to continue indefinitely to increase contribution. Such scarce resources, for example may be:

- labour hours
- levels of labour skills
- machine capacity
- time
- market demand
- components
- raw materials
- cash
- credit facilities.

A limiting factor, or key factor, is anything that limits the activity of the organisation. The organisation has to decide what mix of products or services to provide, given the restricted resources available to it, with its volume of output constrained by the limited resources rather than by sales demand. It can do this by seeking to maximise profit by optimising the benefit it obtains from the limiting factor. Machine time would be an example of a limiting factor for a company if all the machines in the company were operating at full capacity without being able to provide the output required to meet all the sales demand available to the company.

The technique used for decisions involving just one scarce resource assumes that the organisation is aiming to maximise profit. This further assumes that fixed costs are unchanged by the decision to produce more or less of each product. The technique therefore is to rank the products in order of their contribution-maximising ability per unit of the scarce resource. The following two worked examples illustrate this technique. The first example assumes that product demand is unlimited, whilst the second example assumes given levels of product demand.

Worked Example 8.21

Need The Dough, a small village bakery, makes only two types of loaf, small and large. There is unlimited demand for this bread and both products use the same skilled labour of bakers, which is in short supply. The product data are as follows:

	Small	**Large**
Sales price per loaf	£0.71	£0.85
Variable cost per loaf	£0.51	£0.61
Contribution per loaf	£0.20	£0.24
Minutes of skilled labour per loaf	20	30

We can determine the contribution-maximising strategy for Need The Dough.

If we consider the contribution per unit of scarce resource, one hour of skilled labour, we can see that the contribution for each loaf per hour is:

Small loaves earn	£0.60 per labour hour	[60/20 × 20p]
Large loaves earn	£0.48 per labour hour	[60/30 × 24p]

So even though large loaves generate a larger unit contribution of 24p compared to 20p earned by small loaves, the contribution-maximising strategy for Need The Dough is to bake and sell as many small loaves as possible which generate a contribution of 60p, compared with 48p for large loaves, per each hour of scarce labour.

Worked Example 8.22

Felinpot Ltd are potters who make only two products, two ornamental pots called the Bill and the Ben. The product data are as follows:

	Bill	**Ben**
Contribution per pot	£5	£7.20
Volume of special blue clay per pot	1 kg	2 kg
Monthly demand	470	625

In one month the maximum amount of specialist blue clay available is 1,450 kg.
We can determine the contribution-maximising strategy for Felinpot Ltd.

For each pot the contribution per unit of blue clay is:

Bill	£5/1 kg	=	£5	per kg
Ben	£7.20/2 kg	=	£3.60	per kg

The contribution-maximising strategy for Felinpot Ltd should therefore be to make Bill pots in preference to Ben pots, even though the unit contribution of a Ben is greater than a Bill.

Output of Bill pots should be maximised to meet the monthly demand of:

470 pots, using 1 kg × 470 = 470 kg   contribution = 470 × £5   = £2,350

The balance of 980 kg of clay (1,450 kg less 470 kg) should be used to make Ben pots

980 kg/2 kg = 490 pots   contribution = 490 × £7.20   = £3,528

total contribution   = £5,878

Worked Example 8.22 showed that because special blue clay was in short supply, every endeavour should be made to maximise the contribution to Felinpot Ltd for every kilogram of clay used. Regardless of the high level of demand for the other product, the product with the highest contribution per kilogram of special clay used is the one which should be produced to its maximum demand level. All the clay left over from that should then be used to produce the 'less profitable' product in terms of its return per kilogram of special clay.

More complex actual scenarios may be encountered. For example, there may be limited product demand with one scarce resource. The same technique applies whereby the factors are ranked in order of their contribution per unit of scarce resource. Optimum profit is earned from the decision to produce the top-ranked products up to the limit of demand.

Many situations occur where there are two or more scarce resources. The technique of ranking items in order of contribution per unit of limiting factor cannot be used in these situations. In these cases linear programming techniques need to be used – the graphical method or the simplex (algebraic) method – which are beyond the scope of this book.

Progress check 8.11 What are limiting factors and how do they impact on decisions related to product mix?

Summary of key points

- Cost/volume/profit (CVP) analysis may be used to determine the break-even position of a business and provide sensitivity analyses on the impact on the business of changes to any of the variables used to calculate break-even.
- There are a great many limitations to CVP analysis, whether it is used to consider break-even relationships, decision-making or sales pricing.
- Decision-making is of fundamental importance to organisations, for example in the areas of problem solving, planning, control and investment.
- The decision-making process includes identification of relevant costs, and starts with the identification of objectives. Following the implementation of decisions, the process ends with the comparison of actual results with expected outcomes.
- Relevant costs, or incremental or differential costs, arise as a direct consequence of a decision, and may differ between alternative options.
- Marginal costing may be used to assist in shut-down or continuation decisions.
- Make versus buy decisions involve consideration of a wider range of factors than simply the differences in the basic cost.
- Organisations do not have access to unlimited supplies of resources, for example, labour hours, levels of labour skills, machine capacity, time, market demand, components and raw materials, cash – a limiting factor is the lack of any resource which limits the activity of the organisation.
- Product mix decisions are influenced by the scarcity of resources and the availability of limiting factors.

Questions

Q8.1 How may cost/volume/profit (CVP) analysis be used to determine the break-even point of a business?

Q8.2 Are the assumptions on which CVP analysis is based so unrealistic that the technique should be abandoned?

Q8.3 Why is decision-making so important to organisations?

Q8.4 What are short- and long-range decisions, and control decisions?

Q8.5 What are the seven steps used in the decision-making process?

Q8.6 Use some examples to illustrate, and explain what are meant by relevant costs, sunk costs, and opportunity costs.

Q8.7 In what ways may marginal costing provide a better approach to decision-making than absorption costing?

Q8.8 What are the key factors that should be considered in make versus buy decisions?

Q8.9 How should limiting factors be considered if a business is seeking to maximise its profits?

Q8.10 (i) What are scarce resources?

(ii) What factors does an entity need to consider to make optimising decisions related to product mix?

Discussion points

D8.1 'What is all the fuss about decision-making? Surely it's simply a question of adding up a few numbers and the decision makes itself.' Discuss.

Exercises

Solutions are provided in Appendix 3 to all exercise numbers highlighted in colour.

Level I

E8.1 *Time allowed – 15 minutes*

Break-even sales	£240,000
Marginal cost of sales	£240,000
Sales for January	£320,000

What is the profit?

E8.2 *Time allowed – 15 minutes*

Sales for January	£120,000, on which profit is £10,000
Fixed cost for January	£30,000

What is the break-even point?

E8.3 *Time allowed – 15 minutes*

Selling price	£15
Marginal cost	£9
Fixed cost for January	£30,000
Sales for January	£120,000

What is the break-even point and what is the profit?

E8.4 *Time allowed – 30 minutes*

Seivad Ltd plans to assemble and sell 20,000 novelty phones in 2005 at £30 each.

Seivad's costs are as follows:

Variable:		
materials	£10	per phone
labour	£7	per phone
overheads	£8	per phone
Fixed	£70,000 for the year	

You are required to calculate:

(i) Seivad Ltd's planned contribution for 2005.
(ii) Seivad Ltd's planned profit for 2005.
(iii) The break-even sales value.
(iv) The break-even number of phones sold.
(v) The margin of safety for 2005 in sales value.
(vi) The margin of safety for 2005 in number of phones sold.

and

(vii) If fixed costs were increased by 20% what price should be charged to customers for each phone to enable Seivad Ltd to increase the profit calculated in (ii) above by 10%, assuming no change in the level of demand?

E8.5 *Time allowed – 45 minutes*

Eifion plc manufactures two products, A and B. The company's fixed overheads are absorbed on a machine hour basis, and there was full absorption of these costs in 2004. The company made a profit of £1,344,000 in 2004 and has proposed an identical plan for 2005, assuming the same market conditions as 2004. This means that Eifion plc will be working to its capacity in 2005 at the existing production level with machine hours being fully utilised. Last year's actual data are summarised below:

2004	**A**	**B**
Actual production and sales (units)	12,000	24,000
Total costs per unit	£93.50	£126.00
Selling price per unit	£107.50	£175.00
Machine hours (per unit)	7	3.5
Forecast demand at above selling prices (units)	18,000	30,000
Fixed costs	£1,680,000	

Required:

(i) Explain the relevance of limiting factors in the context of product mix decisions.

(ii) Prepare a profit maximisation plan for 2005 based on the data and selling prices shown for 2004.

(iii) Briefly explain what improvements you would suggest to the information about sales over the next three years, and how this may be used to refine the decision-making process.

Level II

E8.6 *Time allowed – 60 minutes*

Hurdle Ltd makes and sells wooden fencing in a standard length. The material cost is £10 per length which requires one half-hour of skilled labour at £10 per hour (which is in quite short supply).

Hurdle Ltd has no variable overheads but has fixed overheads of £60,000 per month. Each length of fencing sells for £28, and there is a heavy demand for the product throughout the year.

A one-off contract has been offered to Hurdle Ltd for them to supply a variation to their standard product.

(a) The labour time for the contract would be 100 hours.
(b) The material cost would be £600 plus the cost of additional special components.
(c) The special components could be purchased from an outside supplier for £220 or could be made by Hurdle Ltd for a material cost of £100 and labour time of 4 hours.

You are required to advise the company:

(i) **whether the special component should be manufactured by Hurdle Ltd or purchased from the outside supplier**

(ii) **whether the contract should be accepted**

and

(iii) **how much should be charged to the customer to enable Hurdle Ltd to make a 20% mark-up on the cost of the contract.**

(Hint: Do not forget to include opportunity costs in the total costs of the contract.)

E8.7 *Time allowed – 60 minutes*

Muckraker Ltd prepares four types of peat mix for supply to garden centres. Thanks to the popularity of Charlie Dimmock and the success of the *Ground Force* television programme, Muckraker's output has increased in successive months and demand continues to increase. For example, total peat production increased from 2,580 kg April to June to 3,460 kg in the third quarter. Muckraker has now reached a crisis because output cannot be increased by more than another 5% from the current workforce, who are working flat out, and which cannot be increased. In the third quarter of its year Muckraker's financial data are as follows:

	Peat A	Peat B	Peat C	Peat D
Peat production kg	912	1,392	696	460
Selling price per kg	£8.10	£5.82	£4.96	£6.84
Cost data per kg				
Direct labour (£10 per hour)	£0.98	£0.65	£0.50	£0.85
Direct materials	£3.26	£2.45	£2.05	£2.71
Direct packaging	£0.40	£0.35	£0.30	£0.35
Fixed overheads	£1.96	£1.30	£0.99	£1.70
Total costs	£6.60	£4.75	£3.84	£5.61

Fixed overheads are absorbed on a direct labour cost basis. Another company, Bogside Products, has offered to supply 2,000 kg of peat B at a delivered price of 80% of Muckraker's selling price. Muckraker will then be able to produce extra peat A in its place up to the plant's capacity.

Should Muckraker Ltd accept Bogside Products' offer?

E8.8 *Time allowed – 60 minutes*

Ceiling Zero plc has manufactured six CZ311 aircraft for a customer who has now cancelled the order. An alternative buyer, Coconut Airways, would be prepared to accept the aircraft if certain agreed modifications were completed within one month. The CZ contracts manager has prepared a costs schedule as a basis for establishing the minimum price that should be charged to Coconut Airways:

	£000	£000
Original cost of manufacture of 6 CZ311 aircraft		
Based on direct costs + 100% overheads charge		6,400
less: Deposit retained when order cancelled		1,000
		5,400
Costs of modification		
Direct materials	520	
Direct labour	200	
		720
Fixed overheads at 75% of direct costs of modification [0.75 × 720]		540
Administration costs at 25% of direct costs [0.25 × 720]		180
Total costs		6,840
The contracts manager has suggested an additional mark up of 25%		1,710
Suggested minimum price to Coconut airways		8,550

Two types of material were used in the original aircraft manufacture:

Melunium could be sold as scrap for reuse for £400,000, but it would take 60 hours of labour at £100 per hour to prepare the melunium for sale. The department required to carry out this work is particularly slack at the moment.

Polylindeme could be sold for £300,000 and would also require 60 hours' preparation by the same department at the same rate per hour. Alternatively, polylindeme could be kept for a year and used on another contract instead of metalindeme which would cost £400,000. To do this, a further 120 hours of labour at £150 per hour would be required in addition to the 60 hours above.

The materials used in the modifications for Coconut Airways were ordered last year at a cost of £840,000. The delivery was late and the realisable value fell to £200,000. Because of this the suppliers of the materials have given CZ a discount of £320,000. CZ cannot use this material on any other contracts.

The direct labour for the modifications is a temporary transfer from another department for four weeks. That department usually contributes £1,000,000 per week to overhead and profits. 75% of that level could be maintained if a special piece of equipment were hired at a one-off cost of £300,000 to compensate for the reduction in labour force.

If the aircraft were not sold, the specifications, plans and patents could be sold for £350,000.

Additional interim managers would need to be hired at £180,000 for the modifications, included in overhead costs. The fixed overhead rate included straight line depreciation (included in overheads at £140,000), staff expenses and lighting. Hand tools will be used for the modifications. No other overheads are affected by the modifications.

CZ's normal profit mark-up is 50%. The contracts manager has reduced this to 25% because it is felt that this is probably what Coconut Airways would be willing to pay.

You are required to redraft the contract manager's schedule to give a more meaningful price and to explain all assumptions and alterations.

E8.9 *Time allowed – 60 minutes*

Use the data for Muckraker Ltd from Exercise E8.7 to calculate the most profitable combination of output of peats A, B, C and D from subcontracting 2,000 kg of one of the products at a price of 80% of its selling price and producing extra quantities of another product up to Muckraker's total capacity.

You should assume that demand for Muckraker's products will be sufficient to meet the extra output, and that Muckraker's levels of quality and delivery performance will be maintained.

E8.10 *Time allowed – 90 minutes*

Mr Threefingers Ltd manufactures three DIY tools, the Rimbo, the Cutzer, and the Brazer. The numbers for the financial year just ended are as follows:

	Rimbo £	Cutzer £	Brazer £	Total £
Sales	100,000	80,000	120,000	300,000
(units)	(10,000)	(4,000)	(10,000)	
Variable costs	60,000	50,000	70,000	180,000
Contribution	40,000	30,000	50,000	120,000
Fixed costs	34,000	36,000	40,000	110,000
Profit/(loss)	6,000	(6,000)	10,000	10,000

£10,000 of the fixed costs of producing Cutzers are costs which would be saved if their production ceased.

Mr Threefingers Ltd is considering a number of options:

(a) Cease production of Cutzers.
(b) Increase the selling price of Cutzers by 15%.
(c) Reduce the selling price of Cutzers by 10%.
(d) Resurrect a tool which was popular 10 years ago, the Thrad, on the following basis:
- use the resources released by ceasing production of Cutzers
- incur variable costs of £48,000 and extra fixed costs of £12,000, for sales of 20,000 units
- sales of 20,000 Thrads, according to market research, could be made at a price of £5 each.

(i) Evaluate the options (a) to (d), stating any assumptions that are made to support your calculations.

(ii) What other factors should be considered by Mr Threefingers Ltd in its decision on which option(s) to adopt?

(iii) Which option(s) would you recommend and why?

9

Budgeting, planning and control

Contents

Learning objectives

Completion of this chapter will enable you to:

- identify budgeting as one part of the strategic management process
- define a budget, its purpose and uses
- recognise the importance of forecasting within the budget process
- outline how a business may apply the budgeting process in practice
- explain the preparation of budgets for planning purposes
- prepare the elements of an operating budget and a financial budget to derive the master budget
- appreciate the motivational and behavioural aspects of budgeting
- explain the preparation of budgets for control purposes and how performance against budget may be evaluated
- use standard costing in the budget process
- use standard costing in performance evaluation and control
- identify the use of flexible budgeting in performance evaluation and control
- prepare flexed budgets in line with changes in activity levels
- explain what is meant by a variance between actual and standard performance
- appreciate the importance of variance analysis in exception reporting
- calculate the individual variances used to explain differences between actual and standard performance
- explain the reasons for variances between actual and standard performance.

Introduction

Chapter 8 looked at decision-making as one application of the management accounting roles of problem solving and attention directing. This chapter looks at a further application of those roles and is concerned with how businesses attempt to plan their activities for the year ahead, or for a shorter period, to enable them to plan and maintain control of the business. Budgeting is the part of the strategic management of the business to do with planning and control. In this chapter we will consider the budget for planning and control purposes.

This chapter considers the role of forecasting in the budget process, and looks at the budget-setting process in detail. The budgeting process will be used to construct a simple budget for a company based on its organisational objectives, and its best estimates of future activities.

We will discuss the motivational aspects of budgeting and identify some of the important conflicts and problems encountered in the budgeting process.

This chapter will explore in greater detail how the costs of units of a product or a process are determined and at how standards may be used in the budgeting process to cost each unit or process. The budgeted unit or process cost is called its standard cost.

This chapter will explain the technique of standard costing and the ways in which actual performance may be measured and compared with the budget through the use of variance analysis. We will look at how, using standard costs, the budget may be flexed to reflect actual levels of activity, and then used to calculate individual variances. Individual variances may then be investigated to explain the reasons for the differences between actual and expected performance.

The process of explaining significant variances from standard continues to be considered as a powerful management tool. Variance analysis is almost exclusively concerned with the comparison of performance against short-term budget targets. Short-term performance is very important. However the achieving, or exceeding, of short-term targets should not be considered in isolation, which may ignore or be to the detriment of longer-term objectives.

Why do we budget?

Many companies believe that the traditional annual budgeting system is unsuitable and irrelevant in rapidly changing markets. Further, they believe that budgets fail to deal with the most important drivers of shareholder value such as intangible assets like brands and knowledge. Some of these companies, like Volvo, Ikea, and Ericsson, have already revised their need for annual budgets as being an inefficient tool in an increasingly changing business environment. Volvo abandoned the annual budget ten years ago. Instead, they provide three-month forecasts and monthly board reports, which include financial and non-financial indicators. These forecasts and reports are supplemented with a two-year rolling forecast, updated quarterly, and four- and ten-year strategic plans updated yearly. It should also be noted that many of the dot.com companies that failed during the 1990s and early 2000s also felt that traditional budget methods were a little old-fashioned and irrelevant.

The accuracy of budgets

We asked FDs two questions: Is the UK and London in particular capable of hosting the 2012 Olympic Games? AND Are budgets drawn up now unrealistic for an event to be held eight years later?

More than three-quarters of finance directors believe it is unrealistic for the 2012 London Olympic finance team to draw up budget plans eight years in advance of the event taking place.

As bid FD Neil Wood prepares the capital and operating budgets as part of the 600-page bid document to be submitted on 14 November, just 16% of the 258 FDs polled in the latest *Accountancy Age*/Reed Accountancy Big Question survey saw any value in doing this now.

Paresh Samat, finance director of Croner Consulting, said the bid team should 'learn the lessons from the rebuilding of the Wembley Stadium. The figures will end up 30% to 40% higher than estimates. Maybe we should go to Japan and learn from their experiences of building an infrastructure from the last World Cup,' he said.

Another FD was even less convinced: 'Whatever you budget for now you need to double the figure that you ask for.'

FDs were, however, more supportive of the UK's and London's ability to host the 2012 Games, with more than two-thirds believing the capital will be able to stage the event. One FD said: 'Having hosted the Commonwealth Games successfully, I do not see why we should not host the Olympics.'

London 2012 says it will have access to £2.2bn of public funds if the bid succeeds – with £1.4bn coming from the National Lottery, £581m from London residents via a local tax and the rest coming from the London Development Agency.

FDs claim Olympic budgeting now is 'unrealistic', by Larry Schlesinger

© *Accountancy Age*, 3 June 2004

The budgeting process is questioned in the article above reproduced from *Accountancy Age*, with particular emphasis on the time spans over which budgets may be realistic and therefore useful. This article, based on a survey of 258 finance directors, considers whether budgets for large projects like the Olympics can be realistic when they are prepared so many years ahead of the events.

There are clearly different views as to whether or not the budget is an effective and essential business tool. However, the majority of the world's most successful companies have attributed a large part of their success to their reliance on traditional formal budgeting systems. The long-term (strategic) and short-term (budget) planning processes are core management tasks that are critically important to the future survival and success of the business. The budget prepared for planning purposes, as part of the strategic planning process, is the quantitative plan of management's belief of what the business's costs and revenues will be over a specific future period. The budget prepared for control purposes, even though it may have been based on standards that may not be reached, is used for motivational purposes to influence improved departmental performance. Monitoring of actual performance against the budget is used to provide feedback in order to take the appropriate action necessary to reach planned performance, and to revise plans in the light of changes.

The following Worked Examples 9.1 and 9.2 illustrate the importance of the preparation of business plans and what can result if there is a lack of preparation for unexpected future events.

The broad picture of planning and control includes budgeting, strategic planning, management control, and operations control. The process involves:

- identification of objectives, involving factors such as profit, market share, value, etc.
- identification of potential strategies using facts as well as opinion
- evaluation of options, including a selection of courses of action and preparation of forecasts
- implementation of long-term plans, and finalising the planning before going on to provide control
- monitoring of actual outcomes, which will highlight whether the budget was too easy or unachievable
- provision of responses regarding actual outcomes against plans through feedback.

Worked Example 9.1

A business, which was involved in providing marquees and hospitality facilities for business entertaining and private parties, began to face a gradual economic downturn. The effect of this was that demand from companies started to decrease as they cut back their entertaining and hospitality budgets. The business had previously been doing very well and the proprietor felt confident of being able to continue to meet overhead payments even with a reduced sales level, because a reasonable bank balance had been built up. The proprietor did not quantify the change in position in a revised financial plan. After a few months the business needed overdraft facilities and began to delay its payments to creditors. The bank manager was not sympathetic since he had received no prior warning of the potential problem. Goodwill with creditors began to diminish. The business failed, but may not have if the proprietor had:

- attempted to quantify the effect of the economic downturn on profit and cash flow
- warned the bank of the problem
- tried to negotiate the overdraft facility

- negotiated favourable terms with creditors.

The careful preparation, and regular revision, of financial plans is vital to be prepared against the risk of unexpected events and changes in circumstances.

Worked Example 9.2

The managing director of a company that manufactured and sold solid wood kitchen and dining room furniture wanted to increase the turnover of the business by 30% in the coming year. She had identified the requirements necessary to fulfil this increase:

- spare capacity in existing retail outlets
- additional new equipment
- one extra employee.

However, the managing director had failed to recognise the cost of financing the increased turnover:

- cash outflow for additional raw materials before cash flowed in from increased sales
- financing costs of additional equipment
- additional wages.

The managing director had focused only on the positive aspects of the expansion:

- increased sales (although sales prices remained constant)
- increased cash flowing into the business.

The business ran into cash flow problems because it did not inform its bankers of its expansion plans and therefore did not submit a business plan (projected profit and loss account and cash flow) or negotiate a new overdraft facility. For any business it is crucial that any major change, whether expansion or diversification, must be quantified financially in revised business plans. Smaller businesses are particularly vulnerable and should prepare projections more frequently than on an annual basis incorporating realistic expectations for existing activities and plans for any changes in the business in order to:

- alert the business owner to risks and difficulties which may arise
- allow time for remedial action to be taken.

Strategic planning

Strategic planning is the process of deciding:

- on the objectives of the organisation
- on changes in these objectives
- on the resources used to attain these objectives
- on the policies that are to govern the acquisition, use and disposition of these resources.

It is not correct to assume that strategic planning is just an extension of budgeting, but there is a close relationship between these processes. A budget is a quantified statement, for a defined period of time, which may include planned revenues, expenses, assets, liabilities and cash flows. A budget provides a focus for the organisation, aids the co-ordination of activities, and facilitates control.

The way in which a typical strategic planning process may be carried out in an organisation is best illustrated in the flow charts in Figs 9.1 and 9.2. The chart in Fig. 9.1 shows how analysis is used to develop strategies and actions. The chart in Fig. 9.2 shows the sequences of each step in the process and the relationship between strategic planning and budgeting.

Budgeting

The broad purposes of budgeting include:

- planning and control, through
  - exception reporting of financial and non-financial indicators, which
  - economises on managerial time, and
  - maximises efficiency
- co-ordination, which
  - assists goal congruence

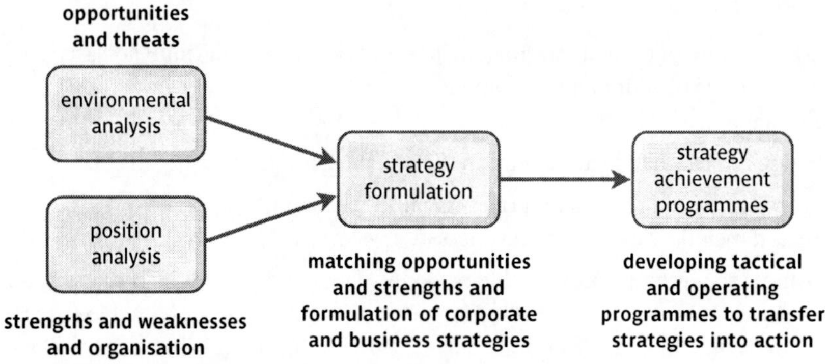

Figure 9.1 The strategic planning process

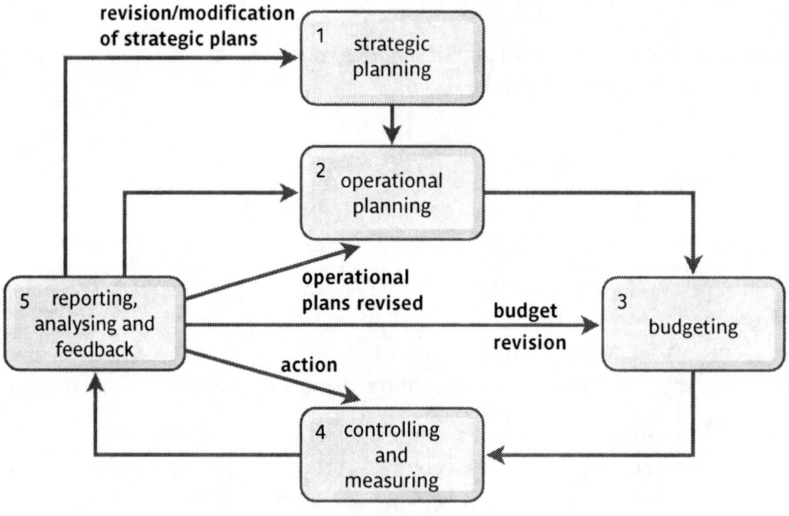

Figure 9.2 The strategic planning relationship with budgeting

- communication, through
  - the feedback process, which should
  - reduce or prevent sub-optimal performance
- motivation and alignment of individual and corporate goals, through
  - participation of many people in the budget-setting process
- evaluation of performance, to
  - facilitate control.

Budgetary control establishes a basis for internal audit by regularly evaluating departmental results. The budget process should ensure that scarce resources are allocated in an optimal way, and so enable expenditure to be controlled. Management is forced to plan ahead so that long-term goals are achieved.

The budget provides a yardstick for performance rather than rely on comparisons with past periods, since when conditions and expectations will have changed. Areas of efficiency and inefficiency are identified through reporting of variances, and variance analysis will prompt remedial action where necessary. Part of the budget process should identify the people responsible for items of cost and revenue so that areas of responsibility are clearly defined.

Planning

Planning and control are two of the most visible ways that financial and non-financial information may be used in the management control process. This is done by:

- setting standards of performance and providing feedback, and therefore
- identifying areas for improvement, by means of
- variance reports.

Planning is the establishment of objectives and the formulation, evaluation and selection of the policies, strategies, tactics and action required to achieve them. Planning comprises long-term/strategic planning, and short-term operational planning. The latter usually refers to a period of one year. With regard to a new retail product, the strategic (long-term) plan of the business, for example, may include the aim to become profitable, and to become a market leader within three years. The short-term operational plan may be to get the product stocked by at least one leading supermarket group within 12 months.

Control

Control and monitoring are the continuous comparison of actual results with those planned, both in total, and for the separate divisions within the organisation, and taking appropriate management action to correct adverse variances and to exploit favourable variances. The UK has seen the growth of 'call centres', and the press have exposed the constant monitoring by management as unpleasantly intrusive. There appears to be a high turnover of staff in these new hi-tech businesses, where they are regarded as cheap labour but do not necessarily meet management targets.

Management control is the process by which managers assure that resources are obtained and used effectively and efficiently in the accomplishment of the organisation's objectives. The UK company Railtrack plc found itself forced into diverting extra resources into rail maintenance during the autumn months of 2000, as it was felt that it was not achieving the basic objective of safety of passengers and employees.

Operational control is concerned with day-to-day activities of organisations, and is the process of assuring that specific tasks are carried out effectively and efficiently. For example, the UK Government decided in the year 2000 to allocate further funds to hospitals for the recruitment of more nurses, to enable the hospitals to carry out specific tasks 'effectively and efficiently'.

Whereas planning is achieved by means of a fixed master budget, control is generally exercised through the comparison of actual costs with a flexible budget. A flexible budget is a budget which, by recognising different cost behaviour patterns, is designed to show changes in variable costs as the volume of activity of the organisation changes. Over the short time-spans that budgets normally cover (one year or six months), fixed costs are assumed to remain unchanged. The mobile telephone market in 2000/2001 is probably one of the best illustrations of a 'high profile' market having the need for flexible budgeting, as the number of units sold in successive periods continued to make the headlines in the media.

Progress check 9.1 **What is budgeting, and how does it fit into the overall strategic planning process?**

Forecasting and planning

The budget is a plan. The planning activity of the budget process should reflect real beliefs of each company's management, reflecting what they think will happen, flexible to changes in circumstances, and providing feedback.

A forecast is not a budget but a prediction of future environments, events, and outcomes. Forecasting is required in order to prepare budgets. This should start with projected sales volumes/market share of current and new products. Examples of forecasts by product, or sector, can be found regularly in the press, for example car sales and mobile telephone sales.

Large companies need to be very sensitive to trends and developments within their forecasting process as mistakes can prove very expensive. For example, a major UK chocolate manufacturer made too many eggs for Easter 2000, which did not sell; its forecasts and therefore its budgets were proved to be very wide of the mark, and the impact on the business was extremely costly.

In order to highlight more clearly some of the issues around forecasting it may be useful to consider it in the context of budgeting in terms of large group plcs, comprising many companies that may be either diversified or within the same industrial sector.

Sales volume projections are required to evaluate turnover and product margins. Marketing policy may or may not be centralised. Centralised marketing information may not always be congruent with individual company expectations and may allow little scope for negotiation.

Sales prices are usually negotiated by individual companies with their customers, to ensure that group margin targets are met. However, in the case of large group companies, relationships with major customers may mean that this is not always an autonomous process, resulting in inevitable acceptance of group agreements in many cases. Whilst this may achieve corporate goals, it may conflict with individual company objectives in trying to meet targeted gross margins. Conversely, commercial managers may try to set sales budgets that may be too easily achievable through understatement of price increase expectations.

Increased market share through new innovation is commonly a primary objective of individual companies. However, new product development, financed out of internally generated funds, involves very large investments and long lead times. This creates competition for resources, and difficulties whilst also trying to achieve group targets for return on investment (ROI). Resources may come off second best, but without any relaxation in product development objectives.

The production manager forecasts production resource requirements, materials and labour, based on sales forecasts, stock-holding policies, and performance improvement targets. The production manager may have an easier job in an expanding rather than a declining market.

Many companies within large groups may be suppliers and customers within the group. The prices to be charged between companies within large groups, transfer prices, are usually set by the parent company and based on pre-determined formulae. Some companies within the group may lose and some companies may gain, the objective being that the group is the overall winner. As a consequence, transfer pricing may provide prices that are disagreed with and cause disputes, which rarely result in acceptable outcomes for individual companies. Optimal pricing for the group must take precedence over individual company requirements to meet group profitability objectives (despite the impact on individual company profit performance bonuses!).

There are groups of companies where materials or components may be supplied from group-nominated suppliers, or certainly from suppliers where unit price is the dominant procurement criterion. Purchase indices are an important performance measure of the purchasing function, but may not relate to total procurement cost. Group purchasing performance objectives may therefore subvert those of the individual companies, which seek to minimise total costs, on which delivery costs, for example, and the impact of foreign currency exchange rate fluctuations may have a significant impact.

The above examples illustrate some important conflicts at the forecasting stage, arising from policy decisions where group goals inevitably dominate individual company goals, which in turn may also lack congruence with individual goals. Quite frequently a subsidiary company must comply with a group instruction, which may result in an apparently successful local product being dropped, in favour of a group-wide product. An example of this was seen in the year 2001 where the group goals of General Motors (USA) were not appreciated by a wide cross-section of the UK community, because so many lost their jobs (and businesses) as a result of Vauxhall cutbacks initiated by the group board of directors.

Forecasting usually relies on the analysis of past data to identify patterns used to describe it. Patterns may then be extrapolated into the future to prepare a forecast. There are many forecasting methods, qualitative and quantitative, with no one best model. It is usually a question of fitting the pattern of historical data to the model that best fits. It could be argued that it is easier to forecast the sales of ice-cream than the sales of CDs by a new band. Apparently, the major music-based groups have also found this a mystery over the years.

Progress check 9.2 **What is the role of forecasting in budgeting?**

Qualitative forecasting

Qualitative forecasting uses expert opinion to predict future events and includes:

- the Delphi method – use of a panel of recognised experts
- technological comparisons – independent forecasters predicting changes in one area by monitoring changes in another area
- subjective curve fitting – for example, similar product life cycles for similar products like CD players and DVD players.

Quantitative forecasting

Quantitative forecasting uses historical data to try to predict the future, and includes univariate models and causal models. Univariate models predict future values of time series when conditions are expected to remain the same, for example exponential smoothing and the use of moving averages.

Causal models involve the use of the identification of other variables related to the variable being predicted. For example, linear regression may be used to forecast sales, using the independent variables of:

- sales price
- advertising expenditure
- competitors' prices.

The major UK retailers have been seen to be highly pro-active in revising their sales prices and their advertising activities (and expenditure) as a result of changes in the marketplace.

Whichever method is used it is important that the basis and the methodology of the forecasting is understood. All assumptions made and the parameters of time, availability of past data, costs, accuracy required, and ease of use must be clearly stated to maintain any sort of confidence in the forecasts.

Progress check 9.3 **Give examples of some of the techniques used to forecast the demand for a product.**

The budget process

The budgeting process normally aims to:

- identify areas of efficiency/inefficiency
- allow people participation
- allocate responsibility to enable performance evaluation through exception reporting of actual versus budget.

Whilst participation may be encouraged, insufficient attention may be given to managers' differing motivational tendencies either to achieve success or to avoid failure. The budget process therefore may not always achieve desired results, nor provide the appropriate rewards for success.

We will use Supportex Ltd in Worked Examples 9.3 to 9.9 to illustrate a step-by-step approach to the budget preparation process.

Sales and gross margin budget

The complete budget preparation process is outlined in Fig. 9.3. Once the sales forecast has been prepared the budgeted gross margin may be calculated. The budgeted gross margin is derived from estimated:

- sales volumes, and prices
- materials usage, and prices
- direct labour hours, and rates
- overhead costs.

Progress check 9.4 What are the decisions to be made and the policies established by a business before embarking on the budget preparation process?

Worked Example 9.3

Supportex Ltd manufactures three only specialist types of lintels: Small; Medium; Large. Supportex has received sales forecasts prepared by its sales manager, Ms Crystal Ball. Taking account of trends in the building industry and an analysis of competitive performance, Crystal has used a linear regression computer model to forecast demand for Supportex's products and sales prices for the year from 1 April 2005. Crystal Ball's sales forecast data are as follows:

Lintel	Demand	Price
Small	5,000	£20
Medium	8,000	£30
Large	6,000	£40

These data can be used to prepare an unphased sales budget for the year ended 31 March 2006.

Sales budget

Lintel	Demand	Price	£ sales
Small	5,000	£20	100,000
Medium	8,000	£30	240,000
Large	6,000	£40	240,000
			580,000

Production budget

The production budget may be prepared by allowing for expected stock movements in the period, based on company policy and targets for improvement. Budgeted materials requirements are based on a bill of materials (BOM), which is the 'list of ingredients and recipe' for each product. The purchasing function ensures that the right materials, components and packaging are procured in the right quantities, at the right time to the right location, in line with production and stockholding requirements.

Budgeted labour requirements are based on standard labour hours required for each product. Conflicts may arise between manufacturing and engineering in respect of estimates of standard hours. Engineering changes may be made continuously, but may not always be reflected in up-to-date bills of materials.

In practice, the calculation of the standard hours required to manufacture each product is not a straightforward process. There is always much debate between managers with regard to how standard labour hours are adjusted in respect of, for example, absenteeism, downtime, training, efficiency, and the extent to which they should be reflected in the standard labour rate. These factors have an obvious impact on the manufacturing director's requirements for direct labour resources for

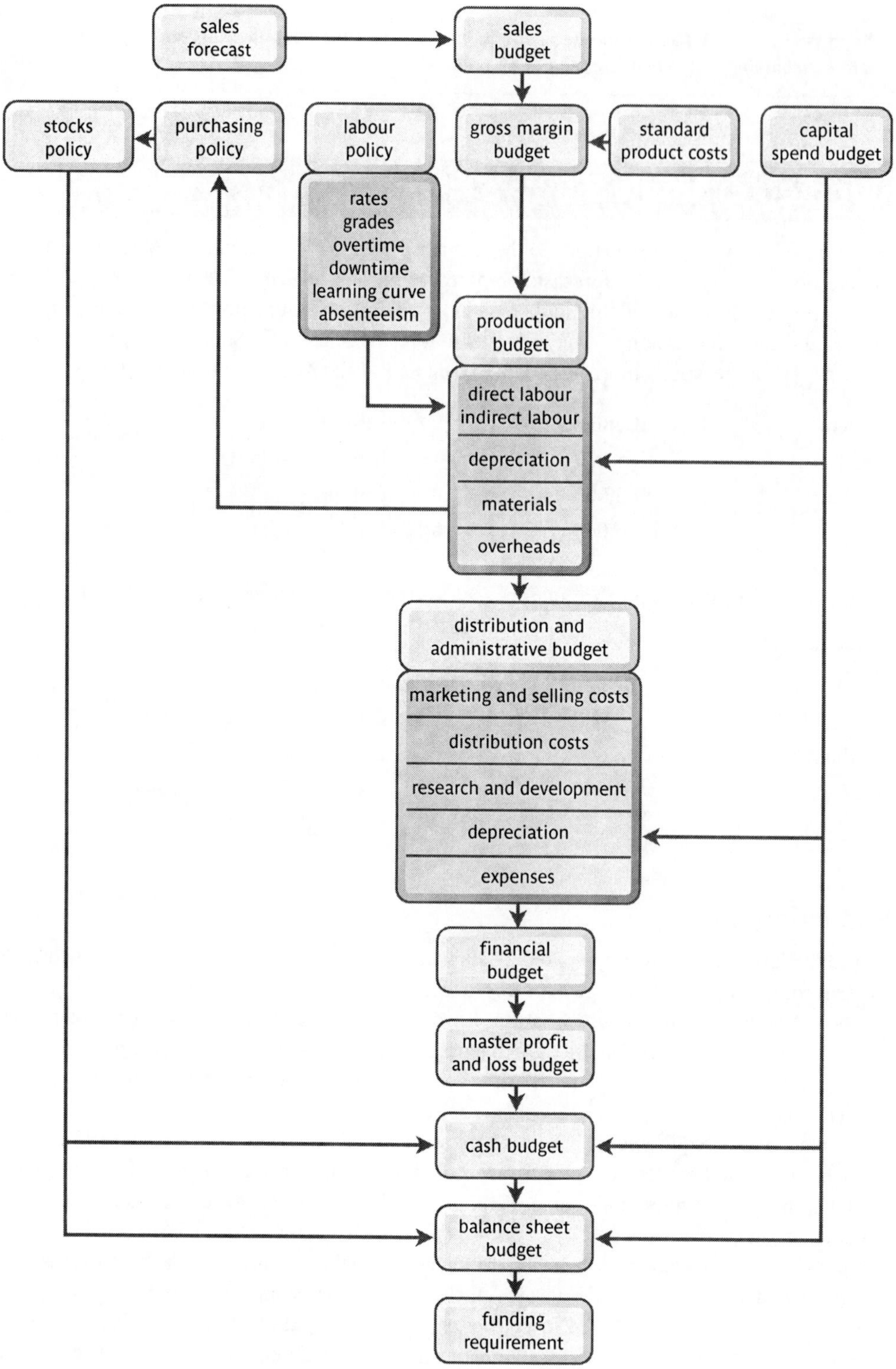

Figure 9.3 Budget preparation flow diagram

given levels of production, inevitably conflicting with the human resources director's headcount objectives.

Many companies have structures comprised of business units, each with responsibility for production areas relating to specific products/customers. Responsibility for estimating budget production overheads and indirect labour requirements is devolved to business unit managers, the remaining above-the-line overheads and indirect labour requirements being provided by quality, purchasing, logistics and maintenance managers. Each manager may also submit his/her capital

Worked Example 9.4

The purchasing manager of Supportex Ltd, Mr Daley, has obtained what he believes are the most competitive prices for materials used to make and package Supportex's products. Supportex's cost prices and the standard quantities used in each product for the budget year are as follows:

Materials

	Labels	**Packaging**	**Rubbers**	**Steels**
Cost prices	£1	£2	£3	£6
Standard quantities				
Small	2	1	1	0.5
Medium	1	1	2	1
Large	2	2	1	1

Material handlers and operators are employed to make the Supportex products. The company's production manager, Ben Drools, has provided the following hourly rates and the standard times used in production:

	Material handlers	**Operators**
Hourly rates	£6	£7.50
Standard minutes		
Small	5	12
Medium	5	20
Large	10	40

Production overheads are forecast at £38,000, which are absorbed into product costs on the basis of direct labour hours.

At 31 March 2005 stock levels have been estimated by Arthur Daley at:

	Quantity		**Quantity**
Finished product		**Materials**	
Small	1,000	Labels	15,000
Medium	1,500	Packaging	10,000
Large	1,000	Rubbers	15,000
		Steels	10,000

The Managing Director has set Ben a target of a 20% reduction in component stocks by 31 March 2006 and the company expects finished goods stock to be up by 10% by the same time.

Unphased budgets for the year ended 31 March 2006 may be prepared for the following:

(i) Production
(ii) Direct labour
(iii) Unit gross margin
(iv) Materials usage and purchases.

(i) Production budget

	Sales units	Stock increases	Production units
Small	5,000	100	5,100
Medium	8,000	150	8,150
Large	6,000	100	6,100

(ii) Direct labour budget

	Production units	Material handlers hours	Operators hours	
Small	5,100	425	1,020	
Medium	8,150	679	2,717	
Large	6,100	1,017	4,067	
Direct labour hours		2,121	7,804	Total 9,925 hours
Direct labour rates		£6/hour	£7.50/hour	
Direct labour cost		£12,726	£58,530	Total £71,256

(iii) Unit gross margin budget

Unit product costs

	Small £	Medium £	Large £
Materials:			
Labels	2	1	2
Packaging	2	2	4
Rubbers	3	6	3
Steels	3	6	6
(a)	£10	£15	£15
Direct labour:			
Material handlers	0.5 [5 × £6/60]	0.5 [5 × £6/60]	1 [10 × £6/60]
Operators	1.5 [12 × £7.50/60]	2.5 [20 × £7.50/60]	5 [40 × £7.50/60]
(b)	£2	£3	£6

Total production overheads				
£38,000 ÷ 9,925				
= £3.8287 per hour	(c)	£1.0848	£1.5953	£3.1906
Total unit production costs				
(a + b + c)	**(d)**	£13.0848	£19.5953	£24.1906
Sales prices	**(e)**	£20	£30	£40
Unit gross margins (e – d)		£6.9152	£10.4047	£15.8094
rounded to		£6.92	£10.40	£15.81

(iv) Materials usage budget

Units	Labels	Packaging	Rubbers	Steels
Small	10,200	5,100	5,100	2,550
Medium	8,150	8,150	16,300	8,150
Large	12,200	12,200	6,100	6,100
Total usage	30,550	25,450	27,500	16,800
Stocks 31 March 2005	15,000	10,000	15,000	10,000
Stocks reduction by 31 March 2006 targeted at 20% of 31 March 2005 levels	3,000	2,000	3,000	2,000

Materials purchases budget

Units	Labels	Packaging	Rubbers	Steels	
Total usage	30,550	25,450	27,500	16,800	
Stock decrease	3,000	2,000	3,000	2,000	
Purchase requirements	27,550	23,450	24,500	14,800	
Unit costs	£1	£2	£3	£6	Total
Purchase requirements	£27,550	£46,900	£73,500	£88,800	£236,750

expenditure requirements, which are then used for subsequent calculation of depreciation, and the assessment of cash flow implications.

Depreciation charged to production overhead is calculated based on existing plant and equipment and the plans for new plant and equipment that have been submitted by managers responsible for production and production support activities. It must be emphasised that the method of determining the depreciation charge is highly subjective, and the marketplace has seen many products last much longer than the most extreme original estimates made by managers. An example has been the Rover Mini car, which was not expected to be in production for over 40 years!

Distribution and administrative budget

The non-production costs of:

- marketing and selling
- distribution
- administration
- research and development

and also planned capital expenditure, are provided by managers responsible for departments such as:

- commercial and marketing
- information technology
- administration
- human resources
- engineering
- product development.

Financial budget

Costs of financing and/or interest receivable from the investment of surplus funds may be estimated for the first draft budget. As the phased profit and loss accounts, capital expenditure, and cash budget become finalised the financial budget can be refined with a little more accuracy.

Master profit and loss budget

The master budget is prepared by pulling together each of the elements outlined above to provide a budgeted:

- trading account
- manufacturing account
- profit and loss account

for the year.

These may then be phased to show expected month-by-month results. The ways in which the various items within the budget are phased are determined by the type of revenue or cost. Some items may be related to the volume of sales, or production levels, whilst others may be spread evenly on a monthly, weekly or daily basis.

The budget preparation procedure described above is usually a negotiation process between budget holders and the budget committee. Conflicts may arise as budgets are very often seen as 'finance' budgets, perceived as a pressure device, with a corresponding demotivating effect on personnel.

Problems ensue due to lack of information, ignorance, and misunderstanding of the budget process (probably through a lack of training), which may result in generally inflated budgets. Judgement is required to identify whether apparently inflated budgets reflect real needs, or some degree of 'padding' due to a fear of cutbacks. Padding relates to the overestimation of budgeted costs (or underestimation of budgeted revenues) by managers with the expectation that their budgets may be cut, so that their final agreed budgets may be at levels that they feel are achievable.

Further conflicts arise between departments within a company, through competition for resources, and also poor communication, resulting in duplication in cost budgets or padding. Examples of costs omitted, or duplicated, are health and safety costs (human resources or manufacturing?), training costs (human resources or decentralised into the operational departments?), and the question of centralised/decentralised costs generally. This often results in each department blaming the other if services are not provided, or if cost targets are not achieved.

Padding may occur where budget holders are allowed to be excessively prudent regarding costs and expenses or achievement of sales. If the company or a sector of its business is expanding, the padding may be tolerated. When competition is fierce or the industry is in decline, then the padding could prove quite harmful and lead to decisions being based on an incorrect cost base. It is inevitable that managers may be prudent when constructing their budgets, and this can take the form of putting a little extra into expense categories that may be difficult to verify, or a little less into certain categories of sales.

The budget preparation process is a continuous process of:

- setting objectives
- forecasting
- draft budget preparation

Worked Example 9.5

Supportex Ltd have budgeted selling and administrative costs of £80,000 for the following year. The overheads and selling and administrative costs include total depreciation budgeted for the year of £23,569. There are not expected to be any financing costs over the coming year.

We will prepare an unphased profit and loss account budget, using absorption costing, for the year ended 31 March 2006.

Profit and loss account master budget

	Small		Medium		Large		Total
	Total	Unit	Total	Unit	Total	Unit	
Sales units	5,000		8,000		6,000		
	£		£		£		£
Sales	100,000	£20	240,000	£30	240,000	£40	580,000
Cost of sales (derived from sales less gross margin)	65,400		156,800		145,140		367,340
Gross margin	34,600	£6.92	83,200	£10.40	94,860	£15.81	212,660
Using unit gross margins from Worked Example 9.4 (iii)							
Selling and administrative costs							80,000
Profit							132,660

- evaluation
- feedback
- forecast and budget revisions.

Within most organisations this process continues, limited by budget preparation timetable constraints, until an acceptable final budget has been achieved.

During the budget process, cost reductions are inevitably requested from all areas within the organisation. This poses obvious dilemmas for all managers. Whilst wanting to co-operate in meeting profitability objectives, they must still maintain the same levels of service for both internal and external customers.

Cash budget

Cash flow is an extremely important element in the budget preparation process. The master profit and loss budget, together with the planned capital expenditure, the outflow of cash on fixed asset acquisitions and investments, may then be used to prepare an initial cash budget. This will also include the impact of the operating cycle:

- materials purchases become stock items held for a period before use, and creditors to be paid out of cash at a later date
- production uses up stock to generate sales which become debtors to be received into cash at a later date
- the more immediate payment of staff costs and other operational expense.

The final cash budget, phased to show monthly cash surpluses or cash requirements, will also include the effect of non-operational events such as cash raised through the issue of shares and loans, and cash paid in respect of taxation and dividends to shareholders.

The calculation of the budgeted cash flow statement, shown in Worked Example 9.6, is carried out by preparing a direct cash flow statement (see Chapter 4). This may be checked by the preparation of a more conventional indirect cash flow statement, as shown in Worked Example 9.7.

Balance sheet budget

The budget balance sheet may be prepared with reference to:

- information relating to sales, costs, etc., from the master profit and loss budget
- the capital expenditure budget
- operating cycle assumptions on stock days, debtor days, creditor days
- the cash budget.

As with the profit and loss budget and cash budget, the balance sheet budget may be phased to show the expected month-by-month financial position of the organisation.

The budget balance sheet as at 31 March 2006 shown in Worked Example 9.8 has been prepared by calculating:

- the effect on fixed assets of depreciation for the year 2005/06
- the closing valuation of stocks at 31 March 2006
- the closing valuation of trade debtors at 31 March 2006
- the cash and bank balance at 31 March 2006
- the closing valuation of trade creditors at 31 March 2006
- the addition to retained earnings, the budgeted profit for the year 2005/06.

Worked Example 9.6

Supportex Ltd have prepared an estimated balance sheet for 31 March 2005 as follows:

	£	£
Fixed assets	362,792	
Stocks	206,669	
Trade debtors	46,750	
Cash and bank	2,432	618,643
Trade creditors	35,275	
Share capital	200,000	
Retained earnings	383,368	618,643

Trade debtors all pay in the month following the month of sale and Arthur Daley has negotiated trade creditors' payments in the second month following the month of purchase. Direct labour, production overheads, and selling and administrative costs are all paid in the month they are incurred. There is no planned capital expenditure for the budget year and trading is expected to be evenly spread over the 12 months, except for month 12 when the changes in stock levels are expected to occur.

We can use this to prepare an unphased cash budget for the year ended 31 March 2006.

Cash budget

Cash inflows from customers:	£	Cash outflows to suppliers:	£
Trade debtors at 31/3/05	46,750	Trade creditors at 31/3/05	35,275
Sales 2005/06	580,000	Purchases 2005/06	236,750
less: Trade debtors at 31/3/06	(48,333)	less: Trade creditors at 31/3/06	(39,458)
(1 month sales)	578,417	(2 months purchases)	232,567
Cash outflows for overheads:		Cash outflow for capital:	zero
Production overheads	38,000	Cash outflow for tax:	zero
Sales and administration	80,000	Cash outflow for dividends:	zero
less: Depreciation	(23,569)	Cash outflow for direct labour:	71,256
	94,431	Cash inflow for shares/loans:	zero

	£	
Inflows from customers	578,417	
Outflows to suppliers	(232,567)	
Outflows for overheads	(94,431)	
Outflow for direct labour	(71,256)	
Budgeted cash flow 2005/06	180,163	[see Worked Example 9.7]
Forecast cash and bank 31/3/05	2,432	
Budgeted cash and bank 31/3/06	182,595	

Worked Example 9.7

An unphased budgeted indirect cash flow statement may be prepared for Supportex Ltd for the year ended 31 March 2006.

Cash flow statement

	£	
Budgeted operating profit 2005/06	132,660	
plus: Depreciation	23,569	
plus: Decrease in stocks	21,334	[206,669 – 185,335] See Worked Example 9.8
less: Increase in debtors	(1,583)	[48,333 – 46,750] See Worked Example 9.6
plus: Increase in creditors	4,183	[39,458 – 35,275]
Budgeted cash flow 2005/06	180,163	See Worked Example 9.6
Forecast cash and bank 31/3/05	2,432	
Budgeted cash and bank 31/3/06	182,595	

The budgeted cash flow figure of £180,163 can be seen to agree with the budgeted cash flow calculated in Worked Example 9.6.

There is an alternative way of deriving the balance sheet that may be used in practice, which also clarifies the links between stock movements and the profit and loss account and its links with the balance sheet. This method requires a calculation of the materials cost of products actually sold (compared with the materials used in production in Worked Example 9.4). It also requires a calculation of the direct labour and production overheads cost of products actually sold (compared with the cash paid out in Worked Example 9.6). The cash paid out for direct labour and overheads in the budget year will be absorbed into the valuation of stock of finished product. Not all that finished product will be sold in the period. Some will have been left in stock at 31 March 2006. The same situation applied at 31 March 2005.

Therefore finished product stocks at 31 March 2006 will need to be adjusted by the amount of direct labour and overheads in their valuation that relates to the difference in the finished goods stock level between 31 March 2005 and 31 March 2006. The balance of what is paid out for direct labour and overheads in the budget year is charged to the profit and loss account.

Funding requirements

The final budget should not be accepted until the projected financial position of the business has been reviewed in terms of the adequacy, or otherwise, of funding. The budget for the forthcoming period may have been based on higher or lower activity than the previous period, or it may include new product development, or other major new projects. Risk analysis and risk assessment is essential to be carried out on each of the uncertain areas of the budget, to determine any requirement for additional funding and to safeguard the future of the business.

Worked Example 9.8

Using the information from the last four Worked Examples 9.4 to 9.7 we can now prepare an unphased balance sheet budget for Supportex Ltd as at 31 March 2006.

Stock valuations at 31 March 2006

	Quantity	£ unit price (see Worked Example 9.4)	£
Finished product			
Small	1,100	13.0848	14,393
Medium	1,650	19.5953	32,332
Large	1,100	24.1906	26,610
Total			73,335
Materials			
Labels	12,000	1.00	12,000
Packaging	8,000	2.00	16,000
Rubbers	12,000	3.00	36,000
Steels	8,000	6.00	48,000
Total			112,000
Budgeted stocks at 31 March 2006			185,335
Fixed assets			
Fixed assets at 31 March 2005			362,792
Budgeted depreciation 2005/06			(23,569)
Budgeted fixed assets at 31 March 2006			339,223
Retained earnings			
Retained earnings at 31 March 2005			383,368
Budgeted profit 2005/06 (see Worked Example 9.5)			132,660
Budgeted retained earnings at 31 March 2006			516,028

Using the budgeted stocks, fixed assets, and retained earnings calculations above, and the budgeted cash and bank balance, trade debtors and trade creditors calculated in Worked Example 9.6, we now have the complete information to construct the budgeted balance sheet as at 31 March 2006:

Balance sheet:

	£	£
Fixed assets	339,223	
Stocks	185,335	
Trade debtors	48,333	
Cash and bank	182,595	755,486
Trade creditors	39,458	
Share capital	200,000	
Retained earnings	516,028	755,486

Worked Example 9.9

The budget balance sheet for Supportex Ltd at 31 March 2006 can be derived by plotting the expected movements for the budget year 2005/06 relating to each type of activity, and totalling across each line from the starting balance sheet 31 March 2005. This is an alternative approach to Worked Example 9.8, which also shows the relationship between sales, costs, cash and the balance sheet.

Materials cost of goods sold

Units	**Labels**		**Packaging**		**Rubbers**		**Steels**	
Small	[5,000 × 2]	10,000	[5,000 × 1]	5,000	[5,000 × 1]	5,000	[5,000 × 0.5]	2,500
Med.	[8,000 × 1]	8,000	[8,000 × 1]	8,000	[8,000 × 2]	16,000	[8,000 × 1]	8,000
Large	[6,000 × 2]	12,000	[6,000 × 2]	12,000	[6,000 × 1]	6,000	[6,000 × 1]	6,000
Total		30,000		25,000		27,000		16,500
Unit costs		£1		£2		£3		£6
Materials cost of sales		£30,000		£50,000		£81,000		£99,000
								Total = £260,000

Direct labour in finished stock increase 31 March 2006

	Stock increases	**Direct labour/unit**	**Stock adjustment**
		£	**£**
Small	100	2	200
Medium	150	3	450
Large	100	6	600
			1,250

Production overhead in finished stock increase 31 March 2006

	Stock increases	**Production overhead/unit** (see Worked Example 9.4)	**Stock adjustment**
		£	**£**
Small	100	1.0848	108
Medium	150	1.5953	239
Large	100	3.1906	319
			666

Sales, materials purchases, depreciation, cash receipts, and cash payments have previously been calculated (see Worked Examples 9.3 to 9.7).

Balance sheet

Figures in £	31/03/05	Sales	Cash recs.	Purchases	Cash pays.	Depn.	Materials cost of sales	Direct labour	Production overheads	31/03/06
Fixed assets	362,792					(23,569)				339,223
Stocks	206,669			236,750			(260,000)	1,250	666	185,335
Trade debtors	46,750	580,000	(578,417)							48,333
Cash and bank	2,432		578,417		(232,567)			(71,256)	(94,431)	182,595
	618,643									755,486
Trade creditors	35,275			236,750	(232,567)					39,458
Share capital	200,000									200,000
Retained earnings	383,368	580,000				(23,569)	(260,000)	(70,006)	(93,765)	516,028
	618,643									755,486

Progress check 9.5 Describe a typical budget preparation process.

Additional funding may be by way of extended overdraft facilities, loans or additional share capital. The appropriate funding decision may be made and matched with the type of activity for which funding is required. For example, major capital expenditure projects would not normally be funded by an overdraft; the type of longer-term funding generally depends on the nature of the project.

Worked Example 9.10

Magic Moments have planned to sell fluffy puppies between October and December to meet the Christmas demand. They have forecast the following sales at £20 each to be received in cash in the month of sale.

	Oct	Nov	Dec	Total
Units	500	750	1,500	2,750

Magic Moments have contracted to buy fluffy puppies at £12 each. They will have to buy 300 in September. Month-end stocks are planned to be:

October 30% of November sales
November 20% of December sales
December zero

Magic Moments must pay for fluffy puppies in the month following purchase.

We will prepare:

- a schedule of opening stocks, purchases, and closing stocks in units for September to December
- a direct cash flow forecast phased for October to January

and then consider how Magic Moments have funded their activities.

Stocks and purchases:

Units	**Sep**	**Oct**	**Nov**	**Dec**
Opening stock	–	300	225	300
Purchases (derived)	300	425	825	1,200
Sales	–	500	750	1,500
Closing stock	300	225	300	–

Cash flow:

Figures in £

		Oct		**Nov**		**Dec**		**Jan**
Opening balance		–		6,400		16,300		36,400
Cash inflow	(500 × £20)	10,000	(750 × £20)	15,000	(1,500 × £20)	30,000		–
Cash outflow	(300 × £12)	3,600	(425 × £12)	5,100	(825 × £12)	9,900	(1,200 × £12)	14,400
Closing balance		6,400		16,300		36,400		22,000

Magic Moments have funded their business through managing their operating cycle. Effectively, their creditors have financed the business.

Regardless of whether higher or lower activity is expected and budgeted for future periods, it is absolutely essential that the company's bankers are kept fully informed of expectations. Bankers do not like surprises. The corporate graveyard is littered with small businesses in particular who have ignored this basic requirement.

Performance evaluation and control

The many uses of budgeting may be summarised as follows:

- a system for optimal allocation of scarce resources, for example a factory capable of a specific process like plate glass manufacture
- a yardstick for performance, better than past performance, since conditions may have changed
- people participation to provide motivation for improved performance and alignment of individual and corporate goals
- improved communication to enable co-ordination of various parts of the business and so avoid sub-optimisation
- thinking ahead to achieve long-term goals and identify short-term problems
- a system of authorisation and for clear identification of responsibility

- internal audit by evaluating efficiency and effectiveness of departmental performance for prompt remedial action as necessary
- a system of control and management by exception reporting.

Prior to budget preparation, targets may be issued, for example, for:

- sales
- gross margin
- return on investment
- stock days
- debtor collection days
- creditor payment days.

Whilst the responsibility for the budget usually rests with a budget committee, for the budget to achieve its aims, it is important for relevant managers to have full participation in the process and receive communication of the guidelines. Uncertainties, limiting factors and constraints, along with all assumptions, must be made available to all managers with budget responsibility.

It is by ensuring that full communication and participation take place that the most effective use may be made of budgeting as a tool of control. Actual departmental results may then be regularly reported against control budgets that have had full acceptance by the relevant managers and are based on up-to-date and realistic standards of performance. The budget is used as a tool for control of the business by monitoring actual performance and comparing how closely it is in line with the plan. For this purpose the overall budget plan is broken down into the individual elements, representing the areas of responsibility of each of the budget holders, which are called **responsibility centres**.

As part of the budgetary process, in order to co-ordinate an organisation's activities, responsibility is assigned to managers who are accountable for their actions. Each manager therefore is in charge of a responsibility centre. A responsibility centre is a department or organisational function whose performance is the direct responsibility of a specific manager. **Responsibility accounting** is the system used to measure and compare actual results against budget for each centre. Costs are traced to the activities causing them, or to the individuals knowledgeable about why they arose, and who authorised them.

There are four main types of responsibility centre, and within each type, the responsibilities of the manager of each centre are defined in a different way:

- cost centre is a production or service location, function, activity or item of equipment for which costs are accumulated – the manager is accountable for costs only
- **revenue centre** is a centre devoted to raising revenue with no responsibility for costs, for example, a sales centre – the manager is responsible for revenues only (revenue centres are often used in not-for-profit organisations)
- **profit centre** is a part of the business that is accountable for both costs and revenues – the manager is responsible for revenues and costs
- **investment centre** is a profit centre with additional responsibilities for capital investment and possibly for financing, and whose performance is measured by its return on investment – the manager is responsible for investments, revenues and costs.

Responsibility must be matched with control, otherwise a manager is more likely to be demotivated. The manager must be able to influence the costs in question over specific time spans. Problems may also arise when costs may be influenced by more than one manager. Many very large businesses have pursued the policy of devolving spending responsibility down through the organisation. Employees are frequently motivated by being given spending responsibility and fully accepting control, which may be supported by sophisticated IT techniques as hardware and software has become more economic, by, for example, file sharing or remote interrogation of files.

Budget holders can only be responsible for controllable costs or revenues within their areas of responsibility. For example, a production manager may be responsible for ensuring that he/she does not exceed the number of direct labour hours allowed within their area of responsibility for a given level of output. Uncontrollable costs, for example the level of depreciation on the machines and equipment used within the production manager's department, may appear within budget holders' areas of activity but cannot realistically be used to measure performance. Further examples of such costs may be business taxes, or rents on property that may have been the subject of long-term agreements.

In a similar way, a budget holder may be responsible for controlling costs of a department that relate to sales volumes or other variable activities. The costs of that department, the variable costs and possibly the fixed costs, will vary according to the level of activity that takes place. For this reason, the budget for control purposes is flexed in line with actual levels of activity to provide more realistic levels of expected costs against which to measure performance.

Progress check 9.6 **Outline the system of responsibility accounting in its various forms and describe what it aims to achieve.**

For control purposes, therefore, the master budget needs to be:

- phased by reporting period – usually by week, calendar month, or four-week periods
- broken down to provide a separate budget for each responsibility centre
- flexed to show the costs (or revenues) expected as a result of changes in activity levels from those planned within the master budget.

We will look at the mechanics of flexed budgets later in this chapter, together with the method of comparison with actual performance. We shall look at the way in which standards are used for this purpose in budget preparation to enable meaningful exception reporting to be provided for analysis of differences, or variances, to the budget plan.

Motivation and the behavioural aspects of budgeting

We have discussed the importance of participation and communication in the budget process and so it can be seen that key aspects of budgeting are behavioural. One of the main objectives is to influence the behaviour of the people in the organisation so that efficiency is maximised and corporate goals are attained. It is important therefore that the evaluation of performance does not degenerate into a blame culture. It follows then that motivation is an important underlying factor in ensuring that achievable budgets are set and that the managers with the responsibility for each of the elements of the budget have a very good chance of achieving their objectives.

The question of motivation is a very large subject in its own right. It is sufficient for our purposes to outline some of the many motivational factors without going into much further detail. Key motivational factors include:

- pay
- bonuses

- feedback of information
- communication and discussion of control reports
- success, and reward for target achievement
- training in the budget process
- the identification of controllable and uncontrollable costs
- the setting of fair, achievable standards
- the avoidance of short-term wins at the expense of long-term considerations, leading to dysfunctional decision-making
- flexibility in meeting the requirements of the budgeting system
- performance appraisal using budgets flexed to actual activity levels
- inclusion of non-financial performance indicators.

Many writers, including Hopwood, Argyris, Hofstede, McGregor, Becker and Green, have identified the various motivational problems which may be encountered in budgeting. The ways they have suggested these problems can be alleviated, and how motivation can be enhanced, is beyond the scope of this book, and may be followed up with further reading.

Progress check 9.7 **As Supportex Ltd's purchasing manager, Arthur Daley is responsible for negotiating the best deals with suppliers. For planning purposes the budget that was prepared for 2005/06 used current materials' prices and suppliers' credit terms that were negotiated by Arthur. Within a control budget, give examples of the type of performance targets that may have been set for Arthur and how these targets may have been set and monitored.**

Within most companies budgeting is a high-profile, formal process, prepared on either a yearly or half-yearly basis. The budget is prepared within the context of a company's strategic management process, and includes current year performance projections. It should ideally emphasise the strategies and priorities of the company and focus on both financial and non-financial performance.

Information provided from the budget process generally falls into the following main categories:

- sales, relating to
  - customers
  - demand volumes
  - market share
  - price index expectations
- product margins
- purchase price index expectations
- overheads
- headcount
- new product development
- capital investment
- working capital
- cash
- non-financial performance indicators, in areas such as
  - product quality
  - staff development
  - delivery performance
  - customer satisfaction.

Many companies have developed dynamic budgeting models, using packaged IT solutions that may link financial and non-financial performance measures.

The major purposes of budgeting may be identified as:

- compelling planning and forcing management to look ahead by
  - setting targets
  - anticipating problems
  - giving the organisation purpose and direction
- formalising the communication of ideas and plans to all appropriate individuals
- co-ordinating activities of different business units and departments
- establishing a system of control, by
  - allocating responsibility
  - providing a plan against which actual performance may be measured and evaluated
- motivating improved performance of personnel.

It may be seen from many job advertisements how motivation is recognised as being extremely important in providing a vital link with individual performance, which in turn links with achievement of corporate budget targets.

The emphasis given to each budget purpose varies, and is very much dependent upon:

- company policy
- the way in which information is provided/received and by whom
- the negotiating skills of each manager with the company's budget team.

Problems of conflict arise out of actual and perceived fulfilment of each of the purposes of the budget. Each area is a minefield of potential problems of conflict. For example, it was revealed in 2005 that the chief executive of a major UK retailer only wanted to hear good news about the company's position in the marketplace. The managers were afraid to give him bad news.

There are basic problems within the process of setting targets. Organisations can be very unforgiving when targets are not achieved. The budget preparation process has become easier to manage with the introduction of powerful IT resources; but it has also resulted in more accuracy required within the estimates and also within a shorter time-frame.

During the budget-setting process, it is essential that individual budget holders 'buy in' to their budgets to enable subsequent meaningful monitoring and evaluation of actual performance. Their budgets, while representing difficult-to-meet targets, must also be achievable to provide the necessary motivation to reach their goals.

Responsibility must be matched with control. Costs that should be considered uncontrollable may not necessarily be treated as such in evaluating individual performance, resulting in discontent and demotivation. Similar conflicts arise if there is insufficient clarification, or if costs are controlled by more than one person; for example, special transport costs incurred to meet production needs through supplier non-performance – a manufacturing or purchasing responsibility?

Performance against budgeted costs at the operating level should be flexed to reflect current activity. This may not always happen, resulting in unfair appraisal of individual performance and misrepresentation of company performance. It is quite obvious that managers have no influence on the basic 'health' of their company's industrial sector; note the examples of mobile telephones (expanding in the UK) and coal (declining in the UK), seen in the latter part of the twentieth century.

Budgeted levels of training, particularly operator quality training, must be evaluated considering short-term profitability performance objectives and longer-term goals of zero defects. The aim must be of course to achieve both! A well-known UK car manufacturer used the pressure of telephone calls from customers direct to the factory floor, to reduce defects in the finished motor cars, especially those going into the export markets. Another UK manufacturer of motor cars required the engines to be signed for by the appropriate engineer, so that the customer could identify who was responsible for that particular engine.

Many materials may be procured in foreign currency. Should the performance of the purchasing department (responsible for supplier selection) reflect the impact of any resultant currency rate variances? Or should performance be measured using standard exchange rates prevailing at the outset, with, say, the finance department (usually responsible for hedging activities) bearing the cost of currency movements?

Major conflicts arise out of management of the operating cycle, the objective being its minimisation, through reduced debtor and stock days and extended creditor days. The company treasurer must respect this objective, while maintaining good relationships with customers and suppliers, and ensuring no threat to operations. The purchasing and manufacturing directors must ensure low stock days, while maintaining buffer stocks to cover disasters and ensuring that schedules are met, through perhaps the use of JIT processes.

When extremely tight time constraints are imposed for the budget-setting process (which is invariably the case in practice) this may conflict with the degree of accuracy possible in reporting. It also means that top management commitment is critical in providing timely:

- direction
- communication
- feedback

required for the budget process.

The final budget is inevitably a quantitative representation of future plans and targets, and the ways in which each company will reach its short-term goals. Whilst increasing attention is now paid to non-financial measures, the focus remains on performance in financial terms. That being so, traditional cost allocation methods continue to distort the way in which product profitability is reported. This, together with the short-term emphasis of the budgeting activity, therefore provides potentially misleading results. It may also have a demotivating effect on managers involved in both commercial and manufacturing activities, which may result in poor performance.

The problems encountered in the budgeting process may be summarised to include:

- the need for good planning
- difficulties with attitudes including lack of motivation, trust and honesty
- the problems in gathering information
- timeliness of the information
- the amount of detail required
- responsibility for the budget and the key performance areas within the budget.

This outline of some of the problems that may be encountered in the budgeting process may appear to give a negative perspective to its use as an instrument of planning and control. However, the conflicts, by their very nature, ideally serve to highlight the important issues and ensure that budgeting is not just a mechanical exercise carried out once or twice a year but a dynamic part of the strategic planning process contributing to successful management of the business.

> Progress check 9.8 **What are the key aims of budgeting and what sort of problems are encountered that may prevent those aims being met?**

The Homer Simpson approach to budgetary control

The business world lost one of its most colourful characters when the board of directors at Rentokil Initial dumped chairman Sir Clive Thompson after more than 20 years with the nation's leading ratcatcher. Once known as 'Mr 20%' for his ability to grow the group's earnings by that amount every year, the senior independent director Sir Brian McGowan let it be known that Sir Clive had recently become too obsessed with meeting short-term targets and had failed to invest in long-term growth.

Now admittedly John Maynard Keynes said that in the long run we're all dead (though someone else once added,'Yes, but not all at the same time!').

Seventies entrepreneur Jim Slater used to say that a long-term investment was a short-term investment that has gone wrong. And, of course, we've all seen project plans that have 'year four' hockey stick projections.

So an overemphasis on the long-term at the expense of keeping on top of the day-to-day business can be just as fatal – but judging by a recent report, that's not the way businesses appear to work. A US study by two universities and the National Bureau of Economic Research demonstrates quite conclusively that senior executives trade off long-term economic value so as to meet short-term earnings targets to satisfy investors. This finding comes two years after PricewaterhouseCoopers castigated companies, saying that many businesses 'confuse short-term shareholder appeasement with effective cost control'.

The bizarre thing is, many businesses know this is going on – surplus cash gets committed before the year-end on a use-it-or-lose-it approach to budgeting, good projects get deferred till a period that has some slack in it – but no one does anything about it. Homer Simpson put it best: 'Marge,' he exclaimed, 'if you're going to get mad at me every time I do something stupid then I'm going to have to stop doing stupid things.' Maybe we could start by encouraging everyone – from line managers to FDs to institutional investors – to regularly ask, 'What stupid things have been done in order to make the company look really clever?'

Management lessons from Homer Simpson, by Andrew Sawers

Standard costing

Although forecasting and budgeting systems should reflect realistic expectations, it is inevitable that differences will arise between actual and expected performance. It is extremely important that the planning and budgeting process includes control systems that enable accurate feedback of actual performance at the right time to the appropriate people within the organisation. Budgetary control systems should ensure that information is regularly communicated and evaluated by key decision-makers in an organisation, so that appropriate action may taken as necessary. Budgetary control systems must provide:

- fast reporting of performance
- quick response in the implementation of remedial actions
- timely revision of forecasts.

As part of the budgeting process, or at any other time when actual costs need to be compared with planned costs, a basis for comparison must be established. Standard costing provides such a basis through the setting of predetermined cost estimates.

A standard cost is defined as the planned unit cost of the products, components or services produced in a period, and it may be determined using many alternative bases. The main uses of standard costs are:

- measurement of business performance
- control of processes
- valuation of stocks
- establishment of selling prices.

Standards may be defined as benchmark measurements of resource usage, set in defined conditions, and can be set on a number of bases:

- on an *ex ante* (before the event) estimate of expected performance
- on an *ex post* (after the event) estimate of attainable performance
- on a prior level of performance by the same organisation
- on the level of performance achieved by comparable organisations
- on the level of performance required to meet organisational objectives.

Standards may also be set at attainable levels which assume efficient levels of operation, but which include allowances for normal loss, waste and machine downtime, or at ideal levels, which make no allowance for the above losses, and are only attainable under the most favourable conditions.

Budgeted costs and standard costs are sometimes used to mean the same thing but this is not always so. All amounts in a budget are budgeted amounts, but not all budgeted amounts are standard amounts. Budgeted costs are usually used to describe the total planned costs for a number of products. Standard amounts relate to a series of specific processes. For example, one of the processes included in production of a bottle of beer, the sticking of the label on to the bottle, is a process that includes the time and the cost of the label.

A standard product specification is a statement containing a full breakdown of the cost elements, which are included in the standard cost of a product or service. For each cost element (direct labour, direct material, overhead) a standard input quantity and standard unit input cost are shown as well as standard cost per unit of output produced.

A bill of materials is a detailed specification, for each product produced, of the sub-assemblies, components and materials required, distinguishing between those items that are purchased externally and those which are manufactured in-house. Having established the quality and other specifications of materials required, the purchasing department estimates costs based on suppliers' prices, inflation, and the availability of bulk discounts, in order to establish direct material unit costs.

The standard direct labour cost is the planned average cost of direct labour, based on the standard time for the job and standard performance. A standard hour is the amount of work achievable, at standard efficiency levels, in one hour. Work study and analysis of the learning curve are techniques that may be used to assist in determining standard hours. The standard time for a job is the time in which a task should be completed at standard performance.

Standard performance is the level of efficiency, which appropriately trained, motivated and resourced employees can achieve in the long run. Initially, the time taken to produce a specific level of output is longer than the time taken after 'normal' employees have been adequately trained and have gained experience of the process. Time taken to achieve specific levels of output will reduce over time, but the amount of the reductions in time will also reduce over time until almost negligible. This is called the learning curve effect, and when time reductions have virtually ceased the curve becomes horizontal. It is that level, where the long-term time for the particular activity has been established, that may be considered standard performance for the activity. The standard direct labour cost is then calculated by multiplying a standard direct labour hour by a standard hourly rate. Direct labour rates per hour are determined with reference to the type of skills to be used, union agreements, inflation and market rates.

Progress check 9.9 What is meant by the standard cost of a product and what type of specifications and analyses are required prior to being able to calculate a standard cost?

A typical standard cost for a unit of a product may be illustrated in the following worked example.

Worked Example 9.11

Applejack Ltd manufactures drums of high grade apple pie filling that uses two types of material, apples and sugar, and requires one grade of direct labour. The company additionally incurs some variable and fixed production overheads, which are absorbed into the unit costs of the product. The standard cost for a drum (one unit) of the product may be represented as follows, where overheads have been absorbed on the basis of direct labour hours:

		£
Direct materials		
Sugar	1 kilo at £2 per kilo =	2
Apples	2 kilos at £3 per kilo =	6
		8
Direct labour		
1 hour at £8 per hour		8
Variable production overhead		
1 hour at £2 per hour		2
Fixed production overhead		
1 hour at £3 per hour		3
Standard full production cost per drum		21

Advantages of standard costs

There are several advantages in using a standard costing system:

- it is a basis for budget preparation
- it may be used in planning and control
- it can be used to highlight areas of strength and weakness
- it can be used in evaluation of performance by comparing actual costs with standard costs and so assisting in implementation of responsibility accounting
- it should result in the use of the best resources and best methods and so increase efficiency
- it may be used as a basis for stock valuation
- it can be used as a basis for pay incentive schemes
- it can be used for decision-making in its estimation of future costs

- it fits in with management by exception, whereby only significant variances (differences between actual and expected results) are investigated, so making effective use of management time
  - control action is immediate because, for example, as soon as materials are issued from stores into production they can be compared with the standard materials which should be required for actual production
  - transfer prices (the prices at which goods or services are transferred from one process or department to another or from one company in the group to another) may be based on standard rather than actual costs to avoid inefficiencies in the form of excess costs.

Disadvantages of standard costs

There are also a number of disadvantages in using a standard costing system, not least of which is the difficulty in the establishment of the standard fixed overhead rate if standard absorption costing is used as opposed to standard marginal costing.

Standard costing requires a great deal of input data, which can prove time-consuming and expensive, as can the maintenance of the cost database. The amount of detail required, together with a lack of historical detail, and lack of experience and further training requirements all add to this administrative burden.

Standard costing is usually used in organisations where the processes or jobs are repetitive. It is important to set accurate standards or else evaluation of performance will be meaningless. If the standard is weak then the comparison is of little value. However, it is difficult to strike a balance in setting accurate standards so that they both motivate the workforce and achieve the organisation's goals. There may be difficulties in determining which variances against standard are significant, and too narrow a focus on certain variances may exclude other useful information.

If performance evaluation is linked to management by exception, which assumes actual equals standard unless variances contradict that, there may be attempts by managers to cover up negative results. Morale may suffer if reprimands follow poor results and managers are not praised for positive results.

Further adverse impacts on behaviour may occur if managers and supervisors feel that they do not have an overall view and are involved only in limited areas, seeing only a small part of the big picture. Responsibility accounting must also ensure that controllable and non-controllable variances are separately identified.

Operating difficulties and frustration may be encountered through, for example, technological and environmental factors, assessment of standards of performance, departmental interdependence, variances reported at the wrong levels, the timing of revisions to standards, over-reaction to results, and the constant need to estimate. It is important to remember that there is a great deal of uncertainty in setting standards costs. This can arise due to inflation, economic and political factors. Standards therefore need to be continually updated and revised – once a year is usually not often enough.

Progress check 9.10 **To what extent do the advantages of the use of standard costing outweigh its disadvantages?**

Types of standard

In addition to current costs there are three types of standard that may be used as the basis for a standard costing system. The use of current standards by definition relates to current circumstances with regard to performance levels, wastage and inefficiencies. It may be observed from the following explanations that 'standard costing' can be seen to be flexible and dynamic. It should not be seen as a straitjacket.

Basic standards are those that remain unchanged since the previous period and probably many previous periods. They may be used for comparison but are likely to be out of date and irrelevant. As business circumstances may change dramatically in the marketplace, so the original basic standard will not reflect the current situation.

Ideal standards are the results expected from perfect performance under perfect conditions. They assume no wastage, or inefficiencies. However, although they may be aimed for they will be impossible to achieve and therefore provide a poor motivational tool.

Attainable standards are the results expected under normal operating conditions, having some allowances for wastage and a degree of inefficiency. Attainable standards should be set to be difficult but not impossible to achieve; they may therefore provide the most challenging targets and give the greatest motivation for achievement.

Progress check 9.11 **What are the different types of standard that may be used as the basis for standard costing and which one may be the most appropriate?**

Flexed budgets

Control budgets need to be revised in line with actual levels of activity to provide more realistic levels of expected costs against which to measure performance. Such a revised budget is called a flexed budget which shows the costs (and revenues) expected as a result of changes in activity levels from those planned within the master budget.

The standards chosen for use in the budget preparation are also used in the revised flexed budget to provide a method of comparison with actual performance. This method allows comparison of costs on a like-for-like basis and so enables meaningful exception reporting of the analysis of variances.

This system of management control uses a closed-loop system. This is a system which allows corrective action using a feedforward or a feedback basis. A feedback control system is shown in Fig. 9.4 and provides the measurement of differences between planned outputs and actual outputs and the modification of subsequent actions or plans to achieve future required results. Figure 9.5 illustrates a feedforward control system which forecasts differences between actual and planned outcomes and implements action before the event to avoid such differences.

Normally, fixed overheads by definition are fixed over the short term regardless of changes in the level of activity, for example units sold, units produced, number of invoices. Equally, direct labour and direct materials costs may be assumed to vary directly with sales. In practice, there is usually a wide band of activity over which direct labour costs may not vary.

Care should be taken in using the above assumptions but we may consider that they hold true for the purpose of illustration of flexed budgets and variance analysis. The variance analysis can be

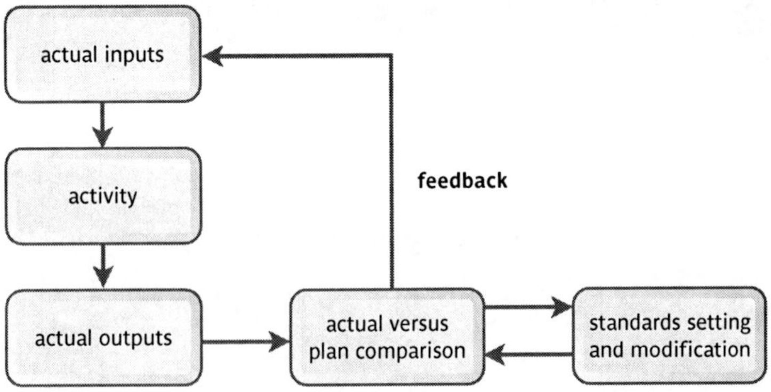

Figure 9.4 Feedback control system

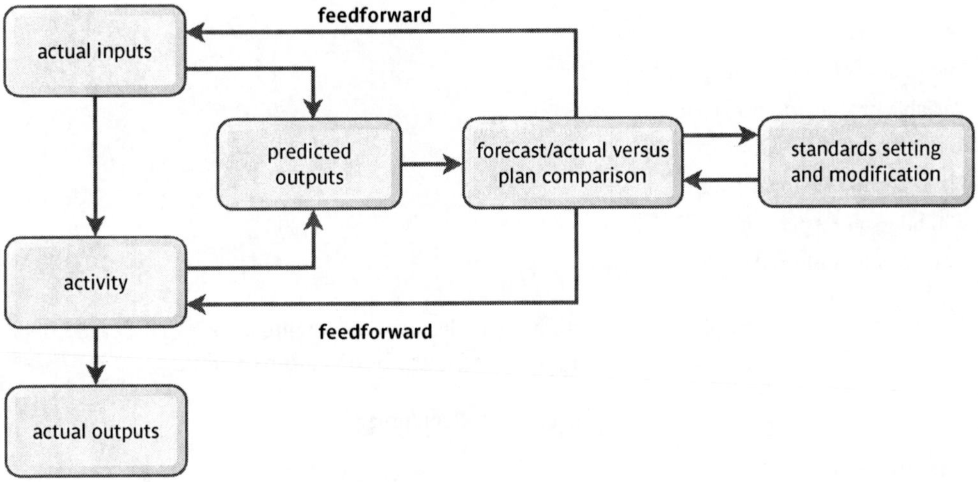

Figure 9.5 Feedforward control system

routine but decisions resulting from the interpretation can be far-reaching. Consider how, following the public's reaction to buying products originating from genetically modified foodstuffs (soya or maize), many UK supermarkets publicly announced they would cease stocking them.

Progress check 9.12 **Describe the way in which flexed budgets are used in a management control system.**

The worked example that follows shows how a straight comparison of actual with budgeted performance may be refined through the preparation of a revised budget flexed in line with the actual activity level.

Worked Example 9.12

Applejack Ltd planned to produce 600 drums of pie filling during September. The budget for September was prepared using the standard costs shown in Worked Example 9.11. Fixed overheads are budgeted at £1,800 for September and absorbed on the basis of direct labour hours.

Budget costs for September

Production		**600 units**
		£
Direct materials		
Sugar	600 kilos at £2 per kilo =	1,200
Apples	1,200 kilos at £3 per kilo =	3,600
		4,800
Direct labour		
600 hours at £8 per hour		4,800
Variable production overhead		
600 hours at £2 per hour		1,200
Fixed production overhead		
600 hours at £3 per hour		1,800
Total production cost		12,600

600 drums of filling were planned to be produced in the month at a manufacturing cost of £12,600.

At the end of September the actual output turned out to be 650 drums as follows:

Actual costs for September

Production		**650 units**
		£
Direct materials		
Sugar	610 kilos at £2.10 per kilo =	1,281
Apples	1,210 kilos at £3.20 per kilo =	3,872
		5,153
Direct labour		
500 hours at £9 per hour		4,500
Variable production overhead		
500 hours at £1.50 per hour		750
Fixed production overhead		
500 hours at £3.60 per hour		1,800
Total production cost		12,203

650 drums of filling were actually produced in the month at a manufacturing cost of £12,203.

The above data can be used to prepare a flexed budget for September as the basis for subsequent variance analysis.

A flexed budget for Applejack Ltd must be prepared for 650 drums output. The flexed budget will use the standard costs shown in Worked Example 9.11 to show what the costs would have been if the budget had been based on 650 drums instead of 600 drums.

Flexed budget costs for September

Production		**650 units**
		£
Direct materials		
Sugar	650 kilos at £2 per kilo =	1,300
Apples	1,300 kilos at £3 per kilo =	3,900
		5,200
Direct labour		
650 hours at £8 per hour		5,200
Variable production overhead		
650 hours at £2 per hour		1,300
Fixed production overhead		
650 hours at £3 per hour		1,950
Total production cost		13,650

If 650 drums of filling had been planned to be produced in the month the standard manufacturing cost would be £13,650.

If we compare the total manufacturing cost from the flexed budget shown in Worked Example 9.12 with the total actual cost for the month, the performance looks even better than the comparison with the total budgeted cost; the total cost is £1,447 [£13,650 – £12,203] less than expected at that level of output. However, whilst the comparison of total cost is favourable, this does not tell us anything about individual performance within each element of the budget; the impacts of the differences between the actual and the flexed budget with regard to:

- amounts of materials used
- materials prices
- direct labour hours
- direct labour rates
- overheads.

The analysis of the detailed variances in respect of each cost can identify each element making up the cost, the unit costs and the unit quantities, and tell us something about whether the individual cost performances were good or bad. Between 2000 and 2003 the UK saw an amazing upward demand for mobile telephones and a decline in the demand for university places (as a percentage of available places). Both sectors would have carried out an 'analysis of the detailed variances' during that year to assist in the determination of conclusions regarding cost performance.

Progress check 9.13 **In what ways does a flexed budget provide a more realistic measure of actual performance than comparison with the original budget?**

Variance analysis

A variance is the difference between a planned, budgeted or standard cost and the actual cost incurred. The same comparisons may be made for revenues. Variance analysis is the evaluation of performance by means of variances, whose timely reporting should maximise the opportunity for managerial action. These variances will be either favourable variances (F) or adverse variances (A). Neither should occur if the standard is correct and actual performance is as expected. A favourable variance is not necessarily good – it may be due to a weak standard. Management by exception assumes that actual performance will be the same as the standard unless variances contradict this.

Detailed variances can identify each difference within the elements making up cost or revenue by looking at unit prices and unit quantities. Variances may be due to:

- measurement errors
- use of standards that are out of date
- operations that are out of control
- random factors.

When variances occur it must then be considered as to whether these variances should be investigated or not. The variances may not be material, or it may not be cost effective to carry out such an investigation.

Calculation of variances

Let's look at the individual variances that occurred for the month of September in Applejack's manufacture of apple pie filling. We will analyse each of the variances and provide a detailed, line-by-line comparison of actual versus budget performance of each of the items that comprise the total actual to budget favourable variance of £397. The simplest way to start to examine the differences is to present the original budget, flexed budget and actual results in three columns for further analysis.

Worked Example 9.13

We saw from Worked Example 9.11 that on the face of it Applejack's performance for September was very good – higher than budget output (650 versus 600 units) at lower than budget costs (£12,203 versus £12,600).

Is it a good performance? If it is, how much of a good performance is it?

To determine how good Applejack's performance was for September we need to provide an analysis of variances to explain the favourable total cost variance of £397 against budget (£12,600 – £12,203).

Applejack Ltd's budget, actual and flexed budget (from Worked Example 9.12) for the production of apple pie filling for the month of September may be summarised as follows:

		Budget		Flexed		Actual	Difference Actual–Flexed
Units		600		650		650	–
		£		£		£	£
Direct materials							
Sugar	(600 × £2)	1,200	(650 × £2)	1,300	(610 × £2.10)	1,281	19
Apples	(1,200 × £3)	3,600	(1,300 × £3)	3,900	(1,210 × £3.20)	3,872	28
		4,800		5,200		5,153	47
Direct labour							
	(600 × £8)	4,800	(650 × £8)	5,200	(500 × £9)	4,500	700
Variable production overhead							
	(600 × £2)	1,200	(650 × £2)	1,300	(500 × £1.50)	750	550
Fixed production overhead							
	(600 × £3)	1,800	(650 × £3)	1,950	(500 × £3.60)	1,800	150
Total cost		12,600		13,650		12,203	1,447

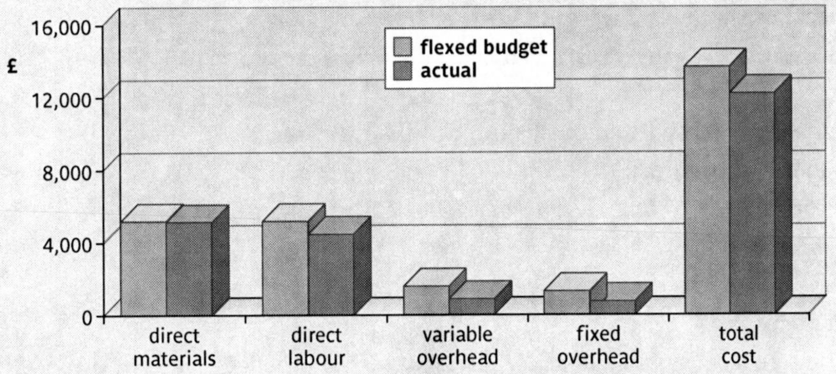

Figure 9.6 Applejack Ltd's actual and flexed budget costs for September

The above graphical representation of each of the cost elements and the total of actual costs compared with the flexed budget for output of 650 units gives a broad picture of Applejack Ltd's good performance.

Let's look at the detailed variances.

We have prepared a flexed budget, which in effect gives us a new starting point against which to compare actual performance more realistically. We have therefore already built in a variance, arising out of the change in volume from 600 drums to 650 drums. At a unit cost of £21 the total of this difference, or variance, is an adverse volume variance of £1,050 (50 × £21).

Volume:

Variance 650 drums less 600 drums at a total unit cost of £21 per drum — £1,050A

We also need to consider the individual cost element variances, between actual costs and the flexed budget costs.

Materials:	
Sugar usage was 40 kilos less than it should have been at a standard cost of £2 per kilo	£80F
The sugar price was 10p more per kilo than standard for the 610 kilos used	£61A
Apples usage was 90 kilos less than it should have been at a standard cost of £3 per kilo	£270F
The apple price was 20p more per kilo than standard for the 1,210 kilos used	£242A
Total materials variance actual versus flexed budget	£47F
Direct labour:	
Hours worked were 150 hours less than they should have been at a standard rate of £8 per hour	£1,200F
The labour rate was £1 more per hour than standard for the 500 hours worked	£500A
Total direct labour variance actual versus flexed budget	£700F
Variable production overhead:	
Hours worked were 150 hours less than they should have been at a standard rate of £2 per hour	£300F
The overhead rate was 50p less per hour than standard for the 500 hours worked	£250F
Total variable production overhead variance actual versus flexed budget	£550F
Fixed production overhead:	
Hours worked were 150 hours less than they should have been at a standard rate of £3 per hour	£450F
Hours worked were 100 less (at £3 per hour) than required to absorb total fixed costs	£300A
Total fixed production overhead variance actual versus flexed budget	£150F
Total variances [£1,050A + £47F + £700F + £550F + £150F] =	£397F
Budget total costs	£12,600
Actual total costs	£12,203
Total variance (favourable)	£397

Several variances are calculated to quantify the difference in activity or volume. Most of the other variances show the impact of:

- differences in prices
  - price variances
  - rate variances
  - expenditure variances

and

- differences in quantities
  - usage variances
  - efficiency variances

between those prices and quantities actually incurred and those which should have been expected at the actual level, or volume of output. The exception to this is the fixed production overhead variance, which is comprised of a fixed production overhead expenditure variance (budget minus actual cost) and a fixed production overhead volume variance.

The total fixed production variance is the difference between:

- the actual cost

and

- the cost shown in the flexed budget.

The two components of the total fixed production volume variance are:

- the fixed production overhead efficiency variance
  - a 'normal' one that calculates the difference between actual and flexed hours at the standard overhead absorption rate
- the fixed production overhead capacity variance
  - calculates the difference between actual and budgeted hours at the standard overhead absorption rate
  - measures the amount by which overheads have been under- or over-absorbed (under-absorbed in the Applejack example), caused by the actual hours worked differing from the hours originally budgeted to be worked.

In the Applejack worked example we have used the absorption costing approach to calculate unit standard costs for the product and therefore in the calculation of variances. Marginal costing may also be used to calculate unit standard costs for the product and calculation of variances. Some of the differences between the variances that are calculated are as one would expect, using contribution instead of profit. Another difference is in respect of production fixed costs, which of course are not absorbed into unit marginal product costs. The fixed production overhead variance using marginal costing is simply the difference between the actual and the budgeted cost.

Progress check 9.14 What does variance analysis tell us about actual performance that a direct analysis of differences to budget cannot tell us?

The hierarchy of variances in Figs. 9.7 and 9.8 show variances using marginal costing principles and variances using absorption costing principles respectively.

A non-accountant will not usually be called upon to calculate variances. However, as a manager, it is important to appreciate clearly the way in which variances are calculated, to be better able to:

- consider their materiality
- investigate the reasons for their occurrence if necessary
- take the appropriate corrective actions.

Explanation of variances is usually part of the day-to-day responsibilities of most budget holding managers. Unless there is knowledge of exactly what a variance represents it is virtually impossible to begin to determine the reason why such a variance occurred. Figures 9.9 and 9.12 include the

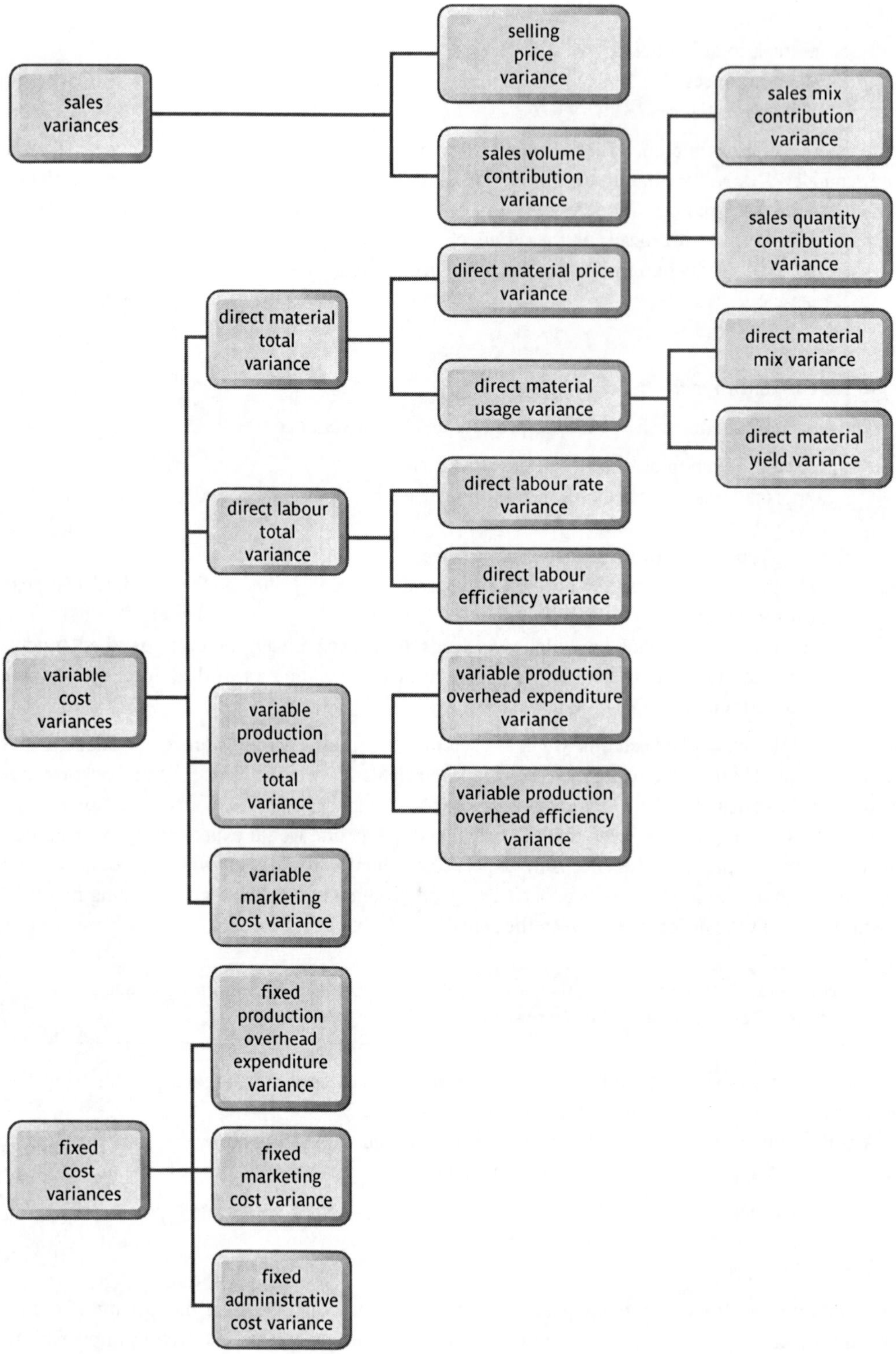

Figure 9.7 Chart of variances using marginal costing principles

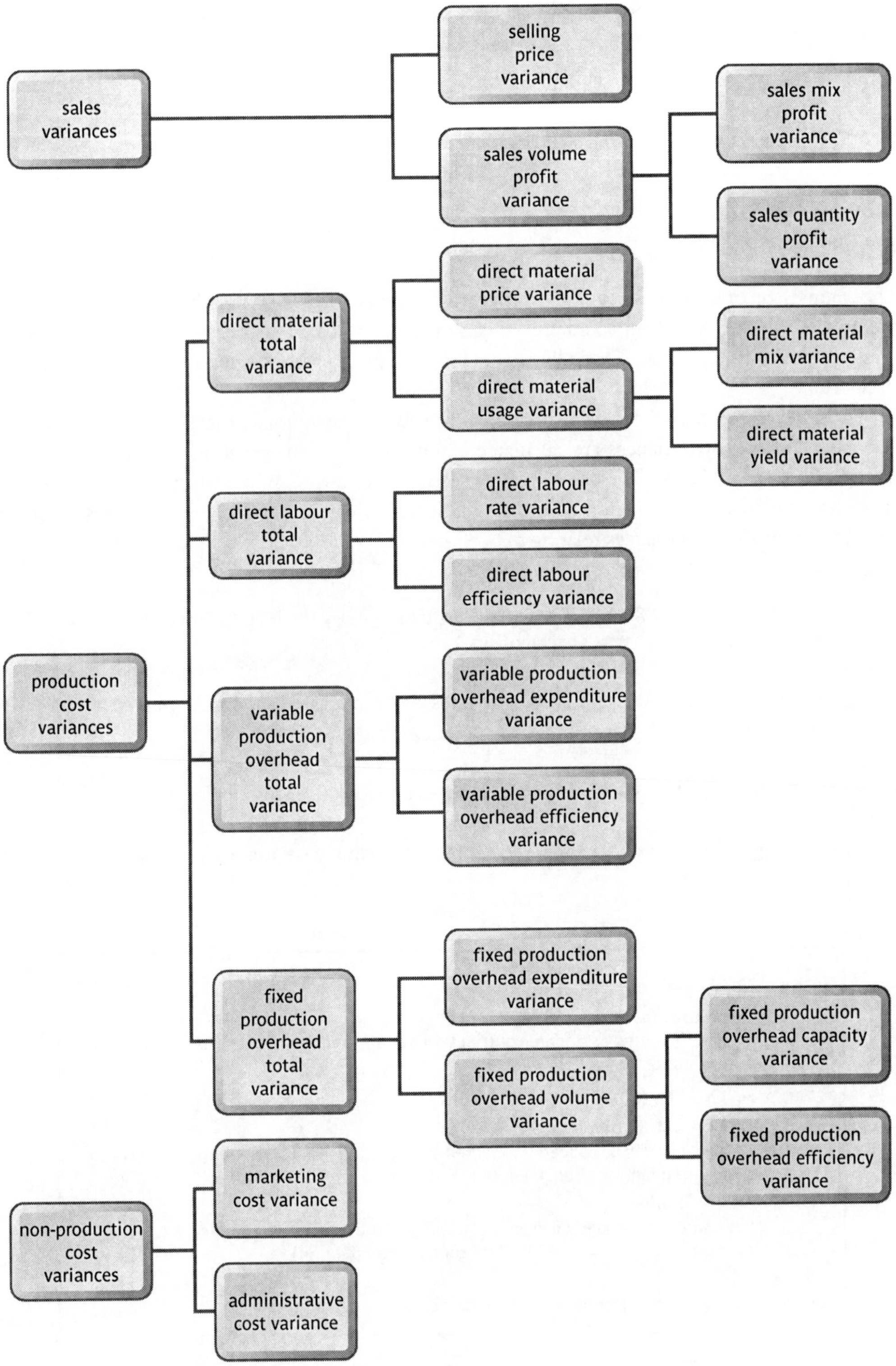

Figure 9.8 Chart of variances using absorption costing principles

detailed formulae for the calculation of variances, on a marginal costing basis. Figures 9.10 and 9.11 include variances that apply to both absorption and marginal costing. Figures 9.13 and 9.14 include the additional variances in respect of absorption costing.

Progress check 9.15 What are the main areas of cost considered in variance analysis?

Operating statements

The comparison of actual costs and revenues with budget is normally regularly reported to management (daily, weekly or monthly) and presented in what is called an operating statement. The operating statement is usually supported by a report explaining the reasons why specific variances have occurred.

Worked Examples 9.15 to 9.21 provide a comprehensive illustration of the preparation of a flexed budget and show how variances are calculated and presented in an operating statement. They also include explanations of possible reasons why the variances occurred. While not including all possible variances that may be considered according to those shown in Figs. 9.7 to 9.14, these worked examples show the key variances relating to:

- sales
  note how the marketing department of a company can use the results, for example, UK supermarkets' consumer products special offers
- labour
  note, for example, how the human resources department of a company may be involved in further investigation if the variances are material
- materials
  note, for example, how company buyers may need to look for new sources
- overheads
  many companies move closer to their customers or to low-cost premises, for example, in order to reduce overheads.

Sales contribution variances

Sales volume contribution
(budgeted sales quantity × standard contribution per unit) – (actual sales quantity × standard contribution per unit)

Which can be split into:

Sales quantity contribution
(budgeted sales quantity × budgeted weighted average standard contribution per unit) – (total actual sales quantity × budgeted weighted average standard contribution per unit)

Sales mix contribution
(actual sales quantity × budgeted weighted average standard contribution per unit) – (actual sales quantity × individual standard contribution per unit)

Sales price
(actual sales quantity × standard selling price per unit) – actual sales revenue

Figure 9.9 Sales variances on a marginal costing basis

Materials variances

Direct material price
(actual quantity of material purchased × standard price) – actual cost of material purchased

Direct material usage
(standard quantity for actual production × standard material cost per unit) – (actual material quantity used × standard cost per unit)

Which can be split into:

Direct material mix
(actual input quantity – standard material input quantity for the output produced) × (standard weighted average cost per input unit – standard cost per input unit)

Direct material yield
(actual material input quantity – standard material input quantity for the output produced) × standard weighted average cost per unit of material input
Or
(actual material input quantity × standard cost per unit) – (total actual material input in standard proportions × standard cost per unit)

Figure 9.10 Direct materials variances

Labour variances

Direct labour rate
(actual hours paid × standard direct labour rate per hour) – (actual hours paid × actual direct labour rate per hour)

Direct labour efficiency
(actual production in standard hours × standard direct labour rate per hour) – (actual direct labour hours worked × standard direct labour rate per hour)

Figure 9.11 Direct labour variances

Overhead variances

Variable production overhead expenditure
actual cost incurred – (actual hours worked × standard variable production overhead absorption rate per hour)

Variable production overhead efficiency
(actual hours worked × standard variable production overhead absorption rate per hour) – (actual production in standard hours × standard variable production overhead absorption rate per hour)

Fixed production overhead expenditure
budgeted fixed production overhead – actual fixed production overhead

Figure 9.12 Overheads variances on a marginal costing basis

Sales profit variances

Sales volume profit
(budgeted sales quantity × standard profit per unit) – (actual sales quantity × standard profit per unit)

Which can be split into:

Sales quantity profit
(budgeted sales quantity × budgeted weighted average standard profit per unit) – (total actual sales quantity × budgeted weighted average standard profit per unit)

Sales mix profit
(actual sales quantity × budgeted weighted average standard profit per unit) – (actual sales quantity × individual standard profit per unit)

Figure 9.13 Sales variances on an absorption costing basis

Overheads variances

Fixed production overhead volume
(actual production in standard hours × standard fixed production overhead absorption rate per hour) – budgeted fixed production overhead

Which can be split into:

Fixed production overhead efficiency
(actual hours worked × standard fixed production overhead absorption rate per hour) – (actual production in standard hours × standard fixed production overhead absorption rate per hour)

Fixed production overhead capacity
(actual hours worked × standard fixed production overhead absorption rate per hour) – (budgeted hours to be worked × standard fixed production overhead absorption rate per hour)

Figure 9.14 Overheads variances on an absorption costing basis

Worked Example 9.14

Dymocks Ltd manufactures large ornamental garden pots, called the El Greco, the standards for which are as follows:

Direct labour	1 hour at £4 per hour
Direct materials	2 kgs at £7.50 per kg
Variable overheads	£3 per direct labour hour
Selling price	£50 per unit

Fixed overheads are budgeted at £4,000 and absorbed on a direct labour hours basis. Dymocks have budgeted to produce and sell 800 Grecos in the month of July.

Using standard costs, the budget for El Grecos for July was:

		£
Sales	800 × £50 per unit	40,000
Direct labour	800 × 1 hour × £4 per hour per unit	(3,200)
Direct materials	800 × 2 kg × £7.50 per kg per unit	(12,000)
Variable overheads	800 × 1 hour × £3 per direct labour hour	(2,400)
Fixed overheads	800 × 1 hour × £5 per direct labour hour	(4,000)
Budgeted profit for July		18,400

The standard profit per unit used in the budget $= \dfrac{£18{,}400}{800 \text{ units}} = £23$ per unit

Actual results for July were:		£
Sales	900 × £48	43,200
Direct labour	850 hours × £3.50 per hour	(2,975)
Direct materials	1,400 kgs × £8 per kg	(11,200)
Variable overheads	actual	(2,750)
Fixed overheads	actual	(5,000)
Actual profit for July		21,275

The flexed budget for July, prepared from this data, can be used to give a summary that compares the actual results for July with the budget and the flexed budget.

The flexed budget for July for sales of 900 units is:

		£
Sales	900 × £50 per unit	45,000
Direct labour	900 × 1 hour × £4 per hour per unit	(3,600)
Direct materials	900 × 2 kg × £7.50 per kg per unit	(13,500)
Variable overheads	900 × 1 hour × £3 per direct labour hour	(2,700)
Fixed overheads	900 × 1 hour × £5 per direct labour hour	(4,500)
Flexed budgeted profit for July		20,700

The July results for Dymocks Ltd may be summarised as follows:

	£ **Budget**	£ **Actual**	£ **Flexed**	£ **Difference** **Actual – Flexed**
Sales	40,000	43,200	45,000	(1,800)
Direct labour	(3,200)	(2,975)	(3,600)	625
Direct materials	(12,000)	(11,200)	(13,500)	2,300
Variable overheads	(2,400)	(2,750)	(2,700)	(50)
Fixed overheads	(4,000)	(5,000)	(4,500)	(500)
Profit	18,400	21,275	20,700	575

The variance or the difference between the budget and the flexed budget of £2,300(F) (£20,700 – £18,400) is only due to volume. The profit variance for sales volume is the only one that will need to be considered between the flexed budget and the budget. All other variances are between actual results and the flexed budget.

Worked Example 9.15

Using the summary of results for Dymocks Ltd for July from Worked Example 9.14 we can prepare an analysis of sales variances, and provide an explanation of why these variances might have occurred.

Sales variances

Sales volume profit

(budgeted sales quantity × standard profit per unit) – (actual sales quantity × standard profit per unit)

measuring the effect of changing sales volumes on profit

(800 × £23) – (900 × £23) = £2,300 (F) (the profit variance of £2,300 noted in Worked Example 9.14)

Sales price

(actual sales quantity × standard selling price per unit) – actual sales revenue

measuring the effect of selling prices different to those budgeted

(900 × £50) – £43,200 = £1,800 (A) (see Worked Example 9.14 summary)

Possible reasons for the above variances:

- selling prices are likely to affect sales volumes
- external factors such as economic recession, changes in demand, or increased competition
- prices not achievable perhaps due to lack of market research or bad planning.

Worked Example 9.16

Using the summary of results for Dymocks Ltd for July from Worked Example 9.14 we can prepare an analysis of materials variances, and provide an explanation of why these variances might have occurred.

Materials variances

Direct material price

(actual quantity of material purchased × standard price) – actual cost of material purchased

(1,400 × £7.50) – £11,200 = £700 (A)

Direct material usage

(standard quantity for actual production × standard material cost per unit) – (actual material quantity used × standard cost per unit)

(1,800 × £7.50) – (1,400 × £7.50) = £3,000 (F)

Total materials variances £2,300 (F) (see Worked Example 9.14 summary)

Possible reasons for the above variances:

- market conditions have changed
- foreign currency exchange rates may have changed (if applicable)
- supplier discounts have been reduced
- changes in the quality levels of materials used
- there may be a supplier invoicing error
- stock control has improved
- the skills of the labour force have changed
- production methods have changed.

Note that materials price variances occur at two points: standard price compared to receipt of goods price; receipt of goods price compared to invoiced price.

Worked Example 9.17

Using the summary of results for Dymocks Ltd for July from Worked Example 9.14 we can prepare an analysis of direct labour variances, and provide an explanation of why these variances might have occurred.

Direct labour variances

Direct labour rate

(actual hours paid × standard direct labour rate per hour) – (actual hours paid × actual direct labour rate per hour)

(850 × £4) – (850 × £3.50) = £425 (F)

Direct labour efficiency

(actual production in standard hours × standard direct labour rate per hour) – (actual direct labour hours worked × standard direct labour rate per hour)

(900 × £4) – (850 × £4) = £200 (F)

Total direct labour variances £625 (F) (see Worked Example 9.14 summary)

Possible reasons for the above variances:

- wage rate negotiations
- changes in the skills of the labour force
- better than expected impact of the effect of the learning curve
- impact of machinery efficiency, levels of maintenance, or use of different materials, with changed levels of quality.

Worked Example 9.18

Using the summary of results for Dymocks Ltd for July from Worked Example 9.14 we can prepare an analysis of variable overhead variances, and provide an explanation of why these variances might have occurred.

Variable overhead variances

Variable production overhead expenditure

actual cost incurred – (actual hours worked × standard variable production overhead absorption rate per hour)

£2,750 – (850 × £3.50) = £225 (A)

Variable production overhead efficiency

(actual hours worked × standard variable production overhead absorption rate per hour) – (actual production in standard hours × standard variable production overhead absorption rate per hour)

(850 × £3.50) – (900 × £3.50) = £175 (F)

Total variable overhead variances £50 (A) (see Worked Example 9.14 summary)

Possible reasons for the above variances may be:

- related to the direct labour variances
- due to a number of individual variances within total variable overheads
- changes in the overhead rate with different levels of activity.

Worked Example 9.19

Using the summary of results for Dymocks Ltd for July from Worked Example 9.14 we can prepare an analysis of fixed overhead variances, and provide an explanation of why these variances might have occurred.

Fixed overhead variances

Fixed production overhead expenditure

budgeted fixed production overhead – actual fixed production overhead

£4,000 – £5,000 = £1,000 (A)

Fixed production overhead volume

(actual production in standard hours × standard fixed production overhead absorption rate per hour) – budgeted fixed production overhead

(900 × £5) – £4,000 = £500 (F)

Total fixed overhead variances £500 (A) (see Worked Example 9.14 summary)

Possible reasons for the above variances:

- due to a number of individual variances within total fixed overheads.

Progress check 9.16 What are the main differences between variance analysis using marginal costing and variance analysis using absorption costing?

Worked Example 9.20

Using the variances calculated for Dymocks Ltd for July we can prepare an operating statement that reconciles the actual profit for July to the budgeted profit for July.

The actual profit for July may be reconciled with the budgeted profit by summarising the variances:

Operating statement

	£	£	£
Budget profit (Worked Example 9.14)			18,400
Sales variances			
Sales volume (Worked Example 9.15)	2,300 (F)		
Sales price (Worked Example 9.15)	1,800 (A)	500 (F)	
Direct materials variances			
Materials price (Worked Example 9.16)	700 (A)		
Materials usage (Worked Example 9.16)	3,000 (F)	2,300 (F)	
Direct labour variances			
Labour rate (Worked Example 9.17)	425 (F)		
Labour efficiency (Worked Example 9.17)	200 (F)	625 (F)	
Variable overheads variances			
Expenditure (Worked Example 9.18)	225 (A)		
Efficiency (Worked Example 9.18)	175 (F)	50 (A)	
Fixed overheads variances			
Expenditure (Worked Example 9.19)	1,000 (A)		
Volume (Worked Example 9.19)	500 (F)	500 (A)	
			2,875 (F)
Actual profit (Worked Example 9.14)			21,275

The reasons for variances

Although not an exhaustive list of possible causes, the following provides the reasons for most of the common variances encountered in most manufacturing and service businesses:

- direct material price: skills of purchasing department, quality of materials, price inflation, supplier discounts, foreign currency exchange rate fluctuations, invoicing errors

- direct material usage: quality of materials, labour efficiency, pilfering, stock control, quality control
- direct labour rate: use of higher or lower skilled labour than planned, wage inflation, or union agreement
- direct labour efficiency: use of higher or lower skilled labour than planned, quality of materials, efficiency of plant and machinery, better or worse than expected learning curve performance, inaccurate time allocation – employees have to learn a new process and then repeat that process for real many times, within times established during the learning curve evaluation
- overhead expenditure: inflation, wastage, resource usage savings, changes in services – many companies are outsourcing basic in-house services, for example accounting
- overhead efficiency: labour efficiency, efficiency of plant and machinery, technological changes
- overhead capacity: under- or over-utilisation of plant capacity, idle time.

Progress check 9.17 **Most of the reasons for materials variances may be identified so that the appropriate corrective actions can be taken. What are the types of action that may be taken?**

Without exploring the detail, we have also already mentioned materials mix and yield variances that show the effects on costs of changing the mix of materials input, and of materials input yielding either more or less output than expected.

Summary of key points

- A budget is a plan and budgeting is one part of the strategic planning process, which is concerned with planning and control.
- Planning budgets are management's belief of what the business's costs and revenues will be over a specified future time period, the budget period.
- Control budgets are used for management motivational purposes and are used in this way to influence improved departmental performance.
- Forecasts are not plans but predictions of the future, which are required as an important prerequisite to the budget process.
- Prior to budget preparation, in addition to forecasting, decisions must be made and policies formulated regarding stock days and purchasing, debtor and creditor days, staff costs, capital expenditure, and standard costs.
- The master profit and loss budget is prepared from each of the elements of the operating budget: sales; production; distribution and administration; and the financial budget.
- The master budget is comprised of the profit and loss budget, cash budget, and balance sheet budget.
- Risk assessment and risk analysis should be applied to the master budget, and it must be closely reviewed in terms of additional funding requirements.
- As part of the control function of the budget, the system of responsibility accounting is used to measure actual results against budget for each of the various types of responsibility centre.
- Control budgets are usually flexed to reflect actual activity levels, and performance against budget provided from exception reporting is evaluated so that corrective actions may be implemented as appropriate.

- The preparation of budgets for planning and control purposes needs the involvement of people to provide realistic plans and the motivation for performance targets to be achieved.
- There are usually many conflicts and problems associated with the budget preparation process in most organisations, the majority of which are concerned with the 'softer' human resources issues of managers' behaviour.
- Standard costing can be used to calculate costs of units or processes that may be used in budgeted costs.
- Not all budgeted amounts are standard amounts, as the latter will be precise by nature, unlike budgeted amounts.
- Standard costing provides the basis for performance evaluation and control from comparison of actual performance against budget through the setting of predetermined cost estimates.
- A flexed budget reflects the costs or revenues expected as a result of changes in activity levels from those planned in the master budget.
- A flexed budget provides a more realistic basis for comparison of actual performance.
- Flexed budgets enable comparison of actual costs and revenues on a like-for-like basis through the calculation of differences, or variances.
- Variances are the difference between planned, budgeted or standard costs (or revenues) and actual costs incurred and may be summarised in an operating statement to reconcile budget with actual performance.
- Variances between actual and standard performance may be investigated to explain the reasons for the differences through preparation of a complete analysis of all variances, or alternatively through the use of exception reporting that highlights only significant variances.

Questions

Q9.1 (i) Why do businesses need to prepare budgets?
(ii) What are they used for?

Q9.2 If there are differences between budgets prepared for planning purposes and budgets prepared for control purposes, what are these differences?

Q9.3 Describe and illustrate the differences between qualitative and quantitative forecasting techniques.

Q9.4 (i) Give some examples of the forecasts that are required to be able to prepare the complete master budget.
(ii) What are the most suitable techniques for each of these forecasts?

Q9.5 Draw a flow diagram to illustrate the budget preparation process.

Q9.6 Explain and illustrate the way in which a business may approach the strategic management process.

Q9.7 (i) What are the internal and external sources of funding for a business?
(ii) How may a business use the budget process to assess its future funding requirements?

Q9.8 How does the assignment of individual budget responsibility contribute to improved organisational performance?

Q9.9 Discuss the ways in which a budget may be used to evaluate performance.

Q9.10 Outline some of the major problems that may be encountered in budgeting.

Q9.11 How is standard costing used in the preparation of budgets?

Q9.12 (i) What are the benefits of using standard costing?
(ii) What type of standard may best ensure that those benefits are achieved?
(iii) How are standards used to achieve those benefits?

Q9.13 Describe and illustrate the technique of flexible budgeting.

Q9.14 (i) What is management by exception?
(ii) How is variance analysis used to support this technique?

Q9.15 (i) Outline the main variances that may be reported using the bases of absorption costing and marginal costing.
(ii) What do these variances tell us about direct labour, direct materials, and overhead costs?

Q9.16 Describe the main reasons why usage and efficiency variances may occur and illustrate these with some examples.

Discussion points

D9.1 'Once I know what the forecast sales are for next year I can tell you how much profit we will make within five minutes, so there's no need for this annual time-wasting and costly budgeting ritual.' Discuss.

D9.2 'The area of budgeting is a minefield of potential problems of conflict.' How can these problems be usefully used as a learning experience to ultimately improve the performance of the business?

D9.3 You are the general manager of a newly formed subsidiary company. The group managing director has declared that he has targeted your company to make a profit of £250,000 in its first year. What assumptions, decisions and policies are concerned with preparing a budget by working backwards from a starting point of budgeted profit?

D9.4 'We set the budget once a year and then compare the actual profit after the end of the financial year. If actual profit is below budget, then everyone needs to make more effort to ensure this doesn't happen the following year.' Discuss.

D9.5 'The standard-setting process is sometimes seen as management's way of establishing targets that demand better and better manufacturing performance.' To what extent do you think that is true, and if it is true how effectively do you think the standard-setting process achieves that objective?

D9.6 To what extent do you think that the techniques of flexed budgets and variance analysis complicate the otherwise simple process of comparing the various areas of actual performance against budget?

D9.7 'Traditional variance analysis tends to focus on cutting costs and increasing output in a way that is detrimental to product and service quality, and the longer-term viability of the business.' Discuss.

Exercises

Solutions are provided in Appendix 3 to all exercise numbers highlighted in colour.

Level I

E9.1 *Time allowed – 15 minutes*

Earextensions plc set up a new business to assemble mobile phones from kits. They planned to make and sell one model only and expected to sell 441,200 units between January and June in their first year of trading. February, March, and April volumes were each expected to be 20% above the preceding month and May, June, and July volumes were expected to be the same as April. The selling price was £50 each.

Cost prices for the parts used in making a phone were as follows:

Electronic assembly	Keypad	Case
£23.30	£1	£2

Operators and assemblers were employed to make the phones with the following hourly rates and standard times used in production:

	Assemblers	Operators
Hourly rate	£10	£8
Standard minutes	3	1.5

Production overheads were forecast at £4.1m, which was incurred on an equal monthly basis and absorbed into product costs on the basis of direct labour hours.

At 31 December the numbers of units in stock were estimated at:

	Quantity		Quantity	
Finished product	zero	**Materials**		
		Electronic assembly	10,000	purchased in December
		Keypad	30,000	purchased in December
		Case	20,000	purchased in December

Materials stock levels at the end of each month were planned to be 50% of the following month's usage. Finished product stock levels at the end of each month were planned to be 20% of the following month's sales.

Earextensions plc have budgeted selling and administrative costs of £4.5m for the six months. The first three months were evenly spread at 60% of the total and the second three months evenly spread at 40% of the total. Production overheads included total depreciation of £50,000 budgeted for six months. Financing costs over the 6 months were expected in line with sales at 0.2% of sales value.

Earextensions plc prepared an estimated balance sheet for its new subsidiary at 31 December as follows:

	£	£
Fixed assets	495,000	
Stocks	303,000	
Trade debtors	–	
Cash and bank	355,000	1,153,000
Trade creditors	303,000	
Loans	450,000	
Share capital	400,000	
Retained earnings	–	1,153,000

Trade debtors were expected to pay in the second month following the month of sale and trade creditors were planned to be paid in the third month following the month of purchase. Direct labour, production overheads, and selling and administrative costs are all paid in the month in which they are incurred. There was no further planned capital expenditure during the first six months.

You are required to prepare a phased sales budget in units and values for the six months January to June.

E9.2 *Time allowed – 30 minutes*

Using the information from Exercise E9.1 prepare a phased finished product stocks and a phased production budget in units for the six months January to June.

E9.3 *Time allowed – 60 minutes*

Nilbog Ltd makes garden gnomes. It uses standard costs and has budgeted to produce and sell 130,000 Fishermen (their top of the range gnome) in 2005. Nilbog's budget for the year is phased over 13 four-week periods, and production and sales are spread evenly in the budget.

Budgeted standards costs and selling prices for the Fisherman are:

		£
Direct materials	3 cu. yds at £3.60	10.80
Direct labour	2 hours at £6.60 per hour	13.20
Variable overheads	2 hours at £2.40 per hour	4.80
Fixed overheads	2 hours at £4.80 per hour	9.60
Standard cost of one Fisherman		38.40
Standard profit		9.60
Standard selling price		48.00

The actual results for period 5, a four-week period, were:

Sales	9,000 Fishermen at £48 each
Production	9,600 Fishermen
Purchase of direct materials	30,000 cu. yards at a cost of £115,200
Direct materials usage	28,000 cu. yards
Direct labour cost	£142,560 over 22,000 hours
Variable overhead	£44,000
Fixed overhead	£100,000

There was no work-in-progress at the start or at the end of period 5. Finished goods and materials stocks are valued at standard cost.

You are required to prepare a flexed budget and an operating statement for Nilbog Ltd for period 5, showing the profit for the period and all standard variances with their detailed calculations, together with an explanation of their likely causes.

E9.4 *Time allowed – 90 minutes*

Cyclops plc is an electronics business that manufactures television sets, and uses a standard costing system. The TV cabinets division of Cyclops manufactures, for sale within the company, the plastic cases for one of their most popular models, the F24. The results for the F24 for October 2004 were as follows:

	Actual	**Budget**
Sales units	61,200	40,800
	£	**£**
Sales	348,840	244,800
Direct labour	133,280	81,600
Direct materials	114,240	81,600
Variable overheads	27,200	16,320
Contribution	74,120	65,280
Fixed overheads	25,000	20,400
Profit	49,120	44,880

The budget had been finalised for 2004 using standard costs for that year.

Sales volumes were increasing and just prior to October the TV cabinets division expected around 50% increase in sales volumes for the month. The division had unused capacity to take up this expected increase in volume. Vimla Patel had recently been appointed as commercial manager and she proposed a 30p selling price reduction per unit, which was effective from 1 October.

Melanie Bellamy, Cyclops' purchasing manager, had negotiated a 4% discount on the standard price of raw materials purchased and used from October. The production manager Graham Brown had been having problems with quality due to the learning curve and some operators who were still receiving training. Training had been completed by the end of September. This meant some increase in operator pay rates but the planned productivity rate was maintained and there was less materials wastage in October. The variable costs of utilities increased in October, primarily due to electricity and gas price increases.

Graham Brown was able to keep stock levels of materials and finished product at the same level at the start and end of October.

You are required to:

- (i) **prepare an operating statement that provides an analysis of the variances between actual and budget for October on a marginal costing basis, highlighting the performance of each of the managers**
- (ii) **give full explanations of why the variances may have occurred**
- (iii) **and (iv) prepare the same analysis and explanations as (i) and (ii) above using absorption costing**
- (v) **explain whether absorption costing provides the best basis for assessment of manager performance.**

Level II

E9.5 *Time allowed – 30 minutes*

Using the information from Exercise E9.1 prepare a unit gross margin budget and a phased direct labour budget for the six months January to June.

E9.6 *Time allowed – 30 minutes*

Using the information from Exercise E9.1 prepare a phased materials stocks, materials usage and purchases budget in units and values for the six months January to June.

E9.7 *Time allowed – 30 minutes*

Using the information from Exercise E9.1 prepare a phased selling and administrative costs budget, and financial budget for the six months January to June, and a phased profit and loss account budget, using absorption costing, for the six months January to June.

E9.8 *Time allowed – 30 minutes*

Using the information from Exercise E9.1 prepare a finished product valuation budget for the six months January to June.

E9.9 *Time allowed – 30 minutes*

An extract from the financial results for 2004 for three of the operating divisions of Marx plc is shown below:

Division	Chico	Groucho	Harpo
Average net operating assets	£7.5m	£17.5m	£12.5m
Operating profit	£1.5m	£1.4m	£2.0m
Administrative expenses	£0.8m	£0.3m	£0.65m
Divisional cost of capital per annum	7%	5%	10%

Required:

(i) **Calculate the ROI for each division for 2004.**

(ii) **Calculate the RI for each division for 2004.**

(iii) **Each division is presented with an investment opportunity that is expected to yield a return of 9%.**

(a) **Which division(s) would accept and which division(s) would reject the investment opportunity if divisional performance is measured by ROI, and why?**

(b) **Which division(s) would accept and which division(s) would reject the investment opportunity if divisional performance is measured by RI, and why?**

E9.10 *Time allowed – 60 minutes*

Using the information from Exercise E9.1 prepare a creditors' budget and a debtors' budget, and a phased cash budget for the six months January to June.

E9.11 *Time allowed – 60 minutes*

Using the information from Exercise E9.1 prepare a phased balance sheet budget for the six months January to June.

E9.12 *Time allowed – 90 minutes*

White Heaven Ltd manufactures a bathroom basin, the Shell, and uses standard costing based on a monthly output of 50,000 units. White Heaven uses two types of direct labour and two items of raw material.

Variable costs include:

- indirect labour costs of materials handlers and stores persons
- maintenance labour costs
- general production overheads.

Fixed costs include:

- supervisory salaries
- other overheads such as
  - factory rent
  - electricity standing charges
  - gas standing charges.

The **ideal** standard cost of a Shell is as follows:

Direct labour	1 hour at £7.20 per hour	grade A
	0.75 hours at £6.00 per hour	grade B
Direct materials	5 kgs at £2 per kg clay	
	3 kgs at £4 per kg glaze	
Indirect labour	0.25 hours at £5.00 per hour	
Maintenance	0.05 hours at £10.00 per hour	
Variable overheads	15% of direct materials cost, plus	
	10% of direct labour cost	
Supervisory salaries	£95,000 per month	
Other fixed overheads	£109,000 per month	

In June 2005 adjustments were agreed as the basis for the following month's **attainable** standard costs:

Grade A labour rates increased by 40p, grade B by 30p and indirect and maintenance labour by 20p

Grade B labour hours increased by 0.05 hours because of process delays due to a tool change problem

Turnover of operators has meant recruiting some inexperienced, untrained operators

10% of grade A operators with 50% efficiency

25% of grade B operators with 60% efficiency

The clay is to be upgraded in quality with the supplier imposing a 10% surcharge

The glaze will be purchased in larger batches with a 12.5% discount but resulting in an increase in variable overheads to 20% of materials cost for this type of material.

For the July output of 49,000 Shells you are required to calculate:

(i) **the ideal standard cost for a Shell**

(ii) **the attainable standard cost for a Shell for July 2005**

(iii) **the total variance between the ideal and attainable standards.**

E9.13 *Time allowed – 90 minutes*

White Heaven Ltd (see Exercise E9.12) actually produced 49,000 Shells during July 2005 and the actual costs for the month were as follows:

Direct labour	52,000 hours at £7.60 per hour	grade A
	43,500 hours at £6.30 per hour	grade B
Direct materials	247,000 kgs at £2.16 per kg	clay
	149,000 kgs at £3.60 per kg	glaze
Indirect labour	12,000 hours at £5.20 per hour	
Maintenance	2,250 hours at £10.20 per hour	
Variable overheads	£251,000	
Supervisory salaries	£97,000	
Other fixed overheads	£110,000	

You are required to:

- **(i) calculate the variances between actual costs for July 2005 and the attainable standard**
- **(ii) prepare an operating statement that summarises the variances**
- **(iii) reconcile the actual cost for July with the expected total attainable cost**
- **(iv) comment on the likely reasons for each of the variances.**

E9.14 *Time allowed – 90 minutes*

Millennium Models Ltd manufactured an ornamental gift for the tourist trade. The standard variable cost per unit was:

Materials price	£0.85 per kg
Unit material usage	2 kgs
Direct labour rate	£4.20 per hour
Standard labour per unit	42 minutes
Selling price per unit	£5.84

Fixed overhead is recovered on the basis of units produced at the rate of £0.82 per unit and Millennium planned to sell 4,300 units in November 2004.

In November 2004 Millennium' s actual performance was:

Units manufactured and sold	4,100
Sales	£24,805
Materials used	6,600 kgs at £0.83
	1,900 kgs at £0.89
Direct labour paid	2,975 at £4.50 per hour
Overheads incurred	£3,800

You are required to:

- **(i) prepare a budget to actual profit reconciliation for November 2004 including an analysis of sales, materials, and labour variances**
- **(ii) calculate the fixed overhead expenditure variance and fixed overhead volume variances for November 2004.**

E9.15 *Time allowed – 90 minutes*

Using the information about Millennium Models Ltd from Exercise E9.14:

- **(i)** **explain what you think are the advantages and disadvantages of the implementation of a standard costing system by Millennium Models Ltd**
- **(ii)** **explain how the analyses of variances may have helped Millennium Models Ltd control the business**
- **(iii)** **prepare a report that explains the variance analysis you have carried out in Exercise E9.14 above and provides explanations of Millennium's performance.**

E9.16 *Time allowed – 90 minutes*

The Stables is a small holiday let business in Wales. The standard variable cost for each holiday let unit (HLU) for one holiday is:

	£
Direct materials (food, cleaning materials and repairs)	120
Direct labour 15 hours at £10 per hour	150
Variable overhead 5 hours at £1 per hour	5

Budgeted costs and sales for the 2004 season are:

Number of holidays	50
Price per holiday	£400
Fixed costs	£2,080

The actual outcome for one HLU for 2004 was:

Number of holidays	52
Total sales revenue	£19,760
Direct materials	£5,928
Direct labour (780 hours at £9 per hour)	£7,020
Variable overhead	£260
Fixed overhead	£1,950

You are required to:

- **(i)** **Prepare a budgeted profit and loss account for one HLU for 2004.**
- **(ii)** **Prepare an actual profit and loss account for one HLU for 2004.**
- **(iii)** **Prepare a flexed budget for one HLU that reflects the amount of actual business for 2004.**
- **(iv)** **Prepare a detailed variance analysis for one HLU that gives possible reasons for each of the variances.**
- **(v)** **Summarise the variances in an operating statement that reconciles the difference between the budgeted profit and the actual profit achieved by one HLU in 2004.**
- **(vi)** **Outline some of the problems with traditional variance analysis and explain how the identification of planning variances may assist in more accurate reporting of operational variances.**

10

Investment decisions

Contents

Learning objectives

Completion of this chapter will enable you to:

- explain what is meant by an investment
- outline the key principles underlying investment selection criteria
- outline the strengths and weaknesses of the five investment appraisal criteria
- explain what is meant by discounted cash flow (DCF)
- consider investment selection using the appraisal criteria of net present value (NPV) and internal rate of return (IRR)
- explain the effects of inflation, working capital requirements, length and timing of projects, taxation, and risk and uncertainty on investment criteria calculations
- evaluate the impact of risk and the use of sensitivity analysis in decision-making.

Introduction

The management accountant is involved with providing financial and non-financial information and analysis to enable managers to evaluate alternative proposals and to make decisions.

In Chapters 8 and 9 we had an introduction into the ways in which accounting and financial information may be used as an aid to decision-making. This chapter looks at the specific area of decision-making that relates to investment. Such decisions may relate to whether or not to invest in a project, or choices between investment in alternative projects which are competing for resources.

We will begin by looking at exactly what an investment is, and outlining the techniques used to decide on whether or not to invest, and how to choose between alternative investments.

We shall evaluate the advantages and disadvantages of the five main investment appraisal criteria used by companies and consider examples that demonstrate their use. The most important of these are the discounted cash flow methods of net present value (NPV), and internal rate of return (IRR). The technique of discounted cash flow (DCF) will be fully explained.

In addition to the initial costs of an investment and the returns expected from it, a number of other factors usually need to be taken into account in investment decision-making. These include, for example, inflation, the need for working capital, taxation, and the length and timing of the project. We will consider the possible impact of these factors and how the effects of risk and uncertainty on the appraisal of investments may be quantified using sensitivity analysis.

Appraisal of an investment is more than an accounting exercise. An investment decision is a crucially significant and important decision for a business. It is usually a highly politically charged area in the management of an organisation, which if mismanaged is capable of destroying shareholder value. Once an investment decision has been made, the project may then be planned and implemented.

What is an investment?

For the accountant an investment appears within the assets section of the balance sheet under fixed assets. For the finance director an investment is any decision that implies expenditure today with the expectation that it will generate cash inflows tomorrow.

Investment decisions are extremely important because they are invariably concerned with the future survival, prosperity and growth of the organisation. The organisation's primary objective of maximisation of shareholder wealth is a basic assumption that continues to hold true. Investments must be made not only to maintain shareholder wealth but more importantly to increase it. To meet the shareholder wealth maximisation objective it is crucial that those managing the organisation make optimal decisions that are based on the best information available and use of the most appropriate appraisal techniques.

At the corporate level, investment (in shares) relates to the amount that shareholders are willing to invest in the equity of a company in the expectation of future cash flows in the form of dividends and enhancement of share price. The level of future dividends and share price enhancement are in turn dependent on the extent to which the company is able to optimise returns on 'real' investment (investment in companies, plant, machinery, working capital) in new products, projects, new business, and so on. There is a great deal of pressure on chief executives to ensure that profitable 'real' investments are made to provide sustained dividend growth and increasing share prices.

Investment decisions faced by companies are therefore financially driven, and so if performance is deemed inadequate or unlikely to meet shareholder expectations, then the pressure becomes even greater to identify alternative, more profitable projects. Decisions are made by managers and not by the management accountant. Levels of authority within the management hierarchy are determined by company policy. Companies normally establish limits at each management level for each type of decision, and the level of expenditure allowed. The approval of one or more directors is normally required for all capital expenditure and for major projects.

Investment may appear in the balance sheet within fixed assets in line with the accountants' definition, for example land, buildings, plant, machinery, etc. It may also appear in the profit and loss account in terms of public relations, staff training, or research and development. In some cases the amount of money gained as a result of making an investment is relatively easy to measure, such as cost savings, capacity increases, etc. In other cases, it may be impossible to measure the gains – company image, education, and so on. The amount of spend may be easily forecast, for example the costs of computerisation of a process to reduce the production of non-quality products. In other projects, such as research and development, costs may be more uncertain.

Regardless, an investment decision is required before spending shareholders' and lenders' funds. The decision made needs to be one that shareholders and lenders would be happy with; it is one that is expected to provide anticipated gains in real terms that greatly exceed the funds spent today, in other words a good return on the money invested. Otherwise the investment should not be made.

Progress check 10.1 **Describe what is meant by investment.**

Investment appraisal criteria

The five main methods used in investment appraisal are shown in Fig. 10.1:

- the accounting rate of return (ARR) for appraising capital investment projects is based on profits and the costs of investment; it takes no account of cash flows or the time value of money

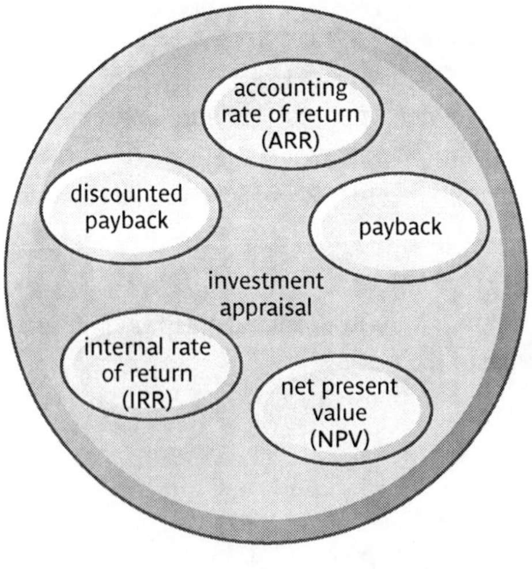

Figure 10.1 The five main investment appraisal criteria methods

- the payback method for appraising capital investment projects is based on cash flows, but also ignores the time value of money
- net present value (NPV) is one of the two most widely used investment decision criteria, which are based on cash flow and the time value of money
- internal rate of return (IRR) is the second of the two most widely used investment decision criteria, which are based on cash flow and the time value of money
- the discounted payback appraisal method is also based on cash flow and the time value of money.

We will look at examples of each of the five appraisal criteria and the advantages and disadvantages of using each of them.

Accounting rate of return (ARR)

ARR is a simple measure which is sometimes used in investment appraisal. It is a form of return on capital employed. It is based on profits rather than cash flows and ignores the time value of money.

ARR may be calculated using:

$$\frac{\textbf{average accounting profit over the project}}{\textbf{initial investment}} \times \textbf{100\%}$$

There are alternative ways of calculating ARR. For example, total profit may be used instead of average profit, or average investment may be used instead of initial investment. It should be noted that in such a case if, for example, a machine originally cost £800,000 and its final scrap value was £50,000 then the average investment is £850,000/2, or £425,000. This is because the investment at the start is valued at £800,000, and the investment at the end of the project is £50,000. The average value over the period of the project is then the addition of these two values divided by two.

It should be noted that the method of calculation of ARR that is selected must be used consistently. However, ARR although simple to use is not recommended as a primary appraisal method. The method can provide an 'overview' of a new project but it lacks the sophistication of other methods (see the following explanations and methods). The impact of cash flows and time on the value of

Worked Example 10.1

Alpha Engineering Ltd is a company that has recently implemented an investment appraisal system. Its investment authorisation policy usually allows it to go ahead with a capital project if the accounting rate of return is greater than 25%. A project has been submitted for appraisal with the following data:

	£000	
Initial investment	100	(residual scrap value zero)
Per annum profit over the life of the project:		
Year		
1	25	
2	35	
3	35	
4	25	

The capital project can be evaluated using ARR.

$$\text{Average profit over the life of the project} = \frac{£25{,}000 + £35{,}000 + £35{,}000 + £25{,}000}{4}$$

$$= £30{,}000$$

$$\text{Accounting rate of return} = \frac{£30{,}000}{£100{,}000} \times 100\% = 30\%$$

which is greater than 25% and so acceptance of the project may be recommended.

money really should be considered in investment appraisal, which we will discuss in a later section about key principles underlying investment selection criteria.

> Progress check 10.2 **What is the accounting rate of return (ARR) and how is it calculated?**

Payback

Payback is defined as the number of years it takes the cash inflows from a capital investment project to equal the cash outflows. An organisation may have a target payback period, above which projects are rejected. It is useful and sometimes used as an initial screening process in evaluating two mutually exclusive projects. The project that pays back in the shortest time may on the face of it be the one to accept.

Worked Example 10.2

Beta Engineering Ltd's investment authorisation policy requires all capital projects to pay back within three years, and views projects with shorter payback periods as even more desirable. Two mutually exclusive projects are currently being considered with the following data:

	Project 1	Project 2	
	£000	£000	
Initial investment	200	200	(residual scrap value zero)

Per annum cash inflows over the life of each project:

	Project 1		Project 2	
Year	Yearly cash flow	Cumulative cash flow	Yearly cash flow	Cumulative cash flow
	£000	£000	£000	£000
1	60	60	100	100
2	80	140	150	250
3	80	220	30	280
4	90	310	10	290

The projects can be evaluated by considering their payback periods.

- Project 1 derives total cash inflows of £310,000 over the life of the project and pays back the initial £200,000 investment three quarters of the way into year three, when the cumulative cash inflows reach £200,000 [£60,000 + £80,000 + £60,000 (75% of £80,000)].
- Project 2 derives total cash inflows of £290,000 over the life of the project and pays back the initial £200,000 investment two thirds of the way into year two, when the cumulative cash inflows reach £200,000 [£100,000 + £100,000 (67% of £150,000)].
- Both projects meet Beta Engineering Ltd's three-year payback criteria.
- Project 2 pays back within two years and so is the preferred project, using Beta's investment guidelines.

Worked Example 10.2 shows how payback may be used to compare projects. The total returns from a project should also be considered, in addition to the timing of the cash flows and their value in real terms. As with ARR, although its use is widespread amongst companies, payback is not recommended as a primary appraisal method. This method can also provide an 'overview' but should be the primary appraisal method used in larger companies or with regard to large projects because it ignores the time value of money.

Progress check 10.3 What is payback and how is it calculated?

Key principles underlying investment selection criteria: cash flow, the time value of money, and discounted cash flow (DCF)

The first two appraisal criteria we have considered are simple methods that have limitations in their usefulness in making optimal capital investment decisions. The three further appraisal criteria are NPV, IRR and discounted payback. Whichever of these three methods is used, three basic principles apply: *Cash is king*, *Time value of money*, and *Discounted cash flow* (DCF) (see pages 373 and 374).

In Chapters 3, 4 and 5 we discussed the differences between cash flow and profit and the advantages in using cash as a measure of financial performance.

We may assume that a specific sum of money may be held in reserve for some unforeseen future need, or used:

- to earn interest in a bank or building society account over the following year
- to buy some bottles of champagne (for example) at today's price
- to buy some bottles of champagne at the price in one year's time, which we may assume will be at a higher price because of inflation.

We may assume that the bank or building society interest earned for one year, or the amount by which the price of champagne goes up due to inflation over one year is say 5%. Then we can see that £100 would be worth £105 if left in the building society for one year, and £100 spent on champagne today would actually buy just over £95 worth of champagne in one year's time because of its price increase.

Cash is king

Real funds can be seen in cash but not in accounting profit.

Interest charges become payable as soon as money is made available, for example, from a lender to a borrower, not when an agreement is made or when a contract is signed.

Time value of money

Receipt of £100 today has greater value than receipt of £100 in one year's time.

There are two reasons for this:

The money could have been invested alternatively in, say, risk-free Government gilt-edged securities – in fact, the actual rate of interest that will have to be paid will be higher than the Government rate, to include a risk premium, because neither companies nor individuals are risk-free borrowers. Generally, the higher the risk of the investment, the higher the return the investor will expect from it.

Purchasing power will have been lost over a year due to inflation.

The percentage rate by which the value of money may be eroded over one year is called the discount rate. The amount by which the value of, say, £100 is eroded over one year is calculated by dividing it by what is called the discount factor

$$\frac{\pounds 100}{(1 + \text{discount rate }\%)}$$

So, for example, we could buy champagne in one year's time worth

$$\pounds 100/(1 + 5\%) \text{ or } \pounds 100/1.05 = \pounds 95.24$$

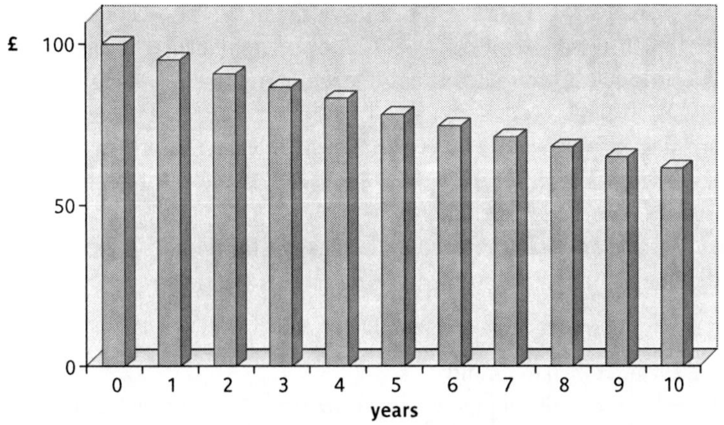

Figure 10.2 Future values of £100 using a discount rate of 5% per annum

If the £95.24 were left for another year, and assuming that prices continued to increase at 5% per annum, we could buy champagne after a further year worth

$$£95.24/(1 + 5\%) \text{ or } £95.24/1.05 = £90.70$$

The yearly buying power continues to be reduced by application of the discount factor (or using the appropriate discount factor if the discount rate has changed). If the money is not used either to earn interest or to buy something, its value therefore normally becomes less and less. The discount factor for each year obviously depends on the discount rate. The successive year-by-year impact on £100 using an unchanging discount rate of 5% per annum may be illustrated using a simple graph showing its cumulative value from the start until the end of 10 years. The graph shown in Fig. 10.2 illustrates the concept of the time value of money.

Discounted cash flow (DCF)

Whichever of the three methods of appraisal is used: NPV; IRR; or discounted payback, a technique of discounting the projected cash flows of a project is used to ascertain its present value. Such methods are called discounted cash flow or DCF techniques. They require the use of a discount rate to carry out the appropriate calculation.

If we consider a simple company balance sheet:

net assets = equity + financial debt

we can see that an investment is an additional asset that may be financed by equity or debt or by both.

Shareholders and lenders each require a return on their investment that is high enough to pay for the risk they are taking in funding the company and its assets. The expected return on equity will be higher than the cost of debt because the shareholders take a higher risk than the lenders. The average cost of these financial resources provided to the company is called the weighted average cost of capital (WACC). An important rule is that the return generated by a new investment undertaken by a company must be higher than the WACC, which reflects the discount rate – the rate of financing the investment. If, say, a company's WACC is 10%, an investment may be accepted if the expected rate of return is 15% or 16%. The importance of WACC and the significance of the debt/equity financial structure of a business will be examined in more detail in Chapter 11 when we look at sources of finance and the cost of capital.

Other discount rates may be used, such as a borrowing interest rate or even the accounting rate of return. However, the cost of capital – the WACC – is usually the hurdle rate, the opportunity cost of funds, that is used to evaluate new investments.

If i represents the cost of capital (the discount rate), and n the number of periods, e.g. years, these can be used to derive a

present value discount factor, which is $1/(1 + i)^n$

where n may have a value from 0 to infinity.
(Note the similarity between this and the way we calculated the future values of £100 illustrated in Fig. 10.2.)

If we consider a project where the initial investment in year 0 is I, and each subsequent year's net cash flows are CF_1, CF_2, CF_3, CF_4 and so on for n years up to CF_n, and the cost of capital is i, then the

present value of the cash flows =

$$-I + CF_1/(1 + i) + CF_2/(1 + i)^2 + \cdots + CF_n/(1 + i)^n$$

The present value of the cash flows using an appropriate cost of capital, or discount rate, is called the net present value or NPV.

Progress check 10.4 What do we mean by discounted cash flow (DCF) and what are the principles on which it is based?

Net present value (NPV)

NPV is today's value of the difference between cash inflows and outflows projected at future dates, attributable to capital investments or long-term projects. The value now of these net cash flows is obtained by using the discounted cash flow method with a specified discount rate.

Worked Example 10.3

An investment of £5,000 is made in year 0. For the purpose of NPV, year 0 is regarded as being today. (The reason for this is that any number to the power of 0 is equal to one.) The investment generates subsequent yearly cash flows of £1,000, £3,000, £3,000, and £2,000. The cost of capital is 10%.

We can evaluate the investment using an NPV approach.

NPV = –£5,000 + £1,000/1.1 + £3,000/1.1^2 + £3,000/1.1^3 + £2,000/1.1^4
NPV = –£5,000 + (£1,000 × 0.91) + (£3,000 × 0.83) + (£3,000 × 0.75) + (£2,000 × 0.68)
NPV = –£5,000 + £910 + £2,490 + £2,250 + £1,360
NPV = +£2,010 which is greater than 0, and being positive the investment should probably be made.

Such an analysis is more usefully presented in tabular form. The discount rates for each year: $1/1.1$, $1/1.1^2$, $1/1.1^3$, $1/1.1^4$, may be shown in the table as discount factor values which are calculated, or alternatively obtained from present value tables (see the extract below from the Present Value table in Appendix 2 at the end of this book).

Rate *r* % **After *n* years**	**1**	**2**	**3**	**4**	**5**	**6**	**7**	**8**	**9**	**10**	**11**	**12**
1	0.99	0.98	0.97	0.96	0.95	0.94	0.93	0.93	0.92	**0.91**	0.90	0.89
2	0.98	0.96	0.94	0.92	0.91	0.89	0.87	0.86	0.84	**0.83**	0.81	0.80
3	0.97	0.94	0.92	0.89	0.86	0.84	0.82	0.79	0.77	**0.75**	0.73	0.71
4	0.96	0.92	0.89	0.85	0.82	0.79	0.76	0.74	0.71	**0.68**	0.66	0.64
5	0.95	0.91	0.86	0.82	0.78	0.75	0.71	0.68	0.65	0.62	0.59	0.57

Tabular format of NPV analysis

Year	**Cash outflows £**	**Cash inflows £**	**Net cash flow £**	**Discount factor**	**Present values £**
0	–5,000		–5,000	1.00	–5,000
1		1,000	1,000	0.91	910
2		3,000	3,000	0.83	2,490
3		3,000	3,000	0.75	2,250
4		2,000	2,000	0.68	1,360
				NPV	+2,010

Progress check 10.5 What is net present value (NPV) and how is it calculated?

Internal rate of return (IRR)

The NPV of a capital investment project is calculated by:

- discounting, using a rate of return, discount rate, or cost of capital, to obtain
- the difference in present values between cash inflows and cash outflows.

The internal rate of return (IRR) method calculates:

- the rate of return, where
- the difference between the present values of cash inflows and outflows, the NPV, is zero.

Through this calculation, the IRR provides the exact rate of return that the project is expected to achieve. An organisation would then undertake the project if the expected rate of return, the IRR, exceeds its target rate of return.

IRR may most easily be determined through interpolation, which assumes a linear relationship between the NPVs of a capital investment project derived using different discount rates. If a project generates a positive NPV of £50,000 using a discount rate of 10% and a negative NPV of £5,000 using a discount rate of 20%, then the IRR (at which point NPV is zero) must be somewhere between 10%

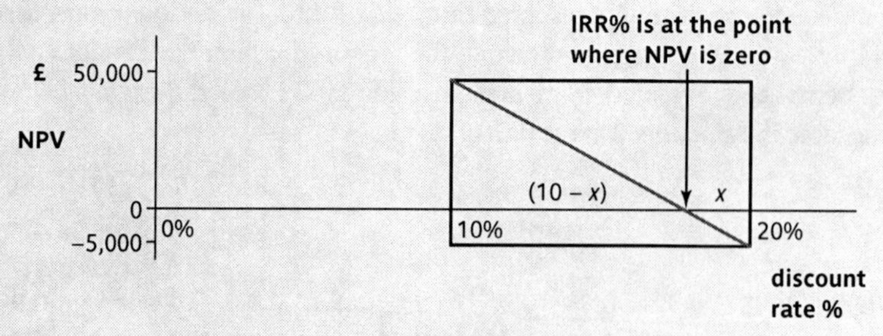

using the algebraic relationships derived from the similar triangles

$$\frac{5,000}{x} = \frac{50,000}{(10 - x)}$$

$$5,000\,(10 - x) = 50,000x$$

divide both sides of the equation by 1,000

$$50 - 5x = 50x$$

$$50 = 50x + 5x$$

$$50 = 55x$$

$$x = 50/55 = 0.91$$

$$\text{IRR} = 20\% - 0.91\% = 19.09\%$$

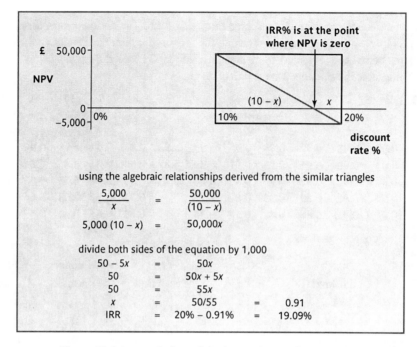

Figure 10.3 Interpolation of the internal rate of return (IRR)

and 20%. The exact rate may be determined graphically or calculated algebraically, as illustrated in Fig. 10.3.

A similar approach may be adopted if both NPVs are positive. For example, if a project generates a positive NPV of £50,000 using a discount rate of 10% and a positive NPV of £20,000 using a discount rate of 15%, then the IRR (at which point NPV is zero) may be extrapolated as shown in Fig. 10.4.

As an alternative to the graphical approach, the calculation of IRR can be carried out manually using a trial and error process, which is a quite laborious task. This may be overcome since IRR can also be determined using the appropriate spreadsheet function in Excel, for example. However, there a couple of further serious difficulties with the use of IRR.

Discount rates of return may change over the life of a project because of changes in the general level of interest rates. The IRR calculated for a project may therefore be greater than expected rates of return in some years and less in other years, which makes a decision on the project very difficult to make. Alternatively, the NPV approach may use different discount rates for each year of a project.

The cash flows of projects do not normally fall into the simple pattern of an outflow at the start of the project followed by positive cash flows during each successive year. Project cash flows may be positive at the start, or may vary between negative and positive throughout the life of a project. Such unconventional cash flow sequences through out each period may lead to a project having no IRR or multiple IRRs. Multiple IRRs makes it impossible to use IRR for decision-making.

Progress check 10.6 **What is the internal rate of return (IRR) and how is it calculated?**

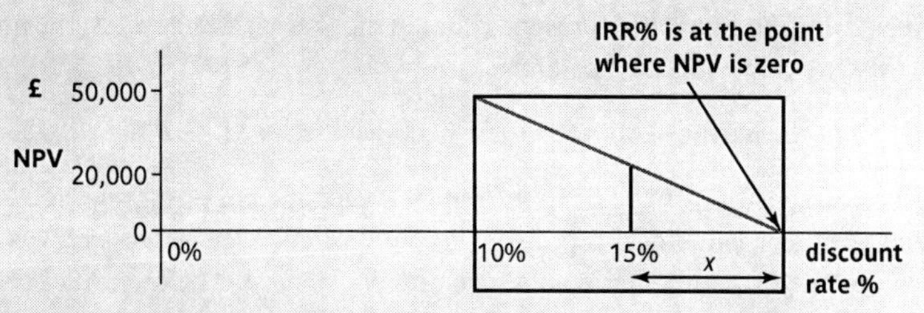

using the algebraic relationships derived from the similar triangles

$$\frac{20{,}000}{x} = \frac{50{,}000}{(5 + x)}$$

$$20{,}000(5 + x) = 50{,}000x$$

divide both sides of the equation by 1,000

$$100 + 20x = 50x$$
$$100 = 50x - 20x$$
$$100 = 30x$$
$$x = 100/30 = 3.33$$
$$\text{IRR} = 15\% + 3.33\% = 18.33\%$$

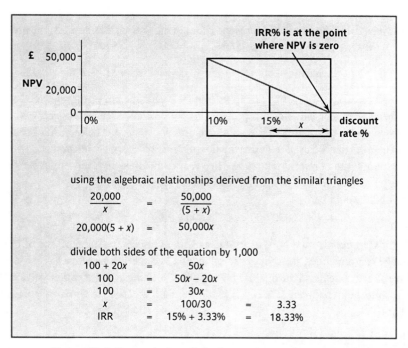

Figure 10.4 Extrapolation of the internal rate of return (IRR)

Worked Example 10.4 illustrates the use of both NPV and IRR, using conventional cash flows.

Worked Example 10.4

Gamma plc is a diversified multinational group that wishes to acquire a computer system costing £600,000, which is expected to generate cash gains of £170,000 per year over five years. The computer system will have a residual value of zero after five years. The suggested cost of capital is 12%. For this example we may ignore taxation. Gamma has a target IRR of 15%. Gamma plc evaluates the computer system investment by considering its IRR.

	£
Yearly cash gains	170,000

Year	Cash outflows £000	Cash inflows £000	Net cash flow £000	Discount factor at 12%	Present values £000
0	−600		−600	1.00	−600.0
1		170	170	0.89	151.3
2		170	170	0.80	136.0
3		170	170	0.71	120.7
4		170	170	0.64	108.8
5		170	170	0.57	96.9
				NPV	+13.7

Alternatively, using the cumulative present values in the Present Value tables, the present value of £1 at 12% over five years is £3.61, therefore

$$NPV = -£600,000 + (£170,000 \times 3.61) = +£13,700$$

The project gives a positive NPV of £13,700 over five years. If Gamma plc used NPV to appraise capital projects then acceptance of this project may be recommended because NPV is positive.

The IRR is the rate of return that would give an NPV of zero. The interpolation technique shown in Fig. 10.3 may be used to derive the internal rate of return of the project.

If we assume a rate of return of 20%, the five-year cumulative discount rate is 2.99 (from the cumulative present value of £1 in the Present Value tables in Appendix 2).

The new NPV would be:

$$-£600,000 + (£170,000 \times 2.99) = -£91,700$$

(Note that if Gamma plc used NPV to appraise capital projects then acceptance of this project would not be recommended at a cost of capital of 20% because it is negative.)

We have already calculated the positive NPV of £13,700 using a cost of capital of 12%. The IRR must be at some point between 20% and 12% (difference 8%). Using a similar calculation to that used in Fig. 10.3:

$$\frac{£91,700}{x} = \frac{£13,700}{(8 - x)}$$

$$£91,700(8 - x) = £13,700x$$

$$(£91,700 \times 8) - £91,700x = £13,700x$$

$$£733,600 - £91,700x = £13,700x$$

$$£733,600 = £13,700x + £91,700x$$

$$£733,600 = £105,400x$$

$$\frac{£733,600}{£105,400} = x$$

$$x = 7.0$$

Therefore, interpolation gives us an IRR of 20% less 7%, which is 13%.

If the Gamma group uses IRR to appraise capital projects then this project may be rejected as the target rate is 15%.

NPV or IRR?

We have looked at the two main capital appraisal methods, which use the DCF technique. Which method should an organisation adopt for the appraisal of capital investment projects? Which is the better method?

IRR is relatively easy to understand, particularly for non-financial managers. It can be stated in terms that do not include financial jargon, for example 'a project will cost £1m and will return 20% per annum, which is better than the company's target of 15%'. Whereas, NPV is not quite so clear, for example 'a project will cost £1,000,000 and have an NPV of £250,000 using the company's weighted average cost of capital of 12%'. But there are major disadvantages with the use of IRR:

- IRR is very difficult to use for decision-making where expected rates of return may change over the life of a project

- if project cash flows do not follow the usual 'outflow at the start of the project followed by inflows over the life of the project' the result may be no IRR, or two or more IRRs, which can lead to uncertainties and difficulties in interpretation
- IRR should not be used to decide between mutually exclusive projects because of its inability to allow for the relative size of investments.

IRR ignores the size of investment projects, because it is a percentage measure of a return on a project rather than an absolute cash return number. Two projects, one with a large initial investment and one with a small initial investment, may have the same IRR, but one project may return many times the cash flow returned by the other project. So, if the projects were judged solely on IRR they would seem to rank equally.

If mutually exclusive projects need to be compared then the following rules for acceptance should apply:

- is the IRR greater than the hurdle rate (usually the WACC)?

If so

- the project with the highest NPV should be chosen assuming the NPV is greater than zero.

A company may be considering a number of projects in which it may invest. If there is a limited amount of funds available then capital rationing is required. This method requires ranking the competing projects in terms of NPV per each £ of investment in each project. Investment funds may then be allocated according to NPV rankings, given the assumption that the investments are infinitely divisible.

Progress check 10.7 What are the disadvantages in the use of internal rate of return (IRR) in the support of capital investment appraisal decisions?

Discounted payback

The discounted payback appraisal method requires a discount rate to be chosen to calculate the present values of cash inflows and then the payback is the number of years required to repay the original investment.

Worked Example 10.5

A new leisure facility project is being considered by Denton City Council. It will cost £600,000 and is expected to generate the following cash inflows over six years:

Year	£
1	40,000
2	100,000
3	200,000
4	350,000
5	400,000
6	50,000

The cost of capital is 10% per annum.

Denton City Council evaluates projects using discounted payback.

Year	Net cash flow	Cumulative net cash flow	Discount factor at 10%	Present values	Cumulative present values
	£000	£000		£000	£000
0	–600	–600	1.00	–600.0	–600.0
1	40	–560	0.91	36.4	–563.6
2	100	–460	0.83	83.0	–480.6
3	200	–260	0.75	150.0	–330.6
4	350	90	0.68	238.0	–92.6
5	400	490	0.62	248.0	155.4
6	50	540	0.56	28.0	183.4
	540		NPV	+183.4	

Taking a simple payback approach we can see that the project starts to pay back at nearly three quarters of the way through year four. The discounted payback approach shows that with a cost of capital of 10% the project does not really start to pay back until just over a third of the way into year five. This method also highlights the large difference between the real total value of the project of £183,400 in discounted cash flow terms, and the arithmetic total of cash flows of £540,000.

Progress check 10.8 What is discounted payback and how is it calculated?

Advantages and disadvantages of the five investment appraisal methods

We have discussed the five capital investment methods and seen examples of their application. The table in Fig. 10.5 summarises each of the methods and the advantages and disadvantages of their practical use in investment appraisal.

It is interesting to note that even ten years ago payback still seemed to be the most popular appraisal method within UK companies, closely followed by IRR! NPV, discounted payback and ARR appeared to be equal third sharing around the same level of popularity (*A Survey of Management Accounting Practices in UK Companies* 1993).

It should be emphasised that the whole area of capital investment appraisal is one that requires a great deal of expertise and experience. In real-life decision-making situations these types of appraisal are generally carried out by the accountant or the finance director. These sorts of longer-term decisions are concerned primarily with the maximisation of shareholder wealth, but they also impact on issues relating to the health and future development of the business. Therefore, such decisions are normally based on qualitative as well as quantitative factors.

	definition	advantages	disadvantages
accounting rate of return (ARR)	average accounting profit over the life of the project divided by the initial or average investment	quick and easy to calculate and simple to use	based on accounting profit rather than cash flows
		the concept of a % return is a familiar one	a relative measure and so no account is taken of the size of the project
		very similar to ROCE	ignores timing of cash flows and the cost of capital
payback	the point where the cumulative value of a project's cash flows becomes positive	easily understood	ignores the timing of cash flows
		considers liquidity	ignores cash flows that occur after the payback point
		looks only at relevant cash flows	ignores the cost of capital, i.e. the time value of money
net present value (NPV)	the total present values of each of a project's cash flows, using a present value discount factor	uses relevant cash flows	its use requires an estimate of the cost of capital
		allows for the time value of money	
		absolute measure and therefore useful, for example, for comparison of the change in shareholder wealth	
		it is additive which means that if the cash flow is doubled then the NPV is doubled	
internal rate of return (IRR)	the discount factor at which the NPV of a project becomes zero	does not need an estimate of the cost of capital	it is a relative rate of return and so no account is taken of the size of the project
		because the result is stated as a % it is easily understood	its use may rank projects incorrectly
			as cash flows change signs –ve to +ve or *vice versa* throughout the project there may be more than one IRR
			it is difficult to use if changes in the cost of capital are forecast
discounted payback	the point where the cumulative value of a project's discounted cash flows becomes positive	easily understood	its use requires an estimate of the cost of capital
		considers liquidity	ignores cash flows that occur after the payback point
		looks only at relevant cash flows	
		allows for the time value of money	

Figure 10.5 Advantages and disadvantages of the five investment appraisal methods

Non-financial measures appear to be as important, if not more important, to businesses in their appraisal of new projects. These may include, for example:

- customer relationships
- employee welfare
- the fit with general business strategy
- competition
- availability of scarce resources such as skills and specialised knowledge.

In addition, there are a number of other important quantitative factors, which are discussed in the next section, that should also be considered in new project appraisal. The impact of taxation, for example, is sometimes forgotten with regard to the allowances against tax on the purchase of capital items and tax payable on profits, and therefore cash flows, resulting from a capital project. The uncertainty surrounding future expectations and the sensitivity of the outcome of a project to changes affecting the various elements of an appraisal calculation, are factors that also require measured assessment.

Progress check 10.9 **Which technique do you think is the most appropriate to use in capital investment appraisal, and why?**

Other factors affecting investment decisions

A number of further factors may have an additional impact on investment criteria calculations:

- the effect of inflation on the cost of capital
- whether additional working capital is required for the project
- taxation
- the length of the project
- risk and uncertainty.

Inflation

If i is the real cost of capital and the inflation rate is I, then the actual (or money) cost of capital *a* may be calculated as follows:

$$(1 + a) = (1 + i) \times (1 + I)$$

Therefore

$$\textbf{actual cost of capital } \boldsymbol{a} = \mathbf{(1 + \boldsymbol{i}) \times (1 + \boldsymbol{I}) - 1}$$

Worked Example 10.6

What is a company's real cost of capital if its actual (money) cost of capital is 11% and inflation is running at 2%?

Real cost of capital

$$i = \frac{(1 + a)}{(1 + I)} - 1$$

$$i = \frac{1.11}{1.02} - 1 = 0.088 \text{ or } 8.8\%$$

This would normally then be rounded to say 9% and forecast cash flows that have been adjusted for inflation may then be discounted using this real cost of capital. Alternatively, if forecast cash flows have not been adjusted for inflation, then these money cash flows would be discounted using the company's actual cost of capital. The result is the same using either method.

Working capital

Any increases in working capital required for a project in addition to the normal investments need to be shown as cash outflows as necessary in one or more years, offset by cash inflows to bring the total to zero by the end of the project.

Worked Example 10.7

Delta Precision plc, a manufacturing company, has the opportunity to invest in a machine costing £110,000 that will generate net cash inflows from the investment of £30,000 for five years after which time the machine will be worth nothing. Cost of capital is 10%. We may ignore inflation and taxation in our evaluation of the project using NPV.

Year	Cash outflows £000	Cash inflows £000	Net cash flow £000	Discount factor at 10%	Present values £000
0	−110		−110	1.00	−110.0
1		30	30	0.91	27.3
2		30	30	0.83	24.9
3		30	30	0.75	22.5
4		30	30	0.68	20.4
5		30	30	0.62	18.6
				NPV	+3.7

The positive NPV of £3,700 would indicate acceptance of this investment.
Suppose that in addition to the above factors, for this project Delta required:

- £20,000 working capital in year 1
- £40,000 working capital in year 2, but then
- zero working capital in years 3, 4 and 5.

The revised cash flows would be:

Year	0	1	2	3	4	5	Total
	£000	£000	£000	£000	£000	£000	£000
Investment	-110						-110
Cash inflows		30	30	30	30	30	150
Working		-20		20			0
capital			-40	40			0
Total	-110	10	-10	90	30	30	40

The total cash flow of the project is still the same at £40,000, but the timings of the cash flows are different.

Year	Net cash flows £000	Discount factor		Present values £000
0	-110	1.00		-110.0
1	10	0.91		9.1
2	-10	0.83		-8.3
3	90	0.75		67.5
4	30	0.68		20.4
5	30	0.62		18.6
			NPV	-2.7

The need for, and the timing of, working capital gives a negative NPV of £2,700 which would now indicate rejection of this investment.

Taxation

In practice, tax must always be allowed for in any capital investment appraisal calculations. The following two examples provide an introduction to this topic, which illustrate the principles.

Worked Example 10.8

Epsilon Ltd is a company that manufactures and distributes consumer products. It is currently considering the acquisition of a machine costing £2,700,000 to market a new product.

The machine will be worth nothing after 10 years but is expected to produce 10,000 units of a product per year during that period, with variable costs of £35 per unit.

The product can be sold for £120 per unit.

Fixed costs directly attributed to this product will be £300,000 per year.

The company's cost of capital is 10%.

We may assume that all costs and revenues are paid and received during each year.

We may further assume that corporation tax is paid in the year that profit is made and calculated at 40% of profit, and that for tax purposes each year's depreciation is equal to capital allowances.

The acquisition of the machine can be evaluated using NPV.

	£000	
Sales revenue	1,200	[10,000 × £120]
Variable costs	(350)	[10,000 × £35]
Depreciation	(270)	[2,700,000 over 10-year life]
Fixed costs	(300)	
Taxable profit	280	
Corporation tax at 40%	(112)	[based on taxable profit plus depreciation less capital allowances]
Profit after tax	168	
Add back depreciation	270	[non-cash flow]
Yearly cash flow	438	

Using the cumulative Present Value tables (see Appendix 2) the present value of £1 at 10% over 10 years is £6.15, therefore:

$$NPV = -£2{,}700{,}000 + (£438{,}000 \times 6.15) = -£6{,}300$$

The NPV is less than 0 and the project is therefore not acceptable.

Corporation tax is normally payable by a company in the year following the year in which profit is earned. If a project lasts for say four years then cash flow in respect of tax must be shown in the fifth year. The length of the project is then effectively five years. Tax payable in respect of operating profit must be shown separately from cash flows in respect of capital allowances. The first investment year is normally shown as year 0 and the first tax allowance year is therefore year one.

Worked Example 10.9

Zeta plc has the opportunity to invest in a machine costing £100,000 that will generate cash profits of £30,000 per year for the next four years after which the machine would be sold for £10,000. The company's after tax cost of capital is 8% per annum.

We may assume:

- corporation tax at 30%
- annual writing down allowances in each year are on the investment reducing balance at 25%
- there will be a balancing charge or allowance on disposal of the machine.

We can consider whether the investment should be made, using an NPV approach.

Capital allowances:

Year	Opening balance	Capital allowance at 25%	Balancing allowance/ (charge)	Closing balance
	£	£	£	£
0	100,000	25,000		75,000
1	75,000	18,750		56,250
2	56,250	14,063		42,187
3	42,187	10,547		31,640
4	31,640	7,910		23,730
	23,730			
Proceeds	10,000		13,730	
Total		76,270	13,730	

Note that the totals of the capital allowances and balancing allowance equal £90,000, the net cost of the machine £100,000 less £10,000.

Next, we can calculate the taxable profit, and the tax payable.

Year	0	1	2	3	4
	£	£	£	£	£
Profits		30,000	30,000	30,000	30,000
Capital allowances	25,000	18,750	14,063	10,547	21,640
Taxable 'profit'	– 25,000	11,250	15,937	19,453	8,360
Tax receivable/ (payable) at 30%	7,500	–3,375	–4,781	–5,836	–2,508

We can now calculate the net cash flows and the present values of the project:

Year	Machine	Profits	Tax	Net cash flow	Discount factor at	Present values
	£	£	£	£	8% pa	£
0	–100,000			–100,000	1.00	–100,000
1		30,000	7,500	37,500	0.93	34,875
2		30,000	–3,375	26,625	0.86	22,897
3		30,000	–4,781	25,219	0.79	19,923
4	10,000	30,000	–5,836	34,164	0.74	25,281
5			–2,508	–2,508	0.68	–1,705
					NPV	+1,271

The positive NPV of £1,271 would indicate acceptance of this investment.

Capital investment decisions take on a wider dimension for international corporations with the consideration of a further factor, the uncertainty associated with foreign currency exchange rate fluctuations. For UK-based companies this has had a particular significance over the past few years with the uncertainty surrounding the UK's adoption of the euro. Foreign currency exchange rate risk is not discussed in this chapter but is an important topic that was introduced in Chapter 2.

> Progress check 10.10 **Why and how should inflation and working capital be allowed for in making capital investment decisions?**

Back in 2001, Nissan's decision to build its new Micra car in Sunderland in the UK illustrated the importance of some of the additional factors that influence investment appraisal decisions. The strength of the £ sterling against the euro had damaged Sunderland's chances of winning the contract. But, the level of Government support and the flexibility of the Sunderland workforce were factors that impacted favourably on the Nissan decision, in addition to their positive initial financial appraisal of the investment. As we can see from the press extract below, the fact that UK had still not joined the euro was now threatening any future new investment in the plant.

The same press extract highlights an additional factor influencing investment decisions – the cost of labour. The labour cost differentials between UK and, for example, China and Eastern Europe have resulted increasingly in companies making new investments in countries like Poland, Czechoslovakia, and China. Despite the receipt from the UK Government of huge grants, interest-free loans and fully-subsidised staff training, Samsung has decided to re-invest in plants in the Far East and Slovakia.

The impact of high UK costs on investments by large foreign companies

Electronics group Samsung yesterday announced it was shutting down its UK manufacturing operation, resulting in the loss of 425 jobs in the north-east.

The South Korean conglomerate said UK labour costs were too high, forcing it to move all of its factories to the Far East and Slovakia.

The Department for Trade and Industry said it would decide whether Samsung should pay back £10.5m of government aid granted it when the two Billingham factories were built for £450m in 1995.

Samsung UK's deputy managing director of manufacturing, John Slider, said the closure was 'the only practical way forward'.

He said: 'It's very sad news. This factory won the gold medal for productivity in the Samsung empire, which is no mean feat. The problem is the expense of the UK. We pay £4.50 to £5.50 an hour, which is not that much over here, but, when you compare that with 50p an hour in China, and £1 an hour in Slovakia, it's clear we can't compete.'

The microwave and flat-panel monitor plant's closure – timetabled for April – threatens another 1,000 jobs with suppliers in the area. It also follows Samsung's closure in 1999 of a nearby factory making fax machines.

Yesterday's move cast further doubt on the Government's policy of attempting to lure large foreign companies to build in the UK with grants and aid. When originally announced at the end of 1994, Michael Heseltine, then President of the Board of Trade, had called the Samsung deal 'a wonderful opportunity'.

The company was promised a total of £58m in grants, provided it created 3,000 jobs in the following five years, but, because employment only reached 1,500 at its peak, it received only £10.5m.

Samsung was also offered a £13m interest-free loan and £20m worth of training provided by a combination of local authorities and quangos. It said yesterday it used £1m of this to build a training centre, and did not take up the loan.

About £11m was also invested by local authorities and English Partnerships in improving the site itself and its transport facilities.

Unions and MPs rounded on Samsung last night, demanding that the grant be repaid in full. Frank Cook, Labour MP for Stockton North, said: 'They were allocated £58m and given every kind of consideration. They had every possible convenience provided for them. They claimed they have only drawn down £10.5m as if they have done us some kind of a favour. Words fail me.'

A DTI spokesman said: 'Offers of this kind include claw-back provisions for the recovery of grant paid where projects run into difficulty or firms withdraw from an investment,' she said. 'The Government has given funding to local agencies to help those affected by today's announcement.'

Another local recipient of government aid, Nissan, has hinted that it might move production abroad. The Japanese car company was most recently awarded £3.26m to build its Micra cabriolet in Sunderland, but its president, Carlos Ghosn, last week threatened to pull the replacement for the Almera from the plant unless the UK joined the euro.

Many of those losing their jobs yesterday live in Prime Minister Tony Blair's Sedgefield constituency. Yesterday he said: 'This is part of the world economy in which we live. There will be occasions when companies close plants.'

High labour cost drives Samsung out of Britain, by Edmund Conway
© *Daily Telegraph*, 16 January 2004

Risk and uncertainty and decision-making – sensitivity analysis

In our earlier discussion on the decision-making process we talked about comparing actual results following implementation of the decision with the expected outcome. Our own experience tells us that actual outcomes usually differ considerably from expected outcomes. In terms of capital investment, the greater the timescale of the project the more time there is for more things to go wrong; the larger the investment, the greater may be the impact.

As a final step in evaluation of the investment in a project it is prudent to carry out some sort of sensitivity analysis. Sensitivity analysis may be used to assess the risk associated with a capital investment project. A project having a positive NPV may on the face of it seem viable. It is useful to calculate how much the NPV may change should there be changes to the factors used in the appraisal exercise. These factors are shown in Fig. 10.6.

Sensitivity may be evaluated through numerical analysis, which is illustrated in Worked Examples 10.10 to 10.14. Sensitivity may also be shown graphically:

- NPV may be plotted on the y vertical axis
- the percentage change in the variable factors, used in the appraisal, may be plotted on the x horizontal axis.

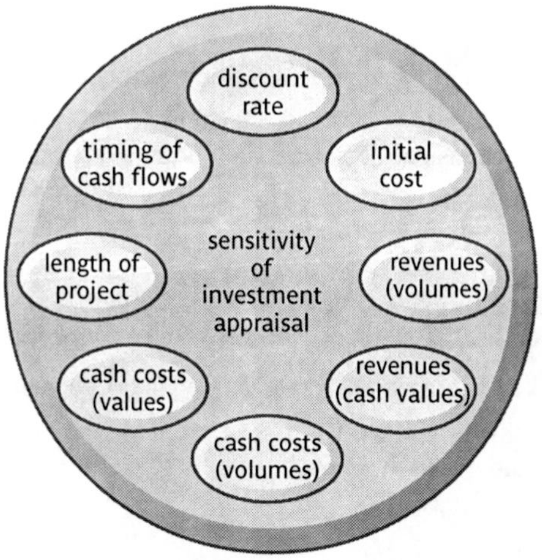

Figure 10.6 Project appraisal factors used in sensitivity analysis

This process may be carried out for each variable, for example:

- sales
- cost savings
- investment
- scrap value.

The most sensitive variable is the one with the steepest gradient.

Worked Example 10.10

Theta Ltd has the opportunity to invest in a project with an initial cost of £100,000 that will generate estimated net cash flows of £35,000 at the end of each year for five years. The company's cost of capital is 12% per annum. For simplicity we can ignore the effects of tax and inflation.

The cumulative present value tables show us the annuity factor over five years at 12% per annum at 3.61 (see Appendix 2).

Therefore the NPV of the project is:

$$-£100,000 + (£35,000 \times 3.61)$$
$$= -£100,000 + £126,350$$
$$\text{NPV} = +£26,350$$

The positive NPV of £26,350 would indicate going ahead with the investment in this project.

We can consider the sensitivity analysis of the project to changes in the initial investment.

Initial investment

The NPV of the project is £26,350. If the initial investment rose by £26,350 to £126,350 (£100,000 + £26,350) the NPV would become zero and it would not be worth taking on the project. This represents an increase of 26.4% on the initial investment.

Worked Example 10.11

Using the data from Worked Example 10.10 we can evaluate the sensitivity of the annual cash flows from the project, using an NPV approach.

We can consider the sensitivity analysis of the project to changes to the annual cash flows.

Annual cash flow

If we again consider what needs to happen to bring the NPV to zero

then $$\text{NPV} = 0 = -£100{,}000 + (a \times 3.61)$$

where a is the annual cash flow

$$a = £100{,}000/3.61$$
$$a = £27{,}700$$

which is a reduction of 20.9% from the original per annum cash flow of £35,000.

Worked Example 10.12

Using the data from Worked Example 10.10 we can evaluate the sensitivity of cost of capital on the project for Theta Ltd, using an NPV approach.

Cost of capital

When the NPV is zero the internal rate of return (IRR) is equal to the cost of capital. If the cost of capital is greater than the IRR then the project should be rejected.

In this example we therefore first need to calculate the cumulative discount factor at which the NPV is zero.

$$\text{NPV} = 0 = -£100{,}000 + (£35{,}000 \times d)$$

Where d is the cumulative discount factor for five years

$$d = £100{,}000/£35{,}000$$
$$d = 2.857$$

The cumulative present value tables show us that the annuity factor over five years of 2.86 represents an interest rate of 22%.

The IRR is therefore approximately 22%, which is an 83.3% increase over the cost of capital of 12%.

Worked Example 10.13

Using the data from Worked Example 10.10 we can evaluate the sensitivity of the length of the project for Theta Ltd, using an NPV approach.

Length of project

The original project was five years for which we calculated the NPV at £26,350. We may consider what would be the effect if the project ended after say four years or three years.

If the project was four years, the cumulative discount factor (from the tables) is 3.04 so the NPV of the project is:

$$-£100{,}000 + (£35{,}000 \times 3.04)$$
$$= -£100{,}000 + £106{,}400$$
$$\text{NPV} = +£6{,}400$$

The positive NPV of £6,400 still indicates going ahead with the investment in this project.

If the project was three years the cumulative discount factor (from the tables) is 2.40 so the NPV of the project is:

$$-£100{,}000 + (£35{,}000 \times 2.40)$$
$$= -£100{,}000 + £84{,}000$$
$$\text{NPV} = -£16{,}000$$

The negative NPV of £16,000 indicates not going ahead with the investment in this project if the length of the project drops below four years, which is the year in which NPV becomes negative. This is a change of 20% (that is a drop from five years to four years).

Worked Example 10.14

Each of the sensitivities that have been calculated in Worked Examples 10.10 to 10.13 may be summarised and we can draw some conclusions about the sensitivity of the project that are apparent from the summary.

The sensitivity analysis that we have carried out is more usefully summarised to show each of the factors we have considered, to show:

- the values used in the original appraisal
- the critical values of those factors
- the percentage change over the original values that they represent.

Factor	Original value	Critical value	% change
Initial investment	£100,000	£126,350	26.4
Annual cash flow	£35,000	£27,700	–20.9
Cost of capital	12%	22%	83.3
Length of project	5 years	4 years	–20.0

We may draw the following conclusions from our sensitivity analysis:

- none of the factors used in the appraisal was critical, their critical values all being +/– 20%
- cost of capital is the least critical factor at 83.3%, which is useful to know since the accuracy of the calculation of cost of capital may not always be totally reliable.

The same technique of sensitivity analysis may be used as an early warning system before a project begins to show a loss. It can be seen from the factors outlined in this section that a board of directors should request a sensitivity analysis on major projects. In the UK, the few years up to 2000 saw several projects concerned with the manufacture of chips for computers become very unprofitable, with timing of cash flows critical to their viability.

However, there are limitations to the use of sensitivity analysis. In the worked examples we have considered we have looked at the effect of changes to individual factors in isolation. In reality two or more factors may change simultaneously. The impact of such changes may be assessed using the more sophisticated technique of linear programming. A further limitation may be the absence of clear rules governing acceptance or rejection of the project and the need for the subjective judgement of management.

Cash flows from investments may be weighted by their probabilities of occurrence to calculate an expected NPV.

Worked Example 10.15

Kappa plc has the opportunity of engaging in a two-year project for a specific client. It would require an initial investment in a machine costing £200,000. The machine is capable of running three separate processes. The process used will depend on the level of demand from the client's final customers. Each process will therefore generate different yearly net cash flows, each with a different likelihood of occurrence. The company's cost of capital is 15% per annum.

The forecast probabilities and net cash flows for each year are:

Process	Probability of occurrence	Per annum cash flow
Process 1	0.5	£150,000
Process 2	0.1	£15,000
Process 3	0.4	£90,000
	1.0	

The total of the probabilities is 1.0, which indicates that one of the options is certain to occur.
Even though one process will definitely be used should Kappa take on the project?

We first need to use the probabilities to calculate the weighted average of the expected outcomes for each year.

Process	Cash flow	Probability	Expected cash flow
	£		£
1	150,000	0.5	75,000
2	15,000	0.1	1,500
3	90,000	0.4	36,000
Expected per annum cash flows			112,500

To calculate the expected NPV of the project we need to discount the expected annual cash flows using the discount rate of 15% per annum.

Year	Expected cash flow	Discount rate	Expected present value
	£		£
1	112,500	0.87	97,875
2	112,500	0.76	85,500
Total	225,000		183,375
Initial investment (year 0)			200,000
Expected NPV			−16,625

The negative expected NPV of £16,625 indicates that Kappa plc should reject investment in this project.

Although the technique of expected net present value is a clear decision rule with a single numerical outcome there are caveats:

- this technique uses an average number which in the above example is not actually capable of occurrence
- use of an average number may cloud the issue if the underlying risk of outcomes worse than the average are ignored
- if the per annum cash flow from process 1 had been £300,000 and the expected NPV had been positive consider the impact on Kappa if, for example, the client had actually required the use of process 2.

Progress check 10.11 Risk and uncertainty increasingly impact on investment decisions. What are these risk factors, and how may we evaluate their impact?

Summary of key points

- An investment requires expenditure on something today that is expected to provide a benefit in the future.
- The decision to make an investment is extremely important because it implies the expectation that expenditure today will generate future cash gains in real terms that greatly exceed the funds spent today.
- '£1 received today is worth more than £1 received in a year's time' is an expression of what is meant by the 'time value of money'.
- The principles underlying the investment appraisal techniques that use the DCF method are cash flow (as opposed to profit), and the time value of money.
- Five main criteria are used to appraise investments: accounting rate of return (ARR); payback; net present value (NPV); internal rate of return (IRR); and discounted payback – the last three being discounted cash flow (DCF) techniques.
- The technique of discounted cash flow discounts the projected net cash flows of a capital project to ascertain its present value, using an appropriate discount rate, or cost of capital.
- Additional factors impacting on investment criteria calculations are: the effect of inflation on the cost of capital; working capital requirements; length of project; taxation; risk and uncertainty.
- There may be a number of risks associated with each of the variables included in a capital investment appraisal decision: estimates of initial costs; uncertainty about the timing and values of future cash revenues and costs; the length of project; variations in the discount rate.
- Sensitivity analysis may be used to assess the risk associated with a capital investment project.
- The techniques of capital investment appraisal require a great deal of expertise and experience, and further training should be received before attempting to use them in real life decision-making situations.

Questions

Q10.1 (i) What is capital investment?
(ii) Why are capital investment decisions so important to companies?

Q10.2 Outline the five main investment appraisal criteria.

Q10.3 Describe the two key principles underlying DCF investment selection criteria.

Q10.4 What are the advantages in the use of NPV over IRR in investment appraisal?

Q10.5 What are the factors that impact on capital investment decisions?

Q10.6 (i) What is meant by risk with regard to investment?
(ii) How does sensitivity analysis help?

Discussion points

D10.1 'I know that cash and profit are not always the same thing but surely eventually they end up being equal. Therefore, surely we should look at the likely ultimate profit from a capital investment before deciding whether or not to invest?' Discuss.

D10.2 'This discounted cash flow business seems like just a bit more work for the accountants to me. Cash is cash whenever it's received or paid. I say let's keep capital investment appraisal simple.' Discuss.

D10.3 'If you don't take a risk you will not make any money.' Discuss.

Exercises

Solutions are provided in Appendix 3 to all exercise numbers highlighted in colour.

Level I

E10.1 *Time allowed – 30 minutes*

Global Sights & Sounds Ltd (GSS) sells multi-media equipment and software through its retail outlets. GSS is considering investing in some major refurbishment of one of its outlets, to enable it to provide improved customer service, until the lease expires at the end of four years. GSS is currently talking to two contractors, Smith Ltd and Jones Ltd. Whichever contractor is used, the improved customer service has been estimated to generate increased net cash inflows as follows:

Year	£
1	75,000
2	190,000
3	190,000
4	225,000

Smith:

The capital costs will be £125,000 at the start of the project, and £175,000 at the end of each of years 1 and 2.

Jones:

The capital costs will be the same in total, but payment to the contractor can be delayed. Capital payments will be £50,000 at the start of the project, £75,000 at the end of each of years one, two and three, and the balance of capital cost at the end of year four. In return for the delayed payments the contractor will receive a 20% share of the cash inflows generated from the improved services, payable at the end of each year. In the interim period, the unutilised capital will be invested in a short-term project in another department store, generating a cash inflow of £60,000 at the end of each of years one, two and three.

It may be assumed that all cash flows occur at the end of each year.

The effects of taxation and inflation may be ignored.

You are required to advise GSS Ltd on whether to select Smith or Jones, ignoring the time value of money, using the appraisal basis of:

(i) **accounting rate of return (ARR), and**

(ii) **comment on the appraisal method you have used.**

E10.2 *Time allowed – 30 minutes*

Using the information on Global Sights & Sounds Ltd from Exercise E10.1, you are required to advise GSS Ltd on whether to select Smith or Jones, ignoring the time value of money, using the appraisal basis of:

(i) payback, and

(ii) comment on the appraisal method you have used.

E10.3 *Time allowed – 60 minutes*

Rainbow plc's business is organised into divisions. For operating purposes, each division is regarded as an investment centre, with divisional managers enjoying substantial autonomy in their selection of investment projects. Divisional managers are rewarded via a remuneration package, which is linked to a return on investment (ROI) performance measure. The ROI calculation is based on the net book value of assets at the beginning of the year. Although there is a high degree of autonomy in investment selection, approval to go ahead has to be obtained from group management at the head office in order to release the finance.

Red Division is currently investigating three independent investment proposals. If they appear acceptable, it wishes to assign each a priority in the event that funds may not be available to cover all three. The WACC (weighted average cost of capital) for the company is the hurdle rate used for new investments and is estimated at 15% per annum.

The details of the three proposals are as follows:

	Project A £000	Project B £000	Project C £000
Initial cash outlay on fixed assets	60	60	60
Net cash inflow in year 1	21	25	10
Net cash inflow in year 2	21	20	20
Net cash inflow in year 3	21	20	30
Net cash inflow in year 4	21	15	40

Taxation and the residual values of the fixed assets may be ignored.

Depreciation is straight line over the asset life, which is four years in each case.

You are required to:

(i) give an appraisal of the three investment proposals with regard to divisional performance, using ROI and RI

(ii) give an appraisal of the three investment proposals with regard to company performance, using a DCF approach

(iii) explain any divergence between the two points of view, expressed in (i) and (ii) above, and outline how the views of both the division and the company can be brought into line.

Level II

E10.4 *Time allowed – 30 minutes*

Using the information on Global Sights & Sounds Ltd from Exercise E10.1, you are required to advise GSS Ltd on whether to select Smith or Jones, using the appraisal basis of:

- (i) **net present value (NPV), using a cost of capital of 12% per annum to discount the cash flows to their present value, and**
- (ii) **comment on the appraisal method you have used.**

E10.5 *Time allowed – 30 minutes*

Using the information on Global Sights & Sounds Ltd from Exercise E10.1, you are required to advise GSS Ltd on whether to select Smith or Jones, using the appraisal basis of:

- (i) **discounted payback, using a cost of capital of 12% per annum to discount the cash flows to their present value, and**
- (ii) **comment on the appraisal method you have used.**

E10.6 *Time allowed – 45 minutes*

Using the information on Global Sights & Sounds Ltd from Exercise E10.1, you are required to advise GSS Ltd on whether to select Smith or Jones, using the appraisal basis of:

- (i) **internal rate of return (IRR), and**
- (ii) **comment on the appraisal method you have used.**

E10.7 *Time allowed – 45 minutes*

In Exercise E10.1 we are told that a 20% share of the improved cash inflow has been agreed with Jones Ltd.

You are required to:

- (i) **calculate the percentage share at which GSS Ltd would be indifferent, on a financial basis, as to which of the contractors Smith or Jones should carry out the work**
- (ii) **outline the other factors, in addition to your financial analyses in (i), that should be considered in making the choice between Smith and Jones.**

E10.8 *Time allowed – 60 minutes*

Alive & Kicking Ltd (AAK) owns a disused warehouse in which a promoter runs regular small gigs. There are currently no facilities to provide drinks. The owners of AAK intend to provide such facilities and can obtain funding to cover capital costs. This would have to be repaid over five years at an annual interest rate of 10%.

The capital costs are estimated at £120,000 for equipment that will have a life of five years and no residual value. To provide drinks, the running costs of staff, etc., will be £40,000 in the first year, increasing by £4,000 in each subsequent year. AAK proposes to charge £10,000 per annum for lighting, heating and other property expenses, and wants a nominal £5,000 per annum to cover any unforeseen contingencies. Apart from this, AAK is not looking for any profit as such from the provision of these facilities, because it believes that there may be additional future benefits from increased use of the facility. It is proposed that costs will be recovered by setting drinks prices at double the direct costs.

It is not expected that the full sales level will be reached until year three. The proportions of that level estimated to be reached in years one and two are 40% and 70% respectively.

You are required to:

(i) **calculate the sales that need to be achieved in each of the five years to meet the proposed targets**

(ii) **comment briefly on four aspects of the proposals that you consider merit further investigation.**

You may ignore the possible effects of taxation and inflation.

E10.9 *Time allowed – 90 minutes*

Lew Rolls plc is an international group that manufactures and distributes bathroom fittings to major building supply retailers and DIY chains. The board of Rolls is currently considering four projects to work with four different customers to develop new bathroom ranges (toilet, bidet, bath, basin, and shower).

Rolls has a limit on funds for investment for the current year of £24m. The four projects represent levels of 'luxury' bathrooms. The product ranges are aimed at different markets. The lengths of time to bring to market, lives of product and timings of cash flows are different for each product range.

The Super bathroom project will cost £3m and generate £5m net cash flows spread equally over five years.

The Superluxury bathroom project will cost £7m and generate £10m net cash flows spread equally over five years.

The Executive bathroom project will take a long time to start paying back. It will cost £12m and generate £21m net cash flows, zero for the first two years and then £7m for each of the next three years.

The Excelsior bathroom project will cost £15m and generate £10m net cash flows for two years.

For ease of calculation it may be assumed that all cash flows occur on the last day of each year.

Projects may be undertaken in part or in total in the current year, and next year there will be no restriction on investment. Lew Rolls plc's cost of capital is 10%.

You are required to:

(i) **calculate the NPV for each project**

(ii) **calculate the approximate IRR for each project**

(iii) **advise on the acceptance of these projects on the basis of NPV or IRR or any other method of ranking the projects.**

(iv) **What are the advantages of the appraisal method you have adopted for Lew Rolls plc?**

(v) **What other factors should be used in the final evaluations before the recommendations are implemented?**

E10.10 *Time allowed – 90 minutes*

A UK subsidiary of a large multinational is considering investment in four mutually exclusive projects. The managing director, Indira Patel, is anxious to choose a combination of projects that will maximise shareholder wealth.

At the current time the company can embark on projects up to a maximum total of £230m. The four projects require the following initial investments:

£20m in project Doh
£195m in project Ray
£35m in project Mee
£80m in project Fah

The projects are expected to generate the following net cash flows over the three years following each investment. No project will last longer than three years.

Project	Doh	Ray	Mee	Fah
Year	£m	£m	£m	£m
1	15	45	15	20
2	30	75	25	25
3		180	60	100

The company's WACC is 12% per annum, which is used to evaluate investments in new projects. The impact of tax and inflation may be ignored.

Advise Indira with regard to the projects in which the company should invest on the basis of maximisation of shareholder wealth, given the limiting factor of the total funds currently available for investment.

11

Financing the business

Contents

Learning objectives

Completion of this chapter will enable you to:

- identify the different sources of finance available to an organisation
- explain the concept of gearing, or the debt/equity ratio
- explain what is meant by the weighted average cost of capital (WACC)
- calculate the cost of equity and the cost of debt
- appreciate the concept of risk with regard to capital investment
- outline the capital asset pricing model (CAPM), and the β factor.

Introduction

This chapter begins with an outline of the types of finance available to organisations to fund their long-term capital investment and short-term requirement for working capital. Financing may be internal or external to the organisation, and either short-term (shorter than one year) or medium- to long-term (longer than one year). Short-term financing is also discussed in Chapter 12, which covers working capital management.

In Chapter 10 we dealt with decisions related to capital investment. This chapter will consider a number of financing options such as leasing and Government grants, but will focus on the main sources of long-term external finance available to an entity to finance such investments: loans (or debt) and ordinary shares (or equity). We shall also discuss gearing or financial structure, which relates to the relationship between the debt and equity of the entity. The appraisal of investment projects by a company inevitably involves calculations, which use some sort of discount rate. The discount rate that is normally used is the company's cost of capital. A company's cost of capital is dependent on the financial structure of the entity, its relative proportions and cost of debt (loans) and equity capital (shares). In Chapter 5 we introduced WACC and in this chapter we will consider its calculation and application.

We will look at how the costs of equity and debt may be determined. One of the fundamental differences between equity and debt is the risk associated with each type of financing and its impact on their cost. The capital asset pricing model (CAPM) is introduced to show how risk impacts on the cost of equity.

Sources of short-term finance

In Chapter 2 we considered some of the various types of business finance when we looked at the balance sheet. Organisations require finance for both short- and medium- to long-term requirements and the financing is usually matched with the funding requirement. Longer-term finance (longer than one year) is usually used to fund capital investment in fixed assets and other longer-term projects. Short-term finance (shorter than one year) is usually used to fund the organisation's requirement for working capital.

Both short- and long-term finance may be either internal or external to the organisation. Internal finance may be provided from:

- retained earnings
- trade credit
- cash improvements gained from the more effective management of working capital.

Retained earnings

Retained earnings are the funds generated that are surplus to:

- the costs of adding to or replacing fixed assets
- the operational costs of running the business
- net interest charges
- tax charges
- dividend payments.

There is statistical evidence, which shows that through the 1990s the majority of capital funding of UK companies continued to be derived from internal sources of finance. However, this is not free. The profit or net earnings generated from the operations of the company belongs to the shareholders of the company. There is a cost, an opportunity cost, which is the best alternative return that shareholders could obtain on these funds elsewhere in the financial markets.

It is the shareholders who decide at the annual general meeting (AGM) how much of those earnings are distributed to shareholders as dividends, the balance being held and reinvested in the business. The retained earnings of the company are increased by net profit less any dividends payable; they are part of the shareholders' funds and therefore appear within the equity of the company. Similarly any losses will reduce the retained earnings of the company. The cost of shareholders' equity is reflected in the level of dividends paid to shareholders, which is usually dependent on how well the company has performed during the year.

Trade credit, together with the more effective management of working capital, will be discussed in Chapter 12.

The main source of external short-term funding is short-term debt.

Short-term debt

Short-term financial debts are the elements of overdrafts, loans and leases that are repayable within one year of the balance sheet date. Short-term finance tends to be less expensive and more flexible than long-term debt. Short-term debt is therefore normally matched to finance the fluctuations in levels of the company's net current assets, its working capital.

Such short-term finance represents a higher risk for the borrower. Interest rates can be volatile, and an overdraft, for example, is technically repayable on demand. The company may finance its operations by taking on further short-term debt, as levels of working capital increase. Because of the higher risk associated with short-term debt, many companies adopting a conservative funding policy may accept a reduction in profitability and use long-term debt to finance not only fixed assets, but also a proportion of the company's working capital. Less risk-averse companies may use short-term debt to finance both working capital and fixed assets; such debt provides increased profitability because of its lower cost.

Sources of long-term finance

Other sources of external finance, which are primarily long-term, include:

- ordinary shares (or equity shares)
- preference shares
- loan capital (financial debt that includes bank loans, debentures, and other loans)
- hybrid finance (for example, convertible loans)
- leasing
- UK Government funding
- European funding.

The two main primary sources of long-term finance available to a company, which are both external, are broadly:

- equity share capital (ordinary shares)
- debt (long-term loans and debentures).

Both types of financing have a unique set of characteristics and rights. The main ones are shown in the table in Fig. 11.1.

Share capital

The capital of a company is called share capital and may comprise ordinary shares and preference shares (although there are other classes of shares, which are not covered in this book). The company determines the maximum share capital that it is ever likely to need to raise and this level is called its

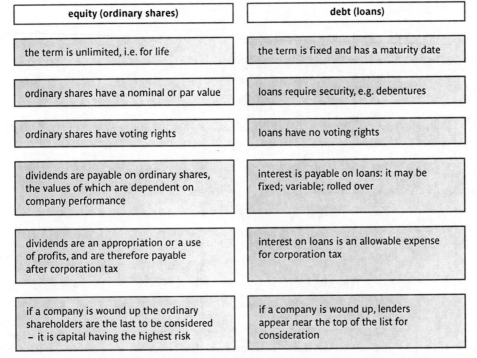

equity (ordinary shares)	debt (loans)
the term is unlimited, i.e. for life	the term is fixed and has a maturity date
ordinary shares have a nominal or par value	loans require security, e.g. debentures
ordinary shares have voting rights	loans have no voting rights
dividends are payable on ordinary shares, the values of which are dependent on company performance	interest is payable on loans: it may be fixed; variable; rolled over
dividends are an appropriation or a use of profits, and are therefore payable after corporation tax	interest on loans is an allowable expense for corporation tax
if a company is wound up the ordinary shareholders are the last to be considered – it is capital having the highest risk	if a company is wound up, lenders appear near the top of the list for consideration

Figure 11.1 Some of the main characteristics and rights of equity capital compared with debt capital

authorised share capital. The amount of shares actually in issue at any point in time is normally at a level for the company to meet its foreseeable requirements. These shares are called the company's issued share capital which, when all the shareholders have paid for them, are referred to as fully paid up issued share capital. Ordinary shares represent the long-term capital provided by the owners of a company, both new and existing.

Rights issues

In a rights issue, the right to subscribe for new shares (or debentures) issued by the company is given to existing shareholders. The 'rights' to buy the new shares are usually fixed at a price discounted to below the current market price (see Worked Examples 11.1 and 11.2). A shareholder not wishing to take up a rights issue may sell the rights.

Worked Example 11.1

A company that achieves a profit after tax of 20% on capital employed has the following capital structure:

400,000 ordinary shares of £1	£400,000
Retained earnings	£200,000

In order to invest in some new profitable projects the company wishes to raise £252,000 from a rights issue. The company's current ordinary share price is £1.80.

The company would like to know the number of shares that must be issued if the rights price is: £1.60; £1.50; £1.40; £1.20.

Capital employed is £600,000 [£400,000 + £200,000]

Current earnings are 20% of £600,000 = £120,000

Therefore, earnings per share (eps) $= \frac{£120{,}000}{400{,}000} = 30\text{p}$

After the rights issue earnings will be 20% of £852,000 [£400,000 + £200,000 + £252,000], which equals £170,400.

Rights price	**Number of new shares £252,000/ rights price**	**Total shares after rights issue**	**Eps £170,400/ total shares**
£	**£**	**£**	**pence**
1.60	157,500	557,500	30.6
1.50	168,000	568,000	30.0
1.40	180,000	580,000	29.4
1.20	210,000	610,000	27.9

We can see that at a high rights issue share price the earnings per share are increased. At lower issue prices eps are diluted. The 'break-even point', with no dilution, is where the rights price equals the capital employed per share £600,000/400,000 = £1.50.

Worked Example 11.2

A company has 1,000,000 £1 ordinary shares in issue with a market price of £2.10 on 1 June. The company wished to raise new equity capital by a 1 for 4 share rights issue at a price of £1.50. Immediately the company announced the rights issue the price fell to £1.95 on 2 June. Just before the issue was due to be made the share price had recovered to £2 per share, the cum rights price.

The company may calculate the theoretical ex-rights price, the new market price as a consequence of an adjustment to allow for the discount price of the new issue.

The market price will theoretically fall after the issue

1,000,000 shares × the cum rights price of £2	£2,000,000
250,000 shares × the issue price of £1.50	£375,000
Theoretical value of 1,250,000 shares	£2,375,000

Therefore, the theoretical ex-rights price is $\frac{£2,375,000}{1,250,000}$ = £1.90 per share

Or to put it another way

Four shares at the cum rights value of £2	£8.00
One new share issued at £1.50	£1.50
	£9.50

Therefore, the theoretical ex-rights price is $\frac{£9.50}{5}$ = £1.90 per share

Long-term debt

Generally, companies try and match their financing with what it is required for, and the type of assets requiring to be financed:

- fixed assets
- long-term projects.

Long-term debt is usually more expensive and less flexible, but has less risk, than short-term debt. Long-term debt is therefore normally matched to finance the acquisition of fixed assets, which are long-term assets from which the company expects to derive benefits over several periods.

Long-term financial debts are the elements of loans and leases that are payable after one year of the balance sheet date. Debt capital may take many forms: loans, debentures, Eurobonds, mortgages, etc. We will look at debentures, but we will not delve into the particular attributes of every type of debt capital. Suffice to say, each involves interest payment, and capital repayment and security for the loan is usually required. Loan interest is a fixed commitment, which is usually payable once or twice a year. But although debt capital is burdened with a fixed commitment of interest payable, it is a tax-efficient method of financing.

Debentures

Debentures and long-term loans are both debt, which are often taken to mean the same thing. However, loans may be either unsecured, or secured on some or all of the assets of the company. Lenders to a company receive interest, payable yearly or half-yearly, the rate of which may vary with market conditions. A debenture more specifically refers to the written acknowledgement of a debt by a company, usually given under its seal, and is secured on some or all of the assets of the company or its subsidiaries. A debenture agreement normally contains provisions as to payment of interest and the terms of repayment of principal. Other long-term loans are usually unsecured.

Security for a debenture may be by way of a floating charge, without attachment to specific assets, on the whole of the business's assets. If the company is not able to meet its obligations the floating charge will crystallise on specific assets like debtors or stocks. Security may alternatively, at the outset, take the form of a fixed charge on specific assets like land and buildings.

Debentures are a tax-efficient method of corporate financing, which means that interest payable on such loans is an allowable deduction in the computation of taxable profit. For example, if corporation tax were at 30%, a 10% debenture would actually cost the company 7%, that is $\{10\% - (10\% \times 30\%)\}$.

Debentures, and other loans, may be redeemable in which case the principal, the original sum borrowed, will need to be repaid on a specific date.

Hybrid finance

Loans may sometimes be required by companies as they move through their growth phase, and for them to finance specific asset acquisitions or projects. Disadvantages of loans are:

- the financial risk resulting from a reduction in the amount of equity compared with debt
- the commitment to fixed interest payments over a number of years
- the requirement of a build up of cash with which to repay the loan on maturity.

Alternatively, if an increase in equity is used for this type of funding, eps (earnings per share) may be immediately 'diluted'. However, some financing is neither totally debt nor equity, but has the characteristics of both. Such hybrid finance, as it is called, includes financial instruments like convertible loans. A convertible loan is a 'two stage' financial instrument. It may be a fixed interest debt or preference shares, which can be converted into ordinary shares of the company at the option of the lender. Eps will therefore not be diluted until a later date. The right to convert may usually be exercised each year at a predetermined conversion rate up until a specified date, at which time the loan must be redeemed if it has not been converted. The conversion rate may be stated as:

- a conversion price (the amount of the loan that can be converted into one ordinary share), or
- a conversion ratio (the number of ordinary shares that can be converted from one unit of the loan).

The conversion price or ratio will be specified at the outset and may change during the term of the loan. Convertibles tend to pay a lower rate of interest than straight loans, which is effectively charging lenders for the right to convert to ordinary shares. They therefore provide an additional benefit to company cash flow and cost of financing.

Progress check 11.1 What makes convertible loans attractive to both investors and companies?

Leasing

Leases are contracts between a lessor and lessee for the hire of a specific asset. Why then is leasing seen as a source of long-term financing? There are two types of leases, operating leases and finance leases, and the answer to the question lies in the accounting treatment of the latter.

Under both types of leasing contract the lessor has ownership of the asset but gives the lessee the right to use the asset over an agreed period in return for rental payments.

An operating lease is a rental agreement for an asset, which may be leased by one lessee for a period, and then another lessee for a period, and so on. The lease period is normally less than the economic life of the asset, and the lease rentals are charged as a cost in the profit and loss account as they occur. The leased asset does not appear in the lessee's balance sheet. The lessor is responsible for maintenance and regular service for assets like photocopiers, cars, and PCs. The lessor therefore retains most of the risk and reward of ownership.

A finance lease relates to an asset where the present value of the lease rentals payable amounts to at least 90% of its fair market value at the start of the lease. Under a finance lease the legal title to the asset remains with the lessor, but the difference in accounting treatment, as defined by SSAP 21, Accounting for Leases and Hire Purchase Contracts, is that a finance lease is capitalised in the balance sheet of the lessee. A value of the finance lease is shown under fixed assets, based on a calculation of the present value of the capital part (excluding finance charges) of the future lease rentals payable. The future lease rentals are also shown as long- and short-term creditors in the balance sheet. The lessee, although not the legal owner, therefore takes on the risks and rewards of ownership.

The leasing evaluation process involves appraisal of the investment in the asset itself, its outright purchase or lease, and an evaluation of leasing as the method of financing. These two decisions may be made separately in either order or they may form a combined decision, and take account of a number of factors:

- asset purchase price and residual value
- the lease rental amounts and the timing of their payments
- service and maintenance payments
- tax
  - capital allowances for purchased fixed assets
  - tax allowable expenses of lease rentals
- VAT (relating to the asset purchase and the lease rentals)
- interest rates (the general level of rates of competing financing options).

Apart from this outline of the process, the evaluation of leasing as a source of finance is beyond the scope of this book.

Stock Exchange listing

In start-up businesses the ordinary shares are usually owned by the founder(s) of the business, and possibly by family and friends, or by investors seeking a gain in their value as the business grows. As a company grows it may decide:

- to raise further equity share capital, in order to finance its growth, at levels much higher than the founders of the business and/or their friends and family are willing or able to afford, or
- to sell its shares by making them publicly available and freely traded, to realise gains in their value for the founders or other investors.

The way that such businesses action these decisions is by making what are termed **initial public offerings (IPOs)** of shares in their companies. This means that shares are offered for sale to the general public and to financial institutions and are then traded (in the UK) on the Stock Exchange or the Alternative Investment Market (AIM).

Floating on the AIM

Shearings, the holiday company and coach operator, is to join the Alternative Investment Market with a potential value of more than £100m.

The company was founded almost 100 years ago. Although it started out as a coach firm, it has expanded to include hotel breaks and cruises.

It now carries more than 500,000 holiday makers to destinations across the globe every year, specialising in customers over 55.

Shearings has been conducting a strategic review since earlier this year.

Although several trade buyers are thought to have expressed an interest, majority shareholder Bridgepoint Capital is understood to favour a stock market listing.

It is being advised by Baird, the broker.

The company is just one of a handful which said yesterday they intended to float on AIM, giving a further boost to London's junior market.

AIM has played host to 80 new admissions since the start of the year, taking the total to more than 831 companies with a market capitalisation of around £22 billion.

The exchange said it had accounted for about 60pc of new listings in Western Europe last year.

Mat Wootton, deputy head of AIM, said the past six months had seen a strong level of activity in the market, with AIM being particularly attractive because of its light regulatory burden.

It has about 25 companies in the pipeline who have expressed their intention to seek admission. AIM celebrates its ninth birthday this month and Mr Wootton said his ambition for the next year would be to improve the efficiency of the secondary market and attract more international companies to the exchange.

But Garry Levin, managing director at Altium, sounded a note of caution.

He said: 'The market is not open for opportunistic companies. The emphasis from fund managers is on quality companies with solid equity growth stories. Only if these are sensibly priced is there an appetite for it.'

Others intending to float include:

- Monkleigh, a new company seeking to develop an integrated event marketing services group
- Libertas Capital, a financial services firm
- US online bookmaker Betonsports
- Plusnet, an internet service provider focusing on broadband services
- Eurocastle Investment, a Guernsey-based investment company dealing primarily in European real estate
- Smallbone, a Devizes-based manufacturer of bespoke kitchens
- Sales technology firm XN Checkout.

However, Wagamama, the Japanese-style noodle bar chain, said it was putting its planned initial public offering on hold to pursue discussions with possible buyers. The company, controlled by private equity firm Graphite Capital, said it had already had a number of approaches.

'We will choose the route that will maximise value for shareholders,' a spokesman said.

Shearings takes fast lane to market, David Litterick

© *Daily Telegraph*, 8 June 2004

The holiday company Shearings (see the press extract above) has expanded from a coach business to a company that provides hotel breaks and cruises to become a company with a value of over £100m. The company carried out a strategic review of its business and considered that its future development may be best served by obtaining a stock market listing on the AIM. The press extract also indicates that a further 25 companies were also currently interested in obtaining an AIM listing.

Ordinary shareholders receive a dividend at a level determined usually by company performance and not as a specific entitlement. The level of dividends is usually based on the underlying profitability of the company (Tesco plc actually advised their shareholders of this relationship in the late 1990s). Preference shareholders receive a dividend at a level that is fixed, subject to the conditions of issue of the shares, and have priority over the ordinary shareholders if the company is wound up. In addition, ordinary shareholders normally have voting rights, whereas preference shareholders do not.

If a company goes into liquidation the ordinary shareholders are always last to be repaid. Ordinary shareholders are paid out of the balance of funds that remain after all other creditors have been repaid.

Additional equity capital may be raised through increasing the number of shares issued by the company through scrip issues and rights issues. A scrip issue (or bonus issue) increases the number of shares with the additional shares going to existing shareholders, in proportion to their holdings, through capitalisation of the reserves of the company. No cash is called for from the shareholders.

UK Government and European funding

Businesses involved in certain industries or located in specific geographical areas of the UK may from time to time be eligible for assistance with financing. This may be by way of grants, loan guarantees, and subsidised consultancy. Funding may be on a national or a regional basis from various UK Government or European Union sources.

By their very nature, such financing initiatives are continually changing in format and their areas of focus. For example, funding assistance has been available in one form or another for SMEs, the agriculture industry, tourism, former coal and steel producing areas, and parts of Wales.

This type of funding may include support for the following:

- business start-ups
- new factories
- new plant and machinery
- research and development
- IT development.

There are many examples of funding schemes that operate currently. For example, the Government, via the DTI (Department of Trade and Industry), can provide guarantees for loans from banks and other financial institutions for small businesses that may be unable to provide the security for conventional loans. Via the various regional development agencies, they may also provide discretionary selective financial assistance, in the form of grants or loans, for businesses that are willing to invest in 'assisted areas'. The DTI and Government Business Link websites, www.dti.gov.uk and www.businesslink.gov.uk, provide up-to-date information of all current funding initiatives.

Progress check 11.2 Describe what is meant by debt and equity and give some examples of each. What are the other sources of long-term, external finance available to a company?

The Welsh Assembly's use of European Structural Funds (ESFs) assists businesses in regenerating Welsh communities. For example, through a scheme called match funding, depending on the type of business activity and its location, ESFs can contribute up to 50% of a project's funding. The balance of the funding is provided from the business's own resources or other public or private sector funding. Websites like the Welsh European Funding Office website, www.wefo.wales.gov.uk, provide information on this type of funding initiative.

Gearing

In Chapter 5 when we looked at financial ratios we introduced gearing, the relationship between debt and equity capital that represents the financial structure of an organisation. We will now take a look at the application of gearing and then consider worked examples that compare the use of debt capital compared with ordinary share capital.

The relationship between the two sources of finance, loans and ordinary shares, or debt and equity gives a measure of the gearing of the company. A company with a high proportion of debt capital to share capital is highly geared, and low geared if the reverse situation applies. Gearing (leverage, or debt/equity) has important implications for the long-term stability of a company because of, as we have seen, its impact on financial risk.

Companies closely monitor their gearing ratios to ensure that their capital structure aligns with their financial strategy. Various alternative actions may be taken by companies, as necessary, to adjust their capital structures by increasing/decreasing their respective levels of debt and equity. An example of one of the ways in which this may be achieved is to return cash to shareholders. In May 2004 Marshalls plc, the paving stone specialist that supplied the flagstones for the newly-pedestrianised Trafalgar Square in London, announced that they were planning to return £75m to shareholders through a capital reorganisation. The reason the company gave for this was that it expected a more efficient capital structure as a result. The company was geared at only 6%, and had generated £5.3m cash in its previous financial year, after dividends and £40m capital expenditure, which its chairman said had reflected its success in growing shareholder value and generating cash.

The extent to which the debt/equity is high or low geared has an effect on the earnings per share (eps) of the company:

- if profits are increasing, then higher gearing is preferable
- if profits are decreasing, then lower gearing or no gearing is preferred.

Similarly, the argument applies to the riskiness attached to capital repayments. If a company goes into liquidation, lenders have priority over shareholders with regard to capital repayment. So, the more highly geared the company the less chance there is of ordinary shareholders being repaid in full.

The many types of short- and long-term capital available to companies leads to complexity, but also the expectation that overall financial risks may be reduced through improved matching of funding with operational needs. The gearing position of the company may be considered in many ways depending on whether the long-term capital structure or the overall financial structure is being analysed. It may also be analysed by concentrating on the income position rather than purely on the capital structure.

Financial gearing relates to the relationship between a company's borrowings, which includes debt, and its share capital and reserves. Concerning capital structure, gearing calculations may be based on a number of different capital values. All UK plcs disclose their net debt to equity ratio in their annual reports and accounts.

The two financial ratios that follow are the two most commonly used (see also Chapter 5). Both ratios relate to financial gearing, which is the relationship between a company's borrowings, which includes both prior charge capital and long-term debt, and shareholders' funds (share capital plus reserves).

$$\text{gearing} = \frac{\text{long-term debt}}{\text{equity} + \text{long-term debt}}$$

$$\text{debt equity ratio, or leverage} = \frac{\text{long-term debt}}{\text{equity}}$$

Worked Example 11.3 illustrates the calculation of both ratios.

Worked Example 11.3

Two companies have different gearing. Company A is financed totally by 20,000 £1 ordinary shares, whilst company B is financed partly by 10,000 £1 ordinary shares and a £10,000 10% loan. In all other respects the companies are the same. They both have assets of £20,000 and both make the same profit before interest and tax (PBIT).

	A	B
	£	£
Assets	20,000	20,000
less 10% loan	–	(10,000)
	20,000	10,000
Ordinary shares	20,000	10,000
Gearing = $\frac{\text{long-term debt}}{\text{equity + long-term debt}}$	$\frac{0}{20{,}000 + 0} = 0\%$	$\frac{10{,}000}{10{,}000 + 10{,}000} = 50\%$
Debt equity ratio = $\frac{\text{long-term debt}}{\text{equity}}$	$\frac{0}{20{,}000} = 0\%$	$\frac{10{,}000}{10{,}000} = 100\%$

Company B must make a profit before interest of at least £1,000 to cover the cost of the 10% loan. Company A does not have any PBIT requirement because it has no debt.

Company A is lower geared and considered less risky in terms of profitability than company B which is a more highly geared company. This is because PBIT of a lower geared company is more likely to be sufficiently high to cover interest charges and make a profit for equity shareholders.

As we have seen, gearing calculations can be made in a number of ways, and may also be based on earnings/interest relationships in addition to capital values. For example:

$$\text{dividend cover (times)} = \frac{\text{earnings per share (eps)}}{\text{dividend per share}}$$

This ratio indicates the number of times the profits attributable to the equity shareholders covers the actual dividends paid and payable for the period. Financial analysts usually adjust their calculations for any exceptional or extraordinary items of which they may be aware.

$$\text{interest cover (times)} = \frac{\text{profit before interest and tax}}{\text{interest payable}}$$

This ratio calculates the number of times the interest payable is covered by profits available for such payments. It is particularly important for lenders to determine the vulnerability of interest payments to a drop in profit. The following ratio determines the same vulnerability in cash terms.

$$\text{cash interest cover} = \frac{\text{net cash inflow from operations + interest received}}{\text{interest paid}}$$

Progress check 11.3 What is gearing? Outline some of the ways in which it may be calculated.

Worked Example 11.4

Swell Guys plc is a growing company that manufactures equipment for fitting out small cruiser boats. Its planned expansion involves investing in a new factory project costing £4m. Chief Executive, Guy Rope, expects the 12-year project to add £0.5m to profit before interest and tax each year. Next year's operating profit is forecast at £5m, and dividends per share are forecast at the same level as last year. Tax is not expected to be payable over the next few years due to tax losses that have been carried forward.

Swell Guys last two years' results are as follows:

	Last year £m	Previous year £m
Profit and loss account for the year ended 31 December		
Sales	18	15
Operating costs	16	11
Operating profit	2	4
Interest payable	1	1
Profit before tax	1	3
Tax on ordinary activities	0	0
Profit after tax	1	3
Dividends	1	1
Retained profit	0	2
Balance sheet as at 31 December		
Fixed assets	8	9
Current assets		
Stocks	7	4
Debtors	4	3
Cash	1	2
	12	9

Creditors due within one year		
Bank overdraft	4	2
Trade creditors	5	5
	9	7
Net current assets	3	2
Total assets less current liabilities	11	11
less		
Long-term loans	6	6
Net assets	5	5
Capital and reserves		
Share capital (25p ordinary shares)	2	2
Profit and loss account	3	3
	5	5

Swell Guys is considering two options:

(a) Issue of £4m 15% loan stock repayable in five years' time

(b) Rights issue of 4m 25p ordinary shares at £1 per share after expenses

For each of the options the directors would like to see:

(i) how the retained profit (derived from operating profit) will look for next year
(ii) how earnings per share will look for next year
(iii) how the capital and reserves will look at the end of next year
(iv) how long-term loans will look at the end of next year
(v) how gearing will look at the end of next year.

(i) Swell Guys plc forecast profit and loss account for next year ended 31 December

Operating profit £5m + £0.5m from the new project

		New debt	New equity
		£m	£m
Operating profit		5.5	5.5
Interest payable	[1.0 + 0.6]	1.6	1.0
Profit before tax		3.9	4.5
Tax on ordinary activities		0.0	0.0
Profit after tax		3.9	4.5
Dividends		1.0	1.5
Retained profit		2.9	3.0

(ii) Earnings per share

$$\frac{\text{Profit available for ordinary shareholders}}{\text{Number of ordinary shares}} \qquad \frac{£3.9\text{m}}{8\text{m}} = 48.75\text{p} \qquad \frac{£4.5\text{m}}{12\text{m}} = 37.5\text{p}$$

(iii) Capital and reserves		**As at 31 December**			
		New debt		**New equity**	
		£m		**£m**	
Share capital (25p ordinary shares)		2.0	(8m shares)	3.0	(12m shares)
Share premium account		0.0		3.0	
Profit and loss account		5.9		6.0	
		7.9		12.0	
(iv) Long-term loans	[6 + 4]	10.0		6.0	

(v) Gearing

$$\frac{\text{long-term debt}}{\text{equity + long-term debt}} \quad \frac{£6\text{m} + £4\text{m}}{£7.9\text{m} + £6\text{m} + £4\text{m}} = 55.9\% \quad \frac{£6\text{m}}{£12\text{m} + £6\text{m}} = 33.3\%$$

Progress check 11.4 **Explain how a high interest cover ratio can reassure a prospective lender.**

The cost of financing and WACC

The weighted average cost of capital (WACC) may be defined as the average cost of the total financial resources of a company, i.e. the shareholders' equity and the net financial debt.

If we represent shareholders equity as E and net financial debt as D then the relative proportions of equity and debt in the total financing are:

$$\frac{E}{E + D} \quad \text{and} \quad \frac{D}{E + D}$$

The cost of equity is the expected return on equity, the return the shareholders expect from their investment. If we represent the return on shareholders' equity as e and the return on financial debt as d, and t is the rate of corporation tax, then we can provide a formula to calculate WACC.The return on shareholder equity comprises both cash flows from dividends and increases in the share price. We will return to how the cost of equity may be derived in a later section in this chapter.

Interest on debt capital is an allowable deduction for purposes of corporate taxation and so the cost of share capital and the cost of debt capital are not properly comparable costs. Therefore this tax relief on debt interest ought to be recognised in any discounted cash flow calculations. One way would be to include the tax savings due to interest payments in the cash flows of every project. A simpler method, and the one normally used, is to allow for the tax relief in computing the cost of debt capital, to arrive at an after-tax cost of debt. Therefore the weighted average cost of capital is calculated from:

$$\text{WACC} = \left\{\frac{E}{(E + D)} \times \boldsymbol{e}\right\} + \left\{\frac{D}{(E + D)} \times d(1 - \boldsymbol{t})\right\}$$

The market value of a company may be determined by its WACC. The lower the WACC then the higher the net present values of its future cash flows and therefore the higher its market value. The determination of the optimum D/E ratio is one of the most difficult tasks facing the finance director.

Worked Example 11.5

Fleet Ltd has the following financial structure:

$e =$	15%	return on equity (this may be taken as given for the purpose of this example)
$d =$	10%	lower risk, so lower than the return on equity
$t =$	30%	rate of corporation tax
$\frac{E}{E+D} =$	60%	equity to debt plus equity ratio
$\frac{D}{E+D} =$	40%	debt to debt plus equity ratio

We can calculate the WACC for Fleet Ltd, and evaluate the impact on WACC of a change in capital structure to equity 40% and debt 60%.

Calculation of WACC for Fleet Ltd with the current financial structure:

$$\text{WACC} = \left\{\frac{E}{(E+D)} \times e\right\} + \left\{\frac{D}{(E+D)} \times d(1-t)\right\}$$

$$\text{WACC} = (60\% \times 15\%) + \{40\% \times 10\%\,(1 - 30\%)\} = 11.8\%$$

If the company decides to change its financial structure so that equity is 40% and debt is 60% of total financing, then WACC becomes:

$$(40\% \times 15\%) + \{60\% \times 10\%\,(1 - 30\%)\} = 10.2\%$$

So it appears that the company has reduced its WACC by increasing the relative weight from 40% to 60% of the cheapest financial resource, debt, in its total financing. However, this is not true because as the debt/equity ratio of the company increased from 0.67 (40/60) to 1.50 (60/40) the company's risk has also increased. Therefore the providers of the financial resources will require a higher return on their investment. There is a well-established correlation between risk and return. So, it is not correct to calculate the WACC using the same returns on equity and debt, as both will have increased.

One of the consequences of this is the problem of calculating an accurate WACC for a company, which is based on its relative proportions and costs of debt and equity capital.

The risks and costs associated with debt capital and equity capital are different and subject to continual change, and may vary from industry to industry and between different types of business. Measurement of the D/E ratio may therefore not be a straightforward task, particularly for diversified groups of companies. Companies in different markets and indeed diversified companies that have trading divisions operating within different markets and producing different products face different levels of risk. If division A operates with a higher risk than division B then the required rate of return of A's investments should be higher than the hurdle rate of return of B's investments. The difference is 'paying' for the difference in risk. This is an important principle but very difficult to implement in practice.

In a later section, we will look at ways in which both the cost of equity and the cost of debt to the company may be determined.

There are many arguments for and against the use of WACC for investment appraisal. Its use is argued on the basis that:

- new investments must be financed by new sources of funds – retained earnings, new share issues, new loans, and so on
- the cost of capital to be applied to new project evaluation must reflect the cost of new capital
- the WACC reflects the company's long-term future capital structure, and capital costs; if this were not so, the current WACC would become irrelevant because eventually it would not relate to any actual cost of capital.

It is argued that the current WACC should be used to evaluate projects, because a company's capital structure changes only very slowly over time; therefore, the marginal cost of new capital should be roughly equal to the WACC. If this view is correct, then by undertaking investments which offer a return in excess of the WACC, a company will increase the market value of its ordinary shares in the long run. This is because the excess returns would provide surplus profits and dividends for the shareholders.

The arguments against the use of WACC are based on the criticisms of the assumptions made that justify the use of WACC:

- new investments have different risk characteristics from the company's existing operations therefore the return required by investors may go up or down if the investments are made, because their business risk is perceived to be higher or lower
- finance raised to fund a new investment
  - may substantially change the capital structure and perceived risk of investing in the company
  - may determine whether debt or equity used to finance the project will change the perceived risk of the entire company, which
  - must be taken into account in the investment appraisal
- many companies raise floating rate debt capital as well as fixed rate debt capital, having a variable rate that changes every few months in line with current market rates; this is difficult to include in a WACC calculation, the best compromise being to substitute an 'equivalent' fixed debt rate in place of the floating rate.

Progress check 11.5 What is WACC and why is it so important?

Cost of debt and equity capital

We have introduced the concept of risk and its correlation with returns on investments. The relationship between risk and return is also one of the key concepts relating to determination of the cost of debt and equity capital. It is an important concept and so we will briefly explore risk a little further, with regard to investments in companies. We shall discuss the cost of debt based on future income flows, that is, interest. We shall similarly discuss the cost of equity based on future income flows, that is, dividends. This will also provide an introduction to the beta factor and the capital asset pricing model (CAPM).

The cost of servicing debt capital, as we have discussed, is the yearly or half yearly interest payment, which is an allowable expense for tax. The cost of repayment of a loan, or debt, depends on the type of loan. Loan capital, a debenture for example, may be irredeemable and traded, with a market value. The cost of capital for a redeemable loan may be calculated using a quite complicated formula.

For our purposes, to demonstrate the principle, we can look at the cost of irredeemable loan capital to a company that may be calculated as follows:

$$d = \frac{i \times (1 - t)}{L}$$

where

d = cost of debt capital
i = annual loan interest rate
L = the current market value of the loan
t = the rate of corporation tax.

By rearranging the formula it can be seen that market value of the debt is dependent on the level of future returns, the interest rate paid, which is determined by the level of risk associated with the investment, and the rate of corporation tax:

$$L = \frac{i \times (1 - t)}{d}$$

Worked Example 11.6

Owen Cash plc pays 12% interest (i) per annum on an irredeemable debt of £1m, with a nominal value of £100. The corporation tax rate (t) is currently 50%. The market value of the debt (L) is currently £90.

What is Owen Cash plc's cost of debt?

d = cost of debt capital

$$d = \frac{i \times (1 - t)}{L} = \frac{12\% \times (1 - 50\%)}{90}$$

$$d = \frac{12\% \times 50\%}{90} = 6.7\%$$

In a similar way, the cost of equity to a company may be determined by looking at future income flows. In the case of equity or ordinary shares this future income is dividends. A difference between this method and the method applied to debt is that there is no tax relief for dividend payments.

The value of an ordinary share may be simply expressed as the present value of its expected future dividend flows.

$$S = v_1/(1 + e) + v_2/(1 + e)^2 + v_3/(1 + e)^3 \ldots v_n/(1 + e)^n$$

where

e = cost of equity capital
v = expected future dividends for n years
S = the current market value of the share

If dividends are expected to remain level over a period of time the formula may be simplified to:

$$S = \frac{v}{e}$$

Therefore, the cost of equity to the company would be:

$$e = \frac{v}{S}$$

Dividends payable on a particular share rarely stay constant from year to year. However, they may grow at a regular rate. This so-called dividend growth model approach to the cost of equity may then be used with the above formula revised as:

$$S = v/(e - G)$$

where G = the expected future dividend growth rate.

The cost of equity may then be stated as:

$$e = \frac{v}{S} + G$$

Worked Example 11.7

Cher Alike plc has 3m ordinary shares in issue that currently have a market price (S) of £2.71. The board have already recommended next year's dividend (v) at 17p per share. The chairman, Sonny Daze, is forecasting that dividends will continue to grow (G) at 4.2% per annum for the foreseeable future.

What is Cher Alike plc's cost of equity?

$$e = \text{cost of equity capital}$$

$$e = \frac{v}{S} + G = \frac{0.17}{2.71} + 4.2\%$$

$$e = 0.063 + 0.042 = 10.5\%$$

The interest rate paid on a loan is known almost with certainty. Even if the debt carries a variable interest rate it is far easier to estimate than expected dividend flows on ordinary shares.

The cost of equity to a company may alternatively be derived using the capital asset pricing model (CAPM). We will look at this approach to risk, and at how some risk may be diversified away by using a spread (or portfolio) of investments.

Progress check 11.6 In broad terms how are the costs of debt and equity determined?

Cost of equity and risk, CAPM and the β factor

Whenever any investment is made there will be some risk involved. The actual return on investment in ordinary shares (equity capital) may be better or worse than hoped for. Unless the investor settles for risk-free securities a certain element of risk is unavoidable.

However, investors in companies or in projects can diversify their investments in a suitably wide portfolio. Some investments may do better and some worse than expected. In this way, average returns should turn out much as expected. Risk that can be diversified away is referred to as unsystematic risk.

Some investments are by their very nature more risky than others. This is nothing to do with chance variations in actual compared with expected returns, it is inherent risk that cannot be diversified away. This type of risk is referred to as systematic risk or market risk. The investor must therefore accept this risk, unless he/she invests entirely in risk-free investments. In return for accepting systematic risk an investor will expect to earn a return which is higher than the return on a risk-free investment.

The amount of systematic risk depends, for example, on the industry or the type of project. If an investor has a balanced portfolio of shares he/she will incur exactly the same systematic risk as the average systematic risk of the stock market as a whole. The capital asset pricing model (CAPM) is mainly concerned with how systematic risk is measured and how systematic risk affects required returns and share prices. It was first formulated for investments in shares on the stock exchange, but is now also used for company investments in capital projects.

Systematic risk is measured using what are known as beta factors. A beta factor β is the measure of the volatility of a share in terms of market risk. The CAPM is a statement of the principles outlined above. An investor can use the beta factor β in such a way that a high factor will automatically suggest a share is to be avoided because of considerable high risk in the past. Consider the impact in January 2001 on the beta factor of Iceland plc caused by the resignation from the board of the major shareholder together with the issue of a profits warning by the company.

The CAPM model can be stated as follows:

the expected return from a security = the risk-free rate of return, plus a premium for market risk adjusted by a measure of the volatility of the security

If

Rs	is the expected return from an individual security
β	is the beta factor for the individual security
Rf	is the risk-free rate of return
Rm	is the return from the market as a whole
(Rm – Rf)	is the market risk premium

$$Rs = Rf + \{\beta \times (Rm - Rf)\}$$

There are many analysts that specialise in the charting of the volatility of shares and markets, and their findings may regularly be found in the UK financial press.

A variation of the above β relationship may be used to establish an equity cost of capital to use in project appraisal. The cost of equity e equates to the expected return from an individual security Rs, and the beta value for the company's equity capital βe equates to beta factor for the individual security β.

So

the return expected by ordinary shareholders, or the cost of equity to the company = the risk-free rate of return plus a premium for market risk adjusted by a measure of the volatility of the ordinary shares of the company

$$e = Rf + \{\beta e \times (Rm - Rf)\}$$

Worked Example 11.8

Bittaboth plc has ordinary shares in issue with a market value four times the value of its debt capital. The debt is considered to be risk free and pays 11% (Rf) before tax. The beta value of Bittaboth's equity capital has been estimated at 0.9 (βe) and the average market return on equity capital is 17% (Rm). Corporation tax is at 50% (t).

We can calculate Bittaboth plc's WACC.

e = cost of equity capital
$e = Rf + \{\beta e \times (Rm - Rf)\} = 11\% + \{0.9 \times (17\% - 11\%)\}$
$e = 0.11 + (0.9 \times 0.06) = 0.164 = 16.4\%$
d = cost of debt capital
which after tax is $i \times (1 - t)$ or $11\% \times 50\% = 5.5\%$

Any capital projects that Bittaboth may wish to consider may be evaluated using its WACC, which may be calculated as:

{equity/(debt + equity) ratio × return on equity} + {debt/(debt + equity) ratio × after tax cost of debt}
$(4/5 \times 16.4\%) + (1/5 \times 5.5\%) = 14.2\%$
14.2% is Bittaboth's weighted average cost of capital (WACC).

It should be remembered that the CAPM considers systematic risk only, and is based on an assumption of market equilibrium.

β factors may be calculated using market and individual companies' information. β values are also obtainable from a variety of sources and are published quarterly by the London Business School.

Progress check 11.7 Describe what is meant by systematic risk and unsystematic risk.

Summary of key points

- Sources of finance internal to a company are its retained earnings, extended credit from suppliers, and the benefits gained from the more effective management of its working capital.
- Short-term, external sources of finance include overdrafts and short-term loans.
- The two main sources of long-term, external finance available to a company are equity (ordinary shares), preference shares and debt (loans and debentures).
- Other sources of long-term, external finance available to UK companies include hybrid finance, leasing, and UK Government and European funding.
- Gearing, or the debt/equity ratio, is the relationship between the two sources of finance, loans and ordinary shares – a company having more debt capital than share capital is highly geared, and a company having more share capital than debt capital is low geared.
- The weighted average cost of capital (WACC) is the average cost of the total financial resources of a company, i.e. the shareholders' equity and the net financial debt, that may

be used as the discount rate to evaluate investment projects, and as a measure of company performance.

- Both the cost of debt and the cost of equity are based on future income flows, and the risk associated with such returns.
- A certain element of risk is unavoidable whenever any investment is made, and unless a market investor settles for risk-free securities, the actual return on investment in equity (or debt) capital may be better or worse than hoped for.
- Systematic risk may be measured using the capital asset pricing model (CAPM), and the β factor, in terms of its effect on required returns and share prices.

Questions

Q11.1 (i) What are the main sources of long-term, external finance available to an organisation?
(ii) What are their advantages and disadvantages?

Q11.2 What are the advantages and disadvantages of convertible loans?

Q11.3 Why may leasing be considered as a long-term source of finance?

Q11.4 What are the implications for a company of different levels of gearing?

Q11.5 What are the advantages and disadvantages for a company in using WACC as a discount factor to evaluate capital projects?

Q11.6 Describe the ways in which the costs of debt and equity capital may be ascertained.

Q11.7 How does risk impact on the cost of debt and equity?

Q11.8 What is the β factor, and how may it be related to WACC?

Discussion points

D11.1 The ex-owner/manager of a private limited company recently acquired by a large plc, of which he is now a board member, said: 'This company has grown very quickly over the past few years so that our turnover is now over £20m per annum. Even though we expect our turnover to grow further and double in the next two years I cannot see why we need to change our existing financing arrangements. I know we need to make some large investments in new machinery over the next two years but in the past we've always operated successfully using our existing overdraft facility, which has been increased as required, particularly when we've needed new equipment. I don't really see the need for all this talk about additional share capital and long-term loans'. Discuss.

D11.2 The marketing manager of a large UK subsidiary of a multinational plc: 'Surely the interest rate that we should use to discount cash flows in our appraisal of new capital investment projects should be our bank overdraft interest rate. I don't really see the relevance of the weighted average cost of capital (WACC) to this type of exercise.' Discuss.

D11.3 In the long run does it really matter whether a company is financed predominantly by ordinary shares or predominantly by loans? What's the difference?

Exercises

Solutions are provided in Appendix 3 to all exercise numbers highlighted in colour.

Level I

E11.1 *Time allowed – 30 minutes*

A critically important factor required by a company to make financial decisions, for example the evaluation of investment proposals and the financing of new projects, is its cost of capital. One of the elements included in the calculation of a company's cost of capital is the cost of equity.

(i) Explain in simple terms what is meant by the 'cost of equity capital' for a company.

The relevant data for Normal plc and the market in general is given below.

Normal plc

Current price per share on the London Stock Exchange	£1.20
Current annual dividend per share	£0.10
Expected average annual growth rate of dividends	7%
β beta coefficient for Normal plc's shares	0.5

The market

Expected rate of return on risk-free securities	8%
Expected return on the market portfolio	12%

(ii) Calculate the cost of equity capital for Normal plc, using two alternative methods:
(a) the Capital Asset Pricing Model (CAPM)
(b) a dividend growth model of your choice.

E11.2 *Time allowed – 30 minutes*

Normal plc pays £20,000 a year interest on an irredeemable debenture, which has a nominal value of £200,000 and a market value of £160,000. The rate of corporation tax is 30%.

You are required to:

(i) **calculate the cost of the debt for Normal plc**
(ii) **calculate the weighted average cost of capital for Normal plc using the cost of equity calculated in Exercise E11.1 (ii) if Normal plc has only ordinary capital of £300,000**
(iii) **comment on the impact on a company's cost of capital of changes in the rate of corporation tax**
(iv) **calculate Normal plc's WACC if the rate of corporation tax were increased to 50%.**

Level II

E11.3 *Time allowed – 30 minutes*

Lucky Jim plc has the opportunity to manufacture a particular type of self-tapping screw, for a client company, that would become indispensable in a particular niche market in the engineering field.

Development of the product requires an initial investment of £200,000 in the project. It has been estimated that the project will yield cash returns before interest of £35,000 per annum in perpetuity.

Lucky Jim plc is financed by equity and loans, which are always maintained as two thirds and one third of the total capital respectively. The cost of equity is 18% and the pre-tax cost of debt is 9%. The corporation tax rate is 40%.

If Lucky Jim plc's WACC is used as the cost of capital to appraise the project, should the project be undertaken?

E11.4 *Time allowed – 60 minutes*

Yor plc is a fast growing, hi-tech business. Its profit and loss account for the year ended 30 September 2004 and its balance sheet as at 30 September 2004 are shown below. The company has the opportunity to take on a major project that will significantly improve its profitability in the forthcoming year and for the foreseeable future. The cost of the project is £10m, which will result in large increases in sales, which will increase profit before interest and tax by £4m per annum. The directors of Yor plc have two alternative options of financing the project:
The issue of £10m of 4% debentures at par, or a rights issue of 4m ordinary shares at a premium of £1.50 per share (after expenses).

Regardless of how the new project is financed, the directors will recommend a 10% increase in the dividend for 2004/2005. You may assume that the effective corporation tax rate is the same for 2004/2005 as for 2003/2004.

Yor plc
Profit and loss account for the year ended 30 September 2004

Figures in £m	
PBIT	11.6
Interest payable	(1.2)
Profit before tax	10.4
Tax on profit on ordinary activities	(2.6)
Profit on ordinary activities after tax	7.8
Retained profit 1 October 2003	5.8
	13.6
Dividends	(3.0)
Retained profit 30 September 2004	10.6

Yor plc
Balance sheet as at 30 September 2004

Figures in £m		
	Fixed assets	
	Tangible	28.8
	Current assets	
	Stocks	11.2
	Debtors	13.8
	Cash and bank	0.7
		25.7
	Current liabilities (less than one year)	

Creditors	9.7
Dividends	1.6
Taxation	2.6
	13.9
Net current assets	11.8
Total assets less current liabilities	40.6
less	
Long-term liabilities (over one year)	
6% loan	20.0
Net assets	20.6
Capital and reserves	
Share capital (£1 ordinary shares)	10.0
Profit and loss account	10.6
	20.6

The directors of Yor plc would like to see your estimated profit and loss account for 2004/2005, and a summary of share capital and reserves at 30 September 2005, assuming:

- **(i) the new project is financed by an issue of the debentures**
- **(ii) the new project is financed by the issue of new ordinary shares**

To assist in clarification of the figures, you should show your calculations of:

- **(iii) eps for 2003/2004**
- **(iv) eps for 2004/2005, reflecting both methods of financing the new project**
- **(v) dividend per share for 2003/2004**
- **(vi) dividend per share for 2004/2005, reflecting both methods of financing the new project**

Use the information you have provided in (i) and (ii) above to:

- **(vii) calculate Yor plc's gearing, reflecting both methods of financing the new project, and compare with its gearing at 30 September 2004**
- **(viii) summarise the results for 2004/2005, recommend which method of financing Yor plc should adopt, and explain the implications of both on its financial structure.**

E11.5 *Time allowed – 90 minutes*

Sparks plc is a large electronics company that produces components for CD and iPod players. It is close to the current year end and Sparks is forecasting profits after tax at £60m. The following two years' post-tax profits are each expected to increase by another £15m, and years four and five by another £10m each.

The forecast balance sheet for Sparks plc as at 31 December is as follows:

	£m
Fixed assets	500
Current assets	
Stocks	120
Debtors	160
	280

Creditors due within one year	
Trade creditors	75
Overdraft	75
	150
Net current assets	130
Long-term loans	150
	480
Capital and reserves	
Share capital (£1 ordinary shares)	220
Share premium	10
Profit and loss account	250
	480

Sparks plc has a large overdraft of £75m on which it pays a high rate of interest at 15%. The board would like to pay off the overdraft and obtain cheaper financing. Sparks also has loan capital of £150m on which it pays interest at 9% per annum. Despite its high level of debt Sparks is a profitable organisation. However, the board is currently planning a number of new projects for the next year, which will cost £75m. These projects are expected to produce profits after tax of £8m in the first year and £15m a year ongoing for future years.

The board has discussed a number of financing options and settled on two of them for further consideration:

1. a 1 for 4 rights issue at £3.00 a share to raise £150m from the issue of 50m £1 shares
2. a convertible £150m debenture issue at 12% (pre tax) that may be converted into 45m ordinary shares in two years' time.

The equity share index has risen over the past year from 4,600 to the current 5,500, having reached 6,250. Sparks plc's ordinary shares are currently at a market price of £3.37. Gearing of companies in the same industry as Sparks plc ranges between 25% and 45%. In two years' time it is expected that all Sparks debenture holders will convert to shares or none will convert.

The rate of corporation tax is 50%. Repayment of the overdraft will save interest of £5.625m a year after tax.

The board requires some analysis of the numbers to compare against the current position:

- **(i) if they make the rights issue**
- **(ii) if they issue debentures**
- **(iii) if the debentures are converted.**

The analysis should show:

- **(a) the impact on the balance sheet**
- **(b) the impact on the profit after tax**
- **(c) earnings per share**
- **(d) gearing**
- **(e) which option should be recommended to the board and why.**

12

Management of working capital

Contents

Learning objectives

Completion of this chapter will enable you to:

- explain what is meant by working capital and the operating cycle
- describe the management and control of the working capital requirement
- outline some of the working capital policies that may be adopted by companies
- implement the systems and techniques that may be used for the management and control of stocks, and optimisation of stock levels
- outline a system of credit management and the control of debtors
- consider the management of creditors as an additional source of finance
- use the operating cycle to evaluate a company's working capital requirement performance
- consider the actions and techniques to achieve short-term and long-term cash flow improvement.

Introduction

Chapters 10 and 11 have been concerned with the longer-term elements of the balance sheet, investments and the alternative sources of funds to finance them. This chapter turns to the shorter-term elements of the balance sheet, the net current assets (current assets less current liabilities) or working capital, which is normally supported with short-term financing, for example bank overdrafts. The chapter begins with an overview of the nature and purpose of working capital.

An emphasis is placed on the importance of good management of the working capital requirement (WCR) for the sustained success of companies. The techniques that may be used to improve the management of stocks, debtors (accounts receivable), and creditors (accounts payable) are explored in detail.

Regular evaluation of the operating cycle may be used to monitor a company's effectiveness in the management of its working capital requirement. Minimisation of working capital is an objective that reduces the extent to which external financing of working capital is required. However, there is a fine balance between minimising the costs of finance and ensuring that sufficient working capital is available to adequately support the company's operations.

This chapter will close by linking working capital to the effective management of cash and by considering some of the ways that both long-term and short-term cash flow may be improved.

Working capital and working capital requirement

The balance sheet is sometimes presented showing assets on the one side and liabilities on the other. This may be said to be a little unsatisfactory since the various categories of assets and liabilities are very different in nature. Cash, for example, is a financial asset and has very different characteristics to fixed assets and stocks.

If we consider the following relationship:

assets = equity + liabilities

it may be rewritten as

fixed assets + stocks + debtors + prepayments + cash
=
equity + financial debt + creditors + accruals

This may be further rewritten to show homogeneous items on each side of the = sign as follows:

equity + financial debt − cash
=
fixed assets + stocks + debtors − creditors − accruals + prepayments

Therefore

equity
=
fixed assets + stocks + debtors − creditors − accruals + prepayments − financial debt + cash

Financial debt comprises two parts:

- long-term debt (payable after one year, in accounting terms)
- short-term debt (payable within one year, in accounting terms)

and so from substitution and rearranging the equation we can see that:

equity + long-term debt
=
fixed assets + stocks + debtors − creditors − accruals + prepayments − short-term debt + cash

Therefore, equity plus long-term financial debt is represented by fixed assets plus, as we saw in Chapter 2, working capital (WC)

WC = stocks + debtors − creditors − accruals + prepayments
− short-term financial debt + cash

Stocks, of course, comprise raw materials, finished product and work in progress (including their share of allocated and apportioned production overheads).

Progress check 12.1 Explain briefly the main components of working capital, using an example of a UK plc.

The need for working capital – the operating cycle

The interrelationship of each of the elements within working capital may be represented in the operating cycle (Fig. 12.1), which was introduced in Chapter 2 when we looked at the balance sheet.

The operating cycle includes:

- acquisition of raw materials and packaging, which are at first stored in warehouses prior to use, are invoiced by suppliers and recorded by the company in trade creditors (or accounts payable), and then normally paid for at a later date

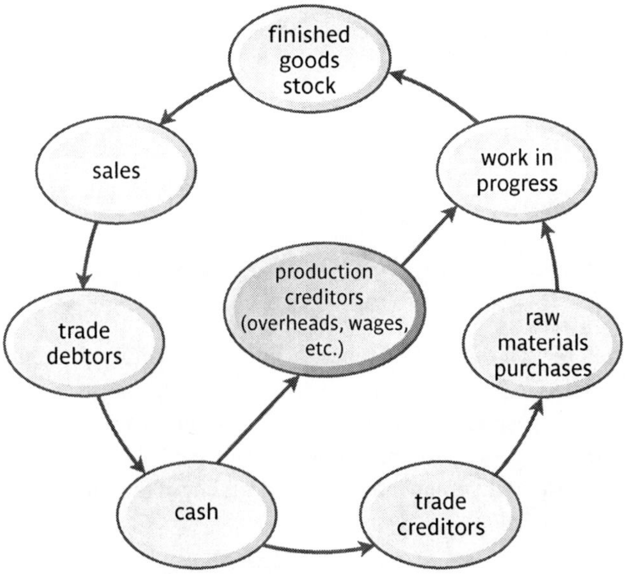

Figure 12.1 The operating cycle

- use of materials and packaging in the manufacturing process to create partly completed finished goods, work in progress, stored as stock in the company's warehouses
- use of materials, packaging, and work in progress to complete finished goods, which are also stored as stock in the company's warehouses
- despatch of finished goods from the warehouses and delivery to customers, who accept the products for which they will pay
- recording as sales by the company its deliveries to customers, which are included in its trade debtors (or accounts receivable) and normally paid by customers at a later date
- use of cash resources to pay overheads, wages and salaries
- use of cash resources to pay trade creditors for production overheads and other expenses
- use of cash resources to pay trade creditors for raw materials.

Worked Example 12.1

We can identify which of the following categories may be included within a company's operating cycle:

- plant and machinery
- trade creditors
- investments in subsidiaries
- cash
- work in progress
- patents
- accounts receivable
- fixtures and fittings

Fixed assets are not renewed within the operating cycle. The following items extracted from the above list relate to fixed assets:

plant and machinery	patents
investments in subsidiaries	fixtures and fittings

The remaining categories therefore relate to the operating cycle, as follows:

trade creditors	cash
work in progress	accounts receivable (trade debtors)

The company therefore uses some of its funds to finance its stocks, through the manufacturing process, from raw materials to finished goods, and also the time lag between delivery of the finished goods or services and the payments by customers of accounts receivable. Short-term funds, for example bank overdrafts, are needed to finance the working capital the company requires as represented in the operating cycle. Many companies use the flexibility of the bank overdraft to finance fluctuating levels of working capital.

Progress check 12.2 How is a company's need for investment in operations explained by the operating cycle?

Working capital requirement (WCR)

We have seen that

equity + long-term debt
=
fixed assets + stocks + debtors – creditors – accruals + prepayments
– short-term debt + cash

From this equation we can see that the total financial resources of the company are equity plus long- and short-term financial debt minus cash. This represents the total money invested in the company, and is called the total investment. Therefore

total investment
=
fixed assets + stocks + debtors – creditors – accruals + prepayments

The total investment in the company can therefore be seen to comprise broadly two elements:

- investment in fixed assets
- investment in operations

where the investment in operations is

stocks + debtors – creditors – accruals + prepayments

which is called the working capital requirement (WCR).

Stated in words, the WCR is telling us something very important: the company has to raise and use some of its financial resources, for which it has to pay, to invest in its operating cycle. These financial resources are specifically for the company to purchase and create stocks, while it waits for payments from its customers. The impact of this is decreased by the fact that suppliers also have to wait to be paid. Added to this is the net effect of accruals and prepayments. Prepayments may be greater than accruals (requiring the use of funds) or accruals may be greater than prepayments (which is a source of funds).

In most manufacturing companies the WCR is positive. The smaller the WCR, the smaller are the total financial resources needed, and the stronger is the company. Some businesses, for example supermarkets, may have limited stocks and zero accounts receivable, but high accounts payable. In such cases WCR may be negative and these companies are effectively able to finance acquisition of fixed assets with funds payable to their suppliers.

Worked Example 12.2

From the balance sheet of Flatco plc for 2005 and the comparatives for 2004 (see Fig. 12.2), we may calculate the working capital requirement for 2005 and the working capital requirement for 2004.

Figures in £000

Working capital requirement:

WCR = stocks + debtors – creditors – accruals + prepayments

WCR for 2005 = 311 + 573 – 553 – 82 + 589 = 838

WCR for 2004 = 268 + 517 – 461 – 49 + 617 = 892

We will use the financial statements of Flatco plc, an engineering company, shown in Figs 12.2 and 12.3, throughout this chapter to illustrate the calculation of the key working capital ratios. The profit and loss account is for the year ended 31 December 2005 and the balance sheet is as at 31 December 2005. Comparative figures are shown for 2004.

Progress check 12.3 **What is meant by working capital requirement (WCR)?**

Working capital (WC)

Working capital (WC) is normally defined as:

current assets – current liabilities

or

WC = stocks + debtors – creditors – accruals + prepayments – short-term debt + cash

Therefore **WC = WCR – short-term debt + cash**

The difference between WC and WCR can be seen to be cash less short-term financial debt.

The financial analyst considers the definitions of long- and short-term in a different way to the accountant, thinking of long-term as 'permanent' or 'stable' and so will consider WC in an alternative way by calculating the difference between the stable financial resources of the company and its long-term use of funds, its fixed assets.

Since

$$\text{equity} + \text{short-term debt} + \text{long-term debt} - \text{cash}$$
$$=$$
$$\text{fixed assets} + \text{stocks} + \text{debtors} - \text{creditors} - \text{accruals} + \text{prepayments}$$

and

$$\text{WC} = \text{stocks} + \text{debtors} - \text{creditors} - \text{accruals} + \text{prepayments} - \text{short-term financial debt} + \text{cash}$$

an alternative representation of working capital is

$$\textbf{WC} = \textbf{equity} + \textbf{long-term debt} - \textbf{fixed assets}$$

Flatco plc
Balance sheet as at 31 December 2005

Figures in £000	**2005**	**2004**
Fixed assets		
Intangible	416	425
Tangible	1,884	1,921
Financial	248	248
	2,548	2,594
Current assets		
Stocks	311	268
Debtors	573	517
Prepayments	589	617
Cash	327	17
	1,800	1,419
Current liabilities (less than one year)		
Financial debt	50	679
Creditors	553	461
Taxation	50	44
Dividends	70	67
Accruals	82	49
	805	1,300
Net current assets	995	119
Total assets less current liabilities	3,543	2,713
less		
Long-term liabilities		
Financial debt	173	-
Creditors	154	167
	327	167
less		
Provisions	222	222
Net assets	2,994	2,324
Capital and reserves		
Capital	1,200	1,000
Premiums	200	200
Profit and loss account	1,594	1,124
	2,994	2,324

Figure 12.2 Flatco plc balance sheet as at 31 December 2005

As a general rule, except in certain commercial circumstances WC should always be positive in the long run because if it were negative then the company would be financing its (long-term) fixed assets with short-term debt. Renewal of such debt represents a major liquidity risk. It is the same thing as, say, financing one's house purchase with an overdraft. Since WC has to be positive and the aim should be for WCR to be as small as possible, or even negative, there is a dilemma as to the acceptability of either positive or negative cash. The answer really depends on the quality of the WCR.

If net cash is negative then short-term debt is higher than the cash balance and so WCR is financed partly with short-term debt. So the question may be asked 'will the company suffer the same liquidity risk as with a negative WC?' If stocks are of high quality champagne, the value of which will probably rise year by year, or if the debtors (accounts receivable) are, say, blue chip companies with no credit risk, then a bank is likely to finance such WCR with no restrictions. If the quality of the WCR is poor the bank is unlikely to finance the WCR with short-term debt. The management and control of each of the elements of WCR: stocks; debtors; creditors, which we will look at in the following sections, must be considered in terms of both their quality and their level.

Flatco plc
Profit and loss account for the year ended 31 December 2005

Figures in £000		**2005**		**2004**
Turnover				
Continuing operations		3,500		3,250
Discontinued operations		–		–
		3,500		3,250
Cost of sales		(2,500)		(2,400)
Gross profit		1,000		850
Distribution costs	(300)		(330)	
Administrative expenses	(155)		(160)	
Other operating costs				
Exceptional items: redundancy costs	(95)		–	
		(550)		(490)
Other operating income		100		90
Operating profit				
Continuing operations	550		450	
Discontinued operations	–		–	
		550		450
Income from other fixed asset investments		100		80
Profit before interest and tax		650		530
Net interest		(60)		(100)
Profit before tax		590		430
Tax on profit on ordinary activities		(50)		(44)
Profit on ordinary activities after tax		540		386
Dividends		(70)		(67)
Retained profit for the financial year		470		319

Figure 12.3 Flatco plc profit and loss account for the year ended 31 December 2005

Progress check 12.4 **What is meant by working capital (WC)? How may it differ in a manufacturing company compared with a supermarket retailer?**

Working capital policy

The financing of its investment in operations, its working capital requirement (WCR), offers a number of options to a company. Choices may be made between internal and external finance. The external financing of WCR is usually provided by bank overdraft. This is because of its flexibility in accommodating the fluctuating nature of net current assets.

Nevertheless, the servicing costs of bank overdrafts, and other short-term funding, are not insignificant and so it is of obvious benefit for companies to maintain their overdraft facility requirements at minimum levels. Such requirements may be reduced by the adoption of appropriate policies with regard to the level of investment in working capital that a company chooses to operate.

The working capital policy adopted will be dependent on individual company objectives that may often be influenced by the type of business and the commercial or industrial sector in which it operates. The choice of objective inevitably presents a conflict between the goals of profitability and liquidity. Working capital policies range between aggressive policies and conservative policies. The former increase profitability through holding low levels of cash and stocks, but run the risk of potential cash shortages and stock-outs. The latter provide greater flexibility, with higher levels of cash and stocks, which provide lower risk at the expense of reduced profitability.

Regardless of the policies adopted, improved management of working capital may have a significant impact on the level of requirement for external financing. Reductions in levels of WCR reduce the requirement for external financing and its associated costs. Maintenance of optimal, and therefore more manageable, levels of WCR increase levels of efficiency and effectiveness and so additionally contribute to increased profitability and a reduction in the requirement for external financing.

Working capital is the 'lubricant' of the investment in operations, enabling the investment in fixed assets to be most effectively exploited. Under-utilised fixed assets can produce extra stocks which then add to the working capital requirement. Good management of their working capital requirement by companies can therefore be seen to be crucially important to both their short- and long-term success.

Progress check 12.5 **Why is the good management of the working capital requirement (WCR) crucial to company success?**

Stocks management

A lean enterprise may be defined as an organisation that uses less of everything to provide more, which results from the control and elimination of waste in all its forms. The Japanese quality expert Taiichi Ohno identified seven main areas of waste (called *muda* by Ohno), which relate to stocks to a large extent in terms of their handling, their movement, and their storage, in addition to the levels held and the proportion of defective and obsolete stocks (see *The Toyota Production System*, Productivity

Press, 1988). These areas of waste emphasise the importance for companies to identify and take the appropriate action for improvement in this aspect of the management of working capital.

Overproduction

- The most serious, which discourages the smooth flow of goods/services and inhibits quality, productivity, communication and causes increases in stocks
- leads to excessive lead and storage times
- lack of early detection of defects
- product deterioration
- artificial work rate pressures
- excessive work in progress
- dislocation of operations and poorer communications
- encourages push of unwanted goods through the system, for example, through the use of bonus systems
- pull systems and *kanban* provide opportunities to overcome overproduction.

Waiting

- Occurs when there is no moving or work taking place
- affects materials, products, and people
- waiting time should be used for training, maintenance or *kaizen* but not overproduction.

Transportation

- Unnecessary movement and double-handling
- may result in damage and deterioration – for example, in 1999 and 2000 the UK car manufacturers Rover and Vauxhall found themselves with unsold or excess stocks being stored for too long in the open air, and were then forced to cut back production because of storage and damage problems
- increased distance means slower communication or feedback of poor quality, therefore slower corrective action.

Inappropriate processing

- Complex solutions to simple procedures
- large inflexible machines instead of small flexible ones – this encourages overproduction to recoup investment, and poor layout leading to excessive transportation and poor communications – the ideal is the smallest machine for the required quality located next to the preceding and succeeding operations
- results from insufficient safeguards, for example, *poka yoke* and *jidoka* – the lack of these lead to poor quality.

Unnecessary stocks

- Leading to increased lead time, space, and costs
- prevents rapid identification of problems
- discourages communication

- all leads to hidden problems, found only by reducing stocks
- results in high storage costs.

Unnecessary motion

- Refers to the importance of **ergonomics** for quality and productivity
- quality and productivity ultimately affected by operators stretching unnecessarily, bending, and picking up, leading to undue exertion and tiredness.

Product defects

- A direct money cost
- and an opportunity to improve, therefore an immediate *kaizen* activity target.

An example of the problems of overproduction resulting in excessive stocks can be seen from the Matalan press extract below. Its immediate effect is to increase the length of the operating cycle and increase the need for further funding, the cost of which has a negative impact on profitability. The other further effects of high stock levels have an additional downward impact on profit from the cost of increased waste in the ways we have examined above.

The result of Matalan being unable to clear its excess stocks following a disastrous Christmas 2004, was fear of a cut in the dividend paid to its shareholders. Many financial analysts downgraded their 2005 profit forecasts for Matalan, and the company saw a large drop in its share price.

Stock levels should be optimised so that neither too little is held to meet orders nor too much is held so that waste occurs. The forecasting of stock requirements must be a part of the management process. In addition, stock level optimisation requires the following:

- establishment of robust stock purchase procedures
- appropriate location and storage of stocks
- accurate and timely systems for the recording, control and physical checks of stocks
- monitoring of stock turnover performance
- implementation of effective stock management and reorder systems.

Progress check 12.6 **Briefly explain how electronic point of sales (EPOS) provides a system of monitoring stock turnover performance.**

The problem of too much stock

Matalan came under pressure yesterday after a leading broker cut its profit forecasts in the light of a year-end round-up meeting with the discount retailer.

After a disastrous Christmas, Matalan warned the City last month that it would make profits of only between £60m and £70m in the year ended February 28.

Yesterday, German bank Dresdner Kleinwort Wasserstein moved its estimate to the lower end of that range, citing concerns that Matalan had been unable to clear excess stock despite heavy discounting.

Dresdner said it had cut its pre-tax profit forecast by 8% to £60.4m and had advised clients to switch into JJB Sports, off 2.5p at 294.

'On our revised estimates, the stock trades on 13.9 times 2005 earnings. This looks expensive relative to the rest of the sector and we therefore maintain our reduce recommendation,' Dresdner said. The bank said it was concerned that the company might have to cut its dividend. Last year Matalan paid a dividend of 8.1p.

Other analysts were not so gloomy. Nick Bubb at Evolution Beeson Gregory said that although he had reduced his profit forecast by a couple of million pounds Matalan had made a good start to the new season. He believes it is possible that he will be upgrading his 2005 forecast when the company reports the full-year figures in May.

Matalan shares closed 7.25p lower at 164p – one of the biggest fallers in the FTSE 250.

Matalan given a dressing down, by Neil Hume

© *The Guardian*, 26 February 2004

Stock purchase

For cash flow (and operational efficiency) purposes it is crucial that efficient and effective sales order, materials procurement and stock control systems are in place and operated by highly trained staff. Authority levels for the appropriate purchasing and logistics managers must be established for both price and quantities, for initial orders and reorders.

Stock location

A variety of options exist for the location of stocks and the ways in which they may be stored. Related items of stocks may be grouped together, or they may be located by part number, or by frequency of pick, or located based on their size or weight.

Stock recording and physical checks

Ideally, all stock transactions should be recorded simultaneously with their physical movement. Stock turnover must be regularly reviewed so that damaged, obsolete and slow moving stock may be disposed of, possibly at discounted sales prices or for some scrap value.

In cash terms, holding on to unsaleable stocks is a 'waste' of the highest order. It uses up valuable space and time and needs people to manage it. It clogs up the system and reduces efficient order fulfilment and represents money tied up in assets of little or no value. Businesses need to move on and dispose of old, obsolete and slow-moving stocks.

Progress check 12.7 **What are the ways in which improvements in a company's management of stocks may contribute to achievement of optimisation of its level of working capital requirement (WCR)?**

It is inevitable that stocks will be required to be physically counted from time to time, to provide a check against stock records. This may be by way of a complete physical count two or three times a year, with one count taking place at the company's financial year end. Alternatively, physical cycle counts may take place continuously throughout the year. This system selects groups of stocks to be counted and checked with stock records in such a way that all stocks are checked two, three, four or more times up to maybe 12 times a year, dependent on such criteria as value or frequency of usage.

Stock ratios

You may recall from the sections in Chapter 5 about financial ratios that one of the efficiency ratios related to stock turnover is a measure used to monitor stock levels:

$$\text{stock days} = \frac{\text{stock value}}{\text{average daily cost of sales in period}}$$

Stock turnover (or stock days) is the number of days that stocks could last at the forecast or most recent usage rate. This may be applied to total stocks, finished goods, raw materials, or work in progress. The weekly internal efficiency of stock utilisation is shown in the following ratios:

$$\frac{\text{finished goods}}{\text{average weekly despatches}} \qquad \frac{\text{raw materials}}{\text{average weekly raw material usage}} \qquad \frac{\text{work in progress}}{\text{average weekly production}}$$

Stock ratios are usually calculated using values but may also be calculated for individual stock lines using quantities where appropriate:

$$\text{stock weeks} = \frac{\text{total stock units}}{\text{average weekly units cost of sales}}$$

Financial analysts usually only have access to published accounts and so they often calculate the stock weeks ratio using the total closing stocks value in relation to the cost of sales for the year.

Worked Example 12.3

From the balance sheet and profit and loss account of Flatco plc for 2005 and the comparatives for 2004, we may calculate the stock turnover for 2005 and the stock days (stock turnover) for 2004.

$$\text{Stock days 2005} = \frac{\text{stock value}}{\text{average daily cost of sales in period}} = \frac{£311}{£2{,}500/365}$$

$$= 45 \text{ days (6.5 weeks)}$$

$$\text{Stock days 2004} = \frac{£268}{£2{,}400/365} = 41 \text{ days (5.9 weeks)}$$

The performance for 2004, 2005 and future years may be more clearly presented in a trend analysis. If 2004 was the first year in the series, then 41 days may be expressed as the base of 100. The 45 days for the year 2005 is then expressed as 110 [45 × 100/41], and so on for subsequent years. Comparison of 110 with 100 more clearly shows its significance than the presentation of the absolute numbers 45 and 41.

ABC and VIN analysis

The appropriate level of control of stocks may be determined through assessment of the costs of control against the accuracy required and the potential benefits. Use of a Pareto analysis (80/20 analysis) allows selective levels of control of stocks through their categorisation into A items, B items, and C items. The ABC method uses Pareto to multiply the usage of each stock item by its value, ranking from the highest to the lowest and then calculating the cumulative result at each level in the ranking.

A items, for example, may be chosen so that the top five stock items make up 60% of the total value. Such items would then be continuously monitored for unit-by-unit replenishment. B items, for example, may be chosen from say 60% to 80% of the total value. Such items would be subject to automated systematic control using cycle counts, with levels of stocks replenished using economic order quantities (see below). C items, for example, may be identified as the 20% of stocks remaining – 'the trivial many' in financial terms. These stocks may be checked by sample counting; because of their low value, more than adequate levels may be held.

Other important factors impact on the choice of stock levels. Total acquisition costs must be considered rather than simply the unit purchase price. There may be requirements to provide items of stock using a just-in-time approach (see the section dealing with JIT later in this chapter). The cost of not having a particular item in stock, even though it may itself have a low cost, may be significant if it is an integral part within a process. Consequently, in addition to ABC categories, stocks are usually allocated vital/important/nice to have (VIN) categories, indicating whether they are:

- vital (V) – out of stock would be a disaster
- important (I) – out of stock would give significant operational problems or costs
- nice to have (N) – out of stock would present only an insignificant problem.

Progress check 12.8 **Describe how stock turnover may be regularly monitored.**

Economic order quantity (EOQ)

A simplistic model called EOQ, or the 'economic order quantity' model, aims to reconcile the problem of the possible loss to a business through interruption of production, or failure to meet orders, with the cost of holding stocks large enough to give security against such loss. EOQ may be defined as the most economic stock replenishment order size, which minimises the sum of stock ordering costs and stockholding costs. EOQ is used in an 'optimising' stock control system.

If

P = the £ cost per purchase order
Q = order quantity of each order in units
N = annual units usage
S = annual £ cost of holding one unit

Then the annual cost of purchasing

= cost per purchase order × the number of orders to be placed in a year
(annual usage divided by quantity ordered per purchase)

Or $P \times N/Q$
Or PN/Q

The annual cost of holding stock

= annual cost of holding one unit in stock × average number of units held in stock
$= 0.5Q \times S$ or $QS/2$

The minimum total cost occurs when the annual purchasing cost equals the annual holding cost,

Or $PN/Q = QS/2$

Cross multiplication gives

$$2PN = Q^2S$$

Or $Q^2 = 2PN/S$

Therefore when the quantity ordered is the economic order quantity:

$$\mathbf{EOQ = \sqrt{2PN/S}}$$

Let's look at a simple example.

Worked Example 12.4

E.C.O. Nomic & Sons, the greengrocers, buy cases of potatoes at £20 per case.

£ cost of one purchase order	P = £5 per order
Number of cases turned over in a year	N = 1,000 cases (units)
Annual £ cost of holding one case	S = 20% of purchase price
Then, S = 20% × £20 = £4	
	$EOQ = \sqrt{2PN/S} = \sqrt{2 \times 5 \times 1{,}000/4}$
	$EOQ = \sqrt{2{,}500}$
The economic order quantity	EOQ = 50 cases of potatoes per order

EOQ illustrates the principle of stock ordering and stock holding optimisation but it is extremely limited. In practice, significant divergences from the EOQ may result in only minor cost increases:

- the optimum order quantity decision may more usually be dependent on other factors like storage space, storage facilities, purchasing department resources, logistical efficiency, etc.
- costs of purchasing and holding stock may be difficult to quantify accurately so the resultant EOQ calculation may be inaccurate
- in periods of changing prices, interest rates, foreign currency exchange rates, etc., continual recalculation is required that necessitates constant updates of all purchasing department and warehouse records of purchases and stocks – computerised systems can assist in providing the answers to some of the financial 'what-ifs' presented by changes in the business environment.

The emphasis over the past couple of decades on stock minimisation or stock elimination systems through the implementation of, for example, JIT, *kanban*, and vendor managed inventory (VMI) has reinforced the disadvantages of holding large stocks. High stock levels reduce the risk of disappointing customers, but it is a costly process not only in the inherent cost of the stock itself, but in the cost resulting from the 'wastes' identified by Shingo and Ohno.

Progress check 12.9 **Outline the basic conflict that might arise between the marketing department and the finance department when discussing the practical application of an economic order quantity (EOQ) system.**

Just in time (JIT)

Just in time (JIT) is sometimes incorrectly referred to as a stock reduction or a zero stock system. JIT is a philosophy that is a response to two key factors: the reduction in product life cycles; the increase in levels of quality required from demanding customers.

JIT is a management philosophy that incorporates a 'pull' system of producing or purchasing components and products in response to customer demand. In a JIT system products are pulled through the system from customer demand back down through the supply chain to the level of materials and components. The consumer buys, and the processes manufacture the products to meet this demand. The consumer therefore determines the schedule.

The JIT system contrasts with a 'push' system where stocks act as buffers between each process within and between purchasing, manufacturing, and sales. In a push system, products are produced to schedule, and the schedule may be based on:

- a 'best guess' of demand
- last year's sales
- intuition.

Some of the key principles and techniques of waste elimination, which in turn support improved stock management, are embraced within the implementation of the JIT process:

- total quality control (TQC), which embraces a culture of waste elimination and 'right first time'
- *kanban* which is a system of signals used to control stock levels and smooth the rate of production, for example using cards to prompt top-up of materials or components driven by demand from the next process
- set-up time reduction for reduced manufacturing batch sizes
- *heijunka*, which is the smoothing of production through levelling of day-to-day variations in schedules in line with longer-term demand
- *jidoka*, or autonomation, where operators are empowered to stop the line if a quality problem arises, avoiding poor quality production and demanding immediate resolution of the problem
- improved production layout
- *poka yoke* (mistake proofing) fail-safe devices, supporting *jidoka* by preventing parts being fitted in the wrong way, so that poor quality is not passed to the next stage in the production process
- employee involvement including self-quality and operator first-line maintenance
- multi-skilling of employees for increased flexibility
- supplier development for higher quality and greater reliability of supply – in the UK, M&S, for example, have publicised their adoption of this practice.

Two other approaches to stock management:

- materials requirement planning (MRP), its development into manufacturing resource planning (MRPII), and
- optimised production technology (OPT)

are sometimes seen as alternatives to JIT, but in fact may be used to complement JIT systems.

Progress check 12.10 Explain briefly what benefits might be gained by both supplier (manufacturer) and customer (national retailer) if they work jointly on optimisation of stock levels and higher quality levels.

Materials requirement planning (MRP)

MRP is a set of techniques, which uses the bill of materials (BOM), stock data and the master production schedule to calculate future requirements for materials. It essentially makes recommendations to release material to the production system. MRP is a 'push' approach that starts with forecasts of customer demand and then calculates and reconciles materials requirements using basic mathematics. MRP relies on accurate BOMs and scheduling algorithms, EOQ analyses and allowances for wastage and shrinkage.

Optimised production technology (OPT)

Optimised production technology (OPT) is a philosophy, combined with a computerised system of shop-floor scheduling and capacity planning, that differs from a traditional approach of balancing capacity as near to 100% as possible and then maintaining flow. It aims to balance flow rather than capacity. Like JIT, it aims at improvement of the production process and is a philosophy that focuses on factors such as:

- manufacture to order
- quality
- lead times
- batch sizes
- set-up times

and has important implications for purchasing efficiency, stock control and resource allocation.

OPT is based on the concept of throughput accounting (TA), developed by Eli Goldratt and vividly portrayed in his book *The Goal* (Gower, 1984). The aim of OPT is to make money, defined in terms of three criteria: throughput (which it aims to increase), and inventory and operating expense, which should at the same time both be reduced. It does this by making better use of limited capacity through tightly controlled finite scheduling of bottleneck operations, and use of increased process batch sizes, which means producing more of a high priority part once it has been set up on a bottleneck machine.

Progress check 12.11 **In the UK there are several low volume car manufacturers. Make an attempt to relate the optimised production technology (OPT) philosophy to their operations.**
(Hint: Research Morgan Cars of Malvern and TVR of Blackpool.)

Factory scheduling is at the root of OPT and the critical factor in OPT scheduling is identification and elimination or management of bottlenecks. OPT highlights the slowest function. This is crucially important in OPT: if one machine is slowing down the whole line then the value of that machine at that time is equivalent to the value of the whole production line. Conversely, attention paid to improving the productivity of a non-bottleneck machine will merely increase stocks.

Progress check 12.12 **What are some of the systems and techniques that may be used to optimise the levels of stocks held by a manufacturing company?**

Debtors and credit management

All companies that sell on credit to their customers should maintain some sort of system of credit control. Improved debt collection is invariably an area that produces significant, immediate cash flow benefits from the reduction of debtor balances. It is therefore an area to which time and resources may be profitably devoted.

Cash flow is greatly affected by the policies established by a company with regard to:

- the choice of customers
- the way in which sales are made
- the sales invoicing system
- the speedy correction of errors and resolution of disputes
- the means of settlement
- the monitoring of customer settlement performance
- the overdue accounts collection system.

These are all areas that can delay the important objective of turning a sale into a debtor and a debtor into cash in the shortest possible time. Each area of policy involves a cost. Such costs must be weighed against the levels of risk being taken.

Customers and trading terms

Sales persons are enthusiastic to make sales. It is important that they are also aware of the need to assess customer risk of the likelihood of slow payment or non-payment. If risks are to be taken then this must be with prior approval of the company and with an estimate of the cost of the risk included within the selling price. Similar limits and authorisations must be in place to cover credit periods, sales discounts, and the issue of credit notes.

Credit checks should always be made prior to allowing any level of credit to a potential new customer. Selling on credit with little hope of collection is a way of running out of cash very quickly and invariably resulting in business failure. The procedure for opening a new account must be a formal process that shows the potential customer that it is something that the organisation takes seriously. Many risky customers may thus be avoided.

Before a new account is agreed to be opened, at least three references should be obtained: one from the customer bank and two from high profile suppliers with whom the customer regularly does business. It is important that references are followed up in writing with requests as to whether there are any reasons why credit should not be granted. A credit limit should be agreed that represents minimum risk, but at a level that the customer can service. It should also be at a level within which the customer's business may operate effectively.

A copy of the latest annual and interim accounts of a potential customer should be requested from the Registrar of Companies. These will indicate the legal status of the company, who the owners are, and its financial strength. These accounts are by their nature historical. If large volumes of business are envisaged then details of future operations and funding may need to be discussed in more detail with the potential customer. If such large contracts involve special purchases then advance payments should be requested to reduce any element of risk.

Having established relationships with creditworthy customers a number of steps may be taken to further minimise risk associated with ongoing trading:

- sale of goods with reservation of title (Romalpa clause) – the goods remain in the ownership of the selling company until they are paid for, and may be recovered should the customer go into liquidation
- credit insurance cover in respect of customers going into liquidation and export risk
- passing of invoices to a factoring company for settlement; the factoring company settles the invoices, less a fee for the service, which therefore provides a type of insurance cover against non-payment – a factoring company can be used as a source of finance enabling short-term funds to be raised on the value of invoices issued to customers.

The measures adopted should be even more rigorous in their application to the supply of goods or services to businesses abroad. This is because of the inevitable distance, different trading conditions, regulations, currencies and legislation.

Progress check 12.13 **What are the ways in which improvements in the management of debtors and credit management may contribute to achievement of optimal levels of working capital requirement (WCR)?**

Settlement methods

Payment collection methods should be agreed with all customers at the outset. The use of cheques, though still popular, is becoming a costly and ineffective collection method. Cash, credit card receipts, and automated electronic transfers are the main methods used by retailers and regular speedy banking is the cornerstone of efficient use of funds. Bankers drafts are the next best thing to cash but should be avoided because of the risk involved through their potential for accidental or fraudulent loss. Electronic mail transfers are frequently used for settlement by overseas companies. These tend to be costly and have been known to 'get lost' in the banking systems. Letters of credit together with sight drafts are frequently used for payments against large contracts.

Extreme care needs to be taken with letters of credit, which are a minefield of potential problems for non-settlement. Letters of credit must be completed providing full details and with the requisite numbers of copies of all supporting documentation. The conditions stipulated must be fully complied with and particularly regarding delivery of goods at the right time at the right location and in the quantity, quality and condition specified.

Electronic collection methods continue to increase in popularity. Direct debit payments are an option where settlement may be made on presentation of agreed sales invoices to the bank. Personal banking is now a feature of the Internet. As its use and level of sophistication continues to be developed, corporate banking transactions conducted through the Internet will inevitably become a major feature. Absolute control is required over both sales and purchase ledger transactions, and all businesses benefit from the strict adherence to administrative routines by the staff involved. Successful control of cash and cheques requires well-thought-out procedures. Examples may be seen in the formal recording that takes place in the systems adopted in high volume businesses.

One of the most acceptable methods is payment through BACS, the bankers' automated clearing services. The BACS method requires customers to register as BACS users and to specify the type of payment pattern they wish to adopt for settlement of their creditor accounts (or payroll). Every week, or two weeks or every month, companies supply details of payments to be made – names of payees and amounts. These are then settled by BACS exactly on the day specified and with only one payment transaction appearing on the bank statement. This means that the problems of cost of individual cheques and the uncertainty of not knowing when each payment will be cleared are avoided.

Cash takings must be strictly controlled in terms of a log and the issue of receipts. Regular physical counts must be carried out and cash banked twice daily or at least once daily. Cheques may be lost in the post, or bear wrong dates, or wrong amounts, or the customer may have forgotten to sign. One person should be nominated to receive and bank cash and cheques. A separate person should maintain the sales ledger in order to maintain internal control.

Sales invoices

The sales invoicing system must ensure that prompt, accurate invoices are submitted to customers for all goods and services that are provided. A control system needs to be implemented to prevent supply without a subsequent sales invoice being issued. An invoicing delay of just one day may result in one month's delay in payment. Incorrect pricing, VAT calculations, invoice totalling, and customer names and addresses may all result in delay. A customer is unlikely to point out an undercharged invoice.

Sales invoices may be routinely followed up with statements of outstanding balances. The credit period offered to customers should obviously be as short as possible. Care should be taken in offering cash discounts for immediate or early payment. This is invariably a disadvantage. Many customers will take the discount but continue to take the extended credit. This is something that may not even be spotted by staff responsible for checking and processing receipts from customers, which effectively results in an unauthorised cost being incurred by the business.

Debtor ratios

Another of the efficiency ratios from the sections in Chapter 5 about financial ratios relates to debtor days, which is a measure used to monitor customer settlement performance.

$$\textbf{debtor days} = \frac{\textbf{accounts receivable} \times \textbf{365}}{\textbf{sales}}$$

Debtor days indicate the average time taken, in calendar days, to receive payment from credit customers. Adjustment is needed if the ratio is materially distorted by VAT or other taxes. Currently, UK sales for exports to countries abroad are not applicable for VAT. Other forms of sales tax may be applicable to sales in those countries.

Worked Example 12.5

From the balance sheet and profit and loss account of Flatco plc for 2005, and the comparatives for 2004, we may calculate the debtor days for 2005 and the debtor days for 2004.

$$\text{Debtor days 2005} = \frac{\text{accounts receivable} \times 365}{\text{sales}} = \frac{£573 \times 365}{£3,500} = 60 \text{ days}$$

$$\text{Debtor days 2004} = \frac{£517 \times 365}{£3,250} = 58 \text{ days}$$

A similar trend analysis to that described in Worked Example 12.3 may be used for greater clarification of performance.

If in 2004, 58 days = 100, then the year 2005 debtor days would = 103.

Progress check 12.14 **Describe how customer settlement performance may be regularly monitored.**

Collection policy

As a great many experienced businessmen may confirm, perhaps the key factor underlying sustained, successful collection of accounts receivable is identification of 'the person' within the customer organisation who actually makes things happen and who can usually speed up the processing of a payment through the company's systems. Payments are usually authorised by the finance director and/or managing director or the accountant. However, 'the person' is the one who prepares payments and pushes them under the nose of the appropriate manager for signature. Cultivation of a good relationship with 'the person' within each customer organisation is an investment that usually pays massive dividends.

The benefit of issue of regular monthly statements of account to customers may be questioned. Most companies pay on invoice and so a brief telephone call to confirm that all invoices have been received, to check on the balance being processed for payment, and the payment date, usually pays greater dividends. Issue of a statement is usually of greater benefit as an *ad hoc* exercise to resolve queries or when large numbers of transactions are involved.

A routine should be established for when settlement of invoices becomes overdue. This process should include having a member of staff who has the specific responsibility for chasing overdue accounts – a credit controller. Chasing overdue accounts by telephone is usually the most effective method. It allows development of good working relationships with customers to enable problems to be quickly resolved and settled.

It is absolutely essential that accurate debtor information is available, up-to-date in terms of inclusion of all invoices that have been issued and allowing for all settlements received, before calling a customer to chase payment. It is also imperative that immediately errors are identified, for example errors in invoicing, they are corrected without delay. These are two of the commonest areas used by customers to stall payment and yet the remedy is within the hands of the company!

An indispensable information tool to be used by the credit controller should be an up-to-date aged debtors report giving full details of all outstanding invoices (see Fig. 12.4). This shows the totals of accounts receivable from all customers at a given date and also an analysis of the outstanding invoices in terms of the time between the date of the report and the dates on which the invoices were issued.

In addition, it is useful to have available the full details of each customers' payment record showing exactly what has been paid and when, going back perhaps one year. To provide an historical analysis and assist in resolving possible customer disputes, computerised systems may be used to hold customer data going back many years, for future retrieval. The friendly agreement of the facts on a customer account on the telephone usually goes a very long way towards obtaining settlement in accordance with agreed terms.

Hannagan plc

Aged debtors As at 30 September 2005

Customer name	total balance	up to 30 days	over 30, up to 60 days	over 60, up to 90 days	over 90 days
		ageing			
	£	£	£	£	£
Alpha Chemicals Ltd	16,827	7,443	8,352	635	397
Brown Manufacturing plc	75,821	23,875	42,398	6,327	3,221
Caramel Ltd	350,797	324,776	23,464	2,145	412
*	*	*	*	*	*
*	*	*	*	*	*
*	*	*	*	*	*
*	*	*	*	*	*
Zeta Ltd	104,112	56,436	43,565	3,654	457
Total	**4,133,714**	**2,354,377**	**1,575,477**	**184,387**	**19,473**
% ageing		**56.96%**	**38.11%**	**4.46%**	**0.47%**

Figure 12.4 Example of an aged debtors report

Perhaps one of the most effective methods of extracting payment from an overdue account is a threat to stop supply of goods or services. If a debt continues to be unpaid then the next step may be a chasing letter that shows that the organisation means business and will be prepared to follow up with legal action. Prior to sending any such letter the facts should be checked and double-checked – people and computers make mistakes! This letter should clearly explain what is expected and what the implications may be for non-compliance with agreed terms. A solicitor's letter should probably be considered, as a rule of thumb, not before an invoice is, say, 60 days overdue from its expected settlement date.

The last resort is to instruct a solicitor to take action against a customer for non-payment. Small debts may be recovered through the small claims court. The costs are low and the services of a solicitor are not necessarily required. Large debts may be recovered by suing the customer for non-payment. This is an expensive and very time-consuming business. The use of the last resort measures that have been outlined should be kept to a minimum. Their use may be avoided through a great deal of preliminary attention being paid to the recruitment of excellent staff, and the establishment of excellent systems, robust internal controls, and a formal credit control system.

Progress check 12.15 **What are some of the ways in which the settlement of accounts receivable from customers may be speeded up?**

Creditors management

The balance sheet category of creditors payable within one year comprises taxes, National Insurance, VAT, etc. and accounts payable to suppliers of materials, goods and services provided to the company (trade creditors). Payments to the Government are normally required to be made promptly, but trade creditors are sometimes considered a 'free' source of finance. This really is not the case, and accounts payable are not free debt as the following worked example illustrates.

Worked Example 12.6

A supplier may offer Justin Time Ltd payment terms of 90 days from delivery date. If Justin Time Ltd alternatively proposes to the supplier payment terms of 60 days from delivery date the supplier may, for example, offer 1% (or 2%) discount for settlement 30 days earlier.

Annual cost of discount:

At 1% discount $\frac{365 \times 1\%}{30} = 12.2\%$ per annum

At 2% discount $\frac{365 \times 2\%}{30} = 24.3\%$ per annum

A discount of 1% for settlement one month early is equivalent to over 12% per annum (and a discount of 2% is over 24% per annum). Consequently, it becomes apparent that the supplier's selling price must have included some allowance for financial charges; accounts payable are therefore not a free debt.

Many companies habitually delay payments to creditors, in order to enhance cash flow, either to the point just before relationships break down or until suppliers refuse further supply. Creditors may be paid slower than the agreed terms to gain a short-term cash advantage but even as a short-term measure this should only be regarded as temporary. It is very short-term thinking and obviously not a strategy that creates an atmosphere conducive to the development of good supplier relationships. A more systematic approach to the whole purchasing/payables system is the more ethical and professional means of providing greater and sustainable benefits. This is an approach followed by the majority of UK plcs, which is now supported by changes in legislation that were introduced during 1999/2000.

With regard to suppliers, overall business effectiveness and improved control over cash flow may be better served by establishment of policies, in much the same way as was suggested should apply to customers, with regard to:

- the choice of suppliers
- the way in which purchases are made
- the purchase invoicing system
- the speedy correction of errors and resolution of disputes
- the means of settlement
- the monitoring of supplier payment performance.

Progress check 12.16 **Explain whether or not trade creditors are a 'free' or even a cheap source of finance for a company, and why.**

Suppliers and trading terms

New suppliers should be evaluated perhaps even more rigorously than customers with particular regard to quality of product, quality and reliability of distribution, sustainability of supply, and financial stability. Appropriate controls must be established to give the necessary purchasing authority to the minimum of managers. This requires highly skilled buyers who are able to source the right quality product for the job at the best total acquisition price (base price, delivery, currency risk, etc.), in the delivery quantities and frequencies required and at the best possible terms. Their authority must be accompanied by rules governing:

- which suppliers may be dealt with
- acceptable ranges of product
- purchase volumes
- price negotiation
- discounts
- credit terms
- transaction currencies
- invoicing
- payment methods
- payment terms.

Terms of trading must be in writing. Most companies print their agreed terms on their purchase orders.

Payment methods

Payments to suppliers should be made in line with terms of trading, but advantages may be gained from cheaper payment methods and providing better control than through the issue of cheques. For example, the payables system may automatically prepare weekly payment schedules and trigger automated electronic payments (for example, BACS) directly through the bank. Alternatively, submission of correct supplier invoices directly to the company's bank may also be used to support automatic payment in line with agreed terms. Provided that adequate controls are put in place to check and monitor such transactions these methods provide a cost-effective method of controlling cash outflows and may be an invaluable aid to cash planning.

Purchase invoices

Integrated purchase order, stock control and payables systems, preferably computerised, should be used to control approval of new suppliers, trading terms, prices, etc. When supplier invoices are received by the organisation they must match completely with goods or services received and be matched with an official order. An efficient recording system should allow incorrect deliveries or incorrect invoices to be quickly identified, queried and rectified. The recording system should verify the credit terms for each invoice.

> Progress check 12.17 **What are some of the ways in which payments to suppliers may be improved to the mutual benefit of the company and its suppliers?**

Creditor ratios

Another of the efficiency ratios, from the sections in Chapter 5 about financial ratios, relates to creditor days, which is a measure used to monitor supplier payment performance.

$$\textbf{creditor days} = \frac{\textbf{accounts payable} \times \textbf{365}}{\textbf{cost of sales}} \quad \textbf{(or purchases)}$$

Creditor days indicate the average time taken, in calendar days, to pay for supplies received on credit. Adjustment is needed if the ratio is materially distorted by VAT or unusual trading terms.

Worked Example 12.7

From the balance sheet and profit and loss account of Flatco plc for 2005, and the comparatives for 2004, we may calculate the creditor days for 2005 and the creditor days for 2004.

$$\text{Creditor days 2005} = \frac{\text{accounts payable} \times 365}{\text{cost of sales}} = \frac{£553 \times 365}{£2{,}500} = 81 \text{ days}$$

$$\text{Creditor days 2004} = \frac{£461 \times 365}{£2{,}400} = 70 \text{ days}$$

A trend analysis may also be calculated in the same way as discussed in Worked Examples 12.3 and 12.5.

Payment policy

The priority for the accounts payable manager must be to maintain the level of payables and cash outflows in line with company policy, but at all times ensuring absolutely no interruption to any manufacturing processes or any other operations of the business. Fundamental to this is the development of good working relationships with suppliers so that problems may be quickly resolved and settled, thus avoiding any threats to supply.

The accounts payable manager must have accurate accounts payable information that is up-to-date in terms of all invoices received, invoices awaited and payments made. In the same way as the credit controller deals with customer queries it is also imperative that the accounts payable manager requests corrections of invoice errors, immediately errors are identified. The accounts payable manager should have access to an up-to-date **aged creditors report** (see Fig. 12.5). This shows the totals of accounts payable to all suppliers at a given date and also an analysis of the balances in terms of the time between the date of the report and the dates of the invoices from suppliers.

The accounts payable manager should also have available detailed reports of all unpaid invoices on each account, and full details of each supplier's payment record showing exactly what has been paid and when, going back perhaps one year. The availability for use of correct, up-to-date information goes a long way to ensuring the avoidance of the build-up of any potential disputes.

Progress check 12.18 **Describe how supplier payment performance may be regularly monitored.**

Hannagan plc					
Aged creditors		**As at 31 December 2005**			
		ageing			
Customer name	total balance	up to 30 days	over 30, up to 60 days	over 60, up to 90 days	over 90 days
	£	£	£	£	£
Ark Packaging plc	9,800	4,355	2,555	455	2,435
Beta Plastics plc	45,337	32,535	12,445	144	213
Crown Cases Ltd	233,536	231,213	2,323	*	*
*	*	*	*	*	*
*	*	*	*	*	*
*	*	*	*	*	*
*	*	*	*	*	*
Zonkers Ltd	89,319	23,213	21,332	12,321	32,453
Total	**3,520,811**	**2,132,133**	**1,142,144**	**123,213**	**123,321**
% ageing		**60.56%**	**32.44%**	**3.50%**	**3.50%**

Figure 12.5 Example of an aged creditors report

Operating cycle performance

The operating cycle, or working capital cycle, which was illustrated in Fig. 12.1, is the period of time which elapses between the point at which cash begins to be expended on the production of a product and the collection of cash from the customer. It determines the short-term financing requirements of the business. For a business that purchases and sells on credit the cash operating cycle may be calculated by deducting the average payment period for suppliers from the average stock turnover period and the average customer's settlement period.

$$\textbf{operating cycle (days)} = \textbf{stock days} + \textbf{debtor days} - \textbf{creditor days}$$

The operating cycle may alternatively be calculated as a percentage using:

$$\textbf{operating cycle \%} = \frac{\textbf{working capital requirement}}{\textbf{sales}}\ \textbf{(stocks + debtors – creditors)}$$

Worked Example 12.8

From the working capital requirement calculated in Worked Example 12.2 and the stock days, debtor days, and creditor days calculated in Worked Examples 12.3, 12.5, and 12.7, we may calculate the operating cycle in days and % for Flatco plc for 2005 and 2004.

Operating cycle days:
Operating cycle 2005 = stock days + debtor days − creditor days
= 45 + 60 − 81 = 24 days
Operating cycle 2004 = 41 + 58 − 70 = 29 days

Operating cycle %:

$$\text{Operating cycle \% 2005} = \frac{\text{working capital requirement}}{\text{sales}}$$

$$= \frac{(£311 + £573 - £553) \times 100\%}{£3{,}500} = 9.5\%$$

$$\text{Operating cycle \% 2004} = \frac{(£268 + £517 - £461) \times 100\%}{£3{,}250} = 10.0\%$$

From this example we can see that Flatco plc's operating cycle has improved by five days from 2004 to 2005, an improvement of 0.5%. The deterioration in debtor days and stock turnover in this example has been more than offset by the increase in creditor days. Despite the overall improvement, this must be a cause for concern for the company who should therefore set targets for improvement and action plans to reduce its average customer collection period and reduce its number of stock days.

Overtrading

We have seen how important to a company is its good management of WCR. Personal judgement is required regarding choice of optimal levels of working capital appropriate to the individual company and its circumstances. This generally leads to the quest for ever-reducing levels of working capital. However, there is a situation called overtrading which occurs if the company tries to support too great a volume of trade from too small a working capital base.

Overtrading is a condition of a business which enters into commitments in excess of its available short-term resources. This can arise even if the company is trading profitably, and is typically caused by financing strains imposed by a lengthy operating cycle or production cycle. Overtrading is not inevitable. If it does occur then there are several strategies that may be adopted to deal with it:

- reduction in business activity to consolidate and give some breathing space
- introduction of new equity capital rather than debt, to ease the strain on short-term resources
- drastically improve the management of working capital in the ways which we have outlined.

This chapter has dealt with working capital, and the working capital requirement (WCR). We have looked specifically at management of the WCR. The appreciation by managers of how working capital operates, and its effective management, are fundamental to the survival and success of the company. Cash and short-term debt are important parts of working capital, the management of which we shall consider in the section that follows.

Progress check 12.19 **How may a company's investment in operations, its operating cycle, be minimised? What are the potential risks to the company in pursuing an objective of minimisation?**

Cash improvement and cash management

We have already discussed how profit and cash flow do not mean the same thing. Cash flow does not necessarily equal profit. However, all elements of profit may have been or will be at some time reflected in cash flow. It is a question of timing and also the quality of each of the components of profit:

- day-to-day expenses are usually immediately reflected in the **cash book** as an outflow of cash
- fixed assets may have been acquired with an immediate outflow of cash, but the cost of these assets is reflected in the profit and loss account through depreciation which is spread over the life of the assets
- sales of products or services are reflected as revenue in the profit and loss account even though cash receipts by way of settlement of sales invoices may not take place for another month or two or more
- some sales invoices may not be paid at all even though the sales revenue has been recognised and so will subsequently be written off as a cost to bad debts in the profit and loss account
- purchases of materials are taken into stock and may not be reflected in the profit and loss account as a cost for some time after cash has been paid to creditors even though credit terms may also have been agreed with suppliers.

Cash flow is therefore importantly linked to business performance, or profit, which may fluctuate from period to period. There is also a significant impact from non-profit items, which may have a more permanent effect on cash resources.

The non-profit and loss account items that affect short-term and long-term cash flow may be identified within each of the areas of the balance sheet (see Fig. 12.6).

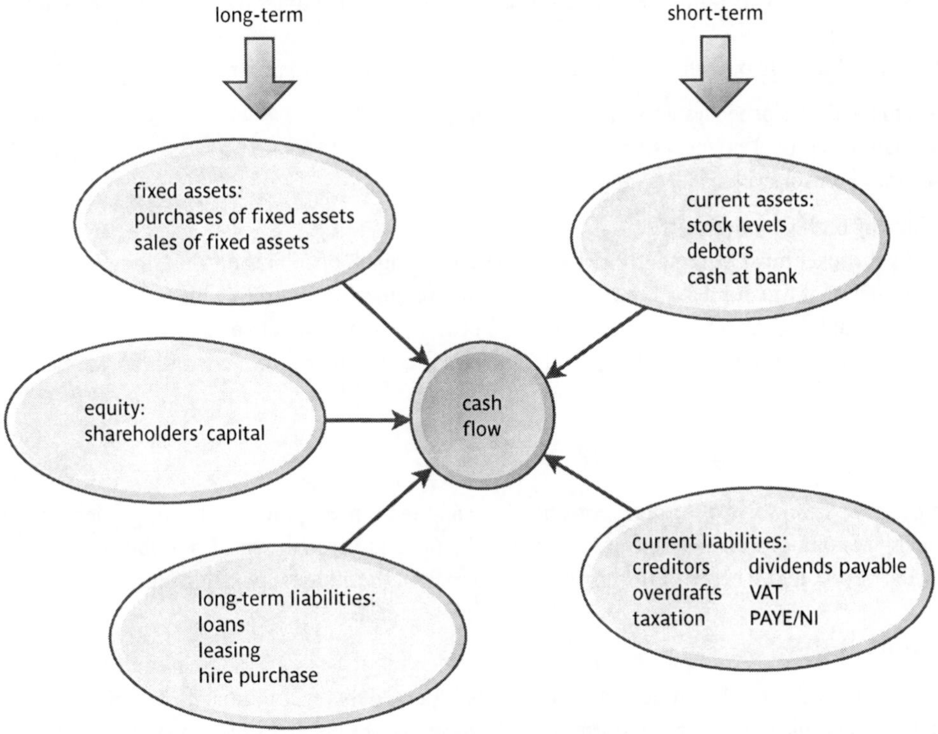

Figure 12.6 Non-profit and loss account balance sheet items that impact on short-term and long-term cash flow

The short-term cash position of a business can be improved by:

- reducing current assets
- increasing current liabilities.

The long-term cash position of a business can be improved by:

- increasing equity
- increasing long-term liabilities
- reducing the net outflow on fixed assets.

We shall consider each of these actions for improvement in the cash position of the business.

> Progress check 12.20 **Profit and cash do not always mean the same thing. In what way therefore does profit impact on cash flow?**

Stock levels

Stock levels should be optimised so that neither too little is held to meet orders nor too much held so that waste occurs. It is a fine balance that requires planning, control and honesty. Many companies either hide or are prepared to turn a blind eye to stock errors, overordering or overstocking because managers do not like to admit their mistakes, and in any case the higher the stock then the higher the reported profit!

For cash flow (and operational efficiency) purposes it is crucial to put in place:

- efficient sales order systems
- materials procurement systems
- stock control systems

operated by highly trained staff.

Stock turnover must be regularly reviewed so that damaged, obsolete and slow-moving stock may be disposed of at discounted sales prices or for some scrap value if possible. In cash terms, hanging on to unsaleable stocks is a 'waste' of the highest order. It uses up valuable space and time and needs people to manage it. It clogs up the system, hinders efficient order fulfilment and represents money tied up in assets of little value.

Debtors

Debtors arise from sales of products or services. The methods employed in making sales, the sales invoicing system, the payment terms, and the cash collection system are all possible areas that can delay the important objective of turning a sale into cash in the shortest possible time.

Cash at bank

Whichever method is used for collection from customers, debts will ultimately be converted into a balance in the bank account. It is important to recognise that the balance shown on the bank statement is not the 'real' balance in the bank account. It is very important to frequently prepare a **bank reconciliation** that details the differences between a company's cash book and its bank statement at a given date. However, it should be noted that the bank statement balance does not represent 'cleared' funds.

Cleared funds are funds that have actually been cleared through the banking system and are available for use. It is this balance, if overdrawn, which is used to calculate overdraft interest. There are software packages which routinely monitor bank charges and many users have obtained a refund from their bank.

The difference between the bank statement balance and the cleared balance is the 'float' and this can very often be a significant amount. The cleared balance information should be received from the bank and recorded so that it can be monitored daily. Cash requirements should be forecast in some detail say six months forward and regularly updated. Cleared funds surplus to immediate requirements should be invested. This may be short-term, even overnight, into, say, an interest-bearing account, or longer-term into interest-bearing investments or the acquisition of capital equipment or even other businesses.

Creditors

Creditors may be paid more slowly than the agreed terms to gain a short-term cash advantage, but even as a short-term measure this should only be regarded as temporary. A more systematic approach to the whole purchasing/payables system is a more ethical and professional approach that may provide greater and sustainable benefits.

Ordering anything from a third party by any individual within the organisation is a commitment to cash leaking out at some time in the future. Tight controls must be in place to give such authority to only the absolute minimum of employees. This authority must be accompanied by rules governing:

- which suppliers may be dealt with
- acceptable ranges of product
- purchase volumes
- price negotiation
- discounts
- credit terms
- transaction currencies
- invoicing
- payment methods
- payment terms.

A tightly-controlled and computerised system of:

- integrated purchase order
- stock control
- payables

must also feature countersigned approval of, for example:

- new suppliers
- terms
- price ranges.

When supplier invoices are received by the organisation they must match absolutely with goods or services received and be matched with an official order. The recording system should verify the credit terms for each invoice. If payment is made by cheque, these should always bear two signatures as part of the control systems.

Cash improvements may be gained from the purchasing and creditors' system in a number of ways. The starting point must be a highly skilled buyer or buyers who are able to source the right quality product for the job at the best total acquisition price (base price plus delivery costs plus allowance for currency risk, for example), in the delivery quantities and frequencies required and at the best possible terms.

Further gains may be achieved from efficient recording systems that allow incorrect deliveries or incorrect invoices to be quickly identified, queried and rectified. Payments should be made in line with terms but advantages may be gained from less costly payment methods and better control than the issue of cheques. For example, the payables system may automatically prepare weekly payment schedules and trigger automated electronic payments directly through the bank.

Alternatively, submission of correct supplier invoices directly to the company's bank may also be used to support automatic payment in line with agreed terms. Provided that adequate controls are put in place to check and monitor such transactions they provide a cost-effective method of controlling cash outflows and cash planning.

Overdrafts

If an overdraft facility is a requirement then the lowest possible interest rate should be negotiated. As with the purchase of any service, it pays to shop around to obtain the best deal. Bank interest charges should be checked in detail and challenged if they look incorrect – all banks make mistakes. Software packages are available to routinely monitor bank charges.

A bank statement should be received routinely by the company weekly, or daily, and should always be thoroughly checked. A detailed monthly schedule of bank charges should be requested from the bank and checked very carefully. These charges should be strictly in line with the tariff of charges agreed at the outset with the bank. In the same way as interest charges, bank charges should be challenged if they look incorrect.

At all times minimisation of both bank interest and bank charges must be a priority. This can be achieved by cash-flow planning and optimisation of the methods of receipts into and payments out of the bank account. If several bank accounts are held they should be seriously reviewed and closed unless they are really essential and add value to the business.

Taxation

Taxation on corporate profit is a complicated and constantly changing area. Tax experts may be engaged to identify the most tax efficient ways of running a business. At the end of the day, if a business is making profits then tax will become payable. Obvious cash gains may be made from knowing when the tax payment dates are and ensuring they are adhered to. Penalties and interest charges for late and non-payment are something to avoid.

VAT

Value added tax (VAT) is probably an area that is even more complicated than corporate taxation. VAT does not impact on the profit of the business. Businesses are unpaid collectors of VAT. If a business is registered for VAT (currently mandatory for businesses with a turnover of £58,000 or more) it is required to charge VAT at the appropriate rate on all goods and services that are vatable. Accurate records must be maintained to account for all such VAT. Such VAT output tax, as it is called, must be paid over to Her Majesty's Customs and Excise every three months or every month, whichever has been agreed.

VAT charged by suppliers, or input tax, may be offset against output tax so that the net is paid over monthly or quarterly. If input tax exceeds output tax, the VAT is refunded by HM Customs and Excise. It is important to note that VAT offices look very carefully at trends on VAT returns. A return that is materially different to the trend will usually result in a visit from a VAT inspector who will carry out an extremely rigorous audit of all accounting records.

It may benefit an organisation to choose to account either monthly or quarterly for VAT. In the same way as corporate taxation, great care must be taken to submit correct VAT returns, and pay VAT on the correct date to avoid any penalties or interest charges.

PAYE/NI

Pay As You Earn (PAYE) taxation and National Insurance (NI) contributions must be deducted at source from payments to employees. Salaries net of PAYE and NI are paid to employees, and the PAYE and NI and a further contribution for employer's NI is then paid to the Inland Revenue. Employees may be paid weekly or monthly and then PAYE and NI is paid over to the Inland Revenue by the 19th of the following month. In exceptional circumstances the IR may allow an odd day's delay. However, as with all other taxes, payment on the due date without fail is the best advice to avoid unnecessary outflows of cash in penalties and interest for non-compliance.

Dividends payable

Dividends are payable to shareholders by companies as a share of the profits. They are not a cost or a charge against profits but are a distribution of profits. There are some factors for consideration regarding cash flow. The timing of dividend payments is within the control of the company. Dividends may therefore be paid on dates that are most convenient in terms of cash flow and it is important to remember to include them in cash planning.

> Progress check 12.21 **Which areas within the profit and loss account, and the balance sheet may be considered to identify improvements to the short-term cash position of a company?**

Worked Example 12.9

An extract from Flatco plc's balance sheet as at 31 December 2005 and 2004 is shown below. From it we can see that trade debtors at 31 December 2004 were £517,000. Sales were £3,250,000 and so debtor days for 2004 were 58 days. Trade debtors at 31 December 2005 were £573,000, sales were £3,500,000 and debtor days for 2005 had worsened to 60 days. Although new cash collection procedures and a reinforced credit control department were introduced in the latter part of 2005, it was too early to see an improvement by December 2005. A report published on the industry for 2004 indicated that the average time customers took to pay was 35 days, with the highest performing companies achieving 25 days.

We will calculate the range of savings that Flatco would expect if it were to implement the appropriate measures to achieve average performance, or if it improved enough to match the best performers. We may assume that sales are more or less evenly spread throughout the year. Flatco's profit before tax for 2004 was £430,000. The average bank interest paid/earned by Flatco plc was 9% per annum.

Flatco plc
Extract of the balance sheet as at 31 December 2005

	2005 £000	2004 £000
Current assets		
Stocks	311	268
Debtors	573	517
Prepayments	589	617
Cash	327	17
	1,800	1,419

	Flatco		Average (derived)		Best (derived)
Debtors	£517,000		£312,000		£223,000
Sales	£3,250,000		£3,250,000		£3,250,000
Debtor days	58		35		25
Gain per annum		[517 – 312]	£205,000	[517 – 223]	£294,000
Interest saved/ earned at 9% per annum			£18,450		£26,460
Improvement to profit before tax		[£18,450 × 100/£430,000]	+4.3%	[£26,460 × 100/£430,000]	+6.2%

Assuming that Flatco plc's new credit control procedures become effective, at current trading levels it should result in a profit improvement for 2006 of between £25,000 and £37,000 per annum.

Shareholders' capital

Shareholders' capital has many advantages in providing a means of improving long-term cash flow. Provision of additional equity by the shareholders immediately strengthens the balance sheet. It also indirectly strengthens the profit position because equity (ordinary shares) does not bear a commitment to pay interest. Additional equity is an investment in future business, which will ultimately result in dividends payable from successful trading.

When owners of the organisation provide additional equity, a personal cost is imposed on them in that the funding is from their own capital. It also may dilute their own stake or percentage of the business. New shareholders or professional risk capitalists may be another source of equity. This carries the same advantages but also the expectation of rewards is much higher than those from interest-bearing loans.